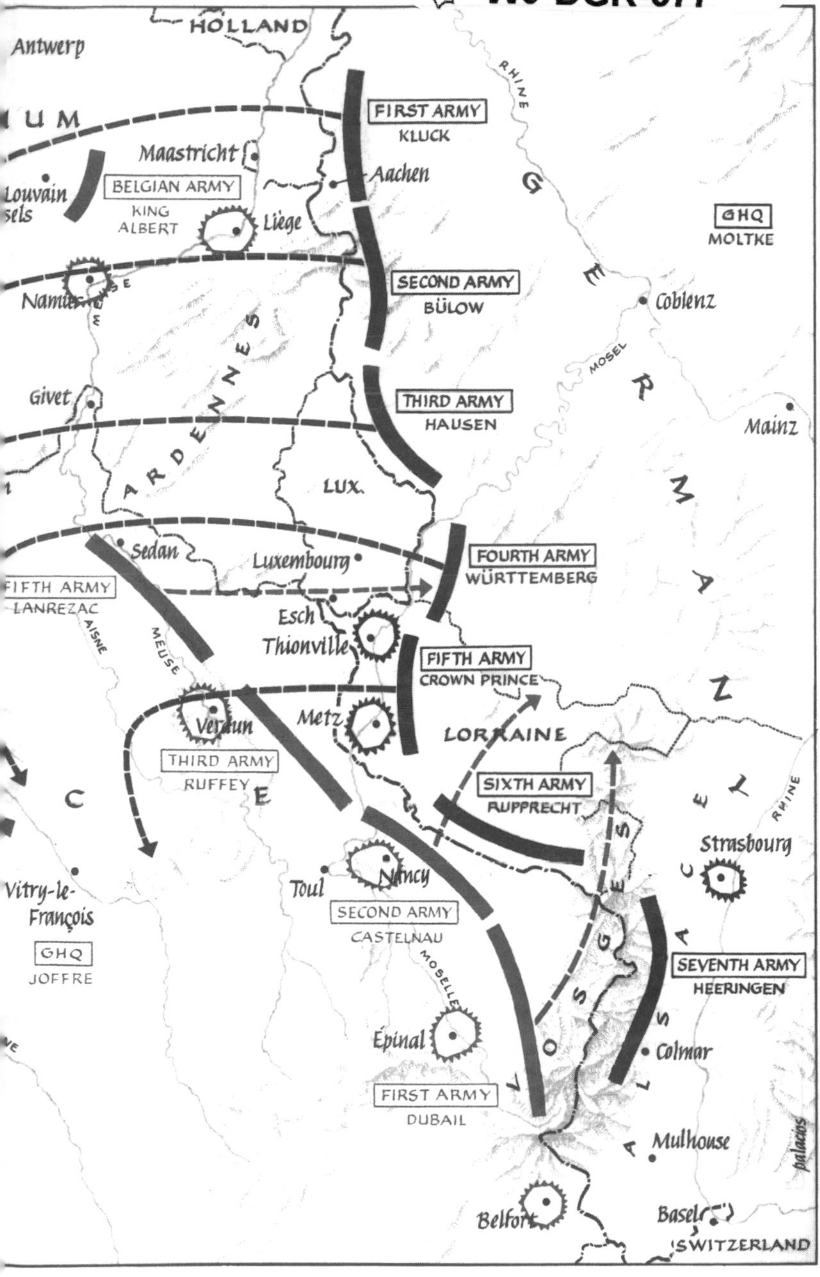
HOLLAND
Antwerp
UM
Maastricht
Louvain
sels
BELGIAN ARMY
KING ALBERT
Liège
Aachen
FIRST ARMY
KLUCK
RHINE
GHQ
MOLTKE
Namur
MEUSE
SECOND ARMY
BÜLOW
Coblenz
ARDENNES
MOSEL
Givet
THIRD ARMY
HAUSEN
Mainz
LUX.
GERMANY
Sedan
Luxembourg
FOURTH ARMY
WÜRTTEMBERG
FIFTH ARMY
LANREZAC
AISNE
MEUSE
Esch
Thionville
FIFTH ARMY
CROWN PRINCE
Metz
Verdun
LORRAINE
THIRD ARMY
RUFFEY
SIXTH ARMY
RUPPRECHT
Strasbourg
RHINE
Toul
Nancy
Vitry-le-François
SECOND ARMY
CASTELNAU
GHQ
JOFFRE
MOSELLE
VOSGES
ALSACE
SEVENTH ARMY
HEERINGEN
Épinal
Colmar
FIRST ARMY
DUBAIL
Mulhouse
palacios
Belfort
Basel
SWITZERLAND

BARBARA W. TUCHMAN

BARBARA W. TUCHMAN

THE GUNS OF AUGUST
THE PROUD TOWER

Margaret MacMillan, *editor*

THE LIBRARY OF AMERICA

The paper used in this publication meets the minimum requirements of the American National Standard for Information Sciences—Permanence of Paper for Printed Library Materials, ANSI Z39.48—1984.

Distributed to the trade in the United States
by Penguin Group (USA) Inc.
and in Canada by Penguin Books Canada Ltd.

Library of Congress Control Number: 2011928609
ISBN 978-1-59853-145-9

Second Printing
The Library of America—222

Manufactured in the United States of America

Barbara W. Tuchman:
The Guns of August, The Proud Tower
is kept in print by a gift from

THE FLORENCE GOULD FOUNDATION

to the Guardians of American Letters Fund,
established by The Library of America
to ensure that every volume in the series
will be permanently available.

Contents

THE GUNS OF AUGUST

"The human heart is the starting point of all matters pertaining to war."

MARÉCHAL DE SAXE
Reveries on the Art of War (Preface), 1732

"The terrible Ifs accumulate."

WINSTON CHURCHILL
The World Crisis, Vol. I, Chap. XI

AUTHOR'S NOTE

This book owes a primary debt to Mr. Cecil Scott of The Macmillan Company whose advice and encouragement and knowledge of the subject were an essential element and a firm support from beginning to end. I have also been fortunate in the critical collaboration of Mr. Denning Miller who in clarifying many problems of writing and interpretation made this a better book than it would otherwise have been. For his help I am permanently grateful.

I should like to express my appreciation of the unsurpassed resources of the New York Public Library and, at the same time, a hope that somehow, someday in my native city a way will be found to make the Library's facilities for scholars match its incomparable material. My thanks go also to the New York Society Library for the continuing hospitality of its stacks and the haven of a place to write; to Mrs. Agnes F. Peterson of the Hoover Library at Stanford for the loan of the Briey *Procés-Verbaux* and for running to earth the answers to many queries; to Miss R. E. B. Coombe of the Imperial War Museum, London, for many of the illustrations; to the staff of the Bibliothèque de Documentation Internationale Contemporaine Paris, for source material; and to Mr. Henry Sachs of the American Ordnance Association for technical advice and for supplementing my inadequate German.

To the reader I must explain that the omission of Austria-Hungary, Serbia, and the Russo-Austrian and Serbo-Austrian fronts was not entirely arbitrary. The inexhaustible problem of the Balkans divides itself naturally from the rest of the war. Moreover, operations on the Austrian front during the first thirty-one days were purely preliminary and did not reach a climax, with effect on the war as a whole, until the Battle of Lemberg against the Russians and the Battle of the Drina against the Serbs. These took place between September 8 and 17, outside my chronological limits, and it seemed to me there was unity without it and the prospect of tiresome length if it were included.

After a period of total immersion in military memoirs, I had hoped to dispense with Roman-numeraled corps, but convention proved stronger than good intentions. I can do nothing about the Roman numerals which, it seems, are inseparably riveted to army corps, but I can offer the reader a helpful RULE ON LEFT AND RIGHT: rivers face downstream and armies, even when turned around and retreating, are considered to face the direction in which they started; that is, their left and right remain the same as when they were advancing.

Sources for the narrative and for all quoted remarks are given in the Notes at the end of the book. I have tried to avoid spontaneous attribution or the "he must have" style of historical writing: "As he watched the coastline of France disappear, Napoleon must have thought back over the long . . ." All conditions of weather, thoughts or feelings, and states of mind public or private, in the following pages have documentary support. Where it seems called for, the evidence appears in the Notes.

CONTENTS

ILLUSTRATIONS

(following page 312)

MAPS

by Rafael D. Palacios

1

A Funeral

SO GORGEOUS was the spectacle on the May morning of 1910 when nine kings rode in the funeral of Edward VII of England that the crowd, waiting in hushed and black-clad awe, could not keep back gasps of admiration. In scarlet and blue and green and purple, three by three the sovereigns rode through the palace gates, with plumed helmets, gold braid, crimson sashes, and jeweled orders flashing in the sun. After them came five heirs apparent, forty more imperial or royal highnesses, seven queens—four dowager and three regnant—and a scattering of special ambassadors from uncrowned countries. Together they represented seventy nations in the greatest assemblage of royalty and rank ever gathered in one place and, of its kind, the last. The muffled tongue of Big Ben tolled nine by the clock as the cortege left the palace, but on history's clock it was sunset, and the sun of the old world was setting in a dying blaze of splendor never to be seen again.

In the center of the front row rode the new king, George V, flanked on his left by the Duke of Connaught, the late king's only surviving brother, and on his right by a personage to whom, acknowledged *The Times*, "belongs the first place among all the foreign mourners," who "even when relations are most strained has never lost his popularity amongst us"—William II, Emperor of Germany. Mounted on a gray horse, wearing the scarlet uniform of a British Field Marshal, carrying the baton of that rank, the Kaiser had composed his features behind the famous upturned mustache in an expression "grave even to severity." Of the several emotions churning his susceptible breast, some hints exist in his letters. "I am proud to call this place my home and to be a member of this royal family," he wrote home after spending the night in Windsor Castle in the former apartments of his mother. Sentiment and nostalgia induced by these melancholy occasions with his English relatives jostled with pride in his supremacy among the assembled potentates and with a fierce relish in the disappearance of his uncle from the European scene. He had come to bury Edward his bane; Edward the arch plotter, as William conceived it, of Germany's encirclement; Edward his mother's brother whom he could neither bully nor impress, whose fat figure cast a shadow between Germany and the sun. "He is Satan. You cannot imagine what a Satan he is!"

This verdict, announced by the Kaiser before a dinner of three hundred guests in Berlin in 1907, was occasioned by one of Edward's continental tours undertaken with clearly diabolical designs at encirclement. He had spent a provocative week in Paris, visited for no good reason the King of Spain (who had just married his niece), and finished with a visit to the King of Italy with obvious intent to seduce him from his Triple Alliance with Germany and Austria. The Kaiser, possessor of the least inhibited tongue in Europe, had worked himself into a frenzy ending in another of those comments that had periodically over the past twenty years of his reign shattered the nerves of diplomats.

Happily the Encircler was now dead and replaced by George who, the Kaiser told Theodore Roosevelt a few days before the funeral, was "a very nice boy" (of forty-five, six years younger than the Kaiser). "He is a thorough Englishman and hates all foreigners but I do not mind that as long as he does not hate Germans more than other foreigners." Alongside George, William now rode confidently, saluting as he passed the regimental colors of the 1st Royal Dragoons of which he was honorary colonel. Once he had distributed photographs of himself wearing their uniform with the Delphic inscription written above his signature, "I bide my time." Today his time had come; he was supreme in Europe.

Behind him rode the widowed Queen Alexandra's two brothers, King Frederick of Denmark and King George of the Hellenes; her nephew, King Haakon of Norway; and three kings who were to lose their thrones: Alfonso of Spain, Manuel of Portugal and, wearing a silk turban, King Ferdinand of Bulgaria who annoyed his fellow sovereigns by calling himself Czar and kept in a chest a Byzantine Emperor's full regalia, acquired from a theatrical costumer, against the day when he should reassemble the Byzantine dominions beneath his scepter.

Dazzled by these "splendidly mounted princes," as *The*

Times called them, few observers had eyes for the ninth king, the only one among them who was to achieve greatness as a man. Despite his great height and perfect horsemanship, Albert, King of the Belgians, who disliked the pomp of royal ceremony, contrived in that company to look both embarrassed and absent-minded. He was then thirty-five and had been on the throne barely a year. In later years when his face became known to the world as a symbol of heroism and tragedy, it still always wore that abstracted look, as if his mind were on something else.

The future source of tragedy, tall, corpulent, and corseted, with green plumes waving from his helmet, Archduke Franz Ferdinand of Austria, heir of the old Emperor Franz Josef, rode on Albert's right, and on his left another scion who would never reach his throne, Prince Yussuf, heir of the Sultan of Turkey. After the kings came the royal highnesses: Prince Fushimi, brother of the Emperor of Japan; Grand Duke Michael, brother of the Czar of Russia; the Duke of Aosta in bright blue with green plumes, brother of the King of Italy; Prince Carl, brother of the King of Sweden; Prince Henry, consort of the Queen of Holland; and the Crown Princes of Serbia, Rumania, and Montenegro. The last named, Prince Danilo, "an amiable, extremely handsome young man of delightful manners," resembled the Merry Widow's lover in more than name, for, to the consternation of British functionaries, he had arrived the night before accompanied by a "charming young lady of great personal attractions" whom he introduced as his wife's lady in waiting, come to London to do some shopping.

A regiment of minor German royalty followed: grand dukes of Mecklenburg-Schwerin, Mecklenburg-Strelitz, Schleswig-Holstein, Waldeck-Pyrmont, of Coburg, Saxe-Coburg, and Saxe-Coburg-Gotha, of Saxony, Hesse, Württemberg, Baden, and Bavaria, of whom the last, Crown Prince Rupprecht, was soon to lead a German army in battle. There were a Prince of Siam, a Prince of Persia, five princes of the former French royal house of Orléans, a brother of the Khedive of Egypt wearing a gold-tasseled fez, Prince Tsia-tao of China in an embroidered light-blue gown whose ancient dynasty had two more years to run, and the Kaiser's brother, Prince Henry of Prussia, representing the German Navy, of which he was Commander in

Chief. Amid all this magnificence were three civilian-coated gentlemen, M. Gaston-Carlin of Switzerland, M. Pichon, Foreign Minister of France, and former President Theodore Roosevelt, special envoy of the United States.

Edward, the object of this unprecedented gathering of nations, was often called the "Uncle of Europe," a title which, insofar as Europe's ruling houses were meant, could be taken literally. He was the uncle not only of Kaiser Wilhelm but also, through his wife's sister, the Dowager Empress Marie of Russia, of Czar Nicolas II. His own niece Alix was the Czarina; his daughter Maud was Queen of Norway; another niece, Ena, was Queen of Spain; a third niece, Marie, was soon to be Queen of Rumania. The Danish family of his wife, besides occupying the throne of Denmark, had mothered the Czar of Russia and supplied kings to Greece and Norway. Other relatives, the progeny at various removes of Queen Victoria's nine sons and daughters, were scattered in abundance throughout the courts of Europe.

Yet not family feeling alone nor even the suddenness and shock of Edward's death—for to public knowledge he had been ill one day and dead the next—accounted for the unexpected flood of condolences at his passing. It was in fact a tribute to Edward's great gifts as a sociable king which had proved invaluable to his country. In the nine short years of his reign England's splendid isolation had given way, under pressure, to a series of "understandings" or attachments, but not quite alliances—for England dislikes the definitive—with two old enemies, France and Russia, and one promising new power, Japan. The resulting shift in balance registered itself around the world and affected every state's relations with every other. Though Edward neither initiated nor influenced his country's policy, his personal diplomacy helped to make the change possible.

Taken as a child to visit France, he had said to Napoleon III: "You have a nice country. I would like to be your son." This preference for things French, in contrast to or perhaps in protest against his mother's for the Germanic, lasted, and after her death was put to use. When England, growing edgy over the challenge implicit in Germany's Naval Program of 1900, decided to patch up old quarrels with France, Edward's talents as

Roi Charmeur smoothed the way. In 1903 he went to Paris, disregarding advice that an official state visit would find a cold welcome. On his arrival the crowds were sullen and silent except for a few taunting cries of "*Vivent les Boers!*" and "*Vive Fashoda!*" which the King ignored. To a worried aide who muttered, "The French don't like us," he replied, "Why should they?" and continued bowing and smiling from his carriage.

For four days he made appearances, reviewed troops at Vincennes, attended the races at Longchamps, a gala at the Opéra, a state banquet at the Elysée, a luncheon at the Quai d'Orsay and, at the theater, transformed a chill into smiles by mingling with the audience in the entr'acte and paying gallant compliments in French to a famous actress in the lobby. Everywhere he made gracious and tactful speeches about his friendship and admiration for the French, their "glorious traditions," their "beautiful city," for which he confessed an attachment "fortified by many happy memories," his "sincere pleasure" in the visit, his belief that old misunderstandings are "happily over and forgotten," that the mutual prosperity of France and England was interdependent and their friendship his "constant preoccupation." When he left, the crowds now shouted, "*Vive notre roi!*" "Seldom has such a complete change of attitude been seen as that which has taken place in this country. He has won the hearts of all the French," a Belgian diplomat reported. The German ambassador thought the King's visit was "a most odd affair," and supposed that an Anglo-French *rapprochement* was the result of a "general aversion to Germany." Within a year, after hard work by ministers settling disputes, the *rapprochement* became the Anglo-French Entente, signed in April, 1904.

Germany might have had an English entente for herself had not her leaders, suspecting English motives, rebuffed the overtures of the Colonial Secretary, Joseph Chamberlain, in 1899 and again in 1901. Neither the shadowy Holstein who conducted Germany's foreign affairs from behind the scenes nor the elegant and erudite Chancellor, Prince Bülow, nor the Kaiser himself was quite sure what they suspected England of but they were certain it was something perfidious. The Kaiser always wanted an agreement with England if he could get one without seeming to want it. Once, affected by English surroundings and family sentiment at the funeral of Queen Victoria, he allowed himself to confess the wish to Edward. "Not a mouse could stir in Europe without our permission," was the way he visualized an Anglo-German alliance. But as soon as the English showed signs of willingness, he and his ministers veered off, suspecting some trick. Fearing to be taken advantage of at the conference table, they preferred to stay away altogether and depend upon an ever-growing navy to frighten the English into coming to terms.

Bismarck had warned Germany to be content with land power, but his successors were neither separately nor collectively Bismarcks. He had pursued clearly seen goals unswervingly; they groped for larger horizons with no clear idea of what they wanted. Holstein was a Machiavelli without a policy who operated on only one principle: suspect everyone. Bülow had no principles; he was so slippery, lamented his colleague Admiral Tirpitz, that compared to him an eel was a leech. The flashing, inconstant, always freshly inspired Kaiser had a different goal every hour, and practiced diplomacy as an exercise in perpetual motion.

None of them believed England would ever come to terms with France, and all warnings of that event Holstein dismissed as "naïve," even a most explicit one from his envoy in London, Baron Eckhardstein. At a dinner at Marlborough House in 1902, Eckhardstein had watched Paul Cambon, the French ambassador, disappear into the billiard room with Joseph Chamberlain, where they engaged in "animated conversation" lasting twenty-eight minutes of which the only words he could overhear (the baron's memoirs do not say whether the door was open or he was listening at the keyhole) were "Egypt" and "Morocco." Later he was summoned to the King's study where Edward offered him an 1888 Uppmann cigar and told him that England was going to reach a settlement with France over all disputed colonial questions.

When the Entente became a fact, William's wrath was tremendous. Beneath it, and even more galling, rankled Edward's triumph in Paris. The *reise-Kaiser*, as he was known from the frequency of his travels, derived balm from ceremonial entries into foreign capitals, and the one above all he wished to visit was Paris, the unattainable. He had been everywhere, even to

Jerusalem, where the Jaffa Gate had to be cut to permit his entry on horseback; but Paris, the center of all that was beautiful, all that was desirable, all that Berlin was not, remained closed to him. He wanted to receive the acclaim of Parisians and be awarded the Grand Cordon of the Legion of Honor, and twice let the imperial wish be known to the French. No invitation ever came. He could enter Alsace and make speeches glorifying the victory of 1870; he could lead parades through Metz in Lorraine; but it is perhaps the saddest story of the fate of kings that the Kaiser lived to be eighty-two and died without seeing Paris.

Envy of the older nations gnawed at him. He complained to Theodore Roosevelt that the English nobility on continental tours never visited Berlin but always went to Paris. He felt unappreciated. "All the long years of my reign," he told the King of Italy, "my colleagues, the Monarchs of Europe, have paid no attention to what I have to say. Soon, with my great Navy to endorse my words, they will be more respectful." The same sentiments ran through his whole nation, which suffered, like their emperor, from a terrible need for recognition. Pulsing with energy and ambition, conscious of strength, fed upon Nietzsche and Treitschke, they felt entitled to rule, and cheated that the world did not acknowledge their title. "We must," wrote Friedrich von Bernhardi, the spokesman of militarism, "secure to German nationality and German spirit throughout the globe that high esteem which is due them . . . and has hitherto been withheld from them." He frankly allowed only one method of attaining the goal; lesser Bernhardis from the Kaiser down sought to secure the esteem they craved by threats and show of power. They shook the "mailed fist," demanded their "place in the sun," and proclaimed the virtues of the sword in paeans to "blood and iron" and "shining armor." In German practice Mr. Roosevelt's current precept for getting on with your neighbors was Teutonized to, "Speak loudly and brandish a big gun." When they brandished it, when the Kaiser told his troops departing for China and the Boxer Rebellion to bear themselves as the Huns of Attila (the choice of Huns as German prototypes was his own), when Pan-German Societies and Navy Leagues multiplied and met in congresses to demand that other nations recognize their "legitimate aims" toward expansion, the other nations answered with alliances, and when they did, Germany screamed *Einkreisung!*—Encirclement! The refrain *Deutschland ganzlich einzukreisen* grated over the decade.

Edward's foreign visits continued—Rome, Vienna, Lisbon, Madrid—and not to royalty only. Every year he took the cure at Marienbad where he would exchange views with the Tiger of France, born in the same year as himself, who was premier for four of the years that Edward was king. Edward, whose two passions in life were correct clothes and unorthodox company, overlooked the former, and admired M. Clemenceau. The Tiger shared Napoleon's opinion that Prussia "was hatched from a cannon ball," and saw the cannon ball coming in his direction. He worked, he planned, he maneuvered in the shadow of one dominant idea: "the German lust for power . . . has fixed as its policy the extermination of France." He told Edward that when the time came when France needed help, England's sea power would not be enough, and reminded him that Napoleon was beaten at Waterloo, not Trafalgar.

In 1908, to the distaste of his subjects, Edward paid a state visit to the Czar aboard the imperial yacht at Reval. English imperialists regarded Russia as the ancient foe of the Crimea and more recently as the menace looming over India, while to the Liberals and Laborites Russia was the land of the knout, the pogrom, and the massacred revolutionaries of 1905, and the Czar, according to Mr. Ramsay MacDonald, "a common murderer." The distaste was reciprocated. Russia detested England's alliance with Japan and resented her as the power that frustrated Russia's historic yearning for Constantinople and the Straits. Nicholas II once combined two favorite prejudices in the simple statement, "An Englishman is a *zhid* (Jew)."

But old antagonisms were not so strong as new pressures, and under the urging of the French, who were anxious to have their two allies come to terms, an Anglo-Russian Convention was signed in 1907. A personal touch of royal friendliness was felt to be required to clear away any lingering mistrust, and Edward embarked for Reval. He had long talks with the Russian Foreign Minister, Isvolsky, and danced the Merry Widow waltz with the Czarina with such effect as to make her laugh, the first man to accomplish this feat since the unhappy woman put on the crown of the Romanovs. Nor was it such a frivolous achievement as might appear, for though it could hardly be said that the Czar governed Russia in a working sense, he ruled as an autocrat and was in turn ruled by his strong-willed if weak-witted wife. Beautiful, hysterical, and morbidly suspicious, she hated everyone but her immediate family and a series of fanatic or lunatic charlatans who offered comfort to her desperate soul. The Czar, neither well endowed mentally nor very well educated, was, in the Kaiser's opinion, "only fit to live in a country house and grow turnips."

The Kaiser regarded the Czar as his own sphere of influence and tried by clever schemes to woo him out of his French alliance which had been the consequence of William's own folly. Bismarck's maxim "Keep friends with Russia" and the Reinsurance Treaty that implemented it, William had dropped, along with Bismarck, in the first, and worst, blunder of his reign. Alexander III, the tall, stern Czar of that day, had promptly turned around in 1892 and entered into alliance with republican France, even at the cost of standing at attention to "The Marseillaise." Besides, he snubbed William, whom he considered "*un garçon mal élevé*," and would only talk to him over his shoulder. Ever since Nicholas acceded to the throne, William had been trying to repair his blunder by writing the young Czar long letters (in English) of advice, gossip, and political harangue addressed to "Dearest Nicky" and signed "Your affectionate friend, Willy." An irreligious republic stained by the blood of monarchs was no fit company for him, he told the Czar. "Nicky, take my word for it, the curse of God has stricken that people forever." Nicky's true interests, Willy told him, were with a *Drei-Kaiser Bund*, a league of the three emperors of Russia, Austria, and Germany. Yet, remembering the old Czar's snubs, he could not help patronizing his son. He would tap Nicholas on the shoulder, and say, "My advice to you is more speeches and more parades, more speeches, more parades," and he offered to send German troops to protect Nicholas from his rebellious subjects, a suggestion which infuriated the Czarina, who hated William more after every exchange of visits.

When he failed, under the circumstances, to wean Russia away from France, the Kaiser drew up an ingenious treaty engaging Russia and Germany to aid each other in case of attack, which the Czar, after signing, was to communicate to the French and invite them to join. After Russia's disasters in her war with Japan (which the Kaiser had strenuously urged her into) and the revolutionary risings that followed, when the regime was at its lowest ebb, he invited the Czar to a secret rendezvous, without attendant ministers, at Björkö in the Gulf of Finland. William knew well enough that Russia could not accede to his treaty without breaking faith with the French, but he thought that sovereigns' signatures were all that was needed to erase the difficulty. Nicholas signed.

William was in ecstasy. He had made good the fatal lapse, secured Germany's back door, and broken the encirclement. "Bright tears stood in my eyes," he wrote to Bülow, and he was sure Grandpapa (William I, who had died muttering about a war on two fronts) was looking down on him. He felt his treaty to be the master coup of German diplomacy, as indeed it was, or would have been, but for a flaw in the title. When the Czar brought the treaty home, his ministers, after one horrified look, pointed out that by engaging to join Germany in a possible war he had repudiated his alliance with France, a detail which "no doubt escaped His Majesty in the flood of the Emperor William's eloquence." The Treaty of Björkö lived its brief shimmering day, and expired.

Now came Edward hobnobbing with the Czar at Reval. Reading the German ambassador's report of the meeting which suggested that Edward really desired peace, the Kaiser scribbled furiously in the margin, "Lies. He wants war. But I have to start it so he does not have the odium."

The year closed with the most explosive faux pas of the Kaiser's career, an interview given to the *Daily Telegraph* expressing his ideas of the day on who should fight whom, which this time unnerved not only his neighbors but his countrymen. Public disapproval was so outspoken that the Kaiser took to his bed, was ill for three weeks, and remained comparatively reticent for some time thereafter.

Since then no new excitements had erupted. The last two years of the decade while Europe enjoyed a rich fat afternoon, were the quietest. Nineteen-ten was peaceful and prosperous, with the second round of Moroccan crises and Balkan wars still to come. A new book, *The Great Illusion* by Norman Angell, had just been published, which proved that war was impossible. By impressive examples and incontrovertible argument Angell showed that in the present financial and economic interdependence of nations, the victor would suffer equally with the vanquished; therefore war had become unprofitable; therefore no nation would be so foolish as to start one. Already translated into eleven languages, *The Great Illusion* had become a cult. At the universities, in Manchester, Glasgow, and other industrial cities, more than forty study groups of true believers had formed, devoted to propagating its dogma. Angell's most earnest disciple was a man of great influence on military policy, the King's friend and adviser, Viscount Esher, chairman of the War Committee assigned to remaking the British Army after the shock of its performance in the Boer War. Lord Esher delivered lectures on the lesson of *The Great Illusion* at Cambridge and the Sorbonne wherein he showed how "new economic factors clearly prove the inanity of aggressive wars." A twentieth century war would be on such a scale, he said, that its inevitable consequences of "commercial disaster, financial ruin and individual suffering" would be "so pregnant with restraining influences" as to make war unthinkable. He told an audience of officers at the United Service Club, with the Chief of General Staff, Sir John French, in the chair, that because of the interlacing of nations war "becomes every day more difficult and improbable."

Germany, Lord Esher felt sure, "is as receptive as Great Britain to the doctrine of Norman Angell." How receptive were the Kaiser and the Crown Prince to whom he gave, or caused to be given, copies of *The Great Illusion* is not reported. There is no evidence that he gave one to General von Bernhardi, who was engaged in 1910 in writing a book called *Germany and the Next War*, published in the following year, which was to be as influential as Angell's but from the opposite point of view. Three of its chapter titles, "The Right to Make War," "The Duty to Make War," and "World Power or Downfall" sum up its thesis.

As a twenty-one-year-old cavalry officer in 1870, Bernhardi had been the first German to ride through the Arc de Triomphe when the Germans entered Paris. Since then flags and glory interested him less than the theory, philosophy, and science of war as applied to "Germany's Historic Mission," another of his chapter titles. He had served as chief of the Military History section of the General Staff, was one of the intellectual elite of that hard-thinking, hard-working body, and author of a classic on cavalry before he assembled a lifetime's studies of Clausewitz, Treitschke, and Darwin, and poured them into the book that was to make his name a synonym for Mars.

War, he stated, "is a biological necessity"; it is the carrying out among humankind of "the natural law, upon which all the laws of Nature rest, the law of the struggle for existence." Nations, he said, must progress or decay; "there can be no standing still," and Germany must choose "world power or downfall." Among the nations Germany "is in social-political respects at the head of all progress in culture" but is "compressed into narrow, unnatural limits." She cannot attain her "great moral ends" without increased political power, an enlarged sphere of influence, and new territory. This increase in power, "befitting our importance," and "which we are entitled to claim," is a "political necessity" and "the first and foremost duty of the State." In his own italics Bernhardi announced, "What we now wish to attain must be *fought for*," and from here he galloped home to the finish line: "Conquest thus becomes a law of necessity."

Having proved the "necessity" (the favorite word of German military thinkers), Bernhardi proceeded to method. Once the duty to make war is recognized, the secondary duty, to make it successfully, follows. To be successful a state must begin war at the "most favorable moment" of its own choosing; it has "the acknowledged right . . . to secure the proud privilege of such initiative." Offensive war thus becomes another "necessity" and a second conclusion inescapable: "It is incumbent on us . . . to act on the offensive and strike the first blow." Bernhardi did not share the Kaiser's concern about the "odium" that attached to an aggressor. Nor was he reluctant to tell where the blow would fall. It was "unthinkable," he wrote, that Germany and France could ever negotiate their problems. "France must be so completely crushed that she can never cross our path again"; she "must be annihilated once and for all as a great power."

King Edward did not live to read Bernhardi. In January, 1910, he sent the Kaiser his annual birthday greetings and the gift of a walking stick before departing for Marienbad and Biarritz. A few months later he was dead.

"We have lost the mainstay of our foreign policy," said Isvolsky when he heard the news. This was hyperbole, for Edward was merely the instrument, not the architect, of the new alignments. In France the king's death created "profound emotion" and "real consternation," according to *Le Figaro*. Paris, it said, felt the loss of its "great friend" as deeply as London. Lampposts and shop windows in the Rue de la Paix wore the same black as Piccadilly; cab drivers tied crepe bows on their whips; black-draped portraits of the late king appeared even in the provincial towns as at the death of a great French citizen. In Tokyo, in tribute to the Anglo-Japanese alliance, houses bore the crossed flags of England and Japan with the staves draped in black. In Germany, whatever the feelings, correct procedures were observed. All officers of the army and navy were ordered to wear mourning for eight days, and the fleet in home waters fired a salute and flew its flags at half-mast. The Reichstag rose to its feet to hear a message of sympathy read by its President, and the Kaiser called in person upon the British ambassador in a visit that lasted an hour and a half.

In London the following week the royal family was kept busy meeting royal arrivals at Victoria Station. The Kaiser came over on his yacht the *Hohenzollern*, escorted by four British destroyers. He anchored in the Thames Estuary and came the rest of the way to London by train, arriving at Victoria Station like the common royalty. A purple carpet was rolled out on the platform, and purple-covered steps placed where his carriage would stop. As his train drew in on the stroke of noon, the familiar figure of the German emperor stepped down to be greeted by his cousin, King George, whom he kissed on both cheeks. After lunch they went together to Westminster Hall where the body of Edward lay in state. A thunderstorm the night before and drenching rains all morning had not deterred the quiet, patient line of Edward's subjects waiting to pass through the hall. On this day, Thursday, May 19, the line stretched back for five miles. It was the day the earth was due to pass through the tail of Halley's comet, whose appearance called forth reminders that it was traditionally the prophet of disaster—had it not heralded the Norman Conquest?—and inspired journals with literary editors to print the lines from *Julius Caesar*:

> When beggars die there are no comets seen;
> The heavens themselves blaze forth the death of princes.

Inside the vast hall the bier lay in somber majesty, surmounted by crown, orb, and scepter and guarded at its four corners by four officers, each from different regiments of the empire, who stood in the traditional attitude of mourning with bowed heads and white gloved hands crossed over sword hilts. The Kaiser eyed all the customs of an imperial Lying-in-State with professional interest. He was deeply impressed, and years later could recall every detail of the scene in its "marvelous medieval setting." He saw the sun's rays filtered through the narrow Gothic windows lighting up the jewels of the crown; he watched the changing of the guards at the bier as the four new guards marched forward with swords at the carry-up and turned them point down as they reached their places, while the guards they relieved glided away in slow motion to disappear through some unseen exit in the shadows. Laying his wreath of purple and white flowers on the coffin, he knelt with King George in silent prayer and on rising grasped his cousin's hand in a manly and sympathetic handshake. The gesture, widely reported, caused much favorable comment.

Publicly his performance was perfect; privately he could not resist the opportunity for fresh scheming. At a dinner given by the King that night at Buckingham Palace for the seventy royal mourners and special ambassadors, he buttonholed M. Pichon of France and proposed to him that in the event Germany should find herself opposed to England in a conflict, France should side with Germany. In view of the occasion and the place, this latest imperial brainstorm caused the same fuss, that had once moved Sir Edward Grey, England's harassed Foreign Secretary, to remark wistfully, "The other sovereigns are so much *quieter*." The Kaiser later denied he had ever said anything of the kind; he had merely discussed Morocco and "some other political matters." M. Pichon could only be got to say discreetly that the Kaiser's language had been "amiable and pacific."

Next morning, in the procession, where for once he could not talk, William's behavior was exemplary. He kept his horse reined in, a head behind King George's, and, to Conan Doyle, special correspondent for the occasion, looked so "noble that England has lost something of her old kindliness if she does not take him back into her heart today." When the procession reached Westminster Hall he was the first to dismount and, as Queen Alexandra's carriage drew up, "he ran to the door with such alacrity that he reached it before the royal servants," only to find that the Queen was about to descend on the other side. William scampered nimbly around, still ahead of the servants, reached the door first, handed out the widow, and kissed her with the affection of a bereaved nephew. Fortunately, King George came up at this moment to rescue his mother and escort her himself, for she loathed the Kaiser, both personally and for the sake of Schleswig-Holstein. Though he had been but eight years old when Germany seized the duchies from Denmark, she had never forgiven him or his country. When her son on a visit to Berlin in 1890 was made honorary colonel of a Prussian regiment, she wrote to him: "And so my Georgie boy has become a real live filthy blue-coated Pickelhaube German soldier!!! Well, I never thought to have lived to see that! But never mind, . . . it was your misfortune and not your fault."

A roll of muffled drums and the wail of bagpipes sounded as the coffin wrapped in the Royal Standard was borne from the Hall by a score of blue-jackets in straw hats. A sudden shiver of sabers glittered in the sun as the cavalry came to attention. At a signal of four sharp whistles the sailors hoisted the coffin on to the gun carriage draped in purple, red, and white. The cortege moved on between motionless lines of grenadiers like red walls that hemmed in the packed black masses of perfectly silent people. London was never so crowded, never so still. Alongside and behind the gun carriage, drawn by the Royal Horse Artillery, walked His late Majesty's sixty-three aides-de-camp, all colonels or naval captains and all peers, among them five dukes, four marquises, and thirteen earls. England's three

Field Marshals, Lord Kitchener, Lord Roberts, and Sir Evelyn Wood, rode together. Six Admirals of the Fleet followed, and after them, walking all alone, Edward's great friend, Sir John Fisher, the stormy, eccentric former First Sea Lord with his queer un-English mandarin's face. Detachments from all the famous regiments, the Coldstreams, the Gordon Highlanders, the household cavalry and cavalry of the line, the Horse Guards and Lancers and Royal Fusiliers, brilliant Hussars and Dragoons of the German, Russian, Austrian, and other foreign cavalry units of which Edward had been honorary officer, admirals of the German Navy—almost, it seemed to some disapproving observers, too great a military show in the funeral of a man called the "Peacemaker."

His horse with empty saddle and boots reversed in the stirrups led by two grooms and, trotting along behind, his wire-haired terrier, Caesar, added a pang of personal sentiment. On came the pomp of England: Poursuivants of Arms in emblazoned medieval tabards, Silver Stick in Waiting, White Staves, equerries, archers of Scotland, judges in wigs and black robes, and the Lord Chief Justice in scarlet, bishops in ecclesiastical purple, Yeomen of the Guard in black velvet hats and frilled Elizabethan collars, an escort of trumpeters, and then the parade of kings, followed by a glass coach bearing the widowed Queen and her sister, the Dowager Empress of Russia, and twelve other coaches of queens, ladies, and Oriental potentates.

Along Whitehall, the Mall, Piccadilly, and the Park to Paddington Station, where the body was to go by train to Windsor for burial, the long procession moved. The Royal Horse Guards' band played the "Dead March" from *Saul*. People felt a finality in the slow tread of the marchers and in the solemn music. Lord Esher wrote in his diary after the funeral: "There never was such a break-up. All the old buoys which have marked the channel of our lives seem to have been swept away."

PLANS

2

"Let the Last Man on the Right Brush the Channel with His Sleeve"

COUNT ALFRED VON SCHLIEFFEN, Chief of the German General Staff from 1891 to 1906 was, like all German officers, schooled in Clausewitz's precept, "The heart of France lies between Brussels and Paris." It was a frustrating axiom because the path it pointed to was forbidden by Belgian neutrality, which Germany, along with the other four major European powers, had guaranteed in perpetuity. Believing that war was a certainty and that Germany must enter it under conditions that gave her the most promise of success, Schlieffen determined not to allow the Belgian difficulty to stand in Germany's way. Of the two classes of Prussian officer, the bullnecked and the wasp-waisted, he belonged to the second. Monocled and effete in appearance, cold and distant in manner, he concentrated with such single-mindedness on his profession that when an aide, at the end of an all-night staff ride in East Prussia, pointed out to him the beauty of the river Pregel sparkling in the rising sun, the General gave a brief, hard look and replied, "An unimportant obstacle." So too, he decided, was Belgian neutrality.

A neutral and independent Belgium was the creation of England, or rather of England's ablest Foreign Minister, Lord Palmerston. Belgium's coast was England's frontier; on the plains of Belgium, Wellington had defeated the greatest threat to England since the Armada. Thereafter England was determined to make that patch of open, easily traversible territory a neutral zone and, under the post-Napoleon settlement of the Congress of Vienna, agreed with the other powers to attach it to the Kingdom of the Netherlands. Resenting union with a Protestant power, burning with the fever of the nineteenth century nationalism, the Belgians revolted in 1830, setting off an international scramble. The Dutch fought to retain their province; the French, eager to reabsorb what they had once ruled, moved in; the autocratic states—Russia, Prussia, and Austria—bent on keeping Europe clamped under the vise of Vienna, were ready to shoot at the first sign of revolt anywhere.

Lord Palmerston outmaneuvered them all. He knew that a subject province would be an eternal temptation to one neighbor or another and that only an independent nation, resolved to maintain its own integrity, could survive as a safety zone. Through nine years of nerve, of suppleness, of never swerving from his aim, of calling out the British fleet when necessary, he played off all contenders and secured an international treaty guaranteeing Belgium as an "independent and perpetually neutral state." The treaty was signed in 1839 by England, France, Russia, Prussia, and Austria.

Ever since 1892, when France and Russia had joined in military alliance, it was clear that four of the five signatories of the Belgian treaty would be automatically engaged—two against two—in the war for which Schlieffen had to plan. Europe was a heap of swords piled as delicately as jackstraws; one could not be pulled out without moving the others. Under the terms of the Austro-German alliance, Germany was obliged to support Austria in any conflict with Russia. Under the terms of the alliance between France and Russia, both parties were obliged to move against Germany if either became involved in a "defensive war" with Germany. These arrangements made it inevitable that in any war in which she engaged, Germany would have to fight on two fronts against both Russia and France.

What part England would play was uncertain; she might remain neutral; she might, if given cause, come in against Germany. That Belgium could be the cause was no secret. In the Franco-Prussian War of 1870, when Germany was still a climbing power, Bismarck had been happy enough, upon a hint from England, to reaffirm the inviolability of Belgium. Gladstone had secured a treaty from both belligerents providing that if either violated Belgian neutrality, England would cooperate with the other to the extent of defending Belgium, though without engaging in the general operations of the war. Although there was something a little impractical about the tail of this Gladstonian formula, the Germans had no reason to suppose its underlying motive any less operative in 1914 than in 1870. Nevertheless, Schlieffen decided, in the event of war, to attack France by way of Belgium.

His reason was "military necessity." In a two-front war, he wrote, "the whole of Germany must throw itself upon *one* enemy, the strongest, most powerful, most dangerous enemy, and that can only be France." Schlieffen's completed plan for 1906, the year he retired, allocated six weeks and seven-eighths of Germany's forces to smash France while one-eighth was to hold her eastern frontier against Russia until the bulk of her army could be brought back to face the second enemy. He chose France first because Russia could frustrate a quick victory by simply withdrawing within her infinite room, leaving Germany to be sucked into an endless campaign as Napoleon had been. France was both closer at hand and quicker to mobilize. The German and French armies each required two weeks to complete mobilization before a major attack could begin on the fifteenth day. Russia, according to German arithmetic, because of her vast distances, huge numbers, and meager railroads, would take six weeks before she could launch a major offensive, by which time France would be beaten.

The risk of leaving East Prussia, hearth of Junkerdom and the Hohenzollerns, to be held by only nine divisions was hard to accept, but Frederick the Great had said, "It is better to lose a province than split the forces with which one seeks victory," and nothing so comforts the military mind as the maxim of a great but dead general. Only by throwing the utmost numbers against the West could France be finished off quickly. Only by a strategy of envelopment, using Belgium as a pathway, could the German armies, in Schlieffen's opinion, attack France successfully. His reasoning, from the purely military point of view, appeared faultless.

The German Army of a million and a half that was to be used against France was now six times the size it had been in 1870, and needed room to maneuver. French fortresses constructed along the frontiers of Alsace and Lorraine after 1870 precluded the Germans from making a frontal attack across the common border. A protracted siege would provide no opportunity, as long as French lines to the rear remained open, of netting the enemy quickly in a battle of annihilation. Only by envelopment could the French be taken from behind and destroyed. But at either end of the French lines lay neutral territory—Switzerland and Belgium. There was not enough room for the huge German Army to get around the French armies and still stay inside France. The Germans had done it in 1870 when both armies were small, but now it was a matter of moving an army of millions to outflank an army of millions. Space, roads, and railroads were essential. The flat plains of Flanders had them. In Belgium there was both room for the outflanking maneuver which was Schlieffen's formula for success as well as a way to avoid the frontal attack which was his formula for disaster.

Clausewitz, oracle of German military thought, had ordained a quick victory by "decisive battle" as the first object in offensive war. Occupation of the enemy's territory and gaining control of his resources was secondary. To speed an early decision was essential. Time counted above all else. Anything that protracted a campaign Clausewitz condemned. "Gradual reduction" of the enemy, or a war of attrition, he feared like the pit of hell. He wrote in the decade of Waterloo, and his works had been accepted as the Bible of strategy ever since.

To achieve decisive victory, Schlieffen fixed upon a strategy derived from Hannibal and the Battle of Cannae. The dead general who mesmerized Schlieffen had been dead a very long time. Two thousand years had passed since Hannibal's classic double envelopment of the Romans at Cannae. Field gun and machine gun had replaced bow and arrow and slingshot, Schlieffen wrote, "but the principles of strategy remain unchanged. The enemy's front is not the objective. The essential thing is to crush the enemy's flanks . . . and complete the extermination by attack upon his rear." Under Schlieffen, envelopment became the fetish and frontal attack the anathema of the German General Staff.

Schlieffen's first plan to include the violation of Belgium was formulated in 1899. It called for cutting across the corner of Belgium east of the Meuse. Enlarged with each successive year, by 1905 it had expanded into a huge enveloping right-wing sweep in which the German armies would cross Belgium from Liège to Brussels before turning southward, where they could take advantage of the open country of Flanders, to march against France. Everything depended upon a quick decision against France, and even the long way around through Flanders would be quicker than laying siege to the fortress line across the common border.

Schlieffen did not have enough divisions for a double envelopment of France à la Cannae. For this he substituted a heavily one-sided right wing that would spread across the whole of Belgium on both sides of the Meuse, sweep down through the country like a monstrous hayrake, cross the Franco-Belgian frontier along its entire width, and descend upon Paris along the Valley of the Oise. The German mass would come between the capital and the French armies which, drawn back to meet the menace, would be caught, away from their fortified areas, in the decisive battle of annihilation. Essential to the plan was a deliberately weak German left wing on the Alsace-Lorraine front which would tempt the French in that area forward into a "sack" between Metz and the Vosges. It was expected that the French, intent upon liberating their lost provinces, would attack here, and it was considered so much the better for the success of the German plan if they did, for they could be held in the sack by the German left wing while the main victory was obtained from behind. In the back of Schlieffen's mind always glimmered the hope that, as battle unfolded, a counterattack by his left wing could be mounted in order to bring about a true double envelopment—the "colossal Cannae" of his dreams. Sternly saving his greatest strength for the right wing, he did not yield to that vaulting ambition in his plan. But the lure of the left wing remained to tempt his successors.

Thus the Germans came to Belgium. Decisive battle dictated envelopment, and envelopment dictated the use of Belgian territory. The German General Staff pronounced it a military necessity; Kaiser and Chancellor accepted it with more or less equanimity. Whether it was advisable, whether it was even expedient in view of the probable effect on world opinion, especially on neutral opinion, was irrelevant. That it seemed necessary to the triumph of German arms was the only criterion. Germans had imbibed from 1870 the lesson that arms and war were the sole source of German greatness. They had been taught by Field Marshal von der Goltz, in his book *The Nation in Arms*, that "We have won our position through the sharpness of our sword, not through the sharpness of our mind." The decision to violate Belgian neutrality followed easily.

Character is fate, the Greeks believed. A hundred years of German philosophy went into the making of this decision in which the seed of self-destruction lay embedded, waiting for its hour. The voice was Schlieffen's, but the hand was the hand of Fichte who saw the German people chosen by Providence to occupy the supreme place in the history of the universe, of Hegel who saw them leading the world to a glorious destiny of compulsory *Kultur*, of Nietzsche who told them that Supermen were above ordinary controls, of Treitschke who set the increase of power as the highest moral duty of the state, of the whole German people, who called their temporal ruler the "All-Highest." What made the Schlieffen plan was not Clausewitz and the Battle of Cannae, but the body of accumulated egoism which suckled the German people and created a nation fed on "the desperate delusion of the will that deems itself absolute."

The goal, decisive battle, was a product of the victories over Austria and France in 1866 and 1870. Dead battles, like dead generals, hold the military mind in their dead grip, and Germans, no less than other peoples, prepare for the last war. They staked everything on decisive battle in the image of Hannibal, but even the ghost of Hannibal might have reminded Schlieffen that though Carthage won at Cannae, Rome won the war.

Old Field Marshal Moltke in 1890 foretold that the next war might last seven years—or thirty—because the resources of a modern state were so great it would not know itself to be beaten after a single military defeat and would not give up. His nephew and namesake who succeeded Schlieffen as Chief of Staff also had moments when he saw the truth as clearly. In a moment of heresy to Clausewitz, he said to the Kaiser in 1906, "It will be a national war which will not be settled by a decisive battle but by a long wearisome struggle with a country that will not be overcome until its whole national force is broken, and a war which will utterly exhaust our own people, even if we are victorious." It went against human nature, however—and the nature of General Staffs—to follow through the logic of his own prophecy. Amorphous and without limits, the concept of a long war could not be scientifically planned for as could the orthodox, predictable, and simple solution of decisive battle and a short war. The younger Moltke was already Chief of Staff when he made his prophecy, but neither he nor his Staff, nor the Staff of any other country, ever made any effort to plan for a long war. Besides the two Moltkes, one dead and the other infirm of purpose, some military strategists in other countries glimpsed the possibility of prolonged war, but all preferred to believe, along with the bankers and industrialists, that because of the dislocation of economic life a general European war could not last longer than three or four months. One constant among the elements of 1914—as of any era—was the disposition of everyone on all sides not to prepare for the harder alternative, not to act upon what they suspected to be true.

Schlieffen, having embraced the strategy of "decisive battle," pinned Germany's fate to it. He expected France to violate Belgium as soon as Germany's deployment at the Belgian frontier revealed her strategy, and he therefore planned that Germany should do it first and faster. "Belgian neutrality must be broken by one side or the other," his thesis ran. "Whoever gets there first and occupies Brussels and imposes a war levy of some 1,000 million francs has the upper hand."

Indemnity, which enables a state to conduct war at the enemy's expense instead of its own, was a secondary object laid down by Clausewitz. His third was the winning of public opinion, which is accomplished by "gaining great victories and possession of the enemy's capital" and which helps to bring an end to resistance. He knew how material success could gain public opinion; he forgot how moral failure could lose it, which too can be a hazard of war.

It was a hazard the French never lost sight of, and it led them to the opposite conclusion from the one Schlieffen expected. Belgium was their pathway of attack too, through the Ardennes if not through Flanders, but their plan of campaign prohibited their armies from using it until after the Germans had violated Belgium first. To them the logic of the matter was clear: Belgium was an open path in either direction; whether Germany or France would use it depended on which of the two wanted war the more. As a French general said, "The one that willed war more than the other could not help but will the violation of Belgian neutrality."

Schlieffen and his Staff did not think Belgium would fight and add its six divisions to the French forces. When Chancellor Bülow, discussing the problem with Schlieffen in 1904, reminded him of Bismarck's warning that it would be against "plain common sense" to add another enemy to the forces against Germany, Schlieffen twisted his monocle several times in his eye, as was his habit, and said: "Of course. We haven't grown stupider since then." But Belgium would not resist by force of arms; she would be satisfied to protest, he said.

German confidence on this score was due to placing rather too high a value on the well-known avarice of Leopold II, who was King of the Belgians in Schlieffen's time. Tall and imposing with his black spade beard and his aura of wickedness composed of mistresses, money, Congo cruelties, and other scandals, Leopold was, in the opinion of Emperor Franz Josef of Austria, "a thoroughly bad man." There were few men who could be so described, the Emperor said, but the King of the Belgians was one. Because Leopold was avaricious, among other vices, the Kaiser supposed that avarice would rule over common sense, and he conceived a clever plan to tempt Leopold into alliance with an offer of French territory. Whenever the Kaiser was seized with a project he attempted instantly to execute it, usually to his astonishment and chagrin when it did not work. In 1904 he invited Leopold to visit him in Berlin, spoke to him in "the kindest way in the world" about his proud forefathers, the Dukes of Burgundy, and offered to re-create the old Duchy of Burgundy for him out of Artois, French Flanders, and the French Ardennes. Leopold gazed at him "open-mouthed," then, attempting to pass it off with a laugh, reminded the Kaiser that much had changed since the fifteenth century. In any event, he said, his Ministers and Parliament would never consider such a suggestion.

That was the wrong thing to say, for the Kaiser flew into one of his rages and scolded the King for putting respect for Parliament and Ministers above respect for the finger of God (with which William sometimes confused himself). "I told him," William reported to Chancellor von Bülow, "I could not be played with. Whoever in the case of a European war was not with me was against me." He was a soldier, he proclaimed, in the school of Napoleon and Frederick the Great who began their wars by forestalling their enemies, and "so should I, in the event of Belgium's not being on my side, be actuated by strategical considerations only."

This declared intent, the first explicit threat to tear up the treaty, dumfounded King Leopold. He drove off to the station with his helmet on back to front, looking to the aide who accompanied him "as if he had had a shock of some kind."

Although the Kaiser's scheme failed, Leopold was still expected to barter Belgium's neutrality for a purse of two million pounds sterling. When a French intelligence officer, who was told this figure by a German officer after the war, expressed surprise at its generosity, he was reminded that "the French would have had to pay for it." Even after Leopold was succeeded in 1909 by his nephew King Albert, a very different quantity, Belgium's resistance was still expected by Schlieffen's successors to be a formality. It might, for example, suggested a German diplomat in 1911, take the form of "lining up her army along the road taken by the German forces."

Schlieffen designated thirty-four divisions to take the roads through Belgium, disposing on their way of Belgium's six divisions if, as seemed to the Germans unlikely, they chose to resist. The Germans were intensely anxious that they should not, because resistance would mean destruction of railways and bridges and consequent dislocation of the schedule to which the German Staff was passionately attached. Belgian acquiescence, on the other hand, would avoid the necessity of tying up divisions in siege of the Belgian fortresses and would also tend to silence public disapproval of Germany's act. To persuade Belgium against futile resistance, Schlieffen arranged that she should be confronted, prior to invasion, by an ultimatum requiring her to yield "all fortresses, railways and troops" or face bombardment of her fortified cities. Heavy artillery was ready to transform the threat of bombardment into reality, if necessary. The heavy guns would in any case, Schlieffen wrote in 1912, be needed further on in the campaign. "The great industrial town of Lille, for example, offers an excellent target for bombardment."

Schlieffen wanted his right wing to reach as far west as Lille in order to make the envelopment of the French complete. "When you march into France," he said, "let the last man on the right brush the Channel with his sleeve." Furthermore, counting on British belligerency, he wanted a wide sweep in order to rake in a British Expeditionary Force along with the French. He placed a higher value on the blockade potential of British sea power than on the British Army, and therefore was determined to achieve a quick victory over French and British land forces and an early decision of the war before the economic consequences of British hostility could make themselves felt. To that end everything must go to swell the right wing. He had to make it powerful in numbers because the density of soldiers per mile determined the extent of territory that could be covered.

Employing the active army alone, he would not have enough divisions both to hold his eastern frontier against a Russian breakthrough and to achieve the superiority in numbers over France which he needed for a quick victory. His solution was simple if revolutionary. He decided to use reserve units in the front line. According to prevailing military doctrine, only the youngest men, fresh from the rigors and discipline of barracks and drill, were fit to fight; reserves who had finished their compulsory military service and returned to civilian life were considered soft and were not wanted in the battle line. Except for men under twenty-six who were merged with the active units, the reserves were formed into divisions of their own, intended for use as occupation troops and for other rear duty. Schlieffen changed all that. He added some twenty reserve divisions (the number varied according to the year of the plan) to the line of march of the fifty or more active divisions. With this increase in numbers his cherished envelopment became possible.

After retiring in 1906 he spent his last years still writing about Cannae, improving his plan, composing memoranda to guide his successors, and died at eighty in 1913, muttering at the end: "It must come to a fight. Only make the right wing strong."

His successor, the melancholy General von Moltke, was something of a pessimist who lacked Schlieffen's readiness to concentrate all his strength in one maneuver. If Schlieffen's motto was "Be bold, be bold," Moltke's was, "But not too bold." He worried both about the weakness of his left wing against the French and about the weakness of the forces left to defend East Prussia against the Russians. He even debated with his Staff the advisability of fighting a defensive war against France, but rejected the idea because it precluded all possibility of "engaging the enemy on his own territory." The Staff agreed that the invasion of Belgium would be "entirely just and necessary" because the war would be one for the "defense and existence of Germany." Schlieffen's plan was maintained, and Moltke consoled himself with the thought, as he said in 1913, that "We must put aside all commonplaces as to the responsibility of the aggressor. . . . Success alone justifies war." But just to be safe everywhere, each year, cutting into Schlieffen's dying request, he borrowed strength from the right wing to add to the left.

Moltke planned for a German left wing of 8 corps numbering about 320,000 men to hold the front in Alsace and Lorraine south of Metz. The German center of 11 corps numbering about 400,000 men would invade France through Luxembourg and the Ardennes. The German right wing of 16 corps numbering about 700,000 men would attack through Belgium, smash the famed gateway fortresses of Liège and Namur which held the Meuse, and fling itself across the river to reach the flat country and straight roads on the far side. Every day's schedule of march was fixed in advance. The Belgians were not expected to fight, but if they did the power of the German assault was expected to persuade them quickly to surrender. The schedule called for the roads through Liège to be open by the twelfth day of mobilization, Brussels to be taken by M-19, the French frontier crossed on M-22, a line Thionville-St. Quentin reached by M-31, Paris and decisive victory by M-39.

The plan of campaign was as rigid and complete as the blueprint for a battleship. Heeding Clausewitz's warning that military plans which leave no room for the unexpected can lead to disaster, the Germans with infinite care had attempted to provide for every contingency. Their staff officers, trained at maneuvers and at war-college desks to supply the correct solution for any given set of circumstances, were expected to cope with the unexpected. Against that elusive, that mocking and perilous quantity, every precaution had been taken except one—flexibility.

While the plan for maximum effort against France hardened, Moltke's fears of Russia gradually lessened as his General Staff evolved a credo, based on a careful count of Russian railway mileage, that Russia would not be "ready" for war until 1916. This was confirmed in German minds by their spies' reports of Russian remarks "that something was going to begin in 1916."

In 1914 two events sharpened Germany's readiness to a fine point. In April, England had begun naval talks with the Russians, and in June, Germany herself had completed the widening of the Kiel Canal, permitting her new dreadnoughts direct access from the North Sea to the Baltic. On learning of the Anglo-Russian talks, Moltke said in May during a visit to his Austrian opposite number, Franz Conrad von Hötzendorff, that from now on "any adjournment will have the effect of diminishing our chances of success." Two weeks later, on June 1st, he said to Baron Eckhardstein, "We are ready, and the sooner the better for us."

3

The Shadow of Sedan

GENERAL DE CASTELNAU, Deputy Chief of the French General Staff, was visited at the War Office one day in 1913 by the Military Governor of Lille, General Lebas, who came to protest the General Staff's decision to abandon Lille as a fortified city. Situated ten miles from the Belgian border and forty miles inland from the Channel, Lille lay close to the path that an invading army would take if it came by way of Flanders. In answer to General Lebas' plea for its defense, General de Castelnau spread out a map and measured with a ruler the distance from the German border to Lille by way of Belgium. The normal density of troops required for a vigorous offensive, he reminded his caller, was five or six to a meter. If the Germans extended themselves as far west as Lille, De Castelnau pointed out, they would be stretched out two to a meter.

"We'll cut them in half!" he declared. The German active Army, he explained, could dispose of twenty-five corps, about a million men, on the Western Front. "Here, figure it out for yourself," he said, handing Lebas the ruler. "If they come as far as Lille," he repeated with sardonic satisfaction, "so much the better for us."

French strategy did not ignore the threat of envelopment by a German right wing. On the contrary, the French General Staff believed that the stronger the Germans made their right wing, the correspondingly weaker they would leave their center and left where the French Army planned to break through. French strategy turned its back to the Belgian frontier and its face to the Rhine. While the Germans were taking the long way around to fall upon the French flank, the French planned a two-pronged offensive that would smash through the German center and left on either side of the German fortified area at Metz and by victory there, sever the German right wing from its base, rendering it harmless. It was a bold plan born of an idea—an idea inherent in the recovery of France from the humiliation of Sedan.

Under the peace terms dictated by Germany at Versailles in 1871, France had suffered amputation, indemnity, and occupation. Even a triumphal march by the German Army down the Champs Elysées was among the terms imposed. It took place along a silent, black-draped avenue empty of onlookers. At Bordeaux, when the French Assembly ratified the peace terms, the deputies of Alsace-Lorraine walked from the hall in tears, leaving behind their protest: "We proclaim forever the right of Alsatians and Lorrainers to remain members of the French nation. We swear for ourselves, our constituents, our children and our children's children to claim that right for all time, by every means, in the face of the usurper."

The annexation, though opposed by Bismarck, who said it would be the Achilles' heel of the new German Empire, was required by the elder Moltke and his Staff. They insisted, and convinced the Emperor, that the border provinces with Metz, Strasbourg, and the crest of the Vosges must be sliced off in order to put France geographically forever on the defensive. They added a crushing indemnity of five billion francs intended to hobble France for a generation, and lodged an army of occupation until it should be paid. With one enormous effort the French raised and paid off the sum within three years, and their recovery began.

The memory of Sedan remained, a stationary dark shadow on the French consciousness. "*N'en parlez jamais; pensez-y toujours*" (Never speak of it; think of it always) had counseled Gambetta. For more than forty years the thought of "Again" was the single most fundamental factor of French policy. In the early years after 1870, instinct and military weakness dictated a fortress strategy. France walled herself in behind a system of entrenched camps connected by forts. Two fortified lines, Belfort-Epinal and Toul-Verdun, guarded the eastern frontier, and one, Maubeuge-Valenciennes-Lille, guarded the western half of the Belgian frontier; the gaps between were intended to canalize the invasion forces.

Behind her wall, as Victor Hugo urged at his most vibrant: "France will have but one thought: to reconstitute her forces, gather her energy, nourish her sacred anger, raise her young generation to form an army of the whole people, to work without cease, to study the methods and skills of our enemies, to become again a great France, the France of 1792, the France of an idea with a sword. Then one day she will be irresistible. Then she will take back Alsace-Lorraine."

Through returning prosperity and growing empire, through the perennial civil quarrels—royalism, Boulangism, clericalism, strikes, and the culminating, devastating Dreyfus Affair—the sacred anger still glowed, especially in the army. The one thing that held together all elements of the army, whether old guard or republican, Jesuit or Freemason, was the *mystique d'Alsace*. The eyes of all were fixed on the blue line of the Vosges. A captain of infantry confessed in 1912 that he used to lead the men of his company in secret patrols of two or three through the dark pines to the mountaintops where they could gaze down on Colmar. "On our return from those clandestine expeditions our columns reformed, choked and dumb with emotion."

Originally neither German nor French, Alsace had been snatched back and forth between the two until, under Louis XIV, it was confirmed to France by the Treaty of Westphalia in 1648. After Germany annexed Alsace and part of Lorraine in 1870 Bismarck advised giving the inhabitants as much autonomy as possible and encouraging their particularism, for, he said, the more Alsatian they felt, the less they would feel French. His successors did not see the necessity. They took no account of the wishes of their new subjects, made no effort to win them over, administered the provinces as *Reichsland*, or "Imperial territory," under German officials on virtually the same terms as their African colonies, and succeeded only in infuriating and alienating the population until in 1911 a constitution was granted them. By then it was too late. German rule exploded in the Zabern Affair in 1913 which began, after an exchange of insults between townspeople and garrison, when a German officer struck a crippled shoemaker with his saber. It ended in the complete and public exposure of German policy in the *Reichsland*, in a surge of anti-German feeling in world opinion, and in the simultaneous triumph of militarism in Berlin where the officer of Zabern became a hero, congratulated by the Crown Prince.

For Germany 1870 was not a final settlement. The German day in Europe which they thought had dawned when the German

Empire was proclaimed in the Hall of Mirrors at Versailles was still postponed. France was not crushed; the French Empire was actually expanding in North Africa and Indo-China; the world of art and beauty and style still worshiped at the feet of Paris. Germans were still gnawed by envy of the country they had conquered. "As well off as God in France," was a German saying. At the same time they considered France decadent in culture and enfeebled by democracy. "It is impossible for a country that has had forty-two war ministers in forty-three years to fight effectively," announced Professor Hans Delbrück, Germany's leading historian. Believing themselves superior in soul, in strength, in energy, industry, and national virtue, Germans felt they deserved the dominion of Europe. The work of Sedan must be completed.

Living in the shadow of that unfinished business, France, reviving in spirit and strength, grew weary of being eternally on guard, eternally exhorted by her leaders to defend herself. As the century turned, her spirit rebelled against thirty years of the defensive with its implied avowal of inferiority. France knew herself to be physically weaker than Germany. Her population was less, her birth rate lower. She needed some weapon that Germany lacked to give herself confidence in her survival. The "idea with a sword" fulfilled the need. Expressed by Bergson it was called *élan vital*, the all-conquering will. Belief in its power convinced France that the human spirit need not, after all, bow to the predestined forces of evolution which Schopenhauer and Hegel had declared to be irresistible. The spirit of France would be the equalizing factor. Her will to win, her *élan*, would enable France to defeat her enemy. Her genius was in her spirit, the spirit of *la gloire*, of 1792, of the incomparable "Marseillaise," the spirit of General Margueritte's heroic cavalry charge before Sedan when even Wilhelm I, watching the battle, could not forbear to cry, "*Oh, les braves gens!*"

Belief in the fervor of France, in the *furor Gallicae*, revived France's faith in herself in the generation after 1870. It was that fervor, unfurling her banners, sounding her bugles, arming her soldiers, that would lead France to victory if the day of "Again" should come.

Translated into military terms Bergson's *élan vital* became the doctrine of the offensive. In proportion as a defensive gave way to an offensive strategy, the attention paid to the Belgian frontier gradually gave way in favor of a progressive shift of gravity eastward toward the point where a French offensive could be launched to break through to the Rhine. For the Germans the roundabout road through Flanders led to Paris; for the French it led nowhere. They could only get to Berlin by the shortest way. The more the thinking of the French General Staff approached the offensive, the greater the forces it concentrated at the attacking point and the fewer it left to defend the Belgian frontier.

The doctrine of the offensive had its fount in the Ecole Supérieure de la Guerre, or War College, the ark of the army's intellectual elite, whose director, General Ferdinand Foch, was the molder of French military theory of his time. Foch's mind, like a heart, contained two valves: one pumped spirit into strategy; the other circulated common sense. On the one hand Foch preached a *mystique* of will expressed in his famous aphorisms, "The will to conquer is the first condition of victory," or more succinctly, "*Victoire c'est la volonté*," and, "A battle won is a battle in which one will not confess oneself beaten."

In practice this was to become the famous order at the Marne to attack when the situation called for retreat. His officers of those days remember him bellowing, "Attack! Attack!" with furious, sweeping gestures while he dashed about in short rushes as if charged by an electric battery. Why, he was later asked, did he advance at the Marne when he was technically beaten? "Why? I don't know. Because of my men, because I had a will. And then—God was there."

Though a profound student of Clausewitz, Foch did not, like Clausewitz's German successors, believe in a foolproof schedule of battle worked out in advance. Rather he taught the necessity of perpetual adaptability and improvisation to fit circumstances. "Regulations," he would say, "are all very well for drill but in the hour of danger they are no more use. . . . You have to learn to think." To think meant to give room for freedom of initiative, for the imponderable to win over the material, for will to demonstrate its power over circumstance.

But the idea that morale alone could conquer, Foch warned, was an "infantile notion." From his flights of metaphysics he would descend at once, in his lectures and his prewar books

Les Principes de la Guerre and *La Conduite de la Guerre*, to the earth of tactics, the placing of advance guards, the necessity of *sureté*, or protection, the elements of firepower, the need for obedience and discipline. The realistic half of his teaching was summed up in another aphorism he made familiar during the war, "*De quoi s'agit-il?*" (What is the essence of the problem?)

Eloquent as he was on tactics, it was Foch's *mystique* of will that captured the minds of his followers. Once in 1908 when Clemenceau was considering Foch, then a professor, for the post of Director of the War College, a private agent whom he sent to listen to the lectures reported back in bewilderment, "This officer teaches metaphysics so abstruse as to make idiots of his pupils." Although Clemenceau appointed Foch in spite of it, there was, in one sense, truth in the report. Foch's principles, not because they were too abstruse but because they were too attractive, laid a trap for France. They were taken up with particular enthusiasm by Colonel Grandmaison, "an ardent and brilliant officer" who was Director of the Troisième Bureau, or Bureau of Military Operations, and who in 1911 delivered two lectures at the War College which had a crystallizing effect.

Colonel Grandmaison grasped only the head and not the feet of Foch's principles. Expounding their *élan* without their *sureté*, he expressed a military philosophy that electrified his audience. He waved before their dazzled eyes an "idea with a sword" which showed them how France could win. Its essence was the *offensive à outrance*, offensive to the limit. Only this could achieve Clausewitz's decisive battle which "exploited to the finish is the essential act of war" and which "once engaged, must be pushed to the end, with no second thoughts, up to the extremes of human endurance." Seizure of initiative is the *sine qua non*. Preconceived arrangements based on a dogmatic judgment of what the enemy will do are premature. Liberty of action is achieved only by imposing one's will upon the enemy. "All command decisions must be inspired by the will to seize and retain the initiative." The defensive is forgotten, abandoned, discarded; its only possible justification is an occasional "economizing of forces at certain points with a view to adding them to the attack."

The effect on the General Staff was profound, and during the next two years was embodied in new Field Regulations for the conduct of war and in a new plan of campaign called Plan 17, which was adopted in May, 1913. Within a few months of Grandmaison's lectures, the President of the Republic, M. Fallières, announced: "The offensive alone is suited to the temperament of French soldiers. . . . We are determined to march straight against the enemy without hesitation."

The new Field Regulations, enacted by the government in October, 1913, as the fundamental document for the training and conduct of the French Army, opened with a flourish of trumpets: "The French Army, returning to its traditions, henceforth admits no law but the offensive." Eight commandments followed, ringing with the clash of "decisive battle," "offensive without hesitation," "fierceness and tenacity," "breaking the will of the adversary," "ruthless and tireless pursuit." With all the ardor of orthodoxy stamping out heresy, the Regulations stamped upon and discarded the defensive. "The offensive alone," it proclaimed, "leads to positive results." Its Seventh Commandment, italicized by the authors, stated: "*Battles are beyond everything else struggles of morale. Defeat is inevitable as soon as the hope of conquering ceases to exist. Success comes not to him who has suffered the least but to him whose will is firmest and morale strongest.*"

Nowhere in the eight commandments was there mention of matériel or firepower or what Foch called *sureté*. The teaching of the Regulations became epitomized in the favorite word of the French officer corps, *le cran*, nerve, or, less politely, guts. Like the youth who set out for the mountaintop under the banner marked "Excelsior!" the French Army marched to war in 1914 under a banner marked "*Cran*."

Over the years, while French military philosophy had changed, French geography had not. The geographical facts of her frontiers remained what Germany had made them in 1870. Germany's territorial demands, William I had explained to the protesting Empress Eugénie, "have no aim other than to push back the starting point from which French armies could in the future attack us." They also pushed forward the starting point from which Germany could attack France. While French history and development after the turn of the century fixed her mind upon the offensive, her geography still required a strategy of the defensive.

In 1911, the same year as Colonel Grandmaison's lectures, a last effort to commit France to a strategy of the defensive was made in the Supreme War Council by no less a personage than the Commander in Chief designate, General Michel. As Vice President of the Council, a post which carried with it the position of Commander in Chief in the event of war, General Michel was then the ranking officer in the army. In a report that precisely reflected Schlieffen's thinking, he submitted his estimate of the probable German line of attack and his proposals for countering it. Because of the natural escarpments and French fortifications along the common border with Germany, he argued, the Germans could not hope to win a prompt decisive battle in Lorraine. Nor would the passage through Luxembourg and the near corner of Belgium east of the Meuse give them sufficient room for their favored strategy of envelopment. Only by taking advantage of "the whole of Belgium," he said, could the Germans achieve that "immediate, brutal and decisive" offensive which they must launch upon France before the forces of her Allies could come into play. He pointed out that the Germans had long yearned for Belgium's great port of Antwerp, and this gave them an additional reason for an attack through Flanders. He proposed to face the Germans along a line Verdun-Namur-Antwerp with a French army of a million men whose left wing—like Schlieffen's right—should brush the Channel with its sleeve.

Not only was General Michel's plan defensive in character; it also depended upon a proposal that was anathema to his fellow officers. To match the numbers he believed the Germans would send through Belgium, General Michel proposed to double French front-line effectives by attaching a regiment of reserves to every active regiment. Had he proposed to admit Mistinguett to the Immortals of the French Academy, he could hardly have raised more clamor and disgust.

"*Les réserves, c'est zéro!*" was the classic dogma of the French officer corps. Men who had finished their compulsory training under universal service and were between the ages of twenty-three and thirty-four were classed as reserves. Upon mobilization the youngest classes filled out the regular army units to war strength; the others were formed into reserve regiments, brigades, and divisions according to their local geographical districts. These were considered fit only for rear duty or for use as fortress troops, and incapable, because of their lack of trained officers and NCOs, of being attached to the fighting regiments. The regular army's contempt for the reserves, in which it was joined by the parties of the right, was augmented by dislike of the principle of the "nation in arms." To merge the reserves with the active divisions would be to put a drag on the army's fighting thrust. Only the active army, they believed, could be depended upon to defend the country.

The left parties, on the other hand, with memories of General Boulanger on horseback, associated the army with *coups d'état* and believed in the principle of a "nation in arms" as the only safeguard of the Republic. They maintained that a few months' training would fit any citizen for war, and violently opposed the increase of military service to three years. The army demanded this reform in 1913 not only to match an increase in the German Army but also because the more men who were in training at any one time, the less reliance needed to be placed on reserve units. After angry debate, with bitterly divisive effect on the country, the Three-Year Law was enacted in August, 1913.

Disdain of the reserves was augmented by the new doctrine of the offensive which, it was felt, could only be properly inculcated in active troops. To perform the irresistible onslaught of the *attaque brusquée*, symbolized by the bayonet charge, the essential quality was *élan*, and *élan* could not be expected of men settled in civilian life with family responsibilities. Reserves mixed with active troops would create "armies of decadence," incapable of the will to conquer.

Similar sentiments were known to be held across the Rhine. The Kaiser was widely credited with the edict "No fathers of families at the front." Among the French General Staff it was an article of faith that the Germans would not mix reserve units with active units, and this led to the belief that the Germans would not have enough men in the front line to do two things at once: send a strong right wing in a wide sweep through Belgium west of the Meuse and keep sufficient forces at their center and left to stop a French breakthrough to the Rhine.

When General Michel presented his plan, the Minister of War, Messimy, treated it "*comme une insanité*." As chairman of the Supreme War Council he not only attempted to suppress it but at once consulted other members of the Council on the advisability of removing Michel.

Messimy, an exuberant, energetic, almost violent man with a thick neck, round head, bright peasant's eyes behind spectacles, and a loud voice, was a former career officer. In 1899 as a thirty-year-old captain of Chasseurs, he had resigned from the army in protest against its refusal to reopen the Dreyfus case. In that heated time the officer corps insisted as a body that to admit the possibility of Dreyfus's innocence after his conviction would be to destroy the army's prestige and infallibility. Unable to put loyalty to the army above justice, Messimy determined upon a political career with the declared goal of "reconciling the army with the nation." He swept into the War Ministry with a passion for improvement. Finding a number of generals "incapable not only of leading their troops but even of following them," he adopted Theodore Roosevelt's expedient of ordering all generals to conduct maneuvers on horseback. When this provoked protests that old so-and-so would be forced to retire from the army Messimy replied that that was indeed his object. He had been named War Minister on June 30, 1911, after a succession of four ministers in four months and the next day was met by the spring of the German gunboat *Panther* on Agadir precipitating the second Moroccan crisis. Expecting mobilization at any moment, Messimy discovered the generalissimo-designate, General Michel, to be "hesitant, indecisive and crushed by the weight of the duty that might at any moment devolve upon him." In his present post Messimy believed he represented a "national danger." Michel's "insane" proposal provided the excuse to get rid of him.

Michel, however, refused to go without first having his plan presented to the Council whose members included the foremost generals of France: Gallieni, the great colonial; Pau, the one-armed veteran of 1870; Joffre, the silent engineer; Dubail, the pattern of gallantry, who wore his kepi cocked over one eye with the "*chic exquis*" of the Second Empire. All were to hold active commands in 1914 and two were to become Marshals of France. None gave Michel's plan his support. One officer from the War Ministry who was present at the meeting said: "There is no use discussing it. General Michel is off his head."

Whether or not this verdict represented the views of all present—Michel later claimed that General Dubail, for one, had originally agreed with him—Messimy, who made no secret of his hostility, carried the Council with him. A trick of fate arranged that Messimy should be a forceful character and Michel should not. To be right and overruled is not forgiven to persons in responsible positions, and Michel duly paid for his clairvoyance. Relieved of his command, he was appointed Military Governor of Paris where in a crucial hour in the coming test he was indeed to prove "hesitant and indecisive."

Messimy, having fervently stamped out Michel's heresy of the defensive, did his best, as War Minister, to equip the army to fight a successful offensive but was in his turn frustrated in his most-cherished prospect—the need to reform the French uniform. The British had adopted khaki after the Boer War, and the Germans were about to make the change from Prussian blue to field-gray. But in 1912 French soldiers still wore the same blue coats, red kepi, and red trousers they had worn in 1830 when rifle fire carried only two hundred paces and when armies, fighting at these close quarters, had no need for concealment. Visiting the Balkan front in 1912, Messimy saw the advantages gained by the dull-colored Bulgarians and came home determined to make the French soldier less visible. His project to clothe him in gray-blue or gray-green raised a howl of protest. Army pride was as intransigent about giving up its red trousers as it was about adopting heavy guns. Army prestige was once again felt to be at stake. To clothe the French soldier in some muddy, inglorious color, declared the army's champions, would be to realize the fondest hopes of Dreyfusards and Freemasons. To banish "all that is colorful, all that gives the soldier his vivid aspect," wrote the *Echo de Paris*, "is to go contrary both to French taste and military function." Messimy pointed out that the two might no longer be synonymous, but his opponents proved immovable. At a parliamentary hearing a former War Minister, M. Etienne, spoke for France.

"Eliminate the red trousers?" he cried. "Never! *Le pantalon rouge c'est la France!*"

"That blind and imbecile attachment to the most visible of all colors," wrote Messimy afterward, "was to have cruel consequences."

In the meantime, still in the midst of the Agadir crisis, he had to name a new prospective generalissimo in place of Michel. He planned to give added authority to the post by combining with it that of Chief of the General Staff and by abolishing the post of Chief of Staff to the War Ministry, currently held by General Dubail. Michel's successor would have all the reins of power concentrated in his hands.

Messimy's first choice was the austere and brilliant general in pince-nez, Gallieni, who refused it because, he explained, having been instrumental in Michel's dismissal he felt scruples about replacing him. Furthermore he had only two years to go before retirement at sixty-four, and he believed the appointment of a "colonial" would be resented by the Metropolitan Army—"*une question de bouton*," he said, tapping his insignia. General Pau, who was next in line, made it a condition that he be allowed to name generals of his own choice to the higher commands which, as he was known for his reactionary opinions, threatened to wake the barely slumbering feud between rightist army and republican nation. Respecting him for his honesty, the government refused his condition. Messimy consulted Gallieni, who suggested his former subordinate in Madagascar, "a cool and methodical worker with a lucid and precise mind." Accordingly the post was offered to General Joseph-Jacques-Césaire Joffre, then aged fifty-nine, formerly chief of the Engineer Corps and presently Chief of the Services of the Rear.

Massive and paunchy in his baggy uniform, with a fleshy face adorned by a heavy, nearly white mustache and bushy eyebrows to match, with a clear youthful skin, calm blue eyes and a candid, tranquil gaze, Joffre looked like Santa Claus and gave an impression of benevolence and naïveté—two qualities not noticeably part of his character. He did not come of a gentleman's family, was not a graduate of St. Cyr (but of the less aristocratic if more scientific Ecole Polytechnique), had not passed through the higher training of the War College. As an officer of the Engineer Corps, which dealt with such unromantic matters as fortifications and railways, he belonged to a branch of the service not drawn upon for the higher commands. He was the eldest of the eleven children of a petit bourgeois manufacturer of wine barrels in the French Pyrénées. His military career had been marked by quiet accomplishment and efficiency in each post he filled: as company commander in Formosa and Indo-China, as a major in the Sudan and Timbuktu, as staff officer in the Railway Section of the War Ministry, as lecturer at the Artillery School, as fortifications officer under Gallieni in Madagascar from 1900 to 1905, as general of a division in 1905, of a corps in 1908, and as Director of the Rear and member of the War Council since 1910.

He had no known clerical, monarchist, or other disturbing connections; he had been out of the country during the Dreyfus Affair; his reputation as a good republican was as smooth as his well-manicured hands; he was solid and utterly phlegmatic. His outstanding characteristic was a habitual silence that in other men would have seemed self-deprecatory but, worn like an aura over Joffre's great, calm bulk, inspired confidence. He had still five years to go before retirement.

Joffre was conscious of one lack: he had had no training in the rarefied realms of staff work. On a hot July day when doors in the War Ministry on the Rue St. Dominique were left open, officers glancing out of their rooms saw General Pau holding Joffre by a button of his uniform. "Take it, *cher ami*," he was saying. "We will give you Castelnau. He knows all about staff work—everything will go of itself."

Castelnau, who was a graduate both of St. Cyr and of the War College, came, like D'Artagnan, from Gascony, which is said to produce men of hot blood and cold brain. He suffered from the disadvantage of family connections with a marquis, of associating with Jesuits, and of a personal Catholicism which he practiced so vigorously as to earn him during the war the name of *le capucin botté*, the Monk in Boots. He had, however, long experience on the General Staff. Joffre would have preferred

Foch but knew Messimy to have an unexplained prejudice against him. As was his habit, he listened without comment to Pau's advice, and promptly took it.

"Aye!" complained Messimy when Joffre asked for Castelnau as his Deputy Chief. "You will rouse a storm in the parties of the left and make yourself a lot of enemies." However, with the assent of the President and Premier who "made a face" at the condition but agreed, both appointments were put through together. A fellow general, pursuing some personal intrigue, warned Joffre that Castelnau might displace him. "Get rid of me! Not Castelnau," Joffre replied, unruffled. "I need him for six months; then I'll give him a corps command." As it proved, he found Castelnau invaluable, and when war came gave him command of an army instead of a corps.

Joffre's supreme confidence in himself was expressed in the following year when his aide, Major Alexandre, asked him if he thought war was shortly to be expected.

"Certainly I think so," Joffre replied. "I have always thought so. It will come. I shall fight it and I shall win. I have always succeeded in whatever I do—as in the Sudan. It will be that way again."

"It will mean a Marshal's baton for you," his aide suggested with some awe at the vision.

"Yes." Joffre acknowledged the prospect with laconic equanimity.

Under the aegis of this unassailable figure the General Staff from 1911 on threw itself into the task of revising the Field Regulations, retraining the troops in their spirit, and making a new plan of campaign to replace the now obsolete Plan 16. The staff's guiding mind, Foch, was gone from the War College, promoted and shifted to the field and ultimately to Nancy where, as he said, the frontier of 1870 "cut like a scar across the breast of the country." There, guarding the frontier, he commanded the XXth Corps which he was soon to make famous. He had left behind, however, a "chapel," as cliques in the French Army were called, of his disciples who formed Joffre's entourage. He had also left behind a strategic plan which became the framework of Plan 17. Completed in April, 1913, it was adopted without discussion or consultation, together with the new Field Regulations by the Supreme War Council in

May. The next eight months were spent reorganizing the army on the basis of the plan and preparing all the instructions and orders for mobilization, transport, services of supply, areas and schedules of deployment and concentration. By February, 1914, it was ready to be distributed in sections to each of the generals of the five armies into which the French forces were divided, only that part of it which concerned him individually going to each one.

Its motivating idea, as expressed by Foch, was, "We must get to Berlin by going through Mainz," that is, by crossing the Rhine at Mainz, 130 miles northeast of Nancy. That objective, however, was an idea only. Unlike the Schlieffen plan, Plan 17 contained no stated over-all objective and no explicit schedule of operations. It was not a plan of operations but a plan of deployment with directives for several possible lines of attack for each army, depending on circumstances, but without a given goal. Because it was in essence a plan of response, of riposte to a German attack, whose avenues the French could not be sure of in advance, it had of necessity to be, as Joffre said, "a posteriori and opportunist." Its intention was inflexible: Attack! Otherwise its arrangements were flexible.

A brief general directive of five sentences, classified as secret, was all that was shown in common to the generals who were to carry out the plan, and they were not permitted to discuss it. It offered very little for discussion. Like the Field Regulations it opened with a flourish: "Whatever the circumstance, it is the Commander in Chief's intention to advance with all forces united to the attack of the German armies." The rest of the general directive stated merely that French action would consist of two major offensives, one to the left and one to the right of the German fortified area of Metz-Thionville. The one to the right or south of Metz would attack directly eastward across the old border of Lorraine, while a secondary operation in Alsace was designed to anchor the French right on the Rhine. The offensive to the left or north of Metz would attack either to the north or, in the event the enemy violated neutral territory, to the northeast through Luxembourg and the Belgian Ardennes, but this movement would be carried out "only by order of the Commander in Chief." The general purpose, although this was nowhere stated, was to drive through to the

Rhine, at the same time isolating and cutting off the invading German right wing from behind.

To this end Plan 17 deployed the five French armies along the frontier from Belfort in Alsace as far as Hirson, about a third of the way along the Franco-Belgian border. The remaining two-thirds of the Belgian frontier, from Hirson to the sea, was left undefended. It was along that stretch that General Michel had planned to defend France. Joffre found his plan in the office safe when he succeeded Michel. It concentrated the center of gravity of the French forces to this extreme left section of the line where Joffre left none. It was a plan of pure defense; it allowed for no seizing of initiative; it was, as Joffre decided after careful study, "foolishness."

The French General Staff, though receiving many indications collected by the Deuxième Bureau, or Military Intelligence, pointing to a powerful German right-wing envelopment, believed the arguments against such a maneuver more telling than the evidence for it. They did not credit the sweep through Flanders, although, in fact, they had been told about it in a dramatic manner by an officer of the German General Staff who in 1904 betrayed to them an early version of the Schlieffen plan. In a series of three rendezvous with a French intelligence officer at Brussels, Paris, and Nice, the German appeared with his head swathed in bandages, revealing only a gray mustache and a pair of piercing eyes. The documents he handed over for a considerable sum revealed that the Germans planned to come through Belgium by way of Liège, Namur, Charleroi, and invade France along the valley of the Oise, by way of Guise, Noyon and Compiègne. The route was correct for 1914, for the documents were authentic. General Pendezac, then Chief of the French General Staff, believed the information "fitted perfectly with the present tendency of German strategy which teaches the necessity of wide envelopment," but many of his colleagues were doubtful. They did not believe the Germans could mobilize enough men to maneuver on such a scale, and they suspected the information might be a feint designed to draw the French away from the area of the real attack. French planning was hampered by a variety of uncertainties, and the greatest of these was Belgium. To the logical French mind it seemed obvious that the Germans would bring England in against them if they violated Belgium and attacked Antwerp. Was it likely the Germans would deliberately do themselves this disservice? Rather, was it not "altogether likely" that, leaving Belgium unviolated, they would return to the elder Moltke's plan of attacking Russia first before the slow Russian mobilization could be completed?

Attempting to fit Plan 17 to one of several hypotheses of German strategy, Joffre and Castelnau believed that the most likely one was a major enemy offensive across the plateau of Lorraine. They expected it to violate the corner of Belgium east of the Meuse. They calculated German strength on the Western Front, without use of reserves in the front line, at twenty-six corps. For this number to be extended in strength on the far side of the Meuse was "impossible," decided Castelnau. "I was of the same opinion," agreed Joffre.

Jean Jaurès, the great socialist leader, thought differently. Leading the fight against the Three-Year Law, he insisted in his speeches and in his book *L'Armée nouvelle* that the war of the future would be one of mass armies using every citizen, that this was what the Germans were preparing, that reservists of twenty-five to thirty-three were at their peak of stamina and more committed than younger men without responsibilities, that unless France used all her reservists in the front line she would be subjected to a terrible "submersion."

Outside the chapel of Plan 17 there were still military critics who argued strongly for the defensive. Colonel Grouard, in his book *La Guerre éventuelle*, published in 1913, wrote: "It is above all the German offensive through Belgium on which we ought to fix our attention. As far as one can foresee the logical consequences of the opening of our campaign, we can say without hesitation that if we take the offensive at the outset we shall be beaten." But if France prepared a riposte against the German right wing, "all the chances are in our favor."

In 1913 the Deuxième Bureau collected enough information on the German use of reserves as active troops as to make it impossible for the French General Staff to be ignorant of this crucial factor. A critique by Moltke on German maneuvers of 1913 indicating that the reserves would be so used came into French possession. Major Melotte, Belgian military attaché in Berlin, noticed and reported the Germans calling up an unusual number of reserves in 1913 from which he concluded that they were forming a reserve corps for every active corps. But the authors of Plan 17 did not want to be convinced. They rejected evidence that argued in favor of their staying on the defensive because their hearts and hopes, as well as their training and strategy, were fixed on the offensive. They persuaded themselves that the Germans intended to use reserve units only to guard communication lines and "passive fronts" and as siege and occupation troops. They enabled themselves to reject defense of the Belgian frontier by insisting that if the Germans extended their right wing as far as Flanders, they would leave their center so thinned that the French, as Castelnau said, could "cut them in half." A strong German right wing would give the French advantage of superior numbers against the German center and left. This was the meaning of Castelnau's classic phrase, "So much the better for us!"

When General Lebas on that occasion left the Rue St. Dominique, he said to the deputy from Lille who had accompanied him, "I have two stars on my sleeve and he has three. How can I argue?"

4

"A Single British Soldier . . ."

BRITAIN'S JOINT military plans with France were begotten in 1905 when Russia's far-off defeats at the hands of the Japanese, revealing her military impotence, unhinged the equilibrium of Europe. Suddenly and simultaneously the government of every nation became aware that if any one of them chose that moment to precipitate a war, France would have to fight without an ally. The German government put the moment to an immediate test. Within three weeks of the Russian defeat at Mukden in 1905, a challenge was flung at France in the form of the Kaiser's sensational appearance at Tangier on March 31. To Frenchmen it meant that Germany was probing for the moment of "Again" and would find it, if not now, then soon. "Like everyone else I had come to Paris at nine o'clock on that morning," wrote Charles Péguy, the poet, editor, mystic, Socialist-against-his-party and Catholic-against-his-church, who spoke, as nearly as one person could, for the conscience of France. "Like everyone else I knew at half-past eleven that, in the space of those two hours, a new period had begun in the history of my life, in the history of this country, in the history of the world."

Of his own life Péguy was not speaking vainly. In August 1914 he was to volunteer at forty-one for military service and be killed in action at the Marne on September 7.

Britain, too, reacted to the challenge of Tangier. Her military establishment was just then being thoroughly overhauled by Lord Esher's Committee. It included, besides himself, the turbulent First Sea Lord, Sir John Fisher, who had been reforming the navy by a series of explosions, and an army officer, Sir George Clarke, known for his modern ideas on imperial strategy. The "Esher triumvirate" had created a Committee of Imperial Defence to govern policy pertaining to war, of which Esher was permanent member and Clarke was secretary, and had endowed the army with a pristine General Staff. Just at the time when the Kaiser was nervously riding a too spirited white horse through the streets of Tangier, the Staff was engaged in a theoretical war game based on the assumption that the Germans would come through Belgium in a wide flanking movement north and west of the Meuse. The map exercise proved to the Director of Military Operations, General Grierson, and to his assistant, General Robertson, that there was little chance of stopping the Germans unless British forces "arrived on the scene quickly and in strength."

At that time independent action in Belgium was what the British contemplated. Mr. Balfour, the Conservative Prime Minister, at once asked for a report on how soon a force of four divisions could be mobilized and landed in Belgium in the event of a German invasion. In the midst of the crisis, while Grierson and Robertson were over on the Continent examining the terrain along the Franco-Belgian frontier, Balfour's government lost office.

Nerves on all sides were stretched tight in the expectation that Germany might take advantage of Russia's catastrophe to precipitate war in the coming summer. No plans for common Anglo-French military action had yet been made. With Britain in the throes of a general election and ministers scattered about the country campaigning, the French were forced to make an unofficial approach. Their military attaché in London, Major Huguet, made contact with an active and eager intermediary, Colonel Repington, military correspondent of *The Times*, who, with a nod from Esher and Clarke, opened negotiations. In a memorandum submitted to the French government, Colonel Repington asked, "May we take it as a principle that France will not violate Belgian territory unless compelled to do so by previous violation by Germany?"

"Definitely, yes," the French replied.

"Do the French realise," asked the Colonel, intending to convey a warning as well as a prognosis, "that any violation of Belgian neutrality brings us into the field automatically in defense of our treaty obligations?" No British government in history ever committed itself to take action "automatically" upon an event, but the Colonel, with the bit in his teeth, was galloping far ahead of the field.

"France has always supposed so," was the somewhat dazed answer, "but has never received an official assurance."

By further leading questions, the Colonel established that France did not think highly of independent British action in Belgium and believed that unity of command—for France on land and Britain at sea—was "absolutely indispensable."

Meanwhile the Liberals had been elected. Traditionally opposed to war and foreign adventure, they were confident that good intentions could keep the peace. Their new Foreign Secretary was Sir Edward Grey, who suffered the death of his wife a month after taking office. Their new Secretary for War was a barrister with a passion for German philosophy, Richard Haldane, who, when asked by the soldiers in Council what kind of army he had in mind, replied, "A Hegelian army." "The conversation then fell off," he recorded.

Grey, warily approached by the French, indicated he had no intention of "receding" from any assurances his predecessor had given to France. Faced with a major crisis in his first week of office, he asked Haldane if arrangements existed for the British to fight alongside the French in the event of an emergency. Haldane looked in the files and found none. His inquiry disclosed that to put four divisions on the Continent would take two months.

Grey wondered if talks between the General Staffs might not now take place as a "military precaution" without committing Great Britain. Haldane consulted the Prime Minister, Sir Henry Campbell-Bannerman. Despite party affiliation, Campbell-Bannerman was personally so fond of things French that he would sometimes take the Channel steamer over and back in one day in order to lunch at Calais. He gave his assent to Staff talks, though with some misgivings about the stress laid on "joint preparations." He thought that coming, as they did, "very close to an honorable understanding," they might destroy the lovely looseness of the Entente. To avoid any such unpleasantness Haldane arranged for a letter to be signed by General Grierson and Major Huguet, stating that the talks did not commit Great Britain. With this formula safely established, he authorized the talks to begin. Thereupon he, Grey, and the Prime Minister, without informing the rest of the Cabinet, left further developments in the hands of the military as a "departmental affair."

From here the General Staffs took over. British officers,

including Sir John French, a cavalry general who had made a great name in the Boer War, attended the French maneuvers that summer. Grierson and Robertson revisited the frontier in company with Major Huguet. In consultation with the French General Staff, they selected landing bases and staging areas along a front from Charleroi to Namur and into the Ardennes, predicated on a German invasion through Belgium.

The "Esher triumvirate," however, fundamentally disapproved of employing the British Army as a mere adjunct of the French and, after the tension of the Moroccan crisis relaxed, the joint planning begun in 1905 was not pushed further. General Grierson was replaced. The dominant view, represented by Lord Esher, favored action, independent of French command, in Belgium where the holding of Antwerp and the adjoining coast was a direct British interest. In the vehement opinion of Sir John Fisher, British action ought to be predominantly naval. He doubted the military capacity of the French, expected the Germans to beat them on land, and saw no purpose in ferrying the British Army over to be included in that defeat. The only land action he favored was an audacious leap onto Germany's back, and he had chosen the exact spot—a "ten-mile stretch of hard sand" along the Baltic coast of East Prussia. Here, only ninety miles from Berlin, the nearest point to the German capital that could be reached by sea, British troops landed by the navy could seize and entrench a base of operations and "keep a million Germans busy." Apart from this action the army should be "absolutely restricted to . . . sudden descents upon the coast, the recovery of Heligoland and the garrisoning of Antwerp." Its plan to fight in France was, in Fisher's opinion, "suicidal idiocy," the War Office was remarkable for its ignorance of war, and the Army should be administered as an "annex to the Navy." Early in 1910 Fisher, at sixty-nine, was simultaneously raised to the peerage and relieved of the Admiralty, but that was to be far from the end of his usefulness.

After the emergency of 1905–1906 had passed, joint military plans with the French made little progress for the next few years. In the interim two men formed a trans-Channel friendship which was to serve as the first cable for the building of a bridge.

Britain's Staff College was then commanded by Brigadier General Henry Wilson, a tall, bony, ebullient Anglo-Irishman with a face which he thought rather resembled that of a horse. Quick and impatient, Wilson was in a constant boil of ideas, humor, passion, imagination and, above all, energy. When serving at the War Office in London, he used to trot around Hyde Park for exercise before breakfast, carrying with him the morning paper to read whenever he slowed down to a walk. Brought up by a succession of French governesses, he could speak French fluently. He was less interested in German. In January 1909 Schlieffen published an anonymous article in the *Deutsche Revue* to protest certain changes made in his plan by his successor, Moltke. The basic outline, if not the details, of the "colossal Cannae" prepared for the envelopment of the French and British armies was revealed and the identity of the author surmised. When a student at Camberley brought the article to the Commandant's attention, Wilson returned it with the casual comment, "Very interesting."

In December 1909 General Wilson took it into his head to visit his opposite number, the commandant of the Ecole Supérieure de la Guerre, General Foch. He attended four lectures and a seminar and was politely invited to tea by General Foch who, though impatient with the interruptions of distinguished visitors, felt he owed this much to his British counterpart. General Wilson, enthusiastic at what he had seen and heard, stayed for three hours' talk. When Foch was finally able to escort his visitor to the door and made what he thought were his final goodbyes, Wilson happily announced that he was returning next day to continue the conversation and see more of the curriculum. Foch could not but admire the Englishman's *cran* and be pleased by his interest. Their second talk opened their minds to each other. Within a month Wilson was back in Paris for another session. Foch accepted his invitation to come to London in the spring, and Wilson agreed to return for the French Staff tour in the summer.

In London when Foch came over, Wilson introduced him to Haldane and others at the War Office. Bursting into the room of one of his colleagues, he said: "I've got a French general outside—General Foch. Mark my words, this fellow is going to command the Allied armies when the big war comes on."

Here Wilson had already accepted the principle of unity of command and picked the man for it although it was to take four years of war and the brink of defeat before events would bear him out.

During repeated visits after 1909, the two commandants became fast friends even to the extent of Wilson being admitted into the French family circle and invited to the wedding of Foch's daughter. With his friend "Henri," Foch spent hours in what an observer called "tremendous gossips." They used to exchange caps and walk up and down together, the short and the tall, arguing and chaffing. Wilson had been particularly impressed by the rush and dash with which studies were conducted at the War College. Officer-instructors constantly urged on officer-pupils with "*Vite, vite!*" and "*Allez, allez!*" Introduced to the classes in the Camberley Staff College, the hurry-up technique was quickly dubbed Wilson's "*allez* operations."

A question that Wilson asked of Foch during his second visit in January 1910, evoked an answer which expressed in one sentence the problem of the alliance with England, as the French saw it.

"What is the smallest British military force that would be of any practical assistance to you?" Wilson asked.

Like a rapier flash came Foch's reply, "A single British soldier—and we will see to it that he is killed."

Wilson, too, wanted to see Britain committed. Convinced that war with Germany was imminent and inevitable, he strove to infuse his own sense of urgency into his colleagues and pupils and himself became totally absorbed by it. In August 1910 came his opportunity. He was named Director of Military Operations, the post from which General Grierson had originated the Staff talks with France. When Major Huguet at once came to see the new Director to bewail the lack of progress since 1906 on the important question of Anglo-French military cooperation, Wilson replied, "Important question! But it is vital! There is no other."

Immediately the joint planning took on new impetus. Wilson could see nothing, go nowhere, but France and Belgium. On his first visit in 1909 he had spent ten days by train and bicycle touring the Franco-Belgian and Franco-German frontier from Valenciennes to Belfort. He had found that Foch's "appreciation of the German move through Belgium is exactly the same as mine, the important line being between Verdun and Namur," in other words, east of the Meuse. During the next four years he repeated his visits three and four times a year, each time making bicycle or motor tours of the old battlefields of 1870 and of anticipated future battlefields in Lorraine and the Ardennes. On each visit he conferred with Foch and after Foch's departure, with Joffre, Castelnau, Dubail, and others of the French General Staff.

Covering the whole wall of Wilson's room in the War Office was a huge map of Belgium with every road by which he thought the Germans could march marked in heavy black. When he came to the War Office, Wilson found that under the new order wrought by "Schopenhauer among the generals," as Haldane was called, the regular army had been thoroughly trained, prepared, and organized to become an expeditionary force at a moment's need, with all arrangements completed to bring it up to war strength upon mobilization day. But of plans to transport it across the Channel, billet it, feed it, move it up to concentration areas in France, align it with the French armies, there were none.

What he felt to be the lethargy of the Staff on this subject sent Wilson into periodic paroxysms of vexation, recorded in his diary: ". . . very dissatisfied . . . no rail arrangements . . . no arrangements for horse supply . . . a scandalous state of affairs! . . . no train arrangements to ports, no staff arrangements to port, no naval arrangements . . . absolutely no medical arrangements . . . horse difficulty has not been solved . . . absolutely nothing exists, which is scandalous! . . . unpreparedness disgraceful . . . horse question in disgraceful state!" Yet by March 1911 out of all this lack of arrangements—and of horses—he had brought a schedule of mobilization by which "the whole of the infantry of six divisions would embark on the 4th day, cavalry 7th day, artillery 9th day."

It was just in time. On July 1, 1911 the *Panther* came to Agadir. Through all the chancelleries of Europe ran the whispered monosyllable, "War." Wilson hurried over to Paris in the same month that the French War Council, ousting General Michel, turned its back forever on the defensive. Together with General Dubail he drew up a memorandum providing, in the event of

British intervention, for an Expeditionary Force of six regular divisions and a cavalry division. Signed by Wilson and Dubail on July 20, it specified a total force of 150,000 men and 67,000 horses which were to land at Havre, Boulogne, and upriver at Rouen between the 4th and 12th days of mobilization, to proceed by rail to a concentration area in the Maubeuge region and to be ready for action on M-13.

In effect, the Dubail-Wilson agreement attached the British Army, in the event that war came and Britain entered it, to the French, placing it where it would prolong the French line and guard the French flank against envelopment. It meant, as Major Huguet gladly recorded, that the French had persuaded Wilson and the British General Staff against a "secondary theatre of operations" and in favor of common action in "the main theatre, that is to say, the French." In fact the British Navy was as much responsible as the French because its refusal to guarantee disembarkation ports above the line Dover-Calais precluded landings closer to, or within, Belgium.

Upon Wilson's return to London the question of the hour, he wrote in his diary, was whether Germany would go to war "with France and us." Consulted by Grey and Haldane over lunch, he presented an emphatic three-point program. "First we *must* join the French. Second, we *must* mobilize the same day as the French. Third, we *must* send all six divisions."

He felt "profoundly dissatisfied" with the two civilians' grasp of the situation, but he was at once given a further opportunity to instruct the government in the facts of war. On August 23 Prime Minister Asquith (Campbell-Bannerman's successor since 1908) convened a secret and special meeting of the Imperial Defence Committee to clarify British strategy in case of war. It lasted all day, with General Wilson expounding the army view in the morning and Fisher's successor, Admiral Sir Arthur Wilson, presenting the navy's view in the afternoon. Besides Asquith, Grey, and Haldane, three other Cabinet members were present: the Chancellor of the Exchequer, Lloyd George; the First Lord of the Admiralty, Mr. McKenna; and the Home Secretary, a young man of thirty-seven, impossible to ignore, who, from his inappropriate post, had pelted the Prime Minister during the crisis with ideas on naval and military strategy, all of them quite sound, had produced an astonishingly accurate prediction of the future course of the fighting, and who had no doubts whatever about what needed to be done. The Home Secretary was Winston Churchill.

Wilson, facing this group of "ignorant men," as he called them, and accompanied by his fellow officer and future chief, Sir John French, "who knows nothing at all about the subject," pinned up his great map of Belgium on the wall and lectured for two hours. He swept away many illusions when he explained how Germany, counting on Russia's slow mobilization, would send the bulk of her forces against the French, achieving superiority of numbers over them. He correctly predicated the German plan of attack upon a right-wing envelopment but, schooled in the French theories, estimated the force that would come down west of the Meuse at no more than four divisions. He stated that, if all six British divisions were sent immediately upon the outbreak of war to the extreme left of the French line, the chances of stopping the Germans would be favorable.

When the Admiral's turn came in the afternoon, the dazed civilians were astonished to discover that the navy's plan had nothing in common with the army's. He proposed to land the expeditionary force not in France, but on that "ten-mile strip of hard sand" upon the northern shores of Prussia where it would "draw off more than its weight of numbers from the German fighting line." His argument was violently combated by the generals. The absence of Lord Fisher nerved Asquith to reject it, and the Army carried the day. Fisher's growls of disgust erupted periodically thereafter. "The overwhelming supremacy of the British Navy . . . is the only thing to keep the German Army out of Paris," he wrote to a friend some months later. "Our soldiers are grotesque in their absurd ideas of war, but, happily, they are powerless. It is Antwerp we shall seize and not go fooling on the Vosges frontier." A certain inescapable logic in the Antwerp idea was to keep tugging at British military plans up to the last minute in 1914 and even afterward.

The meeting of August 1911, like that of the French War Council which had disposed of General Michel a few weeks earlier, was decisive upon British strategy and it had a decisive by-product. A shake-up in the policy-making posts of the navy being decreed, the eager Home Secretary was happily translated into First Lord of the Admiralty where, in 1914, he was to prove indispensable.

Echoes of the secret meeting of the C.I.D. angered the Cabinet members who had been left out and who belonged to the sternly pacifist wing of the party. Henry Wilson learned that he was regarded as the villain of the proceedings and that they are "calling for my head." At this time began the split in the Cabinet which was to be so critical in the ultimate days of decision. The government maintained the disingenuous position that the military "conversations" were, in Haldane's words, "just the natural and informal outcome of our close friendship with France." Natural outcome they might be; informal they were not. As Lord Esher with a certain realism said to the Prime Minister, the plans worked out jointly by the General Staffs have "certainly committed us to fight, whether the Cabinet likes it or not."

There is no record what Asquith replied or what, in his inmost mind, a region difficult to penetrate under the best of circumstances, he thought on this crucial question.

In the following year, 1912, a naval agreement was reached with France as the result of a momentous mission—not to France but to Berlin. In an effort to dissuade the Germans from passing a new Naval Law providing for increases in the fleet, Haldane was sent to talk with the Kaiser, Bethmann-Hollweg, Admiral Tirpitz, and other German leaders. It was the last Anglo-German attempt to find a common ground of understanding, and it failed. As a quid pro quo for keeping their fleet second to Britain's, the Germans demanded a promise of British neutrality in the event of war between Germany and France. This the British refused to give. Haldane returned convinced that Germany's drive for hegemony in Europe would have to be resisted sooner or later: "I thought, from my study of the German General Staff, that once the German war party had got into the saddle, it would be war not merely for the overthrow of France or Russia but for the domination of the world." Coming from Haldane this conclusion had a profound effect upon Liberal thinking and planning. The first result was a naval pact with France by which the British undertook at threat of war to safeguard the Channel and French coasts from enemy attack, leaving the French fleet free to concentrate in the Mediterranean. As this disposed the French fleet where it would not otherwise be, except by virtue of the agreement, it left a distinct obligation upon Britain.

Although the terms of the agreement were not known to the Cabinet as a whole, an uneasy sense prevailed that matters had gone too far. Not satisfied with the "no commitment" formula, the antiwar group insisted that it be put in writing. Sir Edward Grey obliged in the form of a letter to M. Cambon, the French ambassador. Drafted and approved by the Cabinet, it was a masterpiece of ellipsis. The military conversations, it said, left both parties free to decide at any future time "whether or not to assist each other by armed force." The naval agreement "was not based upon an engagement to cooperate in war." At threat of war both parties would "take into consideration" the plans of their General Staffs and "then decide what effect should be given them."

This curious document managed to satisfy everybody: the French because the whole British Cabinet Government had now officially acknowledged the existence of the joint plans, the antiwar group because it said England was not "committed," and Grey because he had evolved a formula that both saved the plans and quieted their opponents. To have substituted a definite alliance with France, as he was urged in some quarters, would "break up the Cabinet," he said.

After Agadir, as each year brought its summer crisis and the air grew heavier with approaching storm, the joint work of the General Staffs grew more intense. Sir Henry Wilson's tours abroad grew more frequent. He found the new French chief, General Joffre, "a fine, manly, imperturbable soldier with much character and determination," and Castelnau "very clever and intelligent." He continued his surveys of the Belgian frontier, cycling back and forth over the various roads and returning always to his favorite battlefield of 1870 at Mars-la-Tour near Metz where, each time he saw the statue "France," commemorating the battle, he felt a pang. On one visit, he recorded, "I laid at her feet a small bit of map I have been carrying, showing the areas of concentration of the British forces on her territory."

In 1912 he examined the new German railway constructions,

all converging on Aachen and the Belgian frontier. In February of that year Anglo-French plans had reached the point where Joffre could tell the Supreme War Council that he counted on the British for six infantry divisions and one cavalry division and two mounted brigades, totaling 145,000 men. *L'Armée "W"* as, in tribute to Wilson, the force was designated by the French, would land at Boulogne, Havre, and Rouen, concentrate in the Hirson-Maubeuge region and be ready for action on the fifteenth day of mobilization. Later in 1912 Wilson attended autumn maneuvers with Joffre and Castelnau and the Grand Duke Nicholas of Russia and afterward went on to Russia for talks with the Russian General Staff. In 1913 he visited Paris every other month to confer with the French Staff chiefs and to join the maneuvers of Foch's XXth Corps guarding the frontier.

While Wilson was tightening and perfecting his arrangements with the French, Britain's new Chief of Imperial General Staff, Sir John French, made an attempt in 1912 to revert to the idea of independent action in Belgium. Discreet inquiries made by the British military attaché in Brussels put an end to this effort. The Belgians were discovered to be adamant in the strict observance of their own neutrality. When the British attaché asked about possible joint arrangements for British landings in Belgium, on the premise of a prior German violation, he was informed that the British would have to wait until their military assistance was requested. The British minister, making his own inquiries, was told that if British troops landed before a German invasion or without a formal Belgian request, the Belgians would open fire.

Belgium's rigid purity confirmed what the British never tired of repeating to the French—that everything depended upon the Germans violating Belgian neutrality first. "Never, no matter on what pretext," Lord Esher cautioned Major Huguet in 1911, "let the French commanders be led into being the first to cross the Belgian frontier!" If they did, England could never be on their side; if the Germans did, they would bring England in against them. M. Cambon, the French ambassador in London, expressed the condition the other way around; only if Germany violated Belgium, was the burden of his dispatches, could France be sure of Britain's support.

By the spring of 1914 the joint work of the French and British General Staffs was complete to the last billet of every battalion, even to the places where they were to drink their coffee. The number of French railroad cars to be allotted, the assignments of interpreters, the preparation of codes and ciphers, the forage of horses was settled or expected to be consummated by July. The fact that Wilson and his staff were in constant communication with the French had to be concealed. All the work on Plan W, as the movement of the expeditionary force was called by both Staffs, was done in utmost secrecy, confined to half a dozen officers alone, who did even the typing, filing, and clerical work. While the military prearranged the lines of battle, England's political leaders, pulling the blanket of "no commitment" over their heads, resolutely refrained from watching them.

5

The Russian Steam Roller

THE RUSSIAN colossus exercised a spell upon Europe. On the chessboard of military planning, Russia's size and weight of numbers represented the largest piece. Notwithstanding her shoddy performance in the war against Japan, thought of the Russian "steam roller" gave comfort and encouragement to France and Britain; dread of the Slav at their backs haunted the Germans.

Although the defects of the Russian Army were notorious, although the Russian winter, not the Russian Army, had turned Napoleon back from Moscow, although it had been defeated on its own soil by the French and British in the Crimea, although the Turks in 1877 had outfought it at the siege of Plevna and only succumbed later to overwhelming numbers, although the Japanese had outfought it in Manchuria, a myth of its invincibility prevailed. The savage cavalry charge of yelling Cossacks was such a fixture in European minds that newspaper artists in August, 1914, were able to draw it in stirring detail without having been within a thousand miles of the Russian front. Cossacks and inexhaustible millions of hardy, uncomplaining *mujiks* willing to die made up the stereotype of the Russian Army. Its numbers inspired awe: 1,423,000 in peacetime strength; an additional 3,115,000 to be called upon mobilization, and a further reserve of 2,000,000 in territorials and recruits to make a total available force of 6,500,000.

It was envisaged as a gigantic mass, initially lethargic, but once thoroughly roused into motion, rolling forward inexorably with, no matter how many losses, endless waves of manpower to fill the places of the fallen. The army's efforts to purge incompetence and corruption since the war with Japan were believed to have brought improvement. "Everyone" in French politics was "immensely impressed by the growing strength of Russia and her tremendous resources and potential power and wealth," Sir Edward Grey noticed when he was in Paris in April 1914 to negotiate a naval agreement with the Russians. He shared the impression himself. "Russian resources are so great," he told President Poincaré, "that in the long run Germany will be exhausted without our helping Russia."

To the French the success of Plan 17, the irresistible march to the Rhine, was to be the proving of their nation and one of the great moments of European history. To ensure their break-through of the German center, they were bent on having the Russians draw off a portion of the German forces opposing them. The problem was to get Russia to launch an offensive upon Germany's rear at the same time as the Germans and French launched theirs on the Western Front, that is, as nearly as possible to the fifteenth day of mobilization. The French knew as well as everyone else that it was physically impossible for Russia to complete mobilization and concentration of her forces in fifteen days, but they wanted her to begin battle on M-15 with whatever she had ready. They were determined that Germany must be forced to fight on two fronts from the first moment in order to reduce the German superiority in numbers against themselves.

In 1911 General Dubail, then Chief of the War Ministry Staff, was sent to Russia to indoctrinate the Russian General Staff with the need for seizing the initiative. Although half the Russian forces in a European war would be concentrated against Austria and only half of those destined to take the field against Germany would be ready by M-15, the spirit in St. Petersburg was bold and willing. Anxious to restore glory to their tarnished arms, and leaving details of planning to look after themselves, the Russians agreed, with more valor than discretion, to launch an offensive simultaneously with France. Dubail obtained a promise that as soon as their front-line forces were in position, without waiting for concentration to be completed, the Russians would attack, crossing the frontier of East Prussia on M-16. "It is at the very heart of Germany that we should strike," acknowledged the Czar in a signed agreement. "The objective for both of us ought to be Berlin."

The pact for an early Russian offensive was hardened and sharpened in annual Staff talks that were a feature of the Franco-Russian Alliance. In 1912 General Jilinsky, Chief of the Russian General Staff, came to Paris; in 1913 General Joffre went to Russia. By now the Russians had succumbed to the spell of *élan*. Since Manchuria they, too, had to compensate for the humiliation of military defeat and the consciousness of military deficiencies. Colonel Grandmaison's lectures, translated into Russian, enjoyed immense popularity. Suffused with the glittering doctrine of *offensive à outrance*, the Russian General Staff improved on its promises. General Jilinsky undertook, in 1912, to have all of the 800,000 men destined for the German front ready by M-15, although Russia's railways were manifestly inadequate to the task. In 1913 he advanced the date of his offensive by two days, although Russia's armament factories were producing less than two-thirds the estimated need of artillery shells and less than half the need of rifle cartridges.

The Allies did not seriously concern themselves with Russia's military defects, although Ian Hamilton, Britain's military observer with the Japanese, had reported them pitilessly from Manchuria. They were: poor intelligence, disregard of cover, disregard of secrecy and swiftness, lack of dash, lack of initiative, and lack of good generalship. Colonel Repington who had pronounced judgment weekly on the Russo-Japanese War in *The Times* arrived at opinions which caused him to dedicate a book of his collected columns to the Emperor of Japan. Nevertheless the General Staffs believed that simply to get the Russian giant in motion, regardless of how he functioned, was all that mattered. This was difficult enough. During mobilization the average Russian soldier had to be transported 700 miles, four times as far as the average German soldier, and Russia had available one-tenth as many railroads per square kilometer as Germany. As a defense against invasion these had been deliberately built on a wider gauge than those of Germany. Heavy French loans to finance increased railroad construction had not yet accomplished their goal. Equal speed in mobilization was obviously impossible; but even if only half the 800,000 Russian troops promised for the German front could be put in position by the fifteenth day for a lunge into East Prussia, however faulty their military organization, the effect of their invasion of German territory was expected to be momentous.

To send an army into modern battle on enemy territory, especially under the disadvantage of different railway gauges, is a hazardous and complicated undertaking requiring prodigies of careful organization. Systematic attention to detail was not a notable characteristic of the Russian Army.

The officer corps was topheavy with a superabundance of aged generals whose heaviest intellectual exercise was card playing and who, to save their court perquisites and prestige, were kept on the active list regardless of activity. Officers were appointed and promoted chiefly through patronage, social or monetary, and although there were among them many brave and able soldiers the system did not tend to bring the best to the top. Their "laziness and lack of interest" in outdoor sports dismayed a British military attaché who, on visiting a frontier garrison near the Afghan border, was appalled to find "not a single tennis court." In the purges after the Japanese war large numbers had resigned or been forced out in an effort to loosen the mass clogging the top. In one year 341 generals, nearly as many as in all the French Army, and 400 colonels had been retired as inefficient. Yet despite improvements in pay and promotion there was a shortage in 1913 of 3,000 officers. Much had been done since the Japanese war to clean away the decay in the army, but the Russian regime was still the same.

"This insane regime," its ablest defender, Count Witte, the premier of 1903–06, called it; "this tangle of cowardice, blindness, craftiness, and stupidity." The regime was ruled from the top by a sovereign who had but one idea of government—to preserve intact the absolute monarchy bequeathed to him by his father—and who, lacking the intellect, energy, or training for his job, fell back on personal favorites, whim, simple mulishness, and other devices of the empty-headed autocrat. His father, Alexander III, who deliberately intended to keep his son uneducated in statecraft until the age of thirty, unfortunately miscalculated his own life expectancy, and died when Nicholas was twenty-six. The new Czar, now forty-six, had learned nothing in the interval, and the impression of imperturbability he conveyed was in reality apathy—the indifference of a mind so shallow as to be all surface. When a telegram was brought to him announcing the annihilation of the Russian fleet at Tsushima, he read it, stuffed it in his pocket, and went on playing tennis. When the premier, Kokovtsov, returning from Berlin in November 1913, gave the Czar a personal report on German preparations for war, Nicholas listened to him with his usual intent, unwavering gaze, "looking straight into my eyes." After a long pause, when the premier had finished, "as if waking from a reverie, he said gravely, 'God's will be done.'" In fact, Kokovtsov concluded, he was simply bored.

At the bottom the regime was based upon an ant-heap of secret police who penetrated every ministry, bureau, and provincial department to such a degree that Count Witte felt obliged each year to deposit the notes and records he was keeping for his memoirs in a bank vault in France for safekeeping. When another premier, Stolypin, was assassinated in 1911 the perpetrators were discovered to be the secret police acting as *agents provocateurs* to discredit the revolutionists.

Between the Czar and the secret police the mainstay of the regime were the *Tchinovniki*, a class of bureaucrats and officials drawn from the nobility who performed the actual business of government. They were responsible to no constitutional body and subject only to arbitrary recall by the Czar, who, bent by the winds of court intrigue and his wife's suspicions, exercised it constantly. Under the circumstances able men did not hold office long, and one who refused it, pleading "poor health," inspired a colleague to comment, "In those days everyone was in poor health."

Simmering with chronic discontent, Russia in the reign of Nicholas II was harassed by disasters, massacres, military defeats, and uprisings culminating in the revolution of 1905. When at that time the Czar was advised by Count Witte that he must either grant the constitution which the people were demanding or restore order under military dictatorship, he was obliged with bitter distaste to accept the first choice because his father's cousin, the Grand Duke Nicholas, commander of the St. Petersburg Military District, refused to accept responsibility for the second. For this default the Grand Duke was never forgiven by the hyper-Bourbons, the Baltic barons of German blood and sympathy, the Black Hundreds—those "anarchists of the right"—and other reactionary groups who manned the ramparts of autocracy. They felt, as did many Germans, including the Kaiser in alternate hours, that the common interests of autocracies, formerly linked in the *Drei-Kaiser Bund*, made Germany a more natural ally of Russia than the democracies of the West. Regarding the liberals within Russia as their first enemy, the Russian reactionaries preferred the Kaiser to the Duma as the French Right of a later day were to prefer Hitler to Léon Blum. Only the growing threat of Germany itself in the last twenty years before the war induced Czarist Russia against her natural inclination to make alliance with republican France. Ultimately the threat even brought her together with England, which for a century had barred her from Constantinople and of whom one of the Czar's uncles, the Grand Duke Vladimir Alexandrovich, said in 1898: "I hope to live long enough to hear England's death rattle. That is the ardent prayer I address to God each day!"

The cohorts of Vladimir dominated a court that was living out its age of Nero, whose ladies enjoyed the thrills of afternoon séances with the unwashed Rasputin. But Russia also had its Democrats and Liberals of the Duma, its Bakunin the Nihilist, its Prince Kropotkin who became an anarchist, its "intelligentsia" of whom the Czar said, "How I detest that word! I wish I could order the Academy to strike it from the Russian dictionary," its Levins who agonized endlessly over their souls, socialism, and the soil, its Uncle Vanyas without hope, its particular quality that caused a British diplomat to conclude that "everyone in Russia was a little mad"—a quality called *le charme slav*, half nonchalance, half inefficiency, a kind of *fin de siècle* fecklessness that hung like a faint mist over the city on the Neva which the world knew as St. Petersburg and did not know was the Cherry Orchard.

Insofar as readiness for war was concerned, the regime was personified by its Minister for War, General Sukhomlinov, an artful, indolent, pleasure-loving, chubby little man in his sixties of whom his colleague, Foreign Minister Sazonov, said, "It was very difficult to make him work but to get him to tell the truth was well-nigh impossible." Having won the Cross of St. George as a dashing young cavalry officer in the war of 1877 against the Turks, Sukhomlinov believed that military knowledge acquired in that campaign was permanent truth. As Minister of War he scolded a meeting of Staff College instructors for interest in such "innovations" as the factor of firepower against the saber, lance and the bayonet charge. He could not hear the phrase "modern war," he said, without a sense of annoyance. "As war was, so it has remained . . . all these things are merely vicious innovations. Look at me, for instance; I have not read a military manual for the last twenty-five years." In 1913 he dismissed five instructors of the College who persisted in preaching the vicious heresy of "fire tactics."

Sukhomlinov's native intelligence was adulterated by levity to cunning and cleverness. He was short and soft, with a cat-like face, neat white whiskers and beard, and an ingratiating, almost feline manner that captivated those like the Czar whom he set himself to please. In others, like the French ambassador, Paléologue, he inspired "distrust at first sight." Ministerial office, both appointment and dismissal, being entirely at the whim of the Czar, Sukhomlinov had won and kept himself in favor by being at once obsequious and entertaining, by funny stories and acts of buffoonery, avoidance of serious and unpleasant matters, and careful cultivation of "the Friend," Rasputin. As a result he proved immune to charges of corruption and incompetence, to a sensational divorce scandal, and to an even more resounding spy scandal.

Smitten in 1906 by the twenty-three-year-old wife of a provincial governor, Sukhomlinov contrived to get rid of the husband by divorce on framed evidence and marry the beautiful residue as his fourth wife. Naturally lazy, he now left his work more and more in the hands of subordinates while, in the words of the French ambassador, "keeping all his strength for conjugal pleasures with a wife 32 years younger than himself." Mme. Sukhomlinov delighted to order clothes in Paris, dine in expensive restaurants, and give large parties. To gratify her extravagances Sukhomlinov became an early and successful practitioner of the art of the expense account. He charged the government traveling expenses at the rate of 24 horse versts *per diem* while actually making his tours of inspection by railroad. Netting a lucrative balance, augmented by inside knowledge of trends on the stock market, he was able to bank 702,737 rubles during a six-year period in which his total salary was 270,000 rubles. In this happy exercise he was aided by an entourage who lent him money in return for military passes, invitations to maneuvers, and other forms of information. One of them, an Austrian named Altschiller who had supplied the evidence for Mme. Sukhomlinov's divorce and who was received as an intimate in the Minister's home and office where documents were left lying about, was revealed after his departure in January 1914 to have been Austria's chief agent in Russia. Another was the more notorious Colonel Myasoedev, reputed to be Mme. Sukhomlinov's lover, who though only chief of railroad police at the frontier was possessor of five German decorations and honored by the Kaiser with an invitation to lunch at Rominten, the imperial hunting lodge just over the border. Not surprisingly Colonel Myasoedev was suspected of espionage. He was arrested and tried in 1912, but as a result of Sukhomlinov's personal intervention was acquitted and enabled to continue in his former duties up to and through the first year of the war. In 1915, when his protector had finally lost office as a result of Russian reverses, he was rearrested, convicted, and hanged as a spy.

Sukhomlinov's fortunes after 1914 are significant. He escaped prosecution at the same time as Colonel Myasoedev only through the influence of the Czar and Czarina, but ultimately, in August 1917, after the Czar had abdicated and the Provisional Government was already crumbling, he too was brought to trial. In the ruin and tumult of that time he was tried less for treason, which was the nominal charge, than for all the sins of the old regime. In the prosecutor's summing up those sins came to one: that the Russian people, having been forced to fight without guns or munitions, suffered a loss of confidence in the government which had spread like a plague, with "terrible consequences." After a month of sensational testimony in which the details of his financial and amorous peculations were brought out, Sukhomlinov was acquitted of treason but found guilty of "abuse of power and inactivity." Sentenced to hard labor for life, he was liberated a few months later by the Bolsheviks and made his way to Berlin, where he lived until his death in 1926 and where in 1924 he published his memoirs which he dedicated to the deposed Kaiser. In a preface he explained that the Russian and German monarchies having been destroyed as enemies during the war, only the rapprochement of the two countries could restore them to power. This thought so impressed the Hohenzollern exile that he wrote out a dedication of his own memoirs to Sukhomlinov but was apparently dissuaded from using it in the published version.

This was the man who was Russia's Minister of War from 1908 to 1914. Embodying, as he did, the opinions and enjoying the support of the reactionaries, his preparation for war with Germany, which was the Ministry's chief task, was something less than wholehearted. He immediately halted the movement for reform of the army which had made progress since the shame of the Russo-Japanese War. The General Staff, after having been given independence in order to further its study of modern military science, was after 1908 once again subordinated to the Minister of War, who had sole access to the Czar. Shorn of initiative and power, it found no able leader or even the consistency of a single second-rate one. In the six years prior to 1914 six different Chiefs of Staff succeeded each other, with effect upon war plans that was hardly systematic.

While Sukhomlinov left work to others, he allowed no freedom of ideas. Clinging stubbornly to obsolete theories and ancient glories, he claimed that Russia's past defeats had been due to mistakes of commanding officers rather than to any inadequacy of training, preparation, or supply. With invincible belief in the bayonet's supremacy over the bullet, he made no effort to build up factories for increased production of shells, rifles, and cartridges. No country, its military critics invariably discover afterward, is ever adequately prepared in munitions. Britain's shell shortage was to become a national scandal; the French shortage of everything from heavy artillery to boots was a scandal before the war began; in Russia, Sukhomlinov did not even use up the funds the government appropriated for munitions. Russia began the war with 850 shells per gun compared to a reserve of 2,000 to 3,000 shells per gun used by the Western armies, although Sukhomlinov himself had agreed in 1912 to a compromise of 1,500 per gun. The Russian infantry division had 7 field-gun batteries compared with 14 in the German division. The whole Russian Army had 60 batteries of heavy artillery compared with 381 in the German Army. Warnings that war would be largely a duel of firepower Sukhomlinov treated with contempt.

Greater only than his aversion to "fire tactics" was Sukhomlinov's aversion to the Grand Duke Nicholas, who was eight years his junior and represented the reforming tendency within the army. Six foot six, of narrow height with handsome head, pointed beard, and boots as tall as a horse's belly, the Grand Duke was a gallant and imposing figure. After the Japanese war he had been named to reorganize the army as chief of a Council of National Defense. Its purpose was the same as that of the Esher Committee after the Boer War, but, unlike its British model, it had soon succumbed to lethargy and the mandarins. The reactionaries, who resented the Grand Duke for his share in the Constitutional Manifesto and feared his popularity, succeeded in having the Council abolished in 1908. As a career officer who had served as Inspector-General of Cavalry in the Japanese war and who knew personally almost the entire officer corps, each of whom on taking up a new post had to report to him as Commander of the St. Petersburg District, the Grand Duke was the most admired figure in the army. This was less for any specific achievement than for his commanding size and looks and manner, which inspired confidence and awe in the soldiers and either devotion or jealousy in his colleagues.

Brusque and even harsh in manner to officers and men alike, he was regarded outside court as the only "man" in the royal family. Peasant soldiers who had never seen him told stories in which he figured as a sort of legendary champion of Holy Russia against the "German clique" and palace corruption. Echoes of such sentiments did not add to his popularity at court, especially with the Czarina, who already hated "Nikolasha" because he despised Rasputin. "I have absolutely no faith in N.," she wrote to her husband. "I know him to be far from clever and having gone against a man of God his work cannot be blessed or his advice good." She continually suggested that he was plotting to force the Czar to abdicate and, relying on his popularity with the army, to place himself on the throne.

Royal suspicions had kept him from the chief command during the war with Japan and consequently from the blame that followed. In any subsequent war it would be impossible to do without him, and in the pre-war plans he had been designated to command the front against Germany, the Czar himself expecting to act as Commander in Chief with a Chief of General Staff to direct operations. In France where the Grand Duke went several times to maneuvers and where he came under the influence of Foch whose optimism he shared, he was extravagantly feted as much for his magnificent presence, which seemed a reassuring symbol of Russian might, as for his known dislike of Germany. With delight the French repeated the remarks of Prince Kotzebue, the Grand Duke's aide, who said his master believed that only if Germany were crushed once for all, and divided up again into little states each happy with its own little court, could the world expect to live in peace. No less ardent a friend of France was the Grand Duke's wife Anastasia and her sister Militza who was married to the Grand Duke's brother Peter. As daughters of King Nikita of Montenegro, their fondness for France was in direct proportion to their natural hatred of Austria. At a royal picnic in the last days of July, 1914, the "Montenegrin nightingales," as Paléologue called the two princesses, grouped themselves beside him, twittering about the crisis. "There's going to be a war . . . there will be nothing left of Austria . . . you will get back Alsace-Lorraine . . . our armies will meet in Berlin." One sister showed the ambassador a jeweled box in which she carried soil from Lorraine, while the other told how she had planted seeds of Lorraine thistles in her garden.

For the event the Russian General Staff had worked out two alternate plans of campaign, the ultimate choice depending upon what Germany would do. If Germany launched her main strength against France, Russia would launch her main strength against Austria. In this case four armies would take the field against Austria and two against Germany.

The plan for the German front provided for a two-pronged invasion of East Prussia by Russia's First and Second Armies, the First to advance north, and the Second south, of the barrier formed by the Masurian Lakes. As the First, or Vilna, Army, named for its area of concentration, had a direct railway line available, it would be ready to start first. It was to advance two days ahead of the Second, or Warsaw, Army and move against the Germans, "with the object of drawing upon itself the greatest possible enemy strength." Meanwhile the Second Army was to come around the lake barrier from the south and, moving in behind the Germans, cut off their retreat to the Vistula River. The success of the pincer movement depended upon concerted timing to prevent the Germans from engaging either Russian wing separately. The enemy was to be "attacked energetically and determinedly whenever and wherever met." Once the German Army was rounded up and destroyed, the march on Berlin, 150 miles beyond the Vistula, would follow.

The German plan did not contemplate giving up East Prussia. It was a land of rich farms and wide meadows where Holstein cattle grazed, pigs and chickens scuttled about inside stone-walled farmyards, where the famous Trakehnen stud bred remounts for the German Army and where the large estates were owned by Junkers who, to the horror of an English governness employed by one of them, shot foxes instead of hunting them properly on horseback. Further east, near Russia, was the country of "still waters, dark woods," with wide-flung lakes fringed by rushes, forests of pine and birch and many marshes and streams. Its most famous landmark was Rominten Forest, the Hohenzollern hunting preserve of 90,000 acres on the edge of Russia where the Kaiser came each year, attired in knickerbockers and feathered hat, to shoot boar and deer and an occasional Russian moose who, wandering innocently over the border, offered itself as target to the imperial gun. Although the native stock was not Teutonic but Slavic, the region had been under German rule—with some Polish interludes—for seven hundred years, ever since the Order of Teutonic Knights established themselves there in 1225. Despite defeat in 1410 by Poles and Lithuanians in a great battle at a village called Tannenberg, the Knights had remained and grown—or declined—into Junkers. In Königsberg, chief city of the region, the first Hohenzollern sovereign had been crowned King of Prussia in 1701.

With its shores washed by the Baltic, with its "King's city" where Prussia's sovereigns had been crowned, East Prussia was not a country the Germans would yield lightly. Along the river Angerapp running through the Insterburg Gap, defense positions had been carefully prepared; in the swampy eastern region roads had been built up as causeways which would confine an enemy to their narrow crests. In addition the whole of East Prussia was crisscrossed by a network of railroads giving the defending army the advantage of mobility and rapid transfer from one front to the other to meet the advance of either enemy wing.

When the Schlieffen plan had been first adopted, fears for East Prussia were less because it was assumed that Russia would have to keep large forces in the Far East to guard against Japan. German diplomacy, despite a certain record for clumsiness, was expected to overcome the Anglo-Japanese Treaty, an unnatural alliance as Germany regarded it, and keep Japan neutral as a constant threat to Russia's rear.

The German General Staff's specialist in Russian affairs was Lieutenant-Colonel Max Hoffmann whose task was to work out the probable Russian plan of campaign in a war with Germany. In his early forties, Hoffmann was tall and heavily built, with a large round head and a Prussian haircut shaved so close to the scalp it made him look bald. His expression was good-humored but uncompromising. He wore black-rimmed glasses and carefully trained his black eyebrows to grow in a dashing upward curve at their outer ends. He was equally careful and proud of his small, delicate hands and impeccable trouser creases. Though indolent, he was resourceful; though a poor rider, worse swordsman, and gluttonous eater and drinker, he was quick-thinking and rapid in judgment. He was amiable, lucky, astute, and respected no one. In intervals of regimental duty before the war he drank wine and consumed sausages all night at the officers' club until 7:00 A.M., when he took his company out on parade and returned for a snack of more sausages and two quarts of Moselle before breakfast.

After graduation from the Staff College in 1898, Hoffmann had served a six-months' tour of duty in Russia as interpreter and five years subsequently in the Russian section of the General Staff under Schlieffen before going as Germany's military observer to the Russo-Japanese War. When a Japanese general refused him permission to watch a battle from a nearby hill, etiquette gave way to that natural quality in Germans whose expression so often fails to endear them to others. "You are a yellow-skin; you are uncivilized if you will not let me go to that hill!" Hoffmann yelled at the general in the presence of other foreign attachés and at least one correspondent. Belonging to a race hardly second to the Germans in sense of self-importance, the general yelled back, "We Japanese are paying for this military information with our blood and we don't propose to share it with others!" Protocol for the occasion broke down altogether.

On his return to the General Staff under Moltke, Hoffmann resumed work on the Russian plan of campaign. A colonel of the Russian General Staff had sold an early version of his country's plan for a high price in 1902, but since that time, according to Hoffmann's not always wholly serious memoirs, the price had gone up beyond the stingy funds allotted to Germany's military intelligence. The terrain of East Prussia, however, made the general outlines of a Russian offensive self-evident: it would have to be a two-pronged advance around the Masurian Lakes. Hoffmann's study of the Russian Army and the factors governing its mobilization and transportation enabled the Germans to judge the timing of the offensive. The German Army, inferior in numbers, could choose either of two ways to meet a superior force advancing in two wings. They could either withdraw, or attack one wing before the other, whichever offered the best opportunity. The stern formula dictated by Schlieffen was to strike "with all available strength at the first Russian army that came within reach."

OUTBREAK

Outbreak

"SOME DAMNED foolish thing in the Balkans," Bismarck had predicted, would ignite the next war. The assassination of the Austrian heir apparent, Archduke Franz Ferdinand, by Serbian nationalists on June 28, 1914, satisfied his condition. Austria-Hungary, with the bellicose frivolity of senile empires, determined to use the occasion to absorb Serbia as she had absorbed Bosnia and Herzegovina in 1909. Russia on that occasion, weakened by the war with Japan, had been forced to acquiesce by a German ultimatum followed by the Kaiser's appearance in "shining armor," as he put it, at the side of his ally, Austria. To avenge that humiliation and for the sake of her prestige as the major Slav power, Russia was now prepared to put on the shining armor herself. On July 5 Germany assured Austria that she could count on Germany's "faithful support" if whatever punitive action she took against Serbia brought her into conflict with Russia. This was the signal that let loose the irresistible onrush of events. On July 23 Austria delivered an ultimatum to Serbia, on July 26 rejected the Serbian reply (although the Kaiser, now nervous, admitted that it "dissipates every reason for war"), on July 28 declared war on Serbia, on July 29 bombarded Belgrade. On that day Russia mobilized along her Austrian frontier and on July 30 both Austria and Russia ordered general mobilization. On July 31 Germany issued an ultimatum to Russia to demobilize within twelve hours and "make us a distinct declaration to that effect."

War pressed against every frontier. Suddenly dismayed, governments struggled and twisted to fend it off. It was no use. Agents at frontiers were reporting every cavalry patrol as a deployment to beat the mobilization gun. General staffs, goaded by their relentless timetables, were pounding the table for the signal to move lest their opponents gain an hour's head start. Appalled upon the brink, the chiefs of state who would be ultimately responsible for their country's fate attempted to back away but the pull of military schedules dragged them forward.

6

August 1: Berlin

At noon on Saturday, August 1, the German ultimatum to Russia expired without a Russian reply. Within an hour a telegram went out to the German ambassador in St. Petersburg instructing him to declare war by five o'clock that afternoon. At five o'clock the Kaiser decreed general mobilization, some preliminaries having already got off to a head start under the declaration of *Kriegesgefahr* (Danger of War) the day before. At five-thirty Chancellor Bethmann-Hollweg, absorbed in a document he was holding in his hand and accompanied by little Jagow, the Foreign Minister, hurried down the steps of the Foreign Office, hailed an ordinary taxi, and sped off to the palace. Shortly afterward General von Moltke, the gloomy Chief of General Staff, was pulled up short as he was driving back to his office with the mobilization order signed by the Kaiser in his pocket. A messenger in another car overtook him with an urgent summons from the palace. He returned to hear a last-minute, desperate proposal from the Kaiser that reduced Moltke to tears and could have changed the history of the twentieth century.

Now that the moment had come, the Kaiser suffered at the necessary risk to East Prussia, in spite of the six weeks' leeway his Staff promised before the Russians could fully mobilize. "I hate the Slavs," he confessed to an Austrian officer. "I know it is a sin to do so. We ought not to hate anyone. But I can't help hating them." He had taken comfort, however, in the news, reminiscent of 1905, of strikes and riots in St. Petersburg, of mobs smashing windows, and "violent street fights between revolutionaries and police." Count Pourtalès, his aged ambassador, who had been seven years in Russia, concluded, and repeatedly assured his government, that Russia would not fight for fear of revolution. Captain von Eggeling, the German military attaché, kept repeating the credo about 1916, and when Russia nevertheless mobilized, he reported she planned "no tenacious offensive but a slow retreat as in 1812." In the affinity for error of German diplomats, these judgments established a record. They gave heart to the Kaiser, who as late as July 31 composed a missive for the "guidance" of his Staff, rejoicing in the "mood of a sick Tom-cat" that, on the evidence of his envoys, he said prevailed in the Russian court and army.

In Berlin on August 1, the crowds milling in the streets and massed in thousands in front of the palace were tense and heavy with anxiety. Socialism, which most of Berlin's workers professed, did not run so deep as their instinctive fear and hatred of the Slavic hordes. Although they had been told by the Kaiser, in his speech from the balcony announcing *Kriegesgefahr* the evening before, that the "sword has been forced into our hand," they still waited in the ultimate dim hope of a Russian reply. The hour of the ultimatum passed. A journalist in the crowd felt the air "electric with rumor. People told each other Russia had asked for an extension of time. The Bourse writhed in panic. The afternoon passed in almost insufferable anxiety." Bethmann-Hollweg issued a statement ending, "If the iron dice roll, may God help us." At five o'clock a policeman appeared at the palace gate and announced mobilization to the crowd, which obediently struck up the national hymn, "Now thank we all our God." Cars raced down Unter den Linden with officers standing up in them, waving handkerchiefs and shouting, "Mobilization!" Instantly converted from Marx to Mars, people cheered wildly and rushed off to vent their feelings on suspected Russian spies, several of whom were pummeled or trampled to death in the course of the next few days.

Once the mobilization button was pushed, the whole vast machinery for calling up, equipping, and transporting two million men began turning automatically. Reservists went to their designated depots, were issued uniforms, equipment, and arms, formed into companies and companies into battalions, were joined by cavalry, cyclists, artillery, medical units, cook wagons, blacksmith wagons, even postal wagons, moved according to prepared railway timetables to concentration points near the frontier where they would be formed into divisions, divisions into corps, and corps into armies ready to advance and fight. One army corps alone—out of the total of 40 in the German forces—required 170 railway cars for officers, 965 for infantry, 2,960 for cavalry, 1,915 for artillery and supply wagons, 6,010 in all, grouped in 140 trains and an equal number again for their supplies. From the moment the order was given, everything was to move at fixed times according to a schedule precise down to the number of train axles that would pass over a given bridge within a given time.

Confident in his magnificent system, Deputy Chief of Staff General Waldersee had not even returned to Berlin at the beginning of the crisis but had written to Jagow: "I shall remain here ready to jump; we are all prepared at the General Staff; in the meantime there is nothing for us to do." It was a proud tradition inherited from the elder, or "great," Moltke who on mobilization day in 1870 was found lying on a sofa reading *Lady Audley's Secret.*

His enviable calm was not present today in the palace. Face to face no longer with the specter but the reality of a two-front war, the Kaiser was as close to the "sick Tom-cat" mood as he thought the Russians were. More cosmopolitan and more timid than the archetype Prussian, he had never actually wanted a general war. He wanted greater power, greater prestige, above all more authority in the world's affairs for Germany but he preferred to obtain them by frightening rather than by fighting other nations. He wanted the gladiator's rewards without the battle, and whenever the prospect of battle came too close, as at Algeciras and Agadir, he shrank.

As the final crisis boiled, his marginalia on telegrams grew more and more agitated: "Aha! the common cheat," "Rot!" "He lies!" "Mr. Grey is a false dog," "Twaddle!" "The rascal is crazy or an idiot!" When Russia mobilized he burst into a tirade of passionate foreboding, not against the Slav traitors but against the unforgettable figure of the wicked uncle: "The world will be engulfed in the most terrible of wars, the ultimate aim of which is the ruin of Germany. England, France and Russia have conspired for our annihilation . . . that is the naked truth of the situation which was slowly but surely created by Edward VII. . . . The encirclement of Germany is at last an accomplished fact. We have run our heads into the noose. . . . The dead Edward is stronger than the living I!"

Conscious of the shadow of the dead Edward, the Kaiser would have welcomed any way out of the commitment to fight both Russia and France and, behind France, the looming figure of still-undeclared England.

At the last moment one was offered. A colleague of Bethmann's came to beg him to do anything he could to save Germany from a two-front war and suggested a means. For years a possible solution for Alsace had been discussed in terms of autonomy as a Federal State within the German Empire. If offered and accepted by the Alsatians, this solution would have deprived France of any reason to liberate the lost provinces. As recently as July 16, the French Socialist Congress had gone on record in favor of it. But the German military had always insisted that the provinces must remain garrisoned and their political rights subordinated to "military necessity." Until 1911 no constitution had ever been granted and autonomy never. Bethmann's colleague now urged him to make an immediate, public, and official offer for a conference on autonomy for Alsace. This could be allowed to drag on without result, while its moral effect would force France to refrain from attack while at least considering the offer. Time would be gained for Germany to turn her forces against Russia while remaining stationary in the West, thus keeping England out.

The author of this proposal remains anonymous, and it may be apocryphal. It does not matter. The opportunity was there, and the Chancellor could have thought of it for himself. But to seize it required boldness, and Bethmann, behind his distinguished façade of great height, somber eyes, and well-trimmed imperial, was a man, as Theodore Roosevelt said of Taft, "who means well feebly." Instead of offering France an inducement to stay neutral, the German government sent her an ultimatum at the same time as the ultimatum to Russia. They asked France to reply within eighteen hours whether she would stay neutral in a Russo-German war, and added that if she did Germany would "demand as guarantee of neutrality the handing over to us of the fortresses of Toul and Verdun which we shall occupy and restore after the war is over"—in other words, the handing over of the key to the French door.

Baron von Schoen, German ambassador in Paris, could not bring himself to pass on this "brutal" demand at a moment when, it seemed to him, French neutrality would have been such a supreme advantage to Germany that his government might well have offered to pay a price for it rather than exact a penalty. He presented the request for a statement of neutrality without the demand for the fortresses, but the French, who had intercepted and decoded his instructions, knew of it anyway. When Schoen, at 11:00 A.M. on August 1, asked for France's reply he was answered that France "would act in accordance with her interests."

In Berlin just after five o'clock a telephone rang in the Foreign Office. Under-Secretary Zimmermann, who answered it, turned to the editor of the *Berliner Tageblatt* sitting by his desk and said, "Moltke wants to know whether things can start." At that moment a telegram from London, just decoded, broke in upon the planned proceedings. It offered hope that if the movement against France could be instantly stopped Germany might safely fight a one-front war after all. Carrying it with them, Bethmann and Jagow dashed off on their taxi trip to the palace.

The telegram, from Prince Lichnowsky, ambassador in London, reported an English offer, as Lichnowsky understood it, "that in case we did not attack France, England would remain neutral and would guarantee France's neutrality."

The ambassador belonged to that class of Germans who spoke English and copied English manners, sports, and dress, in a strenuous endeavor to become the very pattern of an English gentleman. His fellow noblemen, the Prince of Pless, Prince Blücher, and Prince Münster were all married to English wives. At a dinner in Berlin in 1911, in honor of a British general, the guest of honor was astonished to find that all forty German guests, including Bethmann-Hollweg and Admiral Tirpitz, spoke English fluently. Lichnowsky differed from his class in that he was not only in manner but in heart an earnest Anglophile. He had come to London determined to make himself and his country liked. English society had been lavish with country weekends. To the ambassador no tragedy could be greater than war between the country of his birth and the country of his heart, and he was grasping at any handle to avert it.

When the Foreign Secretary, Sir Edward Grey, telephoned him that morning, in the interval of a Cabinet meeting, Lichnowsky, out of his own anxiety, interpreted what Grey said to him as an offer by England to stay neutral and to keep France neutral in a Russo-German war, if, in return, Germany would promise not to attack France.

Actually, Grey had not said quite that. What, in his elliptical way, he offered was a promise to keep France neutral if Germany would promise to stay neutral as against France *and* Russia, in other words, not go to war against either, pending the result of efforts to settle the Serbian affair. After eight years as Foreign Secretary in a period of chronic "Bosnias," as Bülow called them, Grey had perfected a manner of speaking designed to convey as little meaning as possible; his avoidance of the point-blank, said a colleague, almost amounted to method. Over the telephone, Lichnowsky, himself dazed by the coming tragedy, would have had no difficulty misunderstanding him.

The Kaiser clutched at Lichnowsky's passport to a one-front war. Minutes counted. Already mobilization was rolling inexorably toward the French frontier. The first hostile act, seizure of a railway junction in Luxembourg, whose neutrality the five Great Powers, including Germany, had guaranteed, was scheduled within an hour. It must be stopped, stopped at once. But how? Where was Moltke? Moltke had left the palace. An aide was sent off, with siren screaming, to intercept him. He was brought back.

The Kaiser was himself again, the All-Highest, the War Lord, blazing with a new idea, planning, proposing, disposing. He read Moltke the telegram and said in triumph: "Now we can go to war against Russia only. We simply march the whole of our Army to the East!"

Aghast at the thought of his marvelous machinery of mobilization wrenched into reverse, Moltke refused point-blank. For the past ten years, first as assistant to Schlieffen, then as his successor, Moltke's job had been planning for this day, The Day, *Der Tag*, for which all Germany's energies were gathered, on which the march to final mastery of Europe would begin. It weighed upon him with an oppressive, almost unbearable responsibility.

Tall, heavy, bald, and sixty-six years old, Moltke habitually wore an expression of profound distress which led the Kaiser to call him *der traurige Julius* (or what might be rendered "Gloomy Gus"; in fact, his name was Helmuth). Poor health, for which he took an annual cure at Carlsbad, and the shadow of a great uncle were perhaps cause for gloom. From his window in the red brick General Staff building on the Königplatz where he lived as well as worked, he looked out every day on the equestrian statue of his namesake, the hero of 1870 and, together with Bismarck, the architect of the German Empire. The nephew was a poor horseman with a habit of falling off on staff rides and, worse, a follower of Christian Science with a side interest in anthroposophism and other cults. For this unbecoming weakness in a Prussian officer he was considered "soft"; what is more, he painted, played the cello, carried Goethe's *Faust* in his pocket, and had begun a translation of Maeterlinck's *Pelléas et Mélisande*.

Introspective and a doubter by nature, he had said to the Kaiser upon his appointment in 1906: "I do not know how I shall get on in the event of a campaign. I am very critical of myself." Yet he was neither personally nor politically timid. In 1911, disgusted by Germany's retreat in the Agadir crisis, he wrote to Conrad von Hötzendorff that if things got worse he would resign, propose to disband the army and "place ourselves under the protection of Japan; then we can make money undisturbed and turn into imbeciles." He did not hesitate to talk back to the Kaiser, but told him "quite brutally" in 1900 that his Peking expedition was a "crazy adventure," and when offered the appointment as Chief of Staff, asked the Kaiser if he expected "to win the big prize twice in the same lottery"—a thought that had certainly influenced William's choice. He refused to take the post unless the Kaiser stopped his habit of winning all the war games which was making nonsense of maneuvers. Surprisingly, the Kaiser meekly obeyed.

Now, on the climactic night of August 1, Moltke was in no mood for any more of the Kaiser's meddling with serious military matters, or with meddling of any kind with the fixed arrangements. To turn around the deployment of a million men from west to east at the very moment of departure would have taken a more iron nerve than Moltke disposed of. He saw a vision of the deployment crumbling apart in confusion, supplies here, soldiers there, ammunition lost in the middle, companies without officers, divisions without staffs, and those 11,000 trains, each exquisitely scheduled to click over specified tracks at specified intervals of ten minutes, tangled in a grotesque ruin of the most perfectly planned military movement in history.

"Your Majesty," Moltke said to him now, "it cannot be done. The deployment of millions cannot be improvised. If Your Majesty insists on leading the whole army to the East it will not be an army ready for battle but a disorganized mob of armed men with no arrangements for supply. Those arrangements took a whole year of intricate labor to complete"—and Moltke closed upon that rigid phrase, the basis for every major German mistake, the phrase that launched the invasion of Belgium and the submarine war against the United States, the inevitable phrase when military plans dictate policy—"and once settled, it cannot be altered."

In fact it could have been altered. The German General Staff, though committed since 1905 to a plan of attack upon France first, had in their files, revised each year until 1913, an alternative plan against Russia with all the trains running eastward.

"Build no more fortresses, build railways," ordered the elder Moltke who had laid out his strategy on a railway map and bequeathed the dogma that railways are the key to war. In Germany the railway system was under military control with a staff officer assigned to every line; no track could be laid or changed without permission of the General Staff. Annual mobilization war games kept railway officials in constant practice and tested their ability to improvise and divert traffic by telegrams reporting lines cut and bridges destroyed. The best brains produced by the War College, it was said, went into the railway section and ended up in lunatic asylums.

When Moltke's "It cannot be done" was revealed after the war in his memoirs, General von Staab, Chief of the Railway Division, was so incensed by what he considered a reproach upon his bureau that he wrote a book to prove it could have been done. In pages of charts and graphs he demonstrated how, given notice on August 1, he could have deployed four out of the seven armies to the Eastern Front by August 15, leaving three to defend the West. Matthias Erzberger, the Reichstag deputy and leader of the Catholic Centrist Party, has left another testimony. He says that Moltke himself, within six months of the event, admitted to him that the assault on

France at the beginning was a mistake and instead, "the larger part of our army ought first to have been sent East to smash the Russian steam roller, limiting operations in the West to beating off the enemy's attack on our frontier."

On the night of August 1, Moltke, clinging to the fixed plan, lacked the necessary nerve. "Your uncle would have given me a different answer," the Kaiser said to him bitterly. The reproach "wounded me deeply," Moltke wrote afterward; "I never pretended to be the equal of the old Field Marshal." Nevertheless he continued to refuse. "My protest that it would be impossible to maintain peace between France and Germany while both countries were mobilized made no impression. Everybody got more and more excited and I was alone in my opinion."

Finally, when Moltke convinced the Kaiser that the mobilization plan could not be changed, the group which included Bethmann and Jagow drafted a telegram to England regretting that Germany's advance movements toward the French border "can no longer be altered," but offering a guarantee not to cross the border before August 3 at 7:00 P.M., which cost them nothing as no crossing was scheduled before that time. Jagow rushed off a telegram to his ambassador in Paris, where mobilization had already been decreed at four o'clock, instructing him helpfully to "please keep France quiet for the time being." The Kaiser added a personal telegram to King George, telling him that for "technical reasons" mobilization could not be countermanded at this late hour, but "If France offers me neutrality which must be guaranteed by the British fleet and army, I shall of course refrain from attacking France and employ my troops elsewhere. I hope France will not become nervous."

It was now minutes before seven o'clock, the hour when the 16th Division was scheduled to move into Luxembourg. Bethmann excitedly insisted that Luxembourg must not be entered under any circumstances while waiting for the British answer. Instantly the Kaiser, without asking Moltke, ordered his aide-de-camp to telephone and telegraph 16th Division Headquarters at Trier to cancel the movement. Moltke saw ruin again. Luxembourg's railways were essential for the offensive through Belgium against France. "At that moment," his memoirs say, "I thought my heart would break."

Despite all his pleading, the Kaiser refused to budge. Instead, he added a closing sentence to his telegram to King George, "The troops on my frontier are in the act of being stopped by telephone and telegraph from crossing into France," a slight if vital twist of the truth, for the Kaiser could not acknowledge to England that what he had intended and what was being stopped was the violation of a neutral country. It would have implied his intention also to violate Belgium, which would have been *casus belli* in England, and England's mind was not yet made up.

"Crushed," Moltke says of himself, on what should have been the culminating day of his career, he returned to the General Staff and "burst into bitter tears of abject despair." When his aide brought him for his signature the written order canceling the Luxembourg movement, "I threw my pen down on the table and refused to sign." To have signed as the first order after mobilization one that would have annulled all the careful preparations would have been taken, he knew, as evidence of "hesitancy and irresolution." "Do what you want with this telegram," he said to his aide; "I will not sign it."

He was still brooding at eleven o'clock when another summons came from the palace. Moltke found the Kaiser in his bedroom, characteristically dressed for the occasion, with a military overcoat over his nightshirt. A telegram had come from Lichnowsky, who, in a further talk with Grey, had discovered his error and now wired sadly, "A positive proposal by England is, on the whole, not in prospect."

"Now you can do what you like," said the Kaiser, and went back to bed. Moltke, the Commander in Chief who had now to direct a campaign that would decide the fate of Germany, was left permanently shaken. "That was my first experience of the war," he wrote afterward. "I never recovered from the shock of this incident. Something in me broke and I was never the same thereafter."

Neither was the world, he might have added. The Kaiser's telephone order to Trier had not arrived in time. At seven o'clock, as scheduled, the first frontier of the war was crossed, the distinction going to an infantry company of the 69th Regiment under command of a certain Lieutenant Feldmann. Just inside the Luxembourg border, on the slopes of the Ardennes about twelve miles from Bastogne in Belgium, stood a little town known to the Germans as Ulflingen. Around it cows grazed on the hillside pastures; on its steep, cobblestone streets not a stray wisp of hay, even in August harvest time, was allowed to offend the strict laws governing municipal cleanliness in the Grand Duchy. At the foot of the town was a railroad station and telegraph office where the lines from Germany and Belgium crossed. This was the German objective which Lieutenant Feldmann's company, arriving in automobiles, duly seized.

With their relentless talent for the tactless, the Germans chose to violate Luxembourg at a place whose native and official name was Trois Vierges. The three virgins in fact represented faith, hope, and charity, but History with her apposite touch arranged for the occasion that they should stand in the public mind for Luxembourg, Belgium, and France.

At 7:30 a second detachment in automobiles arrived (presumably in response to the Kaiser's message) and ordered off the first group, saying "a mistake had been made." In the interval Luxembourg's Minister of State Eyschen had already telegraphed the news to London, Paris, and Brussels and a protest to Berlin. The three virgins had made their point. By midnight Moltke had rectified the reversal, and by the end of the next day, August 2, M–1 on the German schedule, the entire Grand Duchy was occupied.

A question has haunted the annals of history ever since: What Ifs might have followed if the Germans had gone east in 1914 while remaining on the defensive against France? General von Staab showed that to have turned against Russia was technically possible. But whether it would have been temperamentally possible for the Germans to have refrained from attacking France when *Der Tag* came is another matter.

At seven o'clock in St. Petersburg, the same hour when the Germans entered Luxembourg, Ambassador Pourtalès, his watery blue eyes red-rimmed, his white goatee quivering, presented Germany's declaration of war with shaking hand to Sazonov, the Russian Foreign Minister.

"The curses of the nations will be upon you!" Sazonov exclaimed.

"We are defending our honor," the German ambassador replied.

"Your honor was not involved. But there is a divine justice."

"That's true," and muttering, "a divine justice, a divine justice," Pourtalès staggered to the window, leaned against it, and burst into tears. "So this is the end of my mission," he said when he could speak. Sazonov patted him on the shoulder, they embraced, and Pourtalès stumbled to the door, which he could hardly open with a trembling hand, and went out, murmuring, "Goodbye, goodbye."

This affecting scene comes down to us as recorded by Sazonov with artistic additions by the French ambassador Paléologue, presumably from what Sazonov told him. Pourtalès reported only that he asked three times for a reply to the ultimatum and after Sazonov answered negatively three times, "I handed over the note as instructed."

Why did it have to be handed over at all? Admiral von Tirpitz, the Naval Minister, had plaintively asked the night before when the declaration of war was being drafted. Speaking, he says, "more from instinct than from reason," he wanted to know why, if Germany did not plan to invade Russia, was it necessary to declare war and assume the odium of the attacking party? His question was particularly pertinent because Germany's object was to saddle Russia with war guilt in order to convince the German people that they were fighting in self-defense and especially in order to keep Italy tied to her engagements under the Triple Alliance.

Italy was obliged to join her allies only in a defensive war and, already shaky in her allegiance, was widely expected to sidle out through any loophole that opened up. Bethmann was harassed by this problem. If Austria persisted in refusing any or all Serbian concessions, he warned, "it will scarcely be possible to place the guilt of a European conflagration on Russia" and would "place us in the eyes of our own people, in an untenable position." He was hardly heard. When mobilization day came, German protocol required that war be properly declared. Jurists of the Foreign Office, according to Tirpitz, insisted it was legally the correct thing to do. "Outside Germany," he says pathetically, "there is no appreciation of such ideas."

In France appreciation was keener than he knew.

7

August 1: Paris and London

ONE PRIME objective governed French policy: to enter the war with England as an ally. To ensure that event and enable her friends in England to overcome the inertia and reluctance within their own Cabinet and country, France had to leave it clear beyond question who was the attacked and who the attacker. The physical act and moral odium of aggression must be left squarely upon Germany. Germany was expected to do her part, but lest any overanxious French patrols or frontier troops stepped over the border, the French government took a daring and extraordinary step. On July 30 it ordered a ten-kilometer withdrawal along the entire frontier with Germany from Switzerland to Luxembourg.

Premier René Viviani, an eloquent Socialist orator, formerly chiefly concerned with welfare and labor, proposed the withdrawal. He was a curiosity in French politics, a Premier who had never been Premier before, and was now Acting Foreign Minister as well. He had been in office barely six weeks and had just returned the day before, July 29, from a state visit to Russia with President Poincaré. Austria had waited until Viviani and Poincaré were at sea to issue her ultimatum to Serbia. On receiving this news the French President and Premier had eliminated a scheduled visit to Copenhagen and hurried home.

In Paris they were told German covering troops had taken their places a few hundred meters from the frontier. They knew nothing as yet of the Russian and Austrian mobilizations. Hopes still flourished of a negotiated settlement. Viviani was "haunted by a fear that war might burst from a clump of trees, from a meeting of two patrols, from a threatening gesture . . . a black look, a brutal word, a shot!" While there was still even the least chance of settling the crisis without war, and in order to leave the lines of aggression clear if war came, the Cabinet agreed upon the ten-kilometer withdrawal. The order, telegraphed to corps commanders, was designed, they were told, "to assure the collaboration of our English neighbors." A telegram informing England of the measure went out simultaneously. The act of withdrawal, done at the very portals of invasion, was a calculated military risk deliberately taken for its political effect. It was taking a chance "never before taken in history," said Viviani, and might have added, like Cyrano, "Ah, but what a gesture!"

Withdrawal was a bitter gesture to ask of a French Commander in Chief schooled in the doctrine of offensive and nothing but the offensive. It could have shattered General Joffre as Moltke's first experience of the war shattered him, but General Joffre's heart did not break.

From the moment of the President's and Premier's return, Joffre had been hounding the government for the order to mobilize or at least take the preliminary steps: recall of furloughs, of which many had been granted for the harvest, and deployment of covering troops to the frontier. He deluged them with intelligence reports of German premobilization measures already taken. He loomed large in authority before a newborn Cabinet, the tenth in five years, whose predecessor had lasted three days. The present one was remarkable chiefly for having most of France's strong men outside it. Briand, Clemenceau, Caillaux, all former premiers, were in opposition. Viviani, by his own evidence, was in a state of "frightful nervous tension" which, according to Messimy, who was once again War Minister, "became a permanent condition during the month of August." The Minister of Marine, Dr. Gauthier, a doctor of medicine shoved into the naval post when a political scandal removed his predecessor, was so overwhelmed by events that he "forgot" to order fleet units into the Channel and had to be replaced by the Minister of Public Instruction on the spot.

In the President, however, intelligence, experience, and strength of purpose, if not constitutional power, were combined. Poincaré was a lawyer, economist, and member of the Academy, a former Finance Minister who had served as Premier and Foreign Minister in 1912 and had been elected President of France in January, 1913. Character begets power, especially in hours of crisis, and the untried Cabinet leaned willingly on the abilities and strong will of the man who was constitutionally a cipher. Born in Lorraine, Poincaré could remember as a boy of ten the long line of spiked German helmets marching through Bar-le-Duc, his home town. He was credited by the Germans with the most bellicose intent, partly because, as Premier at the time of Agadir, he had held firm, partly because as President he had used his influence to push through the Three-Year Military Service Law in 1913 against violent Socialist opposition. This and his cold demeanor, his lack of flamboyance, his fixity, did not make for popularity at home. Elections were going against the government, the Three-Year Law was near to being thrown out, labor troubles and farmers' discontent were rife, July had been hot, wet, and oppressive with windstorms and summer thunder, and Mme. Caillaux who had shot the editor of *Figaro* was on trial for murder. Each day of the trial revealed new and unpleasant irregularities in finance, the press, the courts, the government.

One day the French woke up to find Mme. Caillaux on page two—and the sudden, awful knowledge that France faced war. In that most passionately political and quarrelsome of countries one sentiment thereupon prevailed. Poincaré and Viviani, returning from Russia, drove through Paris to the sound of one prolonged cry, repeated over and over, "*Vive la France!*"

Joffre told the government that if he was not given the order to assemble and transport the covering troops of five army corps and cavalry toward the frontier, the Germans would "enter France without firing a shot." He accepted the ten-kilometer withdrawal of troops already in position less from subservience to the civil arm—Joffre was about as subservient by nature as Julius Caesar—as from a desire to bend all the force of his argument upon the one issue of the covering troops. The government, still reluctant while diplomatic offers and counter-offers flashing over the wires might yet produce a settlement, agreed to give him a "reduced" version, that is, without calling out the reservists.

At 4:30 next day, July 31, a banking friend in Amsterdam telephoned Messimy the news of the German *Kriegesgefahr*, officially confirmed an hour later from Berlin. It was "*une forme hypocrite de la mobilisation*," Messimy angrily told the Cabinet. His friend in Amsterdam had said war was certain and Germany was ready for it, "from the Emperor down to the last Fritz." Following hard upon this news came a telegram from Paul Cambon, French ambassador in London, reporting that

England was "tepid." Cambon had devoted every day of the past sixteen years at his post to the single end of ensuring England's active support when the time came, but he had now to wire that the British government seemed to be awaiting some new development. The dispute so far was of "no interest to Great Britain."

Joffre arrived, with a new memorandum on German movements, to insist upon mobilization. He was permitted to send his full "covering order" but no more, as news had also come of a last-minute appeal from the Czar to the Kaiser. The Cabinet continued sitting, with Messimy champing in impatience at the "green baize routine" which stipulated that each minister must speak in turn.

At seven o'clock in the evening Baron von Schoen, making his eleventh visit to the French Foreign Office in seven days, presented Germany's demand to know what course France would take and said he would return next day at one o'clock for an answer. Still the Cabinet sat and argued over financial measures, recall of Parliament, declaration of a state of siege, while all Paris waited in suspense. One crazed young man cracked under the agony, held a pistol against a café window, and shot dead Jean Jaurès, whose leadership in international socialism and in the fight against the Three-Year Law had made him, in the eyes of superpatriots, a symbol of pacifism.

A white-faced aide broke in upon the Cabinet at nine o'clock with the news. Jaurès killed! The event, pregnant with possible civil strife, stunned the Cabinet. Street barricades, riot, even revolt became a prospect on the threshold of war. Ministers reopened the heated argument whether to invoke *Carnet B*, the list of known agitators, anarchists, pacifists, and suspected spies who were to be arrested automatically upon the day of mobilization. Both the Prefect of Police and former Premier Clemenceau had advised the Minister of Interior, M. Malvy, to enforce *Carnet B*. Viviani and others of his colleagues, hoping to preserve national unity, were opposed to it. They held firm. Some foreigners suspected of being spies were arrested, but no Frenchmen. In case of riot, troops were alerted that night, but next morning there was only deep grief and deep quiet. Of the 2,501 persons listed in *Carnet B*, 80 per cent were ultimately to volunteer for military service.

At 2:00 A.M. that night, President Poincaré was awakened in bed by the irrepressible Russian ambassador, Isvolsky, a former hyperactive foreign minister. "Very distressed and very agitated," he wanted to know, "What is France going to do?"

Isvolsky had no doubts of Poincaré's attitude, but he and other Russian statesmen were always haunted by the fear that when the time came the French Parliament, which had never been told the terms of the military alliance with Russia, would fail to ratify it. The terms specifically stated, "If Russia is attacked by Germany or by Austria supported by Germany, France will use all her available forces to attack Germany." As soon as either Germany or Austria mobilized, "France and Russia, without previous agreement being necessary, shall mobilize all their forces immediately and simultaneously and shall transport them as near the frontiers as possible. . . . These forces shall begin complete action with all speed so that Germany will have to fight at the same time in the East and in the West."

These terms appeared unequivocal but, as Isvolsky had anxiously queried Poincaré in 1912, would the French Parliament recognize the obligation? In Russia the Czar's power was absolute, so that France "may be sure of us," but "in France the Government is impotent without Parliament. Parliament does not know the text of 1892. . . . What guarantee have we that your Parliament would follow your Government's lead?"

"If Germany attacked," Poincaré had replied on that earlier occasion, Parliament would follow the Government "without a doubt."

Now, facing Isvolsky again in the middle of the night, Poincaré assured him that a Cabinet would be called within a few hours to supply the answer. At the same hour the Russian military attaché in full diplomatic dress appeared in Messimy's bedroom to pose the same question. Messimy telephoned to Premier Viviani who, though exhausted by the night's events, had not yet gone to bed. "Good God!" he exploded, "these Russians are worse insomniacs than they are drinkers," and he excitedly recommended "*Du calme, du calme et encore du calme!*"

Pressed by the Russians to declare themselves, and by Joffre to mobilize, yet held to a standstill by the need to prove to England that France would act only in self-defense, the French government found calm not easy. At 8:00 next morning, August 1, Joffre came to the War Office in the Rue St. Dominique to beg Messimy, in "a pathetic tone that contrasted with his habitual calm," to pry mobilization from the government. He named four o'clock as the last moment when the order could reach the General Post Office for dispatch by telegraph throughout France in time for mobilization to begin at midnight. He went with Messimy to the Cabinet at 9:00 A.M. and presented an ultimatum of his own: every further delay of twenty-four hours before general mobilization would mean a fifteen- to twenty-kilometer loss of territory, and he would refuse to take the responsibility as Commander. He left, and the Cabinet faced the problem. Poincaré was for action; Viviani, representing the antiwar tradition, still hoped that time would provide a solution. At 11:00 he was called to the Foreign Office to see von Schoen who in his own anxiety had arrived two hours early for the answer to Germany's question of the previous day: whether France would stay neutral in a Russo-German war. "My question is rather naïve," said the unhappy ambassador, "for we know you have a treaty of alliance."

"*Evidemment*," replied Viviani, and gave the answer prearranged between him and Poincaré. "France will act in accordance with her interests." As Schoen left, Isvolsky rushed in with news of the German ultimatum to Russia. Viviani returned to the Cabinet, which at last agreed upon mobilization. The order was signed and given to Messimy, but Viviani, still hoping for some saving development to turn up within the few remaining hours, insisted that Messimy keep it in his pocket until 3:30. At the same time the ten-kilometer withdrawal was reaffirmed. Messimy telephoned it that evening personally to corps commanders: "By order of the President of the Republic, no unit of the army, no patrol, no reconnaissance, no scout, no detail of any kind, shall go east of the line laid down. Anyone guilty of transgressing will be liable to court-martial." A particular warning was added for the benefit of the XXth Corps, commanded by General Foch, of whom it was reliably reported that a squadron of cuirassiers had been seen "nose to nose" with a squadron of Uhlans.

At 3:30, as arranged, General Ebener of Joffre's staff, accompanied by two officers, came to the War Office to call for the mobilization order. Messimy handed it over in dry-throated silence. "Conscious of the gigantic and infinite results to spread from that little piece of paper, all four of us felt our hearts tighten." He shook hands with each of the three officers, who saluted and departed to deliver the order to the Post Office.

At four o'clock the first poster appeared on the walls of Paris (at the corner of the Place de la Concorde and the Rue Royale, one still remains, preserved under glass). At Armenonville, rendezvous of the *haut-monde* in the Bois de Boulogne, tea dancing suddenly stopped when the manager stepped forward, silenced the orchestra, and announced: "Mobilization has been ordered. It begins at midnight. Play the 'Marseillaise.'" In town the streets were already emptied of vehicles requisitioned by the War Office. Groups of reservists with bundles and farewell bouquets of flowers were marching off to the Gare de l'Est, as civilians waved and cheered. One group stopped to lay its flowers at the feet of the black-draped statue of Strasbourg in the Place de la Concorde. The crowds wept and cried "*Vive l'Alsace!*" and tore off the mourning she had worn since 1870. Orchestras in restaurants played the French, Russian, and British anthems. "To think these are all being played by Hungarians," someone remarked. The playing of their anthem, as if to express a hope, made Englishmen in the crowd uncomfortable and none more so than Sir Francis Bertie, the pink and plump British ambassador who in a gray frock coat and gray top hat, holding a green parasol against the sun, was seen entering the Quai d'Orsay. Sir Francis felt "sick at heart and ashamed." He ordered the gates of his embassy closed, for, as he wrote in his diary, "though it is '*Vive l'Angleterre*' today, it may be '*Perfide Albion*' tomorrow."

In London that thought hung heavily in the room where small, white-bearded M. Cambon confronted Sir Edward Grey. When Grey said to him that some "new development" must be awaited because the dispute between Russia, Austria, and Germany concerned a matter "of no interest" to Great Britain, Cambon let a glint of anger penetrate his impeccable tact and polished dignity. Was England "going to wait until French territory was invaded before intervening?" he asked, and suggested that if so her help might be "very belated."

Grey, behind his tight mouth and Roman nose, was in equal anguish. He believed fervently that England's interests required her to support France; he was prepared, in fact, to resign if she did not; he believed events to come would force her hand, but as yet he could say nothing officially to Cambon. Nor had he the knack of expressing himself unofficially. His manner, which the English public, seeing in him the image of the strong, silent man, found comforting, his foreign colleagues found "icy." He managed only to express edgily the thought that was in everyone's mind, that "Belgian neutrality might become a factor." That was the development Grey—and not he alone—was waiting for.

Britain's predicament resulted from a split personality evident both within the Cabinet and between the parties. The Cabinet was divided, in a split that derived from the Boer War, between Liberal Imperialists represented by Asquith, Grey, Haldane, and Churchill, and "Little Englanders" represented by all the rest. Heirs of Gladstone, they, like their late leader, harbored a deep suspicion of foreign entanglements and considered the aiding of oppressed peoples to be the only proper concern of foreign affairs, which were otherwise regarded as a tiresome interference with Reform, Free Trade, Home Rule, and the Lords' Veto. They tended to regard France as the decadent and frivolous grasshopper, and would have liked to regard Germany as the industrious, respectable ant, had not the posturings and roarings of the Kaiser and the Pan-German militarists somehow discouraged this view. They would never have supported a war on behalf of France, although the injection of Belgium, a "little" country with a just call on British protection, might alter the issue.

Grey's group in the Cabinet, on the other hand, shared with the Tories a fundamental premise that Britain's national interest was bound up with the preservation of France. The reasoning was best expressed in the marvelously flat words of Grey himself: "If Germany dominated the Continent it would be disagreeable to us as well as to others, for we should be isolated." In this epic sentence is all of British policy, and from it followed the knowledge that, if the challenge were flung, England would have to fight to prevent that "disagreeable" outcome. But Grey could not say so without provoking a split in the Cabinet and in the country that would be fatal to any war effort before it began.

Alone in Europe Britain had no conscription. In war she would be dependent on voluntary enlistment. A secession from the government over the war issue would mean the formation of an antiwar party led by the dissidents with disastrous effect on recruiting. If it was the prime objective of France to enter war with Britain as an ally, it was a prime necessity for Britain to enter war with a united government.

This was the touchstone of the problem. In Cabinet meetings the group opposed to intervention proved strong. Their leader Lord Morley, Gladstone's old friend and biographer, believed he could count on "eight or nine likely to agree with us" against the solution being openly worked for by Churchill with "daemonic energy" and Grey with "strenuous simplicity." From discussions in the Cabinet it was clear to Morley that the neutrality of Belgium was "secondary to the question of our neutrality in the struggle between Germany and France." It was equally clear to Grey that only violation of Belgium's neutrality would convince the peace party of the German menace and the need to go to war in the national interest.

On August 1 the crack was visible and widening in Cabinet and Parliament. That day twelve out of eighteen Cabinet members declared themselves opposed to giving France the assurance of Britain's support in war. That afternoon in the lobby of the House of Commons a caucus of Liberal M.P.s voted 19 to 4 (though with many abstentions) for a motion that England should remain neutral "whatever happened in Belgium or elsewhere." That week *Punch* published "Lines designed to represent the views of an average British patriot":

> Why should I follow your fighting line
> For a matter that's no concern of mine? . . .
>
> I shall be asked to a general scrap
> All over the European map,
> Dragged into somebody else's war
> For that's what a double entente is for.

The average patriot had already used up his normal supply of excitement and indignation in the current Irish crisis. The

"Curragh Mutiny" was England's Mme. Caillaux. As a result of the Home Rule Bill, Ulster was threatening armed rebellion against autonomy for Ireland and English troops stationed at the Curragh had refused to take up arms against Ulster loyalists. General Gough, the Curragh commander, had resigned with all his officers, whereupon Sir John French, Chief of General Staff, resigned, whereupon Colonel John Seely, Haldane's successor as Secretary of War, resigned. The army seethed, uproar and schism ruled the country, and a Palace Conference of party leaders with the King met in vain. Lloyd George talked ominously of the "gravest issue raised in this country since the days of the Stuarts," the words "civil war" and "rebellion" were mentioned, and a German arms firm hopefully ran a cargo of 40,000 rifles and a million cartridges into Ulster. In the meantime there was no Secretary of War, the office being left to Prime Minister Asquith, who had little time and less inclination for it.

Asquith had, however, a particularly active First Lord of the Admiralty. When he smelled battle afar off, Winston Churchill resembled the war horse in Job who turned not back from the sword but "paweth in the valley and saith among the trumpets, Ha, ha." He was the only British minister to have a perfectly clear conviction of what Britain should do and to act upon it without hesitation. On July 26, the day Austria rejected Serbia's reply and ten days before his own government made up its mind, Churchill issued a crucial order.

On July 26 the British fleet was completing, unconnected with the crisis, a test mobilization and maneuvers with full crews at war strength. At seven o'clock next morning the squadrons were due to disperse, some to various exercises on the high seas, some to home ports where parts of their crews would be discharged back into training schools, some to dock for repairs. That Sunday, July 26, the First Lord remembered later was "a very beautiful day." When he learned the news from Austria he made up his mind to make sure "that the diplomatic situation did not get ahead of the naval situation and that the Grand Fleet should be in its War Station before Germany could know whether or not we should be in the war *and therefore if possible before we had decided ourselves.*" The italics are his own. After consultation with the First Sea Lord,

Prince Louis of Battenberg, he gave orders to the fleet not to disperse.

He then informed Grey what he had done and with Grey's assent released the Admiralty order to the newspapers in the hope that the news might have "a sobering effect" on Berlin and Vienna.

Holding the fleet together was not enough; it must be got, as Churchill expressed it in capitals, to its "War Station." The primary duty of a fleet, as Admiral Mahan, the Clausewitz of naval warfare, had decreed, was to remain "a fleet in being." In the event of war the British fleet, upon which an island nation depended for its life, had to establish and maintain mastery of the ocean trade routes; it had to protect the British Isles from invasion; it had to protect the Channel and the French coasts in fulfillment of the pact with France; it had to keep concentrated in sufficient strength to win any engagement if the German fleet sought battle; and above all it had to guard itself against that new and menacing weapon of unknown potential, the torpedo. The fear of a sudden, undeclared torpedo attack haunted the Admiralty.

On July 28 Churchill gave orders for the fleet to sail to its war base at Scapa Flow, far to the north at the tip of mist-shrouded Orkney in the North Sea. It steamed out of Portland on the 29th, and by nightfall eighteen miles of warships had passed northward through the Straits of Dover headed not so much for some rendezvous with glory as for a rendezvous with discretion. "A surprise torpedo attack," wrote the First Lord, "was at any rate one nightmare gone forever."

Having prepared the fleet for action, Churchill turned his abounding energy and sense of urgency upon preparing the country. He persuaded Asquith on July 29 to authorize the Warning Telegram which was the arranged signal sent by War Office and Admiralty to initiate the Precautionary Period. While short of the *Kriegesgefahr* or the French State of Siege which established martial law, the Precautionary Period has been described as a device "invented by a genius . . . which permitted certain measures to be taken on the *ipse dixit* of the Secretary of War without reference to the Cabinet . . . when time was the only thing that mattered."

Time pressed on the restless Churchill who, expecting the

Liberal government to break apart, went off to make overtures to his old party, the Tories. Coalition was not in the least to the taste of the Prime Minister who was bent on keeping his government united. Lord Morley at seventy-six was expected by no one to stay with the government in the event of war. Not Morley but the far more vigorous Chancellor of the Exchequer, Lloyd George, was the key figure whom the government could not afford to lose, both for his proved ability in office and his influence upon the electorate. Shrewd, ambitious, and possessed of a spellbinding Welsh eloquence, Lloyd George leaned to the peace group but might jump either way. He had suffered recent setbacks in public popularity; he saw a new rival for party leadership arising in the individual whom Lord Morley called "that splendid condottierre at the Admiralty"; and he might, some of his colleagues thought, see political advantage in "playing the peace-card" against Churchill. He was altogether an uncertain and dangerous quantity.

Asquith, who had no intention of leading a divided country into war, continued to wait with exasperating patience for events which might convince the peace group. The question of the hour, he recorded in his passionless way in his diary for July 31, was, "Are we to go in or stand aside. Of course everybody longs to stand aside." In a less passive attitude, Grey, during the Cabinet of July 31 almost reached the point-blank. He said Germany's policy was that of a "European aggressor as bad as Napoleon" (a name that for England had only one meaning) and told the Cabinet that the time had come when a decision whether to support the Entente or preserve neutrality could no longer be deferred. He said that if it chose neutrality he was not the man to carry out such a policy. His implied threat to resign echoed as if it had been spoken.

"The Cabinet seemed to heave a sort of sigh," wrote one of them, and sat for several moments in "breathless silence." Its members looked at one another, suddenly realizing that their continued existence as a government was now in doubt. They adjourned without reaching a decision.

That Friday, eve of the August Bank Holiday weekend, the Stock Exchange closed down at 10:00 A.M. in a wave of financial panic that had started in New York when Austria declared war on Serbia and which was closing Exchanges all over

Europe. The City trembled, prophesying doom and the collapse of foreign exchange. Bankers and businessmen, according to Lloyd George, were "aghast" at the idea of war which would "break down the whole system of credit with London at its center." The Governor of the Bank of England called on Saturday to inform Lloyd George that the City was "totally opposed to our intervening" in a war.

That same Friday the Tory leaders were being rounded up and called back to London from country houses to confer on the crisis. Dashing from one to the other, pleading, exhorting, expounding Britain's shame if the shilly-shallying Liberals held back now, was Henry Wilson, the heart, soul, spirit, backbone, and legs of the Anglo-French military "conversations." The agreed euphemism for the joint plans of the General Staffs was "conversations." The formula of "no commitment" which Haldane had first established, which had raised misgivings in Campbell-Bannerman, which Lord Esher had rejected, and which Grey had embodied in the 1912 letter to Cambon still represented the official position, even if it did not make sense.

It made very little. If, as Clausewitz justly said, war is a continuation of national policy, so also are war plans. The Anglo-French war plans, worked out in detail over a period of nine years, were not a game, or an exercise in fantasy or a paper practice to keep military minds out of other mischief. They were a continuation of policy or they were nothing. They were no different from France's arrangements with Russia or Germany's with Austria except for the final legal fiction that they did not "commit" Britain to action. Members of the government and Parliament who disliked the policy simply shut their eyes and mesmerized themselves into believing the fiction.

M. Cambon, visiting Opposition leaders after his painful interview with Grey, now dropped diplomatic tact altogether. "All our plans are arranged in common. Our General Staffs have consulted. You have seen all our schemes and preparations. Look at our fleet! Our whole fleet is in the Mediterranean in consequence of our arrangements with you and our coasts are open to the enemy. You have laid us wide open!" He told them that if England did not come in France would never forgive her, and ended with a bitter cry, "*Et l'honneur? Est-ce-que l'Angleterre comprend ce que c'est l'honneur?*"

Honor wears different coats to different eyes, and Grey knew it would have to wear a Belgian coat before the peace group could be persuaded to see it. That same afternoon he dispatched two telegrams asking the French and German governments for a formal assurance that they were prepared to respect Belgian neutrality "so long as no other power violates it." Within an hour of receiving the telegram in the late evening of July 31, France replied in the affirmative. No reply was received from Germany.

Next day, August 1, the matter was put before the Cabinet. Lloyd George traced with his finger on a map what he thought would be the German route through Belgium, just across the near corner, on the shortest straight line to Paris; it would only, he said, be a "little violation." When Churchill asked for authority to mobilize the fleet, that is, call up all the naval reserves, the Cabinet, after a "sharp discussion," refused. When Grey asked for authority to implement the promises made to the French Navy, Lord Morley, John Burns, Sir John Simon, and Lewis Harcourt proposed to resign. Outside the Cabinet, rumors were swirling of the last-minute wrestlings of Kaiser and Czar and of the German ultimatums. Grey left the room to speak to—and be misunderstood by—Lichnowsky on the telephone, and unwittingly to be the cause of havoc in the heart of General Moltke. He also saw Cambon, and told him "France must take her own decision at this moment without reckoning on an assistance we are not now in a position to give." He returned to the Cabinet while Cambon, white and shaking, sank into a chair in the room of his old friend Sir Arthur Nicolson, the Permanent Under-Secretary. "*Ils vont nous lâcher*" (They are going to desert us), he said. To the editor of *The Times* who asked him what he was going to do, he replied, "I am going to wait to learn if the word 'honor' should be erased from the English dictionary."

In the Cabinet no one wanted to burn his bridges. Resignations were bruited, not yet offered. Asquith continued to sit tight, say little, and await developments as that day of crossed wires and complicated frenzy drew to a close. That evening Moltke was refusing to go east, Lieutenant Feldmann's company was seizing Trois Vierges in Luxembourg, Messimy over the telephone was reconfirming the ten-kilometer withdrawal, and at the Admiralty the First Lord was entertaining friends from the Opposition, among them the future Lords Beaverbrook and Birkenhead. To keep occupied while waiting out the tension, they played bridge after dinner. During the game a messenger brought in a red dispatch box—it happened to be one of the largest size. Taking a key from his pocket, Churchill opened it, took out the single sheet of paper it contained, and read the single line on the paper: "Germany has declared war on Russia." He informed the company, changed out of his dinner jacket, and "went straight out like a man going to a well-accustomed job."

Churchill walked across the Horse Guards Parade to Downing Street, entered by the garden gate, and found the Prime Minister upstairs with Grey, Haldane, now Lord Chancellor, and Lord Crewe, Secretary for India. He told them he intended "instantly to mobilize the fleet notwithstanding the Cabinet decision." Asquith said nothing but appeared, Churchill thought, "quite content." Grey, accompanying Churchill on his way out, said to him, "I have just done a very important thing. I have told Cambon that we shall not allow the German fleet to come into the Channel." Or that is what Churchill, experiencing the perils of verbal intercourse with Grey, understood him to say. It meant that the fleet was now committed. Whether Grey said he had given the promise or whether he said, as scholars have since decided, that he was going to give it the next day, is not really relevant, for whichever it was it merely confirmed Churchill in a decision already taken. He returned to the Admiralty and "gave forthwith the order to mobilize."

Both his order and Grey's promise to make good the naval agreement with France were contrary to majority Cabinet sentiment. On the next day the Cabinet would have to ratify these acts or break apart, and by that time Grey expected a "development" to come out of Belgium. Like the French, he felt that he could count on Germany to provide it.

8

Ultimatum in Brussels

LOCKED IN the safe of Herr von Below-Saleske, German Minister in Brussels, was a sealed envelope brought to him by special courier from Berlin on July 29 with orders "not to open until you are instructed by telegraph from here." On Sunday, August 2, Below was advised by telegram to open the envelope at once and deliver the Note it contained by eight o'clock that evening, taking care to give the Belgian government "the impression that *all* the instructions relating to this affair reached you for the first time today." He was to demand a reply from the Belgians within twelve hours and wire it to Berlin "as quickly as possible" and also "forward it immediately by automobile to General von Emmich at the Union Hotel in Aachen." Aachen or Aix-la-Chapelle was the nearest German city to Liège, the eastern gateway to Belgium.

Herr von Below, a tall, erect bachelor with pointed black mustaches and a jade cigarette holder in constant use, had taken up his post in Belgium early in 1914. When visitors to the German Legation asked him about a silver ash tray pierced by a bullet hole that lay on his desk, he would laugh and reply: "I am a bird of ill omen. When I was stationed in Turkey they had a revolution. When I was in China, it was the Boxers. One of their shots through the window made that bullet hole." He would raise his cigarette delicately to his lips with a wide and elegant gesture and add: "But now I am resting. Nothing ever happens in Brussels."

Since the sealed envelope arrived, he had been resting no longer. At noon on August 1 he received a visit from Baron de Bassompierre, Under-Secretary of the Belgian Foreign Office, who told him the evening papers intended to publish France's reply to Grey in which she promised to respect Belgian neutrality. Bassompierre suggested that in the absence of a comparable German reply, Herr von Below might wish to make a statement. Below was without authority from Berlin to do so. Taking refuge in diplomatic maneuver, he lay back in his chair and with his eyes fixed on the ceiling repeated back word for word through a haze of cigarette smoke everything that Bassompierre had just said to him as if playing back a record. Rising, he assured his visitor that "Belgium had nothing to fear from Germany," and closed the interview.

Next morning he repeated the assurance to M. Davignon, the Foreign Minister, who had been awakened at 6:00 A.M. by news of the German invasion of Luxembourg and had asked for an explanation. Back at the legation, Below soothed a clamoring press with a felicitous phrase that was widely quoted, "Your neighbor's roof may catch fire but your own house will be safe."

Many Belgians, official and otherwise, were disposed to believe him, some from pro-German sympathies, some from wishful thinking, and some from simple confidence in the good faith of the international guarantors of Belgium's neutrality. In seventy-five years of guaranteed independence they had known peace for the longest unbroken period in their history. The territory of Belgium had been the pathway of warriors since Caesar fought the Belgae. In Belgium, Charles the Bold of Burgundy and Louis XI of France had fought out their long and bitter rivalry; there Spain had ravaged the Low Countries; there Marlborough had fought the French at the "very murderous battle" of Malplaquet; there Napoleon had met Wellington at Waterloo; there the people had risen against every ruler—Burgundian, French, Spanish, Hapsburg, or Dutch—until the final revolt against the House of Orange in 1830. Then, under Leopold of Saxe-Coburg, maternal uncle of Queen Victoria, as King, they had made themselves a nation, grown prosperous, spent their energies in fraternal fighting between Flemings and Walloons, Catholics and Protestants, and in disputes over Socialism and French and Flemish bilingualism, in the fervent hope that their neighbors would leave them to continue undisturbed in this happy condition.

The King and Prime Minister and Chief of Staff could no longer share the general confidence, but were prevented, both by the duties of neutrality and by their belief in neutrality, from making plans to repel attack. Up until the last moment they could not bring themselves to believe an invasion by one of their guarantors would actually happen. On learning of the

German *Kriegesgefahr* on July 31, they had ordered mobilization of the Belgian Army to begin at midnight. During the night and next day policemen went from house to house ringing doorbells and handing out orders while men scrambled out of bed or left their jobs, wrapped up their bundles, said their farewells, and went off to their regimental depots. Because Belgium, maintaining her strict neutrality, had not up to now settled on any plan of campaign, mobilization was not directed against a particular enemy or oriented in a particular direction. It was a call-up without deployment. Belgium was obligated, as well as her guarantors, to preserve her own neutrality and could make no overt act until one was made against her.

When, by the evening of August 1, Germany's silence in response to Grey's request had continued for twenty-four hours, King Albert determined on a final private appeal to the Kaiser. He composed it in consultation with his wife, Queen Elizabeth, a German by birth, the daughter of a Bavarian duke, who translated it sentence by sentence into German, weighing with the King the choice of words and their shades of meaning. It recognized that "political objections" might stand in the way of a public statement but hoped "the bonds of kinship and friendship" would decide the Kaiser to give King Albert his personal and private assurance of respect for Belgian neutrality. The kinship in question, which stemmed from King Albert's mother, Princess Marie of Hohenzollern-Sigmaringen, a distant and Catholic branch of the Prussian royal family, failed to move the Kaiser to reply.

Instead came the ultimatum that had been waiting in Herr von Below's safe for the last four days. It was delivered at seven on the evening of August 2 when a footman at the Foreign Office pushed his head through the door of the Under-Secretary's room and reported in an excited whisper, "The German Minister has just gone in to see M. Davignon!" Fifteen minutes later Below was seen driving back down the Rue de la Loi holding his hat in his hand, beads of perspiration on his forehead, and smoking with the rapid, jerky movements of a mechanical toy. The instant his "haughty silhouette" had been seen to leave the Foreign Office, the two Under-Secretaries rushed in to the Minister's room where they found M. Davignon, a man until now of immutable and tranquil optimism, looking extremely pale. "Bad news, bad news," he said, handing them the German note he had just received. Baron de Gaiffier, the Political Secretary, read it aloud, translating slowly as he went, while Bassompierre, sitting at the Minister's desk took it down, discussing each ambiguous phrase to make sure of the right rendering. While they worked, M. Davignon and his Permanent Under-Secretary, Baron van der Elst, listened, sitting in two chairs on either side of the fireplace. M. Davignon's last word on any problem had always been, "I am sure it will turn out all right," while van der Elst's esteem for the Germans had led him in the past to assure his government that rising German armaments were intended only for the *Drang nach Osten* and portended no trouble for Belgium.

Baron de Broqueville, Premier and concurrently War Minister, entered the room as the work concluded, a tall, dark gentleman of elegant grooming whose resolute air was enhanced by an energetic black mustache and expressive black eyes. As the ultimatum was read to him everyone in the room listened to each word with the same intensity that the authors had put into the drafting. It had been drawn up with great care, with perhaps a subconscious sense that it was to be one of the critical documents of the century.

General Moltke had written the original version in his own hand on July 26, two days before Austria declared war on Serbia, four days before Austria and Russia mobilized, and on the same day when Germany and Austria had rejected Sir Edward Grey's proposal for a five-power conference. Moltke had sent his draft to the Foreign Office, where it was revised by Under-Secretary Zimmermann and Political Secretary Stumm, further corrected and modified by Foreign Minister Jagow and Chancellor Bethmann-Hollweg before the final draft was sent in the sealed envelope to Brussels on the 29th. The extreme pains the Germans took reflected the importance they attached to the document.

Germany had received "reliable information," the note began, of a proposed advance by the French along the route Givet-Namur, "leaving no doubt of France's intention to advance against Germany through Belgian territory." (As the Belgians had seen no evidence of French movement toward Namur, for the excellent reason that there was none, the charge failed to impress them.) Germany, the note continued, being unable to count on the Belgian Army halting the French advance, was required by "the dictate of self-preservation" to "anticipate this hostile attack." She would view it with "deepest regret" if Belgium should regard her entrance on Belgian soil as "an act of hostility against herself." If Belgium should, on the other hand, adopt "a benevolent neutrality," Germany would bind herself to "evacuate her territory as soon as peace shall have been concluded," to pay for any damages caused by German troops, and to "guarantee at the conclusion of peace the sovereign rights and independence of the kingdom." In the original the sentence had continued, "and to favor with the greatest goodwill any possible claims of Belgium for compensation at the expense of France." At the last moment Below was instructed to delete this bribe.

If Belgium opposed Germany's passage through her territory, the note concluded, she would be regarded as an enemy, and future relations with her would be left to "the decision of arms." An "unequivocal answer" was demanded within twelve hours.

"A long, tragic silence of several minutes" followed the reading, Bassompierre recalled, as each man in the room thought of the choice that faced his country. Small in size and young in independence, Belgium clung more fiercely to independence for that reason. But no one in the room needed to be told what the consequences of a decision to defend it would be. Their country would be subjected to attack, their homes to destruction, their people to reprisals by a force ten times their size with no doubt of the outcome to themselves, who were in the immediate pathway of the Germans, whatever the ultimate outcome of the war. If, on the contrary, they were to yield to the German demand, they would be making Belgium an accessory to the attack on France as well as a violator of her own neutrality, besides opening her to German occupation with small likelihood that a victorious Germany would remember to withdraw. They would be occupied either way; to yield would be to lose honor too.

"If we are to be crushed," Bassompierre recorded their sentiment, "let us be crushed gloriously." In 1914 "glory" was a word spoken without embarrassment, and honor a familiar concept that people believed in.

Van der Elst broke the silence in the room. "Well, sir, are we ready?" he asked the Premier.

"Yes, we are ready," De Broqueville answered. "Yes," he repeated, as if trying to convince himself, "except for one thing—we have not yet got our heavy artillery." Only in the last year had the government obtained increased military appropriations from a reluctant Parliament conditioned to neutrality. The order for heavy guns had been given to the German firm of Krupp, which, not surprisingly, had delayed deliveries.

One hour of the twelve had already gone by. While their colleagues began rounding up all Ministers for a Council of State to be held at nine o'clock, Bassompierre and Gaiffier started working on a draft of the reply. They had no need to ask each other what it would be. Leaving the task to them, Premier de Broqueville went to the palace to inform the King.

King Albert felt a responsibility as ruler that made his awareness of outside pressures acute. He had not been born to reign. A younger son of King Leopold's younger brother, he was left to grow up in a corner of the palace with a Swiss tutor of more than ordinary mediocrity. Coburg family life was not joyous. Leopold's own son died; in 1891 his nephew, Baudouin, Albert's older brother, died, leaving Albert heir to the throne at sixteen. The old King, embittered by the loss of his own son and of Baudouin to whom he had transferred his paternal affections, did not at first see much in Albert whom he called a "sealed envelope."

Inside the envelope were enormous physical and intellectual energies of the kind that marked two great contemporaries, Theodore Roosevelt and Winston Churchill, whom otherwise Albert resembled not at all. He was reserved where they were extroverts; yet he shared many tastes, if not temperament, with Roosevelt: his love of the outdoors, of physical exercise, of riding and climbing, his interest in natural science and conservation and his gluttony for books. Like Roosevelt, Albert consumed books at the rate of two a day on any and all subjects—literature, military science, colonialism, medicine, Judaism, aviation. He drove a motorbicycle and piloted a plane. His ultimate passion was mountaineering, which, incognito, he pursued all over Europe. As heir apparent he toured Africa to study colonial problems at firsthand; as King he studied the army or the coal mines of the Borinage or the "Red country" of the Walloons in the same way. "When he speaks the King always looks as if he wished to build something," said one of his Ministers.

In 1900 he had married Elizabeth of Wittelsbach, whose father, the Duke, practiced as an oculist in the Munich hospitals. Their obvious affection for each other, their three children, their model family life in contrast to the unseemly ways of the old regime gave Albert a head start in popular approval when, in 1909, to general relief and rejoicing, he took the place of King Leopold II upon the throne. The new King and Queen continued to ignore pomp, entertain whom they liked, exercise their curiosity and love of adventure where they liked, and remain indifferent to danger, etiquette, and criticism. They were not bourgeois, so much as bohemian royalty.

In military school Albert had been a cadet at the same time as a future Chief of Staff, Emile Galet. A shoemaker's son, Galet had been sent to the school by popular subscription of his village. Later he became an instructor in the War College, and resigned when he could no longer agree with its dauntless theories of the offensive which the Belgian Staff, regardless of the difference in circumstance, had taken over from the French. Galet had also left the Catholic Church to become a strict Evangelical. Pessimistic, hypercritical, and dedicated, he was intensely serious about his profession as about everything else —it was said he read the Bible daily and was never known to laugh. The King heard him lecture, met him at maneuvers, was impressed by his teachings: that offensive for its own sake and under all circumstances was dangerous, that an army should seek battle "only if there is prospect of important success," and that "attack calls for superiority of means." Though still a captain, though a workingman's son, though a convert to Protestantism in a Catholic country, he was chosen by King Albert as his personal military adviser, a post specially created for the purpose.

Since, according to the Belgian constitution, King Albert would become Commander in Chief only after the outbreak of war, he and Galet were unable in the meantime to impose their fears or their ideas of strategy upon the General Staff. The Staff clung to the example of 1870 when not a toe of either the Prussian or French armies had stepped over the Belgian border, although if the French had crossed into Belgian territory they would have had room enough to retreat. King Albert and Galet, however, believed that the huge growth of armies since that time made it clearer each year that if the nations marched again they would spill over onto the old pathways and meet again in the old arena.

The Kaiser had made this perfectly clear in the interview which so stunned Leopold II in 1904. After his return, Leopold's shock gradually wore off, for, as van der Elst, to whom the King reported the interview, agreed, William was such a weathercock, how could one be sure? On a return visit to Brussels in 1910, the Kaiser proved indeed to be most reassuring. Belgium had nothing to fear from Germany, he told van der Elst. "You will have no grounds of complaint against Germany. . . . I understand perfectly your country's position. . . . I shall never place her in a false position."

On the whole, Belgians believed him. They took their guarantee of neutrality seriously. Belgium had neglected her army, frontier defenses, fortresses, anything that implied lack of confidence in the protective treaty. Socialism was the raging issue. Public apathy to what was happening abroad and a Parliament obsessed by economy allowed the army to deteriorate to a condition resembling the Turkish. Troops were ill-disciplined, slack, untidy, avoided saluting, slouched in the ranks, and refused to keep step.

The officers' corps was little better. Because the army was considered superfluous and slightly absurd, it did not attract the best minds or young men of ability and ambition. Those who did make it a career and passed through the Ecole de Guerre became infected with the French doctrine of *élan* and *offensive à outrance*. The remarkable formula they evolved was, "To ensure against our being ignored it was essential that we should attack."

However magnificent the spirit, this formula conformed ill with the realities of Belgium's position, and the doctrine of the offensive sat oddly upon an army staff committed by the duty of neutrality to plan for the defensive only. Neutrality forbade them to plan in concert with any other nation and required of them to regard the first foot put inside their territory as hostile, whether it was English, French, or German. Under the circumstances a coherent plan of campaign was not easily achieved.

The Belgian Army consisted of six divisions of infantry plus a cavalry division. These would have to face the thirty-four divisions scheduled by the Germans to march through Belgium. Equipment and training were inadequate and marksmanship inferior in view of army funds that permitted enough ammunition for only two firing practices of one round per man a week. Compulsory military service, not introduced until 1913, only served to make the army more unpopular than ever. In that year of ominous rumblings from abroad, Parliament reluctantly raised the annual contingent from 13,000 to 33,000 but agreed to appropriate funds for modernizing the defenses of Antwerp only on condition that the cost be absorbed by reducing the conscripts' period of service. No General Staff existed until 1910 when the new King insisted upon creating one.

Its effectiveness was limited by the extreme dissidence of its members. One school favored an offensive plan with the army concentrated at the frontiers upon threat of war. Another school favored the defensive with the army concentrated in the interior. A third group, consisting chiefly of King Albert and Captain Galet, favored a defensive as close as possible to the threatened frontier but without risking the lines of communication to the fortified base at Antwerp.

While the European sky was darkening, Belgium's staff officers wrangled—and failed to complete a plan of concentration. Their difficulty was compounded by their not permitting themselves to specify who the enemy would be. A compromise plan had been agreed on but existed only in outline, without railroad timetables, supply depots, or billets.

In November 1913, King Albert was invited to Berlin as his uncle had been nine years before. The Kaiser gave him a royal dinner at a table covered with violets and set for fifty-five guests, among them Secretary of War General Falkenhayn, Secretary of the Imperial Navy Admiral Tirpitz, Chief of Staff General Moltke, and Chancellor Bethmann-Hollweg. The Belgian ambassador, Baron Beyens, who was also present, noticed that the King sat through dinner looking unusually grave. After dinner, Beyens watched him in conversation with Moltke, and saw Albert's face growing darker and more somber as he listened. On leaving he said to Beyens: "Come tomorrow at nine. I must talk to you."

In the morning he walked with Beyens through the Brandenburg Gate, past the rows of glaring white marble Hohenzollerns in heroic postures, mercifully shrouded by the morning mist, to the Tiergarten where they could talk "undisturbed." At a court ball early in his visit, Albert said, he had received his first shock when the Kaiser pointed out to him a general—it was von Kluck—as the man designated "to lead the march on Paris." Then, prior to dinner the evening before, the Kaiser, taking him aside for a personal talk, had poured forth a hysterical tirade against France. He said France never ceased provoking him. As a result of her attitude, war with France was not only inevitable; it was near at hand. The French press treated Germany with malice, the Three-Year Law was a deliberately hostile act, and all France was moved by an unquenchable thirst for *revanche*. Trying to stem the flow, Albert said he knew the French better; he visited France every year, and he could assure the Kaiser they were not aggressive but sincerely desired peace. In vain; the Kaiser kept insisting war was inevitable.

After dinner Moltke took up the refrain. War with France was coming. "This time we must make an end of it. Your Majesty cannot imagine the irresistible enthusiasm which will permeate Germany on The Day." The German Army was invincible; nothing could stand up to the *furor Teutonicus*; terrible destruction would mark its path; its victory could not be in doubt.

Troubled by what motivated these startling confidences, as much as by their content, Albert could only conclude they were intended to frighten Belgium into coming to terms. Evidently the Germans had made up their minds, and he felt that France should be warned. He instructed Beyens to repeat everything to Jules Cambon, the French ambassador in Berlin, and to charge him to report the matter to President Poincaré in the strongest terms.

Later they learned that Major Melotte, the Belgian military attaché, had been treated to an even more violent outburst by General Moltke at the same dinner. He also heard that war with France was "inevitable" and "much nearer than you think." Moltke, who usually maintained great reserve with foreign attachés, on this occasion "unbuttoned" himself. He said Germany did not want war but the General Staff was "arch-ready." He said "France must absolutely stop provoking and annoying us or we shall have to come to blows. The sooner, the better. We have had enough of these continual alerts." As examples of French provocations, Moltke cited, apart from "big things," a cold reception given in Paris to German aviators and a boycott by Paris society of Major Winterfeld, the German military attaché. The Major's mother, Countess d'Alvensleben, had complained bitterly. As for England, well, the German Navy was not built to hide in harbor. It would attack and probably be beaten. Germany would lose her ships, but England would lose mastery of the seas, which would pass to the United States, who would be the sole gainer from a European war. England knew this and, said the General, taking a sharp turn in his logic, would probably stay neutral.

He was far from finished. What would Belgium do, he asked Major Melotte, if a large foreign force invaded her territory? Melotte replied that she would defend her neutrality. In an effort to find out whether Belgium would content herself with a protest, as the Germans believed, or would fight, Moltke pressed him to be more specific. When Melotte answered, "We will oppose with all our forces whatever power violates our frontiers," Moltke pointed out smoothly that good intentions were not enough. "You must also have an army capable of fulfilling the duty which neutrality imposes."

Back in Brussels, King Albert called at once for a progress report on the mobilization plans. He found no progress had been made. On the basis of what he had heard in Berlin, he obtained De Broqueville's agreement for a plan of campaign based on the hypothesis of a German invasion. He got his own and Galet's nominee, an energetic officer named Colonel de Ryckel, appointed to carry out the work promised for April. By April it was still not ready. Meanwhile De Broqueville had appointed another officer, General de Selliers de Moranville, as Chief of Staff over De Ryckel's head. In July four separate plans of concentration were still being considered.

Discouragement did not change the King's mind. His policy was embodied in a memorandum drawn up by Captain Galet immediately after the Berlin visit. "We are resolved to declare war at once upon any power that deliberately violates our territory; to wage war with the utmost energy and with the whole of our military resources, wherever required, even beyond our frontiers, and to continue to wage war even after the invader retires, until the conclusion of a general peace."

On August 2, King Albert, presiding at the Council of State when it met at 9:00 P.M. in the palace, opened with the words: "Our answer must be 'No,' whatever the consequences. Our duty is to defend our territorial integrity. In this we must not fail." He insisted, however, that no one present should allow himself any illusions: the consequences would be grave and terrible; the enemy would be ruthless. Premier de Broqueville warned waverers not to put faith in Germany's promise to restore Belgian integrity after the war. "If Germany is victorious," he said, "Belgium, whatever her attitude, will be annexed to the German Empire."

One aged and indignant minister who had recently entertained as his house guest the Duke of Schleswig-Holstein, brother-in-law of the Kaiser, could not contain his wrath at the perfidy of the Duke's expressions of friendship and kept up an angry mumbling as chorus to the proceedings. When General de Selliers, the Chief of Staff, rose to explain the strategy of defense to be adopted, his Deputy Chief, Colonel de Ryckel, with whom his relations were, in the words of a colleague, "denuded of the amenities," kept growling between his teeth, "*Il faut piquer dedans, il faut piquer dedans*" (We must hit them where it hurts). Given the floor, he amazed his hearers with a proposal to anticipate the invader by attacking him on his own territory before he could cross the Belgian frontier.

At midnight the meeting adjourned, while a committee of the Premier, Foreign Minister, and Minister of Justice returned to the Foreign Office to draft a reply. While they were at work a motorcar drew up in the dark courtyard beneath the single row of lighted windows. A visit of the German Minister was announced to the startled Ministers. It was 1:30 A.M. What could he want at this hour?

Herr von Below's nocturnal unrest reflected his government's growing uneasiness about the effect of their ultimatum, now irrevocably committed to paper and irrevocably working upon Belgian national pride. The Germans had been telling one another for years that Belgium would not fight, but now when the moment arrived they began to suffer an acute if belated anxiety. A valiant and ringing "No!" from Belgium would peal round the world with effect on the other neutral countries hardly beneficial to Germany. But Germany was not so worried about the attitude of neutral countries as she was about the delay that armed Belgian resistance would inflict upon her timetable. A Belgian Army that chose to fight rather than "line up along the road" would require the leaving behind of divisions needed for the march on Paris. By destruction of railroads and bridges it could disrupt the Germans' line of march and flow of supplies and cause an infinity of annoyance.

Prey to second thoughts, the German government had sent Herr von Below in the middle of the night to try to influence the Belgian reply by further accusations against France. He informed van der Elst who received him that French dirigibles had dropped bombs and that French patrols had crossed the border.

"Where did these events take place?" van der Elst asked.

"In Germany," was the reply.

"In that case I fail to see the relevance of the information."

The German Minister offered to explain that the French lacked respect for international law and could therefore be expected to violate Belgian neutrality. This ingenious exercise in logic somehow fell short of making its point. Van der Elst showed his visitor the door.

At 2:30 A.M., the Council reconvened in the palace to approve the reply to Germany submitted by the Ministers. It stated that the Belgian government "would sacrifice the honor of the nation and betray its duty to Europe" if it accepted the German proposals. It declared itself "firmly resolved to repel by all means in its power every attack upon its rights."

After approving the document without change, the Council

fell into dispute over the King's insistence that no appeal to the guarantor powers for assistance should be made until the Germans actually entered Belgium. Despite vigorous disagreement he carried his point. At 4:00 A.M. the Council broke up. The last Minister to leave turned and saw King Albert standing with his back to the room and a copy of the reply in his hand, staring out of the window where the dawn was beginning to light the sky.

In Berlin, too, a late meeting was being held that night of August 2. At the Chancellor's house, Bethmann-Hollweg, General von Moltke, and Admiral Tirpitz were conferring about a declaration of war on France as they had conferred the night before about Russia. Tirpitz complained "again and again" that he could not understand why these declarations of war were necessary. They always had an "aggressive flavor"; an army could march "without such things." Bethmann pointed out that a declaration of war on France was necessary because Germany wanted to march through Belgium. Tirpitz repeated Ambassador Lichnowsky's warnings from London that an invasion of Belgium would bring England in; he suggested that the entry into Belgium might be delayed. Moltke, terrified by another threat to his schedule, at once declared this to be "impossible"; nothing must be allowed to interfere with the "machinery of transport."

He did not himself, he said, attach much value to declarations of war. French hostile acts during the day had already made war a fact. He was referring to the alleged reports of French bombings in the Nuremberg area which the German press had been blazing forth in extras all day with such effect that people in Berlin went about looking nervously at the sky. In fact, no bombings had taken place. Now, according to German logic, a declaration of war was found to be necessary because of the imaginary bombings.

Tirpitz still deplored it. There could be no doubt in the world, he said, that the French were "at least intellectually the aggressors"; but owing to the carelessness of German politicians in not making this clear to the world, the invasion of Belgium, which was "a pure emergency measure," would be made to appear unfairly "in the fateful light of a brutal act of violence."

In Brussels, after the Council of State broke up at 4:00 A.M. on the morning of August 3, Davignon returned to the Foreign Office and instructed his Political Secretary, Baron de Gaiffier, to deliver Belgium's reply to the German Minister. At precisely 7:00 A.M., the last moment of the twelve hours, Gaiffier rang the doorbell of the German Legation and delivered the reply to Herr von Below. On his way home he heard the cries of newsboys as the Monday morning papers announced the text of the ultimatum and the Belgian answer. He heard the sharp exclamations as people read the news and gathered in excited groups. Belgium's defiant "No!" exhilarated the public. Many expressed the belief that it would cause the Germans to skirt their territory rather than risk universal censure. "The Germans are dangerous but they are not maniacs," people assured one another.

Even in the palace and in the ministries some hope persisted; it was hard to believe that the Germans would deliberately choose to start the war by putting themselves in the wrong. The last hope vanished when the Kaiser's belated reply to King Albert's personal appeal of two days before was received on the evening of August 3. It was one more attempt to induce the Belgians to acquiesce without fighting. "Only with the most friendly intentions toward Belgium," the Kaiser telegraphed, had he made his grave demand. "As the conditions laid down make clear, the possibility of maintaining our former and present relations still lies in the hands of Your Majesty."

"What does he take me for?" King Albert exclaimed in the first show of anger he had allowed himself since the crisis began. Assuming the supreme command, he at once gave orders for the blowing up of the Meuse bridges at Liège and of the railroad tunnels and bridges at the Luxembourg frontier. He still postponed sending the appeal for military help and alliance to Britain and France. Belgian neutrality had been one collective act of the European Powers that almost succeeded. King Albert could not bring himself to sign its death certificate until the overt act of invasion had actually taken place.

9

"Home Before the Leaves Fall"

ON SUNDAY afternoon, August 2, a few hours before the German ultimatum was delivered in Brussels, Grey asked the British Cabinet for authority to fulfill the naval engagement to defend the French Channel coast. No more distressing moment can ever face a British government than that which requires it to come to a hard and fast and specific decision. Through the long afternoon the Cabinet squirmed uncomfortably, unready and unwilling to grasp the handle of final commitment.

In France war came and was accepted as a kind of national fate, however deeply a part of the people would have preferred to avoid it. Almost in awe, a foreign observer reported the upsurge of "national devotion" joined with an "entire absence of excitement" in a people of whom it had so often been predicted that anarchical influences had undermined their patriotism and would prove fatal in the event of war. Belgium, where there occurred one of the rare appearances of the hero in history, was lifted above herself by the uncomplicated conscience of her King and, faced with the choice to acquiesce or resist, took less than three hours to make her decision, knowing it might be mortal.

Britain had no Albert and no Alsace. Her weapons were ready but not her will. Over the past ten years she had studied and prepared for the war that was now upon her and had developed, since 1905, a system called the "War Book" which left nothing to the traditional British practice of muddling through. All orders to be issued in the event of war were ready for signature; envelopes were addressed; notices and proclamations were either printed or set up in type, and the King never moved from London without having with him those that required his immediate signature. The method was plain; the muddle was in the British mind.

The appearance of a German fleet in the Channel would have been no less direct a challenge to Britain than the Spanish

Armada of long ago, and the Sunday Cabinet reluctantly agreed to Grey's request. The written pledge which that afternoon he handed to Cambon read, "If the German Fleet comes into the Channel or through the North Sea to undertake hostile operations against the French coasts or shipping, the British Fleet will give all protection in its power." Grey added, however, that the pledge "does not bind us to go to war with Germany unless the German fleet took the action indicated." Voicing the real fear of the Cabinet, he said that as England was uncertain of the protection of her own coasts, "it was impossible safely to send our military forces out of the country."

M. Cambon asked whether this meant Britain would never do so. Grey replied that his words "dealt only with the present moment." Cambon suggested sending two divisions for "moral effect." Grey said that to send so small a force or even four divisions "would entail the maximum risk to them and produce the minimum of effect." He added that the naval commitment must not become public until Parliament could be informed on the next day.

Half in despair but yet in hope, Cambon informed his government of the pledge in a "very secret" telegram which reached Paris at 8:30 that night. Though it was but a one-legged commitment, far less than France had counted on, he believed it would lead to full belligerency, for, as he later put it, nations do not wage war "by halves."

But the naval pledge was only wrung from the Cabinet at the cost of the break that Asquith had been trying so hard to prevent. Two ministers, Lord Morley and John Burns, resigned; the formidable Lloyd George was still "doubtful." Morley believed the dissolution of the Cabinet was "in full view that afternoon." Asquith had to confess "we are on the brink of a split."

Churchill, always ready to anticipate events, appointed himself emissary to bring his former party, the Tories, into a coalition government. As soon as the Cabinet was over he hurried off to see Balfour, the former Tory Prime Minister, who like the other leaders of his party believed that Britain must carry through the policy that had created the Entente to its logical, if bitter, end. Churchill told him he expected half the Liberal Cabinet to resign if war were declared. Balfour replied that his party would be prepared to join a coalition, although if it came to that necessity he foresaw the country rent by an antiwar movement led by the seceding Liberals.

Up to this moment the German ultimatum to Belgium was not yet known. The underlying issue in the thinking of men like Churchill and Balfour, Haldane and Grey was the threatened German hegemony of Europe if France were crushed. But the policy that required support of France had developed behind closed doors and had never been fully admitted to the country. The majority of the Liberal government did not accept it. On this issue neither government nor country would have gone to war united. To many, if not to most Englishmen, the crisis was another phase in the old quarrel between Germany and France, and none of England's affair. To make it England's affair in the eyes of the public, the violation of Belgium, child of English policy, where every step of the invaders would trample on a treaty of which England was architect and signatory, was required. Grey determined to ask the Cabinet next morning to regard such invasion as a formal *casus belli.*

That evening as he was at dinner with Haldane, a Foreign Office messenger brought over a dispatch box with a telegram which, according to Haldane's account, warned that "Germany was about to invade Belgium." What this telegram was or from whom it came is not clear, but Grey must have considered it authentic. Passing it to Haldane, Grey asked him what he thought. "Immediate mobilization," Haldane replied.

They at once left the dinner table and drove to Downing Street where they found the Prime Minister with some guests. Taking him into a private room, they showed him the telegram and asked for authority to mobilize. Asquith agreed. Haldane suggested that he be temporarily reappointed to the War Office for the emergency. The Prime Minister would be too busy next day to perform the War Minister's duties. Asquith again agreed, the more readily as he was uncomfortably conscious of the looming autocrat, Field Marshal Lord Kitchener of Khartoum, whom he had already been urged to appoint to the empty chair.

Next morning, Bank Holiday Monday, was a clear and beautiful summer day. London was crammed with holiday crowds drawn to the capital instead of the seashore by the crisis. By midday they were so thick in Whitehall that cars could not get through, and the hum of milling people could be heard inside the Cabinet room where the ministers, meeting again in almost continuous session, were trying to make up their minds whether to fight on the issue of Belgium.

Over at the War Office Lord Haldane was already sending out the mobilization telegrams calling up Reservists and Territorials. At eleven o'clock the Cabinet received news of Belgium's decision to pit her six divisions against the German Empire. Half an hour later they received a declaration from the Conservative leaders, written before the ultimatum to Belgium was known, stating that it would be "fatal to the honor and security of the United Kingdom" to hesitate in support of France and Russia. Russia as an ally already stuck in the throats of most Liberal ministers. Two more of them—Sir John Simon and Lord Beauchamp—resigned, but the events in Belgium decided the pivotal Lloyd George to stay with the government.

At three o'clock that afternoon of August 3, Grey was due in Parliament to make the government's first official and public statement on the crisis. All Europe, as well as all England, was hanging on it. Grey's task was to bring his country into war and bring her in united. He had to carry with him his own, traditionally pacifist, party. He had to explain to the oldest and most practiced parliamentary body in the world how Britain was committed to support France by virtue of something that was not a commitment. He must present Belgium as the cause without hiding France as the basic cause; he must appeal to Britain's honor while making it clear that Britain's interest was the deciding factor; he must stand where a tradition of debate on foreign affairs had flourished for three hundred years and, without the brilliance of Burke or the force of Pitt, without Canning's mastery or Palmerston's jaunty nerve, without the rhetoric of Gladstone or the wit of Disraeli, justify the course of British foreign policy under his stewardship and the war it could not prevent. He must convince the present, measure up to the past, and speak to posterity.

He had had no time to prepare a written speech. In the last hour, as he was trying to compose his notes, the German ambassador was announced. Lichnowsky entered anxiously, asking what had the Cabinet decided? What was Grey going to tell the House? Would it be a declaration of war? Grey answered that it would not be a declaration of war but "a statement of conditions." Was the neutrality of Belgium one of the conditions? Lichnowsky asked. He "implored" Grey not to name it as one. He knew nothing of the plans of the German General Staff, but he could not suppose a "serious" violation was included in them, although German troops might traverse one small corner of Belgium. "If so," Lichnowsky said, voicing the eternal epitaph of man's surrender to events, "that could not be altered now."

They talked standing in the doorway, each oppressed by his own urgency, Grey trying to leave for some last moments of privacy in which to work on his speech, Lichnowsky trying to hold back the moment of the challenge made explicit. They parted and never saw each other officially again.

The House had gathered in total attendance for the first time since Gladstone brought in the Home Rule Bill in 1893. To accommodate all the members extra chairs were set up in the gangway. The Diplomatic Gallery was packed except for two empty seats marking the absence of the German and Austrian ambassadors. Visitors from the Lords filled the Strangers' Gallery, among them Field Marshal Lord Roberts, so long and vainly the advocate of compulsory military service. In the tense hush when, for once, no one bustled, passed notes, or leaned over benches to chat in whispers, there was a sudden clatter as the Chaplain, backing away from the Speaker, stumbled over the extra chairs in the aisle. All eyes were on the government bench where Grey in a light summer suit sat between Asquith whose bland face expressed nothing and Lloyd George whose disheveled hair and cheeks drained of all color made him look years older.

Grey, appearing "pale, haggard and worn," rose to his feet. Though he had been a member of the House for twenty-nine years and on the Government bench for the last eight, members on the whole knew little—and the country much less—of his conduct of foreign policy. Questions put to the Foreign Secretary rarely succeeded in trapping Grey into a clear or definitive answer, yet his evasiveness, which in a more adventurous statesman would have been challenged, was not regarded with suspicion. So noncosmopolitan, so English, so county, so reserved, Grey could not be regarded by anyone as a mettlesome mixer in foreign quarrels. He did not love foreign affairs or enjoy his job but deplored it as a necessary duty. He did not run over to the Continent for weekends but disappeared into the country. He spoke no foreign language beyond a schoolboy French. A widower at fifty-two, childless, nongregarious, he seemed as unattached to ordinary passions as to his office. What passion broke through his walled personality was reserved for trout streams and bird calls.

Speaking slowly but with evident emotion, Grey asked the House to approach the crisis from the point of view of "British interests, British honor and British obligations." He told the history of the military "conversations" with France. He said that no "secret engagement" bound the House or restricted Britain's freedom to decide her own course of action. He said France was involved in the war because of her "obligation of honor" to Russia, but "we are not parties to the Franco-Russian alliance; we do not even know the terms of that alliance." He seemed to be leaning so far over backward to show England to be uncommitted that a worried Tory, Lord Derby, whispered angrily to his neighbor, "By God, they are going to desert Belgium!"

Grey then revealed the naval arrangement with France. He told the House how, as a consequence of agreement with Britain, the French fleet was concentrated in the Mediterranean, leaving the northern and western coasts of France "absolutely undefended." He said it would be his "feeling" that "if the German fleet came down the Channel and bombarded and battered the undefended coasts of France, we could not stand aside and see this going on practically within sight of our eyes, with our arms folded, looking on dispassionately, doing nothing!" Cheers burst from the Opposition benches, while the Liberals listened, "somberly acquiescent."

To explain his having already committed Britain to defend France's Channel coasts, Grey entered into an involved argument about "British interests" and British trade routes in the Mediterranean. It was a tangled skein, and he hurried on to the "more serious consideration, becoming more serious every hour," of Belgian neutrality.

To give the subject all its due, Grey, wisely not relying on his own oratory, borrowed Gladstone's thunder of 1870, "Could this country stand by and witness the direst crime that ever stained the pages of history and thus become participators in the sin?" From Gladstone too, he took a phrase to express the fundamental issue—that England must take her stand "against the unmeasured aggrandizement of any power whatsoever."

In his own words he continued: "I ask the House from the point of view of British interests to consider what may be at stake. If France is beaten to her knees . . . if Belgium fell under the same dominating influence and then Holland and then Denmark . . . if, in a crisis like this, we run away from these obligations of honor and interest as regards the Belgian Treaty . . . I do not believe for a moment that, at the end of this war, even if we stood aside, we should be able to undo what had happened, in the course of the war, to prevent the whole of the West of Europe opposite us from falling under the domination of a single power . . . and we should, I believe, sacrifice our respect and good name and reputation before the world and should not escape the most serious and grave economic consequences."

He placed before them the "issue and the choice." The House, which had listened in "painful absorption" for an hour and a quarter, broke into overwhelming applause, signifying its answer. The occasions when an individual is able to harness a nation are memorable, and Grey's speech proved to be one of those junctures by which people afterward date events. Some dissent was still vocal, for, unlike the continental parliaments, the House of Commons was not to be exhorted or persuaded into unanimity. Ramsay MacDonald, speaking for the Laborites, said Britain should have remained neutral; Keir Hardie said he would raise the working classes against the war; and afterward in the lobby, a group of unconvinced Liberals adopted a resolution stating that Grey had failed to make a case for war. But Asquith was convinced that on the whole "our extreme peace lovers are silenced though they will soon find their tongues again." The two ministers who had resigned that morning were persuaded to return that evening, and it was generally felt that Grey had carried the country.

"What happens now?" Churchill asked Grey as they left the

House together. "Now," replied Grey, "we shall send them an ultimatum to stop the invasion of Belgium within 24 hours." To Cambon, a few hours later, he said, "If they refuse, there will be war." Although he was to wait almost another twenty-four hours before sending the ultimatum, Lichnowsky's fear had been fulfilled; Belgium had been made the condition.

The Germans took that chance because they expected a short war and because, despite the last-minute moans and apprehensions of their civilian leaders over what the British might do, the German General Staff had already taken British belligerency into account and discounted it as of little or no significance in a war they believed would be over in four months.

Clausewitz, a dead Prussian, and Norman Angell, a living if misunderstood professor, had combined to fasten the short-war concept upon the European mind. Quick, decisive victory was the German orthodoxy; the economic impossibility of a long war was everybody's orthodoxy.

"You will be home before the leaves have fallen from the trees," the Kaiser told departing troops in the first week of August. A diarist of German court society recorded on August 9 that Count Oppersdorf came in that afternoon and said things could not last ten weeks; Count Hochberg thought eight weeks, and after that, "You and I will be meeting again in England."

A German officer leaving for the Western Front said he expected to take breakfast at the Café de la Paix in Paris on Sedan Day (September 2). Russian officers expected to be in Berlin about the same time; six weeks was the usual allowance. One officer of the Imperial Guard asked the opinion of the Czar's physician whether he should pack at once his full-dress uniform to wear for the entry into Berlin or leave it to be brought by the next courier coming to the front. An English officer who, having served as a military attaché in Brussels, was considered *au courant*, was asked, upon joining his regiment, his opinion of the duration. He did not know, the officer replied, but he understood there were "financial reasons why the Great Powers could not continue for long." He had heard it from the Prime Minister "who told me that Lord Haldane told him so."

In St. Petersburg the question was not whether the Russians could win but whether it would take them two months or three; pessimists who suggested six months were considered defeatists. "Vasilii Fedorovitch (William, son of Frederick, that is, the Kaiser) has made a mistake; he won't be able to hold out," solemnly predicted the Russian Minister of Justice. He was not so very wrong. Germany had not planned on the need to hold out for long and upon entering the war had a stockpile of nitrates for making gunpowder sufficient for six months and no more. Only the later discovery of a method for fixing nitrogen out of the air enabled her war effort to continue. The French, gambling on a quick finish, risked no troops on what would have been a difficult defense of the Lorraine iron basin but allowed the Germans to take it on the theory that they would regain it with victory. As a result they lost 80 per cent of their iron ore for the duration and almost lost the war. The English, in their imprecise fashion, counted vaguely on victory, without specifying when, where, or how, within a matter of months.

Whether from instinct or intellect, three minds, all military, saw the dark shadow lengthening ahead into years, not months. Moltke, foretelling the "long, wearisome struggle," was one. Joffre was another. Questioned by ministers in 1912 he had said that if France won the first victory in a war, German national resistance would then commence, and vice versa. In either case other nations would be drawn in, and the result would be a war of "indefinite duration." Yet neither he nor Moltke, who were their countries' military chiefs since 1911 and 1906 respectively, made any allowance in their plans for the war of attrition which they both foresaw.

The third—and the only one to act upon his vision—was Lord Kitchener, who had no part in the original planning. Hastily recalled to become War Minister on August 4, as he was about to board a Channel steamer to take him to Egypt, he brought forth from some fathomless oracular depths of his being the prediction that the war would last three years. To an incredulous colleague he said it might last even longer, but "three years will do to begin with. A nation like Germany, after having forced the issue, will only give in after it is beaten to the ground. That will take a very long time. No one living knows how long."

Except for Kitchener who, from his first day in office insisted on preparing an army of millions for a war lasting years, no one else made plans reaching ahead for more than three or six months. In the case of the Germans, the fixed idea of a short war embraced the corollary that in a short war English belligerency would not matter.

"If only someone had told me beforehand that England would take up arms against us!" wailed the Kaiser during lunch at Headquarters one day later in the war. Someone in a small voice ventured, "Metternich," referring to the German ambassador in London who had been dismissed in 1912 because of his tiresome habit of predicting that naval increases would bring war with England no later than 1915. In 1912 Haldane had told the Kaiser that Britain could never permit German possession of the French Channel ports, and reminded him of the treaty obligation to Belgium. In 1912 Prince Henry of Prussia had asked his cousin King George point-blank "whether in the event of Germany and Austria going to war with Russia and France, England would come to the assistance of the two latter powers?" King George had replied, "Undoubtedly yes, under certain circumstances."

In spite of these warnings the Kaiser refused to believe what he knew to be true. According to the evidence of a companion, he was still "convinced" England would stay neutral when he went back to his yacht after giving Austria a free hand on July 5. His two *Corpsbrüder* from student days at Bonn, Bethmann and Jagow, whose qualification for office consisted chiefly in the Kaiser's sentimental weakness for brothers who wore the black and white ribbon of the fraternity and called each other *du*, comforted themselves at intervals, like devout Catholics fingering their beads, with mutual assurances of British neutrality.

Moltke and the General Staff did not need Grey or anyone else to spell out for them what England would do, for they already counted on her coming in as an absolute certainty. "The more English the better," Moltke said to Admiral Tirpitz, meaning the more who landed on the Continent the more would be netted in decisive defeat. Moltke's natural pessimism spared him the illusions of wishful thinking. In a memorandum he drew up in 1913 he stated the case more accurately than many Englishmen could have done. If Germany marched through Belgium without Belgian consent, he wrote, "then England will and *must* join our enemies," the more so as she had declared that intention in 1870. He did not think anyone in England would believe German promises to evacuate Belgium after defeating France, and he felt sure that in a war between Germany and France, England would fight whether Germany went through Belgium or not, "because she fears German hegemony and true to her policy of maintaining a balance of power will do all she can to check the increase of German power."

"In the years immediately preceding the war, we had no doubt whatever of the rapid arrival of the British Expeditionary Force on the French coast," testified General von Kuhl, a General Staff officer of the top echelon. The Staff calculated that the BEF would be mobilized by the tenth day, gather at embarkation ports on the eleventh, begin embarkation on the twelfth, and complete the transfer to France on the fourteenth day. This proved to be almost dead reckoning.

Nor was Germany's naval staff under any illusions. "England probably hostile in case it comes to war," the Admiralty telegraphed as early as July 11 to Admiral von Spee on board the *Scharnhorst* in the Pacific.

Two hours after Grey finished speaking in the House of Commons, that event took place which had been in the back of every mind on both sides of the Rhine since 1870 and in the front of most since 1905. Germany declared war on France. To Germans it came, said the Crown Prince, as the "military solution" of the ever-increasing tension, the end of the nightmare of encirclement. "It is a joy to be alive," rejoiced a German paper on that day in a special edition headlined "The Blessing of Arms." Germans, it said, were "exulting with happiness. . . . We have wished so much for this hour. . . . The sword which has been forced into our hand will not be sheathed until our aims are won and our territory extended as far as necessity demands." Not everyone was exulting. Deputies of the left, summoned to the Reichstag, found each other "depressed" and "nervous." One, confessing readiness to vote all war credits, muttered, "We can't let them destroy the Reich." Another kept grumbling, "This incompetent diplomacy, this incompetent diplomacy."

For France the signal came at 6:15 when Premier Viviani's telephone rang and he heard the American ambassador, Myron Herrick, tell him in a voice choked with tears that he had just received a request to take over the German Embassy and hoist the American flag on its flagpole. He had accepted the charge, Herrick said, but not the flag raising.

Knowing exactly what this meant, Viviani waited for the imminent arrival of the German ambassador, who was announced a few moments later. Von Schoen, who had a Belgian wife, entered in visible distress. He began by complaining that on the way over a lady had thrust her head through the window of his carriage and insulted "me and my Emperor." Viviani, whose own nerves were strung taut with the anguish of the last few days, asked if this complaint was the purpose of his visit. Schoen admitted he had a further duty to perform and, unfolding the document he carried, read its contents, which, as he was the "soul of honor" according to Poincaré, were the cause of his embarrassment. In consequence, it read, of French acts of "organized hostility" and of air attacks on Nuremberg and Karlsruhe and of violation of Belgian neutrality by French aviators flying over Belgian territory, "the German Empire considers itself in a state of war with France."

Viviani formally denied the charges which were included less to impress the French government, who would know they had not taken place, than to impress the German public at home that they were the victims of French aggression. He escorted von Schoen to the door and then, almost reluctant to come to the final parting, walked with him out of the building, down the steps, as far as the door of his waiting carriage. The two representatives of the "hereditary enemies" stood for a moment in mutual unhappiness, bowed wordlessly to each other, and von Schoen drove away into the dusk.

In Whitehall that evening, Sir Edward Grey, standing with a friend at the window as the street lamps below were being lit, made the remark that has since epitomized the hour: "The lamps are going out all over Europe; we shall not see them lit again in our lifetime."

*

At six o'clock on the morning of August 4, Herr von Below paid his last visit to the Foreign Office in Brussels. He delivered a note saying that in view of the rejection of his Government's "well intentioned proposals," Germany would be obliged to carry out measures for her own security, "if necessary by force of arms." The "if necessary" was intended to leave an opening for Belgium still to change her mind.

That afternoon the American Minister, Brand Whitlock, who had been called to take over the German Legation, found von Below and his First Secretary, von Stumm, slumped in two chairs, making no effort to pack up and seeming "nearly unstrung." Smoking with one hand and mopping his brow with the other, Below sat otherwise motionless while two aged functionaries with candles, sealing wax, and strips of paper proceeded slowly and solemnly around the room sealing the oaken cupboards which held the archives. "Oh the poor fools!" von Stumm kept repeating, half to himself, "Why don't they get out of the way of the steam roller. We don't want to hurt them but if they stand in our way they will be ground into the dirt. Oh, the poor fools!"

Only later did anyone on the German side ask himself who had been the fools on that day. It had been the day, Count Czernin, the Austrian Foreign Minister, discovered afterward, of "our greatest disaster"; the day, even the Crown Prince mournfully acknowledged long after the fact, "when we Germans lost the first great battle in the eyes of the world."

At two minutes past eight that morning the first wave of field gray broke over the Belgian frontier at Gemmerich, thirty miles from Liège. Belgian gendarmes in their sentry boxes opened fire. The force detached from the main German armies for the assault upon Liège under the command of General von Emmich consisted of six infantry brigades, each with artillery and other arms, and three cavalry divisions. By nightfall they had reached the Meuse at Visé, a name that was to become the first in a series of ruins.

Up to the moment of invasion many still believed that self-interest would divert the German armies around Belgium's borders. Why should they deliberately bring two more enemies into the field against them? As no one supposed the Germans to be stupid, the answer that suggested itself to the French mind was that the German ultimatum to Belgium was a trick. It was not intended to be followed by actual invasion but designed to "lead us into being the first to enter Belgium," as Messimy said, in an order forbidding French troops to cross the line "even by so much as a patrol or a single horseman."

Whether for this reason or some other, Grey had not yet sent England's ultimatum. King Albert had not yet appealed to the guarantor powers for military aid. He, too, feared that the ultimatum might be a "colossal feint." If he called in the French and British too soon, their presence would drag Belgium into the war in spite of herself, and at the back of his mind was a worry that once established on Belgian soil his neighbors might be in no hurry to leave. Only after the tramp of German columns marching on Liège had put an end to all doubt and left him no choice, did the King, at noon on August 4, make his appeal for "concerted and common" military action by the guarantors.

In Berlin, Moltke was still hoping that after the first shots fired for honor's sake the Belgians might be persuaded "to come to an understanding." For that reason Germany's final note had simply said "by force of arms" and for once refrained from declaring war. When Baron Beyens, the Belgian ambassador, came to demand his passports on the morning of the invasion, Jagow hurried forward asking, "Well, what have you to say to me?" as if expecting a proposal. He reiterated Germany's offer to respect Belgian independence and pay for all damages if Belgium would refrain from destroying railroads, bridges, and tunnels and let German troops pass through freely without defending Liège. When Beyens turned to go, Jagow followed him hopefully, saying, "Perhaps there will still be something for us to talk over."

In Brussels one hour after the invasion began, King Albert, in unadorned field uniform, rode to meet his Parliament. At a brisk trot the little procession came down the Rue Royale led by an open carriage in which were the Queen and her three children, followed by two more carriages and, bringing up the rear, the King alone on horseback. Houses along the way were decked with flags and flowers; an exalted people filled the streets. Strangers shook each other's hands, laughing and crying, each man feeling, as one recalled, "united to his fellow by a common bond of love and hate." Wave on wave of cheers reached out to the King as if the people in one universal emotion were trying to say he was the symbol of their country and of their will to uphold its independence. Even the Austrian Minister, who had somehow forgotten to absent himself and with other diplomats was watching the procession from the Parliament windows, was wiping tears from his eyes.

Inside the hall, after members, visitors, and the Queen and court were seated, the King came in alone, tossed his cap and gloves onto the lectern in a businesslike gesture and began to speak in a voice only faintly unsteady. When, recalling the Congress of 1830 that created an independent Belgium, he asked, "Gentlemen, are you unalterably decided to maintain intact the sacred gift of our forefathers?" the deputies, unable to control themselves, stood up with shouts of "*Oui! Oui! Oui!*"

The American Minister, describing the scene in his diary, tells how he watched the King's twelve-year-old heir in his sailor suit, listening with an absorbed face and eyes fixed on his father, and how he wondered, "What are the thoughts in that boy's mind?" Almost as if he had been granted a glimpse into the future, Mr. Whitlock asked himself, "Will this scene ever come back to him in after years? And how? When? Under what circumstances?" The boy in the sailor suit, as Leopold III, was to surrender in 1940 to another German invasion.

In the streets, after the speech was over, enthusiasm became delirious. The army, hitherto contemned, were heroes. The people shouted, "Down with the Germans! Death to the assassins! *Vive la Belgique indépendante!*" After the King had gone, the crowds shouted for the War Minister, ordinarily, regardless of his identity, the most unpopular man in the government by virtue of his office. When M. de Broqueville appeared on the balcony, even that suave man of the world wept, overcome by the fervent emotion shared by everyone who was in Brussels on that day.

*

On the same day in Paris, French soldiers in red trousers and big-skirted dark blue coats, buttoned back at the corners, chanted as they marched through the streets,

> C'est l'Alsace et la Lorraine
> C'est l'Alsace qu'il nous faut,
> Oh, Oh, Oh, OH!

ending with a triumphant yell on the last "Oh!" One-armed General Pau, whose lost limb gave him an extra popularity, rode by wearing the green and black ribbon of the veterans of 1870. Cavalry regiments of cuirassiers with glistening metal breastplates and long black horsehair tails hanging down from their helmets were conscious of no anachronism. Following them came huge crates housing airplanes and wheeled platforms bearing the long narrow gray-painted field guns, the *soixante-quinzes* that were France's pride. All day the flow of men, horses, weapons and matériel poured through the huge arched portals of the Gare du Nord and the Gare de l'Est.

Down the boulevards, empty of vehicles, marched companies of volunteers with flags and banners proclaiming their purpose: "Luxembourg will never be German!" "Rumania rallies to the Mother of the Latin races," "Italy whose freedom was bought with French blood," "Spain the loving sister of France," "British volunteers for France," "Greeks who love France," "Scandinavians of Paris," "Slav peoples at the side of France," "Latin American lives for the mother of Latin American culture." Roars and cheers greeted the banner that proclaimed, "Alsatians going home."

At a joint session of the Senate and Chamber, Viviani, pale as death and looking as if he were suffering physically and mentally, surpassed his own capacity for fire and eloquence in a speech that was acclaimed, like everybody's on that day, as the greatest of his career. He carried with him in his portfolio the text of France's treaty with Russia but was not questioned about it. Ecstatic cheers greeted his announcement that Italy, "with the clarity of insight possessed by the Latin intellect," had declared her neutrality. As expected, the third member of the Triple Alliance, when the test came, had side-stepped on the ground that Austria's attack on Serbia was an act of aggression which released her from her treaty obligations. Relieving

France of the need to guard her southern frontier, Italy's neutrality was worth an extra four divisions, or 80,000 men.

After Viviani had spoken, a speech by President Poincaré, who was precluded by office from attending Parliament in person, was read for him while the whole audience remained standing. France stood before the universe for Liberty, Justice, and Reason, he said, characteristically altering the traditional French trinity. Messages of sympathy and good will from every part of what he pointedly called the "civilized" world were pouring in on her. As the words were being read, General Joffre, "perfectly calm and wholly confident," came to make his farewell to the President before leaving for the front.

Rain was pouring on Berlin as the Reichstag deputies assembled to hear the Kaiser's speech from the throne. Beneath the windows of the Reichstag, where they came for a preliminary meeting with the Chancellor, they could hear the ceaseless clippety-clop of horseshoes on pavement as squadron after squadron of cavalry trotted through the glistening streets. Party leaders met Bethmann in a room adorned by a huge picture which exhibited the gratifying spectacle of Kaiser Wilhelm I trampling gloriously on the French flag. He was shown, together with Bismarck and Field Marshal Moltke, prancing upon the battlefield of Sedan while a German soldier in the foreground stretched a French flag beneath the hoofs of the Emperor's horse. Bethmann expressed concern for unity and exhorted the deputies to "be unanimous" in their decisions. "We shall be unanimous, Excellency," a spokesman for the Liberals replied obediently. The all-knowing Erzberger who, as *rapporteur* of the Military Affairs Committee and a close associate of the Chancellor, was considered to have his ear to Olympus, bustled among his fellow deputies assuring them that the Serbs would be beaten "by this time next Monday" and that everything was going well.

After services in the cathedral the deputies marched in a body to the palace where the entrances were guarded and roped off and credentials were examined at four different stages before the people's representatives were finally seated in the Weisser Saal. Entering quietly, accompanied by several generals, the Kaiser sat down on the throne. Bethmann, in the uniform of the Dragoon Guards, took his speech from the royal portfolio and handed it to the Kaiser, who stood up, looking small beside the Chancellor, and read it, his helmet on his head and one hand resting on his sword hilt. Without mentioning Belgium he declared, "We draw the sword with a clear conscience and with clean hands." The war had been provoked by Serbia with the support of Russia. Hoots and cries of "Shame!" were evoked by a discourse on Russian iniquities. After the prepared speech, the Kaiser raised his voice and proclaimed, "From this day on I recognize no parties but only Germans!" and called upon party leaders, if they agreed with these sentiments, to step forward and shake his hand. Amid "wild excitement" all did, while the rest of the assembly erupted in cheers and shouts of fervent rejoicing.

At three o'clock members reconvened in the Reichstag to hear an address by the Chancellor and to perform the remainder of their duty which consisted first of voting war credits and then adjournment. The Social Democrats agreed to make the vote unanimous, and spent their last hours of parliamentary responsibility in anxious consultation whether to join in a "*Hoch!*" for the Kaiser which they satisfactorily resolved by making it a *Hoch* for "Kaiser, People, and Country."

Everyone, as Bethmann rose to speak, waited in painful expectancy for what he had to say about Belgium. A year ago Foreign Minister Jagow had assured a secret session of the Reichstag steering committee that Germany would never violate Belgium, and General von Heeringen, then War Minister, had promised that the Supreme Command in the event of war would respect Belgium's neutrality as long as Germany's enemies did. On August 4 deputies did not know that their armies had invaded Belgium that morning. They knew of the ultimatum but nothing of the Belgian reply because the German government, wishing to give the impression that Belgium had acquiesced and that her armed resistance was therefore illegal, never published it.

"Our troops," Bethmann informed the tense audience, "have occupied Luxembourg and perhaps"—the "perhaps" was posthumous by eight hours—"are already in Belgium." (Great commotion.) True, France had given Belgium a pledge to respect her neutrality, but "We knew that France was standing ready to invade Belgium" and "we could not wait." It was, he said inevitably, a case of military necessity, and "necessity knows no law."

So far he had his hearers, both the right which despised him and the left which mistrusted him, in thrall. His next sentence created a sensation. "Our invasion of Belgium is contrary to international law but the wrong—I speak openly—that we are committing we will make good as soon as our military goal has been reached." Admiral Tirpitz considered this the greatest blunder ever spoken by a German statesman; Conrad Haussman, a leader of the Liberal party, considered it the finest part of the speech. The act having been confessed in a public *mea culpa*, he and his fellow deputies of the left felt purged of guilt and saluted the Chancellor with a loud "*Sehr richtig!*" In a final striking phrase—and before his day of memorable maxims was over he was to add one more that would make him immortal—Bethmann said that whoever was as badly threatened as were the Germans could think only of how to "hack his way through."

A war credit of five billion marks was voted unanimously, after which the Reichstag voted itself out of session for four months or for what was generally expected to be the duration. Bethmann closed the proceedings with an assurance that carried overtones of the gladiators' salute: "Whatever our lot may be, August 4, 1914, will remain for all eternity one of Germany's greatest days!"

That evening at seven o'clock England's answer, awaited so long in such anxiety by so many, was finally made definitive. That morning the British government had finally screwed its determination to the sticking point sufficiently to deliver an ultimatum. It arrived, however, in two parts. First, Grey asked for an assurance that German demands upon Belgium would not be "proceeded with" and for an "immediate reply," but as he attached no time limit and mentioned no sanctions in case of non-reply, the message was not technically an ultimatum. He waited until after he knew the German Army had invaded Belgium before sending the second notice stating that Britain felt bound "to uphold the neutrality of Belgium and the observance of the treaty to which Germany is as much a party as ourselves." A "satisfactory reply" was demanded by midnight, failing which the British ambassador was to ask for his passports.

Why the ultimatum was not sent the night before, immediately after Parliament made plain its acceptance of Grey's speech, can only be explained by the government's irresolute state of mind. What sort of "satisfactory reply" it expected, short of the Germans meekly retreating across the frontier they had deliberately and irrevocably crossed that morning, and why England agreed to wait for so fanciful a phenomenon until midnight, can hardly be explained at all. In the Mediterranean that night the lost hours before midnight were to be crucial.

In Berlin, the British ambassador, Sir Edward Goschen, presented the ultimatum in a historic interview with the Chancellor. He found Bethmann "very agitated." According to Bethmann himself, "my blood boiled at this hypocritical harping on Belgium which was not the thing that had driven England into war." Indignation launched Bethmann into a harangue. He said that England was doing an "unthinkable" thing in making war on a "kindred nation," that "it was like striking a man from behind while he was fighting for his life against two assailants," that as a result of "this last terrible step" England would be responsible for all the dreadful events that might follow, and "all for just a word—'neutrality'—just for a scrap of paper. . . ."

Hardly noticing the phrase that was to resound round the world, Goschen included it in his report of the interview. He had replied that, if for strategical reasons it was a matter of life or death for Germany to advance through Belgium, it was, so to speak, a matter of life or death for Britain to keep her solemn compact. "His Excellency was so excited, so evidently overcome by the news of our action, and so little disposed to hear reason," that he refrained from further argument.

As he was leaving, two men in a press car of the *Berliner Tageblatt* drove through the streets throwing out flyers which announced—somewhat prematurely, as the ultimatum did not expire until midnight—Britain's declaration of war. Coming after Italy's defection, this last act of "treason," this latest desertion, this one further addition to their enemies infuriated the Germans, a large number of whom immediately became transformed into a howling mob which occupied itself for the next hour in stoning all the windows of the British Embassy. England became overnight the most hated enemy; "*Rassenverrat!*" (race treason) the favorite hate slogan. The Kaiser, in one of the least profound of all comments on the war, lamented: "To think that George and Nicky should have played me false! If my grandmother had been alive she would never have allowed it."

Germans could not get over the perfidy of it. It was unbelievable that the English, having degenerated to the stage where suffragettes heckled the Prime Minister and defied the police, were going to fight. England, though wide-flung and still powerful, was getting old, and they felt for her, like the Visigoths for the later Romans, a contempt combined with the newcomer's sense of inferiority. The English think they can "treat us like Portugal," complained Admiral Tirpitz.

England's betrayal deepened their sense of friendlessness. They were conscious of being an unloved nation. How was it that Nice, annexed by France in 1860, could settle down comfortably and within a few years forget it had ever been Italian, whereas half a million Alsatians preferred to leave their homeland rather than live under German rule? "Our country is not much loved anywhere and indeed frequently hated," the Crown Prince noted on his travels.

While the crowds shrieked for vengeance in the Wilhelmstrasse, depressed deputies of the left gathered in cafés and groaned together. "The whole world is rising against us," said one. "Germanism has three enemies in the world—Latins, Slavs and Anglo-Saxons—and now they are all united against us."

"Our diplomacy has left us no friend but Austria, and it was we who had to support her," said another.

"At least one good thing is that it can't last long," a third consoled them. "We shall have peace in four months. Economically and financially we can't last longer than that."

"One hopes for the Turks and Japanese," someone else suggested.

A rumor had in fact swept the cafés the previous evening when diners heard distant hurrahs shouted in the streets. As a diarist of the time recorded it: "They came nearer. People listened, then jumped up. The hurrahs became louder; they resounded over Potsdamer Platz and reached the proportions of a storm. The guests left their food and ran out of the restaurant. I followed the stream. What has happened? 'Japan has declared war on Russia!' they roared. Hurrah! Hurrah! Uproarious rejoicing. People embraced one another. 'Long live Japan! Hurrah! Hurrah!' Endless jubilation. Then someone shouted, 'To the Japanese Embassy!' And the crowd rushed away carrying everybody with it and besieged the embassy. 'Long live Japan! Long live Japan!' people shouted impetuously until the Japanese Ambassador finally appeared and, perplexed, stammered his thanks for this unexpected and, it would seem, undeserved homage." Although by next day it was known the rumor was false, just how undeserved was the homage would not be known for another two weeks.

When Ambassador Lichnowsky and his staff subsequently left England, a friend who came to say goodbye was struck by the "sadness and bitterness" of the party at Victoria Station. They were blaming officials at home for dragging them into a war with no allies but Austria.

"What chance have we, attacked on every side? Is no one friendly to Germany?" one official asked mournfully.

"Siam is friendly, I am told," a colleague replied.

No sooner had England delivered herself of the ultimatum than fresh disputes broke out in the Cabinet over the question whether to send an Expeditionary Force to France. Having declared themselves in, they began to dispute how far in they should go. Their joint plans with the French were predicated on an Expeditionary Force of six divisions to arrive in France between M-4 and M-12 and to be ready for action on the extreme left of the French line by M-15. Already the schedule was disrupted because the British M-1 (August 5), which had been expected to be two days behind the French, was now three days behind, and further delay would follow.

Mr. Asquith's cabinet was paralyzed by fear of invasion. In 1909 the Committee of Imperial Defence after a special study of the problem had declared that as long as the home army was kept sufficiently strong to make the Germans mount an invasion force of such size that it could not evade the navy, a large-scale invasion was "impractical." Despite its assurance that the defense of the home islands was adequately guaranteed by the navy, Britain's leaders on August 4 could not summon up the courage to denude the islands of the Regular Army. Arguments were put forward for sending fewer than six divisions, for sending them later rather than sooner, even for not sending them at all. Admiral Jellicoe was told his planned escort of the Expeditionary Force across the Channel would not be required "for the present." No button at the War Office automatically put the BEF in motion because the British government could not make up its mind to push it. The War Office itself, without a minister for the last four months, was distracted for lack of a chief. Asquith had progressed as far as inviting Kitchener up to London, but could not yet nerve himself to offer him the post. The impetuous and tempestuous Sir Henry Wilson, whose uninhibited diary was to cause such anguish when published after the war, was "revolted by such a state of things." So was poor M. Cambon who went, armed with a map, to show Grey how vital it was that the French left should be extended by Britain's six divisions. Grey promised to bring the matter to the attention of the Cabinet.

General Wilson, raging at the delay which he ascribed to Grey's "sinful" hesitation, indignantly showed to his friends in the Opposition a copy of the mobilization order which instead of reading "mobilize and embark," read only "mobilize." This alone, he said, would delay the schedule by four days. Balfour undertook to spur the government. He told them, in a letter addressed to Haldane, that the whole point of the Entente and of the military arrangements which had flowed from it was the preservation of France, for if France were crushed "the whole future of Europe might be changed in a direction we should regard as disastrous." Having adopted that policy, the thing to do, he suggested, was "to strike quickly and strike with your whole strength." When Haldane came to see him to explain the nature of the Cabinet's hesitations, Balfour could not help feeling they were marked by "a certain wooliness of thought and indecision of purpose."

That afternoon of August 4, at about the time when Bethmann was addressing the Reichstag and Viviani the Chambre des Députés, Mr. Asquith announced to the House of Commons a "message from His Majesty signed by his own hand."

Mr. Speaker rose from his chair and members uncovered while the Mobilization Proclamation was read. Next, from typewritten copy that trembled slightly in his hand, Asquith read the terms of the ultimatum just telegraphed to Germany. When he came to the words "a satisfactory answer by midnight," a solemn cheer rose from the benches.

All that was left was to wait for midnight (eleven o'clock, British time). At nine o'clock the government learned, through an intercepted but uncoded telegram sent out from Berlin, that Germany had considered itself at war with Britain from the moment when the British ambassador had asked for his passports. Hastily summoned, the Cabinet debated whether to declare war as of that moment or wait for the time limit set by the ultimatum to expire. They decided to wait. In silence, each encased in his private thoughts, they sat around the green table in the ill-lit Cabinet room, conscious of the shadows of those who at other fateful moments had sat there before them. Eyes watched the clock ticking away the time limit. "Boom!" Big Ben struck the first note of eleven, and each note thereafter sounded to Lloyd George, who had a Celtic ear for melodrama, like "Doom, doom, doom!"

Twenty minutes later the War Telegram, "War, Germany, act," was dispatched. Where and when the army was to act was still unsettled, the decision having been left for a War Council called for the following day. The British government went to bed a belligerent, if something less than bellicose.

Next day, with the assault on Liège, the first battle of the war began. Europe was entering, Moltke wrote that day to Conrad von Hötzendorff, upon "the struggle that will decide the course of history for the next hundred years."

BATTLE

10

"Goeben . . . *An Enemy Then Flying*"

BEFORE THE land battle began, a wireless message from the German Admiralty to the German Commander in the Mediterranean, Admiral Wilhelm Souchon, flickered through the air in the pre-dawn hours of August 4. It read: "Alliance with Turkey concluded August 3. Proceed at once to Constantinople." Although its expectations proved premature and it was almost immediately canceled, Admiral Souchon decided to proceed as directed. His command consisted of two fast new ships, the battle cruiser *Goeben* and the light cruiser *Breslau.* No other single exploit of the war cast so long a shadow upon the world as the voyage accomplished by their commander during the next seven days.

Turkey at the time of Sarajevo had many enemies and no allies because no one considered her worth an alliance. For a hundred years the Ottoman Empire, called the "Sick Man" of Europe, had been considered moribund by the hovering European powers who were waiting to fall upon the carcass. But year after year the fabulous invalid refused to die, still grasping in decrepit hands the keys to immense possessions. Indeed, during the last six years, ever since the Young Turk Revolution overthrew the old Sultan "Abdul the Damned," in 1908, and established under his more amenable brother a government by the "Committee of Union and Progress," Turkey had begun to be rejuvenated.

The "Committee," otherwise the Young Turks, led by their "little Napoleon," Enver Bey, determined to remake the country, forge the strength necessary to hold the slipping bonds of empire, fend off the waiting eagles, and retrieve the Pan-Islamic dominion of the days of Ottoman glory. The process was watched with no relish at all by Russia, France, and England, who had rival ambitions in the area. Germany, late on the imperial scene and with Berlin-to-Bagdad dreams of her own, determined to become the Young Turks' patron. A German military mission sent in 1913 to reorganize the Turkish Army caused such furious Russian resentment that only concerted effort by the Powers to provide a face-saving device prevented the affair from becoming that "damned foolish thing in the Balkans" a year before Sarajevo.

From then on, the Turks felt creeping over them the shadow of the oncoming day when they would have to choose sides. Fearing Russia, resenting England, mistrusting Germany, they could not decide. The "Hero of the Revolution," handsome young Enver with his pink cheeks and black mustache worn in upturned points like the Kaiser's, was the only wholehearted and enthusiastic advocate of a German alliance. Like some later thinkers, he believed in the Germans as the wave of the future. Talaat Bey, political "Boss" of the "Committee," and its real ruler, a stout Levantine adventurer who could devour a pound of caviar at a sitting, washed down by two glasses of brandy and two bottles of champagne, was less sure. He believed Turkey could obtain a better price from Germany than from the Entente, and he had no faith in Turkey's chances of survival as a neutral in a war of the Great Powers. If the Entente Powers won, Ottoman possessions would crumble under their pressure; if the Central Powers won, Turkey would become a German vassal. Other groups in the Turkish government would have preferred an alliance with the Entente, if it had been obtainable, in the hope of buying off Russia, Turkey's age-old enemy. For ten centuries Russia had yearned for Constantinople, the city Russians called Czargrad that lay at the exit of the Black Sea. That narrow and famous sea passage, called the Dardanelles, fifty miles long and nowhere more than three miles wide, was Russia's only year-round egress to the rest of the world.

Turkey had one asset of inestimable value—her geographical position at the junction of the paths of empire. For that reason England had been for a hundred years Turkey's traditional protector, but the truth was that England no longer took Turkey seriously. After a century of supporting the Sultan against all comers because she preferred a weak, debilitated, and therefore malleable despot astride her road to India, England was at last beginning to tire of the fetters that bound her to what Winston

Churchill amicably called "scandalous, crumbling, decrepit, penniless Turkey." The Turkish reputation for misrule, corruption, and cruelty had been a stench in the nostrils of Europe for a long time. The Liberals who had governed England since 1906 were the inheritors of Gladstone's celebrated appeal to expel the unspeakable Turk, "the one great anti-human specimen of humanity," from Europe. Their policy was shaped by an image half Sick Man, half Terrible Turk. Lord Salisbury's sporting metaphor after the Crimean War, "We have put our money on the wrong horse," acquired the status of prophecy. British influence at the Porte was allowed to lapse just at the time when it might have proved beyond price.

A request by Turkey for a permanent alliance with Great Britain was turned down in 1911 through the medium of Winston Churchill who had visited Constantinople in 1909 and established "amicable relations," as he conceived them, with Enver and other Young Turk ministers. In the imperial style used for addressing Oriental states, he suggested that although Britain could accept no alliance, Turkey would do well not to alienate British friendship by "reverting to the oppressive methods of the old regime or seeking to disturb the British status quo as it now exists." Superbly surveying the world from his Admiralty post, he reminded Turkey that British friendship would be of value so long as Britain "alone among European states . . . retains supremacy of the sea." That Turkey's friendship or even her neutrality might be of equal value to Britain was never seriously considered by him or any other minister.

In July 1914, with the two-front war looming before them, the Germans suddenly became anxious to secure the ally who could close the Black Sea exit and cut Russia off from her allies and their supplies. An earlier Turkish proposal of alliance that had been left dangling now suddenly looked desirable. The Kaiser in his alarm insisted that "the thing to do now is to get every gun in readiness in the Balkans to shoot against the Slavs." When Turkey began to haggle over terms, and made a show of leaning toward the Entente, the Kaiser in increasing panic directed his ambassador to reply to the Turkish offer "with unmistakably plain compliance. . . . Under no circumstances at all can we afford to turn them away."

On July 28, the day Austria declared war on Serbia, Turkey

formally asked Germany for a secret offensive and defensive alliance to become operative in the event of either party going to war with Russia. Within the same day, the offer was received in Berlin, accepted and a draft treaty signed by the Chancellor telegraphed back. At the last moment the Turks had difficulty bringing themselves to the point of tying the knot that would tie their fate to Germany's. If only they could be sure Germany would win . . .

While they were hesitating England helpfully gave them a push by seizing two Turkish battleships then being built under contract in British yards. They were first-class capital ships equal to the best of Britain's, one of which was armed with 13.5-inch guns. The spirited First Lord "requisitioned"—to use his own word—the Turkish warships on July 28. One, the *Sultan Osman*, had been completed in May and a first installment already paid, but when the Turks wished to bring her home, the British, supplying sinister hints about a Greek plot to attack her by submarine, had persuaded them to leave her in Britain until her sister ship, the *Reshadieh*, was completed and the two could return together. When the *Reshadieh* was ready early in July, further excuses for departure were offered. Speed and gunnery trials were unaccountably delayed. On learning of Churchill's order, the Turkish captain, who was waiting with five hundred Turkish sailors aboard a transport in the Tyne, threatened to board his ships and hoist the Turkish flag. Not without relish the voice at the Admiralty gave orders to resist such an attempt "by armed force if necessary."

The ships had cost Turkey the immense sum—for that time —of $30,000,000. The money had been raised by popular subscription after their defeats in the Balkan Wars aroused the Turkish public to the need of renovating the armed forces. Every Anatolian peasant had supplied his penny. Although not yet known to the public, news of the seizure caused, as Djemal Pasha, the Naval Minister, not excessively put it, "mental anguish" to his government.

England took no pains to assuage it. Grey, when officially informing the Turks of this simple piece of piracy on the Tyne, felt sure Turkey would understand why England found it necessary to take the ships for her "own needs in this crisis." The financial and other loss to Turkey—a matter of "sincere regret" to His Majesty's Government—would, he blandly said, be given "due consideration." Compensation he did not mention. Under the cumulative effect of the "Sick Man" and "wrong horse" concepts, England had come to regard the entire Ottoman Empire as of less account than two extra warships. Grey's telegram of regrets was sent on August 3. On the same day Turkey signed the treaty of alliance with Germany.

She did not, however, declare war on Russia, as she was pledged to do, or close the Black Sea or take any action publicly compromising strict neutrality. Having obtained an alliance with a major power on her own terms, Turkey proved in no hurry to help her new ally. Her uncertain ministers preferred to wait to see which way the opening battles of the war would go. Germany was far away, whereas the Russians and British were a near and ever-present menace. The now certain entry of England in the war was causing serious second thoughts. Afraid of just such a development, the German government instructed its ambassador, Baron Wangenheim, to obtain Turkey's declaration of war on Russia "today if possible," for it was "of the greatest importance to prevent the Porte from escaping from us under the influence of England's action." The Porte, however, did not comply. All except Enver wished to delay an overt act against Russia until the progress of the war revealed some sign of its probable outcome.

In the Mediterranean gray shapes were maneuvering for coming combat. Wireless operators, tensely listening to their earphones, took down operational orders from far-away Admiralties. The immediate and primary task of the British and French fleets was to safeguard the passage from North Africa to France of the French Colonial Corps which, with its three instead of the normal two divisions, and its auxiliary arms, numbered over 80,000 men. The presence or absence of an entire army corps from its designated place in the line could be decisive upon the French plan of battle, and the war, as both sides believed, would be determined by the fate of France in the opening clash with Germany.

Both French and British Admiralties had their eyes fixed on the *Goeben* and *Breslau* as the chief menace to the French troop transports. The French had the largest fleet in the Mediterranean, with a force available for protecting their transports of 16 battleships, 6 cruisers, and 24 destroyers. The British Mediterranean fleet, based on Malta, while lacking dreadnoughts, was headed by three battle cruisers, *Inflexible*, *Indomitable*, and *Indefatigable*, each of 18,000 tons with an armament of eight 12-inch guns and a speed of 27 to 28 knots. They were designed to overtake and annihilate anything that floated except a battleship of the dreadnought class. In addition the British fleet included four armored cruisers of 14,000 tons, four light cruisers of under 5,000 tons, and 14 destroyers. The Italian fleet was neutral. The Austrian fleet, based on Pola at the head of the Adriatic, had eight active capital ships, including two new dreadnoughts with 12-inch guns and an appropriate number of other ships. A paper tiger, it was unprepared and proved inactive.

Germany, with the second largest fleet in the world, had only two warships in the Mediterranean. One was the battle cruiser *Goeben*, of 23,000 tons, as large as a dreadnought, with a recorded trial speed of 27.8 knots equal to that of the British *Inflexible*s and an approximately equal firepower. The other was the *Breslau* of 4,500 tons, a ship on a par with the British light cruisers. Because of her speed, which was greater than that of any French battleship or cruiser, the *Goeben* "would easily be able," according to the dire forecast depicted by the British First Lord, "to avoid the French battle squadrons and brushing aside or outstripping their cruisers, break in upon the transports and sink one after another of these vessels crammed with soldiers." If there was one thing characteristic of British naval thinking prior to the outbreak of war, it was the tendency to credit the German Navy with far greater audacity and willingness to take risks against odds than either the British themselves would have shown or than the Germans in fact did show when the test came.

To be ready to attack the French transports was indeed one reason why the *Goeben* and her consort had been sent to cruise the Mediterranean after their launching in 1912. At the final moment Germany discovered they had a more important function to perform. On August 3 when the Germans realized the need to bring every possible pressure upon the reluctant

Turks to declare war, Admiral Tirpitz ordered Admiral Souchon to Constantinople.

Souchon, a dark, compact, and incisive sailor of fifty, had raised his flag aboard the *Goeben* in 1913. Since then he had steamed the inland seas and straits of his new command, roamed its coasts and capes, rounded its islands, visited its ports, familiarizing himself with the places and personalities with which he might have to deal in the event of war. He had been to Constantinople and met the Turks; he had exchanged courtesies with Italians, Greeks, Austrians, and French, with all but the British, who, he reported to the Kaiser, rigorously refused to allow their ships to anchor in the same ports at the same time as the Germans. Their habit was always to appear immediately afterward in order to wipe out any impression the Germans might have made, or, as the Kaiser elegantly expressed it, "to spit in the soup."

At Haifa when he heard the news of Sarajevo, Souchon immediately felt a premonition of war and a simultaneous concern for his boilers. They had been leaking steam for some time, and the *Goeben* was in fact scheduled to be replaced by the *Moltke* in October and return to Kiel for repairs. Deciding to prepare for the worst at once, Souchon departed for Pola, after telegraphing ahead to the Admiralty to send him new boiler tubes and skilled repairmen to meet him there. Through July the work proceeded feverishly. Everyone in the crew who could wield a hammer was pressed into service. In eighteen days 4,000 damaged tubes were located and replaced. Still the repairs were not finished when Souchon received his warning telegram and left Pola lest he be bottled up in the Adriatic.

On August 1 he reached Brindisi on the heel of Italy where the Italians, making excuses about the sea being too choppy for tenders, refused him coal. Clearly Italy's anticipated betrayal of the Triple Alliance was about to become a fact, depriving Souchon of her coaling facilities. He assembled his officers to discuss what should be their course of action. Their chances of breaking through the Allied screen to the Atlantic, while inflicting what damage they could upon the French transports on their way, depended upon their speed, and this depended in turn upon the boilers.

"How many boilers leaking steam?" Souchon asked his aide.

"Two during the last four hours."

"Damn!" said the Admiral, raging at the fate which crippled his splendid ship at such an hour. He decided to make for Messina where he could rendezvous with German merchant ships from whom he could obtain coal. For the event of war Germany had divided the world's seas into a system of districts, each under a German Supply Officer, who was empowered to assign all vessels in his area to places where German warships could meet them and to commandeer the resources of German banks and business firms for the warships' needs.

All day the *Goeben*'s wireless, as she rounded the Italian boot, tapped out orders to German commercial steamers, calling them into Messina. At Taranto she was joined by the *Breslau*.

"Urgent. German ship *Goeben* at Taranto," wired the British consul on August 2. The view halloo stirred ardent hopes at the Admiralty of first blood for the British Navy; locating the enemy was half the battle. But as Britain was not yet at war, the hunt could not yet be loosed. Ever on the tiptoe of readiness Churchill on July 31 had instructed the commander of the Mediterranean Fleet, Admiral Sir Berkeley Milne, that his first task would be to aid in protecting the French transports "by covering and if possible bringing to action individual fast German ships, particularly *Goeben*." Milne was reminded that "the speed of your Squadrons is sufficient to enable you to choose your moment." However, at the same time, and with a certain ambivalence, he was told "husband your force at the outset" and "do not at this stage be brought to action against superior forces." The last edict was to ring like a buoy's melancholy knell through the events of the next several days.

The "superior force" Churchill had in mind, as he later explained, was the Austrian fleet. Its battleships bore the same relationship to the British *Inflexible*s as the French battleships did to the *Goeben*; that is, they were more heavily armored and armed but slower. Churchill also later explained that his order was not intended "as a veto upon British ships ever engaging superior forces however needful the occasion." If it was not intended as a veto, then it must have been intended for commanders to interpret as they saw fit, which brings the matter to that melting point of warfare—the temperament of the individual commander.

When the moment of live ammunition approaches, the moment to which all his professional training has been directed, when the lives of men under him, the issue of the combat, even the fate of a campaign may depend upon his decision at a given moment, what happens inside the heart and vitals of a commander? Some are made bold by the moment, some irresolute, some carefully judicious, some paralyzed and powerless to act.

Admiral Milne was made careful. A bachelor of fifty-nine, a polished figure in society, a former groom in waiting to Edward VII and still an intimate at court, son of an Admiral of the Fleet, grandson and godson of other admirals, a keen fisherman, deer stalker, and good shot, Sir Archibald Berkeley Milne appeared a natural choice in 1911 for the Mediterranean Command, the most fashionable, if no longer the premier post in the British Navy. He was appointed to it by the new First Lord, Mr. Churchill. The appointment was promptly, if privately, denounced as a "betrayal of the Navy" by Admiral Lord Fisher, former First Sea Lord, creator of the Dreadnought Fleet, the most passionately vital and least laconic Englishman of his time. His cherished project was to ensure the appointment for the war he predicted would break out in October, 1914, of Admiral Jellicoe, the navy's gunnery expert, as Commander in Chief.

When Churchill appointed Milne to the Mediterranean, which Fisher believed put him in line for the post he wanted reserved for Jellicoe, his wrath was tremendous. He lashed out at Winston for "succumbing to court influence"; he roared and fumed and erupted in volcanic disgust for Milne as an "utterly useless commander" and "unfitted to be Senior Admiral afloat and practically Admiralissimo as you have now made him." He referred to him variously as a "backstairs cad," as a "serpent of the lowest type," and as "Sir B. Mean who buys his *Times* second hand for one penny." Everything in Fisher's letters, which always carried flaming admonitions to "Burn this!" —happily ignored by his correspondents—appears ten times life size and must be reduced proportionately if they are to be read in any reasonable relation to reality. Neither a serpent of the lowest type nor a Nelson, Admiral Milne was an average, uninspired ornament of the Senior Service. When Fisher discovered that he was not in fact being considered for Commander in Chief, he turned his fiery attentions upon other matters, leaving Sir B. Mean in untroubled enjoyment of the Mediterranean.

In June 1914 Milne, too, visited Constantinople, where he dined with the Sultan and his ministers and entertained them aboard his flagship without concerning himself, any more than did other Englishmen, about Turkey's possible place in Mediterranean strategy.

By August 1, after receiving Churchill's first warning, he had assembled at Malta his own squadron of three battle cruisers and the second squadron of armored cruisers, light cruisers, and destroyers commanded by Rear Admiral Sir Ernest Troubridge. Early on August 2 he received a second order from Churchill, saying, "*Goeben* must be shadowed by two battle cruisers" and the Adriatic "watched," presumably against the appearance of the Austrian fleet. The specific order to send two battle cruisers after the *Goeben* clearly envisaged combat, but Milne did not obey it. Instead he sent the *Indomitable* and *Indefatigable* along with Troubridge's squadron to watch the Adriatic. Having been informed that the *Goeben* had been seen that morning off Taranto heading southwest, he sent one light cruiser, the *Chatham*, to search the Strait of Messina where he reasoned the *Goeben* would be and where in fact she was. The *Chatham* left Malta at 5:00 P.M., ran through the Strait at seven next morning and reported back that the *Goeben* was not there. The search had missed by six hours, Admiral Souchon having already left.

He had reached Messina the previous afternoon just as Italy declared her neutrality. Again refused coal by the Italians, he was able, however, to take on two thousand tons provided by a German merchant shipping firm. He requisitioned, as a tender, a merchant steamer, the *General* of the German East Africa line, after debarking her passengers who were given the price of a railroad ticket as far as Naples. Having received no orders as yet from his Admiralty, Souchon decided to put himself in a position to taste action at the earliest moment after hostilities should begin and before superior forces could prevent him. In the darkness, at 1:00 A.M. on August 3, he left Messina, heading west toward the Algerian coast where he planned to bombard the French embarkation ports of Bone and Philippeville.

At the same hour Churchill sent a third order to Milne: "Watch on mouth of Adriatic should be maintained but *Goeben* is your objective. Follow her and shadow her wherever she goes and be ready to act upon declaration of war which appears probable and imminent." When he received this, Admiral Milne did not know where the *Goeben* was, the *Chatham* having lost her. He believed she was heading west to attack the French transports, and from a report he had received of a German collier waiting at Majorca he concluded that she would thereafter make for Gibraltar and the open sea. He now detached the *Indomitable* and *Indefatigable* from their watch on the Adriatic and sent them westward to hunt for the *Goeben*. All day of August 3 the *Goeben*, steaming westward from Messina, was followed by her hunters, a day's distance behind.

At the same time the French fleet was steaming across from Toulon to North Africa. It should have left a day earlier, but in Paris on August 2 occurred the unhappy collapse of the Naval Minister, Dr. Gauthier, after he was discovered to have forgotten to send torpedo boats into the Channel. In the uproar that followed, the orders to the Mediterranean fleet suffered. Messimy, the War Minister, became possessed by a need to hasten the arrival of the Colonial Corps. The embarrassed Dr. Gauthier, endeavoring to cover his lapse in the Channel by jumping to the opposite extreme of belligerency, proposed to attack the *Goeben* and *Breslau* before a declaration of war. "His nerves were on edge," President Poincaré thought. The Naval Minister next challenged the War Minister to a duel, but after fervent efforts by their colleagues to separate and calm the combatants, he embraced Messimy in tears and was persuaded to resign for reasons of health.

French uncertainty over the British role, which had not yet been declared, further complicated matters. At 4:00 P.M. the Cabinet managed to compose a more or less coherent telegram to the French Commander in Chief, Admiral Boué de Lapeyrère, which informed him that the *Goeben* and *Breslau* had been sighted at Brindisi, that as soon as he received the signal for the opening of hostilities he was to "stop them," and that he was to protect the transports by covering them, not by convoy.

Admiral de Lapeyrère, a forceful character largely responsible for bringing the French Navy out of its rusty obsolescence, promptly decided to form convoys anyway, since, in his view, the "doubtful" role of the British left him no choice. He started his fires at once and got under way at four o'clock next morning, a few hours after Souchon left Messina. During the next twenty-four hours the three squadrons of the French fleet steamed southward bound for Oran, Algiers, and Philippeville while the *Goeben* and *Breslau* were coming westward toward the same destination.

At 6:00 P.M., August 3, Admiral Souchon's wireless told him that war had been declared on France. He pressed forward, as did the French, but his speed was greater. At 2:00 A.M. on August 4 he was approaching his goal and the climactic moment of fire, when he received Admiral Tirpitz's order to "proceed at once to Constantinople." Unwilling to turn back without, as he wrote, "tasting that moment of fire so ardently desired by us all!" he kept on course until the Algerian coast came in view in the early morning light. He thereupon ran up the Russian flag, approached within range, and opened fire, "sowing death and panic." "Our trick succeeded brilliantly," enthused one of his crew who later published an account of the voyage. According to the *Kriegsbrauch*, or Conduct of War manual issued by the German General Staff, "The putting on of enemy uniforms and the use of enemy or neutral flags or insignia with the aim of deception are declared permissible." As the official embodiment of German thinking on these matters, the *Kriegsbrauch* was considered to supersede Germany's signature on the Hague Convention of which Article 23 prohibited the use of disguise in enemy colors.

After the shelling of Philippeville—and of Bone by the *Breslau*—Admiral Souchon turned back for Messina by the way he had come. He planned to coal there from German merchant steamers before setting course for Constantinople 1,200 miles away.

Admiral de Lapeyrère, hearing of the bombardment by wireless almost at the moment it was happening, assumed the *Goeben* would continue westward, perhaps to attack Algiers next, on her way to break out to the Atlantic. He forced his speed in the hope of intercepting the enemy "if he presented himself." He detached no ships to scout for the *Goeben* because, as he reasoned, if the enemy appeared he would be given battle; if he did not appear he would be of no further immediate concern. Like everyone else on the Allied side, Admiral de Lapeyrère thought of the *Goeben* purely in terms of naval strategy. That she might perform a political mission, profoundly affecting and prolonging the course of the war, neither he nor anyone else ever considered. When the *Goeben* and *Breslau* did not again appear across the French path, Admiral de Lapeyrère did not seek them out. Thus on the morning of August 4 the first opportunity was lost. Another was immediately offered.

At 9:30 that morning the *Indomitable* and *Indefatigable* which had been steaming west all during the night encountered the *Goeben* and *Breslau* off Bone as the German ships were heading east back to Messina. If Grey had sent his ultimatum to Germany the night before, immediately following his speech to Parliament, Britain and Germany would then have been at war and the cruisers' guns would have spoken. As it was, the ships passed each other in silence at 8,000 yards, well within range, and had to be content with training their guns and omitting the customary exchange of salutes.

Admiral Souchon, bent on putting as much distance between himself and the British as he could before hostilities opened, sped off, straining his ship to the last ounce of speed his boilers could attain. The *Indomitable* and *Indefatigable* turned around and made after him, determined to keep in range until war should be declared. Their wireless, like a huntsman's bugle sounding a find, reported the position to Admiral Milne, who immediately informed the Admiralty, "*Indomitable* and *Indefatigable* shadowing *Goeben* and *Breslau*, 37.44 North, 7:56 East."

The Admiralty quivered in an agony of frustration. There, in the same waters that washed round Cape Trafalgar, British ships had the enemy within range—and could not fire. "Very good. Hold her. War imminent," telegraphed Churchill, and rushed off a "most urgent" minute to the Prime Minister and Grey suggesting that if the *Goeben* attacked the French transports, Milne's cruisers should be authorized "at once to engage her." Unfortunately, when reporting their position, Admiral Milne had neglected to say which way the *Goeben* and *Breslau* were going, so that Churchill assumed they were heading west with further evil intent upon the French.

"Winston with all his war paint on," as Asquith put it, "is longing for a sea fight to sink the *Goeben*." Asquith was willing to let him have it, but the Cabinet to which he unfortunately mentioned the matter, refused to authorize an act of war before the ultimatum should expire at midnight. Thus a second opportunity was lost, though it would have been lost anyway because Churchill's order was contingent upon the *Goeben* attacking the French transports, a goal she had already forsaken.

Now began a desperate chase across the calm summer surface of the sea with Admiral Souchon attempting to outdistance his pursuers and the British attempting to keep him in range until midnight. Driving his ship to its utmost, Souchon brought it up to 24 knots. Stokers who ordinarily could not work in the heat and coal dust for longer than two hours at a time were kept shoveling at an increased pace while bursting tubes scalded them with steam. Four died between morning and evening while the pace was maintained. Slowly, perceptibly, the space between prey and pursuers widened. The *Indomitable* and *Indefatigable*, also suffering from boiler trouble and understaffed furnaces, were not keeping up. In the afternoon they were joined in the long, silent chase by the light cruiser *Dublin* commanded by Captain John Kelly. As the hours wore on, the gap increased until at five o'clock the *Indomitable* and *Indefatigable* dropped out of range. Only the *Dublin* followed, keeping the *Goeben* in sight. At seven o'clock a fog descended. By nine, off the coast of Sicily, the *Goeben* and *Breslau* disappeared in the gathering gloom.

At the Admiralty all during that day Churchill and his staff "suffered the tortures of Tantalus." At 5:00 P.M. the First Sea Lord, Prince Louis of Battenberg, observed there was still time to sink the *Goeben* before dark. Restrained by the Cabinet decision, Churchill could not give the order. While the British waited for the midnight signal, the *Goeben* reached Messina and coal.

When dawn broke the British, now at war and free to fire, could not get at her. From the *Dublin*'s last report before contact was lost, they judged she was at Messina, but in the meantime a new obstacle had intervened. An Admiralty order informing Milne of Italy's declaration of neutrality instructed him to "respect this rigidly and not to allow a ship to come within six miles of the Italian coast." The veto, which was designed to prevent some "petty incident" from causing trouble with Italy, was perhaps an excessive caution.

Prohibited by the six-mile limit from entering the Strait of Messina, Admiral Milne put a guard at both exits. As he was convinced that the *Goeben* would again head west, he himself on his flagship *Inflexible*, together with the *Indefatigable*, guarded the exit to the western Mediterranean while only a single light cruiser, the *Gloucester*, commanded by Captain Howard Kelly, brother of the *Dublin*'s commander, was sent to patrol the exit to the eastern Mediterranean.* Also because he wanted to concentrate his strength to the west, Admiral Milne sent the *Indomitable* to coal nearby at Bizerte instead of further east at Malta. Thus none of the three *Inflexibles* was in a place where it could intercept the *Goeben* if she went east.

For two days, August 5 and 6, Milne patrolled the waters west of Sicily with the fixed idea that the *Goeben* intended to break westward. The Admiralty, which likewise could think of no other course for the *Goeben* but to break through Gibraltar or hole up at Pola, did not disapprove his arrangements.

During these two days, until the evening of August 6, Admiral Souchon was coaling against difficulties at Messina. The Italians were insisting on the laws of neutrality that required him to depart within twenty-four hours of his arrival. The coaling, which had to be done from German merchant steamers whose decks had to be ripped up and railings torn away to permit the transfer, was taking three times as long as usual. While the Admiral argued points of law with the port authorities, every man in his crew was pressed into shoveling coal. Though encouraged by extra beer rations, band music, and patriotic speeches by the officers, the men kept fainting from

*The Strait of Messina runs north and south with the northern exit giving on the western Mediterranean and the southern exit on the eastern Mediterranean. For the sake of geographical clarity these are referred to as the western and eastern exits respectively.

exertion in the August heat until blackened and sweat-soaked bodies lay all over the ship like so many corpses. By noon on August 6 when 1,500 tons had been taken on, not enough to reach the Dardanelles, no one was left capable of further effort. "With a heavy heart," Admiral Souchon ordered loading to stop, a rest for all hands, and readiness for departure at five o'clock.

Two messages had reached him at Messina which increased his peril and faced him with a critical decision. Tirpitz's order to go to Constantinople was suddenly canceled by a telegram saying, "For political reasons entry into Constantinople inadvisable at the present time." The reversal was caused by divided counsel in Turkey. Enver had given the German ambassador permission for the *Goeben* and *Breslau* to pass through the mine fields guarding the Dardanelles. Since their passage would clearly violate the neutrality that Turkey was still publicly maintaining, the Grand Vizier and other ministers insisted the permission must be withdrawn.

Tirpitz's second message informed Souchon that the Austrians could give no naval help to Germany in the Mediterranean, and left it up to Souchon to decide for himself where to go in the circumstances.

His boilers, Souchon knew, could not give him the speed necessary to run through the heavy enemy screen in a dash for Gibraltar. He rebelled against holing himself up in Pola, dependent on the Austrians. He decided to make for Constantinople regardless of orders to the contrary. His purpose, in his own words, was quite definite: "to force the Turks, even against their will, to spread the war to the Black Sea against their ancient enemy, Russia."

He ordered steam up for departure at five o'clock. All on board as well as on shore knew the *Goeben* and *Breslau* were preparing to run a gauntlet against heavy odds. All day excited Sicilians crowded the quays selling postcards and last souvenirs to "those about to die" and hawked extras headlined "In the Claws of Death," "Shame or Defeat," "Voyage to Death or Glory."

Expecting to be pursued, Admiral Souchon deliberately chose to leave while it was still light so that he might be seen steering northward as if for the Adriatic. When night fell he planned to change course to the southeast and elude pursuit under cover of darkness. As he lacked enough coal for the whole voyage, everything depended on his being able, unseen, to make rendezvous with a collier which had been ordered to meet him off Cape Malea at the southeast corner of Greece.

When the *Goeben* and *Breslau* came out of the eastern exit of the Strait of Messina they were immediately seen and followed by the *Gloucester*, which was patrolling outside. As the *Gloucester* was a match for the *Breslau* but could have been knocked out of the sea by the heavy guns of the *Goeben* at 18,000 yards, she could do no more than keep the enemy in sight until reinforcements came up. Captain Kelly telegraphed position and course to Admiral Milne who, with all three battle cruisers, was still patrolling west of Sicily, and followed to seaward of the *Goeben*. As darkness fell, toward eight o'clock he changed course to landward in order to keep the *Goeben* in the light of the moon as it rose on his right. The maneuver brought him within range but did not tempt the *Goeben* to fire. In the clear night the two dark shapes, dogged by a third, ran steadily northward, their smokestacks, owing to inferior coal taken on at Messina, blotching the moonlit sky with black clouds, which rendered them visible at a long distance.

Admiral Milne, on learning that the *Goeben* had left Messina by the eastern exit, stayed where he was. He reasoned that if the *Goeben* continued on her given course she would be intercepted by Admiral Troubridge's squadron which was watching the Adriatic. If, as he was inclined to believe, her course was a feint and she should turn west after all, his own battle cruiser squadron would intercept her. No other possibility occurred to him. Only one ship, the light cruiser *Dublin*, was sent east with orders to join Troubridge's squadron.

Meanwhile Souchon, unable to shake the *Gloucester*, could not afford to lead a false course any longer if he was to reach the Aegean on his available coal. Shadowed or not he must alter course to the east. At 10:00 P.M. he turned, at the same time jamming the *Gloucester*'s wavelength in the hope of preventing his change of course from being reported. He did not succeed. Captain Kelly's wireless, signaling the change of course, reached both Milne and Troubridge about midnight. Milne then set out for Malta where he intended to coal and "continue the chase." It was now up to Troubridge, in whose direction the enemy was coming, to intercept him.

Troubridge had taken up his station at the mouth of the Adriatic under orders to "prevent the Austrians from coming out and the Germans from entering." From the *Goeben*'s course it was clear she was heading away from the Adriatic, but he saw that if he steamed south at once he might be able to head her off. Could he, however, hope to engage her on terms offering a valid hope of victory? His squadron consisted of four armored cruisers, *Defence*, *Black Prince*, *Warrior*, and *Duke of Edinburgh*, each of 14,000 tons, with 9.2-inch guns whose range was considerably less than the range of the *Goeben*'s 11-inch guns. The Admiralty's original order, forwarded to him apparently as an instruction by his superior, Admiral Milne, precluded action "against superior forces." Failing to receive any orders from Milne, Troubridge decided to try to intercept the enemy if he could do it before 6:00 A.M. when the first light of dawn in the east would give him favorable visibility and help to equalize the disadvantage of range. He set off at full speed southward shortly after midnight. Four hours later he changed his mind.

As naval attaché with the Japanese during the Russo-Japanese War, Troubridge had learned respect for the efficiency of long-range fire. Besides enjoying the correct lineage from a great-grandfather who had fought with Nelson at the Nile and a reputation as the "handsomest officer in the Navy in his younger days," he "believed in seamanship as a soldier of Cromwell believed in the Bible." Churchill valued him sufficiently to appoint him to the newly created Naval War Staff in 1912. But seamanship and excellence in staff work do not necessarily aid a commander when he faces imminent and deadly combat.

When by 4:00 A.M. Troubridge had not yet found the *Goeben*, he decided he could no longer hope to engage her under favorable circumstances. He believed that in daylight the *Goeben*, if intercepted, could stand off outside his range and sink his four cruisers one after another. While she was engaged in this feat of marksmanship and slaughter, he evidently saw little opportunity for any one of his four cruisers and eight destroyers to reach her by gunfire or torpedo. He decided she was a "superior force" which the Admiralty had said he was not to engage. He broke off the chase, so informed Milne by wireless and, after cruising off the island of Zante until 10:00 A.M., still hoping for one of Milne's battle cruisers to appear, he finally put into the port of Zante preparatory to resuming his watch for the Austrians in the Adriatic. Thus a third opportunity was lost, and the *Goeben*, carrying her tremendous cargo of fate, steamed on her way.

At 5:30 A.M. Milne, still crediting the *Goeben* with intent to turn back to the west, signaled *Gloucester* "gradually to drop astern to avoid capture." Neither he nor the Admiralty yet thought of the *Goeben* as a ship in flight, far more anxious to avoid combat than to court it, and exerting all her skills and speed to reach her distant goal. Rather, under the impression of the Philippeville raid and the years of mounting apprehensions of the German Navy, the English thought of her as a corsair ready to turn and pounce and roam the seas as a commerce raider. They expected to bring her to bay one way or another, but their chase lacked an imperative urgency because, always expecting her to turn, they did not realize she was trying to get away to the East—specifically to the Dardanelles. The failure was less naval than political. "I can recall no great sphere of policy about which the British Government was less completely informed than the Turkish," Churchill admitted ruefully long afterward. The condition was rooted in the Liberals' fundamental dislike of Turkey.

By now it was full daylight of August 7. Only the *Gloucester*, ignoring Milne's signal, was still following the *Goeben* as, rejoined by the *Breslau*, she approached the coast of Greece. Admiral Souchon, who could not afford to meet his collier within enemy view, became desperate to shake off his shadow. He ordered the *Breslau* to drop back in an attempt to ride off the *Gloucester* by passing back and forth in front of her as if laying mines and by other harassing tactics.

Captain Kelly, still expecting reinforcements, became desperate on his part to delay the *Goeben*. When the *Breslau* dropped back to intimidate him, he determined to attack her with intent to force the *Goeben* to turn around to protect her, regardless of whether she was a "superior force" or not. In true damn-the-torpedoes style he opened fire, which was returned by the *Breslau*. As expected the *Goeben* turned and fired too. No hits were scored by anyone. A small Italian passenger steamer en route from Venice to Constantinople, which happened to be passing, witnessed the action. Captain Kelly broke off action against the *Breslau* and dropped back. Admiral Souchon, who could not afford to spend precious coal on a chase, resumed course. Captain Kelly resumed his shadowing.

For three more hours he held on, keeping the *Goeben* in sight until Milne signaled imperatively, forbidding him to continue the pursuit beyond Cape Matapan at the tip of Greece. At 4:30 in the afternoon, as the *Goeben* rounded the Cape to enter the Aegean, the *Gloucester* at last gave up the chase. Free of surveillance, Admiral Souchon disappeared among the isles of Greece to meet his collier.

Some eight hours later, shortly after midnight, having coaled and made repairs, Admiral Milne with the *Inflexible*, *Indomitable*, *Indefatigable*, and the light cruiser *Weymouth* left Malta heading east. Proceeding at 12 knots, perhaps because he thought speed at this stage was a waste of coal, his pursuit was unhurried. At two o'clock next afternoon, August 8, when he was about halfway between Malta and Greece, he was brought to a sharp halt by word from the Admiralty that Austria had declared war on England. Unfortunately the word was an error by a clerk who released the prearranged code telegram for hostilities with Austria by mistake. It was enough to make Milne abandon the chase and take up a position where he could not be cut off from Malta by the possible emergence of the Austrian fleet and where he ordered Troubridge's squadron and the *Gloucester* to join him. One more opportunity was lost.

They remained concentrated there for nearly twenty-four hours until noon next day when, upon learning from an embarrassed Admiralty that Austria had not declared war after all, Admiral Milne once more resumed the hunt. By this time the *Goeben*'s trail, since she was last seen entering the Aegean on the afternoon of August 7, was over forty hours old. Trying to decide in what direction to look for her, Admiral Milne, according to his own later account, considered four possible courses the *Goeben* might take. He still thought she might attempt to escape westward to the Atlantic, or might head south to attack the Suez Canal, or might seek refuge in a Greek port or even attack Salonika—two rather exotic suppositions in view of the fact that Greece was neutral. For some reason he did not credit Admiral Souchon with intent to violate Turkish neutrality; the Dardanelles as a destination did not occur to Admiral Milne any more than it did to the Admiralty at home. His strategy, as he conceived it, was to keep the *Goeben* bottled up in the Aegean "to the north."

"To the north" was, of course, exactly where Souchon was going, but as the Turks had mined the entrance to the Straits he could not enter without their permission. He could go no further until he had coaled and communicated with Constantinople. His collier, the *Bogadir*, was waiting in Greek disguise at Cape Malea as ordered. Fearing to be discovered, he ordered it to make for Denusa, an island farther inside the Aegean. Unaware that the British chase had been discontinued, he lay low all during the day of August 8 and crept in to the deserted coast of Denusa only on the morning of the 9th. Here, all day, the *Goeben* and *Breslau* coaled while steam was kept up in their boilers so that they might depart on half an hour's notice. A lookout post was erected on a hilltop to keep watch for the British who were then five hundred miles away keeping watch for the Austrians.

Admiral Souchon did not dare use his wireless to communicate with Constantinople because a signal strong enough to cover the distance would have at the same time betrayed his location to the enemy. He ordered the *General*, which had followed him from Messina along a more southerly course, to go to Smyrna and from there transmit a message to the German naval attaché in Constantinople: "Indispensable military necessity requires attack upon enemy in Black Sea. Go to any lengths to arrange for me to pass through Straits at once with permission of Turkish Government if possible, without formal approval if necessary."

All day of the 9th Souchon waited for an answer. At one moment his wireless operators picked up a garbled text, but its meaning could not be deciphered. Night came without a reply. By this time Milne's squadron, having discovered the Austrian error, was advancing toward the Aegean again. Souchon decided, if no answer came, to force the Dardanelles if necessary. At 3:00 A.M. of August 10 he heard the wireless signals of the

British squadron as it entered the Aegean. He could wait no longer. Just then a different series of syncopated buzzes came over the earphones. It was the *General*, at last, transmitting the Delphic message: "Enter. Demand surrender of forts. Capture pilot."

Uncertain whether this meant him to make a show of force to save Turkish face or whether he would have to force his way through, Souchon left Denusa at dawn. While all day he steamed north at 18 knots, all day Admiral Milne cruised across the exit of the Aegean to prevent him from coming out. At four that afternoon Souchon sighted Tenedos and the plains of Troy; at five he reached the entrance to the historic and impregnable passageway under the guns of the great fortress of Chanak. With his crew at battle stations and every nerve on board stretched in suspense, he slowly approached. The signal flag, "Send a pilot," fluttered up his mast.

That morning there arrived at Constantinople the small Italian passenger steamer which had witnessed the *Gloucester*'s action against the *Goeben* and *Breslau*. Among its passengers were the daughter, son-in-law, and three grandchildren of the American ambassador Mr. Henry Morgenthau. They brought an exciting tale of the boom of guns, puffs of white smoke, and the twisting and maneuvering of faraway ships. The Italian captain had told them that two of the ships were the *Goeben* and *Breslau* which had just made their notorious exit from Messina. Mr. Morgenthau, having occasion to meet Ambassador Wangenheim a few hours later, mentioned his daughter's story, in which Wangenheim displayed "an agitated interest." Immediately after lunch, accompanied by his Austrian colleague, he appeared at the American Embassy where the two ambassadors "planted themselves solemnly in chairs" in front of the American lady and "subjected her to a most minute, though very polite, cross-examination. . . . They would not permit her to leave out a single detail; they wished to know how many shots had been fired, what direction the German ships had taken, what everybody on board had said and so on. . . . They left the house in almost jubilant mood."

They had learned that the *Goeben* and *Breslau* had escaped the British fleet. It remained to obtain Turkish consent to let them through the Dardanelles. Enver Pasha, who as War Minister controlled the mine fields, was more than willing but he had to play a complicated game vis-à-vis his more nervous colleagues. A member of the German Military Mission was with him that afternoon when another member, Lieutenant Colonel von Kress, was urgently announced. Kress said that the commander at the Chanak reported the *Goeben* and *Breslau* requesting permission to enter the Straits and wanted immediate instructions. Enver replied he could not decide without consulting the Grand Vizier. Kress insisted that the fort required an answer at once. Enver sat perfectly silent for several minutes, and then said abruptly, "They are to be allowed to enter."

Kress and the other officer, who had unconsciously been holding their breaths, found themselves breathing again.

"If the English warships follow them in are they to be fired on?" Kress next asked. Again Enver refused to answer, pleading that the Cabinet must be consulted; but Kress insisted that the fort could not be left without definite instructions.

"Are the English to be fired on or not?" A long pause followed. Finally Enver answered, "Yes."

At the entrance to the Straits, 150 miles away, a Turkish destroyer put out from shore and approached the *Goeben*, watched in tense anxiety by every eye on deck. A signal flag fluttered briefly and was recognized as "Follow me." At nine o'clock that evening, August 10, the *Goeben* and *Breslau* entered the Dardanelles, bringing, as long afterward Churchill somberly acknowledged, "more slaughter, more misery and more ruin than has ever before been borne within the compass of a ship."

Instantly telegraphed round the world, the news reached Malta that night. Admiral Milne, still probing among the Aegean islands, learned it at noon next day. So little did his superiors understand the mission of the *Goeben* that they instructed him to establish a blockade of the Dardanelles "in case the German ships came out."

Prime Minister Asquith's comment on the news was that it was "interesting." But, he wrote in his diary, "as we shall insist" on the *Goeben*'s crew being replaced by Turks who will not be able to navigate her, "it does not much matter." To "insist" appeared to Asquith to be all that was necessary.

Allied ambassadors at once insisted, furiously and repeatedly. The Turks, still hoping to hold on to neutrality as a bargaining counter, decided to ask the Germans to disarm the *Goeben* and *Breslau* "temporarily and superficially only," but Wangenheim, invited to hear this proposal, absolutely refused. After further agitated discussion, one minister suddenly suggested: "Could not the Germans have sold us these ships? Could not their arrival be regarded as delivery under contract?"

Everyone was delighted with this superb idea which not only solved a dilemma but dealt the British poetic justice for their seizure of the two Turkish battleships. With Germany's agreement, announcement of the sale was made to the diplomatic corps, and shortly thereafter the *Goeben* and *Breslau*, renamed the *Jawus* and *Midilli*, flying the Turkish flag and with their crews wearing Turkish fezzes, were reviewed by the Sultan amid the wild enthusiasm of his people. The sudden appearance of the two German warships, as if sent by a genie to take the place of the two of which they had been robbed, put the populace in transports of delight and invested the Germans with a halo of popularity.

Still the Turks postponed the declaration of war for which Germany was pressing. Instead, they themselves began demanding from the Allies an increasing price for their neutrality. Russia was so alarmed by the *Goeben*'s arrival at the doors of the Black Sea that she was willing to pay. Like the sinner who renounces lifelong bad habits when in extremity, she was even ready to renounce Constantinople. On August 13 Foreign Minister Sazonov proposed to France to offer Turkey a solemn guarantee of her territorial integrity and a promise of "great financial advantages at the expense of Germany" in return for her neutrality. He was actually willing to include a promise that Russia would abide by the guarantee "even if we are victorious."

The French agreed and "moved heaven and earth," in the words of President Poincaré, to keep Turkey quiet and neutral and to persuade Britain to join in a joint guarantee of Turkish territory. But the British could not bring themselves to bargain or pay for the neutrality of their onetime protégé. Churchill, at his "most bellicose" and "violently anti-Turk," proposed to the Cabinet to send a torpedo flotilla through the Dardanelles to sink the *Goeben* and *Breslau*. It was the one gesture which might have carried weight with vacillating Turks and the only gesture which could have prevented what ultimately happened. One of the keenest and boldest minds in France had already suggested it on the day the Straits were violated. "We should go right in after them," said General Gallieni; "otherwise Turkey will come in against us." In the British Cabinet Churchill's idea was vetoed by Lord Kitchener, who said England could not afford to alienate the Moslems by taking the offensive against Turkey. Turkey should be left "to strike the first blow."

For nearly three months, while the Allies alternately blustered and bargained and while German military influence at Constantinople daily increased, the groups within the Turkish government disputed and wavered. By the end of October, Germany determined that their endless procrastination must be brought to an end. Turkey's active belligerency, in order to blockade Russia from the south, had become imperative.

On October 28 the former *Goeben* and *Breslau*, under Admiral Souchon's command and accompanied by several Turkish torpedo boats, entered the Black Sea and shelled Odessa, Sevastopol, and Feodosia, causing some civilian loss of life and sinking a Russian gunboat.

Aghast at the *fait accompli* laid at their door by the German Admiral, a majority of the Turkish government wished to disavow it but was effectively prevented. The operating factor was the presence of the *Goeben* at the Golden Horn, commanded by her own officers, manned by her own crew, disdainful of restraint. As Talaat Bey pointed out, the government, the palace, the capital, they themselves, their homes, their sovereign and Caliph, were under her guns. Dismissal of the German military and naval missions which the Allies were demanding as proof of Turkey's neutrality, they were unable to perform. The act of war having been committed in the Turks' name, Russia declared war on Turkey on November 4, followed by Britain and France on November 5.

Thereafter the red edges of war spread over another half of the world. Turkey's neighbors, Bulgaria, Rumania, Italy, and Greece, were eventually drawn in. Thereafter, with her exit to the Mediterranean closed, Russia was left dependent on Archangel, icebound half the year, and on Vladivostok, 8,000 miles from the battlefront. With the Black Sea closed, her exports dropped by 98 per cent and her imports by 95 per cent. The cutting off of Russia with all its consequences, the vain and sanguinary tragedy of Gallipoli, the diversion of Allied strength in the campaigns of Mesopotamia, Suez, and Palestine, the ultimate breakup of the Ottoman Empire, the subsequent history of the Middle East, followed from the voyage of the *Goeben*.

Other sequels were as bitter if less momentous. Meeting the censure of his comrades, Admiral Troubridge demanded a Court of Inquiry which ordered his trial by court-martial in November, 1914, on the charge that "he did forbear to chase H.I.G.M.'s ship *Goeben*, being an enemy then flying." On the basic issue, whether he was justified in regarding the *Goeben* as a "superior force," the Navy, for its own sake, acquitted him. Though he performed further service in the war, he was never again, owing to feeling in the fleet, given a command at sea. Admiral Milne, recalled on August 18 in order to leave the Mediterranean under French command, came home to be retired. On August 30 the Admiralty announced that his conduct and dispositions in regard to the *Goeben* and *Breslau* had been made the subject of "careful examination" with the result that "their Lordships approved the measures taken by him in all respects." Their Lordships, who had been blind to the importance of Constantinople, did not seek a scapegoat.

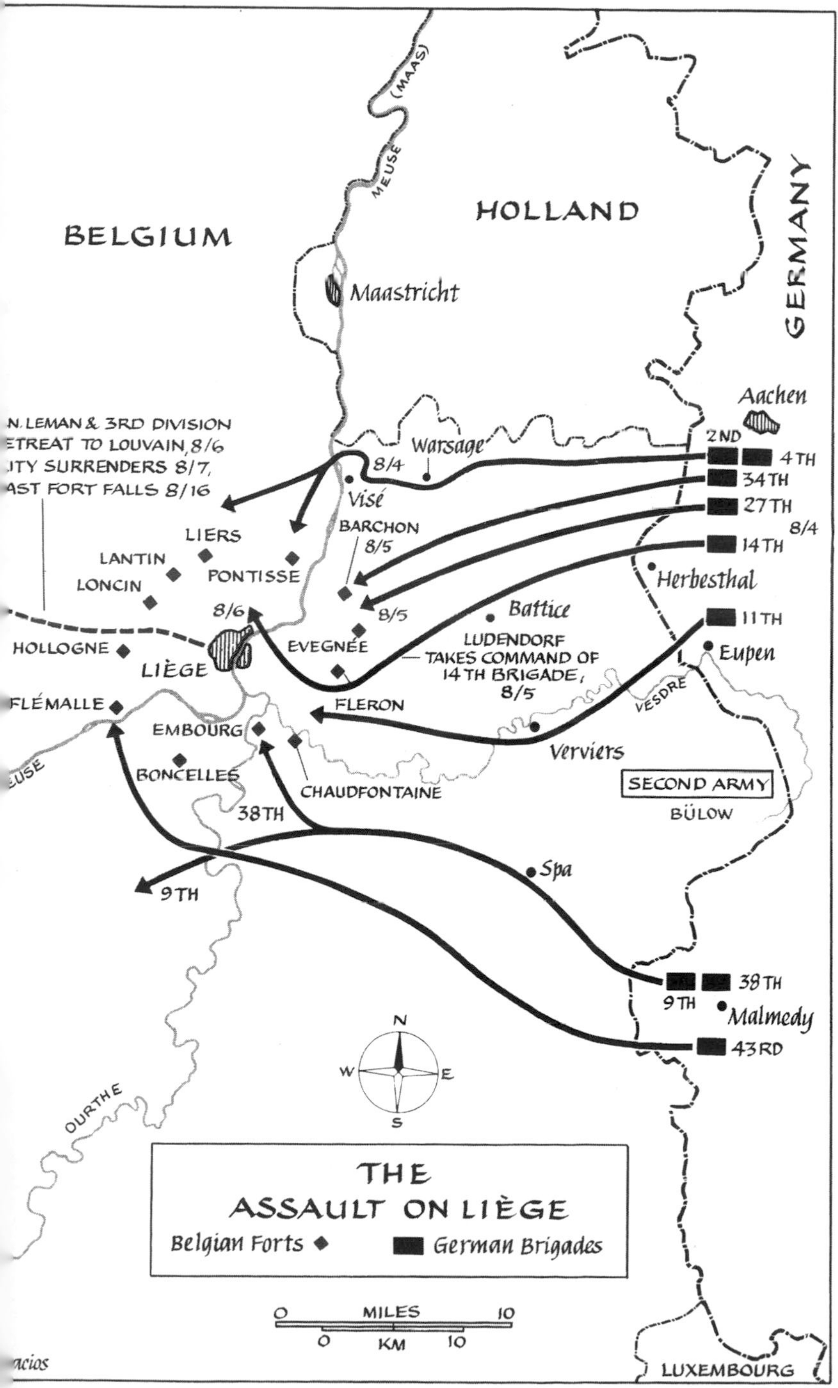

HOLLAND
BELGIUM
GERMANY
(MAAS)
MEUSE
Maastricht
Aachen
N. LEMAN & 3RD DIVISION
ETREAT TO LOUVAIN, 8/6
ITY SURRENDERS 8/7,
AST FORT FALLS 8/16
Warsage
8/4
Visé
2ND
4TH
34TH
27TH
14TH
8/4
BARCHON
8/5
LIERS
LANTIN
PONTISSE
LONCIN
Herbesthal
8/6
8/5
Battice
11TH
EVEGNÉE
LUDENDORF
TAKES COMMAND OF
14TH BRIGADE,
8/5
HOLLOGNE
LIÈGE
Eupen
VESDRE
FLÉMALLE
FLERON
EMBOURG
Verviers
BONCELLES
CHAUDFONTAINE
SECOND ARMY
BÜLOW
EUSE
38TH
Spa
9TH
38TH
9TH
Malmedy
43RD
N
W
E
S
OURTHE
THE
ASSAULT ON LIÈGE
Belgian Forts
German Brigades
0
MILES
10
0
KM
10
LUXEMBOURG
acios

Dover
STRAIT OF DOVER
Dunkirk
Calais
Boulogne
BELGIUM
Ghent
SCHELDT
Waterloo
SCHELDT
LYS
TERR. INF. DIV.
Lille
Nimy
Jemappes
8/21
Mons
MONS CANAL
TERR. INF. DIV.
BEF
8/23
SAMBRE
D'AMADE
FRENCH
Malplaquet
TERR. INF. DIV.
Maubeuge
Le Cateau
Landrecies
SOMME
Amiens
St. Quentin
OISE
Guise
Hirson
Marle
Noyon
Laon
N
W
E
S
Compiègne
AISNE
Soissons
Reims
OISE
SEINE
Pontoise
Château-Thierry
Dammartin
Epernay
MARNE
PARIS
Melun
SEINE
BATTLE OF THE FRONTIERS
AUG. 18-24
German Army FIRST
FIRST Allied Army
palacios

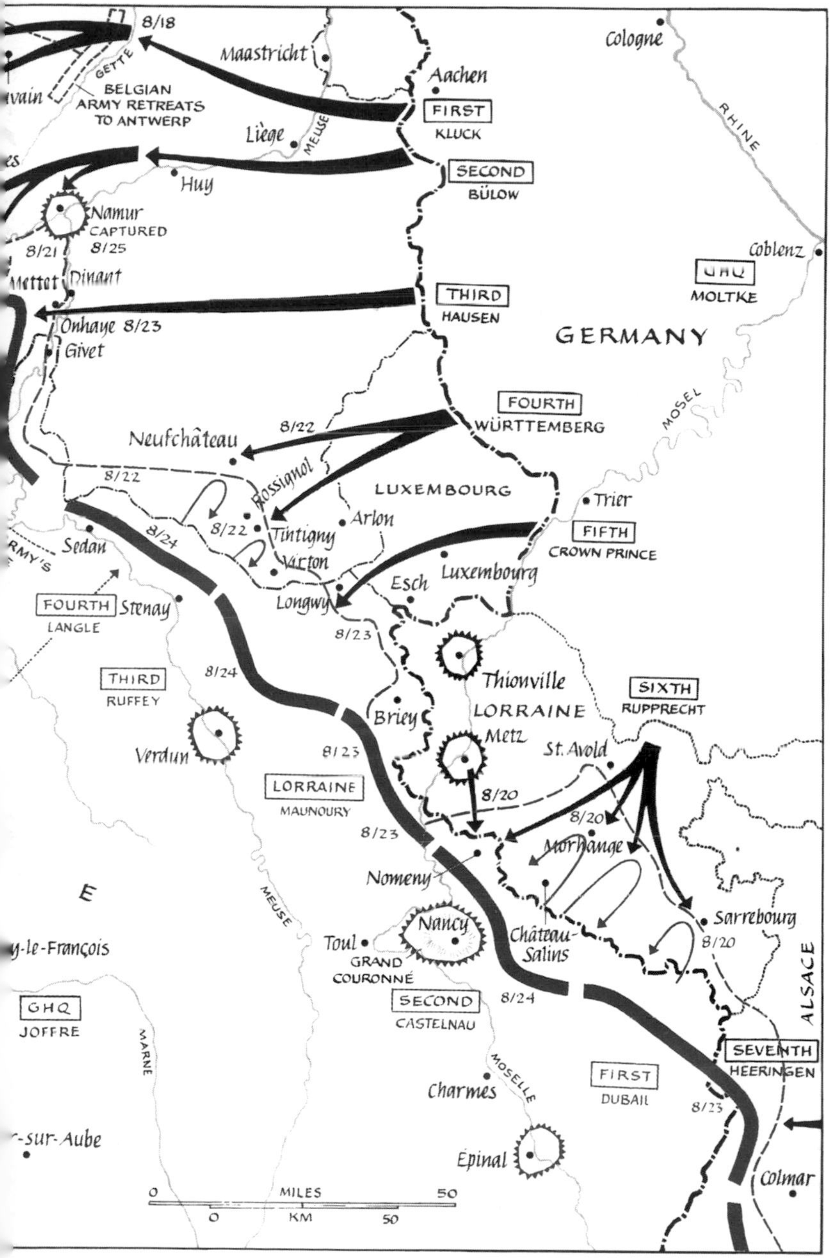

8/18
Maastricht
Aachen
Cologne
GETTE
BELGIAN
ARMY RETREATS
TO ANTWERP
FIRST
KLUCK
Liège
MEUSE
RHINE
SECOND
BÜLOW
Huy
Namur
CAPTURED
8/25
8/21
Coblenz
GHQ
MOLTKE
Dinant
THIRD
HAUSEN
Onhaye 8/23
Givet
GERMANY
MOSEL
FOURTH
WÜRTTEMBERG
8/22
Neufchâteau
Rossignol
8/22
LUXEMBOURG
Trier
8/22
Tintigny
Arlon
FIFTH
CROWN PRINCE
8/24
Sedan
Virton
Luxembourg
Esch
Longwy
FOURTH
LANGLE
Stenay
8/23
Thionville
8/24
THIRD
RUFFEY
LORRAINE
SIXTH
RUPPRECHT
Briey
Metz
St. Avold
Verdun
8/23
LORRAINE
MAUNOURY
8/20
8/20
8/23
Morhange
Nomeny
MEUSE
Sarrebourg
Nancy
Toul
Château-Salins
8/20
GRAND
COURONNÉ
ALSACE
GHQ
JOFFRE
SECOND
CASTELNAU
8/24
MARNE
MOSELLE
SEVENTH
HEERINGEN
FIRST
DUBAIL
Charmes
8/23
Épinal
Colmar
0 MILES 50
0 KM 50

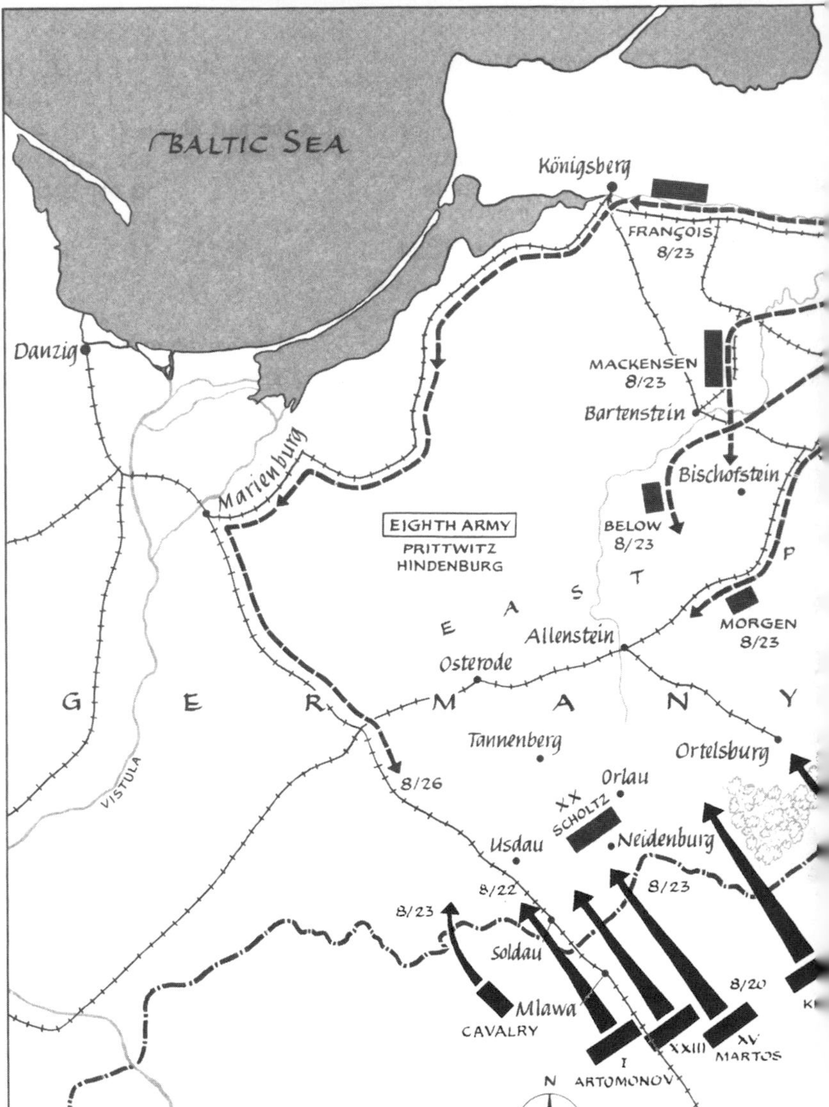

BALTIC SEA
Königsberg
FRANÇOIS 8/23
Danzig
MACKENSEN 8/23
Bartenstein
Marienburg
Bischofstein
EIGHTH ARMY
PRITTWITZ
HINDENBURG
BELOW 8/23
P
T
S
A
E
MORGEN 8/23
Allenstein
Osterode
G E R M A N Y
Tannenberg
Ortelsburg
VISTULA
8/26
Orlau
XX SCHOLTZ
Neidenburg
Usdau
8/22
8/23
8/23
Soldau
8/20
Mlawa
CAVALRY
I ARTOMONOV
XXIII
XV MARTOS
N
W
E
S
P
0 MILES 40
0 KM 40
VISTULA
palacios

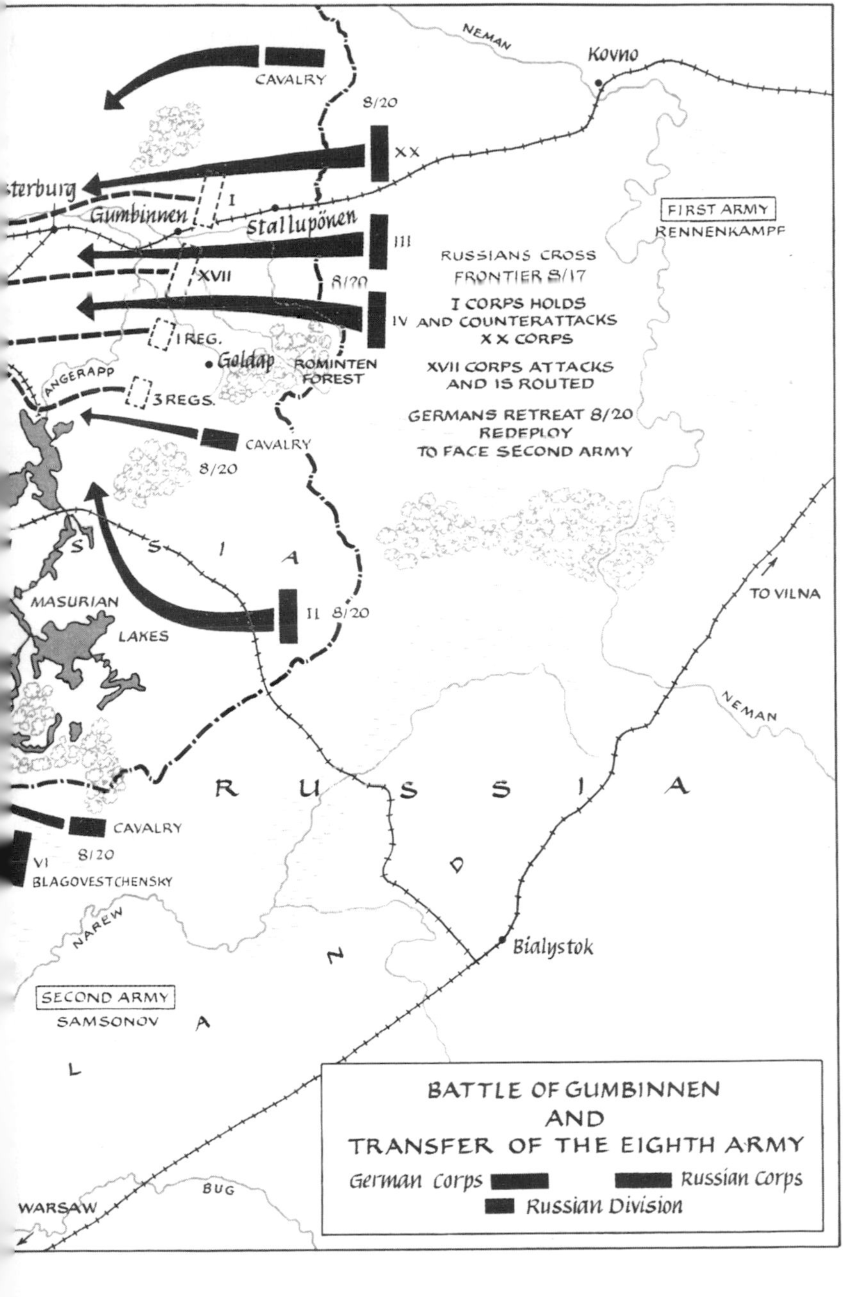

NEMAN
Kovno
CAVALRY
8/20
XX
sterburg
I
Gumbinnen
Stallupönen
III
XVII
8/20
IV
I REG.
Goldap
ROMINTEN FOREST
ANGERAPP
3 REGS.
CAVALRY
8/20
FIRST ARMY
RENNENKAMPF
RUSSIANS CROSS FRONTIER 8/17
I CORPS HOLDS AND COUNTERATTACKS XX CORPS
XVII CORPS ATTACKS AND IS ROUTED
GERMANS RETREAT 8/20 REDEPLOY TO FACE SECOND ARMY
MASURIAN LAKES
II 8/20
TO VILNA
NEMAN
RUSSIA
CAVALRY
8/20
VI
BLAGOVESTCHENSKY
NAREW
POLAND
Bialystok
SECOND ARMY
SAMSONOV
BUG
WARSAW
BATTLE OF GUMBINNEN AND TRANSFER OF THE EIGHTH ARMY
German Corps
Russian Corps
Russian Division

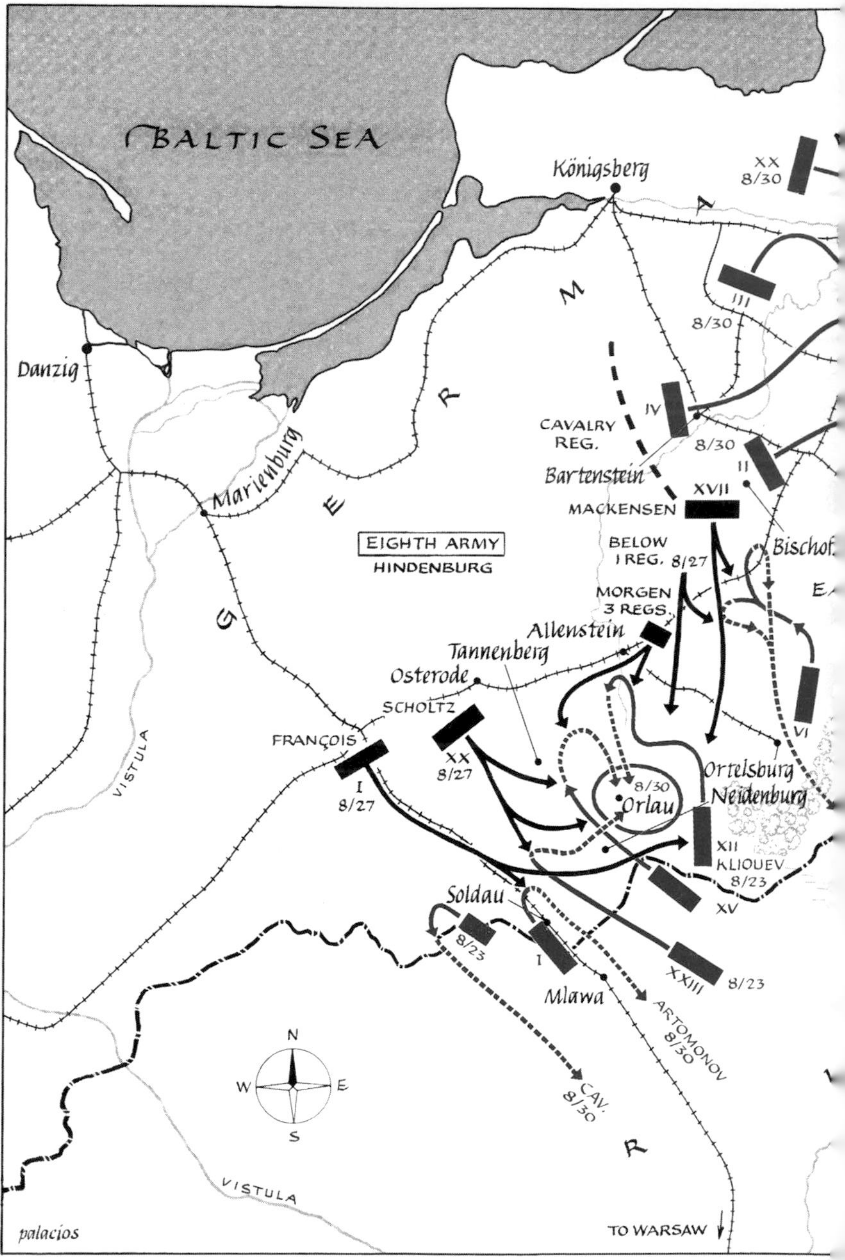
BALTIC SEA
Königsberg
Danzig
Marienburg
G E R M A
EIGHTH ARMY
HINDENBURG
CAVALRY REG.
Bartenstein
MACKENSEN
XVII
BELOW
I REG.
MORGEN
3 REGS.
Allenstein
Tannenberg
Osterode
SCHOLTZ
FRANÇOIS
XX
8/27
I
8/27
Orlau
8/30
Ortelsburg
Neidenburg
XII
KLIOUEV
8/23
XV
Soldau
8/23
I
XXIII
8/23
Mlawa
ARTOMONOV
8/30
CAV.
8/30
R
VISTULA
VISTULA
N
W
E
S
XX
8/30
III
8/30
IV
8/30
II
Bischof.
E
VI
palacios
TO WARSAW

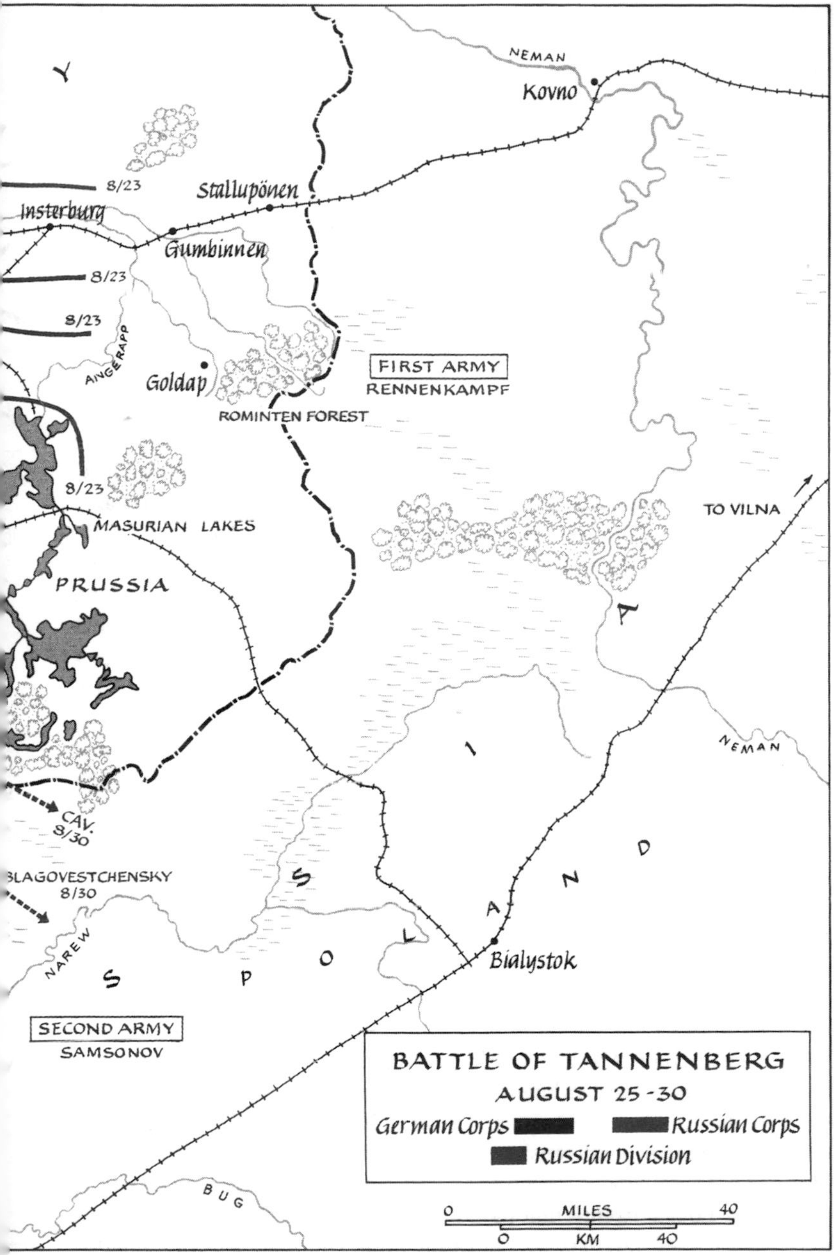

NEMAN
Kovno
Stallupönen
Insterburg
Gumbinnen
8/23
8/23
8/23
ANGERAPP
Goldap
FIRST ARMY
RENNENKAMPF
ROMINTEN FOREST
8/23
MASURIAN LAKES
PRUSSIA
TO VILNA
NEMAN
CAV.
8/30
BLAGOVESTCHENSKY
8/30
NAREW
Bialystok
SECOND ARMY
SAMSONOV
BATTLE OF TANNENBERG
AUGUST 25-30
German Corps
Russian Corps
Russian Division
BUG
0 MILES 40
0 KM 40

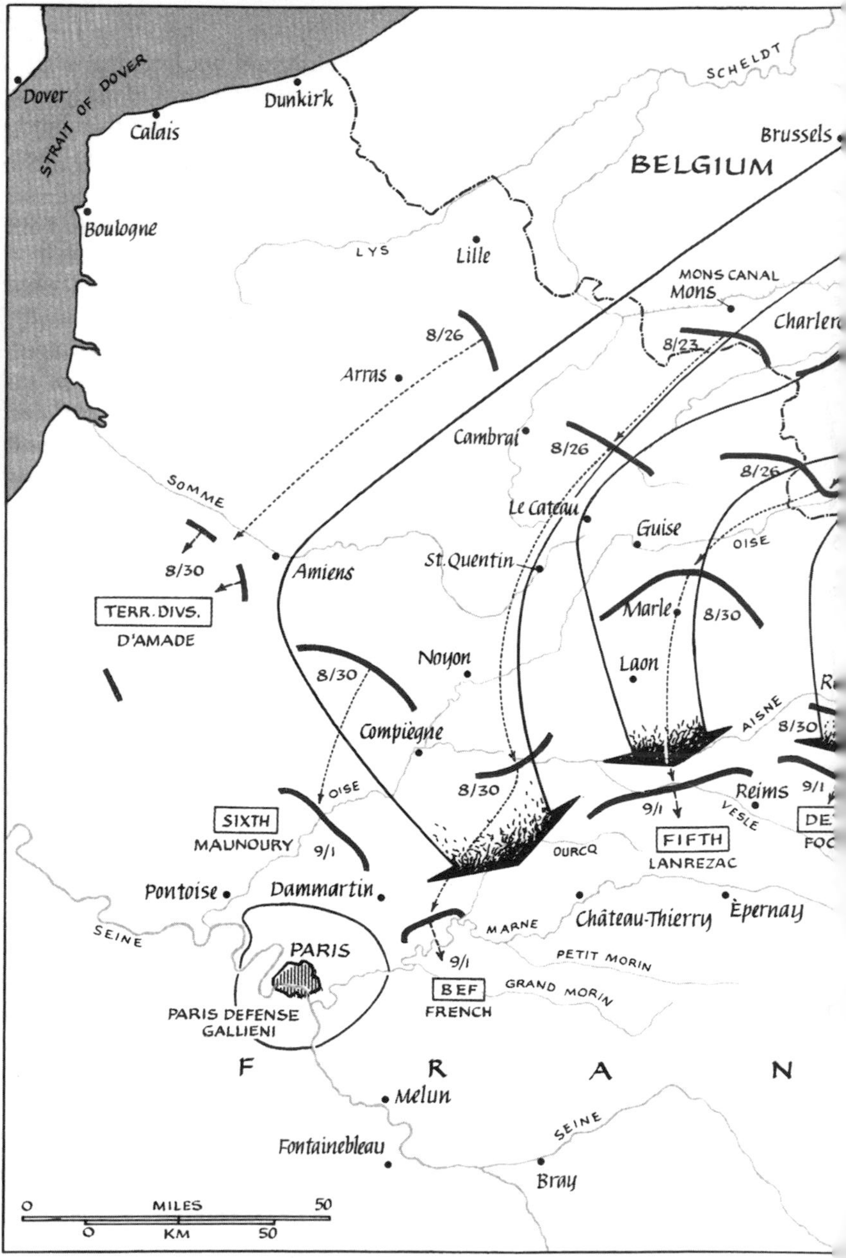

Dover
STRAIT OF DOVER
Calais
Dunkirk
Boulogne
SCHELDT
Brussels
BELGIUM
LYS
Lille
MONS CANAL
Mons
Charlero
8/26
Arras
8/23
Cambrai
8/26
8/26
SOMME
Le Cateau
Guise
OISE
8/30
Amiens
St. Quentin
TERR. DIVS.
D'AMADE
Marle
8/30
Noyon
8/30
Laon
AISNE
8/30
Compiègne
8/30
OISE
Reims
9/1
9/1
SIXTH
MAUNOURY
9/1
VESLE
FIFTH
LANREZAC
OURCQ
Pontoise
Dammartin
Château-Thierry
Épernay
SEINE
MARNE
PARIS
PETIT MORIN
9/1
BEF
FRENCH
GRAND MORIN
PARIS DEFENSE
GALLIENI
F R A N
Melun
SEINE
Fontainebleau
Bray
0 MILES 50
0 KM 50

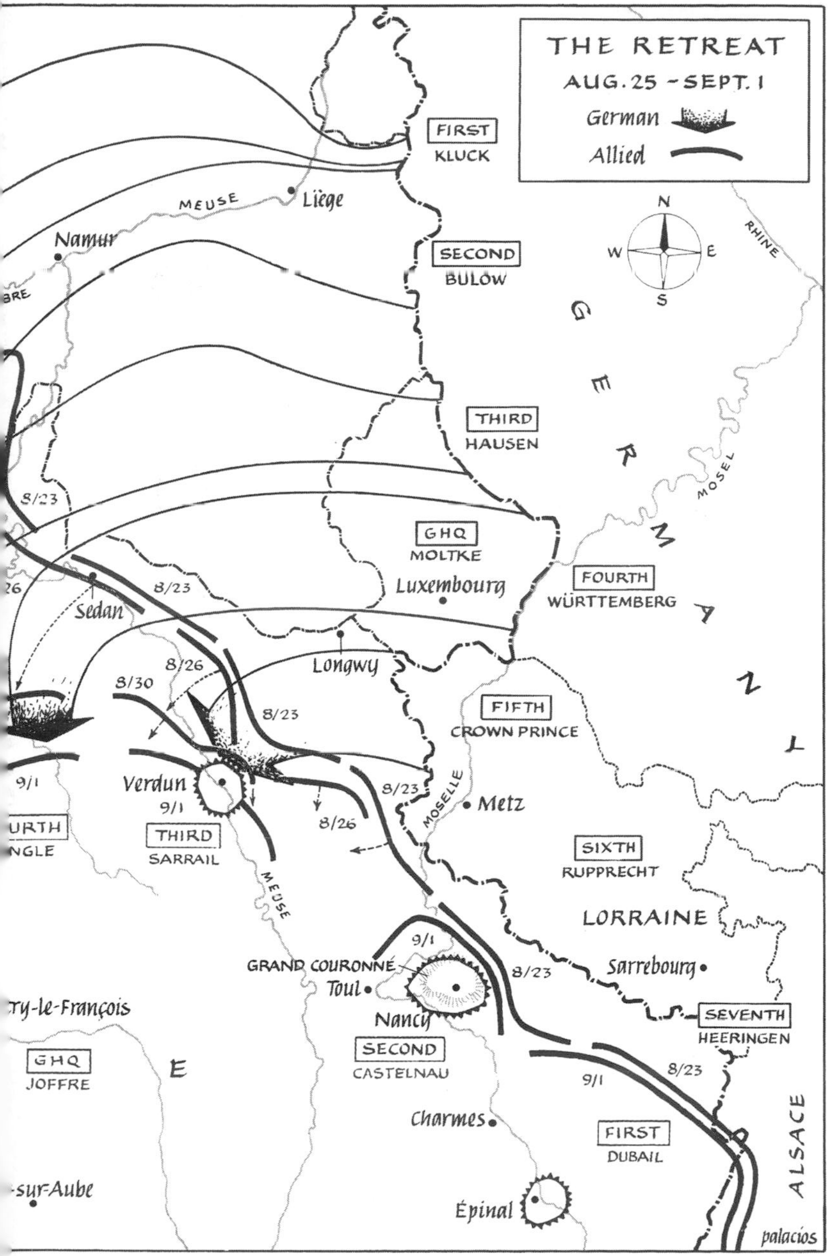
THE RETREAT
AUG. 25 – SEPT. 1
German
Allied
FIRST
KLUCK
SECOND
BULOW
THIRD
HAUSEN
GHQ
MOLTKE
FOURTH
WÜRTTEMBERG
FIFTH
CROWN PRINCE
SIXTH
RUPPRECHT
SEVENTH
HEERINGEN
GERMANY
N
E
S
W
RHINE
MOSEL
MEUSE
Liège
Namur
BRE
Sedan
Luxembourg
Longwy
Verdun
Metz
MOSELLE
LORRAINE
Sarrebourg
GRAND COURONNÉ
Toul
Nancy
Charmes
Épinal
ALSACE
8/23
8/26
8/30
9/1
URTH
NGLE
THIRD
SARRAIL
SECOND
CASTELNAU
FIRST
DUBAIL
GHQ
JOFFRE
E
ry-le-François
-sur-Aube
palacios

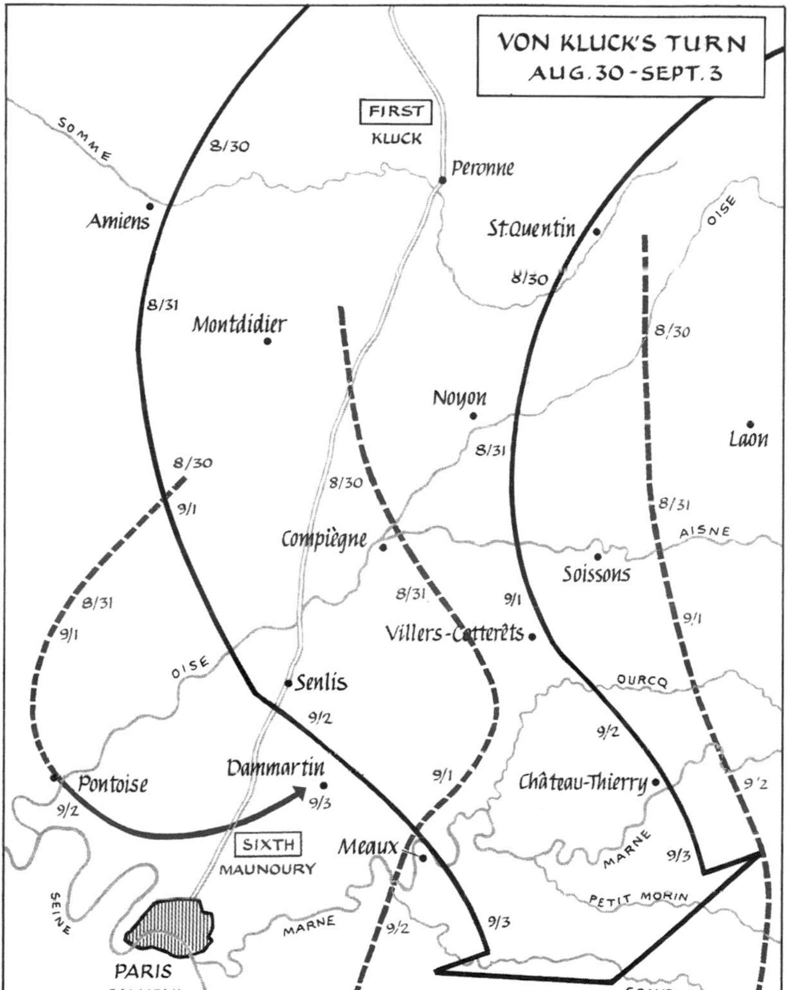
VON KLUCK'S TURN
AUG. 30 - SEPT. 3
FIRST
KLUCK
SOMME
8/30
Peronne
Amiens
St.Quentin
OISE
8/30
8/31
Montdidier
8/30
Noyon
Laon
8/31
8/30
8/30
9/1
8/31
AISNE
Compiègne
Soissons
8/31
8/31
9/1
9/1
9/1
Villers-Cotterêts
OISE
OURCQ
Senlis
9/2
9/2
Dammartin
9/1
Château-Thierry
9'2
Pontoise
9/3
9/2
SIXTH
MAUNOURY
Meaux
MARNE
9/3
SEINE
PETIT MORIN
MARNE
9/2
9/3
PARIS
GALLIENI
GRAND MORIN
9/3
9/3
SEINE
N
W
E
S
Melun
BEF
FRENCH
FIFTH
LANREZAC
0
MILES
20
0
KM
20
Fontainebleau
palacios

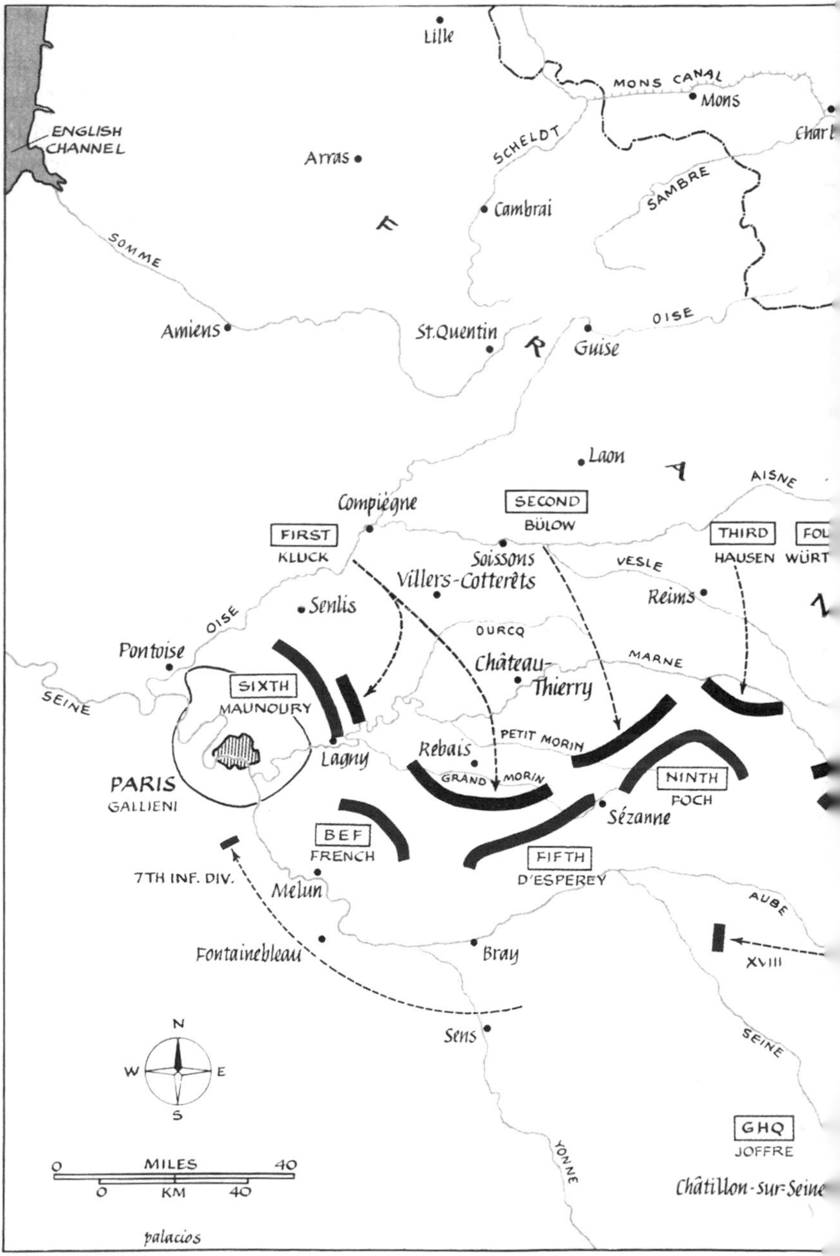
Lille
MONS CANAL
Mons
Charl
ENGLISH CHANNEL
Arras
SCHELDT
SAMBRE
Cambrai
F
SOMME
OISE
Amiens
St.Quentin
R
Guise
Laon
A
AISNE
Compiègne
SECOND
BÜLOW
FIRST
KLUCK
Soissons
THIRD
HAUSEN
WÜRT
VESLE
Villers-Cotterêts
Reims
Senlis
OISE
OURCQ
Pontoise
Château-Thierry
MARNE
SEINE
SIXTH
MAUNOURY
PETIT MORIN
Lagny
Rebais
GRAND MORIN
NINTH
FOCH
PARIS
GALLIENI
Sézanne
BEF
FRENCH
FIFTH
D'ESPEREY
7TH INF. DIV.
Melun
AUBE
Fontainebleau
Bray
XVIII
Sens
SEINE
N
W
E
S
GHQ
JOFFRE
0 MILES 40
0 KM 40
YONNE
Châtillon-sur-Seine
palacios

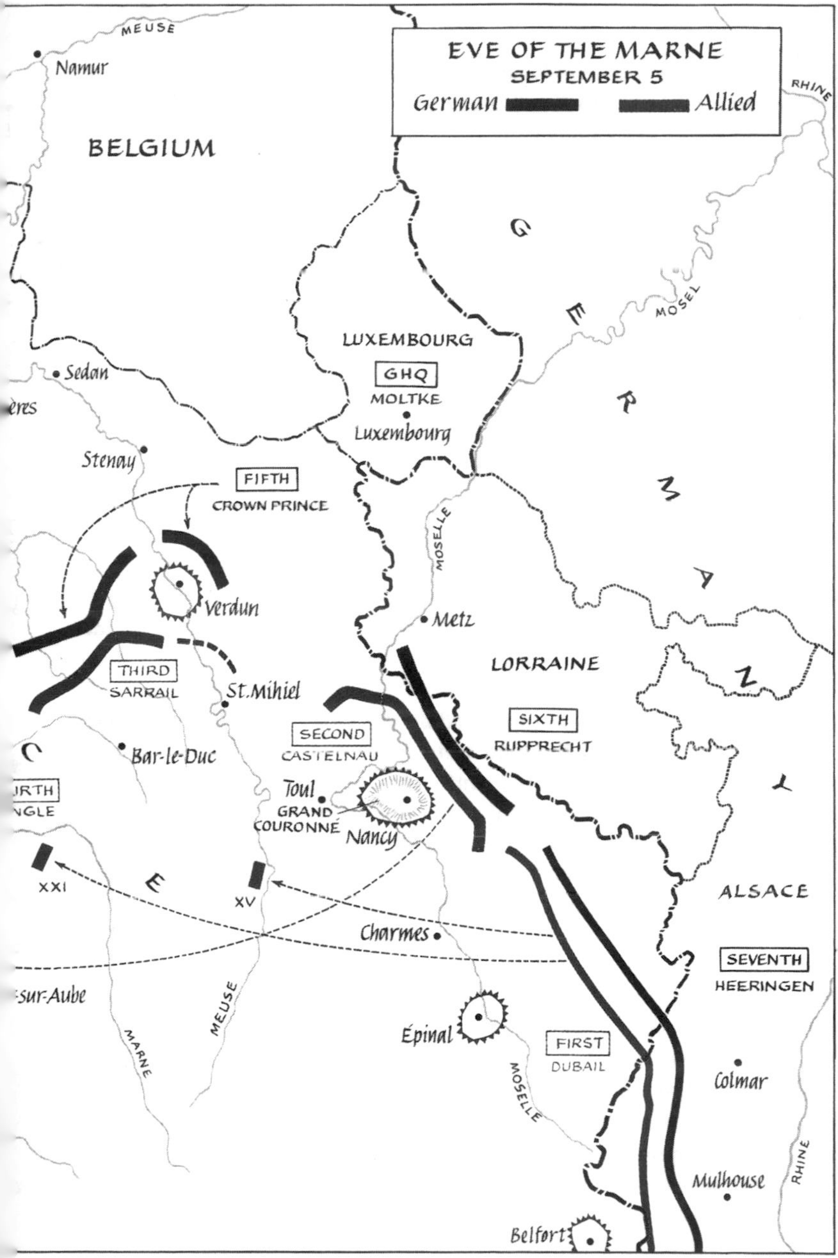
EVE OF THE MARNE
SEPTEMBER 5
German
Allied
MEUSE
Namur
BELGIUM
RHINE
LUXEMBOURG
GHQ
MOLTKE
Luxembourg
MOSEL
Sedan
Stenay
FIFTH
CROWN PRINCE
Verdun
MOSELLE
Metz
LORRAINE
THIRD
SARRAIL
St.Mihiel
SECOND
CASTELNAU
SIXTH
RUPPRECHT
Bar-le-Duc
Toul
GRAND
COURONNE
Nancy
XXI
XV
ALSACE
Charmes
SEVENTH
HEERINGEN
MEUSE
MARNE
Épinal
FIRST
DUBAIL
MOSELLE
Colmar
Mulhouse
Belfort

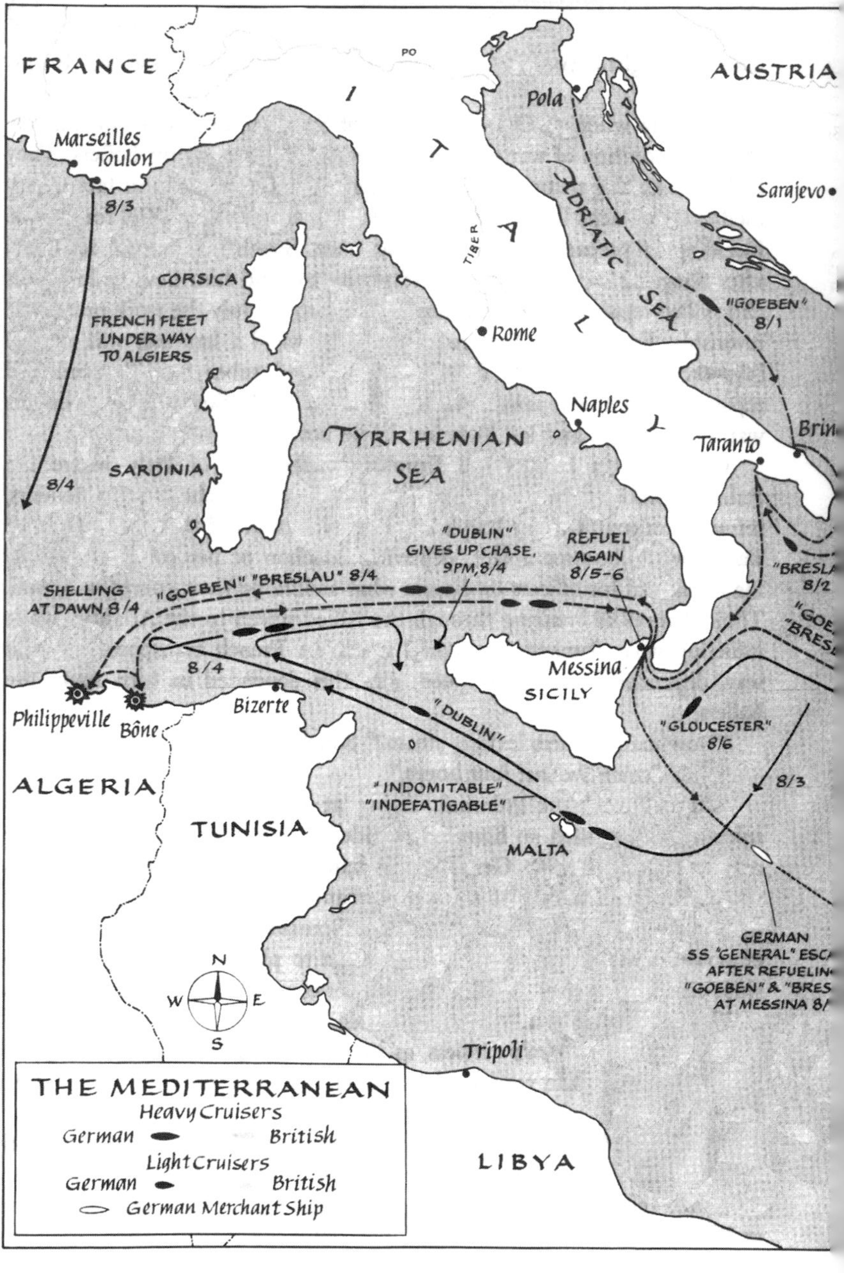

FRANCE
PO
AUSTRIA
Pola
I T A L Y
Marseilles
Toulon
8/3
Sarajevo
ADRIATIC SEA
TIBER
CORSICA
"GOEBEN"
8/1
FRENCH FLEET UNDER WAY TO ALGIERS
Rome
Naples
TYRRHENIAN SEA
Taranto
SARDINIA
8/4
"DUBLIN" GIVES UP CHASE, 9PM, 8/4
REFUEL AGAIN 8/5-6
SHELLING AT DAWN, 8/4
"GOEBEN" "BRESLAU" 8/4
8/4
Messina
SICILY
Philippeville
Bône
Bizerte
"DUBLIN"
"GLOUCESTER"
8/6
8/3
ALGERIA
"INDOMITABLE"
"INDEFATIGABLE"
TUNISIA
MALTA
N
W
E
S
Tripoli
LIBYA
THE MEDITERRANEAN
Heavy Cruisers
German
British
Light Cruisers
German
British
German Merchant Ship

RUSSIA
Sevastopol
UNGARY
RUMANIA
Belgrade
Bucharest
DANUBE
SERBIA
BLACK SEA
BULGARIA
Sofia
Constantinople
Salonika
DARDANELLES
Chanak
Troy
TENEDOS
GREECE
AEGEAN SEA
TROUBRIDGE SQUADRON MISSES "GOEBEN" 8/7, RETURNS TO MALTA 8/8
TURKEY
Smyrna
Athens
CAPE MALEAS
CAPE MATAPAS
ZANTE
REFUELED 8/9
DENUSA
RHODES
"GLOUCESTER" ENGAGES "BRESLAU" 8/7, RETURNS TO MALTA 8/8
CRETE
GERMAN COLLIER "BOGADIR" ORDERED TO DENUSA
MEDITERRANEAN SEA
0 MILES 200
0 KM 200
palacios
Alexandria
EGYPT
NILE

11

Liège and Alsace

WHILE CONCENTRATION of the armies was proceeding, advance groups of the German and French forces moved to the attack as if through a revolving door. The Germans entered from the east and the French from the west. Each opponent's first move was to take place on his own extreme right on the rim of the revolving door's perimeter, three hundred miles apart. The Germans would proceed, regardless of what the French did, to the assault of Liège and the reduction of its ring of twelve forts in order to open the roads across Belgium to the armies of their right wing. The French, equally regardless of what the enemy did, would charge into Upper Alsace in a move, more sentimental than strategic, designed to open the war upon a wave of national enthusiasm and encourage an uprising of the local population against Germany. Strategically its purpose was to anchor the French right on the Rhine.

Liège was the portcullis guarding the gateway into Belgium from Germany. Built upon a steep slope rising 500 feet up from the left bank of the Meuse, moated by the river, here nearly 200 yards wide, surrounded by a 30-mile circumference of forts, it was popularly considered the most formidable fortified position in Europe. Ten years ago Port Arthur had withstood a siege of nine months before surrender. World opinion expected Liège certainly to equal the record of Port Arthur if not to hold out indefinitely.

Seven German armies totaling over 1,500,000 men were being assembled along the Belgian and French frontiers. They ranged in numerical order from the First Army on the German extreme right opposite Liège to the Seventh Army on the extreme left in Alsace. The Sixth and Seventh Armies composed the German left wing of 16 divisions, the Fourth and Fifth Armies the center of 20 divisions, and the First, Second, and Third Armies made up the right wing of 34 divisions which was to move through Belgium. An independent cavalry corps of three divisions was attached to the right wing. The three armies of the right wing were commanded by Generals von Kluck, von Bülow, and von Hausen, all sixty-eight years old of whom the first two were veterans of 1870. The commander of the cavalry corps was General von Marwitz.

As von Kluck's First Army had to travel the farthest, its progress was to regulate the pace of the general advance. Concentrating north of Aachen, it was to take the roads which crossed the Meuse over the five bridges of Liège whose capture was thus the vital first objective upon which all else depended. The guns of the forts of Liège dominated the gap between the Dutch frontier and the wooded and hilly Ardennes; its bridges provided the only multiple crossing of the Meuse; its junction of four railroad lines connecting Germany and Belgium with northern France was essential to the supply of the German armies on the march. Until it was taken and its forts put out of action, the German right wing could not move.

A special "Army of the Meuse" of six brigades commanded by General von Emmich was detached from the Second Army to open the way through Liège. It was expected, unless the Belgians offered serious resistance, to accomplish this while the main armies were still concentrating. In one of his prewar indiscretions, the Kaiser once said to a British officer at maneuvers, "I will go through Belgium like *that*!" cutting the air with a flip of his hand. Belgium's declared intention to fight was, the Germans believed, no more than the "rage of dreaming sheep"—in the words a Prussian statesman once applied to his domestic opponents. When Liège had been taken and the First and Second Armies were on the roads on either side of it at a point level with the city, the main advance would begin.

Henri Brialmont, the greatest fortifications engineer of his time, had built the forts of Liège and of Namur in the 1880's at the insistence of Leopold II. Located on high ground in a circle around each city, they were designed to hold the passage of the Meuse against invaders coming from either direction. The Liège forts were situated on both banks of the river at an average distance of four to five miles from the city and two to three miles from each other. Six were on the east bank facing Germany and six on the west reaching around and behind the city. Like medieval castles sunk underground, the forts showed nothing on the surface but a triangular mound from which protruded the cupolas for the disappearing gun turrets. Everything else was subterranean. Inclined tunnels led to the chambers underground and connected the turrets with the magazines and fire control rooms. The six larger forts and the six smaller *fortins* in between had a total of 400 guns of which the largest were 8-inch (210 mm.) howitzers. In the corners of the triangles were smaller turrets for quick-firing guns and for machine guns which covered the slopes immediately below. A dry moat 30 feet deep surrounded each fort. Each had a searchlight fitted to a steel observation tower which could be lowered underground like the guns. The garrisons of each of the larger forts numbered 400, composed of two companies of artillery and one of infantry. Intended as advance posts to defend the frontier rather than as last-ditch retreats to withstand a siege, the forts depended on the Field Army to hold the spaces in between.

Overconfident in the great work of Brialmont, the Belgians had done little to keep the forts up to date, leaving them to be manned by inadequate garrisons drawn from the oldest classes of reserves with one officer per company. For fear of giving Germany the least excuse to declare Belgium's neutrality compromised, the order to construct trenches and barbed-wire barricades for defense of the intervals between the forts and to raze trees and houses in the way of the guns was not given until August 2. When the attack came these measures were barely begun.

On their part the Germans, believing the Belgians would yield to the ultimatum or at most offer a token resistance, had not brought up the surprise weapon they had in store in the form of gigantic siege cannon of such size and destructive power that it had not been thought possible such guns could be made mobile. One, built by Skoda, the Austrian munitions firm, was a 12-inch (305 mm.) mortar; the other, built by Krupp's at Essen, was a monster of 16.5 inches (420 mm.) which together with its gun carriage was 24 feet long, weighed 98 tons, fired a shell a yard long weighing 1,800 pounds at a range of 9 miles and required a crew of 200 attendants. Until then the largest guns known were Britain's 13.5-inch naval guns and the largest land guns 11-inch fixed howitzers of the coast artillery. Japan, after a six-month failure to reduce Port Arthur, had stripped her coasts of such weapons to use in the siege, but it had taken three more months under their fire before the Russian fortress surrendered.

The German schedule could allow no such period to reduce the Belgian forts. Moltke had told Conrad von Hötzendorff that he expected the decision in the West to take place by the 39th day and had promised to send German troops eastward to help Austria beginning on the 40th day. Although the Belgians were not expected to fight, nevertheless German thoroughness required that every contingency be provided for. The problem was to design the heaviest possible anti-fortification gun that could be transported overland. It had to be a mortar or short-barreled howitzer with high angle of fire capable of lobbing shells onto the tops of the forts and yet, without the rifling of a long barrel, have sufficient accuracy to hit a specific target.

Krupp's, working in iron secrecy, was ready with a model of the 420 in 1909. The sawed-off bloated giant, though fired successfully, proved excessively cumbersome to move. It had to be transported by rail in two sections each requiring a locomotive to pull it. Spur tracks had to be laid to bring the gun to its emplacement pit which, owing to the tremendous downward thrust of the recoil, had to be dug several yards deep and filled with concrete in which the gun was embedded and from which it could only be released by blasting. The emplacement process required 6 hours. For four more years Krupp's worked to construct a gun transportable by road by breaking it down into several sections. In February 1914 such a model was achieved and tested at the Kummersdorf proving ground much to the gratification of the Kaiser, who was invited for the occasion. Further tests over roads with steam and gasoline motors and even multiple horse teams as movers showed that improvements were necessary. A target date of October 1, 1914, was set.

The Austrian Skoda 305s, completed in 1910, had the advantage of superior mobility. Motor-drawn in three sections consisting of gun, mount, and portable foundation, they could travel 15 to 20 miles in a day. Instead of tires, their wheels wore continuous belts of what was then awesomely described as "iron feet." At the point of emplacement the portable steel foundation was set down, the mount bolted to it, and the gun fitted to the mount, the whole process requiring 40 minutes.

Disassembly could be achieved equally quickly, which made the guns proof against capture. They could be swung right or left to an angle of 60 degrees and had a range of 7 miles. Like the 420s they fired an armor-piercing shell with a delayed-action fuse allowing the explosion to take place after penetration of the target.

When war broke out in August, several of the Austrian 305s were in Germany, loaned by Conrad von Hötzendorff until the German model should be ready. Krupp's had in existence at this time five 420s of the railroad model and two of the road model still waiting for the necessary improvements in transportation. Urgent orders to make them ready were issued on August 2. When the invasion of Belgium began, Krupp's was working desperately day and night to assemble guns, mounts, motors, equipment, horse teams for emergencies, mechanics, truck drivers, and artillery personnel who had to be given last-minute training.

Moltke still hoped to get through without needing them. If, however, the Belgians were so misguided as to fight, the Germans expected that the forts could be taken by simple assault. No detail of the assault had been left to chance. Its planning had been the study of an officer who was Schlieffen's most devoted disciple on the General Staff.

Gluttony for work and a granite character had overcome lack of a "von" to win for Captain Erich Ludendorff the right to wear the coveted red stripes of the General Staff whose ranks he entered at the age of thirty in 1895. Although his thick body, his blond mustache over a harsh down-curving mouth, his round double chin, and that bulge at the back of the neck which Emerson called the mark of the beast, characterized Ludendorff as belonging to the opposite physical type from the aristocratic Schlieffen, he modeled himself on Schlieffen's hard, shut-in personality. Deliberately friendless and forbidding, the man who within two years was to exercise greater power over the people and fate of Germany than anyone since Frederick the Great, remained little known or liked. None of the usual reminiscences of friends and family or personal stories or sayings accumulated around him; even as he grew in eminence he moved without attendant anecdotes, a man without a shadow.

Regarding Schlieffen as "one of the greatest soldiers who ever lived," Ludendorff, as a member and ultimately Chief of the Mobilization Section of the General Staff from 1904 to 1913, devoted himself to ensuring the success of his master's plan. Of its soundness, he says, the entire Staff was convinced, for "nobody believed in Belgium's neutrality." In the event of war Ludendorff expected to become Chief of Military Operations, but in 1913, he came into conflict with the then Minister of War, General von Heeringen, and was removed from the Staff to a regimental command. In April 1914 he was promoted to general with orders, upon mobilization, to join the Second Army as Deputy Chief of Staff.* In that capacity, on August 2, he was assigned to Emmich's Army of the Meuse for the attack upon Liège, charged with liaison between the assault force and the parent command.

On August 3 King Albert became Commander in Chief of the Belgian Army—without illusions. The plan he and Galet had drawn up to meet the hypothesis of a German invasion had been frustrated. They had wanted to bring up all six Belgian divisions to take a stand along the natural barrier of the Meuse where they could reinforce the fortified positions of Liège and Namur. But the General Staff and its new chief, General Selliers de Moranville, disinclined to let the young King and the low-ranking Captain Galet dictate strategy, and itself torn between offensive and defensive ideas, had made no arrangements to bring the army up behind the Meuse. In accordance with strict neutrality the six divisions were stationed before the war to face all comers: the 1st Division at Ghent facing England, the 2nd at Antwerp, the 3rd at Liège facing Germany, the 4th and 5th at Namur, Charleroi, and Mons facing France, the 6th and the Cavalry Division in the center at Brussels. General Selliers' plan, once the enemy was identified, was to concentrate the army in the center of the country facing the invader, leaving the garrisons of Antwerp, Liège, and Namur to look after themselves. The impetus of existing plans is always stronger than the impulse to change. The Kaiser could not change Moltke's plan nor could Kitchener alter Henry

*This title, which fits the functions of the post, is used in preference to the German title *Quartiermeister*, which is confusing to English-speaking readers.

Wilson's nor Lanrezac alter Joffre's. By August 3 when King Albert, becoming officially Commander in Chief, took precedence over General Selliers, it was too late to organize deployment of the whole army along the Meuse. The strategy adopted was to concentrate the Belgian Army before Louvain on the river Gette about forty miles east of Brussels where it was now decided to make a defense. The best the King could do was to insist upon the 3rd Division remaining at Liège and the 4th at Namur to reinforce the frontier garrisons instead of joining the Field Army in the center of the country.

As commander of the 3rd Division and Governor of Liège, the King had obtained the appointment in January 1914 of his own nominee, General Leman, the sixty-three-year-old Commandant of the War College. A former officer of Engineers like Joffre, Leman had spent the last thirty years, except for a six-year interval on the Staff of the Engineers, at the War College where Albert had studied under him. He had had seven months to try to reorganize the defenses of the Liège forts without the support of the General Staff. When the crisis came, a conflict of orders broke over his head. On August 1 General Selliers ordered away one brigade of the 3rd Division, a third of its strength. On appeal from Leman the King countermanded the order. On August 3 General Selliers in his turn countermanded the King's order for demolition of the bridges above Liège on the ground that they were needed for movements of the Belgian Army. Again on appeal from Leman, the King supported the General against the Chief of Staff and added a personal letter charging Leman to "hold to the end the position which you have been entrusted to defend."

The will to defend the country outran the means. Of machine guns, the essential weapon for defense, the Belgian Army's proportion per man was half that of the German Army. Of heavy field artillery, needed for the defensive positions between the forts, it had none at all. The planned increase in military service which was intended to bring the Field Army up to 150,000 with 70,000 reserves and the fortress troops to 130,000 by the year 1926, had hardly got under way. In August 1914 the Field Army mustered 117,000 with no trained reserves, all the remaining reserves being used to man the forts. The Civic Guard, a gentlemanly gendarmerie in top hats and bright green uniforms, were pressed into active service; many of its duties were taken over by Boy Scouts. The active army had had no practice in entrenching and hardly any tools to dig with. Transport was lacking as were tents and field kitchens; cooking utensils had to be collected from farms and villages; telephone equipment was negligible. The army marched in a chaos of improvisation.

It marched also, or was borne along, on a crest of enthusiasm, haloed by a mist of illusion. Soldiers, suddenly popular, were overwhelmed by gifts of food and kisses and beer. They soon broke ranks and strolled through the streets, showing off their uniforms and greeting friends. Parents joined their sons to see what war was like. Magnificent limousines, requisitioned as transport, sped by piled with loaves and joints of meat. Cheers roared after them. Cheers greeted the machine guns pulled, like the milk carts of Flanders, by dogs.

Early on August 4, a quiet, clear, luminous morning, seventy miles to the east of Brussels, the first invaders, units of von Marwitz's Cavalry, crossed into Belgium. Coming at a steady purposeful trot, they carried twelve-foot steel-headed lances and were otherwise hung about with an arsenal of sabers, pistols, and rifles. Harvesters looking up from the roadside fields, villagers peering from their windows, whispered "Uhlans!" The outlandish name, with its overtones of the savage Tartar horsemen from whom it derived, evoked Europe's ancestral memory of barbarian invasion. The Germans, when engaged in their historic mission of bringing *Kultur* to their neighbors, showed a preference, as in the Kaiser's use of the word "Huns," for fearful models.

As vanguard of the invasion, the cavalry's mission was to reconnoiter the position of the Belgian and French armies, to watch out for British landings, and to screen the German deployment against similar enemy reconnaissance. On the first day the duty of the advance squadrons, supported by infantry brought up in automobiles, was to seize the crossings of the Meuse before the bridges were destroyed and capture farms and villages as sources of food and forage. At Warsage, just inside the frontier, M. Flechet, the Burgomaster of seventy-two, wearing his scarf of office, stood in the village square as the horsemen clattered over the cobblestones of the Belgian *pavé*.

Riding up, the squadron's officer with a polite smile handed him a printed proclamation which expressed Germany's "regret" at being "compelled by necessity" to enter Belgium. Though wishing to avoid combat, it said, "We must have a free road. Destruction of bridges, tunnels and railroads will be regarded as hostile acts." In village squares all along the border from Holland to Luxembourg the Uhlans scattered the proclamations, hauled down the Belgian flag from the town halls, raised the black eagle of the German Empire, and moved on, confident in the assurance given them by their commanders that the Belgians would not fight.

Behind them, filling the roads that converged on Liège came the infantry of Emmich's assault force, rank after rank. Only the red regimental number painted on helmet fronts broke the monotony of field-gray. Horse-drawn field artillery followed. The new leather of boots and harness creaked. Companies of cyclists sped ahead to seize road crossings and farmhouses and lay telephone wires. Automobiles honked their way through, carrying monocled Staff officers with orderlies holding drawn pistols sitting up front and trunks strapped on behind. Every regiment had its field kitchens on wheels, said to be inspired by one the Kaiser had seen at Russian maneuvers, with fires kindled and cooks standing up stirring the stew as the wagons moved. Such was the perfection of the equipment and the precision of the marching that the invaders appeared to be on parade.

Each soldier carried sixty-five pounds: rifle and ammunition, knapsack, canteen, extra boots, entrenching tools, knife and a multiplicity of implements and kits strapped to his coat. In one bag was his "iron ration" containing two cans of meat, two of vegetables, two packages of hard-tack, one of ground coffee, and a flask of whisky which was only to be opened on permission of an officer and was inspected daily to determine if its owner had cheated. Another bag held thread, needles, bandages and adhesive tape; another held matches, chocolate, and tobacco. Around the officers' necks hung binoculars and leather-bound maps covering the particular regiment's designated line of march so that no German would ever be in the predicament of the British officer who complained that battle is a process which always takes place at the junction of two maps. As they marched, the Germans sang. They sang "Deutschland über Alles," "Die Wacht am Rhein," and "Heil dir im Siegerkranz." They sang when they halted, when they billeted, when they caroused. Many who lived through the next thirty days of mounting combat, agony, and terror were to remember the sound of endless, repetitious masculine singing as the worst torment of the invasion.

General von Emmich's brigades, converging upon Liège from the north, east, and south, discovered when they reached the Meuse that the bridges above and below the city had already been destroyed. When they attempted to cross on pontoons, Belgian infantry opened fire, and the Germans to their astonishment found themselves in actual combat, hit by live ammunition, wounded and dying. They had 60,000 men to the Belgians' 25,000. By nightfall they had succeeded in crossing the river at Visé, north of the city; the brigades attacking from the south were held off; those attacking through the center where the river makes an inward bend reached the line of forts before reaching the river.

During the day as the boots and wheels and hoofs of the German ranks overran villages and trampled fields of ripe grain, the shooting increased and with it the vexation of the German troops, who had been told that the Belgians were "chocolate soldiers." Surprised and enraged by the resistance, the German soldiers in the state of heightened nerves produced by the first experience of combat were immediately susceptible to the first cry of "Snipers"! At once they imagined enraged civilians shooting at them from behind every house and hedgerow. At once they raised the cry, "*Man hat geschossen!*" that was to be the signal for every reprisal upon civilians from Visé to the gates of Paris. From the first day, the figure of the terrible *franc-tireur*, remembered from 1870, which the Germans were to conjure into gigantic proportions, began to take shape.

The spirit of resistance, soon to find its voice in the famous clandestine newspaper *Le Libre Belge*, was barely awake that first morning among the inhabitants of the frontier towns. Their own government, knowing the nature of the enemy, had already distributed notices to be posted in every community ordering civilians to deposit arms with the town authorities and warning that if caught with arms by the Germans they might be subject to the death penalty. The placards instructed the people not to fight or insult the enemy and to remain indoors behind closed windows in order to avoid "any pretext for measures of repression resulting in bloodshed or pillage or massacre of the innocent population." Thus sternly cautioned and awestruck at the sight of the invaders, the people were hardly prepared to try to halt the armored multitudes with individual rabbit guns.

Nevertheless on the first day of the invasion the Germans began the shooting not only of ordinary civilians but of Belgian priests, a more deliberate affair. On August 6, Major-General Karl Ulrich von Bülow,* brother of the ex-chancellor and commander of a cavalry division in the attack on Liège, told a brother officer that he disapproved of "the summary executions of Belgian priests which had taken place on the previous day." The pretext that Belgian priesthood was engaged in a conspiracy to encourage *franc-tireur* warfare—organized within the first twenty-four hours and in defiance of the civil government—was designed for German consumption. For Belgian consumption the executions were meant as an exercise in frightfulness according to the theory developed by the Emperor Caligula: "*Oderint dum metuant*" (Let them hate us as long as they fear us).

On the first day too the Germans shot six hostages taken at Warsage and burned the village of Battice as an example. It was "burned out, completely gutted," wrote a German officer who marched through it a few days later. "One could see through the frameless window openings into the interior of the rooms with their roasted remnants of iron bedsteads and furnishings. Broken bits of household utensils lay scattered about the street. Except for dogs and cats scavenging among the ruins, all sign of life had been extinguished by the fire. In the market square stood the roofless, spireless church." In another place where, he was told, three German Hussars had been shot, "the whole village was in flames, cattle bellowed desperately in barns, half-burned chickens rushed about demented, two men in peasant smocks lay dead against a wall."

*A different person from Generaloberst Karl von Bülow who commanded the Second Army.

"Our advance in Belgium is certainly brutal," Moltke wrote to Conrad on August 5, "but we are fighting for our lives and all who get in the way must take the consequences." He did not have in mind the consequences to Germany. But the process which was to make Belgium the nemesis of Germany had begun.

On August 5 Emmich's brigades opened the attack on the four easternmost forts of Liège with a cannonade by field artillery followed by infantry assault. The light shells made no impression on the forts, and the Belgian guns poured a hail of fire on the German troops, slaughtering their front ranks. Company after company came on, making for the spaces between the forts where the Belgian entrenchments had not been completed. At some points where they broke through, the Germans stormed up the slopes where the guns could not be depressed to reach them and were mowed down by the forts' machine guns. The dead piled up in ridges a yard high. At Fort Barchon, Belgians, seeing the German lines waver, charged with the bayonet and threw them back. Again and again the Germans returned to the assault, spending lives like bullets in the knowledge of plentiful reserves to make up the losses. "They made no attempt at deploying," a Belgian officer described it later, "but came on line after line, almost shoulder to shoulder, until as we shot them down, the fallen were heaped on top of each other in an awful barricade of dead and wounded that threatened to mask our guns and cause us trouble. So high did the barricade become that we did not know whether to fire through it or to go out and clear openings with our hands. . . . But would you believe it?—this veritable wall of dead and dying enabled those wonderful Germans to creep closer, and actually to charge up the glacis. They got no farther than halfway because our machine guns and rifles swept them back. Of course we had our losses but they were slight compared to the carnage we inflicted on our enemies."

The prodigal spending of lives by all the belligerents that was to mount and mount in senseless excess to hundreds of thousands at the Somme, to over a million at Verdun began on that second day of the war at Liège. In their furious frustration at the first check, the Germans threw men recklessly against the forts in whatever numbers would be necessary to take the objective on schedule.

During the night of August 5 Emmich's brigades reassembled on their separate roads for a renewed attack, scheduled to begin at midnight. General Ludendorff, accompanying the 14th Brigade which occupied the center of the German line, found the troops gloomy and "nervous." Ahead the fortress guns loomed fearfully. Many officers doubted that infantry attack could prevail against them. Rumor reported that an entire cyclist company sent out to reconnoiter earlier in the day had been "annihilated." A column taking the wrong road in the darkness bumped up against another, tangled, and came to a confused halt. Ludendorff riding up to find the cause of the trouble discovered the orderly of General von Wussow, commander of the 14th Brigade, leading the General's horse with empty saddle. Von Wussow had been killed by machine-gun fire along the road ahead. Ludendorff with instant boldness seized opportunity by the throat. He took command of the Brigade and gave the signal for attack that was intended to pierce the interval between Fort Fleron and Fort d'Evegnée. As they advanced, men fell under fire and for the first time in his life Ludendorff heard the "peculiar thud of bullets striking human bodies."

Through some quirk in the fortunes of war, the guns of Fort Fleron less than two miles away failed to open fire. In a village where house-to-house fighting developed, Ludendorff ordered up a field howitzer which "fired right and left into the houses" and soon cleared the way through. By two o'clock on the afternoon of the 6th the Brigade had broken through the ring of forts and reached the heights on the right bank of the Meuse from where they could see Liège and its Citadel, an imposing but disused fort, directly across the river. Here they were joined by General von Emmich, but although they waited in increasing anxiety, scanning the roads to north and south, no troops of the other brigades appeared. The 14th discovered itself isolated within the circle of forts. Its field guns were trained on the Citadel and fired as a signal to the other brigades as well as "to intimidate the governor of the fortress and the inhabitants."

Angered at having to waste time and manpower fighting a people who, with ordinary common sense, should have let them pass, the Germans throughout the month of August were obsessed by the goal of "intimidating" the Belgians into giving up their stupid and futile resistance. Under a flag of truce the former German military attaché at Brussels who was personally known to General Leman had been sent the day before to persuade or, failing in that, to threaten him into surrender. Leman was told by the emissary that Zeppelins would destroy Liège if he did not let the Germans through. The parley failed of its purpose, and on August 6 the Zeppelin L-Z was duly sent from Cologne to bomb the city. The thirteen bombs it dropped, the nine civilians it killed, inaugurated a twentieth century practice.

After the bombardment Ludendorff sent another emissary under another flag of truce who also failed to persuade Leman to surrender. Ruse, too, was tried. In an effort to kidnap or kill the commander, a detachment of thirty men and six officers, disguised in unmarked uniforms resembling those of the British, drove up in automobiles to Leman's headquarters on the Rue Sainte-Foi and asked to see the General. His aide, Colonel Marchand, coming to the door, cried, "They are not English; they're Germans!" and was instantly shot down. He was immediately avenged by comrades who, in the spirited and unabashed reporting of 1914, "maddened at the dastardly violation of the rules of civilized warfare, spared not but slew." In the confusion, General Leman escaped to Fort Loncin, west of the city, where he continued to direct the defense.

He realized, now that a German brigade had penetrated between the forts, that he could not expect to hold the city. If the brigades attacking from the north and south also succeeded in breaking through, Liège would be encircled and the 3rd Division cut off from the rest of the army, where it could be trapped and annihilated. Leman's Intelligence had identified units of four German Army corps in the attacking force, which appeared to give Emmich the equivalent of eight divisions against Leman's one. Actually, Emmich's troops were not organized by corps but by detached brigades and now numbered, with the reinforcements hurriedly sent to him, about five divisions. The lone 3rd Division was not enough to save itself or

Liège. On the morning of August 6, General Leman, knowing it was the King's fixed purpose to preserve the Field Army in being and in contact with Antwerp regardless of what happened elsewhere, ordered the 3rd Division to fall back from Liège and join the rest of the army in front of Louvain. It meant that the city, though not the forts, would fall; but even for Liège a division could not be sacrificed, for beyond Liège was the independence of Belgium. Unless the King remained in command of an army on some corner of his own soil, he would be at the mercy not only of his enemies but of his Allies.

Brussels on August 6 went mad with excitement at news of the repulse administered to the Germans the day before. "*Grande Victoire Belge!*" proclaimed newspaper extras. Happy, ardent people crowded the cafés, congratulated one another, boasted of vengeance, stayed up all night to celebrate, and next morning delightedly read to each other a Belgian communiqué which said that 125,000 Germans had "completely failed to make any impression and three army corps engaged in the attack were cut up and useless." Echoing the optimism, the Allied press reported the "German rout complete," with several regiments having surrendered, many prisoners taken, 20,000 German casualties, the defenders everywhere successful, the "invaders decisively checked," and their advance brought to a "standstill." How the withdrawal of the Belgian 3rd Division, briefly mentioned, fitted into this picture was somehow left unexplained.

At Belgian Headquarters in the old Town Hall at Louvain confidence was as high as if the Belgian Army numbered thirty-four divisions and the German six instead of the other way around. The forward group within the General Staff "hummed with wild plans for an immediate offensive."

The King vetoed it at once. He recognized in the size of the force attacking Liège, and in new reports of five German corps now identified, the outlines of the envelopment strategy of Schlieffen. There was still a chance, if he were reinforced by French and English forces in time, of halting the Germans at the river Gette midway between Antwerp and Namur. Already he had sent two urgent appeals to President Poincaré. At this stage he still expected, as did everyone in Belgium, to be joined on Belgian territory by his Allies. "Where are the French? Where are the English?" people everywhere asked one another. In one village a Belgian woman offered a bunch of flowers tied with the English colors to a soldier in a strange uniform which she thought was khaki. In some embarrassment he identified himself as German.

In France, Poincaré and Messimy who in his exuberance had instantly proposed to send five corps to help the Belgians were helpless against Joffre's silent and stubborn refusal to change his plan of deployment by so much as a brigade. Three French cavalry divisions under General Sordet would enter Belgium on August 6 to reconnoiter German strength east of the Meuse, but only the nonappearance of the English, Joffre said, would induce him to extend his left wing. Late on the night of August 5 word came from London that the War Council, after an all-day meeting, had made up its mind to send an expeditionary force, but of only four divisions, plus cavalry, instead of six. Although this was disappointing, it did not induce Joffre to shift any divisions to his left to make up the British deficiency. He was keeping everything for the French offensive through the center. All he sent to Belgium, apart from the cavalry, was a single Staff officer, Colonel Brécard, with a letter to King Albert. It suggested that the Belgian Army should postpone decisive action and retreat upon Namur where it would make contact with the French and, when the French concentration was completed, join in a common offensive. Four French divisions, Joffre said, would be sent to Namur but would not reach there until August 15.

As Joffre saw it, the Belgian Army, ignoring purely Belgian interests for the sake of a common front, should act as a wing of the French Army in conformity with French strategy. As King Albert saw it, with his clearer sense of the danger of the German right wing, if he allowed the Belgian Army to make a stand at Namur it could be cut off from its base at Antwerp by the advancing Germans and pushed out of Belgium over the French border. More intent on holding the Belgian Army on Belgian soil than upon a common strategy, King Albert was determined to keep open his line of retreat to Antwerp. Purely military considerations pointed to Namur; historical and national reasons pointed to Antwerp even at the risk of the army being bottled up there where it could exercise no direct influence upon the war as a whole.

If compelled, the Belgian Army would retreat upon Antwerp, not Namur, the King told Colonel Brécard. Bitterly disappointed Brécard informed Joffre that the Belgians could not be expected to join the French in a combined offensive.

On August 7 the French Government, which had never been consulted about Plan 17 and was now prevented by its requirements from coming to the aid of Belgium, conferred the Grand Cross of the Legion of Honor upon Liège and the Military Medal upon King Albert. The gesture, however inadequate in the circumstances, expressed something of the world's startled admiration of Belgium's fight. She is not only "defending the independence of Europe; she is the champion of honor," declared the President of the French Chamber. She has won "immortal renown" by shattering the superstition that the German armies are invincible, declared *The Times* of London.

While the tributes multiplied, the people of Liège spent the first of the countless nights that twentieth century Europeans were to spend in cellars. Following the day of terror under the Zeppelin raid, Liège was pounded all night by the exploding shells of Ludendorff's field artillery in an attempt to cow the city into surrender. The method was as fruitless as the long-range bombardment of Paris by the Big Berthas in 1918 or the Luftwaffe and V-2 bombings of London one war later.

After the preliminary softening up, Emmich and Ludendorff decided to enter the city without waiting for the other brigades to come up. Meeting no resistance, as the Belgian 3rd Division had by now been withdrawn, the 14th Brigade marched across two bridges which were still undestroyed. Ludendorff, thinking the Citadel had been taken by an advance guard sent ahead for that purpose, drove up the steep winding road in a Staff car with a single adjutant. Reaching the courtyard he found no German soldiers in possession, the advance guard having not yet arrived. He nevertheless unhesitatingly "banged on the gates" and on their being opened to him received the surrender of the Citadel from the remaining Belgian soldiers inside. He was forty-nine, twice the age of Bonaparte in 1793 and Liège was his Toulon.

Down below in the city, General Emmich, not finding Leman, arrested the burgomaster, who was told that Liège would be shelled and burned unless the forts surrendered, and was offered a safe conduct to obtain the surrender from General Leman or the King. He refused, and remained a prisoner. By evening three more German brigades had broken through the ring of forts to join the 14th inside the city.

At six that evening an officer of motor transport tore through the streets of Aachen bringing excited word to Second Army Headquarters that General Emmich was inside Liège and at that moment negotiating with the burgomaster. In the midst of shouts and "*Hochs!*" a telegram from Emmich to his wife was intercepted with the message, "Hurrah, in Liège!" At 8:00 P.M. a liaison officer brought word from Emmich that although General Leman had not been taken, the bishop and burgomaster were prisoners, the Citadel had surrendered, the city was evacuated by Belgian troops, but that he had no information about the forts.

In Berlin, where Supreme Headquarters, or *Oberste Heeresleitung* (hereafter OHL), remained until the end of the concentration period, the Kaiser was ecstatic. At the beginning, when it had appeared that the Belgians were going to fight after all, he had bitterly reproached Moltke, "Now you see you have brought the English down on me without any reason!" but at news of the fall of Liège, he called him his "dearest Julius" and, as Moltke recorded it, "I was rapturously kissed." Still the English continued to worry the Kaiser. On August 10 the American ambassador, Mr. Gerard, who came to present an offer by President Wilson to mediate, found him "despondent." Seated in the garden of the Palace at a green iron table under a sun umbrella with papers and telegraph forms scattered before him and two dachshunds lying at his feet, the Kaiser lamented, "The English change the whole situation—an obstinate people—they will keep up the war. It cannot end soon."

The bitter truth that none of the forts had been taken was learned the day after the fall of the city when Ludendorff came out of Liège to report. He insisted that the siege cannon must be brought into action at once; the Belgians still showed no disposition to surrender. Already the advance of Kluck's First

Army, scheduled to be the first to start, had to be put off from the 10th to the 13th.

Meanwhile at Essen the hideous fat black siege mortars stood immobile while around them surged the frantic struggle to assemble the motor transport and trained gun crews. By August 9 the two road models were ready and that night were loaded onto freight cars to be transported as far as possible by railway to save their treads. The train left Essen on the 10th and reached Belgium by nightfall, but at Herbesthal, twenty miles east of Liège, at 11:00 P.M. came to a dead stop. The railroad tunnel, blown up by the Belgians, was blocked. Furious efforts failed to reopen it. The mammoth guns had to be unloaded and proceed by road. Though they had only eleven miles to cover to come within range of the forts, one breakdown after another thwarted their progress. Motors failed, harness broke, roads were blocked, passing troops had to be pressed into service to help haul them. All day the slow struggle with the two silent monsters went on.

While they were on their way, the German government made a last effort to persuade Belgium to yield passageway through her territory. On August 9 Mr. Gerard was asked to forward a note to his colleague in Brussels for presentation to the Belgian government. "Now that the Belgian Army has upheld its honor by heroic resistance to a very superior force," it said, the German government "beg" the King of the Belgians and his government to spare Belgium "further horrors of war." Germany was ready to make any compact with Belgium consistent with allowing her armies free passageway and would give her "solemn assurances" that she had no intention of taking Belgian territory and would evacuate the country as soon as the progress of war permitted. Both the American ministers in Brussels and at The Hague declined to be the bearer of such a proposal, but through the offices of the Dutch government it eventually reached King Albert on August 12. He refused.

His steadfastness, in view of the enormity of the threat to his country, did not seem entirely believable even to his Allies. No one had expected heroism from Belgium. "Yes," said King Albert after the war, in reply to a French statesman's praise of his conduct, "we were cornered into it." In 1914 the French had their doubts, and on August 8 sent the Under-Secretary of

Foreign Affairs, M. Berthelot, to see the King on the basis of a rumor that he was going to arrange a truce with Germany. Berthelot was charged with the unhappy duty of explaining to the King that France would do everything in her power to help Belgium except interfere with her own plan of operations. Albert tried again to convey to the French his apprehension of the huge right wing that would be coming through Flanders and repeated his warning that the Belgian Army might have to withdraw to Antwerp. It would resume the offensive when, he delicately added, "the approach of the Allied armies makes itself felt."

To the outside world it seemed, as, from his pinnacle of authority, the Military Correspondent of *The Times* announced, that the German force attacking Liège "has been very handsomely beaten." For the moment this was approximately true. The vaunted German Army, which had expected to be so easily victorious over the "dreaming sheep," had failed to take the forts by assault. It came to a pause after August 9 and waited for reinforcements—though not of the human kind. It waited for the siege guns.

In France General Joffre and his staff still had their minds closed as resolutely as ever to Flanders, still focused their thoughts as ardently as ever on the Rhine. The five French armies, totaling approximately the same seventy divisions that the Germans had on the Western Front, were arranged in order from the First Army on the right to the Fifth on the left. Divided by the fortified area of Verdun-Toul, they were concentrated in two groups in much the same proportion as the German armies were grouped on either side of Metz-Thionville. The First and Second Armies, facing the German Seventh and Sixth, in Alsace and Lorraine, together formed the French right wing whose mission was by vigorous attack to throw the Germans opposite them back upon the Rhine while driving a solid wedge between the German left and center.

Farthest to the right was stationed a special assault force like Emmich's at Liège for the opening move into Alsace. Detached from the First Army and composed of the VIIth Corps and 8th Cavalry Division, it was to liberate Mulhouse and Colmar and anchor itself upon the Rhine in the corner where Germany, Alsace, and Switzerland meet.

Next to it was the First Army commanded by handsome General Dubail. Dubail, it was said, did not recognize the impossible, combined indomitable will with unlimited energy, and for some cause hidden in the intricate defiles of French Army politics was not on the best of terms with General de Castelnau, his immediate neighbor on the left. Castelnau had left the General Staff to become commander of the Second Army which held the crucial front around Nancy.

The Third, Fourth, and Fifth Armies were gathered on the other side of Verdun for the great offensive through the German center contemplated by Plan 17. Their deployment extended from Verdun to Hirson. The Fifth Army, which held the open end, faced northeast for offense through the Ardennes, rather than north to meet the descending forces of the German right wing. The position on the Fifth Army's left, centering on the once strong but lately neglected fortress of Maubeuge, was expected to be held by the British, who, it was now learned, were not coming in the full strength originally planned. The deficiency, if it did not unduly worry Joffre and his Staff whose attention was centered elsewhere, hardly reassured the Fifth Army's commander, General Lanrezac.

As he would have to bear the impact of the German right wing, General Lanrezac was all too conscious of the danger of his position. His predecessor in command of the Fifth Army had been Gallieni who, after tours of the terrain and failure to persuade the General Staff to modernize the fortifications of Maubeuge, had not been happy with it. When Gallieni reached the age limit in February 1914, Joffre had appointed Lanrezac, a "veritable lion" whose intellectual gifts he much admired and who had been one of his three choices for Deputy Chief of Staff in 1911. Because of his "keen intelligence" Lanrezac was considered a star at the General Staff, which forgave him his caustic manner and his tendency to bad temper and impolite language for the sake of the clarity, brilliance, and logic of his lectures. At sixty-two he fitted, like Joffre, Castelnau, and Pau, the heavy-mustached, heavy-paunched pattern for French generals.

In May 1914, when each of the generals of the five armies was given the pertinent section of Plan 17 that applied to him, Lanrezac immediately pointed out the dangers to his exposed flank if the Germans came down in strength west of the Meuse. His objections were ignored on the basic General Staff theory that the stronger the German right wing, "so much the better for us." In the last days before mobilization, Lanrezac put his objections in a letter to Joffre which was to become a primary document in the mountain of criticism and controversy that after the war rose over the grave of Plan 17. Lanrezac's tone in the letter, as a fellow officer said, was less a bold challenge of a dominant plan than a professor's critique of a pupil's thesis. It pointed out that the offensive planned for the Fifth Army was based on the assumption that the Germans would come through Sedan when in fact it was more likely that they would come around farther north through Namur, Dinant, and Givet. "Clearly," expounded the professor, "once the Fifth Army is committed to an offensive in the direction of Neufchâteau [in the Ardennes] it will be unable to parry a German offensive further north."

That was in fact the crucial point, but as if to cover himself Lanrezac reduced the force of his argument by adding, "it is noted here merely as a suggestion." Joffre who received the letter on mobilization day, August 1, decided it was "entirely inopportune" and "in the midst of the important events that filled my day," did not answer it. At the same time he dismissed the fears of General Ruffey, commander of the Third Army, who came to express concern about a possible German "parade through Belgium." With characteristic economy Joffre replied "You are wrong." In his opinion it was not for a generalissimo to explain but to give orders. It was not for a general to think but to carry out orders. Once a general had received his orders he should carry them out with a mind at rest, knowing it to be his duty.

On August 3, the day Germany declared war, the generals assembled in a meeting summoned by Joffre, hoping at last to hear him explain the totality of Plan 17 and of the strategy they were to carry out. The hope was vain; Joffre waited in benign silence for remarks. At last Dubail spoke up, saying that the offensive laid out for his army required reinforcements which were not allowed for. Joffre replied with one of his cryptic phrases, "That may be your plan; it is not mine." As no one knew what this meant, Dubail, thinking he had been misunderstood, repeated his remark. Joffre, "with his customary beatific smile," replied in the same words as before, "That may be your plan; it is not mine." The truth was that to Joffre what counted in the immense chaos of war was not the plan but the energy and verve with which it was carried out. Victory he believed would come not out of the best plan but out of the strongest will and firmest confidence, and these, he had no doubt, were his.

On August 4 he established Staff headquarters, known as *Grand Quartier Général* (hereafter GQG), at Vitry-le-François on the Marne, about half way between Paris and Nancy where he would be within roughly equal distance, about eighty to ninety miles, of each of the five army headquarters. Unlike Moltke who during his brief tenure as Commander in Chief never went to the front or visited field armies' headquarters, Joffre was in constant and personal contact with his commanders. Placidly ensconced in the back seat of his car, he would be driven on his rounds at seventy miles an hour by his appointed private chauffeur Georges Bouillot, three times winner of the Grand Prix auto race. German generals having been given a perfect plan to carry out were not expected to need constant guidance. French generals were expected, as Foch said, to think, but Joffre, always suspecting weakness of nerve or other personal failings, liked to keep them under close supervision. After the maneuvers in 1913 his dismissal of five generals from the active list had caused a public sensation and a shudder in every garrison in France; nothing like it had ever happened before. During August, under the terrible test of live ammunition, Joffre was to scatter generals like chaff at the first sign of what he considered incompetence or insufficient élan.

Elan was high at Vitry on the banks of the tranquil tree-bordered Marne shining green and gold in the August sun. In the school building taken over by GQG, an unbridgeable gulf separated Operations, the Troisième Bureau, which occupied the class rooms, from Intelligence, the Deuxième Bureau, which was installed in the gymnasium with the apparatus pushed against the walls and the rings tied up to the ceiling. All day the Deuxième Bureau collected information, interrogated prisoners, deciphered documents, put together ingenious conjectures and passed on its reports to its neighbors. Consistently these indicated German activity west of the Meuse. All day Troisième read the reports, handed them around, criticized, disputed, and refused to believe them if they pointed to conclusions that would require the French to modify their plan of offensive.

Every morning at eight o'clock Joffre presided at meetings of the section chiefs, a majestic and immobile arbiter but never the puppet of his entourage as outsiders, misled by his silence and his bare desk, supposed. He kept no papers on his desk and no map on his wall; he wrote nothing and said little. Plans were prepared for him, said Foch; "he weighs them and decides." There were few who did not tremble in his presence. Anyone who was five minutes late at his mess was treated to a thunderous frown and remained an outcast for the remainder of the meal. Joffre ate in silence with a gourmet's entire devotion to the food. He complained continuously of being kept in the dark by his staff. When an officer referred to an article in the latest issue of *l'Illustration* which Joffre had not seen he cried angrily, "You see, they hide everything from me!" He used to rub his forehead, murmuring "Poor Joffre!" which his staff came to recognize as his way of refusing to do something that was being urged upon him. He was angered by anyone who tried too openly to make him change his mind. Like Talleyrand he disapproved of too much zeal. Without the probing intellect of Lanrezac or the creative intellect of Foch, he was inclined by temperament to rely on those he had chosen for his staff. But he remained the master, almost a despot, jealous of his authority, resentful of the least encroachment upon it. When it was proposed that Gallieni, having been designated by Poincaré as Joffre's successor in case of emergency, should be installed at GQG, Joffre, fearing to be in the shadow of his old commander, would have none of it. "He is difficult to place," he confided to Messimy. "I have always been under his orders. *Il m'a toujours fait mousser*" (He has always made me foam), an admission of some significance in view of the part the personal relationship between Joffre and Gallieni was to play in the fateful hours before the Marne. As a result of Joffre's refusal to have him at GQG, Gallieni was left in Paris with nothing to do.

The long-desired moment when the French flag would be raised again in Alsace had come. The covering troops, waiting among the thick, rich pines of the Vosges, trembled with readiness. These were the remembered mountains with their lakes and waterfalls and the damp delicious smell of the forests where fragrant ferns grew between the pines. Hilltop pastures, grazed by cattle, alternated with patches of forest. Ahead, the shadowed purple line of the Ballon d'Alsace, highest point in the Vosges, was hidden in mist. Patrols who ventured to the top could see down below the red-roofed villages of the lost territory, the gray church spires, and the tiny, gleaming line of the Moselle where, young and near its source, it was narrow enough to be waded. Squares of white potato blossom alternated with strips of scarlet-runner beans and gray-green-purple rows of cabbages. Haycocks like small fat pyramids dotted the fields as if arranged by a painter. The land was at its peak of fertility. The sun sparkled over all. Never had it looked so much worth fighting for. No wonder *l'Illustration* in its first issue of the war showed France in the person of a handsome *poilu* sweeping the beautiful damsel Alsace off her feet into a rapturous embrace.

A proclamation addressed to the inhabitants had already been printed by the War Ministry ready for posting on the walls of liberated towns. Airplane reconnaissance showed the area to be lightly held, almost too lightly thought General Bonneau, commander of the VIIth Corps, who feared he was "walking into a mousetrap." He sent an aide on the evening of August 6 to report to General Dubail that he considered the Mulhouse operation "delicate and hazardous" and was concerned for his right flank and rear. GQG, consulted by Dubail who had expressed similar concern at the meeting of generals on August 3, regarded all doubts as failure of the offensive spirit. Expressed at the start of an operation, a commander's doubts, however valid, too often proved a formula for retreat. In French military doctrine seizure of the initiative was more important than careful appreciation of enemy strength. Success depended upon the fighting qualities of commanders, and to permit caution and hesitation to take hold at the outset would, in the view of Joffre and his entourage, have been ruinous. GQG insisted upon the attack in Alsace being launched as soon as possible. Obeying, Dubail called General Bonneau on the telephone, asked if he was "ready," and on receiving an affirmative answer, ordered the attack for next morning.

At five o'clock on the morning of August 7, a few hours before Ludendorff led his brigade into Liège, General Bonneau's VIIth Corps spilled over the crest of the Vosges, presenting arms as they crossed the frontier, and swept down in a classic bayonet charge upon Altkirch, a town of about 4,000 on the way to Mulhouse. They took Altkirch by assault in a battle lasting six hours with 100 casualties. It was not the last bayonet charge of a war whose symbol was soon to be a mud-filled trench, but it might as well have been. Executed in the finest style and spirit of the *Règlement* of 1913, it seemed the proof of *cran*, the apotheosis of *la gloire*.

The hour, as the French communiqué reported, "was one of indescribable emotion." Frontier posts were torn from the ground and carried in triumph through the town. But General Bonneau, still uneasy, did not push on toward Mulhouse. Impatient at his lack of progress, GQG on the following morning issued an imperative order that Mulhouse be taken and the Rhine bridges destroyed that day. On August 8 the VIIth Corps entered Mulhouse without firing a shot about an hour after the last German troops, withdrawn to defend the frontier farther north, had left it.

The French cavalry in gleaming cuirasses and black horsehair plumes galloped through the streets. Almost dumfounded at the sudden apparition, the people stood at first transfixed in silence or sobbing, then gradually broke into joy. A grand review of the French troops lasting two hours was held in the main square. The bands played "The Marseillaise" and the "Sambre et Meuse." Guns were hung with flowers of red, white, and blue. Joffre's proclamation vaunting his soldiers as "the vanguard of the great work of *revanche* . . . who carry in the folds of their flags the magic words 'Right and Liberty'" was posted on the walls. Chocolates, pastries, and pipes of tobacco were thrust upon the soldiers. From all windows flags and handkerchiefs waved and even the roofs were covered with people.

Not all were welcomers. Many of the inhabitants were Germans who had settled there since 1870. One officer riding through the crowds noticed among them "grave and impassive faces, pipe in teeth, who looked as if they were counting us,"—as indeed they were, and afterward hastened away during the night to report on the strength of the French divisions.

German reinforcements hurriedly sent from Strasbourg were deployed around the city while the French were busy occupying it. General Bonneau, who lacked faith in success from the start, had made what dispositions he could to prevent envelopment. When battle began on the morning of August 9, his left at Cernay fought fiercely and stubbornly all day, but his right, holding too long to an unthreatened sector, was not brought around in time. Finally recognizing the necessity of reinforcements which had worried Dubail from the start, GQG sent up a reserve division, but at this stage to solidify the front two would have been required. For twenty-four hours the battle swayed until 7:00 A.M. on August 10 when the French, pushed back and fearing to be enveloped, withdrew.

Humiliating as it was to the army after the glorious rhetoric of the communiqués and proclamations and the accumulated yearning of forty-four years, the loss of Mulhouse was cruelest upon the inhabitants who were now left subject to German reprisals. Those who had been most enthusiastic in welcoming the French were informed upon by their German fellow citizens with unpleasant consequences. The VIIth Corps retreated to within ten miles of Belfort. At GQG the natural and eternal enmity of Staff officers for field officers flared. Confirmed in his belief of Bonneau's lack of *cran*, Joffre began the roll of heads for which his regime was to become famous. General Bonneau became the first of the *limogés*, so-called because officers relieved of their commands reported at Limoges for rear duty. Blaming "faulty execution," Joffre within three days also dismissed the commander of the 8th Cavalry and another general of division.

Intent upon the original plan of freeing Alsace and pinning German forces to that front, and without regard for reports coming out of Belgium, Joffre took one regular and three reserve divisions and added them to the VIIth Corps to form a special Army of Alsace for renewed action on his extreme right. General Pau was called out of retirement to command it. During the four days while it was assembling, heavy pressures were building up elsewhere. On August 14, the day Pau was to move forward, thirty storks were seen flying south over Belfort, leaving Alsace two months before their usual time.

The French nation was hardly aware of what had happened. GQG's bulletins were masterpieces of the opaque. Joffre operated on the fixed principle that civilians should be told nothing. No journalists were allowed at the front; no names of generals or of casualties or of regiments were mentioned. In order to keep all useful information from the enemy, GQG adopted a principle from the Japanese, to wage war "silently and anonymously." France was divided into a Zone of the Rear and a Zone of the Armies; in the latter Joffre was absolute dictator; no civilian, not even the President, much less the despised deputies, could enter it without his permission. It was his and not the President's name that was signed to the proclamation addressed to the people of Alsace.

Ministers protested that they knew more of the movements of the German armies than of the French. Poincaré, to whom Joffre, considering himself independent of the Minister of War, reported directly, complained he was never told about reverses. On one occasion when a presidential visit to the Third Army was proposed, Joffre issued "strict orders" to its commander "not to discuss with the President any questions of strategy or foreign policy. A report of the conversation must be submitted." All his generals were cautioned against explaining military operations to members of the government. "In the reports I forward," Joffre told them, "I never make known the object of current operations or my intentions."

His system was soon to break down under rising public pressure, but in August, when frontiers fell and nations were invaded and vast armies swayed in what was still a war of movement, and the earth shook under the thud of war from Serbia to Belgium, hard news from the front was rare indeed. History while it was happening in that month, despite a thousand eager chroniclers, was not easily pinned down. General Gallieni dining in civilian clothes at a small café in Paris on August 9 overheard an editor of *Le Temps* at the next table say to a companion, "I can tell you that General Gallieni has just entered Colmar with 30,000 men." Leaning over to his friend, Gallieni said quietly, "That is how history is written."

While the Germans at Liège waited for the siege guns, while the world marveled at the continued resistance of the forts and the London *Daily Mail* quoted a consensus of opinion that they "could never be taken," while the assembling of the armies continued, some men waited in acute anxiety for the pattern of the German offensive to reveal itself. General Gallieni was one. "What is happening behind the German front?" he worried. "What massive concentration is gathering behind Liège? With the Germans one must always expect the gigantic."

The answer to this question was what the French cavalry under General Sordet had been sent to find out. Yet so impetuous was the dash of the cuirassiers that it carried them too far too soon. They crossed into Belgium on August 6, riding along the Meuse to reconnoiter the strength and direction of the German concentration. Covering 110 miles in three days, nearly 40 miles a day, they passed Neufchâteau and reached within nine miles of Liège. As the French did not dismount or unsaddle during halts, the horses were exhausted by the forced pace. After a day's rest, the cavalry continued their reconnaissance in the Ardennes and west of the Meuse as far as Charleroi, but everywhere they were too early to find evidence that the Germans had crossed the Meuse in any great strength, and everywhere active German cavalry screened the concentration of the armies building up behind the German border. The French found themselves foiled of the thrilling cavalry charge that was the traditional way to open wars. Although farther north where they were on the offensive toward Louvain and Brussels, the German cavalry used the shock tactics of the charge, here they avoided a direct fight and kept up an impenetrable screen, supported by cyclist battalions and Jagers in motor transport who held off the French with machine-gun fire.

It was disheartening. Cavalrymen on both sides still believed in the naked sword, the *arme blanche*, despite the experience of the American Civil War when Confederate General Morgan, employing his men as mounted infantry with rifles, would cry, "Here, boys, are those fools coming again with their sabers; give it to them!" In the Russo-Japanese War an English observer, the future General Sir Ian Hamilton, reported that the only thing the cavalry could do in the face of entrenched machine guns was to cook rice for the infantry, causing the War Office to wonder if his months in the Orient had not affected his mind. When Germany's observer in the same war, the future General Max Hoffmann, reported a similar conclusion about the defensive power of entrenched machine guns, Moltke was inspired to comment, "There never was such a crazy way of making war!"

In 1914 the Germans' avoidance of cavalry encounter and their use of machine guns proved an effective screen. Sordet's reports of no large German masses coming down on the French left confirmed GQG in its preconceived ideas. But the outlines of a German right wing envelopment were already becoming clear to King Albert and General Lanrezac who, being in its path, were more disposed to see it. Another of these was General Fournier, governor of the French fortress of Maubeuge. He informed GQG that German cavalry on August 7 had entered Huy on the Meuse and that his reports indicated they were covering an advance of five or six corps. As Huy was the site of the only bridge between Liège and Namur, this enemy force was obviously intending to cross the Meuse. Maubeuge, its governor warned, was in no condition to resist such numbers. To GQG the report of five or six corps appeared as the frightened exaggeration of a defeatist mind. Weeding out the fainthearted was for Joffre in August the most vital requirement for success and he promptly relieved General Fournier of his command. Later, after an investigation, the order was rescinded. Meanwhile it was discovered that it would take at least a fortnight to put Maubeuge in any state of effective defense.

The anxiety of General Lanrezac, who had also received the report from Huy, was increasing. On August 8 he sent his Chief of Staff, General Hély d'Oissel, to impress the threat of a German right wing outflanking movement upon GQG. General Lanrezac's concern was "premature," GQG replied, because such a movement was "out of proportion to the means at the enemy's disposal." Further evidence from Belgium kept coming in, but for each report the "chapel" of Plan 17 found an explanation: the brigades seen at Huy were on "some special mission" or the sources of information were "suspicious." The attack on Liège had for its object "nothing more" than seizure of a bridgehead there. On August 10 GQG felt "confirmed in the impression that the principal German maneuver would not take place in Belgium."

Committed to its own coming offensive, the French General Staff wanted to make sure that the Belgian Army would stand fast until it could be joined by the Fifth Army and the British. Joffre sent another emissary, Colonel Adelbert, with a personal letter from Poincaré to King Albert hoping for "concerted action" by both armies. This officer, who reached Brussels on August 11, received the same answer as his predecessors: that if a German advance straight across Belgium developed as the King foresaw, he would not permit his army to risk being cut off from Antwerp. Colonel Adelbert, an ardent apostle of *élan*, could not bring himself to transmit the King's pessimism to GQG. He was saved the necessity by a battle next day from which the Belgians emerged drenched in glory.

The Uhlans, penetrating toward Louvain, were held up at the bridge at Haelen, by the massed fire of Belgian cavalry under General de Witte. Using his troops as dismounted riflemen supported by infantry, de Witte repeated General Morgan's success in Tennessee. From eight in the morning until six in the evening his steady volleys of rifle fire repelled repeated German charges with lance and saber. Slaughtered Uhlans of von Marwitz's finest squadrons covered the ground until at last a remnant turned back, leaving the field to the Belgians. The glorious victory, heralded by happy correspondents in Brussels as the decisive battle of the war, aroused the Belgian Staff and its French friends to transports of enthusiasm; they saw themselves in Berlin. Colonel Adelbert informed GQG it could regard the "retreat of the German cavalry as final and the projected attack through central Belgium as postponed or even abandoned."

The optimism seemed justified by the continuing stand of the Liège forts. Every morning Belgian newspapers published the triumphant headline, "*Les forts tiennent toujours!*" On August 12, the same day as the Battle of Haelen, the great siege guns the Germans had been waiting for to put an end to that boast, arrived.

Liège was cut off from the outside world; when the great black weapons reached the outskirts within range of the forts, only the local inhabitants saw the advent of the monsters that to one observer looked like "overfed slugs." Their squat barrels, doubled by the recoil cylinders that grew on their backs like tumors, pointed cavernous mouths upward at the sky. By late afternoon of August 12 one of them had been set up and aimed at Fort Pontisse. Its crew, wearing padding over eyes, ears, and mouth, lay flat on their stomachs ready for the firing which was done electrically at a distance of 300 yards. At 6:30 the first detonation thundered over Liège. The shell rose in an arc 4,000 feet high and took 60 seconds to reach its target. When it hit, a great conical cloud of dust, debris, and smoke rose a thousand feet in the air. Meanwhile the Skoda 305s had also been brought up, and began bombardment of other forts, "walked in" upon their targets by artillery observers stationed in church towers and balloons. Men of the Belgian garrisons heard the shells descending with a screaming whistle, felt the detonations coming each time more nearly overhead as the aiming was corrected until, as their terror mounted, the shells exploded upon them with deafening crash and the solid steel heads smashed through the concrete. Over and over the shells came, blowing men to bits, choking them with fumes released by the charge of high explosives. Ceilings fell in, galleries were blocked, fire, gas, and noise filled the underground chambers; men became "hysterical, even mad in the awful apprehension of the next shot."

Before the guns went into action only one fort had been taken by assault. Fort Pontisse withstood forty-five shells in twenty-four hours of bombardment before it was sufficiently shattered to be taken by infantry attack on August 13. Two more forts fell that day, and by the 14th all the forts east and north of the city had fallen. Their guns were destroyed; the roads north of the city were open. The advance of von Kluck's First Army began.

The siege mortars were then moved forward to be trained on the western forts. One of the 420s was dragged through the city itself to take aim on Fort Loncin. M. Célestin Demblon, deputy of Liège, was in the Place St. Pierre when he saw coming around the corner of the square "a piece of artillery so colossal that we could not believe our eyes. . . . The monster advanced in two parts, pulled by 36 horses. The pavement trembled. The crowd remained mute with consternation at the appearance of this phenomenal apparatus. Slowly it crossed the Place St. Lambert, turned into the Place du Théâtre, then along the Boulevards de la Sauveniere and d'Avroy attracting crowds of curious onlookers along its slow and heavy passage. Hannibal's elephants could not have astonished the Romans more! The soldiers who accompanied it marched stiffly with an almost religious solemnity. It was the Belial of cannons! . . . In the Parc d'Avroy it was carefully mounted and scrupulously aimed. Then came the frightful explosion; the crowd was flung back, the earth shook like an earthquake and all the window panes in the vicinity were shattered. . . ."

By August 16 eleven of the twelve forts had fallen; only Fort Loncin still held out. In the intervals of bombardment the Germans sent emissaries under flags of truce to demand General Leman's surrender. He refused. On the 16th Loncin was hit by a shell which exploded in the magazine and blew up the fort from inside. When the Germans entered through a tumble of broken cupolas and smoking concrete they found the apparently lifeless body of General Leman pinned beneath a block of masonry. "Respect the General, he is dead," said an adjutant with blackened face who stood guard over the body. Leman was, however, alive but unconscious. Revived and carried to General von Emmich, he surrendered his sword saying: "I was taken unconscious. Be sure to put that in your dispatches."

"Military honor has not been violated by your sword," replied Emmich, handing it back. "Keep it."

Later, from Germany where he was taken a prisoner, General Leman wrote to King Albert, "I would gladly have given my life, but Death would not have me." His opponents, Generals von Emmich and Ludendorff, were both awarded the blue, white, and gold cross of *Pour le Mérite*, Germany's highest military medal, to hang around their necks.

On the day after the fall of Fort Loncin the Second and Third Armies began their advance, bringing the whole mass of the German right wing into motion on its march across Belgium. As the march had not been scheduled to begin before August 15, Liège had held up the German offensive by two days, not two weeks as the world then believed. What Belgium gave the Allies was neither two days nor two weeks but a cause and an example.

12

BEF to the Continent

Delay in covering the exposed flank on General Lanrezac's left was caused by dispute and disagreement among the British who were to have held that end of the line. On August 5, their first day of war, the General Staff's plan, worked out to the last detail by Henry Wilson, instead of going into action automatically like the continental war plans, had to be approved first by the Committee of Imperial Defence. When the Committee convened as a War Council at four o'clock that afternoon, it included the usual civilian as well as military leaders and one splendid colossus, taking his seat among them for the first time, who was both.

Field Marshal Lord Kitchener was no more happy to be the new Secretary of State for War than his colleagues were to have him. The government was nervous at having in their midst the first active soldier to enter the Cabinet since General Monck served under Charles II. The generals were worried that he would use his position, or be used by the government, to interfere with the sending of an Expeditionary Force to France. No one's apprehensions were disappointed. Kitchener promptly expressed his profound contempt for the strategy, policy, and role assigned to the British Army by the Anglo-French plan.

What exactly was to be his authority, given his position straddling two stools, was not entirely clear. England entered the war with a vague understanding that supreme authority resided in the Prime Minister but with no precise arrangement as to whose advice he was to act on or whose advice was to be definitive. Within the army, field officers despised Staff officers as "having the brains of canaries and the manners of Potsdam," but both groups were as one in their distaste for interference by civilian ministers who were known as "the frocks." The civil arm in its turn referred to the military as "the boneheads." At the War Council of August 5, the former were represented by Asquith, Grey, Churchill, and Haldane, and the army by eleven general officers, including Field Marshal Sir John French,

Commander in Chief designate of the Expeditionary Force; its two corps commanders, Sir Douglas Haig and Sir James Grierson; its Chief of Staff, Sir Archibald Murray, all lieutenant generals; and its Deputy Chief of Staff, Major General Henry Wilson, whose easy faculty for making political enemies had flourished during the Curragh crisis and lost him the higher post. In between, representing no one quite knew what, was Lord Kitchener who regarded the purpose of the Expeditionary Force with deep misgivings and its Commander in Chief without admiration. If not quite as volcanic in expressing himself as Admiral Fisher had been, Kitchener now proceeded to pour the same scorn upon the General Staff's plan to "tack on" the British Army to the tail of French strategy.

Having had no personal share in the military planning for war on the Continent, Kitchener was able to see the Expeditionary Force in its true proportions and did not believe its six divisions likely to affect the outcome in the impending clash between seventy German and seventy French divisions. Though a professional soldier—"The most able I have come across in my time," said Lord Cromer when Kitchener came out to command the Khartoum campaign—his career had lately been pursued at Olympian levels. He dealt in India, Egypt, Empire, and large concepts only. He was never seen to speak to or notice a private soldier. Like Clausewitz he saw war as an extension of policy, and took it from there. Unlike Henry Wilson and the General Staff, he was not trapped in schedules of debarkation, railroad timetables, horses, and billets. Standing at a distance he was able to view the war as a whole, in terms of the relations of the powers, and to realize the immense effort of national military expansion that would be required for the long contest about to begin.

"We must be prepared," he announced, "to put armies of millions in the field and maintain them for several years." His audience was stunned and incredulous, but Kitchener was relentless. To fight and win a European war, Britain must have an army of seventy divisions, equal to the continental armies, and he had calculated that such an army would not reach full strength until the third year of war, implying the staggering corollary that the war would last that long. The Regular Army with its professional officers and especially its NCO's, he considered to be precious and indispensable as a nucleus for training the larger force he had in mind. To throw it away in immediate battle under what he expected to be unfavorable circumstances and where, from the long view, its presence could not be decisive, he regarded as criminal folly. Once it was gone there were no troops properly trained, in his opinion, to take its place.

Lack of conscription was the most striking of all differences between the British and continental armies. The Regular Army was designed for overseas duty rather than for defense of the homeland which was left to the Territorials. Since the Duke of Wellington had laid down the unalterable dictum that recruits for foreign service "must be volunteers," Britain's war effort consequently depended on a volunteer army which left other nations uncertain as to how deeply Britain was, or would be, committed. Although Lord Roberts, the senior Field Marshal, now over seventy, had campaigned strenuously for conscription for years with one lone supporter in the Cabinet, needless to say Winston Churchill, labor was rigorously opposed and no government would have risked office to favor it. Britain's military establishment in the home islands consisted of six divisions and one cavalry division of the Regular Army, with four regular divisions totaling 60,000 men overseas, and fourteen divisions of Territorials. A Reserve of about 300,000 was divided into two classes: the Special Reserve which was barely enough to fill up the Regular Army to war strength and maintain it in the field through the first few weeks of fighting and the National Reserve which was to provide replacements for the Territorials. According to Kitchener's standards the Territorials were untrained, useless "amateurs" whom he regarded with the same unmixed scorn—and with as little justice—as the French did their Reserves, and rated them at zero.

At the age of twenty Kitchener had fought as a volunteer with the French Army in the war of 1870 and spoke French fluently. Whether or not he had, as a result, an extra sympathy for France, he was no extreme partisan of French strategy. At the time of the Agadir crisis he told the Committee of Imperial Defence that he expected the Germans to walk through the French "like partridges," and when invited he refused to take part in any decision the Committee might think fit to take. He sent them word, as Lord Esher recorded it, "that if they imagined he was going to command the Army in France he would see them damned first."

That England in 1914 gave him the War Office and thereby acquired the only man prepared to insist on organizing for a long war was not because of his opinions but because of his prestige. With no talent for the bureaucracy of administrative office and no taste for conforming to the "green baize routine" of Cabinet meetings after being accustomed to a proconsul's simple "Let it be done," Kitchener did his best to escape his fate. The government and generals, more conscious of his faults of character than of his virtues of clairvoyance, would have been glad to let him go back to Egypt but they could not do without him. He was named Secretary for War not because he was considered qualified by the holding of opinions which no one else held but because his presence was indispensable "to tranquilize public feeling."

Ever since Khartoum the country had felt an almost religious faith in Kitchener. There existed between him and the public the same mystic union that was to develop between the people of France and "Papa Joffre" or between the German people and Hindenburg. The initials "K of K" were a magic formula and his broad martial mustache a national symbol that was to England what the *pantalon rouge* was to France. Wearing its bushy magnificence with an air of power, tall and broad-shouldered, he looked like a Victorian image of Richard the Lionhearted except for something inscrutable behind the solemn blazing eyes. Beginning August 7, the mustache, the eyes and the pointing finger over the legend, "Your Country Needs YOU" were to bore into the soul of every Englishman from a famous recruiting poster. For England to have gone to war without Kitchener would have been as unthinkable as Sunday without church.

The War Council, however, put little credence in his prophecy at a moment when everyone was thinking of the immediate problem of sending the six divisions to France. "It was never disclosed," wrote Grey long afterward with perhaps needless bewilderment, "how or by what process of reasoning he made this forecast of the length of the war." Whether because Kitchener was right when everybody else was wrong or because civilians find it hard to credit soldiers with ordinary mental processes or because Kitchener was never able or never deigned to explain his reasons, all his colleagues and contemporaries assumed that he reached his conclusion, as Grey said, "by some flash of instinct rather than by reasoning."

Whatever the process, Kitchener also foretold the pattern of the coming German offensive west of the Meuse. This too he was afterward considered to have arrived at by "some gift of divination" rather than by "any knowledge of times and distances," according to one General Staff officer. In fact, like King Albert, Kitchener saw the assault on Liège casting ahead of it the shadow of Schlieffen's right-wing envelopment. He did not think Germany had violated Belgium and brought England in against her in order to make what Lloyd George had called "just a little violation" through the Ardennes. Having avoided the responsibility of the prewar planning, he could not now propose to withhold the six divisions, but he saw no reason to risk their extinction at a position as far forward as Maubeuge where he expected they would bear the full force of the invading German armies. He proposed that they concentrate instead at Amiens, seventy miles farther back.

Exasperated by this drastic change of plan with its appearance of timidity, the generals were confirmed in their worst expectations. The short, stocky, and florid Sir John French, about to take command in the field, was keyed to a pitch of valor and combativeness. His normally apoplectic expression, combined with the tight cavalryman's stock which he affected in place of collar and tie, gave him an appearance of being perpetually on the verge of choking, as indeed he often was, emotionally if not physically. When appointed Chief of the Imperial General Staff in 1912, he at once informed Henry Wilson that he intended to get the army ready for a war with Germany which he regarded as an "eventual certainty." Since then he had been nominally responsible for the joint plans with France, although in fact the French plan of campaign was practically unknown to him—as was the German. Like Joffre, he had been named head of the Staff without Staff experience or study at Staff college.

The choice, like that of Kitchener for the War Office, was less concerned with innate qualification than with rank and reputation. On the several colonial fields of battle where Britain's military reputations had been made, Sir John had shown courage and resource and what an authority called "a practical grasp of minor tactics." In the Boer War his exploits as a cavalry general, culminating in the romantic gallop through the Boer lines to the relief of Kimberley, earned him fame as a bold commander willing to take risks and a popular repute almost equal to that of Roberts and Kitchener. Since Britain's record against an untrained opponent lacking modern weapons had on the whole not been brilliant, the army was proud of and the government grateful for a hero. French's prowess, aided by social éclat, carried him far. Like Admiral Milne he moved in the Edwardian swim. As a cavalry officer he was conscious of belonging to the élite of the army. Friendship with Lord Esher was no handicap, and politically he was allied with the Liberals who came to power in 1906. In 1907 he was made Inspector General; in 1908, representing the army, he accompanied King Edward on the state visit to the Czar at Reval; in 1912 came his appointment as CIGS; in 1913 he was promoted to Field Marshal. At sixty-two he was the army's second ranking active officer after Kitchener to whom he was junior by two years although he looked older. It was generally understood that he would command the expeditionary force in the event of war.

In March 1914 when the Curragh Mutiny, crashing down upon army heads like Samson's temple, caused him to resign, he seemed to have quixotically brought his career to an abrupt end. Instead he gained added favor with the government which believed the Opposition had engineered the Mutiny. "French is a trump and I love him," wrote Grey appreciatively. Four months later when the crisis came, he was resurrected and on July 30 designated to be Commander in Chief if Britain should go to war.

Untrained to study and with a mind closed to books, at least after his early successes in action, French was less renowned for mental ability than for irritability. "I don't think he is particularly clever," King George V confided in his uncle, "and he has an awful temper." Like his vis-à-vis across the Channel, French was an unintellectual soldier with the fundamental difference that whereas Joffre's outstanding quality was solidity, French's was a peculiar responsiveness to pressures, people, and prejudices. He had, it was said, "the mercurial temperament commonly associated with Irishmen and cavalry soldiers." Joffre was imperturbable in all weathers; Sir John alternated between extremes of aggressiveness in good times and of depression in bad. Impulsive and easily swayed by gossip, he had, in the opinion of Lord Esher, "the heart of a romantic child." He once presented to his former Chief of Staff in the Boer War a gold flask inscribed as a memento of "our long and tried friendship proved in sunshine and shadow." The proved friend was the somewhat less sentimental Douglas Haig who in August 1914 wrote in his diary, "In my own heart I know that French is quite unfit for this great command at a time of crisis in our Nation's history." The knowledge in Haig's heart was not unconnected with a sense that the person best fitted for the command was himself, nor was he to rest until he obtained it.

The destination—and consequently the purpose—of the BEF having been reopened by Kitchener, the Council, who were in Henry Wilson's opinion "mostly entirely ignorant of their subjects . . . fell to discussing strategy like idiots." Sir John French suddenly "dragged in the ridiculous proposal of going to Antwerp," saying that as British mobilization was behind schedule anyway the possibility of cooperating with the Belgian Army should be considered. Haig, who like Wilson kept a diary, "trembled at the reckless way" his chief undertook to change plans. Equally upset, the new CIGS, Sir Charles Douglas, said that as everything had been arranged for landings in France and French rolling stock was set aside to transport the troops forward, any shift at the last moment would have "serious consequences."

No problem so harassed the General Staff as the unfortunate difference in capacity between French and British railroad cars. The mathematical permutations involved in transferring troops from one to the other were such as to make transport officers tremble at any threatened change of arrangements.

Happily for their peace of mind the shift to Antwerp was vetoed by Churchill who two months later was to go there himself and to conceive the bold and desperate landing of two marine brigades and a territorial division in a last-minute, vain effort to save the vital Belgian port. On August 5, however, he said the navy could not protect the troop ships over the longer route across the North Sea to the Scheldt, whereas the passage across the Strait of Dover could be guaranteed absolutely. The navy having had time to prepare for the Channel crossing, he argued that the moment was favorable and urged that all six divisions be sent at once. Haldane supported him, as did Lord Roberts. Dispute now arose over how many divisions should be sent, whether one or more should be retained until the Territorials had further time for training or until replacements could be brought home from India.

Kitchener returned to his idea of staging at Amiens, and received support from his friend and future commander of the Gallipoli campaign, Sir Ian Hamilton who, however, felt it was urgent for the BEF to reach there as soon as possible. Grierson spoke up for "decisive numbers at the decisive point." Sir John French, most forward of the forward, suggested that "we should go over at once and decide destination later." It was agreed to order transports for all six divisions immediately while leaving destination to be settled until a representative of the French General Staff, sent for hurriedly at Kitchener's insistence, could arrive for further consultation on French strategy.

Within twenty-four hours, as the result of an invasion scare that brewed up overnight, the Council changed its mind and reduced the six divisions to four. News of the discussion about the strength of the BEF had leaked out. The influential *Westminster Gazette*, organ of the Liberals, denounced the "reckless" denuding of the country. From the opposite camp Lord Northcliffe came roaring in to protest the departure of a single soldier. Although the Admiralty confirmed the conclusion of the Committee of Imperial Defence in 1909 that no serious invasion was possible, visions of hostile landings on the east coast would not vanish. To the intense disgust of Henry Wilson, Kitchener, who was now responsible for England's safety, brought home to England one division that had been scheduled to embark for France directly from Ireland and detached two brigades from other divisions which he sent to guard the east coast, thus "hopelessly messing up our plans." It was decided to send four divisions and the cavalry at once—embarkation to begin August 9—to send the 4th Division later and to keep the 6th Division in England. When the Council adjourned, Kitchener was under the impression, not shared by the generals, that Amiens had been agreed upon as the staging area.

When Colonel Huguet arrived, hastily sent over by the French General Staff, Wilson informed him of the embarkation times. Although it was hardly a matter to be kept secret from the BEF's French hosts, he incurred Kitchener's wrath and a rebuke for breach of secrecy. Wilson "answered back," having, as he wrote, "no intention of being bullied" by Kitchener, "especially when he talks such nonsense as he did today." So began, or was aggravated, a mutually cherished antipathy that was not to aid the fortunes of the BEF. Wilson, who of all the British officers had the most intimate relation with the French and the ear of Sir John French, was considered bumptious and presumptuous, and was consequently ignored by Kitchener, while in his turn Wilson professed to consider Kitchener "mad" and as "much an enemy of England as Moltke," and instilled his iniquities into the mind of the temperamentally suspicious and excitable Commander in Chief.

From August 6 to 10, while the Germans at Liège were waiting for the siege guns and the French were liberating and losing Mulhouse, 80,000 troops of the BEF with 30,000 horses, 315 field guns, and 125 machine guns were assembling at Southampton and Portsmouth. Officers' swords had been freshly sharpened in obedience to an order that prescribed sending them to the armorer's shop on the third day of mobilization, although they were never used for anything but saluting on parade. But apart from such occasional nostalgic gestures the force, in the words of its official historian, was "the best-trained, best organized and best-equipped British Army that ever went forth to war."

On August 9 embarkation began, the transports departing at intervals of ten minutes. As each left its dock every other ship in the harbor blew whistles and horns and every man on deck cheered. So deafening was the noise that it seemed to one officer that General von Kluck could not fail to hear it behind Liège. However, with the navy confident that they had sealed off the Channel from attack, there was little fear for the safety of the crossing. The transports crossed at night without escort.

Waking at 4:30 in the morning, a soldier was astonished to see the whole fleet of transports with engines stopped, floating on an absolutely glassy sea without a destroyer in sight; they were waiting for transports from other embarkation ports to complete a rendezvous in mid-Channel.

When the first arrivals landed at Rouen they were received with as much rapture, said a French witness, as if they had come to conduct a service of expiation for Joan of Arc. At Boulogne others debarked at the foot of a towering column erected in honor of Napoleon on the spot from which he had planned to launch the invasion of England. Other transports came into Havre where the French garrison climbed on the roofs of their barracks and cheered wildly as their allies came down the gangplanks in the blazing heat. That evening, to the sound of far-off summer thunder, the sun went down in a blood-red glow.

In Brussels next day the British ally was at last glimpsed—though narrowly. Hugh Gibson, secretary of the American Legation, on an errand to the British military attaché, walked into his room unannounced and saw a British officer in field uniform, dirty and unshaven, writing at a desk. Hustled out by the attaché, Gibson asked irreverently if the rest of the British Army was hidden in the building. In fact the location of the British landings was so well kept from the Germans that they were not to know where or when the BEF had arrived until they ran into it at Mons.

In England antipathies among its commanders were coming to the surface. The King on a visit of inspection asked Haig, who was an intimate at court, his opinion of Sir John French as Commander in Chief. Haig felt it his duty to reply that "I had grave doubts whether either his temper was sufficiently even or his military knowledge sufficiently thorough to enable him to be an effective commander." After the King had left, Haig wrote in his diary that Sir John's military ideas during the Boer War had "often shocked me," and added his "poor opinion" of Sir Archibald Murray, an "old woman" who "weakly acquiesces" in orders which his better judgment tells him are unsound in order to avoid scenes with Sir John's temper. Neither, thought Haig, "are at all fitted for the appointments which they now hold." Sir John, he told a fellow officer, would not listen to Murray but "will rely on Wilson which is far worse." Wilson was not a soldier but "a politician," a word which, Haig explained, was "synonymous with crooked dealing and wrong values."

Unburdening himself of these sentiments, the smooth, polished, immaculate, and impeccable Haig, who had friends in all the right quarters and at fifty-three a career of unbroken success behind him, was preparing his way to further success ahead. As an officer who during the campaign in the Sudan had included "a camel laden with claret" in the personal pack train that followed him across the desert, he was accustomed to doing himself well.

On August 11, within three days of departing for France, Sir John French learned for the first time some interesting facts about the German Army. He and General Callwell, Deputy Director of Operations, visited Intelligence, whose chief began telling them about the German system of using reserves. "He kept on producing fresh batches of Reserve Divisions and Extra-Reserve Divisions," wrote Callwell, "like a conjuror producing glassfuls of goldfish out of his pocket. He seemed to be doing it on purpose—one felt quite angry with the man." These were the same facts that the Deuxième Bureau, French Intelligence, had learned in the spring of 1914, too late to impress the General Staff or change its estimate of the German right wing. They also came too late to change the British mind. For a new idea to penetrate and effect a fundamental change in strategy, as well as in all the infinite physical details of deployment, would have required time, far more time than was left.

Next day the struggle over strategy between Kitchener and the generals was fought out at a final meeting of the Council. Besides Kitchener, Sir John French, Murray, Wilson, Huguet, and two other French officers were present. Although Kitchener could not hear, unless with the mind's ear, the exploding shells of the 420s opening the roads through Liège, he asserted that the Germans would be coming through on the far side of the Meuse "in great force." With a sweep of his arm he indicated the German enveloping movement on a huge wall map. If the BEF concentrated at Maubeuge, he argued, it would be swamped before it was ready for battle and be forced into a retreat which would be disastrous for its morale in its first encounter with a European enemy since the Crimea. He insisted on a base further back at Amiens to allow freedom of action.

His six opponents, the three English and three French officers, were equally adamant on keeping to the original plan. Sir John French, coached by Wilson since his own suggestion of a shift to Antwerp, now protested that any change would "upset" the French plan of campaign, and remained determined to go forward to Maubeuge. The French officers emphasized the necessity of filling in the left end of their line. Wilson inwardly raged at the "cowardice" of concentrating at Amiens. Kitchener said the French plan of campaign was dangerous; that instead of taking the offensive, to which he was "entirely opposed," they should wait to counter a German attack. For three hours the wrangle continued until Kitchener, unconvinced, was gradually forced to give way. The plan had been in existence and he had known and fundamentally disapproved of it for five years. Now, with the troops already on the water, it had to be accepted because there was no time to make another.

In a last futile gesture—or a calculated gesture to absolve himself of responsibility—Kitchener, bringing Sir John French along with him, took the issue to the Prime Minister. "Knowing nothing at all about it," as Wilson confided to his diary, Asquith did what might be expected. Presented with Kitchener's views as against the expert and united opinion of the combined General Staffs, he accepted the latter. Reduced to four instead of six divisions, the BEF went forward as arranged. The momentum of predetermined plans had scored another victory.

Kitchener, nevertheless, unlike the French and German ministers of war, retained direction of his country's military effort, and the instructions he now issued to Sir John French for the conduct of the BEF in France reflected his desire to limit its liability in the early stages of the war. Like Churchill who, looking ahead to the vast task of the British Navy, had ordered the Mediterranean fleet both to engage the *Goeben* and avoid engaging "superior forces," Kitchener, looking ahead to the army of millions he had to build, assigned a policy and a mission to the BEF irreconcilable with each other.

"The special motive of the Force under your control," he wrote, "is to support and cooperate with the French Army . . . and to assist the French in preventing or repelling the invasion by Germany of French or Belgian territory." With a certain optimism, he added, "and eventually to restore the neutrality of Belgium"—a project comparable to restoring virginity. As the "numerical strength of the British force and its contingent reinforcement is strictly limited," and keeping this consideration "steadily in view," it will be necessary to exercise "the greatest care towards a minimum of loss and wastage." Reflecting Kitchener's disapproval of French offensive strategy, his order stated that if asked to participate in any "forward movements" in which the French were not engaged in large numbers and in which the British might be "unduly exposed to attack," Sir John was to consult his government first and must "distinctly understand that your command is an entirely independent one and that you will in no case come in any sense under the orders of any Allied general."

Nothing could be more unequivocal. At one stroke Kitchener had canceled the principle of unity of command. His motive was to preserve the British Army as a nucleus for the future; the effect, given a captain of Sir John's temperament, was practically to nullify the order to "support" and "cooperate" with the French. It was to haunt the Allied war effort long after Sir John was replaced and Kitchener himself was dead.

On August 14 Sir John French, Murray, Wilson, and a staff officer, encouragingly named Major Sir Hereward Wake, arrived at Amiens, where the British troops detrained for further advance to the concentration area around Le Cateau and Maubeuge. On that day as they began moving up, Kluck's Army began moving down from Liège. The BEF, marching cheerfully up the roads to Le Cateau and Mons, were greeted enthusiastically along the way with cries of "*Vivent les Anglais!*" The happiness of the welcome gave point to Lord Kitchener's dampening notice to his troops that they might expect to "find temptations, both in wine and women," which they must "entirely resist." The farther north the British marched, the greater was the enthusiasm. They were kissed and decked with flowers. Tables of food and drink were set out and all British offers of pay refused. A red tablecloth with bands of white sewn on it to form the St. Andrew's cross of the Union Jack was flung over a balustrade. The soldiers tossed their regimental badges, caps, and belts to smiling girls and other admirers who begged for souvenirs. Soon the British Army was marching with peasants' tweed caps on their heads and their trousers held up by string. All along the way, wrote a cavalry officer afterward, "we were feted and cheered by the people who were soon to see our backs." Looking back on it, he remembered the advance of the BEF to Mons as "roses all the way."

13

Sambre et Meuse

On the Western Front the fifteenth day brought an end to the period of concentration and preliminary attacks. The period of offensive battle began. The French right wing, opening the offensive into German-occupied Lorraine, took an old embattled path like so many in France and Belgium where, century after century, whatever the power that makes men fight brought legions tramping down the same roads, leveling the same villages. On the road east from Nancy the French passed a stone marker inscribed, "Here in the year 362 Jovinus defeated the Teutonic hordes."

While on the far right the Army of General Pau renewed the offensive in Alsace, the First and Second Armies of Generals Dubail and de Castelnau marched through two natural corridors in Lorraine which determined the French line of attack. One led toward Sarrebourg, objective of Dubail's Army; the other descending from the ring of hills around Nancy called the Grand Couronné, led via Château Salins into a valley terminating in the natural fortress of Morhange, objective of de Castelnau's Army. The Germans had prepared the region against expected French attack with barbed wire, trenches, and gun emplacements. At both Sarrebourg and Morhange they had well-fortified positions from which they could only be dislodged by an attack of irresistible *élan* or bombardment by heavy artillery. The French counted on the first and scorned the second.

"Thank God we don't have any!" replied a General Staff artillery officer in 1909 when questioned about 105 mm. heavy field artillery. "What gives the French Army its force is the lightness of its cannon." In 1911 the War Council proposed to add 105s to the French Army, but the artillery men themselves, faithful to the famous French 75s, remained unalterably opposed. They despised the heavy field cannon as drags upon the mobility of the French offensive and regarded them, like machine guns, as defensive weapons. Messimy as War Minister and General Dubail, then on the General Staff, had forced through an appropriation for several batteries of 105s, but through changes of government and the continued contempt of the artillery corps, by 1914 only a few had been incorporated into the French Army.

On the German side the Lorraine front was held by the Sixth Army of Rupprecht, Crown Prince of Bavaria, and by the Seventh Army of General von Heeringen which on August 9 was placed under Prince Rupprecht's orders. Rupprecht's mission was to hold as many French troops on his front as possible in order to keep them away from the main front opposite the German right wing. He was to accomplish this, according to Schlieffen's strategy, by falling back and drawing the French forward into a "sack" where, having lengthened their line of communications, they could be engaged in battle while the decision took place elsewhere. The essence of the plan was to let the enemy in this sector come on as he showed every disposition to do and, while tempting him into a tactical victory, inflict upon him a strategic defeat.

Like the plan for East Prussia, this strategy involved psychological dangers. In the hour when the trumpets sounded, when his fellow commanders were advancing to victory, it required Rupprecht to accept obediently the necessity of withdrawal, not a pleasing prospect to a vigorous commander with an appetite for glory, especially not to one of semi-royal rank.

Erect and good-looking in a disciplined way, with straightforward eyes and a sensible mustache, Rupprecht had no touch about him of his capricious predecessors, the two King Ludwigs of Bavaria whose several and excessive passions, one for Lola Montez and the other for Richard Wagner, had caused one king to be deposed and the other to be declared mad. He came in fact from a less eccentric branch of the family which had provided the regent for the mad king, and as a direct descendant of Henrietta, daughter of Charles I of England, was legitimist Stuart heir to the English throne. In memory of King Charles, white roses decorated the palace of Bavaria every year on the anniversary of the regicide. Rupprecht had a more current Allied connection in the person of his wife's sister Elizabeth who was married to King Albert of Belgium. The Bavarian Army, however, was thoroughly German. They were "barbarians," reported General Dubail after the first days of battle, who before evacuating a town sacked the houses in which they had been billeted, ripped up the chairs and mattresses, scattered the contents of closets, tore down curtains, smashed and trampled furniture, ornaments, and utensils. These, however, were as yet only the habits of troops sullenly retiring. Lorraine was to see worse.

For the first four days of Dubail's and Castelnau's offensive, the Germans retired slowly according to plan, fighting only rearguard action against the French. Down the broad straight roads bordered with plane trees the French came in their blue coats and red trousers. At every rise in the road they could see great distances over the checkerboard of fields, one green with alfalfa, the next gold with ripe grain, another brown, already plowed for the next crop, others dotted with haystacks in neat rows. The 75s spoke with piercing shriek over the fields as the French entered the territory that had once been theirs. In the first combats against a not too determined German resistance the French were victorious, although the German heavy artillery, when used, tore terrible gaps in their lines. General Dubail on August 15 passed carts bringing back the wounded, pale and mangled, some with limbs blown off. He saw a battlefield of the previous day still strewn with corpses. On the 17th the XXth Corps of de Castelnau's army, commanded by General Foch, took Château Salins and reached within striking distance of Morhange. On the 18th Dubail's army took Sarrebourg. Confidence soared; *offensive à outrance* appeared to have triumphed; the troops exulted and saw themselves on the Rhine. At that moment Plan 17 began to crumble, had, indeed, been crumbling for many days.

On the front opposite Belgium, General Lanrezac had all this time been hammering at GQG for permission to face north into the oncoming German right instead of northeastward for the offensive into the Ardennes against the German center. He saw himself being enveloped by the German forces coming down west of the Meuse whose true strength he suspected, and he insisted on being allowed to shift a part of his army to the left bank of the Meuse into the angle with the Sambre where it could block the German path. Here he could hold a line along the Sambre, the river that rises in northern

France and flows northeast through Belgium, edging the mining district of the Borinage, to join the Meuse at Namur. Along its banks rise cone-shaped slag heaps; coal barges ply its waters coming out of Charleroi, city of the kingly name that ever after 1914 would have for French ears a sound as mournful as Sedan.

Lanrezac bombarded GQG with reports from his own reconnaissance of German units and movements which indicated a mass pouring through on either side of Liège in hundreds of thousands, perhaps 700,000, "maybe even two million." GQG insisted the figures must be wrong. Lanrezac argued that strong German forces would come down on his flank through Namur, Dinant, and Givet just at the time the Fifth Army would be entering the Ardennes. When his Chief of Staff, Hély d'Oissel, whose normally melancholy demeanor was growing daily more somber, came to GQG to plead his case, the officer who received him cried: "What, again! Is your Lanrezac still worrying about being flanked on his left? That won't happen and"—he added, voicing GQG's basic thesis—"if it does, why so much the better."

Nevertheless, though determined to let nothing detract from the main offensive planned to start on August 15, GQG could not be entirely impervious to the mounting evidence of an enveloping maneuver by the German right wing. On August 12 Joffre permitted Lanrezac to move his left corps to Dinant. "High time," Lanrezac muttered caustically, but the move no longer sufficed, he insisted; his whole army must be shifted westward. Joffre refused, insisting the Fifth Army must remain oriented eastward to perform its appointed role in the Ardennes. Always jealous of his authority, he told Lanrezac, "The responsibility of stopping the enveloping movement is not yours." Exasperated, like all men of rapid mind at the blindness of others and accustomed to respect as a strategist, Lanrezac continued to hector GQG. Joffre grew irritated at his constant criticism and contentiousness. He conceived the whole duty of generals was to be lions in action and dogs in obedience, an ideal to which Lanrezac, with a mind of his own and an urgent sense of danger, found it impossible to conform. "My inquietude," he wrote later, "increased from hour to hour." On

August 14, the last day before the opening of the offensive, he went in person to Vitry.

He found Joffre in his office buttressed by Generals Belin and Berthelot, his Chief and Assistant Chief of Staff. Belin, once known for his vivacity, was already showing the strain of overwork. Berthelot, quick and clever, like his opposite number, Henry Wilson, was an inveterate optimist who found it temperamentally difficult to anticipate trouble. He weighed 230 pounds and, having early conceded the victory of August heat over military dignity, worked in blouse and slippers. Lanrezac, whose dark Creole face was already sagging with worry, insisted the Germans would appear on his left just when he would be deep in the Ardennes where the difficult terrain made quick success unlikely and a turnabout impossible. The enemy would be left to complete his enveloping maneuver unopposed.

Speaking in what Poincaré called his "creamy tones," Joffre told Lanrezac that his fears were "premature." He added, "We have the impression the Germans have nothing ready there"—"there" meaning west of the Meuse. Belin and Berthelot repeated the assurance of "nothing ready there" and endeavored at once to soothe and encourage Lanrezac. He was urged to forget about envelopment and think only of the offensive. He left GQG, as he said, "with death in my soul."

On his return to Fifth Army headquarters at Rethel on the edge of the Ardennes he found on his desk a report from GQG Intelligence which compounded his sense of doom. It estimated an enemy force across the Meuse of eight army corps and four to six cavalry divisions—in fact an underestimate. Lanrezac instantly sent an aide with a letter to Joffre calling his attention to these reports "coming from your own headquarters" and insisting that the movement of the Fifth Army to the region between Sambre and Meuse should be "studied and prepared from this moment."

Meanwhile at Vitry another visitor arrived in deep anxiety to try to convince GQG of the danger on the left. When Joffre had refused to have Gallieni at Headquarters, Messimy had given him an office in the War Ministry where all reports were channeled to him. Although these did not include Intelligence reports from GQG which Joffre systematically refrained from sending to the government, Gallieni had gathered enough information to detect the outlines of the great flood pouring down upon France. It was the "terrible submersion" that Jaurès, foreseeing the use of reserves in the front line, had predicted. Gallieni told Messimy he must go to Vitry to make Joffre alter his plans, but Messimy who was nearly twenty years Joffre's junior and stood in awe of him said Gallieni must go himself as one to whom Joffre owed much of his career and whom he could not ignore. That was underestimating Joffre who could ignore anyone he chose. When Gallieni arrived, Joffre gave him only a few minutes and passed him on to Belin and Berthelot. They repeated the assurances they had given Lanrezac. GQG had its mind "closed to the evidence" and refused to consider the German advance west of the Meuse a serious threat, Gallieni reported to Messimy on his return.

Yet that evening, under pressure of increasing evidence, GQG began to waver. Joffre, replying to Lanrezac's last urgent message, agreed to "study" the proposed shift of the Fifth Army and to permit "preliminary arrangements" for the movement, although he still insisted that the menace to Lanrezac's flank was "far from immediate and its certainty far from absolute." By next morning, August 15, it had come much closer. GQG, with every nerve wound up for the great offensive, looked apprehensively to the left. A telephone call was put through to Lanrezac at 9:00 A.M. authorizing him to prepare the movement but not to execute it without direct order of the Commander in Chief. During the day reports reached GQG that 10,000 German cavalry had crossed the Meuse at Huy; then another report came that the enemy was attacking Dinant and had seized the citadel commanding the city from the high rock of the right bank; then a further report that they had forced a crossing but had been met by Lanrezac's Ist Corps pouring down from the left bank who had driven them back across the bridge in fierce combat (in which one of the first casualties was a twenty-four-year-old lieutenant named Charles de Gaulle). This was the corps whose movement across the river had been authorized on August 12.

The menace on the left could no longer be minimized. At 7:00 P.M. Joffre's direct order to move the Fifth Army into the angle of Sambre and Meuse was telephoned to Lanrezac, followed by his written order an hour later. GQG had succumbed —but not wholly. The order—Special Instruction No. 10—changed plans just far enough, it was felt, to meet the threat of envelopment but not so far as to give up the offensive of Plan 17. It acknowledged that the enemy "seems to be making his main effort by his right wing north of Givet"—as if Lanrezac needed to be told—and ordered the main body of the Fifth Army to move northwest "to operate together with the British and Belgian armies against the enemy forces to the north." One corps of the Fifth Army was to remain facing northeast in support of the Fourth Army to whom the chief burden of carrying the offensive into the Ardennes was now transferred. In effect the order stretched out the Fifth Army to the west over a wider front than heretofore without added men to cover it.

Order No. 10 instructed the new spearhead, General de Langle de Cary, commander of the Fourth Army, to make ready for attack "in the general direction of Neufchâteau," that is, into the heart of the Ardennes. To strengthen the fighting quality of his army, Joffre set in motion a complicated exchange of troops between the armies of de Castelnau, Lanrezac, and de Langle. As a result, two corps which had trained under Lanrezac were taken from him and replaced by others new to his command. Although the new units included the two highly valued divisions from North Africa which the *Goeben* had tried to halt, the extra movements and last-minute changes aggravated Lanrezac's bitterness and despair.

While the rest of the French Army charged to the east, he saw himself left to guard France's unprotected flank from the blow he believed was designed to kill her. He saw himself given the heaviest task—though GQG refused to recognize it as such —with the smallest means. His temper was not improved by the prospect of operating in common with two independent armies—the British and Belgian—whose commanders outranked him and were unknown to him. His men must execute in the August heat a march of eighty miles requiring five days, and even if they reached the line of the Sambre before the Germans did he feared it might be too late. By then the Germans would have reached it in too great strength to be stopped.

Where were the British who were supposed to be on his left? So far no one had laid eyes on them. Though he could have learned from GQG exactly where they were, Lanrezac no longer put any faith in GQG and suspected darkly that France was the victim of a perfidious British trick. Either the BEF was a myth or it was playing out a last cricket match before joining the war, and he refused to believe in its existence unless it was seen personally by one of his own officers. Daily scouting parties which included Lieutenant Spears, British liaison officer with the Fifth Army, were sent out to scour the countryside but failed to find any men in khaki, a strange functioning of liaison which Lieutenant Spears in a famous book leaves unexplained. The failure added to Lanrezac's sense of peril. Anxieties pressed upon him. "My anguish," he wrote, "rose to its peak."

At the same time as he issued Order No. 10 Joffre asked Messimy to transfer three Territorial divisions from coast defense to fill the space between Maubeuge and the Channel. He was scraping the bottom of the barrel for a makeshift defense against the German right wing rather than subtract a single division from his cherished offensive. Not yet was he ready to acknowledge that the enemy's will was being imposed on him. Not all the Lanrezacs, Gallienis, and reconnaissance reports in the world could shake GQG's central conviction that the greater the German right wing, the more promising the prospects for the French seizure of initiative through the center.

The German march through Belgium, like the march of predator ants who periodically emerge from the South American jungle to carve a swath of death across the land, was cutting its way across field, road, village, and town, like the ants unstopped by rivers or any obstacle. Von Kluck's Army poured through north of Liège and von Bülow's south of the city, along the valley of the Meuse, toward Namur. "The Meuse is a precious necklace," King Albert had said, "and Namur is its pearl." Flowing through a broad canyon between rocky heights set back a space from the river on either side, the Meuse was a vacationland where in every other August, the traditional month of vacation, families picnicked, little boys swam, men fished from the banks under sun umbrellas, mothers sat in folding chairs knitting, little white sailboats tacked and skimmed, and the excursion boat ran from Namur to Dinant. Part of von Bülow's army was now crossing the river at Huy halfway between Liège and Namur to advance along both banks upon the second of Belgium's famed fortresses. Namur's circle of forts, constructed in the same pattern as those of Liège, was the last bastion before France. With confidence in the iron fist of the siege guns which had done their work so well at Liège and were now being dragged in von Bülow's train toward their second assignment, the Germans expected to be through Namur in three days. On von Bülow's left the Third Army commanded by General von Hausen was advancing upon Dinant so that the two armies were converging upon the angle of the Sambre and Meuse just as Lanrezac's army was heading into it. While in the field Schlieffen's strategy was unrolling on schedule, behind the front a jagged crack appeared in the design.

On August 16 OHL, which had remained in Berlin until the end of the concentration period, moved to Coblenz on the Rhine some eighty miles behind the center of the German front. Here Schlieffen had envisaged a Commander in Chief who would be no Napoleon on a white horse watching the battle from a hill but a "modern Alexander" who would direct it "from a house with roomy offices where telegraph, telephone and wireless signalling apparatus are at hand, while a fleet of autos and motorcycles ready to depart, wait for orders. Here in a comfortable chair by a large table the modern commander overlooks the whole battlefield on a map. From here he telephones inspiring words and here he receives the reports from army and corps commanders and from balloons and dirigibles which observe the enemy's movements."

Reality marred this happy picture. The modern Alexander turned out to be Moltke who by his own admission had never recovered from his harrowing experience with the Kaiser on the first night of war. The "inspiring words" he was supposed to telephone to commanders were never part of his equipment and even if they had been would have been lost in transmission. Nothing caused the Germans more trouble, where they were operating in hostile territory, than communications. Belgians cut telephone and telegraph wires; the powerful Eiffel Tower wireless station jammed the air waves so that messages came through so garbled they had to be repeated three or four times before sense could be made of them. OHL's single receiving station became so clogged that messages took from eight to twelve hours to get through. This was one of the "frictions" the German General Staff, misled by the ease of communications in war games, had not planned for.

The wickedly unobliging resistance of the Belgians and visions of the Russian "steam roller" crashing through East Prussia further harassed OHL. Friction developed in the Staff. The cult of arrogance practiced by Prussian officers affected no one more painfully than themselves and their allies. General von Stein, Deputy Chief of Staff, though admittedly intelligent, conscientious, and hard-working, was described by the Austrian liaison officer at OHL as rude, tactless, disputatious, and given to the sneering, domineering manner known as the "Berlin Guards' tone." Colonel Bauer of the Operations Section hated his chief, Colonel Tappen, for his "biting tone" and "odious manner" toward subordinates. Officers complained because Moltke refused to allow champagne at mess and because fare at the Kaiser's table was so meager it had to be supplemented with private sandwiches after dinner.

From the moment the French attack began in Lorraine, Moltke's resolve to carry through Schlieffen's total reliance upon the right wing began to slip. He and his staff expected the French to bring up their main forces on their left to meet the threat of the German right wing. As anxiously as Lanrezac sent out scouts looking for the British, OHL looked for evidence of strong French movements west of the Meuse, and up to August 17 found none. That vexing problem of war presented by the refusal of the enemy to behave as expected in his own best interest beset them. They concluded from the movement in Lorraine and the lack of movement on the west that the French were concentrating their main force for an offensive through Lorraine between Metz and the Vosges. They asked themselves if this did not require a readjustment of German strategy. If this were the main French attack could not the Germans, by a shift of forces to their own left wing, bring about a decisive battle in Lorraine before the right wing could accomplish it by envelopment? Could they not in fact accomplish a true Cannae, the double envelopment that Schlieffen had held in the back of his mind? Anxious discussions of this alluring prospect and even some preliminary shifting of the weight of gravity toward the left engaged OHL from August 14 to 17. On that date they decided that the French were not massing in Lorraine to the extent believed, and reverted to the original Schlieffen plan.

But once divinity of doctrine has been questioned there is no return to perfect faith. From then on, OHL was lured by opportunity on the left wing. Mentally, Moltke had opened his mind to an alternative strategy dependent on what the enemy would do. The passionate simplicity of Schlieffen's design for total effort by one wing and rigid cleaving to plan regardless of enemy movements was broken. The plan that had appeared so faultless on paper cracked under pressure of the uncertainties, above all the emotions, of war. Having deprived himself of the comfort of a prearranged strategy, Moltke was thereafter tormented by indecisiveness whenever a decision was required. On August 16 Prince Rupprecht required one urgently.

He wanted permission to counterattack. His headquarters at Saint-Avold, a dreary, undistinguished town sunk in a hollow on the edge of the dingy mining district of the Saar, offered no princely amenities, no château for his lodging, not even a Grand Hotel. Westward stretched before him a land of easy rolling hills under wide open skies with no obstacles of importance before the Moselle, and, glowing on the horizon, the prize—Nancy, jewel of Lorraine.

Rupprecht argued that his given task to engage as many French troops as possible on his front could best be accomplished by attacking, a theory exactly contrary to the strategy of the "sack." For three days, from August 16 to 18, discussion raged over the telephone wire, happily all in German territory, between Rupprecht's headquarters and General Headquarters. Was the present French attack their main effort? They appeared to be doing nothing "serious" in Alsace or west of the Meuse. What did this indicate? Suppose the French refused to come forward and fall into the "sack"? Suppose Rupprecht continued to retire, would not a gap be opened up between him and the Fifth Army, his neighbor to the right, and would not the French attack through there? Might this not bring defeat to the right wing? Rupprecht and his Chief of Staff, General Krafft von Dellmensingen, contended that it would. They said their troops were impatiently awaiting the order to attack, that it was difficult to restrain them, that it would be shameful to force retreat upon troops "champing to go forward"; moreover, it was unwise to give up territory in Lorraine at the very outset of the war, even temporarily, unless absolutely forced to.

Fascinated yet frightened, OHL could not decide. A Staff major named Zollner was sent to Sixth Army Headquarters at Saint-Avold to discuss it further in person. He said OHL was considering a change in the planned retirement but could not give up the sack maneuver completely. He returned with nothing settled. Hardly had he gone when an airplane reconnaissance report was received of local French movements backward toward the Grand Couronné which were "immediately interpreted" by the Sixth Army Staff as evidence that the enemy was not coming forward into the sack after all and therefore the best thing to do was to attack him as quickly as possible.

Matters were at a crisis. More telephone conversations ensued between Rupprecht and von Krafft at one end and von Stein and Tappen at the other. Another messenger from OHL, Major Dommes, arrived—this was on August 17—with news that made a counteroffensive appear more desirable than ever. He said OHL was now sure the French were transferring troops to their western wing and were not "tied" to Lorraine; he reported the success of the siege guns at Liège which made the French fortress line look less formidable; he said OHL now believed the English had not yet landed on the Continent and, if a decisive battle could be quickly fought here in Lorraine, they might never come at all. But of course, said Major Dommes, he was obliged by Moltke's instructions to warn of all the hazards of a counteroffensive of which the chief and overwhelming one was that it would be a frontal attack—that anathema of German military doctrine—with envelopment impossible because of the mountains and the French fortresses.

Rupprecht retorted that there was less risk in attack than in further retreat, that he would take the enemy by surprise and might unbalance him, that he and his staff had considered all the risks and intended to master them. Working himself up with another eloquent ode to the offensive spirit of his gallant troops who must not be required to withdraw further, he announced he had made up his mind to attack unless he received a definite order from OHL prohibiting him. "Either let me attack," he shouted, "or issue definite orders!"

Confounded by the Prince's "forceful tone," Dommes hurried away to OHL for further instructions. At Rupprecht's headquarters "we waited, wondering if we would receive the prohibiting order." They waited all morning of the 18th, and when no word had come by afternoon von Krafft telephoned to von Stein demanding to know if an order was to be expected. Once again all the advantages and all the misgivings were thrashed over. Out of patience, von Krafft asked for a Yes or No. "Oh, no, we won't oblige you by forbidding an attack," von Stein replied with something less than the authority of a modern Alexander. "You must take the responsibility. Make your decision as your conscience tells you."

"It is already made. We attack!"

"*Na!*" answered von Stein, using a vernacular expression implying a shrug, "then strike and God be with you!"

Thus the sack maneuver was abandoned. The order was given for the Sixth and Seventh Armies to turn around and prepare for the counteroffensive.

Meanwhile the British, whom the Germans supposed not to have landed, were moving up toward their designated position on the left end of the French line. The continued rapturous greeting of the French populace sprang less from any deep love of the British, their antagonists for centuries, than from an almost hysterical thankfulness at the appearance of an ally in the struggle that was life or death for France. To the British soldiers, kissed, fed, and bedecked with flowers, it seemed like a celebration, a huge party of which they were unaccountably the heroes.

Their pugnacious Commander in Chief, Sir John French, disembarked on August 14 with Murray, Wilson, and Huguet who was now attached to the British command as liaison officer. They spent the night in Amiens and went to Paris next day to meet the President, Premier, and Minister of War. "*Vive le*

Général French!" cried the delirious crowd of 20,000 who packed the square in front of the Gare du Nord and lined the streets. "'Eep, 'eep, 'ooray! *Vive l'Angleterre! Vive la France!*" All along the route to the British Embassy crowds, said to be greater than those who greeted Blériot when he flew the Channel, cheered and waved in happy welcome.

Poincaré was surprised to find his visitor a man of "quiet manner . . . not very military in appearance" with a drooping mustache whom one would take for a plodding engineer rather than the dashing cavalry commander of his reputation. He seemed slow and methodical without much *élan* and, despite his French son-in-law and a summer home in Normandy, able to speak few words of recognizable French. He proceeded to horrify Poincaré by announcing that his troops would not be ready to take the field for ten days, that is, until August 24. This was at a time when Lanrezac already feared that August 20 might be too late. "How we have been misled!" Poincaré wrote in his diary. "We thought them ready down to the last button and now they will not be at the rendezvous!"

In fact a puzzling change had come over the man whose most notable qualification for command, apart from seniority and the right friends, had been until now his military ardor. From the moment he landed in France Sir John French began to exhibit a preference for the "waiting attitude," a curious reluctance to bring the BEF to action, a draining away of the will to fight. Whether the cause was Kitchener's instructions with their emphasis on keeping the army in being and their caution against risking "losses and wastage," or whether it was a sudden realization percolating into Sir John French's consciousness that behind the BEF was no national body of trained reserves to take its place, or whether on reaching the Continent within a few miles of a formidable enemy and certain battle the weight of responsibility oppressed him, or whether all along beneath his bold words and manner the natural juices of courage had been invisibly drying up, or whether, fighting on foreign soil for someone else's homeland, it was simply a feeling of limited liability, no one who has not been in the same position can judge.

What is certain is that from the start Sir John French's meetings with his Allies left them variously disappointed, startled, or outraged. The immediate purpose for which the BEF had come to France—to prevent her being crushed by Germany—appeared to escape him, or at least he seemed to react to it with no sense of urgency. He appeared to think that his independence of command, which Kitchener had so stressed, meant he could "choose his own hours for fighting and his hours of resting," as Poincaré put it, indifferent to the possibility that the Germans might overrun France in the meantime, making any further question of fighting obsolete. As the inescapable Clausewitz had pointed out, an allied army operating under independent command is undesirable, but if unavoidable it is at least essential that its commander "should not be the most prudent and cautious but the most *enterprising*." During the next three weeks, the most critical of the war, the reason for Clausewitz's italics was to become clear.

Next day, August 16, Sir John visited GQG at Vitry where Joffre discovered him to be "firmly attached to his own ideas" and "anxious not to compromise his army." Sir John French in his turn was not impressed, owing perhaps to a British officer's sensitivity to social background. The struggle to republicanize the French Army had produced an unfortunate proportion, from the British point of view, of officers who were not "gentlemen." "*Au fond*, they are a low lot," Sir John wrote to Kitchener some months later, "and one always has to remember the class these French generals mostly come from." Indubitably the French generalissimo was the son of a tradesman.

On this occasion Joffre politely but urgently expressed his desire that the BEF should go into action on the Sambre along with Lanrezac on August 21. Contrary to what he had told Poincaré, Sir John French said he would do his best to meet this date. He requested that, as he was to hold the exposed end of the French line, Joffre should place Sordet's cavalry and two reserve divisions "directly under my orders." Joffre, needless to say, refused. Reporting the visit to Kitchener, Sir John French said he was "much impressed" by General Berthelot and the Staff, who were "deliberate, calm and confident" and exhibited a "total absence of fuss and confusion." He expressed no opinion of Joffre beyond noting that he seemed to realize the value of a "waiting attitude," a curious and self-revealing misjudgment.

The next visit was to Lanrezac. The taut temper at Fifth Army Headquarters appeared in Hély d'Oissel's first greeting to Huguet when he drove up in a car with the long-sought British officers, on the morning of August 17: "At last you're here. It's not a moment too soon. If we are beaten, we'll owe it to you."

General Lanrezac appeared on the steps to greet his visitors whose appearance in the flesh did not dispel lingering suspicions that he was being tricked by officers without divisions. Nothing said in the ensuing half-hour did much to reassure him. Speaking no English and his vis-à-vis no useful French, the two generals retired to confer alone without interpreters, a procedure of such dubious value that to explain it as done out of a mania for secrecy, as suggested by Lieutenant Spears, seems hardly adequate. They emerged shortly to join their staffs, of whom several were bilingual, in the Operations Room. Sir John French peered at the map, put on his glasses, pointed to a spot on the Meuse, and attempted to ask in French whether General Lanrezac thought the Germans would cross the river at that point which bore the virtually unpronounceable name Huy. As the bridge at Huy was the only one between Liège and Namur and as von Bülow's troops were crossing it as he spoke, Sir John French's question was correct if superfluous. He stumbled first over the phrase "cross the river" and had to be prompted by Henry Wilson who supplied "*traverser la fleuve*," but when he came to "*à Huy*," he faltered again.

"What does he say? What does he say?" Lanrezac was asking restively.

". . . *à Hoy*" Sir John French finally managed to bring out, pronouncing it as if he were hailing a ship.

It was explained to Lanrezac that the British Commander in Chief wished to know if he thought the Germans would cross the Meuse at Huy. "Tell the Marshal," replied Lanrezac, "I think the Germans have come to the Meuse to fish." His tone, which he might have applied to some particularly dim-witted question at one of his famous lectures, was not one customarily used toward the Field Marshal of a friendly army.

"What does he say? What does he say?" Sir John French, catching the tone if not the meaning, asked in his turn.

"He says they are going to cross the river, sir," Wilson answered smoothly.

In the mood engendered by this exchange, misunderstandings flourished. Billets and lines of communication, an inevitable source of friction between neighboring armies, produced the first one. There was a more serious misunderstanding about the use of cavalry, each commander wanting the use of the other's for strategic reconnaissance. Sordet's tired and half-shoeless corps which Joffre had assigned to Lanrezac had just been pulled away again on a mission to make contact with the Belgians north of the Sambre in the hope of persuading them not to retreat to Antwerp. Lanrezac was in dire need—as were the British—of information about the enemy's units and line of march. He wanted use of the fresh British cavalry division. Sir John French refused it. Having come to France with only four divisions instead of six, he wished to hold the cavalry back temporarily as reserve. Lanrezac understood him to say he intended employing it as mounted infantry in the line, a contemptible form of activity which the hero of Kimberley would as soon have used as a dry-fly fisherman would use live bait.

Most serious of all was the dispute over the date when the BEF would be ready for action. Although on the previous day he had told Joffre he would be ready by the 21st, Sir John French now reverted, either out of pure pique or from the uncertain state of his nerves, to what he had told Poincaré, that he would not be ready until the 24th. To Lanrezac it was the final affliction. Did the British General suppose the enemy would wait for him? he wondered, although not aloud. Obviously, as he had known from the start, the British were not to be relied on. The interview closed "with flushed faces." Afterward Lanrezac informed Joffre that the British would not be ready "until the 24th at the earliest," that their cavalry were to be used as mounted infantry and "cannot be counted on for any other purpose," and raised the question of possible confusion with the British along the roads, "in the event of retirement." The phrase produced a shock at GQG. Lanrezac, the "veritable lion" of admired aggressiveness, was already considering the possibility of retreat.

Sir John French also received a shock upon arriving at his headquarters, temporarily at Le Cateau, where he learned that the commander of his IInd Corps, his good friend General Grierson, had died suddenly that morning in the train near Amiens. French's request to Kitchener for a particular general to replace Grierson—"please do as I ask you in this matter," he wrote—was refused. Kitchener sent out General Sir Horace Smith-Dorrien with whom French had never got on, both being opinionated men. Like Haig, Smith-Dorrien had no great respect for the Commander in Chief and tended to act on his own initiative. Sir John French took out his resentment of Kitchener's choice in a heightened aversion to Smith-Dorrien and vented it, when all was over, in that sad and twisted document he entitled *1914* which a distinguished reviewer was to call "one of the most unfortunate books ever written."

At Belgian Army Headquariers in Louvain on August 17, the day when Sir John French was meeting Lanrezac and Rupprecht was demanding permission to counterattack, Premier de Broqueville came to discuss with King Albert the question of removing the government from Brussels to Antwerp. Detachments of all arms of von Kluck's army, outnumbering the Belgians four or five to one, were reported attacking the Belgian line at the river Gette 15 miles away; 8,000 troops of von Bülow's army were reported crossing the bridge at Huy, 30 miles away, and heading for Namur. If Liège had fallen what could Namur do? The period of concentration was over, the main German advance was on its way, and as yet the armies of Belgium's guarantors had not come. "We are alone," the King said to de Broqueville. The Germans, he concluded, would probably overrun central Belgium and occupy Brussels and "the final issue of events is still uncertain." It was true that the French cavalry was expected that day in the area of Namur. Joffre, when informing King Albert of their mission, had assured him that in the best opinion of GQG the German units west of the Meuse were merely a "screen." He had promised that further French divisions would soon arrive to cooperate with the Belgians against the enemy. King Albert did not think the Germans at the Gette and at Huy were a screen. The mournful decision for the government to leave the capital was taken. On August 18 the King also ordered a general retreat of the army from the Gette to the fortified camp of Antwerp and the removal of Headquarters from Louvain fifteen miles back to Malines.

The order produced "incredulous dismay" among the forward school of the Belgian General Staff and especially in the bosom of Colonel Adelbert, President Poincaré's personal representative. Energetic and brilliantly qualified for the offensive in war, he was "less so" for diplomatic missions, ruefully admitted the French Minister to Belgium.

"You are not going to retreat before a mere cavalry screen?" exploded Colonel Adelbert. Astounded and angry, he accused the Belgians of "abandoning" the French without warning just at "the precise moment when the French cavalry corps had appeared north of the Sambre and Meuse." The military consequences, he said, would be grave, the moral success to the Germans great, and Brussels would be uncovered to "raids by German cavalry." This was his appreciation of the enemy strength that two days later was to take Brussels with over a quarter of a million men. However wrong his judgment and rude his tongue, Colonel Adelbert's anguish, from the French point of view, was understandable. Retirement to Antwerp meant that the Belgian Army would withdraw from the flank of the Allied line and break off contact with the French on the eve of the great French offensive.

During the day of August 18 the King's decision was changed several times in the agony of indecision between desire to save the Belgian Army from annihilation and reluctance to give up good positions just when French help might be arriving. Before the day was over the King's dilemma was solved for him by Joffre's Order No. 13 of that date which made it clear that the main French effort was to be made in another direction, leaving Belgium to guard the passage west of the Meuse with what assistance could be obtained from the Fifth Army and the British. King Albert hesitated no more. He reconfirmed the order for retreat to Antwerp, and that night the five Belgian divisions were disengaged from their positions on the Gette and withdrawn to the Antwerp camp, which they reached on August 20.

Joffre's Order No. 13 was the "get ready" signal for the great offensive through the German center upon which all French hopes were set. It was addressed to the Third, Fourth, and Fifth Armies and communicated to the Belgians and British. It instructed the Third and Fourth Armies of Generals Ruffey and De Langle de Cary to prepare to attack through the Ardennes and left two alternatives open to the Fifth Army, depending upon final appreciation of German strength west of the Meuse. In one case Lanrezac was to attack northward across the Sambre "in complete liaison with the Belgian and British armies"; in the other case, supposing the enemy engaged "only a fraction of his right wing group" west of the Meuse, Lanrezac was to recross the river and support the main offensive through the Ardennes, "leaving to the Belgian and British armies the task of dealing with the German forces north of the Sambre and Meuse."

It was an impossible instruction. It required Lanrezac's army—not a unit but a heterogeneous mass of three corps and seven separate divisions stretched over an area thirty miles wide—which was then in motion on its way up to the Sambre, to face two ways and in the second alternative to return to the original deployment which Lanrezac had so painfully succeeded in turning it away from only three days ago. It could have paralyzed Lanrezac and left him stock-still, waiting for Joffre to choose one alternative or the other. Instead, the phrase "only a fraction of his right wing" sealed his loss of confidence in GQG. Ignoring the second alternative he pushed on to the Sambre. He would be in position by August 20, he informed Joffre, to counterattack any enemy forces attempting to cross the river between Namur and Charleroi and "to throw them back into the Sambre."

Moving toward that rendezvous his battalions sang the "Sambre et Meuse," a memorial of 1870 and favorite marching song of the French Army:

> The regiment of Sambre and Meuse marched to the cry of Liberty!
> Seeking the path of glory that leads to immortality.
> The regiment of Sambre and Meuse died to the cry of Liberty!
> Writing a page of glory that gave them immortality.

What dictated Order No. 13 was GQG's fixed determination to carry through Plan 17, the bearer of all its hopes for victory by decisive battle. In August when the war was young the idea that it could be brought to a quick finish by decisive battle still prevailed. GQG firmly believed that however strong the German right wing, a French offensive through the German center would succeed in isolating and destroying it. That night Messimy, in "anguish" about the weakly defended frontier below the Sambre, telephoned to Joffre and was told the Generalissimo was asleep. His awe greater than his anguish, Messimy agreed that he should not be awakened. Berthelot said to him comfortingly, "If the Germans commit the imprudence of an enveloping maneuver through northern Belgium, so much the better! The more men they have on their right wing, the easier it will be for us to break through their center."

On that day the German right wing was making its wheel through Belgium with von Kluck's army on the outside advancing upon Brussels, von Bülow's in the middle advancing upon Namur, and von Hausen's on the inside advancing on Dinant. Namur, held by the Belgian 4th Division and garrison troops, stood alone, still generally regarded, despite what had happened at Liège, as an impregnable fortress. Even those who took heed of Liège thought Namur would at least hold out long enough to allow Lanrezac to cross the Sambre, make contact with its defenders, and pin his forces to the rim of Namur's circle of forts. Commandant Duruy, a former military attaché in Brussels who was sent as liaison officer to Namur, gloomily reported to Lanrezac on August 19 that he did not believe the fortress could hold for long. Cut off from the rest of their army, the defenders were low in morale as well as in ammunition. Though his views were disputed by many, Duruy remained adamant in his pessimism.

On August 18 von Kluck's leading troops reached the Gette where they found themselves foiled of the Belgian Army. The destruction of that army was von Kluck's task. He had hoped to accomplish it by driving through between the Belgians and Antwerp and rounding them up before they could reach the safety of their base. He was too late. King Albert's withdrawal saved his army and kept it in being to become a menace to von Kluck's rear when later he turned south for the march on Paris. "They always managed to escape our grasp so that their army has not been decisively beaten nor forced away from Antwerp," von Kluck was obliged to report to OHL.

He must shortly make his southward turn not only with the Belgians at his rear but with a new enemy, the British, in front of him. The Germans had worked it out that the logical place for the British to land would be at the ports nearest to the front in Belgium, and von Kluck's cavalry reconnaissance, with that marvelous human capacity to see what you expect to see even if it is not there, duly reported the British to be disembarking at Ostend, Calais, and Dunkirk on August 13. This would have brought them across von Kluck's front at almost any moment. In fact, of course, they were not there at all but were landing farther down the coast at Boulogne, Rouen, and Havre. The Ostend report, however, caused OHL to worry that as von Kluck made his southward turn his right might be attacked by the British, and if he swung his left to meet them a gap might be opened between his army and von Bülow's. To prevent such danger OHL on August 17 put von Kluck, to his extreme annoyance, under the orders of von Bülow. How it was possible for OHL to act on a report that the British were landing at Ostend and on the same day to tell Rupprecht that the British had not yet landed and might not come at all is one of the curiosities of war which can only be explained by conjecture. Perhaps the staff officers at OHL who dealt with the left wing were a different group from those who dealt with the right wing, and failed to consult each other.

The commanders of the First and Second Armies were both within two years of seventy. Von Kluck, a strange, dark, fierce-looking man, hardly looked his age, in contrast to von Bülow with his white mustache and puffy face who looked more than his. Von Kluck, who had been wounded in the war of 1870 and acquired his ennobling "von" at the age of fifty, had been chosen before the war for the leading role in the march on Paris. His was the army that was supposed to be the hammer-head of the right wing, his that was to regulate the pace of the whole, his that had been given the greatest striking power with a density of 18,000 men per mile of front (about 10 per meter) compared to 13,000 for von Bülow and 3,300 for Rupprecht.

But haunted by the specter of a gap, OHL thought that von Bülow in the center of the right wing would be in the best position to keep its three armies abreast of each other. Von Kluck, bitterly resenting the arrangement, promptly disputed von Bülow's orders for each day's march, causing such havoc, what with the garbled communications, that after ten days OHL was forced to rescind the order—whereupon a gap was indeed to open up, beyond recall.

The Belgians even more than von Bülow tried von Kluck's temper. Their army by forcing the Germans to fight their way through delayed the schedule of march and by blowing up railroads and bridges disrupted the flow of ammunition, food, medicine, mail, and every other supply, causing the Germans a constant diversion of effort to keep open their lines to the rear. Civilians blocked roads and worst of all cut telephone and telegraph wires which dislocated communication not only between the German armies and OHL but also between army and army and corps and corps. This "extremely aggressive guerrilla warfare," as von Kluck called it, and especially the sniping by *franc-tireurs* at German soldiers, exasperated him and his fellow commanders. From the moment his army entered Belgium he found it necessary to take, in his own words, "severe and inexorable reprisals" such as "the shooting of individuals and the burning of homes" against the "treacherous" attacks of the civil population. Burned villages and dead hostages marked the path of the First Army. On August 19 after the Germans had crossed the Gette and found the Belgian Army withdrawn during the night, they vented their fury on Aerschot, a small town between the Gette and Brussels, the first to suffer a mass execution. In Aerschot 150 civilians were shot. The numbers were to grow larger as the process was repeated, by von Bülow's army at Ardennes and Tamines, by von Hausen's in the culminating massacre of 664 at Dinant. The method was to assemble the inhabitants in the main square, women usually on one side and men on the other, select every tenth man or every second man or all on one side, according to the whim of the individual officer, march them to a nearby field or empty lot behind the railroad station and shoot them. In Belgium there are many towns whose cemeteries today have rows and rows of memorial stones inscribed with a name, the date 1914, and the legend, repeated over and over: "*Fusillé par les Allemands*" (Shot by the Germans). In many are newer and longer rows with the same legend and the date 1944.

General von Hausen, commanding the Third Army, found, like von Kluck, that the "perfidious" conduct of the Belgians in "multiplying obstacles" in his path called for reprisals "of the utmost rigor without an instant's hesitation." These were to include "the arrest as hostages of notables such as estate-owners, mayors, and priests, the burning of houses and farms and the execution of persons caught in acts of hostility." Hausen's army were Saxons whose name in Belgium became synonymous with "savage." Hausen himself could not get over the "hostility of the Belgian people." To discover "how we are hated" was a constant amazement to him. He complained bitterly of the attitude of the D'Eggremont family in whose luxurious château of forty rooms, with greenhouses, gardens, and stable for fifty horses, he was billeted for one night. The elderly Count went around "with his fists clenched in his pockets"; the two sons absented themselves from the dinner table; the father came late to dinner and refused to talk or even respond to questions, and continued in this unpleasant attitude in spite of Hausen's gracious forbearance in ordering his military police not to confiscate the Chinese and Japanese weapons collected by Count d'Eggremont during his diplomatic service in the Orient. It was a most distressing experience.

The German campaign of reprisals was not, except individually, a spontaneous answer to Belgian provocation. It had been prepared ahead of time, with usual German care for every contingency, and was designed to save time and men by cowing the Belgians quickly. Speed was essential. It was also essential to enter France with every available battalion; Belgian resistance which required troops to be left behind interfered with this objective. Proclamations were printed in advance. As soon as the Germans entered a town its walls became whitened, as if by a biblical plague, with a rash of posters plastered on every house warning the populace against acts of "hostility." The punishment for civilians firing on soldiers was death, as it was for a variety of minor acts: "Any one approaching within 200 meters of an airplane or balloon post will be shot on the spot." Owners of houses where hidden arms were discovered would be shot. Owners of homes where Belgian soldiers were found hidden would be sent to "perpetual" hard labor in Germany. Villages where acts of "hostility" were committed against German soldiers "will be burned." If such an act took place "on the road between two villages, the same methods will be applied to the inhabitants of both."

In summary the proclamations concluded: "For all acts of hostility the following principles will be applied: all punishments will be executed without mercy, the whole community will be regarded as responsible, hostages will be taken in large numbers." This practice of the principle of collective responsibility, having been expressly outlawed by the Hague Convention, shocked the world of 1914 which had believed in human progress.

Von Kluck complained that somehow the methods employed "were slow in remedying the evil." The Belgian populace continued to show the most implacable hostility. "These evil practices on the part of the population ate into the very vitals of our Army." Reprisals grew more frequent and severe. The smoke of burning villages, the roads clogged with fleeing inhabitants, the mayors and burgomasters shot as hostages were reported to the world by the crowds of Allied, American, and other neutral correspondents who, barred from the front by Joffre and Kitchener, flocked to Belgium from the first day of war. A remarkable group of masters of vivid writing, the Americans included Richard Harding Davis for a syndicate of papers, Will Irwin for *Collier's*, Irwin Cobb for the *Saturday Evening Post*, Harry Hansen for the *Chicago Daily News*, John T. McCutcheon for the *Chicago Tribune*, and others. Securing credentials from the German Army, they followed along with it. They wrote of the debris of sacked houses, the blackened villages in which no human was left but only a silent cat on a shattered doorstep, the streets strewn with broken bottles and broken windowpanes, the agonized lowing of cows with unmilked udders, the endless files of refugees with their bundles and wagons and carts and umbrellas for sleeping on rainy nights along the roadside, of the fields of grain bending over with ripeness and no one to reap them, of the questions asked over and over: "Have you seen the French? Where are the French? Where are the British?" A rag doll lying on the road with its head squashed flat by the wheel of a gun carriage seemed to one American correspondent a symbol of Belgium's fate in the war.

On August 19 as the fusillade of shots cracked through Aerschot twenty-five miles away, Brussels was ominously quiet. The government had left the day before. Flags still decked the streets refracting the sun through their red and yellow fabric. The capital in its last hours seemed to have an extra bloom, yet to be growing quieter, almost wistful. Just before the end the first French were seen, a squadron of weary cavalry riding slowly down the Avenue de la Toison d'Or with horses' heads drooping. A few hours later four motorcars filled with officers in strange khaki uniforms drove by. People stared and raised a feeble cheer: "*Les Anglais!*" Belgium's Allies had come at last —too late to save her capital. On the 19th refugees continued to stream in from the east. The flags were being taken down; the populace had been warned; there was a menace in the air.

On August 20 Brussels was occupied. Squadrons of Uhlans moving with lances at the ready appeared suddenly in the streets. They were but the heralds of a grim parade, almost unbelievable in power and grandeur, that followed. It began at one o'clock with column after column of gray-green infantry, shaved and brushed with freshly shined boots and bayonets glinting in the sun and their ranks closed to eliminate the gaps left by the missing. The cavalry appeared in the same gray-green with black and white pennants fluttering from their lances like horsemen riding out of the Middle Ages. The phalanx of their innumerable hoofs clattering in close order seemed capable of trampling to death anything in their path. Heavy guns of the artillery thundered over the cobblestones. Drums pounded. Hoarse voices in chorus roared the victory song, "Heil dir im Siegeskranz," to the tune of "God Save the King." On and on, more and more, brigade after brigade, they came. Silent crowds watching the parade were stupefied by its immensity, its endlessness, its splendid perfection. The exhibition of equipment designed to awe the onlookers accomplished its object. Drawn by four horses, the kitchen wagons with fires lighted and chimneys smoking were no less astonishing than the trucks fitted out as cobblers' shops with cobblers standing at their benches hammering at bootsoles, and soldiers whose boots were being repaired standing on the running boards.

The parade kept to one side of the boulevards so that staff officers in motorcars and messengers on bicycles could dash up and down the line of march. Cavalry officers provided a varied show, some smoking cigarettes with careless hauteur, some wearing monocles, some with rolls of fat at the back of their necks, some carrying English riding crops, all wearing expressions of studied scorn. Hour after hour the march of the conquerors continued, all through the afternoon and evening, all that night and into the next day. For three days and three nights the 320,000 men of von Kluck's army tramped their way through Brussels. A German Governor-General took possession; the German flag was raised on the Town Hall; the clocks were put on German time; and an indemnity of 50,000,000 francs ($10,000,000) payable within ten days was imposed upon the capital and 450,000,000 francs ($90,000,000) upon the province of Brabant.

In Berlin, upon news of the fall of Brussels, bells rang out, shouts of pride and gladness were heard in the streets, the people were frantic with delight, strangers embraced, and "a fierce joy" reigned.

France on August 20 was not to be deterred from her offensive. Lanrezac had reached the Sambre, and the British were on a level with him. Sir John French after all his seesawing now assured Joffre he would be ready to go into action next day. But there was bad news from Lorraine. Rupprecht's counteroffensive had begun with tremendous impact. Castelnau's Second Army, unbalanced by the loss of the corps which Joffre had transferred to the Belgian front, was retreating, and Dubail reported being severely attacked. In Alsace, against greatly reduced German forces, General Pau had retaken Mulhouse and all the surrounding region, but now that Lanrezac's move to the Sambre had pulled away strength from the central offensive Pau's troops were needed to take their places in the line. In Joffre's sore need the decision was taken to withdraw Pau's forces: even Alsace, the greatest sacrifice, was to be laid on the altar of Plan 17. Although, like the iron mines of Briey, Alsace was expected to be regained with victory, General Pau's despair speaks through the lines of his last proclamation to the people he had just liberated. "In the north the great battle begins which will decide the fate of France and with it that of Alsace. It is there that the Commander in Chief summons all the forces of the nation for the decisive attack. For us in deep chagrin it becomes necessary to leave Alsace, momentarily, to assure her final deliverance. It is a cruel necessity to which the Army of Alsace and its Commander have had pain in submitting and to which they would never have submitted except in the last extremity." Afterward all that remained in French hands was a tiny wedge of territory around Thann where Joffre came in November and said simply, bringing tears to a silent crowd, "*Je vous apporte le baiser de la France.*" Final deliverance of the rest of Alsace was to wait four long years.

On the Sambre where Lanrezac was to take the offensive next day, "The 20th was an exciting day for the troops," in the words of Lieutenant Spears. "There was crisis in the air. Not a man but felt that a great battle was at hand. The morale of the Fifth Army was extremely high. . . . They felt certain of success." Their commander was less so. General d'Amade, commander of the group of three Territorial divisions which Joffre, as a last-minute gesture, had sent around to the left of the British, was also disquieted. In answer to a query he addressed to GQG, General Berthelot replied: "Reports on German forces in Belgium are greatly exaggerated. There is no reason to get excited. The dispositions taken at my orders are sufficient for the moment."

At three o'clock that afternoon General de Langle de Cary of the Fourth Army reported enemy movements across his front and asked Joffre if he should not begin the offensive at once. At GQG the conviction reigned firmly that the greater the movements to the German right, the thinner its center. "I understand your impatience," Joffre replied, "but in my opinion the time to attack is not yet. . . . The more the region [of the Ardennes] is depleted at the moment we pass to the offensive, the better the results to be anticipated from the advance of the Fourth Army supported by the Third. It is therefore, of the utmost importance that we allow the enemy to flow by us to the northwest without attacking him prematurely."

At nine that night he judged the time had come, and issued the order to the Fourth Army to begin the offensive at once. It was the hour of *élan*. To Messimy, Joffre reported as night fell on August 20, "There is reason to await with confidence the development of operations."

14

Debacle: Lorraine, Ardennes, Charleroi, Mons

"It is a glorious and awful thought," wrote Henry Wilson in his diary on August 21, "that before the week is over the greatest action the world has ever heard of will have been fought." As he wrote, the action had already begun. From August 20 to 24 the whole of the Western Front blazed with battle—in reality, four battles—known to history collectively as the Battle of the Frontiers. Beginning on the right in Lorraine where the fighting had been in progress since August 14, results were communicated all along the frontier so that the issue in Lorraine had effect on Ardennes and Ardennes on Sambre-and-Meuse (known as the Battle of Charleroi) and Charleroi on Mons.

By morning of August 20 in Lorraine the First Army of General Dubail and the Second Army of General de Castelnau had battered themselves to bruised and bloody punishment against the prepared defenses of the Germans at Sarrebourg and Morhange. *Offensive à outrance* found its limit too soon against the heavy artillery, barbed wire, and entrenched machine guns of the defense. In prescribing the tactics of assault, French Field Regulations had calculated that in a dash of 20 seconds the infantry line could cover 50 meters before the enemy infantry would have time to shoulder guns, take aim, and fire. All these "gymnastics so painfully practised at maneuvers," as a French soldier said bitterly afterward, proved grim folly on the battlefield. With machine guns the enemy needed only 8 seconds to fire, not 20. The Field Regulations had also calculated that shrapnel fired by the 75s would "neutralize" the defensive by forcing the enemy to keep his head down and "fire into the blue." Instead, as Ian Hamilton had warned from the Russo-Japanese War, an enemy under shrapnel fire if entrenched behind parapets could continue to fire through loopholes straight at the attacker.

Despite setbacks both French generals ordered an advance for August 20. Unsupported by artillery barrage their troops threw themselves against the German fortified line. Rupprecht's counterattack, which OHL had not had the nerve to deny him, opened the same morning with murderous artillery fire that tore gaping holes in the French ranks. Foch's XXth Corps of Castelnau's army formed the spearhead of the attack. The advance faltered before the defenses of Morhange. The Bavarians, whose ardor Rupprecht had been so loath to repress, attacking in their turn, plunged forward into French territory where, as soon as someone raised the cry of "*franc-tireurs!*" they engaged in a frenzy of looting, shooting, and burning. In the ancient town of Nomeny in the valley of the Moselle between Metz and Nancy, fifty civilians were shot or bayoneted on August 20, and what remained of its houses, after half had been shattered by artillery, were burned by order of Colonel von Hannapel of the 8th Bavarian Regiment.

Heavily engaged along its entire front, Castelnau's army was now strongly attacked on its left flank by a German detachment from the garrison of Metz. With his left giving way and all his reserves already thrown in, Castelnau realized all hope of advance was gone, and broke off battle. Defensive—the forbidden word, the forbidden idea—had to be recognized as the only choice. Whether he recognized, as Plan 17's most passionate critic suggests he should have, that the duty of the French Army was not to attack but to defend French soil, is doubtful. He ordered a general retreat to the defensive line of the Grand Couronné because he had to. On his right Dubail's First Army, in spite of severe casualties, was holding its ground and had even made an advance. When its left flank was uncovered by Castelnau's retreat, Joffre ordered the First Army to retire in conformity with its neighbor. Dubail's "repugnance" at having to give up territory taken after seven days of battle was strong, and his old antipathy to Castelnau was not softened by a withdrawal which he felt "the position of my army in no way required."

Although the French did not yet know it, the slaughter at Morhange snuffed out the bright flame of the doctrine of the offensive. It died on a field in Lorraine where at the end of the day nothing was visible but corpses strewn in rows and sprawled in the awkward attitudes of sudden death as if the place had been swept by a malignant hurricane. It was one of those lessons, a survivor realized afterward, "by which God teaches the law to kings." The power of the defense that was to transform the initial war of movement into a four-year war of position and eat up a generation of European lives revealed itself at Morhange. Foch, the spiritual father of Plan 17, the man who taught, "There is only one way of defending ourselves—to attack as soon as we are ready," was there to see and experience it. For four more years of relentless, merciless, useless killing the belligerents beat their heads against it. In the end it was Foch who presided over victory. By then the lesson learned proved wrong for the next war.

On August 21 General de Castelnau heard that his son had been killed in the battle. To his staff who tried to express their sympathy, he said after a moment's silence, in a phrase that was to become something of a slogan for France, "We will continue, gentlemen."

Next day the thunder of Rupprecht's heavy artillery, like the hoofs of an approaching stampede, sounded ceaselessly. Four thousand shells fell on Ste. Geneviève, near Nomeny, in a bombardment lasting seventy-five hours. Castelnau believed the situation so serious as possibly to require retreat behind the Grand Couronné, yielding Nancy. "I went to Nancy on the 21st," Foch wrote afterward; "they wanted to evacuate it. I said the enemy is five days from Nancy and the XXth Corps is there. They won't walk over the XXth without protest!" Now the metaphysics of the lecture hall became the "*Attaquez!*" of the battlefield. Foch argued that with the fortified line at their backs, the best defense was counterattack, and won his point. On August 22 he saw an opportunity. Between the French fortified zones of Toul and Epinal there was a natural gap called the Trouée de Charmes where the French had expected to canalize the German attack. Reconnaissance showed that Rupprecht by taking the offensive toward Charmes was exposing his flank to the Army of Nancy.

Rupprecht's movement had been decided in another of the fateful telephone conversations with OHL. The success of the German left-wing armies in throwing back the French from Sarrebourg and Morhange had two results: it brought Rupprecht the Iron Cross, First *and* Second Class—a relatively harmless result—and it revived OHL's vision of a decisive battle in Lorraine. Perhaps, after all, frontal attack could be mastered by German might. Perhaps Epinal and Toul would prove as vulnerable as Liège, and the Moselle no more a barrier than the Meuse. Perhaps, after all, the two armies of the left wing could succeed in breaking through the French fortified line and in cooperation with the right wing bring about a true Cannae—a double envelopment. As reported by Colonel Tappen, this was the prospect that shone before the eyes of OHL. Like the smile of a temptress, it overcame years of single, wedded devotion to the right wing.

While the idea was being breathlessly discussed by Moltke and his advisers, a call came through from General Krafft von Dellmensingen, Rupprecht's Chief of Staff, who wanted to know whether the attack was to continue or come to a halt. It had always been assumed that once Rupprecht's armies contained the initial French offensive and stabilized their front, they would halt, organize their defenses, and free all available forces to reinforce the right wing. An alternative known as Case 3, however, had been carefully provided which allowed for an attack across the Moselle, but only at the express order of OHL.

"We must definitely know how the operation is to continue," Krafft demanded. "I assume Case 3 is in order."

"No, no!" replied Colonel Tappen, the Chief of Operations. "Moltke hasn't decided yet. If you hold the line for five minutes I may be able to give you the orders you want." In less than five minutes he returned with a surprising answer, "Pursue direction Epinal."

Krafft was "stunned." "In those few minutes I felt that one of the most consequential decisions of the war had been made."

"Pursue direction Epinal" meant offensive through the Trouée de Charmes. It meant committing the Sixth and Seventh Armies to frontal attack upon the French fortress line instead of keeping them available for reinforcement of the right wing. Rupprecht duly attacked with vigor next day, August 23. Foch counterattacked. In the days that followed, the German Sixth and Seventh Armies locked themselves in combat against the French First and Second Armies, backed by the guns of

Belfort, Epinal, and Toul. While they strained, other battles were being fought.

Failure of the offensive in Lorraine did not daunt Joffre. Rather, he saw in Rupprecht's violent counterattack deeply engaging the German left wing the right moment to unleash his own offensive against the German center. It was *after* learning of Castelnau's retreat from Morhange that Joffre on the night of August 20 gave the signal for attack in the Ardennes, the central and basic maneuver of Plan 17. At the same time as the Fourth and Third Armies entered the Ardennes, he ordered the Fifth Army to take the offensive across the Sambre against the enemy's "northern group"—GQG's term for the German right wing. He gave the order even though he had just learned from Colonel Adelbert and Sir John French that support for this offensive from the Belgians and the British would not be forthcoming as expected. The Belgian Army—except for one division at Namur—had broken off contact, and the British Army, according to its commander, would not be ready for three or four days. Besides this change in circumstances, the battle in Lorraine had revealed dangerous errors in fighting performance. These had been recognized as early as August 16 when Joffre issued instructions to all army commanders on the necessity of learning "to await artillery support" and of preventing the troops from "hastily exposing themselves to the enemy's fire."

Nevertheless France was committed to Plan 17 as her only design for decisive victory, and Plan 17 demanded the offensive —now and no later. The only alternative would have been to change at once to defense of the frontiers. In terms of the training, the planning, the thinking, the spirit of the French military organism, this was unthinkable.

Moreover GQG was convinced that the French Armies would have numerical superiority in the center. The French Staff could not release itself from the grip of the theory that had dominated all its planning—that the Germans were bound to be thinned out in the center. In that belief Joffre gave the order for the general offensive in the Ardennes and on the Sambre for August 21.

The terrain of the Ardennes is not suitable for the offensive.

It is wooded, hilly, and irregular, with the slope running generally uphill from the French side and with the declivities between the hills cut by many streams. Caesar, who took ten days to march across it, described the secret, dark forest as a "place full of terrors," with muddy paths and a perpetual mist rising from the peat bogs. Much of it had since been cleared and cultivated; roads, villages, and two or three large towns had replaced Caesar's terrors, but large sections were still covered with thick leafy woods where roads were few and ambush easy. French staff officers had examined the terrain on several tours before 1914 and knew its difficulties. In spite of their warnings the Ardennes was chosen as the place of breakthrough because here, at the center, German strength was expected to be least. The French had persuaded themselves of the feasibility of the ground on the theory that its very difficulty made it, as Joffre said, "rather favorable to the side which, like ourselves, had inferiority of heavy artillery but superiority of field guns." Joffre's memoirs, despite constant use of the pronoun "I," were compiled and written by a staff of military collaborators, and represent a careful and virtually official version of the dominant thinking of the General Staff before and during 1914.

On August 20 GQG, assuming the reported enemy movements across the front to be German units heading for the Meuse, envisaged the Ardennes as relatively "depleted" of the enemy. As Joffre intended to make his attack a surprise, he forbade infantry reconnaissance which might make contact and cause skirmishes with the enemy before the main encounter. Surprise was indeed achieved—but the French took their share of it.

The bottom corner of the Ardennes meets France at the upper corner of Lorraine where the Briey iron region is located. The area had been occupied by the Prussian Army in 1870. The ore of Briey not having then been discovered, the region had not been included in that part of Lorraine annexed by Germany. The center of the iron region was Longwy on the banks of the Chiers, and the honor of taking Longwy had been reserved for the Crown Prince, commander of the German Fifth Army.

At thirty-two, the imperial scion was a narrow-chested, willowy creature with the face of a fox who did not at all resemble his five sturdy brothers whom the Empress at annual intervals had presented to her husband. William, the Crown Prince, gave an impression of physical frailty and, in the words of an American observer, "only ordinary mental calibre"—unlike his father. Like him a poseur, fond of striking attitudes, he suffered from the compulsory filial antagonism usual to the eldest sons of kings, and expressed it in the usual manner: political rivalry and private dissipation. He had made himself the patron and partisan of the most aggressive militarist opinion, and his photograph was sold in the Berlin shops carrying the inscription, "Only by relying on the sword can we gain the place in the sun that is our due but that is not voluntarily accorded to us." Despite an upbringing intended to prepare him for military command, his training had not quite reached the adequate. It included colonelcy of the Death's Head Hussars and a year's service on the General Staff but had not included either a divisional or corps command. Nevertheless the Crown Prince felt that his experience with the Staff and on Staff rides in the last few years "gave me the theoretical grounding for command of large units." His confidence would not have been shared by Schlieffen who deplored the appointment of young, inexperienced commanders. He feared they would be more interested to go dashing off on a "*wilde Jagd nach dem Pour le Mérite*"—a wild hunt after the highest honor—than to follow the strategic plan.

The role of the Crown Prince's Fifth Army, together with the Fourth Army under the Duke of Württemberg, was to be the pivot of the right wing, moving slowly forward at the center as the right wing swung out and down in its great enveloping sweep. The Fourth Army was to advance through the northern Ardennes against Neufchâteau while the Fifth Army advanced through the southern Ardennes against Virton and the two French fortress towns, Longwy and Montmédy. The Crown Prince's headquarters were at Thionville—called Diedenhofen by the Germans—where he dined on a manly soldier's fare of cabbage soup, potatoes, and boiled beef with horseradish, eked out, as concession to a prince, by wild duck, salad, fruit, wine, coffee, and cigars. Surrounded by the "grave and gloomy" faces of the native population and envying the glory won at Liège and the progress of the right wing, the

Crown Prince and his staff waited feverishly for action. At last marching orders came for August 19.

Opposite the Crown Prince's Army was the French Third Army under General Ruffey. A lone apostle of heavy artillery, Ruffey was known, because of his eloquence on behalf of the big guns, as "*le poète du canon.*" He had dared not only to question the omnipotence of the 75s but also to propose the use of airplanes as an offensive arm and the creation of an air-force of 3,000 planes. The idea was not admired. "*Tout ça, c'est du sport!*" exclaimed General Foch in 1910. For use by the army, he had added, "*l'avion c'est zéro!*" Next year at maneuvers General Gallieni by using airplane reconnaissance captured a colonel of the Supreme War Council with all his staff. By 1914 the French Army was using airplanes, but General Ruffey was still regarded as having "too much imagination." Besides, as he showed a disinclination to allow Staff officers to tell him what to do, he had made enemies at GQG before he ever entered the Ardennes. His headquarters were at Verdun, and his task was to throw the enemy back on Metz-Thionville and invest them there, retaking the Briey region in the course of his advance. While he folded back the enemy on the right of the German center his neighbor, the Fourth Army under General de Langle de Cary, would fold them back on the left. The two French armies would cleave their way through the middle and lop off the arm of the German right wing at the shoulder.

General de Langle, a veteran of 1870, had been retained in command despite his having reached the French age limit of sixty-four a month before the war. In appearance a sharp, alert bantam, alive with energy, he resembled Foch, and like him, always looked in photographs as if about to leap into action. General de Langle was ready, indeed aching, to leap now, and refused to be discouraged by disquieting news. His cavalry, in combat near Neufchâteau, had run into heavy opposition and had been forced to retire. A reconnaissance tour by a staff officer in an automobile had brought further warning. The officer had talked at Arlon to a worried official of the Luxembourg government who said the Germans were in the nearby forests "in strength." On the way back the officer's car was fired on but his reports to Fourth Army Headquarters were judged "pessimistic." The mood was one of valor, not discretion. The moment had come to move fast, not hesitate. It was only after the battle that General de Langle remembered that he had disapproved of Joffre's order to attack "without allowing me to take soundings first"; only afterward that he wrote, "GQG wanted surprise but it was we who were surprised."

General Ruffey was more troubled than his neighbor. He took more seriously the reports brought in by Belgian peasants of Germans lodged among the woods and cornfields. When he told GQG his estimate of enemy strength opposing him, they paid no attention to him and did not, or so he was to claim, even read his reports.

Fog was thick from the ground up everywhere in the Ardennes on the morning of August 21. The German Fourth and Fifth Armies had been moving forward on the 19th and 20th, entrenching their positions as they advanced. A French attack was expected, although they did not know when or where. In the dense fog the French cavalry patrols sent ahead to scout the ground "might as well have been blindfolded." The opposing armies, moving forward through the woods and between the hills, unable to see ahead more than a few paces, stumbled into each other before they knew what was in front of them. As soon as the first units established contact and commanders became aware that battle was erupting all around them, the Germans dug in. The French, whose officers in prewar training disdained to give the troops entrenching practice for fear of making them "sticky" and who carried as few picks and shovels as possible, threw themselves into *attaque brusquée* with the bayonet. They were mown down by machine guns. In some encounters the French 75s slaughtered German units who had likewise been taken by surprise.

On the first day the encounters were scattered and preliminary; on the 22nd the lower Ardennes was engulfed in full-scale battle. In separate combats at Virton and Tintigny and Rossignol and Neufchâteau guns roared and flared, men flung themselves at each other, the wounded fell, and the dead piled up. At Rossignol, Algerians of the French 3rd Colonial Division were surrounded by the VIth Corps of the Crown Prince's Army and fought for six hours until the survivors were but a remnant. Their divisional commander, General Raffenel, and a brigade commander, General Rondoney, were both killed.

In August 1914 general officers were casualties like ordinary soldiers.

At Virton the French VIth Corps under General Sarrail took a German corps in the flank with fire from its 75s. "The battlefield afterwards was an unbelievable spectacle," reported a French officer dazed with horror. "Thousands of dead were still standing, supported as if by a flying buttress made of bodies lying in rows on top of each other in an ascending arc from the horizontal to an angle of 60°." Officers from St. Cyr went into battle wearing white-plumed shakos and white gloves; it was considered "chic" to die in white gloves. An unidentified French sergeant kept a diary: "the guns recoil at each shot. Night is falling and they look like old men sticking out their tongues and spitting fire. Heaps of corpses, French and German, are lying every which way, rifles in hand. Rain is falling, shells are screaming and bursting—shells all the time. Artillery fire is the worst. I lay all night listening to the wounded groaning—some were German. The cannonading goes on. Whenever it stops we hear the wounded crying from all over the woods. Two or three men go mad every day."

At Tintigny a German officer also kept a diary. "Nothing more terrible could be imagined," he wrote. "We advanced much too fast—a civilian fired at us—he was immediately shot—we were ordered to attack the enemy flank in a forest of beeches—we lost our direction—the men were done for—the enemy opened fire—shells came down on us like hail."

The Crown Prince, not to be outdone by Rupprecht whose victories at Sarrebourg and Morhange were now known, urged his forces to match "the prodigies of valor and sacrifice" of their comrades. He had moved his headquarters to Esch in Luxembourg just across the river from Longwy and followed the battle on huge maps pinned to the walls. The suspense was torture; telephone communications with Coblenz were awful; OHL was "much too far back"; the struggle was frightful, the losses terrible; Longwy is not yet taken, he said, but "we feel we have checked the enemy's offensive"; French units were reported retreating in disorder, not in planned retreat.

This was so. At the last moment before the battle General Ruffey was enraged to discover that three reserve divisions, altogether about 50,000 men, which formed part of his army were no longer part of it. Joffre had sequestered them, in response to the threat of Rupprecht's offensive, to form a special Army of Lorraine made up of these three divisions and four reserve divisions which he collected elsewhere. The Army of Lorraine under General Maunoury began to take form on August 21 between Verdun and Nancy to back up Castelnau's army and protect the right flank of the advance through the Ardennes. It was one of the last minute rearrangements which proved the saving flexibility of the French Army but at the moment had a negative result. It cut into Ruffey's strength and kept seven divisions immobile at a vital time. Ruffey always claimed afterward that if he had had the extra 50,000 men to whom he had already issued orders he could have won the Battle of Virton. At the time his anger proved too much for tact. When a staff officer from GQG came to his headquarters during the battle, Ruffey exploded: "You people at GQG never read the reports we send you. You are as ignorant as an oyster of all that the enemy has in his bag. . . . Tell the Generalissimo his operations are worse than 1870—he sees absolutely nothing—incapacity everywhere." This was not a message to be welcomed upon Olympus where Joffre and his attendant deities were more inclined to lay the blame on the incapacity of commanders and troops—Ruffey among them.

On the same day, August 22, General de Langle was experiencing a commander's most agonizing moments—waiting for news from the front. Chaining himself "in anguish" to his headquarters at Stenay on the Meuse, twenty miles from Sedan, he received bad reports coming hard upon each other. The instinct to rush to the scene of combat could only be checked by reminding himself that a general must not lose himself among his units but can only direct their movements at a distance. To maintain sangfroid before his staff and "that mastery of himself indispensable to a chief at critical moments" was as difficult.

As the day ended, the terrible casualties of the Colonial Corps became known. Another corps, through mishandling by its commander, as De Langle believed, was in retreat, endangering its neighbors. "Serious check at Tintigny; all troops engaged with unsatisfactory results," he had to report to Joffre, adding that losses and disorganization of his units made it impossible to carry out his orders for August 23. Joffre simply refused to believe it. With serene complacence he reported to Messimy, even after receiving De Langle's report, that the armies had been placed "where the enemy is most vulnerable and so as to assure ourselves of numerical superiority." GQG's work was done. Now it was up to the troops and their commanders "who have the advantage of that superiority." He repeated the assurance to De Langle, insisting that as he had no more than three enemy corps in front of him, he must resume the offensive.

In fact the French Armies in the Ardennes enjoyed no superiority, but the reverse. The Crown Prince's Army included, besides the three corps which the French had identified, two reserve corps with the same numerals as the active corps, as did the Duke of Württemberg's Army. Together they massed a greater number of men and guns than the French Third and Fourth Armies.

Fighting continued during August 23, but by the end of the day it was known the French arrow had broken against its target. The enemy had not been "vulnerable" in the Ardennes after all. Despite the massive strength of his right wing his center had not been weak. The French had not "cut them in half." With the cry of "*En avant!*" with waving sword, with all the ardor on which the French Army prided itself, officers led their companies to the attack—against an enemy who dug in and used his field guns. Field gray merging into the fog and shadows had beaten the too visible *pantalon rouge*; steady, solid methodical training had beaten *cran*. Both French Armies in the Ardennes were in retreat, the Third falling back on Verdun and the Fourth on Stenay and Sedan. Briey's iron ore was not regained and for four more years would serve to forge German munitions for the long war which, without that iron, Germany could not have fought.

As yet on the evening of August 23 Joffre did not realize the full extent of the defeat in the Ardennes. The offensive had been "momentarily checked," he telegraphed to Messimy, but "I will make every effort to renew the offensive."

The Crown Prince's Army on that day passed Longwy, leaving its fortress to be taken by siege troops, and was advancing with orders to head off the French Third Army from Verdun.

The Prince who less than a month ago had been cautioned by his father to obey his Chief of Staff in everything and "do as he tells you" was "deeply moved" on this day of triumph to receive a telegram from "Papa William" awarding him, like Rupprecht, the Iron Cross, First *and* Second Class. The telegram was handed around among the staff to be read by all. Soon the Prince would be handing out medals himself, in a "dazzling white tunic," as an admirer describes him later in the war, walking between two lines of soldiers distributing Iron Crosses from a basket carried by an aide. By that time, an Austrian ally would report, the Iron Cross, Second Class, could only be avoided by committing suicide. Today the "hero of Longwy," as he was soon to be acclaimed, had won glory equal to Rupprecht's; and if, amid the adulation, the ghost of Schlieffen grumbled at "ordinary frontal victories" without envelopment or annihilation or muttered scornful references to a "wild hunt for medals," no one heard him.

Meanwhile on the Sambre, Lanrezac's Fifth Army had been ordered to attack across the river and, "resting on the fortress of Namur," with its left passing by Charleroi, was to take as its objective the enemy "northern group." One corps of the Fifth Army was to be held in the angle of the rivers to protect the line of the Meuse against a German attack from the east. Although Joffre had no authority to command the British, his order requested Sir John French "to cooperate in this action" by advancing "in the general direction of Soignies," that is, across the Mons Canal. The canal is an extension of the Sambre which carries navigation to the Channel by way of the Scheldt. It formed part of a continuous waterway, made by the Sambre from Namur to Charleroi and by the canal from Charleroi to the Scheldt, which lay across the path of the German right wing.

According to the German timetable, von Kluck's Army was to reach the water barrier by August 23, while Bülow's Army, which would have to reduce Namur on the way, would reach it earlier and be across it at about the same time.

According to the British timetable laid down by Sir John French's marching orders, the BEF would also reach the canal on the 23rd, the same day as the Germans. Neither army was yet aware of the coincidence. The heads of the British columns were scheduled to reach the line earlier, that is, by the night of the 22nd. On the 21st, the day Lanrezac was ordered to cross the Sambre, the BEF, which had been expected to "cooperate in the action," was a full day's march behind the French. Instead of fighting together as planned, the two armies, because of the late British start and poor liaison resulting from the unhappy relations of their commanders, were to fight two separate battles, Charleroi and Mons, while their headquarters were only thirty-five miles apart.

In General Lanrezac's heart the doctrine of the offensive was already dead. He could not see the whole picture, so clear now, of three German armies converging upon his front but he could feel their presence. Hausen's Third Army was coming at him from the east, Bülow's Second Army from the north, and Kluck's First Army was advancing against the half-size British Army on his left. He did not know their names or numbers but he knew they were there. He knew or deduced from reconnaissance that greater numbers were coming at him than he could dispose of. Evaluation of enemy strength is not an absolute, but a matter of piecing together scraps of reconnaissance and intelligence to form a picture, if possible a picture to fit preconceived theories or to suit the demands of a particular strategy. What a staff makes out of the available evidence depends upon the degree of optimism or pessimism prevailing among them, on what they want to believe or fear to believe, and sometimes upon the sensitivity or intuition of an individual.

To Lanrezac and to GQG the same reports of German strength west of the Meuse conveyed different pictures. GQG saw a weak German center in the Ardennes. Lanrezac saw a great wave rolling down with the Fifth Army directly in its path. GQG estimated German strength west of the Meuse at 17 or 18 divisions. Opposed they counted Lanrezac's 13 divisions, a separate group of two reserve divisions, 5 British divisions, and 1 Belgian division at Namur, a total of 21 giving what they believed a comfortable superiority in numbers. Joffre's plan was for this force to hold the Germans behind the Sambre until the French Third and Fourth Armies should break through the German center in the Ardennes and then for all together to advance northward and throw the Germans out of Belgium.

The British Staff, dominated in fact if not in rank by Henry Wilson, agreed with GQG's estimate. In his diary for August 20, Wilson put down the same figure of 17 or 18 divisions for the Germans west of the Meuse, and happily concluded, "The more the better, as it will weaken their center." Back in England, far from the front, Lord Kitchener felt anxiety and foreboding. On August 19 he telegraphed Sir John French that the German sweep north and west of the Meuse, about which he had warned him, "seems definitely to be developing." He asked to be kept informed of all reports, and next day repeated the request. In truth, at that moment German strength west of the Meuse was not 17 or 18 divisions but 30: 7 active and 5 reserve corps, 5 cavalry divisions and other units. Von Hausen's Army, which at this time had not yet crossed the Meuse but which formed part of the right wing, was to add another 4 corps or 8 divisions. While for the Battle of the Frontiers as a whole, German numerical superiority was one and a half to one, the right wing's preponderance was nearer two to one.

The focus of this force was Lanrezac's Army, and he knew it. He believed the British, after his disastrous interview with their commander, to be both unready and unreliable. He knew the Belgian defense to be cracking at Namur. One of the new corps assigned to him in the recent exchange of units which was to hold his left flank west of Charleroi had not yet come into position on August 21. If he attacked across the Sambre as ordered, he believed he would be outflanked by the German forces pouring down on his left who would then have nothing between them and Paris. The guiding principle of all that he had ever taught at St. Cyr and the Ecole Supérieure, the principle that trained the French Army, was to "attack the enemy wherever met." He looked at it now, and saw the face of a skeleton.

Lanrezac hesitated. He wrote to Joffre that if he took the offensive north of the Sambre the Fifth Army "may be exposed to giving battle alone," as the British would not be ready to act in liaison with him. If both were to act in unison the Fifth Army must wait until the 23rd or 24th. Joffre replied "I leave you absolute judge of the moment to begin your offensive." The enemy was not so permissive.

Detachments of Bülow's Army whose main force was already attacking Namur plunged down upon the Sambre on August 21 and forced crossings at two points between Namur and Charleroi. Troops of the Fifth Army had been told by Lanrezac that their own offensive waited upon "neighboring armies" and that in the meantime they were to oppose any German attempts to cross the river. Defensive preparations not being in the French military vocabulary, the Xth Corps which held this sector had not dug in or laid wire or otherwise organized the defenses of the south bank, but waited to hurl themselves bodily upon the enemy. "With bugles blowing, drums beating and flags flying," but without artillery preparation, the French now dashed to the assault. After sharp combat they were driven back, and by nightfall the enemy remained in possession of Tamines and another village on the south side of the river.

Over the crack of musketry and crash of shells a deeper sound like that of a gigantic drum could be heard in the distance. The German siege guns had begun the bombardment of the forts of Namur. Dragged down from Liège, the 420s and 305s had been brought within range, cemented into emplacements, and were now pouring their two-ton shells on a second Belgian fortress. The shells came over with "a long singing scream," wrote an Englishwoman who had led a volunteer ambulance corps to Namur. They seemed to be coming directly at the listener wherever he stood and to explode within a yard of him wherever they hit. The town cowered through two days of the terrible sound as destruction thundered out of the sky upon the forts around them. The same effects as at Liège of explosive gases, of concrete crumbled like plaster, of men in the underground chambers driven mad were repeated. Cut off from the rest of the Belgian Army, the garrison troops and the 4th Division felt themselves deserted. Commandant Duruy, Lanrezac's liaison officer at Namur, returned to Fifth Army headquarters to say he did not think the forts would hold out another day without some evidence of French help. "They must see the French troops marching along with colors unfurled and a band playing. There must be a band," he pleaded. Three French battalions—one regiment of some 3,000 men—were sent off that night and joined the defense of Namur next morning. The defense numbered 37,000. The German force engaged in the assault from August 21 to 24 ranged from 107,000 to 153,000 with 400 to 500 pieces of artillery.

On the night of August 21 Sir John French reported to Kitchener that he did not think there would be serious fighting before the 24th. "I think I know the situation thoroughly and I regard it as favorable to us," he wrote. He did not know it as thoroughly as he thought. Next day, as British troops were marching up the road to Mons "in the general direction of Soignies," cavalry patrols reported a German corps marching down the Brussels-Mons road, also making for Soignies. From their position they could be expected to reach the village that night. It seemed unlikely the enemy would wait for Sir John's target date of the 24th. More alarming news was brought by a British aviator who reported another German corps marching down a road far enough to the west to outflank the British left. Envelopment. Suddenly, in startling clarity the menace loomed before British eyes—at least before the eyes of the Intelligence section. The "sweep" Kitchener eternally talked of was no longer an idea, but columns of living men. The staff commanders, under Henry Wilson's influence, discounted it. Wedded, through Wilson, to French strategy they were no more inclined than GQG to accept an alarmist view of the German right wing. "The information you have acquired and conveyed to the Commander in Chief appears to be somewhat exaggerated," they decided, and left marching orders unchanged.

They were conscious of treading on territory of past triumphs. Ten miles south of Mons they passed through Malplaquet on the border between France and Belgium and saw by the roadside the stone monument marking the spot where Marlborough had defeated the armies of Louis XIV and won immortality in a French folk song. Ahead of them between Mons and Brussels lay Waterloo. Returning to that victorious field, almost on the hundredth anniversary of the battle, they could not but feel confident.

As the heads of their columns neared Mons on the 22nd, part of a cavalry squadron scouting the road north of the canal saw a group of four horsemen riding toward them. They looked unfamiliar. At the same instant the strange riders saw the British, and halted. There was a kind of breathless pause before each realized he was looking at the enemy. The Uhlans turned to rejoin the rest of their squadron and galloped back, chased by the British, who caught up with them in the streets of Soignies. In a sharp skirmish the Uhlans were "hampered by their long lances and a good many threw them away." The British killed three or four and left the somewhat restricted field victorious. Captain Hornby, leader of the squadron, was awarded the DSO as the first British officer to kill a German with the new pattern cavalry sword. The war had opened in correct style with the most encouraging results.

First contact having been made on the road to Soignies as expected, the staff commanders were given no cause to change their estimate of the enemy's strength or position. German strength opposing the British was put by Wilson at one or possibly two corps and one cavalry division, which was inferior or at most equal to the BEF's two corps and a cavalry division. Wilson's forceful character, high spirits, and recognized familiarity with the ground and with the French carried greater persuasion than the reports of Intelligence officers—especially as Operations officers traditionally discount estimates by their brother bureau on the theory that Intelligence always assumes the worst. The death of Sir James Grierson, who among the British had been the closest student of German military theory and practice, gave Wilson's theories, which were a duplicate of GQG's, that much greater sway. Battle on the morrow was expected with confidence by the staff and corps commanders if not by Sir John French.

His mood was still murky; his hesitancy almost a replica of Lanrezac's. When General Smith-Dorrien, just arrived in France to replace Grierson, came up on the 21st he was told to "give battle on the line of the Condé Canal." When Smith-Dorrien asked if this meant offensive or defensive, he was told to "obey orders." One factor worrying Sir John French was ignorance of Lanrezac's plan of battle on his right flank and fear of a gap opening between them. He set off in a motorcar on the morning of the 22nd to confer with his unpleasing neighbor; but on being told en route that Lanrezac had gone forward to corps headquarters at Mettet where the Xth Corps was now in the heat of combat, he returned without meeting him. One piece of good news met him at Headquarters. The 4th Division, left behind in England at the start, had arrived in France and was on its way forward. The lengthening shadow of the German advance through Belgium and the withdrawal of the Belgian Army to Antwerp had decided Kitchener to send it over.

General von Kluck was more surprised than the British by the cavalry clash on the road at Soignies. Up to this moment—so effective were French and British security measures—he did not know the British were in front of him. He knew they had landed because he had read the news in a Belgian newspaper which published Kitchener's official communiqué announcing the safe arrival of the BEF "on French soil." This announcement on August 20 was the first England, the world, and the enemy knew of the landing. Kluck still thought they had landed at Ostend, Dunkirk, and Calais, chiefly because he wanted to think so, his intention being to "attack and disperse" the British along with the Belgians before meeting the French.

Now, as he moved down from Brussels, he had to worry about a Belgian sortie from Antwerp at his rear and a possible pounce upon his flank by the British, mysteriously deploying, so he thought, somewhere in Belgium to his right. He kept trying to edge his army westward in order to find and meet the British, but Bülow, in constant fear of a gap, kept issuing orders pulling him inward. Kluck protested. Bülow insisted. "Otherwise," he said, "the First Army might get too far away and not be able to support the Second Army." On discovering the British squarely in front of him at Soignies, Kluck again attempted a shift to the west in order to find the enemy flank. When again prevented by Bülow he protested furiously to OHL. OHL's notion of British whereabouts was even dimmer than the Allies' notion of the whereabouts of the German right wing. "It appears from here that no landings of great importance have taken place," said OHL, and rejected Kluck's proposal. Deprived of the opportunity to envelop the enemy and condemned to frontal attack, Kluck moved wrathfully on Mons. His orders for August 23 were to cross the canal, occupy the ground to the south, and force the enemy back into Maubeuge while cutting off his retreat from the west.

Bülow on that day, August 22, was having as much trouble with Hausen on his left as with Kluck on his right. As Kluck's tendency was to get ahead, Hausen's was to lag behind. With advance units of his army already engaged across the Sambre against Lanrezac's Xth Corps, Bülow planned a battle of annihilation in a great joint attack by his own and Hausen's Army. But on the 22nd Hausen was not ready. Bülow complained bitterly of "insufficient cooperation" from his neighbor. Hausen complained equally bitterly of "suffering" from Bülow's constant demands for help. Deciding not to wait, Bülow threw three corps into a violent attack upon the line of the Sambre.

During that day and the next Bülow's and Lanrezac's Armies grappled each other in the Battle of Charleroi, Hausen's Army joining in by the end of the first day. These were the same two days when the French Third and Fourth Armies were wrestling with disaster in the fog and forest of the Ardennes. Lanrezac was at Mettet to direct the battle, a process which consisted largely of agonized waiting for divisional and corps commanders to report back what was happening to them. They in turn found it hard enough to find out what was happening from units under heavy fire or gripped in combat in village streets or stumbling back exhausted and bleeding with hardly an officer left to make a report. Visual evidence reached Mettet before reports. A car carrying a wounded officer drove into the square where Lanrezac and his staff paced anxiously, too restless to remain indoors. The wounded man was recognized as General Boë, commander of a division of the Xth Corps. With a face the color of ashes and eyes of tragedy, he whispered slowly and painfully to Hély d'Oissel who ran to the car, "Tell him . . . tell the General . . . we held on . . . as long as we could."

On the left of the Xth Corps, the IIIrd Corps in front of Charleroi reported "terrible" losses. The sprawling industrial town lying on both sides of the river having been penetrated by the Germans during the day, the French were fighting furiously to dislodge them. When the Germans attacked in dense formation—as was their habit before they learned better—they made perfect targets for the 75s. But the 75s, which could fire 15 times a minute, were supplied with shells at a rate sufficient for only 2.25 shots per minute. At Charleroi the "Turcos" of the two Algerian divisions, recruited by voluntary enlistment, fought as valiantly as had their fathers at Sedan. One battalion charged a German gun battery, bayoneting the gunners, and returned with two men unwounded out of the battalion's complement of 1,030. Everywhere the French were enraged or demoralized, according to the circumstances in different sectors, by the shelling from batteries they usually could not see or get at. They felt helpless rage at the hawk-shaped German airplanes overhead which acted as artillery spotters and whose flight over their lines was invariably followed by a new burst of shells.

By evening Lanrezac had to report the Xth Corps "forced to fall back" having "suffered severely"; the IIIrd Corps "heavily engaged"; "heavy casualties" in officers; the XVIIIth Corps on the left intact but General Sordet's Cavalry Corps on the far left "greatly exhausted" and also forced to fall back, leaving a gap between the Fifth Army and the British. It proved to be a gap of ten miles, wide enough for an enemy corps. Lanrezac's anxiety was so acute as to move him to send word to Sir John French asking him to relieve pressure on the French by attacking Bülow's right flank. Sir John replied he could not comply, but promised to hold the line of the Mons Canal for twenty-four hours.

During the night Lanrezac's position became further imperiled when Hausen brought four fresh corps and 340 guns into action on the Meuse. He attacked during the night and gained bridgeheads across the river which were counterattacked by Franchet d'Esperey's 1st Corps whose mission was to hold the Meuse along the right side of Lanrezac's front. His was the only corps of the Fifth Army to entrench its position.

Hausen's intention, in compliance with orders from OHL, was to attack southwest toward Givet where he expected to come in upon the rear of Lanrezac's Army, which could then be caught between his and Bülow's forces, and destroyed. Bülow, however, whose units in this sector had taken as severe punishment as they had given, was determined to mount a massive and terminal attack, and ordered Hausen to attack directly westward toward Mettet upon the body of the Fifth Army instead of southwestward across its line of retreat. Hausen complied. This was an error. It engaged Hausen all during August 23 in frontal attack against the strongly held positions and vigorous generalship of Franchet d'Esperey's corps and it left Lanrezac's line of retreat open—an opening through which the opportunity for a battle of annihilation was to slip away.

Through the hot clear hours of August 23 the summer sky was spattered with the greasy black puffs of bursting shells. The French had instantly dubbed them "*marmites*" after the cast-iron soup pot that sits on every French stove. "*Il plut des marmites*" (It rained shells) was all that one tired soldier could remember of the day. In some places the French were still attacking, trying to throw the Germans back across the Sambre; in others they were holding; in still others they were retreating in crippled, broken disorder. The roads were choked with long columns of Belgian refugees, coated with dust, weighted down with babies and bundles, pushing wheelbarrows, dully, tiredly, endlessly moving toward no goal or home or refuge but only away from the awful roar of guns to the north.

The refugee columns passed through Philippeville, twenty miles from Charleroi where Lanrezac had his headquarters that day. Standing in the square, with red-trousered legs apart and hands clasped behind his back, Lanrezac watched them somberly, saying nothing. Above his black tunic his dark face looked almost pale and his fleshy cheeks sunken. He fell "prey to extreme anxiety." Enemy pressure was bending against him from all sides. No guidance came from GQG except to ask his opinion of the situation. Lanrezac felt acutely conscious of the gap made by the retreat of Sordet's cavalry. At noon came the news, foreseen yet still incredible, that the Belgian 4th Division was evacuating Namur. The city dominating the confluence of Sambre and Meuse, as well as the forts on the heights behind it, would soon be in Bülow's hands. No word came from General de Langle de Cary of the Fourth Army to whom Lanrezac had sent a message that morning asking for a maneuver to strengthen the sector where their forces joined.

Lanrezac's staff was urging him to permit a counterattack by Franchet d'Esperey who reported a glittering opportunity. A German force in pursuit of the retreating Xth Corps was presenting its flank to him. Other ardent pleaders urged a counterattack on the far left by the XVIIIth Corps to relieve pressure on the British who on this day at Mons were engaged against the full force of von Kluck's Army. To the disgust of the forward-minded, Lanrezac refused. He remained silent, gave no orders, waited. In the controversy which critics and partisans were to weave for years afterwards over the Battle of Charleroi, everyone pronounced his own version of what went on in the soul of General Lanrezac that afternoon. To some he appeared pusillanimous or paralyzed, to others as a man soberly measuring the chances in an obscure and perilous situation. Left without guidance from GQG, he had to make his own decision.

Late in the afternoon occurred the decisive incident of the day. Troops of Hausen's Army enlarged a bridgehead across the Meuse at Onhaye south of Dinant. Franchet d'Esperey at once sent a brigade under General Mangin to deal with the danger which threatened to take the Fifth Army in the rear. At the same time word at last reached Lanrezac from General de Langle. It could not have been worse. Not only was the Fourth Army not successful in the Ardennes, as an earlier communiqué from GQG had implied, but it was being forced into retreat that would leave unguarded the stretch of the Meuse between Sedan and Lanrezac's right flank. At once the presence of Hausen's Saxons at Onhaye took on added threat. Lanrezac believed—"I was bound to believe"—that this force was the van of an army that would be given liberty of action by de Langle's retreat and would be reinforced if not immediately thrown back. He did not yet know—because it had not happened yet—that General Mangin's brigade in a brilliant charge with fixed bayonets would throw the Saxons out of Onhaye.

On top of this, word came that the IIIrd Corps in front of Charleroi had been attacked, had failed to hold its ground, and was falling back. Commandant Duruy arrived with news that the Germans had taken the northern forts of Namur and entered the city. Lanrezac returned to Corps Headquarters at Chimay where he "received confirmation of the check to the Fourth Army which since morning had been retiring in such a way as to leave the Fifth Army's right completely uncovered."

To Lanrezac the danger on his right "seemed acute." The thought haunted him of that other disaster at the very place where de Langle's Army was now giving way, "where 44 years ago our army was encircled by the Germans and forced to capitulate—that abominable disaster which made our defeat irretrievable—what a memory!"

To save France from another Sedan, the Fifth Army must be saved from destruction. It was now clear to him that the French Armies were in retreat along their whole line from the Vosges to the Sambre. As long as the armies existed the defeat was not irretrievable as it had been at Sedan; the fight could go on. But if the Fifth Army were to be destroyed, the whole line would be unhinged and total defeat follow. Counterattack, however bravely pressed and urgent the need, could not save the situation as a whole.

Lanrezac finally spoke. He gave the order for a general retreat. He knew he would be taken for a "*catastrophard*" who must be got rid of—as indeed he was. His own account tells that he said to one of his officers: "We have been beaten but the evil is reparable. As long as the Fifth Army lives, France is not lost." Although the remark has the ring of memoirs written after the event, it may well have been spoken. Fateful moments tend to evoke grandeur of speech, especially in French.

Lanrezac made his decision, which he believed Joffre would disapprove, without consulting GQG. "Enemy threatens my right on the Meuse," he reported, "Onhaye occupied, Givet threatened, Namur carried." Because of this situation and "the delay of the Fourth Army," he was ordering the retirement of the Fifth Army. With that message vanished the last French hope of defeating the ancient enemy in a short war. The last of the French offensives had failed. Joffre did disapprove—but not that night. In the befogged and bitter hours of Sunday night, August 23, when the whole French plan was collapsing, when no one could be certain what was happening from sector to sector, when the specter of another Sedan haunted minds other than Lanrezac's, GQG neither questioned nor countermanded the Fifth Army's retreat. By his silence Joffre ratified the decision; he did not forgive it.

Afterward the official account of the Battle of Charleroi was to state that General Lanrezac, "thinking himself menaced on his right, ordered a retreat instead of counterattacking." That was when GQG, in need of a scapegoat for the failure of Plan 17, settled upon the commander of the Fifth Army. In the hour when he made his decision, however, no one at GQG suggested to General Lanrezac that he merely "thought" himself menaced on his right without actually being so, as the postwar phrase implied.

Far to the left, since early morning, the British and von Kluck's Army had been locked in a duel over the sixty-foot width of the Mons Canal. The August sun broke through early morning mist and rain, bringing promise of great heat later in the day. Sunday church bells were ringing as usual as the people of the mining villages went to Mass in their black Sunday clothes. The canal, bordered by railroad sidings and industrial back yards, was black with slime and reeked of chemical refuse from furnaces and factories. In among small vegetable plots, pastures, and orchards the gray pointed slag heaps like witches' hats stuck up everywhere, giving the landscape a bizarre, abnormal look. War seemed less incongruous here.

The British had taken up positions on either side of Mons. To the west the IInd Corps commanded by General Smith-Dorrien lined the fifteen-mile stretch of canal between Mons and Condé and filled in a salient formed just east of Mons where the canal makes a northward loop about two miles wide and a mile and a half deep. On the right of the IInd Corps General Haig's Ist Corps held a diagonal front between Mons and the left wing of Lanrezac's Army. The cavalry division commanded by General Allenby, future conqueror of Jerusalem, was held in reserve. Opposite Haig was the dividing line between Kluck's and Bülow's armies. Kluck was keeping as far to the west as he could, and thus Haig's corps was not attacked in the fighting of August 23 that was to become known to history and to legend as the Battle of Mons.

Sir John French's headquarters were at Le Cateau, 30 miles south of Mons. The 5 divisions he had to direct over a front of 25 miles—in contrast to Lanrezac's 13 divisions over a front of 50 miles—hardly required him to be that far back. Sir John's hesitant frame of mind may have dictated the choice. Worried by the reports of his air and cavalry reconnaissance, uncertain of his neighbor, uncomfortable about the zigzag line of the front they shared which opened multiple opportunities to the enemy, he was no more happy about undertaking an offensive than was Lanrezac.

On the night before the battle he summoned the senior staff

officers of both corps and the cavalry division to Le Cateau and informed them that "owing to the retreat of the French Fifth Army," the British offensive would not take place. Except for its Xth Corps, which was not adjacent to the British, the Fifth Army was not in retreat at this time, but Sir John French had to blame someone. The same comradely spirit had moved General Lanrezac a day earlier to blame his own failure to take the offensive on the nonappearance of the British. As Lanrezac had then ordered his corps to hold the line of the Sambre instead of attacking across it, Sir John French now issued orders to hold the line of the canal. Despite Henry Wilson who was still thinking in terms of the great offensive northward that was to throw the Germans out of Belgium, the possibility of a very different kind of movement was conveyed to the commanders. Recognizing it, General Smith-Dorrien at 2:30 A.M. ordered the bridges over the canal to be prepared for demolition. It was a sensible precaution of the kind excluded by the French and, because excluded, the cause of the terrible French casualty rate of August 1914. Five minutes before the battle opened, Smith-Dorrien issued a further order directing the bridges to be destroyed on divisional order "in the event of a retirement being necessary."

At six in the morning when Sir John French gave his last instructions to corps commanders, his—or his staff's—estimate of the enemy strength they were about to meet was still the same: one or at most two army corps plus cavalry. In fact, at that moment von Kluck had four corps and three cavalry divisions—160,000 men with 600 guns—within striking distance of the BEF whose strength was 70,000 men and 300 guns. Of von Kluck's two reserve corps, one was two days' march behind and one had been left behind to mask Antwerp.

At 9:00 A.M. the first German guns opened fire on the British positions, the attack falling first upon the salient made by the loop of the canal. The bridge at Nimy at the northernmost point of the salient was the focus of the attack. Lunging at it in their dense formation, the Germans offered "the most perfect targets" to the British riflemen who, well dug in and expertly trained, delivered fire of such rapidity and accuracy that the Germans believed they faced machine guns. After repeated assault waves were struck down, they brought up more strength and changed to open formations. The British, under orders to offer "stubborn resistance," kept up their fire from the salient despite steadily growing casualties. From 10:30 on, the battle was extended along the straight section of the canal to the west as battery after battery of German guns, first of the IIIrd and then of the IVth Corps, were brought into action.

By three in the afternoon when the British regiments holding the salient had withstood shelling and infantry assault for six hours, the pressure on their dwindling numbers became too strong. After blowing up the bridge at Nimy they fell back, company by company, to a second line of defense that had been prepared two or three miles to the rear. As the yielding of the salient endangered the troops holding the straight section of the canal, these too were now ordered to withdraw, beginning about five in the evening. At Jemappes, where the loop joins the straight section, and at Mariette two miles to the west sudden peril loomed when it was found that the bridges could not be destroyed for lack of an exploder to fire the charges. A rush by the Germans across the canal in the midst of the retirement could convert orderly retreat to a rout and might even effect a breakthrough. No single Horatius could hold the bridge, but Captain Wright of the Royal Engineers swung himself hand over hand under the bridge at Mariette in an attempt to connect the charges. At Jemappes a corporal and a private worked at the same task for an hour and a half under continuous fire. They succeeded, and were awarded the V.C. and D.C.M.; but Captain Wright, though he made a second attempt in spite of being wounded, failed. He too won the V.C., and three weeks later was killed on the Aisne.

During the early evening the delicate process of disengagement was effected under sporadic fire with regiment by regiment covering the withdrawal of its neighbor until all had reached the villages and billets of the second line of defense. The Germans, who appeared to have suffered equally from the day's fighting, made no serious effort to force the undemolished bridges nor showed any appetite for pursuit. On the contrary, through the dusk the retiring British troops could hear German bugles sounding "Cease fire," then the inevitable singing, then silence across the canal.

Fortunately for the British von Kluck's more than double

superiority in numbers had not been made use of. Unable, because of Bülow's hampering orders, to find the enemy flank and extend himself around it, Kluck had met the British head on with his two central corps, the IIIrd and IVth, and suffered the heavy losses consequent upon frontal attack. One German reserve captain of the IIIrd Corps found himself the only surviving officer of his company and the only surviving company commander of his battalion. "You are my sole support," wailed the major. "The battalion is a mere wreck, my proud, beautiful battalion . . ." and the regiment is "shot down, smashed up —only a handful left." The colonel of the regiment, who like everyone in war could judge the course of combat only by what was happening to his own unit, spent an anxious night, for as he said, "If the English have the slightest suspicion of our condition, and counterattack, they will simply run over us."

Neither of von Kluck's flanking corps, the IInd on his right and the IXth on his left, had been brought into the battle. Like the rest of the First Army they had marched 150 miles in 11 days and were strung out along the roads several hours' march to the rear of the two corps in the center. If all had attacked together on August 23, history might have been different. Some time during the afternoon von Kluck, realizing his mistake, ordered the two central corps to hold the British until the flanking corps could be brought up for envelopment and a battle of annihilation. Before that time a drastic change of plan forced itself upon the British.

Henry Wilson was mentally still charging forward with medieval ardor in Plan 17, unaware that it was now about as applicable to the situation as the longbow. Like Joffre who could still insist upon the offensive six hours after receiving de Langle's report of disaster in the Ardennes, Wilson, even after the line of the canal had to be given up, was eager for an offensive next day. He had made a "careful calculation" and concluded "that we had only one corps and one cavalry division (possibly two corps) opposite to us." He "persuaded" Sir John French and Murray that this was so, "with the result that I was allowed to draft orders for an attack tomorrow." At 8:00 P.M., just as his work was completed, it was nullified by a telegram from Joffre which informed the British that accumulated evidence now put the enemy force opposite them at three corps and two cavalry divisions. That was more persuasive than Wilson and at once put an end to any thought of attack. Worse news followed.

At 11:00 P.M. Lieutenant Spears arrived after a hurried drive from Fifth Army headquarters to bring the bitter word that General Lanrezac was breaking off battle and withdrawing the Fifth Army to a line in the rear of the BEF. Spears' resentment and dismay at a decision taken without consulting and without informing the British was like that of Colonel Adelbert on learning of King Albert's decision to withdraw to Antwerp. It still colors Spears' account written seventeen years later.

Lanrezac's retreat, leaving the BEF in the air, put them in instant peril. In anxious conference it was decided to draw back the troops at once as soon as orders could be drafted and delivered to the front. A delay that was to cost lives was due to the strange choice of location for Smith-Dorrien's corps headquarters. They were in a modest private country house called rather grandly the Château de la Roche at Sars-la-Bruyère, a hamlet without telegraph or telephone communication on a back country road difficult enough to find in the daytime, much more so in the middle of the night. Even Marlborough and Wellington had not disdained more convenient if less gentlemanly headquarters on the main road, one in an abbey and the other in a tavern. Smith-Dorrien's orders had to be delivered by car, and did not reach him until 3:00 A.M., whereas Haig's Ist Corps, which had not been in the battle, received its orders by telegraph an hour earlier and was able to prepare its retreat and get under way before dawn.

By that time the two German flanking corps had been brought up, the attack was renewed, and the retreat of the IInd Corps, which had been under fire all day, began under fire again. In the confusion one battalion never received its orders, and fought until it was surrounded and almost all its men were killed, wounded, or taken prisoner. Only two officers and two hundred men got away.

So ended the first day of combat for the first British soldiers to fight a European enemy since the Crimea and the first to fight on European soil since Waterloo. It was a bitter disappointment: both for the Ist Corps which had marched forward through the heat and dust and now had to turn and march back almost without having fired a shot; even more for the IInd Corps which felt proud of its showing against a famed and formidable enemy, knew nothing of his superior numbers or of the Fifth Army's withdrawal, and could not understand the order to retreat.

It was a "severe" disappointment to Henry Wilson who laid it all at the door of Kitchener and the Cabinet for having sent only four divisions instead of six. Had all six been present, he said with that marvelous incapacity to admit error that was to make him ultimately a Field Marshal, "this retreat would have been an advance and defeat would have been a victory."

Wilson's confidence and cheer began to wane, and Sir John French, mercurial at best, plunged into despondency. Though in France barely more than a week, the tensions, anxieties, and responsibility, combined with the iniquities of Lanrezac and culminating in frustration on the opening day of battle, soured him on his command. He ended his report to Kitchener next day with the ominous suggestion, indicating that he already had begun to think in terms of departure, "I think immediate attention should be directed to the defense of Havre." Havre at the mouth of the Seine was nearly a hundred miles south of the original British landing base at Boulogne.

That was the Battle of Mons. As the opening British engagement of what was to become the Great War, it became endowed in retrospect with every quality of greatness and was given a place in the British pantheon equal to the battles of Hastings and Agincourt. Legends like that of the Angels of Mons settled upon it. All its men were valorous and all its dead heroes. The deeds of every named regiment were chronicled down to the last hour and bullet of the fight until Mons came to shine mistily through a haze of such gallantry and glory as to make it seem a victory. Unquestionably, at Mons the British fought bravely and well, better than some French units but no better than many others; no better than the Belgians at Haelen or the Turcos at Charleroi or General Mangin's brigade at Onhaye or the enemy on various occasions. The battle, before the retreat began, lasted nine hours, engaged two divisions, or 35,000 British soldiers, cost a total of 1,600 British casualties, and held up the advance of von Kluck's army by one day. During the Battle of the Frontiers, of which it was a part, 70 French divisions, or about 1,250,000 men, were in combat at different times and places over a period of four days. French casualties during those four days amounted to more than 140,000, or twice the number of the whole British Expeditionary Force in France at the time.

In the wake of Charleroi and Mons, Belgium lay coated with white dust from the shattered walls of its houses and pock-marked with the debris of battles. Muddied hay used by the soldiers as beds trailed in the streets along with abandoned packs and blood-stained bandages. "And over all lay a smell," as Will Irwin wrote, "which I have never heard mentioned in any book on war—the smell of half a million unbathed men. . . . It lay for days over every town through which the Germans passed." Mingled with it was the smell of blood and medicine and horse manure and dead bodies. The human dead were supposed to be buried by their own troops before midnight, but often there were too many and there was too little time, and even less for the dead horses whose bodies, lying unburied for a longer time, became bloated and putrid. Belgian peasants trying to clear their fields of the dead after the armies passed by could be seen bending on their spades like pictures by Millet.

Derelict among the bodies lay the fragments of Plan 17 and bright broken bits of the French Field Regulations: ". . . the French Army henceforth knows no law but the offensive . . . the offensive alone leads to positive results."

Joffre, standing amid the tumbled debacle of all French hopes, with responsibility for the catastrophe resting finally upon him, with the frontiers of France breached, with every one of his armies in retreat or fighting desperately to hold a defensive line, remained magically unperturbed. By immediately casting the blame on the executors and absolving the planners, he was able to retain perfect and unblemished confidence in himself and in France—and in so doing, provide the essential and unique requirement in the calamitous days ahead.

On the morning of the 24th when, as he said, "There is no escaping the evidence of the facts," he reported to Messimy that the army was "condemned to a defensive attitude" and must hold out, resting upon its fortified lines and, while trying to wear down the enemy, wait for a favorable occasion to resume the offensive. He set about at once arranging the lines of retreat and preparing a regrouping of his armies to form a mass capable of renewing the attack from a defensive line he expected to establish on the Somme. He had been encouraged by a recent telegram from Paléologue in St. Petersburg to hope that the Germans would at any moment have to withdraw forces from the Western Front to meet the Russian threat, and on the morrow of his own disaster Joffre waited anxiously for a sound of the Russian steam roller. All that came through was a sibylline telegram reporting that "grave strategic problems" were being settled in East Prussia with promise of "further offensive operations."

Next to re-forming his lines, Joffre's most urgent task was to find the cause for failure. Without hesitancy of any kind he found it in "grave shortcomings on the part of commanders." A few had indeed crumbled under the awful responsibility of command. A general of artillery had to step into the place of the commander of the IIIrd Corps in front of Charleroi when that officer could nowhere be found during the most critical phase of the battle. In the Battle of the Ardennes a divisional general of the Vth Corps committed suicide. Human beings, like plans, prove fallible in the presence of those ingredients that are missing in maneuvers—danger, death, and live ammunition. But Joffre, who would admit no fallibility of plan, would permit none in men. Demanding the names of all generals who had shown weakness or incapacity, he enlarged the list of the *limogés* with ruthless hand.

Acknowledging, like Henry Wilson, no error of theory or strategy, he could only ascribe the failure of the offensive, "in spite of the numerical superiority which I thought I had secured for our armies," to a "lack of offensive spirit." He might better have said "excess" than "lack." At Morhange in Lorraine, at Rossignol in the Ardennes, at Tamines on the Sambre it was not too little but too much *cran* that caused the French failure. In a "Note for All Armies" issued the very day after the debacle, GQG amended "lack" to "false understanding" of the offensive spirit. The Field Regulations, it said, had been "poorly understood or badly applied." Infantry attacks were launched at too great a distance and without artillery support, thus suffering losses from machine-gun fire that might have been avoided. Henceforth when ground was occupied, "it must be immediately organized. Entrenchments must be dug." The "capital error" had been lack of coordination between artillery and infantry which it was an "absolute necessity" to rectify. The 75s must fire at maximum range. "Finally, we must copy the enemy in using airplanes to prepare artillery attacks." Whatever else were French military faults, unwillingness to learn from experience was not one of them—at least not in the realm of tactics.

GQG was less quick to locate failure in its own realm of strategy, even when on August 24 the Deuxième Bureau made a startling disclosure: it had discovered that the enemy's active corps were followed by reserve corps using the same corps number. This, the first evidence of reserve units being used in the front line, revealed how the Germans had managed to be equally strong on the right and center at once. It did not convey to Joffre a suspicion that Plan 17 might have had a fallible basis. He continued to believe it a good plan which had failed through poor execution. When called to testify after the war at a parliamentary inquiry into the cause of the catastrophe that opened France to invasion, he was asked his opinion of the prewar Staff theory that the stronger the German right wing, the better for France.

"But I still think so," Joffre replied. "The proof is that our Battle of the Frontiers was planned just for that and if it had succeeded our way would have been open. . . . What is more, it would have succeeded if the Fourth and Fifth Armies had fought well. If they had it would have meant annihilation of the whole German advance."

In the dark morning of August 1914 when the retreat began it was not the Fourth so much as the Fifth Army and its commander that he chiefly blamed. Although British malice, too, clustered about the head of General Lanrezac, an anonymous spokesman for the British Army ultimately declared that Lanrezac's decision to retreat instead of counterattacking on August 23 spared "another Sedan." Of Lanrezac's earlier insistence on shifting the Fifth Army west of the Meuse to Charleroi, the same spokesman added, "There is no doubt that this change of plan saved the BEF and probably the French Armies also from annihilation."

On August 24 all that was then clear was that the French Armies were in retreat and the enemy advancing with relentless force. The extent of the debacle was unknown to the public until August 25 when the Germans announced the capture of Namur with 5,000 prisoners. The news shocked an incredulous world. *The Times* of London had said Namur would withstand a siege of six months; it had fallen in four days. In accents of stunned understatement it was said in England that the fall of Namur "is generally recognized as a distinct disadvantage . . . and the chances of the war being brought to a speedy conclusion are considerably reduced."

How far reduced, how distant the end, no one yet knew. No one could realize that for numbers engaged and for rate and number of losses suffered over a comparable period of combat, the greatest battle of the war had already been fought. No one could yet foresee its consequences: how the ultimate occupation of all Belgium and northern France would put the Germans in possession of the industrial power of both countries, of the manufactures of Liège, the coal of the Borinage, the iron ore of Lorraine, the factories of Lille, the rivers and railroads and agriculture, and how this occupation, feeding German ambition and fastening upon France the fixed resolve to fight to the last drop of recovery and reparation, would block all later attempts at compromise peace or "peace without victory" and would prolong the war for four more years.

All this is hindsight. On August 24 the Germans felt an immense surge of confidence. They saw only beaten armies ahead; the genius of Schlieffen had been proved; decisive victory seemed within German grasp. In France, President Poincaré wrote in his diary: "We must make up our minds both to retreat and to invasion. So much for the illusions of the last fortnight. Now the future of France depends on her powers of resistance."

Elan had not been enough.

15

"The Cossacks Are Coming!"

ON AUGUST 5 in St. Petersburg Ambassador Paléologue of France drove past a regiment of Cossacks leaving for the front. Its general, seeing the French flag on the ambassador's car, leaned down from his horse to embrace him and begged permission to parade his regiment. While Paléologue solemnly reviewed the troops from his car, the general, between shouts of command to the ranks, addressed shouts of encouragement to the ambassador: "We'll destroy those filthy Prussians! . . . No more Prussia, no more Germany! . . . William to St. Helena!" Concluding the review, he galloped off behind his men, waving his saber and shouting his war cry, "William to St. Helena!"

The Russians, whose quarrel with Austria had precipitated the war, were grateful to France for standing by the alliance and anxious to show equal loyalty by support of the French design. "Our proper objective," the Czar was dutifully made to say with more bravado than he felt, "is the annihilation of the German army"; he assured the French that he considered operations against Austria as "secondary" and that he had ordered the Grand Duke "at all costs to open the way to Berlin at the earliest possible moment."

The Grand Duke in the last days of the crisis had been named Commander in Chief despite the bitter rivalry of Sukhomlinov who wanted the post for himself. As between the two, even the Russian regime in the last days of the Romanovs was not mad enough to choose the German-oriented Sukhomlinov to lead a war against Germany. He remained, however, as War Minister.

From the moment the war opened, the French, uncertain that Russia really would or could perform what she had promised, began exhorting their ally to hurry. "I entreat Your Majesty," pleaded Ambassador Paléologue in audience with the Czar on August 5, "to order your armies to take an immediate offensive, otherwise there is risk of the French army being overwhelmed." Not content with seeing the Czar, Paléologue also called upon the Grand Duke who assured the ambassador that he intended a vigorous offensive to begin on August 14, in keeping with the promise of the fifteenth day of mobilization, without waiting for all his army to be concentrated. Though famous for his uncompromising, not to say sometimes unprintable habits of speech, the Grand Duke composed on the spot a message of medieval chivalry to Joffre. "Firm in the conviction of victory," he telegraphed, he would march against the enemy bearing alongside his own standard the flag of the French Republic which Joffre had given him at maneuvers in 1912.

That a gap existed between the promises given to the French and the preparations for performance was all too apparent and may have been cause for the tears the Grand Duke was reported to have shed when he was named Commander in Chief. According to a colleague, he "appeared entirely unequipped for the task and, to quote his own statement, on receipt of the imperial order spent much time crying because he did not know how to approach his duties." Regarded by a leading Russian military historian as "eminently qualified" for his task, the Grand Duke may have wept less for himself than for Russia and the world. There was an aura about 1914 that caused those who sensed it to shiver for mankind. Tears came even to the most bold and resolute. Messimy opening a Cabinet meeting on August 5 with a speech full of valor and confidence, broke off midway, buried his head in his hands, and sobbed, unable to continue. Winston Churchill wishing godspeed and victory to the BEF, when taking leave of Henry Wilson, "broke down and cried so that he could not finish the sentence." Something of the same emotion could be felt in St. Petersburg.

The Grand Duke's colleagues were not the firmest pillars of support. Chief of Staff in 1914 was General Yanushkevich, a young man of forty-four with black mustache and curly black hair who was chiefly notable for not wearing a beard and whom the War Minister referred to as "still a child." More a courtier than a soldier, he had not fought in the Japanese War although he had served in the same regiment of Guards as Nicholas II, which was as good a reason as any for rapid promotion. He was a graduate of the Staff College and later its commandant, had served on the staff of the War Ministry, and when war broke out had been Chief of Staff for barely three months. Like the German Crown Prince, he was completely under the guidance of his Deputy Chief, the stern and silent General Danilov, a hard worker and strict disciplinarian who was the brains of the Staff. Yanushkevich's predecessor as Chief of Staff, General Jilinsky, had preferred to be relieved of that post and had persuaded Sukhomlinov to appoint him commander of the Warsaw military district. He was now in over-all command, under the Grand Duke, of the Northwest Army Group on the front against Germany. In the Russo-Japanese War he had served with little distinction but no positive error as Chief of Staff to the Commander in Chief, General Kuropatkin, and having survived that grave of reputations had managed to remain in the upper echelons without either personal popularity or military talent.

Russia had made no preparations to meet the advanced date for attack which she had promised to the French. Improvisations had to be arranged at the last moment. A scheme of "forward mobilization" was ordered which skipped certain preliminary stages to gain several days' time. Streams of telegrams from Paris, delivered with personal eloquence by Paléologue, kept up the pressure. On August 6 the orders of the Russian General Staff said it was essential to prepare "for an energetic offensive against Germany at the earliest possible moment, in order to ease the situation of the French but, of course, only when sufficient strength has been made available." By August 10, however, the proviso for "sufficient strength" had been dropped. Orders of that date read, "Naturally it is our duty to support France in view of the great stroke prepared by Germany against her. This support must take the form of the quickest possible advance against Germany, by attacking those forces she has left behind in East Prussia." The First and Second Armies were ordered to be "in position" to advance on M–14 (August 13), although they would have to start without their services of supply, which would not be fully concentrated until M–20 (August 19).

Difficulties of organization were immense; the essence of the problem, as the Grand Duke once confessed to Poincaré, was that in an empire as vast as Russia when an order was given no one was ever sure whether it had been delivered. Shortages of telephone wire and telegraph equipment and of trained signal corpsmen made sure or quick communication impossible. Shortage of motor transport also slowed down the Russian pace. In 1914 the army had 418 motor transport vehicles, 259 passenger cars, and two motor ambulances. (It had, however, 320 airplanes.) As a result, supplies after leaving the railhead had to depend on horse transport.

Supply was hazardous at best. Testimony in trials after the Japanese war revealed bribes and graft running like a network of moles' tunnels beneath the army. When even the Governor of Moscow, General Reinbot, was convicted and imprisoned for venality in letting army contracts, he still wielded enough private influence to obtain not only a pardon but reappointment to a new post. Meeting his commissariat staff for the first time as Commander in Chief, the Grand Duke said to them, "Gentlemen, no stealing."

Vodka, another traditional companion of war, was prohibited. In the last mobilization in 1904 when soldiers came reeling in and regimental depots were a mess of drunken slumbers and broken bottles, it had taken an extra week to straighten out the confusion. Now with the French calling every day's delay a matter of life or death, Russia enacted prohibition as a temporary measure for the period of mobilization. Nothing could have given more practical or more earnest proof of loyal intention to meet French pleas for haste, but with that characteristic touch of late-Romanov rashness, the government, by ukase of August 22, extended prohibition for the duration of the war. As the sale of vodka was a state monopoly, this act at one stroke cut off a third of the government's income. It was well known, commented a bewildered member of the Duma, that governments waging war seek by a variety of taxes and levies to increase income, "but never since the dawn of history has a country in time of war renounced the principal source of its revenue."

In the last hour of the fifteenth day at 11:00 P.M. on a lovely summer evening, the Grand Duke left the capital for field headquarters at Baranovichi, a railroad junction on the Moscow-Warsaw line about midway between the German and Austrian fronts. He and his staff and their families gathered in subdued groups on the station platform in St. Petersburg waiting for the Czar to come to bid farewell to the Commander in Chief. However, the Czarina's jealousy overrode courtesy, and Nicholas did not appear. Goodbyes and prayers were spoken in low voices; the men took their places in the train in silence and departed.

Behind the front the struggle to assemble armies was still in process. Russian cavalry on reconnaissance had been probing German territory since the first day of the war. Their forays succeeded less in penetrating the German screen than in providing an excuse for screaming headlines in German newspapers and wild tales of Cossack brutalities. As early as August 4 in Frankfort on the western edge of Germany an officer heard rumors that 30,000 refugees from East Prussia were coming to be accommodated in that city. Demands to save East Prussia from the Slavic hordes began to distract the German General Staff from the task of trying to concentrate all military effort against France.

At dawn on August 12 a detachment of General Rennenkampf's First Army, consisting of a cavalry division under General Gourko supported by an infantry division, opened the invasion of East Prussia ahead of the main advance and took the town of Marggrabowa five miles inside the frontier. Shooting as they rode through the outskirts and into the empty market square, the Russians found the town undefended and evacuated by German troops. Shops were closed, but the townspeople were watching from the windows. In the countryside the inhabitants fled precipitously ahead of the advancing squadrons before there was any fighting as if by prearrangement. On the first morning the Russians saw columns of black smoke rising along their line of march which, on approach, were discovered to be not farms and homes burned by their fleeing owners but dumps of straw burned as signals to show the direction of the invaders. Everywhere was evidence of the German's systematic preparation. Wooden watchtowers had been built on hilltops. Bicycles were provided for local farm boys of twelve to fourteen who acted as messengers. German soldiers, posted as informers, were found dressed as peasants, even as peasant women. The latter were discovered, presumably in the course of nonmilitary action, by their government-issue underwear; but many were probably never caught, it being impossible, General Gourko regretfully admitted, to lift the skirts of every female in East Prussia.

Receiving General Gourko's reports of evacuated towns and fleeing population and concluding that the Germans were not planning a serious resistance so far east of their base on the Vistula, General Rennenkampf was the more eager to dash forward and the less concerned about his incomplete services of supply. A trim, well-set-up officer of sixty-one with a direct glance and energetic mustache turned up at the corners, he had earned a reputation for boldness, decisiveness, and tactical skill during service in the Boxer Rebellion, as commander of a cavalry division in the Russo-Japanese War, and as leader of the punitive expedition to Chita which ruthlessly exterminated the remnants of the Revolution of 1905. His military prowess was slightly shadowed by German descent and by some unexplained imbroglio which according to General Gourko "left his moral reputation considerably damaged." When in coming weeks his strange behavior caused these factors to be recalled, his colleagues nevertheless remained convinced of his loyalty to Russia.

Disregarding the cautions of General Jilinsky, commander of the Northwest Army Group, who was pessimistic from the start, and hastening the concentration of his three army corps and five and a half cavalry divisions, Rennenkampf opened his offensive on August 17. His First Army of some 200,000 men crossed the frontier along a 35-mile front split by Rominten Forest. Its objective was the Insterburg Gap, a distance of 37 miles from the frontier, or about three days' march at the Russian rate. The Gap was a stretch of open land about 30 miles wide lying between the fortified area of Königsberg to the north and the Masurian Lakes to the south. It was a country of small villages and large farms with unfenced fields and wide ranges of view from the occasional swells of high ground. Here the First Army would come through and engage the main German strength until Samsonov's Second Army, turning the lake barrier from the south, would arrive to deliver the decisive blow upon the German flank and rear. The two Russian armies were expected to join in a common front in the area of Allenstein.

General Samsonov's objective line, on a level with Allenstein, was 43 miles from the frontier, about three and a half or four days' march if all went well. Between his starting point, however, and his goal were many opportunities for the unexpected hazards—what Clausewitz called the "frictions"—of war. Owing to the lack of an east-west railway across Russian Poland to East Prussia, Samsonov's army could not cross the frontier until two days behind Rennenkampf's and would already have been on the march for a week before reaching the frontier. Its line of march was along sandy roads through a waste of undeveloped country spotted with forests and marshes and inhabited by a few poor Polish peasants. Once inside hostile territory there would be few resources of food and forage.

General Samsonov, unlike Rennenkampf, was new to the region and unfamiliar with his troops and staff. In 1877, at the age of eighteen, he had fought against the Turks; he was a general at forty-three; in the Russo-Japanese War he too had commanded a cavalry division; since 1909 he had been in semimilitary employment as governor of Turkestan. Aged fifty-five when the war broke out, he was on sick leave in the Caucasus and did not reach Warsaw and Second Army headquarters until August 12. Communication between his army and Rennenkampf's, as well as to Jilinsky's headquarters in the rear which was to coordinate the movements of both, was erratic. Precision in timing was not in any case a notable Russian virtue. Having played out the campaign in war games in April before the war with most of the same commanders and staff as were to take the field in August, the Russian General Staff was gloomily conscious of the difficulties. Although the war games, in which Sukhomlinov played the role of Commander in Chief, revealed that the First Army had started too soon, when war came the same schedule was adhered to without change. Counting two days for Rennenkampf's head start and four days for Samsonov's march, there would be a period of six days during which the German Army would have to face only one Russian army.

On August 17 General Rennenkampf's two cavalry corps, guarding his flanks on right and left, had orders not only to screen his advance but to cut both branches of the railway in order to prevent the withdrawal of German rolling stock.

Having deliberately used a railroad gauge different from the German as a defense against invasion, the Russians could not bring up their own rolling stock, or use the invaluable network of railroads in East Prussia unless they captured German trains. Naturally, the Germans left little rolling stock behind to be captured. The Russian Army, moving farther and farther from its base into hostile country, began almost at once to outrun its horse-drawn and not fully organized supply train. For communication, lacking the wire to lay their own lines, the Russians were dependent on German telegraph lines and offices, and when these were found destroyed they resorted to sending messages by wireless, in clear, because their divisional staffs lacked codes and cryptographers.

Little reconnaissance or artillery spotting was accomplished by airplane, most of the Air Force having been sent to the Austrian front. At sight of an airplane, the first they had ever seen, Russian soldiers, regardless of its identity, blazed away with their rifles, convinced that such a clever invention as a flying machine could only be German. The enlisted soldier consumed quantities of black bread and tea which were said—though it is not easy to see why—to give him a characteristic odor rather like that of a horse. He was armed with a four-edged bayonet which when mounted on a rifle made a weapon as tall as a man and in hand-to-hand combat gave him an advantage over the German. In firepower and fighting efficiency, however, German preponderance in artillery made two German divisions equal to three Russian. The Russian disadvantage was not helped by the mutual hatred of Sukhomlinov as War Minister and the Grand Duke as Commander in Chief, especially as liaison between front and rear was bad enough and the problem of supply worse. Before the fighting was a month old the shortage of shells and cartridges was already so desperate and the indifference or lethargy of the War Ministry so discouraging that on September 8 the Grand Duke was driven to appeal directly to the Czar. On the Austrian front, he reported, operations would have to be held up until stocks of shells reached 100 per gun. "At present we have only 25 per gun. I find it necessary to request Your Majesty to hasten the shipment of shells."

*

The cry "*Kosaken kommen!*" (The Cossacks are coming!) echoing out of East Prussia weakened Germany's resolve to leave the province with only a minimum defense. The Eighth Army in East Prussia, consisting of four and a half corps, one cavalry division, garrison troops of Königsberg and some territorial brigades, was about equal in numbers to either one of the two Russian armies. Its orders from Moltke were to defend East and West Prussia but not to allow itself to be overwhelmed by superior forces or to be driven into the fortress camp of Königsberg. If it found itself threatened by greatly superior forces, it was to withdraw behind the Vistula, leaving East Prussia to the enemy. Such orders contained "psychological dangers for weak characters," in the opinion of Colonel Max Hoffmann who was now deputy Chief of Operations for the Eighth Army.

The weak character Hoffmann had in mind was the Eighth Army's commander, Lieutenant-General von Prittwitz und Gaffron. As a court favorite Prittwitz had enjoyed a career of rapid promotions because, according to a fellow officer, he "knew how to get the Kaiser's ear at table with funny stories and salacious gossip." Now sixty-six years old and notorious for his girth, he was a German version of Falstaff, "impressive in appearance, conscious to the highest degree of his self-importance, ruthless, even coarse and self-indulgent." Known as *der Dicke* (Fatty), he was without intellectual or military interests and never moved if he could help it. In vain Moltke, who considered him unfit for his assignment, had tried for years to remove him from the designated command of the Eighth Army; Prittwitz's connections were proof against his efforts. The best Moltke could do was to appoint his own Deputy, Count von Waldersee, as Prittwitz's Chief of Staff. In August, Waldersee, suffering from the after effects of an operation, was in Hoffmann's opinion "not up to par," and since Prittwitz never had been, this left Hoffmann in the happy assurance that real power to direct the Eighth Army lay in the hands of the best qualified person, himself.

Anxiety for East Prussia became acute when on August 15 Japan declared for the Allies, freeing large numbers of Russian forces. In making or keeping friends, a task that forever eluded it, German diplomacy had failed again. Japan had her own ideas of her best interests in a European war, and these were well understood by their intended victim. "Japan is going to take advantage of this war to gain control of China," foretold President Yuan Shi-kai. As it proved, Japan used the opportunity of the war while the European Powers were too busy to stop her, to impose the Twenty-one Demands on China and to make the incursions into Chinese sovereignty and territory which were to twist the history of the twentieth century. To start with, the immediate effect of Japan's joining the Allies would be to release Russian forces from the Far East. Conjuring up visions of added Slavic hordes, the Germans now had new cause to be nervous about leaving East Prussia to be held by the lone Eighth Army.

From the beginning General von Prittwitz was having trouble controlling the commander of his Ist Corps, General von François, a bright-eyed officer of Huguenot ancestry, fifty-eight years old, who looked not unlike a German Foch. The Ist Corps was recruited from East Prussia, and its commander, determined that not one Slav should tread on Prussian soil, threatened to upset Eighth Army strategy by advancing too far.

Based on Hoffmann's calculations, the Eighth Army expected Rennenkampf's army to advance first, and anticipated meeting it in battle on August 19 or 20 in the area of Gumbinnen, about twenty-five miles from the Russian frontier, before it reached the Insterburg Gap. Three and a half corps, including François' Ist Corps, and a cavalry division were sent to meet it while the fourth corps was sent southeast to make contact with Samsonov's approaching army. On August 16 Eighth Army headquarters moved forward to Bartenstein, closer to the Insterburg front, where it was discovered that François had already reached and passed Gumbinnen. He believed in taking the offensive at once whereas Hoffmann's strategy was to let Rennenkampf's army come as far west as it could on its first two days' march on the theory that the farther it advanced from its base, the more vulnerable it would be. Hoffmann did not want it halted, but on the contrary allowed to reach the Gumbinnen area as soon as possible so as to give the Germans time to engage it alone before having to turn to face Samsonov.

François' advance beyond Gumbinnen where he had established his headquarters on August 16 threatened to pull the rest of the Eighth Army after him to support his flanks, thus extending itself beyond its powers. Prittwitz on the 16th peremptorily ordered him to halt. François indignantly protested by telephone that the nearer to Russia he engaged the enemy, the less risk to German territory. Prittwitz replied that a sacrifice of part of East Prussia was unavoidable, and dispatched a written order reminding François that he was "sole commander" and again prohibiting further advance. François ignored it. At 1:00 P.M. on August 17, Prittwitz "to his great astonishment" received a message from François that he was already in action in Stalluponen, twenty miles beyond Gumbinnen and only five miles from the Russian frontier.

That morning when Rennenkampf's army crossed the frontier in full force, his IIIrd Corps in the center began its march, more by lack of coordination than by design, several hours ahead of the other two. Russian reconnaissance having located François' forces at Stalluponen, orders were given to attack. Battle was joined a few miles east of the town. General von François and his staff were watching the progress of the fight from the steeple of the Stalluponen church when, "in the midst of this nerve-wracking tension," the church bell suddenly tolled with appalling sound upon their eardrums. The steeple shook with its vibrations, the telescope trembled on its tripod, and infuriated officers let loose a hail of Teutonic oaths upon the head of the unfortunate town councilman who had felt it to be his duty to warn the people of the Russians' approach.

Equal fury raged at Eighth Army headquarters on receipt of the message from François. He was ordered by telephone and telegraph to break off action, and a major-general was rushed off in person to confirm the order. Climbing to the belfry in no less bad temper than already raged there, he shouted at General von François, "The General in Chief orders you to stop the battle instantly and retire upon Gumbinnen!" Furious at the tone and manner, François grandiloquently retorted, "Inform General von Prittwitz that General von François will break off the engagement when he has defeated the Russians!"

Meanwhile a German brigade with five batteries of artillery had been sent around from the German right flank to attack the Russians from the rear. As the early advance of the Russian IIIrd Corps, especially of its 27th Division which was now engaged at Stalluponen, had opened a gap between itself and the neighboring Russian corps on its left, it was unprotected from the German attack. The regiment upon whom the German attack fell, broke and fled, involving the whole 27th Division in retreat and leaving 3,000 prisoners to the Germans. Although the rest of Rennenkampf's army reached the objective line laid down for it that day, the 27th Division had to retire to the frontier to reform, holding up the scheduled advance for the following day. Brimming with victory, François retired that same night toward Gumbinnen, after evacuating Stalluponen, personally convinced of the virtues of disobedience.

Despite the check, Rennenkampf's Army renewed its advance. But as early as August 19 it had begun to feel the drain of incomplete services of supply. Hardly fifteen miles from their own frontier, corps commanders reported supplies not coming up and messages not getting through to each other or to army headquarters. Ahead of them roads were clogged by massive, milling droves of cattle and sheep herded by the fleeing populace. The flight of the people and the retrograde movement of François' corps caused Rennenkampf and his superior, General Jilinsky, commander of the Northwest Front, to believe that the Germans were evacuating East Prussia. This did not suit the Russians, for if the German army retired too soon it would escape destruction by the Russian pincers. Rennenkampf consequently ordered a halt for the 20th, less because of his own difficulties than to entice the enemy forward into battle and allow more time for Samsonov's Second Army to come up for the decisive blow upon the German rear.

General von François was more than willing. With battle in his nostrils once more, he telephoned General von Prittwitz at Eighth Army headquarters on the 19th and clamored for permission to counterattack instead of continuing his retreat. It was a golden opportunity, he asserted, because the Russian advance was loose and scattered. He described feelingly the flight of the inhabitants and passionately urged the shame of yielding the soil of Prussia to the horrid footprint of the Slav. Prittwitz was torn. Intending to fight behind Gumbinnen, the Eighth Army had well-prepared positions along the river

Angerapp. But von François' too early advance had upset the plan and he was now some ten miles on the far side of Gumbinnen, to the east. To allow him to attack there would mean to accept battle away from the line of the Angerapp; the other two and a half corps would be pulled away with him and would be separated further from the XXth Corps sent to watch the approach of Samsonov's army from the south and which might need support at any time.

On the other hand, the spectacle of a German army retiring without serious battle, even if only for twenty miles, especially in full view of a terrified population, was distasteful. The decision was made more difficult when the Germans intercepted Rennenkampf's order to halt. The order was sent to Russian corps commanders by wireless in a simple code which a German professor of mathematics attached to the Eighth Army as cryptographer had no difficulty in solving.

This raised the question: How long would Rennenkampf halt? The time in which the Germans would be free to fight one Russian army without the other was running short; by that evening three of the six days would be gone. If the Germans waited on the Angerapp for Rennenkampf to come against them, they might be caught between both armies at once. Just at this moment, word was received from the XXth Corps that Samsonov's army had that morning crossed the frontier. The second claw of the pincer was advancing. The Germans must either fight Rennenkampf at once, giving up their prepared position on the Angerapp, or disengage and turn against Samsonov. Prittwitz and his Staff decided on the former, and told François to attack next morning, August 20. The only difficulty was that the other two and a half corps, dutifully waiting on the Angerapp, could not be activated in time to catch up with him.

Before dawn von François' heavy artillery opened fire, taking the Russians by surprise; the shelling continued for half an hour. At 4:00 A.M. his infantry moved forward over the stubbled fields in the uncertain dark until they came within rifle distance of the Russian lines. As morning broke, combat spread like a licking fire over the front. Russian field batteries poured shells on the advancing gray lines and saw the white road ahead suddenly turn gray with the bodies of the fallen. A second wave of gray charged, coming nearer. The Russians could make out the spiked helmets. Their batteries fired again, and the wave went down and another came. The Russian guns, supplied with ammunition at a rate of 244 rounds per day, were now firing at a rate of 440 per day. An airplane with black crosses flew over and bombed their artillery positions. The gray waves kept on coming. They were within 500 yards when the Russian guns stuttered and fell silent; their ammunition was used up. François' two divisions cut up the Russian 28th Division, inflicting a casualty rate of 60 per cent, virtual annihilation. François' cavalry with three batteries of horse artillery made a wide sweep around the open Russian end, unopposed by the Russian cavalry which, having no artillery, took itself off, permitting the Germans to fall upon the Russian transport in the rear. These were the fortunes of the corps on Rennenkampf's extreme right; on his center and left matters went very differently.

Here the Russians, warned by the sound of François' predawn cannon, were ready for the attack which came piecemeal over a front 35 miles wide. In the center the German XVIIth Corps did not reach the front until 8:00 A.M., four hours behind François, and on the German right the Ist Reserve-Corps did not arrive till noon. The XVIIth was commanded by General August von Mackensen, another of the group of generals who had fought in 1870 and were now sixty-five or over. The Ist Reserve was commanded by General Otto von Below. They had been behind the Angerapp on the evening of the 19th when they received the unexpected order to join François in an offensive beyond Gumbinnen next morning. Hurriedly assembling his units, Mackensen crossed the river during the night to become entangled on the other side among refugees, wagons, and livestock on the roads. By the time they sorted themselves out and advanced far enough to make contact with the enemy, they had lost the advantage of surprise and the Russians opened fire first. The effect of shelling by heavy guns is devastating, whoever is on the receiving end, and in this, one of the rare cases of 1914, the receivers were Germans. The infantry was pinned to the ground lying face down, not daring to raise their heads; ammunition wagons were blown up; horses were galloping riderless. By afternoon Mackensen's 35th Division broke under the fire. A company threw away its arms and ran; another caught the panic; then a whole regiment, then those on either side of it. Soon the roads and fields were covered with battalions streaming to the rear. Staff and divisional officers and Mackensen himself tore across the front in motors, attempting to stem the rout which continued for fifteen miles before it could be halted.

On Mackensen's right von Below's Ist Reserve Corps could give no help because it had started even later and, by the time it reached its appointed sector at Goldap on the edge of Rominten Forest, was at once heavily engaged by the Russians. The rout of Mackensen's corps in the center uncovered von Below's left flank, forcing him, too, to retire, both in order to cover Mackensen's retreat and to protect himself. On von Below's right the 3rd Reserve Division, commanded by General von Morgen, which had started from the Angerapp last of all did not arrive until evening when all was over, and saw no action. Although the Germans made good their retreat and the Russians had suffered severely against François, the Battle of Gumbinnen was on the whole a Russian victory.

Prittwitz saw his whole campaign undone. A vigorous Russian pursuit through the broken German center could smash through the Insterburg Gap, splitting the Eighth Army and pushing François' corps in the north into refuge within the Königsberg fortified zone which OHL had expressly warned must not be allowed to happen. To save the Eighth Army and hold it together, Prittwitz saw retreat to the Vistula as the only solution. Moltke's last words to him had been: "Keep the army intact. Don't be driven from the Vistula, but in case of extreme need abandon the region east of the Vistula." Prittwitz felt the extreme need was now, especially after a talk over the telephone with Mackensen who vividly described the panic of his troops.

At six o'clock that evening, August 20, he called François and told him that in spite of success on his sector the army must retreat to the Vistula. Thunderstruck, François protested violently, urged reasons for Prittwitz to reconsider, contended that because of their own losses the Russians could not mount an energetic pursuit, besought him to change his mind. He hung up with an impression that Prittwitz was not entirely adamant and had agreed to think it over.

At Headquarters, through a chaos of excited comings and goings and conflicting reports, an astonishing condition began clearly to emerge: there was no pursuit. At Russian headquarters Rennenkampf had given the order to pursue between three and four o'clock that afternoon, but owing to reports of heavy German artillery fire covering Mackensen's retreat had canceled the order at 4:30. Uncertain of the extent of the German rout in the center, he waited. An exhausted staff officer who asked his permission to go to bed was told he might lie down but not undress. He slept for an hour and was wakened by Rennenkampf who stood by his bed smiling and said, "You can take off your clothes now; the Germans are retiring."

Much has been made of this remark by the military historians who swarm over a battle after it is over, especially by Hoffmann who reports it with malicious glee in a rather distorted version. They point out with some truth that when an enemy is retiring is the time to pursue, not to go to bed. Because of the momentous results of the Battle of Tannenberg of which Gumbinnen was a preliminary, the episode of Rennenkampf's halt has raised clouds of fevered explanations and accusations, not omitting references to his German ancestry and the explicit charge that he was a traitor. The more probable explanation was offered a hundred years before the event by Clausewitz. "The whole weight of all that is sensuous in an army," he wrote in discussing the problem of pursuit, "presses for rest and refreshment. It requires exceptional vigor on the part of a commander to see and feel beyond the present moment and to act at once to attain those results which at the time seem to be the mere embellishments of victory—the luxury of triumph."

Whether or not Rennenkampf perceived those ultimate results, the fact was that he could not, or felt he could not, fling himself after the fleeing enemy to pluck the final victory. His supply lines were functioning weakly; to advance further beyond his railhead would be to outrun them altogether. He would be lengthening his lines in hostile territory while the Germans, falling back toward their base, were shortening theirs. He could not use the German railways without capturing their rolling stock, and he had no railroad gangs to alter the gauge. His transport was in chaos after the German cavalry attack; his right-wing cavalry had performed miserably; he had lost most of a division. He stayed where he was.

The evening was hot. Colonel Hoffmann was standing outside the house in which German headquarters was located, debating the battle and the prospects for tomorrow with his immediate superior Major General Grünert with whom he expected to govern the weaker wills of Prittwitz and Waldersee. Just then a message was brought to them. It was from General Scholtz of the XXth Corps reporting that the southern Russian army was now across the frontier with four or five corps and advancing over a front 50 to 60 miles wide. Hoffmann in that disturbing way he had, which no one quite knew whether to take seriously, suggested "suppressing" the report in order to keep it from Prittwitz and Waldersee who in his judgment "had for the moment lost command of their nerves." No other phrase in memoirs of the war attains the universality of "He lost control of his nerves," usually applied to a colleague; in this instance it was doubtless justified. Hoffmann's brief plot was in vain, however, for at that moment Prittwitz and Waldersee came out of the house wearing expressions showing that they too had received the report. Prittwitz called them all indoors and said: "Gentlemen, if we continue the battle against the Vilna Army, the Warsaw Army will advance on our rear and cut us off from the Vistula. We must break off the fight against the Vilna Army and retire behind the Vistula." He was no longer talking of retreat "to" but "behind" the Vistula.

Hoffmann and Grünert instantly disputed the necessity, claiming they could "finish off" battle with the Vilna Army in two or three days and still be in time to face the danger from the south, and until then Scholtz's Corps could "manage for themselves."

Prittwitz harshly cut them off. It was up to him and Waldersee to make the decision. He insisted that the threat of the southern Russian Army was too great. Hoffmann must make the necessary arrangements for retreat behind the Vistula. Hoffmann pointed out that the left wing of the southern army was already nearer to the Vistula than the Germans were and, demonstrating with a compass, showed that the retreat had become impossible. He asked to be "instructed" how to carry it out. Prittwitz abruptly dismissed him and everyone in the

1. General Joffre (center) with General de Castelnau (left) and General Pau.

2. Sir Henry Wilson talking with Foch and Colonel Huguet.

. General Sukhomlinov with staff officers.

4. The Czar and Grand Duke Nicholas.

5. (opposite page) The Kaiser and von Moltke

6. The *Goeben*.

7. Admiral Souchon.

8. King Albert.

9. Field Marshal Sir John French.

10. Prince Rupprecht (left) and the Kaiser.

11. General von François.

12. Colonel Hoffmann.

13. German cavalry officers in Brussels.

14. General Gallieni.

15. Joffre, Poincaré, King George V, Foch, and Haig.

16. General von Kluck.

room and telephoned to OHL at Coblenz announcing his intention to retreat to the Vistula if not behind it. He added that its waters in the summer heat were at low ebb and he was doubtful if he could even hold the river without reinforcements.

Moltke was aghast. This was the result of leaving that fat idiot in command of the Eighth Army, and of his own ill-considered last words to him. To yield East Prussia would be to suffer a tremendous moral defeat and lose the most valuable grain and dairy region as well. Worse, if the Russians crossed the Vistula they would threaten not only Berlin but the Austrian flank and even Vienna. Reinforcements! Where could he get reinforcements except from the Western Front where every last battalion was engaged. To withdraw troops from the Western Front now could mean loss of the campaign against France. Moltke was too shocked or too distant from the scene to think to issue a counterorder. For the moment he contented himself with ordering his staff to find out the facts in direct conversation with François, Mackensen, and the other corps commanders.

Meanwhile at Eighth Army Headquarters Hoffmann and Grünert were trying to persuade Waldersee that retreat was not the only course—was indeed an impossible course. Hoffmann now proposed a maneuver by which the Eighth Army, taking advantage of its interior lines and the use of railways, could so dispose itself as to meet the threat of both Russian armies and, if things developed as he thought they would, be in a position to throw all its weight against one of them.

He proposed, if Rennenkampf's army still did not pursue next day, and he did not think it would, to disengage François' Ist Corps and bring it the long way round by rail to reinforce Scholtz's XXth Corps on the southern front. François would take up a position on Scholtz's right opposite Samsonov's left wing, which, being nearest to the Vistula, was the most threatening. General von Morgen's division which had not been in action at Gumbinnen would also be sent to Scholtz's support by a different set of railway lines. The movement of troops with all their stores, equipment, horses, guns and munitions, the assembling of trains, the boarding at stations mobbed by refugees, the switching of trains from one line to another would be a complex matter, but Hoffmann was sure the German railroad system, on which so much brain power had been expended, would be equal to it.

While this movement was under way, the retreat of Mackensen's and von Below's corps would be directed toward the south for another two days' march so that when successfully disengaged they would be some 30 miles nearer the southern front. From here, if all went well, they would march across the short inner distance to take up a position on Scholtz's left which they should reach not long after François reached his right. Thus the whole army of four and a half corps would be in place to engage the enemy's southern army. The cavalry and Königsberg reserves would be left as a screen in front of Rennenkampf's army.

The success of this maneuver depended entirely upon a single condition—that Rennenkampf would not move. Hoffmann believed he would remain stationary for another day or more to rest and refit and make good his supply lines. His confidence was based not on any mysterious betrayal or other sinister or supernatural intelligence, but simply on his belief that Rennenkampf had come to a halt from natural causes. In any event Mackensen's and von Below's corps would not change fronts for another two or three days. By that time there should be some sign—with the help of further intercepted codes—of Rennenkampf's intentions.

Such was Hoffmann's argument, and he persuaded von Waldersee. Somehow, sometime that night Waldersee either persuaded Prittwitz or allowed Hoffmann to prepare the necessary orders without Prittwitz's approval—the record is not clear. As the Staff did not know that Prittwitz had in the meantime told OHL of his intention to retreat to the Vistula, no one bothered to inform the Supreme Command that the idea of retreat had been given up.

Next morning two of Moltke's staff, after battling the frustrations of the field telephone for some hours, succeeded in talking individually with each corps commander in the East, from whom they gathered that matters were serious but retreat too rash a solution. As Prittwitz seemed committed to retreat, Moltke decided to replace him. While he was talking it over with his deputy, von Stein, Colonel Hoffmann was enjoying the delightful sensation of being right—so far. Reconnaissance showed Rennenkampf's army quiescent; "they are not pursuing us at all." Orders were at once issued for the movement of François' Ist Corps to the south. François, according to his own account, was overcome with emotion and wept when he left Gumbinnen that afternoon. Prittwitz had apparently approved and immediately regretted it. That evening he called OHL again and told von Stein and Moltke that the proposal of his staff to advance against the Warsaw Army was "impossible—too daring." In reply to a question, he said he could not even guarantee to hold the Vistula with his "handful of men." He must have reinforcements. That sealed his dismissal.

With the Eastern Front in danger of collapse, someone bold, strong, and decisive was needed at once to take over the command. How a commander will meet the crises of real war is never certain in advance, but OHL was fortunate in knowing of a staff officer who only a week ago had proved himself in action—Ludendorff, the hero of Liège. He would do for Chief of Staff of the Eighth Army. In the German system of command exercised through a pair, the Chief of Staff was as important as the commanding officer and sometimes, depending on capacity and temperament, more so. Ludendorff was at that moment with von Bülow's Second Army on the outskirts of Namur where, following his success at Liège, he was directing the storming of Belgium's second great fortress. He was on the doorstep of France at a crucial moment—but the need of the Eastern Front was drastic. Moltke and von Stein agreed he must be called. A staff captain was instantly dispatched by motorcar with a letter which reached General Ludendorff at nine next morning, August 22.

"You may be able to save the situation in the East," wrote von Stein. "I know no other man in whom I have such absolute trust." He apologized for drawing Ludendorff away from the threshold of a decisive action "which, please God, will be conclusive," but the sacrifice was "imperative." "Of course, you will not be held responsible for what has already happened in the East but with your energy you can prevent the worst from happening."

Ludendorff left within fifteen minutes in the staff captain's car. Ten miles from Namur he drove through Wavre which "only the day before when I passed through it had been a peaceful town. Now it was in flames. Here also the populace fired on our troops."

At six that evening Ludendorff arrived at Coblenz. Within three hours he was briefed on the situation in the East, was received by Moltke, "who was looking tired," and by the Kaiser, who was "very calm" but deeply affected by the invasion of East Prussia. Ludendorff issued certain orders to the Eighth Army and departed at 9:00 P.M. by special train for the Eastern Front. The orders he issued, besides directing Hoffmann and Grünert to meet him at Marienburg, were for François' Corps to be sent by train to support Scholtz's XXth Corps on the southern front. Mackensen's and von Below's two corps were to complete their disengagement and rest and refit through August 23. These were the same as Hoffmann's orders, thus realizing the ideal of the German War College in which all students, given a problem, come up with the identical solution. It is also possible that Ludendorff saw a telegraphed copy of Hoffmann's orders.

During the drive through Belgium, Ludendorff was told by the staff captain that as new Commander of the Eighth Army OHL had selected a retired general but it was not yet known whether he would accept the post. His name was Paul von Beneckendorff und Hindenburg. Ludendorff did not know him. Before leaving Coblenz later that night, he learned that General von Hindenburg had been located, had accepted the post, and would board the train at Hanover next morning at 4:00 A.M.

After deciding on a Chief of Staff, OHL had turned to the problem of finding a commanding officer. Ludendorff, everybody felt, was certainly a man of undeniable ability, but to complete the pair it would be well to have a regular "von." The names of various retired corps commanders were considered. Von Stein remembered a letter he had received from a former comrade on the outbreak of war, saying, "Don't forget me if, as things develop, a commanding officer is needed anywhere," and promising that the writer was "still robust." Just the man. He came from an old Junker family established in Prussia for centuries. He had served on the General Staff under Schlieffen and risen through all the proper steps to become a corps chief of staff and subsequently a corps commander before retiring at sixty-five in 1911. He would be sixty-eight in two months but he was no older than Kluck, Bülow, and Hausen, the three generals of the right wing. What was wanted in the East, especially after Prittwitz's panic, was a man of no nerves, and Hindenburg, throughout a solid, dependable career had been known for his imperturbability. Moltke approved; the Kaiser gave his consent. A telegram was dispatched to the retired general.

Hindenburg was at home in Hanover when at 3:00 P.M. he received a telegram asking if he would accept "immediate employment." He replied, "I am ready." A second telegram instructed him to leave for the East at once to take command of the Eighth Army. OHL did not bother to invite him to Coblenz for talks. He was instructed to board the train at Hanover and informed that his Chief of Staff would be General Ludendorff who would meet him on the train en route. Hindenburg had just time to be fitted for one of the new field-gray uniforms before departing, much to his embarrassment, in the old blue uniform of a Prussian general.

When the recall of Prittwitz was made public a few days later, the invaluable diarist, Princess Blücher, noted, "A General Hindenburg, quite an old man, has taken his place." Newspaper editors hurriedly scraped together material about the new commander, which was difficult to find since he appeared under "Beneckendorff" in the Army list. They were gratified to discover that he had fought at Sedan where he received the Iron Cross, Second Class, and was also a veteran of the earlier war against Austria in 1866. His Beneckendorff ancestors were among the Teutonic Knights who had settled East Prussia; the name Hindenburg was a product of marriage connections in the eighteenth century. He was a native of Posen in West Prussia, and early in his career, as staff officer to the Ist Corps at Königsberg, had studied the military problems of the Masurian Lake district, a fact that was soon to become the germ of the legend that depicted Hindenburg planning the Battle of Tannenberg thirty years in advance. He had been brought up on his grandparents' estate in Neudeck in West Prussia and remembered having had talks as a boy with an old gardener who had once worked two weeks for Frederick the Great.

He was waiting at the station in Hanover when the train drew in at four in the morning. General Ludendorff whom he had never met "stepped briskly" to the platform to report himself. On the way east he explained the situation and the orders he had already issued. Hindenburg listened and approved. So was born, on the way to the battle that was to make them famous, the combination, the "marriage" expressed in the mystic monogram HL that was to rule imperial Germany until the end. When sometime later he was made a Field Marshal, Hindenburg earned the nickname "Marshal *Was-sagst-du*" because of his habit, whenever asked for an opinion, of turning to Ludendorff and asking, "*Was sagst du?*" (What do you say?)

Characteristically the first person OHL thought to inform of the change in the Eighth Army command was the Director of Railways on the Eastern Front, Major-General Kersten. On the afternoon of August 22, even before the special train had started on its way, this officer came into Hoffmann's office wearing "a very startled expression" and showed him a telegram announcing the arrival next day at Marienburg of an extra train bringing a new Commander and new Chief of Staff. That was how Prittwitz and Waldersee learned of their dismissal. An hour later Prittwitz received a personal telegram placing him and Waldersee on the "unattached list." "He took leave of us," says Hoffmann, "without a single word of complaint of this treatment."

Ludendorff's methods were no more tactful. Although he knew Hoffmann well, having lived in the same house with him in Berlin for four years when both were serving on the General Staff, he nevertheless telegraphed his orders to each of the corps commanders individually instead of through the Eighth Army Staff. This was not necessarily a deliberate effort to be offensive; it was normal for General Staff officers to be offensive. Hoffman and Grünert promptly felt insulted. The reception they tendered the new commanders at Marienburg was, says Ludendorff, "anything but cheerful."

The critical question on which the fate of the campaign hung now had to be faced. Should Mackensen's and von Below's corps remain where they were for defense against a further advance by Rennenkampf or should they be moved south in accordance with Hoffmann's plan to oppose Samsonov's right wing? There was no hope of defeating Samsonov's army except by the whole of the Eighth Army. François' Corps on that day, August 23, was finishing the intricate process of entrainment at five different stations between Insterberg and Königsberg and was now en route to the southern front. It would take another two days of switchings and sidings and equally intricate detrainment before it would be in position to fight. Von Morgen's division was also on its way by a different line. Mackensen's and von Below's corps were halted for the day. Cavalry reconnaissance reported continued "passivity" on the part of Rennenkampf's army. He was only separated from Mackensen and von Below by some thirty to forty miles, and if they were moved south against the other Russian army he could still—if he moved—follow and fall upon their rear. Hoffmann wanted Mackensen and von Below to start on their way at once. Ludendorff, barely thirty-six hours out of Namur and newly arrived in a situation in which a decision either way might be fatal and for which he would be responsible, was uncertain. Hindenburg, barely twenty-four hours out of retirement, was relying on Ludendorff.

On the Russian side the task of timing the pincers to close simultaneously upon the enemy tormented the higher command. So many and various, intractable and obvious were the stumbling blocks that the military chiefs were ridden with pessimism from the start. General Jilinsky, commander of the Northwest Front, whose function was to coordinate the movements of Rennenkampf's and Samsonov's armies, could think of no better way to perform it than by continued instructions to hurry. As Rennenkampf had started first and gone into action first, Jilinsky addressed all his hurry-up orders to Samsonov. At the same time Jilinsky himself was on the receiving end of a chain of ever more urgent pleas from the French. To relieve the pressure upon them in the West the French instructed their ambassador to "insist" upon the "necessity of the Russian armies prosecuting their offensive *à outrance* toward Berlin." From Joffre to Paris, from Paris to St. Petersburg, from St. Petersburg to "Stavka" (Russian General Headquarters at Baranovichi), from Stavka to Jilinsky the demands passed, and Jilinsky passed them all on to General Samsonov, struggling forward foot by foot through sand.

Since commanding a cavalry division in the Russo-Japanese War, this "simple and kindly man," as the British liaison officer with the Second Army called him, had had no experience fitting him to command an army of thirteen divisions. He was working through a staff and divisional commanders unfamiliar to him. Because the Russian Army was not organized on a regional basis, the newly reported reservists, numbering in some cases up to two-thirds of a regiment, were complete strangers to their NCOs and officers. The shortage of officers and the low, often nonexistent, level of literacy among the men did not ease the process of communicating orders down the line. Almost the worst confusion was in the signal corps. At the telegraph office in Warsaw a staff officer discovered to his horror a pile of telegrams addressed to the Second Army lying unopened and unforwarded because no communication had been established with field headquarters. The officer gathered them up and delivered them by car. Corps headquarters had only enough wire to connect with the divisional commands but not enough to connect with Army Headquarters or with neighboring corps. Hence the resort to wireless.

Because of the insistence on haste four days had been cut out of the period of concentration, leaving the organization of the rear services incomplete. One corps had to dole out its shells to another whose supply train had not come up, thus upsetting its own calculations. Bakery wagons were missing. To enable an army to live off the country in hostile territory, requisitioning parties were required to be sent ahead under cavalry escort, but no arrangements for this had been made. Single-horse power proved inadequate to pull wagons and gun carriages over the sandy roads. In some places the horses had to be unharnessed from half the wagons, hitched up in double harness to the other half, moved forward a certain distance, unhitched, brought back, harnessed up to the stranded wagons, and the process begun all over again.

"Hurry up the advance of the Second Army and hasten your operations as energetically as possible," Jilinsky wired on August 19. "The delay in the advance of the Second Army is putting the First Army in a difficult position." This was not true. Samsonov on the 19th was crossing the frontier on schedule, but

Jilinsky was so sure it was going to be true that he was anticipating.

"Advancing according to timetable, without halting, covering marches of more than 12 miles over sand. I cannot go more quickly," Samsonov replied. He reported that his men were on the move for ten or twelve hours a day without halts. "I must have immediate and decisive operations," Jilinsky telegraphed three days later. "Great weariness" of his men made greater speed impossible, Samsonov answered. "The country is devastated, the horses have long been without oats, there is no bread."

On that day Samsonov's XVth Corps commanded by General Martos came up against the German XXth Corps of General Scholtz. Combat was opened. The Germans, not yet reinforced, retreated. About ten miles inside the frontier General Martos captured Soldau and Neidenburg which until a few hours before had been General Scholtz's headquarters. When Cossack patrols entering Neidenburg reported German civilians firing on them from the windows, General Martos ordered a bombardment of the town which destroyed most of the main square. A "small, gray man," he personally felt uncomfortable that night when he found himself billetted in a house whose German owners had departed, leaving behind their family photographs staring at him from the mantelpiece. It was the mayor's house, and General Martos ate a dinner prepared for the mayor and served by his maid.

On August 23, the day Ludendorff and Hindenburg arrived in the East, the Russian VIth and XIIIth corps on the right of General Martos captured more villages; General Scholtz, still alone except for some support from the Vistula garrison behind him, backed up a little farther. Ignoring Rennenkampf's inactivity in the north, Jilinsky continued to rain orders on Samsonov. The Germans on his front were hastily retreating, he told Samsonov, "leaving only insignificant forces facing you. You are therefore to execute a most energetic offensive. . . . You are to attack and intercept the enemy retiring before General Rennenkampf's army in order to cut off his retreat from the Vistula."

This was, of course, the original design, but it was predicated on Rennenkampf's holding the Germans occupied in the north. In fact, on that date Rennenkampf was no longer in contact with the enemy. He began to advance again on August 23 but in the wrong direction. Instead of moving crabwise to the south to link up with Samsonov in front of the lakes, he moved straight west to mask Königsberg, fearful that François would attack his flank if he turned south. Although it was a movement with no relevance at all to the original design, Jilinsky did nothing to alter it. Operating like Rennenkampf in a complete fog as to the German movements, he assumed they were doing what the Russians had planned on their doing—retreating to the Vistula. Accordingly, he continued to push Samsonov forward.

On the evening of August 23, General Martos' Corps, encouraged by the feel of the enemy falling back, moved on from Neidenburg and reached positions within 700 yards of the German lines. Scholtz's Corps was entrenched between the villages of Orlau and Frankenau. The Russians were under orders to take the trenches at all costs. They lay all night in position and crept forward another hundred yards before dawn. When the signal for attack came they took the last 600 yards in three rushes, throwing themselves to the ground under the fire of the German machine guns, surging forward again—and down and up again. As the wave of white-bloused figures with their glistening bayonets closed in, the Germans scrambled from the trenches, abandoned their machine guns, and fled. Elsewhere along the line German superiority in artillery punished the attackers. The Russian XIIIth Corps on Martos' right, owing to a blunder in communications or poor generalship, or both, failed to come to his support, and no great advantage was gained from the engagement. By the end of the day the Germans were in retreat but not routed. The Russians captured two field guns and some prisoners, but their own losses were high, a total of 4,000. One regiment lost 9 out of 16 company commanders. One company lost 120 out of 190 men and all its officers.

Though German losses were less, Scholtz, facing overwhelming numbers, withdrew for some ten miles, establishing his headquarters for the night in the village of Tannenberg. Still harried by Jilinsky who insisted that he must move on to the agreed line where he could cut off the enemy's "retreat," Samsonov issued orders to all his corps—the XXIIIrd on the left, the XVth and XIIIth in the center, the VIth on the right—giving their dispositions and lines of march for the following day. Beyond Neidenberg communications had become ever more feeble. One corps had run out of wire altogether and was relying on mounted orderlies. The VIth Corps did not possess the key to the cipher used by the XIIIth. Consequently, Samsonov's orders were issued by wireless in clear.

Up to this moment, some twenty-four hours since the arrival of Ludendorff and Hindenburg, the Eighth Army had not yet decided whether to bring down Mackensen's and von Below's corps to oppose Samsonov's right wing. Hindenburg and his staff came down to Tannenberg to consult Scholtz who was "grave but confident." They returned to Headquarters. That evening, Hoffmann wrote later, "was the most difficult of the whole battle." While the staff was debating, a signal corps officer brought in an intercept of Samsonov's orders for the next day, August 25. Although this assistance from the enemy did not reveal Rennenkampf's intentions which were the crucial question, it did show the Germans where they might expect to meet Samsonov's forces. That helped. The Eighth Army made up its mind to throw all its strength into battle against Samsonov. Orders went out to Mackensen and von Below to turn their backs on Rennenkampf and march south at once.

16

Tannenberg

HAUNTED BY the knowledge of Rennenkampf at his rear, Ludendorff was in a hurry to come to grips with Samsonov. He gave orders for the first stage of the battle to begin on August 25. It was to be an attack on Usdau by General von François' Ist Corps with intent to envelop Samsonov's left wing. François refused. His heavy artillery and some of his infantry were still detraining from the journey that had brought them the long way around from the Gumbinnen front and had not yet come up. To attack without full artillery support and a full supply of ammunition, he argued, would be to risk failure; if Samsonov's path of retreat were left open he would escape the destruction planned for him. He was privately upheld by Hoffmann and by General Scholtz of the XXth Corps who, although he had been in battle against the Russians on the previous day, assured François over the field telephone that he could hold his ground without immediate support.

Confronted by insubordination on the second day of his new command, Ludendorff in a high temper drove down by car to François' headquarters, bringing Hindenburg and Hoffmann with him. In reply to his insistence François said, "If the order is given, of course I shall attack but my troops will be obliged to fight with the bayonet." To show who was in command Ludendorff brushed aside François' reasons and reissued his orders unchanged. Hindenburg said nothing during the interview and when it was over dutifully drove off with Ludendorff. Hoffmann in another car stopped at the railroad station at Montovo, the nearest place in telephone and telegraph communication with Headquarters. Here a signal corps officer handed him two intercepted Russian wireless messages, both sent in clear, one by Rennenkampf at 5:30 that morning and one by Samsonov at 6:00 A.M. Rennenkampf's orders, giving marching distances for the First Army, revealed that his objective line for the next day would not bring him far enough to threaten the German Army from the rear. Samsonov's orders, following the previous day's battle against General Scholtz, revealed that he had misinterpreted Scholtz's backward wheel as full retreat and gave exact directions and times of movement for the pursuit of what he believed was a defeated foe.

No such boon had been granted a commander since a Greek traitor guided the Persians around the pass at Thermopylae. The very completeness of the messages made Major General Grünert, Hoffmann's immediate superior, suspicious. As Hoffmann tells it, "He kept asking me anxiously over and over if we should believe them? Why shouldn't we? . . . I myself believed every word of them on principle." Hoffmann claimed to have personal knowledge of a private quarrel between Rennenkampf and Samsonov dating from the Russo-Japanese War, in which he had been Germany's observer. He said that Samsonov's Siberian Cossacks, after a brave fight, had been obliged to yield the Yentai coal mines because Rennenkampf's cavalry division had remained inactive despite repeated orders and that Samsonov had then knocked Rennenkampf down in a heated quarrel on the platform of the Mukden railway station. Obviously, he demonstrated triumphantly, Rennenkampf would be in no hurry to come to Samsonov's aid. As it was less a question of aiding Samsonov than of winning—or losing—the campaign, it is arguable whether Hoffmann believed his own tale or only pretended to; he always remained fond of telling the story.

Grasping the intercepted messages, he and Grünert hurried to their car, sped after Hindenburg and Ludendorff, and on overtaking them within a few miles, Hoffmann ordered the chauffeur to draw level and handed over the messages while the cars were in motion. All came to a stop while the four officers studied the situation. It showed that the attack planned for next day in which Mackensen's and Below's corps were to attack Samsonov's right wing could proceed without interference from Rennenkampf. According to differing interpretations by the disputants, it either did or did not show that François could afford to postpone his attack until all his men and material were up. Unwilling to yield an inch of authority, Ludendorff, on returning to Headquarters, reiterated his orders.

At the same time orders were given to carry out the general

plan for double envelopment next day, August 26. On the German left Mackensen's corps, supported by Below's, was to attack Samsonov's extreme right wing which had reached a position—at Bischofsburg with cavalry at Sensburg—in front of the lakes where it could have joined fronts with Rennenkampf if he had been there. His absence left open the flank which the Germans hoped to envelop. In the center Scholtz's XXth Corps, now supported by a Landwehr division and General von Morgen's 3rd Reserve Division, was to renew its battle of the day before. On the German right François as ordered was to open the attack that would envelop Samsonov's left wing.

All orders went out before midnight of August 25. Next morning, the opening day of general battle, Ludendorff was attacked by a fit of nerves when a reconnaissance aviator reported movements by Rennenkampf in his direction. Although Hindenburg felt assured that the Eighth Army "need not have the least hesitation" in leaving only a screen against Rennenkampf, all Ludendorff's anxiety returned. Rennenkampf's "formidable host hung like a threatening thunder cloud to the northeast," he wrote. "He need only have closed with us and we should have been beaten." He began to feel the same fears that had assailed Prittwitz and to hesitate whether to commit all his forces against Samsonov or to abandon the offensive against the Russian Second Army and turn back against the First. The hero of Liège "seems to have lost his nerve a little," happily recorded Hoffmann, who of all military writers is the most prodigal in attributing this weakness to his colleagues. Even Hindenburg acknowledges that "grave doubts" afflicted his companion and at this moment, as he claims, it was he who stiffened his Chief of Staff. In his words, "We overcame the inward crisis."

A different crisis erupted when Headquarters discovered that François, who was still waiting for his artillery, had not begun battle as ordered. Ludendorff imperatively demanded that the attack begin at noon. François replied that the preliminary ground which Headquarters supposed had been taken that morning had not been gained, provoking an explosion and what Hoffmann describes as a "probably unfriendly" reply from Ludendorff. Throughout the day François managed to balk and procrastinate and wait for his own moment.

Suddenly an extraordinary telephone call all the way from OHL in Coblenz broke in upon the argument wtih François. Worried enough, without trouble from Supreme Headquarters, Ludendorff picked up the receiver and ordered Hoffmann to listen in on another receiver to "what they want." To his astonishment he heard Colonel Tappen, Chief of Operations at OHL, propose to send him reinforcements of three corps and a cavalry division. Fresh from the Western Front, Ludendorff, who had worked on the mobilization plans and knew to the last decimal the required density of manpower per mile of offensive, could hardly believe what he heard. Schlieffen's plan depended on using every last man to strengthen the right wing. What could have persuaded OHL to weaken its line by three whole corps at the height of the offensive? Appalled, he told Tappen that the reinforcements were not "positively" needed in the East and would in any event arrive too late for the battle that was already beginning. Tappen said they could be spared.

The origin of this crucial decision was the panic at OHL when the Russians launched their offensive two weeks after mobilization instead of the six weeks on which the German plan was predicated. The saving factor, as Tappen reports it, was the "great victory" on the French frontiers which "aroused in OHL the belief that the decisive battle in the West had been fought and won." Under this impression Moltke decided, on August 25, "in spite of objections put to him," to send reinforcements to save East Prussia from the Russians. The woes of the refugees, the Junker estates left to marauding Cossacks, the tearful pleas of well-born ladies to the Kaiserin to save family lands and fortunes were having their effect. In order to arouse feeling against the Russians, the German government had deliberately distributed the refugees in various cities and succeeded in frightening itself. The President of the East Prussian Bundesrat came to OHL to beg for aid to his homeland. A director of Krupp's wrote in his diary on August 25: "People said on all sides, 'Bah! the Russians will never come to the end of their mobilization. . . . We can remain on the defensive for a long time.' But today everyone thinks quite differently and the talk is all of abandoning East Prussia." The Kaiser was deeply affected. Moltke himself had always worried about the light defense in the East, for, as he wrote before the war, "all the success on the Western Front will be unavailing if the Russians arrive in Berlin."

Two of the corps he now withdrew from the Western Front had been in the fighting for Namur at the junction between the German Second and Third Armies and now, upon the fall of the Belgian fortress, were declared disposable by General von Bülow. With the 8th Cavalry Division they were detached on August 26 and marched—because of the destruction of Belgian railroads—to stations in Germany for transport "as quickly as possible" to the Eastern Front. Another corps had got as far as the railroad station in Thionville when cautionary voices at OHL persuaded Moltke to cancel its orders.

Eight hundred miles to the east General Samsonov was preparing for renewed battle on August 26. On his extreme right his VIth Corps under General Blagovestchensky had duly reached the planned rendezvous area in front of the lakes, but Samsonov had left this corps isolated and detached while he pushed the main body of his army in a more westerly direction. Although this drew it away from Rennenkampf, or from the place where Rennenkampf was supposed to be, it was the right direction, Samsonov thought, to bring him between the Vistula and the Germans supposedly retreating to the west. Samsonov's objective was the line Allenstein-Osterode where he could get astride the main German railway and from where, as he informed Jilinsky on August 23, "it would be easier to advance into the heart of Germany."

It was already apparent that his exhausted and semistarved troops who had barely managed to stumble to the frontier were hardly fit for battle much less for the heart of Germany. Rations were not coming up, the soldiers had eaten up their reserve rations, villages were deserted, hay and oats in the fields were not yet cut, and little could be scraped off the land for men or horses. All the corps commanders were calling for a halt. A General Staff officer reported to Jilinsky's Headquarters the "miserable" provisioning of the troops. "I don't know how the men bear it any longer. It is essential to organize a proper requisitioning service." At Volkovisk, 180 miles east of the battlefront as the crow flies and even farther by roundabout railway connections, Jilinsky was too remote to be disturbed by these reports. He insisted upon Samsonov continuing the offensive "to meet the enemy retreating in front of General Rennenkampf and cut off his retreat to the Vistula."

This version of what the enemy was doing was based on Rennenkampf's reports, and as Rennenkampf had kept no contact with the Germans after the Battle of Gumbinnen his reports of their movements were an amiable fantasy. By now, however, Samsonov realized from evidence of railroad movements and other bits of intelligence that he was facing not an army in full retreat but an army which had reorganized and was advancing toward him. Reports of the concentration of a new enemy force—this was François' Corps—opposite his left flank were coming in. Recognizing the danger to his left, he sent an officer to urge upon Jilinsky the necessity of shifting his army westward instead of continuing north. With a rear commander's contempt for a front commander's caution, Jilinsky took this to be a desire to go on the defensive, and "rudely" replied to the officer: "To see the enemy where he does not exist is cowardice. I will not allow General Samsonov to play the coward. I insist that he continue the offensive." His strategy, according to a colleague, seemed designed for *Poddavki*, a Russian form of checkers in which the object is to lose all one's men.

On the night of August 25 at the same time as Ludendorff was issuing his orders, Samsonov disposed his forces. In the center the XVth and XIIth Corps under General Martos and General Kliouev with one division of the XXIIIrd Corps under General Kondratovitch were to carry the main advance to the line Allenstein-Osterode. The army's left flank was to be held by General Artomonov's Ist Corps supported by the other division of the XXIIIrd Corps. Fifty miles away the isolated VIth Corps held the right flank. The reconnaissance techniques of Russian cavalry being less than competent, Samsonov did not know that Mackensen's Corps, last seen streaming in panic from the field of Gumbinnen, had reorganized and in forced marches, together with Below's Corps, had reached his front and was now advancing upon his right. At first he ordered the VIth Corps to hold its position "with the object of protecting the right flank of the army," and then changed his mind and told them to come down "with all speed" to support the advance of the center upon Allenstein. At the last minute on the morning of the 26th the order was changed to the original duty of remaining in position to protect the right flank. By that time the VIth Corps was already on the march toward the center.

Far to the rear a sense of disaster pervaded the Russian High Command. As early as August 24 Sukhomlinov, the War Minister who had not bothered to build arms factories because he did not believe in firepower, wrote General Yanushkevitch, the beardless Chief of Staff: "In God's name, issue orders for gathering up the rifles. We have sent 150,000 to the Serbs, our reserves are nearly used up and factory production is feeble." Despite the fervor of such gallant officers as the general who cantered to war shouting "William to St. Helena!" the mood of the army chiefs from the beginning was one of gloom. They entered the war without confidence and remained in it without faith. Gossip of the pessimism at Headquarters reached the inevitable ear of the French ambassador in St. Petersburg. On August 26 he was told by Sazonov that Jilinsky "considers that an offensive in East Prussia is doomed to defeat." Yanushkevitch was said to agree and to be protesting strongly against the offensive. General Danilov, Deputy Chief of the Staff, was insisting, however, that Russia could not disappoint France and would have to attack despite "indubitable risks."

Danilov was stationed with the Grand Duke at Stavka, the General Staff Headquarters at Baranovichi. A quiet place in the woods where Stavka was to remain for a year, Baranovichi was chosen because it was the junction of a north-south railway line with the main line between Moscow and Warsaw. Both fronts, the German and Austrian, were superintended from here. The Grand Duke with his personal suite, the chief officers of the General Staff, and the Allied military attachés lived and ate in the railroad cars because it was discovered that the house intended for the Commander in Chief was too far from the stationmaster's house used by the Operations and Intelligence staffs. Roofs were built over the cars to protect them from sun and rain, wooden sidewalks were laid out, and a marquee was erected in the station garden where meals were taken in summer. Pomp was absent and physical shortcomings ignored except for the low doorways against which the Grand Duke had an unfortunate tendency to bump his head. Fringes of white paper had to be fixed over all entrances to catch the Grand Duke's eye and remind him to duck.

Danilov was disquieted by Rennenkampf's obvious loss of contact with the enemy and by failing communications as a result of which Jilinsky appeared not to know where the armies were nor the armies each other. When news reached Stavka that Samsonov had engaged the enemy on August 24–25 and was about to renew the battle, anxiety about Rennenkampf's failure to bring up the other arm of the pincers became acute. On August 26 the Grand Duke visited Jilinsky's headquarters at Volkovisk to insist upon Rennenkampf being urged forward. In his leisurely pursuit begun on August 23, Rennenkampf had passed through the former German positions on the Angerapp which the Eighth Army had abandoned in its great transfer to the south. Evidences of hurried departure confirmed his picture of a beaten enemy. According to the notes of one of his Staff officers, he believed it would be a mistake to push the Germans too rapidly. They might then fall back to the Vistula before they could be cut off by Samsonov. Rennenkampf made no effort to follow closely enough to confirm conjecture by eyesight nor did this omission appear to worry Jilinsky, who accepted Rennenkampf's version without question.

The orders Jilinsky issued to Rennenkampf on the day after the Grand Duke's visit were to pursue an enemy he still assumed to be retreating and to guard against a possible German sortie from the fortress of Königsberg upon his flank. It had been intended to mask Königsberg with six reserve divisions, but these had not yet come up. Now Jilinsky instructed Rennenkampf to blockade Königsberg with two corps until the reserve divisions arrived and with his other two corps to pursue "those enemy troops which do not take refuge in Königsberg and may be supposed to be retreating to the Vistula." "Supposing" the enemy to be retreating, he did not conceive of him threatening Samsonov and did not urge Rennenkampf to hurry to close the junction with Samsonov's right wing as originally planned. He merely told him that the "combined operations" of the First and Second Armies must aim at pressing the retreating Germans toward the sea and away from the Vistula. As the two Russian Armies were neither in contact nor moving toward each other, the word "combined" was hardly applicable.

When morning broke on August 26 Samsonov's VIth Corps began its march toward the center in obedience to orders it did not know had been canceled. One division was under way when the other division received news that enemy forces had been sighted some six miles behind it to the north. Assuming these were troops retreating from Rennenkampf, the Russian divisional commander decided to turn around and attack them. The force was in fact Mackensen's Corps, itself moving forward to attack. It fell upon the Russians, and while they were fighting to save themselves, their fellow division, which had already marched eight miles, was desperately summoned. It marched back again and after covering nineteen miles came up at the end of the day against a second enemy corps, Below's. Contact between the two Russian divisions was lost. The corps commander, General Blagovestchensky, "lost his head" (in this case the formula is applied by a British military critic); the divisional commander, whose group had been in battle all day, suffering 5,000 casualties and the loss of sixteen field guns, ordered retreat on his own initiative. During the night orders and counterorders added to the confusion, units became mixed up on the roads, and by morning the VIth Corps was in a disorganized shambles and continuing to fall back. Samsonov's right wing had been turned.

While this was happening, his center of two and a half corps took the offensive. General Martos was in the middle, heavily engaged. His neighbor on the left, a division of the XXIIIrd Corps, was repulsed and thrown back, exposing his flank. On his right General Kliouev's XIIIth Corps took Allenstein but learning that Martos was in trouble moved to his support, leaving Allenstein to be occupied by the VIth Corps which Kliouev supposed to be on its way. The VIth of course never came, and a gap was left at Allenstein.

A few miles behind the front, at Second Army Headquarters in Neidenburg, General Samsonov was at dinner with his Chief of Staff, General Potovsky, and the British military attaché, Major Knox, when the beaten division of the XXIIIrd Corps poured into the streets. In the mood of fear any sound made them think themselves pursued; an ambulance wagon clattering up raised cries of "Uhlans coming!" Hearing the commotion Samsonov and Potovsky, a nervous individual who wore pince-nez and was known, for some now obscure reason, as the "Mad Mullah," buckled on their swords and hurried out. They saw at firsthand the condition of the troops. The men were "terribly exhausted . . . they had been three days without bread or sugar." "For two days my men received no rations and none of the supplies came up," one regimental commander told them.

Although he had not yet received full news of the disaster to the VIth Corps on the right, Samsonov realized by the end of the day that it was no longer a question of enveloping the enemy but of saving himself from envelopment. He nevertheless decided not to break off battle but to renew it next day with his center corps in an effort to hold the Germans until Rennenkampf should come up to deal them the decisive blow. He sent orders to General Artomonov, commander of the Ist Corps holding the front opposite François on the Russians' extreme left, "to protect the flank of the Army . . . at all costs." He felt sure that "not even a greatly superior enemy can break the resistance of the famous Ist Corps," and added that success of the battle depended on their holding firm.

Next morning, the 27th, the impatiently awaited moment for François' offensive had come. His artillery had arrived. At 4:00 A.M., before it was light, a hurricane bombardment of tremendous impact broke upon positions of the Russian Ist Corps at Usdau. The German High Command, with Hindenburg ponderously calm, Ludendorff grim and tense, and Hoffmann behind them, a mocking shadow, left their temporary headquarters at Löbau, twenty miles away, to take up a position on a hill from which Ludendorff intended to "superintend on the spot" the coordination of François' and Scholtz's corps. Before they could even reach the hill news was brought that Usdau was taken. In the midst of rejoicing the report was almost immediately followed by another denying the first. The roar of the artillery barrage continued. In the Russian trenches the men of the "famous Ist Corps," unfed like their fellows of the XXIIIrd and drained of the will to fight, fled from under the torrent of shells, leaving behind them as many dead as those who got away. By 11:00 A.M. the Russian Ist Corps had abandoned the field, the battle had been won by artillery alone, and Ludendorff, whose premature orders might have lost it, felt that the Russian Second Army was now "broken through."

But it was not beaten, and he found that "in contrast to other wars" the battle had not been won in a day. François' advance was still being held east of Usdau; the two Russian corps in the center, a formidable body of men, were still attacking; the threat of Rennenkampf still hung over his rear. Roads were clogged with refugees and livestock; whole villages were fleeing. German soldiers, too, were exhausted and they too conjured pursuit out of the clatter of hoofs and cried, "They're coming!" which, as it passed down a column, became "The Cossacks are coming!" On returning to Löbau the High Command heard with horrified disbelief a report that François' Corps was fleeing and that "relics" of its units were coming into Montovo. A frantic telephone call ascertained that retreating troops of the Ist Corps could indeed be seen in dispirited groups in front of the railroad station. If François' flank had somehow been turned the battle might be lost, and for one awful moment the prospect of a lost campaign, retreat behind the Vistula, abandonment of East Prussia, rose up as it had before Prittwitz. Then it was discovered that the troops in Montovo belonged to one battalion only that in the fighting beyond Usdau had given way.

Late that day the truth that the Germans were not after all "retreating to the Vistula" but advancing against Samsonov finally penetrated Jilinsky's Headquarters. At last he telegraphed to Rennenkampf that the Second Army was under heavy attack and he should cooperate "by moving your left flank as far forward as possible," but the objectives given were too westerly and not far enough advanced and no mention was made of haste or forced marches.

The battle was in its third day. Two armies, now totally committed, surged and gripped and broke apart and clashed again in confused and separate combats over a front of forty miles. A regiment advanced, its neighbor was thrown back, gaps appeared, the enemy thrust through or, unaccountably, did not. Artillery roared, cavalry squadrons, infantry units, heavy horse-drawn field-gun batteries moved and floundered through villages and forests, between lakes, across fields and roads.

Shells smashed into farmhouses and village streets. A battalion advancing under cover of shellfire disappeared behind a curtain of smoke and mist to some unknown fate. Columns of prisoners herded to the rear blocked the advancing troops. Brigades took ground or yielded it, crossed each other's lines of communication, became tangled up with the wrong division. Field commanders lost track of their units, staff cars sped about, German scout planes flew overhead trying to gather information, army commanders struggled to find out what was happening, and issued orders which might not be received or carried out or conform to realities by the time they reached the front. Three hundred thousand men flailed at each other, marched and tiredly countermarched, fired their guns, got drunk if they were lucky enough to occupy a village or sat on the ground in the forest with a few companions while night came; and the next day the struggle went on and the great battle of the Eastern Front was fought out.

General von François opened battle at dawn on the 28th with another great artillery barrage. Ludendorff ordered him to veer left to relieve the pressure upon Scholtz's Corps, which he believed to be "greatly exhausted." Ignoring him, François held to a straight eastward advance, determined to complete envelopment of Samsonov's flank and cut off his retreat. After his successful disobedience of the day before, Ludendorff now almost pleaded with François to obey orders. The Ist Corps would "render the greatest possible service to the army by carrying out these instructions," he said. Paying no attention, François drove eastward, posting detachments along the roads as he moved to keep the enemy from breaking out.

In anxiety for the center, Ludendorff and Hindenburg waited out the battle at Scholtz's field headquarters in the village of Frögenau, about two miles from an even smaller village, Tannenberg. Orders were date-lined from Frögenau. Ludendorff was again tortured by apprehension about Rennenkampf. Worried about Scholtz's Corps, angered at François, harassed by the "very ineffective field telephone" connecting him with that insubordinate commander and by the absence of any telephone communication at all with Mackensen and Below on his left wing, he was "far from satisfied." Mackensen and Below, confused by conflicting orders to take first this direction and then that, sent a Staff officer by airplane to Headquarters to straighten matters out. He received a "far from friendly reception" because neither corps was in the location it was supposed to be. Toward afternoon, however, both were moving satisfactorily, Mackensen pushing after the broken Russian right wing and Below heading for the gap at Allenstein to attack the Russian center. Now François' progress appeared more justified, and Ludendorff issued revised orders to him to pursue the direction he was already taking.

Just as the conviction of coming victory began to settle warmly over German Headquarters, news came in that Rennenkampf's army was unmistakably on the march. But the day's progress by now gave assurance that he would be too late. In fact, at that night's bivouac, Rennenkampf's nearest corps was still twenty miles from Bischofsburg where Samsonov's VIth Corps had been defeated two days before. Making slow progress in hostile territory, Rennenkampf's furthest advance by the end of the next day, August 29, was some ten miles farther west but no farther south and he had made no contact with Samsonov. None was ever to be made.

The collapse of the "famous Ist Corps" in whose resistance he had put such faith, on top of the collapse of the VIth Corps on his other wing, presaged the end to General Samsonov. Both his flanks were turned; his cavalry, the only arm in which he outnumbered the Germans, having been deployed too wide of the flanks, had played no useful part in the battle and was now isolated; supplies and communications were in complete chaos; only the steadfast XVth and XIIIth Corps were still fighting. At his headquarters in Neidenburg he could hear the sound of François' approaching guns. There seemed to him to be only one thing to do. He telegraphed Jilinsky that he was leaving for the battlefront and then, ordering baggage and wireless apparatus to be sent back to Russia, cut his communications with the rear. The reasons for his decision, it has been said, "he took with him to his grave," but they are not hard to understand. The army that had been given him to command was crumbling under him. He became again a cavalry officer and divisional general and did the thing he knew best. With seven of his Staff on horses commandeered from some Cossacks, he rode off to take personal command under fire, in the saddle where he felt at home.

Outside Neidenburg on August 28 he took farewell of Major Knox. Samsonov was sitting on the ground surrounded by his staff, studying some maps. He stood up, took Knox aside, and told him the situation was "critical." He said his own place and duty were with the army, but as Knox's duty was to report to his government he advised him to return "while there was time." He mounted, turned in the saddle and said with a wistful smile, "The enemy has luck one day, we will have luck another," as he rode away.

Later, General Martos, who was conducting the battle in his sector from a hilltop, had just ordered a column of German prisoners to be led out of the fighting line when to his astonishment the General of the Army came up on horseback with his Staff. Samsonov asked about the retiring column, and on being told they were prisoners he reined his horse close to Martos, leaned over to embrace him and said sadly, "You alone will save us." But he knew better, and that night gave the order for a general retreat of what was left of the Second Army.

The retreat during the next two days, August 29 and 30, was a mounting and inexorable disaster. The two center corps which had fought longest and best, and had advanced the farthest and retreated last, had the least chance to escape and were the most completely netted in the German envelopment. General Kliouev's Corps was still on the offensive when Below broke through the gap on his right at Allenstein and completed the cordon around the Russian center. His corps and that of General Martos thrashed about helplessly in the forests and marshes in futile marches and wrong turnings and vain attempts to regroup and make a stand as the cordon was drawn tighter. In the swampy area where the roads were causeways the Germans posted guards with machine guns at every crossing. The men of Martos' Corps in their last four days were literally starving. Kliouev's Corps covered forty-two miles in their last forty hours without rations of any kind; horses were unfed and unwatered.

On August 29 General Martos and a few of his Staff were attempting to find a way through the forest with an escort of five Cossacks. The enemy was firing all around. Major General Machagovsky, Martos' Chief of Staff, was killed by machine-gun fire. Others in the group were picked off one by one until only one Staff officer and two of his escort remained with the general. Having left his haversack with an aide who was now missing, Martos had had nothing to eat, drink, or smoke since morning. One exhausted horse lay down and died; the men dismounted and led the others. Darkness fell. They tried to guide themselves by the stars but the skies clouded over. Troops were heard approaching and were thought to be friends because the horses pulled toward them. Suddenly a German searchlight blazed through the woods and swung back and forth, searching for them. Martos tried to mount and gallop off but his horse was hit. He fell and was seized by German soldiers.

Later, in a "dirty little hotel" in Osterode where Martos was taken as a prisoner, Ludendorff came into the room and, speaking perfect Russian, taunted him with defeat and boasted that the Russian frontier was now open to German invasion. Hindenburg followed and "seeing me disturbed he held my hands for a long time begging me to calm myself." In awkward Russian with a heavy accent he promised to return Martos' sword, and took his leave with a bow saying, "I wish you happier days."

In the woods north of Neidenburg the debris of Martos' Corps were slaughtered or surrendered. Only one officer of the XVth Corps escaped to return to Russia. About ten miles east of Neidenburg the last of the XIIIth Corps, whose commander, General Kliouev, had also been captured, entrenched themselves in a circle. With four guns captured from a German battery in the woods they held off the enemy all through the night of August 30 until they had no more ammunition left and most of them were dead. The remainder were taken prisoner.

A last Russian attack was made that day, mounted with great vigor by General Sirelius, successor to General Artomonov of the Ist Corps who had been dismissed. Collecting various scattered and still fresh regiments and artillery units which had not been in battle and aggregated about a division, he launched an offensive that broke through François' lines and succeeded in retaking Neidenburg. It came too late and could not be sustained. This last act of the Russian Second Army had not been ordered by General Samsonov, for he was dead.

On the night of August 29 he too, like General Martos, was caught in the net, in a different part of the forest. Riding through the woods that fringed the railroad, he and his companions reached Willenburg, only seven miles from the Russian frontier, but the Germans had arrived there before them. The General and his group waited in the forest until nightfall and then, as it was impossible to proceed over the swampy ground in the dark on horseback, continued on foot. Matches gave out and they could no longer read their compass. Moving hand in hand to avoid losing each other in the dark, they stumbled on. Samsonov, who suffered from asthma, was visibly weakening. He kept repeating to Potovsky, his Chief of Staff: "The Czar trusted me. How can I face him after such a disaster?" After covering six miles, they stopped for a rest. It was then 1:00 A.M. Samsonov moved apart into the thicker darkness under the pines. A shot cracked the stillness of the night. Potovsky knew instantly what it meant. Earlier Samsonov had confided his intention of committing suicide but Potovsky thought he had argued him out of it. He was now sure the General was dead. The Staff officers tried to find the body in the darkness but failed. They decided to wait until dawn, but as the sky began to lighten, German troops were heard approaching. Forsaking their task, the Russians were forced to move on toward the frontier, where they fell in with a Cossack patrol and eventually made their way to safety. Samsonov's body was found by the Germans, who buried it at Willenburg where in 1916, with the help of the Red Cross, his widow was able to retrieve it and bring it back for burial in Russia.

Silence had enveloped the Second Army. At Jilinsky's Headquarters wireless contact was dead; nothing had been heard from Samsonov for two days. Now that it was too late, Jilinsky ordered Rennenkampf's cavalry to break through the German lines at Allenstein and find out what had happened to the Second Army. The mission was never to be accomplished, for already the German Eighth Army, having destroyed one arm of the pincers that was to have crushed them, was turning to deal with the other.

Almost with awe they realized the extent of their victory. The haul of enemy dead and prisoners and captured guns was enormous: 92,000 prisoners were taken, and according to some claims the count was higher. Sixty trains were required to bring them to the rear during the week after the battle. Captured guns were counted variously between 300 and 500 out of the Second Army's total of some 600. Captured horses were driven in herds to corrals hurriedly built to hold them. Although no agreed casualty figure for the dead and missing exists, it was estimated at over 30,000. The XVth and XIIIth Corps by capture or death were wiped out of existence; 50 officers and 2,100 men of these two corps were all that escaped. Survivors of the two flank corps, the VIth and Ist, which retreated earliest, amounted to about a division each, and of the XXIIIrd Corps, to about a brigade.

The victors, too, suffered heavily; after the fatigue and suspense of a six-day battle their nerves were raw. When Neidenberg, which changed hands four times, was retaken by the Germans on August 31, a nervous military policeman shouted "Halt!" at a car driving at high speed across the main square. When the car, which contained General von Morgen, ignored his order, he yelled "Stop! Russians!" and fired. Instantly a volley of fire covered the car, killing the chauffeur and wounding an officer sitting beside the General. The same night, after barely escaping being shot by his own men, von Morgen was awakened by his valet who, crying "The Russians have come back!" ran off clutching the General's clothes. To his "extreme vexation" von Morgen was forced to emerge in the street strapping his revolver over his underclothes.

For all but a few officers it had been their first experience under fire, and out of the excited fancy produced by the fears and exhaustion and panic and violence of a great battle a legend grew—a legend of thousands of Russians drowning in the swamps or sinking up to their necks in bogs and quicksands, men whom the Germans were forced to slaughter with machine guns. "I will hear their cries to my dying day," one officer told an awestruck audience of friends in Germany. "The widely circulated report of Russians driven into the marshes and perishing there is a myth," Ludendorff wrote; "no marsh was to be found anywhere near."

As the extent of the enemy's defeat became clear, the German commanders began to consider that they had won, as Hoffmann wrote in his diary, "one of the great victories in history." It was decided—according to Hoffmann at his suggestion, according to Ludendorff at "my suggestion"—to name the battle Tannenberg in delayed compensation for the ancient defeat suffered there by the Teutonic Knights at the hands of the Poles and Lithuanians. In spite of this second triumph even greater than Liège, Ludendorff could not rejoice "because the strain imposed on my nerves by the uncertainty about Rennenkampf's Army had been too great." He was now able, however, to turn with greater confidence against Rennenkampf with the addition of the two new corps that Moltke was sending from the West.

His triumph owed much to others: to Hoffmann who, though right for the wrong reasons, had been firm in the conviction that Rennenkampf would not pursue and had conceived the plan and drawn up the orders for bringing the Eighth Army down to face Samsonov; to François who by defying Ludendorff's orders ensured the envelopment of Samsonov's left wing; to Hindenburg who steadied Ludendorff's nerves at a critical moment; finally and above all to a factor that never figured in the careful German planning—the Russian wireless. Ludendorff came to depend on the intercepts which his staff regularly collected during the day, decoded or translated and sent to him every night at 11:00 P.M. If by chance they were late, he would worry and appear personally in the signal corps room to inquire what was the matter. Hoffmann acknowledged the intercepts as the real victor of Tannenberg. "We had an ally," he said, "the enemy. We knew all the enemy's plans."

To the public the savior of East Prussia was the nominal commander, Hindenburg. The elderly general dragged from retirement in his old blue uniform was transformed into a titan by the victory. The triumph in East Prussia, lauded and heralded even beyond its true proportions, fastened the Hindenburg myth upon Germany. Not even Hoffmann's sly malice could penetrate it. When, as Chief of Staff on the Eastern Front later in the war, he would take visitors over the field of Tannenberg, Hoffmann would tell them, "This is where the Field

Marshal slept before the battle; here is where he slept after the battle; here is where he slept during the battle."

In Russia the disaster did not penetrate the public mind at once, being blotted out by a great victory won at the same time over the Austrians on the Galician front. In numbers an even greater victory than the Germans won at Tannenberg, it had equal effect on the enemy. In a series of engagements fought from August 26 to September 10 and culminating in the Battle of Lemberg, the Russians inflicted 250,000 casualties, took 100,000 prisoners, forced the Austrians into a retreat lasting eighteen days and covering 150 miles, and accomplished a mutilation of the Austro-Hungarian Army, especially in trained officers, from which it was never to recover. It crippled Austria but could not restore the losses or heal the effects of Tannenberg. The Russian Second Army had ceased to exist, General Samsonov was dead, and of his five corps commanders two were captured and three cashiered for incompetence. General Rennenkampf in the ensuing battle of the Masurian Lakes was chased out of East Prussia, "lost his nerve"—in this case the customary formula was applied by Jilinsky—deserted his army, and drove back across the frontier in a motorcar, thus completing the ruin of his reputation and bringing about his discharge in disgrace and incidentally that of Jilinsky. In a telegram to the Grand Duke, Jilinsky accused Rennenkampf of having decamped in panic. This infuriated the Grand Duke, who considered the primary failure to have been Jilinsky's. He thereupon reported to the Czar that it was Jilinsky "who has lost his head and is incapable of controlling operations," with the result that another actor in the Battle of Tannenberg became a casualty.

The inadequacy of training and materials, the incompetence of generals, the inefficiency of organization were laid bare by the battle. General Guchkov, a subsequent Minister of War, testified that he "reached the firm conviction that the war was lost" after Tannenberg. The defeat gave new vigor to the pro-German groups who began openly to agitate for withdrawal from the war. Count Witte was convinced the war would ruin Russia, Rasputin that it would destroy the regime. The Ministers of Justice and of Interior drew up a Memorandum for the Czar urging peace with Germany as soon as possible on the ground that continuing alliance with democracies would be fatal. The opportunity was offered. German proposals to Russia for a separate peace began shortly afterward and continued through 1915 and 1916. Whether out of loyalty to the Allies and the Pact of London or fear of making terms with the Germans, or insensibility to the lapping tide of Revolution or simple paralysis of authority, the Russians never accepted them. In mounting chaos and dwindling ammunition their war effort went on.

At the time of the disaster General Marquis de Laguiche, the French military attaché, came to express his condolences to the Commander in Chief. "We are happy to have made such sacrifices for our Allies," the Grand Duke replied gallantly. Equanimity in the face of catastrophe was his code, and Russians, in the knowledge of inexhaustible supplies of manpower, are accustomed to accepting gigantic fatalities with comparative calm. The Russian steam roller in which the Western Allies placed such hopes, which after their debacle on the Western Front was awaited even more anxiously, had fallen apart on the road as if it had been put together with pins. In its premature start and early demise it had been, just as the Grand Duke said, a sacrifice for an ally. Whatever it cost the Russians, the sacrifice accomplished what the French wanted: withdrawal of German strength from the Western Front. The two corps that came too late for Tannenberg were to be absent from the Marne.

17

The Flames of Louvain

IN 1915 a book about the invasion of his country was published in exile by Emile Verhaeren, Belgium's leading living poet whose life before 1914 had been a flaming dedication to socialist and humanitarian ideals that were then believed to erase national lines. He prefaced his account with this dedication: "He who writes this book in which hate is not hidden was formerly a pacifist. . . . For him no disillusionment was ever greater or more sudden. It struck him with such violence that he thought himself no longer the same man. And yet, as it seems to him that in this state of hatred his conscience becomes diminished, he dedicates these pages, with emotion, to the man he used to be."

Of all that has been written, Verhaeren's is the most poignant testimony of what war and invasion did to the mind of his time. When the Battle of the Frontiers ended, the war had been in progress for twenty days and during that time had created passions, attitudes, ideas, and issues, both among belligerents and watching neutrals, which determined its future course and the course of history since. The world that used to be and the ideas that shaped it disappeared too, like the wraith of Verhaeren's former self, down the corridors of August and the months that followed. Those deterrents—the brotherhood of socialists, the interlocking of finance, commerce, and other economic factors—which had been expected to make war impossible failed to function when the time came. Nationhood, like a wild gust of wind, arose and swept them aside.

People entered the war with varying sentiments and sets of ideas. Among the belligerents some, pacifists and socialists, opposed the war in their hearts; some, like Rupert Brooke, welcomed it. "Now God be thanked who has matched us with His hour," wrote Brooke, conscious of no blasphemy, in his poem "1914." To him it seemed a time

To turn, as swimmers into cleanness leaping
Glad from a world grown old and cold and weary. . . .

Honour has come back. . . .
And Nobleness walks in our ways again,
And we have come into our heritage.

Germans felt similar emotions. The war was to be, wrote Thomas Mann, "a purification, a liberation, an enormous hope. The victory of Germany will be a victory of soul over numbers. The German soul," he explained, "is opposed to the pacifist ideal of civilization for is not peace an element of civil corruption?" This concept, a mirror image of the essential German militarist theory that war is ennobling, was not very far from the raptures of Rupert Brooke and was widely held at the time by numbers of respectable people, among them, Theodore Roosevelt. In 1914, except for Balkan wars on the fringe, there had been no war on the European continent for more than a generation, and in the opinion of one observer the welcoming attitude toward war owed something to the "unconscious boredom of peace."

Where Brooke was embracing cleanness and nobleness, Mann saw a more positive goal. Germans being, he said, the most educated, law-abiding, peace-loving of all peoples, deserved to be the most powerful, to dominate, to establish a "German peace" out of "what is being called with every possible justification the German war." Though writing in 1917, Mann was reflecting 1914, the year that was to be the German 1789, the establishment of the German idea in history, the enthronement of *Kultur*, the fulfillment of Germany's historic mission. In August, sitting at a café in Aachen, a German scientist said to the American journalist Irwin Cobb: "We Germans are the most industrious, the most earnest, the best educated race in Europe. Russia stands for reaction, England for selfishness and perfidy, France for decadence, Germany for progress. German *Kultur* will enlighten the world and after this war there will never be another."

A German businessman sitting with them had more specific aims. Russia was to be so humbled that never again could the

Slav peril threaten Europe; Great Britain was to be utterly crushed and deprived of her navy, India, and Egypt; France was to pay an indemnity from which she would never recover; Belgium was to yield her seacoast because Germany needed ports on the English Channel; Japan was to be punished in due time. An alliance of "all the Teutonic and Scandinavian races in Europe, including Bulgaria, will hold absolute dominion from the North Sea to the Black Sea. Europe will have a new map and Germany will be at the center of it."

Talk of this kind for years before the war had not increased friendliness for Germany. "We often got on the world's nerves," admitted Bethmann-Hollweg, by frequently proclaiming Germany's right to lead the world. This, he explained, was interpreted as lust for world dominion but was really a "boyish and unbalanced ebullience."

The world somehow failed to see it that way. There was a stridency in the German tone that conveyed more menace than ebullience. The world became "sore-headed and fed-up," wrote Mr. George Bernard Shaw in 1914, with Germany's clattering of the sword. "We were rasped beyond endurance by Prussian Militarism and its contempt for us and for human happiness and common sense; and we just rose at it and went for it."

Some rose at it with a clear sense of the issues, satisfying at least to them; some with only the vaguest notion of the whys and wherefores, some with none at all. Mr. H. G. Wells was one of the first kind. The enemy, he announced in the press of August 4, was German imperialism and militarism, "the monstrous vanity begotten in 1870." The victory of Germany, of "blood and iron, flagwagging Teutonic Kiplingism," would mean "the permanent enthronement of the war god over all human affairs." The defeat of Germany "may"—Mr. Wells did not say "will"—"open the way to disarmament and peace throughout the world." Less clear as to issues was a British reservist who in the train on his way to the depot explained to a fellow passenger, "I'm a'goin' to fight the bloody Belgiums, that's where I'm a'goin'." A third kind, happy to fight without any war aims at all, was Major Sir Tom Bridges, commander of the cavalry squadron which killed the first Germans on the road to Soignies. "There was no hatred of Germany," he said. "We were quite ready to fight anybody . . . and would equally readily have fought the French. Our motto was, 'We'll do it. What is it?'"

Having an old score to settle, the French had no need to explain themselves. The German at their gates was enough. Yet here too was felt the "enormous hope." Bergson believed that although the ultimate success of the Allies would require "terrible sacrifices," out of them would come, along with "the rejuvenation and enlargement of France, the moral regeneration of Europe. Then with the advent of a real peace, France and humanity can resume the march forward, only forward, toward truth and justice."

These were not the public attitudes of statesmen or the group attitudes of masses but the private attitudes of individuals. None were yet as fixed as they were to become. National hatred of Germany had not yet taken hold. Among the first and most memorable of *Punch*'s cartoons on the war was one that appeared on August 12 labeled "No Thoroughfare!" Brave little Belgium is there, a stern small boy in wooden shoes barring the way to the trespasser, Germany, pictured as a fat old bandmaster with a string of sausages hanging out of his pocket. He is ludicrous, not evil. Otherwise, in the early days, the cartoonists' pet was the Crown Prince whom they delighted to draw as an exaggerated fop with pinched waist, high tight collar, rakish cap, and an expression of fatuous vacuity. He did not last. The war becoming too serious, he was replaced by the best known German, the Supreme War Lord, whose name was signed to every order of OHL so that he seemed the author of all German acts—the Kaiser. No longer the prewar mischief-maker and saber rattler, he was now depicted as a dark, satanic tyrant, breathing cruelty and malignancy, expressing brutality in every line. The change began in August and progressed from Bridges' cool statement, "There was no hatred of Germany," to that of Stephen McKenna, who wrote in 1921, "Among those who remember, the name of a German stinks and the presence of a German is an outrage." No pseudo-heroic super-patriot but a sober, thoughtful schoolteacher whose memoirs are a social document of the time, McKenna recorded a change of sentiment that was to prevent any negotiated settlement and keep the fighting going until total victory. What wrought the change was what happened to Belgium.

The turn of events in Belgium was a product of the German theory of terror. Clausewitz had prescribed terror as the proper method to shorten war, his whole theory of war being based on the necessity of making it short, sharp, and decisive. The civil population must not be exempted from war's effects but must be made to feel its pressure and be forced by the severest measures to compel their leaders to make peace. As the object of war was to disarm the enemy, "we must place him in a situation in which continuing the war is more oppressive to him than surrender." This seemingly sound proposition fitted into the scientific theory of war which throughout the nineteenth century it had been the best intellectual endeavor of the German General Staff to construct. It had already been put into practice in 1870 when French resistance sprang up after Sedan. The ferocity of German reprisal at that time in the form of executions of prisoners and civilians on charges of *franc-tireur* warfare startled a world agape with admiration at Prussia's marvelous six-week victory. Suddenly it became aware of the beast beneath the German skin. Although 1870 proved the corollary of the theory and practice of terror, that it deepens antagonism, stimulates resistance, and ends by lengthening war, the Germans remained wedded to it. As Shaw said, they were a people with a contempt for common sense.

On August 23 placards signed by General von Bülow were posted in Liège announcing that the people of Andenne, a small town on the Meuse near Namur, having attacked his troops in the most "traitorous" manner, "with my permission the General commanding these troops has burned the town to ashes and has had 110 persons shot." The people of Liège were being informed so that they would know what fate to expect if they behaved in the same manner as their neighbors.

The burning of Andenne and the massacre—which Belgian figures put at 211—took place on August 20 and 21 during the Battle of Charleroi. Hewing to their timetable, harassed by the Belgians' blowing up of bridges and railroads, Bülow's commanders dealt out reprisals ruthlessly in the villages they entered. At Seilles, across the river from Andenne, 50 civilians were shot and the houses given over to looting and burning. At Tamines, captured on August 21, sack of the town began that evening after the battle and continued all night and next day. The usual orgy of permitted looting accompanied by drinking released inhibitions and brought the soldiers to the desired state of raw excitement which was intended to add to the fearful effect. On the second day at Tamines some 400 citizens were herded together under guard in front of the church in the main square and a firing squad began systematically shooting into the group. Those not dead when the firing ended were bayoneted. In the cemetery at Tamines there are 384 gravestones inscribed *1914: Fusillé par les Allemands.*

When Bülow's Army took Namur, a city of 32,000, notices were posted announcing that ten hostages were being taken from every street who would be shot if any civilian fired on a German. The taking and killing of hostages was practiced as systematically as the requisitioning of food. The farther the Germans advanced, the more hostages were arrested. At first when von Kluck's Army entered a town, notices immediately went up warning the populace that the burgomaster, the leading magistrate, and the senator of the district were being held as hostages with the usual warning as to their fate. Soon three persons of prestige were not enough; a man from every street, even ten from every street were not enough. Walter Bloem, a novelist mobilized as a reserve officer in von Kluck's Army whose account of the advance to Paris is invaluable, tells how in villages where his company was billeted each night, "Major von Kleist gave orders that a man or, if no man was available, a woman, be taken from every household as a hostage." Through some peculiar failure of the system, the greater the terror, the more terror seemed to be necessary.

When sniping was reported in a town, the hostages were executed. Irwin Cobb, accompanying von Kluck's Army, watched from a window as two civilians were marched between two rows of German soldiers with fixed bayonets. They were taken behind the railroad station; there was a sound of shots, and two litters were carried out bearing still figures covered by blankets with only the rigid toes of their boots showing. Cobb watched while twice more the performance was repeated.

Visé, scene of the first fighting on the way to Liège on the first day of the invasion, was destroyed not by troops fresh from the heat of battle, but by occupation troops long after the battle had moved on. In response to a report of sniping, a German regiment was sent to Visé from Liège on August 23. That night the sound of shooting could be heard at Eysden just over the border in Holland five miles away. Next day Eysden was overwhelmed by a flood of 4,000 refugees, the entire population of Visé except for those who had been shot, and for 700 men and boys who had been deported for harvest labor to Germany. The deportations which were to have such moral effect, especially upon the United States, began in August. Afterward when Brand Whitlock, the American Minister, visited what had been Visé he saw only empty blackened houses open to the sky, "a vista of ruins that might have been Pompeii." Every inhabitant was gone. There was not a living thing, not a roof.

At Dinant on the Meuse on August 23 the Saxons of General von Hausen's Army were fighting the French in a final engagement of the Battle of Charleroi. Von Hausen personally witnessed the "perfidious" activity of Belgian civilians in hampering reconstruction of bridges, "so contrary to international law." His troops began rounding up "several hundreds" of hostages, men, women, and children. Fifty were taken from church, the day being Sunday. The General saw them "tightly crowded—standing, sitting, lying—in a group under guard of the Grenadiers, their faces displaying fear, nameless anguish, concentrated rage and desire for revenge provoked by all the calamities they had suffered." Von Hausen, who was very sensitive, felt an "indomitable hostility" emanating from them. He was the general who had been made so unhappy in the house of the Belgian gentleman who clenched his fists in his pockets and refused to speak to von Hausen at dinner. In the group at Dinant he saw a wounded French soldier with blood streaming from his head, who lay dying, mute and apathetic, refusing all medical help. Von Hausen ends his description there, too sensitive to tell the fate of Dinant's citizens. They were kept in the main square till evening, then lined up, women on one side, men opposite in two rows, one kneeling in front of the other. Two firing squads marched to the center of the square, faced either way and fired till no more of the targets stood upright. Six hundred and twelve bodies were identified and buried, including Felix Fivet, aged three weeks.

The Saxons were then let loose in a riot of pillage and arson. The medieval citadel perched like an eagle's nest on the heights of the right bank above the city it had once protected, looked down upon a repetition of the ravages of the Middle Ages. The Saxons left Dinant scorched, crumbled, hollowed out, charred, and sodden. "Profoundly moved" by this picture of desolation wrought by his troops, General von Hausen departed from the ruins of Dinant secure in the conviction that the responsibility lay with the Belgian government "which approved this perfidious street fighting contrary to international law."

The Germans were obsessively concerned about violations of international law. They succeeded in overlooking the violation created by their presence in Belgium in favor of the violation committed, as they saw it, by Belgians resisting their presence. With a sigh of long-tried patience, Abbé Wetterlé, Alsatian delegate to the Reichstag, once confessed, "To a mind formed in the Latin school, the German mentality is difficult to comprehend."

The German obsession had two parts: that Belgian resistance was illegal and that it was organized from "above" by the Belgian government or by burgomasters, priests, and other persons who could be classified as "above." Together the two parts established the corollary: that German reprisals were righteous and legal, regardless of degree. The shooting of a single hostage or the massacre of 612 and the razing of a town were alike to be charged to the Belgian government—this was the refrain of every German from Hausen after Dinant to the Kaiser after Louvain. The responsibility must "fall upon those who incited the population to attack the Germans," Hausen protests constantly. There can be absolutely no doubt, he insists, that the whole population of Dinant and other regions was "animated—by whose order?—by one desire to stop the advance of the Germans." That people could be animated to stop the invader without an order from "above" was inconceivable.

The Germans saw these orders everywhere. Von Kluck claimed that the Belgian government's posters warning its citizens against hostile acts were actually "incitements to the civil population to fire on the enemy." Ludendorff accused the Belgian government of having "systematically organized civilian warfare." The Crown Prince applied the same theory to French civil resistance. He complained that the "fanatical" people of the Longwy region shot at us "treacherously and perfidiously" from doors and windows with sporting guns which had been "sent from Paris for the purpose." Had the royal travels included closer acquaintance with the French countryside where a sporting gun for shooting hare on Sundays was as normal equipment as a pair of pants, he might have known it did not require guns sent from Paris to arm the *franc-tireur*.

German accounts of their experiences in enemy territory become shrill with hysteria on the subject of guerrilla warfare. Ludendorff called it "disgusting." He whose name was soon to become a byword for trickery, violence, and cunning had taken the field, he says, "with chivalrous and humane conceptions of warfare" but *franc-tireur* methods "caused me personally bitter disillusionment." Captain Bloem was haunted by the "monstrous thought" that he might be hit or killed by a bullet fired by a civilian, although until a fortnight ago he had been a civilian himself. During an exhausting march of twenty-eight miles in one day, he reports, not one soldier fell out of line because "the thought of falling into the hands of the Walloons was worse than sore feet"—that other great agony of the march on Paris.

Fear and horror of the *franc-tireur* sprang from the German feeling that civil resistance was essentially disorderly. If there has to be a choice between injustice and disorder, said Goethe, the German prefers injustice. Schooled in a state in which the relation of the subject to the sovereign has no basis other than obedience, he is unable to understand a state organized upon any other foundation, and when he enters one is inspired by an intense uneasiness. Comfortable only in the presence of authority, he regards the civilian sniper as something particularly sinister. To the Western mind the *franc-tireur* is a hero; to the German he is a heretic who threatens the existence of the state. At Soissons there is a bronze and marble monument to three schoolteachers who raised a revolt of students and civilians against the Prussians in 1870. Gazing at it in amazement, a

German officer said to an American reporter in 1914, "That's the French for you—putting up a monument to glorify *franc-tireurs.* In Germany the people would not be allowed to do such a thing. Nor is it conceivable that they would want to."

To put the German soldier in the proper frame of mind, German newspapers were filled from the first week, as Captain Bloem recorded, with stories of the Belgians' "revolting cruelties . . . of armed priests at the head of marauding bands of civilians committing every kind of atrocity . . . of treacherous ambushes on patrols, of sentries found with eyes pierced and tongues cut off." Similar "ghastly rumors" had already reached Berlin by August 11 to be recorded by Princess Blücher. A German officer whom she asked for verification told her that in Aachen at that moment there were thirty German officers lying in the hospital with their eyes put out by Belgian women and children.

Emotions aroused by such stories made it easy by a single cry of "Snipers!" to set the German soldier off on a rampage of pillage, arson, and murder, uninhibited by the officers. *Schrecklichkeit* was intended as a substitute for the occupation troops which the High Command could not afford to divert from the march on Paris.

On August 25 the burning of Louvain began. The medieval city on the road from Liège to Brussels was renowned for its University and incomparable Library, founded in 1426 when Berlin was a clump of wooden huts. Housed in the fourteenth century Clothworkers' Hall, the Library included among its 230,000 volumes a unique collection of 750 medieval manuscripts and over a thousand incunabula. The façade of the Town Hall, called a "jewel of Gothic art," was a stone tapestry of carved knights and saints and ladies, lavish even of its kind. In the church of St. Pierre were altar panels by Dierik Bouts and other Flemish masters. The burning and sack of Louvain, accompanied by the invariable shooting of civilians, lasted six days before it was called off as abruptly as it began.

Everything went smoothly when Louvain was first occupied. The shops did a rush of business. German soldiers behaved in exemplary fashion, bought postcards and souvenirs, paid for all their purchases, and stood in line with the regular customers for haircuts at the barbershop. The second day was more strained. A German soldier was shot in the leg, allegedly by snipers. The Burgomaster urgently repeated his call upon civilians to surrender arms. He and two other officials were arrested as hostages. Executions behind the railroad station became frequent. The endless tramp of von Kluck's columns continued through the city day after day.

On August 25 the Belgian Army at Malines, on the edge of the entrenched camp of Antwerp, made a sudden sharp sortie upon the rearguard of von Kluck's Army, flinging them back in disorder upon Louvain. In the turmoil of retreat a riderless horse clattering through the gates after dark frightened another horse which tried to bolt, fell in harness, and overturned the wagon. Shots rang out, setting off cries of "*Die Franzosen sind da! Die Engländer sind da!*" Later the Germans claimed they had been fired on by Belgian civilians or that civilians had fired from rooftops as signals to the Belgian Army. Belgians claimed that German soldiers had fired on one another in the dark. For weeks and months, even years, after the event that appalled the world, judicial inquiries and tribunals investigated the outbreak, and German accusations were contradicted by Belgian countercharges. Who shot whom was never established and was in any case irrelevant to what followed, for the Germans burned Louvain not as a punishment for alleged Belgian misdeeds, but as a deterrent and a warning to all their enemies—a gesture of German might before all the world.

General von Luttwitz, the new Governor of Brussels, expressed as much next morning. Visited in the course of duty by the American and Spanish Ministers, he said to them, "A dreadful thing has occurred at Louvain. Our General there has been shot by the son of the Burgomaster. The population has fired on our troops." He paused, looked at his visitors, and finished, "And now of course we have to destroy the city." Mr. Whitlock was to hear so often the story of one or another German general being shot by the son or sometimes the daughter of a burgomaster that it seemed to him the Belgians must have bred a special race of burgomasters' children like the Assassins of Syria.

Already word of the flames at Louvain had spread. Stunned

and weeping refugees driven from the city told of street after street set on fire, of savage looting and continuing arrests and executions. On August 27 Richard Harding Davis, star of the American correspondents who were then in Belgium, made his way to Louvain by troop train. He was kept locked in the railroad car by the Germans, but the fire had by then reached the Boulevard Tirlemont facing the railroad station and he could see "the steady, straight columns of flames" rising from the rows of houses. The German soldiers were drunk and wild. One thrust his head through the window of the car where another correspondent, Arno Dosch, was confined and cried: "Three cities razed! Three! There will be more!"

On August 28 Hugh Gibson, First Secretary of the American Legation, accompanied by his Swedish and Mexican colleagues, went to Louvain to see for themselves. Houses with blackened walls and smoldering timbers were still burning; pavements were hot; cinders were everywhere. Dead horses and dead people lay about. One old man, a civilian with a white beard, lay on his back in the sun. Many of the bodies were swollen, evidently dead for several days. Wreckage, furniture, bottles, torn clothing, one wooden shoe were strewn among the ashes. German soldiers of the IXth Reserve Corps, some drunk, some nervous, unhappy, and bloodshot, were routing inhabitants out of the remaining houses so that, as the soldiers told Gibson, the destruction of the city could be completed. They went from house to house, battering down doors, stuffing pockets with cigars, looting valuables, then plying the torch. As the houses were chiefly of brick and stone, the fire did not spread of itself. An officer in charge in one street watched gloomily, smoking a cigar. He was rabid against the Belgians, and kept repeating to Gibson: "We shall wipe it out, not one stone will stand upon another! *Kein stein auf einander!*—not one, I tell you. We will teach them to respect Germany. For generations people will come here to see what we have done!" It was the German way of making themselves memorable.

In Brussels the Rector of the University, Monseigneur de Becker, whose rescue was arranged by the Americans, described the burning of the Library. Nothing was left of it; all was in ashes. When he came to the word "library"—*bibliothèque*—he could not say it. He stopped, tried again, uttered the first syllable, "*La bib—*" and unable to go on, bowed his head on the table, and wept.

The loss, made the subject of a public protest by the Belgian government and officially reported by the American Legation, caused an outcry in the outside world while the fire was still raging. Eyewitness accounts by refugees, reported by all the correspondents, filled the foreign press. Besides the University and Library, "all the noble public buildings," including the Town Hall and St. Pierre with all its pictures, were said to have been destroyed; only later was it found that, though damaged, the Town Hall and the church were still standing. GERMANS SACK LOUVAIN; WOMEN AND CLERGY SHOT blazed the headline in the New York *Tribune* above Davis' story. Under a subhead, "Berlin Confirms Louvain Horror," it carried a wireless statement from Berlin issued by the German Embassy in Washington that, following "perfidious" attack by Belgian civilians, "Louvain was punished by the destruction of the city." Identical with General von Luttwitz's statement, it showed that Berlin had no wish for the world to misunderstand the nature of the gesture at Louvain. Destruction of cities and deliberate, acknowledged war on noncombatants were concepts shocking to the world of 1914. In England editorials proclaimed "The March of the Hun" and "Treason to Civilization." The burning of the Library, said the *Daily Chronicle*, meant war not only on noncombatants "but on posterity to the utmost generation." Even the usually quiet and carefully neutral Dutch papers were stung to comment. Whatever the cause of the outbreak, said the Rotterdam *Courant*, "the fact of destruction remains"—a fact "so terrible that the whole world must have received the news with horror."

The reports appeared in the foreign press of August 29. On August 30 the process of destroying Louvain was terminated. On the same day an official communiqué of the German Foreign Office affirmed that "the entire responsibility for these events rests with the Belgian Government," not forgetting the usual claim that "women and girls took part in the fight and blinded our wounded, gouging their eyes out."

Why did the Germans do it? people asked all over the world. "Are you descendants of Goethe or of Attila the Hun?" protested Romain Rolland in a public letter to his former friend Gerhart Hauptmann, Germany's literary lion. King Albert in conversation with the French Minister thought the mainspring was the German sense of inferiority and jealousy: "These people are envious, unbalanced and ill-tempered. They burned the Library of Louvain simply because it was unique and universally admired"—in other words, a barbarian's gesture of anger against civilized things. Valid in part, this explanation overlooked the deliberate use of terror as prescribed by the *Kriegsbrauch*, "War cannot be conducted merely against the combatants of an enemy state but must seek to destroy the total material and intellectual (*geistig*) resources of the enemy." To the world it remained the gesture of a barbarian. The gesture that was intended by the Germans to frighten the world—to induce submission—instead convinced large numbers of people that here was an enemy with whom there could be no settlement and no compromise.

Belgium clarified issues, became to many the "supreme issue" of the war. In America, said a historian of his times looking back, Belgium was the "precipitant" of opinion and Louvain was the climax of Belgium. Matthias Erzberger, soon to be appointed chief of propaganda when that unhappy necessity forced itself upon Germany, found that Belgium "aroused almost the entire world against Germany." The argument of his counterpropaganda, that Germany's conduct was justified by military necessity and self-defense, was, as he admitted with a certain wry regret, "insufficient."

It did the Kaiser little good to take the offensive ten days after Louvain in a telegram to President Wilson saying "my heart bleeds" for the sufferings of Belgium caused "as a result of the criminal and barbarous action of the Belgians." Their resistance, he explained, had been "openly incited" and "carefully organized" by the Belgian government, compelling his generals to take the strongest measures against the "bloodthirsty population."

It did little good for ninety-three German professors and other intellectuals to issue a Manifesto addressed "To the Civilized World" proclaiming the civilizing effects of German culture and stating, "It is not true that we have criminally violated the neutrality of Belgium. . . . It is not true that our troops have brutally destroyed Louvain." However imposing the signatories—Harnack, Sudermann, Humperdinck, Roentgen, Hauptmann—the mute ashes of the Library spoke louder. By the end of August people of the Allied nations were persuaded that they faced an enemy that had to be beaten, a regime that had to be destroyed, a war that must be fought to a finish. On September 4 the British, French, and Russian governments signed the Pact of London engaging themselves "not to conclude peace separately during the present war."

Thereafter issues hardened. The more the Allies declared their purpose to be the defeat of German militarism and the Hohenzollerns, the more Germany declared her undying oath not to lay down arms short of total victory. In reply to President Wilson's offer to mediate, Bethmann-Hollweg said the Pact of London forced Germany to fight to the limit of her endurance, and therefore Germany would make no proposals as basis for a negotiated peace. The Allies took the same stand. In this position both sides were to remain clamped throughout the war. The deeper both belligerents sank into war and the more lives and treasure they spent, the more determined they became to emerge with some compensating gain.

The gains Germany expected to win with victory were laid down within the first thirty days of battle in a Memorandum presented to the government on September 2 by Matthias Erzberger. Leader of the Catholic Centrum Party and *rapporteur* of the Military Affairs Committee, he was the Chancellor's right-hand man and closest associate in the Reichstag. A shrewd and able opportunist who represented whatever opinion was dominant, he combined energy and intelligence with a political flexibility unseen in Europe since Talleyrand's. It was said of him that he had "no convictions but only appetites." As he was one day to make himself the bearer of Germany's plea for an armistice and to serve in the first Cabinet of the Weimar Republic, so now he drew up a list of war aims that would have made the most extreme Pan-German proud. Bethmann, who relied on him, never failed to wonder where Erzberger obtained all his bright ideas when he himself never seemed to have any.

Germany, according to Erzberger, was to utilize victory to gain control of the European continent for "all time." All demands at the peace table were to be based on this premise for which three conditions were necessary: abolition of neutral states at Germany's borders, the end of England's "intolerable hegemony" in world affairs, and the breaking up of the Russian colossus. Erzberger envisioned a Confederation of European States analogous to the later Mandates system under the League of Nations. Some states would be under German "guidance"; others, such as Poland and the Baltic group annexed from Russia, would be under German sovereignty for "all time," with possible representation but no voting power in the Reichstag. Erzberger was not sure which category Belgium would fit into, but in either case Germany was to retain military control over the entire country and over the French coast from Dunkirk down to and including Boulogne and Calais. Germany would also acquire the Briey-Longwy iron basin and Belfort in Upper Alsace which she had failed to take in 1870. She would also take the French and Belgian colonies in Africa. Morocco, curiously enough, was excepted as likely to be too much of a drain on Germany's strength. No mention was made of England's colonies, which suggests that Erzberger may have been considering a negotiated settlement with England. In reparations the vanquished nations were to pay at least 10 billion marks for direct war costs, plus enough more to provide veterans' funds, public housing, gifts to generals and statesmen, and pay off Germany's entire national debt, thus obviating taxes on the German people for years to come.

Drawn up in the intoxicating days of conquest in August, these war aims on which Germany set her sights were so grandiose as to be irreducible to the level of feasible compromise. On the Allied side in August, the primary war aim was expressed by Foreign Minister Sazonov to Paléologue at a tête-à-tête luncheon in St. Petersburg on August 20. "My formula is a simple one," said Sazonov; "we must destroy German imperialism." They agreed that the war was one for existence and that its objects could be gained only by total victory. Rather rashly for a Czarist minister, Sazonov agreed that sweeping political changes must be made if Kaiserism was not to rise from its ashes. Poland must be restored, Belgium enlarged, Alsace-Lorraine returned to France, Schleswig-Holstein to Denmark, Hanover reconstituted, Bohemia set free from Austria-Hungary, and all of Germany's colonies given to France, Belgium, and England.

These were the map carvings of professional statesmen. Among private people who did not know Schleswig-Holstein from Bohemia, a deep underlying recognition had grown by the time the war was twenty days old that the world was engaged by "the largest human fact since the French Revolution." Though a tremendous catastrophe, it seemed, in August when it was still new, to contain that "enormous hope," the hope of something better afterward, the hope of an end to war, of a chance to remake the world. Mr. Britling in Wells' novel, who, though fictional, was representative, thought it might prove a "huge step forward in human life. It is the end of forty years of evil suspense. It is crisis and solution." He saw "a tremendous opportunity. . . . We can remake the map of the world. . . . The world is plastic for men to do what they will with it. This is the end and the beginning of an age. . . ."

18

Blue Water, Blockade, and the Great Neutral

RISK WAS the least favorite concept of the British Admiralty in 1914. Her fleet was Britain's most prized possession. It was not, as Churchill had woundingly said of the German Navy in 1912, a "luxury fleet"; it was a vital necessity in the exact sense of the word "vital." The British Empire could not survive naval defeat or even loss of naval supremacy through individual ship losses. Its tasks were enormous. It had to prevent invasion of the British Isles; it had to escort the BEF safely to the Continent; it had to bring home troops from India to add to the Regular Army and replace them with Territorials; above all, it had to safeguard seaborne commerce over all the oceans of the world.

Not invasion which had been declared "impracticable" by the Committee of Imperial Defence, but "the interruption of our trade and destruction of merchant shipping" was recognized by the Admiralty as the principal danger. Two-thirds of all Britain's food was imported. Her livelihood depended on a foreign commerce carried in British bottoms that represented 43 per cent of the world's total merchant tonnage and carried more than half of the world's total seaborne trade, as much as carried by all the other nations put together. A besetting fear that fast German steamers would be converted into commerce destroyers haunted the British before the war. At least forty such vessels were expected to be let loose to supplement German cruisers in preying on the precious stream of maritime trade. British fleet units had to be spread out to protect the Suez route to Persia, India, and the Far East, the Cape route around Africa, the North Atlantic route to the United States and Canada, the Caribbean route to the West Indies, the South Atlantic and South Pacific routes to South America and Australia. The ocean crossroads where shipping lanes converged and enemy raiders were most likely to attack were the points of control.

"The whole principle of naval fighting," Fisher said in the naval equivalent of a papal bull, "is to be free to go anywhere with every damned thing the Navy possesses." Translated into practical terms this meant that the navy must be superior everywhere at once or wherever it was likely to encounter the enemy. With its vast commitments the British Navy had all it could do to muster superiority in home waters where a battle of equal strengths was at all costs to be avoided. The common expectation was of one great clash of capital ships in which maritime supremacy might be decided in a single action like the Russo-Japanese battle of Tsushima. Britain could not afford to risk loss of supremacy in such a battle, but the same was not true of the German Navy, which was expected to take chances. The rampant Germany of 1914 whose Kaiser had proclaimed "Germany's future is on the water," whose Navy Leagues had proliferated over the country and raised popular subscriptions for battleships with such slogans as "England the Foe! Perfidious Albion! The Coming War! The British Peril! England's Plan to Fall on Us in 1911!" was credited with an aggressive spirit and a readiness to dare battle at unfavorable odds that could lead to any kind of desperate adventure.

Fear of the unknown but certainly bellicose intentions of the enemy, and particularly fear of the invisible submarine, whose lethal potential loomed more alarmingly each year, made for a highly sensitive state of British naval nerves.

Almost at the farthest point to which the Grand Fleet could sail, almost the last bleak tip of British territory, a remote outpost of the British Isles, north even of the northernmost point of the mainland, Scapa Flow, a natural shelter among the Orkney Islands, was the place belatedly chosen for the fleet's wartime base. At latitude 59 opposite Norway, the Flow was at the top of the North Sea, 350 miles farther north than Heligoland, where the German fleet would come out if it chose to appear, and 550 miles north of the Portsmouth-Havre crossing of the BEF. It was farther away from the German place of sortie than the Germans were from the British transports, supposing they attempted to attack them. It was a position from which the Grand Fleet could guard its own and block Germany's lanes of seaborne commerce through the North Sea and by its presence bottle up the enemy in port or, by coming between him and his base, bring him to action if he put to sea. But it was not ready for occupancy.

Each increase in the size of ships required wider docks and harbors, and the Dreadnought program had suffered from the split personality of the Liberal government. Having allowed itself to be persuaded by the passion of Fisher and enthusiasm of Churchill to adopt the building program, the Liberals compensated for this injury to their antiwar sentiments by parsimony in paying for it. As a result, in August 1914 Scapa was not yet equipped with dry docks or fixed defenses.

The fleet, so alertly mobilized by Churchill, reached there safely by August 1 while the government was still debating whether to fight. The days after the declaration of war were, in the words of the First Lord, a period of "extreme psychological tension." As the moment approached for the crowded troop transports to depart, some action by the enemy in the form of raids on the coast to draw off the fleet or other tactics of provocation, was hourly expected. Churchill thought that "the great naval battle might begin at any moment."

His state of mind was fully shared by Admiral Sir John Jellicoe who, traveling north by train to Scapa Flow on August 4, opened a telegram marked "Secret" and discovered himself Commander in Chief of the Grand Fleet. It was not the appointment, which he had long expected, or any doubts of his own competence that weighed on Jellicoe. Since entering the navy in 1872 when he was twelve and a half years old and four and a half feet high, he had been accustomed to wide recognition of his talents. Displayed on active service and in various offices at the Admiralty, they had earned the consistent, fervent, and resonant admiration of Lord Fisher who picked Jellicoe to "be Nelson . . . when Armageddon comes along." The date had come and Fisher's candidate for Nelsonhood, from the moment he arrived, felt "the greatest anxiety constantly confronting me" over the defenseless nature of the base at Scapa. Lacking land-based guns, booms and nets and fixed mine fields, it was "open to submarine and destroyer attacks."

Jellicoe worried when German trawlers captured on August 5 were found to have carrier pigeons aboard, suspected of being informants for submarines. Fear of mines, which the Germans announced they were sowing without regard for the limits agreed upon for such devices, increased his anxiety. When one of his light cruisers rammed and sank a submarine, the U-15, on August 9 he was more disturbed than cheered, and hurriedly sent all his capital ships out of the "infected area." Once, when inside the Flow, a gun crew suddenly opened fire on a moving object reported to be a periscope and set off a flurry of shooting and a feverish hunt by destroyers, he ordered the entire fleet of three battle squadrons out to sea where it stayed all night in fear of what even the navy's official historian concedes "could have been a seal." Twice the fleet was transferred to safer bases at Loch Ewe on the west coast of Scotland and Loch Swilly on the north coast of Ireland, leaving the North Sea free to the Germans had they known it—and twice brought back. If the Germans had launched a naval offensive at this time, it might have obtained startling results.

Between bouts of nerves and sudden bolts like a horse that hears the rustle of a snake, the British Navy set about its business of laying down a blockade and patrolling the North Sea in a ceaseless watch for the appearance of the enemy. With a battle strength of 24 dreadnoughts and a knowledge that the Germans had 16 to 19, the British could count on a firm margin of superiority, and in the next class of battleships believed themselves "markedly superior to the next eight Germans." But a heavy sense of all that depended on the issue hung over them.

During the week of the passage of the transports, "the Germans have the strongest incentives to action," Churchill warned Jellicoe on August 8. Not so much as a torpedo boat was sighted. Nothing stirred. The enemy's inactivity heightened the tension. On the far-flung oceans his individual warships still at large, the *Goeben* and *Breslau* in the Mediterranean, the *Dresden* and *Karlsruhe* in the Atlantic, the *Scharnhorst*, *Gneisenau*, and *Emden* of von Spee's squadron in the Pacific were making bold raids or bolder escapes, but the High Seas Fleet, lurking motionless behind Heligoland, seemed to presage something more sinister.

"Extraordinary silence and inertia of the enemy may be prelude to serious enterprises . . . possibly a landing this week on a large scale," Churchill warned fleet commanders on August 12. He suggested that the Grand Fleet move down nearer to the "theatre of decisive action." Jellicoe, however, continued his remote patrol in the gray waste of waters between the top of Scotland and Norway, and only once, on August 16, when the transport of the BEF was at its height, ventured below latitude 56. The transports made 137 separate crossings of the Channel from August 14 to 18, while all that time the whole of the Grand Fleet, with its attendant squadrons and flotillas, patrolled in taut expectancy, watching for the white wake of a torpedo, listening for the wireless signal that would say the German fleet had come out upon the seas.

Grand Admiral von Tirpitz, the Fisher of Germany, the father and builder and soul of the German Fleet, "eternal Tirpitz" with his forked white beard like Neptune's who at sixty-five had served continuously as Secretary of the Navy since 1897, longer in one post than any minister since Bismarck, was not allowed to know the war plan for the weapon he had forged. It was "kept secret by the Naval Staff even from me." On July 30 when the operational orders were shown to him he discovered the secret: there was no plan. The navy, whose existence had been a chief factor in bringing on the war, had no active role designed for it when war came.

If the Kaiser had confined his reading to *The Golden Age*, Kenneth Grahame's dreamlike story of English boyhood in a world of cold adults, which he kept on the bed-table of his yacht, it is possible there might have been no world war. He was eclectic, however, and read an American book that appeared in 1890 with the same impact in its realm as the *Origin of Species* or *Das Kapital* in theirs. In *The Influence of Sea Power on History* Admiral Mahan demonstrated that he who controls communications by sea controls his fate; the master of the seas is master of the situation. Instantly an immense vision opened before the impressionable Wilhelm: Germany must be a major power upon the oceans as upon land. The naval building program began, and although it could not overtake England at once, pursued with German intensity it threatened to do so eventually. It challenged the maritime supremacy upon which

Britain depended and knowingly created the likelihood of British enmity in war and consequently the use against Germany of Britain's chief weapon, blockade.

As a land power Germany could have fought any possible combination of continental powers without interruption of her seaborne supplies as long as Britain, the world's greatest merchant carrier, remained neutral. In that sense Germany would have been a stronger power without a navy than with one. Bismarck had disapproved of adulterating power on land by a maritime adventure that would add an enemy upon the sea. Wilhelm would not listen. He was bewitched by Mahan and tangled in the private jealousies of his love and hate for seafaring England which came to an annual peak during the yacht regattas of Cowes week. He saw the navy as his knife to cut through Encirclement. He insisted alternately that hostility to England was the last thing he had in mind and that "a larger fleet will bring the English to their senses through sheer fright." They would then "submit to the inevitable and we shall become the best friends in the world." In vain his ambassadors to England cautioned against the doubtful logic of this policy. In vain Haldane came to Berlin and Churchill warned that the fleet was an Alsace-Lorraine in Anglo-German relations. Proposals for a fixed ratio or a naval holiday were rejected.

Once the challenge had been made, British hostility could fairly be expected. There was a further cost. Built at huge expense, the navy drew money and men—enough to make two army corps—from the army. Unless it had been built to no purpose it had to perform a strategic function: either to prevent the coming of added enemy divisions against its own army or prevent blockade. As the preamble to the German Navy Law of 1900 acknowledged, "A naval war of blockade . . . even if lasting only a year would destroy Germany's trade and bring her to disaster."

As it grew in strength and efficiency, in numbers of trained men and officers, as German designers perfected its gunnery, the armor-piercing power of its shells, its optical devices and range finders, the resistant power of its armor plate, it became too precious to lose. Although ship for ship it approached a match with the British and in gunnery was superior, the Kaiser, who could hark back to no Drakes or Nelsons, could never really believe that German ships and sailors could beat the British. He could not bear to think of his "darlings," as Bülow called his battleships, shattered by gunfire, smeared with blood, or at last, wounded and rudderless, sinking beneath the waves. Tirpitz, whom once he had gratefully ennobled with a "von" but whose theory of a navy was to use it for fighting, began to appear as a danger, almost as an enemy, and was gradually frozen out of the inner councils. His high squeaky voice, like a child's or a eunuch's, that emerged as such a surprise from the giant frame and fierce demeanor was no longer heard. While he remained as administrative head, naval policy was left, under the Kaiser, to a group made up of the Chief of Naval Staff, Admiral von Pohl; the chief of the Kaiser's Marine Cabinet, Admiral von Müller; and to the Commander in Chief of the Navy, Admiral von Ingenohl. Pohl, though supporter of a fighting strategy, was a nonentity who achieved the acme of obscurity possible in Hohenzollern Germany—no mention in Bülow's encyclopedia of gossip; Müller was one of the pederasts and sycophants who decorated the court as advisers to the sovereign; Ingenohl was an officer who "took a defensive view of operations." "I need no Chief," said the Kaiser; "I can do this for myself."

When the moment of Encirclement came, the moment that had haunted his reign, the moment when the dead Edward loomed "stronger than the living I," the Kaiser's instructions read, "For the present I have ordered a defensive attitude on the part of the High Seas Fleet." The strategy adopted for the sharp-edged instrument he had at hand was to exert the influence of a "fleet in being." By staying within an impregnable fortified position, it was to act as a constant potential danger, forcing the enemy to remain on guard against a possible sortie and thereby draining the enemy's naval resources and keeping part of his forces inactive. This was a well-recognized role for the inferior of two fleets, and approved by Mahan. He, however, had later concluded that the value of a fleet-in-being "has been much overstated," for the influence of a navy that elects not to fight tends to become a diminishing quantity.

Even the Kaiser could not have imposed such a policy without good reasons and strong support. He had both. Many Germans, particularly Bethmann and the more cosmopolitan civilian groups, could not bring themselves to believe at the start that England was a really serious belligerent. They cherished the thought that she could be bought off in a separate peace, especially after France had been knocked out. Erzberger's careful avoidance of a grab at England's colonies was part of this idea. The Kaiser's maternal family, the English wives of German princes, the ancient Teutonic ties created a sense of kinship. To have battle and spilled blood and deaths between them would make an arrangement between Germany and England difficult if not impossible. (Somehow in this thinking the blood to be spilled in rounding up the BEF along with the French did not count seriously.) Besides, it was hoped to keep the German fleet intact as a bargaining factor to bring the English to terms, a theory which Bethmann strongly supported and the Kaiser was happy to embrace. As time went on and victory went glimmering, the desire to carry the fleet safe and sound through the war for bargaining purposes at the peace table became even more embedded.

In August the primary enemy seemed not England but Russia, and the primary duty of the fleet was considered to be control of the Baltic—at least by those who wished to postpone the test with England. They said the fleet was needed to guard against Russian interference with seaborne supplies from the Scandinavian countries and against a possible Russian descent upon the German coast. Action against England, it was feared, might so weaken Germany's fleet as to lose command of the Baltic, allow a Russian landing, and lead to defeat on land.

Arguments can always be found to turn desire into policy. Above all else, what nullified the navy in August was confidence in decisive victory by the army and the general belief that the war would not last long enough to make blockade a matter for much concern. Tirpitz with a "right presentiment" had already on July 29, the same day that Churchill mobilized the fleet, requested the Kaiser to place control of the navy in the hands of one man. As he felt that "I have more in my little finger than Pohl in his whole anatomy" (a sentiment expressed privately to his wife, not to the Kaiser), he could only suggest that the proposed office be "entrusted to myself." His proposal was rejected. Although he contemplated resigning, he refrained on the useful grounds that the Kaiser "would not have accepted my resignation." Dragged off to Coblenz with the other ministers, he had to suffer in the triumphant aura of OHL while "the Army has all the successes and the Navy none. My position is dreadful after 20 years of effort. No one will understand."

His High Seas Fleet with its 16 dreadnoughts, 12 older battleships, 3 battle cruisers, 17 other cruisers, 140 destroyers, and 27 submarines remained in port or in the Baltic, while offensive action against England was confined to one sweep by submarines during the first week and to mine-laying. The merchant navy also withdrew. On July 31 the German government ordered steamship lines to cancel all merchant sailings. By the end of August 670 German merchant steamers aggregating 2,750,000 tons, or more than half of Germany's total, were holed up in neutral ports, and the rest, except for those plying the Baltic, in home ports. Only five out of the terrible forty German armed merchant raiders materialized, and the British Admiralty, looking around in dazed surprise, was able to report on August 14: "The passage across the Atlantic is safe. British trade is running as usual." Except for the raiders *Emden* and *Königsberg* in the Indian Ocean and Admiral von Spee's squadron in the Pacific the German Navy and German merchant shipping had retired from the surface of the oceans before August was over.

Another battle, Britain's battle with the United States, the great neutral, had begun. The old issues that caused the war of 1812, the old phrases—freedom of the seas, the flag covers the goods—the old and inevitable conflict between the neutral's right of commerce and the belligerent's right of restraint was back again. In 1908, as an outgrowth of the second Hague Conference, an attempt to codify the rules had been made by a conference of all the nations who were to be belligerents in 1914 plus the United States, Holland, Italy, and Spain. Britain, as the largest carrier of seaborne trade with the greatest interest in the free flow of neutral commerce, was host nation, and Sir Edward Grey the moving spirit and sponsor, though not a delegate. Despite the vigorous presence of Admiral Mahan as chief American delegate, the resulting Declaration of London favored the neutrals' right to trade as against the belligerents' right to blockade. Even Mahan, the maritime Clausewitz, the Schlieffen of the sea, could not prevail against the suave workings of British influence. Everyone was for neutrals and business as usual, and Mahan's objections were overruled by his civilian colleagues.

Goods were divided into three categories: absolute contraband, which covered articles for military use only; conditional contraband, or articles for either military or civilian use; and a free list, which included food. Only the first could be seized by a belligerent who declared a blockade; the second could be seized only if enemy destination was proved; and the third not at all. But after the Declaration had been signed and the delegates had gone home, another British interest raised its head—sea power. Admiral Mahan's flag fluttered up the mast again. His disciples lifted their voices in horror at the betrayal of maritime supremacy, Britain's guarantee of survival. What use was it, they asked, to deny use of the seas to the enemy if neutrals were to be allowed to supply him with all his needs? They made the Declaration of London a *cause célèbre* and mounted a campaign against it in press and Parliament. It would nullify the British fleet; it was a German plot; Balfour opposed it. Although the Declaration had passed the House of Commons, the Lords in a burst of energy allowed it to fail to come to a vote, perhaps their most dynamic act of the twentieth century. By this time the government, having had second thoughts, was glad enough to let the matter lapse. The Declaration of London was never ratified.

Meanwhile new realities of naval power made Britain's traditional policy of close blockade of an enemy's ports obsolete. Up to now the Admiralty had contemplated, in war against a continental power, a close blockade by destroyer flotillas supported by cruisers and ultimately by battleships. Development of the submarine and floating mine and refinement of the rifled cannon enforced the change to a policy of distant blockade. Adopted in the Admiralty War Orders for 1912, it plunged the whole problem once more into confusion. When a ship attempts to run a close blockade, the port she is making for is obvious and the question of destination does not arise. But when ships are intercepted miles away from their destination, as at the top of the North Sea, the legality of arrest under the rules of blockade has to be shown by proof of destination or of the contraband nature of the cargo. The problem bristled like a floating mine with spikes of trouble.

When war broke, the Declaration of London was still the collected testimony of nations on the subject, and on August 6, the second day of war, the United States formally requested the belligerents to declare their adherence to it. Germany and Austria eagerly agreed on condition that the enemy would do likewise. Britain as spokesman for the Allies on naval policy composed an affirmative reply which, by reserving certain rights "essential to the efficient conduct of their naval operations," said Yes and meant No. She had as yet no fixed policy about contraband but only an empiric feeling that the terms of the Declaration of London required some stretching. A report of the Committee of Imperial Defence in 1911–12 had already proposed that ultimate destination of the goods, not the ships, should be made the criterion of conditional contraband so that leather for saddles, rubber for tires, copper, cotton, raw textiles, and paper, all convertible to military use, could not be shipped freely merely because they were consigned to a neutral receiver. If they were then to be sent overland to Germany, no blockade would be worth the expense of maintaining it. The Committee had suggested that the doctrine of continuous voyage should be "rigorously applied."

One of those phrases of mysterious power which appear and disappear in history, leaving nothing quite the same as before, "continuous voyage" was a concept invented by the British in the course of an eighteenth century war with the French. It meant that the ultimate, not the initial destination of the goods was the determining factor. Prematurely buried by the Declaration of London before it was quite dead, it was now disinterred like one of Poe's entombed cats with similar capacity for causing trouble. The War Office had been advised that foodstuffs shipped by neutrals to Holland were going to supply the German Army in Belgium. On August 20 the Cabinet issued an Order in Council declaring that henceforth Britain would regard conditional contraband as subject to capture if it was consigned to the enemy or "an agent of the enemy" or if its ultimate destination was hostile. Proof of destination was to depend not as heretofore on bills of lading but—in a phrase of matchless elasticity—on "any sufficient evidence."

Here was the doctrine of continuous voyage, alive, spitting, and sharp of claw. The practical effect, admitted Britain's ambassador in Washington, Sir Cecil Spring-Rice, was to make everything absolute contraband.

The immense train of results, the massive difficulties of implementing the decision, the halting and boarding and examining of ships, the X-ray of cargoes, the prize courts and legal complexities, the ultimate recourse to unrestricted submarine warfare which Germany would take with its ultimate effect upon the United States were not thought of then by the authors of the Order in Council. When he decided to divorce Catherine of Aragon, Henry VIII did not have in mind the Reformation. When ministers sat around the Cabinet table on August 20 they were concerned with the military necessity of stopping the flow of supplies from Rotterdam to the German Army in Belgium. The Order in Council was submitted to them on military advice and authorized after some discussion of which the only record is Asquith's airy reference in his diary to "a long Cabinet—all sorts of odds and ends about coal and contraband."

The Prime Minister was not the only person unconcerned with odds and ends of this kind. When a German official, foreseeing the change to a long war of attrition, presented Moltke with a memorandum on the need for an Economic General Staff, Moltke replied, "Don't bother me with economics—I am busy conducting a war."

By a nice coincidence the Order in Council, reviving the issue of the War of 1812, appeared exactly on the one hundredth anniversary of the burning of Washington by the British. Happily this odd chance and the Order itself were overlooked by the American public, absorbed in streaming headlines about the fall of Brussels, stranded Americans in Paris, Kaisers and Czars, fleets, Cossacks, Field Marshals, Zeppelins, Western and Eastern Fronts. The United States government, however, was shocked. The soft British preamble to the Order, which affirmed loyalty to the Declaration of London before making its delicate exceptions, failed to obscure their meaning to the lawyer's eye of Robert Lansing, Counselor to the State Department. He drew up a firm and immediate protest which precipitated a long duel extending into months and years of letters and replies, briefs and precedents, interviews between ambassadors, volumes of documents.

To the London *Daily Chronicle* on August 27 there appeared to be a "very real danger" of becoming embroiled with the United States over questions of contraband and the right of search which it understood the United States "strongly resists." This was a problem that had occurred to Sir Edward Grey, and required careful handling. In the beginning when the war was expected to be short and all that mattered was the best means of winning quickly, there seemed little likelihood of time for a serious issue with the United States to arise. After Mons and Charleroi the inescapable truth of a long war rose out of the corpse-strewn battlefields and stared the Allies in the face. In a long war they would have to draw upon the United States for food, arms, and money (no one yet thought of men) and cut Germany off from the same nourishment. Stiffening the blockade of the enemy and maintaining friendship with the great neutral became simultaneously essential—and incompatible. As every added restraint put upon the neutrals' trade with Germany raised another majestic howl from the State Department about freedom of the seas, it became uncomfortably apparent that Britain might ultimately have to decide which of two objects was the more important. For the moment, with instinctive English dislike of absolutes, Sir Edward Grey was able to pick his way from incident to incident, avoiding large principles as a helmsman avoids rocks and being careful not to allow discussion to reach a clear-cut issue that would require either side to take a position from which it could not climb down. His aim from day to day was, he said, "to secure the maximum blockade that could be enforced without a rupture with the United States."

He had a formidable opponent who was nothing if not a man of principle. Rigidly, puritanically attached to neutrality, Woodrow Wilson was driven to take and maintain a stand on traditional neutral rights less for their own sake than because they were part of the neutral's role that he grasped with fierce intensity from the beginning. He had come to office strenuously dedicated to unseating the "Interests" and dollar diplomats entrenched under the portly, protective shadow of Mr. Taft and to achieving the New Freedom in domestic and Latin-American affairs. Knowing that war stifles reform, he was bent on keeping the country out of a foreign adventure that would frustrate his program. But beyond that, he had a grander and ulterior reason. He saw in the war an opportunity for greatness on the world stage. In his first utterance on the war, spoken to a press conference on August 3, he said that he wanted to have the pride of the feeling that America "stands ready to help the rest of the world" and that he believed she could "reap a great permanent glory out of doing it." Thus early, even before the guns went off, he had formulated the role that he wanted the United States, with which he identified himself, to play; the role he clung to with increasing desperation as the hammer of events weakened his grip, that he never, even after the final involvement, abandoned in his heart.

To Wilson neutrality was the opposite of isolationism. He wanted to keep out of war in order to play a larger, not a lesser, part in world affairs. He wanted the "great permanent glory" for himself as well as for his country, and he realized he could win it only if he kept America out of the quarrel so that he could act as impartial arbiter. On August 18, in a famous statement, he commanded his countrymen to be "neutral in fact as well as in name, impartial in thought as well as in action," and explained that the ultimate purpose of neutrality was to enable the United States "to speak the counsels of peace" and "play the part of impartial mediator." In the European conflict he hoped to exercise the duty of "moral judgment," as he said in a later statement. He wanted "to serve humanity," bring to bear the force—the moral force—of the New World to save the Old World from its follies and, by applying "standards of righteousness and humanity," bring the gifts of peace through mediation under the flag that was "the flag not only of America but of humanity."

Once the British Navy had effectively gained control of the Atlantic by the end of August, the duel with the United States over contraband, however earnest, prolonged, and often bitter, remained a shadow duel. For Wilson freedom of the seas was never the overriding issue, and though once, when matters became particularly contentious, he was disturbed by the thought that he might become the second Princeton president after Madison to lead the country to war, he had no wish to push home the quarrel to the ultimate conclusion of 1812. In any case, leaping trade with the Allies, which was taking up more than the slack of lost trade with Germany, dulled the edge of national principle. As long as goods were being absorbed, the United States came gradually to acquiesce in the process begun by the Order in Council of August 20.

From that time on, through control of the high seas by the British fleet, American trade was perforce directed more and more toward the Allies. Trade with the Central Powers declined from $169 million in 1914 to $1 million in 1916, and during the same period trade with the Allies rose from $824 million to $3 billion. To supply the demand American business and industry produced the goods the Allies wanted. To enable them to pay for American supplies, financial credit for the Allies had to be arranged. Eventually, the United States became the larder, arsenal, and bank of the Allies and acquired a direct interest in Allied victory that was to bemuse the postwar apostles of economic determinism for a long time.

Economic ties develop where there is a basis of long-founded cultural ties, and economic interests where there is natural interest. American trade with England and France had always been greater than with Germany and Austria, and the effect of the blockade was to exaggerate an existing condition, not to create an artificial one. Trade follows not only a nation's flag but its natural sympathies.

"A government can be neutral," said Walter Hines Page, the American ambassador in London, "but no *man* can be." As a wholehearted adherent of the Allies, to whom the concept of neutrality was despicable, he spoke feelingly and wrote feelingly in vivid, persuasive letters to Wilson. Although Page's outspoken identification with the Allies estranged the President to the point of turning his back on the man who had been one of his earliest supporters, even Wilson could not make himself neutral in thought as he wanted other men to be. When Grey wrote him a letter of sympathy on the death of Mrs. Wilson on August 6, Wilson, who admired Grey and felt close to him as one who had lost his own wife, replied: "My hope is that you will regard me as your friend. I feel that we are bound together by common principle and purpose." There was no one in the German government to whom he could have said the same.

Wilson's cultural roots and political philosophy, like that of the majority of influential people in American life, went back to English experience and the French Revolution. He tried to repress them for the sake of his ambition to be peacemaker to the world. For three years he struggled, using every means of persuasion he could wield, to bring the belligerents to a negotiated peace, a "peace without victory." Neutrality, on which his efforts depended, was helped by a strong current of Irish or what might be called anti-George III sentiment and by the vociferous pro-German groups from Professor Hugo Münsterberg of Harvard down to the beerhalls of Milwaukee. It might have prevailed had it not been for a factor before which Wilson was helpless, which in shaping American sentiment was the greatest Allied asset—not the British fleet but German folly.

At the outbreak on August 4 the President, writing to a friend, expressed only "utter condemnation" for the conflict across the seas, and made no attempt to distinguish between the belligerents. On August 30, after a month of the war in Belgium, Colonel House recorded that the President "felt deeply the destruction of Louvain. . . . He goes even further than I in his condemnation of Germany's part in this war and almost allows his feeling to include the German people as a whole rather than the leaders alone. . . . He expressed the opinion that if Germany won it would change the course of our civilization and make the United States a military nation." A few days later Spring-Rice reported that Wilson had said to him "in the most solemn way that if the German cause succeeds in the present struggle the United States would have to give up its present ideals and devote all its energies to defense which would mean the end of its present system of government."

Holding these views, Wilson nevertheless stood to the last, a

Casabianca on the burning deck of neutrality. But it was on the planks of a legal, not a felt, neutrality. He could never regard the prospect of an Allied victory as a threat to the principles on which the United States was founded, whereas the prospect of a German victory, especially after Belgium clarified the issues, could not be regarded as anything else. If Wilson, who of all his countrymen had the greatest stake in neutrality, was alienated by German actions, how much more so the average man. The sentiments aroused by Louvain muffled the resentment of Britain's blockade procedures. Each time a British search or seizure or addition to the contraband list aroused new gusts of American wrath, they would be diverted by some convenient act of German frightfulness. Just when Lansing's stiff rebuke of the Order in Council was about to ripen into major controversy, German Zeppelins on August 25 bombed the residential area of Antwerp, killing civilians and narrowly missing the Palace where the Belgian Queen had just moved with her children. As a result Lansing found himself framing a protest against "this outrage upon humanity" instead of a protest against continuous voyage.

In a moment of painful foresight Wilson confided to his brother-in-law, Dr. Axon, who remembered the date as shortly after Mrs. Wilson's funeral on August 12, "I am afraid something will happen on the high seas that will make it impossible for us to keep out of war." It was not what happened on the high seas but what did not happen that became the deciding factor. When Sherlock Holmes called Inspector Gregory's attention "to the curious incident of the dog in the night-time," the puzzled Inspector replied, "The dog did nothing in the night-time."

"That was the curious incident," remarked Holmes.

The German Navy was the dog in the night. It did not fight. Chained up by the fleet-in-being theory and by German belief in an early victory on land, it was not allowed to risk itself in the performance of a navy's function—keeping the sea lanes open to the commerce of its country. Although German industry depended on imported raw materials and German agriculture on imported fertilizer, although German dairy cattle chewed all winter on imported fodder, the Navy made no attempt to protect the flow of supplies. The only battle it fought in August was inadvertent and merely served to confirm the Kaiser's reluctance to risk his "darlings."

This was the Battle of Heligoland Bight on August 28. In a sudden challenge meant to divert German attention from the landing of marines at Ostend, submarine and destroyer flotillas of the British Channel fleet, with battle cruisers in support, steamed into the Bight, home base of the German Navy. Taken by surprise, German light cruisers were ordered out without support of heavier warships. "With all the enthusiasm of the first fight," in Tirpitz's words, they rushed about recklessly in the mist and confusion. In a tangled, dispersed, and haphazard series of combats that lasted all day, British units mistook each other for the enemy and were only saved from what Churchill delicately called "awkward embarrassments" by pure luck. The Germans, who failed to respond to the challenge by ordering the whole fleet to sea, were outnumbered and outgunned. The advantage of the day went to the British. Three German light cruisers, the *Köln*, *Mainz*, and *Ariadne*, and a destroyer were shot to pieces and sunk, three others badly damaged, and more than 1,000 men, including an Admiral and a Commodore, were killed under fire or drowned, and over 200, including Wolf Tirpitz, son of the Grand Admiral, were picked from the water and taken prisoner. The British lost no ships and suffered some 75 casualties.

Horrified at his losses and confirmed in his fear of a test with the British, the Kaiser gave orders that risks were not again to be taken, "the loss of ships was to be avoided," the initiative of the Commander of the North Sea Fleet was to be further restricted, and major movements were not to be undertaken without His Majesty's approval in advance.

Thereafter, while the British Navy built up the blockade walls around Germany, the German Navy watched passively. Straining against his chains the unhappy Tirpitz wrote in mid-September, "Our best opportunity for a successful battle was in the first two or three weeks after the declaration of war." "As time goes on," he predicted, "our chance of success will grow worse, not better." It was the English fleet that was "achieving the full effect of a 'fleet-in-being': extraordinary and increasing pressure on the neutrals, complete destruction of German seaborne trade, the fullest practical blockade."

Eventually forced to combat the situation it had allowed to develop, German naval policy went underwater. In belated effort to break the blockade it took to the U-boats. Spawned in default of the surface navy, the U-boats ultimately fulfilled the condition on the high seas that Wilson had fearfully glimpsed during the first days of the war in August.

19

Retreat

LIKE A swinging scythe the five German armies of the right wing and center cut into France from Belgium after the Battle of the Frontiers. A million Germans were in the invading force whose leading columns, shooting and burning, entered French territory on August 24. No breakthrough was made on the Lorraine front where the two armies of the left wing under Prince Rupprecht continued to struggle in prolonged battle against the furious resistance of Castelnau's and Dubail's armies.

Down the long white highways of northern France, cutting a swath seventy-five miles wide, the German right wing was on the march to Paris with Kluck's Army on the extreme right seeking to envelop the Allied line. Joffre's immediate problem was to halt the retreat of his own armies while at the same time shifting weight to the left to create a force strong enough to check the enemy's enveloping movement and be "capable of resuming the offensive." In the aftermath of catastrophe, "resume the offensive" was the dominant thought at GQG. Within twenty-four hours of the debacle, without taking time to assess what was officially called the "check" to the French Armies, or to rethink strategy in terms of the possible, Joffre issued on August 25 a new General Order, the second of the war. It proposed to create in the path of the German right wing a new Sixth Army formed of forces taken from the unbroken front in Lorraine. Transported by rail to Amiens, on the left of the British, it would, together with the BEF and the Fourth and Fifth French Armies, form the mass that was to resume the offensive. While the Sixth Army was forming, the three retreating French Armies were to try to maintain a continuous front and "arrest or at least delay the advance of the enemy by short and violent counterattacks" carried out by rearguards. As stated in General Order No. 2, Joffre expected the Sixth Army to be in position and ready to join in a renewed offensive by September 2, Sedan Day.

That date glittered too before the oncoming Germans who expected by then to accomplish Schlieffen's goal: envelopment and destruction of the French Armies in a central mass in front of Paris. Throughout the next twelve days another Sedan was in the minds of both sides. They were twelve days in which world history wavered between two courses and the Germans came so close to victory that they reached out and touched it between the Aisne and the Marne.

"Fight in retreat, fight in retreat," was the order dinned into every French regiment during these days. The necessity to hold off pursuit and gain time to regroup and reestablish a solid line gave an urgency to the fighting that had been missing from the offensive. It required rearguard actions that were almost suicidal. The Germans' need to allow the French no time to regroup pushed them on with equal intensity.

In retreat the French fought with competence and emergency-learned skills that had not always been present during the opening battles in Belgium. No longer engaged in a vast and only vaguely understood offensive in mysterious forests on alien soil, they were back on their own soil, defending France. The land they were passing through was familiar, the inhabitants were French, the fields and barns and village streets were their own, and they fought now as the First and Second Armies were fighting for the Moselle and the Grand Couronné. Though defeated in the offensive, they were not a routed army; their line, though dangerously pierced, was not yet broken. On the left in the path of the main German advance the Fifth Army, escaping from disaster at Charleroi and the Sambre, was trying to regather cohesion in retreat. In the center, with their backs to the Meuse, the Third and Fourth Armies fought savage holding actions from Sedan to Verdun against the two armies of the German center, frustrating the enemy's effort to surround them and, as the Crown Prince unhappily admitted, "recovering their freedom of movement." Despite rearguard actions the German advance was too massive to be stopped. Still fighting, the French fell back; holding and delaying where they could but always falling back.

At one place after crossing the Meuse, a battalion of *chasseurs à pied* in General de Langle's Fourth Army was ordered at nightfall to hold a bridge which dynamite charges had failed to blow up. They spent a night of "anguish and horror" watching the Saxons of von Hausen's Army on the opposite bank "burning the town and shooting the inhabitants under our eyes. In the morning flames rose from the village. We could see people running in the streets, pursued by the soldiers. There were shots. . . . At a great distance we could see an endless movement of horsemen who seemed to be searching out our position: far away on the plain appeared dark masses marching." The masses approached and soon along the winding road a German infantry battalion in columns of five came "marching steadily toward us. The road below was filled as far back as one could see with a swarm of troops—columns of infantry preceded by officers on horseback, artillery trains, transport, cavalry—almost a division, marching in perfect order."

"Take aim!" The order was repeated down the line of *chasseurs* in low voices. Silently the men took their places. "Volley fire; aim at the infantry first, each man pick his target!" Company leaders gave the range. "Open fire!" Along the length of the river the fusillade crackled. Down among the Germans there was a sudden stupor. Their companies whirled and eddied; they fled. Horses struggled and reared in harness, wagons crashed. The road was covered with hundreds of corpses. At 8:45 the French ammunition was almost gone. Suddenly from behind on their left came a burst of rifle fire. The enemy had turned their flank. "To the rear, *à la baïonnette!*" Under the thrust of their bayonet charge, the Germans gave way; the French regiment cut its way through.

Hundreds of such combats were fought by rearguards while the armies fell back, attempting to keep a continuous front with each other and reach a line from which the offensive could be renewed. Alongside the soldiers, the civil population joined in the southward-moving mass, on foot and in every kind of conveyance from families in six-horse wagons to old men pushed in wheelbarrows and babies in perambulators. Crowding the roads, they added to the confusion. Staff cars could not get through, officers cursed, messages went undelivered. Jammed between marching groups, commercial trucks and municipal buses, mobilized for army service with their familiar markings painted over with military symbols, moved slowly, carrying the wounded men who lay in blood-soaked silence with shell-torn limbs and eyes filled with pain and the fear of death.

Each mile of the retreat was an agony of yielding further French territory to the enemy. In some places French soldiers marched past their own homes knowing the Germans would enter them next day. "We left Blombay on August 27," wrote a cavalry captain with the Fifth Army. "Ten minutes later it was occupied by the Uhlans." Units that had been in heavy combat marched in silence, out of step, without songs. Haggard men, parched and hungry, some bitter, muttered against their officers or whispered of treason. Every French position had been betrayed to the German artillery spotters, it was said in the Xth Corps of Lanrezac's Army which had lost 5,000 men on the Sambre. "The men drag themselves along, their faces marked by a terrible exhaustion," wrote an infantry captain in this corps. "They have just completed a two days' march of 62 kilometers after a sharp rearguard action." But that night they sleep, and in the morning "it is extraordinary how a few hours' sleep revives them. They are new men." They ask why they are retreating, and the captain makes a sharp speech in "a cold assured voice." He tells them they will fight again "and show the Germans we have teeth and claws."

The cavalry, once so shiny in polished boots and bright uniforms, now stained and muddy, sway in their saddles, dazed with fatigue. "The men's heads hang with weariness," writes an officer of Hussars with the 9th Cavalry Division. "They only half see where they are going; they live as if in a dream. At halts the famished and broken-down horses even before unsaddling, plunge at the hay and devour it voraciously. We no longer sleep; we march by night and face the enemy by day." They learn the Germans have crossed the Meuse behind them, are gaining ground, setting villages in flames as they pass. "Rocroi is a mass of fire and the barns burning in the neighborhood light up the trees of the nearby woods." At dawn the voice of the enemy's cannon begins; "the Germans salute the sun with their shells." Through the incessant crash and thunder the French hear the brave scream of their own 75s. They grip their positions, waiting for the artillery duel to end. A mounted orderly rides up with an order from the commander: retreat. They move on. "I contemplated the green fields and the herds of grazing sheep and I thought, 'What a fortune we are abandoning!' My men recovered their spirits. They found a system of trenches dug by the infantry which they examined with the greatest curiosity as if they were sights offered for the admiration of the tourist."

On August 25 Germans belonging to the Duke of Württemberg's Army penetrated Sedan and shelled Bazeilles, scene of the famous Battle of the Last Cartridge in 1870. The French of de Langle's Fourth Army counterattacked to keep them from crossing the Meuse. "A hot artillery duel began," wrote a German officer of the VIIIth Reserve Corps. "It was such a terrible fracas that the earth trembled. All the old bearded Territorials were crying." Later he fought in a "terrible combat on wooded slopes as steep as roofs. Four assaults with the bayonet. We had to jump over piles of our own dead. We fell back on Sedan with heavy casualties and the loss of three flags."

That night the French blew up all the railroad bridges in the area. Torn between the need to delay the enemy and the thought that tomorrow they might require bridges and railroads themselves for a return to the offensive, the French left destruction of communications to the latest possible moment, sometimes too late.

The greatest difficulty of all was the assignment of each unit, from army corps down to single regiments, each with its own supply train and auxiliaries of cavalry and artillery to its own roads and lines of communication. "Rather than yield a road to the transport wagons, the infantry mark time at the crossroads," complained a supply officer. While falling back, the units had to reform and collect again around their flags, report their losses, receive replacements of men and officers from the depots of reserves in the rear. For one corps alone, the IVth of Ruffey's Army, a total of 8,000 reserves, a quarter of its strength, were sent up to replace losses, company by company. Among the officers, devoted to the doctrine of *élan*, casualties from the rank of general down were severe. One of the causes of the debacle, in the opinion of Colonel Tanant, a staff officer with the Third Army, was that general officers would not direct operations from their proper place in the rear but led from the front; "they performed the function of corporals, not commanders."

But now from bitter experience they had learned revised tactics. Now they entrenched. One regiment, shoveling all day in its shirt sleeves under the hot sun, dug trenches deep enough to shoot from standing up. Another, ordered to entrench and organize the defense of a woods, passed the night without incident and moved on again at four in the morning, "almost sorry to go without a fight . . . for by now we are seized with anger at this continual retreat."

Yielding as little territory as possible, Joffre intended to make his stand as near as he could to the point of breakthrough. The line he laid down in General Order No. 2 was along the Somme, about fifty miles below the Mons Canal and the Sambre. Poincaré wondered whether there was not some self-deception lurking in Joffre's optimism, and there were others who would have preferred a line farther back, allowing time to solidify a front. From the day after the debacle the men in Paris already saw Paris as the front, but Joffre's mind had not traveled back to the capital and there was no one in France to question Joffre.

The government was in a frenzy; ministers, according to Poincaré, in a "state of consternation"; deputies, according to Messimy, in a "panic that painted a livid mask of fear upon their faces." Removed from direct contact with the front, lacking eyewitness evidence, uninformed as to strategy, dependent on the "laconic and sibylline" communiqués of GQG and on rumor, supposition, and conflicting reports, they were responsible to the country and the people while without authority over the military conduct of the war. Underneath the rubbed and polished sentences of Joffre's report Poincaré could make out the sharp edges of the truth—"a triple avowal of invasion, defeat and the loss of Alsace." He felt his immediate duty was to tell the country the facts and prepare the people for the "terrible trials" that lay ahead. That the need to prepare Paris for a siege was even more immediate, he did not yet realize.

Early that morning the nakedness of the capital was made known to Messimy, as Minister of War. General Hirschauer of the Engineers, in charge of the defense works and Chief of Staff to General Michel, the Military Governor of Paris, came to see him at 6:00 A.M. This was several hours before Joffre's telegram arrived, but Hirschauer had learned privately of the disaster at Charleroi and his mind took in the distance from the frontiers to the capital in a single stride. He told Messimy flatly that the defenses of the perimeter were not ready to be manned. Despite elaborate studies with every requirement foreseen, "the fortifications existed on paper but nothing had been done on the ground." Originally the date given for the defense works to be usable was August 25, but such was the faith in the French offensive that it had been put off to September 15. Because of reluctance to begin the property destruction involved in felling trees and razing houses for fields of fire and in digging trenches, no definite order for these major measures had been given. Construction of gun emplacements and infantry posts, laying of barbed wire, cutting of timber for parapets, preparation of storage shelters for ammunition were not even half finished, provisioning of the city barely begun. As Military Governor and responsible for the defenses, General Michel, perhaps permanently discouraged by the rejection of his defensive plan in 1911, had been lackluster and ineffectual. His tenure of command which came into being with the outbreak of war had quickly floundered in anarchy and hesitancy. Confirmed in the poor opinion he had had of Michel in 1911, Messimy had called in General Hirschauer on August 13 with orders to make up the delays and complete the defenses in three weeks. Hirschauer now confessed the task was impossible.

"Palaver is the rule," he said. "Every morning I lose three hours in reports and discussions which have no results. Every decision requires an arbitration. Even as Chief of Staff to the Governor, I cannot, as a simple general of brigade, give orders to the generals of division who command the sectors."

As was his habit Messimy sent at once for Gallieni and was conferring with him when Joffre's telegram came in. Its opening phrase blaming the failure on "our troops who have not shown in the field the offensive qualities expected of them," depressed Messimy inordinately, but Gallieni looked for facts, distances, and place names.

"Briefly," he said without sentiment, "you may expect the German armies to be before the walls of Paris in twelve days. Is Paris ready to withstand a siege?"

Forced to answer No, Messimy asked Gallieni to return later, intending in the meantime to obtain authority from the government to name him Military Governor in place of Michel. At that moment he was "stupefied" to learn from another visitor, General Ebener, GQG's representative at the War Ministry, that Paris was to lose two reserve divisions, the 61st and 62nd, assigned to her defense. Joffre had ordered them north to reinforce a group of three Territorial divisions, the only French troops between the British and the sea where Kluck's right-wing corps were sweeping down. Raging, Messimy protested that, as Paris belonged to the Zone of the Interior rather than the Zone of the Armies, the 61st and 62nd were under his command, not Joffre's, and could not be removed from the Paris garrison without his permission and that of the Premier and the President of the Republic. The order was already "in execution" Ebener replied, adding in some embarrassment that he himself was to go north in command of the two divisions.

Messimy rushed off to the Elysée Palace to see Poincaré, who "exploded" on hearing the news but was equally helpless. To his question what troops were left, Messimy had to reply, one reserve cavalry division, three Territorial divisions, and no active units except a few cadres at the army depots in the area. To the two men it seemed that the government and capital of France were left without means of defense and unable to command any. Only one resource was left—Gallieni.

He was now again asked to supplant Michel as he, instead of Joffre, might have done in 1911. At the age of twenty-one, as a second lieutenant just out of St. Cyr, Gallieni had fought at Sedan and been held prisoner for some time in Germany, where he learned the language. He chose to make his further military career in the colonies where France was "growing soldiers." Although the Staff College clique professed to regard colonial service as "*le tourisme*," Gallieni's fame as the conqueror of Madagascar brought him, like Lyautey of Morocco, to the top rank of the French Army. He kept a notebook in German, English, and Italian called *Erinnerungen of my life di ragazzo*, and never ceased studying, whether it was Russian or the development of heavy artillery or the comparative administrations of the colonial powers. He wore a pince-nez and a heavy gray mustache that was rather at odds with his elegant, autocratic figure. He carried himself like an officer on parade. Tall and spare, with a distant, untouchable, faintly stern air, he resembled no other French officer of his time. Poincaré described the impression he made: "straight, slender and upright with head erect and piercing eyes behind his glasses, he appeared to us as an imposing example of powerful humanity."

At sixty-five, he was suffering from the prostatitis of which, after two operations, he was to die within two years. Bereaved by the death of his wife within the last month, and having renounced the highest post in the French Army three years earlier, he was beyond personal ambition, a man with little time left, as irritably impatient with the politics of the army as with the rivalries of politicians. In the last months before the war when, prior to his retirement in April, the intrigues of the cliques swirled around him, some to have him named Minister of War or Commander in Chief designate in place of Joffre, others to reduce his pension or remove his friends, his diary was filled with disgust for life, for "that miserable thing, politics," for the "clan of *arrivistes*," for unreadiness and inefficiency in the army and with no great admiration for Joffre. "When I was riding I passed him in the Bois today—on foot as usual. . . . How fat and heavy he is; he will hardly last out his three years." Now in France's gravest moment since 1870 he was being asked to take over a botched job, called to defend Paris without an army. He believed it was essential to hold the capital for moral effect as well as for its railroads, supplies, and industrial capacity. He knew well enough that Paris could not be defended from the inside like a fortress, but only by an army giving battle beyond the perimeter, an army that would have to come from Joffre—who had other plans.

"They do not want to defend Paris," he said to Messimy that night when he was formally requested to become Military Governor. "In the eyes of our strategists Paris is a geographical expression—a town like any other. What do you give me to defend this immense place enclosing the heart and brain of France? A few Territorial divisions and one fine division from Africa. That is nothing but a drop in the ocean. If Paris is not to suffer the fate of Liège and Namur it must be covered for 100 kilometers around and to cover it requires an army. Give me an army of three active corps and I will agree to become Governor of Paris; on this condition, formal and explicit, you can count on me for its defense."

Messimy thanked him so effusively, "shaking my hands several times and even kissing me," that Gallieni felt assured "from the warmth of these demonstrations that the place I was succeeding to was not an enviable one."

How he was to extract one active corps, much less three, from Joffre, Messimy did not know. The only active unit he could lay his hands on was the African division mentioned by Gallieni, the 45th Infantry from Algiers, which had been formed, apart from the regular mobilization orders, at the direct instance of the Ministry of War and was just disembarking in the south. Despite repeated telephonic demands for it from GQG, Messimy determined to hang on to this "fresh and splendid" division at all costs. He still needed five more. To force Joffre to supply them in order to satisfy Gallieni's condition meant a direct clash of authority between the government and the Commander in Chief. Messimy trembled. On the solemn and unforgettable Mobilization Day he had sworn to himself "never to fall into the error committed by the War Ministry of 1870" whose interference, at the command of the Empress Eugénie, sent General MacMahon on the march to Sedan. He had carefully examined in company with Poincaré the Decrees of 1913 delimiting authority in wartime, and in all the ardor of the first day had voluntarily assured Joffre that he interpreted them as assigning the political conduct of war to the government and the military conduct to the Commander in Chief as his "absolute and exclusive domain." Further, the decrees, as he read them, gave the Commander in Chief "extended powers" in the country as a whole and "absolute" power, civil as well as military, in the Zone of the Armies. "You are the master, we are your purveyors," he had finished. Not surprisingly Joffre "without discussion" had agreed with him. Poincaré and Viviani's neophyte Cabinet had obediently concurred.

Where was he now to find the authority he had forsworn? Searching almost until midnight back through the Decrees for a legal basis, Messimy grasped at a phrase charging the civil government "with the vital interests of the country." To prevent the capital from falling to the enemy was surely a vital interest of the country, but what form should an order to Joffre take? Through the remainder of an agonized and sleepless night the Minister of War tried to nerve himself to compose an order to the Commander in Chief. After four hours of painful labor in the lonely stretch between 2:00 and 6:00 A.M., he achieved two sentences headed "Order" which instructed Joffre that if "victory does not crown our armies and they are forced to retreat, a minimum of three active corps in good condition must be sent to the entrenched camp of Paris. The receipt of this order is to be acknowledged." Sent by telegram, it was also delivered by hand at eleven next morning, August 25, accompanied by a "personal and friendly" letter in which Messimy added, "the importance of this order will not escape you."

By this time word of the defeat at the frontiers and the extent of the retreat was spreading through Paris. Ministers and deputies were clamoring for someone to blame as "responsible"; public opinion, they said, would demand it. In the antechambers of the Elysée mutterings against Joffre were heard: ". . . an idiot . . . incapable . . . fire him on the spot." Messimy as War Minister was equally favored; "the lobbies are out for your skin," his adjutant whispered. To affirm the "sacred union" of all parties and strengthen Viviani's new and feeble ministry was a necessity in the crisis. Approaches were being made to France's leading political figures to join the government. The oldest, most feared and respected, Clemenceau, the Tiger of France, although a bitter opponent of Poincaré, was the obvious first choice. Viviani found him in a "violent temper" and without desire to join a government he expected to be out of office in two weeks.

"No, no, don't count on me," he said. "In a fortnight you will be torn to ribbons, I am not going to have anything to do with it." After this "paroxysm of passion" he burst into tears, embraced Viviani, but continued to decline to join him in office. A triumvirate made up of Briand, a former premier; Delcassé, the most distinguished and experienced Foreign Minister of the prewar period; and Millerand, a former Minister of War, was willing to join as a group but only on condition that Delcassé and Millerand be given their old portfolios at the expense of the present holders, Doumergue at the Foreign Office and Messimy at the War Office. With this uncomfortable bargain, known so far only to Poincaré, hanging in the air, the Cabinet met at ten o'clock that morning. In their minds ministers heard the sound of guns and saw broken, fleeing armies and spike-helmeted hordes marching south, but attempting to preserve dignity and calm, they followed the routine procedure of speaking in turn on departmental matters. As they reported on bank moratoriums, on disturbance to the judicial process by the call-up of magistrates, on Russian aims in Constantinople, Messimy's agitation mounted. From an early pitch of enthusiasm he was nearing despair. After Hirschauer's disclosures and with Gallieni's twelve days ringing in his ears, he felt that "hours were worth centuries and minutes counted as years." When discussion turned upon diplomacy in the Balkans and Poincaré brought up the subject of Albania, he exploded.

"To hell with Albania!" he shouted, striking the table a terrible blow. He denounced the pretense of calm as an "undignified farce," and when begged by Poincaré to control himself, refused, saying, "I don't know about your time but mine is too precious to waste." He flung in the face of his colleagues Gallieni's prediction that the Germans would be outside Paris by September 5. Everyone began talking at once, demands were made for Joffre's removal, and Messimy was reproached for passing from "systematic optimism to dangerous pessimism." One positive result gained was agreement to the appointment of Gallieni in place of Michel.

While Messimy returned to the Rue St. Dominique to remove Michel a second time from office, his own removal was being exacted by Millerand, Delcassé, and Briand. They claimed he was responsible for the false optimism of the communiqués; he was "overwrought and nervy," and besides, his office was wanted for Millerand. A thick-set, taciturn man with an ironic manner, Millerand was a one-time socialist of undoubted ability and courage whose "untiring energy and sangfroid," Poincaré felt, were badly needed. He saw Messimy becoming "gloomier and gloomier," and since a War Minister who "foresees a great defeat" was not the most desirable colleague, the President agreed to sacrifice him. The ministerial rites would be performed gracefully: Messimy and Doumergue would be asked to resign and become Ministers without Portfolio;

General Michel would be offered a mission to the Czar. These soothing arrangements were not accepted by their intended victims.

Michel stormed when asked by Messimy to resign, protested loudly and angrily and obstinately refused to go. Becoming equally excited, Messimy shouted at Michel that if he persisted in his refusal he would leave the room, not for his own office at the Invalides, but for the military prison of Cherche-Midi under guard. As their cries resounded from the room Viviani fortuitously arrived, calmed the disputants, and eventually persuaded Michel to give way.

Hardly was the official decree appointing Gallieni "Military Governor and Commandant of the Armies of Paris" signed next day when it became Messimy's turn to storm when asked for his resignation by Poincaré and Viviani. "I refuse to yield my post to Millerand, I refuse to do you the pleasure of resigning, I refuse to become a Minister without Portfolio." If they wanted to get rid of him after the "crushing labor" he had sustained in the last month, then the whole government would have to resign, and in that case, he said, "I have an officer's rank in the Army and a Mobilization order in my pocket. I shall go to the front." No persuasion availed. The government was forced to resign and was reconstituted next day. Millerand, Delcassé, Briand, Alexander Ribot, and two new socialist ministers replaced five former members, including Messimy. He departed as a major to join Dubail's army and to serve at the front until 1918, rising to general of division.

His legacy to France, Gallieni, was left "Commander of the Armies of Paris" without an army. The three active corps which were to run like a red thread through the dark and tangled confusion of the next twelve days were not forthcoming from Joffre. The Generalissimo instantly detected in Messimy's telegram "the menace of government interference in the conduct of operations." When he was busy laying hold of every brigade he could find to resume battle on the Somme, the idea of sparing three active corps "in good condition" for the capital appealed to him as little as the idea of submitting to ministerial dictation. Having no intention of doing either, he ignored the War Minister's order.

"Yes, I have the order here," admitted his deputy, General

Belin, rapping his safe, when visited next day by General Hirschauer who had been sent by Gallieni to demand an answer. "The government is taking a terrible responsibility to ask for three corps to defend Paris. It might be the origin of a disaster. What does Paris matter!" Millerand, too, arrived to be told by Joffre that there could be no useful defense of Paris except by the mobile army in the field which was now needed to the last man for the maneuver and the battle that would decide the fate of the country. The distress of the government, the threat to Paris, moved him not at all. The loss of the capital, he said, would not mean the end of the struggle.

In order to dam the open space in front of the German right wing, his immediate aim was to bring the new Sixth Army into position. Its nucleus was the Army of Lorraine, hastily scraped together only a few days before and thrown into the Battle of the Frontiers under General Maunoury, called out of retirement to command it. A svelte, delicate, small-boned veteran of sixty-seven, wounded as a lieutenant in 1870, Maunoury was a former Military Governor of Paris and member of the Supreme War Council of whom Joffre had said, "This is the complete soldier." The Army of Lorraine consisted of the VIIth Corps, the same that had made the first dash into Alsace under the unfortunate General Bonneau, and the 55th and 56th reserve divisions taken from Ruffey's Army, which were displaying, as the reserves did again and again, a dependable valor that was one of the elements to sustain France. On the day they received Joffre's orders for transfer to the west, the 55th and 56th were engaged in a spirited battle to prevent passage of the Crown Prince's Army between Verdun and Toul which proved one of the great feats of the retreat. Just when their firm stand was supporting the flank of a counteroffensive by Ruffey's Army in the vital Briey basin, they were snatched from the field to shore up the failing front on the left.

They were railed to Amiens through Paris, where they were switched to the northern railways, already congested by the demands of the BEF. Although French railroad movements had not been polished by the best brains of the General Staff to the fanatic perfection of the German, the transfer was managed quickly, if not smoothly, by means of a French equivalent for German thoroughness called *le système D*, in which the "D" stands for *se débrouiller*, meaning "to muddle through" or "work it out somehow." Maunoury's troops were already detraining at Amiens on August 26, but it was not soon enough. The front was falling back faster than the new army could be got into position, and on the far end of the line von Kluck's pursuit had already caught up with the British.

If there could have been an observer in a balloon high enough to have a view of the whole French frontier from the Vosges to Lille, he would have seen a rim of red, the *pantalons rouges* of 70 French divisions and, near the left end, a tiny wedge of khaki, the four British divisions. On August 24 these were joined by the newly arrived 4th Division and 19th Brigade from England, making a total of five and a half British divisions. Now that the enveloping maneuver of the German right wing was at last clear, the British found themselves holding a place in the line more important than had been intended for them in Plan 17. They were not, however, holding the end of the line unsupported. Joffre had hurriedly sent Sordet's tired Cavalry Corps to add to a group of three French Territorial divisions under General d'Amade in the space between the British and the sea. These were reinforced by the garrison division of Lille which on August 24 was declared an open city, and evacuated. ("If they get as far as Lille," General de Castelnau had said not so long ago, "so much the better for us.") If Joffre's plan were to work, it was essential that the BEF hold the space between Lanrezac and the newly forming Sixth Army. Under General Order No. 2 Joffre intended the BEF to conform to the general pace of the retreat and, once they reached the Somme at St. Quentin, hold firm.

But that was not now the British intention. Sir John French, Murray, and even Wilson, the once enthusiastic progenitor of the plan, were horrified at the unexpected peril of their position. Not one or two but four German corps were advancing against them; Lanrezac's Army was in full retreat, uncovering their right; the whole French offensive had collapsed. Under these shocks, following immediately upon first contact with the enemy, Sir John French gave way at once to the conviction that the campaign was lost. His one idea was to save the BEF in which were nearly all Britain's trained soldiers and staff. He feared it was about to be enveloped either on his left or on his right, in the gap between him and Lanrezac. Taking justification in Kitchener's order not to risk the army, he thought no further of the purpose that had brought him to France but only of extricating his forces from the danger zone. While his troops were retreating to Le Cateau, the Commander in Chief and Headquarters Staff, on August 25, moved twenty-six miles farther back to St. Quentin on the Somme.

With bitterness the British soldiers who felt proud of their fighting at Mons found themselves caught up in continued retreat. Such was their Commander's anxiety to remove them from the danger of von Kluck's enveloping arm that he gave them no rest. Under a blazing sun the soldiers, without proper food or sleep, shuffled along, hardly awake, and when halted fell asleep instantly, standing up. Smith-Dorrien's Corps fought constant rearguard actions as the retreat from Mons began, and although Kluck's pursuit kept them under heavy artillery fire, the Germans were unable to hold the British to a standstill.

Believing the British to be peculiarly battle-wise "from their experience of small wars," German soldiers felt at a disadvantage, as if they had been Redcoats pitted against Ethan Allen's Green Mountain Men. They complained bitterly that the English "were up to all the tricks of the trade." On the second day, as at Mons, they "again vanished without leaving a trace."

Under pressure some of the British were forced onto unplanned lines of retreat. In an effort to get food to them, General "Wully" Robertson, the Quartermaster General, an unorthodox individual who had risen from private, ordered supplies to be dumped at crossroads. Some failed to be picked up, and German reports of these food dumps confirmed OHL in the impression of a foe in disorganized retreat.

When the British reached Le Cateau by the evening of August 25, the nearest corps of Lanrezac's Army had fallen back to a position on a level with, but no further south than, the BEF. Sir John, however, regarding himself as betrayed by what he called Lanrezac's "headlong" retreat, was in a mood to have nothing more to do with him. Lanrezac, rather than the enemy, seemed to him the cause of all that had gone wrong and, when reporting to Kitchener his troops' unwillingness to retreat, he said, "I shall explain to them that the operations of our Allies are the cause of this." He sent orders for the retreat to continue next day to St. Quentin and Noyon. At St. Quentin, seventy miles from the capital, the signposts begin giving the distance to Paris.

On the afternoon of August 25 when Smith-Dorrien arrived in Le Cateau a few hours ahead of his troops and went to look for the Commander in Chief, Sir John had already left, and only Sir Archibald Murray, his hard-working Chief of Staff, could be found. Usually calm, balanced, and reflective, the opposite of his Chief, Murray would have been an excellent complement for Sir John in an aggressive mood, but as he was by nature cautious and pessimistic, he acted as a stimulus to Sir John's gloom. Now worn, harassed, and overworked, he could give Smith-Dorrien no news of Haig's Corps which was expected to billet that night at Landrecies, twelve miles east of Le Cateau.

As Haig's troops were entering Landrecies, they encountered on the road a body of troops who wore French uniforms and whose officer spoke in French when challenged. Suddenly the newcomers "without the slightest warning lowered their bayonets and charged." They proved to be part of von Kluck's IVth Corps who, like the British, were scheduled to billet that night at Landrecies. In the ensuing skirmish about two regiments and a gun battery were involved on each side, but Haig, in the tension and uncertainty of darkness, thought himself under "heavy attack" and telephoned Headquarters to "send help. . . . Situation very critical."

Hearing such words from the cool Haig, Sir John French and his staff could not do otherwise than believe the Ist Corps to be in the greatest danger. Murray, who had rejoined GHQ at St. Quentin, suffered a collapse from the shock. He was sitting at a table studying a map when an aide brought him a telegram, and a moment later another officer noticed he had slumped forward in a faint. Sir John was equally affected. His uncertain temperament, wildly responsive to others, had long been influenced by that self-possessed and model officer who commanded the Ist Corps. In 1899 Haig had lent him £2,000 to meet his creditors, without which he would have had to leave the army. Now, when Haig called for help, Sir John

French immediately saw envelopment, or worse—penetration by the enemy between the Ist and IInd Corps. Assuming the worst, GHQ sent orders altering Haig's line of retreat for the following day with the result that Haig's Corps was set on a line of march on the opposite side of the Oise from Smith-Dorrien's Corps; direct contact was severed and not regained for the next seven days.

Besides accomplishing the splitting of the BEF, Haig's excited and exaggerated estimate of the attack at Landrecies had an effect out of all proportion to its cause. It deepened the alarm of his old friend and impressionable Commander so that he became more intent than ever upon extricating the British Army at all hazards, and it made him that much more susceptible to the next blow. For, at this moment, as the harrowing night of August 25 paled toward dawn, he received another shock. Smith-Dorrien sent word that the IInd Corps was too closely beset by the enemy to get away and would have to make a stand and fight at Le Cateau. Appalled, the men at GHQ regarded him as as good as lost.

What had happened was that General Allenby, commander of the Cavalry Division on Smith-Dorrien's flank, had discovered during the night that the high ground and ridges he would have to occupy to cover the next day's retreat were held by the enemy. Unable to get in touch with GHQ, he went at 2:00 A.M. to consult Smith-Dorrien. Allenby warned him that the enemy was in a position to attack at the first sign of daylight and that unless the IInd Corps could move "*at once* and get away *in the dark*," it would be forced into battle before it could start the day's march. Smith-Dorrien called in his divisional commanders, who told him that some men were still coming in, many were milling around looking for their units, all were too weary to move before morning. They reported also that roads were clogged with transport and refugees and in some places washed out by the heavy storm. Silence fell in the little room. To move at once was impossible; to stay where they were and fight was a reversal of orders. As his field headquarters had no telephone communication with GHQ, the corps commander would have to decide for himself. Turning to Allenby, Smith-Dorrien asked if he would accept orders from him. Allenby said he would.

"Very well, gentlemen, we will fight," Smith-Dorrien announced, adding that he would ask General Snow of the newly arrived 4th Division to act under him as well. His message embodying the decision was sent off by motorcar to GHQ, where it caused consternation at 5:00 A.M.

Henry Wilson, like the equally ebullient Messimy, had gone in one stride from verve and fervor to defeatism. When the offensive plan, of which on the British side he was the chief architect, collapsed, he collapsed with it, at least momentarily, and with significant effect on his Chief over whose slower mind he exerted considerable influence. Although his gift of optimism, wit, and laughter could not be long repressed and was the only thing to keep Staff spirits afloat in the next days, he was now convinced of coming calamity for which he may have felt responsible.

A messenger was sent off by motorcycle to summon Smith-Dorrien to the nearest telephone. "If you stand there and fight," Wilson said to him, "there will be another Sedan." He insisted from his position twenty-six miles away that the danger could not be so great as to require a stand because "troops fighting Haig cannot fight you." Smith-Dorrien patiently explained the circumstances once more and added that in any event it was impossible to break away as the action had already begun and he could hear the guns firing as he spoke. "Good luck to you," Wilson replied; "yours is the first cheerful voice I have heard in three days."

For eleven hours on August 26 the IInd Corps and General Snow's division and a half fought at Le Cateau a rearguard action such as the French Armies were fighting on this and every other day of the retreat. Von Kluck had given orders for that day to continue "pursuit of the beaten enemy." As the most devoted disciple of Schlieffen's precept to "brush the channel with his sleeve," he was still pulling westward and, to complete the envelopment of the British, ordered his two right-wing corps to make forced marches in a southwestward direction. As a result they were never in action against the British at all on that day, but instead came up against "strong French hostile forces." These were D'Amade's Territorials and Sordet's Cavalry whom Smith-Dorrien had informed of his predicament and who by their demonstrations barred the way around the British flank. The delay caused to the Germans, acknowledged Smith-Dorrien later, "and the brave front shown by these Territorials were of vital importance to us as otherwise it is almost certain we should have had another Corps against us on the 26th."

On von Kluck's left faulty intelligence or poor maneuvering kept another of his corps out of reach so that, although he disposed of superior numbers, he did not in fact have more than three infantry divisions in battle against Smith-Dorrien's three at Le Cateau. He had, however, assembled the artillery of five divisions which opened fire at dawn. From shallow trenches hastily and inadequately dug by French civilians, including women, the British repelled German infantry assaults with their rapid and deadly rifle fire. Nevertheless the Germans, flinging wave after wave of men against them, advanced. In one sector they surrounded a company of Argylls who kept up their rifle fire, "bringing down man after man and counting their scores aloud" while the Germans "kept sounding the British 'Cease Fire' and gesturing to persuade the men to surrender but in vain," until finally the group was rushed and overwhelmed. Other terrible holes were torn in the line. To disengage—the most difficult part of the battle—was yet to be done, and at 5:00 P.M. Smith-Dorrien judged the moment had come. It was then or never. Because of gaps and losses and infiltration by the enemy at certain points, the order to break off and retreat could not be got to all units at the same time. Some stayed in position for many hours longer, firing steadily until taken or until they got away in the dark. One unit, the Gordon Highlanders, never received its orders and, except for a few men who made their escape, ceased to exist as a battalion. Losses for that day alone in the three and a half divisions who fought at Le Cateau were over 8,000 men and 38 guns, more than twice as much as at Mons and equal to the 20 per cent casualty rate that the French suffered in August. Among the missing were some who spent the next four years in German prison camps.

Because of darkness, the fatigue of forced marches, their own heavy losses, and the confusing British habit of "slipping away unseen" in the darkness, the Germans did not immediately pursue. Kluck gave orders to halt until next day, when he expected the enveloping maneuver of his right-wing corps to take effect. For that day Smith-Dorrien's decision to turn and face a superior enemy in a pitched battle had succeeded in preventing the planned envelopment and destruction of the BEF.

On reaching St. Quentin, Smith-Dorrien found GHQ had left there at midday while the battle for the life or annihilation of the BEF was still in progress and had moved to Noyon, twenty miles farther to the rear. Troops in the town were not encouraged to see the army's chiefs depart in automobiles headed south while the guns were firing in the north. In that inevitable judgment of a countryman, "The truth is that on the 26th Lord French and his staff completely lost their heads." Sir Douglas Haig, who had by now recovered his, queried, "No news of II Corps except sound of guns from direction of Le Cateau. Can I Corps be of any assistance?" GHQ was too paralyzed to give him any answer. Failing to hear from Headquarters, Haig tried to reach Smith-Dorrien directly, saying he could hear the sound of battle but, as a consequence of the separation of the two corps, "we could form no idea of how we could assist you." By the time he sent the message the battle was over. Meanwhile GHQ had given up the IInd Corps for lost. Colonel Huguet, still attached as liaison officer, reflected their mood in a telegram he dispatched to Joffre at 8:00 P.M., "Battle lost by the English Army which appears to have lost cohesion."

At 1:00 A.M. Smith-Dorrien, having been in combat for the last four of the six days he had been in France, reached Noyon and found everyone at GHQ in bed asleep. Routed out, Sir John French appeared in his nightshirt and, seeing Smith-Dorrien turn up alive with a report that the IInd Corps was not lost but saved, rebuked him for taking too cheerful a view of the situation. Having had a bad fright, Sir John now gave way to furious anger, the more easily as he had resented Smith-Dorrien's appointment, in place of his own choice, from the beginning. The man did not even belong to the cavalry and had taken it upon himself at Le Cateau to override Staff orders. Although Sir John was forced to acknowledge in his official dispatch* that this had resulted in the "saving of the left wing," he did not soon recover from his fright. The losses of Le Cateau seemed even higher than they were until several thousand of the missing men who had merged with the trudging lines of French refugees and followed the retreat, or had made their way through German lines to Antwerp, thence to England, and back to France, eventually rejoined the army. Total casualties for the BEF's first five days in action proved to be just short of 15,000. They intensified the Commander in Chief's anxiety to bring his army out of the fight, out of danger, out of France.

While the Battle of Le Cateau was in progress, Joffre summoned a meeting at St. Quentin of Sir John French, Lanrezac, and their staffs to explain the instructions of General Order No. 2. When he began with a polite inquiry as to the situation of the British Army, he evoked a tirade from Sir John who said that he had been violently attacked by superior numbers, that he was threatened by envelopment on his left, that his right was uncovered by Lanrezac's headlong retreat, and that his troops were too exhausted to resume the offensive. Joffre, who believed above all in maintaining an appearance of calm before the Staff, was shocked by the Field Marshal's "excited tone." Lanrezac, after hearing Henry Wilson's somewhat softened translation of his chief's remarks, merely shrugged. Unable to issue an order, Joffre expressed the hope that the British Commander would conform to the plan contained in the new General Order of the day before.

Sir John looked blank and said he knew nothing of any such Order. Murray, suffering from his collapse of the night before, was absent. A variety of astonished and quizzical French gazes were turned on Wilson who explained that the Order had been

*The dispatch reads, "The saving of the left wing of the army under my command on the morning of the 26th of August could never have been accomplished unless a commander of rare and unusual coolness, intrepidity and determination had been present personally to conduct the operation." Having evidently written or signed this report in one of the extreme swings of his unreliable temperament, Sir John reverted to antipathy, did not rest until he succeeded in having Smith-Dorrien recalled in 1915, and continued a malevolent vendetta against him publicly in the book he published after the war.

received during the night but not yet "studied." Joffre explained its provisions but with obviously failing confidence. Discussion faltered, pauses grew longer, the embarrassment became painful, and the meeting broke up without having achieved any agreement from the British for combined action. With an impression of the "fragility" of his left wing, Joffre returned to GQG where he was met by fresh news of weakness on all fronts, discouragement in every grade of the army, including the Staff, and finally, at the end of the day, by Huguet's black telegram reporting the English Army as having "lost cohesion."

Von Kluck was under the same impression. His orders for the 27th were to "cut off the British who were in full flight westwards," and he reported to OHL that he was about to round up "all six" British divisions (only five were in France) and "if the English stand on the 27th the double envelopment may yet bring a great success." This brilliant prospect, coming the day after the fall of Namur and coinciding with Bülow's report that his opponent, the French Fifth Army, was also a "beaten enemy," confirmed OHL in the impression of imminent victory. "The German Armies have entered France from Cambrai to the Vosges after a series of continually victorious combats," announced OHL's official communiqué on August 27. "The enemy, beaten all along the line, is in full retreat . . . and is not capable of offering serious resistance to the German advance."

Amid the general enthusiasm von Kluck received his reward. When he rebelled furiously at an order of von Bülow's to invest Maubeuge, which he claimed was von Bülow's duty, and demanded to know if he was to remain subordinate, OHL on August 27 restored his independence. The attempt to keep the three armies of the right wing under one command, which had caused so much friction, was abandoned; but as the rest of the way to victory seemed easy, this did not appear important at the moment.

Von Bülow, however, was exceedingly annoyed. In the center of the right wing, he was constantly bedeviled by his neighbors' refusal to keep in step. Already, he warned OHL, Hausen's delays had caused a "regrettable gap" between the Third and Second Armies. Hausen himself, whose chief concern, second only to his reverence for titles, was a passionate attention to the amenities offered by each night's billets, was equally annoyed. On August 27, his first night in France, no château was available for himself and the Crown Prince of Saxony who accompanied him. They had to sleep in the house of a *sous-préfet* which had been left in complete disorder; "even the beds had not been made!" The following night was worse. he had to endure quarters in the house of a M. Chopin, a peasant! The dinner was meager, the lodgings "not spacious," and the staff had to accommodate itself in the nearby rectory whose curé had gone to war. His old mother, who looked like a witch, hung around and "wished us all at the devil." Red streaks in the sky showed that Rocroi, through which his troops had just passed, was in flames. Happily the following night was spent in the beautifully furnished home of a wealthy French industrialist who was "absent." Here the only discomfort suffered by Hausen was the sight of a wall covered by espaliered pear trees heavy with fruit that was "unfortunately not completely ripe." However, he enjoyed a delightful reunion with Count Münster, Major Count Kilmansegg, Prince Schoenburg-Waldenburg of the Hussars, and Prince Max, Duke of Saxe, acting as Catholic chaplain, to whom Hausen was able to convey the gratifying news that he had just received by telephone the best wishes for success of the Third Army from his sister, the Princess Mathilda.

Hausen complained that his Saxons had been on the march for ten days through hostile country, in the heat and often in battle. Supplies were not keeping up with the advance, bread and meat were lacking, troops had to live off the local livestock, horses had not had enough fodder, and yet he had managed an average march of 23 kilometers a day. In fact, this was the least required of the German armies. Kluck's Army on the rim of the wheel covered 30 kilometers or more a day and in some forced marches 40. He managed this by having the men sleep along the roadside instead of spreading out to left and right, and thus saved 6 or 7 kilometers a day. As German lines of communication stretched out and troops advanced farther from the railheads, food supplies often failed. Horses ate grain directly from unharvested fields and men marched a whole day on nothing but raw carrots and cabbages. As hot, as tired, and with feet as sore as their enemies, the Germans were increasingly hungry but on schedule.

Halfway between Brussels and Paris on August 28, von Kluck was gratified to receive a telegram from the Kaiser expressing "my imperial gratitude" for the First Army's "decisive victories" and his congratulations upon its approach to the "heart of France." That night by the light of bivouac fires regimental bands played the victory song "Heil dir im Siegerkranz" and, as one of Kluck's officers wrote in his diary, "the sound was taken up by thousands of voices. Next morning we resumed our march in the hope of celebrating the anniversary of Sedan before Paris."

On the same day a new and tempting idea presented itself to von Kluck which before the week was over was to leave its mark on history. Reconnaissance showed that the French Fifth Army, retreating in front of Bülow, was moving in a southwesterly direction which would bring it across his line of march. He saw a chance to "find the flank of this army . . . force it away from Paris and outflank it," an objective that now seemed to him of more importance than cutting the British off from the coast. He proposed to Bülow that a "wheel inwards" should be made by their two armies. Before anything could be decided, an officer from OHL arrived with a new General Order to all seven armies.

Inspired by a "universal sense of victory," according to the Crown Prince, OHL nevertheless had become aware of the transfer of French forces from Lorraine and now called for a "rapid advance to prevent assembly of fresh bodies of troops and to take from the country as much as possible of its means of continuing the struggle." Kluck's Army was to advance to the Seine southwest of Paris. Bülow's was to move directly upon Paris. Hausen, the Duke of Württemberg, and the Crown Prince were to bring their armies down to the Marne east of Paris, to Château-Thierry, Epernay, and Vitry-le-François respectively. The breakthrough of the French fortress line by the Sixth and Seventh Armies under Prince Rupprecht was left a little vague but they were expected to cross the Moselle between Toul and Epinal, "if the enemy retires." Speed was "urgently desirable" to leave France no time to regroup and organize resistance. With memories of 1870, OHL ordered "severe measures against the population to break any resistance of *franc-tireurs* as quickly as possible" and to prevent a "national rising." Strong resistance by the enemy was expected on the Aisne and then, falling back, on the Marne. Here OHL, echoing Kluck's newborn idea, concluded, "This may necessitate a wheel of the armies from a southwesterly to a southerly direction."

Apart from this suggestion the Order of August 28 followed the original war plan. However, the German Armies who were to carry it out were no longer the same. They were diminished by five corps, the equivalent of a full field army. Kluck had left behind two reserve corps to invest Antwerp and hold Brussels and other parts of Belgium. Bülow and Hausen had each lost one corps to the Russian front: brigades and divisions equal to another had been left to invest Givet and Maubeuge. In order to cover the same ground as originally planned, with the First Army passing west of Paris, the right wing would have to be stretched more thinly or allow gaps to appear between its component armies. Already this was happening: on August 28 Hausen, pulled to his left by the Duke of Württemberg's Army which was in serious combat south of Sedan and demanding "immediate assistance," could not keep up with Bülow on his right and demanded instead that Bülow cover his right flank. The two corps which should have been at the junction of these two armies were on their way to Tannenberg.

OHL began on August 28 to feel its first twinges of concern. Moltke, Stein, and Tappen discussed anxiously whether to send reinforcements from Rupprecht's armies to the right wing, but could not bring themselves to give up their attempt to smash through the French fortress line. The perfect Cannae that Schlieffen had dreamed of and renounced, the double envelopment by the left wing through Lorraine simultaneously with the right wing around Paris, now seemed possible of achievement. Rupprecht's hammer blows fell on Epinal; his armies stood at the gates of Nancy and pounded on the walls of Toul. Since the reduction of Liège, fortified places had "lost their prestige," as Colonel Tappen said, and every day seemed to be the one that would see Rupprecht break through. Destruction of the Belgian railways made a transfer of divisions impractical anyway, and OHL had convinced itself that a forcing of the Charmes Gap between Toul and Epinal was feasible and would obtain, in Tappen's words, "encirclement of the enemy armies in grand style and in the event of success, an end to the war." In consequence, the left wing under Rupprecht was retained in its full strength of twenty-six divisions, about equal to the diminished numbers of the three armies of the right wing. This was not the proportion Schlieffen had in mind when he muttered as he died, "Only make the right wing strong."

Following the drama in Belgium, the eyes of the world were fixed on the course of the war between Brussels and Paris. The public was hardly aware that all this time a fiercer, longer, more sustained battle to force the eastern doors of France raged in Lorraine. Along eighty miles of front from Epinal to Nancy two German armies swayed against the armies of Castelnau and Dubail in locked and nearly static struggle.

On August 24, having massed 400 guns with additions brought from the arsenal at Metz, Rupprecht launched a series of murderous attacks. The French, now turning all their skills to the defense, had dug themselves in and prepared a variety of improvised and ingenious shelters against shellfire. Rupprecht's attacks failed to dislodge Foch's XXth Corps in front of Nancy but farther south succeeded in flinging a salient across the Mortagne, the last river before the gap at Charmes. At once the French saw the opportunity for a flank attack, this time with artillery preparation. Field guns were brought up during the night. On the morning of the 25th Castelnau's order, "*En avant! partout! à fond!*" launched his troops on the offensive. The XXth Corps bounded down from the crest of the Grand Couronné and retook three towns and ten miles of territory. On the right Dubail's Army gained an equal advance in a day of furious combat. General Maud'huy, divisional commander of the *chasseurs alpins*, reviewing his troops before the battle, had them sing the lionhearted chorus of "La Sidi Brahim,"

> Marchons, marchons, marchons,
> Contre les ennemis de la France!

The day ended with many scattered, crippled units not knowing whether they had taken Clezentaine, their given objective.

General Maud'huy, on horseback, seeing a haggard, sweat-soaked company looking for their billets, flung out his arm in a gesture pointing forward, and called to them, "*Chasseurs!* Sleep in the village you have conquered!"

For three days of bloody and relentless combat the battle for the Trouée de Charmes and the Grand Couronné continued, reaching a pitch on August 27. Joffre on that day, surrounded by gloom and dismay elsewhere and hard put to find anything to praise, saluted the "courage and tenacity" of the First and Second Armies who, since the opening battles in Lorraine, had fought for two weeks without respite and with "stubborn and unbreakable confidence in victory." They fought with every ounce of strength to hold the door closed against the enemy's battering ram, knowing that if he broke through here the war would be over. They knew nothing of Cannae but they knew Sedan and encirclement.

The need to hold the fortress line was vital, but the situation on his left was even more fragile and forced Joffre to take from his eastern armies a principal element of their energy. That element was Foch, symbol of the "will to victory," whom Joffre now needed to stiffen the failing front on the left.

A dangerous gap was widening between the Fourth and Fifth Armies and now extended to thirty miles. It was caused when General de Langle of the Fourth Army, unwilling to let the Germans cross the Meuse without a fight, gripped the high banks south of Sedan and held off the Duke of Württemberg's Army in a fierce three-day struggle from August 26 to 28. His troops' performance in the Battle of the Meuse, De Langle felt, avenged their defeat in the Ardennes. But their stand was made at the cost of losing contact with Lanrezac's Army, whose retreat was continuing with its flank on the side of the Fourth Army uncovered. It was to hold this space that Joffre sent Foch, giving him command of a special army of three corps,* drawn partly from the Fourth Army and partly from the Third Army. On the day he received the order, Foch learned that his only son, Lieutenant Germain Foch, and his son-in-law, Captain Bécourt, had both been killed on the Meuse.

*Known as the Foch Detachment until September 5, when it became the Ninth Army.

Farther west, in the area filled by Lanrezac and the British, Joffre still hoped to pin the front to the Somme, but like the foundations of a sand castle, it kept falling away. The British Commander in Chief would give no promise to stay in the line; his cooperation with Lanrezac was at a minimum; and Lanrezac himself, in whom Joffre was losing faith, seemed no more dependable. Although Joffre flung out generals by handfuls in August, he hesitated to dismiss one of Lanrezac's repute. His Staff was still searching out individuals on whom to blame the failure of the offensive; "I have the heads of three generals in my brief case," reported one Staff officer upon returning from a mission to the front. Lanrezac could not be disposed of so easily. Joffre believed the Fifth Army needed a more confident leader. Yet to remove its commander in the midst of retreat might endanger morale. To an aide he confessed that the problem had already given him two sleepless nights—the only occasion of the war known to have caused this grave disturbance.

Meanwhile the 61st and 62nd reserve divisions from Paris who were supposed to join the new Sixth Army had got lost; their commander, General Ebener, had been looking for them all day but nobody knew what had become of them. Fearing that the Sixth Army's detraining area was about to be overrun, Joffre, in a desperate effort to gain time for it to come into position, ordered the Fifth Army to turn and counterattack. This required an offensive in a westerly direction between St. Quentin and Guise. Colonel Alexandre, Joffre's liaison officer with the Fifth Army, conveyed the order verbally to Lanrezac's headquarters, then at Marle some twenty-five miles east of St. Quentin. At the same time, in an effort to assuage the pique and invigorate the spirit of Sir John French, Joffre sent him a telegram expressing the gratitude of the French Army for the brave assistance of their British comrades. Hardly was it dispatched when he learned the British had evacuated St. Quentin, uncovering Lanrezac's left just at the moment he was supposed to attack. According to another of Huguet's missives of doom, the BEF was "beaten and incapable of serious effort" with three of its five divisions unable to take the field again until thoroughly rested and refitted, that is, "for some days or even a few weeks." As Sir John French was reporting the same thing in almost the same words to Kitchener, Huguet cannot be blamed for reflecting the mood of the British chiefs rather than that of the troops or the facts. On top of his message came one from Colonel Alexandre saying Lanrezac was balking at the order to attack.

Although many of his officers responded with enthusiasm to the order, Lanrezac himself regarded it as "almost insane," and said so. To face the Fifth Army west was to invite attack by the enemy on its open right flank. He believed it was necessary to disengage fully and fall further back to Laon before a firm line could be established and a counterattack made with any chance of success. An attack now in the direction ordered by Joffre required him to turn a semi-disorganized army halfway around in a complicated maneuver, dangerous in view of his position and of the menace on his right. His Chief of Operations, Commandant Schneider, attempted to explain the difficulty to Colonel Alexandre, who expressed astonishment.

"What!" said he, "why, what could be simpler? You are facing north; we ask you to face west to attack from St. Quentin." With a gesture of his hand, five fingers spread out to represent the five corps, he described a right angle turn in the air.

"Don't talk nonsense, *mon colonel*!" burst out Schneider, exasperated.

"Well, if you don't *want* to do anything . . ." Colonel Alexandre said, finishing with a contemptuous shrug which caused Lanrezac who was present to lose his temper and explain at great length and no great tact his opinion of GQG's strategy. By now his confidence in Joffre and GQG was on a par with theirs in him. Having on one wing an independent foreign general who refused to act jointly and on the other an unprotected flank (Foch's detachment did not start forming until two days later, August 29), and being now called upon for a counter-offensive, Lanrezac was under severe stress. His was not a temperament that rose to it. Given a task so fateful for France, and lacking any confidence in Joffre's judgment, he relieved his feelings in the bad temper and caustic abuse for which he had been known even in peacetime. He expounded upon his lack of respect for Joffre whom he called a "sapper," a mere engineer.

"I found General Lanrezac surrounded by a number of

officers," reported a Staff officer from one of the corps who came to see him. "He seemed to be extremely displeased and expressed himself in violent language. He did not mince words in his criticism of GQG and our Allies. He was much irritated against the former and the British. The gist of what he was saying was that all he required was to be left alone, that he would retire as far as was necessary, that he would choose his own time and then he would boot the enemy back where he came from." In Lanrezac's own words, "I suffered an anxiety so awful I did not even try to dissimulate from the Staff." To show anxiety before subordinates was bad enough; to compound the sin by public criticism of GQG and the Generalissimo numbered Lanrezac's days of command.

Early next morning, August 28, Joffre himself appeared at Marle where he found Lanrezac haggard, bloodshot, and objecting with nervous gestures to the plan for a counter-offensive. When Lanrezac insisted again upon the risk of enemy attack from the right while his whole army was facing westward, Joffre suddenly fell into a violent fit of rage and shouted: "Do you wish to be relieved of your command? You must march without discussion. The fate of the campaign is in your hands." This spectacular outburst reverberated as far as Paris, taking on added thunder as it traveled, so that by the time it reached President Poincaré's diary next day it was recorded as Joffre's threat to have Lanrezac shot if he hesitated or disobeyed orders to attack.

Convinced of the error of the plan, Lanrezac refused to move without a written order. Having calmed down, Joffre assented and signed an order drawn up at his dictation by Lanrezac's Chief of Staff. In Joffre's opinion, a commander knowing his orders and his duty could have no further cause for disquiet, and he might have said to Lanrezac what he was one day to say to Pétain when giving him orders to hold Verdun under the heaviest bombardment in history, "*Eh bien, mon ami, maintenant vous êtes tranquille.*"

Something less than tranquil, Lanrezac accepted his task but insisted he could not be ready before next morning. All day while the Fifth Army was being turned sideways in a complicated and intricate transfer of corps across each other's fronts, GQG was constantly calling, telling them to "hurry" until

Lanrezac in a fury ordered his staff not to answer the telephone.

On the same day the British chiefs were hurrying the BEF southward with such urgency that the soldiers were deprived of the rest they needed far more than they needed distance from the enemy. On that day, August 28, a day when von Kluck's columns gave them no trouble, Sir John French and Wilson were in such anxiety to hasten the retreat that they ordered transport wagons to "throw overboard all ammunition and other impediments not absolutely required" and carry men instead. Discarding ammunition meant abandoning further battle. As the BEF was not fighting on British soil, its Commander was prepared to pull his forces out of the line regardless of the effect of withdrawal upon his ally. The French Army had lost the opening battle and was in a serious, even desperate, situation in which every division counted to prevent defeat. But it was neither broken through nor enveloped by the enemy; it was fighting hard, and Joffre was exhibiting every intention of fighting further. Nevertheless, Sir John French, succumbing to the belief that the danger was mortal, had determined that the BEF must be preserved from being involved in a French defeat.

Field commanders did not share the pessimism of Headquarters. Receiving an order that virtually rejected any further idea of fighting, they were dismayed. Haig's Chief of Staff, General Gough, tore it up in anger. Smith-Dorrien, who regarded his situation as "excellent," with the enemy "only in small parties and those keeping at a respectful distance," countermanded the order to his own 3rd and 5th divisions. His message reached General Snow of the 4th division too late. Having received a direct order, addressed "To Snowball from Henry," to "load up your lame ducks and hustle along," he had already carried it out with "very damping effect" on the troops, who were made to think they must be in an extremity of danger and who lost their spare clothing and boots as well.

In dust, heat, and discouragement and fatigue beyond telling the British retreat continued. Trailing through St. Quentin, the tired remnants of two battalions gave up, piled up their arms in the railroad station, sat down in the Place de la Gare, and refused to go farther. They told Major Bridges whose cavalry had orders to hold off the Germans until St. Quentin was clear of troops, that their commanding officers had given the mayor a written promise to surrender in order to save the town further bombardment. Not caring to confront the battalion colonels whom he knew and who were senior to him, Bridges wished desperately for a band to rouse the two hundred or three hundred dispirited men lying about in the square. "Why not? There was a toy shop handy which provided my trumpeter and myself with a tin whistle and a drum and we marched round and round the fountain where the men were lying like the dead, playing the British Grenadiers and Tipperary and beating the drum like mad." The men sat up, began to laugh, then cheer, then one by one stood up, fell in and "eventually we moved off slowly into the night to the music of our improvised band, now reinforced with a couple of mouth organs."

Uncheered by fife or drum Sir John French, seeing only his own sector, was convinced that the Kaiser "in his rancour and hate, has really risked weakness in other parts of the field" in order to concentrate an overwhelming force "to destroy us." He demanded that Kitchener send him the Sixth Division, and when Kitchener said it could not be spared until its place in England was taken by troops from India, he considered this refusal "most disappointing and injurious." In fact for one moment after the shock of Mons, Kitchener had considered using the Sixth Division for a landing on the German flank in Belgium. The old idea, long advocated by Fisher and Esher, of using the BEF independently in Belgium instead of as an appendix to the French line, never ceased to haunt the British. Now it was tried, as it was to be again two months later at Antwerp, in miniature and in vain. Instead of the Sixth Division, three battalions of Royal Marines landed at Ostend on August 27 and 28 in an effort to draw off von Kluck's forces. They were joined by 6,000 Belgians who had followed the French retreat after the fall of Namur and were now sent up to Ostend by sea in British ships but who proved to be in no condition to fight. By this time, the retreat in France having swept the front too far away, the operation had lost its meaning, and the marines were reëmbarked on August 31.

Before that happened Sir John French on August 28 evacuated his forward base at Amiens, which was now menaced by von Kluck's westward sweep, and on the following day gave orders for moving the main British base back from Le Havre to St. Nazaire below the Normandy peninsula. In the same spirit as the order jettisoning ammunition, the move reflected the single urgent desire that now possessed him—to leave France. Partly sharing it, partly ashamed to share it, Henry Wilson, as described by a fellow officer, "walked slowly up and down the room, with that comical, whimsical expression on his face, habitual to him, clapping his hands softly together to keep time, as he chanted in a low tone, 'We shall never get there, we shall never get there.' As he passed me I said, 'Where, Henri?' And he chanted on, 'To the sea, to the sea, to the sea.'"

20

The Front Is Paris

THE GRANDS BOULEVARDS were empty, shop fronts were shuttered, buses, trams, cars, and horse cabs had disappeared. In their place flocks of sheep were herded across the Place de la Concorde on their way to the Gare de l'Est for shipment to the front. Unmarred by traffic, squares and vistas revealed their purity of design. Most newspapers having ceased publication, the kiosks were hung meagerly with the single-page issues of the survivors. All the tourists were gone, the Ritz was uninhabited, the Meurice a hospital. For one August in its history Paris was French—and silent. The sun shone, fountains sparkled in the Rond Point, trees were green, the quiet Seine flowed by unchanging, brilliant clusters of Allied flags enhanced the pale gray beauty of the world's most beautiful city.

In the vast warren of the Invalides, Gallieni grappled with obstructionism and the hesitancy of officials to take the radical measures necessary to make the words "entrenched camp" a reality. He envisaged the camp as a base of operations, not a Troy holed up for siege. From the experience of Liège and Namur he knew that Paris could not withstand shelling by the new heavy siege guns of the enemy, but his plan was not to wait passively to be invested but to give battle—with the army he did not yet have—beyond the outer ring of fortifications. Study of the Balkan and Manchurian wars had convinced him that a system of deep and narrow trenches protected by earth mounds and logs, flanked by barbed wire and "wolf pits"—wide-mouthed holes fitted at the bottom with up-pointed stakes—and manned by trained and determined troops armed with machine guns would be virtually impregnable. These were what he was trying to construct in the stretches between the artillery posts, although he still did not have the army to man them.

Every day, sometimes two and three times a day, with increasing desperation he telephoned GQG demanding the three active corps. He wrote to Joffre, sent emissaries, hammered at the Minister of War and the President, repeatedly warned them Paris was unprepared. By August 29 he had received under his orders so far one naval brigade whose appearance, marching through the streets in white with high-pitched pipe, delighted the populace, if not Gallieni.

He conceived of the work to be done as tripartite: military defense, moral defense, and provisioning. To accomplish each of these tasks it was necessary to be frank with the public. As much as he despised politicians, Gallieni respected the people of Paris who, he considered, could be counted on to behave sensibly in the face of danger. He believed Poincaré and Viviani did not want to tell the country the truth, and suspected them of preparing a "mummery" to deceive the people. His efforts to obtain authority for demolition of buildings obstructing the forts' line of fire were hampered by official reluctance to alarm the population. Each destruction of property required a document signed by both the mayor of the arrondissement and the Chief of Engineers fixing the value of indemnity to the proprietor—a process that was a source of endless harassment and delay. Each decision was enmeshed in a further "byzantine" argument by those who contended that Paris as the seat of government could not be a "fortified camp" to be defended militarily. The issue, as General Hirschauer disgustedly remarked, offered a "magnificent field of controversy," and he feared the proponents of an open city would soon succeed in proving the post of Military Governor itself illegal. "You cannot convince the jurists without a text," he said.

Gallieni provided one. On August 28 the Zone of the Armies was extended to include Paris and the country on both sides down to the Seine with the result that the municipal government of Paris was brought under the authority of the Military Governor. At 10:00 A.M. Gallieni assembled his military and civil cabinets in a Council of Defense which was held with everyone standing up and was over by 10:15. Members were asked not to discuss whether Paris should be defended but simply to attest that the presence of the enemy required the institution of a "state of defense." Documents providing the legal basis were already drawn up and lying on the table. Gallieni invited each person to sign his name and immediately declared the Council adjourned. It was the first and last he held.

Ruthlessly he pursued work on the defenses, sparing no time or pity on demurrers or the irresolute, on weakness or ineptitude. Like Joffre, he liquidated incompetents, on his first day of office dismissing a general of Engineers and another general two days later. All inhabitants of the suburbs, "even the oldest and least capable," were impressed for labor with pick and shovel. An order for 10,000 spades and pickaxes to be collected within twenty-four hours was issued; by evening all had been delivered. When on the same occasion Gallieni ordered 10,000 bowie knives for use as tools his purveyor protested it was impossible because their purchase was illegal. "All the more reason," replied Gallieni, looking at him sharply over his pince-nez, and the knives were obtained.

On August 29 an area around Paris within a radius of about twenty miles, reaching to Melun on the south and Dammartin and Pontoise on the north, was brought under Gallieni's authority. Preparations were made for dynamiting bridges in the area. For those classified as "works of art" and part of the "national heritage" a system of special guards was arranged to ensure that they were not destroyed until the last extremity. All entries to the city, even the sewers, were barricaded. Bakers, butchers, market gardeners were organized and cattle brought in to graze in the Bois de Boulogne. To hasten the assembly of stocks of ammunition, Gallieni requisitioned transport "by all means available," including the taxis of Paris, so soon to become immortal. Assigned to the Artillery Staff of the entrenched camp was one already encased in history, former Captain, now Major Alfred Dreyfus, returned to active service at fifty-five.

At the front the First and Second Armies in Lorraine, under the terrible pressure of Rupprecht's guns, still held fiercely and tenaciously to the line of the Moselle. Their line wavered and bulged, in some places even was pierced by German wedges. Tightly contained by French counterattacks on their flanks, these could not be widened to major openings. The battle went on with Rupprecht's armies probing for the weakest place and Dubail and Castelnau, losing troops to Joffre's demands for the west, uncertain how long they could hold or whether they could hold. In the villages taken by the Germans the events of Belgium were re-enacted. In Nomeny on the outskirts of Nancy, "citizens fired on our troops," declared the German Governor of Metz in a bulletin posted on the walls. "I have therefore ordered as a punishment that the village shall be burned to the ground. Nomeny is thus by now destroyed."

On Castelnau's left where the front turned to the west, Ruffey's Third Army, unbalanced by the removal of Maunoury's divisions, was falling back behind the Meuse below Verdun. Next to it the Fourth Army, which had rested in position on August 28 to prove the retreat was "strategic" and not a rout, was ordered, to the disgust of General de Langle, to resume its retreat on August 29. Further to the left where the pressure against the French line was the greatest, General Lanrezac's Fifth Army was completing the turning maneuver preparatory for the counter-attack on St. Quentin which Joffre had imposed upon its unwilling commander. At the extreme end of the line, Maunoury's Sixth Army was coming into position. Between Maunoury and Lanrezac the BEF was being pulled out by Sir John French despite his knowledge of the battle that would be fought on the morrow.

Almost the process was interrupted by a much-needed deed of Anglo-French cooperation when Haig sent word to Lanrezac that his troops were "perfectly ready to attack and he wished to enter into direct communication and act in concert with the Fifth Army in its planned action at St. Quentin." One of Lanrezac's staff immediately hastened to meet him and found Haig standing picturesquely on a little hill, while an orderly held his horse, beside a lance with fluttering white-cross pennon planted in the ground. Haig said his air reconnaissance reported the enemy moving southwest of St. Quentin, "exposing his flank as he advances."

"Go quickly to your General and give him this information. . . . Let him act. I am anxious to cooperate with him in this attack." The offer, conveyed to Lanrezac, gave him "lively satisfaction" and moved him to "say some nice things concerning Sir Douglas Haig." Arrangements for joint action in the morning were confirmed, subject only to approval by the British Commander in Chief. At 2 A.M. word came from GHQ that

Sir John French refused permission on the ground that the troops were "very tired and must have at least one day's rest," a requirement which, however true of the IInd Corps, was not true of the Ist Corps whose commander himself had reported them fit and ready. Lanrezac exploded with wrath. "*C'est une félonie!*" (It's betrayal!) he shouted, and added what a listener described as "terrible, unpardonable things about Sir John French and the British Army."

Nevertheless next morning, sandwiched between von Bülow who was moving down against him and Joffre who came up to superintend the offensive, Lanrezac had no choice but to attack. From papers found on a captured French officer, Bülow had learned of the coming attack and was not taken off guard. Doubting Lanrezac's mood, Joffre arrived early in the morning at Laon, now Lanrezac's headquarters, to lend him sangfroid out of his own bottomless supply. Laon is built on a high mesa from which the view extends over miles of rolling fields that rise and dip like the swells of a green ocean. Twenty miles to the north in a great semicircle the Fifth Army was drawn up facing northwest toward Guise and St. Quentin. From the tower of the cathedral at the highest point of the town the carved stone heads of cows, instead of gargoyles, gaze in bovine serenity over the landscape. Beneath them in the same silent calm, Joffre sat watching Lanrezac dictate orders and conduct the battle. He stayed for three hours without saying a word until, satisfied that Lanrezac was displaying "authority and method," he felt able to leave for a good lunch at the station restaurant before proceeding with his racing chauffeur on his next errand.

This was to find Sir John French who, he suspected, had his eyes on the Channel coast and "might be getting out of our line of battle for a long time." The place he held in the line between Lanrezac's Army and the gathering Sixth Army of Maunoury was now crucial and yet outside Joffre's power to control. He could not give orders to Field Marshal French as he did to Lanrezac or force him to fight by sitting behind him in silent surveillance. If, however, he could persuade the British to stand still, he hoped to stabilize a front on the Aisne along a line Amiens-Rheims-Verdun and resume the offensive from there. British Headquarters having taken another backward step the day before, Sir John was now established at Compiègne which was forty miles or—for tired armies—about three days' march from Paris. While its neighbor, the French Fifth Army, was fighting all during this day at Guise, lifting enemy pressure, the British Army rested. Having retreated without pursuit the day before, it now, after eight hot days of marching, digging trenches, and fighting engagements great and small, at last came to a halt. The IInd Corps made a short march during the evening hours to bring it across the Oise, but the Ist Corps enjoyed a full day's rest in the Forest of St. Gobain only five miles from where the left wing of Lanrezac's Army, which had been marching and fighting for fourteen days and was no less tired, was engaged in major battle.

When Joffre reached Compiègne he pleaded with the British Commander to stick fast until the offensive could be resumed at a favorable moment. His arguments seemed to produce no effect. He "distinctly saw" Murray tugging at the Field Marshal's tunic as if to prevent him from yielding to persuasion. It was a supererogatory effort, for Sir John French kept saying, "No, no," to Joffre and insisting that in view of his losses his army was in no condition to fight and must have two days to rest and refit. Joffre could not dismiss him on the spot as he would have a French general; he could not even throw a fit of temper to gain his ends as he had with Lanrezac at Marle. With the British backing away from the space between Lanrezac and Maunoury, neither of their armies could hold along the present line and all hope of carrying out General Order No. 2 must be abandoned. Joffre departed, by his own confession, "in very bad humor."

Sir John French's intentions were even more drastic than he admitted to Joffre. Without regard for an ally fighting on the threshold of defeat, he now told his Inspector of Communications, Major General Robb, to plan for a "definite and prolonged retreat due south, passing Paris to the east and west." Even Kitchener's instructions could not be blamed for this. Conceived in deep disapproval of Henry Wilson's commitment to Plan 17, they were designed to restrain a too aggressive Sir John and a too Francophil Wilson from risking the British Army in some French-sponsored scheme of *offensive à outrance* that could lead to annihilation or capture. They were never intended to suggest such a degree of caution as would lead to actual desertion. But the sweat that comes from fear cannot be controlled, and Sir John was now gripped by fear of losing his army and with it his name and reputation.

His troops were not, as he pretended, a broken army unfit for further effort. By their own account they were in no mood to give up. Lieutenant Colonel Frederick Maurice of the 3rd Division Staff said that despite exhaustion, sore feet, and lack of time for cooked meals "the restorative effect of a hot meal, a good night's rest and a bath is little short of marvelous, and these were what our army chiefly needed . . . to enable it to take the field again." Captain Ernest Hamilton of the 11th Hussars said that after its day of rest on August 29 the BEF was "now in perfect trim to turn and fight at any moment." General Macready, Adjutant-General in the BEF, said "all they needed was rest and food to make them ready and eager" to show the Germans what they could do.

Nevertheless Sir John French next day sent Joffre definitive notice that the British Army would not be in condition to take its place in the line "for another ten days." Had he asked for ten days' time out when fighting with his back to London he would not have survived in command. As it was, Sir John French remained Commander in Chief for another year and a half.

That afternoon, on edge to get his men on the move and away from the vicinity of the enemy, he was anxious to have Lanrezac break off his battle and resume the retreat with him shoulder to shoulder, less out of concern for covering Lanrezac's flank than to protect his own. In an effort to obtain an order for the Fifth Army to do this, Henry Wilson called GQG and, finding that Joffre had not returned, spoke to General Berthelot who refused to assume authority but arranged to have Wilson intercept Joffre at the Hotel Lion d'Or in Rheims at 7:30 that evening. At mealtimes Joffre's whereabouts were always known. Wilson, when he found him, argued in vain. All Joffre would say was, "Lanrezac must see it out to the end," without specifying what end he had in mind. When Wilson returned with this news, Sir John decided not to wait, and gave orders for the BEF to resume the retreat next day.

Meanwhile Lanrezac's advance on St. Quentin was meeting

difficulties. A regiment of the XVIIIth Corps, under orders to take a village down the road, advanced under shrapnel falling like hail. Shells "gutted the road and tore branches from the trees in huge pieces," wrote a sergeant who survived.

"It was stupid to lie down; one might as well keep moving. . . . Here and there men lay flat on their stomachs or on their backs. They were dead. One of them, under an apple tree, had all of his face missing; blood drowned his head. On the right drums sounded the bayonet charge followed by the trumpet. Our line advanced marked by the sparkle of the bayonets slanted against a blue sky. The rhythm of the drums quickened. 'Forward!' All the men cried 'Forward!' It was a superb moment. An electric shiver went through my scalp and contracted the roots of my hair. The drums beat in a rage, the hot wind carried the notes of the trumpet, the men shouted—they were transported! . . . Suddenly we were stopped. To charge a village 900 yards away against a solid defense was folly. The order came, 'Lie down, take cover.'"

The attack on St. Quentin was thrown back and, as Lanrezac had anticipated, heavy enemy pressure began to bear down upon his right. Bülow was attacking with all his forces instead of allowing the French to move forward against him so that they might be taken in the rear by the armies of Kluck and Hausen. Believing that the action was no more than the death throes of a broken army, Bülow felt "confident of the outcome." In one sector the French were driven back across the Oise, and a panic developed when the bridges and narrow roads leading off them became jammed. Displaying "the greatest quickness and comprehension," in the words of his least sympathetic observer, Lanrezac quickly ordered abandonment of the action at St. Quentin and a new concentration of effort to redeem the situation on the right at Guise.

Franchet d'Esperey, commander of the Ist Corps, the eager, sturdy little general burned by the suns of Tonkin and Morocco whom Poincaré called "a stranger to depression," was ordered to rally the IIIrd and Xth Corps on his left and right. With the aid of officers riding up and down the front on horseback and bands playing once again the quick bright chords of the "Sambre et Meuse," he reformed the line by 5:30 P.M. Preceded by a well-prepared artillery action, the French moved forward once more to the attack. The bridge at Guise was piled high with ramparts of enemy dead. On the far side resistance was desultory; the French could feel it weakening. "The Germans were running away," wrote an observer, and the French, "frantic with joy at the new and longed for sensation were carried forward in a splendid victorious wave."

At the day's end when the sergeant who had participated in the attack on St. Quentin returned to the village from which he had started that morning, he was met by a friend who had all the news. "He said it had been a great day. Our check didn't matter. The enemy was pushed back, we were the winners. The Colonel was killed by a shell; he died while they were carrying him off. Commandant Theron was wounded in the chest. Captain Gilberti was wounded and would not live. Many of the men were dead or wounded. He repeated it had been a good day because the regiment would sleep two nights in the same place."

The retirement of the Guard Corps—the élite of Bülow's Army—pulled back its neighbors and gave Lanrezac a tactical victory—at Guise, if not at St. Quentin. But he was now alone and exposed, facing north, while his neighbors on both sides, the British and the Fourth Army, each a full day's march ahead of him, were continuing their retreat and further uncovering his flanks at every step. If the Fifth Army were to be saved it must immediately break off battle and rejoin its partners. But Lanrezac could get no directive from Joffre who was not at GQG when Lanrezac telephoned.

"Is the Fifth Army to delay in the region of Guise-St. Quentin at the risk of being captured?" Lanrezac asked General Belin, Joffre's deputy.

"What do you mean, let your army be captured! That's absurd!"

"You do not understand me. I am here at the express orders of the Commander in Chief. . . . I cannot take it upon myself to withdraw to Laon. It is for the Commander in Chief to give me the order to retire." Lanrezac was not going to take the blame this time, as at Charleroi.

Refusing to assume authority, Belin said he would report the question to Joffre as soon as he returned. When Joffre did return, although he appeared still confident, still unruffled, his hopes had suffered a second crash even graver than the debacle at the frontiers because now the enemy was that much deeper into France. He had no way of knowing that Lanrezac's fight had inflicted a sharp check on Bülow's army because the results did not yet show. He could only recognize that the Fifth Army was in truth left in a dangerous position, that the BEF was backing out, and he could "no longer nourish any hope of holding our Allies on the anticipated line of battle." The Sixth Army, while still in the process of forming, was under heavy attack from Kluck's two right-wing corps; the front he had hoped to hold was dissipated; more territory would have to be yielded, perhaps as far as the Marne, perhaps even to the Seine.

During this period, the "most tragic in all French history," as its chief investigator was to call it, Joffre did not panic like Sir John French, or waver like Moltke or become momentarily unnerved like Haig or Ludendorff or succumb to pessimism like Prittwitz. What went on behind that opaque exterior he never showed. If he owed his composure to a failure of imagination, that was fortunate for France. Ordinary men, Clausewitz wrote, become depressed by a sense of danger and responsibility; if these conditions are to "lend wings to strengthen the judgment, there must be present unusual greatness of soul." If danger did not strengthen Joffre's judgment in any way, it did call forth a certain strength of soul or of character. When ruin was all around him, he maintained an even tenor, a stolid control, what Foch, who saw him on August 29, called a "wonderful calm" which held the French Army together in an hour when it most needed the cement of confidence. On one of these days Colonel Alexandre, returning from a mission to the Fifth Army, excused his expression of gloom on the ground of "the bad news I have to bring."

"What!" answered Joffre, "do you no longer believe in France? Go get some rest. You will see—everything will be all right."

That night of August 29 at 10:00 P.M. he issued the order for Lanrezac to retire and blow up the bridges of the Oise behind him. General d'Amade was ordered to blow up the bridges over the Somme at Amiens and fall back, along with Maunoury's Army. On the right the Fourth Army was ordered to retire on

Rheims, and General de Langle, who demanded rest for his troops, was told that rest depended on the enemy. As his final bitter act of the night of August 29, Joffre ordered preparations made for leaving Vitry-le-François, "that headquarters of broken hopes and lost illusions." GQG was to be moved back to Bar-sur-Aube on an eastern tributary of the Seine. The news spread among the Staff, adding, as Joffre disapprovingly noted, to "the general nervousness and anxiety."

Through a Staff failure, Joffre's order to the Fifth Army did not reach Lanrezac till early next morning, causing him a long night of unnecessary agony. Fortunately von Bülow did not renew the combat or, when Lanrezac withdrew, follow after. The results of the battle were as obscure to the Germans as to the French, and Bülow's impressions seem to have been curiously mixed, for he both reported it to OHL as a success and at the same time sent a staff captain to von Kluck to say his army was "exhausted by the battle of Guise and unable to pursue." Ignorant of this, the French—Joffre as well as Lanrezac—were possessed by a single aim: to disengage the Fifth Army and bring it out of danger and into line with the other French Armies before the Germans could outflank it on the left.

Meanwhile the threat to Paris of the oncoming German right wing was evident. Joffre telegraphed Gallieni to lay charges under the bridges of the Seine immediately to the west of Paris and of the Marne immediately to the east and to post platoons of Engineers at each one to make sure that orders to blow the bridges would be carried out. Maunoury's Army, in falling back, would cover Paris and be the natural group to provide the army of three corps Gallieni was demanding. But to Joffre and GQG Paris was still a "geographical expression." To defend it for its own sake and, for that purpose, put Maunoury's Army at Gallieni's disposal and under his orders was not Joffre's intention. Paris, as he saw it, would stand or fall with the result of the battle he intended to fight with the whole field army under his own command. To the men inside Paris, however, the fate of the capital was of more direct interest.

The apparent result of the Battle of St. Quentin and Guise deepened the pall of dismay hanging over them. On the morning of the battle M. Touron, vice president of the Senate and an industrial magnate of the north, rushed into Poincaré's office "like a whirlwind," claiming that the government was "being deceived by GQG" and that our left had "been turned and the Germans are at La Fère." Poincaré repeated the stout assurances of Joffre that the left would hold and that as soon as the Sixth Army was ready the offensive would be resumed, but in the back of his mind he feared that M. Touron might be right. Cryptic messages filtered in, indicating a great battle was in progress. Every hour he received contradictory reports. Late in the afternoon M. Touron burst in again, more excited than ever. He had just been talking over the telephone to M. Seline, a fellow Senator from the Aisne who owned a property near St. Quentin and who had been watching the battle from the roof of his house. M. Seline had seen the French troops advancing and the puffs of smoke and the black shellbursts filling the sky and then, as German reinforcements, like an army of gray ants, were brought up, had seen the French thrown back. The attack had not succeeded, the battle was lost, and M. Touron departed wailing.

The second stage of the battle—at Guise—did not come under the eyes of the Senator on the roof and was even less clear to the Government than to GQG. All that seemed clear was that Joffre's attempt to check the German right wing had failed, that Paris faced siege and might again eat rats as it had forty years before. The possibility of the fall of the capital, the question whether the government should leave, which had been lurking in ministerial minds since the Battle of the Frontiers, was now openly and urgently discussed. Colonel Penelon, liaison officer between GQG and the President, arrived early next morning, his usually smiling face for once somber, and admitted the situation was "intensely serious." Millerand as Minister of War at once advised departure to avoid being cut off from the rest of the country. Gallieni, hastily summoned for his opinion, advised telephoning Joffre. Joffre acknowledged the situation was not good; the Fifth Army had fought well but had not accomplished his hopes; the English "had not budged"; the advance of the enemy could not be slowed and Paris was "seriously menaced." He advised the government to leave so as not, by remaining, to be the means of drawing the enemy upon the capital. Joffre knew well enough that the

German objective was the French Armies, not the government, but as the battlefield neared Paris, the presence of the government in the Zone of the Armies would tend to blur the lines of authority. Its withdrawal would remove a source of interference and leave GQG with enhanced power. When Gallieni on the telephone tried to convince him of the necessity of defending Paris as the material and moral hub of the war effort, and again demanded an army to attack the enemy in the field before the city could be invested, he somewhat vaguely promised to send him three corps though not at full strength and largely made up of reserve divisions. He gave Gallieni the impression that he considered Paris expendable and was still unwilling to deplete his forces for its sake.

Then the President of the Republic, appearing "preoccupied and even dispirited," although as always "cold and reserved," asked Gallieni how long Paris could hold out and whether the government should leave. "Paris cannot hold out and you should make ready to leave as soon as possible," Gallieni replied. Desiring, no less than Joffre, to unsaddle himself of the government, he found the advice painless. Poincaré asked him to return later to explain his views to the Cabinet, which in the meantime assembled and passionately argued the question that a bare ten days ago, when the French offensive was launched, would have seemed unthinkable.

Poincaré, Ribot, and the two socialists, Guesde and Sembat, were for staying, or at least awaiting the outcome of the approaching battle. The moral effect of departure, they contended, could produce despair, even revolution. Millerand insisted upon departure. He said a company of Uhlans might penetrate below Paris and cut the railroads to the south, and the government could not take the risk of being shut up inside the capital as in 1870. This time France was fighting as part of an alliance and it was the government's duty to remain in contact with her Allies and the outside world as well as with the rest of France. Doumergue made a deep impression when he said, "It takes more courage to appear a coward and risk popular disfavor than to risk being killed." Whether the emergency required reconvening Parliament, as was demanded in excited visits by the presidents of the two chambers, provided a subject for further heated dispute.

Fretting with impatience to return to his duties, Gallieni was kept waiting outside for an hour while the ministers argued. Finally called in, he told them bluntly they were "no longer safe in the capital." His stern and soldierly appearance and manner and the "clarity and force" with which he expressed himself made a "profound effect." Explaining that without an army to fight outside the perimeter, he could not ward off assault by the enemy's siege artillery; he warned that Paris was not in a state of defense and "cannot be put in one. . . . It would be an illusion to believe that the entrenched camp could offer a serious resistance if the enemy should appear in the next few days before our line of exterior forts." The formation of an army of four or at least three corps to fight under his orders outside the city as the extreme left wing of the French line was "indispensable." The delay in preparing the defenses, before his appointment as Governor, he charged to influential groups who wanted Paris declared an open city to save it from destruction. They had been encouraged by GQG.

"That's right," Millerand interrupted. "It is the opinion at GQG that Paris should not be defended."

Guesde, the socialist, speaking his first words as minister after a lifetime of opposition, excitedly broke in. "You want to open the gates to the enemy so Paris won't be pillaged. But on the day the Germans march through our streets there will be a shot fired from every window in the working-class quarters. And then I will tell you what will happen: Paris will be burned!"

After hectic debate it was agreed that Paris must be defended and Joffre required to conform, if necessary under pain of dismissal. Gallieni argued against any rash removal of the Commander in Chief at this stage. As to whether the government should go or stay, the Cabinet remained completely at odds.

Leaving the ministers "overcome with emotion and indecision" and, as they seemed to him, "incapable of coming to a firm resolve," Gallieni returned to the Invalides, making his way through the crowds of anxious citizens besieging its doors for permits to leave the city, to take their cars, to close essential businesses, and a thousand other reasons. The buzz of anxiety was louder than usual; that afternoon for the first time a German *Taube* bombed Paris. Besides three bombs on the Quai de Valmy which killed two persons and injured others, it dropped leaflets telling Parisians that the Germans were at their gates, as in 1870, and "There is nothing you can do but surrender."

Daily thereafter one or more enemy planes returned regularly at 6:00 P.M., dropped two or three bombs, and killed an occasional passerby in an effort, presumably, to frighten the population. The fearful went south. For those who remained in Paris during this period, when no one knew if the next day might not bring the spiked helmets marching in, the flights of the *Taube*, always at the *apéritif* hour, provided excitement to compensate for the government's prohibition of absinthe. That night of its first visit Paris was blacked out for the first time. The only "little gleam of light" to pierce the general gloom, Poincaré wrote in his diary, was in the East where, according to a telegram from the French military attaché, the Russian armies were "developing their offensive toward Berlin." In fact they were being cut down and surrounded at Tannenberg, and on that night General Samsonov committed suicide in the forest.

Joffre heard a more accurate version when a German radio message, intercepted at Belfort, told of the destruction of three Russian corps, the capture of two corps commanders and 70,000 other prisoners and announced, "The Russian Second Army no longer exists." This terrible news coming when French hopes were already sinking might have dispirited even Joffre except that it was followed by other news which showed the Russian sacrifice had not been in vain. Intelligence reports revealed the transfer of at least two German corps from the Western Front to the East and were confirmed next day by reports of thirty-two troop trains passing eastward through Berlin. This was Joffre's gleam of light, this the aid for which all France's pressure on Russia had been brought to bear. Even so, it hardly counterbalanced the projected loss of the British whose commander's refusal to remain in contact with the enemy opened the way to envelopment of the Fifth Army. The Fifth was also in danger of being outflanked on its right through the space thinly filled by the Foch Detachment.

Wherever a weak sector needed reinforcement, another sector had to be dangerously depleted. On this same day, August 30, Joffre visited the front of the Third and Fourth Armies to look for forces he could assign to Foch. On the road he passed the retreating columns who had fought in the Ardennes and on the heights of the Meuse. Red trousers had faded to the color of pale brick, coats were ragged and torn, shoes caked with mud, eyes cavernous in faces dulled by exhaustion and dark with many days' growth of beard. Twenty days' campaigning seemed to have aged the soldiers as many years. They walked heavily, as if ready to drop at every step. Emaciated horses, with bones sticking out and with bleeding harness sores, sometimes dropped in the shafts, were hurriedly unharnessed by the artillerymen, and dragged off to the side of the road so as not to obstruct the way. Guns looked old and blistered with barely a few patches of their once new gray paint showing through the mud and dirt.

In contrast, other units, still vigorous, had become confident veterans in the twenty days, proud of their fighting skills and eager to halt the retreat. The ultimate compliment was earned by the 42nd Division of Ruffey's Army which, after holding the rearguard and successfully disengaging, was told by its corps commander, General Sarrail, "You have given proof of *cran.*" When Joffre ordered this division transferred to Foch, General Ruffey protested violently on the ground of an anticipated attack. Unlike General de Langle of the Fourth Army whom Joffre had just found calm, confident, and "perfectly master of himself"—the one essential duty of a commander in Joffre's eyes—Ruffey appeared nervous, excitable, and "imaginative to an excessive degree." As Colonel Tanant, his Chief of Operations, said, he was very clever and full of a thousand ideas of which one was magnificent but the question was which. Like the deputies in Paris, Joffre needed a scapegoat for the failure of the offensive and Ruffey's conduct decided the selection; he was removed that day from command of the Third Army and replaced by General Sarrail. Invited to lunch next day with Joffre, Ruffey blamed his defeat in the Ardennes on the last-minute removal of the two reserve divisions that Joffre had transferred to the Army of Lorraine. If he had had those 40,000 fresh men and the 7th Cavalry Division, Ruffey said, he could have rolled up the enemy's left, and "what a success for our arms we might have won!" In one of his terse and mysterious remarks, Joffre replied, "*Chut, il ne faut pas le dire.*" His tone of voice has been lost, and it will never be known whether he meant, "You are wrong; you must not say that," or "You are right but we must not admit it."

On that Sunday, August 30, the day of Tannenberg, the day the French government was warned to leave Paris, England received a shock, since known as the "Amiens dispatch." Headed, with initial exaggeration, "Fiercest Fight in History," it appeared with awful impact in a special Sunday edition of *The Times* on the front page where, ordinarily, discreet columns of advertising screened readers from the news. Subheads proclaimed, "Heavy Losses of British Troops—Mons and Cambrai—Fight Against Severe Odds—Need for Reinforcements." This last phrase was the key; although the dispatch was to arouse an official storm, provoke a furious debate in Parliament, and earn a scolding from the Prime Minister as a "regrettable exception" to the "patriotic reticence" of the press as a whole, it was in fact published with an official purpose. Instantly seeing its qualities as recruiting propaganda, the Censor, F. E. Smith, later Lord Birkenhead, passed it and urged it upon *The Times*, which published it as a patriotic duty with an appended notice as to the "extreme gravity of the task before us." It was written by a correspondent, Arthur Moore, who had arrived at the front in the midst of the retreat from Le Cateau and the hectic despair at GHQ.

He wrote of a "retreating and a broken army" after the series of engagements "which may be called the action of Mons," of the French retreat on the flank, of the "immediate, relentless, unresting" German pursuit and its "irresistible vehemence," of British regiments "grievously injured" though with "no failure in discipline, no panic and no throwing up the sponge." In spite of everything the men were still "steady and cheerful" but "forced backwards, ever backwards." He told of "very great losses," of "bits of broken regiments," and of some divisions having "lost nearly all their officers." Evidently infected with the mood of GHQ, he wrote rather wildly of the German right wing, "so great was their estimated superiority in numbers that they could no more be stopped than the waves of the sea." Britain, he concluded, must face the fact that the "first great German effort has succeeded" and "the investment of Paris cannot be banished from the field of possibility."

When, in summarizing the need for reinforcements, he spoke of the BEF which "bore the weight of the blow," he laid the foundations of a myth. It was as if the French Army had been an adjunct somewhere in the offing. In fact the BEF was never at any time in the first month in contact with more than three German corps out of a total of over thirty, but the idea that it "bore the weight of the blow" was perpetuated in all subsequent British accounts of Mons and of the "Glorious Retreat." It succeeded in planting in the British mind the conviction that the BEF in the gallant and terrible days of its first month of battle saved France, saved Europe, saved Western civilization or, as one British writer unbashfully put it, "Mons. In that single word will be summed up the Liberation of the World."

Alone among the belligerents Britain had gone to war with no prearranged framework of national effort, no mobilization orders in every pocket. Except for the regular army, all was improvisation and, during the first weeks, before the Amiens dispatch, almost a holiday mood. Up to then the truth of the German advance was concealed by—to use Mr. Asquith's exquisite phrase—"patriotic reticence." The fighting had been presented to the British public—as to the French—as a series of German defeats in which the enemy unaccountably moved from Belgium to France and appeared each day on the map at places farther forward. All over England on August 30 as *The Times* was read at Sunday breakfast tables, people were aghast. "It was as if," thought Mr. Britling, "David had flung his pebble—and missed!"

In the sudden and dreadful realization that the enemy was winning the war, people, searching for hope, seized upon a tale that had cropped up within the last few days and turned it into a national hallucination. On August 27 a seventeen-hour delay in the Liverpool-London railway service inspired the rumor that the trouble was due to the transport of Russian troops who were said to have landed in Scotland on their way to reinforce the Western Front. From Archangel they were supposed to have crossed the Arctic Sea to Norway, thence come by ordinary steamer to Aberdeen, and from there were being carried by special troop trains to Channel ports. Anyone whose train was held up thereafter knowingly attributed the delay to "the

Russians." In the gloom following the Amiens dispatch with its talk of German numbers like "the waves of the sea" and its cry for "men, men and more men," thoughts turned unconsciously toward Russia's limitless manpower, and the phantoms seen in Scotland took on body, gathering corroborative detail as the story spread.

They stamped snow off their boots on station platforms—in August; a railway porter of Edinburgh was known who had swept up the snow. "Strange uniforms" were glimpsed in passing troop trains. They were reported variously to be going via Harwich to save Antwerp or via Dover to save Paris. Ten thousand were seen after midnight in London marching along the Embankment on their way to Victoria Station. The naval battle of Heligoland was explained by the wise as a diversion to cover the transport of the Russians to Belgium. The most reliable people had seen them—or knew friends who had. An Oxford professor knew a colleague who had been summoned to interpret for them. A Scottish army officer in Edinburgh saw them in "long gaily-colored coats and big fur caps," carrying bows and arrows instead of rifles and with their own horses "just like Scottish ponies only bonier"—a description that exactly fitted the Cossacks of a hundred years ago as they appeared in early Victorian mezzotints. A resident of Aberdeen, Sir Stuart Coats, wrote to his brother-in-law in America that 125,000 Cossacks had marched across his estate in Perthshire. An English army officer assured friends that 70,000 Russians had passed through England to the Western Front in "utmost secrecy." At first said to be 500,000, then 250,000, then 125,000, the figure gradually settled at between 70,000 and 80,000—the same number as made up the departed BEF. The story spread entirely by word of mouth; owing to the official censorship nothing appeared in the papers except in the United States. Here the reports of homecoming Americans, most of whom had embarked at Liverpool, which was in a furor of excitement over the Russians, preserved the phenomenon for posterity.

Other neutrals picked up the news. Dispatches from Amsterdam reported a large force of Russians being rushed to Paris to aid in its defense. In Paris people hung about the railway stations hoping to see the arrival of the Cossacks. Passing to the Continent, the phantoms became a military factor; for the Germans, too, heard the rumors. Worry about a possible 70,000 Russians at their backs was to be as real a factor at the Marne as the absence of the 70,000 men they had transferred to the Eastern Front. It was only after the Marne, on September 15, that an official denial of the rumor appeared in the English press.

On the same Sunday as the Amiens dispatch appalled the public, Sir John French composed a report that was an even greater shock to Lord Kitchener. GHQ was then at Compiègne, forty miles north of Paris, and the British troops, relieved of pursuit the previous day, had rested while the enemy was engaged by the French. The Operation Order to the BEF that day, bearing Sir John French's signature, stated that enemy pressure "was relieved by a French advance in force on our right which met with great success in the neighborhood of Guise where the German Guard and Xth Corps were driven back into the Oise." This ready acknowledgment of the facts being totally irreconcilable with what Sir John then wrote to Kitchener, it can only be supposed that he signed it without reading it.

He informed Kitchener of Joffre's request to him to hold fast north of Compiègne, keeping in contact with the enemy, but claimed he was "absolutely unable to remain in the front line" and intended to retire "behind the Seine," keeping "at a considerable distance from the enemy." His retirement would involve an eight-day march "without fatiguing the troops" and passing west of Paris so as to be near to his base. "I do not like General Joffre's plan," Sir John continued, "and would have preferred a vigorous offensive"—a preference he had just refused to exercise at St. Quentin when he forbade Haig to cooperate with Lanrezac in the battle.

Quickly reversing himself in the next sentence, Sir John made it clear that, after ten days of campaign, he was ready to give the French up as beaten and come home. His confidence in the ability of the French "to carry the campaign to a successful conclusion is fast waning," he wrote, and "this is my real reason for moving the British forces so far back." Although "pressed very hard to remain in the front line, even in my shattered condition," he had "absolutely refused to do so" in accordance with "the letter and spirit" of Kitchener's instructions and insisted upon retaining independence of action "to retire on my base" if necessary.

Kitchener read the report, received on August 31, with astonishment mounting to consternation. Sir John French's intention to withdraw from the Allied line and separate the British from the French, with its appearance of deserting them in their most desperate hour, he regarded as "calamitous," from the political as well as the military point of view. As a violation of the spirit of the Entente, it became a question of policy, and Kitchener asked the Prime Minister to summon the Cabinet at once. Before it met he sent off a restrained telegram to Sir John expressing his "surprise" at the decision to retire behind the Seine and delicately phrasing his dismay in the form of a question: "What will be the effect of this course upon your relations with the French Army and on the general military situation? Will your retirement leave a gap in the French line or cause them discouragement of which the Germans could take advantage?" He closed with a reminder that the thirty-two troop trains moving through Berlin showed that the Germans were withdrawing forces from the Western Front.

When Kitchener, after reading Sir John's letter to the Cabinet, explained that retirement behind the Seine might mean loss of the war, the Cabinet was, as Mr. Asquith put it in his muffled way, "perturbed." Kitchener was authorized to inform Sir John of the government's anxiety at his proposed retirement and its expectation that "you will as far as possible conform with the plans of General Joffre for the conduct of the campaign." The government, he added, with care for French's *amour propre*, "have all possible confidence in your troops and yourself."

When OHL had learned of General von Prittwitz's intention to retire behind the Vistula, he was instantly dismissed; but when Sir John French proposed to give up not a province but an ally, the same solution was not applied. The reason may have been that, owing to the ravages left by the Ulster quarrel, there was no replacement upon whom government and army could agree. The government may have regarded dismissal of the Commander in Chief at such a moment as too great a shock for the public. In any event, inspired by Sir John's aura of irritability, everyone—French as well as British—continued to treat him with the utmost tact while in fact retaining very little confidence in him. "Joffre and he have never yet been within a mile of the heart of each other," wrote Sir William Robertson, the British Quartermaster General, to the King's secretary a year later. "He has never really, sincerely and honestly concerted with the French and they consider him as by no means a man of ability or a faithful friend and therefore do not confide in him." This was not a situation propitious for the Allied war effort. Kitchener, whose relations with Sir John had not been cordial since the Boer War, never regained confidence in him after August 31, but it was not until December 1915 that Sir John's own machinations against Kitchener, conducted in a manner, as Lord Birkenhead was to say, "neither decorous, fastidious nor loyal," finally nerved the British government to remove him.

While in London, Kitchener was waiting impatiently for Sir John's reply, Joffre in Paris was mobilizing the aid of the French government to try to keep the British in the front line. Joffre had by now discovered that at least half of Lanrezac's battle—the half at Guise—had been a success. Reports showing that the German Guard and Xth Corps had been "severely handled" and that Bülow's Army was not pursuing, combined with the news of the withdrawal of German troops to the East, encouraged him. He told Poincaré the government might not have to leave after all; he now felt hopeful of checking the German advance in renewed action by the Fifth and Sixth Armies. He sent a letter to the British Commander telling him the Fifth and Sixth now had orders not to yield ground except under pressure. As they could not be expected to stand if there was a gap between them, he "earnestly" requested Field Marshal French not to withdraw and "at least to leave rearguards so as not to give the enemy the clear impression of a retreat and of a gap between the Fifth and Sixth Armies."

Asked by Joffre to exert his influence as President of France to obtain a favorable reply, Poincaré called the British ambassador, who called GHQ, but all the calls and visits of liaison officers were of no avail. "I refused," as Sir John later succinctly summarized his reply, and thereby punctured Joffre's momentary, if illusory, hope.

Sir John's reply to his own government was awaited so anxiously by Kitchener that he had the decoders read it to him word by word as it came through late that night. "Of course," it said, there would be a gap in the French line caused by his retirement, but "if the French go on with their present tactics which are practically to fall back right and left of me, usually without notice, and to abandon all idea of offensive operations . . . the consequences will be borne by them. . . . I do not see why I should be called upon to run the risk of absolute disaster in order a second time to save them." This militant misstatement of the truth, after Joffre had just finished telling him the opposite, was the kind of thing that when his book *1914* was published caused his countrymen to search helplessly for a polite equivalent of "lie" and moved even Mr. Asquith to use the phrase, "a travesty of the facts." Even given Sir John's limitations of character, the mystery remains how, with Henry Wilson on the Staff with his thorough knowledge of the French language and his acquaintance with senior French officers including Joffre himself, the British Commander in Chief could have arrived at the picture he did of French defeatism.

When Kitchener finished reading the telegram at 1:00 A.M., he decided instantly there was only one thing to do and it could not wait for daybreak. He must go to France himself. As senior Field Marshal, he was head of the army and as such considered himself entitled to give orders to Sir John French on military matters as well as on matters of policy in his capacity as War Minister. Hastening to Downing Street he conferred with Asquith and a group of ministers, among them Churchill, who ordered a fast cruiser for his conveyance to be ready within two hours at Dover. He telegraphed Sir John to expect him and, lest his appearance at GHQ embarrass the sensibilities of the Commander in Chief, asked him to select a place of meeting. At 2:00 A.M. Sir Edward Grey was startled out of his sleep by the apparition of Kitchener walking into his bedroom to say he was going to France. At 2:30 he departed by special train from Charing Cross and by morning of September 1 was in Paris.

Looking "irritated, violent, his face congested, sulky and angry," Field Marshal French, accompanied by Sir Archibald Murray, arrived at the British Embassy, the meeting place he had selected. He intended it to emphasize the civilian nature of the conference for he insisted on regarding Kitchener as political head of the army only, with no status other than that of any civilian War Minister. His choler was hardly soothed to find Kitchener in uniform, which Sir John instantly took as an attempt to pull rank on him. In fact, after appearing in frock coat and silk hat on his first day at the war office, Kitchener had discarded civilian clothes for the blue undress uniform of a Field Marshal. Sir John took it as a personal affront. Clothes were a matter of the greatest importance to him and he had a tendency to use them to enhance his own dignity in ways his associates considered unorthodox. He offended King George by his habit of "wearing stars in khaki" and "covering himself with foreign baubles"; and Henry Wilson used to say of him, "He is a nice little man in his bath but when he puts his clothes on you can't trust him; you never know what he will wear."

When the meeting at the British Embassy in the presence of Sir Francis Bertie, Viviani, Millerand, and several officers representing Joffre became increasingly acrimonious, Kitchener asked Sir John to retire with him to a private room. As Sir John's version of what was said there, published after Kitchener was dead, is unreliable, only the results of their conversation are known for certain. They were expressed in a telegram from Kitchener to the government stating that "French's troops are now engaged in the fighting line where they will remain conforming to the movements of the French Army," which would mean retiring east, not west, of Paris. In a copy sent to Sir John, Kitchener said he felt sure this represented the agreement they had come to, but in any event "please consider it an instruction." By "in the fighting line," he said he meant disposing the British troops in contact with the French. In a fatal return to tact he added, "Of course you will judge as regards their position in this respect." Unmollified, the Commander in Chief retired in a sulk now deeper and more paralyzing than before.

During this and the previous day Kluck's Army, advancing by forced marches in its haste to envelop the French before they could take a firm stand, had overtaken Compiègne, crossed the Oise, pushing the Allied retreat before it, and on September 1 was in action against rearguards of the French Sixth Army and the BEF thirty miles from Paris. On that day the dead body of a German officer yielded to the French a piece of vital information.

21

Von Kluck's Turn

"AN AUTOMOBILE drove up," wrote M. Albert Fabre, whose villa at Lassigny, twelve miles north of Compiègne, was commandeered by the Germans on August 30. "From it descended an officer of arrogant and impressive bearing. He stalked forward alone while the officers standing in groups in front of the villa made way for him. He was tall and majestic with a scarred, clean-shaven face, hard features and a frightening glance. In his right hand he carried a soldier's rifle and his left rested on the butt of a revolver. He turned around several times, striking the ground with the butt end of his rifle and then halted in a theatrical pose. No one seemed to dare to approach him and indeed he wore a terrible air." Gazing awestruck at this be-weaponed apparition, M. Fabre thought of Attila and learned that his visitor was "the already too-famous von Kluck."

General von Kluck, the "last man on the right" in Schlieffen's scheme, was at that moment considering a fateful decision. He felt himself close to the crisis on August 30. His troops on the far right had driven back units of Maunoury's Army with success that Kluck thought was definitive. His pursuit in the center had not succeeded in catching up with the British, but the jettisoned piles of coats, boots, and ammunition found along the roadside which the British had dumped in their anxiety to bring away their men confirmed Kluck's opinion of a beaten opponent. On his left a division which he had lent to Bülow to help at the battle of Guise reported the French fleeing from that battle. Kluck was fiercely determined to allow them no time to recover.

Reports of the direction of Lanrezac's retreat indicated that the French line did not extend as far west as had been expected. Kluck believed it could be rolled up north of Paris, making a wide sweep to the west and south of the city unnecessary. The change involved a shift in the direction of his advance from due south to southeast and would have the added advantage of closing the gap between his army and Bülow's. Like everyone else he had begun the campaign assuming that reinforcements would be forthcoming from the left wing. He needed them now to replace the corps he had had to leave in front of Antwerp, the brigade in Brussels, the various units left to guard his ever-lengthening line of communications, not to mention his losses in combat. But reinforcements were not forthcoming. Moltke still had detached none from the left wing.

Moltke had many worries. True to his temperament, "Gloomy Julius" was less elated by the advance of his conquering armies than depressed by the difficulties of the advance. It was now the 30th day, and the schedule called for victory over France between the 36th and 40th days. Although his right-wing commanders continued to report the French and English as "decisively beaten" and their retreat in terms of "rout" and "flight," Moltke was uneasy. He noticed a suspicious lack of the usual signs of rout or disorganized retreat: Why were there so few prisoners? "A victory on the battlefield is of little account," his old chief Schlieffen used to say, "if it has not resulted either in breakthrough or encirclement. Though pushed back the enemy will appear again on different ground to renew the resistance he momentarily gave up. The campaign will go on. . . ."

Despite his concern Moltke did not go forward to investigate for himself but remained fretting at Headquarters, depending on delegates for reports. "It is heartbreaking," he wrote to his wife on August 29, "how little suspicions *der hohe Herr* [the Kaiser] has of the seriousness of the situation. He has already a certain shout-hurrah! mood that I hate like death."

On August 30 as the German Armies approached the climax of their campaign, OHL moved forward from Coblenz to Luxembourg City, ten miles behind the borders of France. They were now in territory emotionally if not officially hostile and which, by reason both of proximity and sentiment, was a hub of Allied rumors. Whispers circulated of the 80,000 Russians coming to help the British and French. OHL was kept busy piecing together indications of a landing somewhere on the Channel coast. The actual landing of 3,000 British marines at Ostend which, by the time the news reached Luxembourg, had swollen to serious and even Russian proportions, added apparent reality to German fears.

Besides the specter of Russians at his back, Moltke was bothered by the gaps in his battle line, especially between the armies of the right wing. There was one of twenty miles between Kluck and Bülow, another of twenty miles between Bülow and Hausen, and a third almost as wide between Hausen and the Duke of Württemberg. Moltke was uncomfortably conscious that the thinning spaces should have been filled by reinforcements drawn from the left wing which he had now committed to total involvement in the battle for the Moselle. He thought guiltily of Schlieffen's insistence that the proper course was to leave the left wing on the defensive with minimum forces and send every division that could be spared to the First and Second Armies. But the vision of a breakthrough of the French fortress line still lured OHL. Vacillating, Moltke on August 30 sent his artillery expert, Major Bauer, to make a personal survey of Rupprecht's front.

At Rupprecht's headquarters Bauer found "everything but concerted plans," and when he drove to the front lines commanders and officers gave him conflicting opinions. Some, pointing to the unmistakable withdrawal of enemy divisions from their front, were confident of imminent success. Others complained of the "difficult wooded mountains" along the Moselle, south of Toul, where the attack was running into trouble. Even if it succeeded the troops would be open to flank attack from Toul and supply lines would be lacking, since all roads and railroads led through the fortified city. Toul would have to be taken first. Back at Sixth Army Headquarters the once-aggressive enthusiasm of Prince Rupprecht had cooled to recognition that he was engaged in a "difficult and unpleasant task."

To Bauer, representing the Supreme Command, the report of French withdrawals from this front was a bad sign, for it meant that the enemy was withdrawing units to reinforce his front opposite the German right wing. He returned to OHL with the conclusion, as he told Moltke, that while the attack on Nancy-Toul and the Moselle line was "not without chances," it required an extended effort that seemed "not justifiable" at this time. Moltke agreed—and did nothing. He could not nerve himself to call off the offensive that had already cost so much. And the Kaiser wanted to ride in triumph through Nancy. No changed orders to the Sixth Army went out; full-scale effort to break the Moselle line continued.

Von Kluck resented the failure to reinforce the marching wing at this critical time. But it was not so much the need to narrow his front as the belief that the French were already beaten and needed only to be rounded up that decided him to make an inward wheel. Instead of brushing the Channel with his sleeve he would brush Paris on the inside in direct pursuit of Lanrezac's Army. That in the process he would be exposing his flank to attack by the garrison of Paris or by Maunoury's forces falling back upon Paris in front of him was a danger he did not ignore but did not estimate highly. He considered the forces so far assembled under Maunoury as negligible. The possibility of their being reinforced he considered also negligible because the French, stumbling backward in the throes of defeat and disaster, must be too disorganized for such a maneuver. Moreover, he assumed that all their available forces were pinned down under the heavy pressure of the Crown Prince's Army around Verdun and of Rupprecht's Armies along the Moselle. One of his own corps, the laggard IVth Reserve, would be enough to leave in front of Paris to guard the flank of his army as it slid across to the east in front of the capital. After all, it had been proved in German war games that garrison forces inside an entrenched camp do not venture out until attacked, and the IVth Reserve, he believed, could contain the tatterdemalion collection of units under Maunoury. Having learned, from a captured letter, of Sir John French's intention to quit the line and retreat behind the Seine, he regarded the BEF, his direct opponent up to now, as of no further account.

Under the German system—in contrast to the French—Kluck as commander in the field was allowed the widest possible latitude for independent decision. Prepared by indoctrination, map exercises, and war games to find the correct solution of a given military problem, a German general was expected automatically to reach it when required. Though a deviation from the original strategy, Kluck's plan to ignore Paris and go after the retreating armies was the "correct" solution now that it appeared to him possible to annihilate the French Armies in the field without enveloping Paris. According to German military theory a fortified camp should not be attacked until the enemy's mobile forces were overwhelmed. These once destroyed, all the other fruits of victory followed. Although the lure of Paris was strong, Kluck determined not to be tempted from the path of proper military procedure.

At 6:30 on the evening of August 30 a message reached him from von Bülow that made up his mind. It requested him to make the inward wheel in order to help Bülow "gain the full advantage of victory" over the French Fifth Army. Whether Bülow was in fact asking for help to exploit a victory gained at St. Quentin or to compensate for a defeat suffered at Guise, is, whatever the words he used, uncertain. His request fitted in with what Kluck wanted to do in any event, and Kluck made his decision. The objectives he gave for the next day's march were no longer due south but southeast toward Noyon and Compiègne in order to cut off the retreat of the French Fifth Army. To already protesting and footsore troops who had not rested since they had begun the advance at Liège sixteen days before, his order of August 31 read, "Again, therefore, we must call upon the troops for forced marches."

OHL, informed that the First Army would begin an inward wheel next morning, hurriedly approved. Unhappy about the gaps, Moltke saw a danger of the three armies of the right wing being unable to support each other in delivery of the final blow. Numbers had fallen below the prescribed density for an offensive, and if Kluck were to adhere to the original plan of a sweep around Paris the front would be stretched out for another fifty miles or more. Seizing upon Kluck's move as a fortunate solution, Moltke telegraphed his approval the same night.

The end was in sight: the scheduled defeat of France by the 39th day in time to turn against Russia; the proof of all German training, planning, and organization; the halfway step to winning the war and mastery of Europe. It remained only to round up the retreating French before they could regain cohesion and renew resistance. Nothing, not the gaps, nor the check to Bülow's Army at Guise nor the fatigue of the men nor any last-minute faltering or error must be allowed to check the last dash to victory. With fierce urgency Kluck drove his army forward. As officers rode up and down the roads and sergeants rasped commands, the war-stained troops wearily formed columns on the morning of August 31 to begin another day of endless foot-slogging. Knowing nothing of maps or place names, they were unaware of the change of direction. The magic word Paris drew them on. They were not told that it was no longer their destination.

Hunger added to their misery. They had outrun their supply lines, which were functioning inadequately owing to the destruction of bridges and railroad tunnels in Belgium. Repairs had not succeeded in keeping railheads up with the advance of the armies; the focal bridge at Namur, for one, was not repaired until September 30. Often the tired infantry after a long day's march found the villages where they expected to billet occupied by their own cavalry. The cavalry, who were supposed to live off the country, were always so anxious about their supply trains and horses' fodder that to secure these they "constantly installed themselves," according to the Crown Prince, a former cavalryman himself, in places meant for the infantry. In a piece of unexpected testimony coming from this source, he added, "They always halted and got in the way of the infantry the moment things in front began to look ugly."

Kluck's Army met an ugly surprise on September 1 when it ran into the heels of the British who unaccountably, since Kluck's communiqué had said they were retreating "in the most complete disorder," were able to turn upon the Germans and offer sharp and punishing combat. In a day of desperate fighting in and around the forests of Compiègne and Villers-Cotterets, the British rearguards held off the enemy while the main body of the BEF, to Kluck's disgust, again got away. Postponing a "much-needed" rest for his troops, Kluck ordered a further march next day, shifting back slightly to the west in the hope of enveloping the British. Again they succeeded in escaping him "just in time," to get across the Marne on September 3. His chance of finishing them off was now gone; having lost time, increased his casualties, and added marching distance, he resumed in no good temper his inward wheel in pursuit of the French.

"Our men are done up," wrote a German officer of Kluck's Army in his diary of September 2. "They stagger forward, their faces coated with dust, their uniforms in rags. They look like living scarecrows." After four days of marching an average of twenty-four miles a day over roads pitted with shellholes and barred by felled trees, "they march with eyes closed, singing in chorus so as not to fall asleep. . . . Only the certainty of early victory and a triumphal entry into Paris keeps them going. . . . Without this they would fall exhausted and go to sleep where they fall." The diary testified to a problem that was becoming increasingly serious in the German advance, especially further east where Bülow's and Hausen's troops were coming through Champagne. "They drink to excess but this drunkenness keeps them going. Today after inspection the General was furious. He wanted to stop this general drunkenness but we managed to dissuade him from giving severe orders. If we used too much severity the Army would not march. Abnormal stimulants are necessary to combat abnormal fatigue." "We will put all that right in Paris," the officer concluded hopefully, he, too, evidently unaware of the new direction of the march.

Through France as through Belgium the Germans left a blackened and defiled path as they passed. Villages were burned, civilians shot, homes looted and torn, horses ridden through rooms, artillery wagons dragged across gardens, latrines dug in the family burial plot of the Poincarés at Nubécourt. Kluck's IInd Corps passing through Senlis, twenty-five miles from Paris, on September 2, shot the Mayor and six other civilian hostages. A stone marker, just outside the town on the edge of a field where they are buried, bears their names:

Eugène Odène	Mayor
Emile Aubert	Tanner
Jean Barbier	Carter
Lucien Cottreau	Café waiter
Pierre Dewerdt	Chauffeur
J-B. Elysée Pommier	Baker's helper
Arthur Régant	Stonecutter

September 2 was a happy day for General von Hausen who found himself billeted in the Château of the Comte de Chabrillon at Thugny on the Aisne. Occupying the countess' bedroom, the General was delighted to discover from examination of her visiting cards that she was *née* Comtesse de

Lévy-Mirepois in her own right, which caused him to sleep with that much extra pleasure in her bed. After dining on pheasant obtained by his supply officers who organized a shoot in the park of the château, Hausen counted the countess' table silver and left an inventory of it with an old man in the village.

That night Moltke, who after a second look had developed qualms about the flank that Kluck's inward wheel was exposing to Paris, issued a new General Order. As in the matter of the left wing, it showed his uncertain hand. It ratified Kluck's turn by ordering the First and Second Armies to "drive the French armies in a southeast direction away from Paris." At the same time it attempted to guard against a possible danger by ordering Kluck's army to follow "in echelon behind the Second Army" and make itself "responsible for the flank protection of the Armies."

In echelon! To Kluck the insult was worse than putting him, as OHL had done before, under Bülow's orders. The grim-visaged Attila with rifle in one hand and revolver in the other, the pace-setter of the right wing, was not going to stay behind anybody. He issued his own orders to the First Army "to continue its advance over the Marne tomorrow [September 3] in order to drive the French southeastward." He considered it sufficient for purposes of protecting the flank exposed to Paris to leave behind him his two weakest units: the IVth Reserve which was minus a brigade left back at Brussels and the 4th Cavalry Division which had suffered heavily in the fight against the British on September 1.

Captain Lepic, an officer of Sordet's Cavalry Corps, was reconnoitering northwest of Compiègne on August 31, the first morning of Kluck's turn, when he saw at a little distance an enemy cavalry column of nine squadrons, followed fifteen minutes later by an infantry column with batteries, ammunition wagons, and a company of cyclists. He noticed they were taking the road for Compiègne rather than the direct southward road for Paris. Unaware that he was the earliest witness of a historic swerve, Captain Lepic was more interested to report that the Uhlans had discarded their distinctive helmets and were wearing cloth caps and that "they ask directions of the local people in bad French, saying '*Englisch, Englisch.*'"

His information about their line of march did not as yet convey any great significance to GQG. The town and château of Compiègne, it was thought, might be attracting the Germans, and they could still take the road from Compiègne to Paris. Nor was Captain Lepic's view of two columns necessarily indicative of Kluck's whole Army.

The French, too, on August 31, knew the campaign was coming to a climax. Their second plan—the plan of August 25 to shift the center of gravity over to the left in an effort to halt the German right wing—had failed. The mission of the Sixth Army which, together with the British and the Fifth Army, was to have made a stand on the Somme, had failed. Now the mission of the Sixth Army, Joffre acknowledged, was "to cover Paris." The British, as he said privately, "*ne veulent pas marcher*," and the Fifth Army, with Kluck in pursuit on its flank, was still in danger of being enveloped. Indeed, alarming news was brought that a spearhead of Kluck's cavalry had already penetrated between the Fifth Army and Paris into the space left open by the British retreat. Clearly, as Colonel Pont, Joffre's Chief of Operations told him, "it seems no longer possible to oppose the right wing with sufficient forces to arrest its enveloping movement."

A new plan was necessary. Survival was the immediate aim. At GQG Joffre with his two deputies, Belin and Berthelot, and the senior officers of the Operations Bureau discussed what was to be done. Into the "chapel" of the offensive the hot wind of events had forced a new idea—"to hold out" until the French Armies could stabilize a line from which to resume the offensive. Meanwhile, it was recognized, the German advance would extend its forces along a tremendous arc from Verdun to Paris. The plan this time, rather than to oppose the marching wing of the German Army, would be to cut it off by an attack upon the German center, reverting to the strategy of Plan 17. Only, now the battlefield was in the heart of France. A French defeat this time would not be a reverse as at the frontiers, but final.

The question was, How soon should the "forward movement" be resumed? At the earliest moment, on a level with Paris, in the valley of the Marne? Or should the retreat continue to a line forty miles farther back behind the Seine? Continuing the retreat meant yielding that much more territory to the Germans, but the barrier of the Seine would provide a breathing spell for the armies to gather strength when not under direct pressure of the enemy. As the Germans' chief aim was to destroy the French armies, so "our chief aim," Belin urged, must be to "keep ourselves alive." To take the "prudent" attitude and reform behind the Seine was now both a national duty and the course best designed to frustrate the aims of the enemy. So Belin argued, eloquently supported by Berthelot. Joffre listened—and next day issued General Order No. 4.

It was September 1, eve of the anniversary of Sedan, and the outlook for France appeared as tragic as it had then. Official confirmation of the Russian defeat at Tannenberg came in from the French military attaché. General Order No. 4, in contrast to the firm tone of the Order that followed the debacle on the frontiers, reflected the shaken optimism of GQG after a week of spreading invasion. It prescribed continued retreat for the Third, Fourth, and Fifth Armies "for some time to come" and set the Seine and Aube as the limit of the movement "without necessarily implying that this limit will be reached." "As soon as the Fifth Army has escaped the menace of envelopment," the armies "will resume the offensive"; but unlike the previous Order it named no specific time or place. Yet it contained the genesis of the future battle, for it spoke of bringing reinforcements from the Armies of Nancy and Epinal to participate in the renewed offensive and said "the mobile troops of the fortified camp of Paris may also take part in the general action."

Upon this as upon every other act and order of the next four days, layers of dispute were to be heaped by the partisans of Joffre and those of Gallieni in a long and painful controversy over the origins of the Battle of the Marne. Unquestionably Joffre had in mind *a* general battle if not *the* battle at the time and place it was actually to occur. The battle that he envisaged would take place when the five pursuing German armies would come "between the horns of Paris and Verdun," and the French Armies would be drawn up in a shallow curve or net stretched across the center of France. Joffre thought he had a week's time to make his arrangements, for he told Messimy, who came to say goodbye to him on September 1, that he expected to resume the offensive on September 8 and anticipated that it would be called "the battle of Brienne-le-Château." A town twenty-five miles behind the Marne, about halfway between that river and the Seine, Brienne had been the scene of a Napoleonic victory over Blücher. It may have seemed an appropriate omen to Joffre. Amid the general gloom of further enforced retreat, under the awful shadow of the approaching enemy, his sangfroid, his appearance of serenity and confidence, once again impressed Messimy.

It did not comfort Paris which saw itself uncovered by a retreat of the armies to the Seine. Joffre called Millerand and gave him an unsparing summary of the military situation. The "accentuated" retreat of the English had uncovered the left flank of Lanrezac's Army so that the retreat must continue until Lanrezac was disengaged. Maunoury had been ordered to fall back on Paris and place himself "in relation" to Gallieni, although Joffre said nothing about putting the Sixth Army under Gallieni's command. Enemy columns were taking a direction slightly away from Paris, which might offer some "respite"; nevertheless he considered it "urgent and essential" that the government quit Paris "without delay," either this evening or tomorrow.

Gallieni, informed of this development by a frantic government, called Joffre who managed to avoid speaking to him but was given his message: "We are in no condition to resist. . . . General Joffre must understand that if Maunoury cannot hold, Paris cannot withstand the enemy. Three active corps must be added to the forces of the fortified camp." Later that afternoon Joffre called back and informed Gallieni that he was putting Maunoury's Army under his orders. They would now become the mobile troops of the fortified camp of Paris. Such troops are traditionally commanded independently of the Field Army and could be withheld from a general battle at the will of the garrison commander. Joffre had no intention of giving them up. In a deft maneuver on the same day he requested the Minister of War to put the fortified camp of Paris and all its forces under his authority as Commander in Chief, "to enable me to use the mobile forces of the garrison in the field if the case arises." Millerand, no less under Joffre's spell than Messimy, so ordered it on September 2.

Meanwhile Gallieni had an army at last. Maunoury's forces which he could now dispose of consisted of one active division belonging to the VIIth Corps, a native Moroccan brigade, and four reserve divisions: the 61st and 62nd under General Ebener which had been taken from Paris originally, and the 55th and 56th Reserves which had fought so valiantly in Lorraine. Joffre agreed to add, since it was not under his control anyway, the first-rate 45th Division of Zouaves from Algiers which was just then detraining in Paris and one active corps from the field army. Like Kluck, he picked a damaged one, the IVth Corps of the Third Army which had suffered disastrous losses in the Ardennes. It was receiving replacements, however, and its transfer from the Third Army's front at Verdun to the Paris front was a reinforcement of which Kluck thought the French incapable. Troops of the IVth Corps, Gallieni was informed, would arrive by train in Paris on September 3 and 4.

Instantly upon receiving Joffre's verbal assignment to him of the Sixth Army, Gallieni drove north to make contact with his new command. How late was the hour was apparent when he passed refugees converging upon Paris in flight from the oncoming Germans, a look on their faces of "terror and despair." At Pontoise, just outside Paris to the northwest where the 61st and 62nd Divisions were coming in, all was disorder and dismay. The troops who had been caught in severe combat as they retreated were wearied and bloody; the local population was in panic at the sound of the guns and at reports of Uhlans in the neighborhood. After talking to General Ebener, Gallieni went on to see Maunoury at Creil on the Oise, thirty miles north of Paris. He gave Maunoury orders to blow up the Oise bridges and to try to delay the enemy's advance as he fell back on Paris and under no circumstances to allow the Germans to get between him and the capital.

Hurrying back to Paris he passed a happier sight than the refugees—the splendid Zouaves of the 45th Algerian marching through the boulevards to take their places at the forts. In their bright jackets and ballooning trousers they created a sensation and gave Parisians something to cheer once again.

But inside the ministries the mood was black. Millerand had passed on the "heart-breaking" facts to the President: "all our hopes are shattered; we are in full retreat all along the line;

Maunoury's Army is falling back on Paris. . . ." As Minister of War, Millerand refused to take responsibility for the government remaining an hour longer than tomorrow evening, September 2. Poincaré faced "the saddest event of my life." It was decided that the entire administration must move to Bordeaux as a unit, leaving none behind in Paris lest the public make invidious comparisons between ministers.

Upon Gallieni's return to the city that evening, he learned from Millerand that all civil and military authority for the foremost city in Europe as it came under siege would be left in his hands. Except for the Prefect of the Seine and the Prefect of Police, "I would be alone." The Prefect of Police, upon whom he would have to depend, had been in office, he discovered, barely an hour. The former Prefect, M. Hennion, on learning that the government was leaving, flatly refused to stay behind, and upon being ordered to remain at his post, resigned "for reasons of health." For Gallieni the exit of the government at least had the advantage of silencing the advocates of an open city; their legal excuse was gone and he was free to defend Paris as a fortified camp. Although he "preferred to be without ministers," he thought that "one or two might have stayed for the sake of appearances." This was hardly fair to those who would have liked to stay, but Gallieni's contempt for politicians was all-inclusive.

Expecting the Germans at the gates in two days, he stayed up all night with his staff, making "all my dispositions to give battle north of the city from Pontoise to the Ourcq," that is, over an area forty-five miles wide. The Ourcq is a small river that feeds into the Marne east of Paris.

Late that night information reached GQG that could have spared the government the necessity of flight. During the day a bag was brought to Captain Fagalde, Intelligence Officer of the Fifth Army. It had been found on the body of a German cavalry officer attached to Kluck's Army who, while riding in an automobile, had been shot and killed by a French patrol. In the bag were papers, including a map smeared with blood which showed the lines of advance for each of Kluck's corps and the point each was to reach at the end of that day's march. The lines for the whole army pointed in a southeasterly direction from the Oise toward the Ourcq.

GQG correctly interpreted Captain Fagalde's find as showing Kluck's intention to slide by Paris between the Sixth and the Fifth Armies in an effort to roll up the left of the main French line. If they also recognized that this meant he would forgo attack on Paris, they took no great pains to impress that view upon the government. When in the morning Colonel Penelon, liaison officer between GQG and the President, brought Poincaré news of Kluck's change of direction he did not bring any suggestion from Joffre that the government need not leave. On the contrary Joffre sent word that the government must go, that Kluck's intentions could not be certain, that his columns were already at Senlis and Chantilly, twenty miles away, and Paris would be under his guns very soon. How far the significance of Kluck's turn was understood by Poincaré or Millerand is hard to say; in the midst of war and crisis nothing is as clear or as certain as it appears in hindsight. Urgency, even panic, was in the air. Once having gone through the agony of coming to a decision, the government found it hard to change. Millerand, in any event, continued adamant for departure.

It was September 2, Sedan Day, and "the hateful moment had come." When he learned that arrangements had been made for the government to leave in the middle of the night instead of by day in the sight of the public, Poincaré's "grief and humiliation" increased. The Cabinet insisted that his presence was legally required at the seat of government; even Mme. Poincaré, who begged to continue her hospital work in Paris as a public gesture, was not allowed to remain. Ambassador Myron Herrick of the United States, his face all "puckered up," came to say goodbye with tears in his eyes.

To Herrick, as to everyone inside the French capital at that moment, "the terrible onslaught of the Germans," as he wrote to his son, "seems almost beyond resistance." He had received a warning from the Germans advising him to leave for the provinces as "whole quarters" of Paris might be destroyed. He was determined to stay, however, and promised Poincaré to protect the museums and monuments of Paris under the American flag as being "in the custody of humanity at large." Already he had formed a plan, fitting the desperate and exalted mood of the hour, that "if the Germans reached the outskirts of the city and demanded its surrender, to go out and talk with their army commander and, if possible, the Kaiser." As custodian of their embassy, at their request, he could demand a hearing. In later days, when friends who had lived through the first week of September in Paris used to count themselves a select number, Gallieni would say, "Don't forget, there was also Herrick."

At seven o'clock Gallieni went to take farewell of Millerand. The War Ministry in the Rue St. Dominique was "sad, dark and deserted" and the courtyard filled with huge moving vans in which the archives were being piled for shipment to Bordeaux. The remainder were burned. The process of packing up created a "lugubrious" atmosphere. Climbing the unlit staircase, Gallieni found the Minister alone in an empty room. Now that the government was leaving, Millerand did not hesitate to allow Paris and everyone in it to come under fire. His orders to Gallieni, who hardly needed to be told, were to defend Paris "*à outrance*."

"Do you understand, *M. le Ministre*, the significance of the words, *à outrance*?" Gallieni asked. "They mean destruction, ruins, dynamiting bridges in the center of the city."

"*À outrance*," Millerand repeated. Saying goodbye, he looked at Gallieni as at a man he was unlikely ever to see again, and Gallieni felt "pretty well persuaded, myself, that I was remaining to be killed."

Some hours later, in darkness and self-imposed secrecy that afflicted many of them with a sense of shame, ministers and members of Parliament boarded the train for Bordeaux, clothing the inglorious moment in a noble statement to the public next morning. "To hold out and fight," it said, must now become the order of the day. France would hold out and fight while on the seas England cut the enemy's communications with the rest of the world and the Russians "continue to advance and carry the decisive blow to the heart of the German empire!" (It was not considered the moment to add news of a Russian defeat.) In order to give the greatest "*élan* and effectiveness" to French resistance, the government, at the demand of the military, was moving "momentarily" to a place where it could remain in unbroken and constant contact with the whole country. "Frenchmen, let us be worthy of these tragic circumstances. We will obtain the final victory—by unfaltering will, by endurance, by tenacity—by refusing to perish."

Gallieni was content with a short sharp notice worded deliberately to dispel rumors that Paris had been declared an open city and to let the people know what to expect. His proclamation appeared on the walls of Paris in the morning:

> "ARMY OF PARIS. CITIZENS OF PARIS.
>
> The members of the Government of the Republic have left Paris to give a new impulse to the national defense. I have received a mandate to defend Paris against the invader. This mandate I shall carry out to the end.
>
> Paris, September 3, 1914
> Military Governor of Paris, Commander of the Army of Paris
>
> *Gallieni.*

The shock to the public was all the greater since GQG's policy of issuing only the least explicit communiqués had left people uninformed as to the seriousness of the military situation. The government appeared to have decamped without due cause. Its nocturnal going off left a painful impression which was not dispelled by what proved to be an extended and tenacious affection for Bordeaux. Puns were made at the expense of the government, calling them "*tournedos à la Bordelaise*," and the crowds who stormed the railway stations in their wake inspired a parody of "The Marseillaise":

> "*Aux gares, citoyens!*
> *Montez dans les wagons!*"

These were "days of anguish" for the Military Government of Paris. With the armies retreating north and east of the city, the problem of how long to hold and when to destroy the eighty bridges in the region caused increasing tension and anxiety. Commanders in each sector, as soon as they had assured passage of their own troops, were anxious to blow up the bridges behind them in order to cut off pursuit. GQG's orders were to let "no bridge fall intact into enemy hands"; at the same time the bridges would be needed for a return to the offensive. Three different commands were operating in the area: Gallieni's, Joffre's and, geographically between them, that of Sir John French whose chief concern since Kitchener's visit was to make a show of his independence of everybody. Engineers of the Paris camp guarding the bridges were beset by a conflict of orders. "A disaster is preparing," reported an officer of Engineers to General Hirschauer.

By nightfall of September 2 the British had reached the Marne and got across next day. Below Compiègne the troops discovered they were marching off their maps, and now it dawned on them that this was not after all a "strategic retreat" as they had been told by their officers. Their bases at Boulogne and Havre had by now been evacuated and all stores and personnel moved down to Saint-Nazaire at the mouth of the Loire.

About a day's march behind them the Fifth Army was still not yet out of danger of envelopment. In the continuing hot weather, retreat and pursuit went on, prey as tired as pursuers. Since the Battle of Guise the Fifth Army had been marching eighteen to twenty miles a day. Along its route groups of deserters pillaged farms and homes and spread panic among the population with tales of German terror. Executions took place. Lanrezac thought no army ever underwent such an ordeal as his. At the same time a British officer said of the BEF, "I would never have believed that men could be so tired and so hungry and yet live." Trying to find a source of encouragement during these days, Henry Wilson said to Colonel Huguet, "The Germans are over-hasty. They urge the pursuit too fast. The whole thing is overdone. They are bound to make a big mistake and then your hour will come."

Up to this point Joffre and his advisers at GQG, although aware of Kluck's inward wheel, did not see in it an important or early opportunity for attack on his flank. Kluck's shift in pursuit of the British on September 2 left them uncertain whether he might not be turning back against Paris. In any event their minds were not on Paris but were fixed on a general battle along the Seine, not to take place until they had reestablished a solid front. After further anxious consultation at GQG, Joffre came to a decision to continue the retreat "several days' march to the rear" of where the armies then stood, which would allow time to bring up reinforcements from his right wing. Despite the risk of weakening the barely held line of the Moselle, he decided to bring over a corps each from the First and Second Armies.

His decision was embodied in secret instructions issued to the army commanders on September 2 which made the Seine and Aube definitive as the line to be reached. The object, Joffre explained, was "to extricate the armies from the enemy's pressure and enable them to reorganize," and when this had been accomplished and reinforcements from the east brought up, "at that moment to pass to the offensive." The British Army would be "asked to participate in the maneuver" and the garrison of Paris "will act in the direction of Meaux," that is, against Kluck's flank. Still omitting a date, Joffre said he would give the signal "within a few days." Commanders were ordered to take "the most draconian measures" against deserters to ensure orderly retreat. Asking each to understand the situation and extend his utmost efforts, Joffre made it clear that this would be the battle "upon which the salvation of the country depends."

Gallieni, receiving the orders in Paris, condemned Joffre's plan because it sacrificed Paris and was "divorced from reality." He believed the pace of the German pursuit would allow the French Armies no time to reach or reform upon the Seine. Scattered reports of Kluck's southeastward march were reaching him, but he had not been informed of the vital confirmation found by Captain Fagalde. On the night of September 2, expecting attack next day, he slept at his Headquarters, which were now established in the Lycée Victor-Duruy, a girls' school across the street from the Invalides. A large building set back behind trees, it was isolated from the public and, having fewer entrances and exits than the Invalides, was easier to guard. Sentinels were posted at the doors, field telephones connected with all divisional headquarters of the fortified camp, offices set apart for the Operations and Intelligence staffs, mess and sleeping quarters arranged, and Gallieni was enabled, with great relief, to move into "a regular field Headquarters just as at the front."

The following morning, September 3, he learned definitely of Kluck's movement toward the Marne, away from Paris.

Lieutenant Watteau, an aviator of the Paris garrison making a reconnaissance flight, saw the enemy columns "gliding from west to east" toward the valley of the Ourcq. Later a second airplane from the Paris camp confirmed the report.

In the staff room of Gallieni's *Deuxième Bureau* an unspoken excitement communicated itself among the officers. Colonel Girodon, an officer wounded at the front who, however, "considered himself fit to do staff work," was lying on a chaise longue with his eyes fixed on the wall map on which colored pins traced the direction of the German advance. General Clergerie, Gallieni's Chief of Staff, entered the room just as another air reconnaissance report from British aviators was brought in. As once more the pins were moved, the track of Kluck's turn appeared unmistakably on the map, and Clergerie and Girodon cried out together: "They offer us their flank! They offer us their flank!"

22

"Gentlemen, We Will Fight on the Marne"

GALLIENI INSTANTLY saw the opportunity offered to the Army of Paris. Without hesitating he made up his mind to launch an attack on the flank of the German right wing at the earliest moment and induce Joffre to support the maneuver by resuming the offensive at once, on the entire front, instead of continuing the retreat to the Seine. Although the Army of Paris, of which Maunoury's Sixth Army was the core, was under Gallieni's command, the camp of Paris with all its forces had been, since the day before, under Joffre's command. To launch the Sixth Army upon the offensive two conditions were necessary: Joffre's consent and support of the Sixth Army's nearest neighbor, the BEF. Both stood between Paris and Kluck's flank, Maunoury north and the British south of the Marne.

Gallieni summoned his Chief of Staff, General Clergerie, to what Clergerie called "one of those long conferences he holds on grave issues—they usually last from two to five minutes." It was now 8:30 P.M. of September 3. They agreed, if Kluck's line of march were maintained next morning, to exert every pressure upon Joffre for an immediate combined offensive. Aviators of the Paris camp were ordered to make early reconnaissance flights, upon which "grave decisions would depend," and to report before 10:00 A.M.

Success of a flank attack, as General Hirschauer warned, "depends on the spearhead penetrating," and the Sixth Army was not the strong sharp instrument Gallieni would have liked. It had reached the positions assigned to it in a generally exhausted condition. Some units had marched thirty-seven miles during the day and night of September 2. Fatigue depressed morale. Gallieni, like his colleagues, considered reserve divisions, of which Maunoury's Army was largely composed, as of "mediocre value." The 62nd Reserve, which had not had a day of rest or one day without combat during the retreat, had lost two-thirds of its officers and had only reserve lieutenants as replacements. The IVth Corps had not yet arrived. Only the "calm and resolution" of the people of Paris—those who did not flee south—was a source of satisfaction.

Von Kluck reached the Marne on the evening of September 3 after Lanrezac's Army, which he was pursuing, and the British on his outer flank, had got across earlier in the day. Between them, in the haste, weariness, and confusion of retreat, and despite, or because of, the rain of telegrams about demolitions, they left bridges intact or only partially destroyed. Kluck held the bridgeheads and, disobeying the order to remain level with Bülow, intended to cross in the morning, continuing his inward wheel in pursuit of the Fifth Army. He had sent three messages to OHL announcing his intention to cross the Marne but as wireless communication with Luxembourg was even worse than with Coblenz, they did not get through until the following day. Out of contact with the First Army for two days, OHL did not know Kluck had disobeyed the order of September 2; by the time they found out, his leading columns were across the Marne.

They had marched twenty-five to twenty-eight miles on September 3. When the soldiers came into their billets, said a French witness, "they fell down exhausted, muttering in a dazed way, 'forty kilometers! forty kilometers!' That was all they could say." In the coming battle many German prisoners were taken asleep, unable to go another step. The heat of the days was terrible. Only the expectation of reaching Paris "tomorrow or the day after" enabled them to march at all, and the officers did not dare undeceive them. In his fever to finish off the French, Kluck, besides wearing out his men, outstripped not only his supply trains but also his heavy artillery. His compatriot in East Prussia, General von François, would not budge until he had at hand all his artillery and ammunition wagons. But François faced battle, whereas Kluck, thinking he faced only pursuit and mopping up, ignored the precaution. He believed the French incapable, after ten days of retreat, of the morale and energy required to turn around at the sound of the bugle and fight again. Nor was he worried about his flank. "The General fears nothing from the direction of Paris," recorded an officer on September 4. "After we have destroyed the remains of the Franco-British Army he will return to Paris and give the IVth Reserve the honor of leading the entry into the French capital."

The order to remain behind as flank guard of the German advance could not be carried out, Kluck bluntly informed OHL as he pushed forward on September 4. A two-day halt, necessary to allow Bülow to catch up, would weaken the whole German offensive and give the enemy time to regain his freedom of movement. Indeed, it was only by the "bold action" of his army that the crossings of the Marne had been opened to the other armies, and "it is now to be hoped that every advantage will be taken of this success." Becoming angrier as he dictated, Kluck demanded to know how it was that "decisive victories" by the "other" armies—meaning Bülow—were always followed by "appeals for support."

Bülow was furious when his neighbor transformed "the echelon in rear of the Second Army prescribed by OHL into an echelon in advance." His troops, too, like most of the German units as they came up to the Marne, were exhausted. "We can do no more," wrote an officer of the Xth Reserve Corps. "The men fall in the ditches and lie there just to breathe. . . . The order comes to mount. I ride bent over with my head resting on the horse's mane. We are thirsty and hungry. Indifference comes over us. Such a life isn't worth much. To lose it is to lose little." Troops of Hausen's Army complained of having "no cooked food for five days in a row." In the neighboring Fourth Army an officer wrote: "We march all day in the broiling heat. With bearded faces and powdered with dust, the men look like walking sacks of flour." That the German advance was being achieved at the cost of the exhaustion and apathy of the troops did not alarm the field commanders. Like Kluck, they were convinced the French could not recoup. Bülow on September 3 reported the French Fifth Army "decisively beaten"—for the third or fourth time—and fleeing "utterly disorganized to south of the Marne."

If not "utterly disorganized," the Fifth Army was distinctly not in good shape. Lanrezac's loss of confidence in Joffre, which he took no trouble to conceal, his quarrels with liaison officers from GQG and his dispute of orders infected his staff, half of whom were at odds with the other half. All were irritated and worried with nerves strained by the long agony of bringing up the rear of the French retreat. General Mas de Latrie of the XVIIIth Corps, which was nearest to the enemy, was expressing "anguish" at the condition of his troops. But however battered, the Fifth Army had got across the Marne with enough distance between itself and the enemy to be considered disengaged, thus fulfilling Joffre's condition for resuming the offensive.

Although Joffre intended to make the effort "within a few days," as he informed the government, he was not specific, and discouragement at GQG was deep. Every day liaison officers returned depressed from their visits to the armies over whom, as one of them said, "blew the winds of defeat." Arrangements were being made to move GQG back another thirty miles to Chatillon-sur-Seine, and the move was carried out two days later, September 5. In ten days France had lost the cities of Lille, Valenciennes, Cambrai, Arras, Amiens, Maubeuge, Mézières, St. Quentin, Laon, and Soissons, as well as coal and iron mines, wheat and sugarbeet areas, and a sixth of her population. A pall descended upon everyone when Rheims, in whose great cathedral every French king from Clovis to Louis XVI had been crowned, was abandoned as an open city to Bülow's Army on September 3. It was not until two weeks later, in the angry aftermath of the Marne, that the bombardment took place which was to make the cathedral of Rheims a symbol to the world like the Library of Louvain.

Joffre who had still shown no sign of nerves, whose appetite for three regular meals remained steady and his ten o'clock bedtime inviolable, faced on September 3 the one task that during this period caused him visible discomfort. He had made up his mind that Lanrezac must go. His stated reasons were Lanrezac's "physical and moral depression" and his "unpleasant personal relations," by now notorious, with Sir John French. For the sake of the coming offensive in which the role of the Fifth Army would be crucial and participation by the British essential, he must be replaced. Despite Lanrezac's firm conduct of the battle of Guise, Joffre had convinced himself that since then Lanrezac had "morally gone to pieces." Besides, he never ceased criticizing and raising objections to orders. This was not necessarily evidence of moral depression, but it annoyed the Generalissimo.

With few personal ideas of his own, Joffre was adept at taking advice, and submitted more or less consciously to the reigning doctrinaires of the Operations Bureau. They formed what a French military critic called "a church outside which there was no salvation and which could never pardon those who revealed the falsity of its doctrine." Lanrezac's sin was in having been right, all too vocally. He had been right from the beginning about the fatal underestimation of the German right wing as a result of which a fair part of France was now under the German boot. His decision to break off battle at Charleroi when threatened with double envelopment by Bülow's and Hausen's armies had saved the French left wing. As General von Hausen acknowledged after the war, this upset the whole German plan which had counted on enveloping the French left, and ultimately caused Kluck's inward wheel in the effort to roll up the Fifth Army. Whether Lanrezac's withdrawal came from fear or from wisdom is immaterial, for fear sometimes *is* wisdom and in this case had made possible the renewed effort Joffre was now preparing. All this was to be recognized long afterward when the French government, in a belated gesture of amends, awarded Lanrezac the Grand Cordon of the Legion of Honor. But in the bitter failure of the first month Lanrezac's *lèse majesté* made him intolerable to GQG. On the day he brought his army across the Marne, he was marked for the Tarpeian Rock.

Lanrezac's mood, after all that had passed, was in reality not the most reliable; unquestionably the mutual distrust between him and GQG, whose so ever the fault, and between him and Sir John French made him a risk as a commander in time of crisis. Joffre felt it necessary to take every possible measure to avoid failure in the coming offensive. Including his dismissals of the next two days, Joffre in the first five weeks stripped the French Army of two army commanders, ten corps commanders and thirty-eight, or half the total number of, divisional generals. New and mostly better men, including three future Marshals, Foch, Pétain, and Franchet d'Esperey, moved up to fill their places. If some injustices were committed, the army was improved.

Joffre set out in his car for Sézanne where Fifth Army Headquarters was located that day. At a prearranged meeting place he conferred with Franchet d'Esperey, commander of the Ist Corps who turned up with his head wrapped in a bath towel because of the heat.

"Do you feel yourself capable of commanding an army?" Joffre asked.

"As well as anyone else," replied Franchet d'Esperey. When Joffre simply looked at him, he shrugged and explained: "The higher one goes, the easier. One gets a bigger staff; there are more people to help." That being settled, Joffre drove on.

At Sézanne he retired alone with Lanrezac and said to him: "My friend, you are used up and undecided. You will have to give up command of the Fifth Army. I hate to tell you this but I have to." According to Joffre, Lanrezac thought for a moment and replied, "General, you are right," and seemed like a man relieved of an overwhelming burden. According to Lanrezac's own account, he protested vigorously and demanded that Joffre cite evidence, but Joffre would only repeat "Hesitant, undecided," and complain that Lanrezac always made "observations" on orders given him. Lanrezac said this could hardly be held against him since events proved all his observations correct, which, of course, was the trouble. But Joffre was obviously not listening. He made "facial expressions indicating I had worn out his patience and his eyes refused to meet mine." Lanrezac gave up the struggle. Joffre emerged from the interview looking, according to his aide-de-camp, "very nervous," a unique occasion.

Franchet d'Esperey was now sent for. Called from his dinner at the first mouthful of soup, he stood up, swallowed off a glass of wine, put on his coat, and left for Sézanne. Held up by a transfer of military supplies taking place unhurriedly at a crossroad, he jumped from his car. So well known in the army was his compact hard figure with a head like a howitzer shell, crew-cut hair, piercing dark eyes, and sharp authoritarian voice, that the men, horses, and vehicles parted as if by magic. In the coming days, as tension and his temper rose, his method of dealing with road-blocks as he dashed from corps to corps was to fire his revolver out of the window of his car. To the British soldiers he eventually became known as "Desperate Frankey." Fellow officers found him transformed from the jovial and friendly, though strict, commander they had known, to a tyrant. He became fierce, peremptory, glacial, and imposed a reign of terror upon his staff no less than upon the troops. Hardly had Lanrezac handed over to him the confidential dossier and relinquished command at Sézanne when the telephone rang and Hély d'Oissel, who answered it, was heard repeating "Yes, General. No, General," with increasing irritation.

"Who's that?" rapped out Franchet d'Esperey, and was told it was General Mas de Latrie of the XVIIIth Corps insisting he could not carry out orders for the next day because of the extreme fatigue of his troops.

"I'll take it," said the new Commander. "Hello, this is General d'Esperey. I have taken over command of the Fifth Army. There is to be no more discussion. You will march; march or drop dead." And he hung up.

September 4 opened with a sense of climax felt in widely separated places; a kind of extra-sensory awareness that great events sometimes send ahead. In Paris, Gallieni felt this was the "decisive" day. In Berlin, Princess Blücher wrote in her diary, "Nothing is talked of but the expected entry into Paris." In Brussels the leaves had begun to fall, and a sudden wind blew them in gusts about the street. People felt the hidden chill of autumn in the air and wondered what would happen if the war were to last through the winter. At the American Legation Hugh Gibson noted a "growing nervousness" at German Headquarters where there had been no announcements of victories in four days. "I am sure there is something big in the air today."

At OHL in Luxembourg tension was at a pitch as the triumphant moment of German history approached. Stretched to the snapping point of endurance, the army was about to complete upon the Marne the work begun at Sadowa and Sedan. "It is the 35th day," said the Kaiser with triumph in his voice to a visiting minister from Berlin. "We invest Rheims, we are 30 miles from Paris. . . ."

At the front the German Armies thought of the final battle in terms of a roundup rather than a combat. "Great news," recorded an officer of the Fifth Army in his diary, "the French have offered us an armistice and are prepared to pay an indemnity of 17 billions. For the time being," he added soberly, "the armistice is being refused."

The enemy was considered beaten, and any evidence to the contrary was unwelcome. A horrid doubt entered the mind of General von Kuhl, Kluck's Chief of Staff, upon the report of a French column near Château-Thierry singing as it marched in retreat. He suppressed his doubts, "as all orders for the new movement had already been given." Apart from a few such instances there was no suspicion, or none that made itself felt upon command decisions, that the enemy was preparing a counter-offensive. Although signs were visible, German Intelligence, operating in hostile territory, failed to pick them up. An Intelligence officer from OHL came to the Crown Prince's headquarters on September 4 to say that the situation was favorable all along the front and that "We are advancing triumphantly everywhere."

One man did not think so. Moltke, unlike Joffre, may have had no confidence in his own star but neither did he have the veil that confidence can sometimes draw before the eyes, and so he saw things without illusion. In this he resembled Lanrezac. On September 4 he was "serious and depressed," and said to Helfferich, the same minister who had just talked to the Kaiser, "We have hardly a horse in the army who can go another step." After a thoughtful pause he went on: "We must not deceive ourselves. We have had success but not victory. Victory means annihilation of the enemy's power of resistance. When a million men oppose each other in battle the victor has prisoners. Where are our prisoners? Twenty thousand in Lorraine, perhaps another ten or twenty thousand altogether. And from the comparatively small number of guns captured, it seems to me the French are conducting a planned and orderly retreat." The inadmissible thought had been spoken.

On that day Kluck's message that he was about to cross the Marne finally reached OHL, too late to stop the movement. The flank Kluck thus exposed to Paris worried Moltke. Reports were coming in of heavy railroad traffic in the direction of

Paris, "apparently the movement of troops." Rupprecht on that day reported the withdrawal of two French corps from his front. It was impossible any longer to avoid the evidence that the enemy's power of resistance had not come to an end.

The transfer of French troops, as Colonel Tappen pointed out, could mean "an attack from Paris upon our right flank for which we had no available reserves." This was a problem of which Moltke, as well as the field commanders, was painfully conscious. Losses sustained in the continuing combats with the French rearguards during the retreat could not be made up by reserves as the French were doing. The holes in the German lines remained and the two corps sent to East Prussia were missed. Moltke was now ready to take reinforcements from the left wing even though Rupprecht had just launched a renewed attack on the Moselle on September 3. It happened that the Kaiser was at Rupprecht's headquarters when Moltke's proposal came through. Certain that this time, at last, the defense of Nancy would be broken, the Kaiser stoutly supported Rupprecht and von Krafft in opposing any diminution of their strength. A man other than Moltke might have insisted, but Moltke did not. Since the unnerving night of August 1, the uncertainties and stresses of the campaign had weakened rather than strengthened his will. Failing reinforcements for the right wing, he decided to halt it.

The new Order, addressed to all the armies, which was drafted that night and issued early next morning, was an open admission of failure of the right wing, failure of the design for victory to which Germany had sacrificed the neutrality of Belgium. Dated September 4, a month from the day Belgium was invaded, it was an accurate appraisal of the situation. "The enemy," it said, "has evaded the enveloping attack of the First and Second Armies and a part of his forces has joined up with the forces of Paris." Enemy troops were being withdrawn from the Moselle front and moved westward "probably in order to concentrate superior forces in the region of Paris and threaten the right flank of the German Army." In consequence "the First and Second Armies must remain facing the eastern front of Paris . . . to act against any operation of the enemy from that area." The Third Army was to continue a southward advance to the Seine and the other armies to carry on under the previous order of September 2.

To halt the marching wing on the very threshhold of victory seemed stark madness to the War Minister, General von Falkenhayn, who within two weeks was to be Moltke's successor as Commander in Chief. "Only one thing is certain," he wrote in his diary for September 5. "Our General Staff has completely lost its head. Schlieffen's notes do not help any further so Moltke's wits come to an end." It was not Moltke's wits but German time that was running out. In the French troop movements Moltke correctly saw a danger developing upon his outer flank and took a proper and sensible measure to meet it. His Order had only one flaw: it was late. Even then it might have been in time had it not been for one man in a hurry—Gallieni.

Reports of the Paris aviators, at daybreak on September 4, showed him it was "vital to act quickly." The rear of Kluck's curved march to the southeast presented a clear target to Maunoury's Army and to the British if a joint attack could be launched in time. At 9:00 A.M., before obtaining Joffre's consent, he sent preliminary orders to Maunoury: "My intention is to send your army forward in liaison with the English forces against the German flank. Make your arrangements at once so that your troops will be ready to march this afternoon as the start of a general movement eastward by the forces of the Paris camp." As soon as he could Maunoury was to come to confer personally in Paris.

Gallieni then set himself to obtain an "immediate and energetic" decision from Joffre. Between them lay the remnants of an old relationship as commander and subordinate. Both were conscious of Gallieni's official designation as Commander in Chief if anything happened to Joffre. Aware that Joffre resisted and resented his influence, Gallieni counted less on persuading him than on forcing his hand. To that end he had already called Poincaré in Bordeaux to say he thought there was a "good opening" for resuming the offensive at once.

At 9:45 he put through a call to GQG, the first of a series of which he was later to say, "The real battle of the Marne was fought on the telephone." General Clergerie conducted the conversation with Colonel Pont, Chief of Operations, as Gallieni would not talk to anyone less than Joffre and Joffre would not come to the phone. He had an aversion to the instrument and used to pretend he "did not understand the mechanism." His real reason was that, like all men in high position, he had an eye on history and was afraid that things said over the telephone would be taken down without his being able to control the record.

Clergerie explained the plan to launch the Sixth Army and all available forces of the Paris camp in an attack on Kluck's flank, preferably north of the Marne, in which case contact could be made on September 6; alternatively on the south bank which would require a day's delay to allow Maunoury to cross over. In either case Clergerie asked for an order to put the Sixth Army on the march that evening. He urged Gallieni's belief that the moment had come to end the retreat and return the whole army to the offensive in combination with the Paris maneuver. GQG was left to come to a decision.

Contrary to GQG's willingness to sacrifice the capital, Gallieni from the beginning was motivated by the conviction that Paris must be defended and held. He viewed the front from the point of view of Paris and with no direct knowledge of the situation of the field armies. He was determined to seize the opportunity Kluck's swerve offered him, believing that his own move must and would precipitate a general offensive. It was a bold, even a rash, design, for without fully knowing the situation of the other armies he could not fairly judge the chances of success. Gallieni did not think there was a choice. It may be he had a great commander's instinctive feel for his moment; it is more likely he felt France would not have another.

At 11:00 A.M. Maunoury arrived for briefing; no answer had yet come from Joffre. At noon Clergerie telephoned again.

Meanwhile in the school at Bar-sur-Aube where GQG was installed, officers of the Operations staff, crowding in front of the wall map, animately discussed Gallieni's proposal for a combined offensive. The terrible trampling of French military hopes in the past month had instilled caution in the hearts of some. Others were as fervent apostles of the offensive as ever and had an answer for every counsel of caution. Joffre was present, listening to their arguments recorded by his aide-de-camp, Captain Muller. "Troops at the end of their strength? No matter, they are Frenchmen and tired of retreating. The moment they hear the order to advance they will forget their fatigue. A gap between the Armies of Foch and de Langle? It will be filled by the XXIst Corps coming from Dubail's Army. Unpreparedness of the armies to attack? Ask the field commanders; you will see how they will answer. Cooperation of the English? Ah, that's more serious. One cannot give their Commander orders; one has to negotiate, and time is short. But the important thing is to seize the occasion, for it is fugitive. Kluck can still repair his mistake, and the movements of the Sixth Army will certainly draw his attention to the dangers to which he has exposed himself."

Without having contributed a word, Joffre went to consult Berthelot in his office and found him opposed to the plan. The Armies could not suddenly face about, he argued. They should complete the planned retreat to a strong defensive line and allow the Germans to penetrate more deeply into the net. Above all, the numerical superiority which was wanted could not be achieved until the two corps coming from the Lorraine front had time to come into position.

Silent, astride a straw-bottomed chair facing Berthelot's wall map, Joffre considered the problem. His plan for an ultimate return to the offensive had always included using the Sixth Army in an attack on the enemy's right flank. Gallieni, however, was precipitating matters. Joffre wanted the extra day for the reinforcements to come up, for the Fifth Army to prepare, and for more time in which to secure the cooperation of the British. When Clergerie's second call came through, he was told that the Commander in Chief preferred attack on the south bank of the Marne, and when Clergerie demurred about the delay he was told "the delay of a day will mean more forces available."

Joffre now faced the greater decision: whether to carry out the planned retreat to the Seine or seize the opportunity—and the risk—and face the enemy now. The heat was overpowering. Joffre went outside and sat down in the shade of a weeping ash in the school playground. By nature an arbiter, he collected the opinions of others, sorted them, weighed the personal coefficient of the speaker, adjusted the scale, and eventually announced his verdict. The decision was always his. If it succeeded his would be the glory; if it failed he would be held responsible. In the problem now before him the fate of France was at stake. During the past thirty days the French Army had failed in the great task for which it had been preparing for the past thirty years. Its last chance to save France, to prove her again the France of 1792, was now. The invader was forty miles from where Joffre sat and barely twenty from the nearest French Army. Senlis and Creil, after Kluck's Army had passed over, were in flames and the Mayor of Senlis dead. If the French turned now before the armies were ready—and failed?

The immediate requirement was to find out whether they could be made ready. As the Fifth Army was in a crucial position, Joffre sent a message to Franchet d'Esperey: "It may be advantageous to give battle tomorrow or the day after with all the forces of the Fifth Army in concert with the British and the mobile forces of Paris against the German First and Second Armies. Please advise whether your army is in a condition to do this with a chance of success. Reply immediately." A similar query was sent to Foch who stood next to Franchet d'Esperey and opposite Bülow.

Joffre continued to sit and think under the tree. For most of the afternoon the ponderous figure in black tunic, baggy red pants, and army-issue boots from which, to the despair of his aides, he had banished the affectation of spurs, remained silent and motionless.

Meanwhile Gallieni, taking Maunoury with him, left Paris at one o'clock to drive to British Headquarters at Melun on the Seine, twenty-five miles to the south. In response to his request for British support he had received a negative reply from Huguet who reported that Sir John French "adopts the counsels of prudence of his Chief of Staff," Sir Archibald Murray, and would not join an offensive unless the French guaranteed defense of the lower Seine between the British and the sea. Driving past the lines of southbound cars fleeing Paris, the two French generals reached British Headquarters at three o'clock. Kilted sentinels presented arms smartly; soldiers were busily typing indoors; but neither the Field Marshal nor his principal officers could be found, and the Staff appeared "confounded" by the situation. After a prolonged search Murray was located.

Sir John French, he said, was away inspecting the troops; he could give no idea when he was expected to return.

Gallieni tried to explain his plan of attack and why British participation was "indispensable," but he could feel all the while the Englishman's "great reluctance to share our views." Murray kept repeating that the BEF was under the formal orders of its Commander in Chief to rest, reorganize, and await reinforcements, and he could do nothing until his return. After more than two hours of discussion during which Sir John French still did not appear, Gallieni succeeded in persuading Murray to write down a summary of the plan of attack and proposals for joint British action which "he did not appear to understand very well." Before leaving he secured a promise that Murray would notify him the moment his Chief returned.

At the same time another Anglo-French conference was taking place thirty-five miles up the Seine at Bray from which Sir John French was also absent. Anxious to repair the frayed relations left by Lanrezac, Franchet d'Esperey had arranged for a meeting with the Field Marshal at Bray at three o'clock. He wore for the occasion the ribbon of a Knight Commander of the Victorian Order. On reaching Bray his car was stopped by a French sentinel who reported an urgent message waiting for the General at the telegraph office. It was Joffre's query about the coming battle. Studying it, Franchet d'Esperey strode up and down the street, waiting in growing impatience for the British. After fifteen minutes a Rolls-Royce drove up with an "enormous Highlander" next to the chauffeur, but instead of the florid little Field Marshal in the back seat, "a tall devil, very ugly with an intelligent, expressive face" emerged. It was Wilson who was accompanied by the British Chief of Intelligence, Colonel Macdonogh. They had been delayed on the way when, seeing a Parisian lady in distress by the roadside Wilson gallantly took time to provide gas for her car and maps for her chauffeur.

The group retired to a room on the second floor of the Mairie with the Highlander posted as sentinel outside. Macdonogh lifted a heavy cloth to peer under the table, opened a door leading to an adjoining bedroom, looked under the bed, punched the quilt, opened the closet, and sounded the walls with his fist. Then, in answer to a question from Franchet d'Esperey about the situation of the British Army, he unfolded a map showing the exact positions, marked in blue arrows, of the enemy on his front and gave a masterly analysis of the movements of the German First and Second Armies. Franchet d'Esperey was impressed.

"You are our ally—I shall keep no secrets from you," he said, and read aloud Joffre's proposal. "I am going to answer that my army is prepared to attack," and, fixing his visitors with eyes of steel, "I hope you will not oblige us to do it alone. It is essential that you fill the space between the Fifth and Sixth Armies." He then outlined a precise plan of action which he had worked out in his head in the brief quarter-hour since receiving the telegram. It was based on the assumption, arrived at independently, of attack by Maunoury's Army north of the Marne on September 6. Wilson, concerting again with an energetic French general as he once had with Foch, readily agreed. Disposition of the two armies, the given line each was to reach by morning of September 6, and the direction of attack were decided. Wilson warned there would be difficulty in obtaining consent from Sir John French and especially from Murray, but promised to do his best. He left for Melun while Franchet d'Esperey sent a report of their agreement to Joffre.

At Bar-sur-Aube, Joffre rose from under his shade tree. Without waiting for the replies of Franchet d'Esperey and Foch, he had made up his mind. He walked into the Operations Bureau and ordered an Instruction drafted "to extend the local action envisaged by the Paris garrison to all the forces of the Allied left." Action was to begin on September 7. Instantly a great calm succeeded feverish discussion. The retreat was over. The moment to turn had come. Everyone fell to work preparing the detailed orders. To reduce the risk of leaks to the enemy it was decided not to issue the orders until the last possible moment.

It was then six o'clock, and at six-thirty Joffre went in to dinner to which he had invited two Japanese officers. While at table word was quietly whispered to him that Franchet d'Esperey had persuaded the British to join an offensive; important papers had arrived from the Fifth Army. Meals were sacred and international courtesy no less, especially as the

Allies were engaged at the time in optimistic negotiations for Japanese military assistance in Europe. Joffre could not interrupt dinner but he committed the impropriety of "hurrying through" it. When he read Franchet d'Esperey's crisp answer it was like being pushed into water and forced to swim. In a tone hardly less abrupt than his "march or drop dead," D'Esperey laid down the precise times, places, and conditions of battle by the three armies, Fifth, Sixth, and British. It could open on September 6; the British Army would "execute a change of direction" on condition that its left was supported by the Sixth Army; the Sixth must reach a certain line along the Ourcq at a certain time, "if not the British will not march"; the Fifth would continue its retreat next day until south of the Grand Morin and be in position on the day after for frontal attack upon Kluck's Army while the British and Maunoury attacked his flank. "Vigorous participation" by Foch's Army against the German Second Army was a necessary condition.

"My army can fight on September 6," Franchet d'Esperey concluded, "but is not in brilliant condition." This was a bare statement of the truth. When later Franchet d'Esperey told General Hache of the IIIrd Corps that attack was set for next morning, Hache "looked as if he had been hit on the head with a club."

"It's mad!" he protested. "The troops are exhausted. They don't sleep or eat—they've been marching and fighting for two weeks! We need arms, ammunition, equipment. Everything is in terrible shape. Morale is bad. I've had to replace two generals of division. The Staff is worth nothing and good for nothing. If we had time to refit behind the Seine. . . ."

Like Gallieni, d'Esperey believed there was no choice. His immediate and bold response, like Gallieni's, proved a deciding factor and one that probably would not have been forthcoming from his predecessor. Other unreliable commanders were also weeded out. General Mas de Latrie was removed that day to be replaced by the dashing General de Maud'huy, taken from Castelnau's Army. By now the Fifth Army had undergone the replacement of its commander, 3 out of 5 corps commanders, 7 out of 13 divisional generals, and a proportionate number of generals of brigade.

Encouraged by the "intelligent audacity" of d'Esperey's

reply, Joffre told the Operations Staff to make the battle orders conform to his conditions of place, although retaining September 7 as the date. He received an equally affirmative reply from Foch who announced himself simply as "ready to attack."

Henry Wilson on reaching British Headquarters found a dismaying answer. Murray, without even waiting for the return of Sir John French, had issued orders for a further retreat of ten to fifteen miles in a southwesterly direction to begin that night—"It is simply heartbreaking." Wilson also found Murray's memorandum of Gallieni's plan. He immediately sent off a wire to Paris saying, "Marshal not yet returned" and reporting the proposed retreat. He seems not to have reported it to d'Esperey, perhaps in the hope of persuading Sir John French to cancel it.

When Sir John returned, he walked into an unnerving confusion of plans and proposals. There was a letter from Joffre written prior to the day's events, proposing British action on the Seine; there was Gallieni's proposal to Murray; there was Wilson's agreement with Franchet d'Esperey; and there was Murray himself earnestly whispering retreat. Bewildered by so many calls for action, and unable to decide which took precedence over what, Sir John took refuge in no action at all. He let Murray's orders stand and informed Huguet for the benefit of all French petitioners that, "owing to the continual changes," he preferred to "restudy the situation before deciding on action."

At about the same hour Gallieni returned to Paris from Melun. He found Wilson's telegram and also one from Joffre sent at 12:20 P.M. confirming the preference expressed over the phone at noon that Maunoury's attack should take place south of the Marne on September 7. This was not new, but together with Wilson's message it seems to have had decisive effect on Gallieni. Time was escaping and Kluck advancing. He saw his moment slipping away, and determined to force the issue. This time he called GQG himself. Joffre tried to evade him by putting Belin on the telephone, but Gallieni insisted on speaking personally to the Generalissimo. According to a record of the conversation made by Joffre's aide-de-camp, Gallieni said, "The Sixth Army had made arrangements to attack north of the Marne and it appeared to him impossible to modify the general direction to which the army was already committed, and he insisted that the attack should be launched without any change in the conditions of time and place already laid down."

Confronted voice to voice by his former superior, Joffre may have felt again the moral authority that a man of Gallieni's commanding temperament exerted. Or, as he afterward claimed, he may have felt forced, though "unwillingly," to advance the general offensive to an earlier day for fear that Maunoury's movements, precipitated by Gallieni, would disclose the whole French maneuver to the enemy. He had assurances of readiness to fight from both Foch and Franchet d'Esperey and he thought the latter, by the spell of his magic energy, had secured a similar commitment from the British. He did not know it had become unpinned. In any event he authorized or acquiesced in attack by the Sixth Army north of the Marne and agreed to begin general action on September 6, "as Gallieni desired." Gallieni instantly, at 8:30 P.M., confirmed his marching orders to Maunoury, who was already moving. At GQG the staff revised the positions of attack to suit the advanced date. At 10:00 P.M., two hours after Moltke signed the Order halting the German right-wing, Joffre signed General Order No. 6.

"The time has come," it began in full consciousness of a historic moment, "to profit by the adventurous position of the German First Army and concentrate against that army all efforts of the Allied Armies of the extreme left." Movements prescribed for the Sixth, Fifth, and British Armies were those of Franchet d'Esperey's reply. Separate orders to join the offensive were issued to the Third and Fourth Armies.

The night was not over. Hardly was the Order signed when word came from Huguet of Sir John French's refusal to ratify any plan for joint action and of his desire to "restudy" the situation. Joffre was stunned. The momentous decision had been taken; orders were on their way; in thirty-six hours the battle to save France would begin. The ally whose participation had been planned for the sake, as Foch once said, of a single dead British soldier, but who had been left by a trick of fate holding a vital place in the line, was backing out once again. Because of the time required for encoding and dispatching, the orders were not intended to reach the armies until next morning. As the only means of persuasion he could think of, Joffre sent a special copy of Order No. 6 by personal messenger to British Headquarters. When the officer reached Melun at 3:00 A.M., the three corps of the BEF had already begun the night march of retreat ordered by Murray that afternoon.

The enemy, too, at dawn of September 5 was on the march too soon. Thrusting forward in his effort to roll up the French flank, Kluck already had his army on the roads before Moltke's orders to turn and face the danger on his flank arrived by wireless at 7:00 A.M. Four corps, spread out over thirty miles of country, were headed for the Grand Morin. Kluck did not stop them. He either did not believe or did not heed the warning about a French concentration of troops on his flank. Assuming that the German Armies "were everywhere advancing victoriously along the whole front"—it was the Germans' habit to believe their own communiqués—he did not think the enemy could have forces available to threaten his flank. He, too, had begun to notice signs that the French retreat was perhaps not altogether disorganized and so felt it all the more urgent that no letup of pressure should give the enemy time to halt and "regain freedom of maneuver as well as offensive spirit." Disdaining Moltke's directive, Kluck advanced with his army, moving his own headquarters twenty-five miles forward to Rebais between the two Morins. By evening troops of the German First Army reached a line within ten to fifteen miles of the BEF and Franchet d'Esperey's Army, with outposts less than five miles apart. It was to be their last day of advance.

A representative from OHL with plenary powers came to Kluck's headquarters that evening. With unhappy experience both of wireless and Kluck's temperament, Moltke sent his Chief of Intelligence, Colonel Hentsch, on a 175-mile drive from Luxembourg to explain in person the reasons for the new Order and to see that it was carried out. To their "amazement," Kluck and his staff learned that Rupprecht's Armies were held up in a deadlocked battle before the French fortress line, as was the Crown Prince's Army before Verdun. Colonel Hentsch described the evidence of French troop movements which had led OHL to calculate that "very strong enemy forces" were being shifted westward in a threat to the German flank. It was under these circumstances that OHL dictated the horrid necessity of retirement. The First Army must return north of the Marne. Though it was little consolation, Colonel Hentsch said "the movement could be made at leisure; no special haste was necessary."

Disturbing confirmation came from the IVth Reserve Corps which had been left as flank guard north of the Marne. It reported encountering and engaging in combat an enemy force of at least two and a half divisions supported by heavy artillery. This was, of course, part of Maunoury's Army moving forward toward the Ourcq. Although the French attack was "successfully repulsed," the Commander of the IVth Reserve had ordered a retreat as soon as it was dark.

Kluck gave in. The extra distance he had dragged his army forward in the last two days since crossing the Marne had now to be retraced. Orders were drafted to begin the retirement of two corps next morning, September 6, with the others following later. After the march he had made from Liège to a level with Paris, it was a bitter moment. If he had stayed in echelon behind Bülow as ordered, if he had even halted his army that morning at seven o'clock, he would have been in position to face the threat to his flank with his whole army together. According to General Kuhl, his Chief of Staff, "Neither OHL nor the First Army Staff had the remotest idea that an immediate offensive by the whole French Army was imminent. . . . Not a sign, not a word from prisoners, not a newspaper paragraph gave warning." If Kluck did not know what lay ahead, there was one thing he could not help but know: to break off pursuit and pull back now, with four days left of the German schedule, was not a prelude to victory.

September 5 seemed a darker day to the Allies. With nothing but defeats so far, their representatives met in London that morning to sign the Pact binding each other "not to conclude any separate peace in the course of the present war."

In Paris, Maunoury asked Gallieni, "In case we should be overwhelmed, our line of retreat will be . . . ?" His eyes clouding over, Gallieni answered, "Nowhere." Preparing for possible disaster, he issued secret orders to each regional commander of the Paris camp to report all resources in his district which must be destroyed rather than fall into the hands of the enemy. Even bridges in the heart of the city like the Pont Neuf and the Pont Alexandre were to be blown up. "A void" must be left in front of the enemy in case he should break through, he told General Hirschauer.

At GQG a report from Castelnau was received which seemed to threaten disaster even before the offensive could begin. Pressure was so severe that he felt he might be forced to evacuate Nancy. Joffre ordered him to hold for another twenty-four hours before making a decision, but agreed that if it then seemed unavoidable, he approved the second line of defense suggested in Castelnau's letter.

In transferring one corps from the Third Army and two corps from the Moselle front, Joffre had taken a grave risk in order to gain this time the numerical superiority which he had not had for the opening offensive. The reinforcements were not yet in the battle line. When it came to informing the government of the decision to fight, Joffre carefully included an alibi for himself in case of failure. His telegram to the President and Premier said, "Gallieni having attacked prematurely, I have given the order to suspend the retreat and, in my turn, resume the offensive." Afterward, at a time when Joffre was systematically trying to minimize Gallieni's role at the Marne and even expunge certain things from the records, this telegram was unearthed by Briand and shown to Gallieni. "That 'prematurely' is worth gold," he said.

On the morning of September 5 Joffre's uncertainty about British intentions became "altogether agonizing." He begged Millerand by telegram to exert the government's influence. The imminent battle "can have decisive results but in case of a reverse can also have the gravest consequences for the country. . . . I count on you to call the Field Marshal's attention to the decisive importance of an offensive without *arrière-pensée*. If I could give orders to the English Army as I could to the French Army in the same position, I would pass immediately to the attack."

At three o'clock that morning Henry Wilson received Order No. 6 from Huguet who, however, did not permit Captain de Galbert, the officer who brought it, to see any of the British chiefs. At the center of every discord during this period, with a curiously malign consistency, the figure of Huguet appears.

Deciding that the situation required someone of higher rank, Captain de Galbert started back at once for GQG. At 7:00 A.M. Wilson took the Order to Sir John French and during the course of the morning persuaded him to cooperate. Meanwhile de Galbert arrived back at GQG at 9:30 with no definite news but with a report that British sentiment seemed "lukewarm" toward an offensive. The Mayor of Melun had told him Sir John French's baggage was being moved back to Fontainebleau.

Joffre felt he must have the British Army in the battle line "at any price," even at the price of motoring the 115 miles to Melun. Sending a telephone message ahead to expect him, he set out with his aide and two staff officers. Despite roadblocks and the ineluctable stop for lunch, his racing chauffeur brought him to the château where Sir John French was quartered by 2:00 P.M.

The Field Marshal was standing at a table waiting for him flanked by Murray, Wilson, Huguet, "looking as usual as if he had lost his last friend," and several other members of his staff. Joffre walked over and for once took the floor at the outset. Instead of his usual laconic sentences, a passionate flood of speech poured forth punctuated by a gesture of his forearms which "seemed to throw his heart on the table." He said the "supreme moment" had arrived, his own orders were given and whatever happened the last company of the French Army would be thrown into the battle to save France. The "lives of all French people, the soil of France, the future of Europe" depended upon the offensive. "I cannot believe the British Army will refuse to do its share in this supreme crisis . . . history would severely judge your absence."

Joffre's fist crashed down on the table. "*Monsieur le Maréchal*, the honor of England is at stake!"

At these words Sir John French, who had been listening with "passionate attention," suddenly reddened. Silence fell on the company. Slowly tears came into the eyes of the British Commander in Chief and rolled down his cheeks. He struggled to say something in French and gave up. "Damn it, I can't explain. Tell him we will do all we possibly can."

Joffre looked inquiringly at Wilson who translated, "The Field Marshal says 'Yes.'" It was hardly needed, for the tears and the tone already carried conviction. Murray hurriedly put in that the British troops were now ten miles farther back than the positions called for in the Order and could start only at 9:00 A.M., not 6:00, as Joffre asked. It was a voice of caution that would continue to make itself felt. Joffre shrugged. "It cannot be helped. I have the Field Marshal's word, that is enough." Tea was then served.

The move of GQG to Chatillon-sur-Seine, planned before the offensive, had been accomplished during his absence. Joffre returned there by evening, about the time Colonel Hentsch was warning von Kluck. Entering the Operations Room to confirm a decision already taken, Joffre said to the assembled officers, "Gentlemen, we will fight on the Marne."

He signed the order that would be read to the troops when the bugles blew next morning. Ordinarily the French language, especially in public pronouncements, requires an effort if it is not to sound splendid, but this time the words were flat, almost tired; the message hard and uncompromising: "Now, as the battle is joined on which the safety of the country depends, everyone must be reminded that this is no longer the time for looking back. Every effort must be made to attack and throw back the enemy. A unit which finds it impossible to advance must, regardless of cost, hold its ground and be killed on the spot rather than fall back. In the present circumstances no failure will be tolerated."

That was all; the time for splendor was past. It did not shout "Forward!" or summon men to glory. After the first thirty days of war in 1914, there was a premonition that little glory lay ahead.

Afterword

THE BATTLE of the Marne, as all the world knows, ended in a German retreat. Between the Ourcq and the Grand Morin, in the four days that were left of their schedule, the Germans lost their bid for "decisive victory" and thereby their opportunity to win the war. For France, for the Allies, in the long run for the world, the tragedy of the Marne was that it fell short of the victory it might have been.

Maunoury's attack on the German flank and von Kluck's turnabout to meet it opened a gap between the German First and Second Armies. The issue of the battle depended on whether the Germans could succeed in crushing the two wings —Maunoury and Foch—before Franchet d'Esperey and the British succeeded in exploiting the gap and pushing through the German center. Maunoury, when almost defeated by Kluck, was reinforced by the IVth Corps, of whom 6,000 detraining in Paris were rushed to the front by Gallieni in taxis, and managed to hold his ground. Foch, pressed hard in the Marshes of St. Gond by Hausen's Army and part of Bülow's, at a critical moment when his right was driven back and his left ceding, gave his famous order, "Attack, whatever happens! The Germans are at the extreme limit of their efforts. . . . Victory will come to the side that outlasts the other!" Franchet d'Esperey pushed back Bülow's right; the British entered the gap too slowly and hesitantly; Colonel Hentsch made his historic reappearance to counsel retreat, and the German Armies withdrew in time to avoid a piercing of their line.

So close had the Germans come to victory, so near the French to disaster, so great, in the preceding days, had been the astonished dismay of the world as it watched the relentless advance of the Germans and the retreat of the Allies on Paris, that the battle that turned the tide came to be known as the Miracle of the Marne. Henri Bergson, who had once formulated for France the *mystique* of "will," saw in it something of a miracle that had happened once before: "Joan of Arc won the Battle of the Marne," was his verdict. The enemy, suddenly halted as if by a stone wall springing up overnight, felt it too.

"French *élan*, just when it is on the point of being extinguished, flames up powerfully," wrote Moltke sorrowfully to his wife during the battle. The basic reason for German failure at the Marne, "the reason that transcends all others," said Kluck afterward, was "the extraordinary and peculiar aptitude of the French soldier to recover quickly. That men will let themselves be killed where they stand, that is a well-known thing and counted on in every plan of battle. But that men who have retreated for ten days, sleeping on the ground and half dead with fatigue, should be able to take up their rifles and attack when the bugle sounds, is a thing upon which we never counted. It was a possibility not studied in our war academy."

Bergson notwithstanding, it was no miracle but the inherent ifs, errors, and commitments of the first month that determined the issue at the Marne. Kluck notwithstanding, faults of German command contributed as much as the verve of the French soldier to the outcome. If the Germans had not withdrawn two corps to send against the Russians, one of the two would have been on Bülow's right and might have filled the gap between him and Kluck; the other would have been with Hausen and might have provided the extra strength to overwhelm Foch. Russia's loyal launching of an unready offensive drew those troops away and was given tribute by Colonel Dupont, French Chief of Intelligence. "Let us render to our Allies," he said, "the homage that is their due, for one of the elements of our victory was their debacle."

Other "ifs" accumulated. If the Germans had not committed too much strength to the attempt at double envelopment by the left wing, if the right wing had not outrun its supplies and exhausted its men, if Kluck had stayed level with Bülow, if, even on the last day, he had marched back across the Marne instead of forward to the Grand Morin, the decision of the Marne might have been different and the six-week schedule for victory over France achieved—might have been, that is, except for the first and decisive "if": if the six-week schedule itself had not been based on a march through Belgium. Quite apart from the effect upon the war as a whole of bringing Britain in, and the ultimate effect on world opinion, the addition of Belgium as an enemy reduced the number of German divisions that came up to the Marne and added five British divisions to the Allied line.

At the Marne the Allies achieved the numerical superiority they had not been able to muster at any one point in the Battle of the Frontiers. The missing German divisions were partly responsible, and the balance was tipped by the added French divisions drawn from the Third Army and from the embattled and unflinching armies of Castelnau and Dubail. All during the retreat while the other armies were giving ground, these two held shut the eastern door of France. For eighteen days they fought an almost continuous battle until, finally acknowledging failure too late, Moltke called off the attack on the French fortress line on September 8. If the French First and Second Armies had given way at any point, if they had weakened under Rupprecht's final onslaught of September 3, the Germans would have won their Cannae and there would have been no opportunity for a French counter-offensive on the Marne, the Seine, or anywhere else. If there was a miracle of the Marne, it was made possible on the Moselle.

Without Joffre no Allied line would have existed to bar the German path. It was his impregnable confidence during the tragic and terrible twelve days of retreat that prevented the French Armies from disintegrating into a shattered and fragmentary mass. A more brilliant, more quick-thinking commander with ideas of his own might have avoided basic initial errors, but after the debacle the one thing France needed Joffre had. It is difficult to imagine any other man who could have brought the French Armies out of retreat, in condition and position to fight again. When the moment to turn came, alone he would have been insufficient. The stand he contemplated at the Seine might well have come too late. It was Gallieni who saw the opportunity and, with a powerful assist from Franchet d'Esperey, provoked the earlier counter-offensive. It was the broken figure of Lanrezac, allowed no share at the Marne, who in saving France from the original folly of Plan 17 made recovery possible. Ironically, both his decision at Charleroi and his replacement by Franchet d'Esperey were equally necessary to the counter-offensive. But it was Joffre, whom nothing could panic, who provided the army to fight it. "If we had not had him in 1914," said Foch, his ultimate successor, "I don't know what would have become of us."

The world remembers the battle ever since by the taxis. A hundred of them were already in the service of the Military Government of Paris. With 500 more, each carrying five soldiers and making the sixty-kilometer trip to the Ourcq twice, General Clergerie figured he could transport 6,000 troops to the hard-pressed front. The order was issued at 1:00 P.M., the hour for departure fixed for 6:00 P.M. Police passed the word to the taxis in the streets. Enthusiastically the chauffeurs emptied out their passengers, explaining proudly that they had to "go to the battle." Returning to their garages for gas, they were ordered to the place of assembly where at the given time all 600 were lined up in perfect order. Gallieni, called to inspect them, though rarely demonstrative, was enchanted. "*Eh bien, voilà au moins qui n'est pas banal!*" (Well, here at least is something out of the ordinary!) he cried. Each with its burden of soldiers, with trucks, buses, and assorted vehicles added to the train, the taxis drove off, as evening fell—the last gallantry of 1914, the last crusade of the old world.

After the incomplete victory of the Marne there followed the German retreat to the Aisne, the race to the sea for possession of the Channel ports, the fall of Antwerp, and the Battle of Ypres where officers and men of the BEF held their ground, fought literally until they died, and stopped the Germans in Flanders. Not Mons or the Marne but Ypres was the real monument to British valor, as well as the grave of four-fifths of the original BEF. After it, with the advent of winter, came the slow deadly sinking into the stalemate of trench warfare. Running from Switzerland to the Channel like a gangrenous wound across French and Belgian territory, the trenches determined the war of position and attrition, the brutal, mud-filled, murderous insanity known as the Western Front that was to last for four more years.

The Schlieffen plan had failed, but it had succeeded far enough to leave the Germans in occupation of all of Belgium and all of northern France down to the Aisne. As Clemenceau's paper was tirelessly to remind its readers, month after month, year after year, "*Messieurs les Allemands sont toujours à Noyon.*" For their presence there, deep within France, the error of Plan

17 was responsible. It had allowed the enemy to penetrate too far to be dislodged by the time the French regathered their strength at the Marne. It permitted the breakthrough that could only be stemmed, and later only contained, at a cost of the terrible drain of French manhood that was to make the war of 1914–1918 the parent of 1940.* It was an error that could never be repaired. Failure of Plan 17 was as fatal as failure of the Schlieffen plan, and together they produced deadlock on the Western Front. Sucking up lives at a rate of 5,000 and sometimes 50,000 a day, absorbing munitions, energy, money, brains, and trained men, the Western Front ate up Allied war resources and predetermined the failure of back-door efforts like that of the Dardanelles which might otherwise have shortened the war. The deadlock, fixed by the failures of the first month, determined the future course of the war and, as a result, the terms of the peace, the shape of the interwar period, and the conditions of the Second Round.

Men could not sustain a war of such magnitude and pain without hope—the hope that its very enormity would ensure that it could never happen again and the hope that when

*In the chapel of St. Cyr (before it was destroyed during World War II) the memorial tablet to the dead of the Great War bore only a single entry for "the Class of 1914." The mortality rate is further illustrated by the experience of André Varagnac, a nephew of the cabinet minister Marcel Sembat, who came of military age in 1914 but was not mobilized in August owing to illness, and found himself, out of the twenty-seven boys in his lycée class, the only one alive by Christmas. According to *Armées Françaises*, French casualties in the month of August alone amounted to 206,515, including killed, wounded, and missing out of total effectives for the armies in the field of 1,600,000. As these figures do not include officers or garrison and Territorial divisions, the number is believed to be nearer 300,000. Most were incurred during the four days of the Battle of the Frontiers. No separate figures have been published for the Battle of the Marne, but if the estimated losses through September 11 are added to those of August, the total through the first thirty days is equivalent to a daily loss of the whole population of a town the size of Soissons or Compiègne. No exact figures can be given because in line with GQG's fixed policy against releasing any information of possible value to the enemy, casualty lists were not published. Nor is it possible to give comparable figures for the other belligerents because they tabulated losses at different intervals and on different bases. When the war was over, the known dead per capita of population were 1 to 28 for France, 1 to 32 for Germany, 1 to 57 for England and 1 to 107 for Russia.

somehow it had been fought through to a resolution, the foundations of a better-ordered world would have been laid. Like the shimmering vision of Paris that kept Kluck's soldiers on their feet, the mirage of a better world glimmered beyond the shell-pitted wastes and leafless stumps that had once been green fields and waving poplars. Nothing less could give dignity or sense to monstrous offensives in which thousands and hundreds of thousands were killed to gain ten yards and exchange one wet-bottomed trench for another. When every autumn people said it could not last through the winter, and when every spring there was still no end in sight, only the hope that out of it all some good would accrue to mankind kept men and nations fighting.

When at last it was over, the war had many diverse results and one dominant one transcending all others: disillusion. "All the great words were cancelled out for that generation," wrote D. H. Lawrence in simple summary for his contemporaries. If any of them remembered, with a twinge of pain, like Emile Verhaeren, "the man I used to be," it was because he knew the great words and beliefs of the time before 1914 could never be restored.

After the Marne the war grew and spread until it drew in the nations of both hemispheres and entangled them in a pattern of world conflict no peace treaty could dissolve. The Battle of the Marne was one of the decisive battles of the world not because it determined that Germany would ultimately lose or the Allies ultimately win the war but because it determined that the war would go on. There was no looking back, Joffre told the soldiers on the eve. Afterward there was no turning back. The nations were caught in a trap, a trap made during the first thirty days out of battles that failed to be decisive, a trap from which there was, and has been, no exit.

SOURCES

THE FOLLOWING list contains only titles cited in the Notes. It is confined to primary sources, including those biographies and special studies, like Ritter's *Schlieffen Plan*, which include primary material. A short list of secondary works is given separately. All titles are given in English or French translation where these exist.

A full bibliography of the subject would fill a book. No other episode in history has been more fully documented by its participants. They seem to have known, while they lived it, that like the French Revolution, the First World War was one of the great convulsions of history, and each felt the hand of history heavily on his own shoulder. When it was over, despite courage, skill, and sacrifice, the war they had fought proved to have been, on the whole, a monument of failure, tragedy, and disillusion. It had not led to a better world. Men who had taken part at the command level, political and military, felt driven to explain their decisions and actions. Men who had fallen from high command, whether for cause or as scapegoats—and these included most of the commanders of August—wrote their private justifications. As each account appeared, inevitably shifting responsibility or blame to someone else, another was provoked. Private feuds became public; public controversies expanded. Men who would otherwise have remained mute were stung to publish, as Sir Horace Smith-Dorrien by Sir John French. Books proliferated. Whole schools of partisans, like those of Gallieni and Joffre, produced libraries of controversy.

Through this forest of special pleading the historian gropes his way, trying to recapture the truth of past events and find out "what really happened." He discovers that truth is subjective and separate, made up of little bits seen, experienced, and recorded by different people. It is like a design seen through a kaleidoscope; when the cylinder is shaken the countless colored fragments form a new picture. Yet they are the same fragments that made a different picture a moment earlier. This is the problem inherent in the records left by actors in past events. That famous goal, "*wie es wirklich war*," is never wholly within our grasp.

Official Government Publications

CARNEGIE ENDOWMENT FOR INTERNATIONAL PEACE, *Diplomatic Documents Relating to the Outbreak of the European War*, 2 vols., ed. James Brown Scott, New York, Oxford, 1916. Contains the official publications of the various Foreign Offices which appeared at intervals after the outbreak, beginning with the hurriedly assembled and highly selective *German White Book* issued on August 4, 1914. Included are the *Austro-Hungarian Red*, *Belgian Grey*, *French Yellow*, *German White*, *British Blue I and II*, *Italian Green*, *Russian Orange I and II* and *Serbian Blue* Books.

FRANCE, Assemblée Nationale, Chambre des Députés, Session de 1919. *Procès-Verbaux de la Commission d'Enquète sur le rôle et la situation de la metallurgie en France: defense du Bassin de Briey*, 1re et 2me parties.

———. *Rapport de la Commission d'Enquète* par M. Fernand Engerand, deputé. 1re partie: "Concentration de la metallurgie française sur la frontière de l'Est." 2me partie: "La perte de Briey."

These hearings (referred to in Notes as "Briey"), at which the principal chiefs of the French General Staff as well as field commanders were called to testify, are the basic source for French military policy in August, 1914. They grew out of the loss of the Briey iron ore basin which became critical as the war went on. Certain sinister underpinnings of the munitions industry with its interlocking Franco-German directorates led a deputy, M. Fernand Engerand, to pursue a persistent investigation into the circumstances of the loss of Briey and this led by natural stages to an investigation of French strategy at the outset of the war. When the war was over, M. Engerand succeeded in getting a Committee of Inquiry appointed of which he was named *rapporteur*. "As our inquiry unrolled with all its illustrious witnesses," he wrote in his Report, it was plain that the truth about the origins and failure of Plan 17 was being "obstinately hidden" from the government and the Chamber of Deputies, but "we have tried to unravel the tangled and hidden threads of this month of August, 1914, the most tragic, perhaps, in all the history of France."

FRANCE, Ministère de la Guerre; Etat-major de l'Armée, Service Historique, *Les Armées Françaises dans la grande guerre*, Tome I, Vols. 1 and 2 and *Annexes*, Paris, Imprimerie Nationale 1922–1925. Referred to in Notes as *AF*. The first volume of the Official History, beginning with the pre-1914 war plans and the Michel incident of 1911, covers the war through the Battle of the Frontiers. The second volume covers the Retreat up to the eve of the Battle of the Marne. The real value is in the two volumes of Annexes containing the texts of orders and communications between GQG and the armies. These are the most vivid and immediate source material of all.

GERMANY, Foreign Office, *Outbreak of the World War*; German documents collected by Karl Kautsky and edited by Max Montgelas and Walther Schucking, translated by Carnegie Endowment, New York, Oxford, 1924. Referred to in Notes as "Kautsky." Assembled and published by the Weimar Government to supplement the original German White Book.

GERMANY, Generalstab, *Kriegsbrauch im Landkriege* (Usages of War on Land), translated as *The German War Book* by J. H. Morgan, London, Murray, 1915.

GERMANY, Marine-Archiv, *Der Krieg zur See, 1914–18*, No. 5, Band 1, *Der Krieg in dem Turkische Gewassen; Die Mittelmeer Division*, Berlin, Mittler, 1928.

GERMANY, Reichsarchiv, *Der Weltkrieg* 1914–18, Band 1, *Die Militärische Operationen zu Lande; Die Grenzschlachten im Westen*, Band 3, *Von der Sambre bis zur Marne*, Berlin, Mittler, 1924.

GREAT BRITAIN, Committee of Imperial Defence, Historical Section, CORBETT, SIR JULIAN, *Naval Operations: History of the Great War Based on Official Documents*, Vol. I, New York, Longmans, 1920. Referred to in Notes as "Corbett."

———, EDMONDS, BRIGADIER-GENERAL JAMES E., *Military Operations: France and Belgium*, 1914, Vol. I and volume of maps, 3rd ed., London, Macmillan, 1933. Referred to in Notes as "Edmonds." This work of superb scholarship is particularly valuable for its selections from German and French sources, showing for a given date the actual situation of the BEF's enemies and allies and how each appeared to the other.

———, FAYLE, C. ERNEST, *Seaborne Trade*, Vol. I, London, Murray, 1920.

GREAT BRITAIN, Foreign Office. *British Documents on the Origins of the War, 1898–1914*, 11 vols., eds. G. P. Gooch and H. W. V. Temperley, London, 1927–38. Referred to in Notes as "BD."

UNITED STATES, DEPARTMENT OF STATE. *Papers Relating to the Foreign Relations of the U. S. Supplements*, World War, 1914, Washington, G.P.O., 1928.

Non-Official Sources

On Belgium

BASSOMPIERRE, BARON ALFRED DE, *The Night of August 2–3, 1914, at the Belgian Foreign Office*, tr., London, Hodder & Stoughton, 1916.

BEYENS, BARON, *Deux Années à Berlin, 1912–14*, 2 vols., Paris, Plon, 1931.

CAMMAERTS, EMILE, *Albert of Belgium*, tr., New York, Macmillan, 1935.

CARTON DE WIART, HENRY (Belgian Minister of Justice in 1914), *Souvenirs politiques*, Brussels, Brouwer, 1948.

COBB, IRWIN S., *Paths of Glory—Impressions of War Written at and near the Front*, New York, Dutton, 1914.

DAVIS, RICHARD HARDING, *With the Allies*, New York, Scribner's, 1914.

DEMBLON, CELESTIN (deputy of Liège), *La Guerre à Liège: Pages d'un témoin*, Paris, Lib. Anglo-Française, 1915.

D'YDEWALLE, CHARLES, *Albert and the Belgians*, tr., New York, Morrow, 1935.

ESSEN, LÉON VAN DER, *The Invasion and the War in Belgium from Liège to the Yser*, tr., London, Unwin, 1917.

GALET, GENERAL EMILE JOSEPH, *Albert, King of the Belgians, in the Great War*, tr., Boston, Houghton Mifflin, 1931. This record by King Albert's personal military adviser and later Chief of Staff, is authoritative, thorough, detailed, and indispensable.

GIBSON, HUGH (First Secretary of the American Legation), *A Journal from Our Legation in Belgium*, New York, Doubleday, 1917.

KLOBUKOWSKI, A. (French Minister in Brussels), "Souvenirs de Belgique," *Revue de Paris*, Sept.–Oct., 1927.

———, "La Résistance belge à l'invasion allemande," *Revue d'Histoire de la Guerre*, July 1932.

MALCOLM, IAN, ed., *Scraps of Paper: German Proclamations in Belgium and France*, New York, Doran, 1916.

MILLARD, OSCAR E., *Burgomaster Max*, London, Hutchinson, 1936.

POWELL, E. ALEXANDER (correspondent of the *New York World* attached to the Belgian forces in 1914), *Fighting in Flanders*, New York, Scribner's, 1914.

SCHRYVER, COL. A. DE, *La Bataille de Liège*, Liege, Vaillant-Carmanne, 1922.

SUTHERLAND, MILLICENT, DUCHESS OF (leader of a volunteer ambulance corps of nurses to Belgium in August, 1914), *Six Weeks at the War*, Chicago, McCluny, 1915.

VERHAEREN, EMILE, *La Belgique sanglante*, Paris, Nouvelle Revue Française, 1915.

WHITLOCK, BRAND, *Belgium: A Personal Narrative*, Vol. I, New York, Appleton, 1910. President Wilson's appointment as Minister to Belgium of the lawyer and former journalist who had won fame as Independent mayor of Toledo for four terms proved fortunate for history. A progressive in politics, outspoken and courageous, Whitlock was also a writer of distinction. His book, together with that of Hugh Gibson who, though a professional diplomat, wrote without wraps, constitute a remarkable record of a fatal month in the history of a nation.

On England and the BEF

ADDISON, CHRISTOPHER (Parliamentary Secretary to Board of Education), *Four and a Half Years: A Personal Diary from June 1914 to January 1919*, London, Hutchinson, 1934.

ANGELL, NORMAN, *The Great Illusion: A Study of the Relation of Military Power to National Advantage*, 4th ed., New York, Putnam's, 1913.

ARMY QUARTERLY, London. Referred to in Notes as *AQ*. This journal's reviews of foreign books on the war, as they came out during the 1920s, provide the most inclusive and informative guide in English to the literature of the First World War.

ARTHUR, SIR GEORGE, *Life of Lord Kitchener*, Vol. III, New York, Macmillan, 1920.

———, *George V*, New York, Cape, 1930.

ASQUITH, EARL OF OXFORD AND, *Memories and Reflections*, 2 vols., London, Cassell, 1928.

ASTON, MAJOR-GENERAL SIR GEORGE, *Biography of the Late Marshal Foch*, London, Hutchinson, 1930.

BACON, ADMIRAL SIR REGINALD, *Life of Lord Fisher*, London, Hodder & Stoughton, 1929.

BEAVERBROOK, LORD, *Politicians and the War, 1914–16*, New York, Doubleday, Doran, 1928.

BERTIE, LORD, *Diary of Lord Bertie of Thame*, Vol. I, London, Hodder & Stoughton, 1924.

BIRKENHEAD, VISCOUNT, *Points of View*, Vol. I, London, Hodder & Stoughton, 1922.

BLAKE, ROBERT, ed., *Haig: Private Papers, 1914–18*, London, Eyre & Spottiswoode, 1952.

BRIDGES, LIEUT.-GENERAL SIR TOM (officer in the 2nd Cavalry Brigade of the BEF and formerly military attaché in Brussels), *Alarms and Excursions*, London, Longmans, 1938.

CALLWELL, MAJOR-GENERAL SIR CHARLES E. (became Director of Operations and Intelligence at the War Office in August, 1914, when Wilson and Macdonogh went to France), *Experiences of a Dug-Out, 1914–18*, London, Constable, 1920.

———, *Field Marshal Sir Henry Wilson: His Life and Diaries*, Vol. I, New York, Scribner's, 1927. All quotations in the text from Wilson's Diaries are from this book, referred to in the Notes as "Wilson."

CHAMBERLAIN, SIR AUSTEN, *Down the Years*, London, Cassell, 1935.

CHARTERIS, BRIGADIER-GENERAL JOHN, *At GHQ*, London, Cassell, 1931.

CHILDS, MAJOR-GENERAL SIR WYNDHAM, *Episodes and Reflections*, London, Cassell, 1930.

CHURCHILL, SIR WINSTON, *The World Crisis, Vol. 1, 1911–1914*, New York, Scribner's, 1928. This is the single most important book among English sources by a person holding key office at the outbreak. Further comment in Notes to Chapter 10. All references to Churchill in the Notes are to this book unless otherwise specified.

———, *The Aftermath*, Vol. 4 of *The World Crisis*, New York, Scribner's, 1929.

———, *Great Contemporaries*, New York, Putnam's, 1937.

CORBETT-SMITH, MAJOR A. (artillery officer in Smith-Dorrien's Corps), *The Retreat from Mons*, London, Cassell, 1917.

CUST, SIR LIONEL, *King Edward and His Court: Some Reminiscences*, London, Murray, 1930.

CUSTANCE, ADMIRAL SIR REGINALD, *A Study of War*, London, Constable, 1924.

DUGDALE, BLANCHE E. C., *Arthur James Balfour*, 2 vols., New York, Putnam, 1937.

ESHER, REGINALD, VISCOUNT, *The Influence of King Edward and Other Essays*, London, Murray, 1915.

———, *The Tragedy of Lord Kitchener*, New York, Dutton, 1921.

———, *Journals and Letters, Vol. 3, 1910–15*, London, Nicolson & Watson, 1938.

FISHER, ADMIRAL OF THE FLEET, LORD, *Memories*, London, Hodder & Stoughton, 1919.

———, *Fear God and Dread Nought: Correspondence of Admiral of the Fleet Lord Fisher of Kilverstone*, 3 vols., ed. Arthur J. Marder, London, Cape, 1952–56–59.

French, Field Marshal Viscount, of Ypres, *1914*, Boston, Houghton Mifflin, 1919. The weight of animus and selective omissions in Sir John French's account makes it impossible to use this record as a reliable source for anything but the author's character.

Gardiner, A. G., *The War Lords*, London, Dent, 1915.

Grey, Viscount, of Fallodon, *Twenty-Five Years*, 2 vols., London, Hodder & Stoughton, 1925.

Haldane, Richard Burdon, Viscount, *An Autobiography*, New York, Doubleday, Doran, 1929. All references are to this book unless otherwise specified.

———, *Before the War*, New York, Funk & Wagnalls, 1920.

Hamilton, Captain Ernest W. (Captain of 11th Hussars in Allenby's Cavalry Division), *The First Seven Divisions*, New York, Dutton, 1916.

Hurd, Sir Archibald, *The German Fleet*, London, Hodder & Stoughton, 1915.

———, *The British Fleet in the Great War*, London, Constable, 1919.

Jellicoe, Admiral Viscount, *The Grand Fleet, 1914–16*, New York, Doran, 1919.

Kenworthy, J. M. (Lord Strabolgi), *Soldiers, Statesmen and Others*, London, Rich & Cowen, 1933.

Lee, Sir Sidney, *King Edward VII*, 2 vols., New York, Macmillan, 1925–27.

Lloyd George, David, *War Memoirs*, Vol. I, Boston, Little, Brown, 1933.

Macready, General Sir Nevil (Adjutant-General in the BEF), *Annals of an Active Life*, Vol. I., London, Hutchinson, n.d.

MacDonagh, Michael, *In London During the Great War: Diary of a Journalist*, London, Eyre & Spottiswoode, 1935.

MAGNUS, SIR PHILIP, *Kitchener*, New York, Dutton, 1959.

MAURICE, MAJOR-GENERAL SIR FREDERICK (staff officer of BEF, 3rd Division, August, 1914) *Forty Days in 1914*, New York, Doran, 1919.

MCKENNA, STEPHEN, *While I Remember*, New York, Doran, 1921.

MILNE, ADMIRAL SIR ARCHIBALD BERKELEY, *The Flight of the Goeben and the Breslau*, London, Eveleigh Nash, 1921.

MORLEY, JOHN, VISCOUNT, *Memorandum on Resignation*, New York, Macmillan, 1928.

NEWTON, THOMAS, LORD, *Lord Lansdowne*, London, Macmillan, 1929.

NICOLSON, HAROLD, *King George the Fifth*, London, Constable, 1952.

———, *Portrait of a Diplomatist: Being the Life of Sir Arthur Nicolson, First Lord Carnock*, Boston, Houghton Mifflin, 1930.

PEEL, MRS. C. S., *How We Lived Then, 1914–18*, London, John Lane, 1929.

REPINGTON, LT. COL. CHARLES À COURT, *The First World War, 1914–18*, Vol. I, Boston, Houghton Mifflin, 1920.

ROBERTSON, FIELD MARSHAL SIR WILLIAM, *From Private to Field Marshal*, Boston, Houghton Mifflin, 1921.

———, *Soldiers and Statesmen, 1914–18*, Vol. I, New York, Scribner's, 1926.

SHAW, GEORGE BERNARD, *What I Really Wrote About the War*, New York, Brentano's, 1932.

SMITH-DORRIEN, GENERAL SIR HORACE, *Memories of 48 Years' Service*, London, Murray, 1925.

SPEARS, BRIG.-GEN. EDWARD L., *Liaison, 1914: A Narrative of the Great Retreat*, New York, Doubleday, Doran, 1931. A spirited, colorful and brilliantly written memoir of war, fascinating in its richness of detail, this is by far the most interesting book in English on the opening campaign in France. When the author's personal prejudices become involved he exercises a certain freedom in manipulating the facts. See Notes to Chapters 15 and 22.

STEED, WICKHAM H. (Foreign Editor of *The Times*), *Through Thirty Years*, New York, Doubleday, Doran, 1929.

TREVELYAN, GEORGE MACAULAY, *Grey of Fallodon*, Boston, Houghton Mifflin, 1937.

WILSON, GENERAL SIR HENRY, see CALLWELL.

On France

ADAM, H. PEARL, *Paris Sees It Through: A Diary, 1914–19*, London, Hodder & Stoughton, 1919.

ALLARD, PAUL, *Les Généraux Limogés pendant la guerre*, Paris, Editions de France, 1933.

BIENAIMÉ, ADMIRAL AMADÉE, *Le Guerre navale: fautes et responsabilités*, Paris, Taillander, 1920.

BRUUN, GEOFFREY, *Clemenceau*, Cambridge, Harvard, 1943.

CHARBONNEAU, COL. JEAN, *La Bataille des frontières*, Paris, Lavanzelle, 1932.

CHEVALIER, JACQUES, *Entretiens avec Bergson*, Paris, Plon, 1959.

CLERGERIE, GÉNÉRAL (Chief of Staff of GMP), *Le Rôle du Gouvernement Militaire de Paris, du 1er au 12 Septembre, 1914*, Paris, Berger-Levrault, 1920.

CORDAY, MICHEL, *The Paris Front*, tr., New York, Dutton, 1934.

DEMAZES, GÉNÉRAL, *Joffre, la victoire du caractère*, Paris, Nouvelles Editions Latines, 1955.

DUBAIL, GÉNÉRAL AUGUSTIN, *Quatres années de commandement, 1914–18: Journal de Campagne*, Tome I, *1ère Armée*, Paris, Fournier, 1920.

Dupont, Général Charles (Chief of Deuxième Bureau in 1914), *Le Haut Commandement allemand en 1914: du point de vue allemand*, Paris, Chapelot, 1922.

Engerand, Fernand (deputy from Calvados and *rapporteur* of the Briey Commission of Inquiry), *La Bataille de la frontière, Aôut, 1914: Briey*, Paris, Brossard, 1920.

———, *Le Secret de la frontière, 1815–1871–1914; Charleroi*, Paris, Brossard, 1918. All references in Notes are to this book unless otherwise specified.

———, *Lanrezac*, Paris, Brossard, 1926.

Foch, Marshal Ferdinand, *Memoirs*, tr. Col. T. Bentley Mott, New York, Doubleday, Doran, 1931.

Gallieni, Général, *Mémoires: défense du Paris, 25 Aôut–11 Septembre, 1914*, Paris, Payot, 1920.

———, *Les Carnets de Gallieni*, eds. Gaetan Gallieni & P.-B. Gheusi, Paris, Michel, 1932.

———, *Gallieni Parle*, eds. Marius-Ary et Leblond, Paris, Michel, 1920. Gallieni died in 1916 before he had completed a finished version of his memoirs. They were supplemented by the *Notebooks*, edited by his son and a former aide, and by the *Conversations*, edited by his former secretaries.

Gaulle, Général Charles de, *La France et son armée*, Paris, Plon, 1938.

Gibbons, Herbert Adams, *Paris Reborn*, New York, Century, 1915.

Giraud, Victor, *Le Général de Castelnau*, Paris, Cres, 1921.

Grasset, Colonel, A., *La Bataille des deux Morins: Franchet d'Esperey à la Marne, 6–9 Septembre, 1914*, Paris, Payot, 1934.

Grouard, Lt.-Col. Auguste, *La Guerre éventuelle: France et Allemagne*, Paris, Chapelot, 1913.

———, *La Conduite de la guerre jusqu'à la bataille de la Marne*, Paris, Chapelot, 1922.

GUARD, WILLIAM J., *The Soul of Paris—Two Months in 1914 by an American Newspaperman*, New York, Sun Publishing Co., 1914.

HANOTAUX, GABRIEL, *Histoire illustrée de la guerre de 1914*, 17 vols., Paris, 1916. Especially useful for its excerpts from French and captured German officers' war diaries.

HIRSCHAUER, GÉNÉRAL, and KLÉIN, GÉNÉRAL (Chief and Deputy Chief of Engineers of Military Government of Paris in 1914), *Paris en état de défense*, Paris, Payot, 1927.

HUDDLESTON, SISLEY, *Poincaré. A Biographical Portrait*, Boston, Little, Brown, 1924.

HUGUET, GENERAL A., *Britain and the War: A French Indictment*, London, Cassell, 1928. The bitterness, which tarnishes the value of Huguet's record, is openly expressed in the title.

ISAAC, JULES, *Joffre et Lanrezac*, Paris, Chiron, 1922.

———, "L'Utilisation des reserves en 1914," *Revue d'Histoire de la Guerre*, 1924, pp. 316–337.

JOFFRE, MARSHAL JOSEPH J.-C., *Memoirs*, Vol. I, tr. Col. T. Bentley Mott, New York, Harper's, 1932. Not a book of personal memoirs, but devoted entirely to the conduct of the war, this is by far the most complete and thorough of the records of any of the major commanders—but it is not Joffre. Compared to his characteristically opaque testimony at the Briey hearings, this is lucid, precise, detailed, explanatory, and comprehensible. It shows every evidence of having been written by a devoted staff working from the official records and suffering from perhaps excessive zeal to make the Commander appear the fount and origin of all decisions. On every page he is made to say such statements as, "The conception which I caused to be set down in Col. Pont's memorandum" (228). Nevertheless, with useful sketch maps and in an admirable translation, this is an essential source, if checked against other accounts.

LANGLE DE CARY, GÉNÉRAL DE, *Souvenirs de commandement, 1914–16*, Paris, Payot, 1935.

LANREZAC, GÉNÉRAL CHARLES, *Le Plan de campagne français et le premier mois de la guerre*, Paris, Payot, 1920.

Libermann, Henri, *Ce qu'a vu en officier de chasseurs à pied. Ardennes belges-Marne-St. Gond, 2 Août–28 Septembre, 1914*, Paris, Plon, 1916.

Marcellin, Leopold, *Politique et politiciens pendant la guerre*, Vol. I, Paris, Renaissance, 1923.

Mayer, Lt.-Col. Emile, *Nos chefs de 1914*, Paris, Stock, 1930.

Messimy, Général Adolphe, *Mes Souvenirs*, Paris, Plon, 1937. There is something about everything in Messimy. As packed with information as Galet's book on Belgium, it is, in contrast, as effervescent, voluble, and uninhibited as Galet's is taciturn and disciplined. The work of a man who was Minister of War at two crucial periods, July 1911 and August 1914, it is, like Galet, Churchill, and the Kautsky documents, an essential source for material not published elsewhere.

Mott, Col., T. Bentley, *Myron T. Herrick, Friend of France*, New York, Doubleday, Doran, 1929. (Chiefly excerpts from diary and letters.)

Muller, Commandant Virgile (aide-de-camp to Joffre), *Joffre et la Marne*, Paris, Cres, 1931.

Palat, Général Barthélmy, *La Grande Guerre sur le front occidental*, Vols. I–IV, Paris, Chapelot, 1920–27.

Paléologue, Maurice, *Un Grand Tournant de la politique mondiale, 1904–06*, Paris, Plon, 1934.

———, "Un Prélude à l'invasion de Belgique," *Revue des Deux Mondes*, October, 1932.

Percin, Général Alexandre (member of Supreme War Council in 1911 and Governor of Lille in 1914), *1914, Les erreurs du haut commandement*, Paris, Michel, 1920.

Pierrefeu, Jean de (a journalist by profession who, as an officer, was attached to GQG to prepare the communiqués for publication), *GQG. Secteur I*, Paris, Edition française Illustrée, 1920.

———, *Plutarque a menti*, Paris, Grasset, 1923.

POINCARÉ, RAYMOND, *Memoirs*, 4 vols., tr. Sir George Arthur, New York, Doubleday, 1926–29. In fact, if not in name, Poincaré was the central figure politically as Joffre was militarily, and his record is invaluable as guide and commentary to the war, French politics, international affairs, and the civil conflict with GQG. The English edition is abridged and has a confusing habit of referring under diary entries of a certain date to events that have not yet happened.

TANANT, GÉNÉRAL (Chief of Operations in the French Third Army), *La Troisième Armée dans la bataille*, Paris, Renaissance, 1923.

VIVIANI, RENÉ, *As We See It*, tr., New York, Harper's, 1923.

WHARTON, EDITH (who was living in Paris in August, 1914), *Fighting France*, New York, Scribner's, 1915.

On Germany

BAUER, COLONEL M. (Chief of Artillery section at OHL), *Der Grosse Krieg in Feld und Heimat*, Tübingen, Osiander, 1921.

BERNHARDI, GENERAL FRIEDRICH VON, *Germany and the Next War*, tr. Allen H. Powles, London, E. Arnold, 1914.

BETHMANN-HOLLWEG, THEODOR VON, *Reflections on the World War*, tr., London, Butterworth, 1920.

BLOEM, WALTER (Reserve Captain of Brandenburg Grenadiers in IIIrd Corps of von Kluck's Army), *The Advance from Mons, 1914*, tr. G. C. Wynne, London, Davies, 1930.

BLÜCHER, EVELYN, PRINCESS, *An English Wife in Berlin*, London, Constable, 1920.

BÜLOW, BERNHARD, PRINCE VON, *Memoirs*, 4 vols., tr., Boston, Little, Brown, 1931–32.

BÜLOW, GENERAL KARL VON *Mon Rapport sur la Bataille de la Marne*, tr. J. Netter, Paris, Payot, 1920.

CLAUSEWITZ, GENERAL CARL VON, *On War*, tr. Col. J. J. Graham, 3 vols., London, Kegan Paul, 1911.

CONRAD VON HÖTZENDORFF, FELDMARSCHALL FRANZ, *Aus Meiner Dienstzeit, 1906–18*, 5 vols., Vienna, Rikola Verlag, 1921–25.

ECKHARDSTEIN, BARON H. VON, *Ten Years at the Court of St. James, 1895–1905*, tr., London, Butterworth, 1921.

ERZBERGER, MATTHIAS, *Souvenirs de guerre*, tr., Paris, Payot, 1921.

FOERSTER, WOLFGANG, *Le Comte Schlieffen et la Grande Guerre Mondiale*, tr., Paris, Payot, 1929.

FRANÇOIS, GENERAL HERMANN VON, *Marneschlacht und Tannenberg*, Berlin, Scherl, 1920.

FREYTAG-LORINGHOVEN, FREIHERR VON, *Menschen und Dinge wie ich sie in meinem Leben sah*, Berlin, Mittler, 1923.

GERARD, JAMES W., *My Four Years in Germany*, New York, Doran, 1917.

GRELLING, RICHARD, *J'Accuse*, tr. A. Gray, New York, Doran, 1915.

HALLAYS, ANDRÉ, *L'Opinion allemande pendant la guerre, 1914–18*, Paris, Perrin, 1919.

HANSSEN, HANS PETER (deputy of Schleswig-Holstein in the Reichstag), *Diary of a Dying Empire*, tr. O. O. Winter, Indiana University Press, 1955.

HAUSEN, GENERAL FREIHERR MAX VON, *Souvenirs de campagne de la Marne en 1914*, tr., Paris, Payot, 1922.

HAUSSMANN, CONRAD, *Journal d'un député au Reichstag*, tr., Paris, Payot, 1928.

HINDENBURG, FIELD MARSHAL PAUL VON, *Out of My Life*, Vol. I, tr., New York, Harper's, 1921.

HOFFMANN, GENERAL MAX, *The War of Lost Opportunities*, tr., New York, International, 1925.

———, *The Truth About Tannenberg*, included in Vol. II of his *War Diaries and Other Papers*, tr. Eric Sutton; Intro. by K. F. Nowak, London, Secker, 1929.

KLUCK, GENERAL ALEXANDER VON, *The March on Paris and Battle of the Marne, 1914*, tr., New York, Longmans, 1920.

KOPP, GEORG (a member of the crew of the *Goeben*), *Das Teufelschiff und seine kleine Schwester*, tr. as *Two Lone Ships, Goeben and Breslau*, by Arthur Chambers, London, Hutchinson, 1931.

KRAFFT VON DELLMENSINGEN, GENERAL (Chief of Staff of Rupprecht's Army), *Die Führung des Kronprinzen Rupprecht von Bayern auf dem linken Deutschen Heeresflügel bis zur Schlact im Lothringen im August, 1914, Wissen und Wehr, Sonderheft*, Berlin, Mittler, 1925.

KUHL, GENERAL HERMANN VON (Chief of Staff of Kluck's Army), *Le grand état-major allemand avant et pendant la guerre mondiale*, tr. & ed. by General Douchy, Paris, Payot, 1922.

KURENBERG, JOACHIM VON, *The Kaiser*, tr. Russell and Hagen, New York, Simon & Schuster, 1955.

LICHNOWSKY, PRINCE KARL, *Memorandum* (published in English under the title *The Guilt of Germany*) with Introduction by Viscount Bryce, New York, Putnam's, 1918.

LUDENDORFF, GENERAL ERICH, *Ludendorff's Own Story, August 1914–November 1918*, Vol. I, tr., New York, Harper's, 1919.

LUDWIG, EMIL, *Wilhelm Hohenzollern*, New York, Putnam's, 1926.

MOLTKE, GENERALOBERST HELMUTH VON, *Erinnerungen-Briefe-Dokumente, 1877–1916*, Stuttgart, Der Kommendetag, 1922.

MÜHLON, WILHELM (a director of Krupp's), *L'Europe devastée: notes prises dans les premiers mois de la guerre*, tr., Paris, Payot, 1918.

RITTER, GERARD, *The Schlieffen Plan, Critique of a Myth*, tr. (contains first published text of many of Schlieffen's papers), London, Oswald Wolff, 1958.

RUPPRECHT, CROWN PRINCE OF BAVARIA, *Mein Kriegstagebuch*, Vol. I, Munich, Deutscher National Verlag, 1929.

SANTAYANA, GEORGE, *Egotism in German Philosophy*, 2nd ed., New York, Scribner's, 1940.

Schindler, Oberleutnant D., *Eine 42 cm. Mörser-Batterie im Weltkrieg*, Breslau, Hoffmann, 1934. The author served as artillery officer with the 420s at Liége and afterward. His book is the only firsthand account of the operation of the siege guns.

Schlieffen, Alfred, Feldmarshall Graf von, *Cannae*, tr., Fort Leavenworth, Command and General Staff School Press, 1936.

Schoen, Freiherr Wilhelm von, *Memoirs of an Ambassador*, tr., New York, Brentano's, 1923.

Souchon, Admiral Wilhelm, *La Percée de SMS Goeben et Breslau de Messine aux Dardanelles* in *Les marins allemands au combat*, ed. Vice-Admiral Eberhard von Mantey, Reichs Marine-Archiv, tr. Capitain R. Jouan, Paris, Payot, 1930.

Stürgkh, General Graf Josef (Austrian representative at OHL), *Im Deutschen Grossen Hauptquartier*, Leipzig, List, 1921.

Tappen, General Gerhard (Chief of Operations at OHL), *Jusqu'à la Marne en 1914* in *Documents allemands sur la bataille de la Marne*, tr. and ed. by Lt.-Col. L. Koeltz of the French General Staff, Paris, Payot, 1930.

Tirpitz, Grand Admiral Alfred von, *My Memoirs*, 2 vols., tr., New York, Dodd, Mead, 1919.

Topham, Anne (governess to the Kaiser's daughter), *Memories of the Kaiser's Court*, New York, Dodd, Mead, 1914. An invaluable view from the inside by an outsider.

Wetterlé, Abbé E. (deputy in the Reichstag from Alsace-Lorraine), *Behind the Scenes in the Reichstag*, tr., New York, Doran, 1918.

Wile, Frederic William, *Men Around the Kaiser*, Philadelphia, Lippincott, 1913.

———, *The Assault: Germany Before—and England After—the Outbreak*, Indianapolis, Bobbs-Merrill, 1916.

Wilhelm, Crown Prince of Germany, *My War Experiences*, tr., London, Hurst, 1922.

———, *Letters from the Kaiser to the Czar*, ed. Issac Don Levine, New York, Doubleday Page, 1920. Generally known as the Willy-Nicky Letters.

WOLFF, THEODOR (editor of the *Berliner Tageblatt*), *Eve of 1914*, tr. E. W. Dickes, New York, Knopf, 1936.

ZEDLITZ-TRUTZSCHLER, ROBERT, GRAF VON, *Twelve Years at the Imperial German Court*, tr., New York, Doran, 1924. A particularly revealing study of the Kaiser by his unhappy Court Chamberlain.

On Russia

AGOURTINE, LÉON, *Le Général Soukhomlinov*, Clichy, l'Auteur, 1951.

ALEXANDRA, EMPRESS OF RUSSIA, *Letters of the Tsaritsa to the Tsar, 1914–16*, ed. and intro. by Sir Bernard Pares, London, Duckworth, 1923.

BOTKIN, GLEB (son of the Czar's physician), *The Real Romanovs*, New York, Revell, 1931.

BUCHANAN, SIR GEORGE, *My Mission to Russia*, Boston, Little, Brown, 1923.

BRUSILOV, GENERAL A. A., *A Soldier's Notebook*, tr., London, Macmillan, 1930.

DANILOV, GENERAL YOURI, *La Russie dans la guerre mondiale*, tr. Col. A. Kaznakov, Paris, Payot, 1927.

———, *Le Premier Généralissime des armées russes: le grand-duc Nicolas*, tr., Paris, Berger-Levrault, 1932.

DOBROROLSKY, GENERAL SERGE (Chief of Mobilization Service in the Ministry of War in 1914), "La Mobilisation de l'armée russe en 1914," *Revue d'Histoire de la Guerre*, 1923, pp. 53–69 and 144–165.

GILLIARD, PIERRE (tutor to the Czar's children), *Thirteen Years at the Russian Court*, tr., New York, Doran, 1922.

GOLOVIN, LIEUT.-GENERAL NICHOLAS N., *The Russian Army in the World War*, tr., New Haven, Yale, 1931.

———, *The Russian Campaign of 1914*, tr. Captain Muntz, A.G.S. Command and General Staff School Press, Fort Leavenworth, Kansas, 1933. The first of these on the organization, and the second on the military operations, of the Russian Army are the outstanding sources on the Russian war effort in the early months.

GOURKO, GENERAL VASILII (BASIL) (Commander of a Cavalry Division in Rennenkampf's Army), *War and Revolution in Russia, 1914–17*, tr., New York, Macmillan, 1919.

GOURKO, VLADIMIR, *Features and Figures of the Past: Government and Opinion in the Reign of Nicholas II*, tr., Stanford University Press, 1939.

IRONSIDE, MAJOR-GENERAL SIR EDMUND, *Tannenberg: The First Thirty Days in East Prussia*, Edinburgh, Blackwood, 1925.

KNOX, MAJOR-GENERAL SIR ALFRED, *With the Russian Army*, London, Hutchinson, 1921.

KOKOVTSOV, COUNT V. N. (Premier, 1911–14), *Out of My Past*, tr., Stanford Univ. Press, 1935.

NIKOLAIEFF, COL. A. M., "Russian Plan of Campaign in the World War, 1914," tr., *Infantry Journal*, September–October, 1932.

PALÉOLOGUE, MAURICE, *An Ambassador's Memoirs*, tr. F. A. Holt, Vol. I, London, Hutchinson, 1923.

RADZIWILL, PRINCESS CATHERINE, *Nicholas II, Last of the Czars*, London, Cassell, 1931.

———, *Sovereigns and Statesmen of Europe*, New York, Funk & Wagnalls, 1916.

RODZIANKO, M. V. (President of the Duma), *Memoirs: Reign of Rasputin*, tr., London, Philpot, 1927.

SAZONOV, SERGEI, *Fateful Years, 1909–16*, tr., New York, Stokes, 1928.

SUKHOMLINOV, VLADIMIR, *Erinnerungen*, Berlin, Hobbing, 1924.

WITTE, COUNT SERGIUS, *Memoirs*, tr., New York, Doubleday, Page, 1921. Among the rash of memoirs inspired by the fall of the Czarist regime, this is the most solid and informative, although Witte's official career ended in 1906.

WRANGEL, BARON NICHOLAS, *Memoirs, 1847–1920*, tr., Philadelphia, Lippincott, 1927.

On Turkey

DJEMAL PASHA, *Memoirs of a Turkish Statesman, 1913–1919*, tr., New York, Doran, 1922.

EMIN, AHMED, *Turkey in the World War*, New Haven, Yale, 1930.

KANNENGIESSER, GENERAL HANS (a member of the German military mission to Turkey in 1914), *The Campaign in Gallipoli*, tr., London, Hutchinson, 1928.

MORGENTHAU, HENRY, *Ambassador Morgenthau's Story*, New York, Doubleday, Page, 1918.

NOGALES, GENERAL RAFAEL DE, *Four Years Beneath the Crescent*, New York, Scribner's, 1926.

Secondary Works

BENSON, E. F., *The Kaiser and English Relations*, London, Longmans, 1936.

BUCHAN, JOHN, *A History of the Great War*, Vol. I, London, Nelson, 1922.

CRAIG, GORDON, A., *The Politics of the Prussian Army, 1640–1945*, New York, Oxford, 1956.

CRUTTWELL, C. R. M., *A History of the Great War, 1914–18*, Oxford Univ. Press, 1936.

DE WEERD, H. A., *Great Soldiers of Two World Wars*, New York, Norton, 1941.

EARLE, EDWARD MEADE, ed., *et al.*, *Makers of Modern Stategy*, Princeton Univ. Press, 1943.

———, *Modern France*, Princeton Univ. Press, 1951.

FLORINSKY, MICHAEL T., *The End of the Russian Empire*, New Haven, Yale, 1931.

FROTHINGHAM, CAPT. THOMAS G., *The Naval History of the World War*, Vol. I., *Offensive Operations, 1914–15*, Cambridge, Harvard, 1925.

GOERLITZ, WALTER, *History of the German General Staff*, tr. Brian Battershaw, New York, Praeger, 1955.

HALÉVY, ELIE, *A History of the English People, Epilogue*, Vol. II, *1905–1915*. London, Benn, 1934.

MAUROIS, ANDRÉ, *Edwardian Era*, tr., New York, Appleton-Century, 1933.

MCENTEE, COL. GIRARD L., *Military History of the World War*, New York, Scribner's, 1937.

MONTEIL, VINCENT, *Les Officiers*, Paris, Editions du Seuil, 1958.

NEAME, LT.-COL. PHILIP, *German Strategy in the Great War* (Lectures at Staff College, Camberley), London, Arnold, 1923.

PONSONBY, ARTHUR, *Falsehood in Wartime*, New York, Dutton, 1928.

RENOUVIN, PIERRE, *The Forms of War Government in France*, New Haven, Yale, 1927.

ROSINSKI, HERBERT, *The German Army*, London, Hogarth, 1939.

NOTES

1. A Funeral

Accounts of the funeral, besides those in the daily press and in memoirs of the period, appear in *The Queen*, *The Sphere*, and *The Graphic* for May 21, 1910; "The Meeting of Nine Kings" by William Bayard Hale in *World's Work* for July, 1910; "An Impression of the King's Funeral" by Mary King Waddington in *Scribner's* for October, 1910; Theodore Roosevelt to David Grey, October 5, 1911, *Letters*, ed. E. E. Morison (Harvard U. P., 1951–54), VII, 409–13.

PAGE	
11	"Grave even to severity": *The Times*, May 21, 1910.
11	"Call this place my home": to Bülow, qtd. Ludwig, 427.
12	"He is Satan": Zedlitz-Trutschler, 177–8. The German press also represented Edward's tour as "having the sole object of forming an alliance against Germany." Lascelles to Grey, April 19, 1907, BD, VI, No. 15.
12	"A very nice boy": Roosevelt to Trevelyan, October 1, 1911, *Letters*, VII, 397.
12	"I bide my time": Lee, I, 477–8.
12	Ferdinand of Bulgaria annoyed other sovereigns: Roosevelt to Grey, *op. cit.*, 409–10. His Byzantine regalia: Sazonov, 230.
13	Prince Danilo and friend: Cust, 111, 249.
14	"You have a nice country": qtd. Maurois, 44.
14	Edward's visit to Paris and reports of Belgian and German envoys: Lee, II, 241–2.
16	"Not a mouse could stir": Lee, II, 11.
16	Compared to Bülow an eel was a leech: qtd. Maurois, 177.
16	Holstein called warnings "naïve": Eckhardstein, 249.
16	Eckhardstein overhears: *ibid.*, 230.
16	Kaiser wanted to go to Paris: Paléologue, *Un Prélude*, 494–5.
17	Kaiser complained to Roosevelt: Roosevelt to Trevelyan, *Letters*, VII, 396.
17	Kaiser told King of Italy: Bülow, II, 355; Benson, 248.
17	Bernhardi, "We must secure": Bernhardi, 81.
17	Huns of Attila: Bülow, I, 418.
17	"Legitimate aims": Hans Delbruck, professor of history at University of Berlin and Germany's leading military historian, qtd. Wile, *Men Around the Kaiser*, 119–22.
18	*Deutschland ganzlich einzukreisen*: *Neue Freie Presse*, April 15, 1907, qtd. Lee, II, 542.
18	Clemenceau on Germany's "lust for power": qtd. Bruun, 116.
18	Clemenceau told Edward: Goschen to Grey, August 29, 1908, BD, VI, No. 100; Steed, I, 287.

PAGE	
18	Czar a "common murderer": Lee, II, 587.
18	"An Englishman is a *zhid*": Witte, 189.
18	Edward waltzed with Czarina: Fisher, *Memories*, 234.
19	Czar only fit "to grow turnips": The Kaiser expressed this opinion to the British Foreign Secretary, Lord Lansdowne, at Queen Victoria's funeral, qtd. Newton, 199.
19	"*Garçon mal élevé*": Benson, 45.
19	"Nicky, take my word for it": October 25, 1895, *Willy-Nicky Letters*, 23.
19	"More speeches, more parades": Botkin, 103.
20	A detail that "escaped his Majesty": qtd. Ludwig, 263.
20	"Lies. He wants war": qtd. Maurois, 256.
20	Kaiser took to his bed: Crown Prince, 98–100.
21	Esher's lectures on *The Great Illusion*: "Modern War and Peace" and "La guerre et la paix" in Esher, *Essays*, 211–28 and 229–61.
21	Germany "receptive" to *The Great Illusion*: *ibid.*, 224. Esher gave copies to the Kaiser, *ibid.*, 55.
21	Bernhardi the first to enter Paris in 1870: Hindenburg, 59. Quotations for Bernhardi's book are from Chapters I, II, IV, V, IX, and X.
23	King Edward's death; quotations from Isvolsky and *Le Figaro* and details of mourning in Paris, Tokyo, and Berlin are from *The Times*, May 8, 1910.
23	Kaiser's arrival at Victoria Station: *The Times*, May 20, 1910.
24	Kaiser impressed by the Lying-in-State: Kaiser's *Memoirs*, 129.
24	Kaiser's proposal to Pichon: Arthur, *George V*, 125.
24	"Other sovereigns so much quieter": Trevelyan, 172.
24	Kaiser denies proposal to Pichon: Kaiser's *Memoirs*, 131.
25	"Amiable and pacific": *The Times*, May 21, 1910.
25	Conan Doyle's account: *ibid.*
25	Queen Alexandra loathed Kaiser: Arthur, *George V*, 126. Her letter to George: Nicolson, *George V*, 40.
26	"There never was such a break-up": Esher, *Journals*, III, 4.

2. "Let the Last Man on the Right Brush the Channel with His Sleeve"

29	"The heart of France": qtd. Buchan, I, 118.
29	"An unimportant obstacle": Goerlitz, 129.
31	"The whole of Germany must throw itself": Schlieffen's Memorandum of 1912, Ritter, 172.
31	The Schlieffen plan: Schlieffen's Memoranda for 1892 and 1912 in Ritter; Schlieffen's *Cannae*, Kuhl's *Generalstab*, Förster.
31	"It is better to lose a province": qtd. by Schlieffen, Ritter, 172.
32	"The principles of strategy remain unchanged": Schlieffen, *Cannae*, 4.
33	Von der Goltz, "We have won our position": qtd. Wile, *Men Around the Kaiser*, 222.

PAGE

34 "Desperate delusion of the will": Santayana, 69.

34 Elder Moltke foretold a long war: Foerster, 21.

34 Younger Moltke, "It will be a national war": *Erinnerungen.*

35 "Belgian neutrality must be broken": General von Hahnke's notes on Schlieffen's Memorandum of 1912, Ritter, 186.

35 "Gaining great victories": Clausewitz, III, 209–10.

36 "The one that willed war more than the other": General Percin in article in *Ere Nouvelle*, January, 1925, qtd. Ponsonby, 55–6.

36 Bülow's conversation with Schlieffen: Bülow, II, 88.

36 Leopold II a "thoroughly bad man": Roosevelt to Trevelyan, October 1, 1911, *Letters*, VII, 369.

36 Kaiser's proposal to Leopold II and Leopold's reaction: Bülow, II, 82–85; Cammaerts, 108–9.

37 Two million pounds sterling: J. V. Bredt, *Die Belgische Neutralität und der Schlieffensche Feldzugsplan*, qtd. *AQ*, July, 1929, 289.

37 "The French would have had to pay for it": Dupont, 23.

37 "Lining up her army along the road": the diplomat was Richard von Kuhlmann, then counselor of the German Embassy in London, later, in 1917, Foreign Secretary, qtd. Cammaerts, 134.

37 "All fortresses, railways and troops": Memorandum of 1912, Ritter, 175.

37 "Lille . . . an excellent target": *ibid.*

38 "Let the last man on the right": qtd. Rosinsky, 137.

38 Schlieffen counted on British belligerency: Ritter, 161–4.

38 Use of reserves in the front line: Isaac, *Reserves*, 335; Foerster, 71.

38 "Only make the right wing strong": Foerster, 70.

39 "Engaging the enemy in his own territory": *Erinnerungen.*

39 "Entirely just and necessary": Tappen, 92.

39 "We must put aside all commonplaces": Cambon (French ambassador in Berlin) to Foreign Minister Pichon, May 6, 1913, *French Yellow Book* No. 3.

40 German spies' reports on Russia: Tirpitz, I, 343.

40 Moltke to Conrad: "Any adjournment": Conrad, III, 670

40 "We are ready and the sooner the better": Eckhardstein, *Lebenserinnerungen*, Vol. III, *Die Isolierung Deutschlands*, Leipzig, 1921, 184.

3. The Shadow of Sedan

Official sources for Plan 17 and its predecessors are *AF*, Tome I, Vol. I, Chaps. 1 and 2 and Joffre, 45–112. Text of the general directive and of the deployment orders to the several armies is No. 8 in Annexes to *AF*, I, I. The leading critics of the Plan are Engerand, General Grouard, and General Percin; the last, being blamed for the evacuation of Lille in August, 1914, had a personal ax to grind.

41 General Lebas's interview with Castelnau: Briey, session of May 23, evidence of M. Vendame, deputy of Lille, who accompanied Lebas; session of July 4, evidence of General Lebas.

PAGE

41 Density of troops per meter for offensive action: Col. Grandmaison had worked it out at 6 to 8 km. per army corps. Engerand, 431.

42 "We proclaim forever the right of Alsatians": Alexandre Zevaes, *Histoire de la Troisième République*, Paris, 1926, 41.

42 Gambetta, "*N'en parlez jamais*": Huddleston, 36.

42 Victor Hugo, "France will have one thought": Zevaes, *op. cit.*, 41.

43 Secret patrols gaze down on Colmar: Monteil, 38.

44 Forty-two ministers in forty-three years: qtd. Craig, in Earle's *Modern Strategy*, 276.

44 "*Oh, les braves gens!*": Pierre de la Gorce, *Histoire du Second Empire*, VII, 343.

45 Foch and doctrine of offensive: the quotations and episode of Clemenceau and Foch are from "Du Picq and Foch" by Stefan T. Possony and Etienne Manteux, Chap. 9 in Earle's *Modern Strategy.*

46 Grandmaison's lectures: Lanrezac, 138, n. 1; Messimy, 72; John Bowditch, "The Concept of Elan Vital," in Earle's *Modern France*, 39–43.

47 Fallières, "The offensive alone": Joffre, 30.

47 Field Regulations of 1913: Drafted by a committee of which General Pau was chairman and which included Hély d'Oissel, later Chief of Staff of the Fifth Army, and Berthelot, later deputy chief of staff under Joffre at GQG. Published as a decree signed by Poincaré on October 28, 1913. Text in Engerand, 445–7.

47 Wilhelm I to Eugénie: Engerand, 592.

48 General Michel's Plan of 1911: *AF*, I, I, 13–14; text of his report is in Annexes to this volume, No. 3, 7–11. Discussion of use of reserves in the front line from Proceedings of the Supreme War Council, July 19, 1911, is Annexe No. 4, 12–17.

48 "*Les réserves, c'est zéro!*": Spears, 218.

49 "No fathers at the front," attributed to Kaiser: Joffre, 61.

50 Michel's proposal and reaction of Supreme War Council: Briey, May 13, 23, and 30, evidence of Michel, Percin, and Messimy; Messimy, *Souvenirs*, 76–8; *AF*, I, I, 13–14.

50 "*Comme une insanité*": Percin, 206.

50 "Reconciling the Army": Messimy, 15. "Incapable of leading their troops": *ibid.*, 93. "Hesitant, indecisive": *ibid.*, 75.

51 "*Chic exquis*": In 1870 the Turco regiments under the command of General Charles Bourbaki inspired a marching song with these words:

> Le chic exquis
> Dont les cœurs sont conquis
> Ils le doivent a qui?
> A Charles Bourbaki.

qtd. De Gaulle, 162.

51 "General Michel is off his head": Briey, May 13, evidence of General Michel.

PAGE

51 Statements on *pantalon rouge* by *Echo de Paris* and Etienne: qtd. Messimy, 118–20.
52 "*Question de bouton*": Percin, 208.
52 "Cool and methodical worker": Messimy, 77.
53 "Take it, *cher ami*": Briey, May 23, evidence of Percin.
53 Joffre would have preferred Foch: Joffre, 12.
54 "You will rouse a storm" and President and Premier "made a face": Messimy, 78.
54 "Get rid of me!": Briey, May 23, evidence of Percin.
54 Joffre's conversation with Alexandre: Demazes, 65.
54 "Cuts like a scar": Foch, *Memoirs*, lxii.
55 "Get to Berlin through Mainz": qtd. Grouard, 5, n. 2.
55 "A posteriori and opportunist": Joffre, 69.
56 "Foolishness": Joffre, 17.
56 German officer betrays Schlieffen plan in 1904: Paléologue, *Un Prélude*, 486–88.
56 General Pendezac: *ibid.*, 514.
57 "Altogether likely": Joffre, 63.
57 Castelnau and Joffre on most likely path of German offensive: Giraud, 25–29.
57 Castelnau, "impossible," and Joffre, "same opinion": Joffre, 64.
57 Deuxième Bureau knew of German use of reserves: "It was known that the German plan of mobilization predicated that 'troops of the reserve will be used as active troops,'" *AF*, I, I, 39. The critique by Moltke is from Isaac, *Reserves*, 335, who also states that a French analysis made in May, 1914, of the German mobilization plan for that year showed the role of reserves as identical with that of the active units. This is confirmed by Joffre in his discussion of the problem, 145–7. Major Melotte's report is from Galet, 22. Joffre (61) is the authority for the belief that the Germans would use reserves only as second-line troops.
58 "I have two stars": Briey, May 23, evidence of Vendame.

4. *"A Single British Soldier . . ."*

59 Péguy, "Like everyone else": from his *Cahiers de la quinzaine*, October 22, 1905, reprinted in his *Notre Patrie*, Paris, 1915, 117–18.
60 General Staff war game of 1905: Robertson, *Private to Field Marshal*, 140; *Soldiers and Statesmen*, I, 24.
60 Huguet-Repington Memorandum: Repington, 6–10.
61 "A Hegelian army": Haldane, 198.
61 Grey and Haldane in crisis of 1906: Grey, I, 72–88; Haldane, 203–04; *Before the War*, 186; BD, III, 212.
61 Campbell-Bannerman, lunch at Calais: Maurois, 129.
61 Campbell-Bannerman on "honorable understanding": Grey, I, 85.

PAGE	
61	Haldane authorizes talks: Grey, I, 76.
61	"Departmental affair": Campbell-Bannerman's phrase, qtd. Repington, 10.
62	Plans of Grierson and Robertson: Tyler, John E., *The British Army and the Continent, 1904–14*, London, 1938, 46.
62	Esher favors action in Belgium: Esher, *Journals*, I, 375–6.
62	Fisher, landing on Prussian coast: *Letters*, III, 47; opinions of army strategy: Bacon, II, 182–3.
63	Wilson, in Hyde Park: Wilson, 51; spoke French: *ibid.*, 2.
63	Wilson's comment, "Very interesting": qtd. *AQ*, July, 1929, 287.
63	Wilson's visit to Foch: Wilson, 78.
63	"I've got a French general": *ibid.*, 79–80.
64	"Tremendous gossips": Aston, *Foch*, 129.
64	Wilson's "allez operations": Wilson, 79.
64	"A single British soldier": *ibid.*, 78.
64	"Important question!": Huguet, 21.
65	Foch's views "same as mine": Liddell Hart, *Foch*, 51: in a letter to the British military attaché, Colonel Fairholme, Foch stated his belief that the principal front would be Epinal to Namur, BD, VI, No. 460.
65	Wilson's diary comments: Wilson, 97–8.
65	Wilson-Dubail agreement: *AF*, I, I, 17–18; BD, VII, No. 640.
66	"Secondary theatre . . . main theatre": Huguet, 8.
66	Wilson's talk with Grey and Haldane: Wilson, 99.
66	Secret meeting of C.I.D., August, 1911: Wilson, 99–102; Churchill, 55–9; Haldane, 226.
67	Fisher, "Overwhelming supremacy": letter of April 28, 1912, *Letters*, II, 456.
68	"Calling for my head": Wilson, 106.
68	"Natural and informal outcome": Haldane, *Before the War*, 183.
68	"Certainly committed us": Esher, *Journals*, III, 61.
68	Haldane's mission to Berlin: 254–262, 292; *Before the War*, 72–86.
68	Naval agreement with France: Churchill, 115–16.
69	Grey's letter to Cambon: Grey, I, 97–8.
69	"Break up the Cabinet": Wilson, 113.
69	Wilson on Joffre and Castelnau: *ibid.*, 105; Wilson laid a piece of map: *ibid.*
70	Joffre counted on six British divisions: Joffre, 50. Haldane put the total number at 160,000: *Before the War*, 189.
70	British military talks with Belgians: BD, III, No. 217 ff.; Bridges (then military attaché in Brussels), 62–63.
70	Esher's warning to Huguet: Huguet, 18; Joffre, 54. Cambon's condition: Dupont, 25.
71	Plan W worked in secret: Wilson, 149.

5. The Russian Steam Roller

PAGE

72 German dread of the Slav: When a German regiment in 1914 learned it was going to the western not the eastern front, there was "general rejoicing. For some indefinable reason the very thought of Russia gave one a shudder." Bloem, 20. The same thought moved a German army doctor to complain to the Duchess of Sutherland (49) how wicked it was of England to join the alliance against Germany "and leave us to those devilish Russians."

72 Numbers in the Russian Army: these and other figures about men and matériel in this chapter are from Golovin's *Army* unless otherwise noted.

72 Grey on Russian power: Grey to Sir F. Bertie, May 1, 1914, BD, X, Part 2, No. 541.

73 Franco-Russian staff talks and facts of Russian mobilization: Messimy, 179–81; Kokovtsov, 370–72; Joffre, 55–60; Golovin, *Campaign*, Chapter III, 45–73.

73 Czar, "At the heart of Germany": Joffre, 23.

74 Grandmaison popular in Russia: Golovin, *Campaign*, 61.

74 Jilinksky's promises in 1912–13: Agourtine, 25.

74 Ian Hamilton's reports: Hamilton, General Sir Ian, *A Staff Officer's Scrap Book*, London, 1907, II, 381.

75 "Not a single tennis court": Knox, xxvii.

75 "This insane regime . . . this tangle of cowardice": Witte, 270, 247.

75 Nicholas II uneducated: A few days before his 22nd birthday, on April 28, 1890, Nicholas wrote in his diary, "Today I finished definitely and forever my education." qtd. Radziwill, *Nicholas II*, 210.

75 Kokovtsov's interview with Czar: Kokovtsov, 456.

76 Stolypin assassinated by police agents: Wrangel, 208.

76 "Everyone in poor health": Witte, 319.

77 "England's death rattle": Paléologue, *Intimate Journal of the Dreyfus Case*, New York, 1957, 180.

77 "How I detest that word": Witte, 190.

77 British diplomat: Sir Arthur Nicolson, British ambassador to Russia, 1906–10. Nicholson, *Diplomatist*, 180.

77 "Difficult to make him work": Sazonov, 286.

78 Sukhomlinov on "vicious innovations": Golovin, *Campaign*, 31, 34.

78 "Distrust at first sight": Paléologue, 83; Poincaré (III, 163) had the same reaction.

78 Sukhomlinov's wife, expenses, associations: Agourtine, 18–22; Vladimir Gurko, 552–3; Knox, 222; Sir Bernard Pares, *A History of Russia*, New York, 1953, 472–77.

79 Sukhomlinov's trial: Agourtine, 56–9.

PAGE

79 "Terrible consequences": qtd. Agourtine, 59.

79 Kaiser's dedication to Sukhomlinov: a facsimile in the autograph of the Kaiser is reproduced in Ludwig, 508.

80 Sukhomlinov's responsibility for the shell shortage: Knox, obituary of Sukhomlinov in *Slavonic Review*, 1926, Vol. 5, 148; also Golovin, *Army*, 12, 32, 43.

80 Sukhomlinov hated Grand Duke; Danilov, 150; Golovin, *Campaign*, 35.

81 Grand Duke only "man" in royal family: Pares, Introduction to *Letters of Tsaritsa*, xxi.

81 "I have no faith in *N*.": *Letters to Tsar*, June 16, 1915, 97.

81 Foch's influence on Grand Duke: Esher, *Tragedy*, 19.

82 Prince Kotzebue's remarks: Danilov, 43.

82 "Montenegrin nightingales": Paléologue, 22–23.

82 Russia's alternate war plans: Ironside, 31–36.

83 March on Berlin: according to Danilov, Deputy Chief of Staff (130), this was the fundamental idea and goal of the Russian High Command throughout the "first period" of the war.

83 Junkers shot foxes: Ellen M. Pain, *My Impressions of East Prussia*, London, 1915.

83 Russian moose shot by the Kaiser: Topham, 254. Her Chapter XIII, "Rominten," is brilliant reporting of the Imperial habits.

84 Germany hoped to keep Japan neutral: Hoffmann, *War of Lost Opportunities*, 5.

84 Hoffmann's habits: K. F. Nowak, Introduction to Hoffmann's *War Diaries*, I, 10, 18.

84 "You are a yellow-skin", recorded by the American correspondent Frederick Palmer, qtd. De Weerd, 71.

85 Russian colonel sold war plans: Hoffmann, *War of Lost Opportunities*, 4.

85 "With all available strength": qtd. Hoffmann, *Diaries*, II, 241.

Outbreak

89 "Some damned foolish thing": recalled by Albert Ballin who quoted it to Churchill (207) in July 1914 when Ballin was sent to London by the Kaiser to persuade the British to stay neutral.

89 Kaiser's "shining armor" speech: in the Vienna Town Hall, September 21, 1910, qtd. Stanley Shaw, *William of Germany*, New York, Macmillan, 1913, 329.

89 German's "faithful support": Bethmann-Hollweg to von Tschirschky (German ambassador in Vienna), Kautsky, No. 15; Kaiser to Emperor Franz Joseph, Kautsky, No. 26.

89 "Dissipates every reason for war": Kaiser's marginal note on copy of Austria's ultimatum to Serbia, Kautsky, No. 271.

89 "Make us a distinct declaration": Bethmann-Hollweg to Pourtalès, Kautsky, No. 490.

6. August 1: Berlin

The central episode in this chapter, General Moltke's traumatic experience with the Kaiser on the night of August 1, is based on Moltke's memoirs, 19–23. All quotations from the Kaiser and Moltke himself during the course of this incident are from this source. An English version was published in *Living Age*, January 20, 1923, 131–34.

PAGE

90 Ambassador instructed to declare war on Russia: Kautsky, No. 542.

90 At 5:30 Bethmann and Jagow: The American correspondent, Frederic William Wile, on his way to the Foreign Office, saw the two ministers as they came out: *Assault*, 82.

90 "I hate the Slavs": Stürgkh, 232.

90 Pourtalès's and Eggeling's reports: Kautsky, Nos. 474 and 521. Eggeling's insistence up to the last moment that Russia could not fight because of artillery and transport deficiencies is reported by Kuhl, 31.

91 "Sick Tom-cat": Kautsky, No. 474.

91 A journalist in the crowd: Wile, *Assault*, 81–2; the Belgian ambassador also describes the scene: Beyens, II, 266.

91 "If the iron dice roll": Kautsky, No. 553.

91 Officers waving handkerchiefs: Wolff, 504.

91 Suspected Russian spies trampled: Hanssen, 22–23.

91 Railway transport required for one Army corps: Reichsarchiv, *Das Deutsche Feldeisenbahnwesen*, Band I, *Die Eisenbahnen zu Kriegsbeginn*, qtd. *AQ*, April, 1928, 96–101.

92 Elder Moltke on a sofa: Fisher, *Memories*, 230.

92 Kaiser's marginalia: Kautsky, Nos. 368 and 596.

92 "Dead Edward": Written on margin of Pourtalès's dispatch, received July 30 at 7:00 A.M. reporting that Russian mobilization could not be canceled, Kautsky, No. 401, English version, Ludwig, 448.

93 Autonomy for Alsace: The alleged proposal by an anonymous "close associate" of Bethmann's is reported by Radziwill, *Sovereigns*, 70, a not too reliable source.

93 German ultimatum to France: Schoen, 192, 197; Messimy, 149.

94 French decoded it: Poincaré, III, 251.

94 "Moltke wants to know": Wolff, 504.

94 Lichnowsky's telegram: Kautsky, No. 562.

94 Dinner in Berlin, 1911: Given by Sir E. Goschen, the British ambassador, in honor of Major-General Wilson, Wilson, 94.

94 Grey's proposal to Lichnowsky: Lichnowsky, 73–74; Grey to Goschen, *British Blue Book*, No. 123; Grey, II, Appendix F, "The Suggestions of August 1, 1914."

95 "*Traurige Julius*": Stürgkh, 24.

95 Moltke's character and habits: Freytag-Loringhoven, 135–7; Bauer, 33;

PAGE

Goerlitz, 143; General Sir Edmund Ironside, "Two Chiefs of General Staff," *Nineteenth Century and After*, February 1926; Wile, *NYT*, October 6, 1914, 2:6.

96 "Very critical of myself": *Erinnerungen*, 307; "Place ourselves under Japan": qtd. Ironside, *op. cit.*, 229; "Quite brutally" about Peking: *Erinnerungen*, 308; "Win the big prize twice": *ibid.*

97 "Build railways": Neame, 2. Elder Moltke's use of railroads, Rosinski, 129.

97 Best brains ended in lunatic asylums: *AQ*, April, 1928, 96.

97 General von Staab: His book, *Aufmarsch nach zwei Fronten*, is analyzed by Commandant Koeltz, "La Concentration allemande et l'incident du premier Aôut, 1914," *Revue d'Histoire de la Guerre*, 1926, 117–130.

97 Erzberger's testimony: Erzberger's *Erlebnisse*, qtd. *AQ*, April, 1922, 80.

98 Telegrams to England: Kautsky, Nos. 578 and 579; to Paris: No. 587; to King George: No. 575.

99 Lichnowsky's second telegram: Kautsky, No. 603. King George's reply to the Kaiser saying "There must be some mistake," No. 612.

99 Invasion of Trois Vierges: Luxembourg Minister of State Eyschen to Jagow, Kautsky, No. 602; Buch, German minister to Luxembourg, to Foreign Office, No. 619; Bethmann-Hollweg to Government of Luxembourg, No. 640.

100 Pourtalès's interview with Sazonov: Sazonov, 213; Paléologue, 48; Pourtalès's report, Kautsky, No. 588.

101 Tirpitz on declaration of war: Tirpitz, I, 363–5. The scene is also described by Bülow (III, 187) as told him by Albert Ballin who was present. Bethmann was pacing up and down while *Geheimrat* Kriege, a conscientious jurist of the Foreign Office, was searching through all the lawbooks for a model. "From time to time the agitated Bethmann would ask him, 'Is that declaration of war on Russia ready yet? I must have my declaration at once!' Ballin asked, 'Why such haste to declare war on Russia, Your Excellency?' and Bethmann answered, 'If I don't, we shan't get the Socialists to fight.'"

101 "Place guilt on Russia": Bethmann to Tschirschky, marked "Urgent," Kautsky, No. 441.

7. *August 1: Paris and London*

102 To leave onus of aggression on Germany: Joffre, 133.

102 10-km. withdrawal: Orders of the War Ministry for the withdrawal are Nos. 22, 25, 26, and 27 in *Annexes* to *AF*, I, I.

102 Viviani, "haunted by fear": Viviani, 194–5.

102 "To assure collaboration": Annexe No. 25.

103 Joffre hounding the Government: Joffre, 123–5; Messimy, 139–50.

103 "Frightful nervous tension": Viviani, 195.

PAGE

103 "Permanent condition": Messimy, 183. The premier's nerves were also remarked by Bertie, 5.

103 Dr. Gauthier "forgot": Messimy, 156.

103 Poincaré could remember as a boy: Poincaré, III, 1.

104 Prolonged cry, "*Vive la France!*": Messimy, 138.

104 "Without firing a shot": *ibid.*, 140.

104 "*Une forme hypocrite*": Messimy, 144.

104 Cambon, England "tepid": Poincaré, II, 242. "No interest to Great Britain": *ibid.*, 264.

105 *Carnet B*: Messimy, 147–8; de Gaulle, 237; Renouvin, 13, 27–8.

106 Isvolsky "very distressed": Poincaré, II, 272.

106 Terms of Franco-Russian Alliance: text in *Livre Jaune, l'Alliance Franco-Russe*, Ministère des Affaires Estrangères, Paris, 1918, 92; also in Joffre, 102. Over the years from 1892 to 1914 the Alliance was the subject of continuing discussion between the contracting parties, especially as to the exact interpretation of its *casus foederis*, and it became gradually encrusted with layers of *aides-mémoires*. According to various English translations, France was obligated to "attack," to "oppose," or to "fight" Germany. In the French text the word is "*attaquer*." For Poincaré's interpretation, see II, 289.

106 "*Du calme, du calme*": Messimy, 183–4.

107 Joffre in "pathetic tone": *ibid.*, 149.

107 Schoen-Viviani talk: Poincaré, II, 265; Schoen's report of Viviani's reply, Kautsky, No. 571.

107 10-km. order reaffirmed, text: *AF*, Annexe No. 26.

107 Foch's corps "nose to nose": Joffre, 129, n. 3.

107 General Ebener comes for mobilization order: Joffre, 128; Messimy, 150.

108 Scenes in Paris after mobilization: Adam, 20; Gibbons, 73; Guard, 9; Wharton, 14.

108 "Played by Hungarians": Wharton, 10.

108 "Sick at heart": Bertie, I, 6–7.

108 Cambon-Grey interview: Poinicaré, II, 264.

109 Grey prepared to resign: "Throughout the whole of this week I had in view the probable contingency that we should not decide at the critical moment to support France. In that event I should have to resign." Grey, II, 312.

109 Grey "icy": Lichnowsky to Jagow, April 13, 1913, qtd. Halévy, 627.

109 "If Germany dominated": Grey, I, 299.

110 Lord Morley on Cabinet divisions: Morley, 4, 5, 10.

110 Caucus of Liberal M.P.s: Addison, 32.

110 Verse from *Punch*: by Owen Seaman, *Punch*, August 5, 122.

111 Lloyd George, "gravest issue": qtd. Halévy, 547.

111 German arms to Ulster: *ibid.*, 548.

111 Churchill and Fleet: Corbett, 25–30; Churchill, 230 ff. Subsequent material on Churchill's role in the crisis and mobilization of the Fleet

PAGE

is from his Chapter IX, "The Crisis," and Chapter X, "Mobilization of the Navy."

112 "Invented by a genius": L. J. Maxse, "Retrospect and Reminiscence," *National Review*, Vol. LXXI, 746.

113 "Splendid condottierre" and "playing the peace-card": Morley, 24.

113 "Are we to go in": Asquith, II, 7.

113 Grey in Cabinet of July 31: Morley, 2.

113 "Cabinet seemed to heave a sigh": *ibid.*, 3.

114 Bankers "aghast" and City "totally opposed": Morley, 5; Lloyd George, 61.

114 Tory leaders: Chamberlain, 94–101; Wilson, 154.

114 Cambon, "*Et l'honneur*": Chamberlain, 101.

115 Grey's telegrams on Belgian neutrality and French reply: *British Blue Book*, Nos. 114, 124, 125.

115 Lloyd George, only a "little violation": Beaverbrook, 15–16.

115 Grey to Cambon, "France must take": Nicolson, *Diplomatist*, 304.

115 "*Ils vont nous lâcher*": *ibid.*, 304–5.

116 Churchill at dinner: Beaverbrook, 22–3.

8. Ultimatum in Brussels

117 Below-Saleske's instructions: Jagow to Below, July 29 and August 2, marked "Urgent and Secret," Kautsky, Nos. 375 and 648.

117 "I am a bird of ill omen": Whitlock, 3.

117 Bassompierre's interview with Below: Bassompierre, 15–16.

119 "Your neighbor's roof": *ibid.*

119 Queen translates appeal to Kaiser: Cammaerts, 405; text of the letter: Galet, 31.

119 Delivery of the ultimatum: Bassompierre, 17; remainder of paragraph and further account of government discussions of ultimatum are from Bassompierre unless otherwise noted.

119 Below seen driving back: Gibson, 9–10.

120 Davignon's optimism and van der Elst's esteem for Germans: Klobukowski, 34–5.

120 Moltke drafted ultimatum: Kautsky, No. 376, n. 1.

120 Text of ultimatum: *Belgian Grey Book*, No. 20.

122 "Sealed envelope": Cammaerts, 39.

123 "As if he wished to build something": *ibid.*, 67.

123 Galet's teachings, career, and temperament: D'Ydewalle, 94.

124 Kaiser's assurance to van der Elst: Cammaerts, 108–9, 115.

124 "To ensure against being ignored": Galet, 8.

125 King Albert's visit to Berlin, 1913: Beyens, II, 38–43; Jules Cambon to Pichon, November 22, 1913, *French Yellow Book*, No. 6; Poincaré, II, 86; Galet, 23.

127 What Moltke said to Major Melotte: Beyens, II, 47–53.

PAGE

128 Galet's memorandum: Galet, 23.

128 Council of State, August 2: Carton de Wiart, 207–9: Galet, 46–50.

128 "If Germany victorious, Belgium will be annexed": qtd. Poincaré, II, 281.

129 German anxiety about Belgian resistance: see notes on Moltke and Jagow for Chapter 9, p. 145.

129 Below's interview with van der Elst: *Belgian Grey Book*, No. 21; Cammaerts, 13

130 King staring out the window: Carton de Wiart, 210.

130 Conference at Bethmann-Hollweg's house: Tirpitz, I, 366–70.

130 Berliners looking nervously at the sky: Hanssen, 14. More sophisticated Germans were skeptical of the reports. Conrad Haussmann (16), noting the lack of precise details, found them "not very convincing."

131 De Gaiffier delivers Belgian reply: Bassompierre, 31, 37; text of the reply, *Belgian Grey Book*, No. 22.

131 Kaiser's reply to King Albert: Galet, 58–9.

131 "What does he take me for?": Cammaerts, 19.

9. "Home Before the Leaves Fall"

132 Grey in Cabinet of August 2: Grey, II, 12.

132 "National devotion" in France: Report by British Consul in Dunkirk, BD, XI, 508.

132 War Book: Corbett, 20–21.

133 Grey's naval pledge to Cambon: Grey, II, Appendix D, 301.

133 Cambon-Grey conversation: Grey to Bertie, BD, XI, 487.

133 Cambon's "secret" telegram: Poincaré, II, 278.

133 Nations do not wage war "by halves": article by Cambon, *Revue de France*, July 1, 1921.

133 Dissolution of the Cabinet: Morley, 4, 17; Asquith, II, 8.

133 Churchill hurries to see Balfour: Dugdale, II, 78.

134 Haldane and Grey receive telegram from Belgium and ask Asquith to mobilize: Haldane, 294–5.

135 Conservatives urge support of France and Russia: Dugdale, II, 79–80; Chamberlain, 99–100.

135 Russia disliked as ally: Morley, 6.

135 Lichnowsky's last interview with Grey: Grey, II, 13.

136 House of Commons awaiting Grey: MacDonagh, 3; *Punch*, August 12, 153.

136 "Pale, haggard and worn": Grenfell, Field Marshal Lord, *Memoirs*, London, 1925, 204.

137 Grey's speech: full text, Grey, II, Appendix D.

137 Lord Derby's whisper: Grenfell, *op. cit.*, 204.

138 Ramsay MacDonald, Keir Hardie, and unconvinced Liberals: NYT, August 4.

PAGE

138 "What happens now?": Churchill, 235.

139 "If they refuse there will be war": Poincaré, IV, 519 (French ed.).

139 "You will be home before the leaves": Blücher, 137.

139 German diarist: *ibid.*, 12, 16.

139 Breakfast in Paris on Sedan Day: Count Häseler, qtd. Grelling, 30.

139 Russian expectations of early victory: Vladimir Gurko, 542; Botkin, 112.

139 English officer asked about duration: Bridges, 74.

140 "Vasilii Fedorovitch": Vladimir Gurko, 542.

140 German stockpile of nitrates: Erzberger, 15.

140 Joffre predicts long war: Joffre, 53.

140 Kitchener's prediction: Birkenhead, 22.

141 "If only someone had told me": qtd. Bernhard Huldermann, *Albert Ballin*, London, 1922, 212.

141 Prince Henry and King George: King George to Grey, December 8, 1912, BD, X, part 2, No. 452. On July 26, 1914, Prince Henry, who was again in England, was told by King George, "I hope we shall remain neutral. . . . But if Germany declares war on Russia and France joins Russia, then I am afraid we shall be dragged into it." Nicolson, *George V*, 245–6.

141 Kaiser "convinced" England would be neutral: Freytag-Loringhoven, qtd. *AQ*, April, 1924, 153.

141 *Corpsbrüder*: Wile, 212.

141 "More English, the better": Kuhl, 34.

141 Moltke's memorandum of 1913: Ritter, 68–9. Even in 1906 Schlieffen envisaged Britain as an enemy with an expeditionary force of 100,000 in Belgium, *ibid.*, 161–4.

142 "We had no doubt whatever" of the BEF: Kuhl, qtd. *AQ*, April, 1922, 166.

142 "England probably hostile": qtd. Frothingham, 60. The German Navy, like the Army, expected Britain to be an enemy: "There was scarcely any possible doubt that England would never countenance a military weakening of France by us," Tirpitz, I, 334.

142 Crown Prince, the "military solution": *My War Experiences*, 5.

142 "The Blessing of Arms": *Alldeutscher Blätter*, August 3, qtd. Hallays, 27.

142 Reichstag deputies depressed: Hanssen, 13, 19.

143 Herrick calls Viviani: Poincaré, II, 284.

143 Schoen brings declaration of war: *ibid.*, 285–8.

143 "The lamps are going out": Grey, II, 20.

144 Below's note, "if necessary": Bassompierre, 37.

144 Whitlock calls on Below: Whitlock, 64; Gibson, 22.

144 "Our greatest disaster": Czernin, *In the World War*, New York, 1920, 16.

144 "We Germans lost the first great battle": Crown Prince, *Memoirs*, 180.

145 Many suspect a trick: Galet, 51; Joffre, 135.

PAGE

145 Messimy's order: Messimy, 289.

145 King Albert's appeal to guarantors: Galet, 63.

145 Moltke hopes for "an understanding": Moltke to Jagow, Kautsky, No. 788.

145 Jagow's interview with Beyens: Beyens, II, 269–72.

146 "Common bond of love and hate": Millard, 35.

146 Austrian minister's tears: Bassompierre, 41.

146 King Albert in Parliament: Galet, 62; Gibson, 13–19; Whitlock, 60.

146 Crowds' enthusiasm: Bassompierre, 40; Millard, 35–7.

147 Foreign volunteers in Paris: Gibbons, 27.

147 Speeches of Viviani and Poincaré: *French Yellow Book*, Nos. 158 and 159; Poincaré, II, 296–7.

148 Joffre "perfectly calm": Poincaré, *ibid.*

148 Scenes in Berlin: Hanssen, 25.

148 Picture of Wilhelm I at Sedan: Wetterlé, 29.

148 Bethmann and Erzberger meet deputies: Haussmann, 16–20.

149 Kaiser's speech in Weisser Saal: *ibid.*, 21; Hanssen, 25; text of speech is in Ralph H. Lutz, *Fall of the German Empire, Documents, 1914–18*, Stanford, 1932, Vol. I.

149 Social Democrats debate "Hoch!": Haussmann, 23.

149 Promises of Jagow and von Heeringen: Erzberger, 231.

149 Bethmann's speech: NYT, August 5, 2:6; full text in Lutz, *op. cit.*

150 British ultimatum: *British Blue Book*, Nos. 153 and 159.

151 Goschen-Bethmann interview: Bethmann, 159, note; Goschen to Grey, *British Blue Book*, No. 160.

152 Stoning British Embassy: Gerard, 137; Beyens, I, 273.

152 "To think that George and Nicky": qtd. Blücher, 14.

152 "Treat us like Portugal": Tirpitz, I, 307.

152 "Not much loved": Crown Prince, *Memoirs*, 81–2.

152 Depressed deputies' comments: Haussmann, 25, 27; Hanssen, 32.

153 Rumor about Japan: Hanssen, 14.

153 "Siam is friendly": Blücher, 6.

154 Cambon visits Grey: Poincaré, II, 293.

154 Wilson's indignation at mobilization order: Wilson, 147, 156; Chamberlain, 103–4.

154 Balfour's letter to Haldane: Dugdale, II, 81.

154 Asquith reads ultimatum to House: *Punch*, August 12, 154; MacDonagh, 78. *Punch*'s correspondent, who was present, says Asquith's statement was received with "a deep-throated cheer . . . fierce in its intensity." *The Times* correspondent (MacDonagh) who was also present says it was received in "complete silence." This illustrates one of the perils of writing history.

155 Cabinet waits for midnight: Lloyd George, 69–71.

155 Moltke, "next 100 years": Conrad, IV, 194.

10. "Goeben . . . *an Enemy Then Flying*"

Sources for all action by, and events aboard, the *Goeben* and *Breslau*, unless otherwise noted, are Souchon, Kopp, and *Krieg zur See*, the official German naval history. Likewise, for action of the British ships, the sources are the official history, Corbett, 56–73 (with two magnificent maps, unfortunately too large to reproduce in these less expansive days), Milne, and Churchill, 236–43 and 265–75. Corbett's account was published first; Milne's was written to dispute Corbett who, he felt, had done him injustice, Churchill's to compose a narrative that, while not too obviously blaming the naval commanders, would show the Admiralty to have been blameless and still claim to be history, not special pleading. This delicate feat of balancing was accomplished by placing the blame for failure to arrest the *Goeben* on accidents of fate; on "the terrible Ifs," in his words. The account is one to read with caution not incompatible with admiration.

PAGE

159 Admiralty wireless to Souchon: *Krieg zur See*, 2. Tirpitz's idea was that Souchon should be placed at the disposal of the Turkish Government "to command the Turkish fleet." Tirpitz to Jagow, Kautsky, No. 775.

160 Enver as advocate of German alliance: Emin, 66–69; Nogales, 26, Morgenthau, 30–34.

160 Talaat's appetite and views: Steed, I, 377; Morgenthau, 20–24; Nogales, 26–28.

160 Churchill on Turkey: *Aftermath*, 374.

161 Churchill's letter rejecting Turkish alliance: Churchill, 524.

161 Kaiser's instructions: These took the form of marginal notes on telegrams from Wangenheim, German ambassador in Constantinople, Kautsky, Nos. 141 and 149. The Kaiser was on his yacht at this time, mid-July, and his marginalia were telegraphed to the Foreign Office as instructions.

161 Turkish-German negotiations for treaty: Emin, 66–8; Djemal, 107–14; correspondence between Wangenheim and Jagow; Kautsky Nos. 45, 71, 117, 141, 144, 183, 285. Draft of the Treaty, signed Bethmann-Hollweg, is No. 320; final text is No. 733; further discussion of terms and implementation, Nos. 398, 411, 508, 517, 726, 836.

162 British seizure of Turkish warships: Churchill, *Aftermath*, 377–8; Djemal, 96, 104, 116; Grey, II, 165–66; Grey's "regrets": *British Blue Book*, II, Nos. 1, 2, 3, and 4.

162 Turkish warships cost $30,000,000: Allen, Whitehead, and Chadwick, *The Great War*, Philadelphia, 1916, II, 374.

163 Turkish ministers' second thoughts: On August 3 Wangenheim reported that Enver would like "to declare war immediately" but the other ministers were against it; Kautsky, No. 795.

165 "Spit in the soup": Souchon, 33.

166 "How many boilers leaking?": Souchon gives the conversation verbatim, 37.

PAGE

166 British Consul's telegram: BD, XI, 480.

166 Churchill's July 31 instructions to Milne: Churchill, 237–8.

166 Not intended "as a veto": *ibid.*, 272.

167 "Betrayal of the Navy": Fisher, *Letters*, II, 451, April 22, 1912.

167 Fisher's wrath: *ibid.*; "succumbing to court influence," 458; "Utterly useless," *ibid.*; "unfitted," 451; "backstairs cad," 360; "serpent," 418; "Sir B. Mean," 447.

168 Churchill's Order of August 2: Churchill, 239; third order to Milne, *ibid.*

169 Gauthier challenges Messimy: Poincaré, II, 279–80.

169 Orders to Lapeyrère and his subsequent actions: Capt. Voitoux, "l'Evasion du Goeben et Breslau," *Revue Politique et Parlementaire*, March and May, 1919. The French role in the failure to arrest the *Goeben*, like the British, became a cause of extreme embarrassment to the government and was investigated in 1916 by a Parliamentary Committee of Inquiry under Admiral Amadée Bienaimé. Its report, implying blame of Admiral Lapeyrère, which he refused to answer, was never published but was analyzed in Admiral Bienaimé's book which gives the impression of making Admiral Lapeyrère the scapegoat for a general dissatisfaction with the navy. Materials collected by the Committee of Inquiry were deposited in 1919 with the Ministry of Marine.

170 "Tasting that moment of fire" and "sowing death and panic": Souchon, 40.

170 *Goeben* flew the Russian flag and "Our trick succeeded": Kopp, 23–4.

171 Milne reports position to Admiralty: Churchill, 239.

171 "Very good. Hold her": *ibid.*

171 Churchill's "urgent" message to Asquith: *ibid.*, 240.

172 "Winston with war paint": Asquith, II, 21.

172 Stokers' deaths: Kopp, 28–31, 53; Souchon, 42.

172 "Tortures of Tantalus": Churchill, 242.

173 Order to respect Italian neutrality and "petty incident": *ibid.*, 241.

174 Two messages from Tirpitz: *Krieg zur See*, 13; Souchon, 47. Turkish hesitations which caused the cancellation are reported by Wangenheim, Kautsky, Nos. 852 and 854.

174 "To force the Turks": Souchon, 47.

174 Sicilian headlines: Souchon, 45.

176 "Prevent the Austrians from coming out": Corbett, 62.

176 Troubridge, "handsomest officer" and "Believed in seamanship": Kenworthy, 32.

177 *Gloucester* ordered to "avoid capture": Milne, 104.

178 Admiralty clerk's error about Austria: Churchill, 275.

179 "Indispensable military necessity.": *Krieg zur See*, 20.

180 "Enter. Demand surrender": *ibid.*

180 Wangenheim's "agitated interest": Morgenthau, 70–71.

PAGE

181 Enver's interview with Col. Kress: Kannengiesser, 25–26.

181 "More slaughter, more misery": Churchill, 271.

181 Admiralty order to blockade Dardanelles: Corbett, 73.

181 Asquith, "We shall insist": Asquith, II, 26.

182 "Sale" of the *Goeben*: Djemal, 119–20; Morgenthau, 76–78. The "sale" and the diplomatic furor aroused by the arrival of the German warships are documented in the reports of the various ambassadors in Constantinople to their governments, especially Giers to the Russian Foreign Office and Sir Louis Mallet to the British, contained in the *Russian Orange Book*, II, and the *British Blue Book, II*, respectively.

182 Sazonov, "Even if we are victorious": Paléologue, 84–85.

182 "Most bellicose" and "violently anti-Turk": Asquith, II, 26, 28.

183 Gallieni's comment: *Gallieni Parle*, 78.

183 Kitchener, "strike the first blow": *ibid.*, 26.

183 Souchon's attack in Black Sea: Emin, 75–76; Giers to Foreign Office, *Russian Orange Book, II*, No. 98; Roberts to Grey, *British Blue Book, II*, No. 178; Memorandum by Sir Louis Mallet, November 20, *ibid.*

184 "He did forbear to chase": article on Troubridge, *DNB.* On the ground that the House of Commons had the constitutional right to review courts-martial, Commander Bellairs, an M.P., made several attempts to force the Admiralty to release the report of the Court, without success. As the finding was acquittal, the Commander said he could see no reason for the Admiralty to keep the report secret, "except to prevent the public from knowing the bad arrangements they made at the outset of the war." April 15, 1919, *Parliamentary Debates*, 5th series, Vol. 114, 2863–71.

184 "Their Lordships approved": article on Milne, *DNB.*

11. Liège and Alsace

Unless otherwise noted, the operations of the Belgian Army in this chapter are based chiefly on Galet, van der Essen, and Cammaerts; of the German Army on Ludendorff's chapter "Liège," 28–46, and on Reichsarchiv, *Weltkrieg*, Vol. I, 108–20, which, rather disproportionately, gives twelve pages to the infantry assault and only one to the work of the siege guns. The assembly, transport, and operations of the guns are taken chiefly from Schindler. Operations of the Army of Alsace are from Dubail and *AF*, I, I, Chapters 4 and 5, 90–154.

185 Encourage an uprising in Alsace: Joffre, 136; Engerand, *Bataille*, 193.

186 "I will go through Belgium": qtd. J. M. Kennedy, *The Campaign Round Liège*, London, 1915.

186 "Rage of dreaming sheep": a remark applied by Baron von Stein to the Tugenbund, qtd. Buchan, 129.

188 Moltke on the 39th day: In correspondence with Conrad in 1909 Moltke at first said he expected to be able to transfer troops to help

PAGE

Austria, after defeating France, "between the 36th and 40th day of mobilization." Conrad, I, 369. Later he thought he could defeat France by the 21st day if she took the offensive and by the 28th day if she fought behind her frontiers. *Ibid.*, 374. Five years later, on May 12, 1914, when Conrad visited Moltke at Karlsbad, Moltke said, "We hope to be finished with France in six weeks from the start of operations or at least to be so far forward that we can turn our main forces to the East." *Ibid.*, III, 669. On this occasion, he specified achieving a decision in the west "on the 39th or 40th day after mobilization." Karl Friedrich Nowak, *Les Dessous de la défait*, Paris, Payot, 1925, 53.

188 Siege guns: In addition to Schindler, whose account is largely concerned with the transport and actual operation of the guns, the technical facts are taken from Army War College, *Study on Development of Large Calibre Mobile Artillery in the European War*, Washington, GPO, 1916, p. 8; *U.S. Field Artillery Journal*, October 1914, p. 591 and January 1915, p. 35; "Austria's Famous 'Skoda' Mortars," *Scientific American*, July 3, 1915.

189 Emerson, mark of the beast: qtd. Whitlock, 126.

190 "One of the greatest soldiers": Ludendorff, 28.

190 "Nobody believed in Belgium's neutrality": *ibid.*, 29.

191 "Hold to the end": Galet, 56.

192 M. Flechet, Burgomaster of Warsage: Hanotaux, III, 84.

193 German proclamations: van der Essen, 52.

194 "Chocolate soldiers": Schryver, qtd. *AQ*, October, 1922, 157.

195 Belgian Government proclamations: Gibson, 31; Cobb, 90.

195 "Summary executions of priests": Bülow, III, 160. General von Bülow was killed the same day. According to rumor at the time, he committed suicide; according to an investigation conducted by Prince Bülow, he was shot by a *franc-tireur*.

195 Six hostages of Warsage shot: Hanotaux, III, 125.

195 Battice "burnt out . . . gutted": Bloem, 27, 29.

196 "Our advance is certainly brutal": Conrad, IV, 193.

196 Belgian officer's account: qtd. *Times History of the War*, I, 336.

197 "To intimidate the governor": Ludendorff, 41.

198 Ultimatum to Leman to surrender: Schryver, 103.

198 Zeppelin attack: *Weltkrieg*, I, 115.

198 Attempt to kidnap Leman: van der Essen, 62.

198 "Spared not but slew": Martin H. Donohue in NYT, August 10.

199 "Hummed with wild plans": Cammaerts, 147.

200 Woman offers flowers by mistake to German: Bloem, 48.

200 Joffre's refusal to divert troops to Belgium: Poincaré, III, 7.

200 Joffre's letter to King Albert and King's reply: Galet, 83–4.

201 Belgium "defending the independence of Europe": M. Deschanel, qtd. *Times*, August 7. So great was the moral effect of Belgium's resistance that even the Irish Nationalist leader, John Redmond, said there

PAGE

was no sacrifice he would not make on behalf of Belgium, *Times History of the War*, I, 357.

202 "Hurrah, in Liège!": Bülow, 22.

202 Kaiser reproaches, then kisses Moltke: Moltke, *Erinnerungen*, 24.

202 Kaiser "despondent": Gerard, 198, 206.

203 German note of August 9: Gibson, 44.

203 "We were cornered into it": Cammaerts, 20.

203 Berthelot's mission and King's reply: Galet, 93–5.

205 Dubail: Engerand, 456–7.

205 Lanrezac "a veritable lion": Spears, 345. One of Joffre's choices: Joffre, 12, 236.

206 Lanrezac's letter criticizing strategy: *AF*, I, I, Annexe 19, 59–60; Lanrezac, 54–56; Engerand, 412–15.

206 Joffre ignored it: Joffre, 130–31.

206 Joffre's reply to Ruffey: Briey, April 15, 1919, evidence of Ruffey.

207 "That may be your plan": *ibid.*, also Dubail, 12, and Lanrezac, 60–61.

207 Chauffeur, Georges Bouillot: NYT, September 20, IV, 3.

207 Joffre's habits and characteristics: Mayer, 40; Pierrefeu, *GQQ*, 96–99.

208 "*Il m'a toujours fait mousser*": *Gallieni parle*, 69.

209 Bonneau's fears: Dubail, 14–20.

210 Entry into Altkirch and parade in Mulhouse: Hanotaux, III, 179, 185–92.

211 "Faulty execution": qtd. Mayer, 35; Joffre, 152, 156.

212 Storks leave Alsace: Poincaré, III, 51.

212 "Silently and anonymously" and Joffre's orders to generals not to discuss strategy: Gallieni, *Mémoires*, 172; Corday, 138; Poincaré, III, 92. Messimy, 243–52, gives a heart-rending account of the Government's "anguish" at being kept uninformed by GQG of events at the front and of its persistent efforts to force Joffre out of his "obstinate mutism." Although his exasperation nerved Messimy at one point to inform his liaison officer with GQG that "this intolerable and even ridiculous situation" could not continue, and to appoint André Tardieu as his own representative at GQG, Joffre calmly continued in his "systematic defiance" of the Government and managed to "seduce" Tardieu to his views.

212 Joffre orders generals not to discuss strategy: Gallieni, *Mémoires*, 172; Corday, 138.

212 "That is how history is written": Gallieni, *Carnets*, 33, n. 1.

213 Gallieni worries: *ibid.*, 32, n. 2.

213 French cavalry's advance: Maurice, 30; Spears, 100. The French cavalry's habits were severely disapproved by British cavalrymen. "They never got off," says Major Bridges, 81.

214 Ian Hamilton, Hoffmann and Moltke's "crazy way": qtd. De Weerd, 72.

214 Fournier's report and dismissal: Poincaré, III, 19; Engerand, 422.

PAGE

214 Lanrezac's anxiety "premature": Joffre, 159.

215 GQG's arguments disposing of German threat: Joffre, 141, 147–8, 150.

215 Col. Adelbert's mission: Galet, 96.

215 Saw themselves in Berlin and German retreat "final": *ibid.*, 100.

216 Siege guns begin bombardment: Schindler, 119; Muhlon, 92; Essen, 77–79; Sutherland, 34, 83, who was in Namur when the same guns shelled those forts ten days later.

217 Demblon describes gun dragged through streets: Demblon, 110–11.

217 Capture of General Leman: Hanotaux, III, 254.

217 "Death would not have me": Cammaerts, 151.

12. BEF to the Continent

Unless otherwise noted, facts about the BEF are from Edmonds and all quotations from Sir Henry Wilson and Haig are from their diaries edited by Callwell and Blake respectively.

219 "Brains of canaries": Philip Gibbs, *Now It Can Be Told.*

219 "Frocks" and "Boneheads": Childs, 134.

220 Kitchener scorns plan to "tack on" BEF: qtd. F. Maurice, *Life of General Rawlinson*, 95.

220 "We must be prepared": qtd. Magnus, 284. On Kitchener's views, see also Esher, *Tragedy*, 31, 38–9.

221 Duke of Wellington: qtd. Hurd, *British Fleet*, 29.

221 "Like partridges": qtd. Magnus, 279.

222 "See them damned first": Esher, *Journals*, III, 58.

222 "Tranquilize public feeling": Arthur, 13.

222 "It was never disclosed . . . by some flash of instinct": Grey, II, 69.

223 War with Germany an "eventual certainty": Wilson, 112.

224 "practical grasp of minor tactics": article on French, *DNB.*

224 "French is a trump": qtd. Trevelyan, 198.

224 "I don't think he is clever": to the Duke of Connaught, May 23, 1915, qtd. Nicolson, *George V*, 266.

225 "Mercurial temperament": qtd. Cruttwell, 23.

225 "Heart of a romantic child": Esher, *Tragedy*, 43.

225 Proceedings of War Council of August 5: Churchill, 248–55; Haldane, 296; Wilson, 158–9; Blake, 68–9; Esher, *Tragedy*, 24.

227 "As much an enemy as Moltke": qtd. Magnus, 302.

227 Officers' swords sharpened: *Memoirs of Field Marshal Montgomery of Alamein*, New York, 1958, 30.

227 "Best-trained . . . best-equipped": Edmonds, 11.

227 It seemed to an officer that Kluck could hear: Childs, 115.

228 A French witness at Rouen: qtd. Poincaré, III, 31.

228 Thunder and blood-red sunset: Childs, 117.

PAGE

228 Haig told a fellow officer: Charteris, 11.

229 Sir John French and Callwell visit Intelligence: Callwell, *Dug-Out*, 17.

229 Proceedings of War Council of August 12: Huguet, 41–2; Wilson, 162–3; Arthur, *Kitchener*, 22.

230 Kitchener's instructions to C. in C.: Edmonds, Appendix 8.

231 "Temptations in wine and women": text in Spears, Appendix XIII.

232 French greetings along the way: Corbett-Smith, 32.

232 "Roses all the way": Bridges, 75.

13. Sambre et Meuse

Spears' narrative, Chapters IV through VIII, is the most vivid and valuable in English for the Sambre and Meuse front if its strong anti-Lanrezac bias and other prejudices are skirted and Lanrezac, Engerand, and other French accounts are read to balance it. All French orders cited are in the *Annexes* to *AF*, I, I.

233 "Thank God we don't have any!": qtd. Monteil, 34; also on the artillery, Dubail, 44; Messimy, 86–87.

234 "Sack" strategy of Rupprecht's Army: Rupprecht, 12, 15.

234 White roses for King Charles: NYT, Obituary of Rupprecht, August 9, 1955.

235 "Barbarians": Dubail, 39.

235 Lanrezac's fears and efforts to shift the Fifth Army to the left: Lanrezac, 67–77.

236 "Maybe even two million": Percin, 105.

236 "What, again!": Lanrezac, 73.

236 "The responsibility is not yours": Pierrefeu, *Plutarque*, 69.

237 "The Germans have nothing ready there": Lanrezac, 78.

237 "Death in my soul": *ibid.*

237 Lanrezac's letter to Joffre on Intelligence report: *ibid.*, 79; Annexe No. 283; Joffre, 159.

238 Gallieni goes to Vitry: Joffre, 158; Messimy, "Comment j'ai nommé Gallieni," *Revue de Paris*, September 15, 1921, 247–61.

238 Joffre agrees to "preliminary arrangements": Annexe No. 270.

239 Special Instruction No. 10: Annexe No. 307.

239 Complicated exchange of troops: Joffre, 164; Engerand, 523–4.

240 Lanrezac suspects a British trick: Spears, 89.

241 "Modern Alexander": Schlieffen's *Cannae*, qtd. Earle, *Modern Strategy*, 194.

241 German wireless garbled and channels clogged: Bauer, 47; Kuhl, qtd. *AQ*, January, 1921, 346.

242 Von Stein, rude, tactless, Berlin Guards' tone: Stürgkh, 24.

242 Tappen's "odious manner": Bauer, 34.

242 Moltke forbade champagne and Kaiser's meager fare: *ibid.*, 46.

242 OHL weighs shift of strategy to left wing: Tappen, 103–4.

PAGE

243 Arguments of Rupprecht and Krafft in favor of attack: Rupprecht, 13–21; these and the following account of events at Sixth Army Hq., visits of Zollner and Dommes, conversations with them and OHL are from Krafft, 12–22.

245 Greetings to Sir John French and Poincaré's reactions: Guard, 23; Poincaré, III, 51.

246 "Waiting attitude": French, 39.

247 "Choose his own hours for fighting": Poincaré, III, 225.

247 Clausewitz, "the most *enterprising*": qtd. Poincaré, III, 169.

247 Sir John's visit to Joffre: Joffre, 161; French, 34–5.

247 "*Au fond*, they are a low lot": qtd. Magnus, 302.

247 Sir John "much impressed": to Kitchener, August 17, French, 39–40.

248 "At last you're here": Huguet, 51.

248 Meeting of Sir John French and Lanrezac and the conversation about Huy: Besides the accounts of the two principals which are of little interest, there are four eyewitness reports of this encounter: Wilson's in Callwell, 164; Spears, 72–82; Huguet, 51, and a postwar speech by Captain Fagalde, Intelligence officer of Lanrezac's staff, to the Forum Club, London, qtd. *AQ*, April, 1925, 35.

249 Misunderstandings about cavalry and date and Lanrezac's report to Joffre: Spears, 80–81; Annexe No. 430.

250 "Please do as I ask you in this matter": French, 40.

250 French and Smith-Dorrien never got on: Bridges, 80.

250 "One of the most unfortunate books": J. W. Fortescue, *Quarterly Review*, October 1919, 363.

250 King Albert's talk with de Broqueville: Galet, 103, 116–19.

250 Germans west of the Meuse a "screen": Galet, 106.

251 "Incredulous dismay": Galet, 122.

251 Col. Adelbert's outburst: Klobukowski, *Résistance belge*; D'Ydyewalle, 109; Galet, 122.

251 Special Instruction No. 13: Annexe No. 430.

252 "Throw them back into the Sambre": Spears, 92.

253 Bethelot to Messimy, "So much the better": Briey, March 28, evidence of Messimy.

253 Commandant Duruy: Spears, 87–8, 94.

254 "They always managed to escape": Kluck, 32.

254 Kluck's cavalry report British at Ostend: Kluck, 18.

255 Kluck's extreme annoyance: Kluck, 22; Bülow, 37.

255 Density figures for German armies: Edmonds, 44.

255 Kluck disputed Bülow's orders: Kluck, 29–30.

255 "Severe and inexorable reprisals": *ibid.*, 25–6.

255 Aerschot, 150 killed: Whitlock, 209; Dinant: Gibson, 326–29. Method of procedure: Gibson, 151; Whitlock, Cobb, *et al.*, see Notes to Chap. 16.

256 Quotations from Hausen: Hausen, 25, 135, 141, 152–3.

PAGE

256 German proclamations quoted: Whitlock, 70–71; 162.
257 "Slow in remedying the evil": Kluck, 26.
257 Rag doll seemed a symbol: Cobb, 79.
258 German entry into Brussels: Gibson, 115; Whitlock, 113, 124–6, 138.
259 A "fierce joy" in Berlin: Blücher, 20.
260 General Pau's farewell: *La France héroïque et ses alliés*, Paris, Larousse, 1916, I, 44. Joffre's speech at Thann: Hinzelen, Emile, *Notre Joffre*, Paris, Delagrave, 1919, 39.
260 Berthelot, "No reason to get excited": Annexe No. 587.
260 "I understand your impatience": Annexe No. 589.
261 "There is reason to await with confidence": Annexe No. 585.

14. Debacle: Lorraine, Ardennes, Charleroi, Mons

262 "It is a glorious and awful thought": Wilson, 165.
262 Field Regulations and "gymnastics so painfully practised": qtd. Lt.-Col. Fliecx, *Les Quatre Batailles de France*, Paris, 1958, 12–13.
263 Plan 17's most passionate critic: Engerand, 473.
263 Dubail's "repugnance": Dubail, 57. Battles of Morhange-Sarrebourg: *AF*, I, I, 176–265, *passim*.
263 Nothing visible but corpses and "God teaches the law to kings": Engerand, 473.
264 "To attack as soon as we are ready": qtd. Edmonds, 507.
264 "We will continue, gentlemen": Giraud, 535.
264 "I went to Nancy on the 21st": Aston, *Foch*, 115.
265 OHL lured by the left wing: Tappen, 15 (German ed.).
265 Case 3 and Krafft's call to Tappen: Rupprecht, 37, n.; Krafft, 47.
266 Joffre's order for attack in Ardennes: Annexes Nos. 592 and 593. Battle of Ardennes: *AF*, I, I, 351–432, *passim*.
266 "Await artillery support": Annexe No. 352.
267 Ardennes favorable to side lacking heavy artillery: Joffre, 66.
267 Joffre's memoirs: Messimy (88) says they were written by "a group of faithful and devoted officers."
268 "Only ordinary mental calibre": Wile, *Men Around the Kaiser*, 69.
268 "Only by relying on the sword": Grelling, 46.
268 "Gave me theoretical grounding": Crown Prince, *War Experiences*, 3.
268 "*Wilde jagd nach dem Pour le Mérite*": qtd. Goerlitz, 158.
268 "Grave and gloomy faces": Crown Prince, *War Experiences*, 12.
269 *Poète du canon* and "too much imagination": Engerand, 483, 488–9.
269 "*Tout ça c'est du sport*": qtd. Monteil, 34.
269 Fourth Army reconnaissance officer is judged "pessimistic": Engerand, 491.
270 "We who were surprised": Langle, 137.
270 GQG ignored Ruffey's reports: Briey, April 15, evidence of Ruffey.
270 "Might as well have been blindfolded": Commandant A. Grasset,

PAGE

Un Combat de rencontre, Neufchâteau, 22 Aôut, 1914, qtd. *AQ*, January, 1924, 390.

271 "Battlefield unbelievable spectacle": qtd. Engerand, 499, 504.

271 French sergeant's diary: qtd. W. E. Grey, *With the French Eastern Army*, London, 1915, 49.

271 German officer's diary: Charbonneau, 54.

271 "Prodigies of valor" and remainder of paragraph: Crown Prince, *War Experiences*, 26, 29–37.

271 Ruffey loses three divisions: Joffre, 166; Briey, April 15, evidence of Ruffey.

272 "You people at GQG . . . ignorant as an oyster": Briey, *ibid.*

272 Langle's "anguish": Langle, 137. "Serious check at Tintigny": Annexe No. 1098.

273 "Advantage of numerical superiority": Annexe No. 1044.

273 Germany could not have fought without Briey ore: A memorandum addressed to the German Supreme Command by Dr. Reichert of the Iron and Steel Association in December 1917 supported a plea for annexation of Briey with the argument that without the ores of this region "the continuation of the war would have been impossible. If we had not possessed Briey we would have been defeated long ago." *Wirtschaftzeitung der Zentralmaechte*, December 17, 1917, qtd. Engerand, 486. The subject is fully discussed in Engerand's *Rapport* on Briey, *première partie.*

273 "Every effort to renew the offensive": qtd. Isaac, *Joffre et Lanrezac*, 87.

274 "Do as he tells you": qtd. *AQ*, April, 1923, 37.

274 Telegram from Papa William: Crown Prince, *War Experiences*, 37.

274 "Dazzling white tunic": Sven Hedin, qtd. Gardiner, 223.

274 Iron Cross could only be avoided by suicide: Stürgkh.

274 Joffre orders Lanrezac to attack and BEF to "cooperate": Annexe No. 695. Battle of Charleroi: *AF*, I, I, 433–480, *passim.*

276 Kitchener's telegram of August 19: Arthur, 29.

276 "Give battle alone": Spears, 127. "I leave you absolute judge": Annexe No. 705.

277 No trenches or fixed defenses: Spears, 105; Engerand, 530–31.

277 "With bugles blowing": Spears, 132.

277 "Long singing scream": Sutherland, 36–9.

277 "There must be a band": Spears, 128.

278 "I know the situation thoroughly": Arthur, 30.

278 "Information . . . exaggerated": Spears, 137, n.

279 Calvalry encounter at Soignies: Bridges, 77.

279 Orders to Smith-Dorrien: Edmonds, preface to Bloem, viii.

280 Kluck intended to "attack and disperse": Kluck, 33.

280 Kluck protests, Bülow insists: Kluck, 37–8, 41–2.

280 "No landings of importance": Bülow, 50.

281 Bülow's and Hausen's complaints: Bülow, 58; Hausen, 165–6, 191–3.

PAGE

281 General Boë: Spears, 144.

281 IIIrd Corps "terrible" losses: Annexe No. 894.

281 2.25 shots per minute: Lanrezac, 135.

282 "Forced to fall back . . . suffered severely" *et seq.*: Annexe No. 876.

282 Lanrezac's request to Sir John French and his reply: Spears, 149–50; Edmonds, 92, n. 2.

283 "*Il plut des marmites*": Engerand, 537.

283 "Prey to extreme anxiety" and all quotations on these pages: Lanrezac, 181, 183–4, 196. General Spears has stated (173) that the retreat of the Fourth Army "was not the reason" for Lanrezac's decision because, according to Spears, Lanrezac did not know of it until next morning, a direct contradiction of Lanrezac's own statement that he had "received confirmation" of it before he made his decision. Writing after Lanrezac was dead, Spears states (173 n.), "There is not the least trace of such a communication." In view of the fact that, as Messimy testified at the Briey hearings, the archives contained 45,000 to 50,000 files of 500 to 1,000 documents each, a probable total of 25 to 30 million pieces, Spears' negative is hardly susceptible of proof. His verdict was conditioned less by the evidence than by his feeling that Lanrezac's retreat "left the British in the lurch" (176).

285 "Thinking himself menaced on his right": Lanrezac, 185; Pierrefeu, *Plutarque*, 74.

287 "Owing to the retreat of the Fifth Army": Edmonds, 68, 72. For the battle of Mons, see also Maurice, 58–76.

287 Smith-Dorrien's orders on bridges: Edmonds, 72, n. 1.

287 "Most perfect targets": Smith-Dorrien, 386.

288 "Stubborn resistance": Edmonds, 77.

288 Efforts to blow the bridges: Hamilton, 28; Edmonds, 86.

289 "You are my sole support" *et seq.*: Bloem, 72–73.

289 Wilson made a "careful calculation" and "persuaded": Wilson, 165.

289 Telegram from Joffre: French, 64; Wilson, 167.

290 Sars-la-Bruyère difficult to find: Smith-Dorrien, 388; and experience of the author in 1959.

291 Wilson blames lack of six divisions: Wilson, 167.

291 "Defense of Havre": Arthur, 36.

292 "Over all lay a smell": qtd. Mark Sullivan, *Our Times*, V, 26.

292 Joffre blames executors and all quotations from following three paragraphs: Joffre, 178, 181, 183–5, 187.

294 Deuxième Bureau discovery about reserves: Joffre, 187.

294 Joffre's postwar testimony: Briey, July 4, evidence of Joffre.

294 Anonymous British spokesman: editor of *Army Quarterly*, April, 1925, 35.

295 Fall of Namur a "distinct disadvantage": NYT from London, August 26, 1:3.

295 "We must make up our minds": Poincaré, III, 88.

15. *"The Cossacks Are Coming!"*

Chief sources for military operations in this chapter are Golovin (all references are to his *Campaign of 1914*), Gourko who was with Rennenkampf's Army, Knox who was with Samsonov's Army, Hoffmann and François who were with the Eighth Army, Danilov and Bauer who were at Russian and German Headquarters, respectively, and finally, Ironside who assembled material from both sides. (Hoffmann's two books are referred to in the Notes as *WLO* and *TaT.*)

PAGE

296 "William to St. Helena!": Paléologue, 65.
296 Czar, "Our proper objective": Golovin, 89.
296 "I entreat Your Majesty": Paléologue, 61.
297 Grand Duke's message to Joffre: Joffre, 140.
297 Grand Duke's tears: The colleague who reported them was General Polivanov, War Minister in 1915–16, qtd. Florinsky, *Russia*, New York, 1958, II, 1320.
297 Tears of Messimy and Churchill: Poincaré, III, 3 and Wilson, 163.
298 Russian mobilization orders: Ironside, 39–50.
299 General Reinbot: Gardiner, 132.
299 "Gentlemen, no stealing": *ibid.*, 133.
299 "Never since the dawn of history": qtd. Florinsky, *End of the Empire*, 38.
300 Rumors in Frankfort of 30,000 refugees: Bloem, 13.
302 Faulty schedule of war games repeated in war: Golovin, 38–9.
303 Russians used wireless in clear: Danilov, 203; Hoffmann, *TaT*, 265.
303 Characteristic odor of a horse: Julius West, *Soldiers of the Tsar*, London, 1915, 8.
303 Two German divisions equal to three Russian: McEntee, 90.
303 "Only 25 shells per gun": Golovin, *Army*, 144.
304 "*Kosaken kommen!*": Gourko, 33.
304 "Psychological dangers": Hoffmann, *WLO*, 17.
304 "How to get the Kaiser's ear": Lt.-Gen. Kabisch, *Streitfragen des Weltkrieges*, qtd. *AQ*, July, 1925, 414.
305 "Japan is going to take advantage": qtd. Stephen King-Hall, *Western Civilization and the Far East*, London, 1924, 160.
305 Prittwitz's orders and François's protest: François, 156; Hoffmann, *WLO*, 17.
306 Scene in the steeple: François, 170–76.
307 Rennenkampf's halt and his reasons: Danilov, 192–3; Golovin, 155.
308 German professor of mathematics: François, 276.
310 Moltke's last words to Prittwitz: François, *Tannenberg, Das Cannae des Weltkrieges*, qtd. *AQ*, January, 1927, 411–13.
310 Prittwitz orders François to retreat to Vistula: François, 190.
311 "You can take off your clothes now": Knox, 88.
311 "The whole weight of all that is sensuous": Clausewitz, I, 224.
312 "Lost command of their nerves": Hoffmann, *WLO*, 20–22.

PAGE

312 Prittwitz and Hoffmann dispute retreat to Vistula: Hoffman, *TaT*, 248.

313 Prittwitz telephones OHL: from Prittwitz's papers, found after his death and published in *Militär Wochenblatt*, April 22 and May 7, 1921, qtd. *AQ*, October, 1921, 88–92.

313 Moltke aghast and his orders: Bauer, 45.

313 Hoffmann proposes maneuver to meet Samsonov: Hoffmann, *WLO*, 23.

315 "They are not pursuing us at all": Hoffmann, *TaT*, 250.

315 "Impossible—too daring": Lt.-Gen. Kabisch, qtd. *AQ*, July, 1925, 416.

315 Circumstances of Ludendorff's appointment: Ludendorff, 49–55.

316 Circumstances of Hindenburg's appointment: Hindenburg, 100–03; John Wheeler-Bennett, *Wooden Titan*, New York, 1936, 14–16; Ludwig, *Hindenburg*, Philadelphia, 1935, 83.

317 Gardener who worked for Frederick the Great: Hindenburg, 8.

318 Hindenburg and Ludendorff meet: Ludendorff, 55; Hindenburg, 103.

318 Marshal *Was sagst du*: Capt. Henri Carré, *The Real Master of Germany*, qtd. NYT, May 19, 1918.

318 "A very startled expression": Hoffmann, *TaT*, 253.

319 French "insist" upon offensive upon Berlin: Paléologue, 102.

320 "Simple and kindly man": Knox, 60.

320 Horses hitched in double harness: Golovin, 183.

320 Jilinsky's orders and Samsonov's protests: Ironside, 126–9.

321 "A small, gray man," Knox, 62.

321 Martos eats the mayor's dinner: Martos Ms. qtd. Golovin, 188.

321 Further orders of Jilinsky to Samsonov: Ironside, 134–5.

323 VII and XIII Corps did not have the same cipher: Golovin, 171.

323 Scholtz "grave but confident": Hoffmann, *TaT*, 261.

323 Intercept of Samsonov's orders: *ibid.*, 265; Ludendorff, 59.

16. Tannenberg

324 François refuses to attack without artillery: Hoffmann, 273–5; (all references in this chapter to Hoffmann are to his *Truth About Tannenberg*).

324 "If the order is given": François, 228.

325 Two intercepted Russian messages: Ludendorff, 59; Hoffmann, 265–68. "He kept asking me anxiously": qtd. Nowak, Introduction to Hoffmann's *Diaries*, I, 18. Hoffmann's account of Rennenkampf-Samsonov quarrel, 314; his handing over the messages while cars in motion, 268.

326 Ludendorff's fit of nerves: Ludendorff, 58; Hindenburg, 115, 118; Hoffmann, 282.

327 Tappen's call from OHL: Hoffmann, 315–16. OHL's reasons: Tappen, 16–19, 110–111. President of the Prussian Bundesrat: Ludwig, 456.

PAGE

Director of Krupp: Muhlon, 113. Kaiser deeply affected: François, 51. Moltke quoted: Memorandum of 1913, Ritter, 68–9.

327 Three corps withdrawn from Belgium: Bülow, 64–5; Hansen, 179.

328 "Advance into the heart of Germany": Ironside, 133.

328 "I don't know how the men bear it": *ibid.*, 130.

329 Jilinsky's orders "to meet the enemy retreating from Rennenkampf": *ibid.*, 134.

329 "To see the enemy where he does not exist": Golovin, 205; *Poddavki*: *ibid.*, 217.

329 Samsonov's orders to VIth Corps: Ironside, 155–7.

330 "In God's name": Agourtine, 34.

330 Army chiefs' pessimism quoted by Sazonov: Paléologue, 104.

330 Description of Stavka: Danilov, 44–46.

331 Notes of Rennenkampf's Staff officer: Ironside, 198.

331 "May be supposed to be retreating to the Vistula": *ibid.*, 200.

332 Blagovestchensky "lost his head": *ibid.*, 157.

332 Samsonov and Potovsky see retreat at first hand: Knox, 68–9; "Terribly exhausted": Ironside, 176.

333 Samsonov's orders to General Artomonov: *ibid.*, 164.

333 Battle of Usdau: Ludendorff, 62–3; Hoffmann, 285–89.

334 Report that François' Corps beaten: Ludendorff, 62.

334 Jilinsky's order, "by moving your left flank": Ironside, 207.

335 Ludendorff begs François to "render greatest possible service": Hoffmann, 305.

335 Ludendorff "far from satisfied": Ludendorff, 64.

336 Mackensen's messenger receives "far from friendly reception": Hoffmann, 310.

336 "He took with him to his grave": Golovin, 254.

337 Samsonov's farewell to Knox: Knox, 73–4.

337 "You alone will save us": Martos Ms., qtd. Golovin, 263.

337 Martos' and Kliouev's corps starving: Kliouev, 245; Knox, 80.

338 Capture of Martos and meeting with Hindenburg and Ludendorff: Martos Ms., qtd. Golovin, 294, 327.

339 "The Czar trusted me" and Samsonov's death: Potovsky Ms., qtd. Golovin, 301; Knox, 82, 88.

340 Prisoners and casualties: François, 243–45.

340 General von Morgen at Neidenberg: François, 240.

340 "I will hear their cries": Blücher, 37.

340 Marshes a myth: Ludendorff, 68; François (245) also calls it a "legend."

341 "One of the great victories": Hoffmann, *Diaries*, I, 41. Naming the battle Tannenberg: Hoffman, 312; Ludendorff, 68. "Strain on my nerves": *ibid.*

341 Ludendorff would go personally to inquire for intercepts: Dupont, 9.

341 "We had an ally": Hoffmann, *Diaries*, I, 41. Tappen (108) also acknowledges that the detailed knowledge of Russian movements

PAGE

obtained from the intercepts "greatly facilitated" German command decisions in East Prussia.

341 "This is where the Field Marshal slept": qtd. De Weerd, 80. Hoffmann remained on the Eastern Front throughout the war, eventually succeeding Ludendorff as Chief of Staff on that front and conducting the German side of the negotiations at Brest-Litovsk. He appears as General Wilhelm Clauss, the central character of Arnold Zweig's novel *The Crowning of a King*, N.Y., 1938.

342 Disgrace of Rennenkampf and Jilinsky: Gurko, 83; Golovin, 386.

342 "Firm conviction that the war was lost": Golovin, *Army*, 24.

342 Ministers' Memorandum urging peace: Richard Charques, *The Twilight of Imperial Russia*, New York, 1959, 216.

343 "We are happy to have made such sacrifices": Knox, 90; Paléologue, 106.

17. The Flames of Louvain

344–47 The quotations on these pages, with three exceptions, are taken from the books by the persons quoted, listed under SOURCES, as follows: Verhaeren, *Dedicace*, unpaged; Cobb, 176–7; Bethmann-Hollweg, 95; Shaw, 37; Bridges, 73; Bergson (Chevalier), 24; McKenna, 158; Clausewitz, I, 5. The statement by Thomas Mann is from his "Reflections of a Nonpolitical Man," 1917, qtd. Hans Kohn, *The Mind of Germany*, New York, 1960, 253–5. H. G. Wells is quoted from NYT, August 5, 3:1. "I'm a'goin' to fight the bloody Belgiums" is from Peel, 21.

348 Placards signed by Bülow: facsimile in Gibson, 324.

348 Massacre at Andenne, Seilles, Tamines: Apart from Belgian sources, the most complete firsthand record of these events is that of the American Minister, Mr. Whitlock, in his chapters xxx, "Dinant"; xxxi, "Namur, Andenne and Elsewhere"; xxxii, "Tamines"; and xxxiii, "*Man Hat Geschossen*." For estimated total of civilians shot in August, see *Encyc. Brit.*, 14th ed., article "Belgium."

349 10 hostages from each street in Namur: Sutherland, 45.

349 Bloem on hostages: 34.

349 Cobb watched from a window: 104.

349 Visé: NYT from Maestricht, August 25, 2:2; Whitlock, 198.

350 Hausen on Dinant: 167–70. 612 dead: Gibson, 329. For description of Dinant after the destruction, Cobb, 409–10.

351 Quotations on these pages are from the works of the persons cited, as follows: Wetterlé, 231; Kluck, 29; Ludendorff, 37; Crown Prince, *War Experiences*, 41–2, 50; Bloem, 28, 32, 20, Blücher, 16, 26.

352 Goethe: qtd. Arnold Zweig, *Crowning of a King*, N.Y., 1938, 306.

353 "That's the French for you": Cobb, 269.

354 Riderless horse sets off panic at Louvain: Whitlock, 152.

PAGE

354 Luttwitz, "A dreadful thing has occurred": *ibid.*

355 Richard Harding Davis: qtd. Mark Sullivan, *Our Times*, V, 29; Arno Dosch in *World's Work*, Oct. and Nov., 1914.

355 Gibson at Louvain: Gibson, 154–172.

355 Monseigneur de Becker: Whitlock, 160.

356 Rotterdam *Courant* and other papers quoted: NYT, August 30.

356 German Foreign Office quoted: *ibid.*, August 31.

357 King Albert quoted: Poincaré, III, 166.

357 *Kriegsbrauch* quoted: 52.

357 Belgium "supreme issue": Wile, *Assault*, 115. "Precipitant": Mark Sullivan, *loc. cit.*

357 Erzberger quoted: 23.

357 Kaiser's telegram: NYT, Sept. 11.

357 Manifesto of the 93 intellectuals: text in *Literary Digest*, Oct. 24, 1914.

358 Bethmann's reply to Wilson: NYT, September 18, 1:4.

358 "No convictions but only appetities": Wetterlé, 144.

358 Bethmann on Erzberger's bright ideas: Bülow, III, 235.

359 Erzberger's Memorandum: Among others to whom Erzberger sent it was Grand Admiral von Tirpitz, who published it after the war in his *Politische Dokumente*, Hamburg, 1926, III, 68–73. See also Karl Epstein, *Matthias Erzberger*, Princeton, 1959, chap. v.

360 "Largest human fact since the French Revolution": Frank H. Simonds in "1914—the End of an Era," *New Republic*, Jan. 2, 1915.

18. Blue Water, Blockade, and the Great Neutral

Sources used for this chapter only:

Baker, Ray Stannard, *Woodrow Wilson, Life and Letters*, Vol. V, N.Y., Doubleday, Doran, 1935

Consett, Rear-Admiral Montagu, *The Triumph of the Unarmed Forces, 1914–18*, London, Williams and Norgate, 1923

Guichard, Lieut. Louis, *The Naval Blockade, 1914–18*, tr., N.Y., Appleton, 1930

House, Edward M., *The Intimate Papers*, ed. Charles Seymour, Vol. I, Boston, Houghton Mifflin, 1926

Page, Walter Hines, *Life and Letters*, Vol. I, ed. Burton J. Hendrick, London, Heinemann, 1923

Parmelee, Maurice, *Blockade and Sea Power*, N.Y., Crowell, 1924

Puleston, Captain William (USN) *High Command in the World War*, N.Y., Scribner's, 1934

Salter, J. A., *Allied Shipping Control*, Oxford U.P., 1921

Siney, Marion C., *The Allied Blockade of Germany, 1914–16*, Univ. of Michigan Press, 1957

Spring-Rice, Sir Cecil, *Letters and Friendships*, ed. Stephen Gwynn, Boston, Houghton Mifflin, 1929.

PAGE

361 "Luxury Fleet": Churchill, 103.

361 Invasion "impracticable": Fisher, *Letters*, II, 504. Report of the "Invasion Committee" of the CID in 1912: Churchill, 158.

361 "Interruption of our trade": qtd. Custance, 104. Trade and tonnage figures: Fayle, 6, 15.

362 "Whole principle of naval fighting": Fisher, *Memories*, 197.

362 "Germany's future is on the water": Kurenberg, 129.

362 Navy League slogans: Wile, *Men Around the Kaiser*, 145–6.

363 "Extreme psychological tension" *et seq.*: Churchill, 276.

363 Jellicoe opened telegram marked "Secret": *DNB*, Jellicoe.

363 Jellicoe "to be Nelson": Fisher, *Letters*, II, 416; III, 33.

363 "Greatest anxiety confronting me": Jellicoe, 92. His chaps. IV and V, "Declaration of War" and "Submarine and Mine Menace in the North Sea," describe this anxiety feelingly on every page.

364 "Infected area": Corbett, 79.

364 "Could have been a seal": *ibid.*, 67.

364 "Markedly superior": Churchill, 261.

364 "Strongest incentives to action": *ibid.*, 276.

364 "Extraordinary silence": *ibid.*, 278.

365 "Kept secret even from me": Tirpitz, II, 87.

365 *Golden Age* on Kaiser's bed-table: Peter Green, *Kenneth Grahame*, N.Y., 1959, 291.

365 Kaiser read Mahan: Kurenberg, 126.

366 "Bring the English to their senses" *et seq.*: Ludwig, 423.

366 Navy Law of 1900 quoted: Hurd, *German Fleet*, 183–4.

367 Kaiser's "darlings": Bülow, I, 198.

367 Tirpitz's squeaky voice: Wetterlé, 218. Müller's characteristics: Ludwig, 465.

367 Ingenohl took a "defensive view": Tirpitz, II, 91. "I need no Chief": Ludwig, 466.

367 "I have ordered a defensive attitude": Ludwig, 465.

368 Tirpitz's request for control, reason for not resigning, and "My position is dreadful": Tirpitz, II, 118–20, 219–20, 223.

369 "Passage of the Atlantic is safe": Corbett, 54.

369 London Conference, Mahan, Declaration: Halévy, 223; Puleston, 130; Siney, 11; Salter, 98–99.

371 U.S. requested adherence and British reply: Secretary Bryan to Ambassador Page, *U.S. For. Rel., 1914*, 215–16, 218–20.

371 CID proposed continuous voyage be "rigorously applied": Siney, 12.

371 Order in Council of August 20: *ibid.*, ff.; Parmelee, 37; Guichard, 17.

372 Spring-Rice quoted: *U.S. For Rel., 1914*, 234.

372 "All sorts of odds and ends": Asquith, II, 33.

372 "Don't bother me with economics": qtd. L. Farago, ed. *Axis Grand Strategy*, N.Y., 1942, 499.

373 "To secure the maximum blockade": Grey, II, 103.

PAGE

374 America "stands ready to help" and "permanent glory": Baker, 2–3.

374 "Neutral in fact" and further quotations in this paragraph: *ibid.*, 18, 24–5, 73.

375 U.S. trade figures: Arthur S. Link, *American Epoch*, N.Y., 1955, 177. Footnote on hidden trade: Consett, *passim*, and figures in *Encyc. Brit.*, 14th ed., article "Blockade."

375 "A government can be neutral": Page, 361.

376 Wilson to Grey: Baker, 55–6.

376 "Utter condemnation": *ibid.*, 62; "Felt deeply the destruction of Louvain": House, 293; "In the most solemn way": Spring-Rice, 223.

377 "This outrage upon humanity": *Lansing Papers*, I, 29–30.

377 "I am afraid something will happen": Baker, 74.

378 "Enthusiasm of the first fight": Tirpitz, II, 91. "Awkward embarrassments": Churchill, 331–35.

378 Kaiser's orders after the battle: Tirpitz, II, 93. What Tirpitz wrote afterward: to Admiral von Pohl, Sept. 16 and Oct. 1, Tirpitz, II, 95–7.

19. Retreat

380 General Order No. 2: *AF*, I, II, 21; Joffre, 189–90.

382 A night of "anguish and horror": Libermann, 37–50.

383 "We left Blombay" and further incidents of French retreat quoted from soldiers' diaries: Hanotaux, V, 221–22; VII, 212, 268; VIII, 76–8.

384 "Corporals, not commanders": Tanant.

385 "Sorry to go without a fight": Hanotaux, VIII, 76.

385 Ministers in "consternation" and "panic": Poincaré, III, 92; Messimy, 364. Events and discussions in Paris during August 25–27 and all direct quotations, unless otherwise noted, are from the following sources: Poincaré, III, 89–99 and 118; Gallieni's *Mémoires*, 20–21, supplemented by his *Carnets*, 17–22, 39–46, Hirschauer, 59–63, and above all from Messimy's helpfully outspoken if confusingly arranged *Souvenirs*, Part Three, Chap. IV, "Nomination de Gallieni comme Gouverneur Militaire de Paris," 206–228; Chap. V. "Le Gouvernement et le G.Q.G.," 229–265 and the last part of Chap. VII, "Le Ministère de la Guerre en Août 1914," the paragraphs entitled, "La panique parlementaire," "la journée du 25 Août," and "la journée du 26 Août," pp. 364–375.

387 "Growing soldiers": Hanotaux, IX, 41. "*Le tourisme*": Monteil, 37.

389 "You are the master": qtd. Renouvin, 83.

392 Joffre detects "menace of government interference": Joffre, 193.

395 "All the tricks of the trade" *et seq.*: qtd. Edmonds, 115.

395 Robertson's food dumps and German reaction: Spears, 221.

395 Lanrezac's "headlong" retreat and report to Kitchener: French, 84; Arthur, 38.

396 Incident at Landrecies: Maurice, 101–02; Hamilton, 52–3; "Without the slightest warning": Edmonds, 134.

PAGE

396 "Send help . . . very critical": Edmonds, 135.

396 Murray's faint: Childs, 124; MacReady, 206; Wilson, 169.

396 Haig's loan of £2,000: Blake, 37.

397 Allenby's warning and decision to fight at Le Cateau: Smith-Dorrien, 400–01.

398 Wilson on telephone to Smith-Dorrien: *ibid.*, 405; Wilson, 168–9.

398 Kluck orders pursuit of "beaten enemy": qtd. Edmonds, 169–70.

398 "Strong French forces": *ibid.*, 211.

399 "Brave front of these Territorials": Smith-Dorrien, 409.

399 Battle of Le Cateau: Edmonds' account, which occupies three chapters and sixty pages, 152–211, has all the relevant information but is too detailed to give a very clear impression. Smith-Dorrien, 400–410, Hamilton, 59–79, and Maurice, 113–14, are more readable. Casualties: Edmonds, 238.

400 "Lord French and staff lost their heads": J. W. Fortescue, *Quarterly Review*, Oct. 1919, 356.

400 Haig offers help to Ist Corps: Edmonds, 291, n. 2.

400 Huguet's telegram: Joffre, 197.

400 Sir John French in his nightshirt: Smith-Dorrien, 411.

401 "Saving of the left wing": *ibid.*, 412.

401 Conference at St. Quentin: Joffre, 195–97; Lanrezac, 209; Huguet, 67; Spears, 233–37.

402 Kluck and Bülow report enemy beaten: Bülow, 64.

402 OHL communiqué: qtd. Edmonds, 204.

402 Friction between German commanders: Bülow, 68–9, 78; Kluck, 51, 63.

403 Hausen's lodgings and complaints: 182, 197–99, 204–5, 215.

403 Kluck's troops slept along roadside: Briey, evidence of Messimy, March 28.

404 Kaiser's telegram: Kluck, 75.

404 "In the hope of celebrating Sedan": qtd. Maurice, 126–7.

404 Kluck proposes "wheel inwards": Kluck, 76.

404 "Sense of victory": Crown Prince, *War Experiences*, 59. OHL General Order of August 28: qtd. Edmonds, 235.

405 OHL deliberations and "an end to the war": Tappen, 105.

406 Battle of the Mortagne: Giraud, 538; *AF*, I, II, 305 ff.

407 General de Maud'huy: Hanotaux, VI, 274.

407 "Courage and tenacity": Joffre, 203.

407 De Langle's battle on the Meuse: De Langle, 20–21, 139; *AF*, I, II, 184–201.

407 Formation of the Foch Detachment: Foch, 41–47.

408 "I have the heads of three generals": Percin, 131.

408 Joffre confessed to sleepless nights: Mayer, 194.

408 61st and 62nd divisions lost: Joffre, 209, 212; Spears, 270, n.

408 Huguet reports BEF "beaten and incapable": Joffre, 203–4.

409 "Almost insane": Spears, 256.

PAGE
409 Schneider and Alexandre: Lanrezac, 218–19; Spears, 256–7.
409 Lanrezac called Joffre a sapper: Mayer, 176.
410 "I suffered an anxiety": Lanrezac, 282.
410 Joffre's rage at Marle: Lanrezac, 225–6; Joffre, 207.
410 Order to Pétain at Verdun: qtd. Pierrefeu, *GQG*, 132.
411 Order to "throw overboard ammunition": text, Edmonds, Appendix 17; Wilson's version: Spears, 254; Gough tore it up: Charteris, 21; Smith-Dorrien countermanded it: Smith-Dorrien, 416–17; "Very damping effect": *ibid.*
412 Toy whistle and drum: Bridges, 87–8.
412 Sir John French and Kaiser: Arthor, 37, 43. On Kitchener's refusal: *ibid.*, 39.
412 Ostend operation: Corbett, 99–100, Churchill, 334–35. Asquith in his diary for August 26 (II, 28–9) records a discussion with Kitchener, Churchill, and Grey about "an idea of Hankey's" (Sir Maurice Hankey, Secretary of the CID) to send 3,000 marines to Ostend which would "please the Belgians and annoy and harass the Germans who would certainly take it to be the pioneer of a larger force." Winston was "full of ardour" about the plan. It was conceived in response to the shock of the news from Mons and the Allied debacle which Churchill received at 7:00 A.M. on August 24 when Kitchener appeared in his bedroom looking "distorted and discolored" as if his face "had been punched with a fist." Saying "Bad news" in a hoarse voice, he handed Churchill Sir John French's telegram reporting the debacle and ending with the ominous proposal to defend Havre. It was hoped by the Ostend operation to draw back some of Kluck's forces to the coast, a move in which it only partially succeeded; but German nervousness about this threat, combined with rumors of Russian landings, contributed to the German decision to retreat at the Marne.
413 "To the sea, to the sea": Macready, 206.

20. The Front Is Paris

414 Sheep in the Place de la Concorde: Guard, 17.
414 Gallieni's plans for defense of Paris: *Carnets*, 46; *Gallieni parle*, 36–42; Hirschauer, 59–63, 93–4, 101, 129. "Byzantine" arguments: *ibid.*, 176.
415 Paris included in Zone of Armies: *AF*, I, II, 585.
415 Gallieni's 15-minute Council of Defense: Hirschauer, 98–99.
416 Work on the defenses, bridges, barricades, taxis, etc.: Gallieni, *Mémoires*, 33–36 and *Gallieni parle*, 52; Hirschauer, *passim*.
416 Reappearance of Dreyfus: Paléologue, *Intimate Journal of the Dreyfus Case*, 309.
417 "Nomeny is thus destroyed": qtd. Poincaré, III, 108.
417 Haig's offer to Lanrezac and Sir John French's refusal: Lanrezac, 229–31; Spears, 264–67. "Terrible, unpardonable" things: *ibid.*, 266.

PAGE

"C'est une félonie!": qtd. Lyon, Laurence, *The Pomp of Power*, N.Y., 1922, 37, n. 22.

418 Joffre at Laon superintends Lanrezac: Joffre, 212; Lanrezac, 239. Battle of St. Quentin-Guise: *AG*, I, II, 67–81.

418 Fears Sir John "might be getting out": Joffre, 213. Conference at Compiègne: *ibid.*, 214; Edmonds, 241.

419 "Definite and prolonged retreat": Edmonds, 241. Maurice quoted, 129; Hamilton quoted, 82–3; MacReady quoted, 105. "Another ten days": Edmonds, 245, Joffre, 217.

420 Wilson sees Joffre at Rheims: Huguet, 75; Wilson, 172.

421 Battle of St. Quentin; French sergeant's account: Sergeant André Vienot, qtd. Hanotaux, VIII, 111–12; Bülow "felt confident": Bülow, 85; captured French orders: McEntee, 65. Lanrezac showed "greatest quickness and comprehension": Spears, 276; Germans were "running away": *ibid.*, 279; Lanrezac-Belin conversation: Lanrezac, 241; Spears, 281–2.

423 "No longer nourish any hope": Joffre, 217.

423 "Most tragic in all French history": Engerand, Briey, *Rapport*. Clausewitz quoted: III, 89. "Wonderful calm": Foch, 42. What Joffre said to Alexandre: Demazes, 65.

424 Preparations to leave Vitry: Joffre, 217. "Broken hopes": Muller, 27.

424 Bülow's mixed report: qtd. Edmonds, 251, n. 4; Kühl, qtd. *AQ*, April, 1927, 157.

424 Defense of Paris not Joffre's intention: According to a lecture given at the Sorbonne in 1927 by Commandant Demazes, a member of Joffre's staff and his biographer, qtd. Messimy, 264.

424 M. Touron: Poincaré, III, 111–12.

425 Cabinet discussions about leaving Paris, visit of Col. Penelon, Joffre's advice, his talk with Gallieni on telephone, Gallieni's talk with Poincaré, Millerand, Doumergue, and Gallieni's advice to Cabinet: Poincaré, III, 115–122; Joffre, 122; Gallieni, *Mémoires*, 37–39; *Carnets*, 48–49.

427 Guesde's outburst: interview with Briand, *Revue de Paris*, Oct. 1, 1930, qtd. *Carnets*, 128, n. 1.

427 Threat to dismiss Joffre: *ibid.* The phrase used by Briand was, "*de lui fendre l'oreille*."

427 Ministers "incapable of firm resolve": Gallieni, *Carnets*, 49.

427 Taube raids: Poincaré, III, 120; Gallieni, *Mémoires*, 40, and *Carnets*, 50; Gibbons, 159. Text of the German proclamation: *AF*, I, II, Annexe No. 1634.

428 German report of Tannenberg and reports of 32 troop trains: Joffre, 222.

429 "You have given proof of *cran*": Hanotaux, VII, 250.

429 Joffre finds De Langle calm, Ruffey nervous: Joffre, 216, 221. Col. Tanant quoted: 22; Ruffey's conversation with Joffre: Engerand, *Bataille*, xv.

430 Amiens dispatch: *The History of the Times*, New York, Macmillan, 1952,

PAGE

IV, Part 1, 222–27. "Patriotic reticence": in Parliament, August 31, qtd. *Times*, Sept. 1, p. 10. "Liberation of the world": Corbett-Smith, 237.

431 The Russian phantoms: D. C. Somervell, *Reign of George V*, London, 1935, 106, 117–18, and R. H. Gretton, *A Modern History of the English People, 1880–1922*, New York, 1930, 924–25, contain many of the stories current at the time. Other references in MacDonagh, 24, Gardiner, 99, Carton de Wiart, 226. Stories told by returning Americans: NYT, Sept. 4, (front page), 5 and 6. Sir Stuart Coats' letter: NYT, Sept. 20, II, 6:3.

433 Operation Order to BEF: Edmonds, Appendix 20.

433 Sir John French's letter to Kitchener: Arthur, 46–7.

434 Kitchener's consternation and telegram to French: *ibid.*, 50; Edmonds, 249.

434 Cabinet "perturbed": Asquith, II, 30. "You will conform": Arthur, 51–52. Robertson's letter: to Lord Stamfordham, June 23, 1915, Nicolson, *George V*, 266. This was at a time when Sir John French was supplying Northcliffe with information for a campaign to blame Kitchener for the munitions shortage. King George went to France to talk to army commanders whom he found, as he wrote to Stamfordham, Oct. 25, 1915, to have "entirely lost confidence" in Sir John French and who assured him the feeling "was universal that he must go." *Ibid.*, 267.

435 Kitchener never regained confidence: Magnus, 292. Birkenhead quoted: 29.

435 Joffre tells Poincaré he has hope, "earnestly" requests BEF to hold, Poincaré exerts influence, Sir John French—"I refused": Joffre, 223; Poincaré, III, 121–22; Edmonds, 249; French, 97.

436 Sir John French's reply to Kitchener: Arthur, 52–4. "A travesty of the facts": Asquith qtd. in *Living Age*, July 12, 1919, 67.

436 Kitchener considered himself entitled to give orders to French: Blake, 34.

436 Kitchener confers at Downing St., wakes Grey: Arthur, 54; Asquith, II, 30.

437 "Irritated, violent": Huguet, 84.

437 Sir John French resents Kitchener's uniform: French, 101. Kitchener wore it customarily: Esher, *Tragedy*, 66; Magnus, 281–2.

437 "Wearing stars in khaki" and "Nice little man in his bath": Sir Frederick Ponsonby, *Recollections of Three Reigns*, New York, 1952, 443–4.

437 Meeting at Embassy: Huguet, 84; French, 101–02.

737 Kitchener's telegram to Government and copy to French: Edmonds, 264.

21. Von Kluck's Turn

439 M. Fabre describes von Kluck: Hanotaux, VIII, 158.

439 Kluck's reasons for turn to southeast: Kluck, 77, 82–84.

PAGE

440 Moltke uneasy: Bauer, 52.

440 Schlieffen, "A victory on the battlefield": qtd. Hanotaux, VII, 197.

440 He has a "shout-hurrah! mood": Moltke, *Erinnerungen*, 382.

440 Rumors in Luxembourg of Ostend landings and of Russians: Tappen, 115.

441 Moltke worries about gaps in right wing: Tappen, 106.

441 Bauer's visit to Rupprecht's front: Bauer, 53 ff.; Rupprecht, 77–79.

442 Kluck's estimate of enemy strength: Kluck, 91; captured British letter: Edmonds, 244.

443 Bülow's request: Kluck, 83; Kluck's order of August 31 for forced march: Bloem, 112; Moltke's approval of inward wheel: Kluck, 83–4; Hausen, 195.

444 Cavalry "always halted": Crown Prince, *War Experiences*, 64.

444 "Much needed" rest and British got away "just in time": Kluck, 90.

444 "Our men are done up": qtd. Maurice, 150–51. General Maurice adds (152) that after the Battle of the Marne when the Germans were in retreat to the Aisne, "Whole parties of officers were captured because they were too intoxicated to move."

445 Latrines dug in Poincaré's burial plot: Poincaré, III, 204.

445 Mayor of Senlis and six others shot: *ibid.*; Gallieni, *Mémoires*, 120. Names on the memorial stone were copied by the author on the site.

445 Hausen's happy night: Hausen, 208–10.

446 Moltke's General Order of Sept. 2: Kluck, 94.

446 Kluck orders advance across Marne: Kluck, 100.

446 Captain Lepic's report: *AF*, I, II, Annexe No. 1772.

447 Sixth Army to "cover Paris": *ibid.*, Annexe No. 1783; Joffre, 225.

447 Sixth Army "*ne veulent pas marcher*": Gallieni, *Mémoires*, 52.

447 Col. Pont, "It seems no longer possible": Joffre, 218–19.

447 Discussion of new plan at GQG with Belin and Berthelot: *ibid.*, 230–33.

448 General Order No. 4: *AF*, I, II, Annexe No. 1792.

449 "The battle of Brienne-le-Château": Messimy, 379.

449 Joffre's call to Millerand, "urgent and essential": Poincaré, III, 126; Joffre, 232.

449 Gallieni's call to Joffre: Gallieni, *Carnets*, 53.

449 Maunoury put under Gallieni and Paris put under Joffre: Because these events were taking place at a time of great tension and also because of later efforts during the quarrel over credit for the Marne, to obscure the question of who was under whose orders, this issue is still not entirely clear. The relevant sources are Joffre, 226, 234–5, 239–42; Gallieni, *Mémoires*, 43, and *Carnets*, 53; Joffre's request to have Paris put under his command is Annexe No. 1785; the order putting Maunoury under Gallieni is Annexe No. 1806; Millerand's order complying with Joffre's request is Annexe No. 1958.

450 Composition of the Army of Paris: *AF*, I, II, 772–4. The 55th and 56th Reserve Divisions who were now to fight for the capital had been

PAGE

withdrawn from Lorraine on August 25, causing General Ruffey, whose flank they were supporting in a counteroffensive in the Briey basin, to break off action. Briey, as Ruffey said in his postwar testimony, was thus "the ransom of Paris." Fighting as a reserve officer with one of these divisions, the 55th, Charles Péguy was killed on September 7.

450 Gallieni visits Ebener and Maunoury: *Mémoires*, 42, 48–9.

450 Millerand reports "heart-breaking" facts; decision of Government to leave: Poincaré, III, 125–27.

451 Gallieni and Prefect of Police: *Mémoires*, 51–52; "preferred to be without ministers": *Parle*, 38; "Made all my dispositions": *Mémoires*, 57.

451 Captain Fagalde's find: Spears, 331–32; his report: *AF*, I, II, Annexe No. 1848.

452 Joffre still urges Government to leave: Poincaré, III, 131.

452 "Hateful moment had come": *ibid.*, 134.

452 Herrick's visit and his plans: *ibid.*, 131; Mott, 155–7, 160–63; *Carnets*, 61.

453 Gallieni's farewell to Millerand: *Mémoires*, 59–64; *Parle*, 49.

453 Proclamations of Government and Gallieni: Hanotaux, IX, 39; *Carnets*, 55.

454 Puns and parody of "Marseillaise": Marcellin, 41.

454 "Days of anguish": Hirschauer, 142.

455 Fifth Army desertions and executions: Lanrezac, 254–56.

455 "I never would have believed": qtd. Edmonds, 283; Germans are "over-hasty": Huguet, 70.

456 Joffre's secret instructions of Sept. 2: *AF*, I, II, 829 and Annexes Nos. 1967 and 1993. Order for reinforcements to be taken from Ist and IInd Armies is Annexe No. 1975.

456 Gallieni believes it "divorced from reality": *Mémoires*, 79; *Parle*, 50.

456 Moves to Lycée Victor-Duruy: *Memoires*, 60–61.

457 Lieutenant Watteau's report: Pierrefeu, *Plutarque*, 102–3.

457 "They offer us their flank!": Hirschauer, 180.

22. *"Gentlemen, We Will Fight on the Marne"*

458 Gallieni decides instantly to attack: *Mémoires*, 95–96; Clergerie, 6–7.

458 "One of those long conferences": Clergerie, 127.

458 Sixth Army of "mediocre value"; "calm and resolution" of people of Paris: *Mémoires*, 75, 76.

459 "Forty kilometers!": qtd. Hanotaux, VIII, 222; German prisoners taken asleep: Briey, March 28, evidence of Messimy; "tomorrow or the day after": qtd. Maurice, 152.

459 "The General fears nothing from Paris": *ibid.*, 153.

460 Kluck's insubordinate letter to OHL of Sept. 4: Kluck, 102.

460 Bülow furious at "echelon in advance": Bülow, 103.

PAGE

460 "We can do no more": qtd. Hanotaux, VIII, 223; "No cooked food": *ibid.*, 276; "Broiling heat": *ibid.*, 279.

460 "Decisively beaten" and "utterly disorganized": Kuhl, 29; Kluck, 102.

461 Joffre plans offensive "within a few days": Annexe No. 2152.

461 "Blew the winds of defeat": Muller, 80.

461 Lanrezac's "physical and moral depression" and further comments: Joffre, 236–7.

462 "A church outside which": Grouard, 114. As Hausen acknowledged: in *Revue Militaire Suisse*, Nov. 11, 1919, qtd. Engerand, *Bataille*, xxi.

462 Joffre's dismissals in first five weeks: Allard, 15.

463 The meeting with Franchet d'Esperey on the road: Grasset, 44; Joffre, 237.

463 The meeting with Lanrezac at Sezanne: Lanrezac, 276–7; Joffre, 237–8; Muller, 104–5; Spears, 377–78. In his lively account Spears says the conversation between the two generals took place outdoors as they walked "up and down the courtyard whilst I watched with fascinated interest." Although this obliging arrangement allowed Spears to write as an eyewitness, it does not fit with the probabilities, for Joffre would hardly have chosen to conduct what was to him the most distressing operation of the war so far, in full view of spectators. In fact he did not. "Lanrezac was in his office. I went in there and remained alone with him," he says specifically.

463 Franchet d'Esperey: Grasset, *passim*; Spears, 398.

464 "March or drop dead": Grasset, 45. The phrase he used was "*Marcher ou crever.*"

464 Sept. 4, a sense of climax: *Gallieni parle*, 53; Blücher, 23; in Brussels people felt a chill: Gibson, 191.

464 Kaiser, "It is the 35th day": Helfferich, *Der Weltkrieg*, Berlin, 1919, Vol. II, 279.

465 French "have offered us an armistice": qtd. Hanotaux, VIII, 279.

465 General Kuhl's doubts: Kuhl, 19.

465 "We are advancing triumphantly everywhere": Crown Prince, *War Experiences*, 69.

465 Moltke to Helfferich: Helfferich, *op. cit.*, 17–18.

465 Reports reach OHL of French troop movements: Tappen, 115.

466 "An attack from Paris": *ibid.*

466 Moltke's order of Sept. 4: full text, Edmonds, 290–91.

467 Falkenhayn quoted: from Zwehl's life of Falkenhayn, qtd. *AQ*, April, 1926, 148.

467 Gallieni's order to Maunoury of Sept. 4: *Mémoires*, 112.

467 "Immediate and energetic decision": *ibid.*, 107.

467 Gallieni tells Poincaré there is a "good opening": The fact of this call was disclosed by Poincaré after the war in an interview with *Le Matin*, Sept. 6, 1920.

PAGE

467 The real battle "fought on the telephone": *Gallieni parle*, 53.

468 Joffre's aversion to telephone: Muller. "I have always disliked using the telephone myself," Joffre, 250.

468 Clergerie's conversation with Col. Pont: *Mémoires*, 119; Joffre, 245.

468 Discussions at GQG: Muller, 85–6; Joffre, 243–4; Mayer, 41.

469 Joffre under the weeping ash: Muller, 87.

470 Joffre's messages to Franchet d'Esperey and Foch: *ibid.*, 91–2; *AF*, I, II, Annexe No. 2327.

470 Gallieni's visit to British Hq.: *Mémoires*, 121–4; *Gallieni parle*, 55; Clergerie, 16.

471 Franchet d'Esperey's meeting with Wilson: Grasset, 51–53; Spears, 400–01; Wilson, 174.

472 Joffre at dinner with the Japanese: Joffre, 249.

473 Franchet d'Esperey's reply: full text in Edmonds, 279.

473 General Hache's protest: Grasset, 74.

473 "Intelligent audacity" and Foch's reply: Joffre, 250.

474 Murray's orders "simply heartbreaking": Wilson, 174.

474 "Marshal not yet returned": Gallieni, *Mémoires*, 128.

474 Sir John French decides to "restudy the situation": Joffre, 252.

474 Gallieni's conversation with Joffre: *Mémoires*, 130; Joffre agreed "unwillingly" and "as Gallieni desired": Joffre, 251.

475 General Order No. 6: *AF*, I, II, Annexe No. 2332.

475 Joffre receives Huguet's message: Joffre, 252.

476 Kluck assumes Germans "everywhere advancing victoriously": Kluck, 106. "Regain freedom of maneuver": *ibid.*

476 Col. Hentsch's visit to Kluck's Hq.: Kluck, 107; report of Commander of IVth Reserve: *ibid.*, 108; Kuhl, "Neither OHL nor the First Army": qtd. Edmonds, 292, n. 2.

477 Gallieni replied "Nowhere": *Gallieni parle*, 57, n. 1. His orders for destruction: *AF*, I, II, Annexe No. 2494; "A void": Hirschauer, 228.

478 "Gallieni having attacked prematurely": *Gallieni parle*, 64; "That is worth gold": *Carnets*, 78, n. 3. (To the present author it seems unnecessary to ascribe all credit for the Marne either to Gallieni as, for example, Captain Liddell-Hart does in *Reputations Ten Years After*, at the cost of making Joffre out a fool, or to Joffre as General Spears does at the cost of making Gallieni out a liar. As Poincaré said long ago, there was credit enough for both.)

478 Joffre's uncertainty "altogether agonizing": Joffre, 252; his telegram to Millerand: *AF*, I, II, Annexe No. 2468.

478 Wilson transmits Order No. 6 to Sir John French: Wilson, 174. Huguet, de Galbert and British "lukewarm": Joffre, 253; Mayor of Melun: Hirschauer, 179.

479 "At any price": Joffre, 252.

479 The meeting at Melun: Joffre, 254; Muller, 106; Wilson, 174; Spears,

PAGE

415–18. The phrase "Threw his heart on the table" is Muller's, as is the description of Huguet which reads in the original, "*qui semble, à son habitude, porter le diable en terre.*" (Unfamiliar to most French friends queried, this phrase was variously translated for me as meaning that Huguet looked satanic, bored, or gloomy. I have adopted the last as proposed by the only person who seemed certain.)

Spears, in his vivid and dramatic account of the meeting, performs another historical sleight of hand. Unwilling to give the reader an impression of British reluctance to fight, he claims that Joffre made the trip to Melun—a six-to-seven-hour round trip by car just before the crucial battle—in order to "thank" Sir John French for his cooperation. Inexplicably, Spears then quotes Joffre as saying, "with an appeal so intense as to be irresistible, '*Monsieur le Maréchal, c'est la France qui vous supplie.*'" This does not sound compatible with thanks.

480 "Gentlemen, we will fight on the Marne": Poincaré, III, 136.

480 Order to the troops for Sept. 6: *AF*, I, II, Annexe No. 2641.

Afterword

481 Foch's order: Aston, *Foch*, 124.

481 Joan of Arc won the battle: Bergson said this on several occasions; Chevalier, 25, 135, 191, 249.

482 Moltke to his wife: *Erinnerungen*, 385–6.

482 Kluck's explanation: Interview given to a Swedish journalist in 1918, qtd. Hanotaux, IX, 103.

482 Col. Dupont's tribute to the Russians: Danilov, *Grand Duke*, 57; Dupont, 2.

483 Numerical superiority: In five Armies present at the Marne, the Germans had about 900,000 men in 44 infantry and 7 cavalry divisions. In six armies the Allies had about 1,082,000 men in 56 infantry and 9 cavalry divisions. *AF*, I, III, 17–19.

483 "If we had not had him in 1914": Aston, *Foch*, 125.

484 The taxis: Clergerie, 134–45; *Gallieni parle*, 56.

485 Footnote: experience of André Varagnac from private information; casualty figures from *AF*, I, II, 825; *AQ*, October 1927, 58–63; Samuel Dumas and K. D. Vedel-Petersen, *Losses of Life Caused by War*, Oxford, 1923, Chap. 1.

486 "All the great words cancelled": in *Lady Chatterley*.

THE PROUD TOWER

Paris Exposition, 1900;
Sirot Collection.

THE PROUD TOWER

A Portrait of the World
Before the War

1890—1914

While from a proud tower in the town
Death looks gigantically down.

From "The City in the Sea"
EDGAR ALLAN POE

CONTENTS

ILLUSTRATIONS

Acknowledgments

TO MR. CECIL SCOTT of The Macmillan Company, a participant in this book from the first outline to the end, I owe a writer's most important debt: for the steady companionship of an interested reader and for constructive criticism throughout mixed with encouragement in times of need.

For advice, suggestions and answers to queries I am grateful to Mr. Roger Butterfield, author of *The American Past*; Professor Fritz Epstein of Indiana University; Mr. Louis Fischer, author of *The Life of Lenin*; Professor Edward Fox of Cornell University; Mr. K. A. Golding of the International Transport Workers' Federation, London; Mr. Jay Harrison of Columbia Records; Mr. John Gutman of the Metropolitan Opera; Mr. George Lichtheim of the Institute on Communist Affairs, Columbia University; Mr. William Manchester, author of *The House of Krupp*; Professor Arthur Marer, editor of the letters of Sir John Fisher; Mr. George Painter, the biographer of Proust; Mr. A. L. Rowse, author of an introduction to the work of Graham Wallas; Miss Helen Ruskell and the staff of the New York Society Library; Mr. Thomas K. Scherman, director of the Little Orchestra Society; Mrs. Janice Shea for information about the circus in Germany; Professor Reba Soffer of San Fernando Valley State College for information on Wilfred Trotter; Mr. Joseph C. Swidler, chairman of the Federal Power Commission; and Mr. Louis Untermeyer, editor, among much else, of *Modern British Poetry*. Equal gratitude extends to the many others who gave me verbal aid of which I kept no record.

For help in finding certain of the illustrations I am indebted to Mr. A. J. Ubels of the Royal Archives at The Hague; to the staffs of the Art and Print Rooms of the New York Public Library; and to Mr. and Mrs. Harry Collins of Brown Brothers.

I would like to express particular thanks to two indefatigable readers of the proofs, Miss Jessica Tuchman and Mr. Timothy Dickinson, for improvements and corrections, respectively; and to Mrs. Esther Bookman, who impeccably typed the manuscript of both this and my previous book, *The Guns of August*.

BARBARA W. TUCHMAN

Foreword

THE EPOCH whose final years are the subject of this book did not die of old age or accident but exploded in a terminal crisis which is one of the great facts of history. No mention of that crisis appears in the following pages for the reason that, as it had not yet happened, it was not a part of the experience of the people of this book. I have tried to stay within the terms of what was known at the time.

The Great War of 1914–18 lies like a band of scorched earth dividing that time from ours. In wiping out so many lives which would have been operative on the years that followed, in destroying beliefs, changing ideas, and leaving incurable wounds of disillusion, it created a physical as well as psychological gulf between two epochs. This book is an attempt to discover the quality of the world from which the Great War came.

It is not the book I intended to write when I began. Preconceptions dropped off one by one as I investigated. The period was not a Golden Age or *Belle Epoque* except to a thin crust of the privileged class. It was not a time exclusively of confidence, innocence, comfort, stability, security and peace. All these qualities were certainly present. People *were* more confident of values and standards, more innocent in the sense of retaining more hope of mankind, than they are today, although they were not more peaceful nor, except for the upper few, more comfortable. Our misconception lies in assuming that doubt and fear, ferment, protest, violence and hate were not equally present. We have been misled by the people of the time themselves who, in looking back across the gulf of the War, see that earlier half of their lives misted over by a lovely sunset haze of peace and security. It did not seem so golden when they were in the midst of it. Their memories and their nostalgia have conditioned our view of the pre-war era but I can offer the reader a rule based on adequate research: all statements of how lovely it was in that era made by persons contemporary with it will be found to have been made after 1914.

A phenomenon of such extended malignance as the Great War does not come out of a Golden Age. Perhaps this should have been obvious to me when I began but it was not. I did feel, however, that the genesis of the war did not lie in the *Grosse Politik* of what Isvolsky said to Aehrenthal and Sir Edward Grey to Poincaré; in that tortuous train of Reinsurance treaties, Dual and Triple Alliances, Moroccan crises and Balkan imbroglios which historians have painstakingly followed in their search for origins. It was necessary that these events and exchanges be examined and we who come after are in debt to the examiners; but their work has been done. I am with Sergei Sazonov, Russian Foreign Minister at the time of the outbreak of the War, who after a series of investigations exclaimed at last, "Enough of this chronology!" The *Grosse Politik* approach has been used up. Besides, it is misleading because it allows us to rest on the easy illusion that it is "they," the naughty statesmen, who are always responsible for war while "we," the innocent people, are merely led. That impression is a mistake.

The diplomatic origins, so-called, of the Great War are only the fever chart of the patient; they do not tell us what caused the fever. To probe for underlying causes and deeper forces one must operate within the framework of a whole society and try to discover what moved the people in it. I have tried to concentrate on society rather than the state. Power politics and economic rivalries, however important, are not my subject.

The period of this book was above all the culmination of a century of the most accelerated rate of change in man's record. Since the last explosion of a generalized belligerent will in the Napoleonic wars, the industrial and scientific revolutions had transformed the world. Man had entered the Nineteenth Century using only his own and animal power, supplemented by that of wind and water, much as he had entered the Thirteenth, or, for that matter, the First. He entered the Twentieth with his capacities in transportation, communication, production, manufacture and weaponry multiplied a thousandfold by the energy of machines. Industrial society gave man new powers and new scope while at the same time building up new pressures in prosperity and poverty, in growth of population and crowding in cities, in antagonisms of classes and groups, in separation from nature and from satisfaction in individual work. Science gave man new welfare and new horizons while it took away belief in God and certainty in a scheme of things he knew.

By the time he left the Nineteenth Century he had as much new unease as ease. Although *fin de siècle* usually connotes decadence, in fact society at the turn of the century was not so much decaying as bursting with new tensions and accumulated energies. Stefan Zweig who was thirty-three in 1914 believed that the outbreak of war "had nothing to do with ideas and hardly even with frontiers. I cannot explain it otherwise than by this surplus force, a tragic consequence of the internal dynamism that had accumulated in forty years of peace and now sought violent release."

In attempting to portray what the world before the war was like my process has been admittedly highly selective. I am conscious on finishing this book that it could be written all over again under the same title with entirely other subject matter; and then a third time, still without repeating. There could be chapters on the literature of the period, on its wars—the Sino-Japanese, Spanish-American, Boer, Russo-Japanese, Balkan—on imperialism, on science and technology, on business and trade, on women, on royalty, on medicine, on painting, on as many different subjects as might appeal to the individual historian. There could have been chapters on King Leopold II of Belgium, Chekhov, Sargent, The Horse, or U.S. Steel, all of which figured in my original plan. There should have been a chapter on some ordinary everyday shopkeeper or clerk representing the mute inglorious anonymous middle class but I never found him.

I think I owe the reader a word about my process of selection. In the first place I confined myself to the Anglo-American and West European world from which our experience and culture most directly derive, leaving aside the East European which, however important, is a separate tradition. In choice of subjects the criterion I used was that they must be truly representative of the period in question and have exerted their major influence on civilization before 1914, not after. This consideration ruled out the automobile and airplane, Freud and Einstein and the movements they represented. I also ruled out eccentrics, however captivating.

I realize that what follows offers no over-all conclusion but to draw some tidy generalization from the heterogeneity of the age would be invalid. I also know that what follows is far from the whole picture. It is not false modesty which prompts me to say so but simply an acute awareness of what I have not included. The faces and voices of all that I have left out crowd around me as I reach the end.

Barbara W. Tuchman

I

THE PATRICIANS

ENGLAND: 1895–1902

I

The Patricians

THE LAST government in the Western world to possess all the attributes of aristocracy in working condition took office in England in June of 1895. Great Britain was at the zenith of empire when the Conservatives won the General Election of that year, and the Cabinet they formed was her superb and resplendent image. Its members represented the greater landowners of the country who had been accustomed to govern for generations. As its superior citizens they felt they owed a duty to the State to guard its interests and manage its affairs. They governed from duty, heritage and habit—and, as they saw it, from right.

The Prime Minister was a Marquess and lineal descendant of the father and son who had been chief ministers to Queen Elizabeth and James I. The Secretary for War was another Marquess who traced his inferior title of Baron back to the year 1181, whose great-grandfather had been Prime Minister under George III and whose grandfather had served in six cabinets under three reigns. The Lord President of the Council was a Duke who owned 186,000 acres in eleven counties, whose ancestors had served in government since the Fourteenth Century, who had himself served thirty-four years in the House of Commons and three times refused to be Prime Minister. The Secretary for India was the son of another Duke whose family seat was received in 1315 by grant from Robert the Bruce and who had four sons serving in Parliament at the same time. The President of the Local Government Board was a pre-eminent country squire who had a Duke for brother-in-law, a Marquess for son-in-law, an ancestor who had been Lord Mayor of London in the reign of Charles II, and who had himself been a member of Parliament for twenty-seven years. The Lord Chancellor bore a family name brought to England by a Norman follower of William the Conqueror and maintained thereafter over eight centuries without a title. The Lord Lieutenant for Ireland was an Earl, a grandnephew of the Duke of Wellington and a hereditary trustee of the British Museum. The Cabinet also included a Viscount, three Barons and two Baronets. Of its six commoners, one was a director of the Bank of England, one was a squire whose family had represented the same county in Parliament since the Sixteenth Century, one—who acted as Leader of the House of Commons—was the Prime Minister's nephew and inheritor of a Scottish fortune of £4,000,000, and one, a notable and disturbing cuckoo in the nest, was a Birmingham manufacturer widely regarded as the most successful man in England.

Besides riches, rank, broad acres and ancient lineage, the new Government also possessed, to the regret of the Liberal Opposition and in the words of one of them, "an almost embarrassing wealth of talent and capacity." Secure in authority, resting comfortably on their electoral majority in the House of Commons and on a permanent majority in the House of Lords, of whom four-fifths were Conservatives, they were in a position, admitted the same opponent, "of unassailable strength."

Enriching their ranks were the Whig aristocrats who had seceded from the Liberal party in 1886 rather than accept Mr. Gladstone's insistence on Home Rule for Ireland. They were for the most part great landowners who, like their natural brothers the Tories, regarded union with Ireland as sacrosanct. Led by the Duke of Devonshire, the Marquess of Lansdowne and Mr. Joseph Chamberlain, they had remained independent until 1895, when they joined with the Conservative party, and the two groups emerged as the Unionist party, in recognition of the policy that had brought them together. With the exception of Mr. Chamberlain, this coalition represented that class in whose blood, training and practice over the centuries, landowning and governing had been inseparable. Ever since Saxon chieftains met to advise the King in the first national assembly, the landowners of England had been sending members to Parliament and performing the duties of High Sheriff, Justice of the Peace and Lord Lieutenant of the Militia in their own counties. They had learned the practice of government from the possession of great estates, and they undertook to manage the affairs of the nation as inevitably and unquestionably as beavers build a dam. It was their ordained role and natural task.

But it was threatened. By a rising rumble of protest from below, by the Radicals of the Opposition who talked about taxing unearned increment on land, by Home Rulers who wanted to detach the Irish island from which so much English income came, by Trade Unionists who talked of Labour representation in Parliament and demanded the legal right to strike and otherwise interfere with the free play of economic forces, by Socialists who wanted to nationalize property and Anarchists who wanted to abolish it, by upstart nations and strange challenges from abroad. The rumble was distant, but it spoke with one voice that said Change, and those whose business was government could not help but hear.

Planted firmly across the path of change, operating warily, shrewdly yet with passionate conviction in defence of the existing order, was a peer who was Chancellor of Oxford University for life, had twice held the India Office, twice the Foreign Office and was now Prime Minister for the third time. He was Robert Arthur Talbot Gascoyne-Cecil, Lord Salisbury, ninth Earl and third Marquess of his line.

Lord Salisbury was both the epitome of his class and uncharacteristic of it—except insofar as the freedom to be different was a class characteristic. He was six feet four inches tall, and as a young man had been thin, ungainly, stooping and shortsighted, with hair unusually black for an Englishman. Now sixty-five, his youthful lankiness had turned to bulk, his shoulders had grown massive and more stooped than ever, and his heavy bald head with full curly gray beard rested on them as if weighted down. Melancholy, intensely intellectual, subject to sleepwalking and fits of depression which he called "nerve storms," caustic, tactless, absent-minded, bored by society and fond of solitude, with a penetrating, skeptical, questioning mind, he had been called the Hamlet of English politics. He was above the conventions and refused to live in Downing Street. His devotion was to religion, his interest in science. In his own home he attended private chapel every morning before breakfast, and had fitted up a chemical laboratory where he conducted solitary experiments. He harnessed the river at Hatfield for an electric power plant on his estate and strung up along the old beams of his home one of England's first electric light systems, at which his family threw cushions when the wires sparked and sputtered while they went on talking and arguing, a customary occupation of the Cecils.

Lord Salisbury cared nothing for sport and little for people. His aloofness was enhanced by shortsightedness so intense that he once failed to recognize a member of his own Cabinet, and once, his own butler. At the close of the Boer War he picked up a signed photograph of King Edward and, gazing at it pensively, remarked, "Poor Buller [referring to the Commander-in-Chief at the start of the war], what a mess he made of it." On another occasion he was seen in prolonged military conversation with a minor peer under the impression that he was talking to Field Marshal Lord Roberts.

For the upper-class Englishman's alter ego, most intimate companion and constant preoccupation, his horse, Lord Salisbury had no more regard. Riding was to him purely a means of locomotion to which the horse was "a necessary but extremely inconvenient adjunct." Nor was he addicted to shooting. When Parliament rose he did not go north to slaughter grouse upon the moors or stalk deer in Scottish forests, and when protocol required his attendance upon royalty at Balmoral, he would not go for walks and "positively refused," wrote Queen Victoria's Private Secretary, Sir Henry Ponsonby, "to admire the prospect or the deer." Ponsonby was told to have his room in the dismal castle kept "warm"—a minimum temperature of sixty degrees. Otherwise he retired for his holidays to France, where he owned a villa at Beaulieu on the Riviera and where he could exercise his fluent French and lose himself in *The Count of Monte Cristo*, the only book, he once told Dumas *fils*, which allowed him to forget politics.

His acquaintance with games was confined to tennis, but when elderly he invented his own form of exercise, which consisted in riding a tricycle through St. James's Park in the early mornings or along paths cemented for the purpose in the park of his estate at Hatfield. Wearing for the occasion a kind of sombrero hat and a short sleeveless cloak with a hole in the middle in which he resembled a monk, he would be accompanied by a young coachman to push him up the hills. At the downhill slopes, the young man would be told to "jump on behind," and the Prime Minister, with the coachman's hands on his shoulders, would roll away, cloak flying and pedals whirring.

Hatfield, twenty miles north of London in Hertfordshire, had been the home of the Cecils for nearly three hundred years since James I had given it, in 1607, to his Prime Minister, Robert Cecil, first Earl of Salisbury, in exchange for a house of Cecil's to which the King had taken a fancy. It was the royal residence where Queen Elizabeth had spent her childhood and where, on receiving news of her accession, she held her first council, to swear in William Cecil, Lord Burghley, as her chief Secretary of State. Its Long Gallery, with intricately carved paneled walls and gold-leaf ceiling, was 180 feet in length. The Marble Hall, named for the black and white marble floor, glowed like a jewel case with painted and gilded ceiling and Brussels tapestries. The red King James Drawing Room was hung with full-length family portraits by Romney and Reynolds and Lawrence. The library was lined from floor to gallery and ceiling with 10,000 volumes bound in leather and vellum. In other rooms were kept the Casket Letters of Mary Queen of Scots, suits of armor taken from men of the Spanish Armada, the cradle of the beheaded King, Charles I, and presentation portraits of James I and George III. Outside were yew hedges clipped in the form of crenelated battlements, and the gardens, of which Pepys wrote that he never saw "so good flowers, nor so great gooseberries as big as nutmegs." Over the entrance hall hung flags captured at Waterloo and presented to Hatfield by the Duke of Wellington, who was a constant visitor and devoted admirer of the Prime Minister's mother, the second Marchioness. In her honor Wellington wore the hunt coat of the Hatfield Hounds when he was on campaign. The first Marchioness was painted by Sir Joshua Reynolds and hunted till the day she died at eighty-five, when, half-blind and strapped to the saddle, she was accompanied by a groom who would shout, when her horse approached a fence, "Jump, dammit, my Lady, jump!"

It was this exceptional person who reinvigorated the Cecil blood, which, after Burghley and his son, had produced no further examples of superior mentality. Rather, the general mediocrity of succeeding generations had been varied only, according to a later Cecil, by instances of "quite exceptional stupidity." But the second Marquess proved a vigorous and able man with a strong sense of public duty who served in several mid-century Tory cabinets. His second son, another Robert Cecil, was the Prime Minister of 1895. He in turn produced five sons who were to distinguish themselves. One became a general, one a bishop, one a Minister of state, one M.P. for Oxford, and one, through service to the government, won a peerage in his own right. "In human beings as in horses," Lord Birkenhead was moved to comment on the Cecil record, "there is something to be said for the hereditary principle."

At Oxford in 1850 the contemporaries of young Robert Cecil agreed that he would end as Prime Minister either because or in spite of his remorselessly uncompromising opinions. Throughout life he never bothered to restrain them. His youthful speeches were remarkable for their virulence and insolence; he was not, said Disraeli, "a man who measures his phrases." A "salisbury" became a synonym for a political imprudence. He once compared the Irish in their incapacity for self-government to Hottentots and spoke of an Indian candidate for Parliament as "that black man." In the opinion of Lord Morley his speeches were always a pleasure to read because "they were sure to contain one blazing indiscretion which it is a delight to remember." Whether these were altogether accidental is open to question, for though Lord Salisbury delivered his speeches without notes, they were worked out in his head beforehand and emerged clear and perfect in sentence structure. In that time the art of oratory was considered part of the equipment of a statesman and anyone reading from a written speech would have been regarded as pitiable. When Lord Salisbury spoke, "every sentence," said a fellow member, "seemed as essential, as articulate, as vital to the argument as the members of his body to an athlete."

Appearing in public before an audience about whom he cared nothing, Salisbury was awkward; but in the Upper House, where he addressed his equals, he was perfectly and strikingly at home. He spoke sonorously, with an occasional change of tone to icy mockery or withering sarcasm. When a recently ennobled Whig took the floor to lecture the House of Lords in high-flown and solemn Whig sentiments, Salisbury asked a neighbor who the speaker was and on hearing the whispered identification, replied perfectly audibly, "I thought he was dead." When he listened to others he could become easily bored, revealed by a telltale wagging of his leg which seemed to one observer to be saying, "When will all this be over?" Or sometimes, raising his heels off the floor, he would set up a sustained quivering of his knees and legs which could last for half an hour at a time. At home, when made restless by visitors, it shook the floor and made the furniture rattle, and in the House his colleagues on the front bench complained it made them seasick. If his legs were at rest his long fingers would be in motion, incessantly twisting and turning a paper knife or beating a tattoo on his knee or on the arm of his chair.

He never dined out and rarely entertained beyond one or two political receptions at his town house in Arlington Street and an occasional garden party at Hatfield. He avoided the Carlton, official club of the Conservatives, in favor of the Junior Carlton, where a special luncheon table was set aside for him alone and the library was hung with huge placards inscribed SILENCE. He worked from breakfast to one in the morning, returning to his desk after dinner as if he were beginning a new day. His clothes were drab and often untidy. He wore trousers and waistcoat of a dismal gray under a broadcloth frock coat grown shiny. But though careless in dress, he was particular about the trimming of his beard and carefully directed operations in the barber's chair, indicating "just a little more off here" while "artist and subject gazed fixedly in the mirror to judge the result."

Despite his rough tongue and sarcasms, Salisbury exerted a personal charm upon close colleagues and equals which, as one of them said, "was no small asset in the conduct of affairs." He gave detailed attention to party affairs and even sacrificed his exclusiveness for their sake. Once he astonished everyone by accepting an invitation to the traditional dinner for party supporters given by the Leader of the House of Commons. He asked to be given in advance biographical details about each guest. At the dinner the Prime Minister charmed his neighbor at table, a well-known agriculturist, with his expert knowledge of crop rotation and stock-breeding, chatted amiably afterward with every guest in turn, and before leaving, beckoned to his Private Secretary, saying, "I think I have done them all, but there was someone I have not identified who, you said, made mustard."

Mr. Gladstone, though in political philosophy his bitterest antagonist, acknowledged him "a great gentleman in private society." In private life he was delightful and sympathetic and a complete contrast to his public self. In public acclaim, Salisbury was uninterested, for—since the populace was uninstructed—its opinions, as far as he was concerned, were worthless. He ignored the public and neither possessed nor tried to cultivate the personal touch that makes a political leader a recognizable personality to the man in the street and earns him a nickname like "Pam" or "Dizzy" or the "Grand Old Man." Not in the press, not even in *Punch*, was Lord Salisbury ever called anything but Lord Salisbury. He made no attempt to conceal his dislike for mobs of all kinds, "not excluding the House of Commons." After moving to the Lords, he never returned to the Commons to listen to its debates from the Peers' Gallery or chat with members in the Lobby, and if compelled to allude to them in his own House, would use a tone of airy contempt, to the amusement of visitors from the Commons who came to hear him. But this was merely an outward pose designed to underline his deep inner sense of the patrician. He was not rank-conscious; he was indifferent to honors or any other form of recognition. It was simply that as a Cecil, and a superior one, he was born with a consciousness in his bones and brain cells of ability to rule and saw no reason to make any concessions of this prescriptive right to anyone whatever.

Having entered the House of Commons in the customary manner for peers' sons, from a family-controlled borough in an uncontested election at the age of twenty-three, and, during his fifteen years in the House of Commons, having been returned unopposed five times from the same borough, and having for the last twenty-seven years sat in the House of Lords, he had little personal experience of vote-getting. He regarded himself not as responsible *to* the people but as responsible *for* them. They were in his care. What reverence he felt for anyone was directed not down but up—to the monarchy. He revered Queen Victoria, who was some ten years his senior, both as her subject and, with chivalry toward her womanhood, as a man. For her he softened his brusqueness even if at Balmoral he could not conceal his boredom.

She in turn visited him at Hatfield and had the greatest

confidence in him, giving him, as she told Bishop Carpenter, "if not the highest, an equal place with the highest among her ministers," not excepting Disraeli. Salisbury, who was "bad on his legs at any time," was the only man she ever asked to sit down. Unalike in every quality of mind except in their strong sense of rulership, the tiny old Queen and the tall, heavy, aging Prime Minister felt for each other mutual respect and regard.

In unimportant matters of state as in dress, Salisbury was inclined to be casual. Once when two clergymen with similar names were candidates for a vacant bishopric, he appointed the one not recommended by the Archbishop of Canterbury, and this being sorrowfully drawn to his attention, he said, "Oh, I daresay he will do just as well." He reserved high seriousness for serious matters only, and the most serious to him was the maintenance of aristocratic influence and executive power, not for its own sake, but because he believed it to be the only element capable of holding the nation united against the rising forces of democracy which he saw "splitting it into a bundle of unfriendly and distrustful fragments."

Class war and irreligion were to him the greatest evils and for this reason he detested Socialism, less for its menace to property than for its preaching of class war and its basis in materialism, which meant to him a denial of spiritual values. He did not deny the need of social reforms, but believed they could be achieved through the interplay and mutual pressures of existing parties. The Workmen's Compensation Act, for one, making employers liable for work-sustained injuries, though denounced by some of his party as interference with private enterprise, was introduced and passed with his support in 1897.

He fought all proposals designed to increase the political power of the masses. When still a younger son, and not expecting to succeed to the title, he had formulated his political philosophy in a series of some thirty articles which were published in the *Quarterly Review* in the early 1860's, when he was in his thirties. Against the growing demand at that time for a new Reform law to extend the suffrage, Lord Robert Cecil, as he then was, had declared it to be the business of the Conservative party to preserve the rights and privileges of the propertied class as the "single bulwark" against the weight of numbers. To extend the suffrage would be, as he saw it, to give the working classes not merely a voice in Parliament but a preponderating one that would give to "mere numbers a power they ought not to have." He deplored the Liberals' adulation of the working class "as if they were different from other Englishmen" when in fact the only difference was that they had less education and property and "in proportion as the property is small the danger of misusing the franchise is great." He believed the workings of democracy to be dangerous to liberty, for under democracy "passion is not the exception but the rule" and it was "perfectly impossible" to commend a farsighted passionless policy to "men whose minds are unused to thought and undisciplined to study." To widen the suffrage among the poor while increasing taxes upon the rich would end, he wrote, in a complete divorce of power from responsibility; "the rich would pay all the taxes and the poor make all the laws."

He did not believe in political equality. There was the multitude, he said, and there were "natural" leaders. "Always wealth, in some countries birth, in all countries intellectual power and culture mark out the man to whom, in a healthy state of feeling, a community looks to undertake its government." These men had the leisure for it and the fortune, "so that the struggles for ambition are not defiled by the taint of sordid greed. . . . They are the aristocracy of a country in the original and best sense of the word. . . . The important point is, that the rulers of a country should be taken from among them," and as a class they should retain that "political preponderance to which they have every right that superior fitness can confer."

So sincere and certain was his conviction of that "superior fitness" that in 1867 when the Tory Government espoused the Second Reform Bill, which doubled the electorate and enfranchised workingmen in the towns, Salisbury at thirty-seven flung away Cabinet office within a year of first achieving it rather than be party to what he considered a betrayal and surrender of Conservative principles. His party's reversal, engineered by Disraeli in a neat enterprise both to "dish the Whigs" and to meet political realities, was regarded with abhorrence by Lord Cranborne (as Lord Robert Cecil had then become, his elder brother having died in 1865). Though it might ruin his career he resigned as Secretary for India and in a bitter and serious speech spoke out in the House against the policy of the party's leaders, Lord Derby and Mr. Disraeli. He begged the members not to do for political advantage what would ultimately destroy them as a class. "The wealth, the intelligence, the energy of the community, all that has given you that power which makes you so proud of your nation and which makes the deliberations of this House so important, will be numerically absolutely overmatched." Issues would arise in which the interests of employers and employed would clash and could only be decided by political force, "and in that conflict of political force you are pitting an overwhelming number of employed against a hopeless minority of employers." The outcome would "reduce to political insignificance and extinction the classes which have hitherto contributed so much to the greatness and prosperity of their country."

A year later, on his father's death, he entered the House of Lords as third Marquess of Salisbury. In 1895, after the passage of nearly thirty years, his principles had not shifted an inch. With no belief in change as improvement, nor faith in the future over the present, he dedicated himself with "grim acidity" to preserving the existing order. Believing that "rank, without the power of which it was originally the symbol, was a sham," he was determined, while he lived and governed England, to resist further attack on the power of that class of which rank was still the visible symbol. Watchful of approaching enemies, he stood against the coming age. The pressures of democracy encircled, but had not yet closed in around, the figure whom Lord Curzon described as "that strange, powerful, inscrutable, brilliant, obstructive deadweight at the top."

The average member of the ruling class, undisturbed by Lord Salisbury's too-thoughtful, too-prescient mind, did not worry deeply about the future; the present was so delightful. The Age of Privilege, though assailed at many points and already cracking at some, still seemed, in the closing years of the Nineteenth Century and of Victoria's reign, a permanent condition. To the privileged, life appeared "secure and comfortable. . . . Peace brooded over the land." Undoubtedly Sir William Harcourt's budget of 1894, enacted by the Liberals during the premiership of Lord Rosebery, Mr. Gladstone's rather inappropriate successor, sent a tremor through many. It introduced death duties—and what was worse, introduced them on a graduated principle from 1 per cent on estates of £500 to 8 per cent on estates of over a million pounds. And it increased the income tax by a penny to eightpence in the pound. Although to soften the blow and equalize the burden it imposed a tax on beer and spirits so that the working class, who paid no income tax, would contribute to the revenue, this failed to muffle the drumbeat of the death duties. The eighth Duke of Devonshire was moved to predict a time which he "did not think can be deferred beyond the period of my own life" when great estates such as his of Chatsworth would be shut up solely because of "the inexorable necessities of democratic finance."

But a greater, and from the Conservative point of view a happier, event of 1894 compensated for the budget. Mr. Gladstone retired from Parliament and from politics. His last octogenarian effort to force through Home Rule had been defeated in the House of Lords by a wrathful assembly of peers gathered for the purpose in numbers hardly before seen in their lifetime. He had split his party beyond recall, he was eighty-five, the end of a career had come. With the Conservative victory in the following year there was a general feeling, reflected by *The Times* that Home Rule, that "germ planted by Mr. Gladstone in our political life which has threatened to poison the whole organism," being now disposed of, at least for the present, England could settle down sensibly to peace and business. The "dominant influences" were safely in the saddle.

"Dominant influences" was a phrase, not of the Conservative-minded *Times*, but strangely enough of Mr. Gladstone himself, who was a member of the landed gentry and never forgot it nor ever abandoned the inborn sense that property is responsibility. He owned an estate of 7,000 acres at Hawarden with 2,500 tenants producing an annual rent roll between £10,000 and £12,000. In a letter to his grandson who would inherit it, the Great Radical urged him to regain lands lost through debt by earlier generations and restore Hawarden to its former rank as a "leading influence" in the county, because, as he said, "society cannot afford to dispense with its dominant influences." No duke could have put it better. This was exactly the sentiment of the Conservative landowners, who were his bitterest opponents but with whom, at bottom, he shared a belief both in the "superior fitness" conferred by inherited ownership of land and in the country's need of it. Their credo was the exact opposite of the idea prevailing in the more newly minted United States, that there was a peculiar extra virtue in being lowly born, that only the self-made carried the badge of ability and that men of easy circumstances were more likely than not to be stupid or wicked, if not both. The English, on the contrary, having evolved slowly through generations of government by the possessing class, assumed that prolonged retention by one family of education, comfort and social responsibility was natural nourishment of "superior fitness."

It qualified them for government, considered in England as nowhere else the proper and highest profession of a gentleman. A private secretaryship to a ministerial uncle or other relative could be either a serious apprenticeship for Cabinet office or merely a genial occupation for a gentleman like Sir Schomberg McDonnell, Lord Salisbury's Private Secretary, a brother of the Earl of Antrim. Diplomacy, too, offered a desirable career, often to persons of talent. The Marquess of Dufferin and Ava, when British Ambassador in Paris in 1895, taught himself Persian and noted in his diary for that year that besides reading eleven plays of Aristophanes in Greek, he had learned by heart 24,000 words from a Persian dictionary, "8,000 perfectly, 12,000 pretty well, and 4,000 imperfectly." Military service in one of the elite regiments of Guards or Hussars or Lancers was an equally accepted role for men of wealth and rank, although it tended to attract the weaker minds. The less wealthy went into the Church and the Navy; the bar and journalism provided careers when earning power was a necessity. But Parliament above all was the natural and desirable sphere for the exercise of "superior fitness." A seat in Parliament was the only way to a seat in the Cabinet, where power and influence and a membership in the Privy Council, and on retirement a peerage, were to be won. The Privy Council, made up of 235 leaders in all fields, though formal and ceremonial in function, was the badge of importance in the nation. A peerage was still the magic mantle that set a man apart from his fellows. Cabinet office was highly coveted and the object of intense maneuvering behind the scenes. When governments changed, nothing so absorbed the attention of British society as the complicated minuet of Cabinet-making. Clubs and drawing rooms buzzed, cliques and alliances formed and re-formed, and the winners emerged proudly wearing fortune's crown of laurel. The prize required hard work and long hours, though rarely knowledge of the department. A minister's function was not to do the work but to see that it got done, much as he managed his estate. Details such as decimal points, which Lord Randolph Churchill when Chancellor of the Exchequer shrugged aside as "those damned dots," were not his concern.

The members of Lord Salisbury's Government, of whom the majority, though not all, enjoyed inherited land, wealth or titles, had not entered government for material advantages. Indeed, from their point of view, it was right and necessary that public affairs should be administered, as Lord Salisbury said, by men unaffected "by the taint of sordid greed." A parliamentary career—which was of course unsalaried—conferred, not gain, but distinction. The House of Commons was the center of the capital, of the Empire, of Society; its company was the best in the kingdom. Ambition led men there as well as duty; besides, it was the expected thing to do. Fathers in Parliament were followed by sons, both often serving at the same time. James Lowther, Deputy Speaker of the House from 1895 to 1905 and afterward Speaker, came from a family which had represented Westmorland constituencies more or less continuously over six centuries. His great-grandfather and grandfather each had sat for half a century and his father for twenty-five years. The representative of a county division in Parliament was usually someone whose home was known for seventy miles around as "The House," whose family had been known in the district for several hundred years and the candidate himself since his birth. Since the cost of candidacy and election and of nursing a constituency afterward was borne by the member himself, the privilege of representing the people in Parliament was a luxury largely confined to the class that could afford it. Of the 670 members in the House of Commons in 1895, 420 were gentlemen of leisure, country squires, officers and barristers. Among them were twenty-three eldest sons of peers, besides their innumerable younger sons, brothers, cousins, nephews and uncles, including Lord Stanley, heir of the sixteenth Earl of Derby, who, after the Dukes, was the richest peer in England. As a junior Government Whip, Stanley was obliged to stand at the door of the Lobby and bully or cajole members to be on hand for a division, though himself not allowed inside the chamber while performing this duty. It was as if he were, wrote an observer, "an Upper Class Servant." To see "this heir to a great and historic name and a vast fortune doing work almost menial" was testimony both to a sense of political duty and the allure of a political career.

The ruling class did not grow rulers only. It produced the same proportion as any other class of the unfit and misfit, the bad or merely stupid. Besides prime ministers and empire-builders it had its bounders and club bores, its effete Reggies and Algies caricatured in *Punch* discussing their waistcoats and neckwear, its long-legged Guardsmen whose conversation was confined to "haw, haw," its wastrels who ruined themselves through drink, racing and cards, as well as its normal quota of the mediocre who never did anything noticeable, either good or bad. Even Eton had its "scugs," boys who, in the words of an Etonian, were "simply not good form . . . and if not naturally vicious, certainly imbecile, probably degenerate." Though a scug at Eton—not to be confused with "swat," or grind—could as often as not turn out to be a Privy Councillor thirty years later, some were scugs for life. One of Lord Salisbury's nephews, Cecil Balfour, disappeared to Australia, over an affair of a forged check, and died there, it was said, of drink.

Despite such accidents, the ruling families had no doubts of their inborn right to govern and, on the whole, neither did the rest of the country. To be a lord, wrote a particularly picturesque exemplar, Lord Ribblesdale, in 1895, "is still a popular thing." Known as the "Ancestor" because of his Regency appearance, Ribblesdale was so handsome a personification of the patrician that John Singer Sargent, glorifier of the class and type, asked to paint him. Standing at full length in the portrait, dressed as Master of the Queen's Buckhounds in long riding coat, top hat, glistening boots and holding a coiled hunting whip, Sargent's Ribblesdale stared out upon the world in an attitude of such natural arrogance, elegance and self-confidence as no man of a later day would ever achieve. When the picture was exhibited at the Salon in Paris and Ribblesdale went to see it, he was followed from room to room by admiring French crowds who, recognizing the subject of the portrait, pointed out to each other in whispers "*ce grand diable de milord anglais.*"

At the opening of Ascot Race Week when Lord Ribblesdale led the Royal Procession down the green turf, mounted on a bright chestnut against a blue June sky, wearing a dark-green coat with golden hound-couplings hanging from a gold belt, he made a sight that no one who saw it could ever forget. As Liberal Whip in the House of Lords, an active member of the London County Council and chief trustee of the National Gallery, he too took his share of government. Like most of his kind he had a sense of easy communion with the land-based working class who served the sports and estates of the gentry. When the Queen presented J. Miles, a groom of the Buck-hounds, with a medal in honor of fifty years' service, Ribblesdale rode over from Windsor to congratulate him and stayed "for tea and a talk" with Mrs. Miles. As he himself wrote of the average nobleman, "the ease of his circumstances from his youth up tends to produce a good-humored attitude. . . . To be pleased with yourself may be selfish or it may be stupid, but it is seldom actively disagreeable and usually it is very much the reverse." Despite a tendency of the Liberal press to portray the peerage as characterized "to a melancholy degree by knock-knees and receding foreheads," the peer still retained, Ribblesdale thought, the respect of his county. Identifying himself with its interests and affairs, maintaining mutually kindly relations toward his tenants, cottagers and the tradesmen of his market town, he would have to seriously misconduct himself before he would "outrun the prestige of an old name and tried associations." Yet for all this comfortable picture, Ribblesdale too heard the distant rumble and thirty years later chose for the motto of his memoirs the claim of Chateaubriand: "I have guarded that strong love of liberty peculiar to an aristocracy whose last hour has sounded."

Midsummer was the time when the London season was at its height and Society disported and displayed itself in full glory. To a titled visitor from Paris it seemed as if "a race of gods and goddesses descended from Olympus upon England in June and July." They appeared "to live upon a golden cloud, spending their riches as indolently and naturally as the leaves grow green." In the wake of the Prince of Wales followed a "flotilla of white swans, their long necks supporting delicate jewelled heads," who went by the names of Lady Glenconner, the Duchess of Leinster and Lady Warwick. The Duchess, who died young in the eighties, was, in the words of Lord Ernest Hamilton, "divinely tall, . . . of a beauty so dazzling as to be almost unbelievable." Her successor, the Countess of Warwick, "the prettiest married woman in London," was inamorata of the Prince of Wales and the cause of a famous fracas in which Lord Charles Beresford almost struck his future sovereign. She shimmered before the eyes of a Society journal as "a goddess with a rounded figure, diaphanously draped, and a brilliant haughty beautiful countenance whose fame had penetrated to the dim recesses of the placid country." She was a Beauty, a magic title of the time that conferred upon its bearer a public character. "Get up, Daisy," cried her mother when their ship docked after a particularly seasick crossing of the Irish Channel which had left her prostrate, "the crowd is waiting to have a look at you."

In and out of Adam doorways in Berkeley and Belgrave Squares the constant procession flowed. No one unless dying ever stayed home. The day began at ten with a gallop in the Park and ended at a ball at three in the morning. At a select spot between the Albert and Grosvenor Gates in Hyde Park, a small circle of all the Society that counted was sure of meeting its members on a morning ride or a late afternoon drive between tea and dinner. London had not lost her Georgian air. Window boxes were bright with flowers in houses and squares lived in by the families whose names they bore: Devonshire House and Lansdowne House, Grosvenor Square and Cadogan Place. Splendid equipages filled the streets. Ladies driving their victorias, with a "tiger" sitting very straight with folded arms in the box, gave an extra flick of the whip to their high-stepping cobs as they passed under approving masculine gaze from club windows. Gentlemen sighed and told each other "what a pretty thing it was to see a lovely woman drive in London behind a well-matched pair." Down another street came trotting the Royal Horse Guards in scarlet tunics and white breeches on black horses with bridles and halter-chains shining and jingling. Tall silhouettes of hansom cabs carried the well-known profiles of statesmen and clubmen on their round of visits to the great houses and to the clubs in Pall Mall and Piccadilly: the Carlton for Conservatives, the Reform for Liberals, the Athenæum for distinction, the Turf for sportsmen, the Travellers' or White's, Brooks's or Boodle's for social converse with like-minded gentlemen. The business of government and empire went on in "the best club in London," the House of Commons, which sat through the season. Its library, smoking room and dining room, its servants, waiters and wine cellars were of a quality befitting the profession of a gentleman. Ladies in wide hats and trailing skirts took tea with members and ministers on the terrace overhanging the Thames where they could look out on the episcopal dignity of Lambeth Palace across the river and gossip about political preferment.

At private dinner tables draped in smilax, with a footman behind each chair, gentlemen in white tie and tails conversed with ladies in clouds of tulle over bare shoulders, wearing stars or coronets in their elaborately piled hair. Conversation was not casual but an art "in which competence conferred prestige." At the opera, made fashionable by its most energetic patroness, Lady de Grey, Nellie Melba sang love duets in her pure angelic soprano with the handsome idol Jean de Reszke. In the Royal Box glowed a vision in low-cut velvet, Lady Warwick, with "only a few diamonds on her Mephistophelian scarlet dress" and a scarlet aigrette in her hair. A battle array of lorgnettes was raised to see what Lady de Grey, her rival as London's best-dressed woman, was wearing. Afterwards at Lady de Grey's parties, called "Bohemia in tiaras," the guests might include Mme Melba herself and the Prince of Wales and—before his fatal year of 1895—Oscar Wilde. Every night there were political receptions lasting till midnight or dances continuing until dawn. At the top of a sweeping curve of staircase the Duchess of Devonshire or Lady Londonderry, the two arbiters of Society, glittering in diamonds, received a brilliant stream of guests while a major-domo in a stentorian orgy of titles announced, "His Grace . . . Her Highness . . . The Right Honorable . . . Lord and Lady . . . Excellency the

Ambassador of . . ." and down in the lamplit square a footman bellowed for some departing Lordship's carriage.

Society was divided into several sets whose edges overlapped and members mingled. At the head of the "fast," or sporting, Marlborough House set was the cigar and paunch, the protruding Hanoverian countenance finished off by a short gray beard, the portly yet regal figure of the Prince of Wales. Eclectic, sociable, utterly bored (as was everyone who suffered under it) by the dull monotony of the royal regimen prescribed by his widowed mother, the Prince opened his circle of the nobility to a variety of disturbing outsiders, provided they were either beautiful, rich or amusing: Americans, Jews, bankers and stockbrokers, even an occasional manufacturer, explorer or other temporary celebrity. Professionally the Prince met everybody: among his personal friends he included some of the country's ablest men, such as Admiral Sir John Fisher, and it was an unkind canard to say he never read a book. True, he preferred Marie Corelli to any living author, yet he read Lieutenant Winston Churchill's first book, *The Malakand Field Force*, with "the greatest possible interest" and kindly wrote the author an appreciative note saying he thought "the descriptions and language generally excellent." But on the whole, in his circle, intellectuals and literary people were not welcome and brains not appreciated, because, according to Lady Warwick, Society, or this section of it, "did not want to be made to think." It was pleasure-loving, reckless, thoughtless and wildly extravagant. The newcomers, especially the Jews, were in most cases resented, "not because we disliked them individually, for some of them were charming and even brilliant, but because they had brains and understood finance." This was doubly disturbing because society most particularly did not want to think about making money, only about spending it.

On the right of the sporting set were the "Incorruptibles," the strict, reactionary, intensely class-conscious long-established families who regarded the Prince's circle as "vulgar" and themselves as upholding the tone of Society. Each family was encircled by a tribe of poorer country cousins who appeared in London once or twice a generation to bring out a daughter, but otherwise had hardly emerged from the Eighteenth

Century. On the left were the "Intellectuals," or "Souls," who gathered in worship around their sun and center, Arthur Balfour, nephew of Lord Salisbury and the most brilliant and popular man in London. As a group they were particularly literate, self-consciously clever and endlessly self-admiring. They enjoyed each other's company in the same way that an unusually handsome man or woman enjoys preening before a mirror. "You all sit around and talk about each other's souls," remarked Lord Charles Beresford at a dinner in 1888. "I shall call you the 'Souls,'" and so they were named. An admiral of the Navy and vivid ornament of the Prince of Wales's set, Lord Charles was not himself one of the Souls, although he had married an unusual wife who wore a tiara with her tea gowns and was painted by Sargent with two sets of eyebrows because, as the painter briefly explained, she *had* two sets, a penciled one above the real.

The men of the Souls all followed political careers and nearly all were junior ministers in Lord Salisbury's Government. A leading member was George Wyndham, who had written a book on French poets and an introduction to North's *Plutarch* and after serving as Mr. Balfour's Parliamentary Private Secretary was named Under-Secretary of War in 1898, despite Lord Salisbury's reluctant remark, "I don't like poets." George Curzon, Under-Secretary for Foreign Affairs and soon to be appointed Viceroy of India, was another Soul, as was St. John Brodrick, a later Secretary for War. Both were heirs to peerages who staged a vain protest against their anticipated fate of enforced removal to the House of Lords. Others were the Tennant connection: Alfred Lyttelton, a champion cricketer who was to become Colonial Secretary and who had been married, before she died, to Laura Tennant; Lord Ribblesdale, who was married to Charlotte Tennant; and the uninhibited third sister, Margot, whose marriage to the outgoing Liberal Home Secretary, Mr. Asquith, was attended by two past prime ministers, Mr. Gladstone and Lord Rosebery, and two future ones, Mr. Balfour and the groom. A particularly admired member was Harry Cust, heir of the Brownlow barony, a scholar and athlete with a blazing wit who on sheer reputation alone, with no previous experience, was asked across the dinner table to be editor of the *Pall Mall Gazette*; he accepted on the spot and served for four years.

Flawed by a "fatal self-indulgence" with regard to women—to whom he was "irresistibly fascinating"—his public career suffered and never fulfilled its early promise.

Society was small and homogeneous and its *sine qua non* was land. For an outsider to break in, it was essential first to buy an estate and live on it, although even this did not always work. When John Morley, at that time a Cabinet minister, was visiting Skibo, where Mr. Andrew Carnegie had constructed a swimming pool, he took his accompanying detective to see it and asked his opinion. "Well, sir," the detective replied judiciously, "it seems to me to savour of the parvenoo."

In the "brilliant and powerful body," as Winston Churchill called it, of the two hundred great families who had been governing England for generations, everyone knew or was related to everyone else. Since superiority and comfortable circumstances imposed on the nobility and gentry a duty to reproduce themselves, they were given to large families, five or six children being usual, seven or eight not uncommon, and nine or more not unknown. The Duke of Abercorn, father of Lord George Hamilton in Salisbury's Government, had six sons and seven daughters; the fourth Baron Lyttelton, Gladstone's brother-in-law and father of Alfred Lyttelton, had eight sons and four daughters; the Duke of Argyll, Secretary for India under Gladstone, had twelve children. As a result of the marriages of so many siblings, and of the numerous second marriages, everyone was related to a dozen other families. People who met each other every day, at each other's homes, at race meetings and hunts, at Cowes, for the Regatta, at the Royal Academy, at court and in Parliament, were more often than not meeting their second cousins or brother-in-law's uncle or stepfather's sister or aunt's nephew on the other side. When a prime minister formed a government it was not nepotism but almost unavoidable that some of his Cabinet should be related to him or to each other. In the Cabinet of 1895 Lord Lansdowne, the Secretary for War, was married to a sister of Lord George Hamilton, the Secretary for India, and Lansdowne's daughter was married to the nephew and heir of the Duke of Devonshire, who was Lord President of the Council.

The country's rulers, said one, "knew each other intimately quite apart from Westminster." They had been at school together and at one of the two favored colleges, Christ Church at Oxford or Trinity College at Cambridge. Here prime ministers —including Lords Rosebery and Salisbury, at Christ Church, and their immediate successors, Mr. Balfour and Sir Henry Campbell-Bannerman, at Trinity—were grown naturally. The forcing house of statesmanship, however, was Balliol, whose mighty Master, Benjamin Jowett, frankly spent his teaching talents on intelligent undergraduates "whose social position might enable them to obtain high offices in the public service." Christ Church, known simply as the "House," was the particular habitat of the wealthy and landed aristocracy. During the youth of the men who governed in the nineties, it was presided over by Dean Liddell, a singularly handsome man of great social elegance and formidable manner who had a daughter, Alice, much admired by an obscure lecturer in mathematics named Charles Dodgson. Activities at the "House" were chiefly fox-hunting, racing, a not too serious form of cricket and "no end of good dinners in the company of the best fellows in the world, as they knew it."

When such fellows in after life wrote their memoirs, the early pages were thick with footnotes identifying the Charles, Arthur, William and Francis of the author's school days as "afterwards Chief of Imperial General Staff" or "afterwards Bishop of Southhampton" or Speaker of the House or Minister at Athens as the case might be. Through years of familiarity they knew each other's characters and could ask each other favors. When Winston Churchill, at twenty-three, wanted to join the Sudan expedition in 1898 over the firm objections of its Commander-in-Chief, Sir Herbert Kitchener, the matter was not beyond accomplishment. Winston's grandfather, the seventh Duke of Marlborough, had been Lord Salisbury's colleague under Disraeli, and Lord Salisbury as Prime Minister listened amiably to the young man and promised his help. When it turned out to be needed on short notice, Winston had recourse to the Private Secretary, Sir Schomberg McDonnell, "whom I had seen and met in social circles since I was a child." Winston found him dressing for dinner and on the errand being explained, "'I'll do it at once,' said this gallant man, and off he went, discarding his dinner party." In this way affairs were managed.

The mold in which they were all educated was the same, and its object was not necessarily the scientific spirit or the exact mind, but a "graceful dignity" which entitled the bearer to the status of English gentleman, and an unshatterable belief in that status as the highest good of man on earth. As such, it obligated the bearer to live up to it. In every boy's room at Eton hung the famous picture by Lady Butler of the disaster at Majuba Hill showing an officer with uplifted sword charging deathward to the cry of "*Floreat Etona!*" The spirit instilled may have accounted for, as has been suggested, the preponderance of bravery over strategy in British officers. Yet to be an Etonian was "to imbibe a sense of effortless superiority and be lulled in a consciousness of unassailable primacy." Clothed in this armor, its wearers were serenely sure of their world and sorry for anyone who was not of it. When Sir Charles Tennant and a partner at golf were preparing to drive and were rudely interrupted by a stranger who pushed in ahead and placed his own ball on the tee, the enraged partner was about to explode. "Don't be angry with him," Sir Charles soothed. "Perhaps he isn't quite a gentleman, poor fellow, poor fellow."

This magic condition was envied and earnestly imitated abroad by all the continental aristocracy (except perhaps the Russians, who spoke French and imitated nobody). German noblemen relentlessly married English wives and put on tweeds and raglan coats, while in France the life of the *haut monde* centered upon the Jockey Club, whose members played polo, drank whiskey and had their portraits painted in hunting pink by Helleu, the French equivalent of Sargent.

It was no accident that their admired model was thought of in equestrian terms. The English gentleman was unthinkable without his horse. Ever since the first mounted man acquired extra stature and speed (and, with the invention of the stirrup, extra fighting thrust), the horse had distinguished the ruler from the ruled. The man on horseback was the symbol of dominance, and of no other class anywhere in the world was the horse so intrinsic a part as of the English aristocracy. He was the attribute of their power. When a contemporary writer wished to describe the point of view of the county oligarchy it was equestrian terms that he used: they saw society, he wrote, made up of "a small select aristocracy born booted and spurred to ride and a large dim mass born saddled and bridled to be ridden."

In 1895 the horse was still as inseparable from, and ubiquitous in, upper-class life as the servant, though considerably more cherished. He provided locomotion, occupation and conversation; inspired love, bravery, poetry and physical prowess. He was the essential element in racing, the sport of kings, as in cavalry, the elite of war. When an English patrician thought nostalgically of youth, it was as a time "when I looked at life from the saddle and was as near heaven as it was possible to be."

The gallery at Tattersall's on Sunday nights when Society gathered to look over the horses for the Monday sales was as fashionable as the opera. People did not simply go to the races at Newmarket; they owned or took houses in the neighborhood and lived there during the meeting. Racing was ruled by the three Stewards of the Jockey Club from whose decision there was no appeal. Three Cabinet ministers in Lord Salisbury's Government, Mr. Henry Chaplin, the Earl of Cadogan and the Duke of Devonshire, were at one time or another Stewards of the Jockey Club. Owning a stud and breeding racehorses required an ample fortune. When Lord Rosebery, having married a Rothschild, won the Derby while Prime Minister in 1894, he received a telegram from Chauncey Depew in America, "Only heaven left." Depew's telegram proved an underestimate, for Rosebery won the Derby twice more, in 1895 and 1905. The Prince of Wales won it in 1896 with his great lengthy bay Persimmon, bred at his own stud, again in 1900 with Persimmon's brother Diamond Jubilee, and a third time, as King, in 1909 with Minoru. As the first such victory by a reigning monarch, it was Epsom's greatest day. When the purple, scarlet and gold of the royal colors came to the front at Tattenham Corner the crowd roared; when Minoru neck and neck with his rival battled it out at a furious pace along the rails they went mad with excitement and wept with delight when he won by a head. They broke through the ropes, patted the King on the back, wrung his hand, and "even policemen were waving their helmets and cheering themselves hoarse."

Distinction might also be won by a famous "whip" like Lord Londesborough, president of the Four-in-Hand Club, who was known as a "swell," the term for a person of extreme elegance and splendor, and was renowned for the smartness of his turnouts and the "gloss, speed and style" of his carriage horses. The carriage horse was more than ornamental; he was essential for transportation and through this role his tyranny was exercised. When a niece of Charles Darwin was taken in 1900 to see Lord Roberts embark for South Africa, she saw the ship but not Lord Roberts "because the carriage had to go home or the horses might have been tired." When her Aunt Sara, Mrs. William Darwin, went shopping in Cambridge she always walked up the smallest hill behind her own carriage, and if her errands took her more than ten miles the carriage and horses were sent home and she finished her visits in a horsecab.

But the true passion of the horseman was expressed in the rider to hounds. To gallop over the downs with hounds and horsemen, wrote Wilfrid Scawen Blunt in a sonnet, was to feel "my horse a thing of wings, myself a God." The fox-hunting man never had enough of the thrills, the danger, and the beauty of the hunt; of the wail of the huntsman's horn, the excited yelping of the hounds, the streaming rush of red-coated riders and black-clad ladies on sidesaddles, the flying leaps over banks, fences, stone walls and ditches, even the crashes, broken bones and the cold aching ride home in winter. If it was bliss in that time to be alive and of the leisured class, to hunt was rapture. The devotee of the sport—man or woman—rode to hounds five and sometimes six days a week. It was said of Mr. Knox, private chaplain to the Duke of Rutland, that he wore boots and spurs under his cassock and surplice and "thought of horses even in the pulpit." The Duke's family could always tell by the speed of morning prayers if Mr. Knox were hunting that day or not.

Mr. Henry Chaplin, the popular "Squire" in Lord Salisbury's Cabinet, who was considered the archetype of the English country gentleman and took himself very seriously as representative in Parliament of the agricultural interest, took himself equally seriously as Master of the Blankney Hounds and could not decide which duty came first. During a debate or a Cabinet he would draw little sketches of horses on official papers. When his presence as a minister was required at question time he would have a special train waiting to take him wherever the hunt was to meet next morning. Somewhere between stations it would stop, Mr. Chaplin would emerge, in white breeches and scarlet coat, climb the embankment, and find his groom and horses waiting. Weighing 250 pounds, he was constantly in search of horses big and strong enough to carry him and frequently "got to the bottom of several in one day." "To see him thundering down at a fence on one of his great horses was a fine sight." On one occasion the only opening out of a field was a break in a high hedge where a young sapling had been planted surrounded by an iron cage 4 feet 6 inches high. "There were shouts for a chopper or a knife when down came the Squire, forty miles an hour, with his eyeglass in his eye seeing nothing but the opening in the hedge. There was no stopping him; neither did the young tree do so, for his weight and that of his horse broke it off as clean as you would break a thin stick and away he went without an idea that the tree had ever been there."

The cost of being a Master who, besides maintaining his own stable, was responsible for the breeding and upkeep of the pack was no small matter. So extravagant was Mr. Chaplin's passion that he at one time kept two packs, rode with two hunts and, what with keeping a racing stud, a deer forest in Scotland and entertaining that expensive friend, the Prince of Wales, he ultimately ruined himself and lost the family estates. On one of his last hunts in 1911, when he was over seventy, he was thrown and suffered two broken ribs and a pierced lung, but before being carried home, insisted on stopping at the nearest village to telegraph the Conservative Whip in the House of Commons that he would not be present to vote that evening.

George Wyndham, who was to acquire Cabinet rank as Chief Secretary for Ireland in 1902, was torn like Mr. Chaplin between passion for the hunt and duty to politics. In Wyndham's case, the duty was not untinged by ambition, since he had every intention of becoming Prime Minister. As he likewise wrote poetry and had leanings toward art and literature, life was for him full of difficult choices. A sporting friend advised him against "sacrificing my life to politics and gave Harry Chaplin as a shocking example of whom better things were expected in his youth." It was hard not to agree and prefer the carefree life when gentlemen came down to breakfast in their pink coats with an apron tied on to protect the chalked white of their breeches, or when on a Christmas night, as Wyndham described it, "we sat down thirty-nine to dinner" and thirty hunted next day. "Today we are all out again. . . . Three of us sailed away [fifty lengths in front of the nearest followers]. The rest were nowhere. We spreadeagled the field. The pace was too hot to choose your place by a yard. We just took everything as it came with hounds screaming by our side. Nobody could gain an inch. These are the moments . . . that are the joy of hunting. There is nothing like it."

Older than fox-hunting, the oldest role of the horseman was in war. Cavalry officers considered themselves the cream of the Army and were indeed more notable for social prestige than for thought or imagination. They were "sure of themselves," wrote a cavalry officer from a later vantage point, "with the superb assurance that belonged to those who were young at this time and came of their class and country." In their first years with the regiment they managed, by a daily routine of port and a weekly fall on the head from horseback, to remain in "that state of chronic numb confusion which was the aim of every cavalry officer." Polo, learned on its native ground by the regiments in India, was their passion and the cavalry charge the sum and acme of their strategy. It was from the cavalry that the nation's military leaders were drawn. They believed in the cavalry charge as they believed in the Church of England. The classical cavalry officer was that magnificent and genial figure, a close friend of the Prince of Wales, "distinguished at Court, in the Clubs, on the racecourse, in the hunting field . . . one of the brightest military stars in London Society," Colonel Brabazon of the 10th Hussars. Six feet tall, with clean and symmetrical features, bright gray eyes and strong jaw, he had a moustache the Kaiser would have envied, and ideas to match. Testifying before the Committee of Imperial Defence in 1902 on the lessons of the Boer War, in which he had commanded the Imperial Yeomanry, General Brabazon (as he now was) "electrified the Commission by a recital of his personal experiences in hand to hand fighting and his theories of the use of the Cavalry Arm in war." These included, as reported by Lord Esher to the King, "life-long mistrust of the weapons supplied to the Cavalry and his preference for shock tactics by men armed with a Tomahawk." Giving his evidence "in a manner highly characteristic of that gallant officer . . . he drew graphic pictures of a Cavalry charge under these conditions which proved paralyzing to the imagination of the Commissioners." They next heard Colonel Douglas Haig, lately chief Staff officer of the cavalry division in the South African War, deplore the proposed abolition of the lance and affirm his belief in the *arme blanche*, that is, the cavalry saber, as an effective weapon.

At home in the country, among his tenants and cottagers, crops and animals, on the estate that dominated the life of the district of which "The House" was the large unit and the village the small, on the land that his family had owned and cultivated and rented out and drawn income from for generations, the English patrician bloomed in his natural climate. Here from childhood on he lived closely with nature, with the sky and trees, the fields and birds and deer in the woods. "We were richly endowed in the surpassing beauty of the homes in which we were reared," wrote Lady Frances Balfour. The stately houses—Blenheim of the Dukes of Marlborough, Chatsworth of the Dukes of Devonshire, Wilton of the Earls of Pembroke, Warwick Castle of the Earls of Warwick, Knole of the Sackvilles, Hatfield of the Salisburys—had three or four hundred rooms, a hundred chimneys, and roofs measured in acres. Others less grand often had been lived in longer, like Renishaw, inhabited by the Sitwells for at least seven hundred years. Owners great and small never finished adding on to or altering the house and improving the landscape. They removed or created hills, conjured up lakes, diverted streams, and cut vistas through their woods finished off by a marble pavilion to fix the eye.

Their homes proliferated. A town house, a family estate, a second country home, a shooting box in a northern county, another in Scotland, possibly a castle in Ireland were not out of the ordinary. Besides Hatfield and his London house on Arlington Street, Lord Salisbury owned Walmer Castle in Deal, the Manor House at Cranborne in Dorsetshire, his villa in France, and if he had been a sporting man, would have had a place in Scotland or a racing stud near Epsom or Newmarket.

There were 115 persons in Great Britain who owned over 50,000 acres each, and forty-five of these owned over 100,000 acres each, although much of this was uncultivatable land in Scotland whose income yield was low. There were some sixty to sixty-five persons, all peers, who possessed both land over 50,000 acres and income over £50,000, and fifteen of these—seven dukes, three marquesses, three earls, one baron and one baronet—had landed incomes of over £100,000. In all of Great Britain, out of a population of 44,500,000, there were 2,500 landowners who owned more than 3,000 acres apiece and had landed incomes of over £3,000.

Income taxes were not payable on incomes under £160 and in this category there were approximately eighteen to twenty million people. Of these, about three million were in white-collar or service trades—clerks, shopmen, tradesmen, innkeepers, farmers, teachers—who earned an average of £75 a year. Fifteen and a half million were manual workers, including soldiers, sailors, postmen and policemen and those in agricultural and domestic service who earned less than £50 a year. The "poverty line" had been worked out at £55 a year, or 21*s.* 8*d.* a week, for a family of five. Indoor servants slept in attics or windowless basements. Agricultural laborers lived in houses for which they paid a shilling a week, and worked with scythe, plow and sickle in the fields from the time when the great horn boomed at five o'clock in the morning until nightfall. When their houses leaked or rotted they were dependent on the landlord for repairs, and unless the landlord took care of them when their earning power came to an end, they went to the workhouse to finish out their days. Estate servants—grooms, gardeners, carpenters, blacksmiths, dairymen and field hands—whose families had lived on the land as long as its owners, gave service that was "wholehearted and passionate. . . . Their pride was bound up in it."

With the opening of the grouse season in August, and until the re-opening of Parliament in January, the great landowners engaged in continuous entertainment of each other in week-long house parties of twenty to fifty guests. With each guest bringing his own servant, the host fed as many as a hundred, and on one occasion at Chatsworth, four hundred extra mouths while his house party lasted. Shooting was the favored pastime and consisted in displaying sufficient stamina and marksmanship, assisted by a loader and three or four guns, to bring down an unlimited bag of small game flushed out of its coverts by an army of beaters. From county to county and back and forth into Scotland, their trail marked by thousands upon thousands of dead birds and hares, the gentry were constantly on the move: for shooting with the Prince at Sandringham, for hunting (in blue and buff instead of scarlet coats) with the Duke of Beaufort's hounds in Wiltshire, for deer stalking amid Scottish lochs and crags and trackless forests ("Keep doon, Squire, keep doon"—his ghillie whispered to Mr. Chaplin, forced to crawl into the open to come within shooting distance of his stag—"ye're so splendidly built about the haunches I'm afeert the deer will be seeing ye"), for Christmas parties and coming-of-age parties and occasional time out at Homburg and Marienbad to purge satiated stomachs and allow the round to begin again.

Morning was the gentlemen's time on the moors; ladies came down to breakfast in hats and at afternoon tea reigned in elaborate and languorous tea gowns of, it might be, "*eau de Nil* satin draped with gold-spangled *mousseline de soie* and bands of sable at hem and neck." Formal dinners followed in full evening dress. All day, herds of servants glided silently about, bringing early morning tea and *The Times*, carrying up bath water and coal for the fireplaces, replenishing vases daily with fresh flowers, murmuring "His Grace is in the Long Library," sounding gongs at meal times and waiting up to uncorset Her Ladyship for bed.

Each guest at the house parties had his name on a card fitted into a brass frame on his bedroom door and a corresponding card beside the bell indicator in the butler's pantry. In assigning rooms the recognized, if unacknowledged, liaisons had to be considered. As long as the partners in these intramural infidelities did nothing to provoke a public scandal by outraged wife or cuckolded husband, they could do as they pleased. The overriding consideration was to prevent any exposure of misconduct to the lower classes. In that respect the code was rigid. Within the closed circle of the ruling class the unforgivable sin was to give away any member of the group; there must be no appeal to the Divorce Court, no publicity that would bring the members as a class into disrepute. If, regrettably, a husband refused absolutely to be complaisant and threatened action, all the arbiters of Society, including, if necessary, the Prince of Wales (despite his own hardly faultless record), rallied to stop him. He must not, they reminded him, sacrifice his class to such exposure. It was his duty to preserve appearances and an unsullied front before the gaze of the vulgar. Subdued, he would obey, even at the cost, in the case of one couple, of not speaking to his wife except in public for twenty years.

In their luxurious and lavish world, self-indulgence was the natural law. Notable eccentrics like the nocturnal Duke of Portland and bad-tempered autocrats like Sir George Sitwell and Sir William Eden were merely representatives of their class in whom the habit of having their own way had gone to extremes. But for the majority it was easy to be agreeable when everything was done to keep them in comfort and ease and to make life for the great and wealthy as uninterruptedly pleasant as possible.

The lordly manner was the result. When Colonel Brabazon, who affected a fashionable difficulty with his *r*'s, arrived late at the railroad station to be informed that the train for London had just left, he instructed the station master, "Then bwing me another." Gentlemen who did not relish a cold wait at a country station or a slow journey on a local made a habit of special trains which cost £25 for an average journey. There were not a few among them who, like Queen Victoria, had never seen a railway ticket. Ladies had one-of-a-kind dresses designed exclusively for them by Worth or Doucet, who devoted as much care to each client as if he were painting her portrait. "So as to be different from other people," the English-born beauty, Daisy, Princess of Pless, had "a fringe of real violets" sewn down the train of her court dress, which was of transparent lace lined with blue chiffon and sprinkled with gold sequins.

Fed upon privilege, the patricians flourished. Five at least of the leading ministers in Lord Salisbury's Government were over six feet tall, far above the normal stature of the time. Of the nineteen members of the Cabinet, all but two lived to be over seventy, seven exceeded eighty, and two exceeded ninety at a time when the average life expectancy of a male at birth was forty-four and of a man who had reached twenty-one was sixty-two. On their diet of privilege they acquired a certain quality which Lady Warwick could define only in the words, "They have an air!"

Now and then the sound of the distant rumble in the atmosphere caused them vague apprehensions of changes coming to spoil the fun. With port after dinner the gentlemen talked about the growth of democracy and the threat of Socialism. Cartoons in newspapers pictured John Bull looking over a fence at a bull called Labour. Most people were aware of problems without seriously imagining any major change in the present order of things, but a few were deeply disturbed. Young Arthur Ponsonby saw every night along the embankment from Westminster to Waterloo Bridge the "squalid throng of homeless, wretched outcasts sleeping on the benches," and broke with the courtier tradition of his father and brother to become a Socialist. Lady Warwick tried to smother nagging doubts about a life devoted to the pursuit of pleasure in "recurrent fits of philanthropy" which she indulged in from "an impelling desire to help put things right and a deep conviction that things as they were, were not right." In 1895, on reading an attack by the Socialist editor Robert Blatchford in his paper the *Clarion* on a great ball given at Warwick Castle to celebrate her husband's accession to the title, she rushed in anger to London, leaving a house full of guests, to confront the enemy. She explained to him how during a hard winter when many were out of work the Warwick celebrations provided employment. Mr. Blatchford explained to his beautiful caller the nature of productive labour and the principles of Socialist theory. She returned to Warwick in a daze of new ideas and thereafter devoted her energy, money and influence to propagating them, to the acute discomfort of her circle.

Lady Warwick was a straw, not a trend. As a nation, Britain in 1895 had an air of careless supremacy which galled her neighbors. The attitude, called "splendid isolation," was both a state of mind and a fact. Britain did not worry seriously about potential enemies, felt no need of allies and had no friends. In a world in which other national energies were bursting old limits, this happy condition gave no great promise of permanence. On July 20, when Salisbury's Government was less than a month old, it was suddenly and surprisingly challenged from an unexpected quarter, the United States. The affair concerned a long-disputed frontier between British Guiana and Venezuela. Claiming that the British were expanding territorially at their expense in violation of the Monroe Doctrine, the Venezuelans had been goading the United States to open that famous umbrella and insist on arbitration. Although the American President, Grover Cleveland, was a man of ordinarily sound judgment and common sense, his countrymen were in a mood of swelling self-assertion and, as Rudyard Kipling pointed out, for purposes of venting chauvinist sentiments, France had Germany, Britain had Russia, and America had Britain, the only feasible country "for the American public speaker to trample upon." On July 20, Cleveland's Secretary of State, Richard Olney, delivered a Note to Great Britain stating that disregard of the Monroe Doctrine would be "deemed an act of unfriendliness toward the United States," whom he described in terms of not very veiled belligerence as "master of the situation and practically invulnerable against any and all comers."

This was truly astonishing language for diplomatic usage; but it was deliberately provocative on Olney's part, because, as he said, "in English eyes the United States was then so completely a negligible quantity" that he felt "only words the equivalent of blows would be effective." Upon Lord Salisbury who was acting as his own Foreign Secretary they failed of effect. He was no more disposed to respond to this kind of prodding than he would have been if his tailor had suddenly challenged him to a duel. Foreign policy had been his métier for twenty years. He had been at the Congress of Berlin with Disraeli in 1878 and had maneuvered through all the twists and turns of that perennial entanglement, the Eastern Question. His method was not that of Lord Palmerston, whom the Prince of Wales admired because he "knew his own mind and put down his foot." Issues in foreign affairs were no longer as forthright as in the days of Lord Palmerston's flourishing, and Lord Salisbury sought no dramatic successes in their conduct. The victories of diplomacy, he said, were won by "a series of microscopic advantages; a judicious suggestion here, an opportune civility there, a wise concession at one moment and a farsighted persistence at another; of sleepless tact, immovable calmness and patience that no folly, no provocation, no blunder can shake." But he regarded these refinements as wasted on a democracy like the United States, just as he regarded the vote as too good for the working class. He simply let Olney's note go unanswered for four months.

When he finally replied on November 26 it was to remark coldly that "the disputed frontier of Venezuela has nothing to do with any of the questions dealt with by President Monroe" and to refuse flatly to arbitrate "the frontier of a British possession which belonged to the Throne of England before the Republic of Venezuela came into existence." He did not even bother to obey diplomacy's primary rule: leave room for negotiation. The rebuff was too much even for Cleveland. In a Message to Congress on December 17 he announced that after an American Committee of Inquiry had investigated and established a boundary line, any British extension over the line would be regarded as "wilful aggression" upon the rights and interests of the United States. Cleveland became a hero; a tornado of jingoism swept the country; "WAR IF NECESSARY," proclaimed the New York *Sun*. The word "war" was soon being used as recklessly as if it concerned an expedition against the Iroquois or the Barbary pirates.

Britain was amazed, with opinion dividing according to party. The Liberals were mortified by Lord Salisbury's haughty tone, the Tories angered at American presumption. "No Englishman with imperial instincts," wrote the Tory journalist and novelist Morley Roberts in the inevitable letter to *The Times*, "can look with anything but contempt on the Monroe Doctrine. The English and not the inhabitants of the United States are the greatest power in the two Americas; and no dog of a Republic can open its mouth to bark without our good leave." If the tone was overdone, the outrage was real. Although the absurdity of the issue was recognized on both sides of the Atlantic, belligerence surged and blood boiled. Aggressiveness born of power and prosperity was near the surface. The quarrel was becoming increasingly difficult to terminate when happily a third force caused a distraction.

No one was more useful as a magnet of other nations' animosities than that catalyst of his epoch, Kaiser Wilhelm II of Germany. Forever spoiling to emphasize his own and his country's importance, to play a role, to strike a pose, to twist the course of history, he never overlooked an opportunity. He hankered to be influential and usually was.

On December 29, 1895, the long-standing conflict between the Boer Republic of the Transvaal and the British of the Cape Colony was broken open by the Jameson Raid. Nominally under British suzerainty but virtually independent, the Boer Republic was a block in the march of British red down the length of Africa and an oppressor of the Uitlanders within its borders. These were British and other foreigners who, drawn by gold, had flocked to, and settled in, the Transvaal until they now outnumbered the Boers, but were kept by them without suffrage and other civil rights, and were seething with grievances. Inspired by imperialism's impatient genius, Cecil Rhodes, Dr. Jameson led six hundred horsemen over the border with intent to bring about an uprising of the Uitlanders, overthrow the Boer government and bring the South African Republic under British control. His troop was surrounded and captured within three days, but his mission released a train of events that was to take full effect four years later.

For the moment it provided the ever alert Kaiser with an opening. He telegraphed congratulations to President Kruger of the Boer Republic on his success in repelling the invaders "without appealing to the help of friendly powers." The implication that such help would be available on future request was clear. Instantly, every British gaze, like spectators' heads at a tennis match, turned from America to Germany, and British wrath was diverted from President Cleveland, always unlikely in the role of menace, to the Kaiser, who played it so much more suitably. In helping to bring on the ultimate encirclement that he most dreaded, the Kruger telegram was one of the Kaiser's most effective efforts. It revealed a hostility that startled the British. From that moment the possibility that isolation might prove more hazardous than splendid began to trouble the minds of their policy-makers.

The year 1895 was prolific of shocks, and one that shook society unpleasantly occurred two months before the Conservatives took office. The trial and conviction of Oscar Wilde under Section 11 of the Criminal Law Amendment Act, for acts of gross indecency between males, destroyed both a brilliant man of letters and the mood of decadence symbolized.

The presumption of decay had been heavily reinforced two years earlier by Max Nordau in a widely discussed book called *Degeneration.* Through six hundred pages of mounting hysteria he traced the decay lurking impartially in the realism of Zola, the symbolism of Mallarmé, the mysticism of Maeterlinck, in Wagner's music, Ibsen's dramas, Manet's pictures, Tolstoy's novels, Nietzsche's philosophy, Dr. Jaeger's woollen clothing, in Anarchism, Socialism, women's dress, madness, suicide, nervous diseases, drug addiction, dancing, sexual license, all of which were combining to produce a society without self-control, discipline or shame which was "marching to its certain ruin because it is too worn out and flaccid to perform great tasks."

Wilde, conforming to the duty of a decadent, was already engaged in destroying himself. In his role of aesthete, voluptuary and wit, he had hitherto been protected by the enamel of success. His incomparable talk enraptured friends as his plays did the public. But his arrogance as artist became overweening and his appetites uncontrolled, so that he grew fat and loose and heavy-jowled and, as a friend remarked, "all his bad qualities began to show in his face." Nor did success satisfy him, for satiety required that he must taste the ultimate sensation of ruin. "I was a problem," he said in sad self-knowledge, "for which there was no solution." He precipitated his own arrest by taking action for libel against the Marquess of Queensberry. The ensuing trials tore away Society's screen of discretion and gave everyone a shuddering look at the livid gleam of vice: panders, male prostitutes, hotel-room assignations with a valet, a groom, a boat-attendant picked up on a beach, and blackmail. No charges were brought against Lord Alfred Douglas, son of the Marquess of Queensberry, the flowery and seductive young man who shared these practices as well as Wilde's company and affections. Nor had there been any charges when Lord Arthur Somerset, a son of the Duke of Beaufort and a friend of the Prince of Wales, had been found in a homosexual brothel raided by the police in 1889. He had been allowed to take himself off and live comfortably after his fashion on the Continent while the Prince had asked Lord Salisbury that he might occasionally be permitted to visit his parents quietly in the country "without fear of being apprehended on this awful charge."

Frank Harris, then editor of the *Fortnightly Review*, thought that the solidarity of the governing class would close protectively around his friend Oscar in the same way. He supposed that aristocratic prejudice was a matter of favoring the exceptional over the common and would operate equally for the lord, the millionaire and the "man of genius." He was mistaken. Wilde had done the unforgivable in forcing public notice of his sin. And as artist-intellectual caught in scarlet depravity he evoked the howl of the philistines and plunged the British public into one of the most virulent of its periodic fits of morality. The judge was malevolent, the public vituperative, the society which he had amused turned its back, cabbies and newsboys exchanged vulgar jokes about "Oscar," the press reviled him, his books were withdrawn from sale and his name pasted out on the playbills advertising *The Importance of Being Earnest*, his brightest diamond, then playing to enchanted audiences. His downfall, said the gentleman-Socialist H. M. Hyndman, "was the most grievous thing I have ever known in the literary world." With it was dissipated, in England, if not on the Continent, the yellow haze of *fin de siècle* decadence.

Lord Salisbury's appointment of a Poet Laureate at the end of the year could not have provided a greater contrast in men of letters or done more to re-enthrone Respectability. Since the death of Tennyson in 1892, the post had remained vacant because neither Mr. Gladstone nor Lord Rosebery, who took their responsibility to literature seriously, could find a worthy successor. Swinburne, owing to his distressing habits and opinions, was, regrettably, "absolutely impossible" (although Mr. Gladstone "admired his genius"), William Morris was a Socialist, Hardy was known so far only by his novels and the younger poetic talents tended to wear the colors of the Yellow Book and the Mauve Decade. The young Anglo-Indian, Rudyard Kipling, in his *Barrack Room Ballads* of 1892, had certainly sounded a virile and imperial note but in a rather rough idiom, and neither he nor W. E. Henley nor Robert Bridges was considered. All other candidates were mediocrities, one of whom, Sir Lewis Morris, offered an opening to what a contemporary called "the most spontaneously witty thing ever uttered in England." Morris, author of an effusion entitled *The Epic of Hades*, who wanted the Laureateship badly, complained to Oscar Wilde in the days before his ruin, "There is a conspiracy of silence against me, a conspiracy of silence. What ought I to do, Oscar?" "Join it," replied Wilde.

On the principle that, like bishops, one Laureate would do as well as another, Lord Salisbury, when he became Prime Minister, appointed Alfred Austin. A journalist of deep Conservative dye, founder and editor of the *National Review*, Austin was also the producer of fervent topical verse on such occasions as the death of Disraeli. When a friend pointed out grammatical errors in his poems, Austin said, "I dare not alter these things. They come to me from above." He was a tiny man—five feet high—with a round face and neat white moustache who, as a contributor of articles expounding Conservative foreign policy which he signed "Diplomaticus," was personally acquainted with the Prime Minister and a frequent visitor to Hatfield. He had begun his career as a correspondent in the war of 1870 by gaining an interview with Bismarck at Versailles, and thirty years later was forced to the painful conclusion that Germany, in her wars of 1859–70, had "unquestionably resorted to means which one could not conceive Alfred the Great or any modern British minister employing." His most popular work so far had been a prose book on English gardens, but within two weeks of his appointment as Laureate, he exceeded expectations with a poem in *The Times* celebrating Dr. Jameson's exploit:

> There are girls in the gold-reef city,
> There are mothers and children too!
> And they cry, Hurry up! for pity!
> So what could a brave man do? . . .
>
> So we forded and galloped forward,
> As hard as our beasts could pelt,
> First eastward, then trending northward,
> Right over the rolling veldt. . . .

Some echo of the hilarity this provoked reaching the Queen, she queried Salisbury, who had to admit that her new Laureate's first effusion was "unluckily to the taste of the galleries in the lower class of theatres who sing it with vehemence." Salisbury never bothered to explain his choice of Austin beyond an off-hand remark once that "he wanted it"; but if the choice did not honor British poetry, it was a shrewd match of the British mood.

The Englishman, as an American observer noticed, felt himself the best-governed citizen in the world even when in Opposition he believed the incumbents were ruining the country. The English form of government "is the thing above all others that he is proud of . . . and he has an unshakeable confidence in the personal integrity of statesmen." Austin reflected that comfortable pride. In the radiant summer of Jubilee Year, 1897, a visitor found him in linen suit and panama hat, sitting in a high-backed wicker chair, on the lawn of his country home enjoying conversation with Lady Paget and Lady Windsor. They agreed that each person should tell what was his idea of heaven. Austin's wish was noble. He desired to sit in a garden and receive a flow of telegrams announcing alternately a British victory by sea and a British victory by land.

It was easy to make fun of Alfred Austin, with his small size, large pomposity and banal verse, and many did. Yet in his Jubilee wish there was something simple and devoted, an assurance, a complete and happy love and admiration for his country, a noncognizance of wrong, which expressed a mood and a condition which, like Lord Ribblesdale's appearance, were to become beyond recapture.

The House of Lords, now that the Conservatives had replaced the Liberals, could lean back comfortably and follow its natural bent, which was to do as little work as possible. In the last years of the Liberals it had roused itself to "stop the rot" induced by Radical legislation and had thrown out an Employers' Liability Bill, a Parish Councils Bill designed to make local government councils more democratic, and finally the Home Rule Bill. In the last speech of his career on March 1, 1894, Gladstone had solemnly warned that differences of "fundamental tendency" between the two Houses had reached a point in the past year which required that some solution would have to be found for "this tremendous contrariety and incessant conflict upon matters of high principle and profound importance." Proposals for reform of the Upper House to redress the imbalance when a Liberal Government was in power and thus remove the grounds of criticism had been many. But now that a state of happy harmony had succeeded conflict, the urgency relaxed, Gladstone's warning was forgotten and the Lords could resume their customary quiescence.

Out of 560 members, many "backwoods" peers, as they were called, never took their seats at all. Others appeared only at times of crisis and hardly more than fifty regularly attended the sessions. It was, said Lord Newton, "the most good-natured assembly that exists," hearing out speakers who would not be listened to for five minutes in the Commons. Its debates were "always polite" and conducted with a restraint which seemed to show "detachment almost amounting to indifference." Party animosity was concealed "under a veil of studied courtesy." It was not a stimulating audience, especially to Liberals, whose leader, Lord Rosebery, complained that "every auditor gives the impression of profound weariness and boredom."

While Lord Salisbury was Prime Minister the House of Lords was entirely under his dominance, although its official ruler was the Lord Chancellor, who acted as Speaker. This office was now held by Lord Halsbury, born a commoner, by name Hardinge Giffard, a member of one of the oldest families in England. Its founder had fought at Hastings and was later created Earl of Buckingham by William Rufus. Although the title died out in the next generation, the family persisted with vigor if not riches and the sprightly Lord Chancellor, seventy-two at this time, lived to be ninety-eight. A stubby Pickwickian figure with short legs, red cheeks, white tufts of hair over his ears and a humorous expression, Lord Halsbury, despite his genial manner, was a hard opponent, implacable at the bar, with a relentless memory. He wore a frock coat, a square-topped derby hat, a "true blue" Tory tie and, according to a younger member of the Upper House, "invariably objected on principle to all change." Owing to meagre family finances, he had been educated at home by his father, a barrister and editor of a high

Tory daily paper, the *Standard*, who gave him lessons in Greek, Latin and Hebrew until 4 A.M. and was so upright that he refused an offer from the Duke of Newcastle, an admirer of his paper, to put his three sons through Oxford. The youngest son went through Merton College nevertheless, rose rapidly to the top of the legal profession, acquiring wealth and friends on the way as well as the accusation from some quarters that he "filled his great office with jolly cynicism" and made unscrupulous use of the Bench for political patronage. However, when from among many rival claimants he was named Lord Chancellor, making him the highest-ranking personage after the royal family and the Archbishop of Canterbury, the "Carlton Club supported him to a man," and Lord Coleridge, the Lord Chief Justice and a Liberal, wrote, "Your politics are of course unintelligible to me but in everything else, as a scholar, a gentleman and a lawyer, there is no one fitter to be our head."

Two high-ranking peers in Lord Salisbury's Cabinet, the fifth Marquess of Lansdowne and the eighth Duke of Devonshire, were both Whigs of pedigree and converts to the Conservatives. Lord Lansdowne, the Secretary for War, was an aristocrat who looked it every inch. Smooth and cold as polished stone, elegant, correct and courteous, he was an obvious choice for the great ceremonial posts and had been Governor-General of Canada at thirty-eight and Viceroy of India at forty-three. His family name was Fitzmaurice. In the Twelfth Century the first of his line had settled in Ireland in county Kerry and the current Marquess was twenty-eighth Lord of Kerry in the direct male line. He was one of those Anglo-Irishmen, said the *Spectator* in commenting on the quality of Lord Salisbury's Government, "who can rule by a sort of instinct." The instinct had flourished in his great-grandfather, the first Marquess, who as Earl of Shelburne had been a secretary of state under George III, and had served briefly as Prime Minister in the last year of the war with the American Colonies. The same instinct carried his grandfather, the third Marquess, to the Home Office and other posts in six governments between 1827 and 1857, after which he had declined to be Prime Minister and had refused a dukedom. The present Marquess seemed to his brother-in-law, Lord Ernest Hamilton, to be "the greatest gentleman of his day," who in any international competition for gentlemen must surely be nominated the British representative.

Senior to, and even grander than, Lansdowne—but wearing the patrician air without self-consciousness—was Spencer Compton Cavendish, eighth Duke of Devonshire, probably the only man in England both secure enough and careless enough to forget an engagement with his sovereign. Edward VII, having informed the Duke that he proposed to dine quietly with him at Devonshire House on a certain day, duly arrived, to the consternation of the household, for the Duke was not at home and had to be hurriedly retrieved from the Turf Club.

He was sixty-two in 1895, tall and bearded, with heavy-lidded eyes in a long Hapsburg face and a straight, lordly, high-ridged nose. Formerly Lord Hartington during his thirty-four years in the House of Commons, he was now Lord President of the Council in Salisbury's Cabinet. He owned 186,000 acres and had an income of £180,000 from land alone, not counting investments. Though famous for his lassitude, he had managed to serve in more Cabinet offices under more governments than any man living: as First Lord of the Admiralty under Lord Palmerston, Secretary for War under Lord John Russell, Postmaster-General, Secretary for Ireland, for India and again for War in successive Gladstone governments. A familiar sight coming down Whitehall was Lord Hartington driving himself to the House in a light phaeton with a careless hold on the reins, a large cigar in his mouth and a collie sitting next to him.

He had played a leading role in growing opposition to Mr. Gladstone in the two crises of the eighties that broke apart the Liberal party: the imperialist issue over General Gordon's expedition to the Sudan and the Irish issue over Home Rule. Though he was not one of the polished and impassioned orators, his speech in 1886 announcing his break with Gladstone made a profound impression. By stating plainly that men could not remain in the false position of continuing to support a government, even of their own party, whose principles they disapproved, he gave, said a member, "a new sense of duty and a new power of action to hundreds of men throughout the country." Henry Chaplin thought the speech ought "to make you Prime Minister for certain." Some years earlier the Queen, in her stubborn effort to avoid the inevitability of Mr. Gladstone, had already asked Lord Hartington to form a government; but he had refused, bowing to Gladstone, who, he knew, would not serve except in first place.

In the opinion of Mr. Balfour, an expert, Lord Hartington was "of all the statesmen I have known . . . the most persuasive speaker," less for his words than for the character behind them. He made every listener feel that here was a man "who has done his best to master every aspect of this question, who has been driven by logic to arrive at certain conclusions, and who is disguising from us no argument on either side. . . . How can we hope to have a more honest guide?" It was this quality, said Balfour, which Hartington possessed "in far greater measure than any man I have ever known," which gave him his great influence with the public, made him indispensable to governments and, whether in the Cabinet, in Parliament, or on the public platform, "gave him a dominant position in any assembly."

The Duke would have preferred to be anywhere else, for he undertook the hard work and confining hours of government office more from duty than desire. But he was requited by the feeling of sovereign and country that he was one of the pillars on which the state reposed. "The Queen cannot conclude this letter," Victoria wrote to him in 1892, "without expressing to the Duke . . . how much she relies on him to assist in maintaining the safety and honor of her vast Empire. All must join" —she finished in simple summary of her faith—"in this great and necessary work."

The Duke joined with no visible zest. "Never angry though often bored," according to one friend, "he takes things very easy indeed," according to another. Some said his lethargy was laziness, others that it was a well-considered reluctance to hurry; in either event it was underlined by a habit of going to sleep in the midst of things. Even his own speeches bored him and once when speaking on the Indian budget he paused, leaned over to the colleague nearest him on the bench, and suppressing a yawn, whispered, "This is damned dull."

His only passion was for his racing stud, although he also maintained, whether from passion, habit or indolence, a thirty-year liaison with "one of the handsomest women in Europe," as she was when the affair began, the domineering, ambitious, German-born Louise, Duchess of Manchester. Her first Duke disappointed her by impoverishing himself, but obedient to his caste, refrained or was persuaded to refrain from bringing any unpleasant public action, leaving his wife and Lord Hartington to enjoy both each other and an unassailable moral and social position. When Manchester died, his widow married the Duke of Devonshire in 1892 just after he had succeeded to his title. Thereafter known as the "Double Duchess," she continued to exercise her formidable talents toward her major goal, that of making her husband Prime Minister.

The Duke did not give her the necessary help. He was not the kind in whom a burning ambition for the highest post erases every other consideration. When, after he had led the Liberal Unionists out of the party, Lord Salisbury twice offered to serve under him, he again refused, not yet prepared for coalition. By 1895, however, the split between moderate and radical Whigs having widened and the habit of voting in concert with the Tories having made a bridge, the Duke with four other Liberal Unionists crossed over it to serve under Lord Salisbury.

This was the Conservative—now Unionist—Government which took office in June, 1895. A delicate situation was expected at Windsor when the Duke and the other former Liberals, arriving as members of Lord Salisbury's Ministry to receive their seals of office, would pass their former colleagues on the way out. To avoid embarrassment, the Queen's Private Secretary tactfully arranged that the outgoing Liberals should deliver up their seals at 11 A.M. while the new ministers waited in another drawing room until their predecessors had left. All would have gone off smoothly but for the Duke, who, arriving late as usual, missed the designated waiting room and met his old associates coming out, who peppered him with taunts about his new friends. "No face was more suited to a difficult situation," wrote a witness, for the Duke, quite unperturbed, "passed through them with his mouth wide open and his eyes half closed."

The Cavendishes stemmed from an ancestor who had been Chief Justice of the Court of King's Bench during the Peasants' Revolt of 1381. His son John was the man who killed Wat

Tyler, for which he was knighted on the spot by Richard II, while the father was seized elsewhere by the mob and beheaded in revenge. Dutifully, if none too enthusiastically, the Cavendishes down through the centuries helped to govern the country. The fourth Duke served briefly as Prime Minister in 1756–57, while Pitt and Newcastle were feuding, but resigned as soon as he could be replaced. His brother, Lord John Cavendish, was twice Chancellor of the Exchequer, in which capacity Edmund Burke praised him for his "great integrity . . . and perfect disinterestedness" but wished that Lord John could be "induced to show a certain degree of regular attendance on business" and be allowed only "a certain reasonable proportion of fox-hunting" and no more. The fifth Duke excelled by marrying the ravishing Georgiana, Duchess of Devonshire, whom Gainsborough painted in a pale shining glow against storm clouds, and Reynolds painted laughing with a full-skirted baby on her knee. Her beauty and irresistible charm came in the same excess as her gambling debts, which cost her husband £1,000,000. Fortunately, the Cavendishes were one of the two or three richest families in the kingdom. When his steward regretted to inform the fifth Duke that his heir, the Lord Hartington of that day, was "disposed to spend a great deal of money," the Duke replied, "So much the better; Lord Hartington will have a great deal of money to spend."

In the Duke of 1895, neither fortune, nor position as eldest son, nor disinclination to exert himself, nor desire to follow his heart upon the turf were enough to outweigh in him "certain hereditary government instincts." He felt that "he owed a debt to the State that must be paid." This sense of obligation, remarked on by all who knew him, originated not only in family estate but also in a consciousness of superior ability. His father, a student of mathematics and the classics, known as the "Scholar" Duke, had educated him at home. Later at Trinity College, Cambridge, despite an idle, sporting, sociable life among the "tufts," Lord Hartington was the only one of his set to take an Honours degree, a second class in the mathematical tripos. He entered Parliament at twenty-four and achieved his first Cabinet office at thirty. His brother, Lord Frederick Cavendish, also undertook a political career, and in 1882, on his first day as Chief Secretary for Ireland, was assassinated in

Phoenix Park in Dublin. The killing of an English minister of the Crown by Irish malcontents created a sensation as great as the death of General Gordon at Khartoum. Whether because of his brother's murder or some other less obvious reason, the Duke made a habit of always carrying a loaded revolver about with him, and this was a constant source of worry to his family. "He was always losing them and buying new ones," wrote his nephew, "and there were no less than twenty of them knocking about Devonshire House when he died."

With the advent of the Duchess, an indefatigable hostess, Devonshire entertainments became the stateliest in Society. Every year on the opening of Parliament, the Duke and Duchess gave a great reception. Every year on Derby Day, Devonshire House, filled with roses and June flowers from the Duke's gardens, was the scene of a sparkling ball. Before the ball, the King gave a dinner to members of the Jockey Club at Buckingham Palace while the Queen came to dine with the Duchess. In Jubilee Year of 1897 the Devonshire fancy-dress ball was the most famous and lavish party of the era. At Chatsworth in Derbyshire, home of the Cavendishes for four hundred years, house parties reached their peak with the annual visit of the Prince and Princess of Wales, which continued when they were King and Queen. Every royal comfort was anticipated and satisfied, including the presence of the King's mistress, Mrs. Keppel, brilliant in diamonds, with whom, according to Princess Daisy of Pless, "the King has his bridge in a separate room while in other rooms people are massed together also of course playing bridge."

Built of the golden stone of the district, Chatsworth was surrounded by an Eighteenth Century park designed by Capability Brown. Luxury was everywhere. Cascades rippled over a series of stone steps six hundred feet long copied after the Renaissance water-landscaping of Italy. A copper willow tree, by an ingenious mechanism, could weep water from every leaf. Elaborate and exquisite garlands of flowers and fruit carved in wood festooned the walls. The library and collection of pictures and sculpture were on a princely scale like the Medicis' and administered almost as a public trust. Curators in the Duke's employ kept them open to scholars and connoisseurs, made new purchases and liberally loaned the treasures to exhibitions. The Chatsworth Memling went to Bruges, its Van Dycks to Antwerp, and all year the house was open to the public, who tramped through the halls in thousands. The Duke liked to watch them, and thinking his face as unknown to them as theirs to him, would stand, unconscious of being recognized, "wondering why the housemaid who acted as guide and the whole party had suddenly stood still and were staring at him." Though racehorses were more to him than books, he once astonished his librarian who was showing him his own first edition of *Paradise Lost* by sitting down and reading it aloud from the first line with simple pleasure, until the Duchess came in and, poking the Duke with her parasol, remarked, "If he reads poetry he will never go for his walk."

He was bored by pomp and hated pomposity. When the King decided to make him a Grand Commander of the new Victorian Order, the Duke, "in his sleepy way," asked the King's Private Secretary, Sir Frederick Ponsonby, what he was supposed to do with "the thing." "Anyone less anxious to receive an order I have never seen. He seemed to think it would only complicate his dressing." At the rehearsal for King Edward's coronation in 1902, at which the appearance of the peers wearing coronets with morning dress produced a comical effect, the Duke arrived late as usual and, with his right hand in his trouser pocket and an inexpressibly bored look on his face, strolled about the stage at the bidding of the Earl Marshal. He liked old baggy, casual clothes, never took the slightest trouble with his guests, deliberately ignored those who might prove tiresome, and once, when a speaker in the House of Lords was declaiming on "the greatest moments in life," the Duke opened his eyes long enough to remark to his neighbor, "My greatest moment was when my pig won first prize at Skipton Fair." His favorite club, after the Turf, was the Travellers', known for exclusiveness and an atmosphere of "solemn tranquillity" in which reading, dozing and meditation took precedence over conversation. For the disagreeable task of speaking at public meetings he trained himself by a method he once revealed to the young Winston Churchill when they were appearing together at a Free Trade meeting in Manchester. "Do you feel nervous, Winston?" asked the Duke, and on receiving an affirmative reply, told him, "I used to, but now, whenever I get up on a public platform, I take a good look around and as I sit down I say, 'I never saw such a lot of damned fools in my life' and then I feel a lot better."

When he chose he could be "the best of company, . . . delightful to talk to," that is, if conditions were right. At a dinner party in 1885 he arrived tired and hungry after a long day in Committee and sulked in silence when the first courses proved to be fancy but insubstantial French dishes instead of the solid fare that he liked. When a roast beef was brought in, he exclaimed in deep tones, "Hurrah! something to eat at last" and thereafter joined in the conversation. A fellow guest, the writer Wilfred Ward, noticed that in every case where he differed from Mr. Gladstone, who was of the company, Lord Hartington "put his finger on the weak point in the logic which Mr. Gladstone's rhetoric tended to obscure." Eighteen years later Ward met the Duke again at the British Embassy in Rome and confronted by a blank face reminded him of the place of their previous meeting. Thereupon the Duke exclaimed with feeling, "Of course I remember. We had nothing to eat." The inadequate French dishes, as Ward told the story, "had dwelt in his mind for nearly twenty years."

After succeeding to the title in 1891, he still returned, unlike Salisbury, to visit the House of Commons and "could generally be seen yawning in the front row of the Peers' Gallery" on the nights of big debates. As Duke he had more work to do than ever. He owned estates in Derbyshire, Yorkshire, Lancashire, Lincolnshire, Cumberland, Sussex, Middlesex and Ireland and personally went over all accounts of his properties and all important questions with his estate agents. He was Lord Lieutenant of Derbyshire, Chancellor of Cambridge University, President of the British Empire League and patron of various clerical livings to which he had to make appointments. He was director or chairman of various companies in which he had investments, including two railway lines, a steel company, a waterworks and a naval construction company. Though he distrusted his knowledge of business, "once he got a grip of a subject," according to one of his staff, "then no one was better able to confute a false argument or to see what the real point was." His mind worked slowly, and if he did not understand a matter at once, he would insist on its being thrashed out all over again until it was clear to him. He performed all his functions while continuing to maintain that he was happiest with his racing stud at Newmarket. Once at Aix-les-Bains he met W. H. Smith, then Conservative Leader of the House of Commons, and promptly sat down to talk politics for half an hour, saying, "it was pleasant in a place like this to have some work to do." It is possible he would have been more bored out of office than in.

To the Conservative Government of 1895 he brought, besides long experience and the prestige of his name and rank, an immense fund of public confidence banked over the four decades of his career. His disinterestedness was beyond question. So obviously was he above private ambition, wrote the editor of the *Spectator*, "that no one ever attributed to him unworthy motives or insinuated that he was playing for his own hand. If anyone had ventured to do so, the country would simply have regarded the accuser as mad." When the Duke took a position, people felt they had been given a lead. He never became Prime Minister or won the Derby but "no one," said *The Times*, "had a greater authority in moulding the political convictions of his countrymen." He remained vaguely puzzled by the extent of his own influence. "I don't see why I should tell the people what I should do if I had the vote," he protested. "They will do what they think right and I shall do what I think right. They don't want me to interfere." And when the Prince, who, no less than his subjects, relied on the Duke's judgment of men and issues, consulted him as arbiter of delicate social matters, he complained, "I don't know why it is but whenever a man is caught cheating at cards the case is referred to me." He had become, through a combination of heritage and character, a keeper of the national conscience. When a Presence was required for a solemn or ceremonial occasion, the solid, rather melancholy dignity of the Duke fulfilled the need. He was, Lord Rosebery said, "one of the great reserve forces of this country."

Among Lord Salisbury's ministers who took their seats in 1895 on the Government Front Bench in the House of Commons were two baronets, the ninth and sixth of their lines, Sir Michael Hicks-Beach, Chancellor of the Exchequer, and Sir

Matthew White Ridley, Home Secretary. The former, tall, thin and austere, was an arch Conservative, a champion of the Church of England and of the landowning class, known as "Black Michael." Tart and sharp-tongued, he once, after reading over a Liberal member's remarks on his budget, said to his secretary succinctly, "Go and tell him he is a pig." Beside them sat the two squires, Mr. Henry Chaplin and Mr. Walter Long, representatives of the landed gentry, the old untitled aristocracy who "scorned a peerage but made it a point of honor to stand for their county at the first general election after they came of age." Mr. Long, President of the Board of Agriculture and youngest member of the Government at forty-one, "never said anything in his life that anybody remembered." He "gently dozes," as an observer saw him, "his arms folded, his head sunk back upon a cushion, his ruddy October face giving a touch of color to the scene," while the older Mr. Chaplin "vigorously, wakefully, alertly guards the Empire against the knavish tricks of the Opposition."

Mr. Chaplin at fifty-four, with his magnificent stature, big handsome head, long nose, prominent chin, sideburns and monocle, was a marked personality, one of the most popular men of his generation, "easily recognizable, familiar to the public. Everyone knew him by sight." He was the visible symbol of the English country gentleman. His post was the Local Government Board, which dealt with the poor law, housing, town planning, public health and municipal government. Its functions were best described by Winston Churchill, who, on being offered the post in 1908, said, "I refuse to be shut up in a soup kitchen with Mrs. Sidney Webb." Chaplin performed its duties and those of M.P. with tremendous gravity. He regarded himself, as did his constituents, as the bulwark of the essential Britain, and used to practice his speeches behind hedges the better to do credit to his role. His jovian thunders, the noble sweep of his arm as he spoke from the Front Bench, said a witness, expressed, not vanity, but "the calm, ineradicable conviction of the ruling class." Undaunted by the most abstruse problems of government, he would tackle the tariff or the Education Bill in the same spirit as a difficult ditch in the hunting field and even undertook the fervent advocacy of bimetallism as a cure for economic ills. Once after a two-hour discourse on this recondite subject, he mopped his brow and leaning over to Mr. Balfour, asked, "How did I do, Arthur?"

"Splendidly, Harry, splendidly."

"Did you understand me, Arthur?"

"Not a word, Harry, not a word."

Arthur Balfour, prince of the Cecil line, nephew of the Prime Minister and his political heir apparent, artist of debate and idol of Society, was the paragon of his party and its official Leader in the House of Commons. He was forty-seven in 1895 and, when his uncle retired in 1902, was to succeed him as Prime Minister. Over six feet tall, he had blue eyes, waving brown hair and moustache, and a soft, bland face that might have seemed vulnerable if it had not been smoothed to an external serenity. His expression was gentle, his figure willowy, his manner nonchalant, but there remained a mystery in his face. No one could tell what banked fires burned behind it or whether they burned or even if they existed.

Rarely seen to sit upright, he reclined in indolent attitudes as close to the horizontal as possible, "as if to discover," wrote *Punch*'s parliamentary correspondent, "how nearly he could sit on his shoulder blades." In him all the gifts of privilege had combined. He had wealth, blue blood, good looks, great charm and "the finest brain that has been applied to politics in our time." He was a philosopher on a serious level whose second major work, *The Foundations of Belief*, published in 1895, was read by the American philosopher William James with "immense gusto. There is more real philosophy in such a book," he wrote to his brother Henry, "than in fifty German ones heaped with subtleties and technicalities."

Although ultimately aloof and detached, Balfour had a winning manner that encircled him with admiration. His charm was of the kind that left everyone feeling happy who talked with him. "Although he was the best talker I have ever known," said John Buchan, "he was not a monopolist of the conversation but one who quickened and elevated the whole discussion and brought out the best of other people." After an evening in his company, wrote Austen Chamberlain, "one left with the feeling that one had been at the top of one's form and really had talked rather well." Political opponents were affected no less than allies. He was the only Conservative to whom Gladstone in debate accorded the term usually reserved for members of his own party, "my honourable friend." Women succumbed equally. "Oh dear," sighed Constance Lady Battersea after a visit to his home in 1895, "what a gulf between him and most men!" Margot Asquith found his "exquisite attention" and "lovely bend of the head," when he talked to her, "irresistible"; so much so that earlier, when she was Margot Tennant, and herself a social star of high voltage, she had "moved heaven and earth," according to Lady Jebb, to marry him. Queried on the rumor of this marriage, Balfour replied, "No, that is not so. I rather think of having a career of my own."

As the eldest son of Lord Salisbury's sister, Lady Blanche Balfour, he was named Arthur for the Duke of Wellington, who acted as his godfather. On the paternal side the Balfours were of ancient Scottish lineage, their fortune having been made in the late Eighteenth Century by Arthur's grandfather, James Balfour, a nabob of the East India Company. James acquired in Scotland an estate of 10,000 acres, at Whittinghame overlooking the Firth of Forth, which became the family home, as well as a deer forest, a salmon river, a shooting lodge, a seat in Parliament and a daughter of the eighth Earl of Lauderdale as wife. A daughter of this marriage, Balfour's aunt, married the Duke of Grafton, so that along with the Salisbury connection, Balfour, as a friend said, "can call cousins with half the nobility of England." His younger brother Eustace subsequently married Lady Frances Campbell, daughter of the Duke of Argyll, granddaughter of the Duke of Sutherland, niece of the Duke of Westminster and sister-in-law of Princess Louise, daughter of Queen Victoria.

Balfour's father, also an M.P., died at thirty-five, when Arthur was seven, leaving Lady Blanche, in whom the Cecil streak of religious feeling was particularly marked, to govern her family of five sons and three daughters. Besides teaching Arthur to admire Jane Austen and her brother's favorite, *The Count of Monte Cristo*, she also communicated the Cecil sense of duty. When her son at Cambridge became enamored of philosophy and wished to make over his inheritance to a brother in favor of the studious life, she scolded him severely for poor spirit in wanting to shirk the responsibilities of his position.

At Trinity College, where Balfour read Moral Science, his failure to take a First did not depress his imperturbable good nature or good spirits. He was, wrote Lady Jebb, the doyen of Cambridge society, "a young prince in his way and almost as much spoiled." Of his four brothers, Frank was a professor of embryology who according to Darwin would have become "the first of English biologists" if he had not been killed climbing in the Swiss Alps at the age of thirty-one; Gerald, superbly handsome, was, according to Lady Jebb, "the most superior man I ever met," although her niece thought him "the most conceited"; Eustace was merely average and Cecil was the bad apple in the barrel, who died disgraced in Australia. But Arthur, decided Lady Jebb, was "the best in a family all of whom are best, . . . a man that almost everyone loves." She thought his nature, however, was "emotionally cold" and that his one essay in love, with May Lyttelton, sister of a Cambridge friend and Gladstone's niece, who died when she was twenty-five and Balfour twenty-seven, had "exhausted his powers in that direction." This was the accepted supposition in later years to explain Balfour's bachelorhood. In fact, it was not so much that he was emotionally cold as that he was warmly attached to his complete freedom to do as he pleased.

Among his friends were two of Trinity's outstanding scholars: his tutor Henry Sidgwick, later Professor of Moral Philosophy, and the physicist John Strutt, later third Baron Rayleigh, a future Nobel prize winner and Chancellor of the University, each of whom married a sister of Balfour. At that time, when to be an intellectual was to be agnostic, Balfour's inherited religious sense caused his Cambridge friends to regard him as "a curious relic of an older generation." His Society friends, on the other hand, when he published his first book, *A Defence of Philosophic Doubt*, in 1879, assumed from the title that Arthur was championing agnosticism, and when his name was mentioned, "they went about looking very solemn." In fact, by expressing doubt of material reality, the book was paradoxically asserting the right to spiritual faith, a position more explicitly stated in his later book, *The Foundations of Belief.* At Whittinghame, which was run for him by his maiden sister, Alice, and shared by his married brothers and their numerous children, he read family prayers every Sunday evening. Steeped in the Hebraism of the

Old Testament, he felt a particular interest in the "people of the Book" and was concerned about the problem of the Jew in the modern world. His niece and biographer in her childhood imbibed from him "the idea that Christian religion and civilization owes to Judaism an immeasurable debt, shamefully ill repaid."

He was the most dined-out man in London. Blandly ignoring the implacable rule that required the Leader of the House to be in his place throughout a sitting, he would often disappear during the dinner hour, reappearing shamelessly some hours later in evening dress. Every diary of the time finds him at house parties and dinner parties: "at the Rothschilds," wrote John Morley, "only Balfour there, *partie carrée*, always most pleasurable." He was one of twenty men at dinner at Harry Cust's, where the talk was so absorbing that when the house caught fire upstairs the dinner continued while the footmen passed bath towels with the port for protection against water from the firemen's hoses; he was at Blenheim Palace with the Marlboroughs in a party including the Prince and Princess of Wales, the Curzons, the Londonderrys, the Grenfells and Harry Chaplin; he was at Chatsworth with the Devonshires in a party including the Duke and Duchess of Connaught, Count Mensdorff, the Austrian Ambassador, the ugly, fascinating and ribald Marquis de Soveral, Ambassador of Portugal, the de Greys, Ribblesdales and Grenfells; he was at Hatfield with the Salisburys in a party including the Duke of Argyll, Mr. Speaker Peel and his daughter, Mr. Buckle of *The Times*, George Curzon and General Lord Methuen; he was at Cassiobury, home of Lord Essex, one Sunday at the end of a brilliant London season, when Edith Wharton, arriving for tea, "found scattered on the lawn under the great cedars the very flower and pinnacle of the London world: Mr. Balfour, Lady Desborough, Lady Elcho, John Sargent, Henry James and many others of that shining galaxy, so exhausted by their social labors of the past weeks . . . that beyond benevolent smiles they had little to give."

Most often Balfour was to be found at Clouds, home of the baronet Sir Percy Wyndham and favored country house of the Souls. Among their congenial company the particular attraction for Balfour was Lady Elcho, one of the three beautiful

Wyndham sisters, with whom, though she was the wife of a friend, Balfour pursued a discreet affair over a period of some twelve years, of which the letters survive. Sargent, when he painted the sisters in 1899, was hampered by no such compelling realism as affected him in the matter of Lady Charles Beresford's eyebrows. The group portrait of Lady Elcho, Mrs. Tennant and Mrs. Adeane, gowned in porcelain whiteness and draped in poses of careless but haughty elegance upon a sofa, is a dazzling dream of feminine aristocracy.

The ladies of the Souls, in conscious reaction to the Victorian feminine ideal, determined to be intellectual, to be slim and likewise to allow themselves a new freedom of private morality. Their only American member, the beautiful Daisy White, wife of Henry White, First Secretary of the American Embassy, was once congratulated by a friend on not allowing herself to be changed by "all those people who have lovers." In this activity the Souls were no different from the more philistine members of the Prince of Wales's set. All were engaged in the same open conspiracy in which Society managed to depart from Victorian morality without deserting propriety. Balfour's liaison with Lady Elcho was for a while serious enough to cause their friends some anxiety. The feelings of the husband, Hugo, Lord Elcho, heir of the Earl of Wemyss and a member, though a silent one, of the same circle, are unknown. The affair, like the Duke of Devonshire's, was the permitted excursion of a person of character and position sufficiently lofty to be above reproach.

When Balfour first entered Parliament at twenty-six from a family-controlled borough, it had been less from personal desire than from ordained fate as an eldest son and a Cecil. By the time he moved into Downing Street in 1895 as First Lord of the Treasury and Leader of the House, in lieu of his uncle, who preferred to live at home, the passion for politics latent in his blood had grown with growing skill and power. Yet it did not disturb his temperamental detachment. When meeting criticism he would regard it, not as something to resent, but as a thing to be examined like an interesting beetle. "Quite a good fellow," he would say of an opponent, "has a curious view, not uninteresting." He was at heart both a conservative who wanted to retain the best of the world he knew and a liberal with, as his sister-in-law remarked, "a sympathetic outlook for all progress." People felt in him "a natural spring of youth," in the words of one friend, and a "freshness, serenity and buoyancy" in the words of another. Later, as Prime Minister, he was the first in that office to go to Buckingham Palace in a motorcar and the first to go to the House of Commons in a Homburg hat.

He thought of himself as belonging to the younger generation of Tories who recognized the necessity of responding to the rising challenge of the working class. Yet bred as they were in privilege they could not, when issues came to a test, range themselves on the side of the invaders. In his first years in Parliament, Balfour had joined the four "Radical" Tories of the Fourth Party led by Lord Randolph Churchill. They occupied the Front Bench below the gangway and Balfour sat with them, because, he said, he had room there for his legs, but the choice indicated a point of view. The Fourth Party were gadflies in the cause of what was called "Tory Democracy," the belief that the rising political power of Labour could be harnessed in partnership with the Tories. If Labour, stated Lord Randolph in 1892, found that it could "obtain its objects and secure its own advantage" under the existing constitution—which it was the Tories' business to preserve—then all would be well; but if the Conservatives stubbornly resisted these demands in "unreasoning and shortsighted support of all the present rights of property," then Labour would be ranged against them. Since the Tories were a minority in the country, it was incumbent on them to enlist in their support "a majority of the votes of the masses of Labour."

Balfour was never thoroughly persuaded of this convincingly worded argument, any more than, when it came to a practical test, was Lord Randolph himself. In the abstract, Balfour believed in democracy and extension of the suffrage and in improvement of working conditions and of the rights of Labour but not at the cost of breaking down the walls of privilege that protected the ruling class. Here was the fundamental difficulty of Tory Democracy. Its advocates thought it possible to meet the demands of the workers while at the same time preserving intact the citadel of privilege, but Balfour suspected the bitter truth of history: that progress and gain by one group is never accomplished without loss of some permanent value of another. He continued to express his belief that Socialism would never get possession of the working classes "if those who wield the collective forces of the community show themselves desirous . . . to ameliorate every legitimate grievance." But when it came to specific acts of amelioration he was not enthusiastic or deeply concerned. "What exactly *is* a 'Trade Union'?" he once asked a Liberal friend. Margot Asquith said to him that he was like his uncle in having a wonderful sense of humor, literary style and a deep concern with science and religion. Was there any difference between them? "There is a difference," Balfour replied. "My uncle is a Tory—and I am a liberal." Yet the fact that his uncle remained undisturbed by Balfour's early association with the Tory "Radicals" and that the perfect confidence between them remained unclouded suggests that there was a basic identity of belief stronger than the difference.

Balfour seemed an enigma to his contemporaries because his nature was paradoxical, his opinions often irreconcilable, and because he did not see life or politics in terms of absolutes. As a result, he was often charged with being cynical, and people who looked at the world from a liberal point of view thought him perverse. H. G. Wells portrayed him as Evesham in *The New Machiavelli.* "In playing for points in the game of party advantage Evesham displayed at times a quite wicked unscrupulousness in the use of his subtle mind. . . . Did he really care? Did anything matter to him?" Winston Churchill, too, once used the word "wicked" in speaking of him to Mrs. Asquith. She thought the secret of Balfour's imperturbability in a crisis was that he did not "really care for the things at stake or believe that the happiness of mankind depends on events going this way or that." Balfour did, in fact, hold certain basic convictions, but he could see arguments on both sides of a matter, which is the penalty of the thoughtful man. On one occasion, arriving for an evening party at a great house whose staircase split in twin curves, he stood at the bottom for twenty minutes trying to work out, as he explained to a puzzled observer, a logical reason for taking one side rather than the other.

In 1887 Salisbury's surprising appointment of his nephew to the difficult and dangerous post of Chief Secretary for Ireland was expected to prove a fiasco. Balfour was then regarded as a languid intellectual whom the press delighted to call "Prince Charming," or even "Miss Balfour." Ireland was seething in its chronic war between landlord and tenant made fiercer by agitators for Home Rule. Police daily evicted tenants unable to pay their rent and were in turn bombarded with stones, vitriol and boiling water by the mob. The memory of Lord Frederick Cavendish's fate five years earlier had been kept fresh by continued assaults and "everybody right up to the top was trembling." Balfour, ignoring threats to his life, astonished both islands. He said he intended to be "as relentless as Cromwell" in enforcing the law and as "radical as any reformer" in redressing grievances with regard to the land. His resolute rule "took his foes by surprise," wrote John Morley, "and roused in his friends a delight hardly surpassed in the politics of our day." It made him a popular celebrity and brought him in one bound to recognition as "Bloody" Balfour in Ireland and as the coming natural leader of his party in England.

In 1891, on the resignation of W. H. Smith as Leader of the House, he succeeded by unanimous choice. As Irish Secretary, his absolute disregard for personal danger had revealed a courage—or absence of fear—that his contemporaries had not suspected. George Wyndham, then serving as Balfour's Private Secretary, wrote from Dublin that the Irish loyalists' admiration for him was "almost comic" and ascribed it to the fact that "great courage being so rare a gift and so large a part of human misery being due to Fear, all men are prepared to fall down before anyone wholly free from fear." Winston Churchill ascribed Balfour's lack of nerves to a "cold nature" but acknowledged him "the most courageous man alive. I believe if you held a pistol to his face it would not frighten him."

The same quality gave him mastery in debate. Sure of his own powers, he feared no opponent or embarrassment. According to Morley, he operated on Dr. Johnson's principle that "to treat your adversary with respect is to give him an advantage to which he is not entitled." He debated with "dauntless ingenuity and polished raillery." Although in public he rarely indulged in hurtful sarcasm, his private epigrams could be sharp. He once said of a colleague, "If he had a little more brains he would be a half-wit." In the House he maintained toward opponents an almost deferential courtesy, and when under bitter attack by the Irish members, would sit quietly with a placid smile, and when he rose to reply, demolish them with words which had the effect "of a bullet on a bubble." Yet it was not done without strain. He confessed to a friend that he never slept well after a rough night in the House. "I never lose my temper but one's nerves get on edge and it takes time to cool." He admired Macaulay, finding his narrative irresistible and his style a delight. His own speeches, delivered without notes, were unstudied yet perfectly finished. Lord Willoughby de Broke, an active young member of the other House, who liked to come over to listen to Balfour, said the pleasure lay in hearing "ideas and arguments being produced in exactly the right sequence without any appearance of premeditation, the whole masterly process of thought, argument and phrasing being carried out with such consummate skill and such perfect ease, that to witness the exercise of the art was sheer delight."

Balfour was careless of facts, unsafe with figures, and memory was not his strong point, but he surmounted this weakness by a technique that never failed to amuse the House. When dealing with a complicated bill he would take care to be flanked by a knowledgeable minister such as the Home Secretary or Attorney-General, and if he floundered over details his colleague could whisper a correction. As described by Sir Henry Lucy, parliamentary correspondent of *Punch*, Mr. Balfour would pause, regard the colleague with a friendly glance tinged with gentle admonition, and say, "Exactly." At the next mistake and whispered correction, he would repeat the performance with a sterner note in his "Exactly," conveying the impression that there was a limit to toleration in these matters and the colleague could be forgiven once but he really must not go on blundering.

Promptness was not one of his virtues and often he would come lounging gracefully in when Questions were almost over. He effected a revolution by changing the Wednesday short sitting of the House to Fridays for the sake of the weekend, an institution which he, in fact, invented to allow time for his golf. "This damned Scotch croquet," as a disgusted sportsman called it, owed its popularity to Balfour's influence. With perfect insouciance and contrary to all custom, he played it even on Sundays except in Scotland and such was his magnetism that

Society followed where he went, and so the custom of the country-house weekend was born. He neither shot nor hunted but in addition to golf played vigorous tennis, bicycled whenever possible, on occasion twenty miles at a stretch, and indulged a guilty passion for the thrilling new experience of the motorcar. His idea of distraction was not everyone's. When visiting his sister, Lady Rayleigh, and asked by her what he would like in the way of entertainment, he replied, "Oh something amusing; get some people from Cambridge to talk science." Music was another enthusiasm. He wrote an essay on Handel for the *Edinburgh Review*, and went on a musical tour of Germany during which he charmed that difficult relict Frau Wagner.

His nonchalance and languid air covered an immense capacity for work. Besides leading the Government in the House of Commons he frequently doubled for his uncle at the Foreign Office. When in 1902 Salisbury retired, Lord Esher felt that his absence would be made up by "the supreme energy of Arthur." To conserve energy Balfour transacted as much business as possible in bed and rarely rose before noon.

He read incessantly: a book on science was propped open on the mantelpiece while he dressed, a detective story lay on his bedside table, the shelves of his private sitting room were stacked with volumes of philosophy and theology, the overflow was piled on the sofa, periodicals littered table and chairs and his sponge was used to support the reading of French novels in his bathtub. He never read the newspapers. Overnight guests found he did not even subscribe to them, a negligence for which he was scolded by Mr. Buckle, editor of *The Times.* Once the journalist, W. T. Stead, in conversation with the Prince of Wales, remarked that Balfour was a good man to have at one's back in a fight but he was a little too indifferent. "Ah," replied the Prince, nodding, "he never reads the papers, you know."

The Prince never cared for Balfour, who, he felt, condescended to him. Queen Victoria on the other hand admired him. On a visit to Balmoral, reported Sir Henry Ponsonby, Balfour discussed matters with the Queen, "showing where he differs from her in a way which makes her think it over. . . . I think the Queen likes him but is a little afraid of him." The younger Ponsonby considered him a great success with the

Queen, "although he never seemed to treat her seriously." The Queen set down her own opinion in 1896 after a talk with Balfour on Crete, Turkish horrors, the Sudan and the Education Bill. She was "much struck by Mr. Balfour's extreme fairness, impartiality and large-mindedness. He sees all sides of a question, is wonderfully generous in his feelings toward others and very gentle and sweet-tempered."

The supremacy and security of that time had not long to endure, and Balfour had weaknesses which, as the century turned over into less indulgent years, were to become apparent. Including the weaknesses, he was in character and attributes the final flower of the patrician and of him might have been said what Proust's housekeeper, Celeste, said on the death of her employer, "When one has known M. Proust everyone else seems vulgar."

Not since Rome had imperial dominion been flung as wide as Britain's now. It extended over a quarter of the land surface of the world, and on June 22, 1897, the Queen's Diamond Jubilee, its living evidence marched in splendid ranks to the Thanksgiving service at St. Paul's. The occasion being designed to celebrate the imperial family under the British Crown, none of the foreign kings who had assisted at the Golden Jubilee in 1887 were this time invited. In their place, carriages of state carried the eleven colonial premiers of Canada, New Zealand, the Cape Colony, Natal, Newfoundland and the six states of Australia. In the parade rode cavalry from every quarter of the globe: the Cape Mounted Rifles, the Canadian Hussars, the New South Wales Lancers, the Trinidad Light Horse, the magnificent turbaned and bearded Lancers of Khapurthala, Badnagar and other Indian states, the Zaptichs of Cyprus in tasseled fezzes on black-maned ponies. Dark-skinned infantry regiments, "terrible and beautiful to behold," in the words of a rhapsodic press, swung down the streets in a fantasy of variegated uniforms: the Borneo Dyak Police, the Jamaica Artillery, the Royal Nigerian Constabulary, giant Sikhs from India, Houssas from the Gold Coast, Chinese from Hong Kong, Malays from Singapore, Negroes from the West Indies, British Guiana and Sierra Leone; company after company passed before a dazzled people, awestruck at the testimony of their own might. At the end of the procession in an open state landau drawn by eight cream horses came the day's central figure, a tiny person in black with cream-colored feathers nodding from her bonnet. The sun shone, bright banners rippled in the breeze, lampposts were decked in flowers and along six miles of streets millions of happy people cheered and waved in an ecstasy of love and pride. "No one ever, I believe, has met with such an ovation as was given me," wrote the Queen in her Journal. "Every face seemed to be filled with real joy. I was much moved and gratified."

Already for some months there had been an aura of self-congratulation in the air, "a certain optimism," said Rudyard Kipling, "that scared me." It moved him to write, and on the morning after the parade the stern warning of "Recessional" appeared in *The Times.* Its impact was immense—"The greatest poem that has been written by any living man," pronounced the distinguished jurist, Sir Edward Clarke. Yet however solemnly people took its admonition, how could they believe, as the ceremonies and salutes continued and top-hatted personages came and went to the Imperial Conference in Whitehall, that all this visible greatness was really "one with Nineveh and Tyre"?

On October 11, 1899, a distant challenge, which had been growing stronger ever since the Jameson Raid, became explicit and the Boer War began. "Joe's War," Lord Salisbury called it in tribute to the aggressive role of the cuckoo in his nest, Mr. Joseph Chamberlain, the Colonial Secretary. Although he had started life as a Radical Liberal among men opposed on principle to imperialism, Mr. Chamberlain had since learned to "think imperially," as he put it. It was a change of mind easily understood in a man with his keen sense of opportunity, for in the last twelve years alone, territories equal to twenty-four times the area of Great Britain had been added to the Empire. On joining the Government of 1895, Chamberlain had chosen the Colonial Office in the conviction that here was the key to empire and "manifest destiny," a categorical imperative that was just then directing American eyes toward Cuba and Hawaii and stimulating Germans, Belgians, French, and even Italians, to join in the scramble for choice cuts of Africa.

Chamberlain was a man of surpassing force, ability, and a

consuming ambition which had never been satisfied. Not born to the landowning class, he had perfected an appearance of authority and poise that was distinctly his own. He had sharp, rather elegant features, eyes that revealed nothing and jet-black hair smoothly brushed. His face was a mask adorned by a monocle on a black ribbon; his tailoring was faultless, adorned by a daily orchid in his buttonhole. Having made sufficient fortune as a manufacturer of screws in Birmingham to retire from business at thirty-eight, he had become Mayor of his city, where his accomplishments in education and other social reforms had won national attention. Wasting no time, he had entered Parliament at forty as member for Birmingham, became a vehement spokesman of the Radicals, denouncing aristocrats and plutocrats as ardently as any Socialist, and quickly achieved Cabinet office as President of the Board of Trade in Gladstone's Ministry of 1880. A hard-hitting, cool and masterful character whose popularity in the Midlands swung many votes, he was a political factor to be reckoned with and saw himself as Gladstone's successor. But the Grand Old Man was in no hurry to have one, and Chamberlain, too impatient to wait, found reason in the Home Rule issue to leave the party with a considerable following. In preparing for the election of 1895 the Conservatives were glad, if nervous, to attach him. He did not share the patrician's indifference to public opinion, but in mannerisms and dress, played up to it, making himself a memorable personality. To the public he was "Pushful Joe" the "Minister for Empire" and the best-known figure in the new Government.

Only Lord Salisbury remained unimpressed. "He has not persuaded himself that he has any convictions," he had written to Balfour in 1886, "and therein lies Gladstone's infinite superiority." Balfour, characteristically, was kinder but plain. "Joe, though we all love him dearly," he wrote to Lady Elcho, "somehow does not absolutely or completely mix, does not form a chemical combination with us." This was not surprising. Chamberlain had not been to public school or the University (that is, Oxford or Cambridge), where, as Lord Esher remarked, "everyone with his capacity learns self-restraint," and was not even a member of the Church of England. He nevertheless moved suavely among his new associates and was seen entertaining to tea on the terrace of the House of Commons a large party that included three duchesses. He could certainly never be accused like Balfour of being too indifferent. Chamberlain was always in the grip of one passionate conviction or another which he would pursue, while he held it, with ruthless intensity. But he lacked a permanent, rooted point of view. Though only five years younger than Salisbury and twelve years older than Balfour, he represented the forces and methods of a new time to which Salisbury's Government was essentially opposed. "The difference between Joe and me," said Balfour, "is the difference between youth and age: I am age." Balfour had behind him the long stability of belonging on top; Joe was the new tycoon in a hurry. The ways in which they did not "mix" were fundamental.

For the present the collaboration between Chamberlain and his new colleagues was mutually loyal. When his hand was suspected behind the Jameson Raid and the Liberals made furious accusations, the Government closed ranks around him and a parliamentary committee of investigation found itself unable to trace anything definite back to the Colonial Office. Joe emerged with power undiminished and aggressiveness undimmed. "I don't know which of our many enemies we ought to defy," he wrote to Salisbury after the Kruger telegram, "but let us defy someone." As the minister in charge of the increasingly inimical negotiations with the Boer Republic, his favorite method, reported Balfour to Salisbury, "is the free application of irritants." While these were taking effect an old defeat was avenged: in 1898 Kitchener retook Khartoum and raised the British flag over the grave of General Gordon. Farther up the Nile, at Fashoda, a French military expedition penetrating the Sudan was confronted eye to eye by the British and, after a period of suspense during which the French recognized realities, withdrew without the firing of a shot. Britain's unpopularity rose with her prestige.

Then came the Boer War. The British Army, on which years of splendid isolation had conferred a certain rigidity, was revealed fully prepared for the Crimean War and it met a series of defeats. The Boers, it turned out, possessed cannon from Krupp's and Creusot and their gunners were often German or French. President Kruger had used the reparations awarded for the Jameson Raid to buy artillery, Maxim guns and large stores of rifles and ammunition in preparation for the ultimate clash of arms. In one "Black Week" of December, 1899, Lord Methuen was defeated at Magersfontein, General Gatacre at Stormberg, and Sir Redvers Buller, the Commander-in-Chief, at Colenso with the loss of eleven guns, leaving Kimberley and Ladysmith invested. At home, people were stunned with unbelief. The Duke of Argyll, who was in his last illness, never rallied from the shock and died murmuring Tennyson's line on the Duke of Wellington, "Who never lost an English gun."

With Black Week went the last time Britons felt themselves unquestionably masters of the earth. And the point was brought home when the Kaiser, a few months later, was able to insist successfully on a German commander for the expedition embarking to punish the Boxers at Peking. True, it was a largely German effort, the main British force being already on the spot, but Salisbury objected on principle. It was a British characteristic, even if unreasonable, he told the German Ambassador, "not to endure the command of a foreigner." But he could not afford at that moment to court a conflict which might result in help for the Boers and was forced to acquiesce.

In the new year, with new vigor, reinforcements and a new commander-in-chief to replace the disastrous Buller, the war gradually came under control. Mafeking was relieved in May, 1900—to the accompaniment of hysterics at home—Lord Roberts entered Pretoria in June and the annexation of the Transvaal was proclaimed on September 1 in the belief that only mopping-up was left. On a wave of renewed self-confidence and good spirits, the Conservatives called for a renewed mandate in what was known as the "Khaki" election in October. Using the slogan, "Every seat won by the Liberals is a seat won by the Boers," they were comfortably returned to office. But though patriotic fervor was dominant, there was a current of antipathy to the war which came not only from "Little Englanders" of the orthodox Gladstone tradition but more particularly, this time, from an uneasy sense of ignoble motive, a glitter of the gold mines of the Rand, an aura of predatory capitalism, commercialism and profit. Opposition to the war provided a cause in which a young M.P., David Lloyd George, made himself known, although he did not go so far as to oppose annexation but only to propose negotiation to stop the war.

There were many inside and outside the Government who awaited the approaching Twentieth Century with certain illusions lost which were never to be restored. Lady Salisbury, shortly before she died in November, 1899, said to a young relative, "The young generation may criticize us as they like; will they ever provide anything as good as what we have known?"

The year 1900, rather than 1899, the Astronomer Royal had decided, after much weighing of the pros and cons, was the hundredth and last year of the Nineteenth Century. The moment of its passing was at hand; the end of the most hope-filled, change-filled, progressive, busiest and richest century the world had even known. Three weeks after it closed, on January 24, 1901, Queen Victoria died, redoubling the general sense of an era's end. Lord Salisbury, tired of office, wanted to go too, but felt he could not until victory, still elusive in South Africa, was won. It came finally in June, 1902, and on July 14 Lord Salisbury stepped down. Again was felt the somber consciousness of something coming to an end: an Authority, a type, a tradition had departed. A French paper, *Le Temps* of Paris, still smarting from the humiliation of Fashoda, said, "What closes today with Lord Salisbury's departure is a whole historic era. It is ironic that what he hands on is a democratized, imperialized, colonialized and vulgarized England—everything that is antithetic to the Toryism, the aristocratic tradition and the High Church that he stood for. It is the England of Mr. Chamberlain, not, despite his nominal leadership, of Mr. Balfour."

Queen Victoria, Lord Salisbury and the Nineteenth Century were gone. A year before she died, the Queen, returning on her yacht from a visit to Ireland, was disturbed by rough seas. After a particularly strong wave buffeted the ship, she summoned her doctor, who was in attendance, and said, in unconscious echo of a distant predecessor, "Go up at once, Sir James, and give the Admiral my compliments and tell him the thing must not occur again."

But the waves would not stand still.

1. Lord Salisbury.

2. Lord Ribblesdale (portrait by Sargent, 1902).

3. The Wyndham sisters: Lady Elcho, Mrs. Tennant, and Mrs. Adeane (portrait by Sargent, 1899).

4. Chatsworth.

5. Prince Peter Kropotkin.

6. Editorial office of *La Révolte*.

7. “Slept in That Cellar Four Years” (photograph by Jacob A. Riis, about 1890).

8. "Lockout" (drawing by Théophile Steinlen; signed "Petit Pierre").

9. Thomas B. Reed.

10. Captain (later Admiral) Alfred Thayer Mahan.

11. Charles William Eliot.

12. Samuel Gompers.

13. The mob during Zola's trial (drawing by Théophile Steinlen).

14. The "Syndicate" (drawing by Forain).

Allégorie

L'Affaire Dreyfus.

15. "Allegory" (drawing by Forain).

Coucou, le voilà!

La Vérité sort de son puits.

16. "Truth Rising from Its Well" (drawing by Caran d'Ache).

2

THE IDEA AND THE DEED

THE ANARCHISTS: 1890–1914

2

The Idea and the Deed

SO ENCHANTING was the vision of a stateless society, without government, without law, without ownership of property, in which, corrupt institutions having been swept away, man would be free to be good as God intended him, that six heads of state were assassinated for its sake in the twenty years before 1914. They were President Carnot of France in 1894, Premier Canovas of Spain in 1897, Empress Elizabeth of Austria in 1898, King Humbert of Italy in 1900, President McKinley of the United States in 1901, and another Premier of Spain, Canalejas, in 1912. Not one could qualify as a tyrant. Their deaths were the gestures of desperate or deluded men to call attention to the Anarchist idea.

No single individual was the hero of the movement that swallowed up these lives. The Idea was its hero. It was, as a historian of revolt has called it, "a daydream of desperate romantics." It had its theorists and thinkers, men of intellect, sincere and earnest, who loved humanity. It also had its tools, the little men whom misfortune or despair or the anger, degradation and hopelessness of poverty made susceptible to the Idea until they became possessed by it and were driven to act. These became the assassins. Between the two groups there was no contact. The thinkers in press and pamphlet constructed marvelous paper models of the Anarchist millennium; poured out tirades of hate and invective upon the ruling class and its despised ally, the bourgeoisie; issued trumpet calls for action, for a "propaganda of the deed" to accomplish the enemy's overthrow. Whom were they calling? What deed were they asking for? They did not say precisely. Unknown to them, down in the lower depths of society lonely men were listening. They heard echoes of the tirades and the trumpets and caught a glimpse of the shining millennium that promised a life without hunger and without a boss. Suddenly one of them, with a sense of injury or a sense of mission, would rise up, go out and kill—and sacrifice his own life on the altar of the Idea.

They came from the warrens of the poor, where hunger and dirt were king, where consumptives coughed and the air was thick with the smell of latrines, boiling cabbage and stale beer, where babies wailed and couples screamed in sudden quarrels, where roofs leaked and unmended windows let in the cold blasts of winter, where privacy was unimaginable, where men, women, grandparents and children lived together, eating, sleeping, fornicating, defecating, sickening and dying in one room, where a teakettle served as a wash boiler between meals, old boxes served as chairs, heaps of foul straw as beds, and boards propped across two crates as tables, where sometimes not all the children in a family could go out at one time because there were not enough clothes to go round, where decent families lived among drunkards, wife-beaters, thieves and prostitutes, where life was a seesaw of unemployment and endless toil, where a cigar-maker and his wife earning 13 cents an hour worked seventeen hours a day seven days a week to support themselves and three children, where death was the only exit and the only extravagance and the scraped savings of a lifetime would be squandered on a funeral coach with flowers and a parade of mourners to ensure against the anonymity and last ignominy of Potter's Field.

The Anarchists believed that with Property, the monarch of all evil, eliminated, no man could again live off the labour of another and human nature would be released to seek its natural level of justice among men. The role of the State would be replaced by voluntary cooperation among individuals and the role of the law by the supreme law of the general welfare. To this end no reform of existing social evils through vote or persuasion was of any use, for the ruling class would never give up its property or the powers and laws which protected ownership of property. Therefore, the necessity of violence. Only revolutionary overturn of the entire malignant existing system would accomplish the desired result. Once the old structure was in rubble, a new social order of utter equality and no authority, with enough of everything for everybody, would settle smilingly upon the earth. So reasonable seemed the proposition that once apprised of it the oppressed classes could not fail to respond. The Anarchist task was to awaken them to the Idea by propaganda of the word and of the Deed, and one day, one such deed would flash the signal for revolt.

During the first and formulative period of Anarchism, beginning around the time of the revolutionary year 1848, its two major prophets were Pierre Proudhon of France and his disciple, Michael Bakunin, a Russian exile who became the active leader of the movement.

"Whoever lays his hand on me to govern me," Proudhon proclaimed, "is a usurper and a tyrant; I declare him to be my enemy. . . . Government of man by man is slavery" and its laws are "cobwebs for the rich and chains of steel for the poor." The "highest perfection" for free society is no government, to which Proudhon was the first to give the name "An-archy." He excoriated government in a passion of contempt. "To be governed is to be watched, inspected, spied on, regulated, indoctrinated, preached at, controlled, ruled, censored, by persons who have neither wisdom nor virtue. It is every action and transaction to be registered, stamped, taxed, patented, licensed, assessed, measured, reprimanded, corrected, frustrated. Under pretext of the public good it is to be exploited, monopolized, embezzled, robbed and then, at the least protest or word of complaint, to be fined, harassed, vilified, beaten up, bludgeoned, disarmed, judged, condemned, imprisoned, shot, garroted, deported, sold, betrayed, swindled, deceived, outraged, dishonored. That's government, that's its justice, that's its morality! And imagine that among us there are democrats who believe government to be good, socialists who in the name of liberty, equality and fraternity support this ignominy, proletarians who offer themselves candidates for President of the Republic! What hypocrisy!"

Proudhon believed that the "abstract idea of right" would obviate the need of revolution and man would be persuaded to adopt the stateless society through reason. What Bakunin added, learning from Russia under Nicholas I, was the necessity of violent revolution. As opposed to his rival, Karl Marx, who maintained that revolution would come only from an industrial proletariat, organized and trained for the task, Bakunin believed that immediate revolution could explode in one of the more economically backward countries—Italy, Spain or

Russia—where the workers, though untrained, unorganized and illiterate, with no understanding of their own wants, would be ready to rise because they had nothing to lose. The task of the conscientious revolutionist was to popularize the Idea among the masses, hitherto bound in ignorance and prejudice by the ruling class. It was necessary to make them conscious of their own wants and "evoke" from them thoughts to match their impulses, thoughts of revolt. When this happened the workers would know their own will and then "their power will be irresistible." Bakunin, however, lost control of the First International to Marx, who believed in organization.

There was an inherent paradox within the body of Anarchism that frustrated progress. Anarchism rejected the political party, which Proudhon had called a mere "variety of absolutism"; yet to bring about a revolution it was necessary to submit to authority, organization and discipline. Whenever Anarchists met to prepare a program, this terrible necessity rose up to face them. Loyal to their Idea, they rejected it. Revolution would burst from the masses spontaneously. All that was needed was the Idea—and a spark.

Each strike or bread riot or local uprising the Anarchist hoped—and the capitalist feared—might be the spark. Mme Hennebau, the manager's wife in Zola's *Germinal*, watching the march of the striking miners under the bloody gleam of the setting sun, saw "the red vision of revolution that on some sombre evening at the end of the century would carry everything away. Yes, on that evening the people, unbridled at last, would make the blood of the middle class flow, . . . in a thunder of boots the same terrible troop, with their dirty skins and tainted breath, would sweep away the old world. . . . Fires would flame, there would be nothing left, not a *sou* of the great fortunes, not a title deed of acquired properties."

Yet each time, as when Zola's miners faced the guns of the gendarmerie, the spark was stamped out. The magic moment when the masses would awaken to their wants and their power did not come. The Paris Commune flared and died in 1871 and failed to signal a general insurrection. "We reckoned without the masses who did not want to be roused to passion for their own freedom," wrote Bakunin, disillusioned, to his wife. "This passion being absent what good did it do us to have been right theoretically? We were powerless." He despaired of saving the world and died, disillusioned, in 1876, a Columbus, as Alexander Herzen said, without America.

Meanwhile in his native land his ideas took root in the Narodniki, or Populists, otherwise the Party of the People's Will, founded in 1879. Because of communal use of land peculiar to the Russian peasant, reformers worshipped the peasant as a natural Socialist who needed only the appearance of a Messiah to be awakened from his lethargy and impelled upon the march to revolution. The bomb was to be the Messiah. "Terrorist activity," stated the Narodniki program, "consisting in destroying the most harmful person in government, aims to undermine the prestige of the government and arouse in this manner the revolutionary spirit of the people and their confidence in the success of the cause."

In 1881 the Narodniki struck a blow that startled the world: they assassinated the Czar, Alexander II. It was a triumphant coup, equal, they imagined, to the battering down of the Bastille. It would shout aloud their protest, summon the oppressed and terrorize the oppressors. Instead it ushered in reaction. The dead Czar, whose crown may have been the symbol of autocracy but who in person was the "Liberator" of the serfs, was mourned by the peasants, who believed "the gentry had murdered the Czar to get back the land." His ministers opened a campaign of savage repression, the public, abandoning all thoughts of reform, acquiesced, and the revolutionary movement, "broken and demoralized, withdrew into the conspirators' cellar." There Anarchism's first period came to an end.

Before the movement burst into renewed bloom in the nineties, a single terrible event which enlarged the stature of Anarchism took place, not in Europe, but in America, in the city of Chicago. There in August, 1886, eight Anarchists were sentenced by Judge Joseph Gary to be hanged for the murder of seven police killed on the previous May 4 by a bomb hurled into the midst of an armed police force who were about to break up a strikers' meeting in Haymarket Square.

The occasion was the climax of a campaign for the eight-hour day, which in itself was the climax of a decade of industrial war centering on Chicago. In every clash the employers fought with the forces of law—police, militia and courts—as their allies. The workers' demands were met with live ammunition and lockouts and with strikebreakers protected by Pinkertons who were armed and sworn in as deputy sheriffs. In the war between the classes, the State was not neutral. Driven by misery and injustice, the workers' anger grew and with it the employers' fear, their sense of a rising menace and their determination to stamp it out. Even a man as remote as Henry James sensed a "sinister anarchic underworld heaving in its pain, its power and its hate."

Anarchism was not a labour movement and was no more than one element in the general upheaval of the lower class. But Anarchists saw in the struggles of labour the hot coals of revolution and hoped to blow them into flame. "A pound of dynamite is worth a bushel of bullets," cried August Spies, editor of Chicago's German-language Anarchist daily, *Die Arbeiter-Zeitung*. "Police and militia, the bloodhounds of capitalism, are ready to murder!" In this he was right, for in the course of a clash between workers and strikebreakers, the police fired, killing two. "Revenge! Revenge! Workingmen to arms!" shrieked handbills printed and distributed by Spies that night. He called for a protest meeting the next day. It took place in Haymarket Square, the police marched to break it up, the bomb was thrown. Who threw it has never been discovered.

The defendants' speeches to the court after sentence, firm in Anarchist principle and throbbing with consciousness of martyrdom, resounded throughout Europe and America and provided the best propaganda Anarchism ever had. In the absence of direct evidence establishing their guilt, they knew and loudly stated that they were being tried and sentenced for the crime, not of murder, but of Anarchism. "Let the world know," cried August Spies, "that in 1886 in the state of Illinois eight men were sentenced to death because they believed in a better future!" Their belief had included the use of dynamite, and society's revenge matched its fright. In the end the sentences of three of the condemned were commuted to prison terms. One, Louis Lingg, the youngest, handsomest and most fervent, who was shown by evidence at the trial to have made bombs, blew himself up with a capsule of fulminate of mercury on the night before the execution and wrote in his blood before he died,

"Long live anarchy!" His suicide was regarded by many as a confession of guilt. The remaining four, including Spies, were hanged on November 11, 1887.

For years afterward the silhouette of the gallows and its four hanging bodies decorated Anarchist literature, and the anniversary of November 11 was celebrated by Anarchists in Europe and America as a revolutionary memorial. The public conscience, too, was made aware by the gallow's fruit of the misery, protest and upheaval in the working class.

Men who were Anarchists without knowing it stood on every street corner. Jacob Riis, the New York police reporter who described in 1890 *How the Other Half Lives*, saw one on the corner of Fifth Avenue and Fourteenth Street. The man suddenly leaped at a carriage carrying two fashionable ladies on an afternoon's shopping and slashed at the sleek and shining horses with a knife. When arrested and locked up, he said, "They don't have to think of tomorrow. They spend in an hour what would keep me and my little ones for a year." He was the kind from which Anarchists of the Deed were made.

Most of them were voiceless or could speak their protest only in the wail of a dispossessed Irish peasant spading his field for the last time, who was asked by a visitor what he wanted. "What is it I am wantin'?" cried the old man, shaking his fist at the sky. "I want the Day av Judgment!"

The poor lived in a society in which power, wealth and magnificent spending were never more opulent, in which the rich dined on fish, fowl and red meat at one meal, lived in houses of marble floors and damask walls and of thirty or forty or fifty rooms, wrapped themselves in furs in winter and were cared for by a retinue of servants who blacked their boots, arranged their hair, drew their baths and lit their fires. In this world, at a luncheon for Mme Nellie Melba at the Savoy, when perfect peaches, a delicacy of the season, were served up "fragrant and delicious in their cotton wool," the surfeited guests made a game of throwing them at passers-by beneath the windows.

These were the rulers and men of property whose immense possessions could, it seemed, only be explained as having been accumulated out of the pockets of the exploited masses. "What is Property?" asked Proudhon in a famous question and answered, "Property is theft." "Do you not know," cried Enrico Malatesta in his *Talk Between Two Workers*, an Anarchist classic of the nineties, "that every bit of bread they eat is taken from your children, every fine present they give to their wives means the poverty, hunger, cold, even perhaps prostitution of yours?"

If in their economics the Anarchists were hazy, their hatred of the ruling class was strong and vibrant. They hated "all mankind's tormentors," as Bakunin called them, "priests, monarchs, statesmen, soldiers, officials, financiers, capitalists, moneylenders, lawyers." To the workers themselves it was not the faraway rich but their visible representatives, the landlord, the factory owner, the boss, the policeman, who were the Enemy.

They could hate but only a few were rebels. Most existed in apathy, stupefied by poverty. Some gave up. A woman with four children who made match boxes at 4½ cents a gross, and by working fourteen hours could make seven gross a day for a total of 31½ cents, threw herself out of the window one day and was carried from the street dead. She was "discouraged," a neighbor said. A young man who had a sick mother and had lost his job was charged in magistrate's court with attempted suicide. The lockkeeper's wife who pulled him out of the river testified how "as fast as I pulled to get him out, he crawled back" until some workmen came to assist her. When the magistrate congratulated the woman on her muscular powers, the courtroom laughed, but an observer named Jack London wrote, "All I could see was a boy on the threshold of life passionately crawling to a muddy death."

The failure of practical attempts at Anarchism in Bakunin's period caused Anarchist theory and practice to veer off in a direction not toward the earth but toward the clouds. In the new period beginning in the nineties, its aims, always idyllic, became even more utopian and its deeds less than ever connected with reality. It became impatient. It despised the puny efforts of Socialists and trade unionists to achieve the eight-hour day. "Eight hours of work for the boss is eight hours too much," proclaimed the Anarchist paper, *La Révolte*. "We know that what is wrong with our society is not that the worker works ten, twelve or fourteen hours, but that the boss exists."

The most prominent among the new Anarchist leaders was Prince Peter Kropotkin, by birth an aristocrat, by profession a geographer, and by conviction a revolutionist. His sensational escape after two years' imprisonment from the grim fortress of Peter and Paul in 1876 had endowed him with a heroic aura, kept bright afterwards during his years of exile in Switzerland, France and England by unrepentant and unremitting preaching in the cause of revolt.

Kropotkin's faith in mankind, despite a life of hard experience, was inexhaustible and unshatterable. He gave the impression, said the English journalist Henry Nevinson, who knew him well, of "longing to take all mankind to his bosom and keep it warm." Kindliness shone from his bald and noble dome ringed with a low halo of bushy brown hair. An ample beard spread comfortably beneath his chin. He was very short, "with hardly enough body to hold up the massive head." Descended from princes of Smolensk who, according to family tradition, belonged to the Rurik Dynasty, which had ruled Russia before the Romanovs, Kropotkin took his place in that long line of "conscience-stricken" Russian nobility who felt guilty for belonging to a class which had oppressed the people for centuries.

He was born in 1842. After service as an officer of Cossacks in Siberia, where he studied the geography of the region, he became Secretary of the Geographical Society, for whom he explored the glaciers of Finland and Sweden in 1871. Meanwhile he had become a member of a secret revolutionary committee, and on this being discovered, his arrest and imprisonment followed. After his escape in 1876—the year Bakunin died—he went to Switzerland, where he worked with Elisée Reclus, the French geographer and a fellow Anarchist, on Reclus' monumental geography of the world. Kropotkin wrote the volume on Siberia and, with Reclus, founded and for three years edited *Le Révolté*, which, after suppression and a rebirth in Paris as *La Révolte*, was to become the best-known and longest-lived Anarchist journal. His stream of convincing and passionate polemics, the prestige of his escape from the most dreaded Russian prison, his active work with the Swiss Anarchists of the Jura—which caused his expulsion from

Switzerland—all topped by his title of Prince, made him Bakunin's recognized successor.

In France, where he came next in 1882, the traditions of the Commune had nourished a militant Anarchist movement of which there was a flourishing group in Lyons. A police raid and a retaliatory bomb causing one death had been followed by the arrest and trial of fifty-two Anarchists, including Kropotkin, on charges of belonging to an international league dedicated to the abolition of property, family, country and religion. Sentenced to prison for five years, Kropotkin had served three, had then been pardoned by President Grévy and, with his wife and daughter, had settled in England, the inevitable refuge of political exiles at the time.

In a small house in Hammersmith, a drearily respectable dormitory of outer London, he continued to write fiery paeans to violence for *La Révolte*, scholarly articles for geographical journals and for the *Nineteenth Century*, to entertain visiting radicals in five languages, to lecture Anarchist club meetings in a cellar off Tottenham Court Road, to thump the piano, and paint, and to charm with his sweet temper and genial manners everyone who met him. "He was amiable to the point of saintliness," wrote George Bernard Shaw, "and with his full beard and lovable expression might have been a shepherd from the Delectable Mountains. His only weakness was the habit of prophesying war within the next fortnight. And he was right in the end." This weakness was in fact an expression of Kropotkin's optimism, for war to him was the expected catastrophe that was to destroy the old world and clear the way for the triumph of Anarchy. The "galloping decay" of states was hastening the triumph. "It cannot be far off," he wrote. "Everything brings it nearer."

This agreeable person, conventionally dressed in the black frock coat of a Victorian gentleman, was an uncompromising apostle of the necessity of violence. Man's progress toward perfection was being held back, he wrote, by the "inertia of those who have a vested interest in existing conditions." Progress needed a violent event "to hurl mankind out of its ruts into new roads. . . . Revolution becomes a peremptory necessity." The spirit of revolt must be awakened in the masses by repeated "propaganda of the deed." This phrase, which became the banner of Anarchist violence, was first used by a French Socialist, Paul Brousse, in 1878, a year which saw four attempts on crowned heads: two on Wilhelm I of Germany and one each on the Kings of Spain and Italy. "The Idea is on the march," Brousse wrote, "and we must seek to inaugurate the propaganda of the deed. Through a royal breast is the way to open the road to revolution!"

The next year at an Anarchist Congress in the Swiss Jura, Kropotkin specifically advocated propaganda of the Deed, if somewhat less explicit as to method. Though never recommending assassination in so many words, he continued during the eighties to urge a propaganda by "speech and written word, by dagger, gun and dynamite." He sounded an inspiring summons in the pages of *La Révolte* to "men of courage willing not only to speak but to act, pure characters who prefer prison, exile and death to a life that contradicts their principles, bold natures who know that in order to win one must dare." Men such as these must form an advance guard of revolution long before the masses were ready, and in the midst of "talking, complaining, discussing," must do the "deed of mutiny."

"A single deed," Kropotkin wrote at another time, "is better propaganda than a thousand pamphlets." Words are "lost in the air like the sound of church bells." Acts are needed "to excite hate for the exploiters, to ridicule the Rulers, to show up their weakness and above all and always to awaken the spirit of revolt." The acts he loftily called for on paper were performed, but not by him.

In the nineties, when he was in his fifties, Kropotkin, though never altering his demand for revolt, subdued a little his enthusiasm for the individual Deed. Although "the revolutionary spirit gains immensely through such deeds of individual heroism," he wrote in *La Révolte* of March, 1891, "nevertheless it is not these heroic acts that make revolutions. Revolution is above all a mass movement. . . . Institutions rooted in centuries of history are not destroyed by a few pounds of explosives. The time for such action has passed and the time for the anarchist and communist idea to penetrate the masses has come." Disclaimers, however, rarely have the same force as the original proposition.

In London, in a restaurant in Holborn during the coal strike of 1893, Kropotkin was arguing with Ben Tillett and Tom Mann, two tough-minded trade unionists. "We must destroy! We must pull down! We must be rid of the tyrants!" shouted Mann.

"No," said Kropotkin in his foreign accent, with the eyes of a scientist gleaming behind his spectacles, "we must build. We must build in the hearts of men. We must establish a kingdom of God."

He had the plans for the kingdom already drawn. After the revolution—which he calculated would take three to five years to accomplish the overthrow of governments, the destruction of prisons, forts and slums and the expropriation of land, industries and all forms of property—volunteers would take inventory of all food stocks, dwellings, and means of production. Printed lists would be distributed by the million. Everyone would take what he needed of the things which existed in plenty and there would be rationing of the things of which there was shortage. All property would be community property. Everyone would draw upon the community warehouse for food and goods according to his needs and would have the right "to decide for himself what he needs for a comfortable life." As there would be no more inheritance, there would be no more greed. All able-bodied males would enter into "contracts" with society through their groups and communes by which they would engage to do five hours' daily work from the age of twenty-one to about forty-five or fifty, each in a labour of his choice. In return, society would guarantee them the enjoyment of "houses, stores, streets, conveyances, schools, museums, etc." There would be no need for enforcement or judges or penalties because people would fulfill their contracts out of their own need of "cooperation, support and sympathy" from their neighbors. The process would work because of its very reasonableness, although even Kropotkin might have noticed that the reasonableness of something is rarely a motive in human affairs.

Shaw, with his unrelenting common sense, picked out the trouble in a Fabian Tract called *The Impossibilities of Anarchism*, published in 1893 and reprinted several times during the next ten years. If man is good and institutions bad, he asked, if man will be good again as soon as the corrupt system ceases to oppress him, "how did the corruption and oppression under which he groans ever arise?" Yet the fact that Shaw felt required to write the Tract was his tribute to the force of the Idea.

The most vexing problem of the Anarchist plan was the question of an accounting of the value of goods and services. According to the theories of Proudhon and Bakunin, everyone would be paid in goods in proportion to what he produced. But this required a body to establish values and do the accounting, an Authority, which was anathema to "pure" Anarchy. As resolved by Kropotkin and Malatesta, the solution was to assume that everyone would *want* to work for the good of the whole, and since all work would be agreeable and dignified, everyone would contribute freely and take from the community storehouse freely without the necessity of accounting.

In proof Kropotkin evolved his theory of "mutual aid" to show that Anarchism had a scientific basis in the laws of nature. Darwin's thesis, he argued, had been perverted by capitalist thinkers. Nature was not, in fact, red in tooth and claw nor animated by the instinct of each living thing to survive at the cost of its fellow but, on the contrary, by the instinct of each to *preserve* the species through "mutual assistance." He drew examples from the ants and the bees and from wild horses and cattle—who form a ring when attacked by wolves—and from the communal field and village life of men in the Middle Ages. He greatly admired the rabbit, which, though defenceless and adapted to nothing in particular, yet survived and multiplied. The rabbit symbolized for him the durability of the meek who, an earlier Preacher had claimed, would inherit the earth.

Although Kropotkin never slackened his lust for the total destruction of the bourgeois world, that world could not forbear to honor him. He was such a distinguished scholar—and besides, a Prince. When he refused membership in the Royal Geographic Society because it was under royal patronage, he was invited anyway to the Society's dinner, and when he refused to rise upon the chairman's toast to "The King!" the chairman promptly rose again to propose "Long live Prince Kropotkin!" and the whole company stood up to join in the toast. When he visited the United States in 1901 and lectured to the Lowell Institute in Boston, he was entertained by its intellectual elite and, not to be outdone, by Mrs. Potter Palmer in Chicago. His memoirs were commissioned by the *Atlantic Monthly*, his books bore the imprint of the most respectable publishers. When *Mutual Aid* appeared, the *Review of Reviews* called it "a good healthy cheerful, delightful book which does one good to read."

Aside from Kropotkin, Anarchist thought was most highly developed in France. Among a wide assortment, some serious and some frivolous, the leaders were Elisée Reclus and Jean Grave. Reclus, with a dark-bearded melancholy face of somber beauty like that of a Byzantine Christ, was the soothsayer of the movement. He had fought on the barricades of the Commune and marched to prison down the dusty blood-stained road to Versailles. He came from a distinguished family of scholars and, besides his work as a geographer, had devoted years to explaining and preaching the Anarchist system through his books and through the journals he edited at one time or another with Kropotkin and Grave. In his lectures at the Université Nouvelle of Brussels, where he held for a time the chair of Geography, he exerted on listeners, wrote one of them, an "irresistible magnetism." He moved from the formation of the earth to the future of man and "affirmed, like Rousseau, his unalterable faith in human goodness once it was released from the blemishes of a society founded on force."

In contrast, Grave came from a working-class family. Once a shoemaker and then, like Proudhon, a typesetter and printer, he had, in the eighties, practiced making fulminate of mercury to blow up the Prefecture of Police or the Palais Bourbon, seat of the French parliament. His book, *The Dying Society and Anarchism*, so persuasively argued the overthrow of the State and offered so many insidious suggestions that it cost him two years in prison. While there he wrote another book, *Society After the Revolution* which he promptly printed himself and published upon his release. Being utopian, it was not considered dangerously subversive by the authorities. In a fifth-floor garret in a working-class street, the Rue Mouffetard, he now edited, largely wrote, and printed on a hand press *La Révolte*, at the same time working on his great history, *Le Mouvement libertaire sous la troisième république*. In a room furnished with a table and two chairs, he lived and worked, dressed invariably in a French workman's long black blouse, surrounded by pamphlets and newspapers, "simple, silent, indefatigable," and so absorbed in his thought and task that "he seemed like a hermit from the Middle Ages who forgot to die eight hundred years ago."

The followers who were the body of the movement never formed a party but associated only in small, localized clubs and groups. A few comrades would pass out notices informing friends that, for instance, "the Anarchists of Marseilles are establishing a group to be called The Avengers and Famished which will meet every Sunday at ———. Comrades are invited to come and bring reliable friends to hear and take part in the discussions." Such groups existed not only in Paris but in most of the large cities and many small towns. Among them were the "Indomitables" of Armentières, the "Forced Labour" of Lille, the "Ever-Ready" of Blois, "Land and Independence" of Nantes, "Dynamite" of Lyons, the "Anti-Patriots" of Charleville. With similar groups from other countries, they occasionally held Congresses, such as the one in Chicago during the World's Fair in 1893, but they neither organized nor federated.

Enrico Malatesta, the firebrand of Anarchism, was an Italian, always carrying the flame to whatever corner of the world there was an Anarchist group. Ten years younger than Kropotkin, he looked like a romantic bandit who might have befriended the Count of Monte Cristo. In fact, he came from a well-off bourgeois family and as a young medical student had been expelled from the University of Naples for participating in a student riot at the time of the Paris Commune. Thereafter he learned the electrician's trade in order to make a living, joined the Italian section of the International, sided with Bakunin against Marx, led an abortive peasant revolt in Apulia, went to prison and then into exile. He tried to direct the Belgian general strike of 1891 away from its petty aim of manhood suffrage because the vote, in his Anarchist credo, was merely another booby trap of the bourgeois state. He was expelled for similar revolutionary efforts from one country after another and condemned to five years on the prison island of Lampedusa, from which he escaped in a rowboat during a storm. When confined to Italy he escaped in a packing case marked "sewing machines." It was loaded on a boat for Argentina, where he hoped to prospect for gold in Patagonia to provide funds for the cause, and where, in fact, he found it, only to have his claim confiscated by the Argentine government.

Not content merely with talking about the coming disappearance of the State, Malatesta was constantly embroiled in practical attempts designed to help it disappear. This caused him to be suspected of deviating from "pure" Anarchism and even of leaning toward Marxism. On one occasion he was shot by an Italian fellow-Anarchist of the extreme *anti-organizzatori* wing. Never discouraged, no matter how many of the insurrections he midwifed were stillborn, Malatesta was always just in or out of prison, fresh from some dramatic escape or desperate adventure, forever an exile without a home or with hardly a room to call his own, always turning up, as Kropotkin said, "just as we saw him last, ready to renew the struggle, with the same love of man, the same absence of hatred for adversaries or jailers."

Their optimism was the outstanding characteristic of these leaders. They were certain that Anarchism because of its rightness must triumph and the capitalist system because of its rottenness must fall, and they sensed a mysterious deadline in the approaching end of the century. "All are awaiting the birth of a new order of things," wrote Reclus. "The century which has witnessed so many grand discoveries in the world of science cannot pass away without giving us still greater conquests. After so much hatred we yearn to love each other and for this reason we are the enemies of private property and the despisers of law."

Kropotkin's benevolent eyes peering at the world around him found encouraging signs everywhere. The increasing number of free museums, free libraries and free parks, for instance, seemed to him to be progress toward the Anarchist day when all private property would eventually become common property. Were not turnpikes and toll bridges becoming free? Were not municipalities providing free water and free street lights? Proof of the Anarchists' contention that the society of the future would no longer be held together by government but by the "free association of men into groups" was, he thought, appearing in such developments as the International Red Cross, the trade unions and even the cartels of shipowners and railroads (elsewhere being denounced as "Trusts" by a rather different type of reformer in America).

As formulated by men like Kropotkin, Malatesta, Jean Grave and Reclus, Anarchism at the end of the century may have attained, in the words of one of its recorders, "a shining moral grandeur," but only at the cost of a noticeable removal from reality. These men had all suffered prison more than once for their beliefs. Kropotkin himself had lost his teeth as a result of prison scurvy. They were not men of the ivory tower except in so far as their heads were in ivory towers. They were able to draw blueprints of a state of universal harmony only by ignoring the evidence of human behavior and the testimony of history. Their insistence on revolution stemmed directly from their faith in humanity, which, they believed, needed only a shining example and a sharp blow to start it on its way to the golden age. They spoke their faith aloud. The consequences were frequently fatal.

Anarchism's new era of violence opened in France just after the hundredth anniversary of the French Revolution. A two-year reign of dynamite, dagger and gunshot erupted, killed ordinary men as well as great ones, destroyed property, banished safety, spread terror and then subsided. The signal was given in 1892 by a man whose name, Ravachol, seemed to "breathe revolt and hatred." His act, like nearly all that followed it, was a gesture of revenge for comrades who had suffered at the hands of the State.

On the previous May Day of 1891, at Clichy, a working-class suburb of Paris, a workers' demonstration led by *les anarchos* carrying red banners with revolutionary slogans was charged by mounted police. In the melee five police were slightly, and three Anarchist leaders severely, wounded. Dragged to the police station, the Anarchists were subjected, while still bleeding and untended, to a *passage à tabac* of uncontrolled savagery, being made to pass between two lines of policemen under kicks and blows and beatings with revolver butts. At their trial, Bulot, the prosecuting attorney, charged that one of them, on the day before the riot, had called on the workers to arm themselves, and told them, "If the police come, let no one fear to kill them like the dogs they are! Down with Government!

Vive la révolution!" Bulot thereupon demanded the death penalty for all three, which, since no one had been killed, was an impossible demand that he might better not have made. It was to start a train of dynamite. For the moment, M. Benoist, the presiding judge, acquitted one defendant and sentenced the other two to five and three years' imprisonment respectively, the maximum allowable in the circumstances.

Six months after the trial, the home of M. Benoist on the Boulevard St-Germain was blown up by a bomb. Two weeks later, on March 27, another bomb blew up the home of Bulot, the prosecuting attorney, in the Rue de Clichy. Between the two explosions the police had circulated a description of the suspected criminal as a thin but muscular young man in his twenties with a bony, yellowish face, brown hair and beard, a look of ill health and a round scar between thumb and first finger of the left hand. On the day of the second explosion a man of this appearance took dinner at the Restaurant Véry in the Boulevard Magenta, where he talked volubly to a waiter named Lhérot about the explosion, which no one in the quarter yet knew had taken place. He also expressed anti-militarist and Anarchist opinions. Lhérot wondered about him but did nothing. Two days later the man returned and this time Lhérot, noticing the scar, called the police. When they arrived to arrest him the slight young man suddenly became a giant of maniacal strength and it required ten men and a terrific struggle to subdue and take him prisoner.

This was Ravachol. He had adopted his mother's name in preference to Koenigstein, the name of his father, who had abandoned his wife and four children, leaving Ravachol at eight years of age as chief breadwinner of the family. At eighteen, after reading Eugene Sue's *The Wandering Jew*, he had lost faith in religion, adopted Anarchist sentiments, attended their meetings, and as a result, was dismissed with a younger brother from his job as a dyer's assistant. Meanwhile, his younger sister died and his elder sister bore an illegitimate child. Although Ravachol found other jobs, they did not pay enough to keep the family from misery. Accordingly, he took to illegal supplements, but with a certain fierce pride of principle. Robbery of the rich was the right of the poor "to escape living like beasts," he said in prison. "To die of hunger is cowardly and degrading. I preferred to turn thief, counterfeiter, murderer." He had in fact been all these and grave robber as well.

At his trial on April 26, 1892, he stated that his motive had been to avenge the Anarchists of Clichy who had been beaten up by the police and "not even given water to wash their wounds," and upon whom Bulot and Benoist had imposed the maximum penalty although the jury had recommended the minimum. His manner was resolute and his eyes had the peculiarly piercing gaze expressive of inner conviction. "My object was to terrorize so as to force society to look attentively at those who suffer," he said, putting volumes into a sentence. While the press described him as a figure of sinister violence and cunning and a "colossus of strength," witnesses testified that he had given money to the wife of one of the imprisoned Clichy Anarchists and bought clothes for her children. At the end of the one-day trial, he was sentenced to imprisonment at hard labour for life. But the Ravachol affair had just begun.

The waiter Lhérot, meanwhile, was winning heroic notoriety by regaling customers and journalists with his story of the Scar, the Recognition and the Arrest. As a result he attracted an unknown avenger who set off a bomb in the Restaurant Véry which killed, not Lhérot, but his brother-in-law, M. Véry, the proprietor. The act was hailed by *Le Père Peinard*, an Anarchist journal given to coarse street argot, with the ghoulish double pun, "*Vérification!*"

By now the police had uncovered a whole series of Ravachol's crimes, including a grave robbery for the jewelry on a corpse, the murder of a ninety-two-year-old miser and his housekeeper, the further murder of two old women who kept a hardware shop—which had netted him forty sous—and of another shopkeeper, which had netted him nothing. "See this hand?" Ravachol was quoted as saying; "it has killed as many bourgeois as it has fingers." At the same time he had been living peaceably in lodgings, teaching the little daughter of his landlord to read.

His trial for these murders opened on June 21 in an atmosphere of terror induced by the avenger's bomb in the Restaurant Véry. Everyone expected the Palais de Justice to be blown up; it was surrounded by troops, every entrance guarded, and jurors, judges and counsel heavily escorted by police. Upon being sentenced to death, Ravachol said that what he had done had been for the "Anarchist idea" and added the prophetic words, "I know I shall be avenged."

Faced with this extraordinary person, at once a monster of criminality and a protector and avenger of the unfortunate, the Anarchist press fell into discord. In *La Révolte* Kropotkin repudiated Ravachol as "not the true, the authentic" revolutionary but the "*opéra-bouffe* variety." These deeds, he wrote, "are not the steady, daily work of preparation, little seen but immense, which the revolution demands. This requires other men than Ravachols. Leave them to the *fin de siècle* bourgeois whose product they are." Malatesta likewise, in the literary Anarchist journal, *l'En Dehors*, rejected Ravachol's gesture.

The difficulty was that Ravachol belonged almost but not quite to that class of Ego Anarchists who had one serious theorist in the German Max Stirner and a hundred practitioners of the *culte de moi*. They professed an extreme contempt for every bourgeois sentiment and social restraint, recognizing only the individual's right to "live anarchistically," which included burglary and any other crime that served the need of the moment. They were interested in themselves, not in revolution. The unbridled operations of these "miniature Borgias," usually ending in gun battles with the police and flaunted under the banner of "Anarchism," added much to the fear and anger of the public, who did not distinguish between the aberrant and the true variety. Ravachol was both. There was in him a streak of genuine pity and fellow feeling for the oppressed of his class which led one Anarchist paper to compare him with Jesus.

On July 11, calm and unrepentant, he went to the guillotine, crying at the end, "*Vive l'anarchie!*" At once the issue was clear. Overnight he became an Anarchist martyr and among the underworld, a popular hero. *La Révolte* reversed itself. "He will be avenged!" it proclaimed, adding its bit to the unfolding cycle of revenge. *L'En Dehors* opened a subscription for the children of an accomplice tried along with Ravachol. Among the contributors were the painter Camille Pissarro, the playwright Tristan Bernard, the Belgian Socialist and poet Emile Verhaeren, and Bernard Lazare (soon to be an actor in the Dreyfus case). A verb, *ravacholiser*, meaning "to wipe out an enemy," became current, and a street song called "La Ravachole," sung to the tune of "La Carmagnole," carried the refrain:

> It will come, it will come,
> Every bourgeois will have his bomb.

Ravachol's significance was not in his bombs but in his execution. Meantime, violence erupted across the Atlantic.

Anarchism, which rejected government in sexual matters as in all others, had its love affairs, and one that was to have explosive effect upon the movement in America was at this time in progress in New York. It began in 1890 at a memorial meeting for the Haymarket martyrs at which the speaker was the German exile Johann Most, with the twisted face and deformed body, who edited the Anarchist weekly *Freiheit* in New York.

An untended childhood accident which caused his facial disfigurement, a scorned and lonely youth spent wandering from place to place, sometimes starving, sometimes finding odd jobs, was natural food for an animus against society. In Most it sprouted with the energy of a weed. In Germany he learned the bookbinder's trade, wrote wrathfully for the revolutionary press, and achieved one term as deputy in the Reichstag in the seventies. Exiled for his revolutionary incitement, he had taken refuge first in England, where he became an Anarchist, founded his journal of fiery sentiments and welcomed the regicide of Alexander II in 1881 with such enthusiasm that he received a prison term of eighteen months. When his comrades, while he was in gaol, applauded equally the assassination of Lord Frederick Cavendish by Irish rebels in Dublin, England's traditional tolerance was outraged at last; *Freiheit* was suppressed and Most, when he emerged, took his paper and his passion to the United States.

Freiheit's incitements and ferocity continued unabated and to one reader seemed like "lava shooting forth flames of ridicule, scorn and defiance . . . and breathing hatred." After working secretly for a time in an explosives factory in Jersey City, Most published a manual on the manufacture of bombs and expounded in uninhibited language in *Freiheit* on the uses of dynamite and nitroglycerine. His goal, like his hate, was generalized and directed toward destruction of the "existing class rule" by "relentless" revolutionary action. Most cared nothing for the eight-hour day, that "damned thing" as he called it, which even if gained would serve only to distract the masses from the real issue: the struggle against capitalism and for a new society.

In 1890 Most was forty-four, of medium height with gray, bushy hair crowning a large head, of which the lower part was twisted to the left by the dislocated jaw. A harsh, embittered man, he was yet so eloquent and impassioned when he spoke at the memorial meeting that his repellent appearance was forgotten. To one female member of the audience, his blue eyes were "sympathetic" and he seemed to "radiate hatred and love."

Emma Goldman, a recent Russian Jewish immigrant of twenty-one, with a rebellious soul and a highly excitable nature, was transported. Her companion of the evening was Alexander Berkman, like herself a Russian Jew, who had lived in the United States less than three years. Persecution in Russia and poverty in America had endowed both these young people with exalted revolutionary purpose. Anarchism became their creed. Emma's first job in the United States was sewing in a factory ten and a half hours a day for $2.50 a week. Her room cost $3.00 a month. Berkman came from a slightly better-class family which in Russia had been sufficiently well-off to employ servants and send him to the *gymnasium*. But economic disaster had overtaken them; a favorite uncle of revolutionary sentiments had been seized by the police and never seen again and Sasha (Alexander) had been expelled from school for writing a Nihilist and atheistic composition. Now twenty, he had "the neck and chest of a giant," a high studious forehead, intelligent eyes, and a severe expression. From the "tension and fearful excitement" of Most's speech about the martyrs, Emma sought "relief" in Sasha's arms and subsequently her enthusiasm led her to Most's arms as well. The tensions of this arrangement proved no different from those of any bourgeois triangle.

In June, 1892, in Homestead, Pennsylvania, the steelworkers' union struck in protest against a reduction of wages by the Carnegie Steel Company. The company had ordered the wage cut in a deliberate effort to crush the union, and in expectation of battle, set about erecting a military stockade topped with barbed wire behind which it planned to operate the mills with three hundred strikebreakers recruited by the Pinkerton Agency. Having become a philanthropist, Andrew Carnegie discreetly retreated for the summer to a salmon river in Scotland, leaving his manager, Henry Clay Frick, to do battle with organized labour. No one was more competent or more willing. A remarkably handsome man of forty-three, with a strong black moustache merging into a short black beard, a courteous controlled manner and eyes which could become suddenly "very steely," Frick came from a well-established Pennsylvania family. He dressed with quiet distinction in dark blue with a hairline stripe, never wore jewelry and when offended by a cartoon of himself in the Pittsburgh *Leader*, said to his secretary, "This won't do. This won't do at all. Find out who owns this paper and buy it."

On July 5 the strikebreakers recruited by Frick were to be brought in to operate the plant. When they were ferried in armored barges across the Monongahela and were about to land, the strikers attacked with homemade cannon, rifles, dynamite and burning oil. The day of furious battle ended with ten killed, seventy wounded, and the Pinkertons thrown back from the plant by the bleeding but triumphant workers. The Governor of Pennsylvania sent in eight thousand militia, the country was electrified, and Frick in the midst of smoke, death, and uproar, issued an ultimatum declaring his refusal to deal with the union and his intention to operate with non-union labour and to discharge and evict from their homes any workers who refused to return to their jobs.

"Homestead! I must go to Homestead!" shouted Berkman on the memorable evening when Emma rushed in waving the newspaper. It was, they felt, "the psychological moment for the deed. . . . The whole country was aroused against Frick and a blow aimed at him now would call the attention of the whole world to the cause." The workers were striking not only for themselves but "for all time, for a free life, for Anarchism"—although they did not know it. As yet they were only "blindly rebellious," but Berkman felt a mission to "illumine" the struggle and impart the "vision of Anarchism which alone could imbue discontent with conscious revolutionary purpose." The removal of a tyrant was not merely justifiable; it was "an act of liberation, the giving of life and opportunity to an oppressed people" and it was the "highest duty" and the "test of every true revolutionist" to die in its cause.

Berkman boarded the train for Pittsburgh bent on killing Frick but surviving long enough himself "to justify my case in court." Then in prison he would "die by my own hand like Lingg."

On July 23 he made his way to Frick's office, where he was admitted when he presented a card on which he had written, "Agent of a New York employment firm." Frick was conferring with his vice-chairman, John Leishman, when Berkman entered, pulled out a revolver and fired. His bullet wounded Frick on the left side of his neck; he fired again wounding him on the right side, and as he fired the third time, his arm was knocked up by Leishman so that he missed altogether. Frick, bleeding, had risen and lunged at Berkman, who, attacked also by Leishman, fell to the floor dragging the other two men with him. Freeing one hand, he managed to extract a dagger from his pocket, and stabbed Frick in the side and legs seven times before he was finally pulled off by a deputy sheriff and others who rushed into the room.

"Let me see his face," whispered Frick, his own face ashen, his beard and clothes streaked with blood. The sheriff jerked Berkman's head back by his hair, and the eyes of Frick and his assailant met. At the police station two caps of fulminate of mercury of the same kind Lingg had used to blow himself up were found on Berkman's person (some say, in his mouth). Frick lived, the strike was broken by the militia, and Berkman went to prison for sixteen years.

All this left the country gasping, but the public shock was as nothing compared to that which rocked Anarchist circles when in *Freiheit* of August, 27, Johann Most, the priest of violence, turned apostate to his past and denounced Berkman's attempt at tyrannicide. He said the importance of the terrorist deed had been overestimated and that it could not mobilize revolt in a country where there was no proletarian class-consciousness, and he dealt with Berkman, now a hero in Anarchist eyes, in terms of contempt. When he repeated these views verbally at a meeting, a female fury rose up out of the audience. It was Emma Goldman, armed with a horsewhip, who sprang upon the platform and flayed her former lover across his face and body. The scandal was tremendous.

That personal emotions played a part both in Most's act and hers can hardly be doubted. Most may have taken his cue from Kropotkin and Malatesta, who already in Ravachol's case had begun to question the value of gestures of violence. But the dedicated Berkman was no Ravachol and it was clearly jealousy of him as a younger rival both in love and in the revolutionary movement that galled Most. His splenetic attack on a fellow Anarchist who had been ready to die for the Deed was a stunning betrayal from which the movement in America never fully recovered.

It had no effect on the public at large, who were aware only of the Anarchists' blows, or *attentats*, as the French called them. Society's fear of the disruptive force within its bowels grew with each attack. In the year after Homestead the fear burst out when Governor John P. Altgeld of Illinois pardoned the three remaining Haymarket prisoners. A strange, hard, passionate man who had been born in Germany and brought to the United States at the age of three months, Altgeld had come from a boyhood of hardship and manual labour. He had fought in the Civil War at sixteen, had studied law, become State's Attorney, judge and finally Governor and had made a fortune in real estate, and was an almost demonic liberal. He had pledged himself to right the injustice done by the drumhead trial as soon as he had the power and he was also not unmotivated by a personal grudge against Judge Gary. As soon as he was elected Governor he set in motion a study of the trial records and on June 26, 1893, issued his pardon along with an 18,000-word document affirming the illegality of the original verdict and sentence. He showed the jury to have been packed and "selected to convict," the judge prejudiced against the defendants and unwilling to conduct a fair trial, and the State's Attorney to have admitted that there was no case against at least one of the defendants. These facts had not been unknown, and in the year between the verdict and the hanging, many prominent Chicagoans, uneasy over the death sentence, had worked privately for pardon and had in fact been responsible for the commutation of the sentence of the three defendants now still alive. But when Altgeld displayed publicly the cloven hoof of the Law, he shook public faith in a fundamental institution of society. Had he pardoned the Anarchists as a pure act of forgiveness, there would have been little excitement. As it was, he was excoriated by the press, by ministers in their pulpits, by important persons of all varieties. The Toronto *Blade* said he had encouraged "the overthrow of civilization." So outraged was the New York *Sun* that it resorted to verse:

> Oh wild Chicago . . .
> Lift up your weak and guilty hands
> From out the wreck of states
> And as the crumbling towers fall down,
> Write ALTGELD on your gates!

Altgeld was defeated for office at the next election. Although there were other reasons besides the pardon, he never held office again before he died at fifty-five in 1902.

Simultaneously with these events the era of dynamite exploded in Spain. There it opened with more ferocity, continued in more savagery and excess and lasted longer than in any other country. Spain is the desperado of countries, with a tragic sense of life. Its mountains are naked, its cathedrals steeped in gloom, its rivers dry up in summer, one of its greatest kings built his own mausoleum to inhabit while he lived. Its national sport is not a game but a ritual of danger and blood-letting. Its special quality was expressed by the deposed Queen, Isabella II, who, on a visit to the capital in 1890, wrote to her daughter, "Madrid is sad and everything is more unusual than ever."

In Spain it was natural that the titans' struggle between Marx and Bakunin for control of the working-class movement should have ended in victory for the Anarchist tendency. In Spain, however, where everything is more serious, the Anarchists organized, with the result that they took root and their power lasted long into the modern period. Like Russia, Spain was a cauldron in which the revolutionary element boiled against a tight lid of oppression. The Church, the landowners, the *Guardia Civil*, all the guardians of the State held the lid down. Although Spain had a Cortes and a facade of the democratic process, in reality the working class did not have open to it the legal means for reform and change which existed in

France and England. Consequently, the appeal of Anarchism and its explosive methods was stronger. But unlike "pure" Anarchism, the Spanish form was collectivist because it had to be. Oppression was too heavy to allow hopes of individual action.

In January, 1892, occurred an outburst which, like the May Day affair at Clichy, was to inaugurate a terrible cycle of deed, retaliation and revenge. Agrarian revolt was endemic in the south where the immense *latifundia* of absentee landlords were farmed by peasants who worked all day for the price of a loaf of bread. Four hundred of them now rose in revolt, and armed with pitchforks, scythes and what firearms they could lay hold of, marched on the village of Jerez de la Frontera in Andalusia. Their object was the rescue of five comrades sentenced to life imprisonment in chains for complicity in a labour affair ten years earlier. The rising was promptly suppressed by the military and four of the leaders garroted, a Spanish form of execution in which the victim is tied with his back to a post and strangled with a scarf which the executioner twists from behind by means of a wooden handle. Zarzuela, one of the condemned, died calling upon the people to "avenge us."

A bulwark of the Spanish government was General Martínez de Campos, whose strong arm had restored the monarchy in 1874. After this he had defeated the Carlists, suppressed an early Cuban insurrection, and served as Premier and Minister of War. On September 24, 1893, he was reviewing a parade of troops in Barcelona. From the front row of the crowds an Anarchist named Pallas, who had been with Malatesta in the Argentine, threw first one bomb and then a second, killing the General's horse, one soldier and five bystanders, but erratically leaving its intended victim, who was thrown under the body of his horse, only bruised. Pallas, as he confessed with pride, had planned to kill the General and "his whole staff." When condemned to death by court-martial he cried, "Agreed! There are thousands to continue the work." He was allowed to take farewell of his children but, for some barbaric reason, not of his wife and mother. Sentenced to be shot with his back to a firing squad, another Spanish variant of usual custom, he repeated the cry of Andalusia, "Vengeance will be terrible!"

It came within weeks, again in the Catalan capital, and in the number of its dead was the most lethal of all the Anarchist assaults. November 8, 1893, almost coinciding with the Haymarket anniversary, was opening night of the opera season at the Teatro Lyceo and the audience in glittering evening dress was listening to *William Tell.* In the midst of this drama of defiance to tyrants, two bombs were thrown down from the balcony. One exploded, killing fifteen persons outright, and the other lay unexploded, threatening to burst at any moment. It caused a pandemonium of "terror and dismay," shrieks and curses and a wild rush for the exits in which people "fought like wild beasts to escape, respecting neither age nor sex." Afterwards, as the wounded were carried out, their splendid dresses torn, blood streaming over their starched white shirt fronts, crowds gathered outside "cursing both Anarchists and police," according to a reporter. Seven more died of their wounds, giving a total of twenty-two dead and fifty wounded.

The answer of the government was as fierce. Police raided every known club or home or meeting place of social discontent. Hundreds, even thousands, were arrested and thrown into the dungeons of Montjuich, the prison fortress seven hundred feet above the sea, whose guns dominate the harbor and city of Barcelona and foredoom any revolt by that chronically rebellious city. So full were the cells that new prisoners had to be kept shackled in warships anchored below. There being in this case no one to admit to the guilt of so many deaths, torture was applied mercilessly to extract a confession. Prisoners were burned with irons or forced with whips to keep walking thirty, forty, or fifty hours at a time and subjected to other procedures indigenous to the country of the Inquisition. By these means information was extorted that led to the arrest in January, 1894, of an Anarchist named Santiago Salvador who admitted to the crime in the Opera House as an act of revenge for Pallas. His arrest was immediately answered by his fellow Anarchists of Barcelona with another bombing, which killed two innocent persons. The government replied with six death sentences carried out in April upon prisoners from whom some form of confession had been extracted by torture. Salvador, who had attempted ineffectively to kill himself by revolver and poison, was tried separately in July and executed in November.

The ghastly tale of the Opera House explosion in Spain excited the nerves of authorities everywhere and caused even the English to question whether allowing Anarchists to preach their doctrines openly was advisable. When, three days later, the Anarchists held their traditional memorial meeting for the Haymarket martyrs, questions were put in Parliament about the conduct of the Liberal Home Secretary, Mr. Asquith, in permitting it, since such meetings required specific approval by the Home Office in advance. Mr. Asquith endeavored to shrug the matter aside as insignificant but was "crushed," according to a reporter, by the Leader of the Opposition, Mr. Balfour, who in his languid way suggested that the right to throw bombs was not an open question for public meetings nor defensible on the ground that society was badly organized. Whether convinced by Balfour or by second thoughts about the Spanish deaths, Asquith in any event reversed himself and announced a few days later that, as "the propagation of Anarchist doctrine was dangerous to the social order," no further open meetings of Anarchists would be permitted.

London's Anarchists at this time were mostly Russians, Poles, Italians and other exiles who centered around the "Autonomie," an Anarchist club, and a second group among Jewish immigrants who lived and worked in desperate poverty in the East End, published a Yiddish-language paper, *Der Arbeiter-Fraint*, and gathered at a club called the "International," in Whitechapel. The English working class, to whom acts of individual violence came less naturally than to Slavs and Latins, was on the whole not interested. An occasional intellectual like William Morris was a torch-bearer; but he was mainly interested in his personal version of a utopian state, and his influence having waned by the end of the eighties, he lost control of *Commonweal*, the journal he had founded and edited, to more militant, plebeian and orthodox Anarchists. Another journal, *Freedom*, was the organ of an active group whose mentor was Kropotkin, and a third, called *The Torch*—edited by the two daughters of William Rossetti—published the voices of Malatesta, Faure and other French and Italian Anarchists.

In 1891 with the appearance of *The Soul of Man Under Socialism* a strange recruit alighted briefly on the movement like a gorgeous butterfly and then flew off. The author of the essay was Oscar Wilde. He had been much moved by the personality of Kropotkin and saw true freedom for the Artist in a society in which, "of course, authority and compulsion are out of the question." Despite his title he objected to Socialism on the same ground as the orthodox Anarchist, namely, that it was "authoritarian." If governments are to be armed with economic power, "if in a word, we are to have Industrial Tyrannies, then the last state of man will be worse than the first." Wilde's vision was of Socialism founded upon Individualism, and when this had set free the true personality of man, the Artist would at last come into his own.

In France meanwhile there had been no pause in the assaults. On November 8, 1892, at the time of a miners' strike against the Société des Mines de Carmaux, a bomb was deposited in the Paris office of the company on the Avenue de l'Opéra. Discovered by the concierge, it was taken out to the sidewalk and carefully carried off by a policeman to the nearest precinct station, in the Rue des Bons Enfants. As the policeman was bringing it in, it burst with a devastating explosion, killing five other policemen who were in the room. They were blown to fragments, blood and bits of flesh were splashed over shattered walls and windows, pieces of arms and legs lay about. Police suspicion centered on Emile Henry, younger brother of a well-known radical orator and son of Fortuné Henry who had escaped to Spain after being condemned to death in the Commune. When Emile Henry's movements during the day were traced, it appeared impossible that he could have been in the Avenue de l'Opéra at the right moment, and for the time being, no arrests were made.

The bomb in the police station threw Paris into a panic; no one knew where the next bomb would hit. Anyone connected with the law or police was regarded by his neighbors—since Parisians live largely in apartments—as if he had the plague and was often given notice to leave by his landlord. The city, wrote an English visitor, was "absolutely paralyzed" with fear. The upper classes "lived again as if in the days of the Commune. They dared not go to the theatres, to restaurants, to the fashionable shops in the Rue de la Paix or to ride in the Bois where Anarchists were suspected behind every tree." People exchanged terrible rumors: the Anarchists had mined the churches, poured prussic acid in the city's reservoirs, were hiding beneath the seats of horsecabs ready to spring out upon passengers and rob them. Troops were assembled in the suburbs ready to march, tourists took flight, the hotels were empty, busses ran without passengers, theatres and museums were barricaded.

The time was in any case one of public rancor and disgust. Hardly had the Republic warded off the Boulanger coup d'état than it was put to shame by the nexus of corruption revealed in the Panama scandal and in the official traffic in decorations. Day after day in Parliament during 1890–92 the chain of Panama financing through loans, bribes, slush funds and sales of influence was uncovered, until, it was said, 104 deputies were involved. Even Georges Clemenceau was smeared by association and lost his seat in the next election.

In proportion as the prestige of the State sank, Anarchism flourished. Intellectuals flirted with it. The buried dislike of government and law that exists in most men is nearer to the surface in some. Like the fat man who has a thin man inside crying to get out, even the respectable have a small Anarchist hidden inside, and among the artists and intellectuals of the nineties his faint cry was frequently heard. The novelist Maurice Barrès, who at one time or another tried every position in the political spectrum as a tribune for his talents, glorified Anarchist philosophy in his *l'Ennemi des Lois* and *Un Homme Libre*. The poet Laurent Tailhade hailed the future Anarchist society as a "blessed time" when aristocracy would be one of intellect and "the common man will kiss the footprints of the poets." Literary anarchism enjoyed a vogue among the Symbolists, like Mallarmé and Paul Valéry. The writer Octave Mirbeau was attracted to Anarchism because he had a horror of authority. He detested anyone in uniform: policemen, ticket-punchers, messengers, concierges, servants. In his eyes, said his friend Léon Daudet, a landlord was a pervert, a Minister a thief, lawyers and financiers made him sick and he had tolerance only for children, beggars, dogs, certain painters and sculptors and very young women. "That there need be no misery in the world was his fixed belief," said a friend; "that there nevertheless was, was the occasion of his wrath." Among painters,

Pissarro contributed drawings to *Le Père Peinard* and several brilliant and savage Parisian illustrators, including Théophile Steinlen, expressed in the Anarchist journals their disgust at social injustice; sometimes, as when the President of France was caricatured in soiled pajamas, in terms unprintable in a later day.

Scores of these ephemeral journals and bulletins appeared, with names like *Antichrist*, *New Dawn*, *Black Flag*, *Enemy of the People*, the *People's Cry*, *The Torch*, *The Whip*, *New Humanity*, *Incorruptible*, *Sans-Culotte*, *Land and Liberty*, *Vengeance*. Groups and clubs calling themselves "Anti-patriots' League" or "Libertarians" held meetings in dimly lit halls furnished with benches where members vented their contempt for the State, discussed revolution, but never organized, never affiliated, accepted no leaders, made no plans, took no orders. To them the State, in its panic over the Ravachol affair, in its rottenness revealed by the Panama affair, appeared to be already crumbling.

In March of 1893 a man of thirty-two named August Vaillant returned to Paris from Argentina, where he had gone in the hope of starting a new life in the New World but had failed to establish himself. Born illegitimate, he was ten months old when his mother married a man not his father, who refused to support the child. He was given to foster parents. At twelve, the boy was on his own in Paris, living by odd jobs, petty theft and begging. Somehow he went to school and found white-collar jobs. At one time he edited a short-lived weekly called *l'Union Socialiste* but soon, like others among the disinherited, gravitated to Anarchist circles. As secretary of a *Fédération des groupes indépendants*, he had some contact with Anarchist spokesmen, among them Sebastien Faure, whose "harmonious and caressing voice," beautiful phrases and elegant manners could make anyone believe in the millennium as long as they were listening to him. Vaillant married, parted from his wife, but kept with him their daughter, Sidonie, and acquired a mistress. Not the footloose or libertarian type, he held together his tiny family until the end. After his failure in Argentina he tried again to make a living in Paris, and like his contemporary Knut Hamsun, then hungrily wandering the streets of Christiania, experienced the humiliation of "the frequent repulses, half-promises, the curt noes, the cherished deluded hopes and fresh endeavors that always resulted in nothing," until the last frustration when he no longer had any respectable clothes to wear when applying for a job. Unable to afford a new pair of shoes, Vaillant wore a pair of discarded galoshes he had picked up in the street. Finally he found work in a sugar refinery paying 3 francs a day, too little to support three people.

Ashamed and bitter to see his daughter and mistress go hungry, disillusioned with a world he never made, he decided to end his life. He would not go silently but with a cry of protest, "a cry of that whole class," as he wrote the night before he acted, "which demands its rights and some day soon will join acts to words. At least I shall die with the satisfaction of knowing that I have done what I could to hasten the advent of a new era."

Not a man to kill, Vaillant planned a gesture that had some logic. He saw the disease of society exemplified by the scandal-ridden Parliament. He manufactured a bomb out of a saucepan filled with nails and with a non-lethal charge of explosive. On the afternoon of December 9, 1893, he took it with him to a seat in a public gallery of the Chambre des Députés. An observer saw a tall gaunt figure with a pale face rise to his feet and hurl something down into the midst of the debate. Vaillant's bomb detonated with the roar of a cannon, spraying the deputies with metal fragments, wounding several but killing none.

The sensation, as soon as the news was known, was enormous, and was made memorable by an enterprising journalist. He asked for comment that night at a dinner given by the journal *La Plume* to a number of celebrities, including Zola, Verlaine, Mallarmé, Rodin and Laurent Tailhade. The last-named replied grandly and in exquisite rhythm, "*Qu'importe les victimes si le geste est beau?*" (What do the victims matter if it's a fine gesture?) Published in *Le Journal* next morning, the remark was soon to be recalled in gruesome circumstances. That same morning Vaillant gave himself up.

All France understood and some, other than Anarchists, even sympathized with his gesture. Ironically, these sympathizers came from the extreme right, whose anti-Republican forces —Royalists, Jesuits, floating aristocracy and anti-Semites— despised the bourgeois state for their own reasons. Edouard

Drumont, author of *La France Juive* and editor of *La Libre Parole*, who was busy raging at the Jews involved in the Panama scandal, produced a piece richly entitled "On Mud, Blood and Gold—From Panama to Anarchism." "The men of blood," he said, "were born out of the mud of Panama." The Duchesse d'Uzès, married into one of the three premier ducal families, offered to give a home and education to Vaillant's daughter (whom Vaillant, however, preferred to leave to the guardianship of Sebastien Faure).

In an angry mood, and determined to finish off the Anarchists once and for all, the government acted to stifle their propaganda. Two days after Vaillant's bomb the Chamber unanimously passed two laws making it a crime to print any direct or "indirect" provocation of terrorist acts or to associate with intent to commit such acts. Although known as *les lois scélérates* (the scoundrelly laws), they were hardly an unreasonable measure, since the preaching of the Deed was in fact the principal incitement. Police raided Anarchist cafés and meeting places, two thousand warrants were issued, clubs and discussion groups scattered, *La Révolte* and *Le Père Peinard* closed down, and leading Anarchists left the country.

On January 10, Vaillant came to trial before five judges in red robes and black gold-braided caps. Charged with intent to kill, he insisted that he had intended only to wound. "If I had wanted to kill I could have used a heavier charge and filled the container with bullets; instead, I used only nails." His counsel, Maître Labori, who was destined for drama and violence in a far more famous case, defended him with spirit as *un exaspéré de la misère*. It was parliament, Labori said, which was guilty, for failing to remedy "the misery of poverty that oppresses one third of a nation." Despite Labori's efforts, Vaillant received the death penalty, the first time in the Nineteenth Century it had been imposed on a person who had not killed. Trial, verdict and sentence were rushed through in a single day. Almost immediately petitions for pardon began to assail President Sadi Carnot, including one from a group of sixty deputies led by Abbé Lemire, who had been one of those wounded by the bomb. A fiery Socialist, Jules Breton, predicted that if Carnot "pronounced coldly for death, not a single man in France would grieve for him if he were one day himself to be victim of a bomb." As incitement to murder, this cost Breton two years in prison and proved to be the second comment on the Vaillant affair which was to end in strange and sinister coincidence.

The government could not pardon an Anarchist attack upon the State. Carnot refused to remit the sentence and Vaillant was duly executed on February 5, 1894, crying, "Death to bourgeois society! Long live Anarchy!"

The train of death gathered speed. Only seven days after Vaillant went to the guillotine, he was avenged by a blow of such seemingly vicious unreason that the public felt itself in the midst of nightmare. This time the bomb was aimed not against any representative of law, property or State, but against the man in the street. It exploded in the Café Terminus of the Gare St-Lazare in the midst, as *Le Journal* wrote, "of peaceful, anonymous citizens gathered in a café to have a beer before going to bed." One was killed and twenty wounded. As later became clear, the perpetrator acted upon a mad logic of his own. Even before he came to trial, the streets of Paris rocked with more explosions. One in the Rue St-Jacques killed a passer-by, one in the Faubourg St-Germain did no damage and a third exploded in the pocket of Jean Pauwels, a Belgian Anarchist, as he was entering the Church of the Madeleine. He was killed and proved to have set off the other two. On April 4, 1894, a fourth exploded in the fashionable Restaurant Foyot, where, though it killed no one, it put out the eye of Laurent Tailhade, who happened to be dining there and who only four months earlier had shrugged aside the victims of a "fine gesture."

Public hysteria mounted. When, at a theatrical performance, some scenery back stage fell with a clatter, half the audience rushed for the exits screaming, "*Les Anarchistes! Une bombe!*" Newspapers took to printing a daily bulletin under the heading, "La Dynamite." When the trial of the bomber of the Café Terminus opened on April 27, the terrible capacity of the Anarchist idea to be transformed from love of mankind to hatred of men was revealed.

The accused turned out to be the same Emile Henry who had been suspected of setting the earlier bomb in the office of the Mines de Carmaux which had ultimately killed the five policemen. Already charged for murder in the Café Terminus, he now claimed credit for the other deaths as well, although no proof could be found. He stated that he had bombed the Café Terminus to avenge Vaillant and with full intention to kill "as many as possible. I counted on fifteen dead and twenty wounded." In fact, police had found in his room enough equipment to make twelve or fifteen bombs. In his cold passion, intellectual pride and contempt for the common man, Henry seemed the "St. Just of Anarchism." A brilliant student who had been admitted to the arcane Ecole Polytechnique and had been expelled for insulting a professor, he had been left to occupy his mind as a draper's clerk at 120 francs a month. At twenty-two he was, along with Berkman, the best educated and best acquainted with Anarchist theory of all the assassins, and of them all, the most explicit.

In prison he wrote a long, closely reasoned account of his experience of the cynicism and injustice of bourgeois society, of his "too great respect for individual initiative" to permit him to join the herd-like Socialists, and of his approach to Anarchism. He showed himself thoroughly familiar with its doctrines and with the writings of Kropotkin, Reclus, Grave, Faure and others, although he affirmed that Anarchists were not "blind believers" who swallowed whole any or all the ideas of the theorists.

But it was when he explained his choice of the Café Terminus that he suddenly set himself apart. There, he said, come "all those who are satisfied with the established order, all the accomplices and employees of Property and the State, . . . all that mass of good little bourgeois who make 300 to 500 francs a month, who are more reactionary than their masters, who hate the poor and range themselves on the side of the strong. These are the clientele of the Terminus and the big cafés of its kind. Now you know why I struck where I did."

In court, when reproached by the judge for endangering innocent lives, he replied with icy hauteur, in words that should have been blazoned on some Anarchist banner, "There are no innocent bourgeois."

As for the Anarchist leaders, he said, who "dissociate themselves from the propaganda of the deed," like Kropotkin and Malatesta in the case of Ravachol, and "who try to make a subtle distinction between theorists and terrorists, they are cowards. . . . We who hand out death know how to take it. . . . Mine is not the last head you will cut off. You have hung in Chicago, beheaded in Germany, garroted at Jerez, shot in Barcelona, guillotined in Paris, but there is one thing you cannot destroy: Anarchism. . . . It is in violent revolt against the established order. It will finish by killing you."

Henry himself took death staunchly. Even the caustic Clemenceau, who witnessed the execution on May 21, 1894, was moved and disturbed. He saw Henry "with the face of a tormented Christ, terribly pale, implacable in expression, trying to impose his intellectual pride upon his child's body." The condemned man walked quickly, despite his shackles, up the steps of the scaffold, glanced around and called out in a raucous strangled cry, "*Courage, Camarades! Vive l'anarchie!*" Society's answer to Henry seemed to Clemenceau at that moment "an act of savagery."

Almost without pause fell the next blow, the last in the French series and the most important in its victim, although the least in its assassin. In Lyons on June 24, 1894, during a visit to the Exposition in that city, President Sadi Carnot was stabbed to death by a young Italian workman with the cry, "*Vive la révolution! Vive l'anarchie!*" The President was driving in an open carriage through crowds that lined the streets, and had given orders to his escort to let people approach if they wanted to. When a young man holding a rolled-up newspaper thrust himself forward from the front row, the guards did not stop him, thinking the newspaper contained a bouquet of flowers for the President. Instead it contained a dagger and, with a terrible blow, the young man plunged it six inches into the President's abdomen. Carnot died within three hours. His wife next day received a letter mailed before the attack and addressed to the "Widow Carnot" which enclosed a photograph of Ravachol inscribed, "He is avenged."

The assassin was a baker's apprentice, not yet twenty-one, named Santo Caserio. Born in Italy, he had become acquainted with Anarchist groups in Milan, the home of political turbulence. At eighteen he was sentenced for distributing Anarchist tracts to soldiers. Following the drift of other restless and troublesome characters, he went to Switzerland and then to

Cette in the south of France, where he found work and a local group of Anarchists which went by the name "Les Coeurs de Chêne" ("Hearts of Oak"). He was brooding over Vaillant's case and the refusal of the President to give a reprieve when he read in the newspapers of the President's forthcoming visit to Lyons. Caserio decided at once to do a "great deed." He asked for a holiday from his job and for twenty francs that were due him, and with the money, bought a dagger and took the train for Lyons. There he followed the crowds until he met his opportunity.

Afterwards, in the hands of his captors and in court he was docile, smiling and calm. His wan and rather common but gentle face looked to one journalist like "the white mask of a floured Pierrot illuminated by two bright little blue eyes, obstinately fixed. His lip was ornamented by a poor little shadow of a moustache which seemed to have sprouted almost apologetically." During his interrogation and trial he remained altogether placid and talked quite rationally about Anarchist principles, by which he appeared obsessed. He described his act as a deliberate "propaganda of the deed." His only show of emotion was at mention of his mother, to whom he was greatly attached and to whom he had been writing letters regularly when away from home. When the gaoler came to wake him on August 15, the day of execution, he wept for a moment and then made no further sound on the way to the guillotine. Just as his neck was placed on the block he murmured a few words which were interpreted by some as the traditional "*Vive l'anarchie!*" and by others as "*A voeni nen*," meaning, in the Lombard dialect, "I don't want to."

When Anarchism slew the very chief of State, it reached a climax in France after which, suddenly, face to face with political realities and the facts of life in the labour movement, it retreated. At first, however, it looked as if the Anarchists would be handed a magnificent opportunity for either propaganda or martyrdom. Charging to the offensive, the Government on August 6 staged a mass trial of thirty of the best known Anarchists in an effort to prove conspiracy between theorists and terrorists. As the known terrorists had already been executed, the only examples the Government could produce were three minor characters of the "burglar" type, none of them Ravachols. Of the leaders, Elisée Reclus had left the country, but his nephew Paul Reclus, Jean Grave, Sebastien Faure and others were in the dock. In the absence of a party or corporate body as defendant, the prosecution was in a difficulty similar to having no *corpus delicti*. Nevertheless it accused what it called the "sect" of aiming at the destruction of the State through propaganda that encouraged theft, pillage, arson and murder "in which each member of the sect cooperates according to his temperament and facilities." In dread perhaps of the irresistible oratory of Faure, the prosecution did all the talking, hardly allowing the defendants to open their mouths and regretting it when they did. Addressing Felix Fenéon, the art critic and first champion of the Impressionists, who was one of the defendants, the presiding judge said, "You were seen talking with an Anarchist behind a lamppost."

"Can you tell me, Your Honor," replied Fenéon, "where is 'behind a lamppost'?"

In the absence of evidence connecting the accused with the deeds, the jury was not impressed and acquitted everyone except the three burglars, who were given prison terms. Once again French common sense had reasserted itself.

The jury's sensible verdict deprived Anarchism of a *cause célèbre*, but a greater reason for the decline that followed was that the French working class was too realistic to be drawn into a movement suffering from self-inflicted impotence. The sterility of deeds of terror was already beginning to be recognized by leaders like Kropotkin, Malatesta, Reclus and even Johann Most. Searching for other means of bringing down the State, they were always tripped up by the inherent paradox: Revolution demands organization, discipline and Authority; Anarchism disallows them. The futility of their position was beginning to make itself felt.

Banished from the meeting of the Socialist Second International in London in 1896, because of their refusal to subscribe to the necessity of political action, Anarchist groups called a Congress of their own in Paris in 1900. They made efforts to arrive at a formula of union which the comrades could accept, but every proposal foundered against the stubborn devotion to singleness of Jean Grave. A second attempt in a Congress at Amsterdam in 1907 produced a short-lived International

Bureau which, for lack of support, soon withered and ceased to function.

Yet in the end there was a kind of tragic sense in the Anarchist rejection of Authority. For, as the Jesuit-educated Sebastien Faure said in a moment of cold realism, "Every revolution ends in the reappearance of a new ruling class."

Realists of another kind during these years began to come to terms with the labour movement. It was the eight-hour day that the French working class wanted, not bombs in parliament or murdered presidents. But it was the Anarchist propaganda of the Deed that woke them to recognition of what they wanted and the necessity of fighting for it. That was why Ravachol, whom they understood, became a popular hero and songs were sung about him in the streets. Ever since the massacres of the Commune, the French proletariat had been prostrate; it was the Anarchist assaults that brought them to their feet. They sensed that their strength lay in collective action, and in 1895, only a year after the last of the *attentats*, there was formed the Confédération Générale de Travail (CGT), France's federation of labour.

Upon the Anarchists, frustrated by their own inherent paradox, it exerted a strong pull. One by one they drifted into the trade unions, bringing with them as much of their doctrine as could be applied. This merger of Anarchist theory and trade-union practice took the form known as Syndicalism, derived from *syndicat*, the French word for trade union. In this altered form, though extremists of the "pure" kind like Jean Grave shunned it, French Anarchism developed during the years 1895–1914.

Its dogma was direct action through the general strike and its new prophet was Georges Sorel. Under his banner the general strike was to replace propaganda of the deed. The overthrow of capitalism, Sorel argued, could only be accomplished when the working class developed a will to power. The use of violence was to be the means of fostering and training the revolutionary will. The Syndicalists continued to abhor the State or anyone willing, like the Socialists, to cooperate with it, and they had no more use than their Anarchist predecessors for half-way reformist measures. The strike was all, the general strike and nothing but the strike. They retained the sinews of the old movement; but something of its soul, its mad marvelous independence, was gone.

In Spain the cycle had far from run its course. On June 7, 1896, during the festival of Corpus Christi in Barcelona, a bomb was thrown into the midst of a religious procession as it was entering the church door led by the Bishop and the Commanding General of Barcelona. The two representatives of the Church and the Army at whom the bombs were aimed escaped injury, but eleven others were killed and forty wounded amid scenes of blood and terror comparable to the slaughter in the Opera House three years before. The Anarchists succeeded in thoroughly frightening the country, if not its Premier, Antonio Canovas del Castillo, who was not a man to tremble.

Recalled in 1895 for his fifth term as Prime Minister, Canovas was a man of "humble origin," as the phrase then was, who had risen—through engineering, journalism, diplomacy and election to the Cortes—to the top post of the Conservative Party. He had been the political arm of the restoration of the crown in 1874. In addition to practicing politics, he wrote poetry, literary criticism, a life of Calderón, a ten-volume history of Spain, and was President of the Royal Academy of History. He collected paintings, rare china, old coins and walking sticks, lived in a sumptuous palace in Madrid, dressed always in black and, like Frick, never allowed jewels "to obtrude their vulgarity" upon his person. Whether considered a man of reaction by the republicans or the ablest statesman of his time by others, he was acknowledged to be the only man who could hold the Conservative Party together and hold Cuba for Spain. Although he had formulated a plan for Cuban autonomy, he had also sent out General Weyler to quell the *insurrectos*, and already a firm hand and stern measures, in contrast to that of his Liberal predecessors, were taking effect. Against the Anarchists Canovas had no compunctions about proceeding ruthlessly.

With his sanction the mass arrests began again. Over four hundred persons were imprisoned, the Government as usual seizing the pretext to proceed against any or all enemies of the regime, whether Anarchists, anti-Clericals, or Catalan Republicans. The cries of agony from Montjuich were heard again, followed by the fearsome report that the Attorney-General would ask the death penalty for no less than twenty-eight out of eighty-four accused persons who were to be tried by court-martial. This was under a law passed by the Cortes after the Opera House explosion, making all crimes committed with explosives subject to court-martial and providing the death penalty for the guilty. Life imprisonment was decreed for those guilty of advocating violence through speeches, articles or pictures. The trial took place behind the stone curtain of Montjuich with only military personnel permitted to be present. Only the sentences were announced: eight condemned to die, of whom four were reprieved and four executed. Seventy-six were sentenced to prison terms ranging from eight to nineteen years, of whom sixty-one were sent to the penal colony of Rio de Oro, the Spanish Devil's Island.

At the same time the outside world learned from a firsthand report of the tortures inflicted at Montjuich upon the prisoners of 1893. Tarrida del Marmol, member of a leading Catalan family and director of the Polytechnic Academy of Barcelona, had, because of his liberal opinions, been caught up in the arrests, and his account, published in Paris in 1897 under the title *Les Inquisiteurs de l'Espagne*, aroused horrified protests. It included a posthumous cry for help in the form of a letter from a fellow prisoner, written before his execution and addressed to "All good men on earth." It told how he had been taken at night from his cell to a cliff over the sea where the guards loaded their guns and threatened to shoot him unless he said everything the lieutenant told him to say. When he refused, his genital organs were twisted and later, back in prison, this torture was repeated while he was hung from the door of his cell for ten hours. He was also subjected to the enforced walking for a period of five days. "Finally I declared everything they wanted and in my weakness and cowardice signed my declaration."

Some time later, in August, 1897, Premier Canovas went for a summer holiday to Santa Agueda, a spa in the Basque mountains. During tranquil days there, he noticed a fair-haired well-mannered fellow guest at the hotel who spoke Spanish with an Italian accent and several times saluted him politely. Canovas was moved to ask his secretary if he knew who the strange young man was and found he was registered as correspondent from the Italian newspaper *Il Popolo*. One morning as the Premier was sitting with his wife on the terrace reading his newspaper, the young Italian suddenly appeared, pulled a revolver from his pocket, and at three yards' distance fired three shots into Canovas' body, killing him instantly. Mme Canovas, in a passion of rage and grief, flew at the man still holding the revolver and struck him in the face with her fan, crying, "Murderer! Assassin!"

"I am not an assassin," replied the Italian sternly. "I am the Avenger of my Anarchist comrades. I have nothing to do with you, Madame."

Upon arrest and examination, his real name proved to be Michel Angiollilo. When in the Italian Army, he had served three terms in the disciplinary battalion for insubordination. On release from the Army he became a printer, a trade with an affinity for Anarchism, either because the Anarchist seeks contact with the printed word or because contact with the printed word leads to Anarchism. In any case Angiollilo was shortly sentenced to eighteen months in prison for printing subversive literature. In 1895, following a futile attempt, along with some Italian Anarchist comrades, to set up a clandestine press in Marseilles, he went to Barcelona and left after the Corpus Christi explosion. He drifted to Belgium and then London, where he bought a revolver with the intention of killing the Spanish Premier for "ordering the mass torture and execution of Anarchists." He returned to Spain, stalked Canovas in Madrid but failed to find his opportunity, followed him to Santa Agueda and found it there. Tried by court-martial a week later, he attempted to expound his Anarchist principles, and when silenced by the Court, shouted, "I must justify myself!" but was not allowed to speak. At his execution by the garrote he refused religious rites and maintained an unbroken sang-froid.

The European press erupted in agitated demand for a concerted effort to suppress the "mad dogs" of Anarchism. There was a sense that the loss of a man of Canovas' stature could be grave for Spain if not, as the *Nation* of New York predicted, a "national disaster." In fact, his death proved to be one of those accidents that give a decisive jerk to the course of events. With Canovas gone, the Liberals succeeded in taking office and soon retreated before the wild howls of Hearst-engendered indignation against "Butcher" Weyler then reverberating from the United States. General Weyler was relieved just when he was close to restoring order and the Cuban insurrection flared up again, providing the imperialists in the United States with the excuse for the most deliberately manufactured war of the century. Had Canovas lived, the excuse might not have been available.

For his death there was a reason; for two of the three that followed within the next three years there was none whatever. They were the product partly of Anarchist propaganda, which supplied the suggestion, but even more of public excitement over Anarchist deeds, which gave assassins promise of heroic notoriety and acted as an intoxicant to unsound minds.

The first death took place by dagger on September 10, 1898, alongside the lake steamer at the Quai Mont Blanc in Geneva. Here met, in mortal junction, as meaningless as when a stroke of lightning kills a child, two persons so unconnected, so far apart in the real world, that their lives could never have touched except in a demented moment. One was the Empress Elizabeth of Austria, wife of the Emperor Franz Joseph, the other Luigi Lucheni, a vagrant Italian workman.

The most beautiful and the most melancholy royal personage in Europe, married and crowned at sixteen, Elizabeth was still, at sixty-one, forever moving restlessly from one place to another in endless escape from an unquiet soul. Renowned for her loveliness, her golden-brown hair a yard long, her slender elegance and floating walk, her sparkling moods when she was the "incarnation of charm," she suffered also from "court-ball headaches," and could not appear in public without holding a fan before her face. She was "a fairies' child," wrote Carmen Sylva, the Queen of Rumania, "with hidden wings, who flies away whenever she finds the world unbearable." She wrote sad romantic poetry and had seen her son's life end in the most melodramatic suicide of the century. Her first cousin, King Ludwig of Bavaria, had died insane by drowning; her husband's brother, Maximilian, by firing squad in Mexico; her sister by fire at a charity bazaar in Paris. "I feel the burden of life so heavily," she wrote her daughter, "that it is often like a physical pain and I would far rather be dead." She would rush off to

England or Ireland to spend weeks in the hunting field riding recklessly over the most breakneck fences. In Vienna she took lessons in the most dangerous tricks of circus riding. At times she adopted frenetic diets, reducing her nourishment to an orange or a glass of milk a day, and when her health could no longer sustain hunting, she indulged in orgies of walking for six or eight hours at a time at a forced pace no companion could keep up with. What she was seeking was plain: "I long for death," she wrote her daughter four months before she reached Geneva.

On September 9 she visited the lakeside villa of the Baroness Adolfe de Rothschild, a remote, enchanted world where tame miniature porcupines from Java and exotic colored birds decorated a private park planted with cedars of Lebanon. As she left her hotel next morning to take the lake steamer, the Italian, Lucheni, was waiting outside on the street.

He had come from Lausanne, where he recently had been reported to the police as a suspicious character. The orderly of a hospital where he had been taken for an injury suffered during a building job had found among his belongings a notebook containing Anarchist songs and the drawing of a bludgeon labeled "*Anarchia*" and underneath, in Italian, "For Humbert I." Accustomed to misfits, radicals and exiles of all kinds, the Swiss police had not considered this sufficient cause for arrest or surveillance.

According to what he told the hospital orderly, Lucheni's mother, pregnant at eighteen with an illegitimate child, had made her way to Paris to give birth among the anonymous millions of a great city. Later she was able to return to Italy, where she left her child in the poorhouse in Parma and disappeared to America.

At nine the boy was a day laborer on an Italian railroad. Later when drafted into a cavalry regiment of the Italian Army, he made a good record and was promoted to corporal. Upon his discharge in 1897, having neither savings nor prospects, he became manservant to his former Captain, the Prince d'Aragona, but on being denied a raise, left in anger. Later he asked to come back, but the Prince, considering him too insubordinate for domestic service, refused. Resentful and jobless, Lucheni took to reading *L'Agitatore*, *Il Socialista*, *Avanti* and other revolutionary papers and pamphlets whose theme at the moment was the rottenness of bourgeois society as demonstrated by the Dreyfus case. A single Samson, they indicated, could bring down the State at a blow. Lucheni, now in Lausanne, sent clippings from these papers with his comments to comrades in his former cavalry regiment. Apropos of a workman killed in a quarrel, he remarked to a friend at this time, "Ah, how I'd like to kill somebody. But it must be someone important so it gets into the papers." He attended meetings of Italian Anarchists who fiercely discussed plans to shake the world by a great deed, of which the favored victim was to be King Humbert of Italy.

Meanwhile the Swiss papers reported the coming visit of the Empress Elizabeth to Geneva. Lucheni tried to buy a stiletto but lacked the necessary 12 francs. In its place he fashioned a homemade dagger out of an old file, carefully sharpened and fitted to a handle made from a piece of firewood. As the Empress and her lady-in-waiting, Countess Sztaray, walked toward the Quai Mont Blanc, Lucheni stood in their path. He rushed upon them with hand upraised, stopped and peered beneath her parasol to make sure of the Empress' identity, then stabbed her through the heart. She died four hours later. Lucheni, seized by two gendarmes, was caught in his great moment by an alert passer-by with a camera. The picture shows him walking jauntily between his captors with a satisfied smile, almost a smirk, on his face. At the police station he eagerly described all his proceedings and preparations and when later it was learned that the Empress had died, expressed himself as "delighted." He declared himself an Anarchist and insisted on its being understood that he had acted on his own initiative and not as a member of any group or party. Asked why he had killed the Empress, he replied, "As part of the war on the rich and the great. . . . It will be Humbert's turn next."

From prison he wrote letters to the President of Switzerland and to the newspapers proclaiming his creed and the coming downfall of the State, and signing himself, "Luigi Lucheni, Anarchist, and one of the most dangerous of them." To the Princess d'Aragona he wrote, "My case is comparable to the Dreyfus case." Yet behind the poor foolish megalomania, even in Lucheni, glowed the Idea, for he also wrote to the Princess that he had learned enough of the world during his twenty-five years in it to feel that "never in my life have I felt so contented as now. . . . I have made known to the world that the hour is not far distant when a new sun will shine upon all men alike."

There being no death penalty in Geneva, Lucheni was sentenced to life imprisonment. Twelve years later, after a quarrel with the warder which resulted in his being given a term of solitary confinement, he hanged himself by his belt.

In the month following the Empress' death, the Kaiser, Wilhelm II, in the course of a widely heralded royal progress to Jerusalem, was the most conspicuous ruler of the moment. Police rounded up all known Anarchists along the route and international excitement reached a peak when an Italian Anarchist was arrested in Alexandria in possession of two bombs, a ticket for Haifa and obviously murderous intent upon the Kaiser. That sovereign had little to fear, however, from the Anarchists of his own country, for the two who had attempted to kill his grandfather were the last and only activists. Otherwise, German Anarchists remained theorists, except for those who got away to America. Germans were not fit for Anarchism, as Bakunin had said with disdain, for with their passion for Authority, "they want to be at once both masters and slaves and Anarchism accepts neither."

The assassins of the President of France, the Premier of Spain, and the Empress of Austria, as well as the would-be assassins of the Kaiser, had all been Italians. Inside Italy itself, in 1897, an Anarchist blacksmith named Pietro Acciarito had attempted to kill King Humbert, leaping upon him in his carriage with a dagger in the identical manner of Caserio upon President Carnot. More alert than Carnot to these occupational hazards, the King jumped aside, escaped the blow, and remarking with a shrug to his escort, "*Sono gli incerti del mestiere*" ("These are the risks of the job"), ordered his coachman to drive on. Acciarito told the police that he would have preferred to have "stuck that old monkey" Pope Leo XIII, but that as he could not get inside the Vatican, he chose to attack the monarchy as the next evil after the papacy.

The hatred for constituted society that seethed in the lower classes and the helplessness of society to defend itself against these attacks was becoming more and more apparent. As usual, the police, in wishful hunt for a "plot," arrested half a dozen alleged accomplices of Acciarito, none of whom in the end could be proved to have had any connection with him. Plots by groups or parties could be dealt with; there were always informers. But how could the sudden spring of these solitary tigers be prevented?

So serious was the problem that the Italian Government convened an international conference of police and home ministry officials in Rome in November, 1898, to try to work out a solution. Secret sessions lasted for a month with no known result except the admirable if negative one that Belgium, Switzerland and Great Britain refused to give up the traditional right of asylum or agree to surrender suspected Anarchists upon demand of their native countries.

In the following year, 1899, there were bread riots in Italy, caused by taxes and an import duty on grain, which the Anarchists saw as another aspect of the war on the poor by the State. The riots spread north and south despite repressive measures and bloody collision between troops and people. In Milan, streetcars were overturned to make barricades, people hurled stones at police armed with guns, women threw themselves in front of trains to prevent the arrival of troops, a state of siege was declared, and all Tuscany put under martial law. The cry that at last the revolution had come brought thousands of Italian workmen back from Spain, Switzerland and the south of France to take part. Control was only regained by the dispatch of half an army corps to Milan. All Socialist and revolutionary papers were suppressed, parliament was prorogued, and although the Government succeeded in re-establishing order, it was only on the surface.

The inoffensive monarch who found himself presiding over this situation had a fierce white moustache, personal courage, a gallant soul and no more noticeable talent for kingship than any of the House of Savoy. Humbert was passionately fond of horses and hunting, totally impervious to the arts, which he left to the patronage of his Queen, and very regular in his habits. He rose at six every morning, attended to the management of his private estates (whose revenues were large and deposited in the Bank of England), visited his stables and drove out in his carriage every afternoon at the same hour over the same route through the Borghese Gardens. Every evening at the same hour he visited a lady to whom he had remained devotedly faithful since before his marriage thirty years earlier. On July 29, 1900, he was distributing prizes from his carriage to athletic competitors in Monza, the royal summer residence near Milan, when he was shot four times by a man who stepped up to the carriage and fired at hardly two yards' distance. The King gazed at him reproachfully for a moment, then fell over against the shoulder of his aide-de-camp, murmured "*Avanti!*" to his coachman and expired.

The assassin, "holding his smoking weapon exultantly aloft," was immediately seized. He was identified as Gaetano Bresci, a thirty-year-old Anarchist and silk-weaver who had come from Paterson, New Jersey, to Italy with intent to assassinate the King. His act was the only instance of Anarchist propaganda of the deed for which there is some evidence, though unproven, of previous conspiracy.

Paterson was a center of Italians and of Anarchism. Certainly the Anarchists of Paterson held many meetings and heatedly discussed a Deed which would be the signal for overthrow of the oppressor. Certainly the King of Italy figured as their preferred target, but whether, as charged in reports after the event, lots were actually chosen to select the person to do the deed, or whether the discussions simply inspired Bresci to act of his own accord, is not certain. The picture of a cabal of Anarchists in a cellar drawing lots to select an assassin was a favorite journalistic imagery of the time.

One imaginative reporter pictured Bresci as having been "indoctrinated" by Malatesta, "the head and moving spirit of all the conspiracies which have recently startled the world by their awful success." He claimed that Malatesta had been glimpsed quietly drinking at an Italian bar in Paterson, but the police found no evidence that Bresci had ever met Malatesta. He had, however, either obtained or been given a revolver in Paterson with which he practiced shooting in the woods while his wife and three-year-old daughter picked flowers nearby. Also, he was given by his comrades, or somehow obtained, money to buy a steerage ticket on the French Line with enough left over to make his way from Le Havre to Italy.

"He was not insane enough to expect that the change of

Government would follow his act," explained Pedro Esteve, editor of the Paterson Anarchist journal, to a reporter. "But how else could he let the people of Italy know that there was any such force in the world as Anarchy?" An amiable and scholarly person whose bookshelves held the works of Emerson next to those of Jean Grave, Esteve accepted as quite reasonable that one of his own readers should go out and express the protest of the masses in a magnificent gesture.

Bresci's comrades sent him a congratulatory telegram in prison and wore his picture on buttons in their coat lapels. They also insisted at a mass meeting in Paterson, attended by over a thousand persons, that there had been no plot. "We don't need to make plots or talk," said Esteve, who was the principal speaker. "If you are an Anarchist you know what to do and you do it individually and of your own accord."

Bresci himself suffered the same fate as other instruments of the Idea. As Italy had abolished the death penalty, he was sentenced to life imprisonment, the first seven years to be spent in solitary confinement. After the first few months he killed himself in prison.

In the United States the newspaper account of King Humbert's assassination was read over and over again by a Polish-American named Leon Czolgosz. The clipping became a precious possession which he took to bed with him every night. Twenty-eight at this time, he was small and slight, with a peculiar fixed gaze in his light-blue eyes. Born in the United States shortly after his parents came to America, he was one of six brothers and two sisters, and lived with his family on a small farm in Ohio. According to his father, he had "the appearance of thinking more than most children," and because of his fondness for reading, was considered the intellectual of the family. In 1893, when he was twenty years old, he had been laid off during a strike in the wire factory where he worked, and afterward, according to his brother, "he got quiet and not so happy." Prayer and the local priest having proved ineffective, he broke away from the Catholic Church, took to reading pamphlets issued by "Free Thinkers" and through these became interested in political radicalism. He joined a Polish workers' circle where Socialism and Anarchism were among the topics discussed, and also, as he said later, "we discussed Presidents and that they were no good."

In 1898 he suffered some undefined illness which left him moody and dull. He gave up work, stayed home, took his meals upstairs to his bedroom, kept to himself, read the Chicago Anarchist paper *Free Society* and Bellamy's utopia, *Looking Backward*, and brooded. He made trips to Chicago and Cleveland, where he attended Anarchist meetings, heard speeches by Emma Goldman and had talks with an Anarchist named Emil Schilling to whom he expressed himself as troubled by the conduct of the American Army, which, after liberating the Philippines from Spain, was now engaged in war upon the Filipinos. "It does not harmonize with the teaching in our public schools about our flag," said Czolgosz worriedly.

As flags were a matter of no respect to Anarchists, Schilling became suspicious of him and published a warning in *Free Society* that the oddly behaved Polish visitor might be an *agent provocateur*. This was on September 1, 1901, and was wide of the mark. Five days later Czolgosz turned up in Buffalo, where, in a receiving line at the Pan-American Exposition, he shot President McKinley. The President died eight days later and was succeeded by Theodore Roosevelt. Thus Czolgosz, on the lowest level of understanding among Anarchist assassins, performed of them all the act with the greatest consequences.

"I killed President McKinley," Czolgosz wrote in his confession, "because I done my duty," and later added, "because he was an enemy of the good working people." He told reporters that he had heard Emma Goldman lecture and her doctrine "that all rulers should be exterminated . . . set me to thinking so that my head nearly split with pain." He said, "McKinley was going around the country shouting prosperity when there was no prosperity for the poor man." And further, "I don't believe we should have any rulers. It is right to kill them. . . . I know other men who believe what I do that it would be a good thing to kill the President and to have no rulers. . . . I don't believe in voting; it is against my principles. I am an Anarchist. I don't believe in marriage. I believe in free love."

The Idea of Anarchism, its vision of a better society, had not come within Czolgosz's ken. Like Caserio, the simple assassin of President Carnot, he was of the type of regicide who becomes obsessed by the delusion that it is his mission to kill the sovereign. This was brought out, shortly after Czolgosz's hurried trial and electrocution on October 29, by Dr. Walter Channing, Professor of Mental Diseases at Tufts, and son of the poet William Ellery Channing. Dissatisfied with the official alienists' report, Channing made his own study and concluded that Czolgosz had been "drifting in the direction of *dementia praecox*" and was a victim of a delusion already isolated and described by a French alienist, Dr. Emanuel Regis, in 1890. According to Dr. Regis, the regicide type is much given to cogitations and solitude and "whatever sane reason he may have possessed gives way to a sickly fixation that he is called on to deal a great blow, sacrifice his life to a just cause and kill a monarch or a dignitary in the name of God, Country, Liberty, Anarchy or some analogous principle." He is characterized by premeditation and obsession. He does not act suddenly or blindly, but on the contrary, prepares carefully and alone. He is a *solitaire*. Proud of his mission and his role, he acts always in daylight and in public, and never uses a secret weapon like poison but one that demands personal violence. Afterwards, he does not seek to escape but exhibits pride in his deed and desire for glory and for death, either by suicide or "indirect suicide" as an executed martyr.

The description fits, but for the delusions to become active there is required a certain climate of protest—and an example. This the Anarchist creed and deeds provided. There may be at any time a hundred Czolgoszes living mute, inactive lives; it took the series of acts from Ravachol to Bresci to inspire one to kill the President of the United States.

The public was by now thoroughly aroused, and the public was composed not only of the rich but of the imitators of the rich. The ordinary man, the petty bourgeois, the salaried employee, associated himself—as Emile Henry knew when he threw his bomb in the Café Terminus—with his employers. His living, as he thought, depended on their property. When this was threatened, he felt threatened. He felt a peculiar horror at the Anarchist's desire to destroy the foundations on which everyday life was based; the flag, the legal family, marriage, the church, the vote, the law. The Anarchist became everybody's enemy. His sinister figure became synonymous with everything wicked and subversive, synonymous, said a professor of political science in *Harper's Weekly*, with "the king of all Anarchists, the arch-rebel Satan." His doctrine, said the *Century Magazine* after the death of McKinley, "bodes more evil to the world than any previous conception of human relations."

The new President, an extraordinarily mixed man equally capable of subtle understanding, courageous action and extremes of banality, saw in the Anarchist simply a criminal, more "dangerous" and "depraved" than the ordinary kind. In his message to Congress on December 3, 1901, Theodore Roosevelt said, "Anarchism is a crime against the whole human race and all mankind should band against the Anarchist." He was not the product of social or political injustice and his protest of concern for the workingman was "outrageous." The institutions of the United States, the President insisted, offered open opportunity "to every honest and intelligent son of toil." He urged that Anarchist speeches, writings and meetings should henceforth be treated as seditious, that Anarchists should no longer be allowed at large, those already in the country should be deported, Congress should "exclude absolutely all persons who are known to be believers in Anarchistic principles or members of Anarchistic societies," and their advocacy of killing should by treaty be made an offense against international law, like piracy, so that the federal government would have the power to deal with them.

After much discussion and not without strong objections to the denial of the traditional right of ingress, Congress in 1903 amended the Immigration Act to exclude persons disbelieving in or "teaching disbelief in or opposition to all organized government." The amendment provoked liberal outcries and sorrowful references to the Statue of Liberty.

Of the dual nature of Anarchism, half hatred of society, half love of humanity, the public was aware only of the first. It was the bombs and explosions, the gunshots and the daggers, that impressed them. They knew nothing of the other side of Anarchism which hoped to lead humanity through the slough of violence to the Delectable Mountains. The press showed them Malatesta, for instance, as the evil genius of Anarchism, "silent, cold, plotting." It did not show him as the man whose philosophy of altruism caused him to deed two houses he inherited from his parents in Italy to the tenants inhabiting them. Since the public likewise knew nothing of the theory of propaganda by the deed, it could make no sense of the Anarchist acts. They seemed purposeless, mad, a pure indulgence in evil for its own sake. The press customarily referred to Anarchists as "wild beasts," "crypto-lunatics," degenerates, criminals, cowards, felons, "odious fanatics prompted by perverted intellect and morbid frenzy." "The mad dog is the closest parallel in nature to the Anarchist," pronounced *Blackwood's*, the dignified British monthly. How was it possible, asked Carl Schurz after the murder of Canovas, to protect society against "a combination of crazy people and criminals"?

That was the unanswerable question. All sorts of proposals were put forward, including the establishment of an international penal colony for Anarchists, or disposal of them in hospitals for the insane, or universal deportation, although it was not explained what country would receive them if every country was engaged in sending them away.

Yet the cry of protest in the throat of every Anarchist act was heard by some, and understood. In the midst of the hysteria over McKinley, Lyman Abbott, editor of the *Outlook* and a spokesman of the New England tradition which had produced the Abolitionists, had the courage to ask if the Anarchist's hatred of government and law did not derive from the fact that government and law operated unjustly. So long, he said, as legislators legislate for special classes, "encourage the spoliation of the many for the benefit of the few, protect the rich and forget the poor," so long will Anarchism "demand the abolition of all law because it sees in law only an instrument of injustice." Speaking to the comfortable gentlemen of the Nineteenth Century Club, he suggested that "the place to attack Anarchism is where the offenses grow." He was echoing a concern that was already expressing itself in movements of reform, in Jane Addams and the social welfare work she inspired from Hull House, in the Muckrakers who within a year or two were to begin exposing the areas of injustice, rottenness and corruption in American life.

With McKinley the era of Anarchist assassinations came to

an end in the western democracies. Even Alexander Berkman in his prison cell recognized, as he wrote to Emma Goldman, the futility of individual acts of violence in the absence of a revolutionary-minded proletariat. This second disavowal sent his correspondent, who still believed, into "uncontrollable sobbing," and left her "shaken to the roots," so that she took to her bed, ill. Although she retained an ardent following, especially among the press, who referred to her as the "Queen of the Anarchists," Anarchist passion on the whole passed, as it had in France, into the more realistic combat of the Syndicalist unions. In the United States it was absorbed into the Industrial Workers of the World, founded in 1905, although in every country there remained irreconcilables who stayed lonely and true to the original creed.

In the two countries on Europe's rim, Spain and Russia, each industrially backward and despotically governed, bombs and assassinations mounted as the world moved into the Twentieth Century. When in Spain a bomb was thrown at King Alfonso and his young English bride on their wedding day in 1906, killing twenty bystanders, it spread a fearful recognition of the deep reservoir of hatred which could have impelled such a deed. The reciprocal hatred of the ruling class was confirmed in 1909, when as a result of an abortive revolt in Barcelona known as "Red Week," the Government executed Francisco Ferrer, a radical and anti-clerical educator, though not a true Anarchist. The case raised storms of protest in the rest of Europe, where, as usual, Spanish iniquities provided a vent for liberal consciences. In 1912 a Spanish Anarchist named Manuel Pardinas stalked the Premier, José Canalejas, through the streets of Madrid and shot him dead from behind as he was looking into the window of a bookstore in the Puerta del Sol. It was a poor choice, for Canalejas, carried into office in the wake of Ferrer's death, was attempting some reforms of the unbridled power of Church and landlords, but it was evidence that in their continuing combat against society, Spanish Anarchists were moved, as Shaw wrote, by "consciences outraged beyond endurance."

In Russia the tradition of revolution was old and deep and as full of despair as of hope. Each generation turned up new fighters in the long war between rebel and despot. In 1887, the year the Haymarket Anarchists were hanged, five students of the University of St. Petersburg were hanged for the attempted murder by bomb of Alexander III. Their leader, Alexander Ulyanov, justified the use of terror at his trial as the only method possible in a police state. He was one of three brothers and three sisters, all revolutionaries, of whom a younger brother, Vladimir Ilyich, swore revenge, changed his last name to Lenin, and went forth to work for revolution.

Increasing unrest during the nineties encouraged the revolutionists to believe that the time was ripening for insurrection. A new Czar who was that most dangerous of rulers, a weak autocrat, marked his accession as Nicholas II in 1895 by flatly dismissing all pleas for a constitution as "nonsensical dreams," thereby causing democrats to despair and extremists to exult. In the cities, strikes by newly industrialized workers followed one upon another. Over all, exerting a mysterious intangible pull, like the moon upon the tides, loomed the approaching moment of the end of the century. There was a sense of an end and a beginning, of "a time to break."

All the groups of discontent felt the need to prepare for a time of action, to gather their strength in parties and to state their program. But there was conflict between the followers of Marxism, with its hard-bitten insistence on organization and training, and the inheritors of the Narodniki tradition, who believed in spontaneous revolution brought on by some deed of terror. As a result, two parties took shape in the years 1897 and 1898, the Marxist Social-Democratic party on the one hand, and on the other, the Populist Socialist-Revolutionaries, whose various groups merged into a definitive party in 1901.

In so far as they accepted organization as a party, the Socialist-Revolutionaries were not Anarchists of the true breed, but they shared the Anarchists' belief that deeds of terror could precipitate revolution. Like them they saw revolution as a sunburst on the horizon under whose benevolent beams the future would take care of itself. The public's identification of Anarchists with Russians stemmed partly from their addiction to the bomb, which, ever since the killing of the Czar in 1881, seemed peculiarly a Russian weapon, and partly from the unconscious syllogism: Russians were revolutionists; Anarchists were revolutionists; ergo, Anarchists were Russians. Orthodox Anarchists, of whom there were small groups who published Russian-language journals in Geneva and Paris, and took their inspiration from Kropotkin, were not a significant force inside Russia.

In 1902 Maxim Gorky put into *The Lower Depths* all the woe, the wretchedness and the despair of Russia. "Man must live for something better!" cries the drunken cardsharp in the play, "something better," and searching for words, for meaning, for a philosophy, he can only repeat, "something better." Toward that end, in the years 1901–03 the Terror Brigade of the Socialist Revolutionaries assassinated the Minister of Education, Bogolepov; the Minister of Interior, Sipiagin, who directed the Secret Police; and the Governor of Ufa, Bogdanovitch, who had put down a miners' strike in the Urals with particular brutality. On July 15, 1904, in the midst of the Russo-Japanese War, they disposed of a second Minister of Interior, Wenzel von Plehve, the most hated man in Russia. An ultra-reactionary, Plehve was if anything even firmer than the Czar in the belief that autocracy must be kept unimpaired by the slightest concession to democratic processes. His sole policy was to smash every possible source of antipathy to the regime. He arrested revolutionaries, suppressed the orthodox "old believers," restricted the *zemstvos*, or village governments, victimized the Jews, forcibly Russified the Poles, Finns and Armenians and, as a result, increased the enemies of Czarism, and convinced them of the need for a final change.

A method he favored for diverting popular discontent was expressed to a colleague in the words, "We must drown the revolution in Jewish blood." Stirred up by his agents, watched tolerantly by the police, Russian citizens of Kishinev during the Passover of 1903 burst into a frenzy of violence against the eternal scapegoat, killing and beating, burning and plundering homes and shops, desecrating synagogues, tearing the sacred Torah from the arms of a white-bearded rabbi whose horror at seeing it defiled by Gentiles was shortened by his death under their clubs and boots. The Kishinev pogrom not only resounded around the world but succeeded in penetrating under the skin of the leader of the Terror Brigade, Evno Azev, who was at the same time an agent of the Secret Police and also happened to be a Jew. Azev took care not to inform on the plan for the assassination of Plehve which duly took place. It made an enormous impression upon everyone in Russia as a terrible blow against the system of which Plehve was the incarnation. So ominous did it seem that the assassin was condemned to hard labour in Siberia for life instead of to death by Plehve's successor, Prince Svyatopolk-Mirsky, in the hope that a mild policy might accomplish something.

Six months later, in January, 1905, occurred the massacre in front of the Winter Palace known as "Bloody Sunday," when troops fired on a crowd of workingmen who had come to petition the Czar for a constitution. About one thousand were killed. The terrorists now made plans to assassinate the Czar and his uncles, the Grand Duke Vladimir, who was held responsible for the massacre, and the Grand Duke Sergei, who was said to be the person with the greatest influence on the Czar. As Governor-General of Moscow, Sergei was known for the merciless brutality of his rule, for a capricious and domineering character and extremes of autocratic temperament bordering on derangement. According to an English observer, he was "conspicuous for his cruelty and renowned, even among the Russian aristocracy, for the peculiarity of his vices." Although in the pay of the police, Azev had to allow the Brigade enough successes to satisfy them and to maintain his position as their chief, without which he would have been of far less value to the police. In February, 1905, Sergei was blown up with a bomb thrown by a young revolutionary named Kaliaev who was left standing alive in the midst of the debris, in his old blue coat with a red scarf, his face bleeding, but otherwise unhurt. All that was left of the Grand Duke and of his carriage and horses was "a formless mass of fragments about eight or ten inches high." That evening when the Czar heard the news he came down to dinner as usual and did not mention the murder, but, according to a guest who was present, "after dinner the Czar and his brother-in-law amused themselves by trying to edge one another off the long narrow sofa."

At his trial in April, 1905, Kaliaev, thin, haggard and with eyes sunken in their sockets, said to the judges, "We are two warring camps, . . . two worlds in furious collision. You, the representatives of capital and oppression; I, one of the avengers of the people." Russia was in the midst of war, outside against the Japanese, and inside against her own people, who were in open revolt. "What does all this mean? It is the judgment of history upon you." When sentence of death was pronounced, Kaliaev said he hoped his executioners would have the courage to carry it out openly and publicly. "Learn to look the advancing revolution straight in the eye," he told the Court. But he was hanged, dressed in black, after midnight in the prison yard and buried beneath the prison wall.

In October the Revolution came; propaganda of the deed, in the murders of von Plehve and the Grand Duke Sergei, had helped to excite the nerves of the masses toward the point of insurrection. Neither organized nor led by the Socialist-Revolutionaries, Social-Democrats or Anarchists, it was the spontaneous revolution Bakunin had believed in and did not live to see. In accordance with Syndicalist theory it erupted out of a general strike by the workers, and during the regime's first fright, succeeded in forcing the concession of a constitution and a Duma. Although these were subsequently withdrawn, and the Revolution, when the regime had recovered its nerve, ferociously suppressed, it heartened the Syndicalists' belief in "direct action" through the general strike, and re-enforced the movement of Anarchists into the industrial unions. In Russia the Terror Brigade accomplished several more deaths before it disintegrated under the shock of the exposure of Azev in 1908. By the time the Premier, Stolypin, was assassinated in 1911 the half-lunatic world of the Romanov twilight had so darkened that it was never clear whether the assassins were genuine revolutionaries or *agents provocateurs* of the police.

However self-limited its acts, however visionary its dream, Anarchism had terribly dramatized the war between the two divisions of society, between the world of privilege and the world of protest. In the one it shook awake a social conscience; in the other, as its energy passed into Syndicalism, it added its quality of violence and extremism to the struggle for power of organized labour. It was an idea which drew men to follow it but because of its built-in paradox could not draw them together into a group capable of concerted action. It was the last cry of individual man, the last movement among the masses on behalf of individual liberty, the last hope of living unregulated, the last fist shaken against the encroaching State, before the State, the party, the union, the organization closed in.

3

END OF A DREAM

THE UNITED STATES: 1890–1902

3

End of a Dream

IN THE United States on the opening of Congress in January, 1890, a newly elected Speaker of the House of Representatives was in the Chair. A physical giant, six feet three inches tall, weighing almost three hundred pounds and dressed completely in black, "out of whose collar rose an enormous clean-shaven baby face like a Casaba melon flowering from a fat black stalk, he was a subject for a Frans Hals, with long white fingers that would have enraptured a Memling." Speaking in a slow drawl, he delighted to drop cool pearls of sarcasm into the most heated rhetoric and to watch the resulting fizzle with the bland gravity of a New England Buddha. When a wordy perennial, Representative Springer of Illinois, was declaiming to the House his passionate preference to be right rather than President, the Speaker interjected, "The gentleman need not be disturbed; he will never be either." When another member, notorious for ill-digested opinions and a halting manner, began some remarks with, "I was thinking, Mr. Speaker, I was thinking . . . ." the Chair expressed the hope that "no one will interrupt the gentleman's commendable innovation." Of two particularly inept speakers, he remarked, "They never open their mouths without subtracting from the sum of human knowledge." It was said that he would rather make an epigram than a friend. Yet among the select who were his chosen friends he was known as "one of the most genial souls that ever enlivened a company," whose conversation, "sparkling with good nature, was better than the best champagne." He was Thomas B. Reed, Republican of Maine, aged fifty. Already acknowledged after fourteen years in Congress as "the ablest running debater the American people ever saw," he would, before the end of the session, be called "the greatest parliamentary leader of his time, . . . far and away the most brilliant figure in American politics."

Although his roots went back to the beginning of New England, Reed was not nurtured for a political career by inherited wealth, social position or landed estate. Politics in America made no use of these qualities, and men who possessed them were not in politics. Well-to-do, long-established families did not shoulder—but shunned—the responsibilities of government. Henry Adams' eldest brother, John, "regarded as the most brilliant of the family and the most certain of high distinction," who made a fortune in the Union Pacific Railroad, "drew himself back" from government, according to his brother. "He had all he wanted; wealth, children, society, consideration; and he laughed at the idea of sacrificing himself in order to adorn a Cleveland Cabinet or get cheers from an Irish mob." This attitude was not confined to the rather worn-out Adamses. When the young Theodore Roosevelt announced his intention of entering politics in New York in 1880, he was laughed at by the "men of cultivated and easy life" who told him politics were "low" and run by "saloon-keepers, horse-car conductors and the like," whom he would find "rough, brutal and unpleasant to deal with."

The abdication of the rich was born out of the success of the American Revolution and the defeat of Hamilton's design to organize the State in the interests of the governing class. Jefferson's principles and Jackson's democracy had won. The founding fathers and the signers of the Declaration had been in the majority men of property and position, but the very success of their accomplishment ended by discouraging men of their own kind from participating in government. With the establishment of universal manhood suffrage, men of property found themselves counting for no more at the polls than the common man; being far outnumbered they retired from the combat. No President after the first six came from a well-established family (unless the Harrisons could be considered to so qualify). Retreating to the comfort of their homes and the pursuits of their class, they left government increasingly to hard-driving newcomers pushing up from below. Such energies as they had they devoted to making money in banking and trade, rather than from the land which they gradually abandoned. The great estates of the Dutch-descended patroons of New York declined first; the Southern plantations went with the Civil War; Boston's old families remained active and prosperous but on the whole aloof from government. The proud

"Hub" had produced no President after the first two Adamses. "The most valuable, most moderate, able and cultivated part of the population," wrote Emerson, in his essay on Politics, "is timid and merely defensive of property."

Forty years later the Englishman James Bryce was struck by the "apathy among the luxurious classes and fastidious minds," and devoted a whole chapter in *The American Commonwealth* to "Why the Best Men Do Not Go into Politics." They lacked a sense of noblesse oblige. The "indifference of the educated and wealthy classes" was due partly, he thought, to the lack of respect in which they were held by the masses. "Since the masses do not look to them for guidance, they do not come forward to give it."

Without land to hold on to, a hereditary governing class had failed to develop, and the absence of such a class bound by a traditional morality left America open to the unrestricted exploits of the "plungers" and plunderers, the builders and malefactors and profiteers—and through them to the corruption of politics. With the great release and surge of enterprise after the Civil War, America was in a period of unprecedented expansion. The population increased by 50 per cent from fifty million to seventy-five million in the years 1880–1900. With opportunity opening on every hand, government in America through the seventies and eighties functioned chiefly to make the country safe—and lucrative—for the capitalist. Government was a paid agent. Its scandals and deals, becoming blatant, had aroused anger and people were demanding reform. But meanwhile gentlemen did not "stoop to politics," as Edith Wharton said of New York "Society." Few of her friends of "the best class" made use of their abilities or rendered the public services they could have. America "wasted this class instead of using it."

With no role in government and no security from the land, the American rich panicked easily. When the financial crisis of 1893 threatened the loss of John Adams' fortune, "he went all to pieces," wrote Henry. "The entire nervous system of Boston seemed to give way and he broke down with a whole crowd of other leading men. I have certainly no reason to think that any of us are stronger than he. My own nerves went to pieces long ago." Although many of his class were stronger-fibered than

Adams, they were a far cry from Lewis Morris, lord of the manor of Morrisania, who, when urged by his brother not to sign the Declaration of Independence because of the consequences to his property, replied, "Damn the consequences, give me the pen!"

Speaker Reed in character, intellect and a kind of brutal independence represented the best that America could put into politics in his time. He was sprung from a rib of that hard northern corner of New England with the uncompromising monosyllabic name. At the time of his birth in 1839 his ancestors had been living in Maine for two hundred years. Through his mother he was descended from a *Mayflower* passenger and through his father's mother from George Cleve, who came from England in 1632, built the first white man's house in Maine and was founder of the Portland Colony and its first Governor. The Reed who married Cleve's great-great-granddaughter came of a fishing and seafaring family. Never landed in a large sense, nor wealthy, these forbears and their neighbors had striven over the generations to maintain a settlement on the rock-ribbed soil, to survive Indian attack and isolation and snowbound winters. The habit of struggle against odds was bred into Thomas Reed's blood. His father, captain of a small coastal vessel, had mortgaged his home to send his son to Bowdoin. To maintain himself at college, Reed taught school, walking six miles to and from his lodgings each day. The sons of Portland families went to Bowdoin, not to satisfy social custom, but to gain a serious education. As most of them were situated in circumstances like Reed's, the semesters were arranged to allow for teaching school in winter. Reed intended himself for the ministry, but sitting up nights on the bed in his attic room reading aloud with a college friend Carlyle's *French Revolution*, Goethe's *Faust* and *Werther*, Macaulay's *Essays* and the novels of Thackeray and Charles Reade, he formed religious convictions that were too individual to submit to a formal creed. After graduating in 1861 he studied law while continuing to teach for $20 a month and "boarding round" in local families.

The Civil War did not engulf him until 1864 when he joined the Navy and saw service of a none too bellicose nature on a Mississippi gunboat. He was commissary officer and would freely admit in later life that he had never been under fire. The usual aura of glory and glitter of gallantry which gradually encrust most wartime memories were no part of Reed's. "What a charming life that was, that dear old life in the Navy," he would say when others took to recalling the war, "when I kept grocery on a gunboat. I knew all the regulations and the rest of them didn't. I had all my rights and most of theirs." He was to repeat the method and gain the same result in Congress.

When admitted to the bar in Maine in 1865, Reed was a tall, strong young man of twenty-five with a square handsome hard-boned face and thick blond hair. During the next ten years he served as City Counsel for Portland, was elected to the state Legislature and then to the state Senate, was appointed Attorney-General for Maine, married, and grew fat. He had two children, a son who died young and a daughter. His hair thinned until he was almost bald, his figure bellied out until, as he walked down the streets of Portland, he resembled "a human frigate among shallops." Silent, impassive, with an inward-turned eye, noticing no one, he moved along with the ponderous, gently swaying gait of an elephant. "How narrow he makes the street look!" a passer-by once exclaimed.

In 1876, Reed, now thirty-six, was elected to Congress in place of Blaine, who moved up to the Senate. As a member of the committee formed to investigate the Democrats' charges of electoral fraud in the Hayes-Tilden election, his cross-examination of witnesses drew spectators for its forensic artistry and made him nationally prominent. In subsequent Congresses he became a member of the all-important Rules Committee and chairman of the Judiciary Committee while session by session perfecting his knowledge of House procedure and parliamentary device.

A body of rules had grown up "calculated better than anything else," as a colleague said, "to obstruct legislation," a body as full of "intricacies and secrets" as the armamentarium of a medieval cabalist. Reed mastered it. "In my opinion there never has been a more perfectly equipped leader in any parliamentary body at any period," said a professional observer, Senator Henry Cabot Lodge, who had served with him for seven years in the House. Reed not only knew parliamentary practice and law but "understood as few men do the theory and philosophy of the system." Whether consciously or not, he was preparing for the time when as Speaker he would be able to impress upon the House a sense that no one on the floor could compete with the Chair in command of the rules.

Even with this he could not have imposed his authority if he had not also been "the finest, most effective debater," in Lodge's opinion, "that I have ever seen or heard." He never used an extra word, never stumbled in his syntax, was never at a loss, never forced to retreat or modify a position. He was instant in rejoinder, terse, forcible, lucid. He could state a case unanswerably, illuminate an issue, destroy an argument or expose a fallacy in fewer words than anyone else. His language was vivid and picturesque. "Hardly time to ripen a strawberry," he said to describe a lapse of two months. He had a way of phrasing things that was peculiarly apt and peculiarly his own. In an argument over which of two fellow members, Berry or Curtis, was the taller, he asked them to stand up and be measured. When Berry uncoiled slowly to his full height, Reed said, "My God, Berry, how much of yourself do you keep in your pockets?" His epigrams were famous. "All the wisdom in the world consists in shouting with the majority" was one. "A statesman is a politician who is dead" was another. He rarely made a gesture when speaking. "When he stood up," said Lodge, "waiting for an opponent to conclude, filling the narrow aisle, with his hands resting upon the desk, with every trace of expression banished from his face and looking as if he had not an idea and barely heard what was being said, then he was most dangerous." After one retort which left its victim limply speechless, Reed, looking about him sweetly, remarked, "Having embedded that fly in the liquid amber of my remarks, I will proceed."

His lucidity and logic were particularly effective under the "five-minute" rule. "Russell," he said to a Representative from Massachusetts, "you do not understand the theory of five-minute debate. The object is to convey to the House either information or misinformation. You have consumed several periods of five minutes this afternoon without doing either."

Reed made his point by narrating, not orating. Once when engaged in his favorite sport of baiting the adjoining chamber for which he felt a profound disrespect, he described a Presidential election fifty years in the future when by Constitutional amendment the President would be selected from among and by the Senators. "When the ballots had been collected and spread out, the Chief Justice who presided was observed to hesitate and those nearest could see by his pallor that something unexpected had happened. But with a strong effort he rose to his feet and through a megaphone, then recently invented by Edison, shouted to the vast multitude the astonishing result: seventy-six Senators had each received one vote."

Discussing economic privilege during a tariff debate he told how, when walking through the streets of New York and contrasting "the brownstone fronts of the rich merchants with the unrewarded virtue of the people on the sidewalk, my gorge rises, . . . I do not feel kindly to the people inside. But when I feel that way I know what the feeling is. It is good honest high-minded envy. When the gentlemen across the aisle have the same feeling they think it is political economy."

When word ran down the corridors that Reed was on his feet, about to speak, gossiping groups dissolved, members hurried to their seats, boredom and inattention vanished as the House listened expectantly for the sculptured prose, the prick of sarcasm and the flash of wit. Every member coveted the notoriety of debating with Reed, but he refused to be drawn by the "little fellows," reserving himself only for those he considered worthy opponents.

Reporters, in the hope of eliciting a witticism, were always asking him for comments on the news of the day. They were not always successful. Asked to comment on a Papal message, he replied, "The overpowering unimportance of this makes me speechless." Asked what was the greatest problem confronting the American people, he replied, "How to dodge a bicycle."

After his first term, his nomination as Representative of Maine's First District was never afterward contested. Elections were another matter and he almost lost the one of 1880 when he refused to compromise or equivocate on free silver despite strong "greenback" sentiment in Maine. He kept his seat on that occasion by only 109 votes. But as his fame grew he generally ran ahead of his ticket in the biennial elections. Even Democrats confessed to "voting for him on the sly." "He suited the taste of New England," said Senator Hoar of Massachusetts.

"The people liked to hear him on public questions better than any other man not excepting Blaine or McKinley." The reason was perhaps the same as that given by an Englishman to explain the secret of Palmerston's popularity: "What the nation likes in Palmerston is his you-be-damnedness!"

Though Reed scorned fence-building and never encouraged familiarity with the public, among intellectual equals "no more agreeable companion ever lived." In the small world that was then Washington's elite he was a jovial and radiant personality, a poker-player, storyteller and sought-after dinner guest. At one dinner party when the conversation turned on gambling, another famous raconteur, Senator Choate of New York, remarked somewhat unctuously that he had never made a bet on a horse or card or anything else in his life. "I wish I could say that," a fellow guest said earnestly. "Why caaan't you?" asked Reed with his peculiar twang. "Choate did."

His table talk was enriched by the resources of a cultivated mind. His favorite poets were Burns, Byron and Tennyson, his favorite novel Thackeray's *Vanity Fair.* He habitually read *Punch*, and Balzac in the original, of whom he said, "There is hardly a book of his which is not sad beyond words." He had learned French after he was forty and kept a diary in that language "for practise." The existence of a national library is owed to Reed, whose persistent and eloquent insistence finally wore out the natural parsimony of the House to secure adequate funds for the Library of Congress.

"No one was ever better to listen to or a better listener," said Lodge, "for his sympathies were wide, his interests unlimited and nothing human was alien to him." "We asked the Tom Reeds to dinner," wrote a young friend of Lodge from New York, "and he was delightful." Shortly afterward Reed, an advocate of civil service reform, obtained for the young man a post in Washington on the Civil Service Commission and thereafter, whenever the new Commissioner needed help on the Hill, Reed was ready to give it. Later when the young man from New York bestrode the national scene, Reed composed probably the most memorable tribute ever made to him: "Theodore, if there is one thing more than another for which I admire you, it is your original discovery of the Ten Commandments." With a little less prescience he had also said,

"Theodore will never be President; he has no political background."

In 1889, however, Theodore Roosevelt proved politically useful to Reed in his intra-party contest against McKinley, Joe Cannon and two others for the Speakership. While ranching and hunting in the Northwest, Roosevelt campaigned vigorously, and with success, to ensure that the four new states which had just entered the Union—Washington, Montana and the two Dakotas—would send Republicans to the next Congress. On his return to Washington he opened personal headquarters in a back room of the old Wormley Hotel where he "rounded up" the new Congressmen's votes for Reed. Although, to the despair of his supporters, Reed refused to fish for votes with the bait of promised committee appointments, he won nevertheless.

He now occupied the highest electoral office in the gift of his party next to the Presidency. "Ambitious as Lucifer," in the opinion of Representative Champ Clark, who knew him well, he did not intend to stop there. He was determined, on taking up the gavel as Speaker, to put into effect a plan on which he had long deliberated, consulting no one, and on which he risked his political future. He knew that the fight would focus upon him the nation's attention and also that if he failed his Congressional career would be over. The stakes were high: he would either break "the tyranny of the minority" by which the House was paralyzed into a state of "helpless inanity," or he would resign.

The system Speaker Reed had decided to challenge was known as the silent—or disappearing—quorum. It was a practice whereby the minority party could prevent any legislation obnoxious to it by refusing a quorum, that is, by demanding a roll call and then remaining silent when their names were called. Since the rules prescribed that a member's presence was established only by a viva voce reply to the roll, and since it required a majority of the whole to constitute a quorum, the silent filibuster could effectively stop the House from doing business.

The recent election of 1888 had been a Republican victory in which for the first time in sixteen years one party controlled both Executive and Congress. But by barely a hair. The dour

Benjamin Harrison was a minority President who had lost to Cleveland in popular vote and sat on that unstable throne so oddly carpentered by the electoral college system. The Republican majority in the House of 168–160 was wafer-thin, only three more than a quorum, which was set at 165. With this the Republicans faced the task of enacting two major pieces of party legislation, the Mills Bill for revising the tariff and the Force Bill directed against the poll tax and other Southern devices to keep the Negroes from voting. The Democrats were prepared to obstruct this legislation and also to prevent a vote on the seating of four Republicans, two of them Negroes, in contested elections from Southern districts.

To Reed the issue was survival of representative government. If the Democrats could prevent that legislation which the Republicans by virtue of their electoral victory could rightfully expect to enact, they would in effect be setting aside the verdict of the election. The rights of the minority, he believed, were preserved by freedom to debate and to vote but when the minority was able to frustrate action by the majority, "it becomes a tyranny." He believed that legislation, not merely deliberation, was the business of Congress. The duty of the Speaker to his party and country was to see that that business was accomplished, not merely to umpire debate.

The Speakership was a post of tremendous influence, still possessed of all the powers which in 1910, in the revolt against Joe Cannon, were to be transferred to the committees. Since the Speaker was ex officio Chairman of the Committee on Rules, whose two Republican and two Democratic members canceled each other out, and since he had the right to appoint all committees, the careers of members and the course of legislation depended upon his will. In Reed's hands was now the "power with responsibility," and notwithstanding a famous dictum, power has other effects than only to corrupt: it can also enlarge the understanding. It sometimes begets greatness. The Speaker's office, which the Washington *Post* called "no less consequential than the Presidency," could be the stepping stone to that ultimate peak. Reed was not the man either to miss his opportunity or to meet it feebly.

He reached his decision to attack the silent quorum, and planned his campaign, alone, partly because no one else would have thought there was a chance of success and partly because he was not sure that even his own party would support him. There were indications that they might not. Because of Reed's known views on the silent filibuster it was clear that quorum-counting would be an issue in the new Congress. REED WILL COUNT THEM, predicted a headline in the Washington *Post*, and the story beneath it said that even Mr. Cannon, Reed's closest lieutenant, was opposed to the attempt. The Democrats were manning their defences. Ex-Speaker Carlisle let it be known that any legislation enacted by a quorum which had not been established by a "recorded vote" would be taken to court as unconstitutional.

Reed, however, had satisfied himself that he would be upheld if it came to law, and on the attitude of his own party he was prepared to gamble. He shrewdly judged that the Democrats in their rage would provoke the Republicans to rally to his support. When the first of the contested elections appeared on the schedule for January 29 he was ready. As expected, the Democrats raised a cry of no quorum and demanded a roll call. It produced 163 yeas, all Republican, two less than a quorum. Reed's moment had come. Without a flicker of expression on the great white moon face, "the largest human face I ever saw," as a colleague described it, without any quickening of the drawling voice, he announced, "The Chair directs the Clerk to record the names of the following members present and refusing to vote," and began reading off the names himself. Instantly, according to a reporter, "pandemonium broke loose. The storm was furious . . . and it is to be doubted if ever there was such wild excitement, burning indignation, scathing denunciation and really dangerous conditions as existed in the House" during the next five days. Republicans were wildly applauding, all the Democrats were "yelling and shrieking and pounding their desks" while the voice of their future Speaker, Crisp of Georgia, boomed, "I appeal! I appeal from the decision of the Chair!" The explosion was "as violent as was ever witnessed in any parliament," a member recalled later. Unruffled, expressionless, the Speaker continued his counting, "Mr. Blanchard, Mr. Bland, Mr. Blount, Mr. Breckinridge of Arkansas, Mr. Breckinridge of Kentucky . . ."

Up jumped the Kentuckian, "famous for his silver hair and

silver tongue." "I deny the power of the Speaker and denounce it as revolutionary!" he called.

The resonant twang from the Chair continued unregarding, "Mr. Bullock, Mr. Bynum, Mr. Carlisle, Mr. Chipman, Mr. Clement, Mr. Covert, Mr. Crisp, Mr. Cummings"—through hisses and catcalls and cries of "Appeal!" irresistibly rolling down the alphabet—"Mr. Lawler, Mr. Lee, Mr. McAdoo, Mr. McCreary . . ."

"I deny your right, Mr. Speaker, to count me as present!" bellowed McCreary.

For the first time the Speaker stopped, held the hall in silence for a pause as an actor holds an audience, then blandly spoke: "The Chair is making a statement of fact that the gentleman is present. Does he deny it?"

He went on with his count, unmoved by the protests, denials, cries of "Order!" that rose to bedlam, through the *S*'s and *T*'s to the end. Then suddenly, seeming to gather all the power of his huge body, projecting all the force of his commanding personality and raising the voice which could fill any hall when he wanted, he announced, "The Chair thereupon rules that there is a quorum present within the meaning of the Constitution."

Tumult even worse than before followed. Breckinridge of Kentucky demanded a point of order on the ground that the Chair had no right to make such a ruling. "The Chair overrules the point of order," declared Reed coolly.

"I appeal the decision of the Chair!" shouted Breckinridge.

"I move to lay the appeal on the table," quickly interposed an alert Republican, Payson of Illinois. As this motion, if carried, would have shut off debate, the Democrats foamed with rage. A hundred of them "were on their feet howling for recognition," wrote a reporter. "Fighting Joe" Wheeler, the diminutive former Confederate cavalry general, unable to reach the front because of the crowded aisles, came down from the rear "leaping from desk to desk as an ibex leaps from crag to crag." As the excitement grew wilder, the only Democrat not on his feet was a huge Representative from Texas who sat in his seat significantly whetting a bowie knife on his boot. When a Republican member said he believed "we should have debate" on such an important matter, Reed allowed it. The debate was to last four days with the Democrats fighting every inch of the way, insisting on readings of every word of the Journal, on appeals and points of order and roll calls, each of which were met by Reed imperturbably counting off the silent members as present and evoking each time further infuriated defiance. Once Representative McKinley, striving to please as usual, inadvertently yielded the floor, and had to be prompted by Reed, "The gentleman from Ohio declines to be interrupted."

"I decline to be interrupted," echoed McKinley valiantly closing the breach.

As implacably at each juncture Reed counted heads and repeated his formula, "A Constitutional quorum is present to do business," the fury and frustration of the Democrats mounted. A group breathing maledictions advanced down the aisle threatening to pull him from the Chair and for a moment it looked to a spectator "as if they intended to mob the Speaker." Reed remained unmoved. Infected by the passion on the floor, visitors and correspondents in the galleries leaned over the railings to shake their fists at the Speaker and join in the abuse and profanity. "Decorum," lamented a reporter, "was altogether forgotten. Members rushed madly about the floor, the scowl of battle upon their brows, . . . shouting in a mad torrent of eloquent invective." They called Reed tyrant, despot and dictator, hurling epithets like stones. Among all the variants on the word "tyrant," "czar" emerged as the favorite, embodying for its time the image of unrestrained autocracy, and as "Czar" Reed, the Speaker was known thereafter. The angrier the Democrats became, the cooler Reed remained, bulking hugely in the chair, "serene as a summer morning." Although his secretary saw him in his private room, during an interval, gripping the desk and shaking with suppressed rage, he never gave a sign in the hall to show that the vicious abuse touched him. He maintained an iron control, "cool and determined as a highwayman," said the New York *Times*.

The secret of his self-possession, as he told a friend long afterward, was that he had his mind absolutely made up as to what he would do if the House did not sustain him. "I would simply have left the Chair and resigned the Speakership and my seat in Congress." He had a place waiting for him for the private practice of law in Elihu Root's New York firm, and "I had made up my mind that if political life consisted in sitting helplessly in the Speaker's Chair and seeing the majority helpless to pass legislation, I had had enough of it and was ready to step down and out." Coming to such a decision, he said, "you have made yourself equal to the worst" and are ready for it. This has a very "soothing" effect on the spirit.

It did more than soothe: it gave him an embedded strength which men who fear the worst, or will yield principles to avoid the worst, can never possess. It endowed him with a moral superiority over the House which members without knowing why could sense in the atmosphere.

Now the Democrats, changing their strategy, decided to absent themselves in actuality, counting on the inability of the Republicans to round up a quorum of themselves alone. As one by one the Democrats slipped out, Reed, divining their intention, ordered the doors locked. At once there followed a mad scramble to get out before the next vote. Losing "all sense of personal or official dignity," Democrats hid under desks and behind screens. Representative Kilgore of Texas, kicking open a locked door to make his escape, made "Kilgore's Kick" the delight of cartoonists.

On the fifth day, the Democrats absented themselves altogether and when a vote was called the Republicans were still short of a quorum. Two of their number were brought in on cots from their sickbeds. There was still one too few. One member was known to be on his way to Washington. Suddenly a door opened, and, as a reporter told it, "there was a flash of red whiskers and a voice saying, 'One more, Mr. Speaker.'" Sweney of Iowa was counted in, the quorum was filled, and the vote recorded at 166–0. The battle was over. Democrats sullenly filed back to their seats. The Rules Committee reported out a new set of rules, composed, needless to say, and imposed by the Chairman. Known thereafter as "Reed's Rules" and adopted on February 14, they provided among other things that (1) all members must vote; (2) one hundred shall constitute a quorum; (3) all present shall be counted; and (4) no dilatory motion shall be entertained and the definition of what is dilatory to be left to the judgment of the Speaker.

Five years later Theodore Roosevelt wrote that in destroying the silent filibuster, Reed's reform was of "far greater permanent importance" than any piece of legislation it brought to enactment at the time. Reed knew this as soon as he had won. In his speech closing the Fifty-first Congress he said that "the verdict of history" was the only one worth recording and he was confident of its outcome "because we have taken here so long a stride in the direction of responsible government."

More immediate than a verdict by history, and, indeed, then widely considered its equivalent, was a portrait by Sargent. Commissioned as a tribute to the Speaker by his Republican colleagues, it was a memorable failure. "He is supposed to be in the act of counting a quorum," a critic observed, "but in fact has just been inveigled into biting a green persimmon."

The death of the silent quorum was discussed in parliamentary bodies all over the world. At home it made Reed a leading political figure and obvious candidate for the Presidential nomination in 1892. But his time had not yet come, as he correctly judged, for when asked if he thought his party would nominate him, he replied, "They might do worse and I think they will."

They did. Reed's "czardom" was still resented and his sarcasm had not made friends. Nor did his disgust for deals, his refusal to woo the public with smiles and handshakes, or politicians with promises, enlarge his circle of supporters. The party regulars preferred to nominate the incumbent Harrison, incorruptible but sour, known as the "White House Iceberg," whom Reed disliked with no concealment whatever. When Harrison appointed as Collector of Portland, Reed's home town, a man Reed despised, he thereafter refused to enter the White House or meet Harrison until the day he died.

When, in 1892, the Democrats won control of the House by so large a majority that they could always assemble a quorum among themselves, they triumphantly threw out Reed's reform. He waited for history, not without some faith, as he used to say, that "the House has more sense than anyone in it." History did not keep him waiting long. In the next Congress, with the Democratic majority reduced by half and split over the currency and other heated issues, Reed enjoyed a delicious revenge. Over and over he demanded roll calls and when Bland of Missouri stormed against this "downright filibuster," he countered instantly, "Downright? You mean upright." His control over his party, as minority leader no less than as Speaker, remained total. "Gentlemen on that side blindly follow him," Speaker Crisp said wistfully. "You will hear them privately saying, 'Reed ought not to do that,' or 'This is wrong,' but when Reed says 'Do it,' they all step up and do it." When at last the Democrats had to give way, and for the sake of their own program, re-adopt his quorum-counting rule, Reed refrained from crowing. "This scene here today is a more effective address than any I could make," he said. "I congratulate the Fifty-third Congress."

In 1890, when the last armed conflict between Indians and whites in the United States took place at Wounded Knee Creek and the Census Bureau declared there was no longer a land frontier, a further test was shaping for Reed. In that year Captain A. T. Mahan, president of the Naval War College, announced in the *Atlantic Monthly*, "Whether they will or no, Americans must now begin to look outward."

A quiet, tight-lipped naval officer with one of the most forceful minds of his time, Alfred Thayer Mahan had selected himself to fill the country's need of "a voice to speak constantly of our external interests." Few Americans were aware that the United States had external interests and a large number believed she ought not to have them. The immediate issue was annexation of Hawaii. A naval coaling base at Pearl Harbor had been acquired in 1887, but the main impulse for annexation of the Islands came from American property interests there which were dominated by Judge Dole and the sugar trust. With the support of the United States Marines they engineered a revolt against the native Hawaiian government in January, 1893; Judge Dole became President Dole and promptly negotiated a treaty of annexation with the American Minister which President Harrison hurriedly sent to the Senate in February. Having been defeated for re-election by former President Cleveland, who was due to be inaugurated on March 4, Harrison asked for immediate action by the Senate in the hope of obtaining ratification before the new President could take office. The procedure was too raw and the Senate balked.

Opposed to expansion in any form, Cleveland was a man of

integrity, as well as shape, similar to Reed's. Once, when mistaken for Cleveland in an ill-lit room, Reed said, "Mercy! Don't tell Grover. He is too proud of his good looks already." Before he had been in office a week, Cleveland recalled the treaty of annexation from the Senate, much to the distress of Reed's young friend, Roosevelt, who felt "very strongly" about "hauling down the flag," as he called it.

The motive of the annexationists had been economic self-interest. It took Mahan to transform the issue into one of national and fateful importance. In the same March that Cleveland recalled the treaty, Mahan published an article in the *Forum* entitled "Hawaii and Our Future Sea Power," in which he declared that command of the seas was the chief element in the power and prosperity of nations and it was therefore "imperative to take possession, when it can righteously be done, of such maritime positions as contribute to secure command." Hawaii "fixes the attention of the strategist"; it occupies a position of "unique importance . . . powerfully influencing the commercial and military control of the Pacific." In another article published by the *Atlantic Monthly* in the same month, Mahan argued the imperative need, for the future of American sea power, of the proposed Isthmian Canal.

Captain Mahan's pronouncements were somehow couched in tones of such authority, as much a product of character as of style, as to make everything he wrote appear indisputable. He was already the author of *The Influence of Sea Power on History*, given originally as lectures at the Naval War College in 1887 and published as a book in 1890. Its effect on the naval profession abroad, if not at home, was immediate and tremendous, and even at home, although it had taken three years to find a publisher, it excited the attention of various thoughtful persons concerned with national policy. Theodore Roosevelt, who as the author at twenty-four of a book on *The Naval War of 1812* had been invited to speak at the Naval War College, heard and became a disciple of Mahan. When *The Influence of Sea Power on History* was published he read it "straight through" and wrote to Mahan that he was convinced it would become "a naval classic." Walter Hines Page of the *Forum* and Horace E. Scudder of the *Atlantic Monthly*, editors in the days when magazines were vital arenas of opinion, regularly gave Mahan space. Harvard and Yale conferred LL.D.'s. Nor were all his professional colleagues traditionalists opposed to things new. His predecessor at the Naval War College, Admiral Stephen Luce, who had selected Mahan to succeed him when Luce himself was named to command the North Atlantic Squadron, brought his squadron to Newport so that his officers could hear the lectures of this new man who, Luce predicted, would do for naval science what Jomini in the days of Napoleon had done for military science. After the first lecture, Luce stood up and proclaimed, "He is here and his name is Mahan!"

What Mahan had discovered was the controlling factor of sea power; that whoever is master of the seas is master of the situation. Like M. Jourdain who spoke prose all his life without knowing it, it was a truth that had been operative for a long time without any of its operators being consciously aware of it, and Mahan's formulation was stunning. His first book was followed and confirmed by a second, *The Influence of Sea Power on the French Revolution*, published in 1892. The original idea had come to him "from within" when, on reading Mommsen's *History of Rome*, "it struck me how different things might have been could Hannibal have invaded Italy by sea . . . or could he, after arrival, have been in free communication with Carthage by water." All at once Mahan realized that "control of the sea was an historic factor which had never been systematically appreciated and expounded." It was "one of those perceptions that turn inward darkness into light." For months, while on leave in 1885, before taking up his duties at the War College, he read at the Astor Place branch of the New York Public Library, following his clue through history in mounting excitement and with every faculty "alive and jumping."

In the United States the building of navies with more than coastal defence capacity was traditionally regarded as a sacrilege against the original idea of America as a nation which could live without aggression and demonstrate a new future to the world. In Europe the nations who had exercised power upon the seas for centuries were suddenly made aware by Mahan of what they had. A commentator signed "Nauticus" remarked that sea power, like oxygen, had influenced the world through the ages, but just as the nature and power of oxygen remained unread until Priestley, "so might sea power but for Mahan."

Ordered to command the flagship of the European Station in 1893 (much against his will, for he would have preferred to stay at home and continue writing), Mahan was received in England with unprecedented honors. He was invited by the Queen to a state dinner at Osborne, dined with the Prince of Wales and was the first foreigner ever to be entertained by the Royal Yacht Club, which gave a dinner in his honor with a hundred guests, all admirals and captains. In London, John Hay, who was visiting there, wrote to him that "all the people of intelligence are waiting to welcome you." Lord Rosebery, then Prime Minister, invited him to a private dinner with just himself and John Morley at which they talked until midnight. He met Balfour and Asquith, visited Lord Salisbury at Hatfield, and dined again with the Queen at Buckingham Palace. Wearing a red academic robe over his dress uniform and sword, he received a D.C.L. from Oxford and an LL.D. from Cambridge, said to be the only man ever to receive degrees from both universities in the same week.

After a temporary escape to the Continent, where, equipped with guidebook, umbrella and binoculars, he traced Hannibal's marches, he was seized upon by his most enthusiastic disciple, Wilhelm II, who invited him to dinner aboard his yacht, the *Hohenzollern*, during Cowes Week. With effect that was to be epochal on world history, *The Influence of Sea Power on History* had planted in the Kaiser the idea that Germany's future was on the sea. By his order, a copy of Mahan's book was placed on every ship in the German Navy and the Kaiser's personal copies in English and German were heavily underlined and bristling with marginal comments and exclamation marks. "I am just now not reading but devouring Captain Mahan's book and am trying to learn it by heart," he informed a friend by telegram in 1894, when Mahan was in Europe. "It is a first class book and classical in all points. It is on board all my ships and constantly quoted by my Captains and officers." The Japanese were no less interested. *The Influence of Sea Power on History* was adopted as a text in Japanese military and naval colleges and all Mahan's subsequent books were translated into Japanese.

The obvious corollary of Mahan's thesis was the peremptory need to develop the American Navy, at that time moribund from neglect. As Cleveland's Secretary of the Navy, William C.

White, said in 1887, it did not have the strength to fight nor the speed to run away, and in Mahan's judgment it was not a match for Chile's Navy, much less Spain's. In 1880, when serious discussion began of an Isthmian Canal, which in the absence of adequate naval power would constitute more of a danger than an asset, he had written, "We must without delay begin to build a navy which will at least equal that of England when the Canal shall have become a fact. . . . That this will be done I don't for a moment hope but unless it is we may as well shut up about the Monroe Doctrine at once."

From then on he continually badgered friends, colleagues and correspondents on this theme. His passion was for naval power, not for ships, as such, for he did not enjoy sea duty and looked nothing at all like a sailor. Well over six feet tall, wiry, thin and erect, he had a long, narrow face with narrowly placed pale-blue eyes, a long, straight, knifelike nose, a sandy moustache blending into a closely trimmed beard over an insignificant chin. All the power of the face was in the upper part, in the eyes and domed skull and the intellectual bumps over the eyebrows. Born the year after Reed, he was fifty in 1890, and though exceptionally reserved and retiring, he was capable, according to his wife, of sudden roars in "his quarter deck voice." His brother called him Alf. He had little sense of humor, a high moral tone and shared the respectable man's horror of Zola's novels, which he forbade his daughters to read. So precise were his scruples that when living on naval property at the War College he would not allow his children to use the government pencils.

His friends and acquaintances were few and his social life, except on the occasion of his tour of duty abroad, virtually nonexistent. External expression of his personality was limited; his life was inner. He was like a steam kettle in which the boiling goes on within an enclosed space and the steam comes out through a single spout. Like Reed he was intensely clear-thinking and definitive in his conclusions. Apropos of a trip ashore at Aden, where he visited a colony of Jews, he wrote, "I am without anti-Semitic feeling. That Jesus Christ was a Jew covers his race for me." In a total of sixteen words he settled to his own satisfaction a problem that had harassed mankind for nineteen centuries and had reopened in his own days full of new trouble and malignance. Samuel Ashe, his lifelong friend since they had been classmates at Annapolis, said, "He was the most intellectual man I have ever known."

In 1890 the Navy at last began to build. On the recommendation of the Policy Board appointed by Harrison's Secretary of the Navy, Benjamin Tracy, Congress reluctantly and not without strong objections from inside and out authorized three battleships, the *Oregon*, *Indiana* and *Massachusetts*, and a fourth, the *Iowa*, two years later. They were the first fruits of Mahan's long campaign. The policy which these ships expressed, though far from being generally accepted at once, represented a fundamental change in the direction in which Mahan was pointing: outward. They meant recognition that America must create a fleet capable of meeting successfully the best that a potential enemy could send against her. Canada was regarded as a hostage to restrain Britain, and the political balance in Europe was considered likely to prevent any potential European enemy from sending its full fleet into American waters. The object was therefore to be supreme in these waters and this meant a fleet capable of protecting the American coasts by taking offensive action against enemy bases anywhere from Newfoundland to the Caribbean. Such was to be the function of the new battleships. They were of the 10,000-ton class, with an average speed of fifteen knots, a coal capacity sufficient for a cruising radius of 5,000 miles at moderate speed, four 13-inch guns, and eight 8-inch guns. In combination of armor and firepower they represented the best in design and construction of the time. At their trials, the *Indiana* in 1895 followed by the *Iowa* in 1896 soberly impressed the British as a match for Britain's first-line ships, of which the latest of the "Majestic" class were 15,000 tons with four 12-inch and twelve 6-inch guns.

The ships lent heart to Mahan's disciples. Roosevelt, still on the Civil Service Commission, was not yet widely heard, but his friend and political mentor, Senator Henry Cabot Lodge of Massachusetts, was the principal political voice in Washington of Mahan's views. Son of a family whose fortune had been made in clipper ships and the China trade, author of various biographies and histories of the Colonial period, Lodge was led into political life through his deep interest in American history. His grandfather and namesake, Henry Cabot, could remember as a boy hiding under the sideboard to watch President George Washington at breakfast in his father's home. Elected to the House in 1886, Lodge made an immediate impression by his frequent and able speeches and proved himself an adroit master of political strategy and tactics. He was shrewd, worldly, forceful and possessed of both energy and intelligence. Along with Roosevelt he was a champion of civil service reform and an inner member of the select group which gathered around the two non-participants, John Hay and Henry Adams, who watched government half wistfully, half cynically from the ringside. Representing the party in opposition, Lodge and Roosevelt had no influence on Cleveland; but they believed and they preached with fervor.

"It is sea power which is essential to every splendid people," Lodge declaimed in the Senate on March 2, 1895. He had a map of the Pacific set up with Britain's bases marked by very visible red crosses and he used a pointer as he talked to make Mahan's point about the vital position of Hawaii. The effect was dramatic and reinforced by the speaker being, as he wrote to his mother, "in desperate earnest." Hawaii must be acquired and the Canal built. "We are a great people; we control this continent; we are dominant in this hemisphere; we have too great an inheritance to be trifled with or parted with. It is ours to guard and extend." As he spoke, Senators came in from the cloakrooms, members of the other House appeared, and also messengers and journalists, until soon the chamber was filled and men were standing around the walls. Lodge could feel he had their "absolute attention. . . . When I sat down everybody crowded around to shake my hand . . . which hardly ever happens in the Senate." In an accompanying article that month in the *Forum*, Lodge stated flatly that once the Canal was built, "the island of Cuba will become a necessity" to the United States. He did not say how the necessity was to be made good; whether the United States was to buy the island from Spain or simply take it. He offered the opinion, however, that small states belonged to the past and that expansion was a movement that made for "civilization and the advancement of the race."

At this juncture History lent a hand. On February 24, 1895,

the Cuban people rose in insurrection against Spanish rule and on March 8 a Spanish gunboat chased and fired on an American merchant vessel, the *Alliance*, which it supposed to be bent on a filibustering errand. This "insult to our flag," as it was called, evoked a burst of comments from prominent members of the Senate Foreign Relations Committee which showed that Lodge had not been speaking only for himself. The American appetite for new territory was making itself felt. Senator Morgan of Alabama, Democratic chairman of the Committee, said the solution was clear: "Cuba should become an American colony." Reed's colleague but not his friend, Senator Frye of Maine, agreed that "we certainly ought to have the island in order to round out our possessions" and added with simple candor, "If we cannot buy it, I for one, should like an opportunity to acquire it by conquest." Another Republican, Senator Cullom of Illinois, expressed even more plainly what was moving inside the American people. "It is time some one woke up," he said, "and realized the necessity of annexing some property—we want all this northern hemisphere." It was not, in 1895, necessary to disguise aggressiveness as something else. As yet the Senators were not talking in terms of support for Cubans rightly struggling to be free, because the *insurrectos*, who were burning American property as enthusiastically as Spanish, had not yet been presented in that light.

With President Cleveland standing robustly against expansion, the exuberant greed of certain Senators had little effect on policy. It was an act by Cleveland himself, at the end of the year, that brought into open explosion the new American mood. His emphatic assertion of the Monroe Doctrine over Venezuela, in defiance of Britain, marked the beginning of a new period in American life as vividly as if a signal flag had been run up to the top of the American flagpole. No question of gain, territorial or otherwise, was involved in Venezuela; it was simply a question of asserting an American right, as it seemed to Cleveland and especially to his exceedingly assertive Secretary of State, Richard Olney. The burst of chauvinism, jingoism and general bellicosity that it touched off startled everyone, though it came less from the common man than from the rich and powerful and vocal. The Union League Club had 1,600 members, proclaimed one of them, and "we are 1,600 to a man behind Mr. Cleveland in this matter. . . . There is absolutely not one dissenting voice." Congratulations from other Republicans, stung to admiration, poured in upon the White House, including one from Theodore Roosevelt. The New York *Times* exaggerated matters in headlines which had no relation to the reports beneath them. PREPARATIONS FOR WAR and COUNTRY IS AROUSED, they ran, or, WANT TO FIGHT ENGLAND: *Army and Navy Men Profess Great Eagerness to Go to War. Talk of Invasion of Canada.* The Army bureau chief who was quoted, far from talking about invading Canada, gave a careful and sober statement of American naval and military inadequacies and stated his belief that America would "make a sorry spectacle at war with England."

The surge of militancy evoked by the Venezuela Message shocked people who still thought of the United States in the terms of its founders, as a nation opposed to militarism, conquest, standing armies and all the other bad habits associated with the monarchies of the old world. This tradition was strongest in New England, and was stronger among the older generation—roughly those who were over fifty in 1890—than among the new. They were closer to Jefferson, who had said, "If there is one principle more deeply rooted in the mind of every American, it is that we should have nothing to do with conquest." They took seriously the Declaration of Independence and its principle of just power deriving from the consent of the governed. They regarded the extension of American rule over foreign soil and foreign peoples as a violation of this principle and a desecration of the American purpose. The original American democracy was to them a torch, an ideal, an example of a brave new world that had set its face against the old. They wanted nothing to do with titles of rank and nobility, knee breeches, orders or any of the other insidious trappings of monarchy, and when in the Navy the title of Admiral was first proposed, an officer fumed, "Call them Admirals? Never! They will be wanting to be Dukes next."

First-generation immigrants who had come to the United States beckoned by the American dream were as deeply devoted to the founding principles as those in whom they had been bred for generations. Some came out of the balked revolution of 1848, seeking Liberty, like Altgeld's father and like Carl Schurz, now sixty-six, who as journalist, editor, Cabinet minister and Senator had been a power and reformer ever since Lincoln's Administration. Some came to escape oppression or poverty and to seek opportunity, like the Scottish weaver who arrived in 1848 with his twelve-year-old son, Andrew Carnegie, or like the Dutch-Jewish cigarmaker who came from a London slum in 1863 with his thirteen-year-old son, Samuel Gompers. Some came, like E. L. Godkin, editor of the *Nation* and the New York *Evening Post*, not as a refugee from oppression, but as a voluntary exile from the old world, lured by America as a living demonstration of the democratic ideal. To them, as to men whose ancestors had come in the 1630's, America was a new principle, and they saw the new militancy as its betrayal.

Godkin, filled with "anxiety about the country," determined to oppose the Venezuela Message even if he should jeopardize his paper with the "half-crazed public." Son of an English family settled since the Twelfth Century in Ireland, where he had been born and brought up, he had served as correspondent for English papers during the Crimean War and the American Civil War. He became editor of the *Nation* when it was founded in 1865 by a group of forty stockholders who supplied $100,000 with the stated purpose of championing the labouring class, the Negro, the cause of popular education and "true democratic principles in society and government." In 1883, while remaining at the *Nation*, he succeeded Carl Schurz as editor of the *Evening Post* and through the medium of these two organs made himself, as William James said, "a towering influence on all thought concerning public affairs."

He was a handsome, bearded, hot-tempered Celt, delighting in combat, brooding in melancholy, vivacious, pugnacious and a muckraker before Roosevelt invented the name. So unrelenting was his pursuit of corrupt practices by Tammany politicians that on one occasion they had him arrested for criminal libel three times in one day. James Russell Lowell agreed with the opinion of an English journalist that Godkin had made the *Nation* "the best periodical in the world," and James Bryce, already famous as the author of *The American Commonwealth*, declared the *Evening Post* to be "the best paper printed in the English language." Closer to home, opinion was hotter.

Governor Hill of New York said he did not care about "the handful of mugwumps" who read the *Evening Post* in New York City. "The trouble with the damned sheet is that every editor in New York State reads it." This was what accounted for Godkin's pervasive influence; that other makers of opinion took their opinions from him—though not, to be sure, all. "What fearful mental degeneracy results from reading it or the *Nation* as a steady thing," wrote Theodore Roosevelt to Captain Mahan in 1893.

In 1895 Godkin was sixty-four and feared the future. The United States, he wrote to a friend, "finds itself in possession of enormous power and is eager to use it in brutal fashion against anyone who comes along without knowing how to do so and is therefore constantly on the brink of some frightful catastrophe." Indeed, as the United States had at this moment exactly one battleship in commission, Godkin was not unwarranted in thinking the Jingoes "absolutely crazy." He believed the new spirit of "ferocious optimism," as he strikingly described it, would lead to eventual disaster.

William James, Professor of Philosophy at Harvard, was equally disquieted. "It is instructive to find," he wrote apropos of Venezuela, "how near the surface in all of us the old fighting spirit lies and how slight an appeal will wake it up. Once *really* waked, there is no retreat." His colleague at Harvard, Charles Eliot Norton, Professor of Fine Arts, who was regarded as the exponent and arbiter of culture in American life, protested the war spirit at a meeting in the Shepard Memorial Church in Cambridge. "The shout of brutal applause, which has gone up from every part of this nation," he said, makes every rational lover of his country feel the "greatest apprehension" for the future.

The white-haired, slender, stoop-shouldered figure, the husky yet musical voice speaking in its Boston Brahmin accent, the charm of that "supremely urbane and gentle presence" was never so at home as when against the herd. Born in 1827, only a year after Jefferson and John Adams died, Norton represented the puritan and militantly liberal conscience of an older generation. He was the son of Andrews Norton, "Unitarian Pope" of New England and Professor of Sacred Literature at Harvard, who had married Catherine Eliot, daughter of a wealthy Boston merchant, and was himself descended through a long line of ministers from John Norton, a Puritan divine who had emigrated to America in 1635.

Like Lord Salisbury, Norton believed in the dominance of an aristocratic class, which to him meant a class founded, not in landowning, but in a common background of culture, refinement, learning and manners. He saw it disappearing and protested regularly against encroaching vulgarity in his lectures. In parody of his manner a student said, "I propose this afternoon to make a few remarks on the hor-ri-ble vul-gar-ity of EVERYTHING." Another of his students at Radcliffe, in her diary for 1895, described him looking "so mildly happy and benignant . . . while he gently tells us it were better for us had we never been born in this degenerate and unhappy age." Norton became one of the first contributors to the *Atlantic Monthly* when it was founded by James Russell Lowell in 1857, was later coeditor with Lowell of the *North American Review*, and was one of the forty stockholders who founded the *Nation*.

Writing to Godkin about the Venezuela Message, Norton thought it made "a miserable end for this century" and had done much to increase the "worst spirit in our democracy, . . . a barbaric spirit of arrogance and unreasonable self-assertion." What disturbed him more bitterly was the "deeper consideration" that the rise of democracy was not proving, after all, "a safeguard of peace and civilization," because it brought with it "the rise of the uncivilized whom no school education can suffice to provide with intelligence and reason." It might have been Lord Salisbury speaking. Norton felt the bitterness of a man who discovers his beloved to be not as beautiful—nor as pure—as he had believed. "I fear that America," he wrote to an English friend, "is beginning a long course of error and wrong and is likely to become more and more a power for disturbance and barbarism. . . . It looks as if the world were entering on a new stage of experience in which there must be a new discipline of suffering to fit men for the new conditions."

Yet his was not the desiccated and disappointed pessimism of Henry Adams, who drifted in and out of Washington and back and forth between Europe and America croaking his endless complaints like a wizened black crow; finding the century "rotten and bankrupt," society sunk in vulgarity, commonness, imbecility and moral atrophy, himself on the verge of "mental extinction" and "dying of ennui"; finding America unbearable and leaving for Europe, finding Europe insufferable and returning to America, finding "decline is everywhere" and everywhere "the dead water of the *fin de siècle* . . . where not a breath stirred the idle air of education or fretted the mental torpor of self-content." The Venezuelan crisis merely confirmed him in the belief that "society today is more rotten than at any time within my personal knowledge. The whole thing is one vast structure of debt and fraud." This was less a judgment on the current mood than a reflection of the rude shaking his nerves had suffered in the financial panic of 1893. Adams, like most people, saw society in his own image and ascribed his own impotence and paralysis to society at large. "Though rotten with decadence," he said of himself in 1895, "I have not enough vitality left to be sensual." The rotten old century, however, was bursting with vitality and he need only have looked at intimates of his own circle in the persons of Lodge and Roosevelt to have found the "ferocious optimism" that Godkin noted all around.

Although a decade older than Adams, Norton would allow himself occasional moments of optimism when he suspected that the loss of the values he loved might be the cost of a compensating gain in human welfare. "There are far more human beings materially well off today than ever before in the history of the world," he wrote in 1896, and he could not resist the thought, "How interesting our times have been and still are!"

The last few years had indeed been full of incident. Cleveland, for all his good will, was beset by hard times. Industrial unrest gripped the nation. Depression followed the panic of 1893. In 1894 Coxey's Army of the unemployed marched on Washington, and the bloody Pullman strike angered and frightened both sides in the deepening warfare of labour and capital. In the Congressional elections that November, the Republicans regained the House with a huge majority of 140 (244–104), and when in December, 1895, the new Fifty-fourth Congress assembled, the familiar great black figure with the great white face was again enthroned in the Speaker's Chair.

Reed was now at the zenith of his power. The dangerous

battle of his first term was long past and the guerrilla warfare of two terms as minority leader over, leaving him with unlimited control. "He commands everything by the brutality of his intellect," said a member. His well-drilled ranks, though occasionally, and as time went on, increasingly, restive, could not break the habit of obedience. When the Speaker waved his hands upward members would stand as one man, and if by chance they rose to claim the floor when he wished them silent, a downward wave made them subside into their seats. "He had more perfect control over the House than any other Speaker," wrote Senator Cullom of Illinois.

Stern on dignity and decorum, he permitted no smoking or shirtsleeves and even challenged the cherished privilege of feet on desk. A member with particularly visible white socks who so far forgot himself as to resume that comfortable posture, received a message from the Chair, "The Czar commands you to haul down those flags of truce."

With no favorites and no near rivals, he ruled alone. Careful not to excite jealousy, he avoided even walking in public with a member. Solitary, the stupendous figure ambled each morning from the old Shoreham Hotel (then on Fifteenth and H Streets), where he lived, to the Hill, barely nodding to greetings and unconscious of strangers who turned to stare at him in the street.

He had a kind of "tranquil greatness," said a colleague, which evolved from a philosophy of his own and left him "undisturbed by the ordinary worries and anxieties of life." Reed gave a clue to it one night when a friend came to discuss politics and found him reading Sir Richard Burton's *Kasidah*, from which he read aloud the lines:

> Do what thy mankind bids thee do,
>   from none but self expect applause,
> He noblest lives and noblest dies
>   who makes and keeps his self-made laws.

Secure in his self-made laws, Reed could not be flustered. Once a Democratic member, overruled by Reed on a point of order, remembered that the Speaker had taken a different position in his manual, *Reed's Rules*. Hurriedly, he sent for the book, leafed through its pages, pounced on the relevant passage and marched to the rostrum in anticipatory triumph to lay it before the Speaker. Reed read it attentively, cast a glance down at the man from his glowing hazel eyes and said with finality, "Oh, the *book* is wrong."

During the Venezuela crisis he said little publicly, kept the Republicans in the House under firm control and trusted to Cleveland's basic antipathy for foreign adventure, which he shared, to withstand the Jingoes' eagerness to annex this and that. Reed was unalterably opposed to expansion and all it implied. He believed that American greatness lay at home and was to be achieved by improving living conditions and raising political intelligence among Americans rather than by extending American rule over half-civilized peoples difficult to assimilate. To him the Republican party was the guardian of this principle and expansion was "a policy no Republican ought to excuse, much less adopt."

The year 1896 was a Presidential one and Reed wanted the nomination. With the Democrats torn by their discords, chances of a Republican victory looked favorable and the nomination was a prize worth fighting for. "He is in excellent health and spirits," reported Roosevelt, and "thinks the drift is his way." Appearing with his moustache shaved off, Reed seemed to one reporter to feel the "necessity of taking himself seriously," which tended to muffle his wit. As a contender for the nomination his position was complicated by the fact that the most vigorous campaigners on his behalf were Lodge and Roosevelt, whose views on expansion were fundamentally opposed to his own, although this had not yet become a touchstone. "My whole heart is in the Reed canvass," said Roosevelt.

Reed would not go out of his way to build up support for himself by the usual methods. When members demanded private appropriation bills for their districts without which they feared they would be unable to cultivate sentiment for his nomination, he was unmoved. "Your bill will not be allowed to come up even with that Reed button in your coat," he said to one member. When the railroad magnate, Collis P. Huntington, of the Southern Pacific, three times asked to see Reed's campaign manager, Representative F. J. Aldrich, Reed said yes, Aldrich might call on him, "But remember, not one dollar from Mr. Huntington for my campaign fund!" Aldrich, who went to see him anyway, confided that Reed would not permit any but a few donations from personal friends and had collected a total of $12,000. Disgusted, Huntington disclosed that Reed's rivals were not so particular about money. "The others have taken it," he said, revealing that he had placed his bets across the board.

Another man was spending money liberally on behalf of a rival candidate. Mark Hanna, the boss of Ohio, had cast a President-maker's eye on Reed in the previous campaign but had found him too sardonic, his oratory too Eastern and his personality hardly amenable. As Henry Adams said, Reed was "too clever, too strong-willed and too cynical" to suit the party chiefs. Since then Hanna had found his affinity in a man the antithesis of Reed—the amiable, smooth-speaking, solidly handsome McKinley, of whom it was said that his strongest conviction was to be liked. He was a man made to be managed. He had never made an enemy and his views on the crucial currency question, as a biographer tactfully put it, "had never been so pronounced as to make him unpopular" either with the silver wing or the gold-standard group. Reed now had cause to regret that in naming McKinley chairman of the Ways and Means Committee he had opened his path to prominence as sponsor of the McKinley Bill on the tariff. Since the Fifty-first Congress, when McKinley had ventured some objections to the Speaker's methods in the matter of the quorum, Reed had had little use for him. He considered him spineless, an opinion to which he gave immortal shape in the phrase, "McKinley has no more backbone than a chocolate eclair."*

Hanna saw in McKinley less an eclair than a kind of Lohengrin and felt sure he could secure his nomination as long as McKinley's rivals remained divided and did not unite behind any one of themselves, especially not behind Reed, the only one who had the stature for the Presidency. Hanna shrewdly judged Reed too inflexible, however, to be willing to bend for the sake of gaining the others' support. He was right. Eastern leaders, finding the Reed camp dry of inducements, pledged

*This has also been ascribed to Roosevelt. It is not certain to whom the credit belongs.

their votes elsewhere. Reed was not making it easy for would-be supporters. When a political chieftain from California asked for a promise of a place on the Supreme Court for a man from his state, Reed refused, saying the nomination was not worth considering unless it were free of any deals whatsoever. The California chieftain was soon to be seen basking in Hanna's entourage. When Governor Pingree of Michigan, who controlled the delegates from his state, came to Washington to see Reed, Aldrich had the greatest difficulty in persuading him to leave the Chair and come down to his office where the Governor was waiting. When at last he did, Pingree held forth on his views on free silver, which were obnoxious to Reed, who immediately said so. "Pingree wanted to be for Reed," reported Aldrich helplessly. "He went away and espoused the cause of McKinley."

Reed could see the trend but he could not have changed himself. "Some men like to stand erect," he once said, "and some men even after they are rich and high placed like to crawl."

When in a masterly speech he tore, trampled and demolished free silver, which was less a question of currency than of class struggle, Roosevelt, filled with enthusiasm, wrote him, "Oh Lord! What would I not give if you were our standard-bearer." At times, however, Roosevelt confessed to being "pretty impatient" with Reed, who would not satisfy his insistence on support of a big navy. "Upon my word," he complained to Lodge, "I do think that Reed ought to pay some heed to the wishes of you and myself." It was a vain hope to express of a man who was not given to "heeding" anyone's wishes. To Lodge's annoyance, Reed also refused "to promise offices from the Cabinet down or spend money to secure Southern delegates." Hanna, well supplied with funds, was busy in the South collecting white and Negro Republican delegates who were for sale. "They were for me until the buying started," Reed said.

He was not sanguine and already, in a letter to Roosevelt before the Convention met, talked of retiring to the private practice of law. "In a word, my dear boy, I am tired of this thing and want to be sure that my debts won't have to be paid by a syndicate [a reference to McKinley's]. . . . Moreover the receding grapes seem to ooze with acid and the whole thing is a farce."

At St. Louis in June, Lodge made his nominating speech. Reed received 84 votes on the first ballot in comparison to 661 for McKinley and the grapes receded beyond reach.

President Cleveland likewise was rejected by the Democratic Convention in favor of an ambitious thirty-six-year-old Congressman from Nebraska, known for his crowd-catching oratory, who treated the Convention to the most memorable rhetoric since Patrick Henry demanded liberty or death. "Clad in the armor of a righteous cause . . . a cause as holy as the cause of liberty. . . . You shall not press down upon the brow of labour this crown of thorns. You shall not crucify mankind upon a cross of gold!" When the hysteria was over, Governor Altgeld turned a "weary face and quizzical smile" to Clarence Darrow and said, "I have been thinking over Bryan's speech. What did he say, anyhow?"

The campaign roused the country to extremes of emotion and reciprocal hate. It was Silver against Gold, the People against the Interests, the farmer against the railroad operator who siphoned off his profits in high freight charges, the little man against the banker, the speculator and the mortgage holder. Among the Republicans there was real fear that a Democratic victory, coming after the violence of Homestead and Pullman, would mean overturn of the capitalist system. Factory owners told their men that if Bryan were elected "the whistle would not blow on Wednesday morning." Even the *Nation* supported McKinley. When he won, business settled back in its seat, reinforced in its rejection of social protest. "Mark Hanna's era," wrote a contemporary looking back, "marked a climax of this easy defiance by the strong. I well remember the charming bulldog manner in which Hanna took up defense of unlimited private monopoly. . . . It was a note that can never be sounded quite so fearlessly again."

The arena was now cleared for a different battle, in which Reed's fate and his country's were to be decided. Cleveland had refused to be budged when Congress passed a resolution which by recognizing the Cuban rebels as belligerents would have permitted the sale to them of arms. The resolution was "only an expression of opinion by the eminent gentlemen who voted for it," he said, and since the power to recognize rested exclusively with the Executive he would regard it "only as advice," which left "unaltered the attitude of this Government." Now he was replaced by McKinley, who, though personally opposed to war with Spain, was unpracticed in the art of living up to his convictions. In Spain Premier Canovas was dead, leaving weaker hands in control. In New York William Randolph Hearst, having bought the *Journal*, was adapting himself to the dictum of the editor of England's first halfpenny paper, the *Daily Mail*, who on being asked what sells a newspaper, replied, "War." Hearst was helping to manufacture a war by horrendous stories of Spanish cruelties, Cuban heroism, American destiny and duty, empurpled by the demands of a circulation battle with Joseph Pulitzer's New York *World*.

A new factor in the world was the victory of Japan over China in their local war of 1895, which caused a sudden recognition of Japan as a rising power in the East and startled Kaiser Wilhelm II into coining a phrase, *die Gelbe Gefahr*—"the Yellow Peril." The rise of Japan gave urgency and cogency to the demand for the Isthmian Canal and to Captain Mahan's contention that Cuba in the Caribbean as well as Hawaii in the Pacific were necessary for the Canal's strategic defence. In a number of articles appearing in 1897 Mahan showed that the Caribbean was a vital military crossroads which could be controlled either from Jamaica or Cuba, and he set about proving professionally and unanswerably that Cuba from the point of view of situation, strength and resources was "infinitely superior."

His voice echoed in the Senate through Lodge, who repeated the argument that the Canal would make Cuba a "necessity." As extra inducement to Senators more materially than strategically minded, he expanded on how that "splendid island . . . still sparsely settled and of almost unbounded fertility" offered great opportunities for the investment of American capital and as a market for American goods. Roosevelt, although he had no such forum, was earnestly pleading the same cause wherever he had a hearing. The vociferous campaign he and Lodge were waging reached an august listener who was not pleased.

President Charles William Eliot of Harvard, the "topmost oak" of New England, speaking in Washington on the much-debated issue of international arbitration, denounced the doctrine of jingoism as "offensive." Associated with countries where there had always been a military class, it was, he said, "absolutely foreign to American society, . . . yet some of my friends endeavor to pass it off as patriotic Americanism." He then laid down firmly the principles which he believed made America different from the old nations. "The building of a navy and the presence of a large standing army mean . . . the abandonment of what is characteristically American. . . . The building of a navy and particularly of battleships is English and French policy. It should never be ours." The American policy was reliance upon strength in peace, whereas Jingoes were a creation "of the combativeness that is in man." He specifically identified Lodge and Roosevelt as Jingoes and privately, it was learned, called them "degenerated sons of Harvard."

Eliot spoke with unmatched authority. Descended from Eliots and Lymans who had been settled in New England since the Seventeenth Century, he belonged to a group who felt themselves the best. "Eliza," protested Mrs. Eliot when a friend joined the Episcopal church, "do you kneel down in church and call yourself a miserable sinner? Neither I nor any of my family will ever do that!" His father, a mayor of Boston and a Congressman, was also, as treasurer of Harvard, a member of the seven-man Corporation, Harvard's governing body, which an English observer called "government by seven cousins." His own quarter of a century as president of Harvard had been an unremitting battle against the traditionalists to transform the college from an Eighteenth Century backwater into a modern university. During that time he had, as President Hyde of Bowdoin said, been "misunderstood, maligned, misrepresented, hated," and Eliot himself confessed that in all his public appearances during those years, "I had a vivid sense that I was addressing a hostile audience." Being a fighter, this did not halt him. He was not naturally an ingratiating man. Over six feet tall, with "an oarsman's back, a grave and sculptured head," he was a "noble presence" born to command. A strawberry birthmark which covered one side of his face and pulled a corner of his lip into a seeming superciliousness had set him apart from boyhood and given him a quality of loneliness. With this to overcome and the additional handicap of being, as Professor of Chemistry, a scientist, he had nevertheless been named president of Harvard at thirty-five. His ideal of behavior, in his own words, was that of "a gentleman who is also a democrat." He was inflexible about what he thought was right. When a star baseball player was left off the Harvard team because of low marks, Eliot was heard to remark that this was no loss because he was a player who resorted to deception. "Why," he explained, "they boasted of his making a feint to throw a ball in one direction and then throwing it in ANOTHER!"

Against the strenuous lethargy of the diehards he succeeded in opening the curriculum to modern studies, introducing the elective system, assembling a faculty that gave Harvard its golden age, raising the Law School and Medical School to prestige and prominence and through his influence modernizing the whole American system of higher education. When in 1894 at the age of sixty he celebrated his twenty-fifth anniversary as president, opposition had given way to respect and admiration. He was suddenly recognized as Harvard's greatest president and the "first private citizen of the country." It was said that the Boston Symphony could not open without him and the sanguine birthmark appeared no longer as a blemish but as "an emblem of triumph over the handicaps of life."

To Roosevelt, then thirty-eight, Eliot himself seemed one of the diehards who refused to understand that America's manifest destiny lay outward. Having imbibed deeply from Mahan, Roosevelt felt urgently the need of his country to equip itself for the role of greatness which the times were shaping. The distaste for that role of many of the influential men of his time made his voice shrill with frustration. "If ever we come to nothing as a nation," he wrote Lodge after learning that they had been called "degenerated sons of Harvard," "it will be because the teaching of Carl Schurz, President Eliot, the *Evening Post* and futile sentimentalists of the international arbitration type" will produce "a flabby timid type of character which eats away the great fighting features of our race."

It was maddening to him that now, when war with Spain was in prospect, just such a flabby timid character was in the White House. Roosevelt was determined that there should be someone inside the Administration alert and capable of making ready for great events. He had set his heart on bringing together the man who understood the new destiny—himself—

with the instrument upon which all depended—the Navy. McKinley's Secretary of the Navy was an easygoing and friendly gentleman and former Governor of Massachusetts, John D. Long. Roosevelt believed that if he himself were appointed Assistant Secretary he could, through superior force of energy and ideas, take over the real command of that office.

So did everyone else. Long somewhat apprehensively said, "Roosevelt has the character, standing, ability and reputation to entitle him to be a Cabinet minister—is not this too small for him?" The only thing against him, Lodge wrote to his friend after seeing McKinley on his behalf, was "the fear that you will want to fight somebody at once." Nevertheless McKinley, persuaded as usual by more forceful characters, appointed Roosevelt on April 5, 1897, and he was confirmed on April 8. S. S. McClure, the exposive and perceptive editor of *McClure's Magazine*, sensed whence the appointment came and where it would lead. "Mahan must be seen and talked to at once," he wrote to his co-editor. "He is the greatest naval biographer and student of this century and his field is going to become more and more popular." An identical twin of his time, McClure knew what his twin would do. "Roosevelt seems big from here," he continued. "Write to him and try to get his naval stuff. Mahan and Roosevelt are just our size." This was indeed so. McClure shared their feeling of power and muscle and largeness of opportunity. When in the last year of the century he wanted Walter Hines Page for an editor, he telegraphed him, "Should see you immediately. Have biggest thing on earth." When Page agreed to come, McClure was jubilant and replied that they would make the strongest editorial combine in the world. "Oh my dear boy, *we* are the people with the years in front of us!"

Now the long-thwarted annexation of Hawaii was revived. Roosevelt in the effort to galvanize McKinley reported to him on April 22 that the Japanese had sent a cruiser to Honolulu. He wrote to Mahan asking him how to solve the political problem of acquiring the islands. "Do nothing unrighteous," was the classic answer, "but take the islands first and solve afterward." If he could have his way, Roosevelt replied, they would be annexed "tomorrow," and Spain turned out of the West Indies and a dozen new battleships built at once, half of them on the Pacific Coast. He reported a regrettable disposition on the part of Congress to stop naval building until finances were firmer. "Tom Reed to my astonishment and indignation takes this view."

Still firm in command of the Republican members, Reed could subdue any unhealthy lust among them for annexation, but as Speaker he was bound to pilot Administration policy through the House. The question was, what was Administration policy: the soft reluctance of McKinley or the "outward" drive of Lodge and Roosevelt powered by the ideas of Mahan and the persuasions of the sugar trust? The answer came in June, when a new treaty of annexation was concluded with the Hawaiian government, signed by McKinley and sent to the Senate for ratification. Although there was little likelihood of assembling two-thirds of the Senate in favor of it, the anti-expansionists were worried. Carl Schurz, whom McKinley, always anxious to please, had earlier assured of his disinterest in Hawaii, faced him with the issue after dinner in the White House, over cigars. Very uncomfortable, McKinley pleaded that he had sent the treaty to the Senate only to get an expression of opinion. Nevertheless, Schurz left with a heart "heavy with evil forebodings." In England the *Spectator* said somewhat nervously that the treaty marked "an end to the historic policy of the Republic since its foundation . . . and will mean its gradual evolution into a less peaceful and possibly militant power."

With regard to Cuba, the country was becoming increasingly excited. Reed regarded the Hearst-fabricated furor over Spain's oppression with contempt and Republican espousal of Cuba's cause as hypocrisy. He saw his party losing its moral integrity and becoming a party of political expediency in response to the ignorant clamor of the mob. Without compunction he suppressed the resolution recognizing the belligerence of the "Republic" of Cuba. He too took to the magazines to argue against expansion—in an article whose title, "Empire Can Wait," became a rallying cry for the opponents of Hawaii's annexation. It spoke the awful name; as yet the outright words "empire" and "imperialism," which connoted the scramble for Africa then at its peak among the European powers, had not been used in the United States. James Bryce, perhaps the only Englishman who could have been allowed to give advice, urged Americans to have nothing to do with a policy of annexation.

America's remote position and immense power, he wrote in the *Forum*, freed her from the burden of armaments crushing the European powers. Her mission in the world was "to show the older peoples and states an example of abstention from the quarrels and wars and conquests that make up so large and lamentable a part of the annals of Europe." To yield to the "earth-hunger" now raging among the European states would be "a complete departure from the maxims of the illustrious founders of the republic." Behind his sober words could be sensed the love a man feels for the object of his life's work and a pleading to America not to contradict the promise that hung about her birth.

Mahan's mind, planning the strategy of a war with Spain, had already leapt beyond Hawaii to the far-off Spanish possession of the Philippines. What motivated him was not earth-hunger but sea power, the controlling idea which had drawn from him the grand orchestral words about the British Navy in the Napoleonic wars: "Those far distant, storm-beaten ships upon which the Grand Army never looked, stood between it and the dominion of the world." At the end of 1897 he entered the rising debate with a book, *The Interest of America in Sea Power*, in which were collected his major articles over the past seven years. He also advised Roosevelt on the appointment of a new commander of the Asiatic Squadron who could be trusted to act with vigor when the test should come. The chosen officer was Commodore George Dewey and his task was foreseen. "Our Asiatic Squadron should blockade and, if possible, take Manila," Roosevelt wrote to Lodge on September 21, 1897, and he took care to obtain the necessary coal to prepare the Asiatic Squadron for action.

On February 15, 1898, the United States armored cruiser *Maine* blew up and sank in the harbor of Havana with the loss of 260 lives. Although the cause of the explosion was never ascertained, it was impossible in the mood of the time to assume other than a dastardly Spanish plot. The proponents of war burst into hysteria; the peace-minded were outshouted. McKinley hung back, but fearful of a split in his party, soon gave way to the clamor. Speaker Reed did not. During the two months in which negotiations aimed at forcing Spain into war were being pursued, he did his best to hold back the wave, limiting time for debate and quashing resolutions recognizing Cuban independence. When Senator Proctor, who owned marble quarries in Vermont, made a strong speech for war Reed commented, "Proctor's position might have been expected. A war will make a large market for gravestones." He was attacked by the pro-war press and his rulings aroused resentment in the House, which, on the whole—like the country—wanted war. "Ambition, interest, land-hunger, pride, the mere joy of fighting, whatever it may be" acknowledged the Washington *Post*, "we are animated by a new sensation. . . . The taste of Empire is in the mouth of the people even as the taste of blood in the jungle."

It was too strong for Reed to control. Asked by reporters one morning at breakfast at the Shoreham for comment on the stampede for war, he showed a letter he had just opened from Governor Morton of New York urging him to step down from the chair to the floor of the House and dissuade the members from intervention. "Dissuade them! The Governor might as well ask me to step out in the middle of a Kansas waste and dissuade a cyclone!" He could not keep the ultimatum to Spain from coming to the floor, and the vote for it in the House of 311 to 6 was a measure of the cyclone. To one of the six Reed said, "I envy you the luxury of your vote. I was where I could not do it."

War was declared on April 25, 1898. Mahan, then in Rome, asked by reporters how long he thought the war would last, replied with what proved dead reckoning, "About three months." Returning at once he was appointed one of the three members of the Naval War Board. Roosevelt sent him a plan of campaign for action in the Philippines and on receiving his comments wrote, "There is no question that you stand head and shoulders above the rest of us! You have given us just the suggestions we want."

On April 30 Commodore Dewey's squadron steamed into Manila Bay and with a day's bombardment, loosed by the classic order, "You may fire when ready, Gridley," destroyed or put out of action the Spanish squadron and shore batteries. Never had the country felt such a thrill of pride. GREATEST NAVAL ENGAGEMENT OF MODERN TIMES was one headline. It faced the country suddenly with a new problem which none but a few had thought of: What to do next? The American people on the whole, as Mr. Dooley said, did not know whether the Philippines were islands or canned goods, and even McKinley confessed "he could not have told where those darned islands were within 2,000 miles." The disciples of Mahan knew well enough where they were and what must become of them. Within four days of Dewey's victory Lodge wrote, "We must on no account let the islands go. . . . The American flag is up and it must stay." Since there had been a Filipino independence movement in existence for thirty years, for which many had fought and suffered prison, exile and death, Senator Lodge's simple solution took little account of the consent of the governed. Its leader was Emilio Aguinaldo, a young man of twenty-eight who had been in exile in Hong Kong. Upon Dewey's victory, he had returned at once to the Philippines.

In America the outbreak of a war to be carried to the enemy and posing no danger to the homeland did not silence its opponents but galvanized them. Suddenly they became an entity with a name: the Anti-Imperialists. Professor Norton, now over seventy, brought upon himself torrents of abuse and threats of violence to his house and person by urging his students not to enlist in a war in which "we jettison all that was most precious of our national cargo." Although a Boston Irish politician proposed to send a lynching party for him and the press called him a "traitor" and even Senator Hoar of Massachusetts denounced him, Norton's grief at his country's course was too great to be contained. At a meeting of the Congregational Church in Cambridge he spoke of how bitter it was that now, at the end of a century which had seen the greatest advance in knowledge and the hope of peace, America should be turning against her ideals and "plunging into an unrighteous war."

Others in Boston spoke out. Moorfield Storey, president of the Massachusetts Reform Club and Civil Service Reform League, and a former president of the American Bar Association, was one; Gamaliel Bradford, a rampant critic of government known for his one-man crusades through a flow of letters to newspapers, was another. The first Story (minus the *e*) had settled in Massachusetts in 1635 and Bradford was descended from the first Governor of the Plymouth Colony. Together they assembled a meeting of protest at Faneuil Hall, and here on June 15, 1898, three days after Aguinaldo in the Philippines issued a declaration of independence, the Anti-Imperialist League was founded. Its president was the eighty-year-old Republican George S. Boutwell, former Senator from Massachusetts and former Secretary of the Treasury under President Grant. Its stated purpose was not to oppose the war as such, but to insist that having been undertaken as a war of liberation, it must not be turned into one for empire. The quest for power, money and glory abroad, the League maintained, would distract from reform at home and bring in its train a strong central government destructive of traditional states' rights and local liberties. Americans had enough to do to solve the problems of municipal corruption, war between capital and labour, disordered currency, unjust taxation, the use of public office for spoils, the rights of the colored people in the South and of the Indians in the West, before taking alien peoples under their rule.

These were the problems that absorbed reformers—many of whom, together with independents and dissenters of various kinds and distinguished Democrats who perforce become the anti-expansion party, now banded together under the banner of the League. Its forty-one vice-presidents soon included ex-President Cleveland; his former Secretary of War, William Endicott; former Secretary of the Treasury, Speaker Carlisle; Senator "Pitchfork Ben" Tillman; President David Starr Jordan, of Stanford; President James B. Angell, of the University of Michigan; Jane Addams; Andrew Carnegie; William James; Samuel Gompers, president of the American Federation of Labor; and numbers of other Congressmen, clergymen, professors, lawyers and writers. The novelist William Dean Howells thought the war "an abominable business." When his friend Mark Twain came home from an extended trip abroad, he too became a member of the League. Besides Godkin's *Evening Post*, its chief voices were the Boston *Herald*, the Baltimore *Sun* and the Springfield *Republican*, while two other Republican papers, the Boston *Evening Transcript* and the Philadelphia *Ledger*, also gave it support.

On the side of the Anti-Imperialists was a strong sentiment, growing out of the troubles with the Negroes after the Civil

War, of reluctance to take on new colored populations. Nothing but more trouble would accrue, said Godkin harshly in the *Nation*, from "dependencies inhabited by ignorant and inferior races" with whom Americans had no union "other than would be necessary for purposes of carpet-baggery and corruption." Carl Schurz used the same argument against the Canal, saying that "once fairly started on a career of aggrandizement" the imperialists would insist that the Canal be bordered on both sides by American territory and would want to annex countries "with a population of 13,000,000 Spanish-Americans mixed with Indian blood" who would flood Congress with twenty Senators and fifty or sixty Representatives. Hawaii, where Orientals greatly outnumbered the whites, posed the same threat.

The Anti-Imperialists did not sweep up with them the Populists and followers of Bryan and those soon to be known as Progressives. While these groups opposed standing armies, big navies and foreign entanglements and were in theory anti-imperialist, anti-militarist and anti-European, they were simultaneously imbued with a fever to fight Spain as a cruel European tyrant stamping out liberty at America's doorstep. Bryan called for war as loudly as Theodore Roosevelt and in sincere flattery, if less promptly, had himself appointed Colonel of the Third Nebraska Volunteers, too late to see action in Cuba. Most vociferous of all was a young lawyer from Indianapolis, already famous at thirty-six as a political orator and soon to become a leader of the Progressives. The taste of empire, the rising blood of nationalism expressed in terms of wide-flung dominion, found in Albert Beveridge its most thrilling trumpet. Like Bryan, he possessed that dangerous talent for oratory which can simulate action and even thought. The war sent Beveridge into transports of excitement.

"We are a conquering race," he proclaimed in Boston in April, even before the victory of Manila Bay. "We must obey our blood and occupy new markets and if necessary new lands. . . . In the Almighty's infinite plan . . . debased civilizations and decaying races" were to disappear "before the higher civilization of the nobler and more virile types of man." Pan-Germans in Berlin and Joseph Chamberlain in England also talked of the mission of the superior race, variously Teutonic or Anglo-Saxon, but Beveridge had nothing to learn from them; it was all his own. He saw in present events "the progress of a mighty people and their free institutions" and the fulfillment of the dream "that God had put in the brain" of Jefferson, Hamilton, John Bright, Emerson, Ulysses S. Grant and other "imperial intellects"; the dream "of American expansion until all the seas shall bloom with that flower of liberty, the flag of the great Republic." It was not so much liberty as trade that Beveridge saw following the flag. American factories and American soil, he said, were producing more than the American people could consume. "Fate has written our policy for us; the trade of the world must and shall be ours. . . . We will cover the ocean with our merchant marine. We will build a navy to the measure of our greatness. . . . American law, American order, American civilization will plant themselves on those shores hitherto bloody and benighted but by those agencies of God henceforth to be made beautiful and bright."

Beveridge was so carried away by the opportunities for greatness that the sword he waved flashed almost too nakedly. He spoke of the Pacific as "the true field of our operations. There Spain has an island empire in the Philippines. . . . There the United States has a powerful Squadron. The Philippines are logically our first target."

During the summer while others volunteered and fought in Cuba and sickened of yellow fever and over five thousand died of disease, Beveridge's personal obedience to the call of blood remained rhetorical. He poured scorn on the Anti-Imperialist arguments. "Cuba not contiguous? Porto Rico not contiguous? The Philippines not contiguous? . . . Dewey and Sampson and Schley will make them contiguous and American speed, American guns, American heart and brain and nerve will keep them contiguous forever! . . . Who dares to halt it now, now when we are at last one people, strong enough for any task, great enough for any glory destiny can bestow?" In the following year Beveridge was elected Senator. "We're a gr-reat people," remarked Mr. Dooley. "An' the best iv it is, we know we ar-re."

Theodore Roosevelt in these months was at the front. Though he held a high and crucial office he had made up his mind in advance to give it up, if war came, for active service. Men like himself, as he wrote privately to a friend, having been taunted with being "armchair and parlor Jingoes, . . . my power for good whatever it may be, would be gone if I didn't try to live up to the doctrines that I have tried to preach." He resigned as Assistant Secretary of the Navy immediately after Manila, declined the command of a volunteer cavalry regiment which was offered him by Secretary of War Alger, but asked to serve as Lieutenant Colonel on condition that the command was given to his friend Colonel Leonard Wood of the regular army. This was done. By June 24, two months later, he was in action at San Juan Hill. By July 3 the land fighting was over, the ebullient Rough Rider was a hero and was triumphantly elected Governor of New York in November.

Meanwhile in a Congress flushed with war, advocates of the annexation of Hawaii saw renewed opportunity. Still unable to muster two-thirds of the Senate, they had decided to resort to annexation by a Joint Resolution, which required only a simple majority. The resolution had been introduced in the Senate on March 16 but Reed had been able to prevent its coming to the floor of the House all during the excitement in April. His ruthless command, commented the Washington *Post* on April 15, made him "the most dangerous antagonist in public life." He was in fact the only man whom the dauntless Beveridge did not care to take on. When urged to write to Reed to persuade him not to oppose expansion, Beveridge replied, "I feel that any effort of mine upon the Gibraltar-like mind and will of the Speaker would be absolutely ineffectual."

After the war reached the Pacific, however, even Reed was finding it hard to maintain his iron control. Exasperated, he told Champ Clark of Missouri he wished Dewey would "sail right away from that place. It will make us trouble for all time to come if he does not." The annexationists argued that if the United States did not take Hawaii, Great Britain would, or alternatively Japan, who was already plotting to gain control by encouraging the influx of Japanese subjects subsidized by their government. Besides, it now lay clearly in the American path. "We need Hawaii just as much and a good deal more than we did California," McKinley told his secretary, George Cortelyou, on May 4. "It is Manifest Destiny."

On May 4 the resolution was introduced in the House. Reed stifled it for three weeks against growing pressure. The excuse that control of Hawaii was necessary for the defeat of Spain in the Pacific he regarded as a pure pretext conceived by the sugar interests and imperialists. In this he was at odds with the President, almost all his party in Congress and with friends outside. "The opposition now comes exclusively from Reed, who is straining every nerve to beat Hawaii," Lodge wrote to Roosevelt. Reed even went to the length of enlisting help from the Democrats. When the future Speaker, Champ Clark, a good friend though a Democrat, asked Reed to put him on the Ways and Means Committee, Reed begged him to go on the Foreign Affairs Committee instead, where he needed Clark's help as "a man who believes as I do and who is a fighter."

"If you put it that way," Clark replied, much affected, "I'll stand by you." He agreed to sacrifice the place he had long coveted to help his party's most uncompromising opponent.

Restiveness in Reed's own party was increasing. On May 24 Republican members of the House took the unusual step of signing a petition for a caucus to consider the resolution. It presented Reed with a frontal challenge of all that he had fought for in his battle against the silent quorum. The fundamental premise of that battle and of Reed's Rules was that the will of the House as expressed by the majority must prevail. Reed knew that from his unassailable height above the floor and with his mastery of procedural techniques he could, with Clark's collaboration, fend off a vote on the Hawaii Resolution, but he could not change sentiment. He knew that his own, the majority, party wanted annexation and that the House on the whole was in favor of it. By summoning all his authority he might frustrate the resolution, but if he did, his success would nullify what he had earlier won: the reform which assured that the House really controlled itself, that no tricks of procedure, no arbitrary rules of a Speaker could obstruct the will of the majority. The purpose of the quorum battle had now come to a test, and with tragic irony, against himself. He would have to choose between his hatred of foreign conquest and his duty as Speaker; between, on the one hand, his own deepest beliefs, and on the other, Reed's Rules.

There was only one choice he could make. Knowing too well the value of what he had accomplished in the Fifty-first

Congress, he bowed to the majority. Debate opened on June 11, and on June 15 the resolution passed by 209 to 91 with practically unanimous Republican support. Reed was not in the Chair. Representative Dalzell, substituting, announced before the vote, "The Speaker of the House is absent on account of illness. I am requested by him to say that were he present he would vote No." Reed had taken a stand, said the *Nation*, "absolutely alone" among his party. "Courage to oppose a popular mania, above all to go against party, is not so common a political virtue that we can afford not to pay our tribute to the man who exhibits it."

Annexation of Hawaii was formally ratified on July 7, four days after the war in Cuba was brought to an end by a naval battle off Santiago. There the Spanish fleet, attempting to run the American blockade, was destroyed by the superior fire of the five so-lately-built battleships, *Indiana*, *Oregon*, *Massachusetts*, *Iowa* and *Texas.* With the surrender of Santiago two weeks later, Spanish rule came to an end, defeated, not by the Cuban insurgents, but by the United States. When it came to negotiation of peace terms, all the passion lavished during the past three years on the cause of Cuban liberty, all the Congressional resolutions favoring recognition of an independent Cuban Republic and disclaiming intention to annex it proved a serious obstacle to Senator Lodge's "necessity." To take Cuba as the fruit of conquest was impossible, however alluring its strategic and mercantile advantages, but a smaller island, Porto Rico, at least was available. Required to renounce Cuba and cede the smaller neighbor, Spain was eliminated from the Western Hemisphere. The degree of Cuba's independence and nature of her relations with the United States was left to be worked out in the presence of an American occupation force. The result was the Platt Amendment of 1901, establishing a virtual American protectorate.

In the meantime preliminary peace terms were signed in Washington on August 12, leaving the even more troublesome question of the Philippines to be negotiated by peace commissioners who were to meet in Paris to conclude a final settlement. Drawing up a balance sheet of the war, Lodge could say with some satisfaction, "We have risen to be one of the great world powers and I think we have made an impression upon

Europe which will be lasting." Mahan writing on the same subject to Mrs. Roosevelt was rather more pompous: "The jocund youth of our people now passes away never to return; the cares and anxieties of manhood's years henceforth are ours."

At home the Anti-Imperialists—through meetings, protests, speeches, articles, petitions, and public conferences—were attempting to hold their country back from plucking the archipelago in the Pacific which seemed to glow with the fatal evil of the apple in the Garden of Eden. Carl Schurz urged McKinley to turn the Philippines over as a mandate to a small power, such as Belgium or Holland, so that the United States could remain "the great neutral power of the world." In France it was the "Dreyfus summer," and Americans, too, in those months felt that their country had reached a moment critical for its character and future. In public and private the debate raged whether to keep the Philippines or turn them over to self-government by the Filipinos. Even the usually hard-headed Mahan caught the fever of righteousness and wrote to an English friend about America's duty to keep the Philippines, "*Deus Vult!* It was the cry of the Crusader and the Puritan and I doubt if man ever utters a nobler."

A three-day conference to consider "some of the most momentous problems in the history of the Republic" was convened at Saratoga in August by leaders in public life both for and against expansion. The favored theme of the expansionists, which called forth their most energetic arguments, was a vision of the vast untapped markets of the Orient with their limitless opportunities for American enterprise. Speaking for the Anti-Imperialists, Henry Wade Rogers, president of Northwestern University and chairman of the Conference on opening day, forcefully made the point that it was not necessary to annex territory in order to trade with it. But he could not summon passion equal to that of Judge Grosscup, notorious as the man who had issued the injunction in the Pullman strike, who delivered an exuberant paean to "the new career of commercial activity upon which I trust we are about to enter." With the Philippines and Hawaii in her hands, the United States would control the path to Asia, a whole continent with "doors swinging inward that will lead us to one half the desirable territory and one third the population of the earth."

Samuel Gompers spoke against conquest of foreign lands not only as a betrayal of American principles but as a danger to the standards of American wage-earners. Strange combinations were wrought in the cause of anti-imperialism. When, at a later meeting in Chicago, Gompers declared that retention of the Philippines would show that "our war was without just cause," Andrew Carnegie sent him a telegram of congratulations saying, "Let us stand together to save the Republic."

President McKinley, after soul-searching and prayer, had arrived at the decision desired by his advisers and popular with his party: the Philippines must be kept. In Paris, Spain's commissioners were given to understand that the time for dickering was over; possession talked. They would have to yield or face renewal of the war. A token payment of $20,000,000 was offered to grease acceptance of the inevitable. On December 10 the Treaty of Paris was signed, transferring sovereignty of the Philippines to the United States, with the $20,000,000 to follow upon ratification. "We have bought ten million Malays at $2.00 a head unpicked," remarked Reed acidly, and in the most prescient comment made by anyone at the time, he added, "and nobody knows what it will cost to pick them."

Although by now it was half expected, Aguinaldo and his forces learned of the settlement in bitterness and anguish, many of them hardly able to believe that their liberators and allies had turned into a new set of conquerors. Without an organized army or modern weapons, they prepared to fight again, while waiting for a still possible default. The strong anti-imperialist current in the United States was known to them and there was hope that the Senate would fail to ratify the treaty.

Reopening on December 5, 1898, the winter session of Congress was dominated by the fight over the treaty, more intense than that over Hawaii. Every vote counted. To gather their two-thirds, the Republicans led by Lodge as chief Whip had to utilize every artifice, every argument, every avenue of pressure upon their own members and whatever Democrats might be amenable, while the anti-expansionists struggled to hold firm just enough Senators to make a third plus one. In the House at this time certain members proposed to Reed a coalition of Democrats and anti-imperialist Republicans in order to pass a House resolution against the treaty which would lead to its defeat in the Senate. Though it was no secret in Washington's inner circles by now that he "despised" the Administration, Reed refused. While he remained its pilot, he was not prepared to lead a revolt against it. His task as Speaker was filled with gall. "Reed is terribly bitter," wrote Lodge to Roosevelt, "saying all sorts of ugly things about the Administration and its policy in private talks so that I keep out of his way for I am fond of him and confess that his attitude is painful and disappointing to me beyond words."

The public was not happy about the Philippine adventure and confused as to its duty. Democrats and Populists especially had felt the war in Cuba to be in the cause of freedom. Now, through some sorcery of fate, the war had turned into a matter of imposing sovereignty over an unwilling people by right of conquest. America had become the new Spain. In this unhappy moment impressive advice was offered through the combined effort of two men with the same extraordinary sensitivity to history-in-the-making. On February 1, 1899, S. S. McClure published in a two-page spread in his magazine an exhortation in verse by Rudyard Kipling addressed to the Americans in their perplexity.

Take up the White Man's burden
Send forth the best ye breed,
Go bind your sons to exile
To serve your captives' need;
To wait in heavy harness
On fluttered folk and wild,
Your new-caught sullen peoples,
Half-devil and half-child. . . .

Take up the White Man's burden
The savage wars of peace,
Fill full the mouth of Famine
And bid the sickness cease. . . .

Ye dare not stoop to less——

The note of righteousness was reinstated; Kipling had struck the perfect combination of noble destiny and unselfish mission. Widely reprinted and quoted, the poem spread across the country within a week, doing much to reconcile the hesitant to the imperial task.

In Washington it appeared as if opponents of the treaty might be successful, for the Republicans lacked one vote to make up the two-thirds for ratification. Suddenly, William Jennings Bryan arrived in Washington and to the amazement of his followers urged them to vote *for* the treaty. As leader of the Democratic party, he fully intended to be the standard-bearer himself in 1900, but he recognized the need of a new standard. Calculating that he could not win on a repetition of the silver issue, he was perfectly prepared to give it up in favor of imperialism, a new crown of thorns. He was sure that retention of the Philippines would be productive of so much trouble as to make a flaming campaign issue—but it must be consummated first. Consequently, he told his party, it would not do to defeat the treaty. This extraordinary reasoning astounded and even shocked those legislators who had thought a principle was involved. Senator Pettigrew, the "silver" Senator of South Dakota, was "so incensed that I finally told him he had no business in Washington on such an errand." In the delicate balance that prevailed, the most important issue since Secession depended on the votes of one or two vacillating Senators. Some were affected when Bryan argued that to ratify the treaty would end the war.

At this point, with the vote scheduled for February 6, with the outcome uncertain, with each side anxiously canvassing and counting every possible aye and nay, the Filipinos rose in their own war of independence. Their forces attacked the American lines outside Manila on the night of February 4. In Washington, although the news intensified the frenzied speculation, no one could be certain what effect it would have. A last-minute petition signed by ex-President Cleveland, President Eliot of Harvard and twenty-two other men of national prominence was addressed to the Senate, protesting against the treaty unless it included a provision against annexing the Philippines and Porto Rico. "In accordance with the principles upon which our Republic was founded we are in duty bound to recognize the rights of the inhabitants . . . to independence and self-government," it said, and pointed out that if, as McKinley had once declared, the forcible annexation of Cuba would be "criminal aggression by our code of morals," annexation of the Philippines would be no less so. Its text was unanswerable but it offered no judgeships, political futures or other coin that Lodge and Bryan were dealing in.

When the Senate voted on February 6, the treaty won by 57–27, with a one-vote margin. It was "the closest, hardest fight I have ever known," said Lodge. In the aftermath one thing on which all agreed was that Bryan had swung the deciding votes. By the time the vote was counted 59 Americans were dead and 278 wounded and some 500 Filipinos were casualties in the Philippines. The cost of picking Malays was just beginning to be paid.

"The way the country puked up its ancient principles at the first touch of temptation was sickening," wrote William James in a private letter. Publicly, to the Boston *Evening Transcript*, he wrote, "We are now openly engaged in crushing out the sacredest thing in this great human world—the attempt of a people long enslaved" to attain freedom and work out its own destiny. The saddest thing for men such as James was the parting with the American dream. America, Norton wrote, "has lost her unique position as a leader in the progress of civilization, and has taken up her place simply as one of the grasping and selfish nations of the present day."

To many others the knowledge of American guns firing on Filipinos was painful. The anger of the Anti-Imperialists deepened and their membership increased to half a million, with branches of the League in Boston and Springfield, in New York, Philadelphia, Baltimore, Washington, Cincinnati, Cleveland, Detroit, St. Louis, Los Angeles, and Portland, Oregon. "We are false to all we have believed in," wrote Moorfield Storey. "This great free land which for more than a century has offered a refuge to the oppressed of every land, has now turned to oppression." Still unwilling to give up, he hoped for leadership from Reed, whom Roosevelt had called "the most influential man in Congress." Writing to Senator Hoar, Storey begged him to "persuade Mr. Reed to come out as he should. He is very sluggish and lacks aggression in great matters. If he would come out I think he might really be the next President."

It was too late. Reed's sluggishness was that of a man for whom the fight has turned sour. Others whose main interest lay in non-political fields could feel as deeply without being shattered. Reed's whole life was in Congress, in politics, in the exercise of representative government, with the qualification that for him it had to be exercised toward an end that he believed in. His party and his country were now bent on a course for which he felt deep distrust and disgust. To mention expansion to him, said a journalist, was like "touching a match" and brought forth "sulphurous language." The tide had turned against him; he could not turn it back and would not go with it.

Like his country, he had come to a time of choice. He could go on to another term as Speaker, but already he could see signs of growing feeling in the House that he was too hostile to the Administration to continue as its principal lieutenant. Joe Cannon and others of his old associates were antagonized by his attitude and his remarks about the President but none dared attempt a contest to unseat him. The President lacked the nerve to come out openly in support of anyone else. Reed knew he could hold his command but it would be a term at bay against a pack snarling at his feet. He became "moody and ugly" in these days and curt to old colleagues whom he saw deserting him.

To retain office as Speaker would be to carry through a policy in the Philippines abominable to him. It would be to continue as spokesman of the party of Lincoln, which had been his home for so long and which had now chosen, in another way than Lincoln meant, to "meanly lose the last best hope of earth." To his longtime friend and secretary, Asher Hinds, he said, "I have tried, perhaps not always successfully, to make the acts of my public life accord with my conscience and I cannot now do this thing." For him the purpose and savor of life in the political arena had departed. He had discovered mankind's tragedy: that it can draw the blueprints of goodness but it cannot live up to them.

In February, 1899, after the vote on the treaty, he made his choice. Although he said nothing publicly at this time, rumors that he intended to withdraw from politics began to appear in the press. When reporters came to ask him about his hostility to the Philippines policy and the Nicaragua Canal bill, he brushed aside their questions with an expression of "fatigue and disgust." In April, after the close of the Fifty-fifth Congress, he authorized an announcement. The unbelievable proved true. Speaker Reed would retire from Congress and after a vacation in Europe would take up the private practice of law in New York as senior partner in the firm of Simpson, Thacher and Barnum.

"Congress without Tom Reed! Who can imagine it!" exclaimed an editorial in the New York *Tribune*. Everywhere was felt a half-frightened sense as of some great landmark being removed, leaving a gaping hole at the feet of observers. The *Times*, never one of his admirers, was moved to a full-column editorial on the "national loss." It felt "there must be something wrong in the political condition" that made such a man leave public life for the private practice of law. Its Washington correspondent called the event a "calamity" for Congress in the degree to which it would reduce the level of ability after the Speaker departed. Godkin in the *Evening Post* mourned the passing from political life of that rare phenomenon, "a mature, rational man."

Reed himself offered no public explanation of his going except to say, in a farewell letter to his constituents in Maine, "Office as a ribbon to stick in your coat is worth no-one's consideration." Cornered in the Manhattan Hotel in New York by reporters who urged that the public would want to hear from him, he replied, "The public! I have no interest in the public," and turned on his heel and walked away.

Military operations in the Philippines swelled in size and savagery. Against the stubborn guerrilla warfare of the Filipinos, the U.S. Army poured in regiments, brigades, divisions, until as many as 75,000—more than four times as many as saw action in Cuba—were engaged in the islands at one time. Filipinos burned, ambushed, raided, mutilated; on occasion they buried prisoners alive. Americans retaliated with atrocities of their own, burning down a whole village and killing every inhabitant if an American soldier was found with his throat cut, applying the "water cure" and other tortures to obtain information. They were three thousand miles from home, exasperated by heat, malaria, tropical rains, mud and mosquitoes. They sang, "Damn, damn, damn the Filipino, civilize him with a Krag . . ." and officers on occasion issued orders to take no more prisoners. They won all the skirmishes against an enemy who constantly renewed himself. A raiding party which missed Aguinaldo but captured his young son made headlines. Reed, coming into his office that morning, said in mock surprise to his law partner, "What, are you working today? I should think you would be celebrating. I see by the papers that the American Army has captured the infant son of Aguinaldo and at last accounts was in hot pursuit of the mother."

Aguinaldo fought for time in the hope that anti-imperialist sentiment in America would force withdrawal of the forces already sickening of their task. The longer the war continued, the louder and angrier grew the Anti-Imperialist protests. Their program adopted at Chicago in October, 1899, demanded "an immediate cessation of the war against liberty." They collected and reported all the worst cases of American conduct in the Philippines and all the most egregious speeches of imperialist greed and set them against the most unctuous expressions of the white man's mission. They distributed pamphlets paid for by Andrew Carnegie, and when the League's executive head, Edward Atkinson, applied to the War Department for permission to send the pamphlets to the Philippines and was refused, he sent them anyway.

Anxious to end the war and placate the "new-caught sullen peoples" and govern creditably, the Administration sent various committees to investigate the atrocities, to find out what the Filipinos really wanted—short of self-government, which they said they wanted—and to report on what form of civil government to give them. In April, 1900, the shy, kindly, three-hundred-pound Judge William Howard Taft was sent out to set up a civil government, armed with a charter drawn up by the new Secretary of War, Elihu Root, which granted the Filipinos a liberal degree of internal autonomy. Since neither they nor the Americans were ready to give up fighting, the attempt was premature, but Taft stayed on, determined to govern in the interest of "the little brown brother" as soon as he was given a chance. When friends at home, concerned for his welfare, sent anxious queries about his health, he cabled Elihu Root that he had been out horseback riding and was feeling fine. "How is the horse feeling?" Root cabled back.

Despite difficulties there was no re-thinking or hesitancy among the dominant Republicans about the new career upon which America was launched. The bill for constructing the Nicaragua Canal was in the Senate and so was Albert Beveridge, more closely allied with the Almighty than ever. "We will not renounce our part in the mission of our race, trustees under God, of the civilization of the world," he said on January 8, 1900. He informed Senators that God had been preparing "the English-speaking and Teutonic peoples" for this mission for a thousand years.

Some of Beveridge's generation found the new image of America repugnant. Hearing the sound of "ignoble battle" coming "sullenly over the Pacific seas," William Vaughn Moody wrote his "Ode in a Time of Hesitation," which appeared in the *Atlantic Monthly* in May, 1900. Are we still the "eagle nation" he asked, or:

> Shall some less lordly bird be set apart?
> Some gross-billed wader where the swamps are fat?
> Some gorger in the sun? Some prowler with the bat?

This was the conscience of the few, felt too by Godkin, who, in his disillusion, said a strange and clairvoyant thing at this time. "The military spirit," he wrote to Moorfield Storey in January, 1900, "has taken possession of the masses to whom power has passed."

As the war passed its first anniversary with the American forces deeply extended, there was one event ahead that might yet bring it to an end: the coming Presidential election. In this the Anti-Imperialists and Aguinaldo placed their hopes. Its earliest oddity was a boom for Admiral Dewey, partly inspired by the desperation of some Democrats to find any candidate other than Bryan. Having concluded after some study of the subject that "the office of President is not such a very difficult one to fill," the Admiral announced he was available but as his wording did not inspire confidence and he seemed vague as to party, his candidacy collapsed. Bryan loomed.

The Anti-Imperialists were caught in an agonizing dilemma. McKinley represented the party of imperialism; Bryan in Carl Schurz's words was "the evil genius of the anti-imperialist cause," loathed for his betrayal in the matter of the treaty and feared for his radicalism. Schurz met with Carnegie, Gamaliel Bradford and Senator Pettigrew at the Plaza Hotel in New York in January, 1900, in an effort to organize a third party so that the American people would not "be forced by the two rotten old party carcasses to choose between two evils." Carnegie subscribed $25,000 on the spot, while the others made up a matching sum. Shortly afterward, members of the steel trust with whom Carnegie was then negotiating the sale of his company told him that if he opposed McKinley the deal would not go through. Preferring United States Steel to a third party, Carnegie withdrew his support, received his shares and retired from business. Schurz and the others, however, held a Liberty Congress at Indianapolis, at which they called on Reed to be their candidate, but neither Reed nor anyone else wanted the vain task of leading a mugwump party. At Kansas City in July the inevitable happened: Bryan was chosen.

Campaigning on imperialism as he had planned, Bryan ranged the country as strenuously as before. He was tarnished, but his magnetism, his passion and his sincerity-of-the-moment still reached through to the people and even across the Pacific. In Bryan, but for whom the Treaty of Paris would have been defeated, the Filipinos placed their faith. "The great Democratic party of the United States will win the next fall election," Aguinaldo promised in a proclamation. "Imperialism will fail in its mad attempt to subjugate us by force of arms." His soldiers shouted the war cry, "Aguinaldo-Bryan!"

In their Chicago platform, anticipating the election, the Anti-Imperialists had said, "We propose to contribute to the defeat of any person or party that stands for the subjugation of any people." There was nothing to do, as a friend wrote to ex-President Cleveland, but "to hold your nose and vote" for Bryan. The modified rapture of such people for the Democratic candidate won them the name thereafter of the "hold-your-nose-and-vote" group. So distasteful to the *Nation* were both candidates that it refused to support either, preferring, as a dissatisfied reader complained, to "sit on a fence and scold at both."

The Republicans had no such difficulties. Although they preferred to be called expansionists rather than imperialists, they were proud of the condition whatever its name, and believed in its goals. Forthright as usual, Lodge said, "Manila with its magnificent bay is the prize and pearl of the East; . . . it will keep us open to the markets of China. . . . Shall we hesitate and make, in coward fashion, what Dante calls the 'great refusal'?" Secretary Hay having pronounced the policy of the Open Door, China's markets were much on men's minds. During the summer of the campaign, the siege of the legations at Peking by the Boxers and the American share in the relief expedition pointed up the far-flung role the country was now playing. Its most convinced and vocal champion was McKinley's new vice-presidential nominee, Theodore Roosevelt, who took the President's place as chief campaigner. Unsure of victory, for the "full dinner pail" was more a slogan than a fact, he campaigned so vigorously and indefatigably that to the public and cartoonists the Rough Rider with the teeth, pince-nez and unquenchable zest appeared to be the real candidate. He derided the specter of militarism as a "shadowy ghost," insisted that expansion "in no way affects our institutions or our traditional policies," and said the question was not "whether we shall expand—for we have already expanded—but whether we shall contract."

The country listened to thousands of speeches and read thousands of newspaper columns raking over every argument for and against imperialism and every aspect of the war in the Philippines. It learned, thanks to the efforts of the Anti-Imperialists, more about the conduct of its own troops than the public usually does in wartime. Dumdum bullets, so thoroughly disapproved (except by the British) at The Hague Peace Conference the year before, were found to have been issued to some American troops. In the end the American people, like the British in their Khaki election of the same year, approved the incumbents. What a people thinks at any given time can best be measured by what they do. McKinley and Roosevelt were elected by 53 per cent of the votes cast and with a greater margin over Bryan than had been received in 1896. Expansion and conquest were accepted and the break with the American past confirmed. Still at war in the Philippines, America moved into the Twentieth Century.

For Aguinaldo, after the election, there was nothing more to hope for. Retreating into the mountains, still fighting, he was captured by trickery in March, 1901, and in captivity in April signed an oath of allegiance to the United States together with a proclamation to his people calling for an end to resistance: "There has been enough blood, enough tears, enough desolation."

Professor Norton voiced the elegy of the Anti-Imperialists. "I reach one conclusion," he wrote to a friend in the month of Aguinaldo's capture, "that I have been too much of an idealist about America, had set my hopes too high, had formed too fair an image of what she might become. Never had a nation such an opportunity; she was the hope of the world. Never again will any nation have her chance to raise the standard of civilization."

Six months later came Czolgosz's shot and McKinley's place was taken by Roosevelt, "that damned cowboy," as Mark Hanna said when he heard the news. The remark was not astute. It was an architect of the new age who now became its President at forty-three.

Reed wrote him a letter of good wishes but the exchange was formal and the gulf remained. Living in New York, Reed formed a congenial companionship with Mark Twain, whose wit and turn of mind and sardonic outlook matched his own. They were guests together on board the yacht of the multi-trust capitalist Henry H. Rogers for a long cruise of which the epic legend survives that Reed won twenty-three poker hands in succession. He visited Washington now and then, once arguing a case before the Supreme Court and entertaining the justices by his rather remarkable style of delivery. He did not revisit the floor of the House but would hold court and see old friends in the office of the Ways and Means Committee. On doctor's orders he succeeded in losing forty pounds but his health was worrisome. In the summer of 1902 he was the central figure at Bowdoin's centennial celebration, where he enjoyed "a rare good time" such as, he said, "we may have again but cannot sanely look for." In December he was back in Washington and while in the Committee Room at the Capitol, was suddenly taken ill. He proved to be in the terminal stage of a chronic nephritis. Five days later, on December 6, 1902, he died, aged sixty-two. Joe Cannon, his successor as Speaker, said of him, "His was the strongest intellect crossed on the best courage of any man in public life that I have ever known." With those two qualities and his "self-made laws," Reed had stood his ground on the swampy soil of politics, uncompromising to the end, a lonely specimen of an uncommon kind, the Independent Man.

4

"GIVE ME COMBAT!"

FRANCE: 1894–99

4

"Give Me Combat!"

"THE PERMANENT glamour of France" was a phrase used by an Englishman of the nineties, Sir Almeric Fitzroy, secretary to the Duke of Devonshire. He felt that every child of Western civilization owed a debt to the country from which "came the impulse that dissolved the old world in agony and gave life and passion to the present." For two years, from the summer of 1897 to the summer of 1899, the agony of that old dissolution returned. Rent by a moral passion that reopened past wounds, broke apart society and consumed thought, energy and honor, France plunged into one of the great commotions of history.

During those "two interminable years" of struggle to secure the retrial of a single individual unjustly convicted, "life was as if suspended," wrote Léon Blum, a future premier, then in his twenties. It was as if, in those "years of tumult, of veritable civil war . . . everything converged upon a single question and in the most intimate feelings and personal relationships everything was interrupted, turned upside down, reclassified. . . . The Dreyfus Affair was a human crisis, less extended and less prolonged in time but no less violent than the French Revolution."

It "would have divided the angels themselves," wrote the Comte de Vogüé, on the opposite side from Blum. "Above the base motives and animal passions, the finest souls in France flung themselves at each other with an equal nobility of sentiments exasperated by their fearful conflict."

The protagonists felt a grandeur in the storm that battered them. Decadence was exorcised in the violence of their feelings and they felt conscious again of "high principles and inexhaustible energies." Hate, evil and fear encompassed them as well as courage and sacrifice. Their combat was epic and its issue was the life of the Republic. Each side fought for an idea, its idea of France: one the France of Counter-Revolution, the other the France of 1789; one for its last chance to arrest progressive social tendencies and restore the old values; the other to cleanse the honor of the Republic and preserve it from the clutches of reaction. The Revisionists, who fought for retrial, saw France as the fount of liberty, the country of light, the teacher of reason, the codifier of law, and to them the knowledge that she could have perpetrated a wrong and connived at a miscarriage of justice was insufferable. They fought for Justice. Those on the other side claimed to fight in the name of *Patrie* for the preservation of the Army as the shield and protector of the nation and of the Church as the guide and instructor of its soul. They assembled under the name of Nationalists and in their ranks sincere men were partners of demagogues and succumbed to methods that were reckless and brutal and terms that were foul, so that the world watched in wonder and scorn and the name of France suffered. Locked in mutual ferocity and final commitment the contenders could not disengage, although their struggle was splitting the country and fostering opportunity for the enemy at their frontiers, which every day the enemy measured.

"We were heroes," proclaimed Charles Péguy, who transmuted and exalted the political movements of his day in mystical terms inherited from Joan of Arc. In 1910 he wrote, "The Dreyfus Affair can only be explained by the need for heroism which periodically seizes this people, this race—seizes a whole generation of us. The same is true of those other great ordeals: wars. . . . When a great war or great revolution breaks out it is because a great people, a great race needs to break out, because it has had enough, particularly enough of peace. It always means that a great mass feels and experiences a violent need, a mysterious need for a great movement, . . . a sudden need for glory, for war, for history, which causes an explosion, an eruption . . ." If the values and forces Péguy saw in the Affair were large, it was because they were those of that time and that experience. The Affair made men feel larger than life.

The *casus belli* was condemnation of a Jewish army officer for treason in behalf of Germany; the object of the battle was on the one hand to prevent, on the other to obtain, a reopening of the case. Because it was weak, the Government employed all its weight on the side of its would-be destroyers to brace and support the original verdict. It was not the stable, respected, solidly embedded government enjoyed by the English, but insecure, thinly rooted in public confidence, flouted and on the defensive. Twice since 1789 the Republic had gone down under resurgent monarchy. Emerging as the Third Republic after 1871, France had revived, prospered, acquired an Empire. She nourished the arts, gloried in the most cultivated capital, and raised, on the hundredth anniversary of the Revolution, the tallest structure in the world, the daring, incredible Tower that soared above the Seine, a signal flag of her vitality and genius.

Always, however, in political life the nation was at odds with itself, galled from within by the unreconciled, unsubdued adherents of the *ancien régime* and Second Empire, oppressed from without by the superior strength of Germany and the sense of unfinished war between them, hankering for *revanche* without the means to achieve it. In 1889 discontent with the Republic came to a head in the attempted coup d'état of General Boulanger supported by all the elements of Counter-Revolution who made up the collective Right—the Church, the two hundred families of business and finance, the displaced aristocracy, the royalists and the followers and sympathizers of these groups. Boulanger's attempt ended in fiasco memorable for the remark of the Premier, Charles Floquet, "At your age, General, Napoleon was dead." Nevertheless his attempt shook the Republic and stirred up both the expectations and the frustrations of the Right.

The arrest, trial, conviction and sentencing of Captain Alfred Dreyfus, an artillery officer assigned to the General Staff, which took place in the months October to December, 1894, was not a deliberate plot to frame an innocent man. It was the outcome of a reasonable suspicion acted on by dislike, some circumstantial evidence and instinctive prejudice. Evidence indicated betrayal of military secrets to Germany by some artillery officer on the General Staff. Dreyfus, besides fitting the requirements, was a Jew, the eternal alien: a natural suspect to absorb the stain of treason. As a person he was not liked by his brother officers. Stiff, silent, cold and almost unnaturally correct, he was without friends, opinions or visible feelings, and his officiousness on duty had already attracted unfavorable attention. These characteristics appeared sinister as soon as he came under suspicion. His appearance, the reverse of flamboyant, seemed the perfect cover for a spy. Of medium height and weight, medium brown hair, and medium age, thirty-six, he had a toneless voice, and unremarkable features distinguished only by rimless pince-nez, the fashionable form of eyeglasses in his milieu. His guilt was immediately presumed. When motive and material proof could not be found, the officers who were charged with the inquiry, especially Major Henry and Colonel du Paty de Clam, made up for it by helpful construction and fabrication. Certain that they were dealing with a vile traitor who had sold secrets of military defence to the traditional enemy, they felt justified in supplying whatever was needed to convict him. The dossier they assembled, later to be known as the "Secret File," was persuasive enough to cause the General Staff chiefs sincerely to believe Dreyfus guilty, but it lacked legal proof. Knowing this, and dealing in a case particularly sensitive because of the involvement of Germany, and fearing the blackmail of the press, the then Minister of War, General Mercier, ordered, and the Government of which he was a member permitted, Captain Dreyfus' court-martial to be held *in camera*. When the questions of the five military judges indicated their doubts, the Secret File was submitted to them and withheld from the defence. Convinced by these documents, the judges reached a unanimous verdict of guilty. The death penalty for political crimes having been abolished in 1848, the sentence was life imprisonment. On the prisoner's refusal to confess and persistence in maintaining his innocence, he was ordered confined to Devil's Island, one of three prison islands off the coast of South America used for desperate criminals. A barren rock two miles long and five hundred yards wide, it was cleared of all but guards to accommodate Dreyfus alone, in a stone hut under perpetual surveillance. The unanimity of the military court seemed confirmed by a published rumor that Dreyfus had confessed, which, as it passed from journal to journal, acquired the force of an official statement and satisfied the public.

The next three years were marked by intense efforts both to uncover and to conceal the truth. The long, painful struggle for judicial review, or "Revision," as it was known, originated in the doubts of a few scattered individuals uneasy about the closed trial, who suspected a miscarriage of justice. They uncovered the illegality of the trial—on the basis of material not having been shown to the defence—and accumulated evidence pointing to the probable true culprit, a raffish and exotic officer, Major Ferdinand Walsin-Esterhazy. Their pressures and pryings caused the officers originally responsible for constructing the case against Dreyfus to try to strengthen its weaknesses. Major Henry of the Counter-Espionage Bureau, which by nature dealt in forgery and extra-legal procedures, forged a letter, supposedly from the Italian military attaché, Major Panizzardi, to his German colleague, incriminating Dreyfus after the event, and on this letter, thereafter, the Army's case hung. Each move in the campaign for Revision set off renewed efforts inside the General Staff to shore up the case and cover past fabrications in the Secret File by new ones. Officers succumbed to the mood of conspirators. There were secret meetings, warnings and blackmailings, clandestine relations between Paty de Clam and Esterhazy, disguises in false beards and dark glasses, and various melodramatic enterprises so deeply entangling the Army in acts it could never explain that by now it could not afford to face a reopening of the case. Anyone agitating for Revision or raising a question of Dreyfus' lawful conviction became *ipso facto* the Army's enemy and by extension the enemy of France.

The Army was not political, not particularly clerical, not exclusively aristocratic or royalist, not necessarily anti-Semitic. Although many of its officers were all these things, the Army as a body was part of the Republic, not, like the Church, its antagonist. Despite the anti-Republican sentiments of individual officers, it accepted its role as an instrument of the state. The Republic, needing the Army, was working to make it a more serious, professionally trained body than the operatic corps of the Second Empire, which from the Crimea to Sedan plunged into battle with more dash than staff work. As a whole, the officer corps was still dominated by the graduates of St-Cyr who came largely from county families still mentally barricaded against the ideas of the Revolution. Its cult was that of a class distinct from civilians, little concerned with or aware of what was going on in the rest of the nation. It was a club loyal to its membership and cultivating its distinctiveness of which the visible mark was the uniform. Unlike British officers, who never wore uniform off duty, French officers before 1900 never wore anything else. Poorly paid, slowly promoted, drearily garrisoned for long stretches in some provincial town, their recompense was prestige: the honors, immunities and cachet of their caste; in short, the esteem in which they were held.

The esteem was great. In the eyes of the people the Army was above politics; it was the nation, it was France, it was the greatness of France. It was the Army of Revolution as of Empire, the Army of Valmy in '92 when Goethe, watching, said, "From this day forth commences a new era in the world's history." It was the Army of Marengo, Austerlitz and Wagram, the *Grande Armée* that Lavisse proudly called "one of the most perfect instruments of war history has ever seen"; the Army of the cuirasse and saber, of the képi and *pantalons rouges*, of Sebastopol and the Malakoff, of Magenta and Solferino, the Army that had made France the greatest military power in Europe until the rise of Prussia, the Army of tragedy as of glory, the Army of the Last Cartridges at Sedan, of the wild cavalry charge that evoked the German Emperor's cry, "*Oh, les braves gens!*" Twenty-five years later, under the never-absent shadow of Germany, the Army was both defender of the nation and instrument of *revanche*. It was the means of restoring, someday, the national glory. Men lifted their hats when the colonel and the colors at the head of a regiment marched by. In the words of a character whom Anatole France was satirizing—though not misrepresenting—the Army "is all that is left of our glorious past. It consoles us for the present and gives us hope of the future." The Army was *les braves gens*.

In the course of the Affair it became the prisoner of its friends—clericals, royalists, anti-Semites, Nationalists and all the anti-Republican groups who made its honor the rallying cry of their own causes, for their own purposes. Caught in the trap of its early commitment to Dreyfus' guilt, and of the forgeries and machinations by its officers to establish that guilt, the Army's honor became synonymous with maintenance of the original verdict. It was a fort to be defended against Revision.

Resistance to Revision was grounded in the belief that to reopen the trial was to discredit the Army and a discredited Army could not fight Germany. "Revision means War," proclaimed the royalist *Gazette de France* and a war fought with a disorganized Army is "*la Débâcle*," the name given to the defeat of 1870. How could soldiers go into battle under officers they had been taught to despise? asked the royalist Comte d'Haussonville. Although he thought the idea of an innocent man in prison "intolerable" and the campaign against the Jews "revolting," nevertheless the Dreyfusard campaign against the Army was worse because it destroyed confidence in the officer corps. It was this fear of what would happen if the Army were weakened by distrust that intimidated the Chamber and turned the populace against Revision. The Army was their guarantee of peace. "France loves peace and prefers glory," it was said, and this sentiment too was mauled by Revision. By casting doubt on the infallibility of the General Staff Revision was equivalent to sacrilege against *la gloire militaire* and anyone favoring it was pro-German if not a traitor.

Mystified by the complexities of documents, facsimiles, trials and the Secret File, the people could not reconcile the idea of forgeries deliberately prepared to convict an innocent man with their idea of the Army which meant parades, uniforms, boots, epaulets, guns and flags. How could officers who rode proudly past on horseback, sword in hand, to the sound of music and drums, be imagined bent over tables in stuffy offices carefully forging handwriting and piecing letters together with scissors and glue? There was nothing brave or military about this, therefore it could only be calumny. The people were patriotic and Republican, believed what they read in the newspapers, loved the Army and hated and feared the "others" —*sans-patrie*, incendiaries, church-burners, Dreyfusards—who, they were told, were sworn to destroy it. They shouted "*Vive l'Armée!*" and "*Vive la République!*" "Down with Dreyfusards!" "Down with the Jews!" "Death to traitors!" "*Vive Mercier!*" and any other form of incantation that would serve to banish evil and reassure their faith.

The Army was personified in terms of the Affair by General Auguste Mercier, who as Minister of War in 1894 had originally ordered Dreyfus' arrest and through the consequence of that act became the idol of the Army's supporters and the symbol of its cause. At parties of the *haut monde*, ladies rose to their feet when General Mercier entered the room. Sixty-one, tall, thin, straight and well groomed, he had strongly carved features, a curved nose framed by the sharp upturned points of a "Kaiser" moustache, and expressionless eyes, usually half-closed except when they opened for a cold, direct glance. A veteran of the campaigns in Mexico and at Metz in 1870, he was welcomed by the Staff, on his appointment as War Minister in 1893, as a true soldier who was not a politician. When the Anarchist, Vaillant, had thrown his bomb in the Chamber, Mercier had sat through the smoke and uproar without moving a muscle except to catch a fragment which had bounced off the seat behind him and hand it to the deputy sitting there, saying without expression, "You can have it back." In character firm, decisive and thoughtful, in manner urbane and reserved, he was invariably polite and never abandoned, as the combat grew vicious, the usage *Monsieur* where others used "*sale bête*" or "*ce salaud*" as prefix to the name of a despised opponent.

In 1894 faced with the existence of treason on his Staff and realizing the legal weakness of the evidence collected against Dreyfus, he had ordered his arrest in the hope of extracting a confession. When this was not forthcoming and while the investigating officers were desperately seeking evidence to strengthen the case, the arrest was leaked to the anti-Semitic paper, *La Libre Parole*, which asserted that Dreyfus would not be tried because Mercier was in the pay of the Jews. Under the goading of this and other papers, Mercier had summoned the military editor of *Figaro* and told him what he sincerely believed: that he had had from the beginning "proofs that cried aloud the treason of Dreyfus" and that his "guilt was absolutely certain." He thereby, before the trial, tied the Army to Dreyfus' guilt and locked the terms of the Affair into a position that could never be broken. The issue was instantly recognized at the time. "Today one must be either for Mercier or for Dreyfus; I am for Mercier," said his parliamentary aide, General Riu, to reporters. "If Dreyfus is acquitted, Mercier goes," wrote the royalist editor, Cassagnac, in *l'Autorité*, adding, since Mercier was a member of the Government, "If Dreyfus is not guilty then the Government is." Thereafter every repetition of the choice only hardened the issue.

At the trial, it was General Mercier who authorized submission of the Secret File and its withholding from the defence—the act that made the trial illegal. Fully recognizing the decisive nature of what he had done, Mercier lived up to it during the next two years, through all the mounting evidence of forgeries and false conviction, with increasingly arrogant and positive assertions of Dreyfus' guilt. Once Dreyfus had been convicted on false evidence, any reopening of the case would reveal the Ministry of War, the General Staff and himself as dishonored; in short, as a colleague said, if in a retrial "Captain Dreyfus is acquitted, it is General Mercier who becomes the traitor." Through every reinvestigation and taking of testimony, the trial of Esterhazy, the trial of Zola, the inquiry of the Court of Appeals, the final trial at Rennes, he beat back the forces of Revision and held the citadel of the false verdict. Angular, haughty, icy-faced, never wavering in self-control even when the whole structure he had built was tottering, he reminded an observer of the character in Dante's Inferno who looked around him with disdain, "as if he held Hell in great contempt."

All the strength, except truth, was on his side. Each time the Dreyfusards brought forward new evidence which they were certain this time must force a retrial, it was quashed, suppressed, thrown out or matched with new fabrications by the Army, supported by the Government, by all the *bien-pensants* or right-thinking communicants of the Church, and by the screams and thunders of four-fifths of the press. It was the press which created the Affair and made truce impossible.

Variegated, virulent, turbulent, literary, inventive, personal, conscienceless and often vicious, the daily newspapers of Paris were the liveliest and most important element in public life. The dailies numbered between twenty-five and thirty-five at a given time. They represented every conceivable shade of opinion, calling themselves Republican, Conservative, Catholic, Socialist, Nationalist, Bonapartist, Legitimist, Independent, absolutely Independent, Conservative-Catholic, Conservative-Monarchist, Republican-Liberal, Republican-Socialist, Republican-Independent, Republican-Progressist, Republican-Radical-Socialist. Some were morning, some evening, some had illustrated supplements. Of four to six pages, they covered, besides the usual political and foreign affairs, news of the *haut monde*, of *le turf*, of fashions, of theatre and opera, concerts and art, the salons and the Academy. All the most admired writers, among them Anatole France, Jules Lemaître, Maurice Barrès, Marcel Prévost, contributed columns and critiques and their novels ran serially across the bottom of the front page. Editors on important issues contributed signed editorials of passionate invective. The press was daily wine, meat and bread to Paris. Major careers and a thousand minor ones were made in journalism. Everyone from Academicians to starving Anarchists made a supplementary living from it. Prominent politicians when out of office turned to journalism for a platform and an income.

Newspapers could be founded overnight by anyone with energy, financial support and a set of opinions to plead. Writing talent was hardly a special requirement, because everyone in the politico-literary world of Paris could write—and did, instantly, speedily, voluminously. Columns of opinion, criticism, controversy, poured out like water. *Le Temps*, Olympian and responsible, led all the rest. Its outsize pages were read by everyone in public life, its reviews decided the fate of a play, its editorials on foreign affairs written by André Tardieu were of such influence that the German Foreign Minister, von Bülow, remarked, "There are Three Great Powers in Europe—and M. Tardieu." Only *Le Temps* in its eminence remained above the battle, although inclining gradually toward Revision. *Figaro*, following it in importance, proved vulnerable. Its editor, Fernand de Rodays, after hearing Dreyfus cry out his innocence on the occasion of his military degradation, believed him. Three years later he published the first evidence against Esterhazy as well as Zola's first articles. Although he was a father and father-in-law of officers, his enraged colleagues of the Nationalist press denounced him as a traducer of the Army and organized a campaign to cancel subscriptions to *Figaro*. The management succumbed and de Rodays was ousted, an affair of such moment that Paris gossip said he had been paid 400,000 francs to support Dreyfus and the management 500,000 to get rid of him.

The blackmail of the Nationalist press, wrote Zola, who suffered its extremes, afflicted France like a "shameful disease which nobody has the courage to cure." The mischief-makers were the privately supported organs of special interests or of individual editors who were likely to be men either of rabid principles or none at all. There was Ernest Judet of *Le Petit Journal*, who led the campaign to smear Clemenceau with the mud of Panama and who, when Clemenceau became Premier in 1906, barricaded his villa at Neuilly as if to defend it against a siege. Devoured by a perpetual terror of Freemasons, Judet carried a loaded revolver and a leaded cane weighing twelve pounds. There was the old royalist, Paul de Cassagnac, who started the fashion in journalism for abuse and insult, and attacked everyone and everything from habit regardless of consistency. There was Arthur Meyer, a converted Jew, son of a tailor, grandson of a rabbi, an ardent Boulangist and royalist who was editor of *Le Gaulois*, which specialized in the doings of the *haut monde*. It was the paper read by the world of the "Guermantes." Meyer's wholehearted adoption of that world's opinions and prejudices took a certain courage or a thick skin, for he was no Charles Swann who melted into his surroundings, but in appearance resembled the anti-Semitic caricatures of Jews. He nevertheless had married into the Faubourg—a dowerless daughter of the Comte de Turenne—was accepted into the circle of the Duchesse d'Uzès, became friend, adviser and confidant of the late Pretender, the Comte de Paris, and set masculine style by the cut of his morning coat and the fold of his cravats.

Henri, Comte de Rochefort, of *l'Intransigeant*, was the kind of journalist whose capacity for mischief is unfettered by doctrine: the more unsettled his convictions, the more brilliant and scathing his pen. A constitutional "anti" described by a friend as "a reactionary without knowing it," a bright-eyed cynic and "aristo" with a pointed white beard and an exuberant laugh, Rochefort combined in his person almost every tendency, no matter how opposite, of the Third Republic. His *Adventures of My Life* filled five volumes. He had been everything from an antagonist of Napoleon III to an associate of General Boulanger and his daily column was the delight of the most impressionable and excitable portion of the public.

Approached by the early Dreyfusards on the theory that he would relish a challenge to prove innocent a condemned man whom everyone believed guilty, Rochefort had been cordial, but was dissuaded from the adventure by his manager, Ernest

Vaughan, on the ground that public opinion would not stand for disrespect of the Army. Rochefort found the other side just as exciting and when Vaughan meanwhile changed his mind, they quarreled, with the historic result that Vaughan departed to found his own paper, *l'Aurore*, and to provide an organ for the Dreyfusards which they had hitherto lacked. Rochefort retaliated with the most mischief-making story of the Affair. He informed his readers that a letter from the Kaiser to Dreyfus existed which the President of the Republic had been forced by threat of war to return to the German Ambassador, Count Münster, but not before it had previously been photographed. *L'Intransigeant* could say with "absolute certainty" on the authority of a high military personage that this was the "secret document" on which Dreyfus had been convicted.

So befuddled was the public mind by the fumes of mystification and intrigue rising from the Affair that the story was widely believed. It haunted efforts for Revision at every turn. It added fuel to the argument that Revision meant war. What acted on public opinion in the Affair was never what happened but what the Nationalist press and whispered rumor said happened. Intervention by Count Münster had indeed taken place for the purpose of officially denying any contact with Dreyfus but the view the public had of this incident was of a virtual ultimatum. The generals, whose thinking for good reason was dominated by the problem of Germany, used this as their excuse for not reopening the verdict and argued it so convincingly they convinced themselves. General Mercier testified he had sat up until midnight with the President and Premier after the interview with Count Münster waiting "to learn if war or peace would be the issue." General Boisdeffre, Chief of General Staff, angrily said to Princess Mathilde Bonaparte, when she argued the innocence of Dreyfus, "How can you say such a thing to me who has seen and held in his hands Dreyfus' own letters to the German Emperor?" Furious, the renowned hostess shouted, "If you have seen such letters they can only be apocryphal. You cannot make me believe in such a thing." Whereupon Boisdeffre strode out of the room in a rage and the Princess, letting out a sigh of relief, exclaimed, "*Quel animal, ce général!*"

What was truth and what people persuaded themselves was

truth became hopelessly blurred. The German Government's several denials of any knowledge of Dreyfus were ignored on the ground that Berlin would not know the names of spies its agents dealt with. On the other hand, the Nationalist papers pictured Germany as affronted to the point of threatening war by France's condemnation of Dreyfus in the face of its denials. Any willingness to consider Revision was denounced as cowardly submission to German pressure—and proof of the power of the "Syndicate."

A creation of the anti-Semitic press, the "Syndicate" represented the Right's idea of evil. It was supposed to be a subterranean fellowship of the Jews, a black and sinister conspiracy whose forces were mobilized to reverse the conviction of Dreyfus and to substitute a Christian as the traitor in his place. Any development in the case unfavorable to the Nationalists could be ascribed to the "Syndicate." Any prominent or respected person who proclaimed himself in favor of Revision was in the pay of the "Syndicate." Evidence of the Army's forgeries was itself forged by the "Syndicate." The Nationalists said it had spent ten million francs since 1895 for corrupting judges and handwriting experts, suborning journalists and ministers. They said its funds supplied by the great Jewish bankers were deposited in the vault of an international bank in Berlin. They said its German adviser was Pastor Günther, the Kaiser's personal chaplain. Its aim was to break down the nation's faith in the Army, reveal its military secrets and, when defenceless, open its gates to the enemy. It was personified by the cartoonists as a fat Jewish-featured figure in rings and watch chains wearing an expression of triumphant malevolence, standing with one foot on the neck of a prostrate Marianne. As the animus of the Affair grew, the "Syndicate" swelled in Nationalist eyes into a monstrous league not only of Jews but of Freemasons, Socialists, foreigners and all other evilly disposed persons. It was said to be drawing on funds from all France's enemies, who were using Dreyfus as an excuse to discredit the Army and divide the nation. The humiliation suffered at Fashoda at the hands of England was seen as engineered by the "Syndicate." The "Syndicate" was everywhere; it embodied the hates and fears of the Right. It was the Enemy.

*

The sudden and malign bloom of anti-Semitism in France was part of a wider outbreak. As a social and political force anti-Semitism emerged in the late Nineteenth Century out of other expanding forces which were building tensions between classes and among nations. Industrialization, imperialism, the growth of cities, the decline of the countryside, the power of money and the power of machines, the clenched fist of the working class, the red flag of Socialism, the wane of the aristocracy, all these forces and factors were churning like the bowels of a volcano about to erupt. "Something very great—ancient, cosmopolitan, feudal, agrarian Europe," as a contemporary said, was dying and in the process creating conflicts, fears and new-found strengths that needed outlet.

A classic outlet was anti-Semitism. As scapegoat to draw off discontent from the governing class, it appeared in Germany under Bismarck in the seventies and in Russia in the eighties. The pogroms of 1881 and the subsequent disabling May Laws awoke in Jews a recognition of Mazzini's dictum, "Without a country you are the bastards of humanity." Anti-Semitism served equally as scapegoat for the propertied class, and its virulence at this time reflected a profound unease under a sense of impending breakup of the old order. Old values were giving way. Anarchist assaults, Socialist agitation, the growing self-consciousness of labour were threatening position and property, and nothing so generates hostility as a threat to possessions. In the West the new antipathy afflicted cultivated men like Balfour's secretary, George Wyndham, and Theodore Roosevelt's particular friend, the English diplomat Cecil Spring-Rice. Henry Adams expressed it rabidly and incessantly: he lived only in the wish to see the end of "infernal Jewry" and all "gold-bugs"; "we are in the hands of Jews who do what they please with our values"; "I read with interest *France Juive*, *Libre Parole* and all"; "I pass the day reading Drumont's anti-Semitic ravings."

In men of this class the sentiment sprang from hatred of the new power of money (although nothing concerned Adams himself more than money), that is, of new "gold-bug" money deriving from stocks and shares and financial operations, in place of the acceptable form deriving from land and rents. The Jewish problem, explained the Duc d'Orléans during the Affair, was one of economic war. The day was approaching when all persons with attachment to the land and thus to their country would have to defend themselves against "the anonymous and vagabond" fortunes of the Jews, who had gorged themselves on the ruin of the Union Générale with the Government as their accomplice. The Union Générale was a Catholic bank founded with the blessing of Pope Leo XIII with the express purpose of attracting the investments of the faithful. On the advice of their priests, the aristocracy invested in it their capital, and modest Catholic families their savings. When, owing to the superior resources and shrewd maneuvers of its rivals, including the Rothschilds, the Union Générale collapsed in 1882, rich and poor Catholics alike lost their funds. The Jews were blamed. The Jewish "question" began to be discussed in the clerical and royalist papers. Secret plots and malignant powers were attributed to them. All the arguments which the Jew had inspired as the perennial stranger who persisted in retaining his own identity were revived. Jews were not Frenchmen; they were aliens within the French body, probably conspiring against France, certainly against the Church; they were promoters of the anti-clerical movement and enemies of Catholic *bien-pensants.*

French anti-Semitism, like its virulent appearances elsewhere in history, required the juncture of an instigator with circumstance. The instigator in this case was the previously unknown Edouard Drumont, who in the wake of the collapse of the Union Générale wrote a two-volume book, *La France Juive*, published in 1886 to instant success. It was a polemic compounded of Rothschilds and ritual murder, not a philosophical treatise like Gobineau's earlier *Essay in Racial Inequality*, which had its greatest appeal across the Rhine where the inhabitants were engaged in constructing a theory of a master race. Drumont's central theme was the evil power of Jewish finance. The book was widely read and reprinted and its author, a hearty, red-faced, thick-bodied man with a bushy black beard, thrived. In 1889 in association with the Marquis de Morès he founded the National Anti-Semitic League to fight "the clandestine and merciless conspiracy" of Jewish finance which "jeopardizes daily the welfare, honor and security of France." At its first big public meeting the Duc d'Uzès, the Duc de Luynes, Prince Poniatowski, the Comte de Breteuil and other members of the aristocracy felt gratified at finding themselves seated next to real workmen from the butcher shops and slaughterhouses who in turn were delighted to find themselves sharing their opinions with noblemen.

After the success of the book and the League, Drumont's next step was inevitably a newspaper. In 1892 he founded *La Libre Parole*, just at the time when the anger of bilked investors in the Panama loan fell upon its two leading promoters, Cornelius Herz and the Baron de Reinach, both Jews. Drumont's paper in foaming philippics and raging pursuit of the evildoers, became a power. It undertook at the same time a campaign to drive Jewish officers out of the Army as a result of which two of them fought duels with Drumont and the Marquis de Morès. The Marquis went to the unusual length of killing his opponent and was charged with foul play but acquitted in court.

When Dreyfus was condemned, *La Libre Parole* explained his motive to the public: revenge for slights received and the desire of his race for the ruin of France. "*A mort! A mort les juifs!*" the crowd howled outside the railings of the parade ground where the ceremony of his degradation took place.

The cry was heard by the Paris correspondent of the Vienna *Neue Freie Presse*, Theodor Herzl, who was standing amongst the crowd. "Where?" he wrote later. "In France. In republican, modern, civilised France, a hundred years after the Declaration of the Rights of Man." The shock clarified old problems in his mind. He went home and wrote *Der Judenstaat*, whose first sentence established its aim, "restoration of the Jewish state," and within eighteen months he organized, out of the most disorganized and fractional community in the world, the first Zionist Congress of two hundred delegates from fifteen countries. Dreyfus gave the impulse to a new factor in world affairs which had waited for eighteen hundred years.

The first Dreyfusard was Bernard Lazare, a left-wing intellectual and journalist who edited a little review called *Political and Literary Conversations* while he earned a living on the staff of the Catholic and Conservative *Echo de Paris.* An Anarchist in politics, a Symbolist in literature, and a Jew, he wore bifocals over shortsighted eyes whose gaze, said his friend Péguy, "was lit by a flame fifty centuries old." Suspecting the verdict from the start, he had learned from the commandant of the prison that Dreyfus, far from having confessed, had never ceased to declare his innocence. With the help of Mathieu Dreyfus, who was convinced of his brother's innocence, and after a prolonged search for evidence, hampered by silence, obfuscation and closed doors, Lazare finally brought out a pamphlet entitled, *A Judicial Error; the Truth About the Dreyfus Case.* Although three thousand copies had been distributed to ministers, deputies, editors, journalists, and other opinion-makers, it had been ignored. Lazare's and Mathieu Dreyfus' visits to men of influence succeeded no better. "They bore us with their Jew," said Clemenceau. Comte Albert de Mun, the eminent Catholic social reformer, refused to see them and the Socialist leader, Jean Jaurès, was cold. The Socialist paper, *La Petite République*, reviewing Lazare's pamphlet, reached the required Marxist conclusion that "strikers are unjustly condemned every day without having committed treason and deserve our sympathies more than Dreyfus." Socialists could see no cause for concern in the Affair. Under the conditions of class war, the misfortunes of a bourgeois were a matter of indifference to them. Their traditions were anti-militarist, and Dreyfus, besides being a bourgeois, was an Army officer. Miscarriage of justice as applied to a member of the ruling class was a twist they were more likely to appreciate than deplore.

But the ripples of doubt started by Lazare spread and the Dreyfusard movement was launched. It caught up Lucien Herr, librarian of the Ecole Normale Supérieure, heart of the academic world. Here the keenest students in the country were prepared by the most learned professors for careers as the future teachers of France. Herr was a believer in Socialism, a friend and preceptor of the student world. During the summer vacation of 1897 he used to ride over every afternoon to discuss ideas with his young friend, Léon Blum. One day he said point-blank, "Do you know that Dreyfus is innocent?" It took Blum a moment to place the name; then he remembered the officer convicted of treason. He was startled, having like most of the public accepted the report of Dreyfus' confession as the official version. Herr's influence was pervasive. "He directed our conscience and our thought," wrote Blum. "He perceived truth so completely that he could communicate it without effort."

Elsewhere men who had been collaborators of Gambetta in the founding of the Third Republic, and to whom the principles for which it stood were sacred, stirred and felt uneasy. Two especially became active: Senator Ranc, a leading Radical and a member of the first Government of the Republic, and the younger Joseph Reinach, who in his twenties had been Gambetta's chief secretary. As the nephew and son-in-law of the venal Baron de Reinach of Panama ill-fame, he had cause for extra sensitivity, although it was less Jewish sympathies than concern for French justice that moved him. They found their champion in a man universally respected, Senator Scheurer-Kestner, Vice-President of the Senate, a founder of the Republic and onetime editor of Gambetta's paper *La République Française.*

As a native of Alsace who after 1871 had chosen to live in France, he had been appointed Senator for life and was regarded as the embodiment of the lost province. A dignified gentleman of substance, old family and quiet elegance, he represented the aristocracy of the Republic. When a reporter from *La Libre Parole* came to interview him and sat himself down in an armchair, "the Duc de Saint-Simon himself," it was said, "could not have been more scandalized" than Scheurer-Kestner, who was outraged at anyone from such a paper entering his house. When he learned that the Army had suppressed evidence showing the man on Devil's Island to be innocent and Esterhazy to be the real author of the document used to convict him, he was horrified.

This evidence had been discovered by an Army officer, Colonel Picquart, who had been appointed new chief of the Counter-Espionage Bureau some months after Dreyfus' conviction. When he presented his findings to the Chief and Assistant Chief of the General Staff, Generals Boisdeffre and Gonse, he met a wall of refusal either to prosecute Esterhazy or release Dreyfus. When Picquart insisted, Gonse asked him why he made such a point of bringing Dreyfus back from Devil's Island.

"But, General, he is innocent!" Picquart replied. He was

told that this was "unimportant," the case could not be reopened, General Mercier was involved, and the evidence against Esterhazy was not definitive. When Picquart suggested that matters would be worse if the Dreyfus family, known to be investigating, turned up the truth, Gonse replied, "If you say nothing no one will know."

Picquart stared at him. "That is abominable, General. I will not carry this secret to my grave," he said, and left the room. Trained as a soldier, as loyal and obedient to the service as any other officer, with no ax to grind, no personal motive, nothing to gain in public notoriety as was to move later actors in the Affair, Picquart acted then and thereafter, at certain risk to his career, from purely abstract respect for justice. He was, if anything, anti-Semitic, and on one occasion, when asked to take Reinach, who was a reserve officer, on his staff during maneuvers, had objected, saying, "I can't stand the Jew." For Dreyfus he cared no more than for Reinach. It was the fact that the Army could knowingly condone punishment of an innocent man that he could not stomach. When he would not desist in his pressure he was transferred to an infantry regiment in Tunisia. Subject to Army discipline he could make no public disclosures, but he contrived a brief return to Paris on leave during which he disclosed the facts to a friend who was a lawyer, and left a sealed report to be given in the event of his death to the President of France. Subsequently, when his disclosure became known, he was recalled, arrested, tried and convicted of misconduct, discharged from the Army, later rearrested and imprisoned for a year.

Meanwhile his information had been given by his lawyer to Scheurer-Kestner, a personal friend, who instantly spoke out, asserting Dreyfus' innocence to fellow Senators and demanding a judicial review. He bore down upon the Government, harassed the Ministers of War and Justice, repeatedly interviewed the Premier and President. They stalled, put him off and promised "inquiries." National elections were due in May, 1898, only eight months off. A retrial would raise a howl by the mischief-making press and involve a public inquiry into Army affairs that, once started, could lead anywhere, with undesirable effects both on Russia, with whom France had recently concluded a military alliance, and on Germany. These matters of state, foreign and domestic, outweighed a question of justice for a solitary man on a distant rock; besides, to men who want to stay in office, the nature of justice is not so clear as to those outside. The ministers allowed themselves to be persuaded by the General Staff, on the strength of Major Henry's forged letter, which they had no reason to suspect, that Dreyfus must be guilty after all and Esterhazy probably an accomplice, or some other sort of unfortunate complication not justifying the terrible disturbance of a retrial.

Scheurer-Kestner hammered in vain. He thereupon published a letter in *Le Temps* informing the public that documents existed "which demonstrate that the culprit is not Captain Dreyfus," and demanding a formal inquiry by the Minister of War to "establish the guilt of another."

At the same time, *Figaro* published letters from Esterhazy to a cast-off mistress, one in facsimile, written during the Boulangist era, which expressed disgust for his own country in startling terms. "If I were told that I would die tomorrow as a Captain of Uhlans sabering Frenchmen, I should be perfectly happy," he had written, and added a wish to see Paris "under a red sun of battle taken by assault and handed over to be looted by 100,000 drunken soldiers." These extraordinary effusions of venom and hate for France in the handwriting of the *bordereau* * on which Dreyfus' guilt hung seemed to the Dreyfusards like a miracle. They thought their battle won. But they learned, as Reinach wrote, that "justice does not come down from heaven; it must be conquered." The journals of the Right immediately denounced the letters as forgeries fabricated by the "Syndicate." Esterhazy himself, a gambler in debt, a speculator on the Bourse, a fashionable and witty scoundrel, married to the daughter of a marquis, a man of sallow and cadaverous countenance with a crooked nose, a sweeping black Magyar moustache, the "hands of a brigand" and the air, wrote an observer, "of an elegant and treacherous gipsy or a great wild beast, alert and master of itself," was now transformed by the Nationalist press into a hero and his innocence made an article of faith.

*The document recovered from the wastebasket of the German military attaché which was the original evidence of treason. It was a list of the information supplied.

To the same degree, Scheurer-Kestner was vilified and the public encouraged to demonstrate on the day he was to make a statement in the Senate. Tall, upright, pale, with high forehead, white beard and the austere air of a Huguenot of the Sixteenth Century, he walked to the tribune with measured step, as if he were mounting a scaffold. Outside in the foggy winter afternoon, crowds filled the Luxembourg Gardens howling against a man of whom they knew nothing. He read his appeal to reason in a slow heavy voice to antagonistic Senators who punctuated his speech with boos and insulting laughter. His reminder that he was the last deputy of French Alsace, which at any other time would have moved them, was met with cold silence, and, when he finished, hostile looks followed his return to the floor. A month later in the annual re-election for officers of the Senate he was defeated for the vice-presidency, the office he had held for nearly the life of the Republic.

His battle aroused the formidable support of Clemenceau, the government-breaker, *l'homme sinistre*, as the Conservatives called him, fearsome in debate, in opposition, in journalism, in conversation and in duels with pistol or épée. He fought a duel with Paul Déroulède over Panama and with Drumont over the Affair. He was a doctor by training, a drama critic who promoted Ibsen, an old and intimate friend of Claude Monet, whose work, he wrote in 1895, was guiding man's visual sense "toward a more subtle and penetrating vision of the world." He commissioned Toulouse-Lautrec to illustrate one of his books and Gabriel Fauré to write music for one of his plays. "Only the artists are on the right path," he said at the end of his life. "It may be they can give this world some beauty but to give it reason is impossible."

Out of office and Parliament since Panama, Clemenceau, when persuaded of the facts about Dreyfus by Scheurer-Kestner, saw the shape of a great cause and seized upon it, though not only as a vehicle of political ambition. To Clemenceau the menace of Germany was the dominant fact of political life. "Who"—he demanded, enraged by Esterhazy's vision of Prussian Uhlans sabering Frenchmen—"who among our leaders has been associated with this man? Who is protecting Esterhazy? . . . To whom have the lives of French soldiers and the defense of France been surrendered?" After Germany came anti-clericalism. "The French Army is in the hands of the Jesuits. . . . Here is the root of the entire Dreyfus case." Every day in *l'Aurore* he cut and thrust at the issues of the Affair, writing 102 articles on it in the next 109 days, and altogether nearly five hundred over the next three years, enough, when collected, to fill five volumes. Through all rang the bell of justice. "There can be no patriotism without justice. . . . As soon as the right of one individual is violated, the right of everyone is jeopardized. . . . The true patriots are we who fight to obtain justice and to liberate France from the yoke of gold-braided infallibility."

The Dreyfusard cause, too, had its opportunists. Urbain Gohier, an ex-monarchist who now professed to be a Socialist, lashed at the Army in *l'Aurore*. Its officers were "generals of debacle," "Kaiserlicks" who knew nothing but "flight and surrender" and brought no victories except over the French; they were "the cavalry of Sodom" with retinues of kept women. "One half of France is slinging invective at the other," worriedly wrote the French-born Princess Radziwill, née de Castellane, from Berlin. Married to Prince Anton Radziwill, the Prussian member of an international family of Polish origin who "loves to talk English while his brother, a Russian, talks French," she had dedicated herself to a goal of Franco-German rapprochement. "No one can see how it will finish," her letter continued, "but it cannot go on like this without real moral danger."

The danger was more than moral. Germany watched carefully the internal conflict that absorbed all France's attention. Her periodic denials of dealings with Dreyfus were designed less in the interest of justice than of aggravating French dissension. Happy in the consciousness of innocence, the Kaiser was not reluctant to inform visitors and royal relatives that France had convicted an innocent man. Through the family international of European royalty the word spread. In St. Petersburg in August, 1897, when the case had not yet become the Affair in France, Count Witte, the leading Russian minister, said to a member of a visiting French mission, "I can see only one thing that could cause great trouble in your country. It is this business of a captain condemned three years ago who is innocent."

The assumption so carelessly taken for granted in St. Petersburg was passionately rejected in the French Chamber in December by a sincere and honorable man of lofty ideals. To Comte Albert de Mun the innocence or guilt of Dreyfus was infused with another meaning; transformed, no less than the bread and wine of the sacrament, into another nature. Belief in Dreyfus' guilt was belief in God.

The fusion of these ideas lay in the condition of chronic war between the Church and the Republic. Since the Revolution, the Church had been on the defensive against the purpose of the Republic, in the words of Jules Ferry, "to organize mankind without God or King." The religious orders, furiously resisting the effort of the Republic to displace them from control of education, saw their hope of survival in restoration of the Catholic monarchy. This was what brought the Church in France into position in the Affair. It was the ally of the Army in its own mind as well as in Republican propaganda, which always linked "the Sword and the Censer." In the Jesuits the Republic saw the militant and aggressive general staff of clericalism who pulled the strings which moved the Dreyfus plot. The Jesuit leader was Father du Lac, confessor of both General Boisdeffre and the Comte de Mun, who were regarded as his mouthpieces.

To Pope Leo XIII, a realist looking on from outside, it seemed possible the Republic was here to stay. After the collapse of the Boulanger coup he could no longer believe that restoration of the monarchy was a serious possibility. Besides, he needed French support in his struggle with the Italian state. In the Encyclical of 1892 he urged French Catholics to reconcile themselves to the Republic, to support, infiltrate and ultimately capture it, in a policy called the *Ralliement.* Catholic progressives rallied, others did not and the Left did not trust the policy. "You accept the Republic," said Léon Bourgeois, leader of the Radicals to a meeting of Ralliés. "Very well. Do you accept the Revolution?" De Mun was one who never had.

When, in the midst of the Affair, de Mun arrived at the peak of a French career—election to the French Academy—he chose Counter-Revolution as the theme of his address. The Revolution, he proclaimed, was "the cause and origin of all the evils of the century"; it was "the revolt of man against God." He believed the ancient ideals and ideas were about to "reappear in our time with irresistible evolution" and revive "the social concepts of the Thirteenth Century." To heal the wounds of social injustice under which the working class suffered and re-Christianize the masses alienated by the Revolution had been the goal of his political career.

As a young cavalry officer out of St-Cyr, de Mun first became acquainted with the lives and problems of the poor through the charitable work of the Society of St-Vincent de Paul in his garrison town. During the Commune, as an aide to General Galliffet, who commanded the battalion that fired on the insurgent Communards, he saw a dying man brought in on a litter. The guard said he was an "insurgent," whereupon the man, raising himself up, cried with his last strength, "No, it is you who are the insurgents!" and died. In the force of that cry directed at himself, his uniform, his family, his Church, de Mun had recognized the reason for civil war and vowed himself to heal the cleavage. He blamed the Commune on "the apathy of the bourgeois class and the ferocious hatred for society of the working class." The responsible ones, he had been told by one of the St. Vincent brothers, were "you, the rich, the great, the happy ones of life who pass by the people without seeing them." To see and discover them de Mun had worked among the poor. "It is not enough to perceive the wrong and know its cause," he said. "We must admit ourselves responsible and confess that society has failed in its duty toward the working class." He determined to enter politics but his candidacy for the Chamber and his activities had been resented in the Army. Forced to choose, he had resigned his commission and broken his sword.

Yet in the Chamber his love for the Army remained and formed the theme of his most stirring speeches. Delivered with the adoration of a disciple and the fire of a champion, they made him known as *le cuirassier mystique*. He was the finest orator of his side, "the Jaurès of the Right," who brought to perfection the carefully taught art of the spoken word. A tall figure of dignified bearing, controlled gestures and exquisite manners, he was incomparable in authority when he rose to his feet. He spoke with force of conviction and conscious architecture of phrase, using his voice like a violin, sonorous and vibrant or muted and trembling, in long harmonious rhythms, sudden broken stops and eloquent perorations. His oratorical duels against two major opponents, Clemenceau and Jaurès, were spectacles of style and drama which audiences attended as they would Sarah Bernhardt playing *l'Aiglon*.

Although diehards accused him of being a Socialist and of encouraging subversive ideas and disturbing the established order, his essential loyalties were those of his class. He had been a supporter of Boulanger and until 1892 a royalist of sufficient stature to have the Comte de Chambord* as godparent for one of his children. When Leo XIII, however, called for the *Ralliement*, although most French royalists were stunned and rebellious, de Mun renounced royalist politics—if not sympathies—to become a leader of the Ralliés. Although his aim was social justice, he rejected Socialism as the "negation of the authority of God while we are its affirmation. . . . Socialism affirms the independence of man and we deny it. . . . Socialism is logical Revolution and we are Counter-Revolution. There is nothing in common between us and between us there is no place for liberalism."

His words defined the chasm, and his position on one side of it was inevitable. It led him in the Affair to embrace the brigands and fight on the terms established by Drumont. It was he who introduced the "Syndicate" into the first debate on the Affair in the Chamber. "What is this mysterious occult power," he demanded, looking directly at Reinach, "that is strong enough to disrupt the entire country as it has for the last two weeks and to throw doubt and suspicion on the leaders of our Army who"—here he stopped as if choked by his strength of feeling—"who may one day have to lead the country against the enemy. This is not a question of politics. Here we are neither friends nor opponents of the Government; here there are only Frenchmen anxious to preserve their most precious possession . . . the honor of the Army!"

His proud manner and thrilling voice brought the deputies to their feet in transports of applause. Reinach felt the entire Chamber swept by an overmastering emotion and incapable of individual reflection. "I felt on my head the hatred of three

*The last Bourbon Pretender, grandson of Charles X, who styled himself Henri V and died in 1883.

hundred hypnotized listeners. I crossed my arms; one word, one movement would have transformed this frenzy into fury. How struggle against a whirlwind?" Jaurès was silent and many of the Left were applauding from "the enthusiasm born of fear." Imperiously de Mun demanded from the Government an unequivocal statement confirming Dreyfus' guilt. The Minister of War, General Billot, obeyed, declaring "solemnly and sincerely, as a soldier and leader of the Army, I believe Dreyfus to be guilty." The Premier followed with an appeal to all good Frenchmen, in the interests of the country and the Army, to support the Government "struggling with such difficulties and harassed by such furious passions." The passions were at once expressed in a duel between Reinach and Alexandre Millerand, a Socialist, who in unprecedented support for the Government by one of his party, denounced the Dreyfusard accusations of the Army as "disloyal."

Other members of the nobility besides de Mun also served as deputies, but always as royalists in opposition. None took any share in the actual business of governing under the Republic. Among them was the Duc de la Rochefoucauld, representing the older nobility ante-dating the Empire, whose money came from Pommeroy champagne and Singer sewing machines and who, as president of the Jockey Club, was the acknowledged leader of the *gratin*, or "crust," of French Society. Others were the Marquis de Breteuil, representing a district in the Hautes-Pyrénées, and his friend the Comte de Greffulhe, whose yellow beard and air of combined rage and majesty caused him to resemble the king in a pack of cards. Possessor of one of the largest fortunes in France and a wife who was the most beautiful woman in Society, he and she served as Marcel Proust's models for the Duc and Duchesse de Guermantes. Another deputy was Count Boni de Castellane, the dandy and arbiter of taste of his circle. Tall and slim, with pink skin, blue eyes and small neat golden moustache, he had married the dour American heiress Anna Gould, and with her dowry built a marble mansion furnished with precious antiques to exhibit the perfection that taste endowed by money could reach. At the party to celebrate its opening a footman in a scarlet cloak was stationed at the curve of the staircase, and when the Grand Duke Vladimir asked, "Who is that Cardinal over there?" the host replied, "Oh, he is only there to make an agreeable effect of color against the marble." Count Boni's assessment of the Affair was that the Jews "in their insensate desire to save a coreligionist" were arrogantly interfering with judicial process and simultaneously, or alternatively, were making Dreyfus "the pretext for a campaign against the Army which doubtless originated in Berlin." In either case they were "insupportable to me." This on the whole represented the view of the *gratin*, who in the words of a notable apostate among them, the Marquis de Galliffet, "continue to understand nothing."

Some among them had literary or other distinctions. Comte Robert de Montesquiou, aesthete extraordinary, lavished on himself silks of lavender and gold, wrote elaborately symbolist poems and epitomized decadence to both Proust and Huysmans in their characters, the Baron de Charlus and Des Esseintes. Montesquiou was what Oscar Wilde would have liked to have been if he had had more money, less talent and no humor. The Prince de Sagan, another notorious pederast who wore a perpetually fresh boutonniere and a perfectly waxed moustache, vied with his nephew, Count Boni, as the high priest of elegance and fought a duel with Abel Hermant, in whose satirical novels of the life of the rich and libertine he considered himself libelled. The Comtesse Anna de Noailles wrote poetry and glided through her lovely rooms in long white floating garments like "the ghost of something too beautiful to be real." At her parties everything was required to focus on her. She did not trouble much about her guests, "merely smiled upon them when they arrived and softly sighed when she saw them going away." The Comte de Vogüé, novelist and Academician, influenced the course of French literature by his studies of Turgenev, Tolstoy and Dostoevski which brought the great Russians to French attention.

These were the outstanding members. The bulk of the other one thousand or so who made up the *gratin* were chiefly distinguished, as one of them said, by "the certitude of a superiority that existed despite appearances to the contrary." Comte Aimery de La Rochefoucauld was noted for "the almost fossil rigidity of his aristocratic prejudices." Disgusted at improper protocol in a certain household, he said to a friend of his own level, "Let us walk home together and talk about rank." Of the

Duc de Luynes he remarked that his family were "mere nobodies in the year 1000." Of the same breed was the Duc d'Uzès, whose ancestor, when the King expressed surprise that none of his family had ever been Marshal of France, replied, "Sire, we were always killed in battle too soon."

The *gratin* were not hospitable; some families however wealthy "never offered so much as a glass of lemonade to their friends." The men considered themselves the only ones of their sex who knew how to dress or make love and exchanged tributes from the famous courtesans. They took their orders from the ranking members of their class and were ardently Anglophile in manners and customs. The Greffulhes and Breteuils were intimates of the Prince of Wales, *le betting* was the custom at Longchamps, *le Derby* was held at Chantilly, *le steeplechase* at Auteuil and an unwanted member was *black-boulé* at the Jockey Club. Charles Haas, the original of Swann, had "Mr" engraved on his calling cards.

At the château of the Duc de Luynes at Dampierre, an English visitor found a veneer of modernity in the automobiles, the billiard room, the London clothes of the men and the chatter of women, "but under this glaze a deadness of the Dead Sea. All the books are safe under lock and key in the library outside the house. In the house there is no book, no newspaper, no writing paper and only one pen." Two sisters—the Duchesses de Luynes and de Brissac—and their friend, the Comtesse de Vogüé, all on the point of becoming mothers, were "splendid creatures," very easy to get on with if one talked of nothing but sport. The host was Lord Chamberlain to the current Pretender. Their kind "are children, arrested in intelligence, who hate Jews, Americans, the present, the past two centuries, the Government, the future and the fine arts."

Under the law of the Republic all Pretenders to the throne lived in exile. Bonapartist hopes were lodged in Prince Victor Napoleon, grandson of Jerome Bonaparte, while legitimist allegiance went to a grandson of Louis-Philippe, the Comte de Paris, of whom Thiers said, "From a distance he looks like a Prussian, from close up like an imbecile." On his death in 1894 he was succeeded by his son, the Duc d'Orléans, a hare-brained young man who in 1890 had dashingly appeared in France with declared intent to "share the French soldier's *gamelle*

[mess]," that is, to do his military service. Being equally celebrated for his romance with the prima donna, Nellie Melba, he was irreverently known thereafter as "Gamelba," a name coined by Rochefort. Before the Affair, his cause seemed moribund; but in the Affair the royalists found a new rallying point, new hope and excitement and in the anti-Semites, new partners and energy. Anti-Semitism became the fashion, although with certain unwanted effects on Society, for parvenus were able to force their way in by virtue of the degree of warmth with which they espoused the new cause. "All this Dreyfus business is destroying society," complained the Baron de Charlus, and the Duchesse de Guermantes found it "perfectly intolerable" that all the people one had spent one's life trying to avoid now had to be accepted just because they boycotted Jewish tradesmen and had "Down with Jews" printed on their parasols.

Important neither in government nor in culture, the *gratin* were important only in providing the background, motive, stimulus and financial backing to reaction. In the Affair the only serious leader to emerge from their class was de Mun. It was he who forced the Government to prosecute Zola for libel of the Army in his public letter, *J'Accuse*, and thus brought on the trial which made the case a national, no longer containable, issue. Had the Government had its way it would have taken no action, for discussion and testimony and above all cross-examination were to be avoided. But led by de Mun, the Right in its wrath demanded revenge and his authority exercised a spell. When no one from the Ministry of War was present in the Chamber to reply to Zola's attack, de Mun demanded that the session be suspended until the Minister of War could be summoned so that nothing should take precedence over defence of the Army's honor. A deputy suggested that the matter could wait while other business continued. "The Army cannot wait!" de Mun declared haughtily. Obediently the deputies filed out until the Minister arrived and afterward, swept up in a passionate oration by de Mun, voted to proceed against Zola.

"A colossus with dirty feet, nevertheless a colossus," Flaubert had called Zola. Although he was probably the most widely read and best-paid French author of the time, the brutal realism of his novels had aroused the disgust and resentment of many. He dug mercilessly into the base, sordid and corrupt elements of every class in society, from the slums to the Senate. Peasants, prostitutes, miners, bourgeois businessmen, alcoholics, doctors, officers, churchmen and politicians were exposed in gigantic detail. Worse, the supposedly beneficent Nineteenth Century itself was exposed in his picture of the terrible impoverishment brought upon the masses by industrialization. The doors of the Academy never opened to him. His account of 1870 in *La Débâcle* infuriated the Army and after *Germinal* he was classed as a champion of the workers against the established order. He was an agnostic who believed in science as the only instrument of social progress. Already, however, a literary reaction against realism and the "bankruptcy of science" was taking place.

In the year before Dreyfus' arrest, Zola's fame had reached its peak upon publication of the final novel in his immense twenty-volume panorama of French life. At a party given by his publisher to celebrate the occasion on the Grand Lac in the Bois de Boulogne, writers, statesmen, ambassadors, actresses and beauties, celebrities of every kind from Poincaré to Yvette Guilbert, were present. Where was he to go from here? The Dreyfus case opened a new road to greatness, but only to a man capable of taking it. It required courage to challenge the State, the training and genius of a great writer to compose *J'Accuse*, and sympathy with suffering to inspire him to act. Zola had known suffering: In his youth he had spent two unemployed years in the garret of a shabby boardinghouse, often so hungry that he set traps for sparrows on the roof and broiled them on the end of a curtain rod over a candle.

His first article on the Affair, after summarizing the evidence against Esterhazy—the handwriting, the *petit bleu*, the Uhlan letters—had asserted, "Truth is on the march and nothing will stop it." When a month later the Army ordered Esterhazy's court-martial, the Dreyfusards, believing this was a roundabout way of succumbing to Revision, were exuberant. In fact, it was a device for dealing with the Esterhazy problem through a trial whose verdict the Army could control. Esterhazy was acquitted and acclaimed by the mob as the "martyr of the Jews." The verdict "came upon us like the blow of a bludgeon," wrote Blum. It was as if Dreyfus had been condemned a second time. The march of truth had, after all, been stopped.

The only way to force the evidence onto the record was to provoke a civil trial. This was the purpose of Zola's open letter addressed to the President of France. He conceived it on the day of Esterhazy's acquittal with deliberate intent to bring himself to trial. He told no one but his wife and did not hesitate. Locking himself in his study, he worked without stopping for twenty-four hours, mastered the intricacies and mysteries of what by now had become one of the most complex puzzles in history and wrote his indictment in four thousand words. He took it over to *l'Aurore* on the evening of January 12, and it appeared next morning under the title suggested by Ernest Vaughan (or, according to another version, by Clemenceau): J'ACCUSE! Three hundred thousand copies were sold, many to Nationalists who burned them in the streets.

In separate paragraphs, each beginning "I accuse," Zola specifically named two Ministers of War, Generals Mercier and Billot, one "as accomplice in one of the greatest iniquities of the century," and the other of "possessing positive proofs of the innocence of Dreyfus and suppressing them." He accused the Chiefs of the General Staff, Generals Boisdeffre and Gonse, as accomplices in the same crime, and Colonel du Paty de Clam (he knew nothing about Major Henry) as its "diabolical author." He accused the War Ministry of conducting an "abominable campaign" in the press to mislead the public and conceal its own misdeeds. He accused the first court-martial of conducting an illegal trial and the Esterhazy court-martial of covering that illegal verdict "on order" as well as of the judicial crime of knowingly acquitting a guilty person. The accusations were made in full awareness of the law of libel "to hasten the explosion of truth and justice. Let them bring me to court. Let the inquiry be in broad daylight. I wait."

The public was aghast; such charges flung at the military leaders of the nation seemed equivalent to an act of revolt. Many Revisionists felt Zola had gone too far. He had inflamed an already heated situation almost unbearably by frightening and angering the middle classes and increasing their support of the Army and their dislike of the Dreyfusards. Following de Mun's resolution next day, the Government announced that Zola would be prosecuted. Hatred, filth and insults were spewed on him by the press and in songs sold on the streets.

He was viciously caricatured. "Pornographic pig" was polite among the names he was called. Packages of excrement were mailed to him. He was burnt in effigy. Placards were distributed reading, "The answer of all good Frenchmen to Emile Zola: *Merde!*" Evoking one of the major emotions of the Affair, the attacks denounced him as a "foreigner," in reference to his Italian father. In fact, Zola had been born in Paris of a French mother and brought up in the home of her parents in Aix-en-Provence.

The Government's suit, filed in the name of General Billot as Minister of War, ignored all the accusations relevant to Dreyfus and confined itself to the single charge that the court-martial of Esterhazy had acquitted him "on order." By this device the presiding judge could exclude any testimony not bearing precisely on that point. In a fiery protest against this procedure, Jaurès thundered in the Chamber at the Government, "You are delivering the Republic to the Jesuit Generals!" at which a Nationalist deputy, the Comte de Bernis, assaulted him physically, causing such an uproar that the military guard was required to restore order.

J'Accuse drew world attention to the Affair and gave it the proportions of heroic drama. That the French Army could be accused of such crimes and the French author best known to the foreign public be attacked in such terms were equally astounding. The world watched with "stupor and distress," wrote Björnstjerne Björnson from Norway. When the trial opened, the Dreyfusards were conscious of that audience. "The scene is France; the theatre is the world," they said. The trial transformed the Affair from the local to the universal.

The writer of his time who most truly touched the universal, Chekhov, was profoundly stirred by Zola's intervention. Staying in Nice at the time, he followed the trial in growing excitement, read all the verbatim testimony and wrote home, "We talk here of nothing but Zola and Dreyfus." He found the anti-Semitic and anti-Dreyfus tirades of the St. Petersburg *New Times*, the leading daily which had published most of his own stories, "simply repulsive" and quarreled with its editor, his old and intimate friend.

Foreign opinion, except as conditioned by feeling about the Jews, saw the issue chiefly as one of Justice and could not understand the obstinate refusal of the French to allow Revision. Foreign hostility itself became a factor in the refusal. "French papers ask why foreign countries take such an interest in the Affair," wrote Princess Radziwill, "as if a question of justice did not interest the whole world." It did, but in France the Affair was not only that. It was not a struggle of the Right against the Left, because men like Scheurer Kestner and Reinach, Clemenceau and Anatole France, were not men of the Left. It was fought in terms of justice and patriotism, but fundamentally it was the struggle of the Right against Reason.

Zola's trial opened on February 7, 1898, and lasted sixteen days. The atmosphere at the Palais de Justice on the Ile de la Cité "smelled of suppressed slaughter," said a witness. "What passion on people's faces! What looks of hatred when certain eyes met!" The courtroom was crammed to the window sills with journalists, lawyers, officers in uniform, ladies in furs. Marcel Proust climbed every day to the public gallery, bringing coffee and sandwiches so as not to miss a moment. Outside the windows Drumont's claque, paid at forty sous a head, hooted and jeered. All the Army officers concerned in the trials and investigations of Dreyfus, Esterhazy and Picquart stood up and swore to the authenticity of the documents, including specifically the Panizzardi letter which was declared to be "positive proof" of Dreyfus' guilt. (The Foreign Minister, already advised by the Italians that it was a forgery, had wanted to call off the trial but the Government had not dared for fear of an Army revolt.) General Mercier, upright, haughty, unmoved, "entrenched in his own infallibility," affirmed on his honor as a soldier that Dreyfus had been rightfully and legally convicted. Attempts by the defence to cross-examine were met over and over again by the presiding judge with the sharp order, "The question will not be put." Statements by Zola or by his lawyer, Maître Labori, or by Clemenceau, who, though not a lawyer, was appearing for *l'Aurore*, were met by inarticulate roars from the packed audience. Zola, appearing nervous and sullen, kept his temper until, tormented beyond endurance, he spat out "Cannibals!"—the word used by Voltaire in the Calas affair. Esterhazy, called to testify, was greeted by the crowd with shouts of "*Gloire au victime du Syndicat!*" On the steps of the court, Prince Henri d'Orléans, cousin of the Pretender, shook the hand of the author of the Uhlan letters and saluted in him the "French uniform."

"Paris palpitated," wrote an English visitor, and he felt a lust for blood in the air. Mobs broke the windows of Zola's house and of the offices of *l'Aurore*. Shops closed, foreigners departed. A wave of anti-Semitic riots organized by Drumont's lieutenant, Jules Guérin, erupted in Le Havre, Orléans, Nancy, Lyon, Bordeaux, Toulouse, Marseilles and smaller towns, and reached a peak in Algiers where the looting and sack of the Jewish quarter lasted for four days, with many beaten and in some cases killed. In Paris an employment office opened where toughs were hired at five francs a day or two francs for an evening to shout, "Down with the Jews! Long live the Army! Spit on Zola!" When Zola left the court on one occasion, in company with Reinach, the crowd flew at them, yelling, "Drown the traitors! Death to the Jews!" and they had to be rescued by police. Thereafter, mounted police escorted Zola's carriage to and from the court every day, and were sometimes forced to charge the screaming mob threatening to assault it. Zola's friend Desmoulins, acting as bodyguard, carried a revolver.

In the Court, despite obstructions and jeers, truth was advancing. Neither Labori, young and vehement, of whom it was said, "He is not an intellect, he is a temperament," nor Clemenceau, hard, merciless, invincible in debate, could be bullied or silenced. The jury was rumored to be inclining toward acquittal. General Boisdeffre, taking the stand, warned, "If the nation does not have confidence in its Army chiefs . . . then they are ready to transfer to others their heavy task. You have only to say the word." It was a threat of collective resignation by the General Staff if the jury acquitted. Boisdeffre made it plain: Zola or us. This was the issue, not the guilt or innocence of Dreyfus, which the jury had to decide. Its members came mostly from the petty bourgeoisie: a tanner, a market gardener, a wine-dealer, a clerk, a landlord and two workmen. With implied threat *La Libre Parole* published their names and business addresses and letters from readers warning of vengeance if the "Italian" were acquitted.

In his closing speech, Zola, constantly interrupted by boos and hissing, swore by his forty years of labour and forty volumes of French literature that Dreyfus was innocent. He had acted to save his country from "the grip of lies and injustice" and though he were condemned, "France will one day thank me for having helped to save her honour." Clemenceau concluded, "Your task, gentlemen of the jury, is to pronounce a verdict less upon us than upon yourselves. We are appearing before you. You will appear before history."

Zola was condemned by a vote of 7–5 and the wonder was that five jurors had the courage to vote for acquittal. Outside, the Place Dauphine was black with people screaming in triumph. "Listen to them, listen to them!" said Zola as he was preparing to leave. "They sound as if they were waiting for someone to throw them meat." Clemenceau told a friend that in case of acquittal he was "quite certain not a single Dreyfusard in the court or corridors would have escaped with his life." Zola received the maximum penalty, a year's imprisonment and a fine of three thousand francs and on rejection of an appeal was persuaded by the insistence of his friends to escape to England. He should have been sent "to join his friend Dreyfus on Devil's Island" was Henry Adams' comment, "with as much more French rot as the island would hold, including most of the press, the greater part of the theatre, all the stockbrokers and a Rothschild or two for example." The sentiments were his own, not paid for like those of the Paris mob which they so accurately reflected.

The trial was a tornado that whirled all the vocal elements of society into its vortex. "Every conscience is troubled," wrote *Le Petit Parisien*. "No one reasons any more; no discussion is possible; everyone has taken up a fixed position." Families divided and even servants. In the most famous of the Caran d'Ache cartoons the father of a large family at dinner commands, "No one is to speak of it!" The next panel shows a wild melee of overturned table, knives and forks flying and chairs used as weapons, under the title, "They spoke of it!"

Organizing their efforts the Dreyfusards formed the League for the Rights of Man, which sponsored protest meetings and sent lecturers around the country. They drew up a petition for Revision which made the schism in society visible and inescapable. Called the "Protest of the Intellectuals," it began appearing day by day in *l'Aurore* with successive signatures. It cut jagged divisions between those who signed and those who refused. The organizers were Marcel Proust and his brother Robert (whose father refused to speak to them for a week in consequence), Elie Halévy and his brother Daniel and their cousin Jacques Bizet, son of the composer, all in their late twenties. Almost the first signature they obtained was their greatest coup: that of "the ultimate flower of Latin genius" and leader of Academicians, Anatole France. "He got out of bed to see us, in his slippers with a head cold," wrote Halévy. " 'Show it to me,' he said, 'I'll sign, I'll sign anything. I am revolted.' " He was a rationalist, revolted by unreason. A cynic and a satirist of human folly, he had sympathy neither for crusades nor for Dreyfus as an individual who, he perceptively suggested, was "the same type as the officers who condemned him; in their shoes he would have condemned himself." But he hated the crowd and out of contradictory spirit was usually to be found against the Government.

He wrote prose clear as a running brook. He had lived in the home and adorned the salon of his mistress, Mme Arman de Caillavet, since 1889, when, after a final quarrel with his wife, he walked out in dressing gown and slippers, carrying on a tray, quill pen, inkstand and current MS, and proceeded down the street to a hotel, sent for his clothes and never went home. Mme Arman exercised over him the tyranny of devotion and when he was lazy locked him up to make him write. His series of novels about the current day centering around M. Bergeret had been appearing serially in the violently right-wing *Echo de Paris* since 1895 and continued to appear there through the Affair, in ironic commentary on the print around them. France's signature enchanted the Revisionists and astonished both sides. He was "altogether one of us"; he should have never sided with "them," lamented Léon Daudet.

On its first appearance the Protest of the Intellectuals had 104 signers and within a month 3,000, among them André Gide, Charles Péguy, Elisée Reclus, Gabriel Monod, scholars, poets, philosophers, doctors, professors and one painter, Claude Monet, from sympathy with Clemenceau. The only political action of Monet's life, his signature caused a quarrel with Degas and they did not speak again for years. Now almost blind, Degas used to have *La Libre Parole* read to him each morning, and regarded with contempt the *arrivistes* of the Republican era. "In my time," he said disdainfully, "one did not arrive."

Artists and musicians, though on the whole politically indifferent, tended if anything toward the Nationalist camp. Debussy sat with Léon Daudet's circle at the Café Weber in the Rue Royale. Puvis de Chavannes was another Nationalist sympathizer.

Professors and teachers from the Sorbonne, the Ecole Normale, the Faculty of Medicine, the secondary schools and provincial universities, signed; many were opposed, many refrained for fear of reprisals. "If I sign," said a school principal to Clemenceau, "that ass Rambaud [the Minister of Education] will send me to rot in the depths of Brittany." The distinguished scientist Emile Duclaux, successor to Pasteur, signed immediately, saying that if they were afraid of revision in the laboratory, truth would never be reached except by accident. Following his lead, scientists entered the Affair and some suffered for it. Professor Grimaux of the Polytechnic, who both signed and testified at Zola's trial, was removed from the chair of chemistry. Heated arguments arose as to whether such great masters as Hugo, Renan, Taine or Pasteur would or would not have signed. Pupils and teachers were at odds, students divided, committees were formed for and against, especially in the provinces where the faculties were under Catholic influence.

Like an ice floe cracking, the intellectual world split over the Protest, and as the Affair progressed, the two halves spread wider and wider apart. Former friends passed each other in silence and any words they might have said "would never have carried across the worlds that lay between them." When Pierre Louÿs, author of *Aphrodite*, took the opposite side from his friend Léon Blum, without further communication they never saw each other again. When the Protest was being circulated, three journalist friends of Léon Daudet tried to persuade him, appealing for three hours over lunch to "my patriotism, my intelligence, my heart." Before the Affair he had dined at the home of the Laboris, where Madame sang the songs of Schumann and no evening could have been more delightful; "he robust and eloquent, she full of talent, charm and good will." He was welcome too in the charming house on the Pont-de-l'Arche of Octave Mirbeau, who owned Van Gogh's "Field of

Iris" and where Madame welcomed one with "affectionate and sumptuous hospitality" and the cuisine was incomparable "from the butter to the wine, from the cooking oil to the soup." After the Affair the word "Nationalist" was to Mirbeau a synonym for "assassin," and Democracy was to Daudet "the poisoned terrain." Soon after Zola's trial Daudet was writing weekly diatribes of unexampled ferocity for *La Libre Parole* and *Le Gaulois.*

Maurice Barrès, the brilliant novelist who combined literature with a political career, was another whom his friends expected to be a Revisionist. Léon Blum asked for his signature feeling perfectly certain of him, but Barrès said he wanted to think it over and when he wrote it was to refuse. Though professing friendship and respect for Zola he said he felt doubtful and in his doubt chose "the instinct of patriotism." Within months he was to find the mystic answer in terms of blood and soil; to explain Zola as a "denaturalized Venetian" and the Jews on the same principle: that they "have no country as we understand it. For us our country is the earth of our ancestors, the land of our dead. For them it is the place of their best interest." Becoming the intellectual leader of the Nationalists, Barrès supplied them with words to pre-empt patriotism for the Right.

A new recruit, small but wickedly effective, in the form of a four-page weekly of caricatures called *Psst!*, was brought out by Forain and Caran d'Ache, who composed it sitting together at a table in the Café Weber. Caran d'Ache drew comic strips of inspired simplification. Forain was an artist whose sharp views of Parisian society were incisive and brilliant in black and white, although his oils evoked Degas' deadly comment, "He paints with his hands in my pockets." His cover design of a Prussian officer standing behind a dark and cynical figure representing the Syndicate and manipulating in front of its face the mask of Zola, compressed in one picture all the elements of the Affair as the Nationalists saw it. Reinach, the favored target of *Psst!*, was usually pictured as an orangutang in a top hat with heavily Jewish features going repeatedly to Berlin to confer with spike-helmeted Prussians. Scheurer-Kestner and other Revisionists appear as hook-nosed Jews in bankers' fur-collared coats, paying out German funds, using the Army képi for a football or picking weeds from the grave of Ravachol as a "bouquet for Zola." Throughout appears a stalwart wooden soldier, standing straight and brave, unwincing among the villains, forever valiant—the Army. The Intellectual is a lanky figure with oversized head, the star of David on his brow and carrying a pen bigger than his body, who registers his "disgust with everything French." The only variation in subject is the occasional appearance of "Oncle Sam" as the "New Gargantua" making a meal of Spain, Hawaii, Porto Rico and the Philippines.

The Affair pervaded life at all hours and places. Going to a new dentist, Léon Blum found a young man with the manner and bearing of a cavalry officer who suddenly said as his patient sat down, "All the same, they will not dare touch Picquart!" Gaston Paris, the scholarly medievalist and Academician, concluded an erudite article on Philip the Good with a stirring invocation to justice which at once categorized him. Paul Stapfer, doyen of the Faculty of Letters at Bordeaux, was suspended because in a funeral oration for a colleague he made a discreet allusion to the Revisionist opinions of the deceased. A tempest blew up in the Légion d'Honneur when it "suspended" Zola and succeeded in angering both the military members who had demanded his ouster and those members who were his partisans. Anatole France and others removed the red ribbon from their coats. At the cafés, Nationalists and Revisionists sat at different tables on opposite sides of the terraces. Whole villages took sides. A resident of Samois, fourteen miles from Paris, said everyone in his village was Dreyfusard while at Francoville, three or four miles away, everyone almost without exception was anti-Dreyfusard.

In February, 1898, at the Dîner Bixio, a dining club of the elect who met for the pleasure of each other's conversation, the Affair found everyone "troubled and grieved"; in March the Marquis de Galliffet said he would not go out or visit on account of it; in May conversation turned for a while to the question, "Did the Americans blow up the *Maine* themselves?" otherwise talk was only of the Affair; in November everyone was depressed: "I cannot remember a dinner so black," wrote one member in his diary.

The opening night of Romain Rolland's play *Les Loups* was a battlefield. He had written it in six days to show the world that

France was torn by "one of the most redoubtable problems that can engage the human conscience, a dilemma worthy of Corneille: whether to sacrifice country or justice." The presence of Colonel Picquart in a box and of Colonel du Paty de Clam in the orchestra brought the audience to a peak of excitement. Picquart after his first arrest had just been discharged from the Army, and came to the theatre as the guest of Edmond Rostand, whose *Cyrano de Bergerac*, produced a few months earlier, had raised him to the height of celebrity. For a decade French theatregoers had languished under the skepticism, symbolism and Ibsenism of the Théâtre Libre. "We needed reassurance, ideals, panache," wrote a critic, "and then came Cyrano! Our thirst was assuaged." Cyrano's spirit was there that night.

When the character representing Picquart in the play confronted his opponent, the audience exploded before he could be heard. "The whole theatre shook from floor to roof." The usual *Vive!*'s and *A bas!*'s reached a fury in which someone was moved to cry, "*A bas la patrie!*" and a thirteen-year-old Anarchist in the balcony squealed, "Down with Christianity!" Rolland thought to himself, "My ideas are lost, but no matter, the play doesn't count. The real spectacle is there in the audience. This is history being acted!"

The carnage continued next day. *Echo de Paris* and *La Presse* dismissed their drama critics, the Collège Stanislas canceled a reception for Mme Rostand, and two papers opened a campaign to boycott *Cyrano*, whose popularity, however, proved stronger than its author's association with Picquart. In his diary Rolland wrote, "I would rather have this life of combat than the mortal calm and mournful stupor of these last years. God give me struggle, enemies, howling crowds, all the combat of which I am capable."

It was the same sentiment Péguy voiced: boredom with peace. Others shared it. That summer, Senator Ranc recalled, one was constantly expecting some surprise attack. "One day we would be warned not to sleep at home for fear of assault by anti-Semitic gangs, the next for fear of arrest by the police. It was exciting; one felt alive; nothing is so good as a time of action, and combat in the consciousness of a cause."

From the day early in the Affair when Joseph Reinach announced to the guests at Mme Emile Straus's salon that Dreyfus had been wrongfully convicted, the polarization of the salons began. Heretofore they had linked the worlds of fashion and intellect, bridged the sharp political divisions between classes and coteries. They were to France what the country-house party was to England. They were the market-place of ideas, the stock exchange of social and political favors united by one absorbing concern: who would obtain the next seat in the Academy, who would don the dark-green uniform and, watched by the elite of Paris, deliver his eulogy of the defunct Immortal whose place he was taking? Now they began to pull apart into separate units, frustrating the unifying and mixing process that had been their greatest contribution.

As a rule each salon had its *grand homme*. Mme Aubernon, doyenne of the hostesses, began with Dumas *fils* and finished with D'Annunzio. Mme Emile Straus, on the other hand, the beautiful Geneviève of the liquid black eyes and ardent glance, attracted too many to concentrate on one. Daughter of the composer Halévy and widow of Georges Bizet before she married Straus, leaving disconsolate a train of adorers, she had assembled at her salon the soul and salt of Paris before the ravages of the Affair. Henri Bergson the philosopher, Réjane the actress, Lord Lytton when he was British Ambassador, Professor Pozzi the surgeon, Henri Meilhac, the librettist of Offenbach's operas, Jules Lemaître, Marcel Prévost, Forain, Proust, and the Princesse Mathilde, who held her own salon on Wednesdays, all came to her Saturday afternoons on the Boulevard Haussmann, bringing still hot the happenings of the Chamber, the Quai d'Orsay, the theatres and the editorial offices. After Reinach's announcement, Lemaître left, allowing himself from then on to adorn only the right-wing salon of the Comtesse de Loynes. Other separations followed.

Mme Arman de Caillavet's Sunday salon on the Avenue Hoche where Anatole France was the permanent star was the Revisionist center. Clemenceau, Briand, Reinach, Jaurès and Lucien Herr were regulars. Mme Arman wanted only writers and politicians and snubbed the nobility except for Mme de Noailles, who was a Dreyfusard and would appear "like an Oriental princess descending from her palanquin . . . to set ablaze the torrent of her words by the fire of her glance."

Anatole France's books lay on all the tables and the Master himself stood in the midst of a crowd coming and going and gathering around him while he discoursed on a chosen theme, interrupting himself to greet arriving guests, bowing to left and right, introducing one to another, bending to kiss the hand of a pale feline figure wrapped in chinchilla, and keeping up the flow of his talk on the poetry of Racine, the paradox of Robespierre or the epigrams of Rabelais.

The Affair superseded Rabelais. At Mme Aubernon's, where guests of both camps were still invited, discussions that touched upon it immediately became impassioned. "This petition of the so-called 'Intellectuals' is preposterous and impertinent," declared Ferdinand Brunetière, editor of the magisterial *Revue des Deux Mondes.* "They have coined the name to exalt themselves above others as if writers, scientists and professors were better than anyone else. . . . What right have they to meddle in a matter of military justice?" Victor Brochard, Professor of Ancient Philosophy at the Sorbonne, replied heatedly, "Justice is based not on courts but on law. . . . To convict a man on evidence not shown to him is not only illegal; it is judicial murder. . . . Today it is not the Generals or Rochefort or the brawlers of *La Libre Parole* or Esterhazy or your Duc d'Orléans who represent the French conscience. It is we, the intellectuals."

Headquarters of the Right was the salon of Mme de Loynes on the Avenue des Champs Elysées, where Jules Lemaître reigned. After an initial career as a demi-mondaine she had married the elderly Comte de Loynes, become a recognized power in the making of Academicians and, in the course of time, governess, mother, sister and presumably mistress to Lemaître, although some unkind gossip said their friendship was platonic. Her guests met at dinner on Fridays in a room furnished in plush with a nude marble Minerva on the mantel and what Boni de Castellane described as a "shoddy" Meissonier on the wall. Lemaître, the celebrated drama critic of the *Journal des Débats*, was an immensely prolix writer who could turn his hand to plays, poetry, short stories, critical essays, biographies and assorted speeches, political pieces, opinion and polemics. His works, when ultimately collected, filled fifty volumes. Though essentially dilettante in spirit, he had saved the French theatre in a famous cry of alarm in the *Revue des Deux Mondes* from being inundated by the heavy waves rolling in from the north—Ibsen, Hauptmann, Sudermann and Strindberg—and had duly entered the portals of the Academy. The fruits of democracy and manhood suffrage he found disillusioning. "The Republic cured me of the Republic," he wrote; "life had already cured me of romanticism." Disenchanted as well with "literary games," he craved the role of a man of action, the restorative of a cause that not merely fluttered the pages of reviews but moved live men to passion. With ceremony and cheers in Mme de Loynes' dining room he was named president of the Ligue de la Patrie Française, organized by the Nationalists to unite the intellectuals of the Right against the "enemies of *la patrie*." Its Committee included among others de Vogüé, Barrès, Forain, Mistral the poet of the Provençal revival, Vincent d'Indy the composer and Carolus Duran the painter. The Ligue de la Patrie attracted 15,000 to its first meeting and gained 30,000 members in the first month. Lemaître was chosen president in order to have an Academician equal to Anatole France, but, given to mockery and grumbling, he lacked the spirit of a leader and after five minutes of argument, if he failed to impose his views, would drop out of the discussion.

As vice-president, the gentle poet François Coppée was no more effective. More or less bludgeoned by his friends into accepting the post, he was wrapped in nostalgia for the past and wrote verse romances about the humble of earlier times. When asked by an English friend, "*Que faites vous, Maître, dans cette galère?*" ("What are you doing in with that bunch?"), he replied, "To tell you the truth, I am not quite sure." He was able to explain, however, a vague feeling that the religion and patriotism which had made France great were vanishing and unless revived would disappear in the rising tide of materialism.

The real energy and leadership of the League was supplied by Barrès, Drumont, Rochefort and Déroulède, leader of the older Ligue des Patriotes. At policy sessions Drumont would laugh uproariously and say, "Those fellows will be the death of me." Rochefort, who listened only to himself, would say impatiently after a long discussion, "Yes, yes, it's sickening—what *canaille*!" and then tell some anecdote that enchanted

Coppée. "Each one of us is serious individually," Lemaître confessed to Mme de Loynes, "but together we become frivolous."

Yet they felt the cause was deadly serious. Behind all the disputes over the *bordereau* and *petit bleu*, wrote Léon Daudet, "could be heard the tramp of the barbarian legions." Dreyfusism was the foreigner at the gates. It was revolution. It was Jews, Freemasons, freethinkers, Protestants, Anarchists, Internationalists. Everyone saw in it his own enemy. Barrès saw everything that was "un-French"; Arthur Meyer saw "an alliance of Anarchism and Dreyfusism" of which "twice monstrous cult" the two priests were Anatole France and Octave Mirbeau. Brunetière saw "individualism . . . the great malady of our time . . . the Superman of Nietzsche, the Anarchist, the *culte de moi*."

The strong man of the Radical Government which took office after the elections of May, 1898, was its Minister of War, Godefroy Cavaignac, a civilian. He was a man of rigid Republican righteousness, a "sea-green incorruptible," who regarded himself as the chastiser of parliamentary corruption. He had initiated the Panama inquiry and loathed Clemenceau. As Minister of War for a six months' tenure in 1895, he had accepted the honesty of the Secret File and firmly believed Dreyfus guilty. The outgoing Premier, Méline, had attempted to deal with the case by denying that any case existed after the rendering of a verdict, but Cavaignac decided to face the issue squarely. He reinvestigated the documents and convinced himself that although Esterhazy was involved, the Dreyfus verdict had been just. He thereupon ordered the arrest of both Esterhazy and Picquart and went to the Chamber determined to bury Revision for good. Grim and commanding, he told the members that Esterhazy had been wrongfully acquitted and would be dealt with as an accomplice but that "I am completely certain of Dreyfus' guilt." He went back over the entire history of the case, rebuilt the structure which the Dreyfusards had bit by bit proved false and in final proof cited Dreyfus' supposed confession and the Panizzardi letter which Méline, who had been Premier until two weeks ago and was sitting in the audience, knew from the Italians was a forgery. When Cavaignac finished the Chamber was on its feet cheering. He had lifted the terrible burden and they voted 545–0 (with nineteen abstentions including the silent Méline) for a national *affichage*, or "posting," of his speech outside every town hall in France. "Now the odious case is buried," said de Vogüé that night at his club. "Now Dreyfus is nailed to his rock until he dies!"

For the Dreyfusards it was an unbelievable blow, an "atrocious moment." A journalist came hot from the Chamber to bring the news to Lucien Herr, who was in his study with Léon Blum. They were struck mute; tears were close to the surface; they sat immobilized by consternation and despair. Suddenly the doorbell rang and Jaurès burst in, brushed aside the gesture of his friends inviting him to mourn and berated them in a tone of triumph. "What, you too? . . . Don't you understand that now, now for the first time we are certain of victory? Méline was invulnerable because he said nothing. Cavaignac talks, so he will be beaten. . . . Now Cavaignac has named the documents and I, yes I, tell you they are false, they feel false, they smell false. They are forgeries. . . . I am certain of it and will prove it. The forgers have come out of their holes; we'll have them by the throat. Forget your funeral faces. Do as I do; rejoice."

Jaurès went out and wrote *Les Preuves* (The Proofs), a series of articles beginning that week in the Socialist paper, *La Petite République*, which stunned its readers and marked the first collaboration of Socialism with a cause of the bourgeois world. Through the Affair the bridge of class enmity was crossed.

Jaurès himself had been a declared Dreyfusard since before Zola's trial. Short, stocky, strong, red-faced and jovial, he radiated the joy of battle. With his big head, rough beard and careless clothes finished off by drooping white socks, he looked like the accepted image of a labour leader. He was not, however, of working-class origin but came from the poorer branch of a respectable bourgeois family, and had been a student at the Ecole Normale, where he excelled in Greek and Latin and the humanities and was a friend and classmate of Henri Bergson and his rival for the highest honors. When waiting to testify at Zola's trial he had paced up and down the corridors with Anatole France reciting Seventeenth Century poetry. In the Chamber when he climbed with heavy, purposeful steps to the tribune and tossed off a glass of red wine before speaking, auditors tensed with expectancy, either worshipful or hostile. He spoke with a "splendid amplitude" in a voice almost too loud which he could easily have lowered and still have been heard in the last rows of any hall but which, as Rolland said, was a sensual pleasure to him when he let it out to the full. He could speak at this pitch for an hour and a half to two hours at a time. Using no notes, he could not be fazed by interruptions which served only to supply him with new inspirations. When heckled he played with his opponent "like a huge cat with a mouse, caressing him, making him jump this way and that, . . . and then with a sharp blow, flattened him with a final word."

He was never a sectarian who put a particular orthodoxy ahead of the ultimate goal, a habit which afflicted the Socialist movement. For Jaurès, who led the Carmaux strike in person, the ultimate aim of working-class power was not a theory but a realizable goal and Socialist unity a necessity for its achievement. Once persuaded of Dreyfus' innocence by Lucien Herr and others, he believed that Socialism, by abstaining from combat against injustice, would diminish itself. By making the cause of justice its own it would place its mark on the ultimate victory, open to itself a new path to power and cover itself with moral glory. The Affair, as he saw it, could become the catalyst of a united front of the Left which the Socialists should lead.

His colleagues in the Socialist party shared his enthusiasm not at all. Moderates like Millerand and Viviani did not want to be mixed up in this "obscure and dangerous" business; the extremists led by Jules Guesde, while personally Dreyfusard, opposed party action as an effort diverting working-class strength from a cause not its own. At a caucus of the party after *J'Accuse*, to decide what action to take if the Right demanded the prosecution of Zola, the moderates squirmed, preferring discretion to valor on the eve of the election. "Why risk our re-election for Zola?" they said. "He is not a Socialist; . . . he is after all nothing but a bourgeois." As the factions argued, Guesde in impatient disgust threw open the window with an ostentatious gesture for fresh air and cried, "Zola's letter is the greatest revolutionary act of the century!" But it was no more than a gesture and he signed the manifesto which declared, "Leave it to the bourgeoisie to tear themselves to bits over *patrie*, law, justice and other words that will remain empty of meaning as long as capitalist society endures." The iniquity of the Affair should be used as a weapon with which to beat the bourgeoisie, not as a cause to "mobilize and immobilize the proletariat behind one faction of the bourgeois world." The Dreyfus case was nothing but a power struggle between two bourgeois factions: on the one hand the clericals and on the other the Jewish capitalists and their friends. Socialists could not support one side against the other without violating the class struggle. "Between de Mun and Reinach," proclaimed Guesde, "keep your complete freedom."

But as de Mun had said, between the two sides there was no room for freedom. "You can hardly imagine how tormented I am!" Jaurès said to Péguy. "Our enemies are nothing—but our friends! They devour me because they are all afraid of not being elected. They pull at the back of my coat to keep me from going to the tribune." Shaking them off, Jaurès refused to remain silent and did indeed lose his seat in the election of May, 1898, although more because of industrialist opposition in his district than because of the Affair. Turning instead to *La Petite République* for a platform, as Clemenceau had to *l'Aurore*, he wrote a daily political column. When he began *Les Preuves* class hatred was so rooted in Socialist tradition that in order to rally the Left in the fight for justice it was necessary to de-class Dreyfus. "He is no longer an officer nor a bourgeois," Jaurès wrote. "In his misery he has been skinned of all class character. . . . He is simply a living witness to the crimes of Authority. . . . He is nothing less than mankind itself." He tore into the evidence, took up each one of Cavaignac's arguments and documents, separated rumor and blackmail, tracked down forgery. The impact of his logic and his strenuous seriousness revived the Dreyfusards. Cavaignac was enraged. At a dinner of the Cabinet he proposed to arrest all the leading Revisionists on a charge of conspiracy against the state and named Mathieu Dreyfus, Bernard Lazare, Ranc, Reinach, Scheurer-Kestner, Picquart, Clemenceau, Zola and others. When one of his colleagues asked sarcastically, Why not the lawyers too, Cavaignac replied, "Of course," and added Labori and Dreyfus' lawyer, Demange.

Nevertheless *Les Preuves* had shaken him. To answer certain of Jaurès' charges, he ordered yet another examination of the documents, this time by an officer not previously involved in the case. Working at night by the light of a lamp this officer noticed that the writing paper of the crucial Panizzardi letter was gummed together from two halves of the same brand of paper ruled in lines of faintly different colors. Colonel* Henry had used the blank parts of two real letters from Panizzardi to construct his document. The crucial letter was a forgery. Alerted by this find, the investigating officer looked further, was led down dark warrens of discrepancies and dutifully reporting his discoveries, laid ruin in the lap of the Minister of War.

Cavaignac, conqueror of the Affair, saw the whole of the case he had presented to the Chamber and the country shattered like glass. Its crux was a fraud; the statement on which he had won national acclaim was a fraud. For a man of his principles, to hush up the discovery was impossible; he had to face the tragedy of being wrong. Not being of the Army made it easier. He ordered the arrest of Colonel Henry, who was taken to Cherche Midi where Dreyfus had been lodged. That night, August 31, 1898, Colonel Henry committed suicide with the razor they had left for him.

Army officers, when they heard the news, were aghast; some wept. It was a stain on the Army's honor "worse than Sedan," said one. Léon Blum, vacationing in Zurich, opened the door of his hotel room at 10 P.M. to the porter who brought the news. "I don't think that ever in my whole life have I felt an equal excitement. . . . The immense, the infinite joy that rushed through me had its sources in the triumph of *reason*. The truth had actually won." This time, at last and for certain, it seemed to the Dreyfusards they had accomplished their task. In a sense they had, for the truth was now disclosed. To impose it was another matter.

Cavaignac resigned and within two weeks his successor, the sixth Minister of War since Dreyfus' arrest, also resigned. The Government, surrendering to what was now unavoidable, submitted the case to the Cour de Cassation (literally, "Court of Breaking"), whose task was to decide whether a given ver-

*He had been promoted.

dict should be upheld or broken. The action, taken as mistrust of the Generals, caused another War Minister to resign. Awaiting the Court's decision whether or not to accept the case, Paris boiled with excitement. If the Court took the case, the Secret File must come under civilian review, which the Army was committed to prevent. In England the sober *Spectator* thought the logic of the situation must lead to an Army coup d'état. In Paris the royalists and wild men of the Rightist leagues, hoping to provoke exactly that, spread rumors of a plot, called meetings, sent out their hired bands to shout in the streets. It was Déroulède's longed-for hour.

An irrepressible agitator, a poet and a deputy, long-legged and long-nosed like Don Quixote, Déroulède saw windmills to charge in every aspect of the Republic. A veteran of 1870, he had founded his Ligue des Patriotes in 1882 to keep alive the spirit of *revanche*. It bore the legend "1870–18——" with the second date left significantly blank and a motto of noble meaninglessness, *France Quand Même*. Déroulède wrote patriotic verse, loathed the royalists as much as the Republic and had "the political vision of a child." To foment a crisis he now joined forces with Jules Guérin, active head of the Anti-Semitic League, which was receiving a subsidy from the Duc d'Orléans, who hoped to ride in on the tail of the crisis. Tension grew when a strike of 20,000 construction workers on the site of the Exposition of 1900 caused the Government to bring in troops to occupy the railroad stations and patrol the boulevards. Word spread of a coup planned for the reopening of the Chamber on October 25. Déroulède and Guérin called for a huge protest meeting in front of the Palais Bourbon to demonstrate "confidence in the Army and abhorrence of traitors."

The Socialists, or a part of them, suddenly discovered the Republic was worth saving. However dedicated to overthrow of the existing system, they did not want it overthrown by the Right. Besides, they were discovering from their local committees that their neutrality in the Affair was compromising them with some of their constituents. "Because we seem to oppose all forms of bourgeois republicanism," wrote a party worker from the provinces, "many people take us for the allies of monarchist reactionaries."

The Socialist leaders, sending out notices by *pneumatique*, called an emergency meeting of their several groups to organize a united front in face of the peril, and such seemed the urgency of the moment that they succeeded in forming a joint, if temporary, Committee of Vigilance. Following proper revolutionary procedure, it decided to hold meetings every night and call upon the people for mass demonstrations. Clashes with the Rightist leagues, riots, even civil war loomed. In awful anxiety the Dreyfusard League for the Rights of Man called upon all Republicans to disdain fracas in the streets, but Jaurès saw Socialist opportunity: "Paris is trembling with resolve . . . the proletariat is organizing." Warned, however, by Guesde that to provoke an outbreak would be playing the game of the Generals, who were believed to be waiting for a riot to seize power, the Committee of Vigilance had second thoughts. Socialists would provoke nothing, it announced. "Revolutionary groups are ready to act or abstain, according to the circumstances."

So certain were the royalists of "the day" that Andre Buffet, *chef de cabinet* for the Duc d'Orléans, telegraphed the Pretender that his presence in nearby Brussels on October 24 was "indispensable." The Duke, who was hunting in Bohemia, replied, "Should I come at once or can I wait here? Urgent business." Adamant, Buffet wired back, "Approach frontier necessary," but the Duke, better advised, stayed away.

The day came, crowds surrounded the Chamber, filled the Place de la Concorde and nearby streets, slogans were shouted, red flags waved. "It seemed like the eve either of a new Commune or of a coup by a dictator." The atmosphere was threatening: troops and police were everywhere. The day passed, however, and the Republic still stood, for the Right lacked that necessary chemical of a coup—a leader. It had its small, if loud, fanatics; but to upset the established government in a democratic country requires either foreign help or the stuff of a dictator. As Clemenceau had harshly said when Boulanger shot himself on the grave of his mistress, inside the "Man on Horseback" was only "the soul of a second lieutenant."

Events rushed on. On October 29 the Cour de Cassation announced it would accept the case and begin its inquiry. VICTOIRE! proclaimed *l'Aurore* in the same type as J'ACCUSE! Revisionists hailed the decision as re-establishing civil power over the military. Then the Court demanded the Secret File. The Minister of War refused and resigned. The Government fell. For the next seven months the Court became the focus of the battle. From this point on, the Right was on the defensive and the Affair entered its period of greatest frenzy. The Court was excoriated by the Nationalist press as the "sanctuary of treason," a "branch of the synagogue," the "lair of Judas," a "combination of Bourse and brothel." The judges were variously "hirelings of Germany," "valets of the synagogue" and "rogues in ermine." Pressures of all kinds were exerted, both sides were accused of corrupting the judges, and the Nationalists succeeded in forcing the case out of the Criminal Chamber, which was considered too favorable, to the united Court of three chambers, which was considered more susceptible to pressure.

A Dreyfusard tempest raged at the same time over Picquart. To keep him from testifying before the Cour de Cassation the Army had transferred him to Cherche Midi preliminary to a court-martial. The League for the Rights of Man organized public protest meetings every night, in the provincial cities as well as in Paris. Jaurès' name and prestige drew 30,000 to a meeting in Marseilles. He, Duclaux the scientist, Anatole France, Octave Mirbeau and Sebastian Faure were the favorite speakers. Workers and bourgeois, students and professors, working women and Society women crowded the halls and overflowed onto the sidewalks, applauded the famous orators and marched together to shout "*Vive Picquart!*" under the prison walls of Cherche Midi. Signatures for a protest on Picquart came in this time not by hundreds but by thousands, including thirty-four members of the Institut de France, a measure, as Reinach said, of the distance covered by truth on the march. Among the new names were Sarah Bernhardt and Hervé de Kerohant, editor of *Soleil*, formerly against Revision, who signed the protest as "Patriot, Royalist, Christian." The historian and Academician Ernest Lavisse felt strongly enough to act, and as his gesture of personal protest, resigned his chair at St-Cyr.

Even the Anarchists, hitherto resolutely contemptuous and indifferent, were swept into the cause. Formerly they had denounced the Dreyfus "parade," in the words of their newspaper,

Le Père Peinard, as a "bunch of dirty types" led by Clemenceau and by "the old exploiter Scheurer-Kestner, the toad Yves Guyot [editor of *Le Siècle*], the hideous Reinach, three malefactors who helped to concoct the *lois scélérates*." Now, however, when their bourgeois enemies cried out the sufferings of the two martyred prisoners of Devil's Island and Cherche Midi, the Anarchists did the same for their own martyrs sent to forced labour in French Guiana. With a new interest in these cases the League for the Rights of Man succeeded in obtaining pardons for five of them.

Some on the Right could no longer keep their heads turned from the truth. Mme de Greffulhe, goddess of the *gratin*, becoming secretly convinced of Dreyfus' innocence, wrote to the Kaiser asking to visit him to ascertain if the Germans really had employed Dreyfus as a spy. The only answer she received was a large basket of orchids. Proust chronicles the change in his character, the Prince de Guermantes, who confesses to Swann that after Colonel Henry's suicide he has begun to read *Le Siècle* and *l'Aurore* secretly every day. He and his wife, unknown to each other, have asked the Abbé to say a mass for Dreyfus and his family, and discovered to each other's astonishment that the Abbé too believes him innocent. Meeting the maid on the staircase carrying breakfast to the Princesse and concealing something under the napkin, the Prince discovers it to be *l'Aurore*.

Below the trapped obstinacy of the Generals, some in the Army were deeply troubled. "Just among ourselves with no outsiders present," an officer said to Galliffet while riding in a train, "we are not as anti-Revisionist as people think. On the contrary we too would like to see the light and see the culprits punished so that if wrongs have been committed the Army will not bear the responsibility." He felt that if Picquart were tried and convicted public opinion would turn against the Army.

The Army's cup of bitterness was filled when in the same week that the Cour de Cassation began its inquiry the order was given withdrawing Colonel Marchand from Fashoda. Jaurès lashed at the imperialist adventure as a crime of capitalism which had frivolously imperiled peace without preparing for the consequence of challenging England. As if his already strong intuitive perceptions had been sharpened by the Affair, he wrote with foreboding, "Peace has been left to the whim of chance. But if war breaks out it will be vast and terrible. For the first time it will be universal, sucking in all the continents. Capitalism has widened the field of battle and the entire planet will turn red with the blood of countless men. No more terrible accusation can be made against this social system." In his time it was still possible to suppose the fault lay in the system, not humanity.

The Affair continued in its frenzy. When Reinach wrote a series of articles in *Le Siècle* accusing Colonel Henry of having had a "personal interest" in ruining Dreyfus, Drumont persuaded Mme Henry to sue him for libel and opened a public subscription in her behalf which became the rallying point for Nationalists of every degree. A banner reading "For the Widow and Orphan of Colonel Henry against the Jew Reinach" was stretched across the windows of the offices of *La Libre Parole* on the Boulevard Montmartre and lit up at night. Within a month fifteen thousand persons had contributed 130,000 francs. Their names and comments provided a history of the Right—of that or any time. Five hundred francs, the top sum, was subscribed by the Countess Odon de Montesquiou, née Bibesco, and thirty sous by a lieutenant "poor in money but rich in hate." There were all varieties of hate, chiefly for Jews, expressed in suggestions for skinning, branding, boiling in oil, burning with vitriol, emasculation and other forms of foul or physical punishment. There was hate for foreigners and intellectuals and even a "500-year-old hate for England" but there were many who gave their francs out of love or pity for the widow and child. An abbé contributed for "defence of eternal law against Judaeo-Christian deceit," a music professor for "Frenchmen against foreigners," a civil servant "who wants God in the schools," an anonymous donor "ruined by a Jew after six months of marriage," a workingman as "the victim of the anarchist capitalists Jaurès and Reinach." There were innumerable "true patriots" and one "Frenchman sick at heart." There were *Vive!*'s for Drumont, Rochefort, Déroulède, Guérin, Esterhazy, the Duc d'Orléans, *l'Empereur*, *le Roi*, the Heroes of Austerlitz and Jeanne d'Arc. Reinach was the chief target;

Dreyfus received hardly a mention. General Mercier subscribed a hundred francs without comment; the poet Paul Valéry three francs "not without reflection."

Suddenly and strangely on top of all the excitement, the President of France, Félix Faure, died. The public sensed something unexplained and the truth in fact was too embarrassing to be told. Proud of his amatory prowess, President Faure died in the performance thereof in a ground-floor room of the Elysée. An aura of something hushed up was added to the atmosphere already charged with aggression and suspicion.

In the election of a new president, held in the midst of hysterical battle over jurisdiction of the Court, Emile Loubet, President of the Senate, a steady, simple Republican and product of peasant stock, won over the Conservative Méline. As Premier at the time of the Panama scandal, Loubet was despised by the Nationalists. They called his election an "insult to France," a "challenge to the Army," a "victory for Jewish treason." Their hired mobs sent to hoot his progress from the Gare St-Lazare to the Elysée raised such a clamor that even the band playing the "Marseillaise" could not be heard. "The Republic will not founder in my hands," said Loubet calmly. "They know it and it maddens them."

The Right in a state of ungovernable excitement was prepared to make it founder. "In a week we will have driven Loubet from the Presidency," boasted Jules Lemaître. The state funeral of Faure was fixed on as the occasion for a coup d'état. The Army must be persuaded to save the country. The "Leaguers" thought they could do it by a cry, a gesture, an occasion, and did not concern themselves with serious organization. Their plan was to intercept the military escort of the cortege while it was returning from the cemetery to its barracks in the Place de la Nation, and lead it to seize the Elysée. Déroulède joined by Guérin led a band of two hundred patriots into the streets, caught hold of the bridle of General Roget, commander of the escort, shouting, "To the Elysée, General! Follow us, General, follow us! To the Place Bastille! To the Hotel de Ville! To the Elysée! Friends await us. I beg you, General, save France, establish a Republic of the people, kick out the *parlementaires!*" The General kept his head and kept moving, the crowd, ignorant but willing, shouted, "Save France! *Vive l'Armée!*," the troops sweeping Déroulède and his followers with them, marched on to the barracks and entered. Déroulède, throwing open his coat to reveal his deputy's scarf, emblem of parliamentary immunity, was nevertheless carted off to the police station to be indicted for insurrection and provide at his trial one more cause for combative passions. The fiasco did nothing to daunt the expectations of the Right. In the following month the Anti-Semitic League received 56,000 francs from the Duc d'Orléans and 100,000 from Boni de Castellane.

Hardly had breath been drawn when the verdict that all France was awaiting was announced by the Cour de Cassation. Forty-six judges in scarlet and ermine declared for Revision. A cruiser was sent to bring Dreyfus back from Devil's Island for retrial. Zola returned from England with an article which *l'Aurore* headlined in the now familiar type, JUSTICE! He saw all factional and party lines now dissipated in one great division separating France into two camps: the forces of reaction and the past against the forces of justice and the future. This was the logical order of battle to complete the task of 1789. With the unquenchable optimism of their age the Dreyfusards hailed the Court's decision as the herald of social justice for the century about to be born. A great burden of shame seemed lifted and replaced by pride in France. "What other country," wrote a correspondent of *Le Temps* at The Hague where the Peace Conference was assembled, "has had the privilege of making the world's heart beat faster as we have for the last three years?" Revision meant not only the triumph of justice but of "the liberty of mankind." Others beside Frenchmen felt this universality. William James, traveling in Europe, wrote as he saw daylight breaking through the Affair, "It may be one of those moral crises that become starting points and high water marks and leave traditions and rallying cries and new faces behind them."

The Nationalists were flung into paroxysms of wrath. Caran d'Ache drew a cartoon showing Dreyfus with a smirk and Reinach with a whip ordering, "Come here, Marianne." On the facing page he drew Zola emerging from a toilet bowl holding a toy Dreyfus, with the caption, "Truth Rising from Its Well."

Fury at the Court's decision was vented the next day on the head of President Loubet when he attended the races at

Auteuil. It was the Sunday of *le Grand Steeple*, the most fashionable event of the season. When the President's carriage drove up to the grandstand, groups of well-dressed gentlemen wearing in their buttonholes the white carnation of the royalists and the blue cornflower of the anti-Semites, and brandishing their canes, shouted in pounding rhythm, "*Dé-mis-sion!* [resign] *Pa-na-ma! Dé-mis-sion! Pa-na-ma!*" Through the howls and threats Loubet took his seat. Suddenly a tall man with a blond moustache, wearing a white carnation and white cravat, later identified as the Baron Fernand de Christiani, detached himself from the group, dashed up the steps two at a time and struck the President on the head with a heavy cane. Ladies screamed. A sudden silence of general stupor followed, then an uproar as the assailant's companions rushed to rescue him from the guards. As some were arrested others converged on the police in yelling groups, striking with their canes. The scene was "*un charivari infernal.*" General Zurlinden, Governor of Paris, telephoned for reinforcements of three cavalry detachments. Loubet, though shaken, apologized for the disturbance to Countess Tornielli, the Italian Ambassadress, in the seat beside him. "It was a place of honor," she replied.

In Loubet's top hat the Republic itself had been assaulted and the public was startled and indignant. Telegrams from committees and municipal councils all over France poured in expressing a loyalty deeper than might have been supposed from the experience of the last years. Loubet announced that as an invited guest he intended to appear at next Sunday's races at Longchamps. Forewarned, the leagues and newspapers of both sides called for demonstrations and assembled their battalions. The Government took extraordinary precautions. Thirty squadrons of cavalry and a brigade of infantry in battle dress were lined up along the route from the Elysée to Longchamps, while at the racecourse itself dragoons of the *Garde Républicaine* armed with rifles were stationed at every ten yards around the course and at every betting window. Mounted police guarded the lawn. More than 100,000 people turned out along the route and at the racecourse, many wearing the red rose boutonniere of the Left. Again the threat of the Right brought out the workers, less, perhaps, to defend the bourgeois state than to defy the representatives of the ruling class.

The presence of more than six thousand guardians of the law prevented a major outbreak, but throughout the day demonstrators clashed, private riots and melees erupted, cries and counter-cries resounded, hundreds were arrested, reporters and police as well as demonstrators were injured. As the crowds flowed back to Paris in the evening the turbulence swept through the cafés; "*Vive la République!*" met "*Vive l'Armée!*" Bottles and glasses, carafes and trays were hurled, tables and chairs became weapons, police charged; anger, broken heads and national animosities mounted. Even outside Paris, in a pension in Brest where officers and professors boarded, "these young men equally animated by love of France" could no longer talk to or understand each other without coming to the point of a duel. It was time, urged *Le Temps*, for a "truce of God."

But it was not to be had. When again the Government fell in the week after Longchamps, the fears and difficulties to be faced in office were now so great that for eight days no one could form a Government. In the vacuum the man who came forward with intent to "liquidate" the Affair was able to impose conditions that would otherwise have been unacceptable. He was René Waldeck-Rousseau, fifty-three, the leading lawyer of Paris and a polished orator, known as the "Pericles of the Republic." A Catholic from Britanny, wealthy and wellborn, he was impressive in manner and British in appearance, with cropped hair and moustache, a taste for hunting and fishing, a talent for watercolors and impeccable clothes. Rochefort called him *Waldeck le pommadé* because he was so well groomed. Admired by the Radicals and approved by the Center, he represented the *juste milieu*.

With the retrial of Dreyfus ahead, the Affair was moving toward climax. To retain office under the terrible buffeting he could expect, Waldeck deliberately chose to form a Government which, by being equally obnoxious to both sides, would cancel the blows of either. He selected a Socialist, Millerand, as Minister of Commerce and a military hero, the Marquis de Galliffet, "butcher" of the Commune, as Minister of War. The tumult in press and parliament that greeted this remarkable expedient was unequalled. "Pure madness . . . absolute lunacy . . . monstrous . . . infamous!" came from both sides. The appointment of Millerand not only infuriated the Right; his acceptance created a scandal and a schism in his own party and in the Socialist International of major proportions and historic significance. Acceptance of office in a capitalist Government was a betrayal comparable to that of Judas. Profoundly saddened, Jaurès begged Millerand to shun the offer, but Waldeck had knowingly selected a man to whom the lure of office was strong. The Socialists now had to face the choice whether or not to support the Waldeck Government when it came to the Chamber for a vote of confidence. If the Government lost, the prospect was chaos. Jaurès was persuaded by Lucien Herr's argument: "What a triumph for Socialism that the Republic cannot be saved without calling on the party of the proletariat!" The Guesde faction, however, clung to the class struggle. Socialists, stated Guesde, "enter Parliament as though we were in an enemy State only in order to fight the enemy class." Jaurès warned that if Socialism persisted in this attitude it would sink to the level of "sterile and intransigent anarchism," but he did not prevail. The Union Socialiste broke apart; twenty-five of the parliamentary members agreed to support the Government; seventeen refused. Guesde enchanted his group with the exciting suggestion that it should greet the new Government's appearance in the Chamber with cries of "*Vive la Commune!*" but, so as not to find themselves allied with the Right, abstain when it came to a vote.

For ten minutes next day they stood hurling "*Vive la Commune! A bas les fusilleurs! A bas l'assassin!*" at the new ministers. The object of it all, General the Marquis de Galliffet, Prince de Martigues, nearly seventy, with red-bronze face and bright eyes, looked mockingly on the scene, half-gratified, half-disgusted. He had fought in the Crimea, Italy, Mexico, Algeria and at Sedan, where he had led his regiment into the last cavalry charge with the reply to his commanding officer, "As often as you like, Sir, as long as one of us is left." Impressed by the great Gambetta's patriotism and fighting spirit, Galliffet became and remained a loyal Republican and openly despised Boulanger. The eyes in his highly colored face were sunk on either side of a nose like the beak of a bird of prey, but his figure was vigorous and young and he still wore "the same air that had made his fortune, as of a bandit chief who feared nothing or a *grand seigneur* who cared for nothing." Despite a silver-plated stomach and a limp from old wounds, he played tennis in the Tuileries Gardens and his love affairs, recounted with sparkle and ribaldry, were the delight of the Bixio. He told how Mme de Castiglione showed him her nude portrait by Baudry, and when he asked if she was really as beautiful as that, she disrobed and posed on the sofa. "The picture was better," Galliffet concluded. He was called the *sabreur de la parole* because he told stories "as if he were charging at the head of his squadron." Devoted to the fighting efficiency of the Army and to Picquart who had served under his command, he had become a Revisionist. For this sin he was cut at the Jockey, and after he became a Minister, resigned from the Cercle de l'Union, less because of his own opinions than because of "imbecile" members who got themselves arrested at Auteuil; as he said, "It's not possible to belong to a club if one has to arrest the members; it's not sociable." Caustic and eccentric, proud of having nothing to live on but his pension after having once been rich, he possessed "courage, effrontery, intelligence, contempt for death and thirst for life."

He needed all these to become Minister of War at the peak of the Affair. Confronting the taunts of the Guesde extremists in the Chamber, he suddenly stood up and barked, "*L'assassin, présent!*" The din became general. Nationalists, Radicals, Center, were shouting insults and shaking fists. Millerand, a lawyer like Waldeck, with gray hair *en brosse*, a lorgnon, a neat black moustache and a precise, aggressive manner, was wilting. His moustache trembled and he looked "like a huge cat caught in a downpour." Galliffet was observed taking down names and explained later, "I thought I'd better invite those chaps to dinner." Waldeck, trying to speak, stood at the tribune for an hour without being heard for more than ten minutes. He fought desperately and succeeded in establishing the Government by a majority of twenty-six.

Galliffet joined it "without illusions," he wrote to Princess Radziwill, because of its promise to pacify France, "if that is still possible. The Rightist papers beg me to do another Boulanger and those of the Left want me to cut off the heads of all the Generals who displease them. The public is an idiot. If I touch a guilty general I am accused of massacring the Army; if

I abstain I am accused of treason. What a dilemma. Pity me." Actually, although he found Loubet "too bourgeois," he was pleased to be a Minister and was very "gay and amusing" at the next meeting of the Bixio. He told a lively story of a rather large but lovely lady of forty-five who visited him at his office to propose a little deal involving 20,000 horses to be bought for the Army. There would be a million in it for him. "A million," he said to her. "That's not much considering the twenty-five million I got from the Syndicate as everyone knows. Go to see Waldeck. He is jealous of me because he only got seventeen million."

Six weeks later, on August 8, 1899, the retrial of Dreyfus by a new court-martial was scheduled to open in the garrison town of Rennes, a Catholic and aristocratic corner of traditionally Counter-Revolutionary Brittany. France quivered in expectation; as each week passed bringing the moment closer, the tension grew. The world's eyes were turned on Rennes. All the important foreign newspapers sent their star correspondents. Lord Russell of Killowen, the Lord Chief Justice of England, came as an observer. All the leading figures in the Affair, hundreds of French journalists and important political, social and literary figures crammed the town. The Secret File was brought from Paris in an iron box on an artillery caisson. No one anywhere talked of anything but the coming verdict. Acquittal would mean for the Dreyfusards vindication at last; for the Nationalists it would be lethal; an unimaginable blow not to be permitted. As if on order they returned to the theme of the first blackmail: Dreyfus or the Army. "A choice is to be made," wrote Barrès in the *Journal*; Rennes, he said, was the Rubicon. "If Dreyfus is innocent then seven Ministers of War are guilty and the last more than the first," echoed Meyer in *Le Gaulois.* General Mercier, leaving for Rennes to appear as a witness, issued his Order of the Day: "Dreyfus will be condemned once more. For in this affair someone is certainly guilty and the guilty one is either him or me. As it is certainly not me, it is Dreyfus. . . . Dreyfus is a traitor and I shall prove it."

At six o'clock on the morning of August 8 the Court convened with an audience of six hundred persons in the hall of the *lycée*, the only room in Rennes large enough to accommodate them. In the front row, next to former President Casimir-Perier, sat Mercier, his yellow lined face as expressionless as ever, and nearby, the widow of Colonel Henry in her long black mourning veil. Dignitaries, officers in uniform, ladies in light summer dresses and more than four hundred journalists filled the rows behind. Colonel Jouaust, presiding officer of the seven military judges, called out in a voice hoarse under the pressure of the moment, "Bring in the accused."

At once every chattering voice was stilled, every mouth closed, people seemed to hold their breath as with one movement every head in the audience turned toward a small door in the wall on the right. Every gaze fastened on it with a kind of shrinking awe as if fearful to look upon a ghost. For the accused was a ghost, whom no one in the room had laid eyes on for almost five years, whom no one there beyond his family, lawyers and original accusers had ever seen at all. For five years he had been present in all their minds, not as a man but as an idea; now he was going to walk through the door and they would look on Lazarus. A minute passed, then another while the waiting people were gripped in silence, an agonized silence, "such a silence as never before could have overtaken a crowd."

The door opened, two guards were seen; between them came forward a thin, worn, desiccated figure, a strange shred of humanity, seeming neither young nor old, with a shrunken face and dried-out skin, and a body looking almost hollowed out but holding itself erect as if not to falter in the last few yards between the door and the witness box. Only the pince-nez familiar from the pictures had not suffered. A movement of "horror and pity" passed through the watchers, and the look bent on him by Picquart whose life he had changed beyond repair was so intense it could be felt by the people in between. Others present whose careers he had changed or broken—Clemenceau, Cavaignac—saw him for the first time.

For four and a half years Dreyfus had hardly spoken or heard a spoken word. Illness, fever, tropical sun, periods of chains and brutality when the frenzy in France was reflected by his gaolers, had enfeebled him. He could barely speak and only slowly understand what was spoken to him. Mounting the three steps to the tribune he staggered momentarily, straightened himself, saluted with impenetrable face, raised his gloved hand to take the oath, removed his hat, revealed the hair turned prematurely white. He remained a statue. He knew nothing of the Affair, the battle of the press, the duels and petitions, riots, street mobs, Leagues, trials, libel suits, appeals, coups d'état; nothing of Scheurer-Kestner, Reinach, the arrest of Picquart, the trial of Zola, the court-martial of Esterhazy, the suicide of Colonel Henry, the attack on the person of the President of France. During the trial, the impression he made on many was unfavorable. Rigidly determined to allow nothing to show that would appeal to pity, he antagonized many who came prepared to pity. G. A. Henty who came like most of the English, believing him to have been framed, left voicing doubts. "The man looked and spoke like a spy . . . and if he isn't a spy I'll be damned if he oughtn't to be one." Henty spoke for the last romantics who expected abstract concepts like Justice to be unequivocal and people who behaved oddly to be spies.

In the end it was not the impression Dreyfus made that determined the outcome any more than it was he who made the Affair: it was the dilemma Mercier had formulated long ago and it was General Mercier among the hundreds of witnesses who dominated the trial. Cold in authority, haughty in self-assurance, he took full responsibility for the original order withholding the Secret File from the defence, which he said was a "moral" decision. When on the witness stand he refused to answer questions he did not like; when not on the stand he intervened without being asked. When the Secret File was under examination he ordered the public excluded and the Court obeyed him. When questioned on the Army's suppression of evidence, the cynicism of his answers, Reinach confessed, "was almost admirable, . . . as if crime might be the source of a kind of beauty." Mercier "has become hallucinated," wrote Galliffet. "He thinks France is incarnated in his person . . . but all the same he is an honorable man."

As the weeks of examination and testimony dragged on with the succession of witnesses personally and passionately involved, the contention of lawyers, the disputes of journalists and observers, the heated feelings of the town, suspense as to the verdict became almost insupportable. In Paris rumors of another coup d'état planned for the day Mercier was to testify caused the Government to raid the homes of a hundred suspects and arrest sixty-five in their beds, including Déroulède but missing Guérin, who got away, barricaded himself in a house in the Rue Chabrol with a cache of munitions and fourteen companions, where he held out against a somewhat lackluster police siege for six weeks. "I don't budge from my office from 7 A.M. to 7 P.M. seven days a week, in order to be prepared for anything," wrote Galliffet.

On August 14 the too eloquent and aggressive Maître Labori, who "looked like Hercules and pleaded like a boxer," was shot outside the court, but not killed, by a young man with red hair who ran away shouting, "I've just killed the Dreyfus! I've just killed the Dreyfus!" The name again had become an abstraction. The attack raised the temperature to the level of madness. Since the assailant had run away with Labori's briefcase and had not been caught, it seemed to the Dreyfusards a deliberate plot and one more proof that the Nationalists would stop at nothing. They denounced their opponents as "murderers," a "General Staff of criminals" and swore that "for every one of ours we shall kill one of theirs—Mercier, Cavaignac, Boisdeffre, Barrès." Wrote Princess Radziwill to Galliffet, "My God, what an end to the century!"

The end of the trial came on September 9 and all the world gasped at the unbelievable verdict. By a vote of 5–2 Dreyfus was condemned again with "extenuating circumstances" which permitted a sentence of five years, already served, instead of a mandatory life sentence. Since there could obviously be nothing extenuating about treason, the rider was provocative to both sides. It had been devised by the prosecution, which realized that it would be easier to obtain a verdict of guilty if the judges did not have on their consciences the prospect of sending Dreyfus back to Devil's Island.

The effect of the verdict was as of some awful disaster. People were stunned. Queen Victoria telegraphed Lord Russell, "The Queen has learned with stupefaction the frightful verdict and hopes the poor martyr will appeal it to the highest judges." "Iniquitous, cynical, odious, barbarous," wrote *The Times* correspondent, bereft of sentence structure. Like an angry Isaiah, Clemenceau demanded, "What remains of the historic tradition that once made us champions of justice for the whole of the earth? A cry will ring out over the world: Where is France?

What became of France?" World opinion suddenly became an issue, more acutely because of the coming International Exposition of 1900. At Evian on Lake Geneva, where many of the *gratin* spent their summer holidays, Proust found the Comtesse de Noailles weeping and crying, "How could they do it? What will the foreigners think of us now?" In the Nationalist camp the same thought was cause for rejoicing. "Since 1870 it is our first victory over the foreigner," exulted *Le Gaulois.*

Strength of feeling everywhere was made plain; the whole world cared. Excitement in Odessa was "simply extraordinary"; there was intense indignation in Berlin, "disgust and horror" in far-off Melbourne, protest meetings in Chicago and suggestions from all quarters for boycott of the Exposition. In Liverpool copies of *The Times* were bought out in minutes and soon sold at a premium. From Norway the composer Grieg wrote refusing an invitation to conduct his music at the Théâtre Chatelet because of his "indignation at the contempt for justice shown in your country." The English, riding at the time a wave of anti-French feeling because of Fashoda, were most indignant of all. Hyde Park rang with protest meetings, newspapers denounced the "insult to civilization," industrial firms and cultural societies urged boycott of the Exposition as a means of bringing pressure on the French Government, travelers were urged to cancel proposed visits, a hotel-keeper in the Lake District evicted a honeymooning French couple and one writer to the editor asserted that even the question of the Transvaal "pales into insignificance before the larger questions of truth and justice." *The Times*, however, reminded readers that many Frenchmen had risked "more than life itself" to prevent the defeat of justice and could not be expected to abandon the struggle to redress the wrong of Rennes.

The fight did in fact go on, but public opinion was worn out. The Affair was one of those situations for which there was no good solution. Waldeck-Rousseau offered Dreyfus a pardon which, despite the fierce objections of Clemenceau, was accepted on grounds of humanity—since Dreyfus could go through no more—and with the proviso that it would not terminate the effort to clear his name. Galliffet issued to the Army an Order of the Day: "The incident is closed. . . . Forget the past so that you may think only of the future." Waldeck introduced an Amnesty Bill annulling all pending legal actions connected with the case and angering both sides: the Right because Déroulède was excluded; the Dreyfusards because Picquart, Reinach and others who had suffered injustice or had been sued could not clear themselves. Waldeck was adamant. "The amnesty does not judge, it does not accuse, it does not acquit; it ignores." Debate nevertheless continued furious and lasted for a year before the bill became law. Animosities did not close over. Positions taken during the Affair hardened and crystallized. Lemaître, who had entered it more for sensation than from conviction, became a rabid royalist; Anatole France moved far to the left.

The battle shifted from the moral to the political; from Dreyfus to the Dreyfusian Revolution. It remained the same battle but the terms changed. The issue was no longer Justice and Revision but the effort of the Government under Waldeck and his successor, Combes, to curb clericalism and republicanize education and the Army. The fight was waged as fiercely as ever over Waldeck's Law of Associations directed against the Religious Orders and over the affair of General André and the *fiches* when it was disclosed that the overzealous Minister of War in 1904 was using reports from Masonic officers on Catholic brother-officers to guide him in matters of promotion. Persistent and unrelenting efforts by Mathieu Dreyfus, Reinach and Jaurès succeeded against all obstacles in achieving a final Revision and a "breaking" of the Rennes verdict by the Cour de Cassation. On July 13, 1906, the eve of Bastille Day, almost twelve years after Dreyfus' arrest and seven years after Rennes, a bill restoring Dreyfus and Picquart to the Army was carried in the Chamber by 442–32, with de Mun still among the negatives. Dreyfus, decorated with the Légion d'Honneur, was promoted to Major and Picquart to General, the ranks they would have reached by the normal course of events. In 1902 Drumont failed of re-election to the Chamber; *La Libre Parole* declined and in 1907 was offered for sale with no takers. Zola died in 1902 and at his funeral Anatole France spoke the just and noble epitaph of the man who "for a moment, . . . was the conscience of mankind." In 1908 Zola's ashes were transferred to the Panthéon. In the course of the ceremony a man named Gregori shot at Dreyfus, wounding him in the arm, and was subsequently acquitted in the Assize Court. In 1906 Clemenceau became Premier and named Picquart his Minister of War. Picquart in the seat of Mercier, "that's something to see!" said Galliffet. "There are some things to console one for not being able to decide to die."

Rennes was the climax. After Rennes neither the fight for Justice nor the struggle of the Right against the Republic was over, but the Affair was. While it lasted, France exhibited, as in the Revolution, political man at his most combative. It was a time of excess. Men plunged in up to the hilt of their capacities and beliefs. They held nothing back. On the eve of the new century the Affair revealed what energies and ferocity were at hand to greet it.

17. British delegation to The Hague, 1899. Front row, from left to right: Ardagh; Fisher; Pauncefote; Sir Henry Howard, Minister to The Hague. Arthur Peel is first on the left in the back row.

Porte Monumentale.

18. PARIS EXPOSITION, 1900.

Palace of Electricity.

19. Alfred Nobel (portrait by E. Osterman).

20. Bertha von Suttner.

21. The Krupp works at Essen, 1912.

22. Richard Strauss, 1905.

23. Friedrich Nietzsche, Weimar, 1900 (drawing by Hans Olde).

24. A beer garden in Berlin.

25. Nijinsky as the Faun (design by Léon Bakst).

26. Arthur James Balfour, about 1895.

27. Coal strike, 1910.

28. Seamen's strike, 1911.

AND LABOUR

29. David Lloyd George, about 1908.

30. August Bebel.

31. Keir Hardie.

32. "Strike" (oil painting by Théophile Steinlen).

33. Jean Jaurès.

5

THE STEADY DRUMMER

THE HAGUE: 1899 AND 1907

5

The Steady Drummer

JOY, HOPE, suspicion—above all, astonishment—were the world's prevailing emotions when it learned on August 29, 1898, that the young Czar of Russia, Nicholas II, had issued a call to the nations to join in a conference for the limitation of armaments. All the capitals were taken by surprise by what *Le Temps* called "this flash of lightning out of the North." That the call should come from the mighty and ever expanding power whom the other nations feared and who was still regarded, despite its two hundred years of European veneer, as semi-barbaric, was cause for dazed wonderment liberally laced with distrust. The pressure of Russian expansion had been felt from Alaska to India, from Turkey to Poland. "The Czar with an olive branch," it was said in Vienna, "that's something new in history." But his invitation touched a chord aching to respond.

Fear of the swelling armaments industry was widespread. Krupp, the colossus of Essen, was the largest single business in Europe. Skoda, Schneider-Creusot, Vickers-Maxim, the distended combines of many mergers, with harsh names that grated on the ear, had interests in every camp, sold their products to customers on every continent and to both sides of every quarrel, profited from every dispute. Each year one or another of them produced a new weapon more efficient in deadliness, which, when adopted by the armed forces of one power, immediately required a matching effort by its rival. Each year the cost mounted and the huge piles of weapons grew until it seemed they must burst in final, lethal explosion.

The Czar's manifesto called for a stop to this process. Addressed to all the governments represented at St. Petersburg, it stated that although the longing for peace had been especially pronounced in the last twenty years, "the intellectual and physical strength of nations, labour and capital alike, have been unproductively consumed in building terrible engines of destruction." Today these were the last word in science, tomorrow they were obsolete and had to be replaced. The system of "armaments *à l'outrance* is transforming the armed peace into a crushing burden that weighs on all nations and if prolonged will lead inevitably to the very cataclysm which it is desired to avert." To arrest this exorbitant competition was now incumbent upon all.

The summons from such a source surpassed the wildest dreams of the friends of peace. It "will sound like beautiful music over the whole earth," said a Viennese paper. Phrases like "a new epoch in civilization," "dawn of a new era," "omen for the new century," appeared in the press of every country. In Belgium the summons was called a "veritable deliverance," an act of "colossal importance" whose author would go down in history as "Nicholas the Pacific." In New York it seemed a possible beginning "of the most momentous and beneficent movement in modern history—indeed in all history." Rome lauded "one of the great documents that honors its century," and Berlin greeted "the new Evangelist on the banks of the Neva" whose goal was noble and beautiful in theory however unrealizable in practice. Humanitarian but utopian was the consensus in London—except for Kipling who uttered dire warning. Britain and Russia were then close to conflict across India's Northwest Frontier, and Kipling's poem "The Bear that Walks like a Man," composed in response to the Czar's manifesto, told a grim allegory of a man maimed and blinded when the bear he hunted stood up as if in supplication and the hunter "touched with pity and wonder" withheld his fire only to have his face ripped away by the "steel-shod paw":

> When he stands up as pleading, in wavering, man-brute guise,
> When he veils the hate and cunning of his little swinish eyes;
> When he shows as seeking quarter, with paws like hands in prayer,
> *That* is the time of peril—the time of the Truce of the Bear! . . .

Suspicion of Russia's motive and cynical speculations were ample. The leading question was, had France, Russia's ally, been consulted in advance? Since disarmament presupposed satisfaction with the status quo and since France was vociferously unreconciled to the loss of Alsace-Lorraine, the action of her ally posed, as *The Times* said, a "most surprising enigma." From the French reaction it was clear she had not been consulted. "*Et l'Alsace-Lorraine?*" was *l'Intransigeant*'s one-line summary. Nevertheless many felt that coming at a time when "the intolerable pretensions and immeasurable ambitions" of Anglo-Saxon imperialism were agitating everyone's nerves and when the maintenance of peace was becoming more and more a "miracle of equilibrium," the proposed conference was welcome.

Each group saw reflected in the Czar's manifesto, as if in a magic mirror, the face of its particular opponent. To Germany it was obvious that if England did not consent to naval disarmament the Czar's gesture would amount to "a sword stroke in water" and a few days later the Kaiser pronounced his decisive dictum, "Our future lies upon the ocean." The British saw the major problem in Germany's naval ambitions. Socialists everywhere were sure that whatever the Russian motive had been, considering the cruelties of Czarist oppression, it was not love of humanity. The German Socialist Wilhelm Liebknecht pronounced it a "fraud." Many peace advocates considered it a response to the Spanish-American War, which seemed to them a prelude to world disaster. Many Europeans were convinced by the taking of the Philippines of the necessity of curbing American expansion. Americans themselves were not averse to the thought that the Czar had been prompted by their victory over Spain. Speaking for the anti-imperialists, Godkin sadly noted that the "splendid summons" came at a time when the United States was more deeply committed to "the military spirit and idea of forcible conquest" than ever before in her history.

The puzzle of motive remained. One explanation widely favored was that Nicholas had acted less for humanity than from a human desire to forestall the Kaiser, who was believed to be planning a similar proclamation, *urbi et orbi*, on his forthcoming visit to Jerusalem.

Colonel Henry's suicide in the Dreyfus Affair soon absorbed public attention and ten days later the world gasped again when the Empress Elizabeth was assassinated by an Anarchist. Americans were preoccupied in welcoming home the regiments from Cuba, and the British with Kitchener's march to Khartoum. From September on, the air darkened with the prospect of war between England and France; Fashoda, as the German Ambassador happily remarked, seemed to have obliterated the memory of Alsace-Lorraine. Peace was crowded out as a sensation.

Not, however, to the dedicated disciples of the peace movement in Europe and America, whom the Czar's summons had electrified. Among the best known of these was Baroness Bertha von Suttner, author of the anti-war novel *Die Waffen Nieder* ("Put Down Your Arms"), which Tolstoy called the *Uncle Tom's Cabin* of its cause. When the Baroness' husband came home waving the newspaper, like Emma Goldman bringing the news of Homestead, she was transported with joy. Letters of congratulation soon poured in from fellow workers in the International Peace Bureau, the Interparliamentary Union, the Peace and Arbitration Association. "Whatever may come of it," wrote Björnstjerne Björnson, "from now on the air is throbbing with thoughts of peace." The fervor of the movement was personified by the Baroness, born Countess Kinsky in 1843 into an aristocratic Austrian family of dwindling fortunes. Too strong-minded and energetic to sink into genteel decay, she had taken a position at the age of thirty as tutor-companion to the daughters of the Von Suttner family and had kindled a glowing and reciprocated passion in the son and heir, seven years her junior. But she was dowerless and they parted in Germanic anguish. "He knelt before me and humbly kissed the hem of my gown: 'Matchless, royally generous-hearted woman, your love has taught me to know a happiness which shall consecrate my life. Farewell!' " At this moment a newspaper advertisement by a "very wealthy, cultured, elderly gentleman living in Paris" who was looking for a mature, educated lady as secretary and manager of his household offered a way out, and the Countess found herself in the employ of the discoverer of dynamite, Alfred Nobel.

A strange, satiric idealist and pessimist, shy, melancholy, almost a recluse, though hardly elderly at forty-three, Nobel had made millions in the manufacture of explosives and was profoundly disturbed by its implications. He seemed less in need of a secretary than of someone to listen to him. "I wish," he told his new employee, "I could produce a substance or a machine of such frightful efficacy for wholesale devastation that wars should thereby become altogether impossible." Despite an immediate sympathy and "the intense intellectual enjoyment" of his society and a tentative hint of something more, the lady succumbed to heartache, left after a week, flew back to the arms of her adorer and eloped with him. After twelve years of marriage and a career as a writer, she discovered—with a sense of revelation—the International Peace and Arbitration Association of London. Its statement of purposes declared that now at the close of the Nineteenth Century the time had come for all men to consult and agree on a means for the peaceful settlement of disputes and the abolition of war. Instantly and passionately a convert, Bertha von Suttner threw herself into the effort to organize branches of the society in Vienna and Berlin. In 1891 her efforts, publicized by the *Neue Freie Presse*, succeeded in Vienna and the manifesto issued on the occasion expressed the ideals of peace advocates everywhere. They believed a new war to be morally impossible because "men have lost some of their former savagery and disregard for life," and physically impossible because new weapons were too destructive. They believed the masses though still dumb yearned for peace. While all governments insisted war must be avoided, all were massing armaments to prepare for it and this "monstrous contradiction" must end.

The Interparliamentary Union, formed in Paris in 1888 to bring together members of the various national parliaments in the cause of peace, now held Congresses each year in different capitals. In the United States the Universal Peace Union named as its chief goals gradual disarmament and a Permanent Court of Arbitration. Stemming from the Geneva settlement of the *Alabama* dispute between the United States and Britain, the arbitration movement was especially strong in these two countries. Its goal was to substitute judicial settlement for war. Its advocates believed that if a workable process could be arranged, at first by treaty between individual nations, later by general treaty, while at the same time war was shown to be so destructive as to be "impossible," man would ultimately rather arbitrate than fight. It was a view based on the premise that man was reasonable and that wars came from quarrels susceptible of settlement by other means. The time was one of belief in moral as well as material progress and did not include the view of war as a clash of forces like the winds that blow.

Nobel was an ardent advocate of arbitration, though not of disarmament, which he thought a foolish demand for the present. He urged establishment of a tribunal and agreement among nations for a one-year period of compulsory truce in any dispute. He turned up in person, though incognito, at a Peace Congress in Berne in 1892 and told Bertha von Suttner that if she could "inform me, convince me, I will do something great for the cause." The spark of friendship between them had been kept alive in correspondence and an occasional visit over the years and he now wrote her that a new era of violence seemed to be working itself up; "one hears in the distance its hollow rumble already." Two months later he wrote again, "I should like to dispose of my fortune to found a prize to be awarded every five years," to the person who had contributed most effectively to the peace of Europe. He thought it should terminate after six awards, "for if in thirty years society cannot be reformed we shall inevitably lapse into barbarism." Nobel brooded over the plan, embodied it in a will drawn in 1895 which allowed man a little longer deadline, and died in the following year.

The cause of arbitration almost scored a triumph in January, 1897, when Britain and the United States signed a treaty, negotiated by Secretary Olney and the British Ambassador, Sir Julian Pauncefote, for the settlement of all except territorial disputes, the memory of Venezuela being still warm. Resenting invasion of its control of foreign affairs, the Senate refused to ratify it by three votes. The defeat seemed a calamity, in Olney's words, "not merely of national but of world wide proportions." It shook the general belief in man's moral progress.

In this belief, fostered in the last ten or fifteen years by signs on every hand of society's improvement, the peace movement had its origins. The marvelous strides of science had brought the human race to a stage of material welfare ready to prove the faith of the Nineteenth Century that the better off man became the less aggressive he would be. Society now had running water and lighted streets, sanitation, preserved and refrigerated food, sewing machines, washing machines, typewriters, lawn-mowers, the phonograph, telegraph and telephone and lately, beginning in the nineties, the extraordinary gift of individual powered mobility in the horseless carriage. It seemed impossible that so much physical benefit should not have worked a spiritual change, that the new century should not begin a new era in human behavior; that man, in short, had not become too civilized for war. Science made all phenomena seem subject to certitudes and laws, and if man's physical world could be understood and controlled, why not his social relations also? "Social conditions are destined to become *different*," Baroness von Suttner wrote with conviction. The younger generation agreed. "We were sincerely persuaded in 1898 that the era of wars was over," wrote Julien Benda, a French intellectual who was thirty-one in that year. "For fifteen years from 1890 to 1905 men of my generation really believed in world peace."

Fear as well as faith impelled the peace movement, fear of the unchained energy of the machine age. The great surge in mechanical energy, the amazing new techniques and tools and new inventions following one upon the other, the fantastic capabilities of electricity, created an uneasy sense that man had gathered into his hands more power than he could control; power that could escape, run wild and destroy him unless put under limits. In 1820 the world disposed of 778 metric tons of mechanical energy (expressed in the coal equivalent of mineral fuels and water power) compared to 15,000,000 metric tons in 1898. Productivity per man had increased in proportion. Countries were swelling in size and strength. The death rate declined markedly, owing to developments in sanitation and medicine, with the result that since 1870 the population of Europe had increased by 100,000,000, as much as its whole population in 1650. In the same period Great Britain had acquired 4,700,000 square miles of territory, France 3,600,000, Germany 1,000,000 and Belgium 900,000, or seventy-seven times her own size. In the United States during the same period the population had more than doubled and the per capita output of manufactures multiplied four times. The profits of Carnegie Steel rose from $6,000,000 in 1896 to $40,000,000 in 1900. A new prime mover, the internal combustion engine, succeeded the steam engine and brought into existence the oil industry. The steam turbine and diesel engine added new motor power; hydro-electric power throbbed in thousands of dynamos. Steamships increased in tonnage, speed and cargo space. Steel, the key product of the age, mushroomed in products and uses through invention of the Bessemer converter. The relative invention rate reached the highest point in history in the nineties. Aluminum and other light metal alloys were developed. The chemical industry created new materials and processes. The method of mass production, using interchangeable parts, known as the "American system," came into use in all industrial countries. Dynamite as a blasting agent made possible massive excavations for quarries and mine shafts and mammoth constructions like the Simplon Railway Tunnel and the Panama Canal. The manufacture of dynamite increased from 11 tons in 1867, the year Nobel first put it on the market, to 66,500 tons in 1897. Big business which was necessary to finance heavy industry formed cartels and trusts with vast financial resources.

Nowhere were the added strengths greater than in weapons and other forces of war. The increase in population made manpower available for huge standing armies, and following the German example, conscription was adopted by all the Continental powers after 1871. To arm and equip mass armies required the efforts of mass industry and the munitions companies gathered under their control raw materials, mines, foundries and transportation. Markets and profits were almost limitless and they responded with fierce vigor to the incentive. In the ten years from the mid-eighties to mid-nineties land warfare was revolutionized by the introduction of the magazine-loading small-bore rifle, the improved Maxim machine gun, and smokeless powder. Together these multiplied the range, rapidity and accuracy of firepower five times or more and changed the nature of battle. Infantry who had fired three rounds a minute at Waterloo could now fire sixteen rounds a minute. The small bore added distance to the trajectory and accuracy to the aim. Development of automatic recoil for field guns equally increased the rate of artillery fire. Above all, smokeless powder, patented by Nobel between 1887 and 1891, opened up and extended the battlefield. It cleared the field of vision, permitted concealment of guns, speeded reloading and increased the range and accuracy of artillery from one thousand to five or six thousand yards. Battle would now spread over vast distances and an army be brought under fire before it could see the enemy. The conditions were laid, if barely yet suspected, for the supremacy of artillery over the rifle. The torpedo and the mine equally extended the range of naval warfare and experiments gave awful promise of the submarine.

Some gloried in the energy coursing through the world's veins; others feared it, and felt with Ibsen, "We are sailing with a corpse in the cargo." The desire for nations to come together in some sort of mutual effort to apply a brake grew increasingly vocal and was loud enough for Lord Salisbury as Prime Minister to give heed to it in 1897. In his Guildhall speech of that year he saw the piling up of arms and the yearly improvement in "instruments of death" culminating, unless prevented, in a "terrible effort of mutual destruction which will be fatal for Christian civilization." Without mentioning disarmament, he said the only hope of preventing the disaster lay in bringing the powers together to act on their differences in a friendly spirit and eventually to "be welded in some international constitution." Never an optimist, Lord Salisbury did not go so far as to suggest that this would abolish war, but limited his hopes to "a long spell of prosperous trade and continued peace."

The Czar was neither more pacific nor more idealistic than Lord Salisbury; he was thirty in 1898, a narrow, rather dull-witted young man of no vision and only one idea: to govern with no diminution of the autocratic power bequeathed by his ancestors. His petty view of things, said Pobiedonostsev, Chief Procurator of the Holy Synod, was the result "of the influence of the many chambermaids who surround his mother." The effort to keep a constitution at bay was the sum of his exertions and he had little political energy or interest left for anything else. Unlike the mettlesome Kaiser, who itched to play a hand every time he read a dispatch, the Czar found world affairs rather mentally taxing. "Indeed," as he wrote his mother during the excitement over Fashoda and the Kaiser's visit to Jerusalem, "many strange things happen in the world. One reads about them and shrugs one's shoulders."

The proposal for a peace conference was not his own idea. It originated for certain practical reasons with the ministers of three critical departments—War, Finance, and Foreign

Affairs—and its genesis lay in the simple condition that Russia was behind in the arms race and could not afford to catch up. General Alexei Kuropatkin, the Minister of War, had learned that Austria, Russia's chief rival, was planning to adopt the improved rapid-fire field gun firing six rounds a minute, already possessed by Germany and France. The Russians, whose field gun fired one round a minute, could not hope to finance the rearming of their entire artillery, because they were already, at great financial strain, engaged in rearming their infantry. If the Austrians could be persuaded to agree to a ten-year moratorium on new guns, Kuropatkin thought, both countries would be spared the expense—and why not? For whether both rearmed or both agreed not to rearm, "the final result, if the two groups went to war, would be the same."

Kuropatkin took his simple but grand idea to the Czar, who could see no flaw, and then to the Foreign Minister, Count Muraviev, who took the precaution of consulting the Finance Minister, Count Witte. Capable, energetic and unusually endowed for a Czarist minister with common sense and a hard head, Witte was trying, against the forces of lethargy, autocracy and erosion, to fit Russia for the modern industrial world. He grudged every ruble spent on arms, detested the interference of war and believed the arms race might become "more irksome than war itself." However, as he pointed out, Kuropatkin's Chinese philosophy of agreeing with the enemy in advance depended on trusting the Austrians, which was impossible, and would be harmful besides, as it would "merely reveal our financial weakness to the whole world." Instead he proposed an international, rather than a bilateral, moratorium on new weapons. He expatiated to Muraviev on the incalculable harm that growing militarism was inflicting on the world and the boon which could be conferred upon humanity by limiting armaments. These "rather trite ideas," as he wrote later, were new to Muraviev and apparently produced on him a profound impression. Within a few days he called a council of ministers to consider an appeal to the powers for a conference. The Czar's approval was obtained. If only the awful pace of the world could be slowed down, he and his advisers felt, and something done "to keep people from inventing things," Russia would benefit.

Just at this moment an impressive six-volume work called *The Future of War* was published in Russia. Its author, Ivan Bloch, and his ideas, were known to Witte, whether or not they influenced him. Bloch was a self-educated man and converted Jew who, not satisfied with making a fortune in railroad contracting, had gone abroad to seek higher education in economics and political science in foreign universities. In Warsaw, on his return from Western Europe, he had become a power in banking and the railroad business, which brought him into contact with Witte, and had published a number of scholarly volumes on industrial and monetary problems before embarking on the major work that was to give him a niche in immortality. His studies and his experience in business filled him with growing apprehension that the limited war of the past was no longer possible. Because conscription could call on a pool of the entire nation, he saw wars of the future absorbing the total energies and resources of the combatant states, who, unable to achieve decisive victory on the battlefield, would fight to exhaustion until they had brought each other down in total ruin. The interdependence of nations in finance, foreign trade, raw materials and all business relations, Bloch believed, meant that the victor could not be separated from the vanquished. The destructive power of modern weapons would mean a vast increase in slaughter. The one-day battle had become a thing of the past. Whole armies would become entrenched for weeks and months at a time; battles would become sieges; noncombatant populations would be drawn in. No modern state could achieve victory without the destruction of its resources and the breakup of society. War had become "impossible except at the price of suicide."

Bloch's conclusions led him to the peace movement (or the process may have been the other way around). To convince society of the danger, he used a persuasion more frightening than war—social revolution. If present conditions continued, he argued, nations faced either exhaustion in the arms race or the catastrophe of war, and in either case "convulsion in the social order." The waste of national resources on a sterile product was accountable for the growing anti-militarism of the masses. Therefore in preparing for war the governments were really "preparing the triumph of the social revolution." If they could be convinced of this, Bloch believed, they would be more willing to find other means than war of settling their disputes. His six volumes were a massive piling-up of facts on firepower, blockade, freight and cargo capacities, casualty rates and every military and economic factor to prove the vulnerability of the modern state. Like Marx, Bloch drew from a given set of circumstances the dogma of an inevitable historical conclusion. He believed that armament expenditure necessarily "exhausted" a nation, as Marx believed that capitalism progressively impoverished the proletariat. Neither Bloch nor any of the peace propagandists considered the degree to which the armament and attendant industries created employment.

Fear of social revolution being an effective argument in Russia, Bloch gained an audience with the Czar and his argument found an echo in the manifesto which was written by Muraviev. The Foreign Minister evidently felt its persuasiveness. In conveying it to the British Ambassador he particularly asked him to emphasize in his report that Russia's initiative for peace would show "the discontented and disturbing classes" that powerful governments sympathized with their desire to see national wealth used productively rather than in "ruinous competition." The Ambassador replied suavely that "it would be difficult to remain insensible to the noble sentiments which had inspired this remarkable document."

"It is the greatest nonsense and rubbish I ever heard of," wrote the Prince of Wales less suavely to Lady Warwick. When indignant he took on something of the tone of his mother. "The thing is simply impossible. France could never consent to it—nor *We*." He decided it was "some new dodge of that sly dog" and "subtle intriguer" Muraviev, who had "put it into the Czar's head." On the whole this expressed the view of the governments. Regarding the proposal with cold distaste, they accepted the invitation—because none wished to be the one to reject it—while expecting nothing to come of it but trouble. As the Austrian Foreign Minister said, it would make it more difficult in future for governments to present new military demands to their parliaments.

Dampened but determined, Muraviev sent out a second circular letter in January, 1899, with an agenda of eight topics. The first proposed an agreement not to increase armed forces or military budgets for a fixed period. The last proposed agreement on the principle of arbitration and the working out of procedures. Topics 2, 3 and 4 dealt with prohibition or restriction of new types of weapons and of predicted means of warfare, such as submarines, asphyxiating gases and the "launching of projectiles from balloons" for which no specific verb existed. Topics 5, 6 and 7 concerned the laws and customs of land warfare and the extension of the Geneva rules of 1864 to naval warfare. Topics 2–7 were resented by the peace propagandists, who wished to abolish war, not alleviate it. They suspected that these topics had been included to stir the interest and require the participation of the governments and their military representatives, as was indeed the case.

Chanceries buzzed, diplomatic pouches bulged with dispatches, ambassadors called on foreign ministers and endeavored in the prescribed conversational minuet to discover the intentions of the government to which they were accredited. Lord Salisbury appeared in a German report as "very skeptical" and the Emperor Franz Joseph as taking an "unfavorable" view and considering any limit on military development "unacceptable." In Rome the Marquis Visconti-Venosta declined to be a delegate to a conference "which was not likely to be attended by any very useful results." Washington would send delegates but would do nothing toward limitation of arms. Belgium awaited the conference with "regret and anxiety," fearing that any alteration in the laws of war would confirm the powers of an invading army or restrict the rights of legitimate defence against invasion. Berlin's reaction seemed expressed in the addition of three army corps to her forces. From capital to capital, reaction varied little: arms limitation was "impractical"; restriction on new developments unwanted; arbitration on matters involving "national honor or vital interest" unacceptable, although perhaps feasible on minor matters. Conduct of war, however, offered room for discussion.

Fearing that all the excited talk of the peace advocates about disarmament had caused misunderstanding of his proposal, Muraviev visited the capitals to explain in personal interviews that what Russia really wanted was simply a ceiling on the status quo. It seemed so sensible. The powers might even agree, he suggested, on a fixed percentage of their population to be called to arms, which would enable them greatly to reduce their armies while "retaining the same chances as before." "Idiot," noted the Kaiser on the margin of this memorandum.

No one was more agitated by the Czar's proposal than Wilhelm II, in whose mind the military function was equivalent to the State as well as to himself, who personified the State. The white cloak and shining helmet he liked to pose in, the sparkle and color of uniforms, the gallop of cavalry, the panoply of regimental colors, the complicated rattle of ordnance, the whole paraphernalia of officer corps and Army, and lately, the brilliant vision of power upon the sea, were all facets of the same jewel—armed force. Everything else, Reichstag, political parties, budgets, votes, were more or less extraneous nuisances—except diplomacy, which was only properly understood by monarchs and invariably bungled at lower levels.

The Kaiser had come to the throne at twenty-nine, in 1888, after his father's sad small reign of ninety days when liberal rule had flickered for a moment in Germany and gone out. His first proclamation on his accession was addressed, not like his father's, "To My People," but, "To My Army." It announced, "We belong to each other, I and the Army; we were born for each other." The relationship he had in mind was explained in advice to a company of young recruits: "If your Emperor commands you to do so you must fire on your father and mother." His sense of personal responsibility for the affairs of Germany and of Europe was expressed in the frequent "I's" and "My's" that bedizened his talk. "There is only one master in the Reich and that is I; I shall tolerate no other." Or, some years later, "There is no balance of power in Europe but me—me and my twenty-five army corps." He was willing, however, to make room for the Almighty who figured as the "ancient Ally of my House." Remarks like these caused heads to shake and people to reflect like the Prince of Wales "how different everything would have been" if the Kaiser's father had lived. Still, the Prince explained, his nephew's speeches did not sound so absurd in German as when translated into English.

The Kaiserin remarked that she had not seen her husband so annoyed for a long time as over the sudden intrusion—into a domain he considered his own—of "Nicky," the Czar, whom he was accustomed to patronize and advise in voluble letters in

English signed "Willy." Whether or not he had planned some similar statement from Jerusalem, the real bite was, as his friend Count Eulenburg said, that he "simply can't stand someone else coming to the front of the stage."

Assuming at a glance that the proposal was one for "general disarmament," and immediately seeing the results in personal terms, the Kaiser dashed off a telegram to Nicky. Imagine, he reproached, "a Monarch holding personal command of his Army, dissolving his regiments sacred with a hundred years of history . . . and handing over his towns to Anarchists and Democracy." Nevertheless he felt sure the Czar would be praised for his humanitarian proposal, "the most interesting and surprising of this century! Honor will henceforth be lavished upon you by the whole world; even should the practical part fail through difficulties of detail." He littered the margins of ensuing correspondence with *Aha!*'s and *!!*'s and observations varying from the astute to the vulgar, the earliest being the not unperceptive thought, "He has put a brilliant weapon into the hands of our Democrats and Opposition." At one point he compared the proposal to the Spartans' message demanding that the Athenians agree not to rebuild their walls; at another he suddenly scribbled the rather apt query, "What will Krupp pay his workers with?"

Germany did not have the motive and the cue for peace that Russia had: straitened circumstances. Under-developed industry was not a German problem. When Muraviev in Berlin told Count Eulenburg that the guiding idea behind the Russian proposal was that the yearly increases would finally bring the nations to the point of *non possumus*, he could not have chosen a worse argument. *Non possumus* was not in the German vocabulary. Germany was bursting with vigor and bulging with material success. After the unification of 1871, won by the sword in the previous decade of wars, prosperity had come with a rush, as it had in the United States after the Civil War. Energies were let loose on the development of physical resources. Germany in the nineties was enjoying the first half of a twenty-five-year period in which her national income doubled, population increased by 50 per cent, railroad-track mileage by 50 per cent, cities sprang up, colonies were acquired, giant industries took shape, wealth accumulated from their enterprises and the rise in employment kept pace. Albert Ballin's steamship empire multiplied its tonnage sevenfold and its capital tenfold in this period. Emil Rathenau developed the electrical industry which quadrupled the number of its workers in ten years. I. G. Farben created aniline dyes; Fritz Thyssen governed a kingdom of coal, iron and steel in the Ruhr. As a result of a new smelting process making possible the utilization of the phosphoric iron ore of Lorraine, Germany's production of coal and steel by 1898 had increased four times since 1871 and now surpassed Britain's. Germany's national income in that period had doubled, although it was still behind Britain's, and measured per capita, was but two-thirds of Britain's. German banking houses opened branches around the world, German salesmen sold German goods from Mexico to Baghdad.

German universities and technical schools were the most admired, German methods the most thorough, German philosophers dominant. The Kaiser Wilhelm Institute was the leading laboratory for chemical research in the world. German science boasted Koch, Ehrlich and Roentgen, whose discovery of the X ray in 1895 was, however, as much a product of his time as of his country, for in 1897–99 in England J. J. Thomson had discovered the electron, and in France the Curies the release of energy by radioactivity. German professors expounded German ideals and German culture, among them Kuno Francke at Harvard, who pictured Germany pulsing with "ardent life and intense activity in every field of national aspirations." He could barely contain his worship of the noble spectacle:

"Healthfulness, power, orderliness meet the eye on every square mile of German soil." No visitor could fail to be impressed by "these flourishing, well-kept farms and estates, these thriving villages, these carefully replenished forests, . . . these bursting cities teeming with a well-fed and well-behaved population, . . . with proud city halls and stately courthouses, with theatres and museums rising everywhere, admirable means of communication, model arrangements for healthy recreation and amusement, earnest universities and technical schools." The well-behaved population was characterized by its "orderly management of political meetings, its sober determination and effective organization of the laboring classes in their fight for social betterment" and its "respectful and attentive attitude toward all forms of art." Over all reigned "the magnificent Army with its manly discipline and high standards of professional conduct," and together all these components gave proof of "the wonderfully organized collective will toward the higher forms of national existence." The mood was clearly not one amenable to proposals of self-limitation.

The sword, as Germany's historians showed in their explanations of the marvelous national rise, was responsible for Germany's greatness. In his *History of Germany in the Nineteenth Century*, published in five volumes and several thousand pages over a period of fifteen years in the eighties and nineties, Treitschke preached the supremacy of the State whose instrument of policy is war and whose right to make war for honor or national interest cannot be infringed upon. The German Army was the visible embodiment of Treitschke's gospel. Its authority and prestige grew with every year, its officers were creatures of ineffable arrogance, above the law, who inspired an almost superstitious worship in the public. Any person accused of insult to an officer could be tried for the crime of indirect *lèse majesté*. German ladies stepped off the sidewalk to let an officer pass.

In 1891 the Alldeutsche Verband (Pan-German League) was founded, whose program was the union of all members of the German race, wherever they resided, in a Pan-German state. Its core was to be a Greater Germany incorporating Belgium, Luxemburg, Switzerland, Austria-Hungary, Poland, Rumania and Serbia which, after this first stage was accomplished, would extend its rule over the world. The League distributed posters for display in shop windows reading, "*Dem Deutschen gehört die Welt*" ("The world belongs to Germans"). In a simple statement of purpose Ernst Hasse, founder of the League, declared, "We want territory even if it belongs to foreigners, so that we may shape the future according to our needs." It was a task his countrymen felt equal to.

Any outbreak of fighting among the nations, as in the Sino-Japanese War of 1895 or the Spanish-American War, stirred in the Germans a powerful desire to mix in. Admiral von Diederichs, in command of the German Pacific Squadron at Manila Bay, was edging for a quick grab at the Philippines, and only Admiral Dewey's red-faced roar, "If your Admiral wants a fight he can have it now!"—silently if conspicuously supported by movements of the British squadron—made him draw back. "To the German mind," commented Secretary Hay, "there is something monstrous in the thought that a war should take place anywhere and they not profit by it." Dewey, understandably, thought they had "bad manners." "They are too pushing and ambitious," he said, "they'll overreach themselves someday."

At the top of the German state was a government essentially capricious. Ministers were independent of Parliament and held office at the will of a sovereign who referred to the members of the Reichstag as "sheepsheads." Since government office was confined to members of the aristocracy and the premise of a political career was unqualified acceptance of Conservative party principles, the doors were closed to new talent. "Not even the tamest Liberal," regretted the editor of the *Berliner Tageblatt*, "had any chance of reaching a post of the slightest distinction." After the Kaiser's dismissal of Bismarck in 1890, no one of active creative intelligence held an important post. The Chancellor, chosen because he was such a relief from Bismarck, was Prince Chlodwig zu Hohenlohe-Schillingsfürst, a gentle-mannered, fatherly Bavarian whose motto, it was said, was: "Always wear a good black coat and hold your tongue." The Foreign Minister was Count Bernhard von Bülow, an elegant gentleman of extreme suavity and self-importance and a manner so well oiled that in conversation and correspondence he seemed always to be rubbing his hands like a rug merchant. He used to scribble notes on his shirt cuffs for fear of forgetting the least of His Majesty's wishes. In an effort to catch the effortless parliamentary manner of Balfour he practiced holding onto his coat lapels before the bathroom mirror, coached by an attaché from the Foreign Office. "Watch," murmured a knowing observer in the Reichstag when Bülow rose to speak, "here comes the business with the lapels."

Behind Bülow in control of foreign policy was the invisible Holstein who in the manner of Byzantine courts exercised power without nominal office. He regarded all diplomacy as conspiracy, all overtures of foreign governments as containing a concealed trick, and conducted foreign relations on the premise of everyone's animosity for Germany. The interests of a Great Power, he explained to Bülow, were not necessarily identical with the maintenance of peace, "but rather with the subjugation of its enemies and rivals." Therefore "we must entertain the suspicion" that the Russian objective was "rather a means to power than to peace." Bülow agreed. His instructions to envoys abroad breathed of pitfalls and plots and treated Muraviev's agenda as if it were a basket of snakes. It would be desirable, he wrote to his Ambassador in London, "if this Peace and disarmament idea . . . were wrecked on England's objections without our having to appear in the foreground," and he trusted the Ambassador to guide the exchange of views with Mr. Balfour toward that end.

Mr. Balfour, the acting Foreign Secretary for Lord Salisbury, was not an entirely suitable victim for Bülow's manipulations. However skeptical of results, the British Government, unlike the German, did not feel threatened by an international conference and did not intend to bear the brunt of wrecking it. Moreover, public enthusiasm could not be flouted in England. In the four months following the Czar's manifesto, over 750 resolutions from public groups reached the Foreign Office welcoming the idea of an international conference and expressing the "earnest hope," in the words of one of them, that Her Majesty's Government would exert their influence to ensure its success "so that something practical may result." The resolutions came not only from established peace societies and religious congregations but from town and shire meetings, rural district committees, and county councils, were signed by the Mayor, stamped with the county seal, forwarded by the Lord Lieutenant. Some without benefit of official bodies came simply from the "People of Bedford," "Rotherhead Residents" or "Public Meeting at Bath." Many came from local committees of the Liberal party, although Conservative groups were conspicuously absent, as were Church of England congregations. All the Nonconformist sects were represented: Baptists, Methodists, Congregationalists, Christian Endeavor, Welsh Nonconformists, Irish Evangelicals. The Society of Friends collected petitions with a total of 16,000 signatures. Bible associations, adult schools, women's schools, the National British Women's Temperance Association, the Manchester Chamber of Commerce, the West of Scotland Peace and Arbitration Association, the Humanitarian League, the Oxford Women's Liberal Association, the General Board of Protestant Dissenters, the Mayor of Leicester, the Lord Mayor of Sheffield, the Town Clerk of Poole, were among the signatories.

Bound volumes of the resolutions signed with a shaky "S." indicated that Lord Salisbury was keeping track of public opinion. A deputation representing the International Crusade of Peace headed by the Earl of Aberdeen and the Bishop of London visited Mr. Balfour, who received them with a graceful speech taking "a sanguine view of the diminution, I will not say the extinction, but the diminution of war in the future" and looking forward to the coming conference as a "great landmark in the progress of mankind," whether or not, he added, it produced any practical results. This was not altogether what Bülow had hoped for.

The epitome of the peace movement was the most ebullient and prolific journalist of an age rich in his kind, William T. Stead, founder and editor of the *Review of Reviews.* Stead was a human torrent of enthusiasm for good causes. His energy was limitless, his optimism unending, his egotism gigantic. As the self-estimated pope of journalism his registered telegraph address was "Vatican, London." During the eighties he had edited the Liberal daily, the *Pall Mall Gazette*, in a series of explosions that made it required reading in public life. "You are too strenuous, too uniformly strenuous," pronounced the Prince of Wales who read it regularly. Stead waded recklessly into crusades ranging from protection of prostitutes to a "Sane Imperialism." They included campaigns against Bulgarian atrocities, Siberian convict life, the desertion of General Gordon at Khartoum, Congo slavery, the labour victims of "Bloody Sunday" in Trafalgar Square, and for baby adoption, village libraries, Esperanto, international scholars' correspondence, and housing for the poor. His most notorious effort, published under the title "The Maiden Tribute of Modern Babylon," described his personal purchase of a thirteen-year-old girl for £5 as a means of dramatizing the procurement of child virgins for prostitution. The articles made a world sensation, and besides causing Stead's trial and imprisonment on a charge of abduction, succeeded in forcing an amendment raising the age of consent from thirteen to sixteen.

Stead visited Russia in 1889, where he interviewed Alexander III and became a champion of Anglo-Russian alliance and thus of everything Russian. He campaigned for a big navy at the instance of his friend Admiral Fisher; collaborated with General Booth on a book, *In Darkest England*; joined Cecil Rhodes in the cause of Imperial Federation and union of the English-speaking world. Deciding to reform Chicago after a visit there in 1893, he exposed its evils and laid out a scheme of regeneration in a book called *If Christ Came to Chicago* and organized a Civic Federation which included labour leaders and Mrs. Potter Palmer to put the scheme into action. During the visit he talked with Governor Altgeld and invited Fielden, one of the pardoned Anarchists, to share a speaker's platform.

The connecting principle running through his causes was belief in man's duty to amend society and extend the British sway. He liked to use the phrase "God's Englishman" and conceived of this figure as a righter of wrongs; anything that added to his power was a benevolent influence. He turned up so often on opposite sides of the same question, as in the case of arms limitation and a big navy, that he was accused of insincerity, although in fact, as of any particular moment, his sincerity was genuine, if nimble.

In 1890 he founded his own journal, the monthly *Review of Reviews*, with the expressed object of making it read throughout the English-speaking world "as men used to read their Bibles . . . to discover the will of God and their duty to their fellow man." Finding a monthly less satisfactory as a political organ, he yearned for a millionaire to back him in a daily of his own and once in Paris told a friend, "I went in to Notre Dame to have a talk with God about it."

Detested by some, he was a friend of the great, including, besides Rhodes and Fisher, James Bryce, Cardinal Manning, Lord Esher, Lord Milner, Mrs. Annie Besant and Lady Warwick, who arranged a tête-à-tête lunch for him with the Prince of Wales. He interviewed sovereigns, cabinet ministers, archbishops and helped all "oppressed races, ill-treated animals, underpaid typists, misunderstood women, persecuted parsons, vilified public men, would-be suicides, hot-gospellers of every sort and childless parents." His talk was a river and as a lecturer he "leaped over the face of the globe as though on a pogo-stick." Besides writing, editing, traveling, interviewing and lecturing, he wrote or dictated some 80,000 letters in his twenty-two years on the *Review of Reviews*, an average of ten a day. He espoused spiritualism and considered himself a reincarnation of Charles II, who through him was making amends for his previous life on earth.

He was short in stature, with high color, bright blue eyes and a reddish beard, and in defiance of black broadcloth wore rough tweeds and a soft felt hat. Strong in good will, he was weak in judgment. If he had possessed that quality in proportion to his qualities of mind and character, said Lord Milner, he would have been "simply irresistible." Seeing in him, in exaggerated form, all the attributes of the English people of his generation, an American journalist summed him up as "the perfect type of Nineteenth Century man." Milner saw him as a cross between Don Quixote and P. T. Barnum, which may have been the same thing.

Naturally a passionate advocate of arbitration, Stead saw it leading to the establishment of an international court of justice and eventually to a United States of Europe. Anticipating the Czar, he had in 1894 suggested an international pledge by the powers not to increase their military budgets until the end of the century. When the Russian proposal burst upon the world, Stead saw the greatest opportunity of his career. He determined at once on a personal tour of the capitals as part of a great campaign to convince people everywhere that the Czar was sincere and to arouse a collective cry of support for the Conference. The tour was to culminate in an interview with the Czar from which he was not deterred by the Prince of Wales's opinion, conveyed through Lady Warwick, that the young ruler, his wife's nephew, was "weak as water, . . . has no character and would not be the slightest use to you." On the way, Stead planned to interview the Pope, the Kaiser and the President of France, as well as King Leopold of the Belgians whom he would persuade to become spokesman of a league of small powers. To ward off possible official interference he called on Mr. Balfour at the Foreign Office, whom he found at first "nonchalant and ironical" but who quickly hardened in response to Stead's rhapsodies. Balfour failed to understand, he said, how Stead could contemplate so lightheartedly "the increasing growth and power of Russia." For their own time it did not matter, "but what of our children? . . . What kind of world will it be when Russia exercises a dominating influence over the whole of south-east Europe?" He did not, however, offer to put any obstacles in Stead's path.

Within a month of the first news, Stead was on his way. In Paris he failed to see President Félix Faure, although he did see Clemenceau, who said "nothing would come of the Conference" and refused to alter his opinion. King Leopold, the Kaiser and Pope Leo XIII likewise avoided him, but Nicholas II, in compliance with a promise which his father had given to Stead ten years ago, granted him not only one audience but three. The Imperial graciousness dazzled Stead, who, being unused to courts, took it for the man's character and did not realize it was the monarch's trade. In any case he was determined to produce a hero. The Czar, he told his readers, was charming, sympathetic, alert, lucid, with a keen sense of humor, hearty frankness, admirable modesty, noble gravity, high resolve, remarkable memory, "exceptional rapidity of perception and wide grasp of an immense range of facts," and all these were at the service of the cause of peace. Stead's paeans to Russia's intentions so far outdistanced her real aims that the Russian ministers complained to the British Government of being "much embarrassed." His articles, however, were manna to the peace movement. Back in London he brought out a new weekly, *War Against War*, organized the International Peace Crusade and did his hyperactive best to strengthen public demand for a Conference that could not, must not fail.

Public opinion was not all of a piece. If the Liberals—and not all of them—shared Stead's enthusiasm, the Conservatives did not. In all peoples there was much of what William Ernest Henley hymned as "the battle spirit shouting in my blood." It was what made Romain Rolland, who was one day to become famous as a pacifist, cry joyously in 1898, "Give me combat!" The materialism of the time, the increasing ease, the power of money to substitute for muscle, produced in many a feeling of distaste or even a seeking for the strenuous, as when young Theodore Roosevelt headed for the Rockies. People felt a need for something nobler and saw it glimmer in the prospect of danger and physical combat, in sacrifice, even death, on the battlefield. The journalist Henry Nevinson felt a martial ardor when he drilled as an officer of the Volunteers and offended his Socialist friends by declaring that he "would not care to live in a world in which there was no war." In later years it seemed to him the ardor had derived partly from ignorance of war and partly from the influence of Kipling and Henley.

Within narrow limits Henley was the Conservatives' Stead, although lacking Stead's elemental force and social conscience. No Teutonic homage to the master race could outshout his celebration of "England, My England," whose "mailed hand" guides teeming destinies, whose "breed of mighty men" is unmatched, whose ships are "the fierce old sea's delight," who is:

> Chosen daughter of the Lord
> Spouse-in-Chief of the ancient Sword.
>
> There's the menace of the Word
> In the song on your bugles blown
> England!
> Out of Heaven on your bugles blown!

This was patriotism gone mad and represented a mood, not a people. In the same mood Americans listened to Albert Beveridge rant, "We are a conquering race . . . we must obey our blood."

Such sentiments were among the indirect results of the most fateful voyage since Columbus—Charles Darwin's aboard the *Beagle*. Darwin's findings in *The Origin of Species*, when applied to human society, supplied the philosophical basis for the theory that war was both inherent in nature and ennobling. War was a conflict in which the stronger and superior race survived, thus advancing civilization. Germany's thinkers, historians, political and military scientists, working upon the theory with the industry of moles and the tenacity of bulldogs, raised it to a level of national dogma. Houston Stewart Chamberlain, Wagner's son-in-law, supplied a racial justification in his *Foundations of the Nineteenth Century*, published in German, which showed that Aryans, being superior in body and soul to other men, had a right to be masters of the earth. Treitschke explained that war, by purifying and unifying a great people, was the source of patriotism. By invigorating them it was a source of strength. Peace was stagnant and decadent and the hope of perpetual peace was not only "impossible but immoral as well." War as ennobling became by extension, in the words of Generals von der Goltz and Bernhardi, a necessity. It was the right and duty of the nobler, stronger, superior race to extend its rule over inferior peoples, which, in the German view, meant over the world. To other nations it meant over colonies. Darwinism became the White Man's Burden. Imperialism acquired a moral imperative.

Darwin's indirect effects reached apotheosis in Captain Mahan. "Honest collision" between nations was "evidently a law of progress," he wrote in one of a series of articles in 1897–99 in which he tried to instruct Americans in their destiny. This one was called "The Moral Aspect of War." In another, "A Twentieth Century Outlook," he wrote that nothing was "more ominous for the future of our race" than the current vociferous tendency "which refuses to recognize in the profession of arms—in war" the source of "heroic ideal." In a private letter he wrote, "No greater misfortune could well happen than that civilized nations should abandon their preparations for war and take to arbitration." His thesis was that power, force, and ultimately war were the factors that decide great issues in a nation's fate and that to depend on anything else, such as arbitration, was an illusion. If arbitration were substituted for armies and navies, European civilization "might not survive, having lost its fighting energy." Yet Mahan believed the Twentieth Century would reveal that man's conscience was improving. He could not have preached power so positively if he had not believed equally in progress. His moral rectitude shines in a photograph taken with his wife and two adult daughters. Four pairs of forthright eyes gaze straight at the camera. Four keel-straight noses, four firm mouths, the ladies' high-necked blouses fastened with bar pin at the throat, the hats perched stiffly on high-piled hair, all express the person "assured of certain certainties," a species soon to be as extinct as Ribblesdale.

The necessity of struggle was voiced by many spokesmen in many guises: in Henri Bergson's *élan vital*, in Shaw's Life Force, in the strange magic jumble of Nietzsche which was then spreading its fascination over Europe. Nietzsche recognized the waning of religion as a primary force in people's lives and flung his challenge in three words: "God is dead." He would have substituted Superman, but ordinary people substituted patriotism. As faith in God retreated before the advance of science, love of country began to fill the empty spaces in the heart. Nationalism absorbed the strength once belonging to religion. Where people formerly fought for religion now they would presumably do no less for its successor. A sense of gathering conflict filled the air. Yeats, living in Paris in 1895, awoke one morning from a vision of apocalypse:

> . . . Unknown spears
> Suddenly hurtle before my dream awakened eyes,
> And then the clash of fallen horsemen and the cries
> Of unknown perishing armies beat about my ears.

Quite unconnected, in the same year, the tap of distant drums sounded in the seclusion of A. E. Housman's rooms:

> On the idle hill of summer
> Sleepy with the flow of streams,
> Far I hear the steady drummer
> Drumming like a noise in dreams.
>
> Far and near and low and louder
> On the roads of earth go by,
> Dear to friends and food for powder,
> Soldiers marching, all to die. . . .
>
> Far the calling bugles hollo,
> High the screaming fife replies,
> Gay the files of scarlet follow:
> Woman bore me, I will rise.

The Hague, as the capital of a small neutral country, was selected as site of the Conference and May 18, 1899, was fixed as the opening day. Advance arrangements stirred up a number of old animosities and current quarrels. China and Japan, Turkey and Greece, Spain and the United States had just finished wars; Britain and the Transvaal were warming up to one which threatened to break out at any moment. As host nation and ardent supporters of the Boers, the Dutch almost strangled the Conference before it could be born by demanding invitations for the Transvaal and Orange Free State. Turkey objected to the inclusion of Bulgaria, and Italy threatened to bolt if inclusion of the Vatican implied its recognition as a temporal power. Seeing "very sinister import" in this, Germany immediately suspected Italy of planning to secede from the Triple Alliance and herself threatened to withdraw from the Conference if any other major power did. These matters being surmounted, the nations proceeded to the naming of delegates.

The choices reflected the ambivalance of the agenda, concerned on the one hand with peace by arbitration and on the other with the conduct of war. Although arbitration had not been mentioned in the Czar's manifesto it had been included in Muraviev's agenda and since then, in the public mind, had become the major goal. The Boston Peace Crusade held meetings every week through March and April demanding that the United States commit itself to the goal of "a permanent tribunal for the Twentieth Century." With Congress in crisis over the vote on the Peace Treaty with Spain, McKinley was urged to appoint President Eliot of Harvard in the hope of soothing anti-imperialist sentiment. As Eliot was unlikely to prove a manageable delegate, McKinley preferred a safer selection in Andrew White, former president of Cornell, now Ambassador in Berlin. Rising from Professor of History to civic eminence, White was a hardworking, high-minded man who believed in all the right things. At The Hague he was soon on friendly terms with the Duke of Tetuan, delegate of the late enemy, Spain, who shared with him "a passion for cathedral architecture and organ music." Alongside White was appointed a delegate certain to act as watchdog of American interests and take a hard-headed view of the proceedings with which by no stretch of anyone's imagination could he be considered in sympathy—Captain Mahan. His name appearing on the list deepened Germany's suspicions of the Conference. "Our greatest and most dangerous foe," noted the Kaiser darkly.

American instructions to the delegates began by rejecting the original purpose of the Conference. Arms limitation "could not profitably be discussed" because American arms were below the level of the European powers anyway and the initiative in this matter could be left to them. As to restrictions on the development of new weapons, it was considered "doubtful if an international agreement to this end could prove effective." The delegates were to support efforts to make the laws of war more humane and they were themselves to propose a specific plan for an arbitration tribunal. They were also instructed to propose the immunity of private property from capture at sea, a seemingly bland suggestion which contained depths of unplumbed trouble.

France named as her chief delegate a former premier and friend of arbitration, Léon Bourgeois, whose term of office in 1895–96 had been taken up in a stubborn effort to enact the graduated income tax against the violent opposition of the Senate. It had only narrowly been defeated. With the Dreyfus Affair threatening a government crisis at any time which might bring Bourgeois back to office, The Hague offered a happy opportunity to remove him from the scene. "Amiable, elegant and eloquent," according to a political colleague if not friend, Bourgeois "cultivated a fine ebony beard and expressed commonplace thoughts in a mellow voice."

Already aroused by the Affair to a mood of super-patriotism, insulted by Russia's failure to consult her in advance, determined to accept no fixing of the status quo, France welcomed the Conference no more than any other nation. "To renounce war is in a sense to renounce one's country," was the comment of a French officer on the Czar's manifesto. Mme Adam, Gambetta's friend and priestess of *revanche*, when invited to hear a lecture by Bertha von Suttner, replied, "I? To a lecture on peace? Certainly not. I am for war." France nevertheless sent to The Hague, as second to Bourgeois, a dedicated apostle of peace, Baron d'Estournelles de Constant. A professional diplomat until the age of forty-three, he had become increasingly disturbed at the trend of international affairs until one day in 1895, shocked by a frivolous threat of war in a minor dispute, he resigned from diplomacy to enter politics and the Chamber in the cause of peace. A handsome man of polished manners he brought to the Conference as an official delegate the fervor and voice of the peace movement.

As initiators, the Russians provided the president of the Conference in the person of their Ambassador to London, Baron de Staal, a nice old gentleman with long white side whiskers and a square-crowned derby. He was described by the

Prince of Wales as "one of the best men that ever lived, . . . who never said anything that was not true," which was useful if not adequate equipment for his task. The real head of the Russian delegation was Feodor de Martens, Professor Emeritus of International Law at the University of St. Petersburg, who allowed no one to forget that he enjoyed a reputation as Europe's leading jurist in his field. He was "a man of great knowledge," said Witte, "but by no means broad-minded." A future Chief of Staff, Colonel Jilinsky was the military delegate.

Count Münster, German Ambassador to Paris, in the wastebasket of whose Embassy the Dreyfus Affair began, looked forward with little pleasure to being his country's chief delegate. "Beating empty air is always a tiresome job," he wrote to a friend. Arms limitation was *ausgeschlossen* ("out of the question"), the favorite German word. Arbitration was important but agreement probably hopeless. To save Russia's face the Conference could not be allowed to end in fiasco and its work must be covered with a "cloak of peace." A courtly white-haired gentleman whom Andrew White regarded as a "splendid specimen" of an old-fashioned German nobleman, Münster had once been stationed in England, had married an English wife and was pleased by nothing so much as being taken for an English gentleman. Besides the military and naval delegates, he had two legal associates, Professor Zorn of the University of Königsberg and Professor Baron von Stengel of the University of Munich, whose chief qualification was a pamphlet he had just published entitled *Eternal Peace* which ridiculed the forthcoming Conference and extolled the virtues of war. Although Stengel said nothing abnormally different from what many in other countries believed, he said it after the German fashion rudely and loudly and the Kaiser's prompt gesture in naming him a delegate needed no thumb to his nose to make the point. Stead, then in Berlin, protested, Bülow oozed explanations and the German comic papers caricatured Stengel as a bull introduced into a bed of tulips.

A kind of magic in the Conference had brought it to reality despite general contempt, and drew from Britain the compliment of a strong delegation. Its chief, Sir Julian Pauncefote, Ambassador to Washington, was, as the negotiator of the world's first arbitration treaty, the outstanding champion of the idea in official life. A calm, heavy-set, unfussed dignitary who reminded people of a polar bear, he accomplished wonders of diplomacy by acting on the principle: "Never give way and never give offence." "I never hesitated to open my whole heart to him," said Secretary Hay, "for he was the soul of honor and of candor." Accompanying him was the recently retired Speaker of the House, Sir Arthur Peel, whose impressive presence in the Chair had quelled the most troublesome members. "When Peel lost his temper it was like a storm at sea," said one of them. "He could put up with a bore but he hated a cad, whether well or ill dressed."

As military and naval delegates Lord Salisbury's government selected two exceptional men from the upper ranks of their respective services. Major General Sir John Ardagh, after winning honors in Hebrew and mathematics at Trinity College, Dublin, had changed from a clerical to a military career. Subsequently he had been an observer in the Franco-Prussian and Russo-Turkish wars, seen active service in Egypt and the Sudan and was now Director of Military Intelligence.

His naval colleague was the most unsubdued individualist of his time, possessed of a vigor and impetus remarkable in any time. Admiral Sir John Fisher was a force of nature entirely directed to the renaissance of British sea power through modernization of the Navy. His only other mania was dancing, which he pursued from hornpipe to waltz at every opportunity, with other officers if necessary when there were no ladies present. Whatever he fought for was a struggle against the weight and lethargy of "the way it has always been" and his career was that of a fierce broom sweeping aside obsolescence in men as well as ships. He demanded oil instead of coal twenty years ahead of his time, substituted training in gunnery for cutlasses, training in engines and engineering for rigging and the handling of sails, introduced destroyers, pioneered in ordnance, armor and battleship design. During the bombardment of Alexandria when an armored train was needed to transport a landing force, he invented one. He had been Commandant of the Torpedo School, Director of Naval Ordnance, Superintendent of Dockyards, Third Sea Lord, Controller of the Navy and was currently Commander-in-Chief of the Atlantic Station.

Born in Malaya, Fisher had a strange flat smooth-shaven face which inspired his enemies, who were innumerable, to hint broadly at Oriental ancestry. On his flagship when he "prowled around with the steady rhythmical tread of a panther, the quarter deck shook and all hands shook with it. When the word was passed, 'Look out, here comes Jack!' everyone stood terribly to attention while the great one passed on and away." Upon the orthodox his flow of ideas had an effect either paralyzing or maddening. When he talked of some new scheme or program he held his companion fixed with a glittering eye and emphasized every sentence with a blow of his fist on his palm. When he wrote letters his emphasis took the form of two, three or four lines under a word and he closed, not "in haste," but "in violent haste!" or with the warning: "Burn this!" He liked to quote Napoleon's maxim, *J'ordonne ou je me tais* ("I command or I keep quiet"), but he was incapable of practicing the second half.

At the moment, in case of war with France over Fashoda, he had conceived a plan to execute a naval raid on Devil's Island and kidnap Dreyfus in order to land him on the coast of France to embarrass the Army and sow dissension. For the motto of one of his destroyers he chose *Ut Veniant Omnes* (Let them all come). His pretended principles of battle were "Give No Quarter, Take No Prisoners, Sink Everything, No Time for Mercy, *Frappez vite et frappez fort, l'Audace, l'audace, toujours l'audace*," but this was intended more for moral effect than as serious tactics. When Lord Salisbury appointed him naval delegate to The Hague he remarked that there was no doubt Jacky Fisher would fight at the Peace Conference. "So I did," wrote Fisher afterwards, "though it was not for peace."

The Hague proved an inspired choice. The charm of the Huis ten Bosch (House in the Woods), summer palace of the House of Orange, where the Conference met, the pleasant half-hour's drive from the seashore Scheveningen, where many of the delegates stayed, the hospitality of the Netherlands Government and smiling welcome of its people, the summer weather and flowered countryside, could not fail to refresh the most cynical spirits. Black-and-white cows grazed peaceably along the roadside, canals reflected the radiant sky, the docile wings of windmills turned and sailboats moved seemingly over meadows, on waterways hidden by the tall grass. The once quiet town, a "gracious anachronism" of brick houses and cobblestone streets, bustled with welcome. Flags of all the nations decorated the staid hotels, windows were polished, doorsteps scrubbed, public buildings burnished and refurbished. Brought to animated life by its visitors, The Hague seemed to wake like a Sleeping Beauty from its Seventeenth Century slumbers.

The Huis ten Bosch was a royal château of red brick with white window frames set in a park on the outskirts of the town. Its windows opened on lawns and rose gardens, fountains and marble nymphs. In the woods which gave the place its name delegates could walk and talk between sessions along avenues of magnificent beeches where birds sang and the sun glinted through the leaves.

Plenary sessions were held in the central hall three stories high, hung with golden damask and frescoed with the triumphs of past Prince Stadtholders on throne and horseback. From the ceiling painted cupids, naked Venuses, and Death as a leering skeleton looked down upon the newly installed rows of green-baize desks seating 108 delegates from 26 countries. Black coats predominated, varied by military uniforms, by the Turks' red fezzes and the blue silk gown of the Chinese delegate. The real work of the Conference took place in the subcommittees which met in the many small salons rich in Delft and Meissen, Chinese wallpaper and pale Persian carpets. Every day the Dutch hosts served a bountiful luncheon with fine wine and cigars under the crystal chandeliers of the White Dining Room, where the delegates could meet and talk informally. The taste and dignity of all the arrangements, the choice liqueurs, the beauty of the surroundings, the evening balls and receptions gradually began to mellow the mood of disdain in which the Conference began.

No such body had ever assembled "in a spirit of more hopeless skepticism as to any good result," Andrew White believed when he arrived. The great Professor Mommsen of Germany, most admired historian of his time, predicted the Conference would be remembered as "a printer's error in the history of the world." Even some of Baroness von Suttner's friends were less than hopeful. Prince Scipio Borghese, whom she invited to be present as an observer, replied that nothing would be more charming than to spend time with "*un groupe du high-life pacifique*," but unfortunately in May he would have to attend his sister's wedding in the depths of Hungary. During De Staal's opening address, spoken in a voice alternately quavering and firm, the president dropped his wooden gavel, which was immediately, almost eagerly, seized upon as an ill omen. De Staal's "deplorable" Russian ignorance of parliamentary procedure and his happy-go-lucky way of adopting rules and motions seemed to White to presage "hopeless chaos."

The Conference divided itself into three Commissions: on Armaments, on the Laws of War, and on Arbitration, which in turn divided into subcommittees. The chairman of the First Commission was Auguste Beernaert, former premier and chief delegate of Belgium, who had once been called by King Leopold II "the greatest cynic in the kingdom." A worldly politician in his early career, he had been the King's right-hand man in the vast enterprise of the Congo as well as in Leopold's efforts to fortify the Belgian frontier against invasion. Late in life, however, Beernaert had suffered a personality change and become a pacifist and regular attender of peace congresses. As President of the Belgian Chamber he still exercised political power. Professor de Martens of Russia was chairman of the Second Commission and Léon Bourgeois of the Third.

Delegates were uncomfortably aware of the conscience of the world over their shoulder in the person of a large "*groupe du high-life pacifique*" who had descended upon The Hague as observers. Expecting nothing but failure, the Conference had decided upon closed sessions from which the press was rigidly excluded. It proved a hopeless maneuver, since the press was led by W. T. Stead in person, acting as correspondent for the *Manchester Guardian*. Through importunate interviews and his myriad personal connections he was able to publish a daily chronicle of the Conference on a special page made available to him by the *Dagblad*, leading newspaper of The Hague. The delegates devoured it, all the other correspondents depended on it and the peace propagandists spread its news abroad to their home societies. Succumbing to the inevitable the Conference opened its meetings to the press.

Leading the observers was Baroness von Suttner, acting as correspondent for the *Neue Freie Presse* of Vienna. Convinced that May 18 was an "epoch making date in the history of the world," she earnestly dispensed tea and talk to the delegates and conferred on strategy with D'Estournelles, Beernaert and her other friends. Ivan Bloch came from Russia with trunks full of copies of his book for distribution. He gave lectures with lantern slides for the public and receptions for the delegates combining excellent suppers with pictures and charts on the development of firearms. Dr. Benjamin Trueblood, Quaker secretary of the American Peace Society, came from Boston, and Charles Richet, editor of *La Revue Scientifique* and director of the French Peace Society, from Paris. The Queen of Rumania under her pen name, Carmen Sylva, sent a poem. Mme Selenka of Munich brought a pacifist petition signed by women of eighteen countries; a Belgian petition with 100,000 and a Dutch petition with 200,000 signatures were submitted. Andrew White found himself inundated by people with "plans, schemes, nostrums, notions and whimsies of all sorts" and by floods of pamphlets and books, letters, sermons and telegrams, petitions, resolutions, prayers and blessings. Yet behind the cranks he sensed evidence of a feeling "more earnest and widespread than anything I had dreamed."

Count Münster on the other hand was disgusted. "The Conference has brought here the political riffraff of the entire world," he wrote to Bülow, "journalists of the worst type such as Stead, baptized Jews like Bloch and female peace fanatics like Mme de Suttner. . . . All this rabble, actively supported by Young Turks, Armenians, and Socialists into the bargain, are working in the open under the aegis of Russia." He saw Stead as "a proved agent in the pay of Russia" and the proceedings on the whole as a Russian plot to nullify Germany's military advantage. Even in his native land, however, the "rabble" found an echo when a committee of Reichstag deputies, professors and writers urged support of the aims of the Conference. Although opposed to any arrangement that could "even to infinitesimal degree lower Germany's position among nations," it hoped for some result to relieve Europe of the burden of armament taxation and to prevent the outbreak of wars.

Feeling themselves the cynosure of the world's hope, the delegates began to feel the stirring of a desire not to disappoint it. After the first two weeks of work, reported Pauncefote, they "became interested in spite of themselves." Some, at least, began to want to succeed, from "*amour-propre*" as van Karnebeek, the Netherlands delegate, said, if from nothing else. Some, affected by the coming together of so many nations, began to look ahead to "a federation of the nations of Europe. . . . That is the dream that begins to rise at The Hague. Europe must choose either to pursue the dream—or anarchy."

For arbitration some hope sprouted but for arms limitation, whether of present forces, budgets or new weapons, there was none. Despite the desperate efforts of the Russians and the warm support of the small states and many civilian delegates, every proposal for restriction or moratorium was shown to be "impractical" by the military delegates of the major powers. The issue came to a head when Colonel Jilinsky of Russia urged a five-year moratorium in a peroration calling on the nations to rid themselves of the burden that was crushing the life out of Europe. Eloquently supporting him, General den Beer Portugael of the Netherlands pictured the governments "bound together like Alpine climbers by the rope of their military organizations" and tottering toward the edge of the abyss unless they could halt by a "supreme effort." Rising to his feet, the German military delegate, Colonel Gross von Schwartzkopf, cut through the eloquence as if by a stroke of cold steel. The German people, he said, were "not crushed beneath the weight of armament expenditures. . . . They are not hastening toward exhaustion and ruin." On the contrary their prosperity, welfare and standard of living were rising. Carried away by his subject, Colonel Schwartzkopf did not shrink from taking upon Germany the duty of opposing the moratorium, saving any of the other major powers that awkward task. When it became clear that Germany would be a party to no moratorium of any kind and consequently that there was not the least chance of its being approved, the other nations were happy to vote in favor of submitting it for further consideration to a subcommittee. In this way, wrote Sir John Fisher, explaining his vote to his government, Russian feelings would be spared and the public would not feel that England was blocking full *discussion* of the proposal.

In committee at The Hague, Fisher behaved himself with surprising circumspection; unofficially he remained normal. "The humanizing of war!" he exploded. "You might just as well talk of humanizing Hell!" His reply to a "silly ass" who talked about "the amenities of civilised warfare and putting your prisoners' feet in hot water and giving them gruel," was considered unfit for publication. In Stead's autograph book he wrote, "The supremacy of the British Navy is the best security for the peace of the world." He stayed at the Hotel Kurhaus in Scheveningen which from his description appeared to suit him admirably: "Such a rush always going on. Band plays at breakfast and at lunch and at dinner!!! Huge boxes arrive continuously and the *portier* rushes about like a wild animal. Railway, telegraph and post offices in the hotel!" Among the naval delegates Fisher was treated with worshipful respect, and his promotion in the midst of the Conference to Commander-in-Chief of the Mediterranean Station "fetched all the foreigners very much," including even Baroness von Suttner who regretted his absence from a ball given by De Staal since he was one of the "jolliest dancers." He was called the "Dancing Admiral," and as he was personally most gracious and put on no airs, "no man at The Hague," reported Stead, "was more popular." His contact with the German delegates convinced Fisher that Germany, not France, was going to be Britain's opponent. He learned from the German naval delegate that all British ships would be useless in war as the Germans expected to sink them by hordes of torpedo boats.

Britain was favorably disposed to naval limitation as it would have curbed the German naval program and preserved the status quo. Her support depended, however, on finding a formula for inspection and control which Fisher reported was "absolutely unrealisable." He did not think highly of a Russian suggestion that the good faith of governments might be relied on. Russia should have said straight out, remarked the French delegate rather pitilessly, that her real aim was simply the assurance of peace for three years. The Germans would again hear of no limitation and Japan, according to a British report, "will only listen when she has reached the standard of the great naval powers, that is to say, never."

The United States' position was made unequivocal by its hard realist, Captain Mahan, privately if not in the public meetings. His government, he told the British, would on no account even discuss naval limitation; on the contrary, the coming struggle for the markets of China would require a "very considerable" increase in the American squadron in the Pacific, which would affect the interests of at least five powers. In every commission and discussion Mahan made his presence felt like a voice of conscience saying "No"; it was, however, a conscience operating not in behalf of peace but in behalf of the unfettered exercise of belligerent power. He had "the deepest seriousness of all," wrote one observer.

It led him to oppose his own government's traditional position in favor of the immunity of private property at sea. What had been good for the United States as a weak neutral, Mahan believed, would no longer be good for her as a Great Power. The right of capture was the essence of sea power, especially of British sea power, with which he believed America's interests were now united. He looked ahead to the rights of the belligerent rather than back to the rights of the neutral.

When White, according to instructions, attempted to have the matter put on the agenda, Fisher carried the opposition for Mahan. Take the case of neutral coal, he suggested: "You tell me that I must not seize these colliers. I tell you that nothing that you, or any power on earth, can say will stop me from seizing them or sending them to the bottom, if I can in no other way keep their coal out of the enemy's hands." For the opposite reason Germany, of course, supported the American proposal of immunity from capture. For once in favor of something, Count Münster jumped at the chance to put "our powerful influence behind this principle" and Bülow was delighted to approve a measure so obviously "in the interests of humanity in general." Both were pulled up short by their own naval delegate, Captain Siegel, whose reasoning suggested the mind of a chess-player trained by a Jesuit. The purpose of a navy, he pointed out to his government, was to protect the seaborne commerce of its country. If the immunity of private property were accepted, the Navy's occupation would be gone. The public would demand reduction in warships and refuse to support naval appropriations in the Reichstag. In short, Captain Siegel made it clear that if the German Navy was to have a *raison d'être*, property must be left open to seizure, even in the interest of the enemy.

Discussions of this kind stimulated and absorbed the participants. The conduct of war was so much more interesting than its prevention. When the restriction of new weapons or prohibition of as yet undeveloped ones came up for discussion, the military and naval men, as alert as Captain Siegel, keenly defended their freedom of enterprise. The Russian proposal that the powers should agree "not to radically transform their guns or increase their calibres for a certain fixed period" was allowed to founder on the problem of inspection and control. Sir John Ardagh pointed out there would be nothing to prevent a state from constructing rifles of a new pattern and storing them in arsenals until needed. This caused a Russian delegate, M. Raffalovitch, to reply hotly that "public opinion and parliamentary institutions" should be adequate safeguard. Considering the source, this was not impressive. Mahan raised the same objection to proposals for limiting the calibre of naval guns, thickness of armor plate and velocity of projectiles. Any form of international control, he said, would be an invasion of sovereignty, to which all the delegates at once agreed.

In the debate on extending the rules of the Geneva Red Cross Convention of 1868 to naval warfare, the question was raised of rescuing sailors from the water after battle. This was the occasion that evoked Fisher's explosion about feeding prisoners gruel. When the debate was over his chief was able to report, "Thanks to the energetic attitude and persistent efforts of Sir John Fisher all provisions of the original articles which were likely in any way to fetter or embarrass the free action of the Belligerents have been carefully eliminated."

An ominous issue developed on the rights of defense of an unarmed population against armed invasion. Ardagh proposed an amendment changing the "liberty" of a population to oppose the invader to its "duty" to do so, adding, "by all legitimate means of the most energetic and patriotic resistance"—which won him the enthusiastic response of the small powers. Colonel Schwartzkopf "opposed it tooth and nail," supported for once by the Russians. "If anything was required to show the need for some article of the kind," Ardagh reported, it was the "bitter resistance" of the Germans and Russians which accomplished the amendment's defeat. This committee then turned its attention more successfully to such questions as the treatment of spies and prisoners of war; the prohibition of poison; treachery and ruses; the bombardment of undefended towns; and rules governing flags of truce, surrender, armistice and occupation of hostile territory.

In the committee on limiting new weapons the negative trend had become somewhat embarrassing. Everyone was therefore delighted to fall upon the question of dumdum, or expanding, bullets, which offered an opportunity both to outlaw something and to vent the general anti-British feeling of the time. Developed by the British to stop the rush of fanatical tribesmen, the bullets were vigorously defended by Sir John Ardagh against the heated attack of all except the American military delegate, Captain Crozier, whose country was about to make use of them in the Philippines. In warfare against savages, Ardagh explained to an absorbed audience, "men penetrated through and through several times by our latest pattern of small calibre projectiles, which make a small clean hole," were nevertheless able to rush on and come to close quarters. Some means had to be found to stop them. "The civilized soldier when shot recognizes that he is wounded and knows that the sooner he is attended to the sooner he will recover. He lies down on his stretcher and is taken off the field to his ambulance, where he is dressed or bandaged by his doctor or his Red Cross Society according to the prescribed rules of the game as laid down in the Geneva Convention.

"Your fanatical barbarian, similarly wounded, continues to rush on, spear or sword in hand; and before you have had time to represent to him that his conduct is in flagrant violation of the understanding relative to the proper course for the wounded man to follow—he may have cut off your head." Behind the flippant words Ardagh was making the point that war was a bitter business and, more politely than Fisher, was ridiculing the notion that it could be civilized. Unimpressed, the delegates voted 22–2, against the unyielding opposition of Britain supported by the United States, to prohibit the use of the dumdum bullet.

Unanimity, elusive so far, was at last achieved on one topic: the launching of projectiles or explosives from balloons. Here was something, almost untried, that almost everyone was willing to ban, especially the Russians, for whom the prospect of adding a new dimension to warfare was altogether too much.

As Colonel Jilinsky almost plaintively put it, "In the opinion of the Russian Government the various means of injuring the enemy now in use are sufficient." As regards air warfare, most of the delegates were willing to agree and a permanent prohibition was voted. The committee congratulated itself. Then suddenly at the next meeting Captain Crozier, having had serious second thoughts after consultation with Captain Mahan, raised an objection. They were proposing to ban forever, he said, a weapon of which they had no experience. New developments and inventions might soon make airships dirigible, enabling them to be steered by motor power over the area of battle and to take part at a critical moment with possibly decisive effect, thus in the long run sparing lives and shortening the conflict. Would it be in the humanitarian interest to prevent such a development? Instead of permanent prohibition, Captain Crozier proposed a five-year ban at the end of which period they would have a better idea of the capabilities of airships. This time impressed, the delegates agreed.

A proposed ban on the use of asphyxiating gas failed of unanimity by one vote—Captain Mahan's. He stubbornly refused to withdraw his negative on the ground that the United States was averse to restricting "the inventive genius of its citizens in providing weapons of war." Nothing had yet been done toward inventing it, and if it were, Mahan believed that gas would be less inhuman and cruel than submarine attack, which the Conference had not outlawed. Against his lone negative, nevertheless, the delegates adopted a ban on asphyxiating gas.

In the world outside The Hague, Chinese nationalists under the name "Righteous Fists," or Boxers, were attacking foreigners in Pekin, Boers and British had reached the edge of war in South Africa, Americans had launched war upon Filipinos, there were labour riots in Italy, police shot and killed demonstrators in Spain, a parliamentary crisis over manhood suffrage exploded in Belgium and everyone was talking about the assault on the French President at the races. "How bored Europe would be if it were not for France," patriotically reflected the correspondent of *Le Temps.* M. Bourgeois rushed home to try his hand in the crisis but decided after all not to undertake the burden of government, and, as Jaurès commented rather sourly, "the angel of arbitration flies back once more to The Hague, to return when the danger is over."

Amid the charms of the Huis ten Bosch, the prospect of a largely negative outcome, so lightly assumed at the start, began to cause anxiety about the public reaction, especially that of the Socialists, society's "awful conscience." If the Conference were to end in mere pious but empty ceremony, it was feared, the Socialists would triumphantly denounce the failure as further evidence of the impotence of governments and declare themselves the true representatives of humanity against its masters. Delegates quoted to each other Baron d'Estournelles' story that when he left Paris, Jaurès had said to him, "Go on, do all you can at The Hague, but you will labour in vain. You can accomplish nothing there, your schemes will fail and we shall triumph." Through the summer, as one delegate said, the Socialists prowled around The Hague like a cat around a bird cage. In Amsterdam they organized a mass meeting of three thousand which denounced the pretended efforts of the governments and declared peace could never be achieved except through the organization of the masses against the capitalists.

"Why does no one write over the door of the Conference, *Mene, Tekel, Upharsin*?" asked the anonymous correspondent of *Le Temps* who left such a vivid record of that summer. Watching Dutch fishermen's children playing in the streets and pairs of smiling girls who strolled by coquettishly, he wrote, "If this great assembly does not achieve its purpose, the stupid rivalries of states may one day mow down these young people and lay their corpses by millions on the battlefields."

Hope for the Conference now lay in the Arbitration Commission. The chief delegates of the major powers, Pauncefote, White, Bourgeois, Münster, de Staal, all sat on this commission; its labours were the center of attention; its members, drawn forward by the pull of public opinion, really worked; discussions were animated and strong feelings generated. The British, Russians and Americans had each come with a draft proposal for a permanent tribunal; Pauncefote's plan, which did not require obligatory submission of disputes, was accepted as the basis for discussion. Count Münster, flanked by his two professors, declared from the start that Germany was utterly opposed to arbitration of any kind in any form. The whole idea was nothing but "humbug," he told White, and "injurious" to Germany because his country, as he was not shy in explaining, "is prepared for war as no other country is or can be" and could mobilize in ten days, faster than France or Russia or any other power. To submit to arbitration a dispute which might lead finally to war would simply give rival powers time to catch up and cancel Germany's advantage of rapid mobilization. "Exactly," noted the Kaiser in the margin of Münster's report, "that's the object of this whole hoax."

The Kaiser invariably became frenetic at the mere mention of arbitration, which he saw an incursion on his personal sovereignty and as a plot to deprive Germany of the gains achieved by her matchless military organization. Nevertheless, with Pauncefote, White and Bourgeois determined to achieve something, the Commission persisted in the effort to hammer out some form of tribunal. The civilian delegates laboured against the heavy resistance of their own governments and military colleagues, who were deeply disturbed at the least hint of the compulsory principle. No one wanted to give up an inch of sovereignty or an hour of military advantage and at times the outlook seemed hopeless. On a day when the wind blew from the sea, Baroness von Suttner wrote in her diary, "Cold, cold are all hearts—cold as the draft that penetrates the rattling windows. I feel chilled to the bone."

But the necessity of presenting some result to the public was overriding, and tentatively, bit by bit, a tribunal, though puny, began to take shape. Any suggestion of giving it authority over disputes involving "honor or vital interest" caused it to totter toward collapse. The Austrian delegate saw no objection to a tribunal which could decide on minor matters of dispute "such as for instance the interpretation of a Postal or Sanitary commission," but he resolutely rejected anything more. The Balkan delegates in a group—Rumania, Bulgaria, Serbia and Greece—created a crisis when they threatened to walk out if a provision for "investigating commissions" was retained. With utmost difficulty, one agreement at time, the tribunal's powers and procedures were defined—but not unanimously.

Germany would agree to nothing. The other nations who equally disliked the idea without wishing to say so could rely on Münster's daily negative vote to do their work for them. A tribunal without Germany's adhesion, White wrote despairingly, would seem to the world "a failure and perhaps a farce." He argued earnestly and daily with the German delegates to convince them that their obstruction would only result in the Czar becoming the idol of the plain people of the world and the Kaiser the object of its hatred. They had no right to allow their "noble and gifted" sovereign to be put in this position. He repeated D'Estournelles' story of what Jaurès had said, and when this seemed to make an impression he repeated it in a letter to Bülow and sought out Stead and told him to use it "in every way." Stead complied with such zest that Professor Zorn complained of the "terrorism of the Stead-Suttner press" and warned his government that to abstain from all collaboration raised the danger of Germany being denounced as the "sole troubler of peace." From St. Petersburg the German Ambassador warned Bülow that if the Conference brought forth nothing the Czar would be personally insulted and the world would ascribe the "responsibility and odium of failure to us."

Pressure began to tell. Münster was wavering when a despatch arrived from Berlin stating that the Kaiser had declared himself "strongly and finally" against arbitration. In desperation White persuaded Münster to send Zorn to Berlin and he himself sent Frederick Holls, secretary of the American delegation, to present the issue in person to the Kaiser and his ministers. Friday's scheduled meeting of the Arbitration Commission was postponed until they could report back on Monday. Returning to his hotel White found a visitor, "of all men in the world," Thomas B. Reed, whose "bigness, heartiness, shrewdness" and fascinating conversation helped him to pass the anxious weekend.

In Berlin the Kaiser eluded the interviewers but not a report from Bülow which regretfully advised that the "very popular" idea of arbitration had taken hold of the Conference, won the support of the English, Italians, Americans and even the Russians, leaving Germany in isolated opposition. The margin grew lurid with the Kaiser's disgust. "I consented to all this nonsense only in order that the Czar should not lose face before Europe," he scribbled. "In practice however I shall rely on God and my sharp sword! And I shit on all their decisions."

This evidently being recognized as His Majesty's gracious consent, word that Germany would sign the arbitration agreement was received at The Hague two days later. At last something would come of the Conference and the awful spectre of nullity and a Socialist triumph receded. Delegates worked mightily to draw up a convention of sixty-one articles, while applying "a zeal almost macabre" to removing any trace of compulsory character. They were ready for a final vote in the closing week of the Conference when it was suddenly frustrated by, of all people, the Americans. Delegates were stunned. Deeply embarrassed, White announced that his delegation could not sign Article 27, the particular contribution of the French, which required signatories to consider it their "duty" to remind parties to a dispute of the existence of the tribunal.

White's painful predicament was the work of Captain Mahan, who was in turn reacting indirectly to Stead. Under the influence of Stead's over-enthusiastic reports, the *Manchester Guardian* had hailed the draft of the Arbitration Convention as a great pacific instrument which if it had been operative in 1898 would have required the European powers to bring Spain and the United States to arbitration and would have prevented the war between them. Reading the article, Mahan was appalled. The "honest collision" might have been missed. For the future he saw a net of entanglements spreading before America's unwary feet. Summoning his fellow delegates he insisted that Article 27 would commit the United States to interfere in European affairs and vice versa, and if signed, would lead the Senate to refuse to ratify the tribunal. Mesmerized and convinced by his implacable logic, White and the others on the delegation submitted, although all their careful work was risked. If the Americans refused to sign a part of the agreement, other nations might back out and the whole delicately assembled structure fall apart. Urgently White tried to persuade the French to drop Article 27 or at least qualify the word "duty." Bourgeois and D'Estournelles refused to change so much as a comma. Fiasco loomed. Closing ceremonies were scheduled for the following day, July 29. In desperate maneuvers White sought a compromise. At the last minute the Americans arranged to sign under a qualifying phrase disclaiming any obligation to "intrude, mingle or entangle" themselves in European politics. By forceps and barely breathing, Arbitration was pulled into the world.

Total results of the Hague Conference were three Conventions: on Arbitration; Laws and Customs of War on Land; and Extension of the Geneva Rules to Maritime Warfare; three Declarations: on Projectiles from Balloons, Asphyxiating Gases, and Expanding Bullets; six "Wishes" for future accomplishment; and a Resolution. The last expressed the opinion of the Conference that limitation of military expenditures and of new types of weapons was "highly desirable for the moral and material benefit of humanity" and should be the subject of "further study" by the states. It was a pious dirge for all that was left of the original Russian purpose, yet the delegates did not seem ready to bury the Hague idea. However cynically they had come and however stunted their product, most of them could not but feel a sense of having participated in something important and a desire that the foundations they had laid should not be lost. They registered the feeling in a "Wish" for a Second Conference at some future date—although the idea did not please everyone. Count Münster crustily departed saying he had no desire to see international conferences perpetuate themselves like "bad weeds."

Three months after the Peace Conference, Britain went to war in South Africa. The Dreyfus Affair had distracted attention from the Conference, one ex-delegate commented sadly, and now the Boer War seemed to contradict it. Its unconscious epitaph was left to Andrew White in the form of a reluctant tribute paid to his difficult colleague, Captain Mahan: "When he speaks, the millennium fades."

By the time the Second Conference met in 1907, again at The Hague, war, revolution, new alliances, new governments, new leaders and most notably a new century had intervened. The Twentieth was already unmistakably modern, which is to say it was absorbed in pursuit of the material with maximum vigor and diminished self-assurance; it had forgotten decadence and acquired doubt. Mechanical energy and material goods were redoubling and dominant, but whether beneficent had somehow become a question. Progress, the great certainty of the Nineteenth, no longer appeared so sure.

People felt awe at the turn of the century, as if the hand of God were turning a page in human fate. Cannons were fired at midnight in Berlin to mark the moment and one listener heard the sound "with a kind of shiver: one knew all that the Nineteenth Century had carried away; one did not know what the Twentieth would bring."

To begin with, it brought violence. The new century was born brawling, in the Boxer Rebellion, in the Philippines, in South Africa, although the brawls were still on the periphery. In 1900 France was restless and so filled with frustrated rage that *Punch* predicted her first act on the day after the International Exposition closed would be to declare war on England, "for they have been held in for so long it will be necessary to do something desperate at once." In 1900 the Kaiser exhorted German troops embarking on the punitive expedition to Pekin to emulate Huns in ruthlessness. In the course of the Boxer Rebellion he experienced the inconvenience of too much zeal in the munitions business. Learning that a German gunboat had suffered seventeen hits in a duel with Chinese forts equipped with the latest Krupp cannon, he sent Fritz Krupp an angry telegram: "This is no time when I am sending my soldiers to battle against the yellow beasts to try to make money out of so serious a situation."

Money and bigness governed. Morgan in 1900 bought out Carnegie to form with Rockefeller and a hundred other firms the corporate colossus, U. S. Steel, the world's first billion-dollar holding company. King Leopold of Belgium, the Morgan of Europe, a builder too big for his country, created a money-making empire out of the Congo while British and Americans, busy killing Boers and Filipinos, loudly deplored his methods. Three hundred men, it was said, "all acquainted with each other, controlled the economic destiny of the Continent."

In 1900 Oscar Wilde, a bloated ruin at forty-four, died in Paris, and Nietzsche, aged fifty-five and mad, died at Weimar. "Then in 1900," wrote W. B. Yeats, "everybody got down off his stilts; henceforth no one went mad; nobody committed suicide; nobody joined the Catholic Church or if they did I have forgotten. Victorianism had been defeated." Some welcomed, some regretted the defeat but the fact was clear. As if to mark the event, the Queen herself incredibly was no more.

The year 1900 conveyed a sense of forces and energy running away with the world. Henry Adams felt moved to evolve a "Law of Acceleration" in history. He felt as if he could never drive down the Champs Elysées without expecting an accident or stand near an official without expecting a bomb. "So long as the rate of progress held good, these bombs would double in force and number every ten years. . . . Power leaped from every atom. . . . Man could no longer hold it off. Forces grasped his wrists and flung him about as though he had hold of a live wire or a run away automobile."

Adams' choice of simile was apt, for the automobile was one of the century's two most potent factors of future social change; the other was man's unconscious. Although unrecognized in potential, it too was formulated in 1900, in a book, *The Interpretation of Dreams*, by a Viennese doctor, Sigmund Freud. Although the book attracted little attention and it took eight years to sell out the edition of six hundred copies, its appearance was the signal that Victorianism indeed was dead.

The International Exposition of 1900 covering 277 acres in the heart of Paris displayed the new century's energies to fifty million visitors from April to November. If they could not for this Exposition equal the Eiffel Tower of the last, the French built with the same *élan* a new miracle of engineering and beauty in the Pont Alexandre III, whose low graceful arch spanned the Seine in a single leap. It was considered "peerless in all the world" and the two new permanent exhibition buildings on the right bank, the Grand and Petit Palais, were unanimously acknowledged to be "suitable and grand." Not so the Porte Monumentale, or main gate, in the Place de la Concorde, built of what appeared to one observer to be lath, plaster, broken glass, putty, old lace curtains and glue. At its top, instead of a traditional goddess of Progress or Enlightenment, a plaster Parisienne in evening gown welcomed the world with open arms. Although considered gay and chic by some, the gate was generally deplored as the epitome of the new vulgarity of the new century. Multicolored electric lights played on towering electrically powered fountains at night; the new Metro was opened in time; a track for automobile testing and racing was built at the Expo annex at Vincennes. Of all the wonders the public's favorite was the *trottoir roulant*, a double moving sidewalk circling the grounds, one half of which moved twice as fast as the other. In the temporary buildings, the architects, striving for sensation, had achieved what seemed exciting originality to some and "a debauch of stucco" to others. Industrial exhibits in the Palaces of Machinery, Electricity, Civil Engineering and Transportation, Mining and Metallurgy, Chemical Industries and Textiles, displayed all the extraordinary advances of the past decade.

Of the national pavilions the most popular was the Russian, an exotic Byzantine palace with a Trans-Siberian Railway exhibit in which the visitor could sit in a sumptuous railway carriage and enjoy a moving panorama of the scenery. The Viennese was a fantasy of *Art Nouveau* with fretwork balconies in the form of curling vines and the sinuous lines of the new style curving through ceramics and furniture. The United States had the greatest number of exhibits but Germany's show was the most imposing, clearly superior in quality and arrangement. It affirmed an intense will to surpass every other exhibitor. Germany's dynamos were the largest, the spire of her pavilion the tallest, its searchlight the brightest, its restaurant the most expensive. The Kaiser himself, it was rumored, had commanded the finest china and silver, the most delicate glassware, the most luxurious service, so that one felt in the presence, as one visitor said, of a real style "William the Second."

In all the Exposition the two largest single exhibits were Schneider-Creusot's long-range cannon and Vickers-Maxim's collection of ferocious, quick-firing machine guns. Beholders gazed at them with solemn thoughts. An English correspondent in particular was moved to philosophize on the real meaning of the Exposition for the new era it introduced. Schneider's great gun seemed to him to hold the world collected in Paris under its threat and to mark the passage of war from a realm of sport to a realm of science in which the making of weapons absorbed the ingenuity of mankind. If a lull ever came, he wrote, the arts of peace might revive, "but meanwhile the Paris Exhibition has taught us that the triumph of the modern world is purely mechanical."

The triumphs continued. In 1900 Max Planck broke the chains of classical Newtonian physics to formulate the quantum theory of energy. In Switzerland in 1905 Albert Einstein obtained his doctorate at the University of Zurich with a dissertation on a new theory of relativity. In 1901 wireless telegraphy spanned the Atlantic and Daimler supplanted the horseless carriage with a vehicle distinctly a motorcar. In 1903 a motorized dirigible flying machine flew at Kitty Hawk. But no epoch is all of a piece. To some the almost daily new miracles accomplished by science and mechanics still carried, not a threat as to Henry Adams, but a promise of progress in social justice. "It seemed merely a matter of decades," thought Stefan Zweig, a young intellectual of Vienna, "before the last vestiges of evil and violence would finally be conquered."

In 1900 the German Naval Law precipitated the abandonment of isolation by England. Providing for nineteen new battleships and twenty-three cruisers in the next twenty years, it made explicit Germany's challenge to British supremacy at sea, the fulcrum of Britain's existence. It convinced Britain that she needed friends. In 1901 the Hay-Pauncefote Treaty put a bottom under good relations with the United States. In 1902 the isolation of self-sufficient strength, once so splendid and confident, was ended forever by a formal alliance with Japan. In 1903 the new King of England, Edward VII, prepared the ground for reconciliation with France by a visit of ceremony to Paris carried out with tact and aplomb. In 1904 the new policy culminated in an Anglo-French Entente, disposing of old quarrels, establishing a new friendship and fundamentally defining the balance of Europe.

At the same time, England set about refitting her physical forces to meet a world full of new challenges. Her Army having been revealed in action as something less than in step with modern times, Balfour, now Prime Minister, set up a Committee of Imperial Defence to formulate strategy and reorganize and modernize the armed forces. He appointed Sir John Fisher as one of its three members and would have appointed Captain Mahan to succeed Lord Acton as Regius Professor of Modern History at Cambridge but that King Edward objected on the ground that English historians were available. For all his rarefied pose, Balfour's appreciation of the two hard-headed veterans of The Hague revealed a bent parallel to theirs. In 1904 he appointed Fisher First Sea Lord. The new head of the Navy had momentous plans in mind.

In the same year, Russia went to war with Japan, soon to become mired in a series of losing campaigns marked by the surrender of Port Arthur in January, 1905, and a humiliating, although not decisive, defeat at the Battle of Mukden in March. Three weeks later the alarm bell rang for Europe in Morocco.

To Germany's intense resentment, the Anglo-French Entente had recognized a French sphere of influence in Morocco. Now that Russia could not come to France's aid, Bülow and Holstein determined on a test of strength that would expose the weakness, as they believed, of the Entente. On March 31, 1905, the Kaiser stunningly, if nervously, descended upon Tangier in a challenge that every nation recognized. Europe shook under the impact and the gesture succeeded too well. It completed the work of the Kruger telegram, convincing Germany's neighbors of her ultimate belligerent intent and of the need for more specific preparations than a mere Entente. "Roll up the map of Europe," Pitt had said in despair ninety-nine years before when Napoleon won at Austerlitz. In a different spirit England unrolled it now. She entered into military conversations with France, underpinning their partnership with arms and envisioning, for the first time since Waterloo, an expeditionary force to the Continent in aid of a specific ally against a specific enemy.

In May, 1905, the Russian Baltic Fleet met its fatal rendezvous in the Straits of Tsushima in the world's first head-on clash of modern capital ships on the high seas. Though the Russian fleet was annihilated, its defeat did not end the war, thus proving Bloch's thesis, though few realized it, that against the total resources of a nation, victories on the battlefield were no longer decisive. Japan's victory startled the Old World and warned the New. Three months after Tsushima, in July, 1905, the President of the United States offered to mediate between Russia and Japan, less to save the Russians than to halt the Japanese, who seemed to him to have gone far enough. Accepting the offer, the parties came to Portsmouth, New Hampshire, in August to negotiate a peace treaty under the aegis of the President of the United States. It was a significant moment in Western history. For McKinley or Cleveland or Harrison to have played such a role would have been unimaginable, but a new strength and a new man were now at work.

"Theodore with all thy faults . . ." was the one-line editorial in which the New York *Sun* had expressed its Presidential preference in the election of the previous year. Its candidate, now President in his own right, was exuberantly in charge of a country booming with prosperity. With industry stimulated by the Spanish-American War, the depression, unemployment and savage labour troubles of the nineties had subsided and the bitter class feeling of the McKinley-Bryan campaign of 1896 was dulled by the full dinner pail. The Progressives, who were the new Left, were expansionist and believed America's direction was "onward and upward." President Roosevelt leading the march settled the coal strike, "took" Panama, began the building of the Canal, challenged the trusts, slapped the name "muckrakers" on crusading journalists, bullied the Kaiser out of Venezuela, and when a presumed American citizen was kidnaped by bandits in Morocco, sent the American Fleet to the rescue with the resounding demand (phrased by John Hay): "We want Perdicaris alive or Raisuli dead!"

"The President is in his best mood," said his friend Jules Jusserand, the French Ambassador, "he is always in his best mood." He had the mental energy of a geyser and the flaws of Everyman. His Attorney-General, Philander Knox, rather admired the way the President ignored his advice and once remarked, "Ah, Mr. President, why have such a beautiful action marred by any taint of legality." President Eliot still did not admire him, although when Roosevelt came to Cambridge in 1905 for his twenty-fifth reunion Eliot had felt obliged to invite him to stay at his house. On his arrival, perspiring and in need of a wash, Roosevelt pulled off his coat, rolled it up and flung it across the bedroom so violently it knocked a pillow to the floor, took a large pistol from his pocket and slammed it on the dresser. After washing up, "he came rushing downstairs as if his life depended on it," and when Eliot asked, "Now, are you taking breakfast with me?" replied, "Oh no, I promised Bishop Lawrence I would take breakfast with him—and good gracious!"—clapping his right hand to his side—"I've forgotten my gun!" Retrieving it, the President of the United States rushed off to see the Bishop while the president of Harvard, horrified by violation of a Massachusetts law against carrying pistols, muttered, "Very lawless; a very lawless mind."

The pistol represented, perhaps, less a lawless mind than the creed of the time that life was a fight. No one felt it more deeply than Roosevelt. He despised Tolstoy's "foolish theory that men should never make war," for he believed that "the country that loses its capacity to hold its own in actual warfare will ultimately show that it has lost everything." He was infuriated when the peace advocates equated progress in civilization with "a weakening of the fighting spirit"; such a weakening, as he saw it, invited the destruction of the more advanced by the less advanced. He confused the desire for peace with physical cowardice and harped curiously on this subject: "I abhor men like [Edward Everett] Hale and papers like the *Evening Post* and the *Nation* in all of whom there exists absolute physical dread of danger and hardship and who therefore tend to hysterical denunciation and fear of war." He deplored what seemed to him, as he looked around, a "general softening of fibre, a selfishness and luxury, a relaxation of standards" and especially "a spirit such as that of the anti-imperialists." "That's my man!" the Kaiser used to say whenever Roosevelt's name was mentioned.

No President had a more acute sense of his own public relations. When Baron d'Estournelles came in 1902 to beg him to do something to breathe life into the Arbitration Tribunal, Roosevelt listened. "You are a danger and a hope for the world depending on whether you support aggression or arbitration," d'Estournelles said. "The world believes you incline to the side of violence. Prove the contrary."

"How?" the President asked.

"By giving life to the Hague Court." Roosevelt promptly instructed Secretary Hay to find something to submit for arbitration and Hay obligingly uncovered an old quarrel between the United States and Mexico over church property, the first dispute to activate the Tribunal. Having been Secretary of State during the Hague Conference and sympathetic to arbitration, Hay wanted to build up the prestige of the Tribunal and now arranged to divert to it the dispute over Venezuela's debts. Fearing that the President might accept a German proposal to act as individual mediator in this affair, he strode up and down the room exclaiming, "I have it all arranged, I have it all arranged. If only Teddy will keep his mouth shut until tomorrow noon!" That objective being happily accomplished, the Tribunal received another important case.

Arbitration treaties between individual countries slowly made progress. England and France agreed on one when they joined in the Entente of 1904 and Norway and Sweden concluded another when Norway, without the firing of a shot, became an independent state in 1905—an event hailed in itself as evidence that man was making progress. Two other international disputes of the time, the Dogger Bank affair between Russia and England and the affair of Venezuela's debts, were referred to the Arbitration Tribunal, whose existence proved an invaluable means of saving face and satisfying public opinion. The Hague idea seemed to be putting on flesh.

In the summer of 1904 the Interparliamentary Union, meeting at the St. Louis Fair, adopted a resolution asking the President of the United States to convene a Second Peace Conference to take up the subjects postponed at The Hague and to carry arbitration forward toward the goal of a permanent court of international law. At the White House, Roosevelt accepted the resolution in person, as well as a visit from Baroness von Suttner, who had a private talk with him on "the subject so dear to my heart." She found him friendly, sincere and "thoroughly impressed with the seriousness of the matter discussed." According to her diary he said to her, "Universal peace is coming; it is certainly coming—step by step." As the most unlikely remark of the epoch, it illustrates the capacity of true believers to hear what they want to hear.

Roosevelt felt the glamour of a world role and as convener of the Peace Conference considered himself no less fitted than the Czar. Accordingly on October 21, 1904, Hay instructed American envoys to propose that the nations reconvene at The Hague. That the Second Conference, like the First, was called while a war was in progress need not, he suggested, be considered an ill omen.

The nations accepted on condition that the Conference should not be convened until the Russo-Japanese War was over. No sooner was it over, however, than the Moroccan crisis erupted. Again President Roosevelt played a decisive role and was able to exercise his influence, this time privately, to persuade the Kaiser to agree to an international conference on Morocco. Held at Algeciras in January, 1906, with the United States as a participant, it proved to be a discomfiture for Germany, leaving her more bellicose than before. International tensions were not eased.

Three months before Algeciras, in October, 1905, the keel of *H.M.S. Dreadnought*, first of her class, was laid. With guns and armor plate manufactured by separate ordnance firms, she was ready for trials in an unprecedented burst of speed and secrecy, a year and a day later, achieving the greatest of military advantages—surprise. Designed by Fisher, the *Dreadnought* was larger, swifter, more heavily gunned than any battleship the world had ever seen. Displacing 18,000 tons, carrying ten 12-inch guns, and powered by the new steam-turbine engines, it made all existing fleets, including Germany's, obsolete, besides demonstrating Britain's confidence and capacity to rebuild her own fleet. Germany would now not only have to match the ship but dredge her harbors and widen the Kiel Canal.

In Fisher's mind, as in Clemenceau's, there was but one adversary. Half jokingly in 1904 he shocked King Edward by suggesting that the growing German Fleet should be "Copenhagened," that is, wiped out by surprise bombardment, evoking the King's startled reply, "My God, Fisher, you must be mad!" At Kiel in the same year, the Kaiser upset Bülow by publicly ascribing the genesis of his Navy to his childhood admiration of the British Fleet, which he had visited in company with "kind aunts and friendly admirals." To give such sentimental reasons for a national development for which the people were being asked to pay millions, Bülow scolded, would not encourage the Reichstag to vote credits. "Ach, that damned Reichstag!" was the Kaiser's reply.

Invitations to The Hague meanwhile had been reissued not by Roosevelt but by the Czar, who felt the necessity of regaining face. The upstart American republic had intervened enough. In September, 1905, as soon as his war was over, the hint was conveyed to Washington that he wished the right to call the Conference himself. Roosevelt amiably relinquished it. The Treaty of Portsmouth, which in a few months was to bring him the Nobel Peace Prize, had, he felt, been enough of a good thing. "I particularly do *not* want to appear as a professional peace advocate . . . of the Godkin or Schurz variety," he wrote to his new Secretary of State, Elihu Root.* His withdrawal did not please the peace advocates. Russia, as one of them said, was "not in the van of civilization." This became strikingly apparent upon the outbreak of the Russian revolution of 1905. Forced by the crisis to grant a constitution and a parliament, the Czar repudiated the action as soon as his regime regained control, and dissolved the Duma to the horror of foreign liberal opinion.

The time seemed not on the whole propitious for a Peace Conference, but one encouraging development was a change of government in England which brought the Liberals, the traditional party of peace, to power. The new Prime Minister, Sir Henry Campbell-Bannerman, known to all as C.-B., was a solid round-headed Scot of a wealthy mercantile family who had made himself unpopular in Court and in Society by denouncing British concentration camps in the Boer War as "methods of barbarism." Nevertheless, King Edward, forced to become acquainted, discovered him to be indeed, as a mutual friend had promised, "so straight, so good-tempered, so clever and so full of humor" that it was impossible not to like him. C.-B. had the wit, tact and worldly wisdom that the King appreciated and the two gentlemen, who had a number of tastes in common, soon found each other congenial. They both went annually to Marienbad for the cure, they both loved France and shared a special friendship with the Marquis de Galliffet. Though a Liberal, C.-B. was, to the royal surprise, "quite sound on foreign politics." He spoke the most fluent French of any Englishman, delighted to shop in Paris, to eat French food and read French literature, Anatole France being one of his favorites.

As an old-fashioned Liberal automatically disposed to disarmament,† C.-B. in his first public speech as Prime Minister

*Hay had died in July, 1905.

†Limitation of armaments rather than disarmament was the question at issue, but the single word, being less awkward, was generally used at the time and the usage has been followed here.

somewhat rashly pledged his party to work for it at the coming Conference, although the Czar's invitation, as opposed to 1898, had conspicuously omitted to mention the subject. Nevertheless, C.-B. boldly took it on, as well as a pledge to work for a permanent court of arbitration. "What nobler role," he asked, "could this great country assume than to place itself at the head of a League of Peace?" This may have somewhat overstepped the view of a hard bloc within his own Cabinet composed of Asquith, Haldane and Grey, who as Liberal Imperialists were not altogether as peace-minded as himself. With unexpected toughness at seventy, C.-B. had withstood their attempt to elbow him into the House of Lords so as to obtain leadership of the Commons for Asquith. He detested them all and was enjoying his triumph.

Soon the relentless dilemma that attaches to office caught up with his Government. After years of excoriating the Tories as warmongers, the Liberals now suddenly found themselves responsible for the country's safety. Although committed by election pledges to reduction of military and naval expenditure, once the General Election confirmed them in office they were not anxious to repudiate the work of modernizing the armed forces which the Tories had begun. C.-B. referred to the members of the Committee of Imperial Defence, Fisher, Lord Esher, and Sir George Clark, presumably in that order, as Damnable, Domineering and Dictatorial; but he had inherited them, not to mention the dreadnought program. Haldane, as Secretary for War, undertook to cut £3,000,000 from the Army estimates while at the same time, through sweeping reforms, achieving a more efficient fighting arm, as Fisher had done in the Navy. He created a General Staff and a reserve force called the Territorials. Officers' Training Corps were formed in the public schools and universities and supplied with arms, ammunition and instructors by the government. Young men responded with enthusiasm. The calling bugle and screaming fife worked their magic, though chiefly upon the officer class. Recruitment of private soldiers for the Territorials dwindled after the first few years.

H.M.S. Dreadnought was commissioned in 1906, a strange triumph for the Liberals, and Fisher was demanding construction of three more dreadnoughts for 1907. He threatened, if refused, to resign and take three other members of the Board of Admiralty with him. The Liberal dilemma was painful but not beyond solution. By insisting that the Navy was defensive (which, considering the nature of blockade, was arguable), the Government managed to give Fisher his dreadnoughts and absolve the Liberal conscience at the same time.

Once more the nations found themselves committed to go to The Hague and intensely disliking the prospect. All through 1906 and half of 1907 they put off the uncomfortable day while pursuing desultory discussions of agenda. The Russian program, circulated in April, 1906, proposed arbitration and laws of war as subjects for discussion while continuing to ignore disarmament. Emerging from foreign defeats and domestic revolution, Russia was concerned with replenishing, not reducing, armaments and had called the Conference only to retrieve the initiative from the United States. As far as Izvolsky, the current Russian Foreign Minister, was concerned, disarmament was "a craze of Jews, Socialists and hysterical women." Since the advent of the Liberals in England, however, the question of disarmament could not be escaped. To put it on the agenda after the burial of 1899 was like propping up a dead man; not to put it on was to admit hopelessness and invite public condemnation. At a meeting of the Interparliamentary Union in London in April, 1906, C.-B. urged the delegates to insist at home "in the name of humanity" on their governments going to The Hague with serious intent to decrease military and naval budgets. The meeting was hardly a happy one, for on opening day, as delegates crowded around to congratulate the proud members of the youngest parliament, word came that the Czar had dissolved the Duma. C.-B., who was to give the address of welcome, was so shocked that he challenged the Imperial decision with the words, "Under one form or another the Duma will revive. In all sincerity, we can say, 'The Duma is dead; long live the Duma!'" His outspokenness earned an official Russian protest.

As to disarmament the Kaiser let it be known that if it was brought up for discussion in any form, his delegates would leave the Conference which in any case he "devoutly hoped would not take place." He was already being blamed at home by the militant Pan-Germans and Crown Prince's party for yielding at Algeciras instead of fighting, and German diplomats hinted to other ambassadors that he might even be deposed if Germany were forced to agree to any form of arms limitation arising from the Conference. During one of the periodic visits of King Edward required by royal relations, with usually disastrous results, uncle and nephew discussed the forthcoming Conference while remaining for once reasonably amiable, perhaps because on this subject they were not far apart. The King "entirely disapproved" of the Conference, the Kaiser wrote to Roosevelt, "and himself took the initiative of telling me that he considered it a 'humbug.'" According to his report, King Edward said it was not only useless, since in case of need nobody would feel bound by its decisions, but even dangerous as likely to produce more friction than harmony.

To Roosevelt it was apparent that modern Germany, "alert, aggressive, military and industrial, . . . despises the Hague Conference and the whole Hague idea." His anxiety at the time was lest the British Liberal Government would "go to any maudlin extreme at the Hague Conference." He told the new British military attaché, Count Gleichen, a cousin of the King, that he hoped Haldane and Grey would not let themselves be "carried away by sentimental ideas." He was afraid they might be "swayed by their party in that direction . . . but don't let them do it." He talked fully to Gleichen of his current idea for a limitation on the size of battleships rather than on naval budgets. Unaware that his proposed top limit of 15,000 tons was already outdated by the monstrous hulk then lying in Portsmouth dockyard, Roosevelt explained that he wanted to see the British Navy remain in the same relative position vis-à-vis the navies of Europe and Japan as at present. Conveying the message to the King, Gleichen added that he had found lunch at Roosevelt's home in Oyster Bay "extremely meagre," and with only two Negro servants in attendance and no one to meet him at the station, arrangements rather primitive altogether.

Once the *Dreadnought* was commissioned, the United States Navy could not lag behind and two of the new class were authorized by Congress at Roosevelt's request in January, 1907. The Navy, he wrote to President Eliot, was an "infinitely more potent factor for peace than all the peace societies" and the

Panama Canal far more important than The Hague. With regard to the Conference he added, "My chief trouble will come from the fantastic visionaries who are crazy to do the impossible."

One of these was Andrew Carnegie, whose company, when he sold it in 1900 to Morgan for $250,000,000 in bonds, was producing one-fourth of all the steel in the United States and as much as all of England. Less shy than Nobel, Carnegie was now devoting his profits, while he was still alive, to the welfare of humanity. Next to providing libraries which presumably might make men wiser, he hoped also to make them more pacific, and had agreed on the urging of Andrew White to donate a building for the Arbitration Tribunal at The Hague.

He was now busily engaged between the White House and Whitehall in an effort to promote the cause of the Conference, but Roosevelt had lost interest after the British refused to consider his proposal of a limit on the size of battleships. However, Roosevelt managed to avoid commitments by telling highly placed correspondents what they wanted to hear. He was in correspondence with the sovereigns of both Germany and England, whom he addressed easily as "My Dear Emperor William" and "My Dear King Edward."

By now scarcely any public official except C.-B. and Secretary Root wanted disarmament on the agenda. Root thought it should be discussed even if nothing were accomplished, because, he said, results are never achieved without a number of failures: "failures are necessary steps toward success." C.-B. too felt the world must keep on trying. Though a childless man whose wife, his closest companion, had just died and who himself was within a year of his death, he continued his own efforts. In March, 1907, he took the unusual course for a Prime Minister of publishing an article on a current question of policy. Under the title "The Hague Conference and the Limitation of Armaments," it appeared in the first issue of a new liberal weekly, the *Nation* (of London). Although armaments and engines of war had increased since the First Conference, he wrote, so had the peace movement, which was now "incomparably stronger and more constant." He thought disarmament should be given a chance to make the same progress as arbitration, which now had acquired a "moral authority undreamt of in 1898." Britain, he pointed out, had already reduced military and naval expenditures (which was true if the program for the new dreadnoughts was left out of account) and would be willing to go further if other nations would do likewise. Admittedly this would not affect Britain's naval supremacy, since it would freeze the status quo, but the Prime Minister insisted on the thesis that the British Navy was not a challenge to any state or group of states. The argument was narrow steering between the rocks of conscience and the shoals of political reality and it pleased nobody. The Germans took it as proof of a British plot in concert with France and Russia to force the issue at The Hague before Germany could make good *H.M.S. Dreadnought*'s lead. Bülow announced publicly in the Reichstag that Germany would refuse to discuss disarmament at the Conference. King Edward was equally irritated by the Prime Minister's espousal of disarmament, as bad as his support of women's suffrage. "I suppose he will support the Channel Tunnel Bill next week!" he said in disgust, but from that particular horror C.-B. refrained.

As Foreign Secretary, Sir Edward Grey professed himself ready at all times to budgetary limitation at The Hague. Haldane talked earnestly to the American diplomat, Henry White, of the need for reducing armaments and had gone to Germany in 1906 to feel out possible ground for an agreement. But the hard fact behind the talk was that neither the British Government nor any other had any intention of limiting its freedom to arm as it pleased. The only person to mention the role of the munitions manufacturers was the King of Italy, who suggested that disarmament would cause "an outburst of opposition" among them and he was sure the Kaiser would never consent to "clipping the wings of Krupp." When, on behalf of Russia, Professor de Martens toured the capitals to gather opinions as Muraviev, now dead, had done before, the American Ambassador in Berlin summarized the matter flatly: "De Martens does not believe and nobody believes . . . there is the slightest likelihood of any steps toward practical reduction of armaments being taken at the next Hague Conference."

These were the private exchanges of diplomats, but peace could not be so rudely handled before the public, at least not in England and the United States. It was not a question of the great mute unknown passive mass. Who knew what opinion lay there? Mass opinion when formed would blow with the winds of circumstance and more likely with the loud circumstance of war than with peace. The vocal opinion, however, of the thinking public—especially of the peace movement—would be outraged by exclusion of disarmament from the Hague agenda. Peace Congresses meeting annually—at Glasgow in 1901, Monaco in 1902, Rouen and Le Havre in 1903, Boston in 1904, Lucerne in 1905, Milan in 1906—passed resolutions demanding that governments make some serious effort to reach a truce on armaments. Baroness von Suttner, who had been awarded the Nobel Peace Prize in 1905, and her colleagues in the peace societies and at the annual Lake Mohonk conferences in America, agitated as energetically as ever. In 1907 Jane Addams published a book, *Newer Ideals of Peace*, incurring Roosevelt's displeasure but adding a respected voice to the chorus.

Carnegie, seizing on C.-B.'s idea of a League of Peace or League of Nations, as he variously called it, decided the Kaiser was the man to establish it because "I think he is the man responsible for war on earth." Having several times been invited to visit by the Kaiser, who liked millionaires, he now set forth to convince him of his duty. By letter in advance he explained how the Kaiser could earn in history the title of the "Peacemaker" and added in a covering letter to the American Ambassador, "He and our President could make a team if they were only hitched up together in the cause of Peace." At Kiel, on his arrival in June, 1907, he dined twice with the Kaiser and was invited to a third audience with results eerily echoing the interviews of Stead with the Czar and Baroness von Suttner with Roosevelt. Carnegie found his monarch "a wonderful man, so bright, humorous, and with a sweet smile. I think he can be trusted and declares himself for peace. . . . Very engaging—very; can't help liking him." Once out of reach of the sweet smile, Carnegie remembered his mission and wrote back urging a great gesture by the Kaiser at The Hague to convince the world that he was in reality the "apostle of peace."

Words and gestures of this kind were a habitual weakness of the peace advocates, with effect on the public, if any, that could only be deceptive. At the same time, political leaders told the public only what sounded virtuous and benign, while reserving the hard realities for each other. Only one man tried to instruct the public to take an honest look at war. Mahan, now an Admiral, continued to publish articles on the necessity of the free exercise of fighting strength and especially, in anticipation of the Conference, on the danger of a renewed demand for immunity of private property at sea. The military function seemed to him to need protection from the uncomprehending view of the layman. "The prepossession of the public mind in most countries," he wrote worriedly to Roosevelt after a tour abroad, was such that the question of war was "in danger of being misjudged and 'rushed.'"

It was this prepossession that required both the British and American governments to support inclusion of disarmament on the agenda. Neither Grey nor Roosevelt believed discussion would lead to any practical result and in talks with foreign ambassadors both explained that they were obliged to insist on it for "the sake of public opinion." Germany, Austria and Russia were determined to exclude it for fear that discussion might somehow trap them into an unwanted position. After months of intricate diplomatic negotiation, the Conference was finally announced without disarmament on the agenda and with so many reservations included in the various acceptances that it seemed probable the Conference might break up as soon as it met. Great Britain, the United States and Spain reserved the right to bring disarmament up for discussion; Germany, Austria and Russia reserved the right to abstain or withdraw if it were mentioned, and other nations reserved a variety of rights in between.

So burdened, the nations assembled on June 15, 1907. The first decade of the new century, now three quarters old, was already marked by three characteristics: a bursting economy, a burst of creative vigor in the arts, and the sound of steady "drumming like a noise in dreams." For all who did not hear it there were many who did, not all with dread. In the German Navy it was the custom of officers to drink to "The Day." At a spa near Bayreuth a group of German students and young naval officers made friends with a visiting Englishman and "in the friendliest and most amiable fashion discussed with me the coming struggle between our two countries." They argued that every empire had its day. England's decline must come as had that of Spain, Holland and France. Who should fill the throne but the strong, wise, noble and gifted nation whose development had been the outstanding factor of the Nineteenth Century and who now stood "poised for heroic enterprise." Germany seemed not the only one so poised. The new aggressive powers exhibited by Japan and the United States convinced Europe that these nations were approaching a clash. Following the furor caused in Japan by the California Exclusion Act, both these nations believed it themselves. "The tendency is toward war," wrote Secretary Root, "not now but in a few years' time."

The prospect was viewed by many of the ruling class more matter-of-factly than tragically. Lord Lansdowne, opposing the Old Age Pensions Bill in the House of Lords, said it would cost as much as a great war and the expense of the South African War was a better investment. "A war, terrible as are its consequences, has at any rate the effect of raising the moral fibre of the country" whereas the measure under debate would weaken it. And if the prospect of war appalled the spokesmen of the working class, violence as such did not. Georges Sorel in his *Reflections on Violence* in 1908 claimed that proletarian violence exercised in the interest of class war was a "fine heroic thing," a civilizing agent that could save the world from barbarism.

The Second Conference was larger in size, longer in duration and more voluminous in results than the First, but otherwise not very different. It lasted through October—for four months instead of two—and produced thirteen conventions, as compared to the previous three. Because the United States had insisted on the presence of the Latin-American states, much to the distaste of the European powers, 44 nations and 256 delegates were present as compared to 26 and 108 at the First Conference. The larger number made it necessary to meet in the Ridderzaal, seat of the Netherlands Parliament in the center of The Hague, rather than in the Huis ten Bosch in its lovely park. Many of the delegates were the same as before; many of the notable ones of 1899 were missing. Bourgeois of France and Beernaert of Belgium again headed their respective delegations, but Münster, Pauncefote and De Staal were dead;

Andrew White had not returned; Mahan and Fisher were absent in body if not in spirit. The new president was again a Russian, M. Nelidov, an elderly diplomat like his predecessor whose voice and manner revealed his lack of sympathy with the Conference and who, being in ill health most of the time, left command of the Russian delegation to the pompous Professor de Martens who himself suffered from gout and was often confined to his room. The Russian delegation seemed divided among itself with its members quartered in separate hotels.

Baron d'Estournelles, who was to share the Nobel Peace Prize with Beernaert two years later, was again present for France, and Professor Zorn, looking yellow and emaciated, from Germany. Among the newcomers were Count Tornielli, representing Italy, whose wife had been seated next to President Loubet on the terrible day at Auteuil, and the notorious Marquis de Soveral, who represented Portugal. An intimate friend of King Edward, he was known as the "Blue Monkey" in London Society where it was said, "he made love to all the most beautiful women and all the nicest men were his friends." A whole block of newcomers was provided by the "impeccable dandies" of Latin America.

Pauncefote's firm presence was missed. When he died in 1902 Roosevelt sent his body home to England in a cruiser, saying, "I did not do it because he was Ambassador but because he was a damned good fellow." His place was taken, if not filled, by a judge, Sir Edward Fry, a tiny, unworldly Quaker of eighty-two, yet not so unworldly as to want to yield control of the British delegation to his associate, Sir Ernest Satow, an experienced diplomat, formerly minister to Pekin, who spoke French fluently which Fry did not.

Dominating the Conference were the chief delegates of the United States and Germany: Mr. Joseph Hodges Choate, who at seventy-five with white chin whiskers seemed to personify the Nineteenth Century, and Baron Marschall von Bieberstein, suave and up to date, who though only ten years younger was clearly a man of the new age. Choate was genial and shrewd, famous as a raconteur, Ambassador to England from 1899 to 1905 and a lawyer by profession whose brilliant defence of the rights of property before the Supreme Court in 1895 held off the income tax for another eighteen years. He owned a summer home at Stockbridge designed by Stanford White. His white hair gleaming beneath a glossy silk hat became a landmark of the Conference.

Baron Marschall, Ambassador to Constantinople, a huge handsome man with two *alt-Heidelberg* dueling scars on his cheek, wore "a mask of haughty intelligence that seemed to despise the *ensemble* of human folly." He played chess and the piano, cultivated roses, and smoked tiny cigarettes endlessly, occasionally flicking the fallen ash from the silk lapel of his coat with a gesture that seemed to say he treated human issues with no more compunction. He despised public opinion which he said was whatever the newspapers chose to make it. A government that could not control the press was not worth its salt. The best way to control a newspaper, he advised, was by "banging the door in its face." Equally firm were his opinions on his fellow delegates: De Martens was a "charlatan . . . with an explosive lack of tact"; Barbarosa of Brazil was the "most boring"; Fry was "a good old man completely lacking in experience of modern life"; Tornielli was "gentle and pacific"; Tsudzuki of Japan was a "superior" person who had studied in Germany, spoke German and "felt the utmost veneration for His Majesty"; the Russian military delegate, Colonel Michelson, who made a speech saying that war was terrible and everything should be done by mediation to prevent it, was guilty of talk which might have been understandable coming from Baroness von Suttner but coming from a colonel was a "scandal"; Choate was "the most striking personality" among the delegates with "extraordinary intelligence, profound legal knowledge and great political ability."

Baron Marschall himself shook the Conference when in the course of discussion on a proposal to restrict mine-laying he warned against the folly of making laws for the conduct of war which might be rendered useless by "the law of facts." The implications to be drawn from this excited wide press comment, including a letter to *The Times* from the Poet Laureate. Too indignant for poetry, Alfred Austin wrote that Marschall's words were a plain warning of future German aggression of which all her neighbors—Holland, Belgium, France and Austria—should take note. Britain "duly forewarned" should adopt military conscription and the Laureate closed with a line borrowed from his predecessor, Lord Tennyson: "Form! Form! Riflemen, Form!"

As before, peace advocates converged from all quarters upon The Hague, including Bertha von Suttner and Stead, who had once again appointed himself independent *rapporteur*. Again he published a chronicle of the proceedings, personalities, disputes and private deals, this time in the form of a four-page daily newspaper, the *Courrier de la Conférence*. Bloch was dead but Andrew Carnegie took his place and laid the cornerstone for the new Peace Palace, to which he had donated $1,250,000. It was agreed that all member nations should contribute materials representing their finest products for the building that was to express "universal good will and hope." As before, Socialists, and this time Anarchists and Zionists as well, held their international Congresses in Amsterdam during the Conference to capture some of the world limelight for their causes. The Dutch pastor and pacifist Domela Nieuwenhuis, who managed to combine Anarchism with religion and remain sincere, denounced Carnegie impartially with the delegates as a merchant of death who built a Temple of Peace, while accepting orders for munitions "even from the Japanese," an accusation accurate in spirit if not in time. "Let all workers regardless of nationality strike on the declaration of war and there will be no war!" Nieuwenhuis cried out.

The work of the Conference was organized as before in Commissions—on Arbitration, Rules of War on Land, Rules of War at Sea—with an additional Fourth Commission—on Maritime Law. Bourgeois and Beernaert were chairmen as before of the First and Second Commissions, Tornielli of the Third and De Martens of the Fourth. At the opening session Nelidov's address of welcome aroused no enthusiasm; the first days were gloomy, arrangements and assignments confused and acoustics in plenary session so poor that on one occasion delegates disputed energetically whether the last speaker had addressed them in English or French.

Carrying out their insistence that disarmament must be discussed if only to prove to the public its impracticability and their own honest intentions, the British brought the question to the floor. None of the nations walked out, because Sir Edward Grey's explanations in advance, however foggy, had conveyed a sufficiently clear impression that the matter would not be uncomfortably pursued; nor was it. Sir Edward Fry made a grave and moving presentation of the case, describing the appalling increase in engines of death and moved a resolution calling for "further serious study" in the same phrase of postponement as had been used in 1899. Nelidov agreed that if arms limitation was not ripe in 1899 it was not more so in 1907, and the delegates adopted Fry's resolution without a vote. The matter was disposed of in a total of twenty-five minutes. Stead raged at the "miserable and scandalous debacle" and even Secretary Root concluded that Grey's support had been merely a gesture to "satisfy English public opinion."

Although the world grew bored after Fry's "funeral oration" as Marschall called it, and even the journalists lost interest, the Conference settled down to serious work on the laws and techniques of war. When busied in drafting and disputing the problems of their trade—the rights and duties of neutrals, the recovery of international debts by force, the rules for opening hostilities—all matters which took war for granted as a fact of human life, the delegates became absorbed. Indeed, they worked harder than at the First Conference, as if war was not only a fact of life but an imminent fact. Committee meetings were held twice a day, lengthy documents had to be read, expert opinions examined, new drafts prepared, and endless confidential talks held to work out compromises. "Never since my examination for the bar have I worked so hard as in the last six weeks," Marschall reported to Bülow.

The launching of projectiles or explosives from balloons was reconsidered, and again avoiding any extremes of self-denial, the delegates renewed the prohibition for another limited term of five years. Neutral territory, a matter on which the Belgians were particularly sensitive, was agreed to be inviolable and a convention of twenty-five articles was worked out establishing rules of procedures in case it were violated. As a result of Japan's treacherous opening of hostilities against Russia by surprise attack in 1904, new and interesting discussions were held on this subject. They culminated in a convention whose signatories agreed not to open hostilities without previous unequivocal warning in the form of a declaration of war or ultimatum accompanied by a conditional declaration of war.

Another convention of fifty-six articles was adopted redefining the laws and customs of land warfare. As a result of the Venezuela affair in 1902 a convention against the use of force to collect international debts except if the debtor had refused arbitration was agreed on. This represented one definite advance in international law.

Naval warfare was the subject of the fiercest struggle, with the right of capture of seaborne commerce as the central issue. As the basic weapon of blockade, Britain was determined to preserve the right of capture free of any restrictions. Germany was equally determined to restrict it by international prize court and other interferences. The use of submarines and underwater contact mines as weapons against blockade Germany was determined to defend and Britain to restrict. On the immunity of private property, Grey, at least, had learned Mahan's lesson if the American delegation had not. He instructed his delegates that Britain could not assent to a principle which "if carried to its logical conclusion would entail the abolition of commercial blockade." He added a reason, in his tortured way, which would certainly not have occurred to Mahan. Britain could not agree to anything, he wrote, which might "so limit the prospective liability of war as to remove some of the considerations which now restrain the public from contemplating it." Translated into simpler language, this meant that Britain could not agree to anything which might, by limiting the damages of war, cause people to enter on it more lightly. With the British Liberals it was obligatory to find a moral reason to fortify a natural policy of self-interest, a practice no one carried to higher perfection or more obscure expression than Sir Edward Grey.

Eight conventions on naval warfare were ultimately reached establishing rules, rights and restrictions for every possible means of injuring the enemy. It took thirteen articles to prohibit the use of underwater contact mines unless harmless one hour after being laid; another thirteen articles to regulate naval bombardment of shore establishments; fifty-seven articles to govern an international prize court. Other conventions dealt with the right of capture, the nature of contraband, the rights and duties of neutrals at sea but so unsatisfactorily that all these questions were resumed at a conference of naval powers in London in the following year.

On arbitration, the motive power, now that Pauncefote was gone, was chiefly American, with Secretary Root, a lawyer by profession, supplying the energy behind Choate. Root's object was to transform the tribunal established in 1899 from an optional court for litigants who agreed to arbitration into a Permanent Court of International Justice with permanent judges deciding issues of international law by "judicial methods under a sense of judicial responsibility." President Roosevelt supported the aim without strong conviction, confessing to Root midway through the Conference that "I have not followed things at The Hague." To his friend Speck von Sternberg, the German Ambassador, he expressed himself more forcibly as, for some reason, he habitually did to Germans. He could not take a proper interest in the Hague proceedings, he told Speck, because he was so "utterly disgusted" with the nonsense chattered by professional peace advocates.

The American proposal for a Permanent Court ran into strong opposition, one obstacle being Brazil's insistence that all forty-four nations be represented on it. The idea of having decisions made for them "by decayed Oriental states like Turkey or Persia . . . or a half-breed lawyer from Central or South America," in the words of one commentator, disgusted the major European powers. The crux, however, was once more compulsory arbitration. On this, reported Marschall to Berlin, would depend the final answer, "Was it a Peace Conference or a War Conference that took place in 1907?" Since his own country utterly rejected the compulsory principle, presumably he faced the answer. He did not, however, fall into the error made by his predecessors of strenuous isolation. Instead, as Choate said, he was devoted to the principle of arbitration while opposing every practical application of it. The Conference attempted to work out a list of innocuous subjects for compulsory submission on which everyone could agree, but it failed of adoption when eight nations voted against it. In the end a Convention on the Pacific Settlement of International Disputes was adopted containing ninety-six articles of which the compulsory principle was not one. Consequently, no Court of Justice could be established.

One last point of contention remained: a Third Conference. Believers in the Hague idea wished to see the principle of the interdependence of nations established in the form of a permanent organization and periodic meetings. The day of nations as separate sovereign units was past and before breaking up they wanted a commitment to meet again. Non-believers, chiefly the major European powers, wanted no further limitation of their freedom of action and no more invasions of sovereignty by insistence on compulsory peaceful settlement. They resisted commitment to a Third Conference, more particularly because pressure for it came from the Americans. Secretary Root, faithful to his precept that successive failures were necessary to success, and believing that each of the Conferences had accomplished something toward making possible the next, had instructed Choate to obtain a resolution for a Third Conference. By committing the nations now, he intended also to wrest initiative and control from Russia. Choate fought hard against the reluctance of the other delegates which remained unbending until he threatened Nelidov that if no agreement were reached he would move the resolution publicly in plenary session. Opposition gave way. The delegates adopted a resolution recommending that the next Conference be held "within a period analogous to that which had elapsed since the preceding Conference," namely, eight years.

To have achieved this much, Root wrote to Roosevelt, was at least progress "toward making the practice of nations conform to their professed desire for peace." The desire was real enough. Twice it had brought the nations to The Hague. Twice man's inherent desire to police himself had wrestled against opposite tendencies. The goal of a new international order in which nations would be willing to give up their freedom to fight in exchange for the security of law was still ahead. The advance toward it taken at The Hague, as Choate said later, was necessarily "gradual, tentative and delicate."

He hoped for further progress at the next Conference in 1915.

6

"NEROISM IS IN THE AIR"

GERMANY 1890–1914

6

"Neroism Is in the Air"

THE BOLD bad man of music at the turn of the century, innovator in form, modern and audacious in concept, brilliant in execution, not immune to vulgarity, and a barometer of his native weather, was Richard Strauss. His every new work, usually conducted at its premiere by himself, crammed the concert halls with a public eager to be excited and music critics eager to whip their rapiers through the hot air of their profession. In the ten years from 1889 to 1899, when he was between twenty-five and thirty-five, Strauss produced six works, *Don Juan*, *Tod und Verklärung*, *Till Eulenspiegel*, *Also Sprach Zarathustra*, *Don Quixote* and *Ein Heldenleben*, which created a new form—or, as the critics said, "formlessness." Called tone poems, the compositions were rather condensed operas without words. At the premiere of *Don Juan* the audience called the composer back five times in an effort to make him play the piece all over again. At the premiere of *Heldenleben*, the passage depicting battle enraged some listeners to the point of leaving the hall and caused others to "tremble as they listened while some stood up suddenly and made violent gestures quite unconsciously." If to some Strauss was a sensationalist and corrupter of the pure art of music and to others the prophet of a new musical age, even the "inventor of a new art," one thing was clear: he retained for Germany the supremacy of music which had culminated in Wagner. He was "Richard II."

In one sense this made him the most important man in German cultural life, for music was the only sphere in which foreigners willingly acknowledged the superiority that Germans believed was self-evident. German Kultur in German eyes was the heir of Greece and Rome and they themselves the best educated and most cultivated of modern peoples, yet foreigners in their appreciation of this fact fell curiously short of perfect understanding. Apart from German professors and philosophers, only Wagner excited their homage, only Bayreuth, seat of the Wagner Festspielhaus, attracted their visits. Paris remained Europe's center of the arts, pleasure and fashion, London of Society, Rome of antiquity and Italy the lure of travelers seeking sun and beauty. The new movements and impulses in literature—Naturalism, Symbolism, social criticism; the towering figures—Tolstoy, Ibsen and Zola; the great novels from Dostoyevsky to Hardy: all originated outside Germany. England after its great Victorian age was again in the nineties pulsing with new talent—Stevenson, Wilde and Shaw, Conrad, Wells, Kipling and Yeats. Russia again produced in Chekhov a matchless interpreter of man. Painters bloomed in France. Germany in painting had little but Max Liebermann, leader of the Secessionists, whose secession, however, took him no further than the presidency of the Prussian Academy of Fine Arts. In literature her outstanding figures were the playwright Gerhart Hauptmann, an offshoot of Ibsen, and the poet Stefan George, an offshoot of Baudelaire and Mallarmé.

In music, however, Germany had produced the world's masters and seen the procession crowned by Wagner whose dogma of a fusion of the arts became a cult in which foreigners eagerly joined. Wagner Societies from St. Petersburg to Chicago contributed funds to provide the Master's music dramas with a fitting home, and the "Bayreuth Idea" created intellectual ferment beyond Germany's borders. Germans believed their sovereignty of music would continue forever without serious challenge from any other country. While many of them, like the Kaiser, detested Strauss's modernity, his pre-eminence appeared to them happy proof that German musical supremacy was maintained.

Not only the major cities but every German city or town of substantial size had its opera house, concert hall, music academy, orchestral society and musical *Verein* of one kind or another. Hardly a German did not belong to a choral society or instrumental ensemble and spend his evenings practicing Bach cantatas over several steins of beer. Frankfurt-am-Main, a town of under 200,000 in the nineties, about the size of The Hague, Nottingham or Minneapolis, boasted two colleges of music, with distinguished teaching staffs and pupils from many countries, a new opera house, "one of the handsomest in Europe," which gave performances six nights a week, a Museum Society

Orchestra of 120 players which gave concerts of symphonic and chamber music, two large choral societies also prolific in concerts, and in addition was host to numerous recitals by visiting artists. Besides activity of comparable kind in Berlin, Munich, Cologne, Dresden, Leipzig, Stuttgart and other cities, music festivals lasting as much as a week in honor of some composer or special occasion were held widely and often.

The season at Bayreuth since Wagner's death had acquired an oppressive atmosphere of obligatory reverence. The cab taking a visitor to the Festspielhaus displayed a card pinned over the seat labeled "Historical!" indicating that the Master had sat there. Performances opened with a blast of trumpets as if commanding the audience to prepare for devotions. At intermission sausages and beer were consumed, followed by another trumpet blast; after the second act more sausages and beer and more trumpets and the same procedure after the third act. The faithful absorbed the Master's works "as if they were receiving Holy Communion," reported the young Sibelius, who came in 1894 eager for a great experience and could not leave soon enough. By 1899 when Thomas Beecham, aged twenty, arrived, he found there was a rift in the cult. Malcontents were proclaiming the decadence of the Festival, criticizing the reign of the widow, Frau Cosima, and clamoring for the removal of the son, Siegfried, as director. They said his management was feeble and uninspired, singers were poor and performances shoddy, while the group loyal to "Wahnfried," the Wagners' house, countered with charges of intrigue and jealousy.

By now Strauss was the new Hero, so acknowledged in his self-portrait in music, *A Hero's Life*. Reared in and accustomed to comfort, clad in the correct clothes of a diplomat, slender and six foot three inches tall, with broad shoulders and well-cared-for hands, a soft unlined face, a mouth shaped like a child's under a flaxen moustache and a cap of curly flaxen hair already receding from a high forehead, Strauss looked neither Promethean like Beethoven, nor poetic like Schumann, but simply like what he was: a successful prosperous artist. His works had been performed since he was twelve; as a conductor he was engaged by all the leading orchestras. He was self-possessed, conscious of superiority and comfortably rather than offensively arrogant, a consequence of being Bavarian rather than Prussian.

Bavaria's last King, Ludwig II, who adored Wagner and died mad, had sided with Austria against Prussia in 1866, and Munich's culture was oriented more toward Vienna than Berlin. Munich fostered the arts and considered itself the modern Athens, as opposed to the Sparta of Prussia, whose Junkers, like their ancient prototypes, despised culture as well as comfort. Bavarians, as Germany's southerners—and largely Catholic—enjoyed the pleasures of life, physical as well as aesthetic. In Munich, Stefan George was high priest of a cult of *l'art pour l'art* and beginning in 1892 edited for his worshipful disciples the literary review *Blätter für die Kunst*, which sought the German answer to questions of art, soul and style. Humor found a corner in Munich, where the satiric journal *Simplicissimus*, founded in 1896, and the comic journal *Lustige Blätter* were published. In Munich the *Überbrettl*, a form of satiric café entertainment, flourished and mocked Berlin.

As a native of Munich, Strauss belonged to a culture antipathetic to Prussia, but as a German aged seven in 1871, he grew up parallel with the new nationalism of the German Empire. Born in 1864, five years younger than the Kaiser, Dreyfus and Theodore Roosevelt, he came of a family which combined beer and music, his native city's leading occupations, in that order. His grandfather was a wealthy brewer whose musically inclined daughter married Franz Strauss, first horn of the Munich Court Orchestra and professor at the Royal Academy of Music. He was said to be the only man of whom Wagner was afraid. Although he played Wagner's music "lusciously," he hated it and his emphatic objections to its demands on his instrument accomplished on one occasion the unique feat of rendering the Master speechless. Before a rehearsal of *Die Meistersinger* Wagner begged the conductor, Hans Richter, to play over the horn solo himself for fear Franz Strauss would declare it unplayable. Although Franz Strauss never became reconciled to his son's dissonances and departures from classical form, Richard Strauss used no instrument to more marvelous capacity than the horn, as if in tribute to the man who, when asked how he could prove the boast that he was the best horn player in the world, replied, "I don't prove it, I admit it."

Strauss's parents began his musical education at the piano when he was four and he began composing at six. He could read and write musical notation before he knew the alphabet. While at school he studied violin, piano, harmony and counterpoint with the conductor of the Court Orchestra. With the "superfluous vitality" that was to remain one of his most notable characteristics, he produced at the same time a flow of songs, instrumental solos and sonatas. When he was twelve his *Festival March* (Op. 1) was performed by his school and later published. Performance of his compositions at public concerts began with three of his songs when he was sixteen, a *String Quartet in A* (Op. 2) when he was seventeen and a *Symphony in D minor* (Op. 3) played by the Munich Music Academy to an enthusiastic audience in the same year. At eighteen, he wrote a suite for winds which received the accolade of a commission for another work of the kind from Hans von Bülow, leader of the ducal Orchestra of Meiningen and the outstanding conductor of the day. Trained by Bülow, the Meiningen was the jewel of German orchestras, whose members learned their parts by heart and played standing up like soloists. Strauss wrote a *Serenade for Thirteen Winds* which Bülow invited him to conduct at a matinee concert without a rehearsal. The twenty-year-old composer led the performance "in a state of slight coma," having never conducted in public before. Becoming Bülow's protégé, he appeared with him as solo pianist in a Mozart concerto and at the age of twenty-one was appointed music director of the Meiningen, where he studied conducting under its recognized master. In composition his adored model at the time was Mozart, and Strauss's early quartets and orchestral pieces composed before he was twenty-one were works of great charm and style in the classical tradition.

The musical world of the eighties was immersed in the party politics of classical versus romantic. New works were heard less for themselves than as upholders of the one or followers of the other. Composers, critics and public revolved in a perpetual war dance around the rival totem poles of Brahms and Wagner. To his partisans Brahms, who died in 1897, was the last of the great classicists, Wagner was anti-Christ and Liszt a secondary Satan. *Lisztisch* was their last word of contempt. Wagnerians on the other hand considered Brahms stuffy and tradition-ridden and their own man a combined prophet, Messiah and Napoleon of music. Strauss, as his father's son and a disciple of Mozart, was anti-Wagner, but under Bülow became converted. Even Wagner's seduction of his wife could not dim Bülow's admiration for the seducer's operas. Strauss was affected also by the preaching of Alexander Ritter, first violinist of the Meiningen, who enjoyed extra prestige as husband of Wagner's niece and convinced Strauss that *Zukunftsmusik* (Music of the Future) belonged to the successors of Berlioz, Liszt and Wagner. "We must study Brahms," he asserted, "long enough to discover that there is nothing in him."

Strauss felt Ritter's influence "like a storm wind." It combined with the experience of a trip to Italy, whose sun and warmth acted on him as it had on Ibsen and other northerners, to inspire *Aus Italien*, his first work in a new form. It was called a "Symphonic Fantasia" of four movements which bore descriptive titles: "In the Campagna"; "Among the Ruins of Rome"; "By Sorrento's Strand"; "Scenes of Popular Life in Naples." The second movement was subtitled "Fantastic pictures of vanished splendor; feelings of melancholy and splendor in the midst of the sunny present": and was marked *allegro molto con brio*, an odd way to express melancholy but *molto con brio* was to be characteristic of Strauss.

Aus Italien picked up where Liszt and Berlioz left off. They also had experimented in narrative and descriptive music, though within traditional patterns of theme and development. These requirements sometimes stretched program music into strange shapes, as in the case of the German composer J. J. Raff, in whose *Forest Symphony*, according to one critic, the shades of evening in the finale fell three times. Strauss avoided this problem by discarding traditional patterns. He described without developing, tantalizing the listener with a series of dazzling glimpses but no resolution. The result, at the first performance of *Aus Italien*, conducted by the composer in Munich, was hisses and catcalls, "general amazement and wrath."

Refusing to be diverted from the path he had chosen, Strauss next produced an orchestral work on the theme of Macbeth, as

Berlioz had done on King Lear and Liszt on Hamlet. Not the drama's events but the conflict within Macbeth's soul was his subject, expressed in the rich polyphony and fertility of musical idea which were to create his renown. Meanwhile on Bülow's resignation he had succeeded as conductor of the Meiningen Orchestra and in 1889 moved to Weimar as conductor in the post Liszt had held thirty years before. Combining classics with "madly modern" works, including Liszt's as yet unappreciated tone poems, he presented fresh and exciting programs which drew large audiences. In a discussion with a friend who declared his preference for Schumann and Brahms, Strauss replied, "Oh, they are only imitators and will not survive. Apart from Wagner there is really only one great master and that is Liszt."

At Weimar on November 11, 1889, he conducted the premiere of his own *Don Juan*. Its theme, as stated by Nicholas Lenau, author of the poem on which it was based, was not that of a "hot-blooded man eternally pursuing women," but of a man's "longing to find a woman who is to him incarnate womanhood and to enjoy in one all the women on earth, whom he cannot, as individuals, possess. Because he does not find her, although he reels from one to another, disgust at last seizes hold of him and this disgust is the Devil that fetches him."

In adopting this theme Strauss committed himself fully to the business of making music perform a non-musical function: making it describe characters, emotions, events and philosophies, which is essentially the function of literature. He was forcing instrumental music by itself, without singers or words, to do the work of opera or what Wagner called "music drama." Given the task, no one was better equipped to accomplish it. With his knowledge, gained from conducting, of the capacities of every instrument, his bursting talent and overflow of ideas, his mastery of the techniques of composition, Strauss, like a circus trainer, could make music, like a trained seal, perform dazzling miracles against nature. *Don Juan* proved an enthralling seventeen minutes of music with its snatches of amorous melody, its headlong passion, its marvelous song of melancholy by the oboe, its frenzied climax and strange end on a dissonant trumpet note of disenchantment. Its undeveloped themes, however, were disconcerting and its episodic form sacrificed musical to narrative sequence. Bülow nevertheless pronounced it an "unheard of success." Eduard Hanslick, the grand panjandrum of musical criticism who wrote for the *Neue Freie Presse* and other papers of Vienna and detested everything that was not Brahms or Schumann, denounced it as "ugly" with only shreds of melody and no development of musical idea.

The feuds of music were personified by Hanslick, who had worn out the world "ugly" on Wagner through a thousand repetitions until Wagner conferred immortality on him as the unpleasant Beckmesser in *Die Meistersinger*. Hanslick pursued Bruckner, a symphonic follower of Wagner, with such virulence that when the Emperor Franz Joseph granted Bruckner an audience and asked if there was anything he could do for him, Bruckner could only mutter, "Stop Hanslick." Strauss now emerged as another of the new breed to be scotched, and as each new work of his appeared, Hanslick and his school warmed to new degrees of invective.

But Strauss was on his way. Bülow dubbed him "Richard II" and the next year he produced a more ambitious work, *Tod und Verklärung* (Death and Transfiguration). In this a dying man in his final fever relives his life from the innocence of childhood through the struggles and frustrations of maturity to the death agony. At the end comes "the sound of heavenly spaces opening to greet him with what he had yearningly sought on earth." Based on an idea rather than on a literary text (although his mentor, Alexander Ritter, wrote a poem to fit the music *ex post facto*), it escaped the traps of the too specific and soared on great sweeping melodies supported by orchestral splendors. Strauss was twenty-five and had made Liszt look like an amateur.

He continued to conduct, to encourage and perform the works of contemporaries and to compose his first opera, *Guntram*, which was rejected as imitation Wagner by a public already saturated with the real thing. No rigid partisan, Strauss conducted *Hänsel und Gretel* with as much enthusiasm as *Tristan und Isolde*. When Humperdinck, then an obscure teacher at the Frankfurt Academy, sent him the score, Strauss was delighted with it and wrote the composer, "My dear friend, you are a great master who has bestowed on our dear Germans a work which they can hardly deserve." His introduction of the opera at Weimar made Humperdinck famous overnight and rich soon afterwards.

In 1894 Strauss moved on to Munich as conductor of the Court Opera and following the death of Bülow led the Berlin Philharmonic concerts for the winter season of 1894–95. In the same year he was guest conductor at Bayreuth. "So young, so modern, yet how well he conducts *Tannhaüser*," sighed Cosima Wagner. The summers Strauss devoted to his own compositions, working best, as he said, when the sun shone. During the concert season he appeared as guest conductor in different German cities and toured with the Berlin Philharmonic throughout Europe. In the years 1895–99 he conducted in Madrid and Barcelona, Milan, Paris, Zurich, Budapest, Brussels and Liège, Amsterdam, London and Moscow. Limitless in energy, he once conducted thirty-one concerts in thirty-one days. On the podium, making no show of extravagant gesture or muscular contortions, he used a firm, decided simple beat, a few hard angular movements and signaled for crescendo with a hasty bend of the knee joints. "He conducts with his knees," said Grieg. Tyrannical in his demands on the players, he was generous in praise of a well-performed solo no matter how short, and would step down from the podium to shake hands with the player when the piece was over. He was no longer the "shy young man with a large head of hair" whom Sibelius, then a young music student in Berlin, had seen rise from a seat in the audience to acknowledge the applause at one of the early performances of *Don Juan*. His hair was already receding and it is doubtful if he had ever been shy. Now in his early thirties and with Bülow gone he was the most renowned conductor and exciting composer in Germany.

Between 1895 and 1898 he brought out three more new works which carried the symphonic poem to more daring feats of description and more boldly original subject matter than had so far been attempted in music. The marvels of polyphonic complexity were more stunning, the unresolved discords more disturbing and the uses of music in some places seemed deliberately provocative.

Nothing so clever, so comic, so flashing and surprising as *Till Eulenspiegel's Merry Pranks* had ever been heard. The brisk twinkling motif of the horn carries the medieval folk hero,

Germany's Peer Gynt, on his picaresque progress, with every kind of instrumental device portraying his adventures as he gallops through the marketplace scattering pots and pans, disguises himself as a priest, makes love, and comes to a bad end in court with a long drum roll announcing the death sentence. An impudent twitter of the clarinet voices his final defiance on the gallows and a faint trill carries off his last breath as his feet swing in air. Strauss's program notes this time were more specific: "That was an awful hobgoblin," he noted over one passage, or, "Hop! on horseback in the midst of the market women," or, *"Liebegluhend"* (Burning with Love). The Till motif, becoming familiar as it came and went in different disguises, charmed the audience. It was music full of enchanting tricks, like the performance of a superlatively witty and nimble magician. It delighted if it did not move. It expressed a bubbling imagination and unsurpassed skill, though not of course to Hanslick, who, using the favorite censure of outraged orthodoxy, pronounced it "the product of decadence."

For his next subject Strauss moved to the core of his time. By 1896, the world had discovered Friedrich Nietzsche. Living in solitude, disillusionment and chronic drug-blurred battle against insomnia, this other German had produced a body of work around the central idea of the Superman, which was to reverberate down the corridors of his country's life. Responding early to its influence, Strauss determined to make *Also Sprach Zarathustra* the subject of a tone poem.

Nietzsche's alluring concept of "rule by the best," of a new aristocracy which would lead humanity to a higher plane, of man rising to superior fulfillment to become *Übermensch*, seduced the imagination of Europe. It stirred both the yearning hope of human progress as well as the beginning disillusionment with democracy. Nietzsche rejected the democratic idea of equal rights for all men as hampering natural leaders from realizing their full capacities. Where Lord Salisbury had feared democracy as leading to political, and Charles Eliot Norton to cultural, debasement, Nietzsche saw it as a ball and chain holding man back from his highest attainment. He saw the dominant weight of mass tastes, opinions and moral prejudices as a "slave morality." Mankind's leaders should live by a "master morality" above common concepts of good and evil. The goal of human evolution was the *Übermensch*, the higher man, the "artist-genius" who would be to ordinary man as ordinary man was to the monkey.

Through *Also Sprach Zarathustra* and its sequels, *Beyond Good and Evil*, *The Will to Power* and the final *Ecce Homo*, Nietzsche roamed wildly. His ideas rolled and billowed like storm clouds, beautifully and dangerously. He preached Yes to the promptings of energy as good *per se*, regardless of conflict with conventional morality. Law and religion which discouraged such promptings frustrated man's progress. Christianity was a sop for the weak, the meek and the poor. The Superman had no need of God but was a law unto himself; his task was self-fulfillment not self-denial; he shook off the chains of tradition and history as the intolerable burden of the past. Nietzsche stated his credo, not in logical declarative language, but in a kind of prose poetry like the Psalms, meandering and obscure, full of mountain tops and sunrises, the singing of birds and dancing of girls, perorations to Will, Joy and Eternity and a thousand colored metaphors and symbols carrying Zarathustra on his soul's quest toward the goals of humankind.

When he published in the eighties no one listened. Despising the Germans for their failure to appreciate his work, Nietzsche drifted to France, Italy and Switzerland, working himself up, as Georg Brandes said, "to a positive horror of his countrymen." It was a foreigner, Brandes, a Dane and a Jew, who discovered him and whose articles on him, translated and published in the *Deutsche Rundschau* in 1890 introduced him to Germany and began the spread of his fame. By this time Nietzsche was mad and Max Nordau, the author of *Degeneration*, discovering this, naturally seized on him as a prime example of his case and lavished on him some of his most excoriating pages. Since Nordau's book was translated and read all over Europe and in the United States, it helped to make Nietzsche known. He was lauded as a seer, denounced as an Anarchist, examined and discussed by the reviews, English and French as well as German. His aphorisms were quoted as verse titles and chapter headings, he became the subject of doctoral dissertations, the model of a train of imitators, the focus of a whole literature of adulation and attack. Because of his abuse of the Germans as vulgar, materialist and philistine, he was particularly welcomed in France, but this did not prevent his becoming a cult in his native land. The sap was rising in Germany and Germans responded eagerly to Nietzsche's theory of the rights of the strong over the weak. In his writings these were hedged about with a vast body of poetic suggestion and exploration, but taken crudely as positive precepts they became to his countrymen both directive and justification. By 1897 the "Nietzsche Cult" was an accepted phrase. In a bedroom in Weimar a man leaning against a pillow, staring at an alien world out of sad lost eyes, had bewitched his age.

To the "artist-geniuses" of real life *Zarathustra* was irresistible. In Paris when a friend read passages of it to the peasant-born sculptor Rodin, one of the great movers of art forms of his time, he became so interested that he returned every evening until the whole book had been read aloud. At the end, after a long silence, he said, "What a subject to put into bronze!" Under the same thrall Strauss saw the subject in music and in fact Nietzsche himself had written that the whole of *Zarathustra* "might be considered as music." It was not Strauss's intention to set Nietzsche's text to music but, modestly, "to convey musically an idea of the development of the human race from its origin through the various phases of evolution, religious as well as scientific, up to Nietzsche's idea of the *Übermensch*." The whole was to be his "homage to the genius of Nietzsche."

When it became known that Germany's most advanced composer was at work on a tone poem inspired by Germany's most advanced philosopher, admirers grew nervous and enemies sharpened their pens. The finished piece, composed over a period of seven months in 1896 and scored for thirty-one woodwinds and brasses, timpani, bass drum, cymbals, triangle, glockenspiel, two harps and organ beside the usual strings, took thirty-three minutes' playing time, almost twice as long as *Till*, and was performed under the composer's baton within three months of its completion. Trumpets sounded the opening, swelling into an immense orchestral paean by the whole ensemble which seemed to depict less the sunrise stated in the program notes than the creation of the world. Its magnificence was breathtaking. The end came with twelve strokes of a low bell gradually dying away to a pianissimo trembling of strings and winds and ending in the famous "enigma" of a B major chord in the treble register against a dark mysterious C in the bass. In between there was again the Strauss wizardry of polyphonic effect and enough musical ideas for a dozen pieces: "Science" was expressed by a fugue containing the twelve tones of the chromatic scale and the Dance theme of girls in a meadow, introduced by high flutes in a halting waltz rhythm, seemed to catch all the joy and freshness of a green world. It was, however, more Viennese than Bacchic and somehow cheapened by bells and triangles. Three days after the premiere *Zarathustra* was performed again in Berlin and within the year in all the major German cities as well as in Paris, Chicago and New York, evoking from critics new excesses of both savagery and eulogy. To Hanslick it was "tortured and repulsive," to the American James Huneker "dangerously sublime," to the eminent musicologist Richard Batka "a milestone in modern musical history" and Strauss "pre-eminently the composer of our time."

In Germany because of the plethora of performances, with a festival every week and continuing operas, concerts, choral societies and chamber music, success was almost too easy; orchestras were ready to grasp a composition the instant it was finished. "*There is too much music in Germany*," wrote Romain Rolland in italics. As an observer deeply interested both in music and in Germany, he explained: "This is not a paradox. There is no worse misfortune for art than a superabundance of it." Germany, Rolland thought (not without French bias), "has let loose a flood of music and is drowning in it," a situation which did not leave Strauss unaffected. Early prominence and now pre-eminence in his field and confident mastery of his medium afflicted him with a desire to dazzle, and in his next composition, *Don Quixote*, he let his affinity for realism run unreined.

Realism was a German passion. Brünhilde at Bayreuth was always accompanied by a live horse which, affected by equine stage fright or the galloping music of the Valkyrie, invariably misbehaved in the middle of the stage to the relish of the German audience if not of visiting foreigners. The painter Philip Ernst, father of Max Ernst, when painting a picture of his garden omitted a tree which spoiled the composition and then, overcome with remorse at this offence against realism, cut down the tree. When Strauss used a wind machine in *Don Quixote* to represent the turning sails of the windmills, people could not be blamed for wondering if this were not carrying literalism to inartistic excess. His muted brasses representing the bleating of sheep aroused the critics' scorn, although it could not be denied that he conveyed with extraordinary skill not only the sound of bleating but a sense, almost a view, of the crowded mass of animals moving and shoving against each other.

The critics' blasts only added to Strauss's notoriety and drew greater crowds to his concerts. At thirty-four, admitted the English critic Ernest Newman, he was "the most talked of musician in the world." Although the Kaiser disapproved of his music, the German capital could not afford to do without him. Six months after the premiere of *Don Quixote* he was offered and accepted the conductorship of the Berlin Royal Opera.

Berlin meant Prussia, the natural enemy of Munich and Bavaria. The North German regarded the South German as easy-going and self-indulgent, a sentimentalist who tended to be deplorably democratic, even liberal. In his turn, the South German regarded the North German as an arrogant bully with bad manners and an insolent stare who was politically reactionary and aggressively preoccupied with business.

Architecturally, Berlin, Europe's third largest city, was new and not beautful. It belonged in style to what in America was called the Gilded Age. Its main public buildings, streets and squares, built or rebuilt since 1870 to house suitably the new national grandeur, were heavily pretentious and florid with gilding. Unter den Linden, a mile long with a double avenue of trees, was laid out with obvious intent to be the biggest and most beautiful boulevard in Europe. It ended naturally in an Arch of Triumph at the Brandenburg Gate. The gate led in turn to the famous Sieges Allee in the Tiergarten, with its glittering marble rows of helmeted Hohenzollerns in triumphant attitudes. When the statues were raised at the Kaiser's direction, Max Liebermann, who had a studio overlooking the Tiergarten, lamented, "All I can do is to wear blue goggles but it is a life sentence." The imposing Reichstag building was of maximum size to make up for its minimum powers. Along the Leipzigerstrasse and Friedrichstrasse, department stores and the head offices of banks and mercantile houses bulged with the rich excitement of business that was growing daily. The city was spotlessly clean and the population so orderly that a Berlin landlady's bill included three pfennings for sewing on a trouser button and twenty for removing an inkstain. Police were efficient, though an English visitor found them "extremely rough and even brutal." The lure of vice was aggressively flaunted, food was uninteresting, ladies unfashionable. Prussian thrift stifled elegance. Berlin women of the middle class wore homemade clothes with plaid blouses, muddy-brown skirts, sack coats like traveling rugs, square-toed boots and nondescript hats that went with everything and matched nothing. They had stout figures, raw complexions and wore their hair pulled back and pinned in a braided coil.

Society, owing to the lack of intercourse between its rigidly maintained categories, was stiff and dull. Unless ennobled by a *von*, businessmen, merchants, professional men, literary and artistic people were not *hoffähig*, that is, not received at court and did not mix socially with the nobility. Nor did they mix among each other. Every German belonged to a *Kreis*, or circle of his own kind whose edges were not allowed to overlap those of the next one. The wife of a Herr Geheimrat or Herr Doktor did not speak to the wife of a tradesman, nor she to the wife of an artisan. To congregate or entertain or marry outside of *Kreis* borders invited disorder, the thing Germans feared most. Perhaps to compensate for social monotony, some Germans, according to one report, ate seven meals a day.

Since the unification of Germany had been accomplished under the leadership of Prussia, the ruling caste was drawn from the landowning Junkers, or Prussian nobility, who were numerous, poor and backward. Looked down on by the Catholic nobility of Württemberg and Bavaria as coarse, tasteless and unfitted for social leadership, the Junkers made up in assertiveness what they lacked in education. They dominated the Army, which in Germany dominated the State, and in the wake of Bismarck, their greatest exponent, filled most of the government offices though not the business life of the capital, which was grasping and intense. Though an anti-commercial class, they were its willing agents and their Government was the most frankly commercial in Europe. The Kaiser, who admired money, included in his circle the wealthier and more cosmopolitan non-Prussian nobility. Court life was notable for minute rules of behavior and immense state dinners accompanied by very loud music. Jews, unless converted, were not received, with the occasional exception of a Court Jew, like the Kaiser's friend Albert Ballin. Although the Jews numbered about one per cent of the population, anti-Semitism was fashionable, stimulated by their rapid progress in science and the arts, business and the professions after legal emancipation was confirmed for the Empire in 1871. Despite the emancipation, however, professing Jews were excluded from political, military and academic posts and from the ranks of the *von*, an exclusion which, fortunately for Germany, did not make them feel any less devotedly German. Bleichroder, the banker who gave Bismarck the necessary credit for the Franco-Prussian War; Ballin, the developer of maritime trade; Emil Rathenau, founder of the Allgemeine Elektrizitäts-Gesellschaft, which electrified Germany; Fritz Haber, discoverer of the process for fixing nitrogen from the air, which made Germany independent of imported sources of nitrogen for explosives, were all born Jews and among them were responsible for a major proportion of Germany's booming energies. The German ruling class was likewise supported by an intensely industrious middle and lower class who applied themselves earnestly and worked incessantly, taking few holidays. They were better educated on the whole than those of other countries. Prussia had enforced full-time school attendance for children from seven to fourteen since the 1820's and by the nineties had two and a half times as many university students in proportion to the population as England.

The sovereign who ruled over this thriving people was busy and dynamic like them, but more restless than thorough. He was into everything and alert to everything, sometimes with useful results. When the Barnum and Bailey Circus played Germany in 1901, the Kaiser, hearing about the remarkable speed with which trains were loaded, sent officers to observe the method. They learned that instead of loading heavy equipment separately on each freight car from the side, the circus people laid connecting iron treads through the whole length of the train on which all equipment, loaded from one end, could be rolled straight through. By this means three trains, of twenty-two cars each, could be loaded in an hour. The circus technique promptly went to feed the insatiable appetite for speed of the German mobilization system. The Kaiser's observers also noted the advantages of the great circus cooking wagons over stationary field kitchens, and adopted them for the Army so that meals could be cooked on the move.

The Kaiser took immense care always to wear appropriate uniform for every occasion. When the Moscow Art Theatre played Berlin, he attended the performance in Russian uniform. He liked to arrange military pageants and festivals, especially the annual spring and autumn parades of the Berlin garrison on the huge Tempelhof Field, where formations of 50,000 troops, equivalent to several divisions, could maneuver. He felt himself no less an authority on the arts, on which he held decided if not advanced views. When Gerhart Hauptmann, author of *The Weavers*, a gloomy working-class drama, was designated by the judges to receive the Schiller Prize in 1896, the Kaiser awarded it instead to Ernst von Wildenbruch, a favorite of his own who produced historical dramas in the style of *William Tell*. When the Rhodes scholarships were established, the Kaiser nominated Germany's candidates, "vulgar rich people," according to a member of Balliol, "who don't have a good effect at all." One shot a deer in Magdalen College park and had to be recalled by the embarrassed monarch's order. The Kaiser liked to think of himself, as he explained in his speech dedicating the Sieges Allee in 1901, as an "art-loving prince . . . around whom artists could gather" and in whose reign the arts could flourish as in classical times "in the direct intercourse of the employer with the artist." As the employer in this case, he had given to the sculptors of the statues "clear and intelligible tasks" and "ordered and defined" their work but thereafter left them free to carry out his ideas. He could now take pride in the results, which were "untainted by so-called modern tendencies."

Art, he announced, should represent the Ideal. "To us Germans great ideals, lost to other peoples, have become permanent possessions" which "only the German people" can preserve. He cited the educational effect of art upon the lower classes, who after a hard working day could be lifted out of themselves by contemplation of beauty and the Ideal. But, he sternly warned, "when art descends into the gutter as so often nowadays, choosing to represent misery as even more unlovely than it is already," then art "sins against the German people." As the country's ruler he felt deeply hurt when the masters of art "do not with sufficient energy oppose such tendencies."

The theatre too, he explained in 1898, should contribute to culture of the soul, elevate morals and "inculcate respect for the highest traditions of our German Fatherland." So that the Royal Theatre, which he invariably referred to as "my theatre," should perform this function, he arranged a series of his favorite historical dramas for working-class attendance at suitable prices. He was a stickler for accuracy of detail in scenery and costumes and, for a ballet-pantomime on Sardanapalus, ransacked the museums of the world for information on Assyrian chariots.

He liked to attend and even personally direct rehearsals at the Royal Opera and Royal Theatre. Driving up in his Imperial black and yellow motorcar, he would establish himself at a big business-like table in the auditorium, furnished with a pile of paper and array of pencils. An aide in uniform stood alongside and held up his hand whenever the Kaiser signed to him, whereupon the performance halted, the Kaiser with gestures explained what improvements he wanted, and the actors tried again. He referred to the actors as "*meine Schauspieler*," and once when one of them, Max Pohl, was suddenly taken ill, he said to an acquaintance, "Fancy, my Pohl had a seizure yesterday." The acquaintance, thinking he meant a pet dog who had had a fit, commiserated, "Ach, the poor brute."

In music the Kaiser's tastes were naturally conservative. He liked Bach, the greatest of all, and Handel. As regards opera, to which he was devoted if it was German, he would say, "Gluck is the man for me; Wagner is too noisy." At performances he stayed to the end and frequently commanded concerts at the Palace, whose programs he arranged himself and whose rehearsals he attended, expecting them to have been rehearsed previously and everything to run smoothly. On a trip to Norway he summoned Grieg to an audience at the

German Legation and having assembled an orchestra of forty players, placed two chairs in front for himself and the composer, who was requested to conduct the *Peer Gynt Suite.* During the music the Kaiser continually corrected the composer's tempi and expression and swayed his body in "oriental movements" in time to Anitra's dance which "quite electrified him." Next day the whole performance was repeated by a full orchestra on board the Imperial yacht, *Hohenzollern.*

Admiration for the Kaiser during the early part of his reign was a national cult. After the prolonged rule of his grandfather, Wilhelm I, followed by the painful three months' reign of a dying man, the advent of a young and vigorous monarch who obviously relished his role and played up to the glamour of a king was welcomed by the nation. His flashing eye and martial attitudes, his heroic poses enhanced by all that brilliant dress and stirring music could add, thrilled his subjects. Young men went to the court hairdresser to have their moustaches turned up in points by a special curling device; officers and bureaucrats practiced flashing their eyes; employers addressed their workers in the Kaiser's most dynamic style, as did Diederich, title character of Heinrich Mann's harsh satire of Wilhelmine Germany, *Der Unterthan* (The Loyal Subject): "I have taken the rudder into my own hands," he says on inheriting the family factory. "My course is set straight and I am guiding you to glorious times. Those who wish to help me are heartily welcome; whoever opposes me I will smash. There is only one master here and I am he. I am responsible only to God and my own conscience. You can always count on my fatherly benevolence but revolutionary sentiments will be shattered against my unbending will." The workers stare at him dumb with amazement and his assembled family with awe and respect.

The first half of the Kaiser's reign which began in 1888 coincided with the first flush of the Nietzschean cult. The monarch's ceaseless activity in every kind of endeavor made him seem to be the universal man, as if, rightfully in Germany, crowning the century of her greatest development, *Übermensch* had appeared, where else but at the head of the nation. Hero-worship was the natural consequence. Diederich in the novel sees the Kaiser for the first time at the head of a mounted squadron as he rides out with a face of "stony seriousness" to meet a workers' demonstration at the Brandenburger Tor. Transported by loyalty, the workers, who have been shouting "Bread! Work!" now wave their hats and cry, "Follow him! Follow the Emperor!" Running alongside, Diederich stumbles and sits down violently in a puddle with his legs in the air, splashed with muddy water. The Kaiser, catching sight of him, slaps his thigh and says to his aide with a laugh, "There's a royalist for you; there's a loyal subject!" Diederich stares after him "from the depths of his puddle, open-mouthed."

In Diederich, who is always brutalizing someone beneath him while sucking up to someone above him, Mann savagely portrayed one aspect of his countrymen—the servility which was the other side of the bully. The banker Edgar Speyer, returning to his birthplace in Frankfurt-am-Main in 1886 after twenty-seven years in England, found that three victorious wars and the establishment of Empire had created a changed atmosphere in Germany that was "intolerable" to him. German nationalism had replaced German liberalism. Great prosperity and self-satisfaction acted, it seemed to him, like a narcotic on the people, leaving them content to forego their liberty under a rampant militarism and a servility to Army and Kaiser that were "unbelievable." University professors who in his youth had been leaders of liberalism "now kowtowed to the authorities in the most servile manner." Oppressed, Speyer gave up after five years and returned to England.

What Speyer observed, Mommsen attempted to explain. "Bismarck has broken the nation's backbone," he wrote in 1886. "The injury done by the Bismarck era is infinitely greater than its benefits. . . . The subjugation of the German personality, of the German mind, was a misfortune that cannot be undone." What Mommsen failed to say was that Bismarck could not have succeeded against the German grain.

In the nineties, as a convinced believer in *Übermensch*, Strauss shared the general admiration for the Kaiser. Personal experience as conductor of the Berlin Royal Opera modified it. After conducting a performance of Weber's tuneful *Der Freischütz*, one of the Kaiser's favorites, he was summoned to the Imperial presence. "So, you are another of these modern composers," stated the Kaiser. Strauss bowed. Mentioning a contemporary,

Schillings, whose work he had heard, the Kaiser said, "It was detestable; there isn't an ounce of melody." Strauss bowed and suggested there was melody but often hidden behind the polyphony. The Kaiser frowned and pronounced, "You are one of the worst." Strauss this time merely bowed. "All modern music is worthless," repeated the royal critic, "there isn't an ounce of melody in it." Strauss bowed. "I prefer *Freischütz*," stated the Kaiser firmly. Strauss deferred. "Your Majesty, I also prefer *Freischütz*," he replied.

If the Kaiser was not the hero he had supposed, Strauss was not long in finding a better one—himself. This seemed a natural subject for his next major work, unbashfully entitled *Ein Heldenleben* (A Hero's Life). Since *Aus Italien* his subjects had never been moods or pictures, sunken cathedrals or pastoral scenes, but always Man: Man in struggle and search, seeking the meaning of existence, contending against his enemies and against his own passions, engaged in the three great adventures: battle, love and death. Macbeth, Don Juan, the nameless hero of *Tod und Verklärung*, Till, Zarathustra, Don Quixote, were all voyagers on the soul's journey. A portrait of the artist now joined their company.

Strauss's personal experience of the two first of the three great adventures had been adequate if not epic. He had had battles with critics which left wounds, and in 1894 he had married. Pauline de Ahna, whom he met when he was twenty-three, was the daughter of a retired General and amateur baritone who gave local recitals of Wagnerian excerpts. Following his lead, the daughter had studied singing at the Munich Academy but had made little progress professionally until Strauss fell in love with her and combined instruction with courtship so effectively that in two years he introduced her to the Weimar Opera in leading soprano roles. She sang Elsa in *Lohengrin*, Pamina in *The Magic Flute*, Beethoven's Fidelio and the heroine of Strauss's own opera *Guntram*. Once, when rehearsing Elisabeth in *Tannhäuser*, she fell into an argument with him over tempo, and shrieking "frightful insults," threw the score at his head and rushed off to her dressing room. Strauss followed and members of the orchestra listened in awe to sounds of feminine rage audible through the closed door, followed by prolonged silence. Wondering which of the two, conductor or prima donna, might have killed the other, a delegation of trembling players knocked on the door and when Strauss opened it the spokesman stammered that he and his colleagues, shocked by the soprano's behavior, felt they owed it to the honored Herr Kapellmeister to refuse in future to play in any opera in which she had a role. "That distresses me," Strauss replied, smiling, "as I have just become engaged to Fräulein de Ahna."

The pattern of this occasion was retained in marriage. The wife shrieked, the husband smiled and evidently enjoyed being bullied. At parties Frau Strauss did not permit him to dance with other ladies. At home she practiced housewifery with "ruthless fanaticism," requiring her husband to wipe his feet on three different doormats before entering his own house. Every guest of no matter what age or rank was greeted by the order, "Wipe your feet." Floors were as clean as table tops and servants who failed to leave the contents of linen closets in mathematically perfect rows were pursued by the inevitable shrieks of wrath. Enthusiastically submitting to, as well as inflicting, punishment, Frau Strauss engaged the daily services of a masseuse of the violent school during whose visits Strauss was obliged to go for a walk to avoid hearing the tortured screams of his wife. She bore him one child, a son, Franz, born in 1897, who at once expressed the family tradition of *molto con brio* by "screaming like hell," according to a proud report to the child's grandparents.

When to her husband's accompaniment Frau Strauss sang his songs, which usually ended with a long coda on the piano, she flourished a large chiffon handkerchief which she would fling down with a gesture at the end to keep the audience's eyes on her instead of on the pianist. To guests she would explain in detail, while Strauss listened with an indulgent smile, how and why her marriage was a shocking *mésalliance*. She should have married that dashing young Hussar; now she was tied to a man whose music was not even comparable to Massenet's. During a visit to London when Strauss conducted *Heldenleben* and a toast was proposed in his honor at a dinner at the Speyers', his wife excitedly interrupted, "No, no!"—pointing to herself—"no, no! to Strauss *de Ahna*." Strauss merely laughed and seemed to an observer to enjoy his wife's claim of precedence.

She was responsible for his orderly habits. His worktable was a model of neatness, with sketches and notebooks arranged, filed and indexed as scrupulously as the records of a law firm. His handwriting was exquisitely clear and his scores "miracles of calligraphy," with hardly an erasure or correction. His songs might be dashed off at odd moments, sometimes during the intervals of concerts or operas when he was conducting, but his longer pieces were composed only at his summer home, first at Marquardstein in Upper Bavaria, later at his second home near Garmisch. Here in his studio he worked regularly from breakfast to lunch and often, or so he told an interviewer, through the afternoon and evening until one or two o'clock in the morning. He enjoyed writing his incredibly intricate scores, often so complicated in their excessive subdivision of groups and interweaving of melodies that the theme was beyond the reach of the listener's ear. Discernible to the eye of an expert score-reader who would marvel at the mathematical ingenuity of the scheme, such music was called *Augenmusik* (eye music) by the Germans. When complimented on his skill Strauss said it was nothing compared to that of a new young man in Vienna, Arnold Schönberg, who required sixty-five staves for his scores and had to have his music paper specially printed. Strauss's own facility was such that he said to a visitor, "Go right on and talk for I can write this score and talk at the same time." A symphonic poem took him three or four months, with scoring usually completed in Berlin between rehearsals and conducting engagements.

Visitors at the summer home were met by arrangements which exhibited a talent for organization on the part of Frau Strauss not inferior to that of the late Field Marshal von Moltke. A speaking tube was fixed to the gate under a sign telling the visitor to ring a bell and then put his ear to the tube. A voice over the tube demanded his name and if found acceptable, informed him the gate was now unlocked. Another sign instructed him how to open it and to be sure to close it behind him.

Frau Strauss did not permit dawdling. If her husband should be found on occasion wandering aimlessly around the house, she would command, "*Richard jetzt gehst componieren!*" (Go ahead and compose!), and he would obey. If he worked too hard she would say, "Richard, put down that pencil!" and he would put it down. When he conducted the first performance in Vienna of his second opera, *Feuersnot*, Frau Strauss attended in the box of the Austrian conductor-composer Gustav Mahler and fumed throughout, as Frau Mahler recalled: "Nobody could like this trash; we were liars to pretend, knowing as well as she did that there wasn't an original note in it. Everything was stolen from Wagner and a dozen others better than her husband." The Mahlers sat in silent embarrassment not daring to agree, for "this shrew was quite capable of twisting the words in our mouths and suddenly screaming that we had made all those comments." After enthusiastic applause and many curtain calls, Strauss, beaming, came to the box and asked, "Well, *Pauksel*, what do you think of my success?"

"You thief!" she screamed. "You have the nerve to show yourself? I'm not going with you. You're rotten." Hurriedly pushed into Mahler's office, she continued her berating behind closed doors until Strauss stumbled out followed by his mate who announced in awful tones that she was returning to the hotel and "I sleep alone tonight."

"Can't I walk with you at least?" Strauss begged humbly.

"All right—ten steps behind me!" and she stalked off followed by the hero of the evening at a respectful distance. Later, looking subdued and exhausted, he rejoined the Mahlers for a late supper and spent the remainder of the evening with pencil and paper figuring out the royalties in the event of a major or minor success. Making money interested him as much as any aspect of his profession.

Strauss composed *Ein Heldenleben* in the summer of 1898, describing it as "a largish tone poem . . . with lots of horns, always expressive of the heroic." When finished it played for forty minutes, longer than any of his previous works. Artists had often portrayed themselves before, but Strauss, reflecting the national mood, was probably the first to name his self-portrait a Hero. He conducted the premiere himself on March 3, 1899, which, considering the provocative title, the nature of the music and the program notes, displayed considerable bravado. *Heldenleben* was divided into six sections, dealing with "The Hero," his "Adversaries," his "Consort," his "Battle," his "Works of Peace" and finally his "Escape from the World and

Fulfillment of Life." In form it was an expanded sonata on a vast scale with recognizable statements of theme, development and recapitulation. After the Hero is proclaimed by the horns in a proud theme rising to fortissimo, the woodwinds introduce the Adversaries in busy, sniggering music that as plainly says "critics" as the bleating brasses in *Don Quixote* said "sheep." The Consort is played by solo violin in a series of cadenzas, alternately seductive and shrewish, with outspoken not to say painfully frank marks of expression on the score, among them, "*Heuchlerisch schmachtend*" (Hypocritically gushing), plus "frivolously," "haughtily," "affectionately," and at the last, in a passionate and moving love duet, "tenderly and lovingly." Meanwhile three trumpeters have tiptoed off stage and suddenly from a distance sound the call to arms. With fiercely scurrying stings, rattling kettledrums, fanfares of brasses and thunder of bass drums, the battle rages in a confused crescendo of noise that, not unlike real war, sounds as if all the generals had blundered. To the ears of 1899 it sounded "hideous." Through the turmoil the Hero's theme returns triumphantly. His Works of Peace, making the autobiographical point unmistakable, are themes from the composer's earlier works. The Hero's final apotheosis is accomplished to muted solemn music which in later program notes Strauss designated as "funeral rites with flags and laurel wreaths lowered on a hero's grave."

Listening to the second performance at Cologne a few weeks later, Romain Rolland, fresh from his own exhilarating battle at the opening of *Les Loups*, was transported with excitement. Although some auditors hissed and some members of the orchestra even laughed at the music, "I clenched my teeth and trembled and my heart saluted the young Siegfried resurrected." In the "tremendous din and uproar" of the battle music, Rolland heard "the storming of towns, the terrible charge of cavalry which makes the earth tremble and our hearts beat." He thought it "the most splendid battle that has ever been painted in music." There were gulfs in which the musical idea disappeared for a time but emerged again, sometimes mediocre in melodic sentiment but grand in "harmonic and rhythmic invention and orchestral brilliance." Strauss seemed to Rolland to express a will "heroic, dominating, eager and powerful to a sublime degree." Touched too by the Nietzschean spirit,

Rolland found this the reason why "Strauss is noble and at the present quite unique. One feels in him the force that has dominion over men." In the midst of admiration, however, Rolland also felt French and could not resist drawing political lessons. Now that Strauss, he decided, like Germany, had "proved his power by victory, his pride knows no limit." In him as a man "of vital energy, morbidly overexcited, unbalanced but controlled by an effort of will power," the Frenchman saw reflected the face of Germany. Nevertheless Rolland became his friend and celebrator.

He had met Strauss for the first time eight years before in Bayreuth and again in January, 1899, when Strauss conducted *Zarathustra* in Paris. It was the Dionysus of Nietzsche let loose. "Aha!" Rolland wrote then, "Germany as the All-Powerful will not keep her balance for long. Nietzsche, Strauss, the Kaiser—giddiness blows through her brain. Neroism is in the air!" Rolland thought he could detect in the reiterated theme of Disgust in the tone poems and in the deaths that concluded them, a German "sickness hidden beneath the strength and military tautness." He heard it again in *Heldenleben*.

When on this occasion he called on Strauss at his apartment in Charlottenburg, Berlin's fashionable suburb, he found him more Bavarian than Nietzschean, with "a certain humorous buffoonery, paradoxical and satirical like that of Till Eulenspiegel." Like Till he delighted to scandalize the philistines. He alternated between energy and bouts of "laziness, softness and ironic indifference." Though cordial and well-behaved toward Rolland, he could be short with others, scarcely listening to what was said to him and occasionally muttering, "*Was? Ach, so so.*" He behaved badly at table, sitting with his legs crossed at the side, holding his plate under his chin to eat and stuffing himself with sweets. In the drawing room he might lie down on a sofa, punching the cushions with his fists, and "insolently indifferent to those around him," fall asleep with his eyes open.

It was difficult to decide whether he was Till or Superman. In an article for the *Revue de Paris* Rolland presented him as "the artist-type of this new Germany, the reflection of a heroic pride close to delirium, of a Nietzschean egoism which preaches the cult of force and disdain for weakness." But he had to admit the picture was overdrawn. Rolland suffered from the same difficulty as Matthew Arnold's niece in Max Beerbohm's cartoon who was forced to ask, "Why, Uncle Matthew, oh why, will you not be always wholly serious?" Strauss would not live up to his image either and was quite prepared to admit it. "You're right," he wrote to Rolland. "I'm no hero; I haven't got the necessary strength; I'm not made for battle. . . . I don't want to make the effort. At the moment all I want is to make sweet and happy music. No more heroics." The fact was that in the surrounding Nietzschean ethos, *Heldenleben* had seemed like the thing to do; it reflected the national mood more than his own.

Strauss was a string plucked by the *Zeitgeist.* Although he had never known any but the most comfortable bourgeois circumstances, he sensed and expressed the revolutionary rumble of the working class in two of his finest songs so effectively that one, "Der Arbeitsmann" (The Workingman) became an anthem of the Socialist party. Another, "Das Lied des Steinklopfers" (Song of the Stonecutter), was his own favorite among his songs. When these were sung by Germany's leading concert baritone, Ludwig Wüllner, with the composer at the piano, they had such dramatic power that "hearing these grim defiant sounds," wrote a critic, "was like hearing the Marseillaise of tomorrow." Of another of his songs for the male voice, the "Nächtlicher Gesang" (Night Song), it was said that it could "make one shudder in broad daylight."

In *Heldenleben*, however, convinced admirers began to detect evidence of a deep-seated flaw in the composer. Ernest Newman believed Strauss had enriched music with more new ideas than anyone since Wagner and had "put into music a greater energy, a greater stress of feeling and a greater weight of thinking than any other composer of the day." Yet he did not seem able to restrain an unworthy desire to "stagger humanity." His technical facility and command over ideas was such that he could do anything he wanted and there was no limit to his inventiveness, but he could not keep it within bounds. Newman would willingly have left the hall during the "sniggering, snarling and grunting" of the Adversaries in *Heldenleben*, which he considered "freak" music like the sheep in *Don Quixote.* He felt a failure of taste, a streak of vulgarity in a man willing to spoil "two of the finest scores of the Nineteenth Century" with such "monstrosities" as these. Such reactions merely stimulated Strauss to further freaks as a sign of his contempt for what were claimed to be the "eternal" laws of beauty in music. The fact that he insisted on making the critics pay for their seats, causing "screams of agony" all over the Continent, did not help matters.

To the younger critics Strauss's discords and dissonances were not as distressing as his freaks. Lawrence Gilman, an American, thought the dissonance of the Battle music, like that depicting the mental confusion of Don Quixote, was "eloquent and meaningful" and quite different from that other kind achieved, as Whistler said, "by the simple expedient of sitting on the keyboard." Apart from the freaks there were enough marvels of music in Strauss's work to have put him above the sneers and carping; it was the non-musical aspect of his work—that is, the didactic realism of his program notes—which kept him in the center of critical furor. In the same spirit in which Philip Ernst, having omitted the tree from his picture, decided it must be cut down, Strauss insisted on painting the tree and then hanging a sign on it saying, "This is a tree." As a result critics leaped to take issue, as when Newman said of a trombone passage in *Zarathustra* labeled "Disgust," which followed "Delights and Passions," that "it no more suggests disgust than it does the toothache." It was no defence by his friends to insist that Strauss wanted his music to be listened to as music and that he added the program notes only under the urgent pressure of colleagues and publishers. An artist certain of his standards would not have made the concession and in any case the literary labels were in his mind and scribbled on his scores when he composed.

In France Claude Debussy, too, was writing descriptive music. Rather than literal and narrative, like that of Strauss, it was elusive and shimmering, after the manner of the Impressionists in painting and the Symbolists in poetry. The Symbolist credo was to suggest, not to name, an object. Where Strauss stated, Debussy suggested. "If people insist on wanting to understand what happens in a symphonic poem, we may as well give up writing them," he said. Literal meaning was a matter of equal unconcern to Sibelius. When asked by a friend after listening to a recording of his Fourth Symphony what it really meant, he said after a short pause, "Play the record again."

Debussy, however, admired Strauss, who was two years his junior, and acknowledged that the *Verklärung* (Transfiguration) in *Tod und Verklärung* "takes place before our very eyes." When he heard *Till Eulenspiegel* in 1903 he thought its flouting of musical laws amounted almost "to an hour of music in a lunatic asylum. . . . You do not know whether to roar with laughter or groan with pain and you are filled with wonder when you find anything in its customary place." Nevertheless he thought it a work of "genius" and was awed by its "amazing orchestral assurance" and the "mad rhythm that sweeps us along from beginning to end and forces us to share in the hero's pranks." What impressed him most about *Heldenleben*, which he also heard in 1903, was its "cyclonic energy." The listener is no longer master of his emotions: "I say again that it is impossible to withstand his irresistible domination." Debussy's own orchestral prelude, *L'Après-midi d'un Faune*, based on Mallarmé's poem, and his *Nocturnes* for orchestra, which appeared in the nineties, led Strauss to return the compliment. Debussy was "a remarkable and altogether unique genius," he said, "within his own limited domain."

Strauss was always rather surprised when someone else produced work of high quality. "I had no idea that anyone except myself was capable of writing such good music as this," he remarked "charmingly and characteristically" to Beecham on hearing a work of Delius. He never listened to Puccini and did not know *Manon* from *Tosca*, or *Butterfly* from *Bohème*, although Puccini's works were exactly contemporary with his own. Italian opera was not highly regarded in Germany. He was generous, however, in performing the works of other contemporaries. Unable to conduct modern music at the Berlin Royal Opera while the Kaiser's taste held sway, he founded an orchestra of his own, the Tonkünstler, to encourage "progressive principles" in music. Subsidized by private patrons, the Tonkünstler played all Liszt's tone poems in chronological order as well as Strauss's own works and introduced to Berlin performances of Tchaikovsky, Bruckner, Hugo Wolf, Elgar and, if not Debussy, at least his predecessors, Charpentier and d'Indy. Once in London on a visit to the National Gallery in company with Edgar Speyer and Edward Elgar, the group stopped in front of Tintoretto's "St. George and the Dragon" while Speyer remarked, "Here we have a revolutionary who broke ground at the very end of the glorious Venetian period. Shall we say that Tintoretto was to painting what our friend Richard Strauss is today to music?" Much struck by this remark, Strauss returned to the painting on their way back through the rooms, studied it again and exclaimed, "Speyer is right. I am the Tintoretto of music!"

From this height he could afford, and did not stint, encouragement of less renowned colleagues. On hearing a performance in Düsseldorf in 1902 of Elgar's *Dream of Gerontius*, based on a poem by Cardinal Newman, Strauss proposed a toast "to the welfare and success of the first English Progressive, Meister Edward Elgar, and of the young progressive school of English composers." Such tribute from Strauss startled the musical world and aroused the usual critics' uproar which it amused him to provoke. Though disliking the terms of the compliment all England was impressed and flattered. Strauss was no less appreciative of the ultra-modern Schönberg, whose experiments in atonality so impressed him that he arranged for the young composer to be given the Liszt Fellowship and appointment as Professor of Composition in the Stern Academy in Berlin. On the occasion of the premiere of Mahler's *Third Symphony* in Cologne in 1902, Strauss decided its success by going up to the platform and applauding ostentatiously. From 1900 on, as president of the Allgemeiner Deutscher Musikverein, founded by Liszt, he invited foreign composers to conduct their new works at the Society's festivals. Sibelius, whom he invited to present his *Swan of Tuonela* in 1900, found him "extraordinary amiable." When Strauss himself took the podium at these concerts he was greeted by the orchestra with a threefold fanfare and by the audience rising to its feet.

In England and the United States his renown was large and his appearances lionized. A Strauss Festival lasting three days was held in London in 1903 at which all his works from *Aus Italien* to *Heldenleben* were played. Strauss liked the English "very much," as he once told Rolland. For one thing they made traveling comfortable in places like Egypt, so that "you can always be sure of finding clean rooms and modern conveniences." For Strauss this proved they were a superior people and, according to the Nietzschean formula, they and not the Boers should have had Germany's sympathy during the South African War. "The Boers are a barbarian people, backward, still living in the Seventeenth Century. The English are very civilized and very strong. It's a thoroughly good thing that the strong should triumph."

In London he could enjoy the hospitality of Edgar Speyer, head of the syndicate which owned Queen's Hall and manager of its orchestra, who with his wife, a professional violinist before her marriage, made their home at Grosvenor Square a center of musical and artistic society. Here he could meet Henry James or Debussy, listen to Mme Grieg sing her husband's songs and enjoy a sumptuous dinner in company with John Sargent, to whom painting was a profession but music and food a matter of love. Noticing a gypsy band which had been wandering around London playing Spanish music, Strauss proposed that it be hidden in the garden to play during one of the Speyer parties, with results that tantalized Sargent, who was torn between his dinner and the need to run to the window to discover the source of the music.

In America, Strauss's compositions had been known and played ever since Theodore Thomas, conductor of the Chicago Symphony, had performed his *Symphony in F minor* in 1884 and the German-born Emil Paur of the Boston Symphony had played *Aus Italien* in 1888. Thomas and Paur, who later moved to the New York Philharmonic, continued to play Strauss's works as they came out, and in 1904 an American premiere was arranged for his newest work, *Sinfonia Domestica*, as the feature of a Strauss Festival to be held in New York. The composer was invited to conduct the new piece as well as a subsequent concert of his works in Chicago. Thomas, a fervent admirer over twenty years, considered him at this point in his career "the greatest musician now living and one of the greatest musical pioneers of all times."

With the new wealth of American business tycoons overflowing their coffers, the United States was developing a whole new audience and source of support for music and the arts. It was a time of exuberant expenditure and large ideas. When the rector of Trinity Church in New York wanted a new pulpit, he asked the senior partner of the leading architectural firm, McKim, Mead and White, to design him something "big, broad, ample and simple but rich in the right places." When the same McKim built the Boston Public Library a plaque was put up honoring the "splendid amplitude" of his genius. Splendid amplitude was in the air. Louis Tiffany designed for himself a house with a palatial flight of stairs leading up, between walls with complete Sudanese Negro huts built into them, to a hall so vast the ceiling was invisible in the dim light. In the center of the hall a black chimney soared to infinity, four immense fireplaces blazed, each with flames of a different color, mysterious light glowed through hanging Tiffany glass lamps and an invisible organist played the prelude from *Parsifal.*

The several major American orchestras subsidized by copper kings, railroad barons and their kind provided an important extra source of concert fees and royalties. Strauss was delighted to come and the concertgoing American public breathlessly awaited the "most eminent of living composers," who, they were told by *Harper's Weekly*, uttered "imaginings of overpowering significance" and touched "the margin of the sublime."

Sinfonia Domestica, it was apparent on first performance, touched the ridiculous. Although it was performed by the composer's wish without program notes so that it could be listened to "purely as music," Strauss had already told an interviewer that it illustrated "a day in my family life" in the form of a triple figure representing "Papa, Mama and Baby." At the premiere it was presented only as Introduction and Scherzo, Adagio, Double Fugue and Finale, but, as usual, the composer soon obliged with an official analysis for subsequent performances which indicated the baby in its bath, the parents' happiness, the quarrels of aunts and uncles over family resemblances—"Just like his Papa!" "Just like his Mama!"—and similar stuff. Although there was tender melody of Strauss's finest in the cradle song and love duet, the dominant impression is of thumping and screaming and raucous confusion suggesting a maddened circus. If this is German home life, German history becomes understandable. Even longer than *Heldenleben*, the work astonished and offended most listeners. "If all the sacred elephants in India were driven into the Ganges at the same moment," said a renowned but unnamed conductor to Beecham when the piece was played in London some months later, "they could not have made half as much noise as that one little Bavarian baby in its bath." Gurgling bath water and ringing alarm clock were not what Wagner had meant by "the stuff of music." The vulgarity of the new century seemed suddenly confirmed by its most eminent composer. Strauss missed the point. "I do not see why I should not compose a Symphony about myself," he told Rolland. "I find myself quite as interesting as Napoleon or Alexander."

His choice of two world conquerors was indicative. In music the German assumption of superiority was by this time beginning to annoy other peoples. "German musicians always put a German arrival on a pedestal so that they can idolise it," wrote Grieg to Delius in 1903. "Wagner is dead but they must have something to satisfy their patriotism and they would rather have ersatz than nothing at all." In 1905 at a music festival in Strasbourg, capital of formerly French, now German, Alsace, the stated purpose was to bring French and Germans together through art. In a three-day program, however, only two French works were performed, while the first day of concerts began with Weber and ended with Wagner, the second day was devoted to Brahms, Mahler and Strauss and the last day entirely to Beethoven. The selection from Wagner of the last scene from *Die Meistersinger*, in which Hans Sachs denounces foreign insincerity and frivolity, suggested to one auditor a certain "lack of courtesy."

The world's increasing irritation with Germany appeared in the eagerness with which foreign critics seized upon evidence of a decline in Strauss's inspiration. Everyone jumped on *Sinfonia Domestica*. Newman was astonished that "a composer of genius should have fallen so low" and Gilman revealed the degree to which Germany was getting on the nerves of other nations. Quoting Matthew Arnold to the effect that Teutonism tends insistently toward the "ugly and ignoble," he wrote that "only a Teuton with a Teuton's failure of tact" could have contrived *Domestica*.

The *Zeitgeist* did not call for Papa, Mama and Baby. A restlessness fermenting under the superabundant materialism was producing in artists a desire to shock; to rip and slash the thick quilt of bourgeois comfort. Attuned as always, Strauss responded. *Sinfonia Domestica* had shocked by banality, but now he felt a need to unnerve and appall and went straight from Bavarian family life to a theme of depraved and lascivious passion—*Salome*, in Oscar Wilde's version.

A drama as lush and gruesome as Wilde trying hard could make it, *Salome* was a pursuit of sensation for its own sake, an effort to produce what Baudelaire called "the phosphorescence of putrescence." The original play, written in French in 1891, went into rehearsal in London a year later with Sarah Bernhardt in the title role, but performance was banned by the Lord Chamberlain on the ground that its presentation of St. John the Baptist was sacrilege. Upon publication (with copies for the author's friends bound in "Tyrian purple and tired silver"), the play was denounced by *The Times* as "an arrangement in blood and ferocity, morbid, bizarre, repulsive and very offensive." In 1894 an English translation by Lord Alfred Douglas appeared, illustrated with luscious evil by the truest decadent of them all, Aubrey Beardsley. Three of his drawings, considered indecent by the publishers, had to be withdrawn. In 1896, when Wilde was in Reading Gaol, *Salome* was produced in Paris by the actor-manager Lugné-Poë at his Théâtre de l'Oeuvre, with himself as Herod but without Bernhardt. The quintessence of decadence was overripe and it was not a success. In Germany, however, *Salome* matched a craving for the horrendous and found its place. First produced in Breslau in 1901, its real success came in 1902 with a production by Max Reinhardt at his Kleines Theater in Berlin, where Strauss saw it.

More a poem than a play, Wilde's *Salome* was an exercise in purple, an orgy in words, which succeeded on paper but embarrassed on the stage. It offered the spectacle of Salome pouring out her hot erotic pleas to the eyes, the hair, the limbs, the body and the love of Iokanaan, of King Herod avid for his stepdaughter, of her voluptuous dance to excite his lust and win her ghastly desire, of the black Executioner's huge arm rising from the pit holding the bearded bloody head of the Prophet who had scorned her, of her necrophilic raptures addressed to the head on the platter and her final conquest of its dead lips, of Herod's climactic order of horror and remorse, "Kill that woman!" and of her death crushed beneath the shields of his soldiers. Performed in flesh and blood it delighted the Berlin audience. Wilde's moonlit fantasia, in Germany, came into its own and enjoyed a phenomenal run of two hundred performances.

The undercurrent of morbidity in Germany, which Rolland had already noticed, grew more apparent in the first decade of the new century. It increased in proportion as Germany's wealth and strength and arrogance increased, as if the pressure of so much industrial success and military power were creating an inner reaction in the form of a need to negate, to expose the worms and passions writhing within that masterful, prosperous, well-behaved, orderly people. It was as if Bismarck had perforce produced Krafft-Ebing. Indeed Krafft-Ebing's *Psychopathia Sexualis* which appeared in 1886 provided a well of lurid resource on which the German drama, then the most vigorous form of national literature, could draw.

The theatre ranked with music and opera as a German pleasure and, beginning in the nineties, broke out in a surge of problem plays stemming from Ibsen and in new styles of acting and experiments in stagecraft. Proclaiming the doctrine of Realism and Naturalism, the Freie Bühne (Independent Theatre) of Berlin, copied after the Théâtre Libre of Paris, opened in 1889 with Ibsen's *Ghosts* followed by Hauptmann's first play, *Before Dawn*. Theatres sprouted and multiplied. Society's masks were torn off and the "beast in man," Zola's objective, was enthusiastically exposed. Besides Ibsen, Strindberg's cruel *Miss Julie*, Tolstoy's *Powers of Darkness*, Zola's *Therèse Raquin*, the symbolist and neo-romantic dramas of Maeterlinck, D'Annunzio and von Hofmannsthal, the social plays of Ibsen's disciple Shaw, the worldly satires of Arthur Schnitzler of Vienna and a proliferation of German tragedies were performed. Student stage societies revived *Oedipus Rex* and Euripides, the Modern Touring Company took the new drama to the provinces, and a people's theatre, the Freie Volksbühne, followed by the Neue Freie Volksbühne, allied it to Socialism. In Munich, the Intimes Theater was founded in 1895 by Ernst von Wolzogen, librettist of Strauss's opera *Feuersnot*. To achieve the same intimate atmosphere for experimental plays, Reinhardt founded the Kleines

Theater in 1902, where, besides *Salome*, he produced Maxim Gorky's awful look at society's dregs, *The Lower Depths*.

Tragedy was the staple of the German theatre. Social comedies with happy endings were not a German genre. German fun was confined to buffoonery, either painful or coarse. Their tragedies were not so much curative, like Ibsen's, nor compassionate, like Chekhov's, but obsessively focused on mankind's cruelty to man, on his bent toward self-destruction and on death. Death by murder, suicide or some more esoteric form resolved nearly all German drama of the nineties and early 1900's. In Hauptmann's *Hannele* the child heroine dies of neglect and abuse in an almshouse, in his *Sunken Bell* Heinrich's wife drowns herself in a lake and he drinks a poisoned goblet, in *Rose Bernd* the title character, seduced and deserted, strangles her newborn child, in *Henschel* the title character hangs himself after betraying his dead wife by marrying a tart who lets his child die of neglect, in *Michael Kramer* a sensitive son is driven to suicide by an overbearing father, a popular theme in Germany rich in such fathers. In Sudermann's *Magda* only the father's fatal stroke prevents his shooting himself and his daughter, who needless to say is illegitimately pregnant, the invariable fate of the German heroine. An endless succession of them were driven in the grip of this circumstance to hysteria, insanity, crime, prison, infanticide and suicide. In Sudermann's *Sodoms Ende*, which varies the pattern if not the end, a dissolute young artist, corrupted by the wife of a banker, drives his foster sister to suicide and dies himself of a hemorrhage. In Wedekind's *Frühlings Erwachen* (Spring's Awakening), first effort of a playwright who was to exceed all the rest, the discovery of sex by adolescents conflicting with the prurience of adults produces total catastrophe: the fourteen-year-old heroine, being with child, dies, apparently of a mismanaged abortion; the boy is expelled from school and sent to a reformatory by his parents; his friend, unable to bear life, commits suicide and reappears in a graveyard with his head under his arm in a closing scene of opaque symbolism. In the course of the action a third boy, in a scene of explicit auto-eroticism, addresses a passionate love declaration to the picture of a naked Venus which he then drops down the toilet. First produced in 1891, the play was a sensational success and in book form went into twenty-six editions.

Born in the same year as Strauss, Wedekind was a writer of satanic talent who had been an actor, journalist, circus publicity agent, singer of grisly ballads for *Überbrettl* and while on the staff of *Simplicissimus* served a term in prison for *lèse majesté*. "I have the imagination of disaster and see life as ferocious and sinister" exactly described him, though it was Henry James who said it of himself. *Frühlings Erwachen*, if taken as a plea for sex education, at least had a social message and a quality of pity, but thereafter Wedekind saw nothing but the ferocious and sinister. In the same years in which Freud was carefully arriving at his discovery of the subconscious, Wedekind saw an awful vision of it and stripped off every covering to show it as purely malignant. From 1895 on, his plays plunged into a debauch of the vicious and perverse which seemed to have no argument but that humanity was vile. *Erdgeist* (Earth Spirit) and its sequel, *Die Büchse der Pandora* (Pandora's Box), take place in a world of pimps, crooks, harlots, blackmailers, murderers and hangmen surrounding the heroine, Lulu, who represents sensuality incarnate both heterosexual and lesbian. Her adventures proceed through brothels and dives, seduction, abortion, sadism, necrophilia and nymphomania in what a contemporary critic called "a torrent of sex foaming over jagged rocks of insanity and crime." It was sex, not creative in its primal function, but destructive, producing not life but death. Lulu's first husband dies of a stroke, her second, bedeviled by her perfidy, cuts his own throat, her third on discovering her infidelity committed with his son is killed by her. After prison, degradation and prostitution, she ends, logically, slashed to death by a Jack the Ripper in a final lethal explosion of that erotic power which Shaw, a very different playwright, was celebrating at the same time as the Life Force.

The all-pervasive influence of Nietzsche was at work. Shaw's *Man and Superman* distilled from it a philosophic idea, but the Germans took Nietzsche literally. His rejection of conventional morality, which he meant as a steppingstone to a higher ground, they embraced as a command to roam the gutter.

Sudermann quoted Nietzsche's words, "Only in the savage forest of vice can new domains of knowledge be conquered." As the domain of art if not knowledge, the same forest had lured the French decadents and the aesthetes of England in the movement that was abruptly terminated by Wilde's trial. In Germany the movement, carrying over into the new century, was pushed to new limits by Wedekind with a kind of frustrated ferocity. It was a form of rebellion against the overwhelming material success of the country, a sense of something wrong beneath the twelve-course dinners, the pomp of military parades, the boasts of "blood and iron." Wedekind and his kind were *Schwarzseher*, seers of black, of the black in man. They were a trend feeble in comparison with the dominant mood of self-confident power and pugnacity, yet who felt intimations of disaster, of a city ripe for burning, of Neroism in the air.

Strauss's antennae picked up whatever was in the air and he fixed unerringly on *Salome*—as the subject of an opera, not a tone poem. Using more instruments than ever, he composed a score of tremendous difficulty and exaggerated dissonance with the orchestra at times divided against itself, playing in two violently antagonistic keys as if to express the horror of the subject by horrifying the ear. Instruments were twisted to new demands, cellos made to reach the realm of violins, trombones to cavort like flutes, kettledrums given figures of unprecedented complexity. The musical fabric was dazzling. Strauss could write for the voice with no less virtuosity than for orchestra and the singers' parts seemed to grow more eloquent as the drama deepened in depravity. Salome's final song to the severed head thrilled listeners with a sinister beauty that did justice to Wilde's words:

> "Ah! wherefore didst thou not look at me, Iokanaan! If thou hadst seen me thou hadst loved me. I am athirst for thy beauty; I am hungry for thy body and neither the floods nor the great waters can quench my passion. . . . Ah! I have kissed thy mouth, Iokanaan, I have kissed thy mouth."

When Berlin and Vienna refused performance, like London, on the ground of sacrilege, Strauss's great admirer, Ernst von Schuch, conductor of the Dresden Royal Opera, presented it there on December 9, 1905. The production, in a single act lasting an hour and forty minutes without interruption, spared the audience's sensibilities nothing. Iokanaan's head, made up in realistic pallor of death with appropriate gore, was held in full view; Salome's seven veils were ritually discarded one by one while Herod leered. Death under the soldiers' shields supplied a punishing catharsis. The audience responded with unbounded enthusiasm extending to thirty-eight curtain calls for cast and composer. In subsequent performances in other German cities *Salome* went on to huge success and, for Strauss, large financial reward not adversely affected by bans and censorship troubles. In Vienna owing to the objections of the Archbishop the ban held, but in Berlin over the strenuous objections of the Kaiserin a compromise was reached of the kind applied by the Church to the Song of Solomon. Performance was allowed on condition that the star of Bethlehem should appear in the sky as Salome died, presumably indicating the posthumous triumph of the Baptist over unnatural passion.

Kaiser Wilhelm nevertheless remained unhappy. Despite an affinity for coarse physical jokes practiced upon his courtiers to their intense embarrassment, his moral views were more Victorian than Edwardian and he was married to a model of German bourgeois respectability. The Kaiserin Augusta, known as Dona, was a plain, amiable woman who provided her husband with six sons and a daughter, had no interests outside her family and wore large feathered hats on every occasion, even when yachting. They were her husband's choice since his annual birthday present to her was invariably twelve hats selected by himself which she was obliged to wear. Her one mark on history was her insistence on a double bed in which she so often kept her husband awake with family discussions which made him irritable next day, that Chancellor Bülow suggested separate bedrooms for the good of the State. But against her conviction that a good German husband and wife should sleep together, his proposal was in vain. Already offended by Strauss's earlier opera *Feuersnot*, whose theme, bawdily expressed, was the necessity of a maiden yielding her virginity to restore fire to a village, the Kaiserin had caused its cancellation, at which the Intendant of the Royal Opera had resigned in protest. The Kaiser himself had removed the imperial coat of arms from the

Deutsches Theater when it performed Hauptmann's *Die Weber* to a cheering Socialist demonstration in the mid-nineties. A decade had passed since then and to suppress on moral grounds an opera by Germany's leading composer would now have subjected the Kaiser to the sharp-tongued wit of *Kladderadatsch* and other irreverent journals. Accepting the compromise the Kaiser said, "I am sorry Strauss composed this *Salome.* It will do him a great deal of harm," upon which Strauss said that it had enabled him to build his new villa at Garmisch.

Outside Germany where taste was more prudish, *Salome* became "the storm center of the musical world." In New York a tense audience at the Metropolitan Opera on January 22, 1907, awaited the rise of the curtain with "foreboding," soon amply fulfilled. The music, when critics could tear their attention from portrayal of "a psychopathic condition literally unspeakable in its horror and abnormality," was acknowledged marvelous but perverted to means that "sicken the mind and wreck the nerves." The opera's theme, not humanly representative as the material of music should be, was considered variously "monstrous," "pestilential," "intolerable and abhorrent," "mephitic, poisonous, sinister and obsessing in the extreme." Its "erotic pathology" was unfit for "conversation between self-respecting men," and the Dance alone "ought to make it impossible for an Occidental woman to look at it." Rising in "righteous fury" the press agreed that popularity in Germany settled nothing for America and the Metropolitan bowing to the storm withdrew the production.

London did not even attempt it until three years later. A license was at first refused but this was overcome with the help of Mrs. Asquith, who invited Beecham, conductor at Covent Garden, for a visit in the country to enlist the help of the Prime Minister. By playing for him the march from *Tannhäuser* on the piano, the only piece of music Mr. Asquith knew, and assuring him that to like it was not a sign of philistinism, and by explaining that Strauss was "the most famous and in common opinion the greatest of living composers," Beecham won his support. In consultation with the Lord Chamberlain, changes in the text were worked out transforming all Salome's expressions of physical desire into pleas for spiritual guidance and, as extra precaution against sacrilege, requiring her final song to be sung to an empty platter.

In *Salome* Strauss had found his lode but where was there another Wilde? One appeared, and with a subject which promised to outdo *Salome*. Hugo von Hofmannsthal, a young poet and prodigy of Vienna, was already famous at twenty-six when he first met Strauss, ten years his senior, in 1900. The grandson of an Italian lady and a converted Jew ennobled as a baron, he embodied Vienna's cosmopolitan strains. When at sixteen and still a student in the gymnasium, he read his first verse play to Arthur Schnitzler, the listener felt he had "encountered a born genius for the first time in my life." Two years later, in 1892, under the pseudonym "Loris," he enraptured *Jung Wien*, the literary avant-garde of Vienna, with two verse plays, *Gestern* (Yesterday) and *Der Tod des Tizian* (Titian's Death), whose worldly knowledge and sophisticated weariness led Hermann Bahr, leader of the young literati, to suppose the author must be a titled diplomat of fifty. He was incredulous to find him a boy of eighteen, "a strange youth . . . fired by the slightest stimulus, but only with his intellect, for his heart remained cold." Self-indulgent, already a man of the world, "yet terribly sad in his precocious worldliness," Hofmannsthal was a combination of Edwardian Werther and Viennese Dorian Gray. Like Wilde an artist in language, he played on German as on a harp and in 1893, his next drama, *Tod und der Tor* (Death and the Fool), confirmed in him a poet who could raise his native language to the harmony of Italian. When words are used for their own sake the result may be musical but the thought murky. In 1905 Hofmannsthal concluded an essay on Wilde, in perfect if unconscious emulation of his subject, "He who knows the power of the dance of life fears not death. For he knows that love kills." To his contemporaries he seemed "absolute poetic perfection come into being." As an acolyte, for a time, of the circle which genuflected to Stefan George in Munich, von Hofmannsthal was absorbed in problems of symbol and paradoxes of "the truth of masks." As a Viennese he did not escape the pessimism that infused the capital of the oldest empire in Europe.

In Vienna, the *Kaiserstadt*, seat of the Congress that had

pasted Europe together after Napoleon, the time was twilight. As the center of a centuries-old mixture of races and peoples and the unwilling allegiances of restless nationalities, the capital of Austria-Hungary had too many problems of political life too difficult to cope with—and so turned its attention to other matters: to culture and connoisseurship, dalliance if not love, refinement of manner above everything and seriousness in nothing but music. The tempo was easygoing, the temper flippant, the mood hedonism and a nonchalant fatalism. It was the land of the Lotus-Eaters, the "Capua of the Mind." Its Emperor was seventy-five in 1905 and had been holding together his difficult domains through a reign of fifty-seven years. Its sad wandering Empress was dead by an Anarchist's knife. Its court had retreated to the aristocratic purity of sixteen quarterings for every member. It was a place where something was visibly coming to an end; everyone knew it and no one spoke of it.

Vienna looked down on Berlin as parvenu and crude and expressed its feeling in a popular song:

Es gibt nur eine Kaiserstadt
Es gibt nur ein Wien,
Es gibt nur ein Räubernest
Und das heisst Berlin.*

In the city of Beethoven, music and opera were king and the man in the street discussed the rival merits of the bands who played in the Prater. Art and the artist were esteemed. In politics, in government, in morals, Vienna was "affably tolerant of all that was slovenly, . . . in artistic matters there was no pardon; here the honor of the city was at stake." That honor was maintained by the bourgeoisie and the cultivated Jews, who were the new patrons of art. Franz Joseph had never read a book and nursed an antipathy to music. The nobility not only kept its distance from artistic and intellectual life but feared and contemned it. They had, however, the most accom-

*There's only one King's City,
Vienna's its name;
There's only one Robber's Nest,
Berlin is the name.

plished social manners in Europe, and when Theodore Roosevelt was asked what type of person he had found most sympathetic on his European travels, he replied, "the Austrian gentleman."

In internal affairs the strongest political sentiment was anti-Semitism, which was outspoken but more routine than heated. Karl Luger, the handsome blond-bearded Mayor of Vienna and head of the Christian Socialist party, was the leading anti-Semite, though more officially than personally. "I myself decide who is a Jew," he used to say. Known as *der schöne Karl*, he was the most popular man in the city and his funeral in 1910 was a major event. Despite their handicap the Jews, who represented 10 per cent of Vienna's population, were fertilizers of its culture. They played a prominent part in press, theatre, music, literature, finance, medicine and the law. They supplied the conductor of the Vienna Court Opera and the country's leading composer in Gustav Mahler as well as Vienna's truest mirror in Arthur Schnitzler.

A doctor like Chekhov, Schnitzler was marked by the same melancholy underlying a tone of irony and mockery. Except in his tragedy of *Professor Bernhardi*, the Jewish doctor who was assimilated but never enough, Schnitzler's heroes were philanderers, seekers for meaning in love and art and life, but always, as became Vienna, a little listlessly. They were charming, good-natured, clever and sophisticated; voices of the wit, inconstancy, politeness and unscrupulousness of the Viennese soul—and of its lassitude. The hero of *Der Weg ins Freie* (The Road to the Open), six months after returning from a "melancholy and rather boring" tour of Sicily with his mistress before a final parting, reminds himself that since then he has done no real work, not even written down "the plaintive adagio which he had heard in the waves breaking on the beach on a windy morning in Palermo." He is obsessed by a feeling of the "dreamlike and purposeless character of existence." Discussing a heated debate in the Landtag he replies to a question, "Heated? Well, yes, what we call heated in Austria. People were outwardly offensive and inwardly indifferent."

Hofmannsthal after his first meeting with Strauss sent him a verse play for a ballet which he had written on discovering

"Dionysian beauty" in the wordless gesture of the dance. Not so dedicated to pure art as not to value an association with Strauss, he hoped the Master would set his libretto to music. Strauss, however, was at the moment too busy with *Feuersnot* and other projects. Pursuing the Dionysian trail, Hofmannsthal began to make notes on Greek themes, on the relation of the supernatural to the bestial, on "phallic exuberance" and the "pathology and criminal psychology" of the tragedies then enjoying revival on the stage. Here he found, not the marble purity of the conventional classical Greece known to the Nineteenth Century, but Nietzsche's vision of a demonic Greece in whose sins and hates and forbidden bloodstained passions was the birth of tragedy, the earliest statement of man's compulsive drive toward ruin. The central tragedy, which Aeschylus, Sophocles and Euripides all had dramatized, was the chain of guilt in the house of Atreus from the sacrifice of Iphigenia to the murder of Agamemnon to the revenge of Electra and Orestes in their ultimate act of matricide. Hofmannsthal followed, but his *Elektra* turned out to be closer to Poe than Euripides, a nightmare of Gothic horror rather than a drama of man's fate.

His stage directions describe a palace courtyard at sunset where "patches of red light glimmering through the fig tree fall like bloodstains on the ground and walls." His characters surpass Salome in extravagant utterances of torment and desire, in ghastly longing for the double slaying of Clytemnestra and Aegisthus, in recollections of Agamemnon's gaping wounds, in sexual images of hatred appearing as a bridegroom, "hollow-eyed, breathing a viperous breath," whom Electra takes into her bed that it might teach her "all that is done between man and wife." Crazed with mutual hate, mother and daughter circle each other like mad dogs. Electra is a maniacal fury, feeding the vulture of revenge on her body, groveling in the dust of Agamemnon's grave at sundown, the hour when she "howls for her father" and sniffs among the dogs for the buried corpse. Clytemnestra is almost putrescent, with "a sallow bloated face" and heavy eyelids which she can only keep open by a "terrible effort." Dressed in purple, covered in jewels and talismans, she leans on an ivory cane, her train carried by "a yellow figure with the face of an Egyptian and the posture of a serpent." Sick with terror, evil dreams and an old lust, she is obsessed by the need to spill blood and drives herds of animals to the sacrifice in the hope that if the right blood flows she will be relieved of the nameless horror of her nightmares. It is no word, no pain that chokes her; it is nothing, yet so terrifying that her soul "hungers to hang itself and every nerve cries for death."

> Can one decay alive like a rotten corpse?
> Can one fall apart if one is not even ill?
> Fall apart wide awake like a dress eaten by moths?

She seems an allegory of Europe and the play a climax of the *Schwarzseher*, an apocalyptic vision of disaster. When, desperate for surcease from her dreams, Clytemnestra demands to know from Electra who must bleed and die that she may sleep at last, Electra cries in exaltation, "What must bleed? Your own throat! . . . and the shadows and torches shall envelop you in their black and scarlet net."

The play was produced by Max Reinhardt in Berlin in 1903, the year after *Salome*. Hofmannsthal was alert to its possibilities. To serve as a libretto for an opera by Strauss was then considered "to reach the summit of contemporary fame," and he repeatedly urged *Elektra* on Strauss as his next project. Though attracted, Strauss hesitated because of its similarity to *Salome* and cast about for some other theme of human nature driven to dreadful extremes. "Something like a really wild Cesare Borgia or Savonarola would be just what I am yearning for," he wrote to Hofmannsthal in March, 1906. Following a visit to The Hague, where he was haunted by Rembrandt's "Saul and David," he suggested a "raving Saul" as a possible subject. Ten days later he suddenly proposed, "How about a subject from the French Revolution for a change?" Hofmannsthal, with his drama already written, kept returning to *Elektra* and, although the marks of Wilde on it were obvious, he insisted that it was really very different. Eager for collaboration, he was persuasive and Strauss succumbed. Meanwhile, with one foot in the dominant camp, he composed five highly colored military marches for the Kaiser which won him the Order of the Crown, Third Class.

While Strauss was at work on *Elektra* a major scandal revealing rottenness in high places became public. The Eulenburg affair concerned homosexuals in the immediate circle of the Kaiser, but it was less their habits than the layers disclosed of malice, intrigue and private vendetta which shed a lurid glow on Germany. Three years earlier Fritz Krupp, head of the firm, on being accused by the Socialist paper *Vorwärts* of homosexual acts with waiters and valets, committed suicide. This time the central figure was Prince Philipp Eulenburg, former Ambassador to Vienna from 1894 to 1902, a suave and cultivated aristocrat who was the Kaiser's oldest and closest friend, sang songs to him beautifully at the piano, and gave him intelligent advice. As the only courtier to exercise on the whole a beneficent influence on the sovereign, he was naturally the object of the jealousy of Bülow and Holstein, who suspected the Kaiser of intention to make him Chancellor. Initiator of the scandal was Maximilian Harden, the feared and fearless editor of the weekly *Die Zukunft*, of which it was said that everything rotten and everything good in Germany appeared in its pages. Cause and motive had to do with Germany's diplomatic defeat at the Algeciras Conference which set off waves of recrimination among ministers, culminating in the removal of the spidery Holstein. He blamed Eulenburg, although in fact his removal had been secretly engineered by Bülow. Rabid for revenge, Holstein, who for years had kept secret police files on the private habits of his associates, now joined forces with Harden to ruin Eulenburg, whose influence on the Kaiser, Harden believed, was pacific and therefore malign. With Holstein's files at his disposal, Harden opened a campaign of innuendo naming three elderly Counts, all A.D.C.'s of the Kaiser, as homosexuals and gradually closing in on the friendship of Eulenburg with Count Kuno Moltke, nicknamed Tutu, "the most delicate of generals," commander of a cavalry brigade and City Commandant of Berlin. The Kaiser ditched his friends instantly and forced Moltke to sue Harden for libel, which was just what Harden wanted in order to ruin Eulenburg. Through four trials lasting over a period of two years, from October, 1907, to July, 1909, evidence of perversion, blackmail and personal venom was spread before a bewildered public. Witnesses including thieves, pimps and morons told of "disgusting orgies" in the Garde du Corps regiment and testified to abnormal acts of Eulenburg and Moltke twenty years in the past. A celebrated specialist in pathological conditions discoursed on medical details, Moltke's divorced and vindictive wife was called to testify, charges of subornation and perjury were added, Chancellor Bülow was himself accused of perversion by a half-crazed crusader for the legal rights of homosexuals and forced to sue, the verdict of the first trial in favor of Harden was reversed by a second trial and re-reversed in a third at which Eulenburg, now ill, disgraced and under arrest, was brought to court in a hospital bed. The public felt uneasily that justice was being tampered with, readers of *Die Zukunft* were given an impression of perversion everywhere and the prestige of Kaiser and court sank. At the same time in Vienna the Emperor's brother, Archduke Ludwig-Viktor, known as Luzi-Wuzi, became involved in a scandal with a masseur.

In England the three trials of Oscar Wilde had blazed and been put out within two months; the establishment turned its back on him and destroyed him. In Germany the establishment itself was on trial. In the midst of it, in October, 1908, came the tremendous gaffe of Kaiser Wilhelm's interview on foreign affairs in the *Daily Telegraph*, in which his more than usually indiscreet opinions, carelessly allowed to pass by Bülow, aroused the fury and hilarity of nations and questions as to his sanity at home. Some even demanded his abdication. Bülow, maneuvering neatly as he thought, virtually apologized in the Reichstag for his sovereign who never forgave him. Hurt and indignant, the Kaiser retired to the estate of his friend Prince Fürstenberg, where, in the course of an evening's festivities, Count Hülsen-Haeseler, chief of the Military Cabinet, appeared in a pink ballet skirt and rose wreath and "danced beautifully," affording everybody much entertainment. On finishing he dropped dead of heart failure. Rigor mortis having set in by the time the doctors came, the General's body could only with the greatest difficulty be divested of its ballet costume and restored to the propriety of military uniform. It had not been a happy year for the Kaiser, although six months later he at least had the satisfaction of forcing the resignation of Bülow.

Damage to the image of the ruling caste caused its members to swagger more than ever. As the Kaiser's prestige slipped, the trend of the extreme militants grew in favor of the Crown

Prince, a strutting creature whose flatterers told him he resembled Frederick the Great, as indeed, facially, he did. In the eternal duel of reigning monarch and eldest son, Wilhelm II and "little Willy" felt required to outdo each other in bombast. "I stand in shining armor" and similar pronouncements of the Kaiser were of this period. The nation's mood of conscious power could absorb unlimited bombast. Germans knew themselves to be the strongest military power on earth, the most efficient merchants, the busiest bankers, penetrating every continent, financing the Turks, flinging out a railroad from Berlin to Baghdad, gaining the trade of Latin America, challenging the sea power of Great Britain, and in the realm of intellect systematically organizing, under the concept *Wissenschaft*, every branch of human knowledge. They were deserving and capable of mastery of the world. Rule by the best must be fulfilled. By this time Nietzsche, as Brandes wrote in 1909, held "undisputed sway" over the minds of his countrymen. What they lacked and hungered for was the world's acknowledgment of their mastery. So long as it was denied, frustration grew and with it the desire to compel acknowledgment by the sword. Talk of war became a commonplace. When the Kaiser's troublesome Rhodes scholars got drunk they threatened Oxford colleagues "with invasion and castigation at the hands of the German Army." In 1912 General Bernhardi, the leading military theorist of his day, proclaimed the coming necessity in a book of indisputable authority and conviction whose title was *Germany and the Next War*.

The other Germany, the Germany of intellect and sentiment, the liberal Germany which lost in 1848 and never tried again, had withdrawn from the arena, content to despise militarism and materialism and sulk in a tent of superior spiritual values. Its representatives were a caste of professors, clergy, doctors and lawyers who regarded themselves as the *Geistaristokratie* (aristocracy of the mind) superior to the vulgar rich, the vulgar nobility and the vulgar masses. Unconcerned with social problems, unengaged in politics, they were satisfied with an indoor liberalism which fought no battles and expressed itself in abstract opposition to the regime, in contempt for the Kaiser and in the anti-militarist cartoons of *Simplicissimus*. They were personified by a professor of philosophy, Georg Simmel, whose lectures in a room overlooking Unter den Linden coincided with the hour of the changing of the guard. At the first sound of the military band Professor Simmel would abruptly stop talking and stand motionless in "an attitude of arrogant disgust and stoical suffering until the barbaric noise had faded away." Only then would he resume his lecture.

At the centenary celebration of the University of Berlin in 1910, the two Germanys met when the academic community found itself invaded by their fierce-moustachioed monarch in the golden cuirass and golden-eagled helmet of the Garde du Corps, with retinue in gorgeous uniform, heralded by the terrific blasts of a trombone choir. Satisfied that the Kaiser "looked even worse than his caricatures," the audience consoled itself with the thought that such an intrusion could not trouble their halls again for another hundred years.

Strauss completed the score of *Elektra* in September, 1908, with his publishers taking it from him page by page. Anticipating the prospect of another *succès de scandale*, they paid $27,000 for it, almost double the $15,000 paid for *Salome*, making Strauss's income from music in 1908 $60,000. The German public's appetite for sensation had become a habit and four cities competed for the honor of the premiere. Grateful to Schuch, Strauss gave it to Dresden, which in honor of the occasion scheduled a Strauss festival to include *Salome*, *Feuersnot*, *Sinfonia Domestica* and two performances of *Elektra*—five evenings of Strauss in succession.

Rehearsals of the new opera took place in a atmosphere of uproar; everything was larger, noisier, more violent than life. The score called for the biggest orchestra yet, sixty-two strings including eight bass cellos, forty-five winds including six bass trumpets and a contra-bass tuba, six to eight kettledrums as well as a bass drum, in all a total of about one hundred and twenty. The opera was performed in a single act lasting two hours without intermission with Electra on stage the entire time. Her part was longer than Brünhilde's in all of *The Ring* put together and her vocal intervals were considered "unsingable." The role of Clytemnestra was created by Mme Schumann-Heink, who, finding it "such a desperate one that it nearly killed me," never sang it again. In places where she was required to sing over the orchestra at fortissimo, Strauss, listening from the stalls, would scream over the din and crash, "Louder, louder, I say! I can still hear the Heink's voice!"

For a legendary drama set in 1500 B.C. he wanted everything to be "exact and realistic," insisting on real sheep and bulls for Clytemnestra's sacrifice. "*Gott in Himmel!* Strauss, are you mad?" howled the stage director in terror. "Imagine the cost! And the danger! What will they do when your violent music begins?" They would stampede, crash into the orchestra, kill the musicians, even wreck valuable instruments. Strauss was adamant. Von Schuch was called in to add his protest. Only after terrific arguments was Strauss persuaded to yield on the bulls and be content with sheep. Equally realistic in his music, he virtually took the role of words away from von Hofmannsthal. The tinkling of Clytemnestra's bracelets is heard in the percussion; when Chrysothemis speaks of a stormy night the storm rages in the orchestra; when the beasts are driven to sacrifice the noise of their hoofs makes the listener want to get out of the way; when the slippery pool of blood is described the orchestra gives a picture of it. The composer's mastery of his technical resources seemed superhuman and his breaking of musical laws more reckless than ever. As he put it, "I went to the uttermost limits of harmony and psychic polyphony and of the receptive capacity of present day ears."

When the evening came for the premiere on January 25, 1909, an international audience was assembled including opera directors from every country on the continent and, according to a possibly overwhelmed reporter, "200 distinguished critics." "All Europe is here," the hotel porter said proudly to Hermann Bahr, who came from Vienna.

Without overture or prelude the curtain rose as the orchestra thundered out Agamemnon's theme like the hammer of doom pounding on the great lion gate of Mycenae. No opera had ever opened so stunningly before. When the curtain fell after two hours of demonic intensity the audience sat for some seconds in stupefied silence until the "Straussianer" recovered and began to applaud. An opposition group hissed but most of the audience was too cowed to do anything until the claque won the upper hand and wrung curtain calls and ultimately cheers for the composer. The brutality of the libretto and the outrages upon musical form provoked the usual controversy. To some the music of *Elektra* seemed no longer music. "Indeed, many serious minded people consider Richard Strauss insane," wrote one benumbed listener. But on second hearing and at further performances which followed Berlin, Munich and Frankfurt within four weeks of the premiere, the mastery of Strauss's score in conveying dread and impending horror leading up to the final murder was undeniable.

Listening to the music Hermann Bahr felt it expressed something sinister about the present time, a pride born of limitless power, a defiance of order "lured back toward chaos," and a yearning in Chrysothemis for some simple tranquil feeling. Though deeply disturbed he felt it had been a "marvelous evening" and returned to Vienna excited and uplifted. This was what Nietzsche had prescribed.

When it reached London a year later, in February, 1910, notoriety preceded it and musical warfare raged before a note had been heard. Strauss came himself to conduct two performances at a fee of £200 for each. The *Daily Mail* critic was struck by the sobriety of his gestures. "A tall pale man with smooth brow" whose steel-blue eyes flashed from time to time at singers or musicians, he conducted with head immobile and elbows as if riveted to his body. "He seemed a mathematician writing a formula on a blackboard neatly with supreme knowledge." After the performance *The Times* found the opera "unsurpassed for sheer hideousness in the whole of operatic literature," while the *Daily Telegraph* reported that "Covent Garden had never previously witnessed a scene of such unfettered enthusiasm." The rising controversy created a public demand that required Beecham to extend his season. From his point of view it was, excepting the death of King Edward VII some months later, "the most discussed event of the year." The truth was that by this time it could no longer be heard outside Germany without political overtones. George Bernard Shaw, believing that anti-German hysteria was responsible for the attacks on *Elektra*, leaned backward to the opposite extreme: In an article in the *Nation* he wrote that if once he could have said that "the case against the fools and the money changers who are trying to drive us into war with Germany consists in the single word, Beethoven, today I should say with equal confidence, Strauss." He called *Electra* "the highest achievement of the highest art" and its performance "a historic moment in the history of art in England such as may not occur again in our lifetime."

Strauss recognized that in the style of *Salome* and *Elektra* he had gone as far as he could go. Suddenly, as after *Heldenleben*, having enough of the grand manner, he decided to give the public a comic opera for a change, in the style of Mozart's *Marriage of Figaro*, to prove that Strauss could do anything. As librettist Hofmannsthal approved and early in 1909 was at work drafting an "entirely original" scenario set in Eighteenth-Century Vienna, "full of burlesque situations and characters" with opportunity for lyrical melody and humor. On receiving the opening scene, Strauss found it delightful and replied, "It will set itself to music like oil and melted butter." Collaborating by correspondence through 1909 and the first half of 1910, librettist and composer constructed a new opera to be called *Der Rosenkavalier*.

The juvenile lead was to be sung by a woman dressed as a man. *Hosenrolle* (trouser parts) for women were a convention which Mozart himself had used for Cherubino but the Hofmannsthal-Strauss concept of Octavian was a rather different matter, not devoid of a desire to titillate. When Strauss's prelude to the opera describes with characteristic realism the pleasures of the sex act and the curtain rises on the Marschallin and her young lover still in bed, the discovery that both are women was likely to produce in the audience a peculiar sensation of which the authors were certainly aware. The idea was originally Hofmannsthal's. Strauss later claimed that the device was necessary because no man young enough to sing Octavian would have had the experience necessary to be an accomplished actor. "Besides," he added more frankly, "writing for three sopranos was a challenge." He met it, especially when the three sing together in the last act, with exquisite song. In *Elektra* the men's parts had been of small account and in *Rosenkavalier* the only male part was that of a coarse lecher who appears either as unpleasant or ridiculous. Baron Ochs represented the German idea of the comic. As Strauss wrote to Hofmannsthal during the composition, he missed "a genuinely comic situation—

everything is merely amusing but not comic." He wanted the audience to laugh; "Laugh! not just smile or grin."

The inevitable animals made their appearance in the form of a dog, a monkey and a parrot. When Strauss demanded from Hofmannsthal a love scene between Sophie and Octavian to which he could write a duet "much more passionate, . . . as it reads now it is too tame, too mannered and timid," Hofmannsthal replied pettishly that these two young creatures "have nothing of the Valkyrie or Tristan and Isolde about them" and he wished to avoid at all costs having them "burst into a kind of Wagnerian erotic screaming." This was hardly tactful and incompatibilities of temperament between composer and librettist were becoming evident. A touch of Tristan in fact appeared, not to mention some borrowing from Mozart and even from Johann Strauss. With bland anachronism a Viennese waltz, unknown in the Eighteenth Century, was a main theme.

By April, 1910, the full score of Act II was already at the printer before Strauss had received the libretto for Act III. Its situations contrived for the Baron's embarrassment turned out to have been adapted by von Hofmannsthal from *The Merry Wives of Windsor*, with the difference that, unlike Falstaff, Ochs remained unrelievedly unlikable. By the end of summer the opera was finished and on January 26, 1911, two years after *Elektra*, *Rosenkavalier* had its premier at Dresden. It was rarely to be off the opera stage thereafter. Composer and librettist endowed it with all the shimmer of super-civilized Vienna. It glistened like the silver rose that was its symbol. All Strauss's skill, resourcefulness and audacity—and his duality—were in the score. His highest gift of musical expressiveness could convey the bustle of an Eighteenth-Century levee, the delicious discovery of young love, the comic terror of the duel, the sweet sadness of the Marschallin's renunciation, and at the same time be used for coarse jokes and bottom-pinching humor. He gave the world a silver rose, beautiful, glittering and tarnished.

In 1911 Strauss was at the peak of the musical world, the most famous composer alive, "one of those," wrote a biographer of musicians, Richard Specht, "without whom we can no longer imagine our spiritual life." Although he and Hofmannsthal set to work at once on another opera, *Ariadne auf Naxos*,

Strauss had reached his own peak and the palm was already passing.

In 1908 in Paris the Russian Ballet company of Sergei Diaghilev burst like a gorgeous tropical bird upon the Western world. Its season was a triumph of wild throbbing exotic splendor, another "flash of lightning out of the North." Instead of the tired routines of classical ballet it brought fresh excellence of music by contemporary Russian composers, new librettos, imaginative choreography and brilliant modern stage design, all assembled like a bed of jewels to set off a blaze of dancing that was virile and superb. The male dancer was the star, no longer a mere *porteur* to lift the ballerina, but a wind who brought vitality and zest sweeping onto the stage. Above all the rest was one, Vaslav Nijinsky. When he appeared with an astonishing leap into the air and seemed almost to pause there, people felt the excitement of perfection and knew they were seeing the greatest *ballon* dancer who ever lived. He was an angel, a genius, an Apollo of motion. He took possession of all hearts. The whole ensemble took Paris by storm. Devotees predicted the downfall of opera. "It was as if," wrote the Comtesse de Noailles, "something new had been added to the creation of the world on its seventh day."

New movements in the arts were erupting everywhere. At the Salon d'Automne in 1905 and 1906 the *Fauves* (Wild Beasts) led by Matisse exhibited in riotous color and distorted line their credo of painting independent of nature. In 1907–8 Picasso and Braque, discovering essential reality in geometrical forms, created Cubism. In its terms Léger celebrated the machine and a train of other artists followed. In Germany the new idea broke out in a school of Expressionists who searched for emotional impact through exaggeration or distortion of nature. Two Americans broke old molds: Frank Lloyd Wright at home and Isadora Duncan, who, touring Europe in the years 1904–8, introduced emotion into the dance. Rodin, speaking for his own métier but voicing a new goal for all the arts, had already said, "Classical sculpture sought the logic of the human body; I seek its psychology." Seeking it too, Marcel Proust in 1906 shut himself up in a cork-lined room to embark upon *Remembrance of Things Past*. Thomas Mann took up the search in *Death in Venice*. In Bloomsbury, Lytton Strachey prepared a new kind of biography. The Moscow Art Theatre demonstrated a new kind of acting. The Irish Renaissance flowered in Yeats and in J. M. Synge, who in *Riders to the Sea* and *The Playboy of the Western World* proved himself the only writer since Shakespeare to produce an equally fine tragedy and comedy. The time vibrated with a search for new forms and new realms. When on July 25, 1909, Blériot flew the Channel, confirming what the Wrights had begun, he seemed to mark a wiping out of frontiers, and everyone in Europe felt in his triumph "a soaring of feelings no less wonderful than that of the planes."

All the fever and fecundity of the hour seemed captured by the Russian Ballet. That it should come out of Imperial Russia, considered at once barbaric and decrepit, was as surprising as had been the summons to disarmament by the Czar. A great interest in things Russian aroused by the Franco-Russian Alliance and the Exposition of 1900 had inspired the enterprising Diaghilev to bring an exhibition of Russian art to Paris in 1906. Paintings and sculpture, ikons, priestly brocades and the jeweled marvels of Fabergé lent by the Imperial and private collections and by museums filled twelve rooms under the patronage of the Grand Duke Vladimir, Ambassador Izvolsky of Russia and Mme Greffulhe. The next year Diaghilev brought Russian music in a series of dazzling concerts with Rimsky-Korsakov conducting his own work, Rachmaninoff playing his own piano concerto, Josef Hofmann playing a concerto by Scriabine, and the magnificent basso Chaliapin singing excerpts from Borodin's *Prince Igor* and Moussorgsky's *Boris Godunov*. Building on the enthusiastic welcome, Diaghilev planned a greater triumph in a season of ballet and Russian opera. The Imperial Russian Ballet lent its leading artists, Anna Pavlova, Nijinsky, Adolph Bolm and Tamara Karsavina, with Michel Fokine as choreographer. For stage design and costumes, Diaghilev obtained the gorgeous and barbaric talent of Léon Bakst, supplemented by outstanding painters, Soudeikine, Roerich, Alexandre Benois and others. The sensation of the first season was *Cleopatra*, whose music was a melange from at least five Russian composers. Russian themes mingled with Egyptian and Persian and even the original sorceress of the Nile could not have matched the ravishing beauty and figure of Ida Rubinstein borne on a palanquin surrounded by a whirling bacchanal of veils and rose leaves arranged to conceal the fact that as a dancer she was as yet barely trained. Paris found her almost "too beautiful, like strong perfume."

Every year for the next six years the Ballet returned with new and exuberant productions which revolutionized choreography and stage design. Music was dignified by a full orchestra, with Pierre Monteux engaged as conductor. Additional operas—Moussorgsky's *Khovantschina*, Rimsky's *Sadko* and *Ivan the Terrible*—besides *Prince Igor* and *Boris Godunov*, were added to the repertoire. Pavlova later left the company, but in 1909 in *Les Sylphides* she seemed to dancing "what Racine is to poetry," while Karsavina was "the exquisite union of classic tradition and revolutionary artistry." For the music of this ballet two of Chopin's piano compositions, *Nocturne* and *Valse Brillante*, were orchestrated by a pupil of Rimsky-Korsakov, Igor Stravinsky, then twenty-six, whom Diaghilev had commissioned after hearing his first performed orchestral work in St. Petersburg in 1908. In contrast to the classical delicacy of *Sylphides*, Fokine staged the savage Polovtsian dances from *Prince Igor* with Tartar-Mongol themes echoing in the music and a wild Asiatic horde of dancers against a scene in dull grays and reds, of low round-topped tents and rising columns of smoke stretching toward the infinite horizon of the steppe.

Emotion long absent from the ballet was infused by the voluptuous physical spectacles and intoxicating colors of Bakst. Houris of the Sultan's harem from the *Arabian Nights*, bacchantes from a Greek vase, Russian boyars in boots, harlequins and colombines of the Commedia dell'Arte, forest creatures in maroon, green and gold suggesting "the sparkling beauty of spotted pythons," tennis-players in modern dress took over the stage. Bakst inspired Paul Poiret and five years of women's fashions. When planning Rimsky-Korsakov's *Schéhérazade* with his associates, the red-haired Bakst in his elegant and scented clothes jumped on a chair and explained, in his guttural accent with explicit gestures, how the Sultan's bodyguard should cut everyone to pieces: "*everyone*, his wives and all their Negro lovers!" For *Schéhérazade* he designed a setting to suggest "dreadful deeds of lust and cruelty" which Fokine interpreted enthusiastically in a dance of Negro slaves whom the Sultan's wives persuade the eunuchs to liberate from their golden cages and who fling themselves upon the willing harem in an orgiastic dance of "spasms of desire." The sexual theme was a favorite of the Ballet. For *Thamar*, the Caucasian queen, a Cleopatra *à la russe*, Bakst designed a medieval castle above a river into whose waters rejected lovers fell to their doom. In her various roles as temptress the delicate and flower-like Karsavina conveyed vice, as the critics said, "with a great deal of verisimilitude."

When Rimsky died in 1908 Stravinsky composed a *Chant Funèbre* for a memorial concert in St. Petersburg. More than ever impressed, Diaghilev asked him to write the music for a ballet based on the Russian fairy tale of Prince Ivan and the Firebird. Set in a wood with a wicked wizard and twelve princesses under a spell, it evoked from the composer an imaginative score of mixed rhythms, graceful melody and a weird electric dance of demons. With Bolm as the Prince and Karsavina as the Firebird, it was performed in June, 1910, the first work of Stravinsky in his own right to be heard outside of Russia. Debussy rushed backstage to embrace him. The audience was delighted to appreciate music that was contemporary without being uncomfortable and Diaghilev was congratulated on every hand. He at once commissioned another ballet for the following season. When Stravinsky played for him a piece for piano and orchestra which he had already written on the adventures of Petrouchka, "the immortal and unhappy puppet, hero of every fair in every country," Diaghilev was enchanted. Together they worked out the scenes of the ballet, the carnival in the public square, the crowds and booths, the magician with his tricks, the gypsies and trained bear, the puppet show whose dolls come to life, the vain love of Petrouchka for the Dancer and his death at the hands of his rival, the Moor.

Petrouchka was music of power and vitality, close to the Russian people, with folk tunes and echoes of the hurdy-gurdy, humor and satire and poignant grief. Like Strauss, Stravinsky scorned development of themes but in a tradition he had inherited from the Russian "Five" rather than from Germany. Almost contrary to the nature of music, which traditionally depended on development and repetition, Stravinsky was terse and direct, aiming, as he said, "at straightforward expression in its simplest form. I have no use for 'working-out' in dramatic music. The one essential thing is to feel and convey one's feelings."

In this *Petrouchka* succeeded and Paris acknowledged what Debussy's embrace had already recognized: the appearance of an original and major composer. Nijinsky as the puppet broke the audience's heart. Thrown by his master into a black box, rushing about waving his stiff arms in the air, pathetic in love and frantic in jealousy, his performance was a triumph just in time for the London season.

England greeted the Russian Ballet with a fervor equal to France. In the brilliant Coronation summer of 1911 "it was exciting to be alive." The heat broke records, festivities were at a peak, airplanes landed on country lawns, everybody was stimulated by the thrill of flight but the Russian Ballet "crowned all." It restored the dance to its "primal nobility," wrote Ellen Terry. It was a revelation in the harmony of the arts. Society, intellectuals, everyone with any pretensions to taste, flocked to Covent Garden "night after night, entranced." Nijinsky enraptured all who came: as the uncouth puppet, as the Negro slave in silver trousers of *Schéhérazade*, as Pierrot in a candle-lit garden chasing dancers dressed as butterflies to music by Schumann, as the Blue God rising from a lotus in a Chinese pool to music by Proust's friend Reynaldo Hahn, as the ghost of a rose in a costume of petals, flying out of a window in a famous leap that made people say his element was the air. Speaking no English and hardly any French, he became the darling of the dinner parties, speechless but smiling.

Impelled by triumph, like Strauss, to try for new sensation, Diaghilev in the season of 1912 succeeded in shocking Paris. He produced two new ballets by French composers. Maurice Ravel's *Daphnis et Chloé*, written for the occasion, was acknowledged by Stravinsky "one of the finest things by a French composer." Debussy's *L'Après-midi d'un Faune*, whose music was already known, was a scandal for non-musical reasons. Nijinsky was the Faun in skin-fitting tights painted in animal spots, with a tiny tail, a wig of tight curls made of gold cord, and two little curling horns. In a ballet lasting twelve minutes he chased nymphs in Greek gowns and, as the last escaped him, leaving behind her veil, fell upon it in a movement of sexual consummation. The choreography in this case was Nijinsky's own. The curtain fell upon hoots, whistles, and insults mixed with cries of "*épatant!*" and "*Bis, bis!*" Obliging, the company danced the ballet over again to "indescribable chaos." Next morning Gaston Calmette, the editor of *Figaro*, published a signed editorial on his front page under the title "Un Faux Pas" denouncing "the extraordinary exhibition of erotic bestiality and shameless gesture" and demanding its suppression in subsequent performances. Agreeing, if less excitedly, *Le Gaulois* found the final gesture "*de trop*," while *Le Temps* with customary dignity expressed the "justified discontent" of the French people at this "regrettable adventure." A report quickly circulated that the Prefect of Police at Calmette's request had issued an injunction against further performance. In clubs, salons, cafés and lobbies of the Chamber no one talked of anything else; Paris momentarily was again in two camps. The excitable Russian Ambassador, M. Izvolsky, wanted to know if *Figaro* was attacking the Franco-Russian Alliance. Next day *Le Matin* published a letter from Rodin defending Nijinsky for restoring "freedom of instinct and human emotion" to the dance. The controversy transferred itself to Rodin, whose supporters issued a manifesto in which Jules Lemaître and Maurice Barrès were now on the same side as Anatole France and Octave Mirbeau along with ex-President Loubet, former premiers Clemenceau, Léon Bourgeois and Briand, Ambassador Izvolsky and Baron d'Estournelles. Forain, unreconstructed, published in *Figaro* an anti-Rodin cartoon. With every ticket for the second performance sold at a premium, the offending gesture was suppressed, leaving the Faun merely gazing on the veil with doleful regret.

In Vienna that season, where owing to a current Balkan War the mood was anti-Slav, a fiasco was barely averted. At rehearsals the orchestra of the Viennese Royal Opera, which could play anything put before it with accomplished ease, played the Russian music with ostentatious disapproval and deliberate mistakes. Monteux was helpless and when the enraged Diaghilev commented out loud on the behavior of these "pigs," the musicians downed their instruments and left the stage. Only by extracting an apology from Diaghilev next day was the crisis resolved. In Berlin the Kaiser attended a performance of

Cleopatra and *Firebird*. Preferring the former, he summoned Diaghilev and told him he would send his Egyptologists to see it, apparently under the impression that Bakst's fantastic decor was authentic and the Russian potpourri a revelation of the real music of Ptolemaic Egypt.

Strauss too came to the performance and afterward complimented Stravinsky, adding a characteristic piece of advice. Referring to the muted mysterious opening of *Firebird*, where the Prince rides into the enchanted wood, he said, "You make a mistake in beginning your piece pianissimo; the public will not listen. You should astonish them by a sudden crash at the start. After that they will follow you and you can do what you like."

To capture Strauss for the Ballet was an obvious next task, and the Ballet's prestige in turn had already interested von Hofmannsthal, who opened negotiations. After obtaining Diaghilev's financial terms, he suggested to Strauss a ballet on Orestes and the Furies with Nijinsky portraying the hero's "terrible deed and terrible suffering" and the Furies "bursting forth horribly and triumphantly" in a dance of destruction at the end. It was hardly a fresh idea but Hofmannsthal wrote temptingly that it would provide the occasion for "wonderful, somber, grandiose music. . . . Think it over and please don't refuse." He enclosed a note of the terms which Diaghilev "takes the liberty of submitting to you." When Strauss promptly rejected the idea, Hofmannsthal hurriedly offered instead a libretto for a ballet based on Joseph and Potiphar's Wife which he had already written in collaboration with Count Harry Kessler, a German littérateur, amateur in politics and patron of the arts who like other Germans of liberal ideas had no place in official life. Applying pressure to Strauss, Hofmannsthal wrote that if he refused, Diaghilev—who liked the libretto—would commission a Russian or French composer. This worked. "Joseph is excellent," Strauss replied. "I'll bite. Have already started sketching it out."

Trouble soon developed. The libretto as conceived by its two sophisticated authors was a metaphysical version of the story of the Baptist and Salome, with Joseph as a God-seeker "whose secret is that of growth and transmutation, whose holiness is that of creating and begetting, whose perfection is that of things which have not yet been." He is confronted by a sensual woman who is ruined "by perception of the divine which she cannot conquer." These were not the most suitable ideas to express in music, much less the dance. Squirming, Strauss complained, "The chaste Joseph isn't at all up my street and if a thing bores me I find it difficult to set to music." He complained that Joseph in the ballet did nothing but resist the Queen's advances; "this God-seeker is going to be a hell of an effort." Hofmannsthal explained carefully that Joseph's resistance was "the struggle of man's intensified intellectuality" against woman's urge to drag him down, a clarification which did little to relieve Strauss's boredom with his task. His first sketches, which he played for Hofmannsthal in December, 1912, left his collaborator "disturbed" and conscious that "there is something wrong between the two of us which in the end will have to be brought into the open." For the time being he implored Strauss not to feel constrained by the demands of the dance but to write "unrestrained pure Strauss" expressing his own personality "with every conceivable freedom in polyphony and modernism in a manner as bold and bizarre as you may wish." Joseph remained chaste, however, and Strauss uninspired. In the meantime Diaghilev had another premiere ready for the season of 1913.

It was *Le Sacre du Printemps* (The Rite of Spring) by Stravinsky. Its theme was elemental, the rejuvenation of earth in spring. The form was a celebration of pagan rites in which a sacrificial maiden dances herself to death to renew the life of the soil. In contrast to the tired sophistry of *Joseph*, Stravinsky's scenario was simply a framework for dancers and music. He opened not with a bang, as Strauss had advised, but with a slow trembling of woodwinds as if to suggest the physical mystery of budding. As the curtain rose on tribal games and dances, the music became vibrant and frenetic with primeval rhythms, the chant of trumpets, the driving beat of machinery, jazz metres and pitiless drums never before used with such power and abandon. It rose in intensity and excitement to a blazing climax and all the promise of a new age. It was the Twentieth Century incarnate. It reached at one stride a peak of modern music that was to dominate later generations. It was to the Twentieth Century what Beethoven's *Eroica* was to the Nineteenth, and like it, never surpassed.

The premiere conducted by Monteux on May 28, 1913, created almost a riot in the theatre. The abandonment of understood harmony, melody and structure seemed musical anarchy. People felt they were hearing a blasphemous attempt to destroy music as an art and responded with howls and catcalls and derisive laughter. Counter-demonstrators bellowed defiance. One young man became so excited he began to beat rhythmically with his fists on the head of an American in the audience whose own emotion was so great that "I did not feel the blows for some time." A beautifully gowned lady in a box stood up and slapped the face of a man hissing in an adjoining box. Saint-Saëns indignantly rose and left the hall; Ravel shouted, "Genius!" The dancers could not hear the music above the uproar and Nijinsky, who had choreographed the ballet, stood in the wings pounding out the rhythm with his fists and shouting in despair, "*Ras, Dwa, Tri!*" Monteux threw desperate glances to Diaghilev who signed to him to keep on playing and shouted to the audience to let the piece be heard. "Listen first, hiss afterwards!" screamed Gabriel Astruc, the French manager, in a rage. When it was over the audience streamed out to continue their battle in the cafés and the critics to carry it to the press, but as the music had hardly been heard, opinion was largely emotion. Not until a year later when the music was played again in Paris as a concert in April, 1914, was it recognized for what it was. With the performance of the *Sacre*, filling out a decade of innovation in the arts, all the major tendencies of the next half-century had been stated.

That summer Strauss completed *Joseph*. Meeting with Diaghilev and Bakst in Venice, Hofmannsthal planned a production that was to be "the most lavish and beautiful imaginable." It was to be set not in Egypt but in the Venice of Tintoretto and Veronese because as Count Kessler explained, "Too scrupulous an accuracy can but impede the freedom of imagination."

Already busy with several new works, Strauss was news. When in July he finished *Ein Deutsches Motette* for chorus and orchestra it was considered worth a cable dispatch to the New York *Times*. For the opening of a new concert hall in Vienna in November he composed a *Festival Prelude* scored for a bigger orchestra than ever: one hundred and fifty musicians including eight horns, eight drums, six extra trumpets and an organ. It was suitable to a year of national chest-thumping in celebration of the hundredth anniversary of the defeat of Napoleon at Leipzig and the simultaneous twenty-fifth anniversary of the Kaiser's reign.

For the Centenary a book called *Germany in Arms* was published with an introduction by the Crown Prince, who wrote: "It is the holy duty of Germany above all other peoples to maintain an army and a fleet ever at the highest point of readiness. Only then, supported by our own good sword, can we preserve the place in the sun which is our due but which is not willingly granted to us." Although the "gigantic conflagration" of nations, once started, would not be easily extinguished, this should not deter the German hand from the sword, "for the sword will remain the decisive factor till the end of the world."

More factually Karl Helfferich, director of the Deutsche Bank, published a survey of *Germany's Economic Progress and National Wealth, 1888–1913* which supplied overwhelming figures of the "impetuous and triumphant upward movement" of the last twenty-five years. Helfferich showed that the population had increased by more than a third, that Germany's excess of births over deaths was greater than any other country's except Russia, that economic opportunity and demand for labour had expanded faster than the population, that productivity of German workers and percentage of population gainfully employed had increased, that upward was the word for statistics on production, transportation, consumption, capital aggregation, investments, savings-bank deposits and every other factor of economic life. Helfferich's pages groaned under such phrases as "enormous development," "vast progress," "prodigious expansion," "gigantic increase."

That year an Englishman traveling in Alsace-Lorraine asked a waiter in Metz what nationality he considered himself. "*Muss-Preussen*" (Obligatory Prussian) the man replied, and for the rest of the journey the Englishman was heard by his traveling companion to mutter at intervals, "*Muss-Preussen*—we're all going to be *Muss-Preussen* before long."

Fear of the same ancient sin of pride that had prompted Kipling to write "Recessional" in the year of Britain's Jubilee now afflicted an occasional thoughtful German. Walther Rathenau, introspective and literary heir of the Allgemeine Elektrizitäts-Gesellschaft, published a long poem called "Festal Song" in *Die Zukunft* whose tone was a protest against the organized enthusiasm worked up for the Centenary. He too saw an apocalyptic vision and headed his poem with a text from Ezekiel, "Also thou son of man, thus saith the Lord God unto the land of Israel, 'An end, the end is come upon the four corners of the land. Now is the end come upon thee; it watcheth for thee; behold it is come.'" Rathenau quoted no more but readers who turned to Ezekiel would have found the judgment upon Tyre: "With thy wisdom and thy understanding thou hast gotten thee riches and hast gotten gold and silver into thy treasure and by thy traffick hast thou increased thy riches and thine heart is lifted up because of thy riches and thou hast said I am a God. . . . Therefore I will bring strangers upon thee, the terrible of nations and they shall draw their swords against the beauty of thy wisdom . . . and bring thee down into the pit and thou shalt die the deaths of them that are slain in the midst of the seas."

Voices like that of Rathenau, who did not have quite the courage to sign his own important name but used a pseudonym, were not heard. Such was German national sentiment that when Hauptmann's *Festspiel* in honor of the Centenary was produced by Max Reinhardt it was attacked by the Nationalists and closed on demand of the Crown Prince because it stressed liberation rather than the sword which had accomplished it. The mood culminated at Zabern, a small Alsatian town where ill-feeling between the German garrison and the natives provoked German officers to assault and arrest civilians. Becoming a *cause célèbre* the incident increased foreign hostility to Germany. When Colonel Reuter, the commanding officer of Zabern, was court-martialed and acquitted, the power of the Army over the rights of the citizen became a major political issue in Germany. If Army officers were put beyond the law, said a member of the Center party in the Reichstag, "then *finis Germaniae*." He was cheered by the majority, but Colonel Reuter received the Order of the Red Eagle, Third Class, and a congratulatory telegram from the Crown Prince saying, "Keep it up!"

*

The combination of Richard Strauss and Russian Ballet, awaited as a major event, was scheduled for May, 1914, with the composer conducting. Attempting to sum up his career so far, Lawrence Gilman in January found the same baffling duality in Strauss which had so often troubled historians of his country. His best work, Gilman wrote, as in the opening of *Zarathustra*, the finale of *Don Quixote*, the love passage in *Heldenleben*, the recognition of Orestes and Electra, was music of "terrifying cosmic sublimity" and *Elektra*, his masterpiece, would someday be recognized as "among the supreme things of music." Yet he could achieve "a degree of bad taste that passes credibility, be commonplace with a blatancy that sets teeth on edge" and irritate by his "staggeringly complacent habit" of writing music without point or coherence, reason or logic. He always stirred the waters, coming up now with something precious, now with mud, but the activity was indisputable. Gilman, who had not yet heard the *Sacre*, concluded that Strauss was "unequalled in music as an awakener, . . . the most dynamic, the most reckless, the most preposterous of all composers, . . . the most commanding music maker since Wagner."

Strauss arrived in Paris for rehearsals in April. Nijinsky, for whom the part had been created, was not to play it, having been banished from the company by Diaghilev in a jealous fury because of his marriage. A new young dancer from the Imperial Ballet, Léonide Massine, slim, barely seventeen, with great brown eyes, replaced him. Ida Rubinstein was the Queen and the Spanish painter José Maria Sert supplemented the designs of Bakst. In a Palladian hall with fountains, pillars of gold, marble floors, and ewers of crystal piled with fruit, Potiphar's wife in scarlet brocade was surrounded by slaves in pink and gold and a bodyguard of gigantic mulattoes in black plumes holding golden whips. Animal life was present in a brace of Russian wolfhounds. A variety of exotic dancers endeavor to relieve the Queen's "almost passionate weariness of life" in vain, until a shepherd boy, Joseph, is carried in asleep wrapped in yellow silk and who, on waking, dances his search for the divine, instantly arousing the Queen from passionate weariness to passionate desire. Her most strenuous efforts at seduction are repulsed, she denounces Joseph, guards prepare his torture and death and he is saved by an Archangel who carries him off to the sound of heavenly music while Potiphar's wife strangles herself with her rope of pearls.

Although the libretto was widely ridiculed and the music was considered second-rate Strauss, the production was so sumptuous and lascivious that everyone enjoyed it and the evening ended happily in a gala supper at Larue's given by the composer for his friends who had come from Germany, Austria and Italy for the premiere. After feasting on early strawberries and exquisite wines, each guest was presented by the waiter with his share of the bill.

The company went to London at the end of May for a two-month season of "extraordinary success." Chaliapin was declared "supreme" as Ivan the Terrible, Rimsky's last opera, *Coq d'Or*, and Stravinsky's new one, *The Nightingale*, were acclaimed and the "ultra-modern" *Joseph*, to be given on June 23 with the composer again conducting, aroused eager expectations. At rehearsals with Karsavina, who had replaced Ida Rubinstein, Strauss demonstrated how he wanted her to perform her dance of seduction. Starting from the far corner of her dressing room and singing the music "he would run, trampling heavily across the room, to the sofa representing the couch of Joseph."

On the night of the performance Drury Lane was crowded to the last seat by a bejewelled and brilliant audience "keyed up to concert pitch for a memorable event." To a young man among them, jostled by bare shoulders and gay laughter, everyone seemed to know one another as if at "an enormous but exclusive party." In the presence of the Prime Minister and Mrs. Asquith, the Russian company and the renowned composer, it seemed "an occasion of almost international importance." As applause filled the house the young man, leaning forward from his seat in the dress circle, could see the tall "world-weary" German composer take up his stand before the orchestra, "pink and imperturbable."

If the music won no new laurels, Strauss's visit was personally satisfying. He conducted the Queen's Hall Orchestra in a program of his own and Mozart's music, which was considered one of the finest concerts of the season. On June 24 wearing the "most beautiful of all the Doctors' robes," the crimson silk and cream-colored brocade of a Doctor of Music, he received an honorary degree from Oxford.

A month later on July 25 the Russian Ballet closed its season with a joint performance of Strauss's *Joseph* and Stravinsky's *Petrouchka*. At the same hour that evening in Belgrade the Serbian reply to an Austrian ultimatum was rejected by the Austrian Ambassador, who announced the severance of relations and left for home.

7

TRANSFER OF POWER

ENGLAND: 1902–11

7
Transfer of Power

Lord Salisbury, who had died in 1903, was not on hand to see the workings of democracy in the first major election of the new century, but he would not have been surprised. A new segment of society was rising, not yet to take the patricians' place, but by its pressure and through its surrogates to push them aside. The age of the people was under way.

It revealed itself in the cry "Pigtail!" which echoed through the constituencies in the General Election of 1906 with virulence equal to its irrelevance. No issue proved more exploitable than "Chinese Slavery" and the Liberals played it up as designedly as the Tories had used patriotic slogans in the Khaki Election of 1900. The slaves in question were indentured Chinese labour imported with the consent of the Unionist government to mine gold in South Africa. Billboards flamed with pictures of Chinese in chains, Chinese being kicked, Chinese being flogged. Sandwich men dressed as Chinese slaves paraded the streets. Cartoons showed the ghosts of British soldiers killed in the Boer War pointing to the fenced compounds where the Chinese were lodged and asking, "Did we die for this?" Working-class audiences were told the Tories would introduce Chinese labour into England if they won and pictures of a pigtailed coolie in a straw hat were labeled "Tory British Workingman." Thrown on a lantern screen at political meetings, the pictures, reported Graham Wallas, a Liberal sympathizer, aroused "an instantaneous howl of indignation against Mr. Balfour." The audience could not have told whether it howled from humanitarian indignation or fear of the competition of cheap labour. Underlying both these sentiments Wallas thought he detected a fear of the alien symbolized by the alien pigtail. The hideous yellow faces aroused "an immediate hatred of the Mongoloid racial type and this hatred was transferred to the Conservative party." In the howl of the audience he heard the force of the irrational in public affairs.

New men were appealing to a new electorate; were called

forth, as was the yellow press, by the existence of a new electorate. People were more literate and to that extent more reachable and more gullible. The ha'penny *Daily Mail* had a circulation of over half a million, more than ten times that of *The Times.* Motorcars enabled candidates to reach a wider audience and the growth of cities made audiences larger. The force of the irrational was not necessarily wrong; it could just as well be right for the wrong reasons. It was not necessarily confined to what Matthew Arnold called the Populace, but the effect was greater because there were more of them.

When Arthur Balfour smoothly succeeded Lord Salisbury as Prime Minister after the end of the Boer War in 1902, the waves of change were already lapping at his feet. Business was good but competition from abroad was cutting into British supremacy in foreign commerce, moving into her markets, taking the lead in new industries. At home upper-class life was still delightful, but unemployment, hunger and want, all the ills, injustices and inequities collectively known as the Social Problem, were pressing against the ramparts of privilege in a tide of discontent impossible to ignore or repress. The demands of a new age were requiring from government more action, more imagination, more positive intention and measures than formerly. The Liberals, who now looked forward to their chance after ten years out of office, believed they could supply the need.

They were not a coherent group and never had been. Their dominant philosophy, as of liberalism anywhere, favored change and reform, but it was cut into by a thousand fissures of ideas and social background. In person the Liberals ranged from Whig aristocrats like Lord Rosebery to country gentlemen like Sir Edward Grey to men of business wealth like Campbell-Bannerman to landless intellectuals like Asquith and Morley to a unique and alien upstart from the Celtic fringe like Lloyd George. Some were Little Englanders who regarded Empire, in the words of John Bright, as "a gigantic system for providing outdoor relief for the aristocracy"; some were as fervent imperialists as the Tories. Some were Church of England, some Nonconformist, some Home Rulers, some unalterably opposed to Home Rule. Some were ardent Radicals dedicated to redistribution of wealth and political power, some were magnates of industry absorbed in making fortunes. Those who were liberals from conviction rather than from family tradition or political expedient felt that between themselves and the Tories existed "a gulf as wide as any in previous time"; the gulf, as Herbert Samuel put it, between "the quietist and the reformer." Filled with the zeal of the reformer, Samuel believed that the principles of Liberalism "are nothing else than the application to public affairs of the religious spirit itself." Some Liberals were sincere, some were opportunists, some were demagogues, some like Lloyd George all three at once. They were the outs, eager for office, ready to answer the demands of a new time.

Their opponents were split among themselves, harassed by a series of domestic quarrels which had reopened since the Boer War with a peculiar vehemence. All the hatred and jealousy of Nonconformity for the Establishment blew up into a national tempest over the Education Act of 1902. Sponsored and largely drafted by Balfour himself, the Act added secondary to primary education as an obligation of the state with the object of making it available to all and of bringing all schools up to a uniform standard. Like the Compulsory Education Act of 1870 it had an economic motive: the recognition that unless the nation undertook to raise the level of schooling, it would continue to fall behind in the competition for markets. In effecting progress, the Act was perhaps the most important of the decade but its method was partisan. By favoring and, in fact, giving financial support to the schools of the Established Church—that is, the Church of England—while the Board Schools under local control were abolished, the Act infuriated the Nonconformists, who were traditionally Liberals. It supplied a cause to reunite the Imperialist and Radical wings of the Liberal party which had divided over the Boer War and Home Rule. Debate in the Commons took on the animus peculiar to the war of High Church against Low Church, Methodist clergymen wrote outraged letters to the papers, the Act was called "the greatest betrayal since the Crucifixion," protest meetings assembled in villages and leagues were formed pledged to non-payment of school taxes with all the fervor of Roundheads refusing ship money to King Charles. Lloyd George, already the champion of Welsh Disestablishment, encouraged the leagues with histrionic oratory. In throwing themselves into a revival of religious battle, people seemed to be on the hunt for excitement, as if the Boer War had created a taste for it while supplying its physical experience to less than two per cent of the population.

The cry "Votes for Women!" promised further trouble and those who raised it frankly called themselves "militants." They organized under the leadership of Mrs. Pankhurst in 1903 in opposition to the Suffrage group led by Mrs. Fawcett which believed in obtaining the vote by persuasion. Their first experiments in militancy, confined to heckling and unfurling banners at political meetings, while not yet serious, were one more evidence, as Lady Frances Balfour wrote, of "new winds blowing hard through society."

At the same time, mine-owners of the Rand were demanding license to import Chinese labour when African labour, finding enough work after the war to satisfy a low appetite, could not be obtained for the mines. Contract labour had horrid connotations from which the Government shrank, but the mine-owners were insistent, else they could not reopen, investments were tied up, Rand shares tumbled, and as the *Economist* frankly stated, it was a matter of *£.s.d.* "If the people of England and elsewhere who own Transvaal mining shares to the value of £200,000,000 want to get their money back with interest, then they will have to tackle this labour question in the right spirit."

The Government reluctantly consented, the Chinese were brought in and lodged in compounds; the Liberals, who had themselves introduced contract labour in British Guiana, now thundered in awful wrath. The Chinese compounds were no worse than England's dark satanic slums, where one water faucet and one privy often served twenty-five families, where beds were rented for three and the space under them for two. But humanitarian instincts grow fiercer in proportion to the distance by which their causes are removed and it is always easier to build Jerusalem in Africa than at home. Moreover the Chinese labour issue carried the smell of money which had hung about the Boer War from the start. It devalued the moral content which the imperialists liked to attach to the cause of Empire.

On top of these issues Joseph Chamberlain wrought havoc with Tariff Reform. When he launched his campaign for Protection he aroused against his party the fundamental British sentiment of laissez-faire, raised among the people old memories of hated Corn Laws and fears of a rise in food prices, handed the Liberals another issue in the cry "Free food!" and split his party between the old and the new Conservatives, between land and money. Manufacturers and businessmen, exponents of what H. G. Wells called "commercialized imperialism with all its push and energy," favored Protection. As an imperialist and businessman himself, Chamberlain saw it as a means of drawing together the mother country and all its dependencies in a vast Imperial tariff system which would stimulate trade within the Empire and prosperity at home, strengthen Imperial bonds, increase revenues for social legislation, and, not least, provide an issue of which he would be the hero. In the British Cabinet he was what Germany was among the nations: dynamic, ambitious, conscious of power and ability, fitted in his own mind for the top place and galled that it was held by another. Tariff Reform was his usurpation of the office he had missed. It wrecked the Cabinet. Chamberlain himself resigned, the better to carry his campaign to the country. Five Free Traders, including the Duke of Devonshire and the Chancellor of the Exchequer, also resigned. In the ranks a vigorous new M.P., Winston Churchill, waving the banner of Free Trade, crossed over to join the Liberals amid cries of "Rat!" from the Tories. Interminable debates raged over preferential duties, bounties, dumping, and other fiscal mysteries. The public, barely comprehending, took sides, Free Food leagues sprang up alongside the anti-school-tax leagues; the British people were rapidly becoming as contentious as the French.

As Prime Minister, Mr. Balfour, still suave, effortless, unaddicted to political dogma, refused to take a firm position, partly because he saw no firm ground on which to take one and partly because he believed a strategy of steering between extremes was the best way to hold his party together and his Government in office. He saw no virtue in a doctrinaire persistence in Free Trade and he could see advantages to British industry in some form of selective tariff, although he had no wish to swallow Chamberlain's program whole. The one thing he firmly believed was that continued direction of England's affairs by the Conservative party was more important than either Free Trade or Protection and this he was determined to maintain. Amid quarreling colleagues, resigning ministers, party apostasies, he eluded all pressures and coolly told the House that he would be ill performing his duty "if I were to profess a settled conviction where no settled conviction exists." He infused the issues with such philosophic doubt and infused his doubt with such authority as almost to mesmerize members on both sides. When called upon to explain his relations with Free Traders and Protectionists within his own party he "indulged the House with a brilliant display of disdainful banter." Exploiting all his parliamentary dexterity, he maneuvered the Government through session after session for more than two years, seeming almost to find amusement in the difficulty of his task. But the performance left his followers uneasy. They wanted the leader of their party to lead and instead, as Harry Cust said, "he nailed his colors to the fence."

Balfour's purpose, however, was serious. He wanted to retain office as long as he could in order to consolidate the Entente and the work of the Committee of Imperial Defence especially after the Tangier Crisis of 1905. He had given the order for rearming the artillery with a new quick-firing gun, the 18-pounder, and he was determined, as he explained later, "not to go out of office until we were so far committed to the expenditure that no Liberal Government could have withdrawn from that position." Relentless, Chamberlain persisted in his campaign. Balfour's dancing on eggs grew increasingly difficult as the exasperation of his own party and the impatience for office of the Opposition mounted.

Overshadowing all was the Social Problem. Investigations and reports appearing all at once after 1900 made harshly visible the fact and the consequences of extreme inequality in possession of material goods. In B. S. Rowntree's *Poverty: A Study of Town Life*, 1901, in the last volume of Charles Booth's *Life and Labour of the People of London*, 1903, in L. Chiozza Money's *Riches and Poverty*, 1905, in reports of the Royal Commission on Labour and in the Fabian Society's studies of the destitute, diseased and insane, evidence accumulated that the richest country in the world rested on a foundation of one-third of its population living "in chronic poverty, unable to satisfy the primal needs of animal life." Chiozza Money showed that economic inequality was particularly wide in England. In France, whose population was about the same, there were twice as many small estates between £500 and £10,000 as in England, but in the United Kingdom three times as many large estates over £50,000 and four times as many over £250,000 as in France.

The investigators produced the facts: sleep, diet, sanitation, privacy, even respiratory air, were inadequate for basic human needs. Professor Huxley had calculated that 800 cubic feet of air space per person was the ideal. Even the Poor House provided 300. In the slums people lived three to a bedroom of 700 cubic feet or, with children, eight and nine in a space of 1,200 cubic feet. Vermin lived with them, a piece of paper on the floor served as a toilet, fish on Sundays was the weekly protein for a family of eight, at two and a half ounces per portion. Children were stunted and pale, with rotting teeth, and if they went to school, sat dully at their desks or fell asleep. Ignorance and apathy as much as ill health were poverty's product; the slums were sloughs of wasted lives. Overcrowding in country villages was often as bad. In an Oxfordshire cottage a family of eight slept in two beds with a pair of thin blankets among them, in a Yorkshire cottage husband and wife and five daughters shared two beds and an attic floor, in Somerset a mother and three children slept in one room, five children of both sexes up to the age of nineteen in another.

For unskilled and unorganized labour, working conditions matched the slums. At the Shawfield Chemical Works in Glasgow in 1897, year of the Diamond Jubilee, workmen received 3*d.* or 4*d.* an hour for a twelve-hour day, seven days a week, spent amid poisonous vapors without a lunch-hour rest. They ate lunch standing at the furnaces and if they took Sunday off were fined the next day's wages. Lord Overtoun, owner of the Works, a philanthropist who gave £10,000 a year to charity, was a leading member of the Sunday Observance and Sunday Rest Societies. In other industries workers could be arrested for taking a day off without permission. If they applied for it, the request could be refused; if they took it anyway they could be, and often were, hauled off to a day in gaol. Skilled workers organized in England's craft unions, the oldest in Europe, were better off. Numbering about one-fifth of all adult male workers, a larger proportion than in any other country, they had their own insurance and pension systems backed by large funds and they benefited from lower prices in their own cooperatives. Nevertheless, vis-à-vis capital, they were still on the defensive and the dark persistent presence of unemployment at their backs made them vulnerable.

England's economy since 1900 had recovered from the depression of the nineties and was on the whole prosperous, active and expanding. Shippers and shipbuilders, bankers and millowners were busy, coal mines were operating to capacity, and although in chemical, electrical and other new industries the British were not as enterprising as some foreign competitors, most businesses, despite ups and downs, were doing well. Yet the gap in distribution of profits was growing not less but greater. While the rich lived at an acme of luxury and leisure, the purchasing power of wages was falling and human material deteriorating. The minimum height for recruits for the British Army was lowered from five feet three inches in 1883 to five feet in 1900.

Something was wrong with the system. Somehow the great mechanical and material achievements of the recent past had twisted society out of shape. In the United States, where the process was accelerated, Thorstein Veblen was moved to make his inquiries into business enterprise and the Muckrakers to their searches in the slums and stockyards and the files of Standard Oil. In England, reformers, writers, crusading journalists, Fabians, Socialists, Radical Liberals were impatient for the remedy. The shrill cries of H. G. Wells warned that material progress without planning would lead to a future, as he depicted it in *When the Sleeper Wakes* in 1899, of higher buildings, bigger towns, wickeder capitalists, more downtrodden and desperate labour, a future where "everything was bigger, quicker, more crowded" . . . in short an "exaggeration of contemporary tendencies." Like a blue jay incessantly pecking and cawing at the ills of civilization, he demanded in *Anticipations* in 1900 and *A Modern Utopia* in 1905 the New Republic of a planned society and fervently expounded the possibilities for improvement which science had put in the hands of man.

Peace, Retrenchment and Reform which had satisfied as the Liberal creed for so long were no longer adequate. The optimistic Liberalism of the Nineteenth Century was past. An "indignant pessimism" inspired Charles Masterman's *From the Abyss* in 1902 and *In Peril of Change* in 1905. A young Liberal journalist, literary editor of the *Daily News*, devoutly High Church in religion, married to a Lyttelton whose uncle was a member of Balfour's cabinet, he was one of the new kind of Liberal, puzzled and disturbed by trends which betrayed the promise of the Nineteenth Century. Another was the lonely economist J. A. Hobson, author of *The Social Problem*, 1901. He saw the brilliant hopes of early Liberalism overcast by the doctrine of survival of the fittest and the energy for progress absorbed in material growth. Political Economy having failed to solve the Social Problem, he believed a new social science was needed to "furnish a satisfactory basis for the art of social progress." Hobson fixed on unemployment as the crux of the matter. He saw it as a waste of human resources and included in that waste the idle rich, of whom 250,000 males between the ages of twenty and sixty-five, according to a census of 1891, were without trade or profession. Under-consumption, the corollary of unemployment, was the chief source of trouble and he saw imperialism, not as the white man's burden nobly shouldered, but as the economy's drive to compensate for markets missing at home. Hobson's views, expressed in *The Psychology of Jingoism* in 1901 and *Imperialism* in 1902, were influential but offensive both to the imperialists and to the Fabians, who believed in imperialism. He was never offered a chair either by the major universities or by the London School of Economics, founded by the Fabians in 1894, to establish that new social science which was his goal.

What the Fabian Society wanted was Socialism without Marx or revolution, something like Macbeth without murder—an intellectual, respectable, gradual, factual, practical, "gas and water" English Socialism powered by the brains, hard work and infinite attention to detail of the Webbs and the brilliant common sense of Shaw. Founded in the eighties, expounding plans and arguments through the Fabian Tracts, it was an intellectual lobby bent on guiding existing political institutions toward the ultimate goals of Socialism. Fabians were the B's in

Beatrice Webb's division of people into A's (aristocrats, artists and anarchists) and B's (benevolents, bourgeois and bureaucrats). They sought no working-class base but preferred to operate, as William Morris said, by "gradually permeating cultivated people with our own aspirations" and gradually influencing government toward their goals. They made splendid progress among those of their own kind but remained a scholastic regiment of seven or eight hundred, aloof from the people for whom they toiled. In England persons of the educated classes did not and could not penetrate the unions. Discrediting the Marxian dogma of mandatory class war, the Fabians believed that labourers and employees must gain their ends within the capitalist system because it was the employers' surplus capital which gave them work. In his lectures "disproving" Marx, Shaw, a tall, reedy, red-haired figure, emphatic, provocative and bold, held listeners spellbound as he poured out ideas in crisp, sharp sentences, unfaltering for an hour and a half. In *Major Barbara*, which opened in December, 1905, with Mr. Balfour in the audience, Shaw spoke through the mouth of the munitions magnate, Undershaft, on "the crime of poverty." "What you call crime is nothing: a murder here and a theft there. What do they matter? They are only the accidents and illnesses of life: there are not fifty genuine professional criminals in London. But there are millions of poor people, abject people, dirty people, ill-fed, ill-clothed people. They poison us morally and physically: they kill the happiness of society: they force us to do away with our own liberties and to organize unnatural cruelties for fear they should rise against us and drag us down into their abyss. Only fools fear crime: we all fear poverty."

The Webbs attacked the crime with mountainous reports and the English lubricant of social intercourse and conversation. Coldly bent on improving society, they were essentially authoritarians, impatient with the democratic process. They favored Protection, Joseph Chamberlain (with whom Beatrice had once contemplated marriage) and anything which strengthened the State and brought in revenue for more sewers, soup kitchens and unemployment insurance. They had no use for the Liberals, who understood neither the imperial nor Socialist demands of the new age, and had little faith in a Labour party of the untutored which would be incapable of imposing its will. What was needed was a strong party with no nonsense and a business-like understanding of national needs which would take hold of the future like a governess, slap it into clean clothes, wash its face, blow its nose, make it sit up straight at table and eat a proper diet. This could only be the Conservative party, regenerated by Chamberlain, advised by Mr. and Mrs. Webb, bestowing upon England the iron blessings of Tory Socialism.

Orthodox Socialism was represented by the Socialist Democratic Federation led by H. M. Hyndman, a wealthy product of Eton and Trinity College, Cambridge, which he had attended in the same year as the Prince of Wales. As devout in Marxism as it was detached from the working class, the SDF expressed all the fiercest revolutionary doctrines of continental Socialism, but, lacking followers, remained a voice without a body. "I could not carry on," said Hyndman, "unless I expected the revolution at ten o'clock next Monday morning." Presumably it was to drop from the sky, because in Hyndman's scheme the workers did not figure as initiators. "A slave class cannot be freed by the slaves themselves," he pronounced. "The leadership, the initiative, the teaching, the organization, must come from those who are born into a different position and are trained to use their faculties in early life." He complained of the peculiarly British technique by which the ruling class absorbed rising labour leaders who proved only too willing to sell out to the dominant minority (that is, the Liberals) after they had "obtained their education from well-to-do Socialists who have been sacrificing themselves for their sake." The tone suggests some justification for the friends who said that Hyndman, a cricketer, had adopted Socialism out of spite against the world because he was not included in the Cambridge eleven. Along with Robert Blatchford, editor of the *Clarion*, and other earnest spirits, Hyndman in meetings, articles, journalism and oratory, relentlessly pursued that Monday morning which he could not have survived and the British working class did not want.

In 1901 occurred a decisive moment in the shifting balance of political power. The Taff Vale judgment by the House of Lords, acting in its capacity as a court of appeal, held trade unions liable for the damage caused by strikes, thus putting in jeopardy their pension and benefit funds. It proved to be that act of the ruling class which convinced the English working class of the need for political representation. Until then English labour believed in fighting its battles against employers by direct action through trade unions rather than by political action through Parliament. Giving its political allegiance to the Liberals, English labour could not be drawn into support of a Socialist party and disapproved of class war. "The English working class," said Clemenceau, "is a bourgeois class." Continental comrades found the English Trade Union Congresses dull and uninspired because the members were not interested in debating ideas but only in immediate gains. To the French, said one visitor, such gains were the gathering of strength for the social revolution; to the British worker they were ends in themselves while "fundamental principles and eternal verities irritate him." He was not interested in a new social system, as Morley said, "but of having a fairer treatment in this one."

In 1892 the eternal verities found a voice in a Scottish miners' organizer with the zeal of a prophet. Keir Hardie, then thirty-six, was a short handsome man with smoldering brown eyes and hair brushed back from a domed forehead. Born in a one-room cottage on a Lanarkshire coal field and brought up with two adults and nine children in that room, where somehow his mother taught him to read, he went to work as a baker's errand boy at the age of seven. On one weekly payday, with his father out of work, his mother in bed with a newborn child and no food in the house, the family's small and only breadwinner walked the two miles to his place of employment in the rain, to arrive for the second day in a row fifteen minutes late. "You are wanted upstairs by the Master," said the girl behind the counter. Entering the room where the employer and his family sat around a mahogany breakfast table set with steaming coffee and hot rolls, he was told he was dismissed and, as a reminder against lateness, his week's wages were forfeit. On his empty way out the maid in silent pity gave him a roll.

Hardie believed in class war to the end. Liberals to him were no different from Tories but just another face of the employing class. When he stood for the first time as an independent labour candidate from mid-Lanark in 1888, the Liberal candidate—Sir George Trevelyan—explained to him how unfortunate it was that they should fight each other to the benefit of the Tories and proposed that if Hardie withdrew, the Liberals would assure him a safe seat and election expenses at the next general election and pay him as M.P. a yearly salary of £300. Hardie, who had never earned anything approaching that sum, refused. Although he lost on this occasion, receiving only 617 votes out of a total of 7,000, four years later he was elected as an independent from South West Ham. When he took his seat in the House wearing tweeds and a cloth cap, unlike others of his class who put on respectable black broadcloth when they mixed in the world, it was as if the red flag had been raised at Westminster. He never succumbed to the capitalist embrace. During a debate on the unemployed he sat listening in growing rage while no word of sympathy for the starving was uttered and finally burst out, "You well-fed beasts!" On another occasion when a member was denouncing the unemployed as lazy vagabonds who did not want to work, Hardie suggested that an equal number of vagabonds could he seen "every day on Rotten Row in top hats and spats." When he addressed meetings, standing like a statue in hewn granite of the emancipated worker, with head thrown back and body erect, he seemed to express the "equality, freedom and triumphant self-reliance" which he wanted to infuse in the working class. With no salary or political funds to draw on, he supported himself, his wife and three children on what he could earn from journalism, the maximum he ever made being £210 a year.

In 1889 the desperate dockers' strike for 6*d.* an hour started the movement to organize the unskilled in industry-wide unions. It continued through the nineties with organizers moved by a sense of "religious necessity" and workers whom it was difficult to persuade that arbitration paid them better than "the fierce strikes in which their repressed emotions sought outlet."

The dockers' strike waged in the heart of London had thrust the realities of labour's battles under the eyes of capital and swept young men like Herbert Samuel into politics. Appalled by conditions among the strikers and by the sweatshops and squalid homes he saw in Whitechapel when canvassing there for his brother's candidacy for the LCC (London County Council), he decided "from that moment" that the House of Commons was "my objective and to take part in social legislation my aim." The strike also brought to prominence a rampant trade unionist, John Burns of the Amalgamated Engineers, union of the locomotive drivers, who was known as the "Man with the Red Flag" from his habit of carrying that item with him whenever he addressed meetings. Although the dockers were not his union, he took over management of the strike to help its leaders, Tom Mann and Ben Tillett. He kept on excellent terms with the police, organized food lines and procured the settlement which won the "dockers' tanner"—to the distress of Kropotkin, who thought a critical moment had been missed. "If Burns with 80,000 men behind him does not make a revolution," he wrote, "it is because he is afraid of having his head cut off." Burns, however, despite a period of vociferous Socialism, was too English to be revolutionary and never shared Hardie's refusal to compromise with capitalism. He preferred to fight labour's cause through whatever alliances suited the situation, and when elected to the LCC, collaborated with the Liberals. His hatred of Keir Hardie, according to Beatrice Webb, "reaches the dimensions of mania."

At the Trades Union Congress of 1893 Hardie generated enough support, against the opposition of Burns, to form an Independent Labour Party of which he was named chairman. Its declared Marxian purpose was to secure public ownership of "all means of production, distribution and exchange" and, lest there be any mistake, "to take charge of the revolution to which economic conditions are leading us." Not unnaturally financial support from the craft unions was shy. Two years later in the general election of 1895, which brought in Lord Salisbury's Government, the ILP failed to elect a single one of its twenty-eight candidates. It was "the most costly funeral since Napoleon's," commented Burns, not without satisfaction in which he was joined by Mrs. Webb. For Labour to act independently and insist on three-cornered contests, she declared, was "suicide." Yet the Conservative editor J. L. Garvin suspected that despite the fiasco the ILP might well prove to be "an increasingly powerful and disturbing factor in English politics."

At the same time, employers' associations—formed to resist the demands of labour—increased in number and joined in agreements to employ non-union labour. To create a "reserve" in case of strikes they organized Free Labour Registries, which were simply lists of strikebreakers under another name. In 1897 they were able to defeat the old and powerful Amalgamated Engineers in its strike for the eight-hour day which lasted thirty weeks. Taking the offensive by lockouts, they succeeded against other unions in re-establishing piecework and repudiating overtime pay. On occasion the Government lent troops in their support. Leaving nothing to chance, the associations in 1898 formed the Employers' Parliamentary Council to smother any nascent legislation unfavorable to their interests.

In 1900, reluctantly edging toward the political arena, a number of trade unions, representing about one quarter of the total membership, joined with the ILP and Hyndman's group to form a Labour Representation Committee for the election of political candidates. The Fabian Society lukewarmly and temporarily joined also. As Secretary, the Committee chose Ramsay MacDonald, a thirty-four-year-old Scot who emerged from obscure beginnings to be a founder of the ILP and was recognized for an astute political sense. On discovering that the intellectuals were not, after all, to control policy, Hyndman's group pulled out and the Fabians, finding the endeavor "not in our line," never played a role. Coal and Cotton and the older craft unions remained hostile. Of the committee's fourteen candidates put up for the general election of 1900, only two, Hardie and John Burns, were elected.

Then came the "staggering blow" of Taff Vale. On the strength of the decision other employers began to sue for damages, the unions lost case after case; with their funds held liable, the long-acknowledged right of strike was nullified and all the hard-won gains of collective bargaining suddenly vulnerable. Discouraged and disillusioned in the old principle of direct action, the unions faced into politics, determined to reverse Taff Vale in the only way possible: through Parliament. Union membership in the Labour Representation Committee more than doubled in two years and with union treasuries opening up, the Committee won three by-elections in 1902 and 1903, including one three-cornered contest at Durham.

Will Crooks, a former cooper and borough councilman, born in a workhouse, Arthur Henderson of the Ironfounders, and David Shackleton, a weaver, took their places in the House called "the best club in London."

Here indeed were new winds blowing through society. Yet they did not as yet seriously ruffle the class represented by the Tories. Its prevailing mood remained on the whole complacent. Tory philosophy accepted a surplus labour force as the fulcrum of the profit system, an economic law of nature not to be disturbed by legislation. Upper-class life continued so comfortable and pleasant that it was difficult to feel any urgency about reforming what *The Times* imperturbably called "imperfections of the Social Order." When Keir Hardie in 1901 moved the first Socialist resolution ever presented to the House of Commons and spoke for twenty minutes on how the menace of the profit system, responsible for the Boer War, the Boxer Rebellion and the London slums, could be remedied by common ownership of land and capital, "Mr. Balfour, coming back from dinner, smiled pleasantly on the Speaker, doubtless calculating that things as they were would last his time."

By 1905 with a general election looming, concessions were necessary. Wooing the labour vote the Conservatives appointed a Royal Commission on Trades Disputes to report on the question of re-establishing the principle of non-liability. It even allowed a Trades Disputes Bill, which would have reversed Taff Vale, to go through committee and pass two readings in the House, though it did not go so far as to enact it. It faced unemployment sufficiently, if not very boldly, to enact an Unemployed Workmen's Act which established Labour Bureaus to register the unemployed and to help them find work and to pay compensation in certain cases. The Act applied, however, only to London and its spirit was one of limited patching. The Tories had no really remedial program to offer because they did not want one.

As a minority party the Liberals needed the support of labour to win, especially to win by a large enough margin to free them of the Irish incubus. For them the appearance of independent labour candidates in the field could mean disaster. Faced with the danger of three-cornered contests which could only take away their votes, the Liberals now needed not merely support but alliance. Labour in the person of Ramsay MacDonald was ready to listen. In 1903 he and Herbert Gladstone, Chief Liberal Whip, worked out a secret pact by which the Liberals agreed not to contest thirty-five seats in return for the voting alliance of those labour M.P.'s elected. Keir Hardie, who was not consulted, would have regarded the arrangement as not only betrayal but superfluous. The Liberals would eventually discover, in his opinion, that without the working-class vote they were helpless; at that point they would either come to Labour or "go the Tory way."

In mid-January, 1906, spread over a period of two weeks, as was then the custom, the General Election took place. Chinese slavery, Protection vs. Free Trade, the school tax, Taff Vale, all the issues aired over three years, resounded again. Chinese labour on the hills of Wales? roared Lloyd George rhetorically, "Heaven forbid!" The voice of the demagogue and the force of the irrational merely reinforced a general sense that the Tories had been in power too long and this time the demagogue and the irrational were right. People wanted a change and they got one.

The Liberals won in a gigantic landslide. They returned to Parliament with the unprecedented margin of 513–157. Not all of this was their own. Labour won a total of 53 seats, of whom 29 were elected by the Labour Representation Committee, and organized themselves in the House for the first time as a recognized party with their own Whips. The remaining 24 were trade-union representatives called Lib-Labs who accepted the Liberal Whip and did not affiliate with the Labour Party until 1909. All 53 voted with the 377 Liberals, as did 83 Irish, giving the victorious party an absolute, almost unwieldy majority of 356. Even without the Irish and Labour, their own majority of 220 made them free of ties to any group. For the first time they had what Gladstone always wanted, that "hideous abnormality," as one Tory called it, a Liberal majority independent of the Irish vote.

The Labour accomplishment was even more startling and its implication was not missed. A friend of Sir Almeric Fitzroy who lost his seat in Lancashire attributed his defeat to the uprising of Labour and did not believe that the tariff and other issues played much part in the outcome but rather "the conviction, for the first time born in the working classes, that their social salvation is in their own hands."

In recognition of the new arrival on the political scene, John Burns was named President of the Local Government Board, becoming the first workingman ever to hold Cabinet rank. "I congratulate you, Sir Henry," he replied when Campbell-Bannerman, the new Prime Minister, offered him the post, "it will be the most popular appointment that you have made," as in fact it proved. After a week's enjoyment of the ruling-class embrace, Burns told Beatrice Webb, "I am a different man from what I was a week ago." His enjoyment of Cabinet office was so patent that he reminded Sir Edward Grey of a sentence from the naturalist Gilbert White, "In June the tortoise grows elate and walks on the tips of his toes."

For the Tories the result was the most overwhelming electoral defeat of a party in living memory. In the debacle even Balfour lost his seat, as did his brother Gerald, two members of his Cabinet, Alfred Lyttelton and St. John Brodrick, his cousin Lord Hugh Cecil, and, "saddest fate of all," as *Punch* lamented, Henry Chaplin, Squire of England, after thirty-nine years as M.P. All subsequently found seats in by-elections but in the meantime the "new Demos" reigned in fat triumphant majority.

During the hectic days of canvassing in Manchester before the election, Balfour, with his extraordinary capacity for detachment, took time out to seek an answer to an older if less immediate question than whether or not he would return as Prime Minister. In 1903 Joseph Chamberlain had been asked by Theodor Herzl on behalf of the Zionists for support in obtaining a colonization charter for the Sinai peninsula. Unable to persuade the British authorities in Egypt, Chamberlain, who saw the Jews as enterprising agents of colonization, offered them Uganda in East Africa as a substitute for Palestine. In the time of agony of the Russian pogroms, when East European Jews were desperately seeking an escape from Europe, the Zionist Congress nevertheless refused the offer, and Balfour wanted to know why. Long concerned with the idea "that Christian religion and civilization owes to Judaism an immeasurable debt," he held the Uganda question in the back of his mind and in the heat of the election campaign questioned his political agent, a Mr. Dreyfus, about it. Dreyfus offered to bring along a friend and ardent Zionist, born in the Russian pale, Dr. Chaim Weizmann, then a thirty-two-year-old instructor of chemistry at Victoria University in Manchester. Balfour at his election headquarters in a Manchester hotel set aside fifteen minutes for his visitor and stayed to listen for over an hour. Weizmann was nervous at the prospect of explaining to the renowned statesman in his shaky English all the history and hopes, the divisions and crosscurrents of his people in fifteen minutes. "I plunged into a long harangue on the meaning of the Zionist movement . . . that nothing but a deep religious conviction expressed in modern political terms could keep the movement alive and that this conviction had to be based on Palestine and Palestine alone. Any deflection from Palestine was—well, a form of idolatry. . . . I was sweating blood and trying to find some less ponderous way of expressing myself. . . . Suddenly I said: 'Mr. Balfour, supposing I were to offer you Paris instead of London, would you take it?'

"He sat up, looked at me and answered: 'But Dr. Weizmann, we have London.'

" 'That is true,' I said, 'But we had Jerusalem when London was a marsh.' He leaned back and continued to stare at me. . . . I did not see him again until 1914." Of the future Declaration that was to bear his name, Balfour said at the end of his life that "on the whole [it] had been the thing he looked back upon as the most worth his doing."

On the morning after his electoral defeat, Balfour visited a friend who for the first time in his life saw him "seriously upset." However, he went to bed with a book, came down to lunch next day "quite rested and cheerful," played golf in the afternoon and again on the day following, appeared thoroughly to enjoy himself and showed no curiosity about the continuing election results, "not even looking at a newspaper." He ascribed the defeat to the rise of Labour and to the public's desire for a change. Real issues had played little part, he noticed, audiences having refused to listen to argument.

Behind his carefree golf Balfour had been thinking. "The election of 1906 inaugurates a new era," he wrote the next day to the King's secretary, Francis Knollys, and the sudden emergence of a Labour party was its salient fact. It was the bid for power of a raw claimant. In letters to several friends on this and the following day, Balfour opened his mind: something more was going on than the "ordinary party change. . . . What has occurred here has nothing to do with any of the things we have been squabbling over for the last three years." Campbell-Bannerman "is a mere cork dancing on a torrent which he cannot control" and the full significance of the drama could not be understood unless it was seen in terms "of the same movement which has produced massacres in St. Petersburg, riots in Vienna and Socialist processions in Berlin." His mind traveling ahead to the implications of this new development, Balfour wrote, at that moment of swollen Liberal victory, "It will end, I think, in the break-up of the Liberal Party." More enlivened than depressed by the new terms of battle, he assured Knollys that he had no intention of withdrawing from politics, because "I am so profoundly interested in what is *now* going on."

More clearly than most he sensed the beginnings of a transfer of power, not a mere political transfer from the in-party to the outs but one more profound, to a new class which, though as yet far from the possession of power, by its pressure on the possessors was causing upheaval in the components of society.

Meanwhile he had no seat. "I am certainly not going to go about the country explaining that I am honest and industrious like a second footman out of a place," he remarked. A seat in the City of London being found for him, he returned to the House as Leader of the Opposition.

Others besides Balfour glimpsed in Liberalism's victory the portents of its dissolution. To the Socialists this was the Marxian imperative. Robert Blatchford predicted that the Liberal party would try to carry out "a half-hearted policy in the hope of not estranging any of its moderate followers." If they attempted really remedial social legislation they would lose the support of their capitalist backers, who would defect to the Tories. If they did nothing in social reform they would lose the support of the Radicals who elected them. In either case this would be their last Government. "The most certain of all aids to our cause is the inevitable disintegration of the Liberal Party."

The Parliament of 1906 convinced the Tories of the rise of Socialism with its explicit threat to the existence of Privilege. Until now the landed aristocracy and squirearchy had believed that they could speak for the people, that their national interest was the same, that in that sense they were one. They believed in the benevolent working of Tory Democracy as long as it did not interfere with the existing order. They thought of the populace in terms of the rural and servant class whom they knew. George Wyndham, Chief Secretary for Ireland in Balfour's Cabinet, a dithyrambic true-blue Tory who retained his seat in 1906, believed he had won, as he wrote his mother, "because the working men love me. I won by their hearts. . . . All my song has been the brotherhood of the Empire for us all, fair terms for the Foreigner, and the glory of Empire for our children with a little straight talk for Christianity in our schools. . . . I have opened my heart to all their hearts and we just love each other. I won on Toryism, Empire and Fiscal Reform. The Irish voted for me, the Fishermen voted for me, the Soldiers voted for me, the Artisans voted for me! Simply because we liked each other and love the traditions of the past and the Glory of the future."

Wyndham's charming Eighteenth Century picture, whatever the case in his own constituency, was for England, as for the rest of the world in 1906, as dead as the Prince Regent. The agricultural class was disappearing, seeping into the cities, and between the industrial proletariat which was replacing it and the patricians, there was no love or common interest. Wyndham and his kind knew nothing of miners and millhands and people who lived in long monotonous rows of urban houses. "Fancy," said Winston Churchill, born in Blenheim Palace, when canvassing with a friend in Manchester they entered a particularly drab street, "living in one of those streets, never seeing anything beautiful, never eating anything savoury—*never saying anything clever*!" The partakers of that fate were the new voters.

Among the 377 Liberal M.P.'s, 154, or 40 per cent, were businessmen, 85 were barristers and solicitors, 69 were "Gentlemen," 25 were writers and journalists, 22 were officers and the remaining 22 included university professors, teachers, doctors and champions of causes. Among the defeated Tories the largest category was still Gentlemen, representing 30 per cent, followed by businessmen at 25 per cent and officers 20 per cent. Almost half the House, to the number of 310, were new men who had never sat in Parliament before. A noble lord on visiting the newly assembled body was relieved to find that few were in "unconventional dress," but *Punch*'s veteran correspondent Sir Henry Lucy found the tone, character and social behavior of the House "revolutionized." The Irish were a rough group notable for bad manners which they exercised deliberately, uncowed by the traditions of the House. Since it was English they hated it, and since the Liberal majority had no need of them, they had no bargaining value and could do little but take out their frustration in noise and nuisance value to impede any legislation that was not Home Rule. Their old, hard-fought, ever-foiled battle to unseat English rule and govern themselves was not helped but swamped by the size of the Liberal victory.

When Balfour returned, the hostile majority openly showed their dislike of him as leader and symbol of the defeated party. New members, according to Austen Chamberlain, were "intolerant and rude to him . . . jeered at him and constantly interrupted him." Unmoved, debonair as ever, he remained master of debate and was able within a year to re-establish his ascendancy and win the respect of his opponents who "felt he gave distinction to the House." Although many of the new Government were his personal friends, the man who sat in his old place, facing him across the Speaker's table, was not. Campbell-Bannerman was impervious, as a colleague said, to the "historic charm" of Balfour; "he simply could not see it." Early in the session he tried to puncture its spell. Required to state his party's position on a resolution against Tariff Reform, Balfour managed an evasion as ambiguous as of old, exasperating the Prime Minister. "Enough of this foolery!" C.-B. burst out. His predecessor was "like the old Bourbons—he has learnt nothing. He comes back with the same airy graces, the same subtle dialectics, the same light and frivolous way of dealing with a great question but he little knows the temper of the new House of Commons if he thinks these methods will prevail here. I say enough of this foolery!" It was a doughty effort, widely quoted, but it did not dispel the Balfour aura.

The real temper of the new House was represented by a different kind of man than either Balfour the patrician or C.-B. the old-fashioned Liberal. The two dominant figures of the new Government, each of whom was to serve in succession as Prime Minister, were both men for whom government was not an inherited function but a professional career. They were H. H. Asquith, son of a Nonconformist Yorkshire wool merchant, and David Lloyd George, son of a Welsh schoolteacher. In background and temperament totally dissimilar, they had both made their way to Parliament through the practice of law.

The most dynamic of the new ministers, Lloyd George had been named President of the Board of Trade, not one of the chief Cabinet posts but one that gave him Front Bench rank. In him A. G. Gardiner, editor of the *Daily News* and a particularly perceptive student of political character, saw "the portent of a new age—the man of the people in the seat of power." If not yet in ultimate power, Lloyd George was obviously on his way to it and his purpose was as clear as that of a fox in a hen coop. He was forty-two, eleven years younger than Asquith and eleven years older than Churchill. Sent to Parliament in 1890 by a borough in Wales in the cause of Welsh nationalism, he was a Nonconformist dedicated to Disestablishment and a Radical dedicated to social reform. His political bible as a young man was *Les Misérables*, which he carried with him in a shilling paper edition whenever he traveled. His stand against the Boer War at the risk of professional boycott and actual assault took moral as well as physical courage. He had strong political principles but no scruples. Small and handsome, fearless, ruthless, and honey-tongued, with bright blue eyes, brown moustache and intense vitality, he constantly pursued and attracted women and adroitly avoided the occasional legal consequences. As a public speaker he was the Bernhardt of the political platform who ravished audiences with Celtic lilt and strong emotion. In public no rhetoric for him was too theatrical, no rabble-rousing too extreme; in office, however, he was circumspect and shrewd, conscious, as he used to say, that "England is based on commerce," and that no party could live by appeal to Labour alone. His greatest gift was an acute, intuitive, unerring sense of what the moment demanded, coupled with the conviction that he was the man to supply it. He "swooped down on opportunity like a hawk," and with it in his grasp, was a man whom the party leaders could not choose but use, even if like Chamberlain among the Tories, he was a cuckoo who would use them.

Ahead of him as Chancellor of the Exchequer was Asquith and coming up fast from behind, Winston Churchill, who had been given a sub-Cabinet post as Under-Secretary for the Colonies in reward for coming over from the Tories. Asquith was a professional intellectual machine who worked by training and judgment of what was expedient rather than by any fundamental primal belief. He was implacable in logic, irrefutable in debate. "Go and bring the sledgehammer," ordered C.-B. on one occasion when Balfour was delicately slitting the Liberals to ribbons, and Asquith was duly sent for. A brilliant First at Oxford, to which he had won a scholarship, he was the finest product, wrote Gardiner, of the Balliol system, which avoids excessive zeal and "distrusts great thoughts even if it thinks them." He understood everything and originated nothing. Firm but passionless he might have been a judge and was a perfect chairman of the board. After a successful early career as a barrister, he no sooner became a Cabinet minister under Gladstone in 1892 than he was marked as the coming man even though he was so unaccustomed to Society that he used to give his arm to his own wife to take her in to dinner. That difficulty was rectified when she died and Margot Tennant, with an eye for coming men, decided to marry him. He fitted smoothly into the elite; he "has no egotism, no jealousy, no vanity," said a woman friend. He dominated by intellect but he did not excite or stir reaction. The public could never form a picture of or pin a label on him and he remains for history a man without a face.

The Government included a number of peers, none of them great landowners, among whom were the aged Marquess of Ripon, who later resigned, Lord Tweedmouth, who became mentally "unhinged" and also eventually resigned, and Lord Crewe, Rosebery's son-in-law, who "horrified" the current Prince of Wales (later King George V) by his habit of wearing a jacket instead of a morning coat in the House of Lords. The only representative of the great aristocracy was the renegade Tory, Winston Churchill. Not Free Trade alone had brought him over to the Liberals. By 1904 when he changed parties he knew the Tories were on their way out. Craving office, he did not want to wait and besides he could not afford to. Although the grandson of a duke, he had to make a living. Journalism and authorship would pay but not with the kind of opportunity he wanted. In America a man of his energy would have chosen business, but for an Englishman of his inheritance Government was the one career for the exercise of greatness.

Recognizing the challenge of the social problem, he believed the Liberals could meet it and he wanted to play a major share. Apart from ambition he was moved by his deep devotion and love for his old childhood nurse, Mrs. Everest. Through her he felt personally the fate of the old unemployed person, "so many of whom have no one to look after them and nothing to live on at the end of their lives." In 1904 he saw opportunity, seized it, made the right choice for the time and won his chance. From then on in all his speeches he preached Liberalism as the "cause of the left-out millions" to which the working class should attach themselves rather than to a destructive Socialism. Once in office he knew that unless the Liberals could win the trade-union vote away from the rising Labour party, they must eventually collapse. He set out to earn it, forming a team with Lloyd George to draft and enact legislation on wages and hours, pensions and social insurance. In a speech at Glasgow in October, 1906, he outlined a program virtually adopting the Fabian idea of a welfare state and far ahead of anything intended by the Government of which he was a minor member. "We want to draw a line below which we will not allow persons to live and labour," he announced boldly and went on to propose the state as a "reserve employer" of labour, the establishment of minimum standards and state ownership of railways. Beatrice Webb was very gratified: "Winston has mastered the Webb scheme," she noted in her diary, and having done that he could be classified as "brilliantly able."

The most outright opportunist called forth to match the new times appeared in Tory ranks. He was F. E. Smith, a new M.P. aged thirty-three, who was one day to become Lord Chancellor under the name Lord Birkenhead. His maiden speech in 1906 was the most sensational parliamentary debut of his time. Like Asquith a barrister and self-made, he too had won a scholarship to Oxford, where, as a star of the Union, he learned every trick, gambit and lunge of debate. An adventurer without connections among the great territorial interests, he was prepared to fight his way up by intelligence, audacity, driving ambition and sheer gall. When he stood up to speak for the first time in the House of Commons amid the dispirited remnants of the Tory debacle, members saw "a young man, elaborately dressed, slim and clean-shaven with a long hatchet face, scornful eye and hair oiled and smooth." Standing with his hands in his pockets and a look of contempt on his face, he began in a suave, self-assured voice a speech of "brilliant insolence and invective." It was so biting in tone and practiced in delivery that listeners hardly noticed the lack of subject matter. The speech was a series of sneers, sarcasm and personal allusion tossed into Liberal laps like firecrackers. The Tories sat up, startled and delighted. When the speaker quoted a slightly twisted version of Lloyd George's electioneering reference to Chinese slavery on the hills of Wales and Lloyd George interrupted from the Front Bench "I did not say that," Smith was undaunted. "Anticipating a temporary lapse of memory," he said smoothly, "I have in my hand the *Manchester Guardian* of January 16," and after reading the quoted remark, added with thrilling insolence, "I would rather accept the word of its reporter than that of the right honorable gentleman."

The whole performance was a triumph of calculated purpose. Smith saw that what was needed at that moment was attack to give heart to the defeated side. From then on he was a growing power. Lacking the keel of a considered philosophy of government, he traveled fast but without direction. His brains were as notable as Lansdowne's manners; they went to his head, said Margot Asquith. Ideas and principles did not interest him but only the play of material forces, and he was supremely confident of his ability to manipulate them. A legend later went the rounds that when he was at Oxford he and Sir John Simon had tossed to decide which party each should join since no party could contain them both. While probably untrue, the fact that it was told and considered apt was indicative. After one of Churchill's speeches addressed to the labour vote, Smith said publicly, "The Socialists had better not cheer the name of Mr. Churchill for he will most likely steal their clothes when they go bathing—if they do bathe, which I doubt." It was a sneer of an unforgivable kind and one which meant a new kind of man was on his way up. Churchill's retort, "Mr. Smith is invariably vulgar," did not prevent them from becoming the best of friends.

Change of government re-established the terms of an old conflict. When the Liberals held the Commons, the Conservatives, if they felt really threatened, could fall back on the veto power of the House of Lords, as they had done in 1893 to block Gladstone's Home Rule Bill. Between the proponents of Change and the proponents of Things-as-they-are, between the policy of Reform and the policy of Hold-fast, another clash was bound to come, as Lord Salisbury had foreseen. Stating its essence he had said, "We have so to conduct our legislation that we shall give some satisfaction to both Classes and Masses. This is especially difficult with the Classes because all legislation is rather unwelcome to them as tending to disturb a state of things with which they are satisfied." When the disturbance became too threatening the House of Lords would balk, not because they were lords but as the reserve defenders of Things-as-they-are. Repeated use of the Veto to block the will of the Commons would precipitate a constitutional crisis. "As long as I am there," Lord Salisbury had said, "nothing will happen; I understand my lords thoroughly. But when I go, mistakes will be made: the House of Lords will come in conflict with the Commons."

Balfour made the first move even before Parliament met. In a speech at Nottingham on the night of his electoral defeat he said it was the duty of all Conservatives to ensure that their party "should still control, whether in power or in Opposition, the destinies of this great Empire." Asquith afterward saw in this a claim to reassert the power of the Conservatives through the House of Lords. Whether it was or not, the event soon followed. In April, 1906, the Liberal Government introduced a new Education Bill of their own to cancel the objectionable features of the Act of 1902. It abolished state support of denominational schools. At this the High Church party reacted as furiously as the Nonconformists had done in 1902. The issue was at once recognized as the opening of battle between the two Houses of Parliament. "Possibly the ministers feel," wrote

Lord Esher, "that *all* their legislation will be nullified by the House of Lords and the sooner they have to stand up and fight the better."

Balfour, following his uncle's line of thought, feared that the Lords would let themselves be provoked into making mistakes. He at once suggested to Lord Lansdowne, Conservative leader of the upper House, that the Government's strategy would be to send up bills with more extreme provisions than needed, trusting to the Lords to amend or reject them until they had built up a case against themselves. Then the Liberals would appeal to the country for a mandate to limit the Veto. Never before, he warned, had the Lords been called on to play a role "at once so important, so delicate or so difficult."

The tone of debate in the Lords on the Education Bill showed no sign of caution and their temper was not improved when they received from the Commons a Plural Voting Bill designed to end the ancient usage whereby owners of land in more than one constituency had more than one vote. "Something will happen," said Lloyd George almost visibly rubbing his hands. "There will be a great game of football on that field before long, I can assure you." In December, fulfilling his anticipation and Lord Salisbury's foreboding, the Lords threw out both the Education and the Plural Voting Bills. Significantly, however, they did not interfere with the equally, if not more, unpalatable Trades Disputes Bill, although the Liberals would have been only too pleased if they had. This bill, reversing the Taff Vale judgment, had been introduced in the Commons and passed against the real wish of the Government and over the objections of several ministers because of the pressure of Labour joined by the Radical members. "We could not resist the numbers pledged to it," Haldane, the Liberal Minister of War, admitted. Cautiously steered by Lansdowne, the Lords let the bill pass because they did not wish to antagonize the working class and cement its alliance with the Liberals.

Making the most of the rejection of the other two bills, Asquith denounced the situation as "intolerable" and warned that a way must be found "by which the will of the people expressed through their elected representatives will be made to prevail."

His challenge was explicit and the house of Lords was waking up. The home of England's 544 hereditary peers, including twenty-two dukes, and of the bishops and law lords who sat with them was a high, dark oak-paneled chamber ninety feet long filled by two banks of red leather benches. Stained-glass windows held portraits of royalty since the Conquest. Walls and ceiling were thick with elaborately carved gothic molding and heraldic emblems. Between the windows, statues of the barons of Magna Carta, inadvertent founders of the parliamentary system, looked down a little grimly on what they had wrought. At one end of the chamber under a golden canopy were twin thrones for the King and Queen flanked by tall candelabra standing like guardsmen at attention. Below the throne the Lord Chancellor presided on the Woolsack, a square cushioned bench. Crossbenches in the aisle accommodated princes of the royal family and peers not affiliated with party. Sovereigns and judges in scenes from English history lent their shadowy presence in murals on the upper walls. The light was subdued, the general tone one of dignified somnolence.

Now the prospect of assault began to fill the benches usually sparsely dotted with forty or fifty peers. Lansdowne encouraged his followers to speak, paid attention when they did and supported their efforts with the gracious manner of the grand seigneur which characterized him. Lord Curzon adorned debate with speech "so infinitely superior to that of the ordinary peer that it is quite difficult to believe that he is ever in the wrong." The Liberals' new Lord Chancellor, Lord Loreburn, lent an invigorating presence and paid the House the compliment of always being wide awake when he was on the Woolsack. He was the former Sir Robert Reid, known as "Fighting Bob," a Scot, a famous cricketer who had bowled for Oxford, a Radical strongly opposed to the Liberal Imperialists and a "fiery orator" in the Commons who now lectured the Opposition "in tones that almost made the sinner weep," and advanced "the most contentious proposition with the most entrancing plausibility." In the rhythm of Gibbon and the gallantry of Lord Tolloller bowing to Lord Mountararat in *Iolanthe*, Lord Curzon acknowledged Lord Loreburn as "courtesy personified, persuasiveness incarnate and dignity enthroned."

On the crossbenches sulked the Liberals' last Prime Minister, Lord Rosebery, who had resigned the leadership and as an

Imperialist and opponent of Home Rule had announced, when C.-B. became party leader, that "emphatically and explicitly and once and for all I cannot serve under that banner." Acknowledged since Eton days for his brilliance, wit and charm, Rosebery, having won the Derby and married a Rothschild fortune, was too used to success to be an accommodator, and remained—in Morley's phrase—"a dark horse in a loose box." When he sulked he could turn "an eye like a fish" on his friends and wither them with biting sarcasm; when he charmed he encircled himself in adoration. His variability caused the public to lose trust in him and recalled to A. G. Gardiner the story of a rustic who, being asked if Wordsworth was not very fond of children, replied, "Happen he was but they wasna verra fond o' him."

During the years of crisis over Home Rule, Rosebery had been leader of the movement for reform of the House of Lords by some modification of the hereditary principle and had three times brought forward proposals toward that goal in the hope that self-reform would ward off attacks on the veto power. The reform movement was now revived with Lord Curzon as the leading spirit. Even Mr. Churchill, who liked to have a hand in everything, contributed his suggestion in an article for the *Nation* entitled "A Smooth Way With the Peers." He proposed a system by which peers should be appointed for each session to reflect the same majority as in the House of Commons at the time, not however to exceed 250. This would exclude the "frivolous, lethargic, uninstructed or disreputable elements." Most of the proposed reforms contemplated some system by which the peers would elect from among themselves those specially qualified by ability or services. But many preferred the simple principle which once had moved Lord Melbourne to say he liked the Garter "because there was no damn merit about it." Balfour sympathized. He advised Lansdowne to "avoid the fatal admission that the ancient ground of hereditary qualification is insufficient to qualify for the upper House. If it is not sufficient qualification it is no qualification at all. . . . I think it a fact that the accident of birth is more easily defended on what some people call its naked absurdity than birth plus services." The Government did nothing to encourage reform of the Lords because it did not want them reformed; it wanted an issue and an excuse to limit the Veto.

Faced with these exciting possibilities Lloyd George became quite impatient with his constituents' single-minded attention to Welsh nationalism and tactlessly told them, "I will say this to my fellow countrymen. If they find the Government moving its artillery into position for making an attack on the Lords, Welshmen who worry the Government into attending to anything else until the citadel has been stormed ought to be pushed into the guardroom." The military language was curious and the speech so much resented that its careless author had to hurry to Wales to declare with hand on heart, "Am I going to sell the land that I love? God knows how dear to me is my Wales!"

In June, 1907, Campbell-Bannerman told the Commons that the time had come to challenge the pretensions of the peers, supported as they were by Mr. Balfour, "at the winding of whose horn the portcullis of the House of Lords comes rapidly down." Lloyd George's choice of metaphor was equally picturesque. The House of Lords, he said, was not the watchdog of the Constitution but "Mr. Balfour's poodle." C.-B. moved a resolution stating that in order to give effect to the "will of the people, the power of the other House to alter or reject Bills passed by this House must be restricted by law" so that, within the lifetime of any one Parliament, the final decision of the Commons should prevail. The Labour party immediately offered an amendment proposing to abolish the House of Lords altogether. In introducing a resolution rather than a bill, the Government's purpose was clearly propaganda rather than action and after the resolution was adopted—without the Labour amendment—nothing further was done.

That summer the Second Hague Conference assembled. In April of the following year, 1908, C.-B., expecting death, resigned and died within a month. Succeeding to the premiership Asquith remodeled the Cabinet more nearly in his own image. Four of a very able group of under-secretaries were promoted to Cabinet rank, among them Walter Runciman, son of a wealthy shipowner, Herbert Samuel, son of a Jewish banking family and like Asquith a First at Balliol, and Reginald

McKenna, son of a London civil servant who had taken a superior degree in mathematics at Cambridge. His appointment as First Lord of the Admiralty in place of Lord Tweedmouth prompted Morley to recall that when he had proposed a certain name to Gladstone for that post in 1892, Gladstone with great solemnity and a wave of his hand said, "Well, for the Admiralty I think we require what is called a *gentleman*!" And "Here we are," sighed Lord Esher, looking over the new Cabinet, "overwhelmed by the middle classes."

The most important change in the Cabinet was Lloyd George's promotion to fill Asquith's place as Chancellor of the Exchequer while his own vacated place as President of the Board of Trade was filled by Winston Churchill, fourth of the under-secretaries to be promoted. Churchill's career almost ended at this point when he had to fight a by-election at Manchester owing to a custom then in force which obliged an M.P. raised to Cabinet rank to have his seat confirmed by the electorate. In a hard contest, harassed by Suffragettes, Churchill lost, to the screaming delight of the Tory press. His defeat proved that the balance was already swinging back from the abnormal Liberal victory of 1906 and it made more urgent the Liberals' need of the labour vote. At Dundee, where Churchill was immediately offered another seat, he insisted that only with the workers' support could the Liberals have the strength to put their legislation through the House of Lords against the growing forces of Tory reaction. "With your support we shall overwhelm them. . . . Ah, but we must have that support."

As it proved, none of the social legislation carried through by the energetic team of Lloyd George and Churchill was blocked by the House of Lords. A Coal Mines Act establishing the eight-hour day for miners, a Trade Boards Act establishing minimum wages for piecework in the sweated trades, a Workman's Compensation Act establishing employers' liability for industrial accidents and the Old Age Pensions Act were passed and the team began work on the National Insurance Bill for unemployment and health insurance which was to be the crown of the Liberals' welfare legislation. None was obstructed by the House of Lords for the same reason that the Trade Disputes Act had not been. The oncoming conflict with the Commons, however, was not diverted.

All the challenges, resistances and emotions of the conflict were stuffed like gun-cotton into a new piece of legislation, the Licensing Bill. The darling object for twenty-five years of Liberal temperance reformers, mostly Nonconformists, who wished to reduce the drinking of the lower classes, the Bill was the Government's election debt to the Nonconformist voters. It was designed to reduce the number of public houses by thirty thousand over fourteen years by canceling their licenses according to a fixed ratio of population. Since the public houses were owned by the brewing and distilling companies, the Bill was strenuously opposed by the vested interests, not to mention the drinking public. Every property owner allied himself with the distillers; the Bill took on an aspect as sinister as Home Rule, as threatening as Socialism. Balfour declared it to be a direct attack on the rights of property and Conservatives responded to it much as the working class had responded to Chinese slavery. A special meeting of Conservative peers was called at Lansdowne House in Berkeley Square. The country peers, or "Backwoodsmen," as they were known, who were never consulted on anything outside the affairs of their own counties, were summoned. Some had never spoken in the House, some had never even been inside it, and, mistaking Lansdowne House for the House of Lords itself, thought the Bill was being decided then and there. "Some of us . . . met each other fresh from the hunting field and were able to compare notes about the past season and discuss possible winners of the spring handicaps." All agreed the Bill must be rejected, and "adjourned for a good lunch at the Carlton Club."

In this case they had the country with them, as was shown in a by-election at Peckham fought on the Licensing issue. It turned what had been a Liberal majority of two thousand into a Conservative majority of the same amount. For the moment it was not popularity but the principle of the thing that concerned the Liberals. The high-handed disposal of the bill by caucus in Lansdowne House enraged them. In November, 1908, when the bill was formally rejected by the House of Lords, Churchill, "perfectly furious," revealed in a private conversation that the Liberals' answer had already been decided. "We shall send them up such a Budget in June," he said, "as shall terrify them; they have started the class war and they had better be careful." In fact the Licensing Bill had nothing to do with the class war, nor was it the class war alone, but the accumulating pressures of a new age which were the cause of Liberal discomfiture.

By 1909, the year of the great Budget battle, Liberalism had run into the realities of a world grown too difficult for the building of Jerusalem. The Liberal program was not winning the working class. On the contrary Labour and Liberals were drawing apart. Labour, impressed by the extent of its own power as revealed in the election of 1906, was becoming more aggressive; strikes had begun again as soon as the unions recovered their freedom of action by the Trade Disputes Act. Liberals of the employing class responded like employers. No pact operated now, and in two three-cornered by-elections in 1907 Labour won. The victory of Victor Grayson, a raving Socialist, in the West Riding of Yorkshire raised frightening prospects. A former theological student with a gift for oratory and a fondness for drink, he preached Socialism as the deliverance of the poor with a fervor that swept through the mill towns like fire. His wild antics in the House twice caused his suspension and attracted attention all over Europe. The Kaiser was reported to have proposed invading England with an Army corps or two, proclaiming that he had come not as an enemy but as Victoria's grandson to deliver England "from the Socialist gang which is ruling the country." In cooperation with King Edward he would dissolve Parliament and re-establish autocratic monarchy as a feudatory of Germany.

Englishmen were increasingly conscious of the threat of Germany. "The danger now is," wrote Lord Esher to a friend in 1908, "that in Europe we have a competitor the most formidable in numbers, intellect and education with which we have ever been confronted." The necessity of facing that danger was one more blow to the Liberal creed. Traditional pacifist Liberalism was violated when Asquith and his fellow Imperialists in the Cabinet, who controlled foreign policy, agreed to give Sir John Fisher four new Dreadnoughts. Conservatives, dissatisfied, shouted the slogan, "We want eight and we won't wait." Haldane's Territorial Army was equally resented by the pacifists of his party, who claimed that it would cost too much and drain money from social reform. With the King's strong support it was enacted over their objections. "We are certainly living in hard times," mourned King Edward, "but yet I hope that peace may be maintained—but only because Europe is *afraid* to go to war."

The topic of invasion occupied both the official and the public mind. The Committee of Imperial Defence anointed an Invasion Inquiry in 1908 and summoned the ex-Prime Minister to give his views on the evidence it had collected. Balfour spoke for an hour in a closely reasoned and "luminous" exposition, "quite perfect in form and language," which according to Esher, a member of the committee, so "dumbfounded" Asquith, Grey, Haldane and Lloyd George that none of them could think of a single question to ask him. "The general opinion was that no finer exposition of this question has ever been made."

The Committee's conclusion that a successful invasion could not be mounted was not known to the public, which felt an awful fascination in the topic. Erskine Childers had raised it in an absorbing novel *The Riddle of the Sands*, in 1903 and William Le Queux more emphatically if less artistically in a novel called *The Invasion of 1910* which ran as a serial in the *Daily Mail* in 1906 and was advertised through London by sandwich-men dressed in Prussian blue uniforms and spiked helmets. In 1909 Guy du Maurier's play *An Englishman's Home*, which dramatized an invasion by the forces of "the Emperor of the North," opened at Wyndham's Theatre and played to packed houses for eighteen months. The idea of invasion became almost a psychosis. Living at Rye on England's south coast Henry James felt "exposed," as he nervously wrote a friend in 1909. He worried that "when [he did not say 'if'] the German Emperor carries the next war into this country, my chimney pots, visible to a certain distance out at sea, may be his very first objective."

The prospect of war negated everything that orthodox Liberalism stood for, yet the Government had to adapt to it. Meanwhile the sex war raged at home. The Suffragette movement, which Charles Masterman believed to be an "outlet for suppressed energy," released a curious surge of sex hatred, a mutual "blaze of antagonism," as H. G. Wells called it, which fitted the other strangely violent quarrels afflicting England in the first decade of the Twentieth Century. Wells thought the main impulse of the Suffragettes—that swarm of "wildly exasperated human beings"—was "vindictive," an outburst against man's long arrogant assumption of superiority. Their open warfare followed almost immediately upon the advent of the Liberals, prompted by repeated postponements and refusal of the Government to introduce a bill of enfranchisement. Unable to obtain any satisfaction by legal means, the women resorted to tactics which were essentially "propaganda of the deed" and, like their prototype, anarchic in spirit. They turned up at every political meeting despite all doorkeepers' precautions and drowned out the speakers by ringing bells and shrieking for the vote. They besieged the Houses of Parliament and offices of Whitehall, attacked ministers on their doorsteps, in one case knocking down Mr. Birrell, the Minister of Education, and kicking him in the shins, broke department-store windows with hammers, set fires in mail boxes, penetrated the House and stopped proceedings by chaining themselves to the grill of the Ladies' Gallery and keeping up the incessant shout, "Votes for Women!"

In 1909 under the Liberal Government occurred the first forcible feeding of imprisoned Suffragettes, a peculiarly revolting process in which both the victims, who invited it by hunger strikes, and the officials who performed it, writhed like animals. It was accomplished by means of rubber tubes passed through the mouth, or sometimes the nostrils, to the stomach. While the prisoner was strapped in a chair and held down by guards or matrons, liquid food was forced down the tubes by stomach pumps. Outside in the streets Suffragettes marched with placards proclaiming, "Stop Forcible Feeding!" and one threw herself at the King's feet in the midst of a court reception crying, "Your Majesty, won't you please stop torturing women!" Inside the prisons the Suffragettes persisted in the hunger strikes which provoked the treatment. The irrational was gaining ground.

Put off again and again by Asquith's promises to carry through Enfranchisement, which he made to secure quiet and never kept, the feminists in the years after 1909 slashed pictures in the National Gallery and set fires in cricket pavilions, racecourse grandstands, resort hotels and even churches. They interrupted services in St. Paul's and Westminster, forced petitions on the King at court, engaged in "painful and distressing" struggles with police, forcing their own arrest and imprisonment. They endured starvation and pain with mad fortitude, invited humiliation, brutality and finally, when Emily Davidson threw herself under the hoofs of the horses in the Derby of 1913, even death. Although these extremes were not reached until the period 1910–14, the practice and the spirit were already strong by 1909.

Men, otherwise decent citizens, reacted in the ugly spirit of a Saturday night drunkard beating his wife. When a meeting addressed by Lloyd George in the Albert Hall in December, 1908, was broken up by militants who, shouting "Deeds not words!" tore off their coats to reveal themselves dressed in prisoner's gowns, the stewards, according to the *Manchester Guardian*, "went mad with fury and rushed upon the women, ejecting them with nauseating brutality, knocking them against seats, throwing them down steps, dragging them out by the hair." In other instances of the kind they were deliberately struck in the breast. Possibly the fury was provoked by woman's abandonment of feminine lures and her substitution of attack as a means of gaining her desires, which seemed to unsex her. It touched fundamentals. "These termagants, these unsexed viragoes, these *bipeds*!" thundered a Nonconformist minister, expressing more than all the editorials. The strange physical fury generated by the women's struggle for the vote was the most unsettling phenomenon of the Liberal era.

By 1909 a gathering pessimism converged upon the Liberals and those allied with them. "A thousand sad and baffling riddles" had somehow replaced the simple verities of politics, wrote Masterman, now a member of the Government as Under-Secretary of the Home Office. In 1909 he published *The Condition of England*, a book of profound discouragement. He saw the world divided vertically "between nation and nation armed to the teeth" and horizontally between rich and poor. "The future of progress is still doubtful and precarious. Humanity at best appears as a shipwrecked crew which has taken refuge on a narrow ledge of rock beaten by wind and wave; we cannot tell how many, if any at all, will survive when the long night gives place to morning."

Around him Masterman saw a complacent society reposing in an illusion of security but "of all the illusions of the opening of the Twentieth Century perhaps the most remarkable is that of security." Instead of security he saw "gigantic and novel forces of mechanical invention, unheavals of people, social discontents . . . vast implements of destruction placed in the hands of a civilization imperfectly self-controlled" in which "material advance has transcended moral progress."

James Bryce, another member of the Liberal Government as Chief Secretary for Ireland and since 1907 as Ambassador to Washington, found discouragement in the central theme of his life, the democratic process. In a series of lectures he delivered at Yale in 1909 on "Hindrances to Good Citizenship," he admitted that the practice of democracy had not lived up to the theory. The numbers who could read and vote had increased twenty times in the last seventy years but "the percentage of those who reflect before they vote has not kept pace either with popular education or with the extension of the suffrage." The "natural average man" was not exhibiting in public affairs the innate wisdom which democracy had presumed he possessed. He was more interested in betting at the races than in casting his vote. Old evils of class hatred, corruption, militarism, had recurred and new evils emerged. Although the world was undeniably better off than it had been, the faith of the Nineteenth Century in the ultimate wisdom of government of the people, by the people, had met "disappointment." For the man who once described himself as "almost a professional optimist," the Yale lectures were a painful confession.

The philosophers of Liberalism, looking around them, were making the equally painful discovery that laissez-faire, essence of the Liberal creed, had not worked. It had produced the evils of sweated labour, unemployment and destitution which Liberalism, unready for the wholehearted state intervention of the Fabian dream, could not cope with. In three years of office the Liberal Government, after coming to power in a new century with the greatest mandate in party history, had not been able to give shape to the great promise of 1906. By 1910 the number of men involved in strikes was the highest for any year since 1893. "We began slowly to lose what we had of the confidence" of working people, admitted Haldane, and "this gradually became apparent." J. A. Hobson and L. T. Hobhouse, the economic and moral philosophers of social planning, had come to the conclusion that neither man nor society was operating properly. In *The Crisis of Liberalism*, published in 1909, Hobson wrote that if Liberalism could not transform its role into a more positive one, then "it is doomed to the same sort of impotence as has already befallen Liberalism in most continental countries."

Hobhouse and a number of other investigators were concerned with man's curious refusal to behave rationally in what seemed his own best interest. The low level on which the populace reacted politically, the appeal of the sensationalist press and the new phenomenon of mass interest in spectator sports were disturbing. Henri Bergson's idea of man as moved by a force which he called *élan vital* had stimulated a new science of social psychology to probe the role of emotions and instinct as the basis of human conduct. One of the most influential of English studies of the mental processes at work in public affairs was Hobhouse's *Democracy and Reaction*, published in 1904. An Oxford don whose deep interest in the labour movement led him to leave the University for the staff of the *Manchester Guardian*, Hobhouse found that the average man "has not the time to think and will not take the trouble to do so if he has the time." His opinions faithfully reflect "the popular sheet and shouting newsboy. . . . To this new public of the streets and tramcars it is useless to appeal in terms of reason."

This was the public which had shouted "Pigtail!" and the phenomenon of herd behavior suddenly was recognized as an entity. The Columbus of this discovery was a surgeon, Wilfred Trotter, who named the phenomenon, gave it status as a subject for scientific study and quietly concluded his first voyage in sociology with a sentence as pessimistic as any ever written. "A quiet man," as a friend described him, with a wide variety of interests in philosophy, literature and science, Trotter, who was 36 in 1908, was to be judged thirty years later "the greatest surgeon of the present century in this country." He had "the head and face of a scholar redeemed from austerity by a smile of great charm and sincerity." In his two essays on "The Herd Instinct" in the *Sociological Review* in 1908 and 1909 he found man's social behavior springing from that same dark and sinister well of the subconscious whose uncovering marked the end of the Victorian age. He saw the subconscious as a force lacking "all individuality, will and self-control." It was "irrational, imitative, cowardly, cruel . . . and suggestible." Because of man's innate desire for group approval, he is at the mercy of this irrational force and vulnerable to the herd reaction. Unlike Kropotkin who in *Mutual Aid* assumed the herd instinct to be benevolent, Trotter considered it a factor for danger because its operation was unconscious and irrational. "It needs but little imagination to see," he concluded, "how great are the probabilities that after all man will prove but one more of nature's failures."

The herd instinct occupied two other investigators in 1908, William McDougall in *Social Psychology* and Graham Wallas in *Human Nature in Politics.* Wallas' life and thought were directed toward *The Great Society*, the title of a book he published in 1914. With Shaw and the Webbs he was the fourth of the Fabian junta until he resigned in 1904 in protest against its support of Tariff Reform. A member of the LCC, chairman of the London School Board, a founder of, and professor of political science at, the London School of Economics, Wallas in his own words was "a working thinker." He was described by Wells as a "rather slovenly, slightly pedantic, noble-spirited man" in moustache and pince-nez whose lectures, though slow and fussy, were "penetrating and inspiring." To another student, G. D. H. Cole, he was "the most inspiring lecturer I have ever heard." In *Human Nature in Politics* he examined the evidence showing that man did not act according to rational assumptions. His hope was that the new methods of psychology and sociology would light the way toward more enlightened behavior in humanity's self-interest.

Wallas did not want to accept the implications of Darwinism which seemed to condone and accept as inevitable the native aggressiveness of human nature and to condemn mankind to ruthless struggle as a condition of progress. Yet he foresaw that, unless the irrational was controlled, nations would engage in a series of inter-empire wars until only England and Germany or America and China remained, and then finally, after a "naval Armageddon in the Pacific, only one Empire will exist" and the inhabitants of the globe, reduced by half, would have to begin all over again. Already the process seemed to be on the way with "Germany and ourselves marching towards the horrors of world war" merely because, having made entities of Nation and Empire, "our sympathies are shut up within them."

Lloyd George's Budget of 1909 was the fuse, deliberately lit, of one of the great quarrels which made the Liberal era, in the words of a participant, "so unprecedentedly cantankerous and uncomfortable." With Liberal prestige sinking, party leaders were aware that without a popular issue they might not win the next election. People were already beginning to calculate, Gardiner wrote, "when the election would come and by how much the Liberals would lose."

As Chancellor of the Exchequer Lloyd George had to provide £16,000,000 of additional revenue for 1909, one-third toward the eight Dreadnoughts to which the Government had agreed, and two-thirds for implementing the Old Age Pensions Act. He chose to obtain it by a tax-the-rich program which, while neither unsound nor confiscatory, was framed as provocatively as possible with intent to goad the Lords to reject it so as to create an issue of Peers vs. People. The Budget raised the income tax on a graduated scale from 9*d.* to 1*s.* 2*d.* in the pound with an extra supertax of 6*d.* on incomes over £5,000. (Already when the Liberals' first budget had raised the income tax to 11*d.* in the pound, a daughter of the Duke of Rutland recalled, "We all thought Papa would die. He looked too ashen to recover.") The new Budget raised death duties to a maximum of 10 per cent on estates of £200,000 or over, it added a tax on motors and petrol which at this date affected only the rich, and also on tobacco and alcohol of which the last was to prove a political mistake.

It was none of these measures but a tax of one-fifth the value on "unearned increment" of land when it was sold or passed by death, plus an annual tax of a halfpenny in the pound on undeveloped land and mineral rights, which aroused the whole of the landowning class in furious resentment, as it was intended to. The land clauses required registration and valuation of property, which to the landowner was no less than the bailiff's foot in the door, the State's trespass on a man's private property. Lloyd George pressed it home in public mockery and appeals to the populace as blatant as when Mark Antony wept over Caesar's wounds. Personifying the enemy as "the Dukes," he told a working-class audience of four thousand at Limehouse in London's East End, "A fully equipped Duke costs as much to keep up as two Dreadnoughts . . . is just as great a terror and lasts longer." When the Government wanted money to pay for the Dreadnoughts, he went on, "we sent the hat around among the workmen. They all brought in their coppers." Yet when "the P.M. and I knock at the doors of Belgravia" and "ask the great landlords to give something to keep the aging miners out of the workhouse, they say, 'Only a ha'penny, just a copper' and they turn their dogs on us and every day you can hear them bark. . . . It is rather hard that an old workman should have to find his way to the gates of the tomb bleeding and footsore through the brambles and thorns of poverty. We cut a new path for him, an easier one, a pleasanter one, through fields of waving corn."

For a minister of the Crown it was a performance that no one but Lloyd George could have given without blushing. If the Prime Minister was embarrassed by it he gave no sign, a point which disturbed King Edward, who let it be known that he "cannot understand how Asquith can tacitly allow" speeches that would "not have been tolerated by any Prime Minister until the last few years."

Furor exploded over the Budget exactly as its authors wished. Conservative leaders roared in protest. Lord Lansdowne called Lloyd George a "robber gull." Mr. Chaplin denounced the Budget as the first step in a Socialist war against property, the Law Society declared a land tax unjust and unworkable, a meeting of City men headed by Lord Rothschild protested the valuation of property by "irresponsible tribunals" such as those which had "cost one Stuart his head and another his throne." The Duke of Norfolk announced he would have to sell a Holbein which he had lent to the National Gallery, the Earl of Onslow put up for sale parts of his Surrey estate, and Kipling in a hysterical poem, "The City of Brass," portrayed England riddled by hatemongers and crushed by tributes levied "on all who have toiled or striven or gathered possession," until without a defender "it passed from the roll of the Nations in headlong surrender!" No less a Cassandra, Lord Rosebery said the measure was "not a Budget but a revolution." Underlying it was the "deep, subtle, insidious danger of Socialism" and Socialism was the "end of everything . . . of faith, of family, of property, of monarchy, of Empire." His speech, addressed to a meeting of businessmen in Glasgow, was read next morning "with the greatest joy at every country house party in England, Scotland and Wales."

A new Labour M.P., Philip Snowden, himself one day to be Chancellor of the Exchequer, said it was necessary to make the rich poorer in order to make the poor richer and the Budget was the beginning of democratic government. Balfour retorted that "you cannot abolish poverty by abolishing riches" and "let them not associate democracy with robbery." The Duke of Rutland, close to apoplexy, proposed that all Labour M.P.'s should be gagged. As rage mounted, the King was forced to confess that the "foolish and *mean* speeches and sayings" of landowners and capitalists were causing immense harm.

Everyone including the common people was aware that the Veto, not the Budget, was the stake. When Minoru won the Derby that summer one man among the cheering crowd shouted, "Now King, you have won the Derby—go home and dissolve the bloody Parliament!" Churchill speaking at Leicester in September welcomed the struggle as likely to "smash" the Veto if the Lords rejected a Finance Bill. Balfour stripped the issue down to the land valuation clauses, which as "compulsory registration" were, he claimed, illegal in a finance bill; "How dare you describe it as a Finance Bill?" In fact, as Lord Salisbury had once pointed out over an earlier budget, there was no constitutional bar to the Lords throwing out a Finance Bill—only a practical one: they could not throw out the Government of the day along with it. To reject a budget and leave the Government in power would amount to deadlock. The Government's recourse, if driven, would be to advise the King to create enough peers to provide a Liberal majority in the House of Lords, as many as five hundred if necessary, a deluge that would drown the hereditary peerage. Nevertheless the mood of the Conservatives was against compromise. Act boldly, said Lord Milner, and "Damn the consequences." This, with Balfour's concurrence and under his guidance, was the decision.

"The whole political world is convulsed with excitement," wrote Beatrice Webb in her diary, as to whether or not the Lords would throw out the Budget. Debate opened in the House of Lords on November 22 and lasted for ten days. Peeresses and visitors, including the King of Portugal, packed the galleries, aged peers came down from the country who "could not even find their way to the Houses of Parliament"; altogether four hundred members took their seats, the largest number to assemble since the rejection of Home Rule. Noble members, from the ancient ex-Lord Chancellor, Lord Halsbury, to young Lord Willoughby de Broke, spokesman of the country group, proclaimed their duty to the country to reject the Bill. As a Liberal, Lord Ribblesdale admitted his distaste for Lloyd George as "half pantaloon, half highwayman," but he did not see anything really socialistic about the Budget, nor did he think the country would be seriously affected by "the sobs of the well-to-do." If it came to a division he would vote with the Government.

Lord Rosebery, after all his horrors, advised passing the Budget rather than risk "the very existence of a Second Chamber." The climax was Lord Curzon's speech, which one deeply moved peer said was the finest ever heard in the House in forty years. The Government, Curzon said, proposed to introduce any measure it liked and, provided it could be covered with the label of a Finance Bill, force the Lords to pass it—"a revolutionary and intolerable claim" amounting to Single Chamber government. Despite the consequences, he advised rejection in the hope of bringing about a reformed House of Lords acting as an "essential feature" of the Constitution and not "a mere phantom rendered equally impotent and ridiculous."

The division was called on December 1, 1909, the Lords filed solemnly into the lobbies, the vote to reject was 350–75. Next day amid loud enthusiasm in the Commons, the Prime Minister, declaring a breach of the Constitution had taken place, announced the Government would appeal to the country and called for a dissolution. Customarily recumbent on the Opposition Front Bench, Mr. Balfour, who had a cold, coughed, tapped his chest, took a pill and sniffed a restorative.

While preparing for the new election, Asquith's Government drew up a Parliament Bill for abolition of the Lords' Veto which they expected to introduce upon being returned to office. It provided that on bills certified by the Speaker as Finance Bills the Veto should be abolished and that other bills, if passed by three successive sessions of the Commons, should become law with or without the consent of the Lords. Talk flew around London about creation of peers; everyone from poets to tea merchants, "even Hilaire Belloc," as Wilfrid Blunt noted maliciously, saw visions of the coronet descending upon his own head. Asquith meanwhile dropped hints of guarantees already secured from the King which were without foundation.

In the period of campaigning before the election in January, 1910, it became clear that Lloyd George, for all his oratorical forays against the Dukes, had failed. The public could not get excited about the peers; Haldane confessed that 40 per cent of the electorate were doubtful and 20 per cent "highly detached," in short, returning to normal. To Alfred Austin, vacationing in the south of France, the election was deadly serious. Since his district was safely Conservative, he felt exonerated from the need to go home to cast his vote, "but I had the results telegraphed to me, every day, from the Carlton Club." At home, wrote Beatrice Webb, "we are all awaiting breathlessly the issue of the great battle." The issue proved unfortunate for all. The Liberals were returned but with a majority so reduced as to put them back in the grip of the Irish. Labour, crippled by the Osborne judgment of 1908 which declared the use of union funds for political purposes illegal, lost ten seats. The Conservatives gained 105 seats, enough to have been a victory but for the low point from which they started. Both sides were caught in a trap. To put the Budget through now, the Liberals needed the Irish votes and the Irish disliked the Budget because of the tax on whiskey. The price of their support was Asquith's promise to carry through abolition of the Lords' Veto in order to clear the way for Home Rule. During four years in office the Liberals had not once introduced a Home Rule Bill, but this now became, as Speaker Lowther said, "the crux which dominated the whole situation." No longer hopeless suppliants, the Irish appeared "sinister and powerful" and the connection between the two issues was made "direct, obvious and unmistakable." Whether they liked it or not the Government was now committed to carry the battle to its ultimate conclusion—a creation of peers or at least the King's promise to create them. Events from this point on rose to a pitch of bitterness unsurpassed since the Reform Bill.

Asquith formally introduced the Parliament Bill in February, 1910, with the announcement that if the Lords failed to pass it he would advise the Crown to take the necessary steps. Then ensued a turmoil of negotiations and intrigue, of pressures on and advices to the King, of inter- and intra-party bargaining behind the scenes, of visits and consultations in country houses, of conferences with the Archbishop of Canterbury. Almost unnoticed, the Budget, cause of it all, was passed, as Lansdowne had promised if the Liberals won the election. But the Budget by now was forgotten, replaced as an issue by the Parliament Bill dragging along behind it its ridiculous shadow of five hundred artificial peers. Though it absorbed for months the efforts, passions and utmost political skills of Crown, Ministers and Opposition, it was a spurious issue. No basic question of human rights and justice was involved as in the Dreyfus Affair. The Liberals insisted that the issue was the power of the Lords to frustrate the will of the Commons, yet, in fact, as Herbert Samuel admitted, "It is true they let through almost all our social legislation" except for the Education and Licensing Bills, one of which had been a composite of compromises satisfactory to no one and the other hardly a question on which to shatter the British constitution. What drove the Liberals forward in the full rage of attack was the need to vindicate themselves for their failing program and for selling their honor to the Irish. They felt justified because their view of the House of Lords, as expressed by Masterman, was that of an institution which would only "allow changes it profoundly dislikes when compelled by fear. . . . It can do little but modify, check or destroy other men's handiwork. It has no single constructive suggestion of its own to offer to a people confronting difficult problems."

What impelled the Conservatives in their equal rage of resistance was a determination to preserve the last rampart of privilege. To lose the Veto or to lose the Conservative majority in the House of Lords meant to lose their last check upon the advance of the besieging classes. They looked on the attainment of power by the Populace, wrote Masterman, who saw their point of view too, as the Deluge. "They see our civilization as a little patch of redeemed land in the wilderness; preserved as by a miracle from one decade to another" and the rise of the Populace as the rush of a crowd upon a tranquil garden, "tearing up the flowers by the roots . . . strewing the pleasant landscape with torn paper and broken bottles." Their resistance, however, was weakened by a split in their ranks. As leader of the party, Balfour held to a policy of warding off at all costs a creation of peers large enough to saddle the House of Lords with a permanent Liberal majority. This in his mind was "revolution." Loss of the Veto, that is, acceptance of the Parliament Bill, he considered a lesser evil. Opposed to this view a group of "Diehard" peers was beginning to form, taking its name from a famous regiment. Its symbol and champion was that "antique bantam of a fighting breed," Lord Halsbury, and its active organizer was Lord Willoughby de Broke, nineteenth baron of his line, one of the eighteen members of the House of Lords whose title was created before 1500. Before succeeding to it he had served in the House of Commons, and besides political flair, possessed "unbounded energy and a marked talent for forcible and humorous oratory." At forty-two he was a personality of ingenuous charm whose father's dying wish was that his son should do everything he could "to prevent motor cars being used for any purpose connected with hunting," and whose great-grandfather "had never tired of voting against the Reform Bill and died many a silent death in the last ditch, or in the last lobby, in defense of the existing order." Willoughby de Broke looked on industrialism and democracy as forces which had "reacted hideously on the nation at large," talked in hunting and racing metaphor and dashed about like a foxhound to rally the Backwoodsmen. In a circular letter addressed to them, Lord Halsbury urged each peer "to take your stand on your Constitutional hereditary right and stoutly resist any tampering with it."

In the midst of tense maneuvering around the throne, King Edward suddenly and unexpectedly died. Extreme Tories claimed the wickedness of the Government had caused his death and regarded the Liberals as regicides. There was a general sense as of an anchor slipping away and of a recognized order of things gone. People somehow felt that the familiar royal bulk had stood between England and change, between England and outside menaces. A song sung by the charwoman in *Pelissier's Follies* of 1909 was widely popular:

> There'll be no wo'ar
> As long as there's a King like good King Edward
> There'll be no wo'ar
> For 'e 'ates that sort of thing!
> Mothers needn't worry
> As long as we've a King like good King Edward.
> Peace with 'Onner
> Is his Motter
> So God Sive the King!

When he died people expected times would now get worse. "I always felt," said one Edwardian, "that he kept things together somehow."

In verse for the occasion the Poet Laureate urged Englishmen to cease their "fateful feuds" and "fractious clamors" and declare "a truce of God." In an effort to spare the new King a crisis at the moment of his ascending the throne, the parties agreed to try to reach a settlement in a Constitutional Conference attended by four leaders from each side including Asquith and Lloyd George, Balfour and Lansdowne. Through twenty-one meetings during the summer and fall of 1910 they discussed and bargained, tried out the idea of popular referendum and came close to an agreement only to founder finally over Home Rule. The Conference at least demonstrated that the Parliament Bill itself was something less than a fundamental issue, but statesmen would not or could not disengage themselves from the combat. Lloyd George, who was nothing if not a realist, tried. Principles being now thoroughly muddied, he approached Balfour with a proposal for a Coalition which, being free of the pressures of party extremists on both sides, might solve both the Veto and the Irish questions. He did not really want creation of peers any more than Balfour, he admitted amiably, because "looking into the future, I know that our glorified grocers will be more hostile to social reform than your Backwoodsmen." Since it is believed that Lloyd George made his first overture to Balfour without informing Asquith, it is possible he also had in mind ditching the Prime Minister as he was ultimately to do six years later. When Asquith was informed of the proposal he neither joined nor enjoined it but remained in the background, faithful to his motto, "Wait and see."

Believing that the British system of government depended on the check and balance of two parties and that a Coalition was warranted only in case of national emergency, such as war, Balfour refused. He did not really believe the Liberals could force the King to give them the necessary promise and in any case he considered there was less "real public mischief" in the Parliament Bill than in the creation of peers. Further he believed that if sufficient Conservative peers abstained from voting, the number of new peers created could be kept to a minimum short of the "revolution" of a permanent Liberal majority.

When Conference and Coalition both had failed, a General Election once more was called, in December, 1910, the second within a year. With public apathy unshaken, the results, except for a Liberal loss of two seats, were identical with those of the previous election. The country, as Wilfrid Blunt wrote, "cares too little about abolishing the House of Lords to make a revolution for it."

By judicious bullying before the election, Asquith had succeeded in obtaining the fateful promise of creation of peers from King George, who was confused by the conflicting advice and devious maneuvers of his advisers. The horrid prospect of England's hereditary peerage submerged by a "battalion of emergency noblemen," all Liberals, pleased no one and the prospect of the world's laughter and ridicule even less. Nevertheless the Government went ahead partly because it was impossible to stop and partly because they believed that when it came to a test the Lords would prefer to lose their Veto than to be doubled by the middle class. At some undated stage in the proceedings Asquith drew up, or caused to be drawn up, a list of some 250 names for wholesale ennobling which, though it included Sir Thomas Lipton, did not altogether deserve Lloyd George's sneer about glorified grocers. On the list along with Lipton were Asquith's brother-in-law, H. J. Tennant, as well as his devoted admirer and future biographer, J. A. Spender; also

Sir Edgar Speyer, Bertrand Russell, General Baden-Powell, General Sir Ian Hamilton, the jurist Sir Frederick Pollock, the historians Sir George Trevelyan and G. P. Gooch, the South African millionaire Sir Abe Bailey, Gilbert Murray, J. M. Barrie, Thomas Hardy, and Anthony Hope, author of *The Prisoner of Zenda*.

In February, 1911, the Parliament Bill was reintroduced in the Commons to the accompaniment of "a great roar of cheering which had in it not only a note of triumph but of resolution, determination." "We are in grim earnest," wrote Herbert Samuel, and if the Lords reject the Bill, "nothing could suit us better." Passed by the Commons in May, the Bill was duly sent for consideration to "another place."

In June began the great transport strike which opened a new period of deep industrial warfare. It marked the change from individual "trades disputes" to action according to the Syndicalist pattern in which workers struck not against a particular employer but against a whole industry. Unskilled labour had become disgusted with the political methods which won them no wage increases and revolted against the leadership of the Labour party, which once inside Westminster had become absorbed in the parliamentary game, with MacDonald gradually displacing Keir Hardie. Mass labor wanted hard gains in more pay and recognition of its unions by employers. It was clamoring for direct action and growing increasingly aggressive. Assaults on mine-owners' property had marked the strike of thirty thousand coal-miners in the Rhondda Valley of Wales a few months previously. Ben Tillett and Tom Mann, leaders of the first great dockers' strike, in 1889, were now preaching the doctrine of Syndicalism derived from Sorel and the French CGT, which combined belief in revolution with trade unionism and rejected political action in favor of the final weapon of the general strike. Mann and Tillett succeeded in organizing thirty-six unions of seamen, firemen, cooks and stewards, dockers and teamsters into a National Transport Workers' Federation. When shipowners refused to negotiate with it, the strike was called in June. It was to last seventy-two days and involve 77,000 men. As it spread from London to Liverpool, Hull, Cardiff, Bristol and Southampton, all traffic stopped in nearly every port and riots, looting and arson followed in its wake. "It is revolution!" exclaimed an excited employer to a Board of Trade official. "The men have new leaders, unknown before; and we don't know how to deal with them."

At this juncture, on July 1, the German gunboat *Panther* arrived at Agadir in Morocco, precipitating an international crisis which teetered for several weeks on the imminent brink of war. In August, in the midst of the crisis, four railway unions joined the seamen and dockers' strike, threatening a total stoppage of all transport. The Home Secretary, Winston Churchill, supplied military convoys to keep essential trains running and sent troops to strike centers. There were inevitable clashes; soldiers in Liverpool opened fire, killing two strikers and wounding two hundred. For appealing to the soldiers not to shoot at British workers even if ordered, Tom Mann was imprisoned on a charge of inciting the troops to mutiny. Although the strike was settled on emergency terms, owing to the foreign crisis, others of equal intensity followed during the next three years. After the gunfire at Liverpool, trade-union votes turned increasingly toward their own representatives, ending the alliance with Liberalism. In the clang of the realities of class war, Churchill's earnest plea to labour in 1908, "Ah, but we must have that support!" echoed now with the faint ironic note of a faraway horn. Dividing from labour, Liberalism's road to the political wilderness was open.

Against this background, Coronation Summer, the hottest in a generation, bloomed in the golden fullness of an open rose. There were dinner parties and extravagant receptions every night, garden parties every afternoon, country house parties every weekend, glitter and picnics and fancy dress balls. Even the heat was "splendid—such a summer as comes seldom in England." The Henley Regatta was held in ideal weather and clear days were on hand for every rite of the season, polo at Ranelagh, the Eton-Harrow cricket match at Lords, the Gold Cup at Ascot. Neither the prospect of war, a general transport strike nor even creation of peers could subdue the high spirits of the festivities. Newspapers used the language of crisis and indignant noblemen growled at "nothing short of revolution" but a guest came to a masquerade ball at Claridge's flippantly wearing a peer's mantle and coronet with "No. 499" pasted on it. Lady Curzon was crowned Queen of Beauty at a Tournament of Knights organized by Mrs. Cornwallis-West, Churchill's mother, with tickets at £20 apiece. The Russian Ballet made its London debut at Covent Garden, Pavlova and Nijinsky danced at private parties, including one in a garden under a blue sky at Strawberry Hill, once the home and gothic extravaganza of Horace Walpole. Its new owner, Lady Michelham, owned nineteen yards of pearls and gave a dinner for sixty guests after the dance in the garden, at which the entrées were served in the form of lighthouses, lit up inside and surrounded by ortolans representing sea gulls with a surf of white sauce breaking over them. At a house party at Blenheim, the Duke, his cousin Winston, Neil Primrose, son of Lord Rosebery, and F. E. Smith played cards till dawn in a tent by candlelight on upturned barrels. "What shall we play for, F. E.?" asked Marlborough. "Your bloody palace, if you like," Smith answered, although what he staked himself is not recorded.

Yet it was not the same, not the England of Jubilee year. The strikes were a reminder of the rising pressure of the working class, as Agadir was a reminder of the pressure of Germany. The assurance of a time characterized in English memory long afterward in terms of "the golden sovereigns, the sense of honor, the huge red blocks on the map," was gone. The gaiety was "feverish," the fancy dress ball of the season was given by F. E. Smith, not by the Duchess of Devonshire (the Duke had died in 1908), and in London the last horse-drawn bus had disappeared from the streets; motor-taxis, of which there had been none at the turn of the century, now outnumbered horsecabs 6,300 to 5,000.

The upper class still found life and each other immensely agreeable. At a party given by Mrs. Hwfa Williams and entertained by the wit of the Marquis de Soveral, the conversation was so generally enjoyed that the guests who had come to lunch stayed until one o'clock in the morning. It may have been enjoyment or they may have stayed from boredom, the boredom of having nothing else to do. The laughter, the fun, the practical jokes, the undeniable high spirits of privileged life of the time were the other face of ennui. The endless talk "at luncheon, tea and dinner, at dances and gatherings far into the night," Masterman believed, was the talk "of a society desirous of being interested, more often finding itself bored, filled with a resolute conviction that it must 'play the game,' and that this is the game to be played." They were "an aggregation of clever, agreeable, often lovable people . . . trying with desperate seriousness to make something of a life spared the effort of wage-earning." Writing in 1909 he did not call it the boredom of peace, yet when he wrote of "the present Roman peace which has come upon the western races of Europe," it was almost with a reluctant sigh.

During the first week of July the House of Lords amended the Parliament Bill so as to cancel abolition of the Veto and to except Home Rule from legislation which could become law without their consent. On July 18 Asquith officially informed Balfour by letter that he was in possession of the King's promise to create peers, that the amendments were unacceptable and that he proposed to make a statement to the Commons that unless the Lords passed the bill in its original form he would ask the Crown to take appropriate measures. The Diehards flung themselves furiously into organizing resistance like settlers preparing a stockade against the Indians. "Let them make their peers," declared Lord Curzon at a Diehard meeting, "we will die in the last ditch before we will give in!" To those who did not sympathize they were known as "Ditchers" thereafter. Among them were the new Marquess of Salisbury, his brother-in-law the Earl of Selborne, and, in the Commons, his younger brother Lord Hugh Cecil, Austen Chamberlain, George Wyndham and the two adventurers, Sir Edward Carson and F. E. Smith. During that hot July, Lord Willoughby de Broke worked feverishly canvassing all the peers, arranging meetings and obtaining speakers. On July 12, fifty-three peers including five dukes signed a letter to Lord Lansdowne stating that unless the amendments were retained they would vote to reject the Parliament Bill at its final reading "even though the consequence be the creation of peers."

Balfour and Lansdowne, whom the King begged not to force him to the loathsome expedient, summoned a Shadow Cabinet of the Opposition of which a majority, though not all, were willing to follow their recommendation to surrender, that is, to let the Parliament Bill pass without a division, since to die in the last ditch, while upholding principle, would not prevent abolition of the Veto. Unless the Government were bluffing, the result would only be creation of peers *and* loss of the Veto. But the Ditchers were adamant. To call for a division, said Lord Halsbury, was his "solemn duty to God and country." Assuming that the "Hedgers," as the followers of Balfour and Lansdowne were now called, abstained, the Ditchers needed enough votes to outnumber the seventy-five Liberal peers. Willoughby de Broke believed he had sixty and hoped for eighty.

Once more a meeting was called at Lansdowne House in an effort to arrive at a concerted policy between Hedgers and Ditchers. Curzon had now come around to Balfour's view but old Lord Halsbury grimly maintained he "would divide, even if alone, rather than surrender." Balfour was urged to call another meeting of the Shadow Cabinet but he was becoming irritated and impatient with the "theatrical" attitude of the Diehards, especially of the commoners such as Smith and Chamberlain. The most he would do was to write a public letter to *The Times* addressed to a "perplexed peer" advising the necessity of passing the Bill. The Ditchers replied that the Bill would establish Single Chamber government and they could not absolve themselves from responsibility "for a contemplated revolution merely by abstention." As the climax of their campaign they organized a great banquet in honor of Lord Halsbury for which the demand for tickets exceeded the capacity of the hall. Amid gladiatorial speeches and toasts Lord Halsbury, appearing "very unwell, anxious and tired," expressed the determination of his group to fight to the end and received a tremendous ovation. Lord Milner, whose "Damn the consequences" might be said to have started the train of events, was a logical addition to the company. Among other speakers Austen Chamberlain denounced Asquith as having "tricked the Opposition, entrapped the Crown and deceived the people."

On July 24, the day when the Prime Minister was scheduled to make his announcement to the Commons, the Ditchers' supporters in that House, led by Lord Hugh Cecil and F. E. Smith, organized a protest which culminated in the "most violent scene in the Commons within living memory." All the anger and frustration of a class on the defensive exploded in a demonstration of hatred and hysteria. Smith entered it from love of attack, Lord Hugh from passionate sincerity. In him all the Cecils' hatred of change was concentrated without the cooling Cecil skepticism so notable in his cousin Arthur. All his convictions were white hot. He saw doom in modern materialist society, in the turning away from Church and land and in democracy's turning away from "natural" leaders. Tall and stooped like his father as a young man, with a somber, narrow face, he had his father's habit of twisting and turning his long hands and looked and behaved like Savonarola. Churchill, at whose wedding in 1908 he had been best man, wrote that in Cecil "I met for the first time a real Tory, a being out of the Seventeenth Century." In private conversation he was "so quick, witty and unexpected that it was a delight to hear him," and in the House he held members "riveted in pin-drop silence for more than an hour" with a discourse on the difference between Erastians and High Churchmen. Considered by Asquith "the best speaker in the House of Commons and indeed anywhere," he was in gift of speech as in opinions an English Albert de Mun.

Once when Gladstone visited Hatfield, Hugh, then a small boy, burst into his bedroom and hit him with his fists, crying, "You're a bad man!"

"How can I be a bad man when I am your father's friend?" asked Gladstone, who had not dominated a thousand debates for nothing. But this opponent was not to be sidetracked into debate; he dealt in finalities. "My father is going to cut off your head with a great big sword" was his answer.

The sword was now drawn against Mr. Asquith. At three in the afternoon, in a House already buzzing with excitement, with every seat taken and members standing in the gangway, clustered in dense groups like bees, and galleries packed with onlookers, the Prime Minister entered, looking flushed and a little nervous. Liberals rose to their feet waving their order papers and cheered for three minutes, drawing "fierce ejaculations" from the Opposition, who cheered in their turn when Balfour came in. As Asquith rose to speak he was interrupted before he could pronounce an audible sentence by shouts of "Traitor!" and "Redmond!" in reference to the Irish sword hanging over his head, followed by a low steady murmur of "Divide! . . . 'vide! . . . 'vide!"* which began, grew, died away, and each time Asquith opened his mouth, began again. Standing on the Opposition front bench below the gangway, his eyes blazing, his bony ungainly body swaying to the rhythm of his cries, his face ashen and contorted by "tremendous passion," Hugh Cecil faced him, possessed by a fanaticism which allowed him to believe that any tactic, however discreditable, was justified for the sake of the cause. Asquith looked at his screaming foes with scorn and wonder, his eyes coming to rest on Cecil with the fascinated gaze of someone held by the pacing of a caged tiger. In the galleries excited ladies stood on their chairs. Sir Edward Grey, with a grim face, moved over next to Asquith as if to protect him. Balfour, lounging opposite, watched his own followers with a look of amazed disgust. Several times Asquith tried to read his statement but nothing he said could be heard over the shouts of " 'vide! 'vide!" "Who killed the King?" and "Dictator!" What few words he managed to make heard only enraged his opponents and evoked more howls. Despite every effort of the Speaker the demonstrators refused to subside. For three-quarters of an hour Asquith stood his ground until finally "white with anger" he folded up his speech and sat down.

When Balfour rose to speak the Liberals did not retaliate, but when F. E. Smith, who was believed to be the instigator, stood up he was met by pandemonium. To have exaggerated the intensity of passion in the House that afternoon, wrote *The Times'* correspondent, would have been impossible. Again the Speaker was helpless, and finally after the session had lasted two hours and amid continued shouts and an isolated cry from the Labour benches, "Three cheers for the Social Revolution!" he adjourned the House as a "disorderly assembly," for the first time in its history.

The brawling and abuse of the "Cecil scene," as it came to be known, astonished everyone. No Prime Minister had ever before been so disrespectfully treated. The press overflowed with indignant comment and letters pro and con. Many felt

*The call for a vote, which is taken by division, that is, a physical separation of members into their respective lobbies.

that the scene had been directed as much against Balfour's leadership as against Asquith. Blunt recorded that F. E. Smith, George Wyndham and Bendor (the Duke of Westminster) were "in the highest possible spirits at the commotion they have caused and consider they have forced Balfour's hand."

Publication next day of Asquith's unheard statement marked the point of no recall and the Conservative leaders had to face the possibility that the insurgents would actually bring about the "revolution" that Balfour most wished to avoid—creation of a permanent Liberal majority in the Lords. If the Diehards could muster more than seventy-five, creation of peers must follow—unless the Government was bluffing. Was it bluffing? Many still believed so; no one could be sure. Nor did anyone know how many peers would actually vote with the Diehards. In this crucial situation Lansdowne and the Hedgers had to undertake the terrible necessity of finding a number of Conservative peers who would sacrific principle if not honor to vote with the Government for the bill they detested. It was the only way to prevent a possible Diehard majority. How many would be needed for the sacrifice and how many would have the courage at the last moment to perform it was another of the painful uncertainties of the situation.

On August 10, the day for drinking the hemlock, the temperature reached a record of a hundred degrees and tension at Westminster was even higher, for, unlike previous political crises, the outcome was in suspense. By 4:00 P.M. the House of Lords had filled to the last seat with the greatest attendance ever known, with visitors' galleries jammed and peers standing in passages and doorways. They wore morning coats with wing collars, ascots, spats and light waistcoats and after the dinner recess many appeared in white tie and tails. The Diehards wore white sprigs of heather sent by the Duchess of Somerset, while many of the Hedgers wore red roses. As Halsbury marched to his seat with the air of a knight entering the lists he seemed to an observer to be accompanied by an almost audible sound of jingling spurs. In a shrill appeal to conscience he demanded defeat of the Bill. Lord Curzon spoke for the majority and afterward sat "pale and angry" while Lord Selborne sprang to the table and "in strident tones with dramatic gestures" fiercely renewed the intention to die in the last ditch. New suspense was injected by the speech of the Liberal leader, Lord Crewe, whose reference to the King's "natural reluctance" and whose own unhappy conclusion, "The whole business, I frankly admit, is odious to me," reinvigorated a belief that the Government was bluffing. Anxious counts and recounts took place. Of six peers who sat at the same table during the dinner recess, two of whom, Lord Cadogan and Lord Middleton, were former Conservative Cabinet members, not one had made up his mind how to vote. When, on reassembling, one of the "sacrificial" peers, Lord Camperdown, announced his intention to vote with the Government, the Duke of Norfolk, enraged, replied that if any Conservative peer voted for the Bill, he and his group would vote with the Diehards. Lord Morley, whose peerage was barely three years old, nevertheless felt "deeply moved" when obliged to make explicit the Government's intention to follow defeat of the Bill by "a large and prompt creation of peers." Upon request he repeated the statement. A pall settled on the chamber. The Archbishop of Canterbury urged members not to provoke an act that would make their House and indeed the country a "laughing stock." Lord Rosebery, whose vacillations had confused everyone but who had been expected to abstain, suddenly jumped up from the crossbenches and announced, in "this last, shortest and perhaps most painful speech of my life," that he would vote with the Government. Since, whatever the outcome, "the House of Lords, as we have known it, disappears," he said he intended never to enter its doors again, and he never did.

At 10:40 P.M. amid "intense excitement" the division was called. Abstaining peers who could find room squeezed onto the steps of the throne where they could remain without voting while the rest of the abstainers led by Lord Lansdowne left the chamber. The two groups, as they gathered to file out in two streams into the lobbies on either side of the chamber, appeared to the tense watchers in the galleries about equal in number. Counting was done by tellers with white wands who tapped the shoulder of each peer as he returned from the division lobby. Slowly the streams reappeared while from the open doors the tellers could be heard counting aloud, "one, two, three, four. . . ." For a quarter of an hour which seemed like a full hour the process continued. During an accidental pause in the Government stream, the undaunted Lord Halsbury was heard to whisper, "There! I knew we should beat them!" Lord Morley waited anxiously for the sight of the bishops' lawn sleeves, feeling certain that they would vote with the Government. The procession came to an end. The tellers brought their count to the Chief Whip, Lord Herschell, who handed the results on a piece of paper to the Lord Chancellor. Amid profound silence Lord Loreburn rose from the Woolsack, shook back the panels of his wig and in clear tones announced the result: for the Bill, 131; against, 114; majority, 17. Unable to contain her emotion Lady Halsbury hissed loudly from the Peeresses' Gallery. No cheers or enthusiasm came from the victors except for M.P.'s who dashed off with the news to their own House, where it was greeted with roars of triumph. The Lords left at once and in five minutes their hall was empty. Thirty-seven Conservative peers plus the two archbishops and eleven bishops had voted with the Government and those of them who appeared that night among a tumultuous gathering at the Carlton Club were greeted with cries of "Shame!" and "Judas!"

"The floodgates of revolution are opened," bawled Lord Northcliffe's *Daily Mail* next morning, but no waters poured through. With the Veto abolished the way was open for a Home Rule Bill which the Government introduced in the following session. In the event, the victory over the Lords proved irrelevant. Opposition to Home Rule merely shifted its ground and, in the fresh form of the Ulster rebellion, provoked a new and sterner crisis in which the existence of the Parliament Bill was immaterial. Ultimately it took a greater upheaval than abolition of the Veto to lift the Irish incubus off English politics.

Some weeks later Sir Edward Grey remarked to Winston Churchill, "What a remarkable year this has been: the heat, the strikes, and now the foreign situation."

"Why," said Winston, "you've forgotten the Parliament Bill," and a friend who recorded the conversation added, "and so he had and so had everybody."

On the morning after the vote in the House of Lords, the heat wave and the transport strike, which seemed about to become a general strike and to threaten a "real danger of social revolution," absorbed the country's attention. A chagrined peer could find "no evidence anywhere that the Constitutional crisis had agitated the country." On the same day a measure of perhaps greater significance passed the House of Commons: a Payment of Members Bill by which M.P.'s would henceforth receive an annual salary of £400. It had long been bitterly fought by the Conservatives and determinedly sought by Labour. Non-payment was regarded by the Labour party as depriving the working class of the right to be represented in Parliament by men from their own ranks. Especially was payment needed after the Osborne judgment cut off the use of union funds for members' salaries. To its opponents, Payment of Members marked the passing of politics as a gentleman's profession and as such was "more disastrous" even than the Parliament Bill. It would introduce a new and "intolerable type of professional politician," complained Austen Chamberlain. It would remove the "last check upon the inrush of mere adventurers," said *The Times*, then owned by that supreme adventurer Lord Northcliffe, and it would encourage the "invasion" of unpaid forms of public service "now efficiently carried on by men who can afford to be disinterested." For the patrician, free of pecuniary greed and partaking in government from a sense of civic duty, the point was valid but obsolete; society's needs had grown beyond him, nor had he ever been disinterested in defending the ramparts of his caste. Payment of Members measured another advance in the transfer of power.

The next act followed logically: Balfour resigned the leadership of the Conservative Party, which he had held in the House of Commons for twenty years. His announcement, made on November 8, 1911, after returning from a vacation in Bad Gastein, caused a political "sensation." Although a movement for his ouster under the slogan B.M.G. (Balfour Must Go) had taken shape, inspired by the insurgent wing under the influence of F. E. Smith and Austen Chamberlain, it had been expected that he would fight for control. But the final stages of the Veto crisis, the wildness of a meaningless battle, the preference of the Ditchers for gesture over thought, the rising influence of adventurers such as Smith, whom he detested, and the challenge to his own leadership displayed by the uncouth tactics of the Cecil scene, had accumulated in Balfour to the point of irritated indifference. Almost as a gesture of contempt he had not waited for the issue of the final vote in the House of Lords but left for Bad Gastein the day before. During his stay among "the cataracts, the pines and the precipices" he thought things over and reached a decision. He was sixty-three, his interest in philosophy was still strong and to face the necessity of returning to a fight for control, first of the party, then of the country, against the trends of a new age did not appeal to him. He belonged to a tradition in which government was the function of the patrician, whereas already, as he said in his speech of resignation, the demand upon administrators and legislators had become so heavy that the affairs of state must devolve upon those who were prepared "to be politicians and nothing but politicians, to work the political machine as professional politicians." The rush of the crowd upon the tranquil garden, as Masterman had depicted the rise of the Populace, was under way and Balfour was too much the philosopher to fight it.

His succession went to neither of the two chief contenders, Walter Long, representing the landed gentry, nor Austen Chamberlain, who canceled each other out, but to Bonar Law, a Glasgow steel manufacturer, born a Canadian, who read the newspapers regularly, ate meals of vegetables, milk and rice pudding and had the backing of another of the adventurers, his fellow Canadian Max Aitken, soon to be Lord Beaverbrook.

Balfour's departure inspired floods of press comment and political gossip and an impeccable tribute from Asquith to "the most distinguished member of the greatest deliberative body in the world." George Wyndham, rather more sour if more genuine, thought Balfour's refusal to fight was in character, arising from indifference which came from taking "too scientific a view of politics." "He knows," said Wyndham, "that there was once an ice age and that there will be an ice age again."

8

THE DEATH OF JAURÈS

THE SOCIALISTS: 1890–1914

8

The Death of Jaurès

SOCIALISM WAS international. Its name as an organized movement, the Second International Workingmen's Association, said so. Its anthem, "The International," affirmed it and promised besides that "tomorrow the International will be the human race." Its founding Congress of 1889 had as joint presidents a Frenchman and a German, Edouard Vaillant and Wilhelm Liebknecht. Its membership at its height represented the Socialist parties of thirty-three nations and would-be nations, including Germany, France, England, Austria, Hungary and Bohemia, Russia, Finland, Holland, Belgium, Spain, Italy, Sweden, Norway, Denmark, Serbia, Bulgaria, India, Japan, Australia and the United States. Its flag was a solid red representing the blood of Everyman. Its essential thesis was that the class solidarity of workingmen transcended national frontiers in a horizontal division of society. Its holiday set aside the first of May to demonstrate proletarian brotherhood. Its slogan was "Workers of the World, Unite!"

Whether or not miners, factory hands, farm labourers, servants and other members of the working class, in whose interest Socialism existed, felt themselves to be international, their leaders believed it, practiced it, counted on it. At the Amsterdam Socialist Congress which took place in 1904 during the Russo-Japanese War, the Russian and Japanese delegates, Plekhanov and Katayama, were seated side by side. When the two men clasped hands, all 450 delegates rose to their feet in a tribute of thunderous applause. When Plekhanov and Katayama each made a speech declaring that the war had been forced upon his country by capitalism and was not a matter of the Japanese people fighting the Russian people, they were listened to in "almost religious silence" and sat down amid cheers.

Socialism was equally predicated on the concept of class war and on its eventual outcome, the destruction of capitalism. It regarded both the ruling class and the bourgeoisie as the enemy. The sentiment was reciprocated. The word "Socialist" had a ring of blood and terror, like "Jacobin" of the old days. During the quarter century following its founding in Paris in 1889 on the hundredth anniversary of the French Revolution, the Second International inspired growing apprehension in the ruling class. Vienna was "paralyzed with fright" when Viktor Adler, the Austrian Socialist leader, called for a one-day general strike and mass demonstrations throughout the Empire on the first May Day to demonstrate the workers' united strength. When Adler announced a workers' parade down the chestnut-bordered Prater where usually only the carriages of the wealthy appeared, the rich and their allies trembled, expecting the rabble would set houses on fire, plunder shops, and commit unimaginable atrocities on their march. Merchants let down their iron shutters, parents forbade children to go out of doors, police were posted at every street corner, troops were held in reserve. The bourgeoisie saw spreading before their feet what Henry George had called in *Progress and Poverty* "the open-mouthed, relentless hell which yawns beneath civilized society." They were made aware of the rising threat "of the House of Want upon the House of Have."

When the Second International was founded, the twelve-hour day and seven-day week were normal for unorganized labour. Sunday rest and the ten- or nine-hour day were the hard-won privileges of skilled labour in the craft unions, which represented barely one-fifth of the labour force. In 1899 Edwin Markham, struck by the bent brute figure of Millet's "Man with the Hoe," expressed both society's fear and responsibility in a poem named for the picture:

> Through this dread shape humanity betrayed,
> Plundered, profaned and disinherited,
> Cries protest to the Judges of the World,
> A protest that is also prophecy. . . .
>
> How will the Future reckon with this Man?
> How answer his brute question in that hour
> When whirlwinds and rebellion shake the world?
> How will it be with the kingdoms and the kings—
> With those who shaped him to the thing he is—
> When this dumb Terror shall reply to God
> After the silence of the centuries?

In 1899, when poetry still spoke to the public, Markham's poem caused a sensation. Newspapers throughout America reprinted it, editorials discussed it, clergymen used it as a text, school children studied it, debating societies debated it, and commentators called it "the cry of the *zeitgeist*" and, next to Kipling's "Recessional," the most "meaningful poem of the age."

The public conscience which responded to an artist's vision and a poet's words was frightened and angry when confronted with the real thing. When in 1891 the textile workers of Fourmies, a small industrial town in northern France, organized a May Day demonstration for the eight-hour day, police charged their parade and in the ensuing melee killed ten people, including several children. "Take care!" warned Clemenceau in the Chamber. "The dead are strong persuaders. One must pay attention to the dead. . . . I tell you that the primary fact of politics today is the inevitable revolution which is preparing. . . . The Fourth Estate is rising and reaching for the conquest of power. One must take sides. Either you meet the Fourth Estate with violence or you welcome it with open arms. The moment has come to choose."

There was little disposition toward open arms. When the Socialist leaders and unions of Belgium, after two previous bloody attempts, succeeded in 1893 in organizing a general strike for equal manhood suffrage, the essential precondition for the conquest of power, soldiers killed twelve before the strike ended. When the Pullman strike in the United States in 1894 stopped trains and the mail, Judge William Howard Taft of Cincinnati, far from a ferocious man, wrote to his wife, "It will be necessary for the military to kill some of the mob before the trouble can be stayed. They have only killed six . . . as yet. This is hardly enough to make an impression." Here was the class war in operation.

Socialism's ultimate aim was the abolition of private property and the redistribution of the world's goods to provide everybody with enough. The goal was the same as that of Anarchism; what caused the permanent conflict between the two groups was that the Socialists believed in organization and political action to achieve it.

Collective ownership was the answer of both to the terrible

riddle posed by the Nineteenth Century: that the greater the material progress, the wider and deeper the resulting poverty. Marx drew from the riddle the central theme of his system: that this inherent contradiction within capitalism would bring about its breakdown. He proved it from the economic analysis of history. The effect of the Industrial Revolution had been to transform the worker from an independent producer who owned his own tools into a factory hand, a propertyless, destitute member of society, dependent for his livelihood on the capitalist who owned the means of production. Through the capitalist's accumulation of profits derived from the surplus value of the worker's product, the exploiters were becoming richer and the exploited poorer. The process could only end in the violent collapse of the existing order. Trained in class consciousness and prepared for this event, the working class would, at the moment of ripeness, rise in revolution to usher in the new order.

This Marxian doctrine of *Verelendung* (pauperization, or increasing misery) and *Zusammenbruch* (collapse) was the religious formula of Socialism, equivalent to "God is One" of another religion. It afflicted Socialism and the labour movement with a chronic schism between the necessity of collapse and revolution on the one hand and the possibility of gradual reform of the existing order on the other. As a schism between the future Absolute and the present Possible, it was present from birth, when the founders of 1889 split into two Congresses over the issue whether to permit cooperation with the bourgeois political parties. The true Marxists accused the French Possibilists of lying in wait at the Paris railroad stations to lead unsuspecting delegates from the provinces to the wrong Congress. Throughout the next twenty-five years the schism affected every act, decision and formulation of policy in the working-class movement, dividing negotiated gains from uncompromising class war, pragmatists from theorists, trade unions from parliamentary parties, the workers themselves, who wanted improvements in wages, hours and safety today, from the leaders, who agitated in their behalf for political power tomorrow.

The Marxian premise built into Socialism a chronic dilemma as well as a schism. As a movement on behalf of the working class it needed working-class support, which could only be obtained by showing practical results. Yet every practical result slowed or arrested the process of impoverishment. When walking with a friend who reached in his pocket to give money to a beggar, Johannes Miquel in his youth an ardent Socialist, stopped him, saying, "Don't delay the Revolution!" This was the logical extreme of Marxism. Any reform inferred a common ground between the contesting classes; revolution assumed the absence of it. If there was no common ground, what then was the use of anything short of revolution? Orthodox Socialists skirted this gaping hole in the creed by contending that reforms should continue to be wrung from the possessing class in order to strengthen the workers for the final struggle. The several national parties always stated a minimum program of reforms to be obtained within the existing system and a maximum program for the destruction of capitalism and triumph of the class struggle. Increasingly the moderates, or "opportunists," as their opponents called them, concentrated on the minimum program and the acquisition of political power necessary to put it through, while the orthodox refused to concede that any interim successes interfered with the truth of "increasing misery."

On the final necessity of revolution the Socialist party programs were imprecise. They glossed over it both in order to appeal to the voters and because it remained a disputable point. Socialism was not a hard gemlike doctrine impervious to modification, but varied, depending on time, country, situation and faction. Whether or not a Socialist believed in revolution was largely a matter of temperament. For some it was "nothing if not revolution." For others what counted was the Socialist millennium, however achieved. For the orthodox Marxist, in any case, collapse was ineluctable and Capitalism not a system to be modified but an Enemy to be destroyed, a living tyrant armed with the weapons of its class: courts, army, judges, legislature, police, injunctions, lockouts.

Property had lasted too long, filling the world with wickedness, turning men against each other. The time for overturn had come. The social evils produced by capitalism—poverty, ignorance, racial prejudice and war, which was just another form of capitalist exploitation—would be wiped out and replaced by social harmony. Freed from false patriotism, workingmen linked by their underlying brotherhood would no longer fight each other. Freed from the greeds and frustrations imposed by capitalism, every individual could pursue "the unimpaired development of his personality," being guaranteed under the collective system sufficient means and liberty to achieve it.

As the chariot of a new and higher order of life, Socialism seemed to its advocates to carry a sacred trust and to impose upon them a moral duty to be worthy of the ideal. Because he believed drinking was disgracing and destroying the working classes, Viktor Adler adopted total abstinence to set a personal example. Socialism was the repository of the big words. When, as a student in Brussels, Angelica Balabanov, a young Russian revolutionary, listened to Socialist orators in the Belgian Parliament, "Parliament seemed to me then a sacred place where Science, Truth and Justice . . . were to conquer the forces of Tyranny and Oppression for the working class."

The goal gave an excitement, a meaning, a glow to Socialist lives which for many of them substituted for the usual drives of personal ambition and profit. Party militants and organizers in the early days worked for nothing. Since there was no money in the movement, there could be no corruption. Since it could offer no livelihood or gain, its leaders tended to be idealists. It was a cause, not a career. It gave its disciples something to work for and infused a passion which could be understood across the barrier of language. At one Socialist Congress the Spanish leader Pablo Iglesias spoke so eloquently in his native tongue that although the audience did not understand a word, they burst into frequent applause. To the workers who increasingly voted for it, in millions after the turn of the century, Socialism gave self-respect and an identity. A workingman could feel himself no longer an ignored anonymous member of a herd but a citizen with a place in society and a political affiliation of his own. Unlike Anarchism, Socialism gave him a party to belong to and, since the nettle of revolution did not have to be grasped, an acceptable way to reach the goal instead of by way of the lawless deed.

The cause drew men like the Italian Amilcare Cipriani, one of the founders of the Congress of 1889. Type of the eternal rebel, he had fought with Garibaldi's Red Shirts and as a volunteer in the Cretan insurrection against Turkey and turned up in Brussels to join the comrades in the general strike of 1893. "Magnificent in cape and soft felt hat, with black beard streaked with grey and eyes of flame," he carried a handbag in which "there were doubtless more explosives than toilet articles . . . ready to fight in any corner of the world for the cause of Revolution."

It drew men of troubled conscience from the upper class, like the American Robert Hunter, married to a daughter of the banker and philanthropist Anson Phelps Stokes. Like others of his class, Hunter was startled by the articles of the Muckrakers and moved to seek a remedy for social injustice. He saw his first vision of the poor in settlement-house work, discovered Socialism, and at the age of twenty-eight in 1904 wrote a small classic, *Poverty*. With the undulled emotion of his time he described a valley in Italy "so smiling and peaceful, with a thousand terraced gardens on its exquisite slopes, under sides that enrapture the soul; and with men, women and children whose faces with big eyes and sunken cheeks lacerate the heart. . . . Great God, is not the Valley of the Tirano all the school that Italy needs for Socialism? . . . The faces are with you when you eat and your food sickens you. . . . Any man with a heart would become a Socialist in Italy."

Valleys of the Tirano in every country made Socialists out of intellectuals who saw them and workers who were born in them. What both had in common was faith that man had it in his power to make things better. The obstacles were massive; the House of Have was old and strong and entrenched. But the grievances of the working class were rising and were concerned as much with social inequality as with pure want. The workers resented disparity in suffrage, due to property qualifications. They resented the unequal working of compulsory military service, from which the privileged could be exempted; the bias of the law, which worked one way for the rich and another for the poor; the layers of hereditary privilege of all kinds, which the ruling class took for granted. Socialism was making the workers' wants conscious and articulate. The apathy of the masses which had disillusioned Bakunin and caused Lassalle to rail at "the damned wantlessness of the poor" was passing. They were beginning to know what they wanted, though on the whole it was not revolution. Socialism's inclusion of that goal was what gave it fervor and impetus, as in the case of Julius Braunthal, who joined the Austrian Socialist party at the age of fourteen "for the sake of the Revolution." But revolution appealed more to intellectuals who had no doubt of their capacity to manage society than it did to the working class.

Like a crack in a plank of wood which cannot be sealed, the difference between the worker and the intellectual was ineradicable in Socialism. Organized Socialism bore the name Workingmen's Association but in fact it was never any such thing. It was a movement not of, but on behalf of, the working class, and the distinction remained basic. Although it spoke for the worker and made his wants articulate, goals and doctrine were set, and thought, energy and leadership largely supplied by, intellectuals. The working class was both client and ultimately, in its mass strength, the necessary instrument of the overthrow of capitalism. As such it appeared as Hero; it was sentimentalized. In the illustrations for an English pamphlet commemorating the London Congress of 1896, the workingmen appeared as handsome strong-muscled Burne-Jones figures in smocks accompanied by indomitable women with long limbs and rippling hair. They were not the same race as Zola's soiled figures, harsh, hungry, consumptive and alcoholic. The reality was neither all one thing nor the other; neither all *lumpenproletariat* nor curly-bearded, clenched-fisted revolutionist. The working class was no more of a piece than any other class. Socialist doctrine, however, required it to be an entity with a working-class mind, working-class voice, working-class will, working-class purpose. In fact, these were not easily ascertainable. The Socialist idealized them and to be idealized is to be overestimated.

Owing to its internal quarrels, the founding Congress of 1889 did not lay down a body of doctrine to which the member parties were obliged to subscribe. Agreement went no farther than four resolutions which established four objectives as proper Socialist aims short of the maximum program: the eight-hour day; universal equal manhood suffrage; substitution of citizens' militias for standing armies; observance of May Day for a show of working-class strength.

While the first was the essential demand of the clientele, the second was fundamental to the whole Socialist purpose and program. The vote was the one means by which the masses could translate numbers into power; their only means to equalize the power of capital. For the same reason, the ruling class resisted it. Equal manhood suffrage at this date existed only in France and the United States, and only in national elections, not local government, in Germany. In most other countries the propertyless were disqualified or plural votes were given to taxpayers, university graduates and fathers of families. Socialists demanded the one-man-one-vote principle.

May Day, last of the four resolutions, was agreed on in response to a message from the American Federation of Labor, which planned to open its campaign for the eight-hour day on May 1, 1890. It was adopted at the suggestion of a French trade unionist, but the result was divisive because the Germans refused to commit themselves to a gesture likely to anger officialdom and evoke reprisals.

Nevertheless it was the Germans who spoke with most authority in the International. As the oldest and largest of the Socialist parties, the German party enjoyed the greatest prestige and, by virtue of the fact that Marx was a German, regarded itself as the Petrine rock, not to mention the Vatican, of Socialism. In 1890, released from the anti-Socialist law, it won 1,400,000 votes, nearly 20 per cent of the total, and thirty-five seats, in the elections for the Reichstag, a victory that dazed Socialists in the rest of the world. In practice, the German Social-Democratic party, as a result of its successes among the voters and its close ties with the trade unions, adapted itself to the possible. In theory it remained stoutly Marxist and at its Erfurt Congress in 1891 restated the Marxian view of history as official.

The Erfurt Program reaffirmed that the middle class, small businessmen and farmers, were being squeezed out, sinking along with the proletariat into increasing misery, and that the greater the masses grew in number, increasing the pool of labour, the sharper became the division between exploiters and exploited. Since the ultimate solution of public ownership could only be accomplished through the conquest of political power, the program of the party must be to gain political control, using trade unions as the source of votes but maintaining direction of policy in the party.

The Erfurt order for political action stamped its image upon the Second International, though not without the furious resistance of the Anarchists and their friends whose split with the Marxists on this issue had broken up the First International. Although not invited to the Congress of Zurich in 1893, the Anarchists arrived anyway, whereat August Bebel, the German chairman, a master of Marxian abuse, harangued them for having "neither program nor principles." In Zurich, "accustomed to German methods," he had no difficulty in having them expelled by force. In protest against such methods, Amilcare Cipriani resigned as a delegate. The Anarchists retired to conduct a diminutive counter-Congress in a café while the majority unanimously adopted a resolution recognizing the "necessity of organizing the workers for political action." Only those parties and groups accepting this principle could henceforth call themselves Socialists and take part in Congresses of the International. Not wishing to cut themselves off from their foundations, they made an exception for trade unions, which in future were to be admitted without being required to subscribe to the political principle. According to the Belgian delegate Emile Vandervelde, these difficult problems were solved in an atmosphere of "profound calm." It seemed anything but calm to a young British trade-union delegate, J. R. Clynes of the cotton workers, who had never been abroad before. He was astonished at the "verbal orgies" and violence of the Latin and Slav delegates and at the flareups of hostility in which one delegate flourished a knife and "everyone was yelling and struggling." Among Socialists, human bellicosity found its vent in factionalism whose vehemence Clynes tactlessly ascribed to "national rivalries and hatreds growing out of past wars."

Going for a swim in the Lake of Zurich Clynes saw "a ruddy beard on the surface of the water floating gently towards me" which proved to be attached to Bernard Shaw, also a delegate to the Congress, representing the Fabian Society. Having already discounted Marx and revolution, Shaw did not spare his contempt, in his reports of the Congress, for Wilhelm Liebknecht's duping of his followers with the "rhetoric of the barricade." The German leaders, he decided thereafter, were forty years out of date. At sixty-seven, Liebknecht, founder of the party in 1875, was now its elder statesman. Descended from a long line of university professors reaching back to the Eighteenth Century, he had been imprisoned for his role in the bourgeois revolution of 1848, and afterwards lived in exile in England for thirteen years, where he studied with Marx. When he died in 1900 a crowd of an estimated hundred thousand mourners and spectators lined the streets along the route of his four-hour funeral procession.

By all but Shaw the German party was considered the hope of Socialism, bearer of the torch in the country from which Marx expected revolution to come. Everyone was impressed by its size and strength, its wonderful organization, its twenty-eight secretaries and organizers, its training program for party workers, and its mounting membership. In the elections of 1893 the Social-Democrats increased their votes to 1,750,000, close to 25 per cent of the total, more than those of any other single party. Since it was against principle to join forces with any bourgeois party, the Social-Democrats in the Reichstag remained, despite their numbers, a relatively impotent group in what was in any case an impotent body. The fact of their existence, however, exerted a silent pressure which made the Government more reasonable toward concessions. The Kaiser, who in the first careless rapture of his dismissal of Bismarck had lifted the anti-Socialist law in 1890, recovered quickly. By 1895 he had decided that the Social-Democrats were a "gang of traitors" who "do not deserve the name of Germans" and by 1897 that the party "which does not stop attacking the person of the All-Highest Ruler must be rooted out to the last stump." In 1895 Liebknecht was arrested on a charge of *lèse-majesté* for a speech of which Shaw said that it could have been made "by Mr. Arthur Balfour to the Primrose League tomorrow with the approbation of England." But this was no special mark of repression, since it could happen to anyone in Germany.

National tended to outweigh class traits among the German Socialists: they were more obedient than bold. For all its size the party did not venture to play host to an International

Socialist Congress on German soil until 1907. Despite fiery speeehes its leaders were prudent in action; they restricted May Day demonstrations to the evening so as not to interfere with work. Work stoppage, said Liebknecht, was general strike and "a general strike is general nonsense." In Munich no May Day demonstration was permitted until 1901 and then only on condition that it took place outside city limits and did not form crowds in the streets on the way. Columns of Socialists, "their pockets bulging with radishes," accompanied by wives and children, marched briskly in dead silence through the city to a beer garden on the outskirts where they drank beer and munched their radishes and struck a Russian exile as "not at all resembling a May Day celebration of working-class triumph."

They were better off, however, than any Russian worker. Under the heavy throb of German industrial expansion, employment was increasing faster than the population. Unions, under these conditions, were successful in raising wages. Social legislation, originally bestowed from above by Bismarck to weld labour to his state, was the most advanced of any country. By 1903, 18,000,000 workers were insured against accident, 13,000,000 against old age and 11,000,000 against illness, with a total annual expenditure of $100,000,000 in social welfare benefits. Laws regulated wages, hours, time off, grievance procedures, safety measures, and the number of factory windows and toilets. With characteristic thoroughness Germany's rulers wanted to ensure physical efficiency, leaving as little as possible to chance and bringing everything possible under orderly rule. Professor Delbrück in 1897 publicly supported the right of collective bargaining on the ground that labour peace was necessary for national unity and national defense. To keep labour quiet by judicious concessions was considered the best method of smothering the Social-Democrats, whom the possessing class regarded with increasing enmity and fear.

August Bebel, the party's dictator, was believed by the bourgeoisie to be a kind of "shadow-Kaiser." A small-boned, narrow little man with white hair and goatee, he had been born in a barracks in 1840, the same year as Czar Reed. His father was an Army corporal and his mother a domestic servant. Taking up the carpenter's trade, he had joined the labour movement in the days of Lassalle; and on a charge of incitement to treason had been sentenced to four years in prison, a punishment fruitful in producing Socialists. In prison Bebel read much, received visits from Liebknecht and wrote a magisterial history of *Woman and Socialism*. His brains, Mommsen said, if divided among a dozen Junkers from east of the Elbe, were enough to make each of them shine among his peers. In the Reichstag, where he had debated Bismarck in "savage accents," Bebel was the spokesman of poverty and misery, loved and admired by the workers, who felt him to be a comrade. He would remain "the deadly enemy of this bourgeois society and this political order" until it was destroyed, he proclaimed at a party Congress in 1903. This was traditional verbiage. In fact, Bebel had no great illusions about the mass of his followers. "Look at those fellows," he said in 1892 to a correspondent of the London *Times* as they watched a march of a battalion of Prussian Guards; "80 per cent of them are Berliners and Social-Democrats but if there was trouble they would shoot me down at a word of command from above."

Of the outstanding figures of the Second International only he and Keir Hardie were of working-class origin. Karl Kautsky, fourteen years younger than Bebel, thinker and writer of the party and formulator of the Erfurt Program, whose commentaries on doctrine provided the text of endless discussion, was the son of intellectuals, a painter and a novelist. Viktor Adler of Austria was a doctor, Emile Vandervelde was the son of wealthy parents whom he described as "models of bourgeois virtue," and Jaurès of France came from the petty bourgeoisie.

As a doctor, Adler knew the human damage caused by undernourishment, overwork and squalor. He wanted to lead the workers to a new existence of "health, culture, liberty and dignity." Born of a wealthy Jewish family of Prague, he had studied medicine in order to treat the poor. Dressed in rags like a bricklayer, he investigated conditions in the Viennese brickyards where workers lived in company barracks guarded like prisons, five or six families to a dormitory room, and were paid in chits valid only in company stores. Before founding the Austrian party in 1889 he traveled in Germany, England and Switzerland to study workers' lives and social legislation which might be introduced in Austria. He was a short, scraggy, rather fragile figure with bushy hair and moustache, gold-rimmed spectacles, a pale face and one shoulder bent forward. Next to music he loved Ibsen and Shelley. Accepting revolution as the ultimate goal, he believed interim reforms were necessary in order to fit the worker physically and intellectually for his destiny. The struggle to secure these reforms against that "despotism mitigated by slovenliness," as he described the Hapsburg regime, was often discouraging and gradually wore down the edge of Adler's faith. Trotsky, who knew him in the early 1900's, found him a skeptic who had come to tolerate everything and adapt himself to everything.

In Belgium, whose population was the densest in Europe and where the process of industrialization had been fierce and rapid, the life of the working class was, in the words of one observer, an "inferno." Textile factories, steel mills, mines, quarries, docks and wharves used up labour as a mill grinds grain. Twenty-five per cent of all workers earned less than the equivalent of forty cents a day; another 25 per cent earned between forty and sixty cents. An investigation in Brussels showed 34 per cent of working-class families living in a single room. The Belgian illiteracy rate was the highest in northern Europe because child labour was used to such an extent that few had a chance to go to school. Concerned with "something more profound than doctrine," the labour movement had founded the Belgian Workers' Party in 1885 without the usual schisms because it could not afford them. The most solidified, disciplined and serious of the European Socialist parties, it was markedly proletarian though led by the ardent Vandervelde. A lawyer by training, an eloquent and admired speaker and prolific writer on labour problems, Vandervelde was "gushed" over by female Socialists who found him "charming and physically attractive." Together with the unions, the party organized a system of cooperatives where workers bought Socialist bread and Socialist shoes, drank Socialist beer, arranged for Socialist vacations, and obtained a Socialist education at the Université Nouvelle, where the French Anarchist and geographer Elisée Reclus lectured. Founded by Vandervelde and others in 1894, the same year the Fabians founded the London School of Economics, the Belgian school capped a Socialist world created inside a capitalist society.

By virtue of the extended suffrage won with workers' lives, the Belgian Workers' Party in 1894 elected twenty-eight deputies to the most bourgeois parliament in Europe. The advent of this solid bloc "firmly and recklessly prepared to take up arms against every institution of the existing regime" created a thrill of fear in the ruling class and a sudden vision among the faithful that Belgium might be the land where Socialism would first be realized. When a second attempt by general strike to win suffrage on the one-man-one-vote principle was called in 1902, many in the movement were reluctant to risk the gains that had been made, but the militants prevailed. Still aggressive and strong, the ruling class suppressed the strike by "murderous fusillade" in the streets of Louvain. Eight strikers were killed and it took the party many years to recover from the defeat.

If Germany had Marx, France had her Revolution and her Commune. Her Socialism was more spirited but, owing to its extreme factionalism, less solid and therefore less authoritative than Germany's. The Marxist matrix was the French Workers' Party, founded by Jules Guesde in consultation with Marx and Engels in 1879. Two years later Paul Brousse seceded to form the Possibilists on the principle that the emancipation of the workers was possible without revolution. Edouard Vaillant, heir of the old Communard Blanqui, headed a separate Socialist Revolutionary Party from which an extreme wing split off called the Allemanists for its leader, Jean Allemane. Guesde was the self-appointed keeper of the Marxian conscience, tirelessly preaching against backsliders and false idols. With thin black hair worn almost to his shoulders, the face of an emaciated Jesus and a pince-nez on his long didactic nose, he was a zealot who never for an instant relaxed total battle against the capitalist system. "Torquemada in eyeglasses" was a contemporary's epithet and Zola described him talking "with a whole range of passionate gesticulations and a perpetual cough." For Guesde nothing short of revolution was of any value; no touch of cooperation with the enemy classes permissible. He was an Impossibilist. He belonged to that category of Marxists rendered gloomy by their own prophecies of catastrophe. Mankind, absorbed by materialist districtions, was deteriorating. Postponed much longer, Socialism might not come in time to save it. "What will we Socialists do with a humanity so degraded?" he asked during the Dreyfus Affair. "We will come too late; the human material will be rotten when the time comes to build our house."

In 1893 Socialists in France, as in Belgium, won an impressive electoral victory: over half a million votes sending thirty-seven deputies to the Chamber. Dominant among them was the newly famous thirty-four-year-old Jean Jaurès, whose championship of the Carmaux strike in his home district of the Tarn had aroused sympathies all over France. The miners of Carmaux, an area of old and bitter labour disputes, succeeded in 1892 in electing as mayor the secretary of their union, a Socialist, who, upon being refused time off to perform his political duties, took it anyway and was thereupon dismissed from his job by the company. It was a blow at the intent of the vote, an insult to the suffrage understood by every heir of the Revolution. When the miners struck in protest, Jaurès, the former professor of philosophy, made himself their adviser, leader and spokesman. His opponent, the Marquis de Solages, master of Carmaux, owner of iron mines, glass works, timber forests, a title and a seat in parliament, was the epitome of capitalism with whom Jaurès fought an endless duel, through strikes and elections, that lasted most of his life. As a candidate of the French Workers' Party, elected from Carmaux, Jaurès entered the Chamber.

Short and heavy set, a "robust caryatid" with a "jubilant and humorous" face, Jaurès glowed with the warm vitality of the South. "Everything interested him, everything excited him," said Vandervelde. With his voice which had the volume and range of an organ, his command of debate, his formidable intelligence, inexhaustible energy and unquenchable enthusiasm, he drew leadership upon himself. When he spoke he was in constant motion with bearded head thrown back or body thrust aggressively forward and short arms flailing. "His shoulders trembled and his knees shook under the burden of his thought. All the force of his immense culture and conviction were poured into words to guide the multitude who believed in him toward a better future." He seemed to combine the solidity of earth with the mobility of fire. His phrasing was so admired that even political opponents would go to hear him as they would to hear Mounet-Sully speak Racine. Hearing him discuss astronomy at a dinner party, a guest wrote, "The walls of the room seemed to dissolve: we swam in the ether. The women forgot to re-powder their faces, the men to smoke, the servants to go in search of their own supper." Remy de Gourmont said, "Jaurès thinks with his beard," but the man who wrote *Les Preuves* and had been in youth the glory of the Ecole Normale thought more clearly than most. Although the French Socialist movement had no official chief, since it was constantly splitting and subdividing, uniting and splitting again, Jaurès, gradually replacing Guesde, came to be accepted as its leader.

He was the authentic Socialist, not in doctrine, but in the essence of the idea and the cause. He believed that man was good, that society could be made good and the struggle to make it so was to be fought daily, by available means and within present realities. He fought it wherever it appeared: in the Fourmies fusillade, at Carmaux, in the *lois scélérates*, over the bill for the income tax, in the Dreyfus Affair. His Socialism did not stem from Marx; it was, he declared simply, "the product of history, of endless and timeless sufferings." His Latin thesis for his doctorate was on the origins of German Socialism beginning with Luther, *De primis socialismi germanici lineamentis apud Lutherum, Kant, Fichte et Hegel.* Elected to the Chamber first as a Republican in 1885, when he was twenty-six and its youngest member, he had become discouraged with politics and had returned to the academic life as professor at the University of Toulouse, where his lectures were soon thronged by workmen and bourgeois townsmen as well as students and faculty. The labour struggles of Toulouse and the Tarn drew him back into public life and he announced himself a Socialist in 1890. Edouard Vaillant once said he never knew any kind of revolution Jaurès was not in favor of, but Jaurès' idea of revolution was rather of taking over than of overthrowing the State. His Marxism was fluid: he was a patriot as much as an internationalist and believed in individual freedom no less strongly than in collectivism. "We Socialists also have a free spirit; we also feel restive under external restraint," he said. If Socialist society of the future did not allow men to "walk and sing and meditate under the sky" whenever they chose, it would be unacceptable. He denied the Marxist concept of the bourgeois state as one in which the working class had no share. He saw the working class not as an outsider at the door waiting to take over but as part of the State now, needing to make itself felt now and needing to use the middle class as an ally in the struggle to reform society toward the realization of the Socialist ideal.

His faith had the strength of an engine. "Do you know how to spot an article by Juarès?" asked Clemenceau. "Very simple; all the verbs are in the future tense." Nevertheless, of all Socialists he was the most pragmatic, never a doctrinaire, always a man of action. He lived by doing, which meant advance and retreat, adaptation, give and take. A formal dogma that might have closed off some avenue of action was not possible for him. He was always the bridge, between men as between ideas. He was a working idealist.

Elected with him as Socialist deputies in 1893 were Alexandre Millerand, a hardheaded lawyer; René Viviani, renowned more for his moving oratory than for its content; and another lawyer, Aristide Briand, youngest of the group, the F. E. Smith of the Socialists, whose brains, ability and ambition were to prove stronger than his convictions. Briand "knows nothing and understands everything," said Clemenceau, adding that if he were ever accused of stealing the towers of Notre Dame, he would choose Briand to defend him. The Socialist deputies in the parliament of 1893–98 made their ideas and aims and immediate demands known to the country. Among themselves they had managed to agree in 1896 on a minimum definition known as the St-Mandé Program, formulated by Millerand, which stated that "a Socialist is one who believes in the collective ownership of property." It established as essential Socialist goals the nationalization of the means of production and exchange, one by one as each became ripe; the conquest of political control through universal suffrage; and international cohesion of the working class. In the Chamber they demanded as interim reforms the eight-hour day, the income and inheritance tax, old-age pensions, municipal reform, health and safety regulations in factories, mines and railroads. With Jaurès in the van, with Guesde in his piercing voice making the bourgeoisie tremble as he expounded the implacable march of Marxian history toward collapse, with the conservative defense led by de Mun, and with all the speeches reported in the papers, the debate developed into a great tournament of ideas which made Socialism from then on a main current of French life.

French trade unions, infused by the fierce Syndicalist rejection of political action, federated in the Confédération Générale du Travail in 1895 and kept aloof from Socialism. The antagonism reached a climax at the London Congress of the Second International in 1896, the most "tumultuous and chaotic" of all, when armed with mandates from the French unions the Anarchists (among them Jean Grave, representing the steelworkers of Amiens) made their last claim to membership in the Socialist family. The French factions split apart in frenzied antagonism over the issue, and when they caucused before the plenary session a "pandemonium of savage clamor" could be heard through the closed doors. After six days of strife during which the old quarrel between Marx and Bakunin was fought all over again, the Congress ended by excluding the Anarchists once and for all. A phase of Socialism had come to an end. Few doubted that new issues would not arise to divide the right and left wings of Socialism and keep open the schism between the Absolute and the Possible.

Before that expectation was fulfilled, Socialism in the United States took on a new dimension when the use of injunction in the Pullman strike made a Socialist out of Eugene Victor Debs. Named for Eugène Sue and Victor Hugo by his father, an émigré from Alsace, Debs was brought up on *Les Misérables*, the bible of father and son. He went to work as a railroad fireman at fourteen, founded the Brotherhood of Locomotive Firemen, and resigned from it in 1892 when he was thirty-seven to organize all railwaymen in an industrial union, the American Railway Union. When in 1893 and 1894 the Pullman Company cut wages by 25 to 33⅓ per cent without lowering rents in company houses and while continuing to pay dividends to investors, Debs called a sympathy strike on all trains carrying Pullman cars. More than a hundred thousand men came out in what developed into the greatest strike effort yet seen in the United States. Mobilizing all the powers of capital, the owners, representing twenty-four railroads with a combined capital of $818,000,000, fought back with the courts and the armed forces of the Federal government behind them. Three thousand police in the Chicago area were mobilized against the strikers, five thousand professional strikebreakers were sworn in as Federal deputy marshals and given firearms; ultimately six thousand Federal and state troops were brought in, less for the protection of property and the public than to break the strike and crush the union. A regular Army colonel, drunk in a Chicago club, wished he could order every man in his regiment to take aim and fire at every "dirty white ribbon," the emblem of the strikers.

Although the union had agreed to furnish necessary men for the mail trains, delivery of the mail was made the pretext for an injunction, the most sweeping ever granted. As the arm of the State used in support of property, injunction was capitalism's most formidable weapon and the most resented. Attorney-General Olney, who had been a lawyer for railroads before entering the Cabinet and was still a director of several lines involved in the strike, persuaded President Cleveland of the necessity. The United States District Attorney in Chicago drew up the injunction with the advice of Judges Grosscup and William Wood of the Federal Circuit Court, who then mounted the bench to confirm their own handiwork. When Governor Altgeld refused to request Federal troops, the judges certified the need of them in order to justify the injunction. It was war, proclaimed Debs, between "the producing classes and the money power of the country." Refusing to obey the injunction, he was arrested along with several associates, imprisoned without bail, tried and sentenced in 1895 to a term of six months.

After his arrest the strikers, by then more or less starving, gave up. Thirty had been killed, sixty injured and over seven hundred arrested. In rehiring, Pullman imposed yellow-dog contracts, requiring every worker to relinquish his right to join a union. The American Railway Union was destroyed but the strike had made a hero of Debs and a villain of injunction. It showed that strikes could not be won when government sided with capital; therefore labour must attain political power.

Debs pondered the lesson in prison. He read *Progress and Poverty*, Bellamy's *Looking Backward*, *Fabian Essays*, Blatchford's *Merrie England* and Kautsky's commentary on the Erfurt Program. He received a visit from Keir Hardie. He became convinced that the cause of the working class was hopeless under capitalism, and when, in the election of 1896, the forces of Mark Hanna and McKinley defeated Bryan and Populism, his conviction was confirmed. Capitalism, too strong to be reformed, must be destroyed. In return, the ruling class felt no less strongly about "Debs the revolutionist." While campaigning for McKinley, Theodore Roosevelt said in a private conversation, "The sentiment now animating a large proportion of our people can only be suppressed as the Commune was suppressed, by taking ten or a dozen of their leaders out, standing them against a wall and shooting them dead. I believe it will come to that. These leaders are plotting a social revolution and the subversion of the American Republic."

Debs announced his conversion to Socialism in a manifesto in the *Railway Times* of January 1, 1897, saying, "The time has come to regenerate society—we are on the eve of a universal change." In association with other labour leaders and adopting the form of the name used in Germany, he founded the American Social Democracy, which became the party of native American Socialism. In its early years, with less than four thousand members, it was kept alive by the gold watch of Debs's brother Theodore, pawned periodically to keep the party newspaper going. Whenever Theodore Debs appeared in the doorway of a pawnshop in the Loop, its old German proprietor would call over his shoulder to the girl at the cash register, "Giff the Socialist chentleman forty dollars." The political period of American Socialism still lay ahead, when in the first twelve years of the new century, under changed conditions, Debs was to be four times his party's candidate for President and campaign across the country on board the railwaymen's Red Special.

For the moment, his rival was the Socialist Labor Party, drawn chiefly from the foreign born and existing largely on paper and in the mind of its fanatic dictator, Daniel De Leon. Born in Curaçao of Dutch-Jewish parents and educated in Germany, De Leon was convinced that only he was fitted to lead the class struggle. He had come to the United States at twenty-two, and having taken a law degree at Columbia and held a lectureship there in Latin-American history, he was scorned by union opponents as the "professor." Besides keeping up hot and incessant propagation of Socialist ideas in his weekly *The People*, De Leon ran for the New York State Assembly, for Congress and in 1891 for Governor without visible result. To draw organized labor into political action he launched the Socialist Trade and Labor Alliance, whose chief function was to excite the rage of the craft-union leader, Sam Gompers. Political action in Gompers' eyes was the devil's pitchfork and of De Leon he said that "no more sinister force" had ever appeared in Socialism. In 1901 a large faction of the Socialist Labor Party, opposing De Leon's "dictatorship," seceded, under Morris Hillquit and Victor Berger, to join Debs's group, which now renamed itself the Socialist Party of America.

Socialism's inveterate opponent, Gompers was the prototype of regular as opposed to revolutionary trade unionism. He was the outstanding exponent of the view that labour's fight must be carried on within, not against, the capitalist system. Dwarfish and stocky, "almost grotesque," with a huge head and heavy coarse features, he was, though ugly, an impressive personality who dominated any meeting in which he took part. When launched on one of his anti-Socialist tirades in the Federation, an old opponent in the Typographers' Union who enjoyed heckling him used to call from the floor, "Give 'em hell, Sam; give 'em hell." Sam never slackened in the effort. Having rejected the Old World, he deeply distrusted the Socialist tradition, though well grounded in it. As a young man in the cigarmaking trade, which, paying by the piece, allowed one worker to read aloud while the others made up his quota, he read Marx, Engels, and Lassalle to his fellow workers. "Learn from Socialism" but "don't join," advised his mentor, an exiled Swedish Marxist. "Study your union card, Sam," he would say, "and if the idea doesn't square with it, it ain't true."

With faith in the new society of America, Gompers rejected the pessimism of the Marxian premise. He believed unalterably that labour should keep out of politics, while using its power to bargain directly with employers. Regulation of wages, hours and working conditions should be achieved by union activity, not by legislative enactment. He founded the Federation in 1881, when he was thirty-one, in a room ten by eight with a kitchen table for a desk, a crate for a stool and tomato boxes supplied by a friendly grocer for files. By 1897 it had 265,000 members, by 1900 half a million, by 1904 a million and a half. When Bryan, angling for the union vote in 1896, promised that if elected he would appoint Gompers to his Cabinet, Gompers stood up to announce that under "no circumstances" would he ever accept any political office. He refused to allow the AF of L to come out in support of Bryan and Populism because, as he said, "these middle-class issues" diverted labour from its own interest, which was the union and nothing else.

As his power grew, he shaved off his walrus moustache, adopted pince-nez, a Prince Albert coat and a silk hat, and like John Burns, enjoyed hobnobbing with the great, negotiating with Mark Hanna or August Belmont. Yet he never made money for himself and was to die a poor man. While repudiating the class struggle he remained profoundly class conscious. "I am a working man. In every nerve, in every fibre, in every aspiration I am on the side which will advance the interests of my fellow working men." The task for union members was to "organize more generally, combine more closely, unite our forces, educate and prepare ourselves to protect our interests, that we may go to the ballot box and cast our votes as American freemen, united and determined to redeem this country from its present political and industrial misrule, to take it from the hands of the plutocratic wreckers and place it in the hands of the common people." This in effect was practical Socialism. So was his reaction fifteen years later when on a tour of Europe he saw visitors appalled at an exhibit of slum conditions in Amsterdam. He recorded their shock that any human being would stand this "gross insult" from civilization: "Why not revolt against it somehow?" Socialism was essentially the movement of those who felt impelled to "revolt against it somehow," and Gompers, as Morris Hillquit used to say, was a Socialist without knowing it.

In Europe in 1899 a new issue exploded in the ranks of Socialism when Waldeck-Rousseau, seeking a wide base for the Government that was to "liquidate" the Dreyfus Affair, offered Cabinet office to Millerand, who accepted. Never before had a Socialist stepped over the invisible barrier into the bourgeois camp to cooperate with any part of it. Although Jaurès had led, pushed and persuaded the Socialists, or a faction of them, to join the bourgeois Dreyfusard groups in the battle to save the Republic, to enter a bourgeois government was another matter. Millerand's case raised the fundamental issue of cooperation which from here on grew more pressing as with each year the Socialists played a greater role in national life. The dilemma presented itself: whether to remain condemned to an orthodox if sterile purity waiting for the final overthrow of capitalism, or to cooperate with the bourgeois parties left of center, supporting them against reaction and spurring them toward reforms. The question carried the further implication: whether Socialist goals might not, in the long run, be attained by way of reform?

While *le cas Millerand* threw French Socialists into a turmoil, the same issue rose up in Germany, not in the flesh, but, as befitted Germans, in theory. It came from the most impeccable origins, promulgated by a man of the inner circle, a protégé of Marx and Engels, a friend and associate of Liebknecht, Bebel and Kautsky and a member of the founding Congress of 1889. It was as shocking as if one of the apostles had disputed Jesus. The name of the man who presumed to revise Marx was Eduard Bernstein, and his new doctrine, as if not quite daring to give itself a name, came to be called simply Revision. A bank clerk as a young man, Bernstein, at the age of nineteen, had gone into exile in Switzerland in 1878, the year of Bismarck's anti-Socialist law. From here he edited the party paper, *Sozialdemokrat*, so effectively as to win the approval of Marx and the accolade of Engels, who called it "the best the party has had." In 1888 the German Government paid it the compliment of bringing pressure on the Swiss to expel the staff. Bernstein moved to London, where, like the Master, he spent his time in the reading room of the British Museum and made no attempt to return to Germany after the repeal of the anti-Socialist law in 1890. Though still under indictment for sedition, he could have appealed his case, but he was writing a book on the English Revolution according to the Marxian interpretation and besides he found the atmosphere of London sympathetic. This was symptomatic of his trouble. During these years he acted as correspondent for the new party paper, *Vorwärts*, and for Kautsky's *Neue Zeit*. Headquarters of German Socialism in London was Engels' house in Regent's Park, where the exiles gathered for evenings of discussion around a table generously laden with thick sandwiches and beer and, at the proper season, Christmas pudding. On Engels' death in 1895 Bernstein and Bebel were named his literary executors.

The following year, as if restraint had been lifted by Engels' death, Bernstein's first heretical articles appeared. He was forty-six in 1896, an outwardly decent, respectable figure with rimless glasses and thinning hair who looked as if he might have been a bank teller all his life, rising perhaps to branch manager. His only noticeable feature was a long flaring independent nose. Acquainted with the Fabians—in fact, a good friend of Graham Wallas—he had for a long time felt a prejudice against them for their willingness to work within the capitalist order. At the same time the workings of democratic government in England impressed him and he could not resist the surrounding evidence that capitalism was somehow not approaching imminent collapse. Despite glaring inequalities of wealth and the "increasing misery" Marx had predicted, paradoxically the system was undeniably strong, even aggressive. The world seemed unfairly caught in a relentless spiral of prosperity, with results which seeped down to counteract the "increasing misery" in the form of increased employment. In London and in exile Bernstein suffered the disadvantages of independent thought and became increasingly prey to the suspicion that history was not following the path that Marx had charted. She had disobeyed the German *diktat.* Hegel had laid it down; Marx had hardened it; but history, with a Mona Lisa smile, had gone her own way, eluding the categorical imperative.

Like a man beginning to doubt the Biblical story of Creation, Bernstein was assailed by the agonies of failing faith. He became moody and irritable and at one point even applied for a job in a bank in the Transvaal. Eleanor Marx wrote to Kautsky that Bernstein was in bad spirits and making enemies. But intellectual courage won. From 1896 to 1898 he submitted a series of articles on "Problems of Socialism" to the *Neue Zeit* which instantly provoked outcries and tirades. The German Socialist world was thrown into an orgy of controversy, heightened when Bernstein embodied his ideas in an address which he sent to the German party's Congress at Stuttgart in

October, 1898, and subsequently enlarged into a book, *Die Voraussetzungen des Sozialismus* (The Evolution of Socialism), published in March, 1899.

It set forth the facts contrary to Marx: the middle class was not disappearing; the number of propertied persons was increasing, not decreasing. In Germany the working class was not sinking in progressive impoverishment but slowly making gains. Capital was not accumulating among a diminishing number of capitalists but was rather being diffused over a wider ownership through the medium of stocks and shares. Increased production was not all being consumed by capitalists but was spreading into increased consumption by the middle class and even, as they earned more, by the proletariat. In Germany the consumption of sugar, meat and beer was going up. The wider the spread of money, the less chance of any single economic crisis bringing about a final crash. If Socialists waited for that, Bernstein warned, they might wait indefinitely. In short, the grim twins, *Verelendung* and *Zusammenbruch*, were shadows.

In place of the Marxian dialectic, Bernstein suggested a capitalist economy capable of indefinite expansion and ability to adjust itself so as to rule out the supposedly inevitable breakdown. In that case the existing order was here to stay. If breakdown and revolution were not, after all, inescapable, then the Socialist goal might be an ethical democratic society based on the support of all classes, rather than on the proletariat alone. If revolutionary aims were abandoned, Bernstein declared, carried away on a wave of optimism, the working class could win the support of the bourgeoisie for reforms within the existing order.

The implication for "Millerandism" was clear. If capitalism and Socialism were not, after all, to be a stark choice of one or the other, if society was to continue with some of this and some of that, then there was no further point in Socialists excluding themselves from a role in government.

Revision meant in effect abandonment of the class struggle. It was a stake plunged into the heart of Socialism. Bernstein did not shrink. The workers, he brazenly suggested, were not, as Marx assumed, a coherent, homogeneous "class," conscious of themselves as "the proletariat" or likely to become so. They were divided between rural and urban, skilled and unskilled, factory and home, with different interests and different levels of earning power. Many were hostile or indifferent to Socialism and tended to share bourgeois morals and habits rather than sharing Socialist contempt for the bourgeois.

If class was not, after all, the primary loyalty of the worker, then it followed that his interests like those of any citizen were bound up with the national interests of his country. Here was the terrible horizon of Revision. Bernstein even banished the cruel edict of the *Communist Manifesto*: "the worker has no Fatherland." When every workingman had the vote, he said, as in Germany, he acquired political rights and responsibilities and must therefore think in terms of the national interest.

Revision tore Socialism apart. Bernstein's open formulation of the case rallied adherents long troubled by their own doubts. Party leaders rushed to attack the heretic. He was accused of being "English." Kautsky refuted every argument in a book, *Bernstein and the Social-Democratic Program*, which was intended to dispose of him but somehow did not. Dispute swelled and penetrated every meeting, newspaper and policy committee. Charged with ignoring the final goal of Socialism, Bernstein made the shocking reply, "I confess openly I have little interest in what is generally called 'the final goal of Socialism.' This goal, whatever it may be, is nothing to me; the movement [for social progress] everything." He decided to come home to defend himself in person. Friends interceded for him with the Government, and Chancellor von Bülow, calculating that he would be a disruptive influence, allowed the indictment against him to lapse. Returning in 1901, Bernstein was elected to the Reichstag in a by-election in 1902. He became the editor of a Revisionist journal and the oracle of a Revisionist faction which sprang up within the party and continued to grow.

The appeal of Revision was that it offered an end to Socialist isolation, opened the door to participation and also to ambition. It allowed Socialists to feel themselves part of their country, however contrary the feeling was to the command of the prophet. It recognized another reality: that imperceptibly, in a way Marx had not foreseen, a transfer of power between classes was in fact taking place, like water seeping through a dam.

Revision had a fault which Viktor Adler noted. It was said of Adler that like Montaigne he should have adopted a pair of scales for his emblem and the motto "*Que sais-je?*" because he always looked for some evil in anything good and some good in anything evil. In a letter to Bernstein he wrote that he had brought into the open doubts which all Socialists felt at one time or another but that in the end Adler himself would side with the Revolutionaries because Revision carried the mortal danger that "Socialists would lose sight of Socialism."

In the French Socialist world, at the same time, the quarrels let loose by *le cas Millerand* were even more ferocious and divisive than those in Germany. Distressed though he had been at Millerand's acceptance of office, Jaurès, when forced to take a stand, supported collaboration as against no collaboration at all. At the French party's Congress in Paris in December, 1899, he denied that it would lead to personal corruption, as charged by the Marxists. Since, he argued, it was impossible to predict when the capitalist collapse would come, it was necessary to work for reforms while preparing the way. "We must not fight from a futile distance," he said, "but from the heart of the citadel." Enraged orations by his opponents filled the hall. "Tall, thin, desiccated, his eyes ablaze like black fire," Guesde preached the purity of Marxism and was citing Liebknecht when one excited Ministerialist, as the supporters of Millerand were called, shouted, "Down with Liebknecht!" The shock that passed over the faces of the Guesdists, a delegate said later, was as if someone had shouted "Down with God!" in Notre Dame. After three days of intense fracas the proposition was put, "Yes or no, does the class struggle permit a Socialist to enter a bourgeois government?" The vote was for No but was immediately followed by another vote permitting Ministerialism under exceptional circumstances. With Jaurès pleading for unity the Congress managed to close under a patched-up formula in which underlying antagonisms were unresolved. Two parties thereafter emerged: Guesde, Vaillant and Marx's son-in-law, Paul Lafargue, formed the Socialist Party of France committed to "no compromise with any fraction of the bourgeoisie" and to the destruction of capitalism. Jaurès, Millerand,

Briand and Viviani formed the French Socialist Party committed to a reform program for "immediate realization."

Throughout the world in every Socialist party headquarters and meeting hall where the red flag stood dustily in a corner, Revision and *le cas Millerand* widened old schisms. While doctrinaire Socialists clung to original principles, the Revisionists were discovering that Socialism, like politics, was the art of the possible. More divided than ever, the Second International assembled for its fifth Congress in Paris in September, 1900, in the midst of the Exposition. With the city full of visitors and the center of world attention, Socialist leaders were anxious to prevent an open rupture. Kautsky contrived a resolution which, while refusing to approve Millerand's action, did not condemn it. Delegates called it the Kaoutchouc (india-rubber) Resolution because it was so elastic. Pounded in debate, slashed by the furious swordplay of De Leon, it occupied almost the entire time of the Congress. At one point a German delegate, Erhard Auer, let slip a regret that the opportunity for a *cas Millerand* was not likely to offer itself to German Socialists. Exposing a basic fact of life in his country, the remark caused an outburst of applause, hisses and outraged discussion in the corridors. Eventually, under the expert piloting of Jaurès, bent as ever on unity, the Kautsky Resolution was passed over the heads of an intransigent minority. Jaurès' theme, as at his own Congress, was: "We are all good revolutionaries; let us make that clear and let us unite!" But the fact was something less than the wish.

With the Boer War, the war in the Philippines and the Boxer Rebellion in progress, delegates found it easy to unite on a resolution put forward by Rosa Luxemburg stating that capitalism would collapse as a consequence, not of economic conditions, but of imperialist rivalries. Recommending Socialist parties to work against war by organizing and educating youth to carry on the class struggle, by voting against military and naval estimates and by anti-militarist protest meetings, the resolution was passed unanimously along with another denouncing the recent Hague Conference as a fraud.

The only concrete accomplishment of the Congress was a decision to establish a permanent organization in the form of a

Bureau in Brussels of which Vandervelde was named chairman and Camille Huysmans, another Belgian, secretary. It was to pass interim resolutions, prepare agenda for Congresses and hold emergency meetings, if necessary, to which member nations would each send two delegates. As the budget allocated to it was minuscule, the Bureau, as time went on, did not acquire great prestige or executive power, and except as a mail drop, served chiefly to emphasize that the sinews of internationalism were slender.

Revision continued to cut deep inroads. Jaurès, while defending collaboration as a fact of political life, refused to accept Bernstein's revision of theory. In the controversy between Bernstein and Kautsky, he told a Socialist Student Conference in 1900, "I am, on the whole, with Kautsky." Bernstein was wrong, he said, about the proletarian and bourgeois classes merging at their edges. Between the class that possesses the means of production and the class that does not "there *is* a definite line of demarcation," although of course there were intermediate shadings; and from these, Jaurès, once more the professor, launched himself happily on the wings of philosophic discourse. "One goes from white to black, from purple to red, from night to day by these imperceptible transitions which allowed Heraclitus to say that in day there is always some night and in night some day. . . . In fact, it is a characteristic of extremes that they are approached by intermediary nuances. . . ." Jaurès sailed on, holding his audience entranced until with a snap he came back to the issue. However "radically antagonistic" the classes, that did not mean there could be no contact or cooperation, and he closed with a final appeal for Socialist unity "amid loud applause, prolonged acclamations and cries of *Vive Jaurès!*"

As one of the four vice-presidents of the Chamber after his re-election in 1902, Jaurès practiced cooperation daily, becoming virtual leader of the left bloc of the parties which supported the Government in its battles against the Army and the religious orders. Life was pushing him toward Revision. He attended garden parties at the British Embassy and a banquet in the Elysée Palace for the King and Queen of Italy in 1903. At the Bordeaux Congress of his party that year he argued that the State was not, as Guesde maintained, an impenetrable bloc to stand or be overthrown, but penetrable by reforms. As these were gained, one by one, the workers' state would one day be discovered to have replaced the bourgeois state and "we shall be aware of having entered the zone of Socialism as navigators cross into the zone of a new hemisphere, though there is no rope stretched across the ocean to mark it." But he acknowledged that the problem of reconciling collaboration with class struggle was "complicated." In their party Congress at Dresden that year the Germans were finding it painfully so.

The issue came to a head in the great "knee-breeches" debate. The Social-Democrats were fresh from an electoral victory in which they had polled over three million votes to win eighty-one seats in the Reichstag. To maintain rigid Marxian apartness under these circumstances, Bernstein argued, was senseless. He urged the party to assume the prerogatives of its strength, namely, to accept one of the vice-presidencies of the Reichstag which was its due. Since this required paying an official call upon the Kaiser in court costume, the problem provided matter for days of passionate dispute. Imagine Socialists dressed up in knee-breeches, stockings and buckled shoes! scolded Bebel. To make the Socialist party *hoffähig* (acceptable at court) was an insult to the entire working class. Bernstein suggested that the issue was less a question of what Socialists wore than of what they did in Parliament, but the debaters were too absorbed in the awful yet alluring prospect of knee-breeches to listen to him.

The debate on Revision continued for three days with fifty speakers participating. Bernstein's expulsion was demanded by a group led by Rosa Luxemburg, whose small, frail body contained an outsize passion for revolution. Born in Poland in 1870, the daughter of a Jewish timber merchant, she was not good-looking save for a pair of fine black eyes. She had a limp, a deformed shoulder, a powerful intellect and a strong, clear voice. Retaining always a slight Polish accent, she was a formidable orator whose eloquence so aroused an Inspector of Police, posted at one of her meetings, as to make him forget his official status and applaud loudly. Rosa sent him a note saying, "It is a pity that a man as sensible as you should be in the police but it would be a greater pity if the police should lose so human an example. Don't applaud any more."

With Karl Liebknecht, son of Wilhelm, she represented the militant revolutionary left wing, centered in Leipzig, whose organ was the *Leipziger Volkzeitung*, edited by Franz Mehring. As the party increased in size and influence and its writers and advocates inevitably mixed in bourgeois circles, she led the resistance to growing respectability. For Revision, or "parliamentary and trade-union cretinism" as she called it, with its "comfortable theory of a peaceful passage from one economic order to another," she had only burning contempt. She believed in the revolutionary instinct and creative revolutionary energy of the unorganized masses which were to erupt spontaneously when history required it. The task of the party, as she saw it, was to educate, guide and inspire the masses in anticipation of the historic crisis, not to soften the revolutionary impulse through reform.

Between the Radicals and the Revisionists, the General Council of the party arbitrated, maintaining its balance without too much difficulty. As one of the leaders, Georg Ledebour, said, the party was 20 per cent radical, 30 per cent revisionist and the rest "will follow wherever Bebel goes." Bebel arranged the usual compromise. Without expelling Bernstein, the Dresden Congress defeated his motion for cooperation and passed a resolution reaffirming the policy of class struggle "which we have triumphantly pursued hitherto," and "decisively" rejecting any policy or tactics of "accommodation to the existing order." Thus the largest Socialist bloc in Europe maintained fidelity to Marx on paper while the facts of Revision continued to flourish.

Revisionists were not blind to the implications of abandoning the primacy of the class struggle. Nationalism was in the air and they felt its invigorating force. As Socialists they wanted to participate in national life, not to stay shut out, waiting for the promised collapse which never came. In the *Socialist Monthly* Bernstein used the English experience of imperialism and its relation to employment to argue that the fate of the working class was "indissolubly tied up" with the nation's external affairs, that is, with its foreign markets. Labour's interest, he said forthrightly, lay in a "*Weltpolitik* without war."

While the Germans disputed at Dresden, Revision cut a historic schism among the Russian Social-Democrats, who held their own party Congress of sixty members that year in London. No *cas Millerand* or even knee-breeches appeared on their horizon, nevertheless they split between Bolsheviks and Mensheviks over the issue of collaboration in the future. The former insisted on revolution and dictatorship of the proletariat in one leap with no interim accommodation; the latter believed this could not be achieved until Russia had first passed through a bourgeois stage of parliamentary government during which Socialists would have to collaborate with the liberal parties.

As a member of the Second International, the Russian party was perennially represented at international Congresses by its founder, Georgi Plekhanov, who had lived so long in exile that he had lost touch with affairs inside his own country. Apart from him, the other Russians in exile had little or no contact with the Socialists in whose countries they lived. Absorbed in their own fierce factional quarrel they held their own Congresses with little role in the International. Moving through London, Paris, Geneva and Munich, Plekhanov's rival, Lenin, leader of the Bolshevik faction, relentlessly poured out his denunciations of "opportunism" and "social-chauvinism." Now and then he visited the Bureau at Brussels, but no one, wrote Vandervelde, paid much attention to this "little man with the narrow eyes, rusty beard and monotone voice, forever explaining with exact and glacial politeness the traditional Marxist formulas."

Elsewhere the facts of political life were making a necessity of Revision whether the Marxists liked it or not. Industry was expanding, bringing with it a rise in trade-union membership which increased the lever of pressure in the hands of the working class. While the battle of capital and labour continued as fiercely as ever, the working class through the Socialist parties was enlarging its representation in every European Parliament. In Italy, where the peasants' unions and agricultural cooperatives were strongly Socialist, the party increased from 26,000 votes and 6 seats in Parliament in 1892 to 175,000 votes and 32 seats in 1904. In France, Jaurès' party, followed by the imprecations of Guesde and his followers, was performing a role in national life, and Jaurès himself was emerging as the real if not nominal leader of the Government's majority in the Chamber. In the Socialist world he moved forward to challenge the domination of the great German monolith at the next Congress of the International, held in Amsterdam in August, 1904.

The duel of Jaurès and Bebel made the Amsterdam Congress remembered by everyone present as the most stimulating of all the meetings of the Second International. Five hundred delegates attended, of whom about two hundred at any one time understood the language of the speaker. The platform was draped in red stamped with a gold monogram of the initials I.S.C., which, with the *S* twining around the *I* bore a startling resemblance to a well-known symbol of capitalism. Overhead a banner bore in Dutch the device on which everyone could still agree, *Proletaariers van alle Landen, Vereinigt U!* (Workers of the World, Unite!)

Factions were multiple. Britain had four delegations: the ILP led by Keir Hardie, the Socialist-Democratic Federation by Hyndman, the Labour Representation Committee by Shackleton, and a Fabian group. France had three delegations and the United States two, with the inevitable De Leon casting his scorn on all. He disapproved of the "social and picnic" aspect of the Congress, of delegates rustling papers and conversing and walking about during speeches, visiting with foreign friends, introducing one to another, arriving and departing and slamming doors. He pronounced Jaurès an "unqualified nuisance in the Socialist movement," Bebel its "evil genius," Adler "absurd," Vandervelde a "comedian," Hyndman "too dull" to understand what was going on, the British trade unionists "disastrous," Shackleton a "capitalist placeman," and Jean Allemane a "flannel-mouthed blatherskite." The only party which did not betray the working class by "revisionist flapdoodlism" was his own, whose attitude at all times was "sword drawn, scabbard thrown away."

Cooperation was the question to be settled, placed on the agenda by demand of Guesde. Bebel's object was to impose the Dresden Resolution of the German party upon the International. It provided, he said, the correct guidance for Socialists at all times in all circumstances since it stated the fundamental antagonism between the proletarian and the capitalist state. He took occasion to cite the growing strength of the German party. Jaurès retorted that if Socialists were as strong as that in France, they would "make something happen." Between the appearance of German strength and the reality of their influence, he said, launching upon a major offensive, there was a startling contrast. Why? Because "there is no revolutionary tradition among your workers. They never conquered universal suffrage on the barricades. They received it from above." All the deputies in the Reichstag were powerless, for the Reichstag was itself powerless in any case. It was the very helplessness of the German Socialists which enabled them to take an uncompromising stand on doctrine. What weighed most heavily upon Europe now was not the bold attempt of French Socialists to play a part in their national life, "but the tragic impotence of German Social Democracy." Passionately he defended his main thesis: that Socialists without abandoning principle must be the "marching wing" of democratic progress, even if necessary in liaison with bourgeois parties.

"Certainly Germany is a reactionary, feudal, police state, the worst governed country in Europe" except for Turkey and Russia, Bebel replied, "but we scarcely need anyone from the outside to tell us how dismal our conditions are." Jaurès' policy, he said, would corrupt the proletariat. The Dresden Resolution was the only safe guide. Shrilly Rosa Luxemburg denounced Jaurès as "*der grosse Verderber*" (the great corrupter). When he stood up to reply, asking who would translate for him, she answered, "I will, if you like, Citizen Jaurès." Looking around with a broad smile Jaurès said, "You see, Citizens, even in battle there is collaboration."

Refusing to give up the principle of class war, the majority voted for the Dresden Resolution against Jaurès, combining, as Vandervelde said, doctrinal enmity with personal sympathy. "We remembered the Dreyfus Affair" and the "magnificent ardor" of Jaurès' great battle against the accumulated forces of reaction, but the majority could not nerve themselves to cut the umbilical cord to Marx. In a final effort to close the rifts of Revision, the Congress adopted a last resolution stating it to be "indispensable" to have only one Socialist party in each country henceforth. All who claimed the name of Socialist must work for unity in the interest of the working classes of the world, to whom they would be responsible for "the mortal consequences of a continuance of their divisions."

A problem that had not yet been their main concern made a tentative appearance at Amsterdam. With the echo of the Russo-Japanese War in their ears, delegates discussed working-class responsibility to society in the event of another war and the feasibility of a general strike. German Marxist ardor cooled at the very word. To talk general strike was one thing; to get the unions to act on it quite another. So far as the German trade unions were concerned, the "political mass strike," as they called it, was anathema. If the Fatherland were attacked, said Bebel, old as he was, he with every other Social-Democrat would shoulder a rifle and fight to defend his country. Looking very grave, Jaurès said to Vandervelde on their way out, "I think, my friend, I am going to apply myself to the study of military questions."

On his return home, as a loyal Socialist in obedience to the Amsterdam decision, he moved back toward a rapprochement with Guesde, reuniting the two parties in the following year as the Socialist Party, French Section of the Workers' International, commonly called, from its French initials, the SFIO. It declared itself to be "not a party of reform but a party of class struggle and revolution" and verbally repudiated collaboration. Although this was a defeat for his position, Jaurès did not make a fetish of words. He let doctrine follow action and could the more easily concede formula to Guesde since he himself was the real leader of the union. Cooperation for him was not an end in itself but an avenue of action.

For some it proved indeed the corrupter in a political sense. In 1906, the same year in which the ILP entered the House of Commons and John Burns the Cabinet, French Socialists polled 880,000 votes and won fifty-four seats in the Chamber. Briand, who had been active in the matter of disestablishing the religious schools, was offered the post of Minister of Education. He accepted and in the ensuing bitterness left the party. A few months later Viviani followed him into office as Minister of Labour. Together with Millerand, who now called himself an Independent Socialist, they held a succession of offices from now on, with Briand reaching the premiership within three years and Viviani five years later. Carrying cooperation to its logical extreme, they became, as Ambassador Izvolsky said, "reasonable through the exercise of power."

In 1905 the great Marxist event, Revolution, suddenly took place—in the wrong way in the wrong country. Russia had not reached the highly industrialized stage which Marx had predicated as necessary for collapse. The rising was not the work of a self-conscious disciplined proletariat but simply of exasperated human beings. No one was surprised that it failed, but the most extraordinary aspect of its passage was that it left Socialism virtually untouched.

All over the world people were horrified by the Cossacks' shooting down of workers on their march to the Winter Palace with their petition to the Czar. When news of the "fiendish massacre" was heard at a Trade Union Congress in Liverpool, the immediate reaction was to raise a fund of £1,000 for the families of the murdered men. When the Russian workers' protest became a general strike in October, forcing the regime in its fright to grant a Constitution, the event created a profound impression as a triumph of the working class. Workers in Europe held mass meetings, cheered and waved red flags. "Long live the Russian Revolution! Long live Socialism!" shouted Italian peasants fifteen hundred miles from St. Petersburg. But no spark from the Russian fire ignited a general conflagration. The long-awaited spontaneous uprising had occurred, but no Western working class was prepared to overthrow capitalism. Only the Austrian Socialists alertly used the example to bring to a climax their campaign for universal suffrage.

Seizing the opportunity to work on the fright inspired in the rulers by Russian events, Viktor Adler in Vienna proclaimed a general strike for November 28. He worked on the preparations for a month in advance. One party member in a factory where the workers were not Socialists could not bring them to join; no one would talk about the Revolution or the proposed strike or "touch a political subject with a ten-foot pole." The demonstration, however, was a success. In Vienna, the Mariahilferstrasse was black with thousands of marchers packed so tightly that it took an hour to cover the half mile to the Ringstrasse, where the parade was joined by even greater crowds from other districts of the city. The tramp of the masses, the clenched fists, the red flags, raised again the terrible vision of Mme Hennebau in *Germinal.* The Austrian regime, frightened by the demonstrations, yielded the promise of manhood suffrage, which went into effect in 1907, virtually the only positive result of the Russian rising.

German Social-Democrats, too, arranged demonstrations for reform of the electoral system in Prussia, which was organized according to the tax roll. The great number of small taxpayers at the base who paid the same total amount as the fewer middle third and as the very few rich at the top were not permitted to elect more than one-third of the local representatives. The Socialists always elected their full third of the municipal councils, but even when they had the votes, could never win control. Nor, confirming Jaurès' taunt, could they win it on the barricades. Against the steel of the Prussian government, their demonstrations won no improvements.

One effect of the Russian revolution was to lose the Socialists' votes. In the German election of 1907 middle-class voters represented by the Progressive party, which previously, when it came to a choice, had supported the Social-Democrats in preference to the reactionary parties, voted for the Conservative candidate. They were influenced too by heavy propaganda of the Navy and Pan-German Leagues, who wanted the election to register an overwhelming mandate for nationalism and imperialism. In the "Hottentot Election," as it was called from the current war in Germany's African colonies, the Socialists for the first time since 1890 lost seats.

Leon Trotsky, despairing at the repression under which the Russian revolution now seemed "hopelessly and permanently trampled," was struck by the lack of interest among the European Socialists. Meeting Kautsky in 1907, a small, delicate man with clear blue eyes and snow-white hair and beard who looked like "a very kind grandpapa" though only fifty-three, he found him "hostile to the transfer of revolutionary methods to German soil." On paper, revolution had a lovely glow; the reality in the streets was less welcome. The abortive experience in Russia revealed that the Western working class on the whole wanted no part of it. As a result, Revision was encouraged and

Revision signified the further from class, the nearer to nationalism.

Industrial war did not slacken. Labour after 1905 listened increasingly to the Syndicalist teaching of direct action. Its source and influence was strongest in France, where Anarchists had long vigorously denounced the parliamentary method as a sham which diverted the labour movement from revolutionary aims to political issues and favored the leadership of intellectuals. In Syndicalist eyes the Socialist politicians, as members of a national parliament, became essentially part of the bourgeois world, taking on its codes and losing touch with the working class. Syndicalists insisted class war was economic, not political, and should be waged by strike, not debate. With the increasing infiltration of the Anarchists, the trade union movement adopted revolutionary Syndicalism and direct action as its official doctrine at the CGT Congress of 1906. Direct action against employers consisted of the strike, the slowdown, boycott and sabotage; against the State it included propaganda, mass demonstration, resistance to militarism and to patriotism, a delusion fostered by the capitalists to perpetuate their power. Every gain by the workers was to be considered as strengthening them for the final battle and for the supreme last act of the class war—the general strike, the "revolution of folded arms" which, paralyzing the bourgeois world, would emancipate the working class and win control of the means of production.

In Italy where suppression of the labour movement by police and troops had long been brutal and the gulf of mutual hatred and fear between the classes was deep, the general strike was twice attempted under Syndicalist leadership, in 1904 and 1906, at a cost of savage strife and workers' lives. In France the defeat of one strike after another during the years of Clemenceau's Radical Government from 1906 to 1909 revealed the gap between Syndicalist preaching of the general strike and the actual power of the workers. Labour in France was still largely agricultural and a large share of industry was conducted in small non-union enterprises. CGT membership was not a major proportion of all industrial labour and, reflecting the old antagonism between Anarchists and Socialists, was more frequently at odds with the party than united in mutual support.

Employers fought back violently with dismissals and lockouts against CGT efforts to organize new trades and were frequently abetted by the use of troops, which Clemenceau claimed were necessary to prevent violence against non-strikers. In the strikes by miners of the Nord in 1906, by dockers at Nantes and by vineyard workers of the Midi in 1907, by construction workers in 1908, troops were dispatched by the Government in each case with a resulting total of 20 killed and 667 wounded. Strikes by postal workers and teachers were stamped out by threat of permanent dismissal on the ground that civil servants had no right to organize or strike against the government. CGT officials who had organized them were arrested on charge of incitement to rebellion. Against the stubborn resistance of employers a maximum limit of an eleven-hour day had been enacted in 1900, and a Sunday rest law and old-age pensions in 1906, but against the strike wave in the Clemenceau years, the hard hand of the Government behind the employer reflected Clemenceau's unsentimental dictum, "France is founded on property, property, property." The state's intervention nourished anger and disillusion. The Radical Government's recourse to violence, said Jaurès in 1909, and "its failure to reform society have produced a public lassitude, a muffled grumbling, an undercurrent of discontent. . . ." In the same year, a similar discontent with the Liberal Government in England was creating the same climate of restiveness.

In the United States the employers' counter-offensive also gathered force, backed by court decisions which used the Sherman Anti-Trust Act to outlaw picketing, boycott and strikes as restraint of trade. Like the hilltop signal fires of ancient times, Syndicalism sent its message across the Atlantic and it flared into existence in America with the founding of the Industrial Workers of the World in 1905. Created by Debs and "Big Bill" Haywood of the Western Federation of Miners in strange alliance with De Leon, the IWW was, by European standards, an impossible combination of Syndicalism and Socialism. It preached the doctrine of direct action, while Debs, its hero, campaigned as Socialist candidate for the Presidency of the United States.

American Socialism, like Russian, since it had no representatives in Congress and no role in government even at the municipal level, was protected from the temptations of collaboration. Debs by now had completely espoused the doctrine of class war to the end. Workers must be revolutionaries, not compromisers with the existing order. Their object was not merely to raise wages but to abolish the wage system. He saw Syndicalism as taking over the revolutionary spirit of original Socialism and as offering the means to achieve the promised goal through the trade-union methods in which he had grown up. In a letter to thirty trade-union leaders in December, 1904, he invited them to join in discussing "ways and means of uniting the working people of America on correct revolutionary principles." At its opening convention in Chicago on June 27, 1905, attended by miners, lumbermen, railwaymen, brewery workers and other industrial unions and Socialist factions, the IWW declared itself to be "the Continental Congress of the working class" which would unite skilled and unskilled in one great industrial union to overthrow capitalism and establish a Socialist society. Declaring for the ultimate weapon of Syndicalism, its slogan was "One big Union and one big Strike." According to Haywood—a one-eyed giant and "a bundle of primitive instincts"—the IWW would go down into the gutter to reach the "bums" and migratory workers and bring them up along with the whole mass of labour to a "decent plane of living." Scorning collective bargaining, agreements and political effort, it would work through propaganda, boycott, sabotage and the strike. Government, politics, elections were the bunk; the country should be run by the unions.

The IWW's rejection of political action set off a series of schisms and secessions which flew like woodchips from an ax. Debs was violently attacked by some Socialist colleagues for splitting the labour movement. De Leon broke away in 1908 and continued from his diminished outpost to fight for pristine principle. For Debs the goal was everything and any method which led to it, political as well as direct action, acceptable. Despite the Syndicalist principles of the IWW he ran again for President as the candidate of the Socialist party in 1908. In meetings across the country Haywood and others raised money in pennies and nickels to rent a locomotive and sleeping car to carry Debs on his campaign. Passing locomotive engineers tooted their whistles as the Red Special with red banners streaming from its roof and rear platform went by. Debs had a way of making people believe in the attainability of Socialism. Without brass bands or loud-speakers, his voice, smile and outstretched arms were enough. He "actually believes that there can be such a thing as the brotherhood of man," said a hard-bitten organizer who confessed himself pained when any-one else called him Comrade. "But when Debs says Comrade, it's all right. He means it." Families in wagons with red flags stuck in the whip sockets came for miles across the prairies to greet the Red Special at railroad stops. Torchlight parades in the towns, mass meetings, children with bouquets of red roses, created an illusion in which Debs himself began to believe. Socialists, he wrote to a friend, are "thick as grasshoppers out here" and the farmers "are revolutionary to the core and ripe and ready for action." The "plutes" would get a shock when the votes were counted. But the total vote proved disappointing: 400,000, no more than in 1904.

In 1910 on the wave of the general Reform movement in the United States, Victor Berger, the first Socialist to win a seat in Congress, was elected from Milwaukee together with a Socialist city attorney, Socialist comptroller, two Socialist judges and twenty-one Socialist aldermen out of thirty-five. In 1911 a Socialist mayor was elected in Schenectady and by 1912 the party had elected mayors in fifty-six municipalities. But these were victories of Revision and the successful candidates were intellectuals—lawyers, editors, ministers—not workingmen. The labour movement at both wings, IWW and AF of L, refused to enter politics. In 1912 when the major parties engaged in a three-cornered contest for the Presidency, Debs ran again. Again it seemed, as Victor Berger wrote in the Milwaukee *Leader*, that Socialism was the coming order and "we are speeding toward it with the accelerating velocity of a locomotive." Touring New York's Lower East Side, Debs stood on a truck which "slowly plowed its way through a roaring ocean of people as far as the eye could see all up and down dark tenement streets." The vote was 900,000, double that of the time before, though only 6 per cent of the total. The IWW won its greatest victory that year in Lawrence, Massachusetts, where it organized a strike of textile workers against a pay cut. It fed and maintained an entire town of workers and their dependents for two months and won a wage increase. But the bitter and brutal defeat of the Paterson strike shortly afterwards began the decline of American Syndicalism.

In Germany Syndicalist doctrine of the general strike took little hold. Like other German institutions the unions were too orderly to be attracted by a measure which was the negation of all order and duty. The working class, whom Kuno Francke in 1905 lauded as so "well-behaved," shared the attachment to authority and obedience which in Germany seemed overdeveloped, as if, without its protection, some old Teutonic savagery, some inner Hun, might break out. The German Socialists were realistic about the general strike. Bebel opposed its use for political purposes because, he said, it could only be organized under extraordinary conditions to the accompaniment of a revolutionary state of mind among the workers. Among his countrymen, as he was only too aware, this was missing. When the Radicals of the party at its Mannheim Congress in 1906 proposed a *Massenstreik* in case of war, Bebel rejected it as futile. In the event of war, he said, the military would take over law and order, resistance would be folly and chauvinist fever in any event would grip the masses. Bebel, at least, never fed on, or encouraged, illusions.

At Mannheim a crucial if quiet struggle for power took place with results decisive for German and, through it, for world Socialism. Kautsky offered a resolution intended to subordinate the trade unions to the party in matters of policy. Their task, as Kautsky defined it, was to defend and improve the lot of the worker until the final advent of Socialism. Since the task of the party was achievement of the long-term maximum goal, its decisions must predominate.

During the past decade membership in the German unions had increased from 250,000 to 2,500,000, with funds in proportion. Unlike the French, they were in close communion with the party and its chief source of votes. Sam Gompers on his tour of Europe in 1909 was impressed by the cash benefits the unions paid in strikes and lockouts, by their organization and discipline, and by the improved conditions and increased wages they had won. Day labourers earned three marks and skilled labour six marks a day, or about thirty-six shillings or eight or nine dollars a week. Mealtimes were regulated, fines and penalties posted on the bulletin board, the right to organize was recognized by the government except for servants and farm labour; child labour under thirteen was outlawed and between the ages of thirteen and fourteen was restricted to six hours a day. Gratified that such progress disproved the Marxist theory of "increasing misery," Gompers was inspired to a paean of optimism by the status of the German worker, who appeared to him to live in an age of "the greatest production, the most wealth, the highest general intelligence and the best reasons for hope for his class that the history of the world has recorded." Even if, in his anti-Marxist enthusiasm, Gompers overstated the case, the German worker was clearly acquiring a stake in the existing order. The effect was not conducive to revolutionary ardor in the unions. The fear that they were becoming too embedded in the existing order inspired Kautsky's resolution to subordinate them to the political control of the party.

His motion was firmly defeated by the majority at Mannheim for fear of offending the trade unions. It was all very well to let Kautsky formulate theory, but when it came to practical matters the General Council of the party was nothing if not realistic. Defeat of the resolution meant, in effect, a victory for the trade unions. Since Kautsky's analysis had been correct, it also meant, in the country of dominant Socialist influence, preference for the existing order over the final goal. Bernstein's onetime heresy "I care nothing for the final goal . . ." was now canonical. After Mannheim, day-to-day activity became increasingly practical and revisionist, even while party declarations at Congresses and ceremonial occasions continued to reiterate the Marxist formulas.

Nationalism came in with the rising Revisionist tide. In the Reichstag on April 25, 1907, shortly before the opening of the Hague Conference, a Socialist deputy, Gustav Noske, made the trend explicit in a speech which caused a sensation. It was a "bourgeois illusion," he announced, to suppose that all Socialists believed in disarmament. While they looked forward to peace in the future, international economic conflicts at present were too strong to permit disarming. Socialists would resist just as vigorously as the gentlemen on the right any attempt by another nation to press Germany to the wall. "We have always demanded an armed nation," he said to the astonished gasps of his colleagues and the equally astonished delight and applause of the Right. Indignantly repudiated by Kautsky, who with considerable courage said that in the event of war, German Social-Democrats would regard themselves as proletarians first and Germans second, Noske nevertheless found many followers.

In Germany as in England the topic of coming conflict between the two countries was fashionable, fomented by the Navy League's slogans, "The Coming War!" "England the Foe!" "England's Plan to Fall on Us in 1911!" and the Pan-German accompaniment, "To Germany belongs the world!" In every country as the air thickened with talk of war, the instinct of patriotism swelled. Older, deeper, more instinctive than any class solidarity, it was not something easily eradicated on the say-so of the *Communist Manifesto.* Unhappily for world brotherhood, the worker felt he had a fatherland like anybody else.

In strident dispute, a voice, expressing the opposite tendency from Noske in Germany, was raised in France. It came from the Socialist Gustave Hervé, a shrieking prophet of anti-patriotism and anti-militarism. Once a follower of Déroulède, he had swung to the opposite extreme and attained national notoriety by his declaration during the Dreyfus Affair that as long as military barracks existed he would hope to see the tricolor flag planted upon the dunghill in their courtyards. This led to his dismissal as a teacher and trial for incitement to mutiny in which he was successfully defended by Briand. Regarding the mystique of *patrie* as a Moloch sucking workers into its armored jaws where they shed each other's blood, Hervé continued his campaign against army and country, undaunted by further trials and a term in jail. "We shall reply to the mobilization order by revolt!" he screamed. "Civil war is the only war that is not stupid." At the French Socialist party Congress of 1906, in the midst of the first Moroccan crisis, and again at the Congress of 1907, he embodied these sentiments in a resolution. All the Syndicalist intellectuals, devotees of Sorel, Bergson and Nietzsche, rallied to his support. They were the cultists of the "myth" of the general strike, not the men who would be called upon to practice it, for these were not present. The CGT did not come to congresses of the SFIO, and in any case it designed the general strike for purposes of revolution, not prevention of war.

Representing the diehard Marxists, Guesde led the opposition to Hervé on the ground that since war was inherent in the capitalist system and the predecessor of its death-throes, it was futile, and for Socialists self-defeating, to prevent it.

Jaurès, as the party's leading figure, had to guide the Congress to a position. With his faith that a good society was within man's grasp, he saw war as the great wrecker; not the opportunity of the working class, but the enemy of the workingman. To prevent it was to become, in the years ahead, his primary aim. He had long maintained that the general strike, unless well organized both as to means and ends, was "revolutionary romanticism," yet at the same time it was the only way the working class could make its power felt to prevent a threatened war. He was also inclined to support it because, in maintaining the precarious unity of the SFIO, it was important to make concessions to the Syndicalist-minded wing. No less a man of this world than Bebel, Jaurès remained also an idealist and dealt with the problem of the general strike by persuading himself that if war loomed, somehow the masses would be stirred by the necessary fervor to rise in spontaneous and effective protest without previous planning or organization. In this one area, a crucial one, Jaurès came closest to thinking "with his beard." He agreed to a resolution less explicit than Hervé's, but committing French Socialism to all forms of agitation against war, including parliamentary action, public meetings, popular protests, "even the general strike and insurrection."

It was rhetoric, but Jaurès believed or persuaded himself that "ceaseless agitation" could make it come true. He did not content himself with hoping but practiced agitation at Socialist mass meetings and on speaking tours throughout France. From this time on, at Toulouse, Lille, Dijon, Nîmes, Bordeaux, Guise, Reims, Avignon, Toulon, Marseille, and of course Carmaux, "at every railroad station in France, it seemed, Jaurès descended from a train at one time or another, suitcase in hand, the great salesman of peace." Abroad too, in London, in Brussels and other foreign capitals, his voice poured forth as if trying physically to lift his listeners to a fervor that could be translated into action if need arose. On one trip to England in company with Vandervelde they visited Hatfield, home of the Cecils, which Jaurès said interested him more than Oxford.

The problem of war, the effort to reconcile the trends between the extremes of Hervé and Noske dominated Socialism from now on. It came to a head at once at the next Congress, convened for the first time on German soil, in August, 1907. Although the working class of Berlin was a stronghold of Socialism, the party's leaders did not venture to hold the Congress in the capital under the nose of the Kaiser. The site they chose was Stuttgart, capital of Württemberg in South Germany. Eight hundred and eighty-six delegates representing twenty-six nations or nationalities assembled in the largest auditorium of the city. Among them were Ramsay MacDonald from England, De Leon and Big Bill Haywood from the United States, Plekhanov, Lenin, Trotsky and Alexandra Kollontay for the various Russian factions, Mme Kama of India, the "Red virgins," Rosa Luxemburg and Clara Zetkin, and among the polyglot translators, Angelica Balabanov from Italy accompanied by a "violently protesting bullish young man with a dark face," Benito Mussolini. As a demonstration of Socialist strength an outdoor demonstration was held on the opening day, a Sunday, in a field outside the city. Workingmen and their families came from all around, filling the streets leading to the field where a dozen red-draped platforms had been set up for the speakers. Bands played and choral societies sang Socialist hymns while vigilant police watched over the proceedings from two captive balloons. By 2 P.M. a crowd of fifty thousand had gathered to listen to the Socialist celebrities amid "extraordinary enthusiasm but no disorder." In his speech Bebel congratulated the British proletariat on its recent brilliant success at the polls, remarking with perhaps a touch of envy that while the Government had cleverly made John Burns a member of the Cabinet, he was sure it had not succeeded in changing the party's fighting tactics. Loud cheers greeted Jaurès' speech, delivered in German. Though he could memorize a German translation of his speech after one reading or recite long passages of Goethe by heart, he could not command enough colloquial German to engage a hotel room.

Afterwards in the hall amid the admirable German arrangements everyone, understandably, had a sense of deliberating under the eyes of the police. When Harry Quelch, an English delegate, disrespectfully referred to the Hague Conference, then in session, as a "thieves' supper," Chancellor von Bülow, who was not notably respectful toward the Conference himself, brought pressure on the Württemberg government to have him expelled. Immediately ill at ease, Bebel did not even protest. Quelch's empty chair was kept filled with flowers during the remaining sessions.

While the Congress divided as usual into committees on suffrage, women, minorities, immigration, colonialism and other problems, the Committee on Anti-militarism was the focus of attention. The duty of the working class in the face of rising militarism and threat of war, placed on the agenda by the French, unleashed five days of debate. In an opening tirade, Hervé again proposed mass disobedience to mobilization, in effect insurrection. Since this could be transformed into revolution, it was supported by the German Radicals led by Rosa Luxemburg and Karl Liebknecht, but the official weight of the party, from old Marxists like Bebel and Kautsky to new nationalists of the Noske variety, shifted solidly to the right. Debating "within earshot, so to speak, of the Wilhelmstrasse," as Vandervelde put it, the Germans muted their customary verbal tornadoes, though not only from discretion; the shift was ideological. Some admittedly, some still pretending otherwise, they were aligning themselves with the national mood, accommodating to the facts of life in an era of national expansion from which the worker derived material benefits. "It is not true that workers have no Fatherland," declared Georg von Vollmar, a leading Revisionist; "the love of humanity does not prevent us from being good Germans." He and his group, he said, would not accept an internationalism that was anti-national.

Jaurès proposed the same resolution as had just been adopted by the French Congress, emphasizing "agitation" and including the general strike as a last resort.

To expect an effective general strike without planning or organization was equivalent to expecting an army to march without orders, billets, supply depots, transport, food or ammunition. Even if the Second International could have agreed on a general strike, it had no power to give orders to its national components, each of whom would have had to organize the strike of its own people separately. Unless the action were simultaneous and international, the workers who accomplished it most effectively would only be opening their own country to defeat. As Guesde was forever pointing out, a general strike could only be made effective by the best organized and disciplined labour force. If successful its only result would be to lay open the more modern countries to military defeat by the backward. The dilemma was awful and insoluble. Jaurès kept it at bay because he thought of the general strike more as an idea to kindle the masses than as a real possibility. Walking with Bernstein in one of Stuttgart's parks, he tried to convince him of the inspiriting value of a declaration in favor of the strike. "All my objections concerned its impracticality," Bernstein said later, "but he kept coming back to the *moral* effect of such a commitment." As Clemenceau was to say long afterwards, it was Jaurès' fate "to preach the brotherhood of nations with such unswerving faith . . . that he was not daunted by the brutal reality of facts."

Bebel opposed the general strike as totally impractical. Tied to the unions, as the French party was not, the German party looked at the strike from the union point of view. Though every member may have been a good Socialist, the unions had no wish to lose their funds in a reckless gesture against the power of the State. Financial reserves to maintain a general strike even in peacetime were not available. To oppose defence of the Fatherland in a nation seized by war fever, Bebel said, would put the Socialists in an impossible position. Even Kautsky agreed. A strike was impossible without consent of the unions, he pointed out. Privately he and like-minded friends comforted themselves, like Jaurès, with the belief that somehow, if war came, the "infuriated" workers would rise against it.

Where was the voice of the worker, the man directly concerned, in all this talk of strike? It was not heard. The worker was at home concerned with the job, the boss, the broken window, the ailing child, tonight's supper, tomorrow's holiday. If he thought about a strike it was for wages; if he thought about war it was as some vague grand happening with an aura of excitement and valor. He thought less of striking against it than of marching to it, to smite the foreigner and protect his country. Bebel knew him. "Do not fool yourselves," he said to an English delegate, and repeated his old assertion that the instant the Fatherland declared itself in danger, "every Social-Democrat will shoulder his rifle and march to the French frontier."

If Bebel was still the Pope of Socialism it was as a secular Pope; the moral torch had passed to Jaurès, "the greatest hope of the Second International," in the words of Vandervelde's opening speech. He was brimming with energy, plunged into a great campaign against war, delighted to be in Germany. Seizing a huge foam-crowned mug at a country beer garden, he said, "Beer! Vandervelde, German beer!" with a fresh enthusiasm that his companion found irresistible. One night, returning from an outing via medieval Tübingen, he insisted on getting out in the pouring rain and darkness, although nothing could be seen, to stand in front of the illustrious University.

Bebel threw the weight of the party against an explicit commitment to the general strike less because he was convinced it was impractical than because he feared reprisals by his Government, perhaps even renewal of the anti-Socialist law. Grown middle-aged and successful since Engels' warning, "Legality kills us," his party had no desire to go underground again. In addition to the conflicting French resolutions, he had also to contend against the Radicals of his own party assisted by a formidable partner. Pointing him out to a friend, Rosa Luxemburg said, "That's Lenin. Observe his obstinate self-willed skull." Together she and he were determined that any resolution taken by the Congress on militarism should remind the working class of its duty to transform war into revolution. In private sessions Lenin engaged in prolonged negotiations with Bebel, who insisted that there should be "nothing in the resolution that would enable the public prosecutor in Berlin to outlaw the party." After many rewordings and discussions which Lenin found overlong but rich in dialectic, a satisfactory formula was worked out and tacked on to the main resolution.

As drafted by a committee under Bebel's direction, the final result managed to accommodate all points of view, short of Hervé's insurrectionary strike, in a form calculated neither to alarm the public prosecutor in Berlin nor alienate any important section of the Congress. Bebel had prevailed. The resolution did not mention general strike. It reaffirmed the class struggle, the nature of war as inherent in capitalism and the demand for citizen armies to replace standing armies, but stated that "the International is not in a position to prescribe in a rigid form the action to be taken by the working class against militarism." It recommended the usual "ceaseless agitation" and declared in favor of arbitration and disarmament. The addition sponsored by Lenin and Rosa Luxemburg, pruned to respectability, pledged the working classes and their parliamentary representatives to exert their utmost efforts to prevent the outbreak of war "by using the means which seem most effective to them"; if war should nevertheless break out they were to work for its speedy termination and meanwhile "exploit the crisis with all their strength thereby to hasten the abolition of capitalism."

In 1909 a people suddenly rose in a strike against war with tragic results. It was not an organized movement but, as in the Russian rising of 1905, a spontaneous outbreak. Red Week in Barcelona, called by the Spaniards *la semana tragica*, was a mass protest against the conscription of soldiers for a campaign in Morocco which was considered by the workers a war in the interests of the Riff mine-owners. A strike initiated by the Labour Federation of Barcelona became overnight an outpouring of the people themselves, especially the women, against war, rulers, reaction, the Church and all the elements of an oppressive regime. Stamped out in gunfire and blood, the rising aroused Socialist wrath over the trial and execution of one man, Francisco Ferrer, but excited no concern for the problems or techniques of revolt.

In the same year, a general strike was called by the National Federation of Labour in Sweden in protest against the increasing use of lockouts by employers. Involving nearly 500,000 strikers and lasting a month, it was broken by the Government's threat of permanent dismissal and loss of pensions and by the success of the upper classes in organizing brigades to carry on essential services. Activity was easier to organize than the inactivity of folded arms.

In the same year, the shadow of war moved nearer when Austria-Hungary annexed Bosnia-Herzegovina in a challenge which Russia, not yet recovered from her troubles, had to swallow, the more so as the Kaiser proclaimed his stand in "shining armor" at his ally's side. Austrian Socialists could not resist a thrill of national pride. The Socialist *Arbeiter-Zeitung* of Vienna published a series of chauvinist articles which caused the Serbian bourgeois press malicious joy in pointing out that international solidarity of the working class was not so solid as supposed.

In England the anti-German wave swept up Blatchford, who for all his Socialism had, as an old soldier, supported the Boer War. With Hyndman he now conducted a campaign for conscription in his paper, the *Clarion*. Branding them as betrayers of Socialism, Keir Hardie still believed "absolutely that organized labour would never take part in another orgy of workmen's blood." Nor was he alone. The mystique of the working class standing as one, in heroic consciousness of itself, was strong. Sam Gompers, born to the working class himself like Hardie, and concerned all his life with workingmen and their affairs, believed in it. When he came to Europe to attend an international Trade Union Congress in 1909, the primary impression he took away was "the fact of the solidarity today in the sentiment of the masses of Europe." Still the unconscious Socialist, he believed the struggle of the workers for their rights would take precedence "over wars between nations in which working men have no cause." He knew and stated in another context that a general strike was "impossible in the current stage of organized labour"; nevertheless he too felt sure of a "deep seated resolve" among his class to refuse to take military duty's last step of shooting down their fellow workers. The spirit of the international trade-union congresses where delegates talked and broke bread together would, he wrote, spread back through their reports to all organized workers, who would understand and refuse to kill each other. "Even the unorganized" would read the accounts and listen to the returning delegates and take up this spirit of refusal. Statesmen knew very well that their next order, "To the front!" would be followed by "mass demonstrations for peace"—Gompers did not venture to say mass disobedience. "It is the general consensus of opinion," he concluded, "that the final obstacle to a war of nations in Europe today is the determined adverse attitude of the workers in the different countries."

Gompers was as practical and toughminded as any man who ever lived, but the age he lived in was sentimental. That, like Jaurès, he could believe in a final Halt! accomplished by "mass demonstrations" showed the extent to which the idea of the working class as Hero had taken hold.

His purpose in coming to Europe was to affiliate the AF of L with the International Federation of Trade Unions. If any action by organized labour was to make itself felt against war, this was the only body which could supply it, supposing it possessed both the will and the means. It had neither. Founded in 1903 at the suggestion of English and French unions but opposed by the Germans, it represented twenty-seven federations of trades or industries with a membership of over seven million in nineteen countries. The figures were more imposing than its real functions, which were chiefly secretarial. It kept member unions informed of trade conditions and did its best to frustrate employers' efforts to recruit foreign strikebreakers. To conciliate the large and well-financed German unions, its headquarters were in Germany and Carl Legien, chief of the German National Federation of Trade Unions, was its Secretary. At its biennial Congresses, political and social questions, usually brought forward by the French, were not welcomed. In 1909 the Federation raised a strike aid fund of $643,000 for the Swedish general strike, most of it coming from the German and Scandinavian unions and very little from the British, French or American. Solidarity was less than total. With German influence strong and with a non-political orientation, it was not a body to interest itself in ideas of an international general strike.

One of its strongest units was the International Transport-workers' Federation of seamen, dockers and railwaymen. Founded in 1896, it represented forty-two unions in sixteen countries with a membership of 468,000. It was on the ITF that Keir Hardie, who like Jaurès had become primarily concerned with the problem of war, rested his hopes of an international strike in the event of war. If the transport workers alone, or together with the miners' International, downed tools, he believed they could stop a war. Here again the problem was simultaneous action in all countries, but Hardie's fervor carried him over that and he brought his proposal forward at the next Socialist Congress, held in Copenhagen in August, 1910.

As host city to the International in 1910 Copenhagen was a symbol of the importance Socialism had reached. The Danish Socialist Party, one of the strongest of the small countries, controlled the municipal government of the capital. The committee, determined to impress the world by its organization and efficiency, gave magnificent receptions and a Socialist mayor delivered the address of welcome. Replying in a voice of "ripe sonority which makes hearts vibrate," Vandervelde expressed the delegates' sense of a great occasion when "a free people, masters of their City Hall, welcomes the Red International." Socialist voters in the world now numbered eight million. French Socialists were fresh from an electoral victory in May in which they had won over a million votes and increased their deputies from 54 to 76. Although it was not a matter for unmixed pride, Briand, still calling himself an Independent Socialist, was actually Premier. Socialism seemed to have reached a stage to exercise effectively the "awful conscience" of mankind.

At Copenhagen it spoke through Keir Hardie, who proposed a resolution jointly with Edouard Vaillant of France, recommending that "the affiliated Parties and Labour organizations consider the advisability and feasibility of the general strike, especially in industries that supply war material, as one of the methods of preventing war and that action be taken on the subject at the next Congress." When proposing it, Hardie acknowledged that the workers were not ready to strike against war but he clung to the hope that they would be ready when the time came. "We must give them a great lead," he said. His resolution was supported by Vandervelde and by Jaurès, who was the more disposed to be sympathetic because he was in the midst of an effective effort, which partly depended on acceptance of the general strike, to draw the CGT closer to the SFIO. Further, his concern over the bureaucratic trend of the German party led him increasingly to consider the need for mass tactics.

The Germans and Austrians were solidly opposed to Hardie's motion on the same ground as before: that to advocate a strike in the event of war might lead to prosecution for treason and confiscation of funds. Bebel, ill and growing old, was absent, but even without him German pressure secured a negative vote. As a compromise the resolution was referred to the Bureau in Brussels for reconsideration at the next Congress. To go on record even to this extent worried the Germans. They were only reluctantly persuaded to agree by Vandervelde's argument that if they refused, the British and French might pursue the plan independently. A resolution on anti-militarism was passed, virtually the same as that of Stuttgart, with the addition that organized labour in member countries "shall consider whether a general strike should not be proclaimed if necessary in order to prevent the crime of war." As nervously if not quite as quickly as capitalists had disposed of Disarmament at The Hague, Socialists disposed of the general strike.

Within weeks hard proof was given of labour's inability to win a transport strike. In France in October Premier Briand broke a general strike of railwaymen against all private and state-operated lines by conscripting the workers into the army for a period of three weeks, making absence from work subject to a charge of military desertion. On the excuse of national defense, Briand defended his action as dictated by a patriotic conscience. Even to an old Socialist his conscience did not dictate pressure on the companies for the wage increase the railwaymen were demanding.

History had reached 1910. The transfer of power to a new class whose signals Balfour had seen in the British general election of 1906 was a process in the making, not a fact. In a test of strength, as in the French railway strike, labour could not command real power. International action was hallucination. While the Socialists kept on talking about it and believing in it, they were dealing more in a hope and a theory than in flesh and bones. One genuine attempt at international working-class action was made at this time. While the Socialists in Copenhagen were discussing a possible general strike in war industries, the very men who would be crucial to it, the International Transportworkers (ITF), by nature the most international of the unions, were also in session in Copenhagen. Once during the Boer War pro-Boer Dutch members had urged an international boycott of British shipping but the ITF leaders had flatly turned down the proposal on the ground that it was just not possible at that stage to interest workers in an international movement for political purposes. Direct trade union purposes were another matter. Now in 1910 they decided to call an international strike of their own in the following year for redress of grievances against the shipowners.

The active instigators were the British delegates, Ben Tillett and Havelock Wilson, while the German delegate, Paul Müller, was strongly opposed, just as his compatriots were simultaneously opposing Keir Hardie's proposal at the Socialist congress. A seamen's strike at the present moment, Müller said, would be "absolutely insane" and would certainly end disastrously. The masters would triumph, the union leaders would lose their influence, the men would become destitute and would ultimately have to sue for peace on their knees. Since a shipping strike, like a strike against war, would operate to the advantage of the shipping trade in the countries whose unions did not go out, and since the Germans and British were rivals in shipping, the international principle was vital. Heavy pressure brought Herr Müller around and the Congress voted unanimously for a seamen's strike against the "brutal and callous" refusal of the shipowners in all countries to discuss the unions' demands for a conciliation board. All agreed that the strike "must and would be international."

At subsequent meetings of the seamen's committee at Antwerp in November and the following March, the British stated they would definitely strike in 1911 and the Belgians, Dutch, Norwegians and Danes pledged their support. The Germans, now claiming that they had no reason to strike, backed out. The date was set for June 14. In the meantime the Danes and Norwegians retired, the former because they had succeeded in winning a favorable five-year agreement and the latter because, on their demands being turned down, they felt themselves too weak to enforce them. In what developed into the great Transport strike of Coronation summer, the British struck anyway, along with the Belgians and Dutch, whose action was overshadowed by the dramatic British effort. Sympathetic action in other Continental ports was organized by the ITF, which prevented recruitment of strikebreakers and helped the British seamen win their demands. As a whole, however, the strike solidarity originally contemplated was not reached. As if in preview, the ITF endeavor of 1911 showed what might be expected of the working class in international action.

Socialism with steadfast heart remained, nevertheless, predicated in the event of war on a "rising" of the workers of the world. In this it shared the tendency of the age to clothe reality in sentimental garments. The public of the time was not represented by those doctors, writers and social psychologists who were beginning to look at man without illusions. These were the advance guard, as were "seers of black" like Wedekind. The public preferred the rosy view: the perfect pearly nudes of Bouguereau, the impossibly handsome Gibson girls—creatures that never were on land or sea. So, in their own way, did the Socialists.

The rosy view predominated in Germany, where in the general election of 1912 the Social-Democrats won an astounding 35 per cent of the total vote, amounting to 4,250,000 votes and 110 seats. The party was growing so fast and seemed so powerful that to other Socialists it appeared "irresistible" and the moment near and certain when the Socialist movement in Germany would "include the majority of the people and burst the fetters of the feudal-capitalist state." The existence of so many Social-Democrats in the country meant a proportionate increase of their numbers in the armed forces, leading to a time, surely, when it would be impossible for the Army to be used against the workers.

But the discrepancy between size and actual influence which Jaurès had brought into the open at the Amsterdam Congress remained, indeed grew more noticeable as the size of the party swelled. The uses to which the German parliamentary Socialists put their electoral triumph of 1912 were not impressive. When the Government that year increased its forces by three Army corps, they opposed the enabling bill but did not venture so far as to oppose the tax which was to pay for it. When one of their number, Philipp Scheidemann, was elected First Vice-President of the Reichstag, his announcement that he would not join in the official call on the Kaiser touched off a new version of the knee-breeches debate. All the parties, not only the Socialists, took part. The vital question at issue was whether Scheidemann would make the call if the Second Vice-President were absent and whether Bebel had or had not agreed that the Socialists could join in the customary cheers for their Sovereign. In the upshot, Scheidemann's principles caused his election to be cancelled, thus averting serious problems.

Within the body of Social-Democracy, Revision was keeping pace with the growing nationalism of the country. Socialism's very success turned its sights away from the maximum program, toward the minimum and the possible. The red dawn of revolution receded. Believers repeated the Marxist formulas with untamed ardor, but conviction had passed to those who were still "illegals"—the Russians. At a meeting of the Leipzig left-wingers, a visiting Austrian Socialist referred to his hosts as revolutionaries. "We revolutionaries?" interrupted Franz Mehring. "Bah! *Those* are the revolutionaries," he said, nodding at Trotsky, who was a guest.

For Jaurès the overriding task had become the need to forge and impose a policy for preventing war in terms compatible both with the defence of France and faith in Socialism. In his country too, nationalism, *revanche*, the belligerent spirit, was rising. The pressure of Germany was omnipresent, the shadow of Sedan lengthening. To logical extremists like Guesde, peace and the interests of the working class were not necessarily equivalent, but to Jaurès they were. He now believed that the only way consistent with Socialism to meet the threat of war was through a citizen army. When the whole nation was an army of reserves, with everyone having taken six months' basic training, and with officers drawn from the ranks, the nation could not be drawn into belligerency in the interest of capitalist warmongers. In a war of defence aginst invasion only such an army of the whole nation, he argued, could hope to repel the terrible "submersion" that German use of reserves in the front line was preparing.

Jaurès' campaign was not merely Socialist oratory. As in *Les Preuves* in the Dreyfus Affair, he set about demonstrating the practicability of his case, studying and working out, over a period of three years, the means of reorganizing the military establishment. He embodied the results in a bill submitted to the Chamber in November, 1910, and in a book of seven hundred pages, *l'Armée Nouvelle*, published in 1911. Preaching his cause tirelessly in the Chamber, in *l'Humanité*, the Socialist paper of which he was founder and director, in meetings and lectures, he was thunderously abused as a "traitor," pro-German and "pacifist" by the cohorts of the Right, particularly by the vituperative *Action Française*.

The Balkans, where the interests of Russia and Austria clashed, was, as everyone knew, the hot-box of Europe. When in October, 1912, the Balkan League of Serbia, Bulgaria, Greece and Montenegro, encouraged by Russia, declared war on Turkey, it seemed the awful moment had come. In Belgrade, Trotsky watched the 18th Serbian Infantry marching off to war in uniforms of the new khaki color. They wore bark sandals and a sprig of green in their caps, which gave them a look of "men doomed for sacrifice." Nothing so brought home to him the meaning of war as those sprigs of green and bark sandals. "A sense of the tragedy of history took possession of me, a feeling of impotence before fate, of compassion for the human locust."

To demonstrate the unity of the workers of the world against war, the Bureau in Brussels convened an emergency Congress to meet in Basle on the Swiss border between France and Germany on November 24 and 25. Five hundred and fifty-five delegates hastened to Basle from twenty-three countries. A manifesto drawn up in advance by the Bureau was voted unanimously, proclaiming "readiness for any sacrifice" against war, without specifying what. Addresses by Keir Hardie, Adler, Vandervelde and all Socialism's most inspiring orators culminated in a speech by Jaurès, tacitly acknowledged by now the most influential figure of the movement. Bebel, though present, was in decline and making what proved to be his last international appearance.

Jaurès spoke from the pulpit of the Cathedral, given over to the Congress by the ecclesiastical authorities despite bourgeois fears of "dangerous" consequences. The sound of the church bells, he said, reminded him of the motto of Schiller's "Song of the Bells": *Vivos voco, mortuos plango, fulgura frango* (I summon the living, I mourn the dead, I break the furnaces). Leaning forward urgently, he spoke to the upturned faces: "I call on the living that they may defend themselves from the monster who appears on the horizon. I weep for the countless dead now rotting in the East. I will break the thunderbolts of war which menace from the skies."

As it happened, these particular thunderbolts were broken by capitalist statesmen who summoned a Conference in London in December, 1912, which limited and, when reconvened in the following May, settled the war before it could expand into conflict between Russia and Austria.

In March, 1913, in a measure directly contrary to Jaurès' campaign, France acted to enlarge her Army by restoring the period of military service from two years to three. Jaurès threw all his energies into battle against it and in favor of the nation-in-arms. For the next six months the Three-Year Law was the dominant fact of French life. Enactment became the rallying cry of nationalism and resistance to it the symbol of the Left. Jaurès denounced the measure in the Chamber as "a crime against the Republic" and drew a crowd of 150,000 to an open-air protest meeting. Leadership of the opposition marked him as the outstanding spokesman for peace. As such he was made the object of further attack as a pacifist and pro-German. After seven weeks of furious debate, the Law was enacted on August 7. Persisting, as he had done through six years of embittered struggle after Rennes until Dreyfus and Picquart were reinstated, Jaurès now led the movement for repeal.

Bebel died that year at seventy-three. In a procession lasting three days, workers and Socialists from many countries filed past the coffin surrounded by hundreds of wreaths and bunches of red flowers. Leadership of the party went to his chosen successor, Hugo Haase, a lawyer and deputy from Königsburg. In August, 1913, in the presence of Andrew Carnegie, and representatives of forty-two states affiliated with the Permanent Court of Arbitration, the Peace Palace was opened at The Hague in what *The Times* called "the happiest circumstances." A survey of French student life in 1913 remarked that the word "War" had a fascination which "the eternal warrior instinct in the heart of man keeps reviving."

Working-class strength continued to grow. Union membership in Germany and Great Britain each reached three million by 1914 and one million in France. The Socialists of Denmark were the largest single party; in Italy Socialists increased their seats in parliament from 32 to 52 in the election of 1913; in France from 76 to 103 in the election of April, 1914. Belgian Socialists, besides electing 30 deputies and seven senators, held 500 municipal council seats. Long frustrated by the stubborn resistance of the ruling class to equal suffrage, they felt themselves strong enough at last to enforce their demand by a general strike. Against impatient radicals who wanted immediate action, Vandervelde and his associates insisted on long and careful preparation; even so, although 400,000 workers joined the strike and stayed out for two weeks, they could not prevail and the strike failed.

The Tenth Congress of the Second International was scheduled for August, 1914, in Vienna, to mark the fiftieth anniversary of the founding of the First International and the twenty-fifth of the Second. Faith in its purpose and its goal were high. In May a Franco-German Committee of Socialist deputies, including Jaurès and Hugo Haase, met at Basle to discuss measures for rapprochement between their countries. Their intention was good but its limit was talk. In England Keir Hardie in the midst of a speech to a conference of the ILP in April turned suddenly to face rows of children from Socialist Sunday Schools, seated behind the platform. Speaking directly to them, he pictured the loveliness of the world of nature and of the world of man as it could become. He spoke of how unnecessary were war and poverty and how he had tried to pass on to them a better world and how, although he and his associates had failed, they, the children, could yet succeed. "If these were my last words I would say them to you: Live for that better day."

At the end of June, news that Serbian patriots had assassinated the Archduke Franz Ferdinand, heir to the Austrian throne, in an obscure town in the annexed territory of Bosnia, provided a sensation of the kind to which Europe was accustomed. It passed without causing undue public alarm. Then suddenly, a month later, on July 24, with terrible impact, came the announcement that Austria had delivered an ultimatum to Serbia of such "brutality," in the words of *Vorwärts*, the German Socialist paper, that "it can be interpreted only as a deliberate attempt to provoke war." Full-scale crisis opened beneath Europe's feet. Would it be another like Agadir and the Balkan

War, hot with challenge and maneuver but finally fended off? People waited in desperate hope. "We relied on Jaurès," wrote Stefan Zweig long afterwards, to organize the Socialists to stop the war.

Socialist leaders consulted. To wait to make a demonstration at Vienna a month hence might be too late. A readiness, a sense of gathering belligerence, could be felt in the atmosphere. The Bureau of Brussels summoned an emergency meeting of leading members for July 29. Jaurès, Hugo Haase, Rosa Luxemburg, Adler, Vandervelde, Keir Hardie and representatives of the Italian, Swiss, Danish, Dutch, Czech and Hungarian parties and of the several Russian factions, about twenty in all, assembled with a "sense of hopelessness and frustration." What could they do? How could they make the will of the working class felt? What indeed was that will? No one asked that question for none doubted that it was for peace, but one answer had already been given two days earlier in Brussels at a congress of trade unions attended by Léon Jouhaux, head of the CGT, and Carl Legien, the German trade-union chief. Jouhaux tried anxiously to find out what the German unions would do. The French, said Jouhaux, would call a strike if the Germans would, but Legien remained silent. In any case no plans had been prepared.

All week the Socialist press of every country roared against militarism, urged the working class of all nations to "stand together," to "combine and conquer" the militarists, to engage in "ceaseless agitation" as planned by the International. *La Bataille Syndicaliste*, organ of the French unions, stated: "Workers must answer the declaration of war by a revolutionary general strike." Workers poured out to mass meetings, listened to exhortations, marched and shouted, but of desire to strike there was no sign as there had been no plan.

On a rainy day in Brussels the Socialist leaders met in a small hall of the Maison du Peuple, the proud new building of the Belgian labour movement with its theatre, offices, committee rooms, café and shops of the cooperatives. As they met they learned that Austria had declared war on Serbia but that other nations were not yet engaged. The hope that somehow the workers would rise—the "somehow" to which they had clung for so long—was all that remained. Each delegate hoped his neighbor would bring news of some great spontaneous outbreak in his country expressing the workers' No! Adler's speech brought no hope of a rising in Austria. Haase, too restless to sit still, reported protests and mass meetings in Germany and assured his colleagues that "the Kaiser does not want war; not from love of humanity but from cowardice. He is afraid of the consequences." Jaurès gave an impression of "one who, having lost all hope of a normal solution, relies on a miracle." Hardie was certain that the British transport workers would call a strike but his confidence was assumed. A few weeks earlier he had written, "Only the binding together of the Trade Union and the Socialist movements will ever put the workers into a position of controlling Governments, thus bringing war to an end." The one country where such binding had taken place was Germany. The delegates talked all day but the only decision reached was to advance the date and change the place of the Vienna Congress to August 9 in Paris, there to resume discussion.

That evening a mass meeting was held in the Cirque Royale crowded by Belgian working people from all parts of the city and its suburbs. As the leaders mounted the platform Jaurès stood with his arm around Haase's shoulders in a gesture which denied the enmity of Germany and France. When he spoke at the climax of the meeting his eloquence mounted until the hall shook with the force of it. He was "quivering, so intense was his emotion, his apprehension, his eagerness to avoid somehow the coming conflict." When he had finished, the crowd, on waves of enthusiasm, poured into the streets to form a parade. Carrying white cards inscribed "*Guerre à la guerre!*" they alternately shouted the slogan and sang "The International" as they marched.

Next day, as the delegates departed, Jaurès, taking leave of Vandervelde, reassured him. "It will be like Agadir—ups and downs—but it is impossible that matters will not be settled. Come, I have a few hours before my train. Let's go to the Museum and see the Flemish primitives." But Vandervelde, who was leaving for London, could not go and never saw Jaurès again. On the train returning to Paris, exhausted from the strain, Jaurès fell asleep. A companion, Jean Longuet, looking at his "wonderful face," was "suddenly overcome with a feeling . . . that he was dead. I froze with fright." On arrival, however, Jaurès woke up and, still persisting, went to the Chamber to talk among the deputies and to the office of *l'Humanité* to write a column for the morning.

Angelica Balabanov and other delegates who left Brussels by another train were breakfasting in the station restaurant at Basle next morning when two comrades of the German Central Committee rushed by in obvious excitement. "There is no doubt about war now," said one of the delegates who had just talked with the Germans outside. "They came here to put the money of the German party in safe-keeping." In Berlin that day Chancellor Bethmann-Hollweg assured the Prussian Ministry of State that there was "nothing particular to fear from the Social-Democratic party" and "there would be no talk of a general strike or of sabotage."

In Paris on July 31, the day of Germany's ultimatum to Russia and declaration of *Kriegsgefahr*, or preliminary mobilization, the public was tense with the knowledge that France stood on the edge of war. The Cabinet was in continuous session, the German Ambassador arrived and departed ominously from the Foreign Office, the life of the country was in suspense. Jaurès led a Socialist deputation to the office of the Premier, his former comrade, Viviani, and returned to organize party pressure in the Chamber. At 9 P.M. he left the office of *l'Humanité*, worn out from anxiety, to have dinner with a group of colleagues at the Café Croissant around the corner in the Rue Montmartre. As he sat eating and talking with his back to the open window, a young man who had been following him since the previous evening appeared in the street outside. Filled, as was later ascertained, with the demented zeal of the superpatriot, he pointed a pistol at the "pacifist" and "traitor" and fired twice. Jaurès slumped to one side and fell forward across the table. Five minutes later he was dead.

The news licked through Paris like a flame. Crowds gathered so quickly in the street outside the restaurant that it took the police fifteen minutes to open a passage for the ambulance. When the body was carried out a great silence fell. As the ambulance clanged away, escorted by policemen on bicycles, a sudden clamor arose, as if to deny the fact of death, "*Jaurès! Jaurès! Vive Jaurès!*" Elsewhere people were stupefied, numb with sorrow. Many wept in the streets. "My heart is breaking," said Anatole France when he heard. Informed at its night session by a white-faced aide, the Cabinet was stunned and fearful. Visions rose of working-class riots and civil strife on the eve of war. The Premier issued a public appeal for unity and calm. Troops were alerted but next morning, in the national peril, there was only deep grief and deep quiet. At Carmaux the miners stopped work. "They have cut down a mighty oak," said one. In Leipzig a Spanish Socialist student at the University wandered blindly through the streets for hours; "everything took on the color of blood."

The news of Jaurès' death appeared in the papers on Saturday, August 1. That afternoon Germany and France mobilized. Before evening, groups of reservists, carrying bundles and bouquets of flowers, were marching off to the railway stations as civilians waved and cheered. Enthusiasm and excitement were equal in every country. In Germany on August 3, Socialist deputies held a caucus to decide whether to vote for war credits. Only a few days ago *Vorwärts* had scorned the pretence of a defensive war. But now the Government talked of the Russian peril and French aggression. Bernstein, the reviser of Marx, assured them that the Government planned to build a "golden bridge" for the Socialists and as proof cited the fact that the Foreign Ministry had extended official condolences in the great loss they had suffered by the death of Jaurès. Of the total of 111 Socialist deputies, only 14, including Haase, Rosa Luxemburg, Karl Liebknecht and Franz Mehring, were opposed, but they obeyed the strict discipline of the majority. Next day the Social-Democrats voted unanimously with the rest of the Reichstag for war credits.

The Kaiser announced, "Henceforth I know no parties, I know only Germans." In France M. Deschanel, President of the Chamber, delivering Jaurès' eulogy before a standing assembly, said, "There are no more adversaries here, there are only Frenchmen." No Socialist in either parliament disputed these statements of the primary loyalty. Léon Jouhaux, head of the CGT, declared, "In the name of the Syndicalist organizations, in the name of all the workers who have joined their regiments and those, including myself, who go tomorrow, I declare that we go to the field of battle willingly to repel the aggressor."

Before the month was out Vandervelde joined a wartime coalition Government in Belgium and Guesde a Government of "sacred union" in France. Guesde a minister! The tribal pull of patriotism could have had no stronger testimony.

In England where there was less sense of national danger than on the Continent, Keir Hardie, Ramsay MacDonald and a few Liberals spoke out against the decision to fight. Elsewhere there was no dissent, no strike, no protest, no hesitation to shoulder a rifle against fellow workers of another land. When the call came, the worker, whom Marx declared to have no Fatherland identified himself with country, not class. He turned out to be a member of the national family like anyone else. The force of his antagonism which was supposed to topple capitalism found a better target in the foreigner. The working class went to war willingly, even eagerly, like the middle class, like the upper class, like the species.

Jaurès was buried on August 4, the day the war became general. Overhead the bells he had invoked at Basle tolled for him and all the world, "I summon the living, I mourn the dead."

Afterword

THE FOUR years that followed were, as Graham Wallas wrote, "four years of the most intense and heroic effort the human race has ever made." When the effort was over, illusions and enthusiasms possible up to 1914 slowly sank beneath a sea of massive disillusionment. For the price it had paid, humanity's major gain was a painful view of its own limitations.

The proud tower built up through the great age of European civilization was an edifice of grandeur and passion, of riches and beauty and dark cellars. Its inhabitants lived, as compared to a later time, with more self-reliance, more confidence, more hope; greater magnificence, extravagance and elegance; more careless ease, more gaiety, more pleasure in each other's company and conversation, more injustice and hypocrisy, more misery and want, more sentiment including false sentiment, less sufferance of mediocrity, more dignity in work, more delight in nature, more zest. The Old World had much that has since been lost, whatever may have been gained. Looking back on it from 1915, Emile Verhaeren, the Belgian Socialist poet, dedicated his pages, "With emotion, to the man I used to be."

REFERENCES

BIBLIOGRAPHY AND NOTES

THE BIBLIOGRAPHY, arranged according to chapter, is confined (with one or two exceptions) to those sources cited in the Notes and is not intended to be either systematic or thorough. It is simply a list of what I used, often of what I stumbled on, weighted heavily toward primary personal accounts. It is noticeably light on secondary interpretative studies. When I needed their guidance I used those as nearly contemporary to their subjects as possible, not because they are better books than today's but because they are closer in spirit to the society and the time of which I was writing. Modern scholarship, nevertheless, has given me a firm underpinning in many places, notably Halévy's great and reliable encyclopedia of English affairs, Pinson's and Kohn's studies of Germany, Morison's edition of Roosevelt's letters and two superbly informative biographies of subjects who were at the heart and core of their age, Goldberg's *Jaurès* and Mendelssohn's *Churchill*. Each, while focusing on an individual, is a detailed history of his surrounding period, amply and carefully documented. In a narrower field Ginger's *Debs* and in a still more restricted one Painter's *Proust* achieve the same result.

Several remarkable investigations made at the time I could hardly have done without: Bateman's study of landed income in England, Jack London's and Jacob Riis's studies of the poor, and Quillard's study of the contributors to the Henry Subscription. Certain novelists, such as V. Sackville-West, Anatole France, and Proust, were invaluable as social historians, as were certain memoirists: Blum and Daudet on opposite sides, Lady Warwick, Sir Frederick Ponsonby, Lord Esher, Wilfrid Blunt, Baroness von Suttner, Stefan Zweig, and especially Vandervelde, who alone among the Socialists provided an intimate personal view of his milieu, of the kind in which the ruling class is so prolific. Even more valuable, perhaps, are those occasional individuals endowed both with a peculiar extra insight into their time and a gift for expressing it; who illumine what is happening around them by a sudden flash of understanding: Romain Rolland is one, Masterman another. Although less central to this book, Trotsky, as revealed in his matchless phrase about the Serbian infantry, has that same mysterious ability to perceive—almost to feel—the historical meaning of the moment and to convey it in words.

Of all the sources listed, the outstanding work is unquestionably

Reinach's (of which more is said in the Notes to Chapter 4); the most consistently informative and brilliant writer is A. G. Gardiner; the most striking fact to emerge from the assembled bibliography is the absence (except for Henry Adams, whom I find disagreeable) of first-rate memoirs by an American.

In an effort to keep the Notes to manageable length, I have given a reference *only* for those statements whose source is not obvious. When no reference is given, the reader may assume that any act or quotation by, or statement made to, a person whose memoirs or other work appears in the Bibliography, was taken from that person's account. For example, in Chapter 4, should a reader wish to know what is my source for the statement that Léon Blum and his friend Pierre Louÿs took opposite sides in the Affair and thereafter never saw each again, he should check the Bibliography under the names of the participants in the episode and, in this case, on finding a book by Blum, assume that Blum was my authority. When Mme Melba's guests throw peaches out the window or Lord Ribblesdale is quoted on the status of a lord, it may be assumed that the work of each cited in the Bibliography is the authority. Often, as when Strauss visits Speyer or makes a passing remark to Beecham, the source is the memoirist, not the principal. In general, when no reference is given, the name of the person mentioned in a particular conversation, correspondence or incident is the key to the source. While this method requires anyone interested to find the page number in the original book for himself, it has the advantage of not perpetuating mistakes, and any other method would have stretched out the Notes to a length equal to the text.

In cases where a book has served in several places it is listed under the chapter of its primary concern. *DNB* refers to the *Dictionary of National Biography*, DAB to the American ditto, *The Times* to the London newspaper, *NYT* to the *New York Times*. An asterisk denotes a source of particular value or interest.

1. The Patricians

Bibliography

ADAMS, WILLIAM SCOVELL, *Edwardian Heritage, 1901–6*, London, Muller, 1949.

ASQUITH, EARL OF OXFORD AND, *Fifty Years of British Parliament*, 2 vols., Boston, Little, Brown, 1926.

ASQUITH, MARGOT (Countess of Oxford and Asquith), *Autobiography*, Vols. I and II, London, Butterworth, 1920.

AUSTIN, ALFRED, *Autobiography*, 2 vols., London, Macmillan, 1911.

BALFOUR, LADY FRANCES, *Ne Obliviscaris*, 2 vols., London, Hodder & Stoughton, n.d.

*BATEMAN, JOHN, *The Great Landowners of Great Britain and Ireland*, 4th ed., London, Harrison, 1883.

BATTERSEA, CONSTANCE, LADY, *Reminiscences*, London, Macmillan, 1922.

BENNETT, ARNOLD, *Journals*, 3 vols., New York, Viking, 1932.

BENSON, E. F., *As We Were*, New York, Longmans, 1930.

BIRKENHEAD, FIRST EARL OF, *Contemporary Personalities*, London, Cassell, 1924.

BLUNT, WILFRID SCAWEN, *My Diaries*, 2 vols., New York, Knopf, 1921.

BUCHAN, JOHN, *Pilgrim's Way* (English title: *Memory hold-the-door*), Boston, Houghton Mifflin, 1940.

CARPENTER, RT. REV. WILLIAM BOYD, *Some Pages of My Life*, New York, Scribner's, 1911.

CECIL, LADY GWENDOLYN, *Life of Robert, Marquis of Salisbury*, 4 vols., London, Hodder & Stoughton, 1921–32.

CHAMBERLAIN, SIR AUSTEN, *Down the Years*, London, Cassell, 1935.

CHANDOS, VISCOUNT (OLIVER LYTTELTON), *Memoirs*, London, Bodley, 1962.

CHURCHILL, RANDOLPH SPENCER, *Fifteen Famous English Homes*, London, Verschoyle, 1954.

———, *Lord Derby*, London, Heinemann, 1959.

CHURCHILL, WINSTON S., *A Roving Commission: My Early Life*, New York, Scribner's, 1930.

COOPER, LADY DIANA (MANNERS), *The Rainbow Comes and Goes*, Boston, Houghton Mifflin, 1958.

CREWE, MARQUESS OF, *Lord Rosebery*, New York, Harper, 1931.

CURZON, LORD, *Subjects of the Day*, New York, Macmillan, 1915.

DUGDALE, BLANCHE E. C., *Arthur James Balfour*, 2 vols., New York, Putnam's, 1937.

ESHER, VISCOUNT REGINALD, *Journals and Letters*, ed. Maurice V. Brett, 3 vols., London, Nicholson & Watson, 1934–48.

FITZROY, SIR ALMERIC, *Memoirs*, 2 vols., London, Hutchinson, n.d.

FORD, FORD MADOX, *Return to Yesterday*, New York, Liveright, 1932.

*GARDINER, A. G. (editor of the *Daily News*), *Pillars of Society*, New York, Dodd, Mead, 1914.

*———, *Prophets, Priests and Kings*, London, Dent, 1914 (new edition, first published 1908).

*HALÉVY, ÉLIE, *A Histoy of the English People in the 19th Century*, Vol. V, 1895–1905; Vol. VI, 1905–14, New York, Barnes & Noble, 1961.

HAMLTON, LORD ERNEST, *Forty Years On*, New York, Doran, 1922.

HAMILTON, LORD FREDERICK, *The Days Before Yesterday*, New York, Doran, 1920.

HARRIS, FRANK, *Oscar Wilde, His Life and Confessions*, New York, The Author, 1916.

HOLLAND, BERNARD (former private secretary to the Duke), *Life of the Duke of Devonshire*, London, Longmans, 1911.

JEBB, LADY, *With Dearest Love to All: The Life and Letters of Lady Jebb*, ed. Mary Reed Bobbitt, London, Faber, 1960.

KENNEDY, A. L., *Salisbury, 1830–1903: Portrait of a Statesman*, London, Murray, 1953.

KIPLING, RUDYARD, *Something of Myself*, London, Macmillan, 1951.

LAMBTON, HON. GEORGE, *Men and Horses I Have Known*, London, Butterworth, 1924.

LEE, SIR SIDNEY, *King Edward VII*, 2 vols., New York, Macmillan, 1927.

LESLIE, SHANE, *The End of a Chapter*, New York, Scribner's, 1916.

LONDONDERRY, MARCHIONESS OF, *Henry Chaplin: A Memoir*, London, Macmillan, 1926.

LOWELL, ABBOTT LAWRENCE, *The Government of England*, 2 vols., New York, Macmillan, 1908.

LUCY, SIR HENRY, *Diary of a Journalist*, New York, Dutton, 1920.

———, *Memories of Eight Parliaments, 1868–1906*, London, Heinemann, 1908.

LYTTELTON, EDITH, *Alfred Lyttelton*, London, Longmans, 1917.

MACKINTOSH, ALEXANDER (a parliamentary correspondent for the provincial press), *From Gladstone to Lloyd George*, London, Hodder & Stoughton, 1921.

MAGNUS, SIR PHILIP, *Edward VII*, New York, Dutton, 1964.

———, *Gladstone*, New York, Dutton, 1954.

MARSH, EDWARD, *A Number of People*, New York, Harper, 1939.

MELBA, NELLIE, *Melodies and Memories*, New York, Doran, 1926.

MIDLETON, EARL OF (ST. JOHN BRODRICK), *Records and Reactions*, London, Murray, 1939.

MONEY, SIR LEO GEORGE CHIOZZA, M.P., *Riches and Poverty*, 10th rev. ed., London, Methuen, 1911.

MORLEY, JOHN, VISCOUNT, *Recollections*, 2 vols., New York, Macmillan, 1917.

MOUNT, CHARLES MERRILL, *John Singer Sargent*, London, Cresset, 1957.

NEVILL, RALPH, *London Clubs*, London, Chatto and Windus, 1911.

NEVINS, ALLAN, *Henry White*, New York, Harper, 1930.

NEVINSON, HENRY W., *Changes and Chances*, New York, Harcourt, Brace, 1923.

———, *More Changes and Chances*, New York, Harcourt, Brace, 1925.

NEWTON, LORD, *Lord Lansdowne*, London, Macmillan, 1929.

———, *Retrospection*, London, Murray, 1941.

NICOLSON, HAROLD, *Helen's Tower*, London, Constable, 1937.

NORDAU, MAX, *Degeneration*, tr., New York, Appleton, 1895.

PLESS, DAISY, PRINCESS OF, *Better Left Unsaid*, New York, Dutton, 1931.

PONSONBY, ARTHUR, *The Camel and the Needle's Eye*, London, Fifield, 1910.

———, *The Decline of Aristocracy*, London, Unwin, 1912.

*PONSONBY, SIR FREDERICK, (First Lord Syonsby), *Recollections of Three Reigns*, New York, Dutton, 1952.

PONSONBY, SIR HENRY, *His Life from His Letters*, ed. Arthur Ponsonby, New York, Macmillan, 1943.

RAVERAT, GWEN, *Period Piece*, New York, Norton, 1952.

RIBBLESDALE, THOMAS, LORD, *Impressions and Memories*, London, Cassell, 1927.

RONALDSHAY, EARL OF, *Life of Lord Curzon*, 3 vols., London, Benn, 1928.

RUSSELL, GEORGE W. E., *Prime Ministers and Some Others: A Book of Reminiscences*, New York, Scribner's, 1919.

*SACKVILLE-WEST, V., *The Edwardians*, London, Hogarth, 1930.

SITWELL, SIR OSBERT, *Left Hand, Right Hand*, Boston, Little, Brown, 1944.

———, *Great Morning*, London, Macmillan, 1948.

STRACHEY, JOHN ST. LOE (editor of the *Spectator*), *The Adventure of Living*, New York, Putnam's, 1922.

VICTORIA, QUEEN, *Letters*, ed. G. E. Buckle, Vol. III, 1896–1901, New York, Longmans, 1932.

*WARWICK, FRANCES, COUNTESS OF, *Life's Ebb and Flow*, New York, Morrow, 1929. (Notes refer to this book unless otherwise stated.)

———, *Discretions*, New York, Scribner's, 1931.

WHARTON, EDITH, *A Backward Glance*, New York, Appleton-Century, 1934.

WILDE, OSCAR, *Letters*, ed. Rupert Hart-Davis, New York, Harcourt, Brace, 1964.

WILLOUGHBY DE BROKE, RICHARD GREVILLE VERNEY, LORD, *The Passing Years*, Boston, Houghton Mifflin, n.d.

WILSON-FOX, ALICE, *The Earl of Halsbury, Lord High Chancellor*, London, Chapman & Hall, 1929.

*WYNDHAM, GEORGE, *Life and Letters*, ed. J. W. MacNeil and Guy Wyndham, 2 vols., London, Hutchinson, n.d.

YOUNG, KENNETH, *Arthur James Balfour*, London, Bell, 1963.

Notes

PAGE

568 "An almost embarrassing wealth": H. H. Asquith, I, 273, 275.

569 "Nerve storms": Kennedy, 353.

569 Family threw cushions: Frances Balfour, I, 311.

570 "Poor Buller": Young, 168; talking to Lord Roberts: Russell, 54–55.

570 Horse an "inconvenient adjunct": Cecil, I, 176.

570 He told Dumas *fils*: *The Times*, Aug. 24, 1903.

570 "Jump on behind": Kennedy, 241.

571 Pepys on Hatfield garden: q. R. Churchill, *Fifteen Homes*, 74.

571 "Jump, dammit . . . !": *ibid.*, 71.

571 "Quite exceptional stupidity": Cecil, I, 1.

572 Birkenhead on the Cecils: Birkenhead, 177.

572 Disraeli quoted: Mackintosh, 50–51.

572 "That black man": *ibid.*

572 Morley, "blazing indiscretion": q. H. H. Asquith, II, 277.

572 " 'Every sentence,' said a fellow member": Ribblesdale, 173.

572 "I thought he was dead": *National Review*, "Lord Salisbury: His Wit and Humor," Nov., 1931, 659–68.

573 "When will all this be over?": Carpenter, 237.

573 Colleagues complained: Cecil, III, 177.

573 "Just a little more off here": Ribblesdale, 174.

573 His charm "no small asset": Hicks-Beach, q. Cecil, III, 178.

573 "I think I have done them all": *National Review*, *op. cit.*, 665.

574 Gladstone quoted: Mackintosh, 50–51.

574 "Not excluding the House of Commons": Lucy, *Eight Parliaments*, 114.

575 Queen Victoria quoted: Carpenter, 236.

575 "Bad on his legs": F. Ponsonby, 67.

575 "Oh, I daresay": Benson, 164.

575 "Splitting it into a bundle": *Quarterly Review*, Oct., 1883, 575.

575 Articles in *Quarterly Review*: quotations in this and the following two paragraphs are from Cecil, I, 149, 157–60, 196.

577 Speech against Disraeli's policy: July 5, 1867, *Hansard*, 3rd Series, Vol. 188, 1097 ff.

577 "Grim acidity": Gardiner, *Prophets*, 150.

577 "Rank without power": Cecil, II, 5.

577 Curzon quoted: Ronaldshay, I, 282.

577 "Secure and comfortable": Buchan, 75.

578 Duke of Devonshire on Harcourt's Budget: *Annual Register*, 1894, 121.

578 "Germ planted": *The Times*, July 17, 1895, leader.

578 "Dominant influences": q. Magnus, *Gladstone*, 433.

579 Dufferin taught himself Persian: Nicolson, 246.

PAGE

580 "Those damned dots": Leslie, 30–31.
581 Stanley "an Upper Class Servant": T. P. O'Connor, q. R. Churchill, *Derby*, 45.
581 Eton's "scugs": Willoughby de Broke, 133.
581 Cecil Balfour forged a check: Young, 11.
581 Sargent asked Ribblesdale to sit: Mount, 418.
582 "*Ce grand diable*": Ribblesdale, xvii.
582 "A race of gods and goddesses": Clermont-Tonnerre (*see* Chap. 4), I, 175.
583 "Divinely tall": E. Hamilton, 7.
583 Gentlemen sighed and told each other: Sackville-West, 122.
584 "Bohemia in Tiaras": Benson, 157.
585 Prince of Wales to Churchill: W. Churchill, 155.
586 "I shall call you the 'Souls': q. Nevins, 81.
586 Two sets of eyebrows: Melba, 226.
586 "I don't like poets": Wyndham, I, 67.
587 Harry Cust's "fatal self-indulgence": Margot Asquith, q. Nevins, 81.
587 Lord Morley's detective: Fitzroy, II, 463.
587 "Brilliant and powerful body": W. Churchill, 89.
587 "Knew each other intimately": Willoughby de Broke, 180.
588 Jowett's choice of undergraduates: Newton, *Lansdowne*, 6.
588 "No end of good dinners": Willoughby de Broke, 30.
589 "Effortless superiority": Leslie, 43.
589 "Poor fellow, poor fellow": Marsh, 183.
589 "Born booted and spurred": Gardiner, *Prophets*, 214.
590 "When I looked at life from the saddle": Warwick, *Discretions*, 78.
590 Chauncey Depew's telegram: Robert Rhodes James, *Rosebery*, London, 1963, 355.
590 "Even policemen were waving their helmets": Lee, II, 421.
591 Londesborough's "gloss, speed and style": Sitwell, *Left Hand*, 154.
591 "Because the carriage had to go home": Raverat, 178.
591 Blunt's sonnet: "On St. Valentine's Day."
591 Duke of Rutland's chaplain: Cooper, 20.
591 Squire Chaplin in the hunting field: Lambton, 133; Londonderry, 227, 240.
593 "Sure of themselves": Sitwell, *Great Morning*, 10, 121–22.
593 Colonel Brabazon described: W. Churchill, 67; testimony quoted: Esher, I, 362.
595 Figures on income and acreage: Bateman, *passim*.
595 The "poverty line": set by B. S. Rowntree at 21*s*. 8*d*. for a family of five. In *Poverty, A Study of Town Life*, 1901.
596 "*Eau de Nil* satin": Warwick, 230.
597 "Then bwing me another": W. Churchill, 68.
598 "Squalid throng of homeless outcasts": A. Ponsonby, *Camel*, 12.

PAGE

599 Kipling on venting chauvinism: *American Notes* (*see* Chap. 3), 45.

599 "Knew his own mind and put down his foot": Whyte (*see* Chap. 5), II, 115.

599 "A series of microscopic advantages": q. *Monthly Review*, Oct., 1903, "Lord Salisbury," 8.

600 Morley Roberts: q. Peck (*see* Chap. 3), 428.

602 "All his bad qualities": Hyndman (*see* Chap. 7), 349.

602 "I was a problem": to More Adey, Nov. 27, 1897, *Letters*, 685.

602 Lord Arthur Somerset: Magnus, *Edward VII*, 214–15.

603 Swinburne "absolutely impossible": H. Ponsonby, 274.

604 "Join it": Hyndman (*see* Chap. 7), 349.

604 "I dare not alter these things": Marsh, 2.

604 Austin on Germans and Alfred the Great: q. Adams, 76, n. 3.

605 Salisbury on Austin's poem: Victoria, *Letters*, 24.

605 An American observer quoted: Lowell, II, 507.

605 Austin's Jubilee wish: Blunt, I, 280.

606 Lord Newton on the Lords: *Retrospection*, 101.

606 Rosebery complained: Crewe, 462.

606 Halsbury "invariably objected": Newton, *Lansdowne*, 361; "jolly cynicism": Gardiner, *Prophets*, 197; Carlton Club: Wilson-Fox, 122; Lord Coleridge: *ibid.*, 124.

607 "Rule by a sort of instinct": q. Halévy, V, 23, n. 2.

608 "Greatest gentleman of his day": Newton, *Lansdowne*, 506.

608 "A new sense of duty": Holland, II, 146. All quotations, anecdotes and other material about the Duke are from this source unless otherwise specified.

609 "Take things very easy": H. Ponsonby, 265.

609 "This is damned dull": Mackintosh, 113.

609 Duchess "one of the handsomest women": F. Hamilton, 201.

610 "No face was more suited": F. Ponsonby, 52.

611 "Certain hereditary governmental instincts" and "a debt to the State": Esher, I, 126.

612 "He was always losing them": H. Ponsonby, 265 n.

613 Duke at coronation rehearsal: Lucy, *Diary*, 193.

613 "Do you feel nervous, Winston?": R. Churchill, *Fifteen Homes*, 105.

614 "The best of company": F. Ponsonby, 294.

615 *Spectator* and subsequent quotations in this paragraph: Strachey, 406 and 398; Holland, II, 211, n. 1; *The Times*, Mar. 25, 1908.

616 "Go and tell him he is a pig": Mackintosh, 91.

616 "A point of honor to stand for their county": Sir George Otto Trevelyan, q. A. Ponsonby, *Decline*, 101.

616 Long and Chaplin described: Gardiner, *Pillars*, 217; *Prophets*, 212.

616 "Calm, ineradicable conviction": Gardiner, *Prophets*, 213.

617 "How did I do, Arthur?": Londonderry, 171.

617 "Sit on his shoulder blades": q. Young, 100.

617 "The finest brain": q. Chamberlain, 206.
617 William James: letter of Apr. 26, 1895, *The Letters of William James*, ed. H. James, Boston, 1920.
618 "Oh dear, what a gulf": Battersea, Diary for Sept. 6, 1895.
618 "Lovely bend of the head": Margot Asquith, I, 166.
618 "No, that is not so": Margot Asquith, I, 162.
619 Darwin on Frank Balfour: Young, 8.
619 Cambridge friends: Esher, I, 182; society friends: Russell, 63.
620 Balfour on Judaism: Dugdale, I, 324.
620 Harry Cust's dinner: Bennett, I, 287.
621 Daisy White congratulated: Nevins, 81.
621 "Quite a good fellow": Frances Balfour, II, 367; "A sympathetic outlook": *ibid.*, II. 93.
622 "A natural spring of youth": *ibid.*; "a freshness, serenity": Fitzroy, I, 28.
622 Lord Randolph: *Life of Lord Randolph Churchill*, by Winston Churchill, II, 459–60.
623 Balfour on Socialism: q. Halévy, V, 231.
623 "What exactly *is* a 'Trade Union'?": Lucy Masterman (*see* Chap. 7), 61.
623 "My uncle is a Tory": Margot Asquith, I, 154.
623 Churchill used the word "wicked": Blunt, II, 278.
624 "Relentless as Cromwell": Young, 105.
624 Morley, "took his foes by surprise"; q. Russell, 66.
624 "The most courageous man alive": Blunt, II, 278.
624 Debated with "dauntless ingenuity": Morley, I, 225–27.
624 "If he had a little more brains": q. Buchan, 156.
625 "A bullet on a bubble": Andrew White (*see* Chap. 5), II, 430.
625 "I never lose my temper": q. Morley, I, 227.
625 "This damned Scotch croquet": Lyttelton, 204.
626 Reply to Lady Rayleigh: Fitzroy, II, 491; charmed Frau Wagner: Esher, I, 312.
626 "Supreme energy of Arthur": *ibid.*, 340.
626 "He never reads the papers": Whyte (*see* Chap. 5), II, 120.
626 Prince felt Balfour condescended: Halévy, VI, 231.
626 The Queen admired him: F. Ponsonby, 69.
627 Queen "much struck": Journal, Sept. 11, 1896, Victoria, 74.
627 Proust's housekeeper: q. Havelock Ellis (*see* Chap. 4), 377.
628 Queen Victoria, "No one ever": q. Hector Bolitho, *Reign of Queen Victoria*, 366.
628 Kipling, "a certain optimism": Kipling, 147.
628 Sir Edward Clarke, "The greatest poem": q. Amy Cruse, *After the Victorians*, London, 1938, 123.
628 "Joe's War": Kennedy, 315.
628 Salisbury on Chamberlain: Dugdale, I, 67.
629 Balfour to Lady Elcho: Young, 129.
630 Entertaining three duchesses: Frances Balfour, II, 211.

PAGE
630 "The difference between Joe and Me": q. Julian Amery, *Life of Joseph Chamberlain*, IV, 464.
630 "Let us defy someone": q. Adams, 78.
631 Duke of Argyll: Frances Balfour, II, 318.
631 Salisbury to German Ambassador: Hatzfeld to Foreign Office, July 31, 1900, *Grosse Politik* (*see* Chap. 5), XVI, 76.
632 Lady Salisbury: Frances Balfour, II, 290.
632 *Le Temps*, "What closes today?": q. *The Times*, July 15, 1902.
632 "Go up at once, Sir James": Blunt, I, 366.

2. The Idea and the Deed

Bibliography

ARCHER, WILLIAM, *The Life, Trial and Death of Francisco Ferrer*, New York, Moffat, Yard, 1911.

BARNARD, HARRY, *Eagle Forgotten: The Life of John Peter Altgeld*, Indianapolis, Bobbs-Merrill, 1938.

BERKMAN, ALEXANDER, *Prison Memoirs of an Anarchist*, New York, Mother Earth Publishing Co., 1912.

BRENAN, GERALD, *The Spanish Labyrinth*, Cambridge, University Press, 1950.

CHANNING, WALTER, "The Mental Status of Czolgosz, the Assassin of President McKinley," *American Journal of Insanity*, October, 1902, 233–78.

CHARQUES, RICHARD D., *The Twilight of Imperial Russia*, London, Phoenix, 1958.

CORTI, COUNT EGON, *Elizabeth, Empress of Austria*, New Haven, Yale Univ. Press, 1936.

**Crapouillot, Numéro Spécial, l'Anarchie*, Paris, January, 1938.

CREUX, V. C., *Canovas del Castillo, sa carrière, ses œuvres, sa fin*, Paris, Leve, 1897.

DAVID, HENRY, *History of the Haymarket Affair*, New York, Farrar & Rinehart, 1936.

*ELTZBACHER, PAUL, *Anarchism*, tr. S. T. Byington, New York, Benjamin Tucker, 1908.

GOLDMAN, EMMA, *Living My Life*, Vol. I, New York, Knopf, 1931.

HAMSUN, KNUT, *Hunger*, New York, Knopf, 1921.

HARVEY, GEORGE, *Henry Clay Frick*, New York, Scribner's, 1928.

HUNTER, ROBERT, *Poverty*, New York, Macmillan, 1904.

ISHILL, JOSEPH, *Peter Kropotkin*, New Jersey, Free Spirit Press, 1923.

———, ed., *Elisée and Elie Reclus, in Memoriam*, New Jersey, Oriole Press, 1927.

KERENSKY, ALEXANDER, *The Crucifixion of Liberty*, New York, John Day, 1934.

KROPOTKIN, PRINCE PETER, *The Conquest of Bread*, New York, Putnam's, 1907.

———, *Mutual Aid*, London, Heinemann, 1902.

*———, *Paroles d'un révolté*, Paris, Flammarion, 1885.

———, "Anarchism," in *Encyclopedia Britannica*, 11th ed.

*LONDON, JACK, *People of the Abyss*, New York, Macmillan, 1903.

*MAITRON, JEAN, *Histoire du mouvement anarchiste en France, 1880–1914*, Paris, Société Universitaire, 1951.

MALATESTA, ENRICO, *A Talk Between Two Workers*, tr., 8th ed., London, Freedom Press, n.d.

MALATO, CHARLES, "Some Anarchist Portraits," *Fortnightly Review*, September, 1894.

MILIUKOV, PAUL, SEIGNOBOS, CHARLES, and EISENMANN, L., *Histoire de Russie*, Vol. III, Leroux, n.p., n.d.

MIRSKY, D. S., *Russia: A Social History*, London, Cresset, 1931.

NEVINSON, HENRY W., *The Dawn in Russia: Scenes in the Russian Revolution*, New York, Harper, 1906.

NICOLAEVSKY, BORIS, *Azev, the Spy*, tr. George Reavey, New York, Doubleday, Doran, 1934.

*NOMAD, MAX, *Apostles of Revolution*, Boston, Little, Brown, 1939.

———, *Rebels and Renegades*, New York, Macmillan, 1932.

PILAR, PRINCESS OF BAVARIA, and CHAPMAN-HUSTON, MAJOR D., *Alfonso XIII: A Study of Monarchy*, New York, Dutton, 1932.

REGIS, DR. EMMANUEL, *Les Régicides dans l'histoire et dans le présent*, Paris, Masson, 1890.

*RIIS, JACOB A., *How the Other Half Lives*, New York, Scribner's, 1890.

*SAVINKOV, BORIS V., *Memoirs of a Terrorist*, tr. Joseph Shaplen, New York, Boni, 1931.

SOREL, GEORGES, *Réflexions sur la violence*, Paris, Pages Libres, 1908.

VIZETELLY, ERNEST ALFRED, *The Anarchists*, London, John Lane, 1911.

WOODCOCK, GEORGE, and AVAKUMOVIC, IVAN, *The Anarchist Prince: A Biographical Study of Prince Kropotkin*, London, Boardman, 1950.

Three useful books have appeared since this chapter was written: *Anarchism*, by George Woodcock, *The Anarchists*, by James Joll, and *The Anarchists*, an anthology, edited by Irving L. Horowitz.

Notes

I have not thought it necessary, in this chapter, to give separate references for each incident and quotation since they group themselves, according to subject, into easily identifiable sets of sources, as follows:

For the conditions of the poor, Riis, London, Hunter and Chiozza Money (*see* Chap. 1) were my chief contemporary sources. For the ideas and theories of Anarchists of all countries and for excerpts from their writings, Eltzbacher was particularly useful. For French Anarchism all quotations, unless otherwise stated, are from Maitron or Malato (himself one of the French Anarchists of the time), supplemented by *Crapouillot* and Vizetelly. For Emma Goldman and Alexander Berkman their own memoirs are the sources for all quotations. For Johann Most the chapter on him in Nomad's *Apostles* was the chief source. In the sections on Spanish Anarchists the quotations are taken chiefly from contemporary reports in the American press, as noted. For Czolgosz the essential primary source is Channing. For the Russians, Savinkov, himself a member of the Terror Brigade, and Nicolaevsky are primary (and indeed so fascinating that my first version of the Russian incidents, having grown altogether out of proportion, had to be condensed to a fifth of its original length).

Facts and quotations not covered by the foregoing, and which seem to require a specific reference, are separately noted.

PAGE

635 "A daydream of desperate romantics": Nomad, *Rebels*, 13.

637 Proudhon, "Whoever lays his hand on me": from his *Confessions of a Revolutionary*. "To be governed is to be . . .": from his *Idée générale de la révolution au vingtième siècle*, Epilogue.

637 "Abstract idea of right": Bakunin said this was Proudhon's point of departure, q. Nomad, *Apostles*, 15.

638 "Their power will be irresistible": q. Eltzbacher, 138.

638 "We reckoned without the masses": q. Nomad, *Apostles*, 205.

639 "The gentry had murdered the Czar" and "Broken and demoralized": Kerensky, 44–45.

640 Henry James, "sinister anarchic underworld": from his Preface to *Princess Casamassima*, his novel with Anarchist characters first published in 1886. Johann Most is said to have inspired the conception of the unseen Anarchist leader Hoffendahl in the novel. Another literary exercise in the theme was Joseph Conrad's rather shallow story "An Anarchist," published in *Harper's Weekly* for Aug., 1906, of which the chief point seems to be that Anarchists are people of "warm hearts and weak heads." It was followed in 1907 by his novel *The Secret Agent*, dealing with plot and conspiracy. Neither James nor Conrad was concerned with the underlying social origins or social philosophy of Anarchism.

640 August Spies quoted: David, 332–39.

641 "I want the Day av Judgment!": a story told by Robert Blatchford, q. London, 298.

641 "What is Property?": the title of his second treatise, *Qu'est ce que la propriété?* 1840.

642 "All mankind's tormentors": from his *Dieu et l'Etat*, 2nd ed., 1892, 11.

642 Woman who made match boxes and young man in the river: Riis, 47 and London, 205–07.

PAGE

642 "Eight hours of work": q. Maitron, 186.

643 Nevinson on Kropotkin: *Changes and Chances* (*see* Chap. 1), 125.

644 Shaw on Kropotkin: q. Woodcock, 225.

644 "Galloping decay" of states: *Paroles*, 8–10..

644 "Inertia of those who have a vested interest": *Paroles*, 275–76.

645 Brousse, "The Idea is on the march": q. *Crapouillot*, 15.

645 "By dagger, gun and dynamite": q. *ibid.*, 15.

645 "Men of courage . . . the deed of mutiny": *Paroles*, 285.

645 "A single deed . . .": *ibid.*, 285.

645 *La Révolte* of March, 1891; q. Maitron, 240.

646 Argument with Ben Tillett and Tom Mann: Ford (*see* Chap. 1), 110.

646 Plans for Anarchist society: Kropotkin's *Revolutionary Studies, Conquest of Bread, l'Anarchie dans l'évolution social.* Malatesta's *Talk Between Two Workers.*

646 Shaw: Tract No. 45, read to the Society Oct. 16, 1891, published July, 1893.

647 Royal Geographic Society's dinner: Woodcock, 227.

648 Elisée Reclus, "irresistible magnetism": Vandervelde (*see* Chap. 8), 37.

649 Jean Grave, "simple, silent, indefatigable": Malato, 316.

649 Malatesta's adventures: Nomad, *Rebels*, 1–47.

650 "Just as we saw him last": Ishill, *Kropotkin*, 40.

650 "All are awaiting the birth": *ibid.*, 9.

651 "A shining moral grandeur": Victor Serge in *Crapouillot*, 5.

651 "Breathe revolt and hatred": Malato, 317.

654 Kropotkin and Malatesta repudiate Ravachol: in *La Révolte*, Nos. 17 and 18, Jan., 1892, and *l'En Dehors*, Aug. 28, 1892, q. Maitron, 204, 221.

654 "Miniature Borgias": Nomad, *Rebels*, 26.

658 The shooting of Frick: in addition to Berkman, Harvey's *Frick* and *Harper's Weekly*, Aug. 6, 1892.

659 Altgeld and the pardon: Barnard, 217, 246; *NYT*, June 28, 1893.

660 "Madrid is sad . . .": Pilar, 50.

661 Pallas' attempt on Martínez de Camos: Creux, 295–96; *Crapouillot*; *NYT*, Sept. 25, 30, 1893.

662 Barcelona Opera House bombing: *NYT*, Nov. 9, Dec. 20, 1893, Jan. 3, 1894.

662 Montjuich tortures: Brenan, 168, n. 1.

663 Asquith-Balfour exchange on the Anarchists: *Spectator*, Nov. 18, 1893, 706, Dec. 2, 791; *NYT*, Nov. 11, 1893.

664 Paris "absolutely paralyzed": Ford (*see* Chap. 1), 107.

665 Laurent Tailhade, "a blessed time": Nomad, *Apostles*, 11.

665 Octave Mirbeau: Daudet (*see* Chap. 4), 70.

665 "That there need be no misery": Suttner (*see* Chap. 5), 1, 313.

666 President caricatured in soiled pajamas: in *Père Peinard*, July 4, 1897.

666 Sebastian Faure's "harmonious voice": Malato, 316.

PAGE

667 "*Qu'importe les victimes . . .*": q. Maitron, 217. (This is frequently quoted as *Qu'importe les vagues humanités pourvu que le geste soit beau?* but this seems to have a ring of the morning after.)

668 Duchesse d'Uzès: Maitron, 215.

671 Clemenceau on Henry's execution: in *La Justice*, May 23, 1894, q. Maitron, 226.

672 Trial of the Thirty, Felix Fénéon: Roman (*see* Chap. 4), 59, 95.

674 "Every revolution ends . . .": q. Nomad, *Apostles*, 6.

675 Corpus Christi bomb: *NYT*, June 9, Nov. 25, Dec. 2, 22, 1896.

675 Canovas: Pilar, 40; Millis (*see* Chap. 3), 80–81; *Nation*, Aug. 12, 1897; *Review of Reviews*, Nov., 1897.

676 Letter from prisoner of Montjuich: q. *Crapouillot.*

677 Angiolillo: Creux, 301–15; Nomad, *Rebels*, 23.

678 Empress Elizabeth and Luigi Lucheni: Corti, 456–93.

681 Plot to assassinate the Kaiser: *Spectator*, Oct. 22, 1898; *NYT*, Oct. 15/16, 1898.

681 Bakunin, Germans not fit for Anarchism: Nomad, *Apostles*, 169, n. 5.

682 International Conference of Police in Rome: Maitron; Vizetelly, 238.

683 King Humbert and Gaetano Bresci: *Outlook*, Aug. 10, 1900; *Harper's Weekly*, Aug. 4, 1900; *NYT*, Aug. 3, 1900; *Review of Reviews*, Sept., 1900, 316–22.

684 Czolgosz: Channing; Nomad, *Apostles*, 298–99; *NYT*, Sept. 9, 1901.

687 *Harper's* and *Century* quoted: *Harper's Weekly*, Dec. 23, 1893, Aug. 28, 1897. "The Assassination of Presidents," by J. M. Buckley, in *Century*, Nov., 1901.

687 Roosevelt on Anarchists: *NYT*, Dec. 5, 1901.

688 *Blackwood's*: July, 1906, 128, apropos of attempt on King Alfonso.

688 Lyman Abbott: *Outlook*, Feb. 22, 1902.

689 Assassination of Canalejas: *Literary Digest*, Nov. 23, 1912; *Living Age*, Dec. 12, 1912.

689 "Outraged beyond endurance": in his Preface to *Major Barbara*, dated June, 1906, apropos of the attempt on King Alfonso.

690 Russian Socialist-Revolutionaries: in addition to Savinkov and Nicolaevsky, general background from Charques, Miliukov and Kerensky.

691 Plehve, "We must drown the revolution": Miliukov, 1056.

692 Grand Duke Sergei "conspicuous for his cruelty": Nevinson.

692 "A formless mass 8 or 10 inches high": Savinkov, 106–7.

692 Czar and brother-in-law on the sofa: Bülow (*see* Chap. 5), II, 178.

3. End of a Dream

Bibliography

There are two full-length biographies of Reed, one by Samuel McCall, who served with him in Congress and was later Governor of Massachusetts, and one by Professor Robinson, both listed below. Among friends, reporters, Congressional colleagues and other contemporaries who wrote about him are the following:

BROWMAN, W. H., "Thomas Brackett Reed," *New England Magazine*, April, 1890.

DAY, HOLMAN F., "Tom Reed Among His Neighbors," *Saturday Evening Post*, January 3, 1903.

DE CASSERES, BENJAMIN, "Tom Reed," *American Mercury*, February, 1930.

FULLER, HERBERT B., *Speakers of the House*, Boston, Little, Brown, 1909.

HINDS, ASHER C., "The Speaker of the House of Representatives," *American Political Science Review*, May, 1909.

KNIGHT, ENOCH, "Thomas Brackett Reed: An Appreciation," *New England Magazine*, April, 1904.

LEUPP, FRANCIS E., "Personal Recollections of Thomas Brackett Reed," *Outlook*, September 3, 1910.

*LODGE, HENRY CABOT, "Thomas Brackett Reed," reprinted in *The Democracy of the Constitution and Other Essays*, New York, Scribner's, 1915.

*MCCALL, SAMUEL, *The Life of Thomas Brackett Reed*, Boston, Houghton Mifflin, 1914.

MCFARLAND, HENRY, "Thomas Brackett Reed," *American Review of Reviews*, January, 1903.

PORTER, ROBERT P., "Thomas Brackett Reed of Maine," *McClure's*, October, 1893.

*ROBINSON, WILLIAM A., *Thomas B. Reed, Parliamentarian*, New York, Dodd, Mead, 1930.

ROOSEVELT, THEODORE, "Thomas Brackett Reed and the 51st Congress," *Forum*, December, 1895.

Other Sources

ADAMS, HENRY, *The Education of Henry Adams*, Boston, Houghton Mifflin, 1918.

———, *Letters*, ed. Worthington Chauncey Ford, 2 vols., Boston, Houghton Mifflin, 1930–38.

ALEXANDER, DE ALVA STANWOOD, *History and Procedure of the House of Representatives*, Boston, Houghton Mifflin, 1916.

BARRY, DAVID S., (Washington Correspondent of New York *Sun* and Providence *Journal*), *40 Years in Washington*, Boston, Little, Brown, 1924.

BISHOP, JOSEPH BUCKLIN, *Theodore Roosevelt and His Times*, 2 vols., New York, Scribner's, 1920.

BOWERS, CLAUDE G., *Beveridge and the Progressive Era*, Boston, Houghton Mifflin, 1932.

BRYCE, JAMES, *The American Commonwealth*, 3 vols., London, Macmillan, 1888.

*CLARK, CHAMP, *My Quarter Century of American Politics*, 2 vols., New York, Harper, 1920.

CROLY, HERBERT, *Marcus Alonzo Hanna*, New York, Macmillan, 1912.

CULLOM, SENATOR SHELLY M., *Fifty Years of Public Service*, Chicago, McClurg, 1911.

DUNN, ARTHUR WALLACE, *From Harrison to Harding*, 2 vols., New York, Putnam's, 1922.

DUNNE, FINLEY PETER, *Mr. Dooley in Peace and War*, Boston, Small, Maynard, 1898.

FOULKE, WILLIAM DUDLEY, *A Hoosier Autobiography*, Oxford Univ. Press, 1922.

FUESS, CLAUDE MOORE, *Carl Schurz, Reformer, 1829–1906*, New York, Dodd, Mead, 1932.

GARRATY, JOHN A., *Henry Cabot Lodge: A Biography*, New York, Knopf, 1953.

GODKIN, EDWIN LAWRENCE, *Life and Letters*, ed. Rollo Ogden, 2 vols., New York, Macmilllan, 1907.

GOMPERS, SAMUEL, *70 Years of Life and Labour*, 2 vols., London, Hurst & Blackett, 1925.

GRIFFIN, SOLOMON B., *People and Politics Observed by a Massachusetts Editor*, Boston, Little, Brown, 1923.

HARRINGTON, FREDERICK, "The Anti-Imperialist Movement in the United States," *Miss. Valley Hist. Rev.*, September, 1935.

HOAR, SENATOR GEORGE FRISBIE, *Autobiography of 70 Years*, 2 vols., New York, Scribner's, 1905.

HOWE, M. A. DEWOLFE, *Moorfield Storey: Portrait of an Independent*, Boston, Houghton Mifflin, 1932.

JAMES, HENRY, *Charles William Eliot*, 2 vols., Boston, Houghton Mifflin, 1930.

KIPLING, RUDYARD, *American Notes*, New York, Munro's, 1896.

KOHLSAAT, H. H., *From McKinley to Harding: Personal Recollections of Our Presidents*, New York, Scribner's, 1923.

LANZAR, MARIA C., "The Anti-Imperialist League," *Philippine Social Science Revue*, August and November, 1930.

LODGE, HENRY CABOT, ed., *Selections from the Correspondence of Theodore Roosevelt and H. C. Lodge*, 2 vols., New York, Scribner's, 1925.

LONG, JOHN D., *The New American Navy*, 2 vols., New York, Outlook, 1903.

LYON, PETER, *Success Story: The Life and Times of S. S. McClure*, New York, Scribner's, 1963.

MCELROY, ROBERT, *Grover Cleveland*, 2 vols., New York, Harper, 1925.

MAHAN, CAPTAIN ALFRED THAYER, *The Influence of Sea Power on History*, New York, Sagamore Press, 1957.

———, *From Sail to Steam* (autobiography), New York, Harper, 1907.

———, *The Interest of America in Sea Power*, Boston, Little, Brown, 1897. (Collected articles from *Atlantic Monthly*, *Harper's Monthly*, *Forum* and *North American Review*, 1890–97.)

MILLIS, WALTER, *The Martial Spirit*, Boston, Houghton Mifflin, 1931.

MITCHELL, EDWARD P., *Memoirs of an Editor*, New York, Scribner's, 1924.

NORTON, CHARLES ELIOT, *Letters*, ed. Sara Norton and M. A. DeWolfe Howe, 2 vols., Boston, Houghton Mifflin, 1913.

PECK, HARRY THURSTON, *Twenty Years of the Republic*, New York, Dodd, Mead, 1906.

PERRY, R. B., *Thought and Character of William James*, Harvard Univ. Press, 1948.

PETTIGREW, SENATOR RICHARD F., *Imperial Washington, 1870–1920*, Chicago, Kerr, 1922.

PLATT, THOMAS COLLIER, *Autobiography*, New York, Dodge, 1910.

POWERS, SAMUEL LELAND, *Portraits of Half a Century*, Boston, Little, Brown, 1925.

PRINGLE, HENRY F., *Theodore Roosevelt*, New York, Harcourt, 1931.

PULESTON, CAPTAIN WILLIAM D., *Mahan*, Yale Univ. Press, 1939.

ROOSEVELT, THEODORE, *An Autobiography*, New York, Scribner's, 1920.

*———, *The Letters*, ed. Elting E. Morison, Vols. I and II, Harvard Univ. Press, 1951.

SCHURZ, CARL, *Reminiscences*, Vol. III (continued by Frederic Bancroft), New York, McClure, 1908.

SPRING-RICE, CECIL, *The Letters and Frendships*, ed. Stephen Gwynn, 2 vols., Boston, Houghton Mifflin, 1929.

STEALEY, ORLANDO O., *Twenty Years in the Press Gallery*, New York (author), 1906.

STOREY, MOORFIELD, *The Conquest of the Philippines by the United States*, New York, Putman's, 1926.

SULLIVAN, MARK, *Our Times*, Vols. I and II, New York, Scribner's, 1926.

TAYLOR, CHARLES CARLISLE, *The Life of Admiral Mahan*, New York, Doran, 1920.

VANDERBILT, KERMIT, *Charles Eliot Norton*, Harvard Univ. Press, 1959.

VILLARD, OSWALD GARRISON, *Fighting Years*, New York, Harcourt, 1939.

WOLFF, LEON, *Little Brown Brother*, New York, Doubleday, 1961.

Notes

All biographical facts, anecdotes and quotations by or about Reed are from Lodge, McCall or Robinson except where otherwise stated. All quotations from Roosevelt are from the Morison edition of his *Letters*, for which I have given the dates and dispensed with volume and page references.

PAGE

697 "Out of whose collar": De Casseres. The following quotations in this paragraph, in order, are from Clark, I, 287; Leupp; McCall, 248; Dunn, I, 165; Foulke, 110; Porter. "The ablest running debater" was said by Rep. John Sharp Williams, Democratic Leader of the House;

PAGE

"the greatest parliamentary leader" by Lodge; "far and away the most brilliant" by Clark, II, 10.

698 Henry Adams on his brother John: Sept. 1, 1894, *Letters*, II, 55.

699 Bryce, "apathy . . .": III, 326–28.

700 Lewis Morris, "Damn the consequences": "Biographical Sketches of the Four Signers from New York," *Americana*, Aug., 1914, 627.

701 "A human frigate" and "How narrow": Day.

701 "Calculated . . . to obstruct legislation": Rep. Frye of Maine.

702 "All the wisdom": Clark, I, 286.

703 "Voting for him on the sly": Porter.

704 Palmerston's popularity: Peck, 276.

704 Choate anecdote: Barry, 142.

704 On Balzac: Porter.

704 "We asked the Tom Reeds": Lodge, *Corres.*, I, 77, 120.

704 "Theodore, if there is one thing more than another": q. George Stimpson, *A Book About American Politics*, New York, 1952, 342.

705 "Theodore will never be President": Leupp.

705 "Ambitious as Lucifer": Cullom, 243.

706 "It becomes a tyranny": Dunn, I, 35.

707 "The largest human face": Clark, I, 277–78.

707 "The Chair directs": All remarks by the Speaker and Representatives in the account of the Quorum fight are from the *Congressional Record*, 51st Congress, First Session.

707 "Pandemonium broke loose": Dunn, I, 27. Reporters and other eye witnesses quoted on the Quorum fight are Dunn, I, 24–32; Peck, 200–02; Fuller, 219–21. The New York *Times* gave the story four columns on page 1 on both Jan. 30 and 31.

710 Reed's Rules: Fuller, 228.

711 Roosevelt on Reed's reform; *Forum*, Dec., 1895.

711 "Biting a green persimmon": Mount (*see* Chap. 1), 192. Sargent had difficulty with the portrait and destroyed his first version. "His exterior somehow does not correspond with his spirit. What is a painter to do? . . . I could have made a better picture with a less remarkable man. He has been delightful." Reed claimed that he liked it although "I am willing to admit that the picture is not so good-looking as the original." The portrait now hangs in the Speaker's Lobby in the Capitol. As it seems to the author to convey little of Reed's personality, it is not reproduced here.

711 "They might do worse": Brownson.

711 "White House Iceberg": Platt, 215.

711 "The House has more sense": Alexander, 27.

712 "Look outward": "The United States Looking Outward," Dec., 1890.

712 "A voice . . . of our external interests": Puleston, 133. All subsequent biographical facts, anecdotes and quotations by or about Mahan are from Puleston unless otherwise stated.

PAGE

713 "Don't tell Grover": Clark, I, 281–82.

713 Roosevelt read it "straight through": May 12, 1890, *Letters*, I, 221.

714 Origin of "Sea Power": Mahan, *From Sail to Steam*, 276–77.

715 Kaiser on Mahan: q. Taylor, 131.

715 Secretary White: Fuller, 211.

716 Mahan on the Jews: *From Sail to Steam.*

718 Lodge in "desperate earnest": q. Garraty, 52.

719 Comments of Senators Morgan, Frye and Cullom: Millis, 29.

719 Union League Club, *NYT*, Dec. 18, 1895.

720 "Admirals? Never!": q. Taylor, 12.

721 "A towering influence": q. Godkin, I, 221.

721 Lowell on the *Nation*: Godkin, I, 251; Bryce on the *Evening Post*: *ibid.*, 232; Governor Hill: Villard, 123.

721 Godkin on the United States in 1895: *Life and Letters*, II, 187, 202.

722 William James on "fighting spirit": to Frederic Myers, Jan. 1, 1896, Perry, 244.

722 Norton, "shout of brutal applause": *NYT*, Dec. 30, 1895.

722 "Supremely urbane": Daniel Gregory Mason, "At Home in the Nineties," *New England Quarterly Review*, Mar., 1936, 64.

723 Students on Norton: William D. Orcutt, *Celebrities on Parade*, 41; Josephine Preston Peabody, *Diary and Letters*, 73.

723 Norton to Godkin and to English friend: q. Vanderbilt, 211; to Leslie Stephen, Jan. 8, 1896, *Letters*, II, 236.

724 Henry Adams: "dead water of the *fin de siècle*" is from *The Education*, 331. Other quotations in this paragraph are from the *Letters*, Vol. II, in order, as follows: Sept. 9, 1894, 55; Aug. 3, 1896, 114; Apr. 1, 1896, 103; Apr. 25, 1895, 68; July 31, 1896, 111; Feb. 17, 1896, 99; Sept. 25, 1895, 88.

724 Norton, "How interesting our times": to S. G. Ward, Apr. 26, 1896, *Letters*, II, 244.

725 "The Czar commands you": Fuller, 238.

725 "Tranquil greatness": Powers.

725 Reading Richard Burton: Stealey, 413.

726 "A policy no Republican": Knight.

726 Roosevelt on Reed campaign: Oct. 18, 1895; Dec. 27, 1895; Jan. 26, 1896.

726 Reed's campaign: Robinson, 326–34; Griffin, 344; Platt, 313.

727 Henry Adams on Reed: to Brooks Adams, Feb. 7, 1896, *Letters*, II, 96.

727 "Chocolate eclair": Robinson, 362, calls it Reed's "alleged" statement. Kohlsaat, 77, gives it to Roosevelt and Peck says it was a "favorite saying" of Roosevelt although this does not exclude its having originated with Reed. To the present author it bears the stamp of Reed's picturesque turn of phrase.

728 Roosevelt to Reed: McCall, 228; to Lodge: Mar. 13, 1896.

728 "In a word, my dear boy": Pringle, 159.

PAGE

729 Altgeld to Darrow: q. Ginger (*see* Chap. 8), 188.

729 "The whistle would not blow": *ibid.*, 191.

729 "Mark Hanna's era": Norman Hapgood, *The Advancing Hour*, 1920, 76–77.

730 What sells a newspaper, "War": Kennedy Jones, q. Halévy (*see* Chap. 1), V, 9.

730 Eliot's speech in Washington: New York *Evening Post*, May 18, 1896.

731 "Degenerated sons of Harvard": Roosevelt to Lodge, Apr. 29, 1896.

731 Eliot characterized: In addition to James's biography, the sources used were:

BROWN, ROLLO WALTER, *Harvard Yard in the Golden Age*, New York, 1948.

HOWE, M. A. DEWOLFE, *Classic Shades*, Boston, 1928.

MORISON, SAMUEL ELIOT, *Three Centuries of Harvard*, Harvard Univ. Press, 1937.

SEDGEWICK, ELLERY, *The Happy Profession*, Boston, 1946.

731 "Eliza, do you kneel . . .": James, I, 33–34; "Misunderstood": Morison, 358; "I had a vivid sense": Brown, 27; "An oarsman's back": Sedgewick, 371–72; "A noble presence": Howe, 185; "A gentlemen who is . . .": *ibid.*; "Throwing it in ANOTHER!": James, II, 69; "First private citizen": *ibid.*, 92; "An emblem of triumph": Sedgewick, 371–72.

732 "If ever we come to nothing": Apr. 29, 1896.

733 Secretary Long on Roosevelt: Bishop, I, 71; Lodge to Roosevelt: Mar. 8, 1897, q. *ibid.*

733 McClure to co-editor: Lyon, 148; to Page: *ibid.*, 167.

733 "Do nothing unrighteous": q. Puleston, 182; Roosevelt's reply: May 3, 1897.

734 Schurz's visit to McKinley: Fuess, 350.

734 *Spectator* on the Treaty: June 19, 1897.

734 "Empire Can Wait": *Illustrated American*, Dec., 1897.

734 Bryce in the *Forum*: Dec., 1897, "The Policy of Annexation for America."

735 "Far distant, storm-beaten ships": from his *Influence of Sea Power on the French Revolution*.

736 Reed on Senator Proctor: Dunn, I, 234.

736 "The taste of Empire": q. Morison and Commager, *Growth of the American Republic*, II, 324.

736 "Dissuade a cyclone": *NYT*, Apr. 7, 1898.

736 Roosevelt to Mahan: Mar. 21, 1898.

737 Mr. Dooley on the Philippines: Dunne, 43. When Mr. Dooley asked Hinnissy if he could tell where the Philippines were, Hinnissy, representing public opinion, replied, "Mebbe I cudden't, but I'm f'r takin' thim in, annyhow." Mr. Dooley wasn't so sure. "Th' war is still goin' on; an' ivry night, whin I'm countin' up the cash, I'm askin' mesilf will I annex Cubia or lave it to the Cubians? Will I take Porther Ricky or

PAGE

put it by? An' what shud I do with the Ph'lippeens? Oh, what shud I do with thim?": *ibid.*, 46–47.

737 McKinley on the Philippines: Kohlsaat, 68.

737 Lodge, must not "let the islands go": to Henry White, May 4, 1898, Nevins (*see* Chap. 1), 136.

737 Norton, "We jettison . . .": text of the speech in *Letters*, II, 261–69. The politician who proposed lynching was the Hon. Thomas J. Gargan.

737 The Anti-Imperialists: Lanzar, Harrington, Howe, Fuess.

738 "An abominable business": *Mark Twain–Howells Letters*, Harvard Univ. Press, 1960, II, 673, n. 4. See also Mark Twain's "To The Person Sitting in Darkness," *North American Review*, Feb., 1901.

739 Godkin on "inferior races": Mar. 24, 1898, 216.

739 Carl Schurz, same argument: Schurz, 441.

739 Beveridge's speeches: Bowers, 68–70, 76; Storey, 38; W. E. Leuchtenberg, "Progressivism and Imperialism, 1898–1916," *Miss. Valley Hist. Rev.*, Dec., 1952.

740 "We're a gr-reat people": Dunne, 9.

741 Roosevelt, "my power for good": Mar. 29, 1898.

741 Beveridge on Reed: to George W. Perkins, May 31, 1898, Bowers, 71.

742 "Opposition exclusively from Reed": May 31, 1898, Lodge, *Corres.*, I, 302.

742 Reed begged Clark: Dunn, I, 289.

743 Lodge, "one of the great world powers": to Henry White, Aug. 12, 1898, Nevins' *White*, 137.

744 Mahan, "the jocund youth" and "*Deus Vult!*": Puleston, 201.

744 Schurz, "the great neutral power": Fuess, 354.

744 Saratoga conference: *NYT*, Aug. 20, 1898.

745 Carnegie, "Let us stand together": Harvey, *Gompers* (*see* Chap. 8), 89–90.

746 Reed "terribly bitter": Dec. 20, 1898, Lodge, *Corres.*, I, 370.

747 Bryan and the Treaty: Dunn, I, 283; Hoar, I, 197; II, 110; Pettigrew, 206. The dealing in judgeships and other bribes by the Republicans is discussed in W. S. Holt, *Treaties Defeated by the Senate*, Johns Hopkins, 1933, 171, and in Garraty, *Lodge*, 201–2.

748 "Closest, hardest fight": *ibid.*

748 William James: *Letters*, II, 289; Perry, 240.

748 Norton, "lost her unique position": Nov. 18, 1899, *Letters*, II, 290.

748 Moorfield Storey, "We are false": Howe, 221.

748 "Most influential man": Mar. 3, 1898, *Letters*, II, No. 976.

748 Storey to Hoar: Howe, 218–19.

749 "Touching a match": *NYT*, Apr. 23, 1899.

749 "Moody and ugly": Dunn, I, 298.

749 "Fatigue and disgust": *NYT*, Feb. 21, 1899.

750 *Tribune*: q. Robinson, 380; *Times*, Apr. 19 and 23, 1899.

PAGE

750 Godkin on Reed: *Letters*, II, 239, 241.

750 "The public!": *NYT*, Apr. 20, 1899.

751 "How is the horse feeling?": Pringle, *Life and Times of William Howard Taft*, 1939, I, 236.

752 Beveridge, "We will not renounce": q. Wolff, 303.

752 Godkin, "the military spirit": *Life and Letters*, 243.

752 Admiral Dewey on the Presidency: Sullivan, I, 311.

752 "Evil genius": Fuess, 366.

753 Third party and Plaza Hotel meeting: Pettigrew, 320–21; Fuess, 362–63.

753 Aguinaldo on the election: Wolff, 252.

753 "Hold your nose": Lanzar, 40.

753 *Nation*'s dissatisfied reader: Oct. 18, 1900, 307.

754 Lodge on Manila; q. Wolff, 304.

755 Roosevelt on expansion: *ibid.*, 332.

755 Dumdum bullets; *ibid.*, 305.

755 Norton's elegy: to S. G. Ward, Mar. 13, 1901, Vanderbilt, 217. An effort to heal the breach between the Anti-Imperialists and the Administration was made by Senator Hoar in the spring of 1901, with embarrassing results. As President of the Harvard Alumni Association, he offered an honorary LL.D. to McKinley without consulting the Harvard Corporation. Although President Eliot regarded McKinley as a "narrow-minded commonplace man" (James, II, 118), the Corporation gave its approval. But when the Board of Overseers, which contained a number of Anti-Imperialists, was asked for its concurrence a storm was raised, led by Moorfield Storey and Wendell Phillips Garrison. Bitter feeling developed, debate was "very sharp," and Theodore Roosevelt, thrown into a frenzy, and denouncing Storey as a "scoundrel," marshaled the votes of the waverers by mail. Leaked to Godkin, who published it in the *Nation*, Apr. 25, 1901, the opposition in the Overseers became known to McKinley. Although the Board finally voted for his degree, reportedly by 26 to 3, he did not appear at Commencement, with the result that the LL.D., which could not be conferred in absentia, was not conferred at all. Roosevelt, *Letters*, III, Nos. 2010, 2012; Howe, 177; *NYT*, May 3 and 9, 1901.

755 "That damned cowboy": Kohlsaat, 100.

755 Twenty-three poker hands: A. B. Paine, *Mark Twain*, III, 1163.

755 Joe Cannon said of him: q. McFarland.

4. "Give Me Combat"

Bibliography

Barclay, Sir Thomas, *Thirty Years: Anglo-French Reminiscences, 1876–1906*, Boston, Houghton Mifflin, 1914.

*Barrès, Maurice, *Scènes et doctrines du nationalisme*, Paris, Plon, 1925.

Benda, Julien, *La Jeunesse d'un clerc*, Paris, Gallimard, 1936.

Bertaut, Jules, *Paris, 1870–1935*, New York, Appleton-Century, 1936.

*Blum, Léon, *Souvenirs sur l'affaire*, Paris, Gallimard, 1935.

Bordeaux, Henry, *Jules Lemaître*, Paris, Plon, 1920.

Boussel, Patrice, *L'Affaire Dreyfus et la presse*, Paris, Colin, 1960.

Brunetière, Ferdinand, *Après le procés: réponse à quelques "intellectuels,"* Paris, Perrin, 1898.

Cambon, Paul, *Correspondence, 1870–1924*, 3 vols., Paris, Grasset, 1940.

Castellane, Marquis Boni de, *How I Discovered America*, New York, Knopf, 1924.

*Chapman, Guy, *The Dreyfus Case: A Reassessment*, New York, Reynal, 1955.

Claretie, Jules, "Souvenirs du dîner Bixio," *La Revue de France*, June 15, July 1 and 15, August 1 and 15, 1923.

Clemenceau, Georges, *Contre la justice*, Paris, Stock, 1900.

Clermont-Tonnerre, Elisabeth (de Gramont), Duchesse de, *Mémoires*, 3 vols., Paris, Grasset, 1928.

*Daudet, Léon, *Au temps de Judas: souvenirs de 1880 à 1908*, Paris, NLN, 1920.

DELHORBE, CECIL, *L'affaire Dreyfus et les ecrivains français*, Paris, Attinger, 1932.

ELLIS, HAVELOCK, *From Rousseau to Proust*, Boston, Houghton Mifflin, 1935.

FRANCE, ANATOLE, *M. Bergeret à Paris*, Paris, Calmann-Lévy, 1902.

GARD, ROGER MARTIN DU, *Jean Barois*, Paris, Gallimard, 1921.

GARRIC, ROBERT, *Albert de Mun*, Paris, Flammarion, 1935.

GIRAUD, VICTOR, *Les maîtres de l'heure* (Jules Lemaître), Vol. II, Paris, Hachette, 1919.

GOLDBERG, HARVEY, *The Life of Jean Jaurès*, Univ. of Wisconsin Press, 1962.

GUILLEMINAULT, GILBERT, ed., *La belle epoque*, 3 vols., Paris, Denoël, 1957.

HERZOG, WILHELM, *From Dreyfus to Petain*, tr. Walter Sorell, New York, Creative Age Press, 1947.

HYNDMAN, H. M., *Clemenceau*, New York, Stokes, 1919.

IBELS, H. G., *Allons-y!: Histoire contemporaine*, Paris, Stock, 1898.

JAURÈS, JEAN, *Les preuves: affaire Dreyfus*, Paris, *La Petite République*, 1898.

LETHEVE, JACQUES, *La Caricature et la presse sous la Troisième République*, Paris, Colin, 1961.

LONERGAN, W. F. (correspondent of the *Daily Telegraph*), *Forty Years of Paris*, New York, Brentano's, 1907.

MARTET, JEAN, *Le tigre* (Clemenceau), Paris, Albin Michel, 1930.

MASUR, GERHARD, *Prophets of Yesterday*, New York, Macmillan, 1961.

MEYER, ARTHUR, *Ce que mes yeux ont vu*, Paris, Plon, 1912.

———, *Ce que je peux dire*, Paris, Plon, 1912.

*PAINTER, GEORGE D., *Proust: The Early Years*, Boston, Little, Brown, 1959.

PALÉOLOGUE, MAURICE, *An Intimate Journal of the Dreyfus Case*, New York, Criterion, 1957.

PÉGUY, CHARLES, "Notre jeunesse," *Cahiers de la Quinzaine*, 1910. (This was a reply to Daniel Halévy's essay on the Affair written at Péguy's invitation and published by him in the *Cahiers de la Quinzaine*. It is reprinted in English translation by Alexander Dru in *Temporal and Eternal*, New York, Harper, 1958.)

POUQUET, JEANNE SIMON, *Le Salon de Mme Arman de Caillavet*, Paris, Hachette, 1926.

PROUST, MARCEL, *A la recherche du temps perdu*, Paris, Gallimard, 1921–27.

*QUILLARD, PIERRE, *Le monument Henry: liste des souscripteurs*, Paris, Stock, 1899.

RADZIWILL, PRINCESS CATHERINE, *France Behind the Veil*, New York, Funk & Wagnalls, 1914.

*RADZIWILL, PRINCESS MARIE, *Lettres au Général de Robilant*, Vol. II., 1896–1901 (the Appendix contains her correspondence with General de Galliffet), Bologna, Zanichelli, 1933.

**REINACH, JOSEPH, *Histoire de l'affaire Dreyfus*, 7 vols., Paris, Charpentier, 1901–11.

ROLLAND, ROMAIN, *Mémoires*, Paris, Albin Michel, 1956.

ROMAN, JEAN, *Paris fin de siècle*, New York, Arts, Inc., 1960.

SOREL, GEORGES, *La révolution dreyfusienne*, Paris, Rivière, 1911.

VIZETELLY, ERNEST ALFRED, *Emile Zola*, London, John Lane, 1904.

———, *Paris and Her People*, New York, Stokes, n.d. (1918).

ZEVAÈS, ALEXANDRE, *L'affaire Dreyfus: quelques souvenirs personnels*, *La Nouvelle revue*, January, February, March, 1936, Vols. 141 and 142.

ZOLA, EMILE, *La vérité en marche* (collected ed.), Paris, Bernouard, 1928.

Notes

Since my purpose in this chapter was not to retell the story of the Dreyfus Affair but rather to show French society reacting to it, I have not thought it necessary to document the historical events of the case unless they are controversial or obscure. The basic and essential source is still Reinach's stupendous work overflowing with facts, texts, documentation, insights, comments, eyewitnessed scenes, character portraits of the leading figures he knew and his own direct experiences, such as the moment in the Chamber during de Mun's speech when "I felt on my head the hatred of three hundred hypnotized listeners." Everything that anyone said or did connected with the Affair he made it his business to collect and record, including, besides obvious matters, thousands of peripheral details such as Scheurer-Kestner's disgust with the reporter or Count Witte's flash of clairvoyance. As a major actor in, not merely an observer of, the events, Reinach was vilified, calumniated, and caricatured more than anyone excepting Zola. Under these circumstances to have put together a work of such historical value is a feat perhaps unequaled, certainly unsurpassed, in historiography. The reader may take it that any statement or quotation in this chapter not otherwise accounted for is to be found in Reinach, to be located through his Index, which occupies the entire seventh volume.

The most thoughtful expression of the Nationalist point of view is Barrès' while the most vivid and vicious is Daudet's. The best modern account—reliable, objective and of readable length—is Chapman's. For the riots at Auteuil and Longchamps I relied on the contemporary press.

PAGE

759 "Would have divided the angels themselves": in *Journal des débats*, Mar. 8, 1903, on death of Gaston Paris, q. Barrès, 9.

761 "At your age, General": q. Lonergan, 76.

764 Lavisse on the Grande Armée: *Histoire de France contemporaine*, III, 379.

764 Anatole France, "all that is left": The character is M. Panneton de la Barge in *M. Bergeret à Paris*, 65–70.

765 Comte de Haussonville quoted: Paléologue, 147.

765 "France loves peace and prefers glory": said by Albert Vandal, member of the French Academy, q. *Figaro*, Sept. 25, 1898.

765 Ladies rose for General Mercier: Proust, *Guermantes*, II, 150. The Duchesse de Guermantes caused a sensation at the soirée of the Princesse

PAGE

de Lignes by remaining seated when other ladies rose. It was this action which helped to defeat the Duc for the Presidency of the Jockey Club.

766 "You can have it back": Reinach, I, 2.

766 "If Dreyfus is acquitted, Mercier goes": Paléologue, 44.

767 Observer reminded of Dante: *ibid.*, 198–99.

768 Bülow, "There are Three Great Powers": C. Radziwill, 298.

768 Gossip on de Rodays bribed: Radziwill, *Letters*, 106.

768 Zola, a "shameful disease": *l'Aurore*, May 13, 1902, q. Boussel, 216.

769 Ernest Judet's fear of Clemenceau: Daudet, 43.

769 Arthur Meyer's career: C. Radziwill, 297–307.

770 Rochefort and Kaiser's supposed letter: Blum, 78–80; Boussel, 157–59. The story of the letter appeared in *l'Intransigeant*, Dec. 13, 1897.

770 Boisdeffre and Princess Mathilde: Radziwill, *Letters*, 133–35. Princess Radziwill told the story to the Kaiser who commented, "It's a good thing for me that such a man heads the French General Staff . . . and all I wish is that they leave him where he is."

771 The "Syndicate": The Right's conception of the Syndicate is expressed in all seriousness by Daudet, 11–17, and satirized by Anatole France in Chapter 9 of *M. Bergeret*. The *Dépêche de Toulouse* on Nov. 24, 1897, affirmed the existence of a *Syndicat D.* and its expenditure of 10,000,000 francs: q. Boussel, 138. Other charges from *Libre Parole, l'Intransigeant, Jour, Patrie, Eclair, Echo de Paris* given with dates by Reinach, III, 20; also "Le Syndicat," *l'Aurore*, Dec. 1, 1897, in Zola, 13–19.

772 "Something very great": Count Harry Kessler, q. Masur, 297.

772 Henry Adams on reading Drumont: July 27 and Aug. 4, 1896, *Letters*, 110, 116.

773 "Clandestine and merciless conspiracy": q. Herzog, 30.

773 Duc d'Uzès felt gratified: *ibid.*, 31.

775 "They bore us with their Jew": q. Goldberg, 216.

775 Socialist review of Lazare's pamphlet: Zevaès, v. 141, 21.

776 "The Duc de Saint-Simon himself": Reinach, II, 618, n. 1.

778 Esterhazy, "hands of a brigand"; "elegant and treacherous": C. Radziwill, 326–27; Benda, 181.

779 Scheurer-Kestner like a 16th-century Huguenot: Rolland, 290.

779 Crowds in the Luxembourg gardens: described by Clemenceau in 1908 in a speech dedicating a statue to Scheurer-Kestner.

779 Clemenceau on Monet: q. J. Hampden Jackson, *Clemenceau and the Third Republic*, New York, 1962, 81.

779 "Only the artists": Martet, 286.

779 Clemenceau on Esterhazy, Jesuits, justice: q. Boussel, 143; Reinach, III, 265. The degree to which contemporary attention was focused on the Affair may be judged from Clemenceau's five volumes of collected articles: *L'Iniquité* (162 articles from *l'Aurore* and *La Justice* up to July, 1898); *Vers la Réparation*, 1899 (135 articles from *l'Aurore*, July–Dec.,

PAGE

1898); *Des Juges*, 1901 (40 articles from *l'Aurore*, Apr.–May, 1899); *Injustice Militaire*, 1902 (78 articles from *l'Aurore*, Aug.–Dec., 1899); *La Honte*, 1903 (65 articles from *La Dépêche de Toulouse*, Sept., 1899–Dec., 1900).

780 "Generals of debacle" *et seq.*: Reinach, III, 258.

780 Anton Radziwill "loves to talk English": Spring-Rice (*see* Chap. 3), I, 184.

780 Witte, "I can see only one thing": Reinach, II, 542, n. 1.

781 Jules Ferry, "to organize mankind": q. Goldberg, 39.

781 Léon Bourgeois to the Ralliés: q. Chapman, 23.

781 De Mun's speech to the Academy: Mar. 10, 1898. Reprinted in his *Discours politiques et parlementaires*.

782 De Mun's career: Garric, *passim*; on Socialism, *ibid.*, 94.

785 Galliffet, "continue to understand nothing": to Princess Radziwill, Sept. 22, 1899, 342.

785 Comtesse de Noailles, "too beautiful to be real" and "merely smiled": C. Radziwill, 337–38.

785 "Certitude of superiority": Clermont-Tonnerre, 113.

785 Aimery de la Rochefoucauld: "fossil rigidity" was Proust's phrase for the Prince de Guermantes, for whom de Rochefoucauld served as a model. "Mere nobodies in the year 1000": q. Painter, 189.

786 Duc d'Uzès, "we were always killed": Painter, 200.

786 *Gratin* not hospitable: Clermont-Tonnerre, 113.

786 English visitor of Duc de Luynes: Wyndham (*see* Chap. 1), I, 346, 480.

786 Thiers on Comte de Paris: q. Spender, *Campbell-Bannerman* (*see* Chap. 5), II, 59.

787 Gamelba: Lonergan, 120–21.

787 "All this Dreyfus business" and "Perfectly intolerable": Proust, *Guermantes*, I.

787 "Colossus with dirty feet": Flaubert, *Correspondence*, Apr. 18, 1880.

790 "Pornographic pig," "Merde!" and other reactions: du Gard, 8.

790 Björnson, "stupor and distress": Reinach, III, 314.

790 "The scene is France": q. Herzog, 144.

790 Chekhov on Zola's trial: Ernest J. Simmons, *Chekhov: A Biography*, Boston, 1962, 412–13.

791 "Smelled of suppressed slaughter": Paléologue, 131.

792 "Paris palpitated": Hyndman (*see* Chap. 7), 301.

792 Zola's trial: Paléologue, 131–33; Hyndman, *Clemenceau*, 176–77; Vizetelly, 430–56; *et al.*

792 Labori "not an intellect": q. Chapman, 175.

793 Zola, "Listen to them!": Guilleminault, I, 189.

793 Clemenceau, "not a single Dreyfusard": Hyndman (*see* Chap. 7), 301.

793 Henry Adams on Zola verdict: Feb. 26, 1898, *Letters*, 151.

794 Anatole France got out of bed: from unpublished diary of Daniel Halévy, q. Delhorbe, 95–96.

PAGE

794 "Altogether one of us": Daudet, 66.

794 Monet quarreled with Degas: Stephen Gwynn, *Claude Monet*, New York, Macmillan, 1934, 92.

794 Degas read *Libre Parole*: Chapman, 182; on *arrivistes*: q. George Slocombe, *Rebels of Art: Manet to Matisse*, New York, 1939, 158.

795 Debussy and Puvis de Chavannes: Painter, 356; Reinach, III, 248, n. 2.

795 "If I sign" said a school principal: Clemenceau in *l'Aurore*, Jan. 18, 1898.

795 Emile Duclaux, Revision in the laboratory: Reinach, III, 169.

796 "He paints with his hands in my pockets": René Gimpel, *Carnets*, Paris, 1963.

797 Gaston Paris: Reinach, IV, 150, n. 5; Paul Stapfer: Zevaès, v. 141, 202.

797 Whole villages took sides: Barclay, 135.

797 Dîner Bixio: Claretie. All anecdotes of Dîner Bixio are from this source.

797 Opening of "Les Loups": Rolland, 291–95.

798 "We needed reassurance, ideals": Adolphe Brisson on "l'Aiglon," in *Figaro*, Mar. 13, 1900.

798 Ranc, "warned not to sleep at home": q. Reinach, IV, 151.

799 The salons: Bertaut, 163–73; Wharton (*see* Chap. 1), 261, 273; Painter, 130, 201, 281; for Mme Straus, see esp. Bertaut, Painter, 110–16, Paléologue; for Mme Arman, esp. Pouquet, *passim*; Clermont-Tonnerre, I, 4–5, 13; Blum, 98; for Mme Aubernon: Paléologue, 114; Suttner (*see* Chap. 5), I, 282–84; for Mme de Loynes: esp. Meyer, *Ce que je peux dire*, 250–53, 287; Castellane, 195.

801 Lemaître, "The Republic cured me": q. Giraud, 72.

801 "*Que faite vous, Maître?*": Barclay, 142.

801 Meetings of Ligue des Patriotes: Meyer, *Ce que je peux dire*, 253–63; Daudet, 89–90.

803 De Vogüé, "Now the odious case": Paléologue, 151.

803 Reciting 17th-century poetry: Goldberg, 226.

804 His "splendid amplitude": Rolland, 298; "Like a huge cat with a mouse": *ibid.*

804 Socialists on Zola's trial: Jaurès' *Œuvres*, VI, 197, q. Goldberg; Reinach, III, 255, IV, 148; Zevaès, v. 141, 97, 199.

805 Jaurès, "how tormented I am": q. Goldberg, 220.

807 "Because we seem to oppose": from a letter of Nov. 7, 1898, in the Guesde Archives, Amsterdam, q. Goldberg, 243.

808 Socialist Committee of Vigilance: Zevaès, v. 141, 203.

808 André Buffet telegraphed Pretender: Details of the right-wing conspiracy and its financing were obtained from evidence at the subsequent trial of Déroulède, Reinach, IV, 332–42.

808 "Eve of a new Commune": Radziwill, *Letters*, 155.

808 "Soul of a second lieutenant": André Maurois, *The Miracle of France*, New York, 1948, 404.

PAGE

809 "Sanctuary of treason," *et seq.*: Paléologue, 187–90.

809 Anarchists on Dreyfus "parade": Boussel, 170–72: Maitron (*see* Chap. 2), 307–18.

810 Mme de Greffulhe wrote to the Kaiser: André Germain, *Les clés de Proust*, 1953, 43. (I am indebted for this source to Mr. George D. Painter, the biographer of Proust.)

810 Change in the Guermantes: recorded in *Sodome* and *La Prisonnière*.

810 An officer said to Galliffet: Claretie, 50.

811 Jaurès, "If war breaks out": q. Goldberg, 245.

811 Contributors to the Henry Subscription: Quillard, *passim*.

812 Loubet's election: Paléologue, 203; "The Republic will not founder": q. Chapman, 254.

812 Lemaître on driving Loubet out: q. Goldberg, 247.

813 Anti-Semitic League funds: Reinach, IV, 573, n. 4; V, 113, 254, n. 1, from evidence at Déroulède trial.

813 *Le Temps*, "What other country": June 6, 1899.

813 William James, "one of those moral crises": June 7, 1899, *Letters*, II, 89.

813 The attack on Loubet at Auteuil: *Figaro*, June 5, 1899.

814 Next Sunday at Longchamps: *Le Temps*, June 12/13, 1899. Henri Léon, the Nationalist leader and cynic in *M. Bergeret à Paris*, describes how hooligans yelled "*Pa-na-ma! De-mis-sion!*" under his orders. "I beat time for them and they yell the separate syllables. It was really done with taste."

816 Lucien Herr's argument: from *Vie de Lucien Herr*, by Charles Andler, q. Goldberg, 254.

816 Socialists split on support for Government: Zevaès, v. 142, 47.

816 Marquis de Galliffet, silver-plated stomach: Castellane, 99; "air of a bandit chief": Reinach, V, 168–69; on arresting members of his club: Radziwill, *Letters*, 340; "courage and effrontery": Reinach, *loc. cit.*

817 Millerand, "cat in a downpour": Suarez (*see* Chap. 8), I, 259.

817 "Invite those chaps to dinner": from Louis Thomas, *Le Général de Galliffet*, 1910, 247 (supplied by Mr. Painter).

818 Rennes trial: eyewitness accounts by Marcel Prévost, New York *Herald*, Aug. 8/9; Severine and others, q. in Reinach, V; Barrès, 146; Zevaès, v. 142, 53; Benda, 211; London *Times*, New York *Tribune*, Aug. 8/9. Evidently it is a rule that discrepancies in observation increase with intensity of emotion: Dreyfus' hair was "white" according to *The Times*, "auburn-grey" according to the *Tribune*; his moustache "jet black" according to *The Times*, "frankly red" according to the *Tribune*.

820 G. A. Henty: Hyndman, 184.

821 Galliffet, "I don't budge from my office": Radziwill, *Letters*, 340.

821 Labori "looked like Hercules": Meyer, *Mes Yeux*, 152.

821 "I've just killed the Dreyfus": Paléologue, 241.

821 Queen Victoria's telegram: Reinach, V, 544.

PAGE

821 Clemenceau: In *l'Aurore*, Sept. 10, 1899.

822 Comtesse de Noailles weeping: Painter, 299.

822 Foreign reaction to Rennes verdict: *The Times*, Sept. 12, 13, 14, 1899; Barclay, 162.

822 Grieg's "Indignation": Finck, *Grieg* (*see* Chap. 6), 104.

824 Galliffet, "That's something to see": Lonergan, 369.

5. The Steady Drummer

Bibliography

Official publications of the proceedings of the two Peace Conferences at The Hague are the following:

FRANCE, MINISTÈRE DES AFFAIRES ETRANGÈRES, Documents Diplomatiques, *Conférence internationale de la Paix*, 1899, Paris, Imprimerie Nationale, 1900.

———, *Deuxième conférence internationale de la paix*, 1907, Paris, Imprimerie Nationale, 1908.

*GERMANY, AUSWARTIGEN AMT, *Die grosse politik der europäischen Kabinette*, Berlin, 1924–25. Band 15: *Rings um die Erste Haager Friedenskonferenz*. Band 23: *Die Zweite Haager Friedenskonferenz*. (Referred to in Notes as *GP*.)

GREAT BRITAIN, FOREIGN OFFICE, *Correspondence respecting the Proposal of HM the Emperor of Russia for a Conference on Armaments*, Russia, No. 1 (1899), Cd. 9090, London, HMSO.

———, *Correspondence respecting the Peace Conference held at The Hague in 1899*, Misc. No. 1 (1899), Cd. 9534, London, HMSO. (The material in these two volumes is referred to in the Notes as F.O. 83, 1695-6-7-8-9 and 1700. These are the reference numbers for the autograph originals in the Public Record Office which I consulted in preference to the published version.)

———, *Correspondence respecting the Second Peace Conference held at The Hague in 1907*, Misc. No. 1 (1908), Cd. 3857, London, HMSO.

———, *Further Correspondence*, Cd. 4174, Misc. No. 5 (1908).

HAGUE, THE, *The Proceedings of The Hague Peace Conference*, 4 vols.

Translation of the official texts (originally published by the Netherlands Ministry of Foreign Affairs), prepared in the Division of International Law of the Carnegie Endowment for International Peace; ed. James Brown Scott, Oxford Univ. Press, 1920–21, Vol. I, 1899; Vol. II, III, IV, 1907.

UNITED STATES, *The Hague Peace Conferences of 1899 and 1907*, ed. James Brown Scott, 2 vols., Baltimore, Johns Hopkins Press, 1909. The second volume contains the instructions to and reports of the American delegates and the correspondence in 1904 and 1906 relating to the calling of the Second Conference.

Other Sources

ADAM, PAUL, "Physionomie de la conférence de la Haye," *Revue de Paris*, August 1, 1907, 642–72.

BACON, ADMIRAL SIR REGINALD HUGH, *The Life of Lord Fisher of Kilverstone*, 2 vols., London, Hodder & Stoughton, 1929.

BERGENGREN, ENK, *Alfred Nobel*, tr., London, Nelson, 1962.

BLOCH, IVAN S., *The Future of War*, tr., with a "Conversation with the Author" by W. T. Stead, Boston, Ginn, 1902.

BÜLOW, BERNHARD, PRINCE VON, *Memoirs*, 4 vols., Boston, Little, Brown, 1931–32.

CHIROL, SIR VALENTINE, *Fifty Years in a Changing World*, New York, Harcourt, 1928.

CHOATE, JOSEPH HODGES, *The Two Hague Conferences*, Princeton Univ. Press, 1913.

CURTI, MERLE, *Peace or War: The American Struggle, 1636–1936*, New York, Norton, 1936.

DAVIS, CALVIN DE ARMOND, *The United States and the First Hague Peace Conference*, Cornell Univ. Press, 1962.

DILLON, E. J., *The Eclipse of Russia*, New York, Doran, 1918.

FISHER, JOHN ARBUTHNOT, LORD, *Records*, London, Hodder & Stoughton, 1919.

FISHER, JOHN ARBUTHNOT, LORD, *Fear God and Dread Nought: Correspondence of Lord Fisher*, ed. Arthur J. Marder, Vol. 1, 1854–1904, Harvard Univ. Press, 1952; Vol. 2, 1904–14, London, Cape, 1956.

FULLER, J. F. C., *Armament and History*, New York, Scribner's, 1945.

HENDRICK, BURTON J., *The Life of Andrew Carnegie*, 2 vols., Garden City, Doubleday, 1932.

HULL, WILLIAM I., *The Two Hague Conferences*, Boston, Ginn, 1908.

JESSUP, PHILIP G., *Elihu Root*, 2 vols., New York, Dodd, Mead, 1938.

LEMONON, ERNEST, *La Seconde Conférence de le Paix*, Paris, 1908.

MOWAT, ROBERT B., *Life of Lord Pauncefote*, Boston, Houghton Mifflin, 1929.

NEF, JOHN J., *War and Human Progress*, Harvard Univ. Press, 1950.

NOWAK, KARL FRIEDRICH, *Germany's Road to Ruin*, New York, Macmillan, 1932.

PALMER, FREDERICK, *With My Own Eyes*, Indianapolis, Bobbs-Merrill, 1932.

PINSON, KOPPEL S., *Modern Germany*, New York, Macmillan, 1954.

SPENDER, J. A., *The Life of Sir Henry Campbell-Bannerman*, 2 vols., Boston, Houghton Mifflin, 1924.

STEAD, W. T., "Character Sketch: Lord Fisher," *Review of Reviews*, February, 1910.

*SUTTNER, BERTHA VON, *Memoirs*, 2 vols., Boston, Ginn, 1910.

TATE, MERZE, *The Disarmament Illusion*, New York, Macmillan, 1942.

**Temps, Le*, Reports of Special Correspondent at The Hague.

USHER, ROLAND, *Pan-Germanism*, Boston, Houghton Mifflin, 1913.

*WHITE, ANDREW D., *Autobiography*, 2 vols., New York, Century, 1905.

*WHYTE, FREDERIC, *Life of W. T. Stead*, London, Cape, 1925.

WITTE, COUNT SERGEI, *Memoirs*, New York, Doubleday, 1921.

WOLFF, THEODOR (editor of *Berliner Tageblatt*), *The Eve of 1914*, tr. E. W. Dickes, New York, Knopf, 1936.

Notes

As primary sources for what was said and what occurred at The Hague, I used the delegates' reports to their Governments contained in the Foreign Office Correspondence and *Grosse Politik*; the account in diary form by Andrew White in his *Autobiography*, and the reports of the Special Correspondent of *Le Temps*. Written while events were still hot, these make livelier reading than the tedious verbatim proceedings, collected and edited afterward. (*Le Temps'* correspondent signed himself X or sometimes XX, suggesting the possibility of two different people. Inquiries to *Le Monde*, successor of *Le Temps*, and to the Archivist of the Quai d'Orsay failed to penetrate his anonymity.) Unless otherwise stated all quotations by the delegates are from these sources; specific references are given only where it seems important. All material relating to Baroness von Suttner, including Nobel's letters, is from her *Memoirs*. All quotations from Roosevelt are from his *Letters* (*see* Chap. 3).

PAGE

827 "The Czar with an olive branch": *Neue Freie Presse*, q. *Figaro*, roundup of press comment, Aug. 30, 1898.

828 "It will sound like beautiful music" and other press quotations in this paragraph: *ibid.*; also *The Times* and *Le Temps*, roundup of foreign press comment, same date.

829 Kipling: The poem was first published in *Literature*, Oct. 1, 1898.

829 "A sword stroke in water": q. *Figaro*, Aug. 31, 1898. "Our future": Nowak, 237.

829 Liebknecht: Suttner, II, 198.

829 Godkin, "splendid summons": *Evening Post*, Aug. 29, 1898.

832 Olney on defeat of Arbitration Treaty: Mowat, 171.

833 Julien Benda: (*see* Chap. 4), 203.

833 Figures on world's mechanical energy: W. S. and E. S. Woytinsky, *World Population and Production*, New York, 1953, 930, Table 394.

835 "We are sailing with a corpse": q. Masur (*see* Chap. 4), 237.

835 Salisbury's Guildhall speech: *The Times*, Nov. 10, 1897.

835 Czar and his mother's chambermaids: q. David Shub, *Lenin*, 72.

835 Czar's letter to his mother: *Secret Letters of the Last Czar*, ed. E. J. Bing, New York, 1938, 131.

PAGE

836 Kuropatkin and genesis of Peace Conference: Witte, 96–97; Report of German Ambassador Radolin to Chancellor Hohenlohe, July 13, 1899, *GP*, XV, No. 4350; Dillon, conversation with Kuropatkin, 275–77.

836 "Keep people from inventing things": q. White, II, 70.

837 "Except at the price of suicide," *et seq.*: Bloch, xxxi, lxii, 349, 355–56.

838 British Ambassador's report: Sir Charles Scott to Salisbury, Aug. 25, 1898, Cd. 9090.

838 "It is the greatest nonsense": Warwick, 138.

839 Diplomatic reactions: *GP*, XV, Nos. 4223, 4224, 4236, 4237, 4248, 4249; also Foreign Office, Plunkett from Brussels, Jan. 11, 1899; Rumbold from Vienna, Feb. 3, 1899.

840 Kaiser, "Idiot": *GP*, XV, No. 4233.

840 "To My People": Pinson, 279; "When your Emperor commands": *ibid.*, 278; "There is only one master": *ibid.*; "Me and my 25 army corps": q. Bernadotte Schmitt, *The Coming of the War, 1914*, New York, 1930, I, 29; "Ally of my House": q. Chirol, 275.

840 Prince of Wales, "how different" and not so absurd: q. White, II, 113–14.

840 Kaiserin on Kaiser's annoyance: Bülow, I, 275; Eulenberg quoted: *ibid.*

841 Kaiser's telegram to Czar and subsequent comments: *GP*, XV, Nos. 4222, 4216, 4228, 4231.

841 Muraviev told Eulenberg: *ibid.*, 4231.

842 Kuno Francke pictured Germany: "German Ideals of Today," *Atlantic Monthly*, Dec., 1905.

843 Pan-German program and "We want territory": *Encyc. Brit.*, "Pan-Germanism."

843 Admiral Dewey, on German bad manners: Palmer, 115.

844 Hay, "To the German mind": q. A. L. P. Dennis, in S. F. Bemis, ed., *American Secretaries of State*, IX, 124.

844 "Sheepsheads": Pinson, 278.

844 "Not even the tamest Liberal": Wolff, 310.

844 "Always wear a good black coat": q. Pinson, 286.

844 Bülow and the lapels: Nowak, 226.

844 Holstein's explanation and Bülow's instructions: *GP*, XV, Nos. 4255, 4217, 4245-6-7.

845 Public resolutions: F.O. 83, 1699.

846 Balfour, "A sanguine view": *ibid.*

846 Stead: All the material on Stead in these pages is from Whyte's biography with the exception of the story about Charles II, which is from Esher, I, 229; the Prince of Wales's opinion of the Czar as "weak as water," which is from Warwick, 136; and the Russian complaint of being "embarrassed," which was relayed by Ambassador Sir Charles Scott, Jan. 14, 1899, F.O. 83, 1699.

849 Henley, "the battle spirit": from "Rhymes and Rhythms," No. XVI, first published in *Poems*, 1898.

PAGE

850 Nevinson: *Changes and Chances* (*see* Chap. 1), 130.
851 Mahan, "no greater misfortune": q. Puleston (*see* Chap. 3), 171.
851 "Assured of certain certainties": T. S. Eliot, "Preludes."
852 Yeats' poem: in his autobiography, *The Trembling of the Veil*, ch. 18.
853 Boston Peace Crusade "permanent tribunal": Davis, 62.
853 McKinley urged to appoint Eliot: *ibid.*, 68.
853 Kaiser on Mahan, "Our greatest foe": *GP*, XV, n. to 4250.
854 Bourgeois, "amiable, elegant": Zevaès (*see* Chap. 4), v. 141, 202; "cultivated fine beard": Suarez (*see* Chap. 8), I, 420.
854 "To renounce war": General Barail, q. *Figaro*, Aug. 31, 1898.
854 Mme Adam, "I am for war": Suttner, II, 233.
855 "Beating empty air": q. Davis, 88.
855 Baron Stengel's pamphlet: Drummond to F.O., Apr. 6, 1899; Tate, 230, n. 44.
856 "Never give way": Mowat, 300; "soul of honor": *ibid.*, 295.
856 "When Peel lost his temper": Birrell (*see* Chap. 7), 126–27.
856 Fisher: the material in these three paragraphs is from Bacon's biography except for the last line, "So I did," which is from Fisher's *Records*, 55.
857 The Hague during the Conference: chiefly from reports by the correspondent of *Le Temps*, May 10, 20, 24, 25; *Figaro*, May 20; White, Mowat, Suttner. The Huis ten Bosch was visited by author in 1963.
858 "A printer's error": q. Davis, 86.
859 Beernaert "greatest cynic": Neal Ascherson, *The King Incorporated*, London, 1963, 142.
860 Münster, "political riff-raff": *GP*, XV, 4327.
860 Reichstag deputies: *The Times*, May 11, 1899.
861 Fisher, "humanizing of war!" *et seq.*: Stead, *Review of Reviews*, Feb., 1910, 117.
862 Hotel Kurhaus: *Letters*, I, 142.
862 Stead on Fisher: q. Bacon, I, 121.
862 He learned from German naval delegate: *ibid.*, 128, 177.
863 "Deepest seriousness": q. Taylor (*see* Chap. 3), 99.
863 Fisher on neutral coal: Bacon, I, 128.
863 Captain Siegel's argument: *GP*, XV, 4274.
865 Ardagh's speech on dumdums: June 14, F.O. 83, 1695.
867 "The angel of arbitration": q. Reinach (*see* Chap. 4), V, 173, n. 2.
867 Society's "awful conscience": Hunter (*see* Chap. 8), 30.
867 D'Estournelles' story of Jaurès: White, 300.
868 Kaiser, "this whole hoax": *GP*, XV, 4276.
868 Efforts to persuade Germany on arbitration: White, II, 265–313. Pauncefote Memorandum, June 19, F.O. 83, 1695, and other reports in F.O. 83, 1700; *GP*, XV, 4276, 4280, 4284, 4317, 4320, 4349.
869 Kaiser's disgust, "I consented . . .": *GP*, XV, 4320.
870 "Zeal almost macabre": *Le Temps*, editorial, July 27.
870 Mahan blocks arbitration: Puleston (*see* Chap. 3), 211; White, 338–41.

PAGE

872 As if the hand of God: Clynes (*see* Chap. 7), 98; "With a kind of shiver": M. Radziwill, *Letters* (*see* Chap. 4), Jan. 2, 1900, 237.

872 Kaiser to Fritz Krupp: from the Krupp archives, q. William Manchester, "The House of Krupp," *Holiday*, Dec., 1964, 110.

872 Three hundred men "all acquainted": q. Kessler (*see* Chap. 8), 121.

872 "Then in 1900," wrote Yeats: Introduction to *Oxford Book of Modern Verse*.

873 Henry Adams expecting a bomb: *Education*, 494–95.

873 Exposition: *l'Illustration* and *Le Monde Illustré*, *passim* through the summer; *Outlook*, Sept. 8, Nov. 10, 1900, Jan. 5, 1901; *Harper's Monthly*, Sept., 1900; *Blackwood's*, July, 1900; *Nation*, June 28, 1900.

875 "It seemed merely a matter of decades": Zweig (*see* Chap. 6), 3.

875 Balfour wished to appoint Mahan Regius Professor: Magnus, *Edward VII*, 306.

877 Jusserand and Philander Knox on Roosevelt: Jules Jusserand, *What Me Befell*, Boston, 1934, 241; Sullivan (*see* Chap. 3), II, 438 n.

877 Roosevelt's visit to Eliot: James, *Eliot* (*see* Chap. 3), II, 159.

878 Roosevelt, "foolish theory": to Spring-Rice, Dec. 21, 1907, VI, 871; "weakening of fighting spirit": *ibid.*; "I abhor men like Hale": to Speck von Steinberg, July 16, 1907, V, 721; "General softening of fibre": to Whitelaw Reid, Sept. 11, 1905, V, 19.

878 Kaiser, "That's my man!": Bülow, I, 658.

878 D'Estournelles' visit to Roosevelt: Suttner, II, 390–91.

879 Hay, "I have it all arranged": Tyler Dennett, *John Hay*, New York, 1933, 346.

880 Fisher proposes to "Copenhagen" German fleet: Bacon, II, 74–75.

880 "Ach, that damned Reichstag!": Bülow, II, 36–37.

880 Czar's hint conveyed to Washington: Roosevelt to Carl Schurz, Sept. 15, 1905, V, 30–31. The letter to Root, Sept. 14, 1905, V, 26.

881 C.-B., "so straight, so good-tempered": Lee (*see* Chap. 1), II, 442.

882 C.-B., "What nobler role": at Albert Hall, Dec. 21, 1905, Spender, II, 208.

882 Damnable, Domineering and Dictatorial: Bacon, I, 207.

883 Izvolsky, "a craze of Jews": *GP*, XXIII, 7879.

883 C.-B., "Long live the Duma!": C.-B. delivered the speech in French, Spender, II, 264.

883 Kaiser hoped Conference "would not take place": *GP*, XXIII, 7815. On King Edward's visit: *ibid.*; also 7823, 7825–26.

884 "Alert, aggressive, military": to Oscar Straus, Feb. 27, 1906, V, 168.

884 "Maudlin extreme": to Reid, Aug. 7, 1906, V, 348; talk with Count Gleichen: Lee, II, 437. Another visitor who found American amenities less than satisfactory was Count Witte. During his mission to the Portsmouth Peace Conference he said the only decent meal he had had in America was on board Morgan's yacht (Witte, 169).

884 Navy "more potent factor for peace": Sept. 22, 1906, V, 421.

PAGE

885 Carnegie agreed to donate Peace palace: Hendrick, II, 164.
885 Root, "failures are necessary steps": Jessup, II, 70.
885 First issue of the *Nation*: Mar. 2, 1907.
886 "I suppose he will support": Lee, II, 467.
886 Sir Edward Grey and all other diplomatic exchanges: Nevins (*see* Chap. 1), 249, 252, 258–59; Hull, 49–50; U. S., Scott, Vol. II; *GP*, XXIII, 7750, 7869, 7927, 7986.
887 Carnegie's visit to Kaiser: Hendrick, II, 299–318.
888 Mahan, "prepossession of the public mind": Puleston (*see* Chap. 3), 270, 280.
888 German officers drank to "The Day": Usher, 1.
888 Visiting Englishman at spa near Bayreuth: Buchan (*see* Chap. 1), 55.
889 Root, "tendency is toward war": Jessup, II, 25.
889 Lansdowne on Old Age Pensions: *The Times*, July 21, 1908.
890 Marquis de Soveral: Warwick, *Discretions*, 20; also F. Ponsonby, 216 (*both* Chap. 1).
890 "A damned good fellow": q. Mowat, 297.
891 Baron Marschall's appearance and habits: Gardiner, *Pillars* (*see* Chap. 1), 160–68; Barclay (*see* Chap. 4), 281. His opinions of delegates: to Bülow, July 28, 1907, *GP*, XXIII, 7961.
891 Austin's letter to *The Times*: Oct. 17, 1907.
892 Domela Nieuwenhuis: Adam, 655.
893 Fry's speech and comments: Hull, 72–74; White, II, 291.
893 Proceedings of the Conference: Scott, I, 110, *et seq.* Baron Marschall's report to Bülow, *GP*, XXIII, 7963; Grey's instructions on limiting "prospective liability" is No. 11 in F.O. correspondence, Cd. 3857.
895 Roosevelt, "I have not followed": July 2, 1907, V, 700; "Utterly disgusted": July 16, 1907, V, 720–21.
895 "Decayed Oriental states": M. W. Hazeltine, "The Second Peace Conference," *North American Review*, Nov., 1907.
895 "Was it a Peace Conference?": q. Choate, 40.
896 "Gradual, tentative, and delicate": Choate, 22.

6. "Neroism Is in the Air"

Bibliography

ALDRICH, RICHARD (music critic of the New York *Times* for this period), *Concert Life in New York, 1902–23*, New York, Putnam's, 1941.

BAUMONT, MAURICE, *L'Affaire Eulenberg et les Origines de la guerre mondiale*, Paris, Payot, 1933.

Beecham, Sir Thomas, *A Mingled Chime*, New York, Putnam's, 1943.

———, *Frederick Delius*, New York, Knopf, 1960.

Bertaux, Felix, *A Panorama of German Literature, 1871–1931*, tr., New York, Whittlesey, 1935.

Bigelow, Poultney, *Prussian Memories, 1864–1914*, New York, Putnam's, 1915.

Brandes, Georg, *Friedrich Nietzsche*, New York, Macmillan, n.d.

Cladel, Judith, *Rodin*, New York, Harcourt, 1937.

*Del Mar, Norman, *Richard Strauss*, New York, Free Press of Glencoe, 1962.

Dukes, Ashley, *Modern Dramatists*, Chicago, Sergel, 1912.

Ekman, Karl, *Jean Sibelius*, New York, Knopf, 1938.

Finck, Henry T., *Grieg and His Music*, London, John Lane, 1909.

*———, *Richard Strauss*, Boston, Little, Brown, 1917.

———, *Success in Music*, New York, Scribner's, 1909.

Gilman, Lawrence, *Nature in Music and Other Studies*, London, John Lane, 1914.

Gooch, G. P., *Germany*, New York, Scribner's, 1925.

Grigoriev, S. L. (stage manager for Diaghilev), *The Diaghilev Ballet, 1909–29*, London, Penguin Ed., 1960.

Hamburger, *see* Hofmannsthal.

Haskell, Arnold L. (director of the Covent Garden Royal Ballet), *Diagileff*, New York, Simon & Schuster, 1935.

Helfferich, Karl, *Germany's Economic Progress and National Wealth, 1888–1913*, Berlin, Stilke, 1913.

Hofmannsthal, Hugo von, *Selected Plays and Libretti*, ed. Michael Hamburger, New York, Bollingen-Pantheon, 1963.

HUNEKER, JAMES, *Overtones*, New York, Scribner's, 1904.

JEFFERSON, ALAN, *The Operas of Richard Strauss in Britain*, London, Putnam's, 1963.

KARSAVINA, TAMARA, *Theatre Street*, London, Constable, 1948.

KESSLER, COUNT HARRY, *Walter Rathenau*, London, Howe, 1929.

KOHN, HANS, *The Mind of Germany*, New York, Scribner's, 1960.

LAWTON, MARY, *Schumann-Heink*, New York, Macmillan, 1928.

LEHMANN, LOTTE, *Five Operas and Richard Strauss*, New York, Macmillan, 1964.

LOWIE, ROBERT HARRY, *Toward Understanding Germany*, Univ. of Chicago Press, 1954.

MAY, ARTHUR J., *The Hapsburg Monarchy*, Harvard Univ. Press, 1951.

MILLER, ANNA IRENE, *The Independent Theatre in Europe, 1887 to the Present*, New York, Long & Smith, 1931.

NEMIROVITCH-DANTCHENKO, VLADIMIR, *My Life in the Russian Theatre*, Boston, Little, Brown, 1936.

NEWMAN, ERNEST, *Richard Strauss*, London, John Lane, 1908. (With a valuable Memoir by Alfred Kalisch.)

NIJINSKY, ROMOLA, *Nijinsky*, New York, Simon & Schuster, 1934.

POLLARD, PERCIVAL, *Masks and Minstrels of New Germany*, Boston, Luce, 1911.

*ROLLAND, ROMAIN, *Correspondance; fragments de Journal* (No. 3 in *Cahiers Romain Rolland*), Paris, Albin Michel, 1951.

———, "Souvenirs sur Richard Strauss," in *Les Œuvres Libres*, Nouv. Serie, No. 27, Paris, 1948. (Much of this duplicates material in the *Correspondance* and *Journal* and parts of both appear in Rolland's *Musicians of Today*, New York, Holt, 1914.)

ROSENFELD, PAUL, *Musical Portraits*, New York, Harcourt, 1920.

———, *Discoveries of a Music Critic*, New York, Harcourt, 1936.

Schoenberner, Franz, *Confessions of a European Intellectual*, New York, Macmillan, 1946.

Shaw, George Bernard, *The Sanity of Art* (originally published 1895), New York, Boni, 1907.

Shaw, Stanley, *William of Germany*, New York, Macmillan, 1913.

Sokolova, Lydia, *Dancing for Diaghilev*, New York, Macmillan, 1961.

Speyer, Edward, *My Life and Friends*, London, Cobden-Sanderson, 1937.

*Strauss, Richard, and Hofmannsthal, Hugo von, tr., *Correspondence*, London, Collins, 1961.

Stravinsky, Igor, *Autobiography*, New York, Simon & Schuster, 1936.

Terry, Ellen, *The Russian Ballet*, London, Sidgwick, 1913.

Thomas, Rose Fay, *Memoirs of Theodore Thomas*, New York, Moffat, Yard, 1911.

Thompson, Oscar, *Debussy, Man and Artist*, New York, Dodd, Mead, 1937.

Tovey, Donald Francis, *A Musician Talks*, 2 vols., Oxford Univ. Press, 1941.

Van Vechten, Carl, "The Secret of the Russian Ballet" and "Igor Stravinsky: A New Composer," in *Music After the Great War and Other Studies*, New York, Schirmer, 1915.

Werfel, Alma Mahler, *And the Bridge Is Love*, New York, Harcourt, 1958.

Wood, Sir Henry, *My Life of Music*, London, Gollancz, 1938.

Wylie, I. A. R., *The Germans*, Indianapolis, Bobbs-Merrill, 1911.

*Zweig, Stefan, *World of Yesterday*, New York, Viking, 1943.

Notes

All biographical facts about Strauss not otherwise identified and all quoted comments about him by German critics and musicologists are from Finck. Separate references for comments or anecdotes by Rolland, Beecham, Newman, Mme Mahler (Werfel), Speyer, Stravinsky and others whose works are listed above are given *only* when the source is not obvious. By good fortune the celebration by major orchestras of Strauss's centenary in 1964, the year in which this chapter was written, enabled me to hear all his major works within the space of several months. Many of the program notes for these concerts, though ephemeral and therefore not listed in the Bibliography, were useful.

PAGE

899 "Tremble as they listened": Rolland, *Journal*, 125.

900 Frankfurt's musical life: Speyer, 79.

901 Bayreuth: Stravinsky, 60; Beecham, 55; Ekman, 125.

904 Shades of evening fell three times: Grove's *Dictionary of Music*, "Program Music."

905 "Oh, they are only imitators": q. Speyer, 143.

906 "Stop Hanslick": Werner Wolff, *Anton Bruckner*, New York, 1942, 103.

907 "So young, so modern": q. *Current Biography*, 1944, "Strauss."

909 "Positive horror of his countrymen": Brandes, 113.

910 Rodin on Nietzsche: Anne Leslie, *Rodin*, New York, 1937, 200.

911 "*Too much music in Germany*": *Souvenirs*, 232–33.

911 Brünhilde's horse: Haskell, 156.

911 Philip Ernst: *Current Biography*, 1942, "Max Ernst."

912 North and South Germans: Wylie, 29–38.

912 Max Liebermann on statues: Frederic William Wile, *Men Around the Kaiser*, Philadelphia, 1913, 168.

913 Berlin landlady's bill: Zweig, 113.

913 "Extremely rough": Chirol (*see* Chap. 5), 266.

913 Berlin women: Wylie, 192–93.

913 Seven meals a day: However unlikely, this was the report of the American Ambassador, James W. Gerard, *My Four Years in Germany*, New York, 1917, 56.

914 Number of university students in Prussia: Charles Singer, *et al.*, *A History of Technology*, Oxford Univ. Press, 1958, V, 787–88.

914 Barnum and Bailey's circus: Dexter Fellows, *This Way to the Big Show*, New York, 1936, 22; H. L. Watkins, *Barnum and Bailey in the Old World, 1897–1901*, 45. (I am indebted for these references to Mrs. Janise Shea.)

915 Kaiser at the Moscow Art Theater: Nemirovitch-Dantchenko. Material in this and the following four paragraphs is chiefly from the chapter "The Kaiser and the Arts" in the book by Stanley Shaw. The prize to Wildenbruch is from Lowie, 41; the Rhodes scholars from the *Letters*

PAGE

of Cecil Spring-Rice, II, 119; the adventure with Peer Gynt from Finck's *Grieg*, 145–46.

918 "Bismarck has broken": q. Kohn, 187–88.

918 Strauss's interview with the Kaiser was told to Rolland, q. Del Mar, 280–81.

919 Strauss becomes engaged: *ibid.*, 121–22.

920 Frau Strauss, character and habits: Lehmann, chaps. 2 and 3.

920 "Screaming like hell": Del Mar, 182.

920 Toast at the Speyers': Wood, 216.

921 "*Jetzt gehst componieren*": q. William Leon Smyser, in *The New Book of Modern Composers*, ed. David Ewen, New York, 1961, 396. "Put down that pencil": q. F. Zweig, *Stefan Zweig*, New York, 1946, 103.

924 "Neroism is in the air": *Journal*, Jan. 22, 1898, 118.

925 "Arbeitsmann" as Socialist anthem: Pinson (*see* Chap. 5), 262.

926 Made critics pay for seats: Huneker, in *NYT*, Nov. 24, 1912.

926 Debussy, "If people insist": Thompson, 183.

926 Sibelius, "Play the record again": Told by William Golding, q. Maurice Dolbier, in New York *Herald Tribune*, Apr. 21, 1964.

927 Debussy on Strauss: Thompson, 182–83.

927 Strauss on Debussy: Caesar Searchinger, "Richard Strauss As I Knew Him," *Saturday Review of Literature*, Oct. 29, 1949.

929 Sargent and gypsy band: Mount (*see* Chap. 1), 217.

929 Thomas, "the greatest musician": Thomas, 502.

930 "Big, broad, ample and simple": Charles Moore, *The Life and Times of Charles Follen McKim*, Boston, 1929, 85.

930 Tiffany's house: Werfel, 47–48.

930 "A day in my family life": Gilman, *Harper's Weekly*, Mar. 9, 1907.

930 "All the sacred elephants in India": Beecham, *Delius*, 129.

931 Grieg to Delius: *ibid.*, 129.

931 "Lack of courtesy" at Strasbourg: Rolland, 213.

932 "Tyrian purple and tired silver": Wilde to Frances Forbes Robertson, Feb. 23, 1893, *Letters* (*see* Chap. 1), 333.

932 *Salome* denounced by *The Times*: q. *ibid.*, 335 n.

932 Beardsley's drawings: *ibid.*, 344, n. 3.

935 "See life as ferocious and sinister": to A. C. Benson, June 29, 1896, *Henry James: Letters to A. C. Benson*, London, 1930, 35.

935 "A torrent of sex": Horace B. Samuel, *Modernities*, London, 1914, 135.

937 Star of Bethlehem: Del Mar, 281.

937 Kaiserin's hats: Mary Ethel McAuley, *Germany in War Time*, Chicago, 1917, 183; double bed: Palmer (*see* Chap. 5), 222; canceled *Feuersnot*: Del Mar, 236.

938 Kaiser on *Salome* and Strauss's reply: Del Mar, 281.

938 *Salome* in New York: *Outlook*, Feb. 9, 1907; Gilman, *Harper's Weekly*, Feb. 9, 1907; Aldrich, 172–79.

938 *Salome* in London: Beecham, 161, 168–73.

PAGE

939 Von Hofmannsthal: Zweig, 46–48; Hamburger, xxvii; Bertaux, 95.

940 "Capua of the Mind": Bertaux, 92.

940 "*Es gibt nur eine Kaiserstadt*": May, 309.

940 "Affably tolerant" and Franz Joseph never read a book: Zweig, 19, 21.

941 Roosevelt on the "Austrian gentleman": q. Wharton (*see* Chap. 1), 277.

941 Karl Luger: Zweig, 105; May, 311.

942 Hofmannsthal's notes on Greek themes: Hamburger, xxxii. The common assumption that Hofmannsthal's *Elektra* was influenced by Freud is historical conclusion-jumping for which there is no evidence. Ernest Jones, Freud's biographer, points out (*Freud*, I, 360, and II, 8) that the publication of *The Interpretation of Dreams* in Nov., 1899, awakened no interest in Viennese intellectual circles. Although Hofmannsthal owned a copy, there is no evidence when he acquired it and his correspondence does not discuss it. Hamburger, xxxiii.

943 "Summit of contemporary fame": Dukes, 68.

943 Eulenburg affair: Baumont; Wolff (*see* Chap. 5).

945 Hülsen-Haeseler's death: Zedlitz-Trutzschler, Robert, Graf von, *Twelve Years at the Imperial German Court*, New York, 1924. The episode is discussed in every biography of the Kaiser.

946 Rhodes scholars: Spring-Rice, II, 119.

946 Professor Simmel: Schoenberner, 55–56.

947 University of Berlin centenary: *ibid.*, 58.

947 Strauss's income in 1908: Finck, *Success in Music*, 14.

947 *Elektra* rehearsals: Schumann-Heink (Lawton, 322–25). According to this version, Strauss said, "I still can't hear the Heink's voice," meaning, presumably, that he was addressing his "Louder!" to her. Finck, on the other hand, who says he obtained the story directly from Schumann-Heink herself, gives it the other way around, and his version is the one generally repeated. To the present author, it is a puzzle why Strauss should have wanted to drown out the singer's voice in a part he himself had composed, but since I am not the first to find his actions occasionally baffling, I have given the accepted version of the incident.

948 Premiere of *Elektra*: Arthur Abell, in *Musical Courier*, Feb. 17, 1909; Hermann Bahr's article, q. Rosenfeld, *Discoveries*, 141–42.

949 *Elektra* in London: Finck, 252–53; Beecham, 147; Jefferson, 22; GBS in the *Nation*, Mar. 19, 1910.

950 Strauss's explanation for female Octavian: Lehmann, chap. 2.

952 Comtesse de Noailles, "something new": q. Haskell, 184.

952 Rodin, "classical sculpture": q. Albert E. Elsen, *Rodin*, New York, Museum of Modern Art, 1964.

953 "A soaring of feelings" on Blériot's triumph: Zweig, 196.

954 Quoted descriptions of Rubinstein, Pavlova, Karsavina: Haskell, 188.

954 Bakst jumped on a chair: Grigoriev, 39.

956 *Schéhérazade*: Terry, 41–44.

PAGE

955 Karsavina, vice "with verisimilitude": Van Vechten, 81.

955 Premiere of *Firebird*: Unless otherwise stated, Stravinsky is the source for this and other performances of his works for the Ballet.

956 "It was exciting to be alive" and "night after night entranced": Leonard Woolf, *Beginning Again*, New York, 1963–64, 37.

956 Premiere of *Faun*: Nijinsky, 172–74; Cladel, 218–21; *Le Gaulois*, May 30; *Le Temps*, May 31; *Figaro*, May 29–31; *Current Lit.*, Aug., 1912, "The Faun That Has Startled Paris."

957 Incident in Vienna: Nijinsky, 194–95.

958 Kaiser on *Cleopatra*: Stravinsky, 67.

960 Premiere of *Sacre*: Stravinsky, 72; Nijinsky, 202; *Figaro*, May 31; *Le Temps*, June 3; *Le Gaulois*, June 1, 1913; Van Vechten (*q.v.*) was the American who was hit on the head.

960 Kessler, "too scrupulous an accuracy": q. *Lit. Digest*, June 20, 1914.

961 Crown Prince's book: q. *The Times*, May 1, 1913.

961 "*Muss-Preussen*": Ford (*see* Chap. 1), 402–3.

962 Rathenau's "Festal Song": *Zukunft*, Oct. 26, 1912, 128–36. The poem was signed "Herwart Raventhal."

962 Zabern, "*finis Germaniae*" and "Keep it up!" (*Immer feste darauf!*): Wolff (*see* Chap. 5), 341–44. Full accounts of the Zabern affair are given by J. Kaestlé, *l'Affaire de Saverne*, Strasbourg, n.d., and Charles D. Hazen, *Alsace-Lorraine Under German Rule*, New York, 1917.

963 Gilman in January: *North American Review*, Jan., 1914.

964 Ballet's London season of 1914: *Annual Register*, Part II, 73.

964 Night of the performance at Drury Lane: Siegfried Sassoon, *The Weald of Youth*, 245.

964 Strauss at Oxford: *The Times*, June 25, 1914.

7. Transfer of Power

Bibliography

(in addition to those listed for Chapter 1)

BIRKENHEAD, EARL OF, *Contemporary Personalities*, London, Cassell, 1924.

BIRKENHEAD, SECOND EARL OF, *F. E., Earl of Birkenhead*, by his son, London, Eyre & Spottiswoode, 1960.

BIRRELL, AUGUSTINE, *Things Past Redress*, London, Faber, 1937.

BROCKWAY, FENNER, *Inside the Left*, London, Allen & Unwin, 1942.

Bryce, James, Viscount, *The Hindrances to Good Citizenship* (Yale Lectures), Yale Univ. Press, 1909.

Clynes, John Robert, *Memoirs*, Vol. I, London, Hutchinson, 1937.

Fulford, Roger, *Votes for Women*, London, Faber, 1957.

Gardiner, A. G., *Portraits and Portents*, New York, Harper, 1926.

Hearnshaw, F. J. C., ed., *Edwardian England, 1901–10*, London, Benn, 1933.

Hobson, John Atkinson, *The Social Problem*, London, Nisbet, 1901.

Hughes, Emrys, *Keir Hardie*, London, Allen & Unwin, 1956.

Hyndman, Henry M., *The Record of an Adventurous Life*, New York, Macmillan, 1911.

Jenkins, Roy, *Mr. Balfour's Poodle*, London, Heinemann, 1954.

Jones, Thomas, *Lloyd George*, Harvard Univ. Press, 1951.

*Masterman, C. F. G., *The Condition of England*, London, Methuen, 1909.

Masterman, Lucy, *C. F. G. Masterman: A Biography*, London, Nicholson, 1939.

*Mendelssohn, Peter de, *The Age of Churchill, 1874–1911*, London, Thames & Hudson, 1961.

Nicolson, Harold, *King George the Fifth*, London, Constable, 1952.

Nowell-Smith, Simon, ed., *Edwardian England, 1901–14*, Oxford Univ. Press, 1964.

Pankhurst, E. Sylvia, *The Suffragette*, New York, Sturgis, 1911.

———, *The Suffragette Movement* (re-issue), London, Longmans, 1932.

Pope-Hennessy, James, *Lord Crewe: The Likeness of a Liberal*, London, Constable, 1955.

Samuel, Herbert, *Grooves of Change* (English title: *Memoirs*), Indianapolis, Bobbs-Merrill, 1946.

———, *Liberalism*, London, Richards, 1902.

Somervell, D. C., *The Reign of George the Fifth*, New York, Harcourt, 1935.

Spender, J. A., *Life of H. H. Asquith*, 2 vols., London, Hutchinson, 1932.

Trotter, Wilfred, *Instincts of the Herd in Peace and War*, London, Allen & Unwin, 1916 (also Oxford Univ. Press, 1953, with a Foreword by F. M. R. Walshe).

Ullswater, Viscount (James Lowther), *A Speaker's Commentaries*, 2 vols., London, Arnold, 1925.

Wallas, Graham, *Human Nature in Politics*, Boston, Houghton Mifflin, 1909 (also 3rd ed., New York, Knopf, 1921).

Webb, Beatrice, *Our Partnership*, London, Longmans, 1948.

Wells, H. G., *Experiment in Autobiography*, New York, Macmillan, 1934.

Williams, Mrs. Hwfa (Florence), *It Was Such Fun*, London, Hutchinson, 1935.

Notes

(For all sources not listed above, see Chap. 1)

PAGE

969 Chinese Slavery: Lyttelton, 320–21; Pope-Hennessy, 69; Wallas, 127; Hearnshaw, 94.

970 Yellow press: the phrase was in use in England at that time: Lucy Masterman, 216.

970 "Outdoor relief for the aristocracy": q. Cecil, I, 167.

971 Education Act, "greatest betrayal": q. Adams, 123.

972 *Economist*, a matter of *£.s.d.*: q. Adams, 103.

PAGE

972 One water faucet and one privy: This and subsequent facts about the living conditions of the poor are from the chapter "Domestic Life," by Marghanita Laski, in Nowell-Smith.

972 Contract labour in British Guiana: Alfred Lyttelton speaking in the House of Commons, March 21, 1904, demonstrated that these contracts, negotiated under Gladstone and Rosebery, were for longer duration (five years as against three) and more severe conditions than the South African contracts. (Hansard, IV series, v. 132, 283 ff.).

973 Cries of "Rat!": Mackintosh, 222.

973 Balfour on Tariff issue: Fitzroy, I, 191, 220; Spender, *C.-B.*, II, 102.

974 Cust quoted: Sir Ronald Storrs, *Memoirs*, 37.

974 "Not to go out of office": Young, 232.

975 "In chronic poverty": Hobson, 12.

975 Conditions at Shawfield Chemical Works: Hughes, 91.

975 Hauled off to a day in gaol: Gompers (*see* Chap. 8), 29–30.

976 Army lowered minimum height: Nowell-Smith, 181.

976 Wells depicted it: *Autobiography*, 550.

978 A's and B's: Lord Beveridge, *Power and Influence*, 66–67.

978 William Morris, "gradually permeating": Hunter (*see* Chap. 8), 97.

978 Beatrice Webb contemplated marrying Chamberlain: Margaret Cole, *Beatrice Webb*, New York, 1946, 21.

979 "I could not carry on": q. Hesketh Pearson, *Shaw*, 68; "A slave class": Hyndman, 397.

979 Hyndman, a Socialist from spite: White (*see* Chap. 5), I, 98.

980 Clemenceau, "a bourgeois class": q. Hyndman, 300.

980 "Eternal verities irritate him": Hunter, 120.

980 Keir Hardie: Hughes, *passim*; Brockway, 17–18.

981 "Well-fed beasts" and "Every day in Rotten Row": Hunter, 230.

981 "Religious necessity" and strikes as "outlet": Clynes, 83, 85.

982 "If Burns with 80,000 men": q. Webb, 23.

982 ILP's declared aims: Hughes, 66–67.

982 "Most costly funeral" and Garvin quoted: Hughes, 76.

983 Fabians, "not in our line": Edward Pease, q. Halévy, V, 263, n. 2.

984 "Imperfections of the Social Order": Aug. 23, 1902.

984 "Mr. Balfour, coming back from dinner": Parliamentary correspondent of the *Daily News*, q. Hughes, 113.

985 MacDonald-Gladstone secret pact: Mendelssohn, 322.

985 "Go the Tory way": Hughes, 69.

985 "Hideous abnormality": Willoughby de Broke, 249.

986 Burns congratulates C.-B.: Webb, 325; reminds Grey: q. Lucy Masterman, 112.

987 Balfour and Weizmann: Dugdale, I, chap. 19; Chaim Weizmann, *Trial and Error*, New York, 1949, chap. 8.

987 Friend saw him "seriously upset": Newton, *Retrospection*, 146–47.

PAGE

987 Balfour's letters on Election results: Letter to Knollys, q. in full in Lee, II, 449; others in Esher, II, 136; Young, 255.

988 "Like a second footman": Dugdale, II, 49.

988 Blatchford predicted: q. *The Times*, Jan. 19, 1906.

989 "*Never saying anything clever!*": Marsh, 150.

989 Categories of new M.P.'s: Jenkins, 7.

990 Few in "unconventional dress": Newton, *Retrospection*, 149; Irish members' bad manners: *ibid.*, 99.

990 C.-B. impervious to Balfour's charm: Birrell, 243.

991 "England is based on commerce": q. Gardiner, *Prophets*, 136.

992 "Bring the sledgehammer": Gardiner, *Prophets*, 54.

992 Took his own wife into dinner: Blunt, II, 300.

992 "No egotism, no vanity": q. Gardiner, *Pillars*, 122.

993 Churchill motivated by Mrs. Everest: *Roving Commission*, 73. All subsequent statements by Churchill, unless otherwise noted, are from Mendelssohn.

993 F. E. Smith: Gardiner, *Pillars*, 95–103; *Portraits*, 122–28.

995 Salisbury on coming clash of Lords and Commons: Margot Asquith, 157; H. H. Asquith, *Fifty Years*, I, 174.

995 Conservatives "should still control": *The Times*, Jan. 16, 1906.

996 Balfour warns Lansdowne: Newton, *Lansdowne*, 354.

996 "Something will happen": at Llanelly, Sept. 29, 1906, Lee, II, 456.

997 Curzon "so infinitely superior": Newton, *Retrospection*, 161.

997 Loreburn: Willoughby de Broke, 260; Curzon, *Subjects of the Day*, 228.

998 Rosebery, "eye like a fish": F. Ponsonby, 382.

998 Churchill, in the *Nation*: Mar. 9, 1907.

998 Balfour on "hereditary qualification": q. Young, 266.

999 "Portcullis" and "poodle": These phrases graced the debate on the Lords' rejection of the Licensing Bill, June 24, 1907.

1000 Morley recalled Gladstone saying: q. Esher, II, 303.

1001 "Backwoodsmen" meet at Lansdowne House: Willoughby de Broke, 246–47.

1001 Churchill "perfectly furious": Lucy Masterman, 114.

1002 Victor Grayson: Brockway, 24–25; Halévy, VI, 105.

1002 Kaiser's proposal to save England: Blunt, II, 210.

1003 King Edward on "hard times": q. Magnus, 417.

1003 Invasion psychosis: I. F. Clark, "The Shape of Wars to Come," *History Today*, Feb., 1965.

1003 Henry James, chimney pots: Jan. 8, 1909, *Letters*, ed. Percy Lubbock, New York, 1920, II, 121.

1003 Suffragettes: In addition to Pankhurst and Fulford, the list of Suffragette assaults is most conveniently found in successive volumes of the *Annual Register*. The Albert Hall meeting is quoted from Nevinson, *More Changes*, 321–25, as is also "Those *bipeds*!": 306.

1005 A gathering pessimism: Masterman, 84, 120, 289; Bryce, 15, 39, 228;

PAGE

Hobson and Hobhouse, q. C. H. Driver, “Political Ideas,” in Hearnshaw; Trotter described: *DNB*; quoted: 47; Wallas described: Wells, 509, 511; Cole, 222; quoted: 284–85.

1009 “Cantankerous and uncomfortable”: *DNB*, Lowther.

1009 “We all thought Papa would die”: Cooper, 11.

1010 The Limehouse speech: July 30, 1909. The King’s displeasure was expressed in a letter to Lord Crewe, q. in full, Pope-Hennessy, 72–73. Other reactions and comments chiefly from the *Annual Register*. Rosebery’s Glasgow speech in Crewe, 511–12; Kipling’s poem appeared in the *Morning Post*, June 28, 1909, and only once since, in the *Definitive Edition* of his Verse, London, Hodder & Stoughton, 1940. “Foolish and *mean* speeches”: q. Magnus, 431.

1011 “Now King, you have won the Derby”: Fitzroy, I, 379.

1011 Balfour and Salisbury on Finance Bill: Dugdale, II, 56; *Annual Register*, 1909, 118.

1012 Lords debate the Budget, *et seq.*: As the English love nothing so much as a political crisis, the literature on the Budget–Parliament Bill crisis is so extensive that it cannot be missed, or even avoided. In the recent publication of *Churchill As I Knew Him*, by Lady Violet Bonham-Carter, Asquith’s daughter, it is still going on. Every biography or autobiography of the principal figures involved and every political memoir of the period discuss it, the major sources being: Newton’s *Lansdowne*, Young’s *Balfour*, Spender’s *Asquith*, Lee’s *Edward VII*, Nicolson’s *George V*, Wilson-Fox’s *Halsbury*, Pope-Hennessy’s *Crewe*, Ronaldshay’s *Curzon*, Crewe’s *Rosebery*, Willoughby de Broke’s *Memoirs* and Roy Jenkins’ book on the whole affair, *Mr. Balfour’s Poodle*. The major parliamentary debates were quoted fully in *The Times* as well as verbatim in Hansard, and the big scenes were described at length and in detail in the daily and periodical press. For material in the following pages, therefore, references are given *only* for odd items whose source might be hard to locate.

1013 Haldane on public apathy: q. *Annual Register*, 245.

1013 Speaker Lowther on the Irish: Ullswater, II, 85; “sinister and powerful” and “direct, obvious”: Morley, II, 349–50.

1015 “Antique bantam”: from a poem by an admirer which appeared in the *Morning Post*, q. Pope-Hennessy, 123.

1016 Charwoman’s song: Sitwell, *Great Morning*, 57.

1016 “He kept things together somehow”: Sackville-West, 307.

1016 Laureate’s poem: Austin, II, 292.

1016 “Our glorified grocers”: Lucy Masterman, 200, told to her by Lloyd George.

1017 Asquith’s list: Spender, *Asquith*, I, Appendix.

1018 “We are in grim earnest”: *Grooves of Change*, 39.

1018 Transport strike, “it is revolution!” q. Halévy, VI, 456.

1019 Tom Mann imprisoned: Clynes, 154.

PAGE

1019 Even the heat was "splendid": Sir Edward Grey, *Twenty-Five Years*, London, 1925, I, 238.

1020 Lady Michelham's party: Williams, 192–93.

1020 "Your bloody palace": Birkenhead, 175.

1020 "The golden sovereigns": Cyril Connolly, reviewing Nowell-Smith, *The Sunday Times*, Oct. 18, 1964.

1020 Last horse-drawn bus and preponderance of motor-taxis: Somervell, 28; Nowell-Smith, 122.

1021 Hugh Cecil: Churchill, 201; also Churchill's *Amid These Storms*, New York, 1932, 55; also Gardiner, *Pillars*, 39.

1022 The Cecil scene: besides accounts in the daily press there are illustrations of the scene in *Punch*, Aug. 2 and 16; and *Illus. London News*, July 29.

1024 "Disorderly assembly," for the first time: *The Times*, parl. corres., July 25, 1911.

1026 Of six peers at dinner, none had made up his mind: Midleton, 275.

1027 "You've forgotten the Parliament Bill": Christopher Hassall, *Edward Marsh*, London, 1959, 173–74.

1027 "A real danger" and chagrined peer: Newton, *Retrospection*, 187.

1029 Balfour, "nothing but politicians": q. Young, 315.

1029 Asquith's tribute: Guildhall speech, Nov. 9, *Fifty Years*, II, 129–31.

1029 Wyndham, "ice age": Blunt, II, 339.

8. The Death of Jaurès

Bibliography

BALABANOFF, ANGELICA, *My Life as a Rebel*, New York, Harper, 1938.

BEER, MAX, *The General History of Socialism and Social Struggles*, Vol. II, New York, Russell & Russell, 1957.

BERNSTEIN, EDOUARD, *My Years of Exile*, New York, Harcourt, 1921.

BRAUNTHAL, JULIUS, *In Search of the Millennium*, London, Gollancz, 1945.

COLE, G. D. H., *A History of Socialist Thought*, Vol. III, *The Second International, 1889–1914*, Parts I and II, London, Macmillan, 1956.

COLEMAN, MCALISTER, *Eugene V. Debs*, New York, Greenberg, 1930.

DELEON, DANIEL, *Flashlights of the Amsterdam Congress*, New York, Labor News, 1929.

DESMOND, SHAW, *The Edwardian Story*, London, Rockliff, 1949.

DULLES, FOSTER RHEA, *Labor in America*, New York, Crowell, 1960.

(L'EGLANTINE), *Jean Jaurès; feuilles eparses*, Brussels, l'Eglantine, 1924.

FISCHER, LOUIS, *The Life of Lenin*, New York, Harper, 1964.

FYFE, HAMILTON, *Keir Hardie*, London, Duckworth, 1935.

GAY, PETER, *The Dilemma of Democratic Socialism: Bernstein's Challenge to Marx*, New York, Collier, 1962.

GINGER, Ray, *The Bending Cross: A Biography of Eugene Debs*, Rutgers Univ. Press, 1949.

*GOLDBERG, HARVEY, *The Life of Jean Jaurès*, Univ. of Wisconsin Press, 1962.

GOMPERS, SAMUEL, *Labour in Europe and America*, New York, Harper, 1910. (For autobiography, *see* Chap. 3.)

HARVEY, ROWLAND HILL, *Samuel Gompers*, Stanford Univ. Press, 1935.

HENDERSON, ARCHIBALD, *Bernard Shaw*, New York, Appleton, 1932.

HILLQUIT, MORRIS, *Loose Leaves from a Busy Life*, New York, Macmillan, 1934.

*HUNTER, ROBERT, *Socialists at Work*, New York, Macmillan, 1908.

INTERNATIONAL SOCIALIST CONGRESS, *Proceedings*; published variously. Nos. 1, 1889, Paris, and 3, 1893, Zurich, are in German, entitled *Protokoll*. No. 4, 1896, London, is in English; Nos. 2 and 5–8 are in French, entitled *Compte rendu analytique*. No. 5 was published by the *Cahiers de la Quinzaine*, Paris, 1901.

JAURÈS, JEAN, *Bernstein et l'évolution de la méthode socialiste* (text of lecture delivered to Socialist Student Conference, February 10,

1900. Erroneously dated 1910). Paris, Socialist Party pamphlet, 1926.

JOLL, JAMES, *The Second International, 1889–1914*, London, Weidenfeld, 1955.

KLEENE, G. A., "Bernstein vs. 'Old-School' Marxism," *Annals of Am. Academy*, November, 1901, 1–29.

KRUPSKAYA, NADEZHDA K., *Memories of Lenin*, 2 vols., tr., New York, International, 1930.

LORWIN, LEWIS, L., *Labor and Internationalism*, New York, Brookings, 1929.

———, *The International Labor Movement*, revised ed. of the above, New York, Harper, 1953.

MANN, TOM, *Memoirs*, London, Labour Publishing Co., 1923.

ORTH, SAMUEL P., *Socialism and Democracy in Europe*, New York, Holt, 1913.

ROSENBERG, ARTHUR, *The Birth of the German Republic, 1871–1918*, New York, Russell & Russell, 1962.

SCHORSKE, CARL E., *German Social Democracy, 1905–17*, Harvard Univ. Press, 1955.

STEWART, WILLIAM, *J. Keir Hardie*, London, ILP, 1921.

SUAREZ, GEORGES, *Briand, sa vie, son œuvre*, Vols. I and II, Paris, Plon, 1938.

TROTSKY, LEON, *My Life*, New York, Scribner's, 1930.

*VANDERVELDE EMILE, *Souvenirs d'un militant socialiste*, Paris, Denoël, 1939.

VAYO, JULIO ALVAREZ DEL, *The Last Optimist*, New York, Viking, 1950.

Notes

Unless otherwise stated all quotations by Jaurès are from Goldberg, by Debs from Ginger, by Bernstein from Gay, by Gompers, in the case of biographical facts, from his autobiography, and in the case of comments on European labour, from his *Labour in Europe and America*; by Vandervelde, DeLeon and others, following the principle already established, from their own works.

PAGE

1033 In "almost religious silence": Hunter, 319.

1034 Vienna "paralyzed with fright": Zweig (*see* Chap. 6), 61; Braunthal, 56.

1035 Comments on Markham's poem: Sullivan (*see* Chap. 3), II, 236–47.

1035 Clemenceau on Fourmies: Alexandre Zevaès, *Histoire de la 3me République*, Paris, 1926, 342.

1035 Taft on the Pullman strike: *DAB*, Taft.

1036 Marxists accused the French Possibilists: Joll, 33.

1037 "Don't delay the revolution!": Bülow (*see* Chap. 5), I, 672. Miquel in later life became a Conservative and Minister of Finance, 1890–1900.

1037 "Nothing if not revolution": DeLeon, 192.

1038 Applause for Pablo Iglesias: Hyndman, 396.

1038 Cipriani described: Vandervelde, 44.

1039 Hunter on the Valley of the Tirano: in *Socialists at Work*, 55.

1039 "Damned wantlessness of the poor": The phrase was circulating at the time without a clear claim as to authorship. Minus the adjective it appeared anonymously in a Fabian Tract of 1884, *Why Are the Many Poor?*, and has been ascribed by Professor Gay in his book on Bernstein to William Morris. As *Verdammte Bedürfnislosigkeit* it was quoted by Shaw in his Preface to *Major Barbara*, without attribution but suggesting a German origin. Although some German scholars are reluctant to specify an origin, the attribution to Lassalle is made on the authority of George Lichtheim in a letter to the author.

1040 English pamphlet on Congress of 1896: Walter Crane, *Cartoons for the Cause, 1886–96*, London, 1896.

1042 Zurich Congress: Vandervelde, 144.

1043 Shaw on Liebknecht: Henderson, 220.

1043 Kaiser on the Socialists: Michael Balfour, *The Kaiser and His Times*, London, 1964, 159.

1043 "By Balfour to the Primrose League": Joll, 76.

1044 "General Strike is general nonsense": *ibid.*, 53, n. 2.

1044 May Day in Munich: Krupskaya, I, 67.

1044 Bebel a "shadow-Kaiser": Rosenberg, 44.

1045 Mommsen on Bebel: Hunter, 227; "savage accents": *ibid.*, 226; "deadly enemy": q. Pinson, 212; "Look at those fellows": Chirol (*see* Chap. 5), 274.

1045 Adler characteristics: Braunthal, Trotsky, Balabanoff, Joll, 38; "Despotism mitigated by slovenliness": Braunthal, 52.

PAGE

1046 “More profound than doctrine”: Hunter, 134.

1046 Vandervelde “gushed” over: Balabanoff, 15.

1047 “Firmly and recklessly”: Vandervelde, 46.

1047 “Torquemada in eyeglasses”: Nomad, *Rebels* (*see* Chap. 2), 65.

1048 “What will we Socialists do . . . ?”: Goldberg, 226.

1048 Jaurès, “Jubilant and humorous”: Hyndman, 398; “His shoulders trembled” and discussed astronomy at dinner party: Severine, in *l’Eglantine*, 7–8; “Thinks with his beard”: Clermont-Tonnerre (*see* Chap. 4), II, 251.

1049 Vaillant on Jaurès: Hunter, 79.

1050 Clemenceau, “all the verbs”: Roman (*see* Chap. 4), 91.

1051 The London Congress: Vandervelde, 145.

1052 Army Colonel in a Chicago club: Ginger, 139.

1052 Injunction advised by Grosscup and Wood: Allan Nevins, *Grover Cleveland*, New York, 1932, 618.

1053 Roosevelt on “shooting”: Pringle (*see* Chap. 3), 164.

1053 Theodore Debs’s gold watch: Coleman, 201.

1054 “Almost grotesque”: Hillquit, 93.

1054 “Give ’em hell, Sam”: Harvey.

1055 “These middle class issues”: q. Dulles, 181.

1055 “I am a working man”: Hillquit, 95.

1059 “I confess openly . . .”: Braunthal, 91; Gay, 74.

1060 It was said of Adler: DeLeon, 37; his letter to Bernstein: Braunthal, 100.

1060 “Tall, thin, desiccated” and “Down with Liebknecht!”: Goldberg, 262.

1061 Erhard Auer’s regret: DeLeon, 66–67.

1063 Knee-breeches debate at Dresden: Gay, 232, n. 39.

1063 Rosa Luxemburg: Balabanoff, 22; Vayo, 61.

1064 Georg Ledebour’s estimate: Trotsky, 215.

1064 Dresden Resolution: Pinson, 215–16.

1064 “*Weltpolitik* without war”: *ibid.*, 214.

1066 Amsterdam Congress: Vandervelde, 152–62; DeLeon, *passim.*

1068 Bebel would shoulder a rifle: Vandervelde, 161.

1069 Izvolsky on Briand and Viviani: Goldberg, 455.

1069 “Fiendish massacre”: Clynes, 103.

1069 Italians hail Russian Revolution: Balabanoff, 54.

1069 Austrian suffrage strike: Braunthal, 64–68.

1072 “Property, property, property”: q. Goldberg, 363.

1073 Debs’s letter of December, 1904: Coleman, 227–28.

1073 “Bundle of primitive instincts”: q. Dulles, 211.

1074 “Slowly plowed its way”: Ernest Poole, q. Ginger, 281.

1075 Mannheim Congress: Schorske, 56.

1076 Noske’s speech in Reichstag: Pinson, 215.

1077 Hervé; “We shall reply . . .”: D. W. Brogan, *France Under the Republic*, 429.

PAGE
1078 "At every railroad station": M. Auclair, *La Vie de Jean Jaurès*, q. Goldberg, 381.
1079 Hatfield visit: Vandervelde, in *l'Eglantine*, 38–40.
1079 Mussolini described: Desmond, 207.
1079 Police in balloons over Stuttgart: *The Times*, Aug. 19 and 20, 1907.
1080 Quelch incident: Balabanoff, 82; Trotsky, 205.
1080 Georg von Vollmar quoted: Pinson, 215–16.
1081 Clemenceau on Jaurès' fate: in *l'Homme Libre*, Aug. 2, 1914.
1081 "Infuriated" workers would rise: Braunthal, 106.
1082 "Do not fool yourselves": Desmond, 206.
1082 Jaurès at Tübingen: Vandervelde, 167.
1082 "That's Lenin": q. Fischer, 58.
1082 Lenin's parleys with Bebel: Supplied to the author by Louis Fischer from Lenin's "The International Socialist Congress at Stuttgart," *Works*, 5th ed., Moscow, 1961, XVI, 67–74, 514–15.
1082 Stuttgart Resolution: Beer, II, 156.
1084 *Arbeiter-Zeitung* of Vienna: q. Trotsky, 211.
1084 Blatchford and Hyndman for conscription: Halévy (*see* Chap. 1), VI, 395.
1084 Hardie believed "absolutely": Clynes, 25.
1086 "Ripe sonority": report in *Le Peuple*, q. Vandervelde, 170.
1086 8,000,000 Socialist voters: *The Times*, Aug. 31, 1910.
1086 Hardie at Copenhagen: Cole, 83–84; Hughes, 197–98; Stewart, 302.
1087 ITF and Boer War: Information supplied by K. A. Golding, Research Secretary, ITF, London.
1088 ITF strike of 1911: Prior discussion of the strike at Copenhagen in 1910 from *The Times*, Aug. 25–29. Subsequent developments from Mr. Golding.
1089 German Socialism appeared "irresistible": Braunthal, 46.
1089 Scheidemann debate: *The Times*, Feb. 19, Mar. 9, 1912.
1090 "We revolutionaries?": Trotsky, 213.
1091 Basle Cathedral, "dangerous" consequences: *Annual Register*, 1912, 367.
1091 Jaurès' speech: Joll, 155.
1092 A survey of French student life: *Les Jeunes Gens d'Aujourd'hui*, q. Wolff (*see* Chap. 5), 275.
1093 "If these were my last words": Brockway, 39.
1093 *Vorwärts* on Austrian ultimatum: Vayo, 78.
1094 "We relied on Jaurès": Zweig (*see* Chap. 6), 199.
1094 Jouhaux's proposal to Legien: Joll, 162.
1094 *La Bataille Syndicaliste*: *ibid.*, 161.
1094 Brussels Conference: Balabanoff, 4, 114–18; Vandervelde, 171; Stewart, 340; Joll, 164.
1095 Hardie, "Only the binding together": Fyfe, 136.
1095 Jean Longuet quoted: Goldberg, 467.
1096 Bethmann-Hollweg: Joll, 167.

PAGE

1096 Jaurès' death: *Humanité*, *Figaro*, *Echo de Paris*, Aug. 1/2.

1097 Spanish Socialist in Leipzig: Vayo, 81.

1097 Bernstein, "golden bridge": Hans Peter Hanssen, *Diary of a Dying Empire*, Indiana Univ. Press, 1955, 15.

1097 Kaiser, Deschanel, Jouhaux: *The Times*, *Echo de Paris*, Aug. 5.

Afterword

1099 Graham Wallas: Preface to 3rd ed. of *Human Nature in Politics*, 1921.

1099 Emile Verhaeren: *La Belgique sanglante*, Paris, 1915, *Dédicace*, unpaged.

Overleaf:
August 1914 (collection unknown)

APPENDIX

How We Entered World War I

On April 2, 1917, the United States as a new contender entered the tournament of world power from which we have not since, despite wishful attempts, been able to withdraw. Up to then, notwithstanding our hearty belligerence in the Spanish American War, we were not regarded as one of the Great Powers, either by them or, on the whole, by ourselves. American participation in the Great War was the beginning of our majority in world affairs.

In the half-century that has since elapsed, a fundamental shift of the international balance has taken place, with the sites of power spreading outward from Europe to the periphery. The governing seat vacated by the collapse of Britain has been taken—not without kicking and protesting against our fate—by this country. Risen from newcomer to one of the world's two dominant powers in fifty years, we are once again at war, no longer fresh and untrained but an old hand, skilled, practiced, massively equipped, sophisticated in method, yet infirm of purpose, and without a goal that anyone can define. Is this the destiny to which that first experience has led us? How did the United States become involved and had she a choice? "God helping her," said President Wilson on that April 2 fifty years ago, "she can do no other." Could we have done other?

The Great War has never been for us so embedded a part of our national tradition as the Civil War or World War II. It is somehow less "ours." The average person thinks of it in terms of air aces who flew in open cockpits, a place called Château-Thierry, a song called "Over There," a form of transport called "40 and 8," and a soldier in leggings who became President Truman—but what it means in our history he could not easily say. When this writer in 1955 proposed to a prospective publisher a book on the Zimmermann telegram, a major factor in precipitating America's involvement, the advice received was to abandon the idea because it was the "wrong war"; the public was interested only in the Civil and the Second. This was in fact a justifiable assessment, much the same as that reached by a historian in 1930 who, a decade after the end of the war, found the American people still "irritated and bewildered" by it.

These words, which describe so aptly our attitude toward the war in Vietnam, establish a link between the two experiences. The first experience was governed by an old illusion, and the present experience by a new one. World War II, on the other hand, with the imperative of Pearl Harbor supplying an understood cause and purpose, did not sow doubt and self-mistrust. It was clear why we had got in and what was the end in view. But as will certainly be the case with Vietnam, so for twenty years after World War I historical controversy raged over how and why we got into it, and the question is still being probed and re-examined.

The revisionists of the 1920s and '30s, fueled by post-war disillusion, discarded the accepted view of our involvement as the unavoidable consequence of German aggression toward neutral shipping, in favor of conspiracy theories of one kind or another. They discovered the causative factor in British propaganda, capitalist profit, and other concealed and sinister forces. Burrowing into statistics of trade and finance, private correspondence, and all manner of inner workings, the revisionists brought to light much significant material and fresh insights. But their self-accusatory thesis required a compensatory leaning-over-backward in favor of Germany, and just as they were most vigorously making their case, Germany, returning to the offensive under Hitler, unmade it for them.

Since then, as is the circular fashion of history, counter-revision is leading the way back to what was obvious at the start. The somersaults of revisionists—whether it be that Roosevelt plotted Pearl Harbor or that the Third Reich, as held by England's antic historian A. J. P. Taylor, was pushed into aggression by the democracies—enjoy the notoriety of the sensational, but the facts roll over them in the end.

On the outbreak of war in 1914 the prevailing American attitude was one of self-congratulation that it was none of our affair; and there was a fixed intention that it should not become so. In classic summary—appropriately from a small town in the heart of the Midwest—the *Plain Dealer* of Wabash, Indiana, stated: "We never appreciated so keenly as now the foresight of our fathers in emigrating from Europe." Newspaper cartoons habitually depicted Uncle Sam separated by a large body of water from a far-off, furiously squabbling group of little figures, in one case reminding himself that the chance of his life was to "sit tight, keep his hands in his pockets and his mouth shut"; in another case standing shoulder to shoulder with President Wilson with backs firmly turned on Europe's gore-dripping "barbarians."

The belief in our safe isolation was reinforced by Wilson, who, bent on pursuing the New Freedom through domestic reform, was irritated by the threatened interference with his program from overseas. He declared in December 1914 that the country should not let itself be "thrown off balance" by a war "with which we have nothing to do, whose causes cannot touch us." (The familiar ring can be traced to a more famous echo twenty-five years later in Neville Chamberlain's reference to Czechoslovakia as "a far-away country of which we know nothing.")

For Wilson it was justifiable in August 1914 to ask the American people to be "impartial in thought as well as in action . . . neutral in fact as well as name." But by December, when the expectation of a short war had vanished at the Marne and the armies were locked in the deadly stalemate of the trenches, the war was already touching us. Forced to recognize that American business could not be held immobile, Wilson had already in October reversed his earlier ban on loans to belligerents. This was the foundation for the economic tie which thereafter in ever-increasing strength and volume attached the United States to the Allies. By permitting extension of commercial credit it enabled the Allies to buy supplies in America from which the Central Powers, by virtue of Allied control of the seas, were largely cut off. It opened an explosive expansion in American manufacture, trade, and foreign investments and bent the national economy to the same side in the war as prevailing popular sentiment.

For the country on the whole was as pro-Allied in sympathy as it was anti-belligerent in wish. The President shared the sentiment. "I found him," wrote Colonel House after the first month of war, "as unsympathetic with the German attitude as is the balance of the country." Counselor Von Haniel of the German Embassy in Washington, trying to disabuse his principals of certain illusions, reminded them that American feeling was the outgrowth of a natural connection with England "in history, blood, speech, society, finance, culture," and that "in the present case commercial instinct and sentiment point in the same direction." He had hit upon the essence of the situation.

At the same time as he lifted the ban on loans, Wilson agreed to permit unrestricted trade in munitions, contrary to an earlier proposal for their embargo. The two measures were not taken in the Allied interest (although they were to work to the Allies' advantage) but in the American interest—for the Administration, no less than Von Haniel, knew the strength of the country's "commercial instinct" and feared that an embargo would turn Allied orders to Canada, Australia, and Argentina. To ban loans and embargo munitions would have been to give realistic expression to the isolation that the people and their President believed they enjoyed. But it would have closed off the wealth of unlimited orders, and Americans did not wish to suffer for their neutrality. Rather they hoped to make a good thing of it. With these two economic measures taken before the war was three months old, the fact, if not the illusion, of isolation was dead.

In February 1915 Germany declared a submarine blockade of Britain, to be carried out by a policy of "unrestricted" undersea warfare, which meant attack without warning on merchant ships found in the war zone. As a violation of traditional neutral rights to freedom of the seas, this was, said Wilson, outraged, "an extraordinary threat to destroy commerce." An American President was obliged to resist it even though a quarrel would heighten the risk of involvement. Quarrels with the British were continuous over their incursions on freedom of the seas in the form of the Declaration of London, the doctrine of continuous voyage, elaboration of contraband, the right of search, Prize Court procedures, and other annoyances which together added up to that old conflict between the belligerent's right to blockade and the neutral's right to trade. But Britain's measures, however infuriating to legalists of the State Department, did not threaten life or touch the public mind or seriously hamper the flow of goods, of which by far the major share was directed to the Allies in any case.

By contrast, acquiescence in the role claimed for the U-boat would have meant the end of overseas trade. The explicit threat to neutral civilian lives meant either that Americans must stay off the public highway of the ocean or the American government must exert enough pressure, without tipping the precarious balance of neutrality into open rupture, to make the Germans draw back. Either way, with this development, the war had not only touched but entangled us.

During the next two years German activities on the seas, in Belgium, and in the plots of spies and saboteurs in the United States operated relentlessly to weaken American neutrality, with results that would have been the same with or without Allied propaganda.

Germany's violation of Belgium's guaranteed neutrality, the opening act of the war, had aroused American indignation and put Germany in the wrong from the start. It established the image of bully in the public mind. This was no sudden reversal, for the image of the kindly German professor personified by Dr. Bhaer, who married Jo in *Little Women*, had long since given way, under the influence of Wilhelmine Germany, to the arrogant Prussian officer. Initial American indignation would doubtless have subsided into indifference if, before the first month was out, it had not been re-excited and confirmed by the burning of Louvain and its ancient library. The horror engendered by this act was profound, for the time, it must be remembered, was on the far side of the gulf of 1914–18, when people permitted themselves simple and sentimental reactions and society was believed to be advancing in moral progress.

With the American Minister to Belgium, Brand Whitlock, former reform mayor of Toledo, remaining in Brussels in constant contact between the occupying power and the population, Americans felt a particular concern for Belgium's misfortunes, from the shooting of hostages to the developing starvation that evoked the Hoover Relief Commission. The Bryce Report on atrocities issued by England and signed, not by accident, by the Englishman best known to the United States, the former Ambassador to Washington and author of *The American Commonwealth*, fell on prepared ground. It gave rise to many exaggerated atrocity stories, but it was not British propaganda that staged the trial and execution of Edith Cavell. This shooting of a woman, a nurse, a humanitarian, accomplished with the unfailing German affinity for the act that would most successfully outrage world opinion, sealed the concept of the Hun.

Above all, the mass deportations, begun in 1916, of ultimately three hundred thousand Belgians to forced labor inside Germany aroused more anger than anything since the *Lusitania*. Whether or not because of sensitivity on the subject of slavery, Americans—at least of that day—found something peculiarly shocking about citizens of a white Western nation being carried off to forced labor. The revulsion, reported Von Haniel, "is general, deep-rooted and genuine."

The sinking in May 1915 of the Cunard Line's *Lusitania*, which carried, in addition to a full complement of non-combatant passengers, a part-cargo of small-arms ammunition, besides enhancing German "frightfulness," had brought to a head the issue of submarine warfare. Regarded by the Germans as a munitions carrier using its non-combatant status as protection, the ship was sunk without warning; that is, without ordering passengers off in lifeboats before loosing the torpedo. Of the nearly 2,000 persons aboard, 1,195 were lost, including 124 Americans. In the previous week two American ships had been attacked with two American deaths.

Thus the rights of both neutrals and non-combatants were at stake. Tense and protracted negotiations followed in which Wilson's almost impossible task was to force Germany to acknowledge these rights without the ultimate threat of war, which was the last thing he wanted. He had to pick his way along a narrow ridge between the precipice of war on one side and that of abdication of neutral rights, as advocated by his Secretary of State, William Jennings Bryan, on the other. Representing the pacifist position that no interest was worth defending at the risk of war, Bryan became spokesman of the demand that Americans be warned not to (or, as some insisted, forbidden to) travel on belligerent ships.

In this demand was crystalized a central issue that transcended the matter of American trade or neutral rights. The real issue was our position as a great power. The United States could not allow the U-boats to keep her nationals off the sea lanes without forfeiting the respect of other nations, the confidence of her own citizens, and her prestige before the world. She could not forbid her own people to exercise their rights, Wilson wrote to Senator Stone, chairman of the Foreign Relations Committee and a leading isolationist, "without conceding her own impotence as a nation." This was the crux, the more so as to concede impotence now would undercut the ambition which the President already had in mind: to mediate the war and save the world from its own wickedness.

Wilson rejected the proposal to keep American citizens off belligerent ships as a gesture "both weak and futile" which, by revealing the United States' posture to be one of "uneasiness and hedging," would "weaken our whole position fatally." Bryan, finding his insistent and reiterated advice as Secretary of State overridden, accordingly resigned to become thereafter a trumpeting voice of the pacifist wing. While his going relieved Washington's diplomatic dinners from the temperance of grape juice, imposed by the Secretary's edict, it hardly eased matters for Wilson, who had still to make good his stand against the submarine without going to war. The pressure of the dilemma brought forth those memorable words: "There is such a thing as a nation being so right that it does not need to convince others by force that it is right. . . . There is such a thing as a man being too proud to fight."

Although the speech aroused tirades of disgust by the interventionists at Wilson's "poltroonery," it reasserted the strength of the "sit-tight" sentiment in the nation which the *Lusitania* had so nearly dissipated.

Wilson, in note after note to Berlin, fencing, countering, reiterating, rejecting, ultimately won his point. After another ship crisis over the sinking of the *Arabic* in August 1915, with the loss of forty-four lives, including two Americans, he extracted a German promise not to sink without warning. But the whole issue was revived again by the sinking of the *Ancona* in November and the *Sussex* in March 1916, and was only resolved by Germany's renewal of her promise upon the President's notice that without it the United States would have no recourse but to sever relations. In fact, this result was due less to Wilson's firmness than to Germany's recognition that she had too few submarines to sink enough shipping to make the risk of American belligerency worthwhile. Her shipyards meanwhile worked round the clock to correct that inadequacy.

Each time during these months when the torpedo streaked its fatal track, the isolationist cry to keep Americans out of the war zones redoubled. When a resolution to that effect was introduced in Congress by Senator Gore of Oklahoma and Representative McLemore of Texas in February 1916, Champ Clark of Missouri, Speaker of the House, led a delegation to the White House to inform Wilson that it would pass two to one. After absorbing four and a half million words of debate, it was, however, ultimately tabled, although not without 175 votes in its favor.

As the war lengthened and hates and sufferings increased, with repercussions across the Atlantic, American public opinion lost its early comfortable cohesion. The hawks and doves of 1916, equivalent to the interventionists and isolationists of the 1930s, were the preparedness advocates and the pacifists, with the great mass of people in between still stolidly, though not fanatically, opposed to involvement.

The equivalency to the present, however, is inexact because of the sharp ideological reversal in our history that took place after 1945. The attitude of the American people toward foreign conflict in the twentieth century has been divided between those who regard the enemy or potential enemy as a threat to American interests and way of life and are therefore interventionists, and those who recognize no such danger and therefore wish us to stay at home and mind our own business. Who belongs to which group is decided by the nature of the enemy. When, as in the years before 1945, the enemy was on the right, our interventionists by and large came from the left. When, as in the years since 1945 the Soviet Union and Communist China replaced the right-wing powers of Germany and Japan as our opponents, American factions switched roles in response. The right has become interventionist and the left isolationist. Former advocates of America First, who used to shriek against engagement outside our frontiers, are now hawks calling for more and bigger intervention (otherwise escalation). Former interventionists who once could not wait to fight the Fascists now find themselves doves in the unaccustomed role of isolationists. It is this regrouping which has made most people over twenty-five so uncomfortable.

In 1916 ideologies of right and left were less determining. The most vigorously anti-German interventionists came from the upper and educated classes especially on the East Coast, where Prussian militarism (the term then in use) was regarded as the ultimate foe of democracy which could not be allowed to triumph. President Emeritus Eliot of Harvard, "the topmost oak of New England," declared the defeat of the Central Powers to be "the only tolerable result of this outrageous war." Chief Justice White of the Supreme Court said, "If I were thirty years younger, I would go to Canada to enlist."

Distinguished clergymen like Henry Van Dyke and Lyman Abbott felt no less warmly, and the president of the American Historical Association, William Roscoe Thayer, announced in response to Wilson's original advice to be impartial in thought, that only a "moral eunuch" could be neutral in the sense implied by the "malefic dictum" of the President. The new Secretary of State, Robert Lansing, was convinced that a German victory "would mean the overthrow of democracy in the world" by the forces of military despotism, an opinion shared by his Republican predecessor, Elihu Root, not to mention by the President's closest adviser, Colonel House, and his bitterest despiser, ex-President Theodore Roosevelt.

The opinions of the articulate East, however, were more influential than representative. The rest of the country, with its center of gravity a thousand miles from any ocean, still bore the stamp "Keep out of it." Isolationism naturally centered in, although was not confined to, the largely Republican Midwest, with its "hyphenated" settlements of German-Americans in Milwaukee, Chicago, St. Louis, and other cities, its Populist traditions, and its agrarian radicals called sons-of-the-wild-jackass. The home states of congressional isolationist leaders tell the tale: Speaker Champ Clark and Senator Stone of Missouri, Senators Hitchcock and Norris of Nebraska, La Follette of Wisconsin, Gore of Oklahoma, and, from the South, Vardaman of Mississippi and Representative Claude Kitchin, chairman of the Ways and Means Committee, from North Carolina.

Ideological divisions cut across the geographical. Progressives and Socialists, though hating the autocracies, were largely (though by no means all) isolationist, partly because they did not want war to interfere with domestic reform and partly from inherited dislike of Europe. They shunned foreign entanglements with the Old World from whose quarrels and standing armies and reactionary regimes their fathers had escaped to the promise of America. Regardless of background or position, they all joined in one dominant argument: Sentiment for war was manufactured for profit by bankers and businessmen. David Starr Jordan, pacifist president of Stanford, pictured Uncle Sam "throwing his money with Morgan & Co. into the bottomless pit of war," La Follette denounced profiteers as the real promoters of preparedness, and Eugene Debs, leader of the Socialist party, declared he would rather be shot as a traitor than "go to war for Wall Street."

Foreseeing that we might, and believing that we should, enter the war, pro-Allied groups opened a preparedness campaign in 1915. Supported by the Army and Navy Leagues, they formed committees for national security and American rights, organized parades, distributed books, films, and leaflets identifying preparedness with patriotism, introduced a bill in Congress to expand the Reserve into a continental army of 400,000, and called for a congressional appropriation of $500 million to build an "adequate Navy." As the agitation mounted, vociferously led by Theodore Roosevelt, the administration forces took alarm lest in resisting it, in a diehard grip on neutrality, they allow a partisan issue to develop in which the Republicans would become the party of patriotism and the Democrats be identified with "weakness."

Wilson accordingly embraced preparedness, marched straw-hatted in parades, supported the Army Bill for increasing the Regulars from 80,000 to 140,000 and the Reserves to 400,000, and approved a five-year program of naval construction to provide 10 battleships, 16 cruisers, 50 destroyers, and 100 submarines. He undertook a speaking tour through the Midwest on behalf of the Army Bill, but failed to persuade the hard core of isolationists of the need for adequate armed forces. This outcome was not surprising since he balanced every eloquent plea to prepare "not for war but for adequate national defense" with an equally eloquent avowal of his and the country's "deep-seated passion for peace."

In the spring of 1916 debate raged in Congress and country over the Army Bill. Progressives thundered against militarism as the spawn of capitalist greed and the destroyer of the American dream. Interventionists insisted America must join in the battle of the democracies against tyranny (a cause embarrassed by the inconvenient alliance of the Czar) if political freedom was to survive anywhere. Preparedness parades grew louder and longer, a mammoth example on Fifth Avenue lasting twelve hours with 125,000 civilian men and women marchers, two hundred brass bands and fifty drum corps, thousands of cheering observers on the sidewalks, and floodlights on the last squadrons as they marched on into the night. Impervious, a majority of Republican Representatives in the House voted to warn American citizens off armed merchant ships, indicating their firm preference for discretion over neutral rights.

A stunning and unexpected testimony to the depth of pacifist feeling emerged at the Democratic convention at St. Louis in June. Wilson's managers had planned to make patriotism the theme, with bands concentrating on the national anthem instead of "Dixie" and bursts of "spontaneous" enthusiasm for the flag. These demonstrations proved uninspired, but the keynote speech of ex-Governor Martin Glynn of New York, which argued that the American tradition was to stay out of war whatever the provocation, produced a frenzied outburst and a "delirium of delight." Designed to appeal to the peace sentiment, it had been approved in advance by the President, who, no less than any other practicing politician in search of re-election, was interested in consensus. As Glynn cited each historical precedent, his audience took up the chant, "What did we do? What did we do?" and the speaker roared in reply, "We did not go to war!" Delegates cheered, waved flags, jumped on their seats. When Glynn, becoming somewhat dismayed at what he had aroused, tried to slide over his prepared text, they yelled, "No! No! Go on! Give us more! More! More!" They danced about the aisles, "half mad with joy . . . shouting like schoolboys and screaming like steam sirens."

Glynn had shown that pacifism, instead of being something not quite manly, was right, patriotic, and American. The effect was "simply electrifying." Convention leaders were appalled. Chairman McCombs hastily scribbled on a sheet of paper, "But we are willing to fight if necessary," signed his name, and passed it to Glynn, who nodded and called back, "I'll take care of that." But by now fascinated with his own effect on the crowd, he never did. Political plans were deranged. Wilson's campaign was revised to make peace the main issue; the Republicans, repudiating Roosevelt, nominated Hughes on a platform of "straight and honest neutrality" and lost in November to the slogan promoted by Wilson's managers, "He kept us out of war."

It was this use of the peace sentiment which accomplished the close victory through a notably sectional vote of the Western states in new alliance with the South. It enabled Wilson to recover for the Democratic party what Bryan had three times failed to win, the support of the majority of predominantly agricultural states.

The final four months leading up to U.S. belligerency began with Wilson's concerted effort through December and January to end the war through mediation. His concept of a "peace without victory," although called by Senator La Follette "the greatest message of the century," did not appeal to the belligerents. Since neither side wanted the American President to arrange the terms of a settlement and each was bent on total victory, Wilson's attempt to negotiate a peace failed.

In the meantime Germany, having built up a fleet of two hundred submarines, took the decision to risk American hostility for the sake of an all-out effort to end the war her way. On January 31, 1917, she formally notified Washington of intent to resume unrestricted submarine warfare beginning next day. All neutral ships would be "forcibly prevented" from reaching England. A single exception in the form of one U.S. passenger ship a week would be allowed provided that it carry no contraband, dock only at Falmouth and only on a Sunday, be marked by three vertical stripes each a meter wide painted alternately white and red, and fly at each mast a large flag checkered white and red.

At the prospect of funnels "striped like a barber's pole and a flag like a kitchen tablecloth," the American historian J. B. McMaster could hardly contain his indignation. The insult implied in such orders addressed to the major neutral indicated that Germany had no doubts of America's answer. "We are counting on the probability of war with the United States," Field Marshal von Hindenburg had said at Supreme Headquarters when the decision was taken, but "things cannot be worse than they are now. The war must be brought to an end by whatever means as soon as possible." Headquarters had convinced itself that in the time before the submarine could knock out the Allies, American military assistance would "amount to nothing." But the civilian Chancellor Bethmann-Hollweg believed the entry of America meant "*finis Germaniae*."

In the vortex of the conflict, America had become, willing or not, a major power: as arsenal and bank of the Allies, to whose cause our economy no less than our political system was now attached, and as obstacle, so long as we continued to supply the Allies, to any German hope of victory. To yield freedom of the seas now after two years' hard-fought maintenance of the principle was incompatible with first-class status. Wilson was left with no choice but to declare the long-avoided rupture of relations. At once pacifist groups were roused to feverish action in mass meetings to demand that American ships stay out of war zones, while interventionists agitated equally loudly for the arming of our ships and the aggressive assertion of American rights.

As ships piled up in home ports, American commerce threatened to come to a standstill affecting the entire national economy. The Cabinet grew seriously alarmed. Although Wilson possessed the executive authority to arm ships, he was reluctant to take the step that would inevitably start the shooting. He preferred to ask Congress for authorization, thus touching off the great debate and filibuster on the Armed Ship Bill. In the midst of it came the revelation of the telegram from German Foreign Minister Arthur Zimmermann inviting Mexico into alliance as a belligerent. As a scheme to keep U.S. forces occupied on their own border, it offered to help Mexico regain her lost territories of Texas, Arizona, and New Mexico. Intercepted and decoded by British naval intelligence and made available to this country, the telegram was released to the press on March 1 in the hope of influencing "the little band of willful men" in the Senate. It failed of that purpose, but aroused the American public more than anything since the outbreak of war. As a proposed assault on U.S. territory, it convinced Americans of German hostility to this country.

On March 9 Congress adjourned without passing the bill. The President issued the order for arming ships anyway and waited for the "overt act." It came on March 18 in the torpedoing without warning of three American merchant ships with heavy loss of life. Conveniently at this moment the overthrow of the Czar by the preliminary revolution in Russia purified the Allied cause, and the advent of the great new convert to democracy under the Kerensky regime brought a glow of enthusiasm to liberal hearts. At the same time the relentlessly mounting toll of the submarine was making a graveyard of the Atlantic and raising a serious prospect of the Allies' defeat.

For two more weeks the President hesitated in his agony, afflicted by his sense, as he had said earlier that month, that "matters outside our life as a nation and over which we had no control . . . despite our wish to keep free of them" were drawing the country into a war it did not want. "If any nation now neutral should be drawn in," he had said in November, "it would know only that it was drawn in by some force it could not resist."

This is as just a statement of the truth as any. We were not artificially maneuvered to a fate that might have been otherwise; what engulfed us were the realities of world conflict. In the latest of a long train of scholars' examinations, Ernest May of Harvard in his *The World War and American Isolation, 1914–17*, published in 1959, concluded, "Close analysis cannot find the point at which he [Wilson] might have turned back and taken another road."

On April 2 Wilson went to Congress to ask for its formal acceptance of "the status of belligerent that has been thrust upon it." He put the blame specifically on submarine warfare: "a war against all nations." He said "neutrality is no longer feasible or desirable" when the peace of the world and freedom of its people are menaced "by the existence of autocratic governments backed by force which is controlled wholly by their will, not by the will of the people."

The validity of this proposition was somewhat weakened by

the fact that he had believed neutrality feasible and eminently desirable in coexistence with these same nations for nearly three years. "A steadfast peace," he now discovered, "can never be maintained except by a partnership of democratic nations." Citing the Zimmermann telegram as evidence of hostile purpose, he said there could be no assured security for the democracies in the presence of Prussian autocracy, "this natural foe of liberty." And so to the final peroration: "The world must be made safe for democracy . . . the right is more precious than peace."

Nothing that Wilson said about the danger to democracy could not have been said all along. For that cause we could have gone to war six months or a year or two years earlier, with incalculable effect on history. Except for the proof of hostility in the resumed submarine campaign and the Zimmermann telegram, our cause would have been as valid, but we would then have been fighting a preventive war—to prevent a victory by German militarism with its potential danger to our way of life—not a war of no choice. Instead, we waited for the overt acts of hostility which brought the war to us.

The experience was repeated in World War II. Prior to Pearl Harbor the threat of Nazism to democracy and the evidence of Japanese hostility to us was sufficiently plain, on a policy level, to make a case for preventive war. But it was not that plain to the American people, and we did not fight until we were attacked.

In our wars since then the assumption of responsibility for the direction, even the policing, of world affairs has been almost too eager—as eager as it was formerly reluctant. In what our leaders believe to be a far-sighted apprehension of future danger, and before our own shores or tangible interests have been touched, we launch ourselves on military adventure half a world away with the result that the country, as distinct from the government, does not feel itself fighting in self-defense. Korea was thoroughly unpopular and Vietnam—where we have gone a step further into a purely preventive war, to contain Chinese communism—even more so. In the circumstances the instinct of the country is uneasy, consciences troubled, and counsels divided.

Two kinds of war, acquisitive and preventive, make hard

explaining and the last more so than the first. Although the first might be considered less moral, so far in human experience abstract morality has not notably determined the conduct of states and a good, justifiable reason like need, or irredentism, or "manifest destiny," can always be found for taking territory. Besides, acquisitive wars tend to be short, sharp, and successful and success never needs explaining. But it is never possible to prove a preventive war to have been necessary, for no one can ever tell what would have happened without it. Given the gap in modern power and organized resources between China and ourselves, our exaggerated fear of Chinese communism, both as threat to us and in its appeal to the rest of Asia, seems unwarranted by a "clear and present danger." In the grip of a new illusion we have not waited, as in World Wars I and II, for the enemy's shot to be aimed at us.

In April 1917 the illusion of isolation was destroyed. America came to the end of innocence, and of the exuberant freedom of bachelor independence. That the responsibilities of world power have not made us happier is no surprise. To help ourselves manage them, we have replaced the illusion of isolation with a new illusion of omnipotence. That screen, too, must fall.

Where once we saw ourselves self-contained and free to stand apart, we now see ourselves as if endowed with some mission to organize the world in our image. Militarily we could knock out Hanoi, and doubtless Peking, too, tomorrow, but we cannot raise a clean new democracy on nuclear ashes. Whatever our material or political power, it is not enough for omnipotence. We cannot mold the non-Western world to our desires nor require its acceptance of our concepts of political freedom and representative government. It is too late in history to export to the nations of Asia and Africa with unschooled and undernourished populations in the hundreds of millions the democracy that evolved in the West over a thousand years of slow, small-scale experience from the Saxon village moot to the Bill of Rights. They have not had time to learn it and history is not going to give them time. Meanwhile we live on the same globe. The better part of valor is to spend it learning to live with differences, however hostile, unless and until we can find another planet.

CHRONOLOGY

NOTE ON THE TEXTS

NOTES

INDEX

Chronology

1912 Born Barbara Wertheim in New York City on January 30, the second child of Maurice Wertheim and Alma Morgenthau. (Father, born 1886, known to family and friends as "MW," is vice president and secretary of the United Cigar Manufacturers' Company, a firm co-founded by his father. Mother, born 1887, trained as a singer, is the daughter of Henry Morgenthau Sr., a German-Jewish lawyer born in Mannheim who immigrated to the United States as a boy and amassed a fortune in real estate before entering public service as a diplomat; as ambassador to Turkey from 1913 to 1916 he will do much to publicize Turkish atrocities being committed against Armenians. Sister Josephine Alma, the couple's first child, was born in 1910.) Family lives at 43 East 70th St. in Manhattan and spends summers and weekends at estate in Cos Cob, Connecticut.

1913 Father leaves position at United Cigar Manufacturers' Company and serves on the New York State Industrial Board, working primarily on drafting a new state labor law.

1914 Sister Anne Rebe is born on April 20. Family travels to Turkey to see Ambassador Morgenthau. On August 7, on board the Italian passenger steamer *Sicilia* off the coast of Greece, the young Wertheim girls and their mother witness a naval engagement between the British light cruiser *Gloucester* and the German battle cruiser *Goeben* and light cruiser *Breslau* that ends when the German ships escape toward the Dardanelles (an episode Tuchman later writes about in *The Guns of August*). Arriving at Constantinople three days later, mother is questioned about what she saw by the German and Austrian ambassadors, and afterwards remarks, "I never felt so important in all my life." Tuchman will later claim to have a distinct memory of her visit to Constantinople, despite her age. Father travels to Palestine to oversee the distribution of $50,000 in gold bullion raised by the American Jewish Committee in response to an appeal for aid by Morgenthau, and in October submits a report about the effects of the early months of World War I on the Jewish population. Family returns to New York toward the end of the year.

1915 Father joins the investment banking firm of Hallgarten & Company.

1917–18 After the United States enters the war in April 1917 father serves on the Treasury Department's National War Savings Committee, promoting the sale of war savings stamps. As treasurer of the American-Persian Relief Committee, he leaves in July 1918 for several months on an aid mission through present-day Iran, Iraq, and elsewhere in the Middle East.

1919–28 Barbara is enrolled at the Walden School, a recently founded progressive day school at 88th Street and Central Park West. Develops an early interest in history from "when I was about six" through reading children's historical fiction (Lucy Fitch Perkins, G. A. Henty), then moves on to novelists such as Alexandre Dumas, Arthur Conan Doyle, Walter Scott, and Jane Porter. Mother champions modern music, patronizing groups such as the International Composers' Guild and the League of Composers and contributing art and financial support to the magazine *Modern Music*. Father is one of the cofounders of the Theatre Guild in 1919; the girls are taken to Broadway premieres of the Guild's productions and, during Guild meetings at their home (as Barbara and Anne will later recall) they hear "the raised voices from the dining room . . . the shrieks of argument and laughter, and the often stormy departures as the choice of plays and performers for the new season was being decided." (Father later becomes a serious art collector and tournament chess player.) Barbara enjoys swimming and riding at Cos Cob estate. The family's French governess, Mlle. Thouvenel, reads to her from the plays of Racine and Corneille and instructs her in French, particularly during a three-month absence from school because of illness at age fifteen. Having been a partner since 1919, father leaves Hallgarten to found his own investment banking firm, Wertheim & Company, in 1927.

1929–32 Parents divorce in 1929. Barbara enrolls at Swarthmore College but is soon unhappy there; resists taking the required course in chemistry and is angered to discover that none of the campus sororities will accept Jewish pledges. When she announces her intention to leave Swarthmore, she is summoned to meet with the college president, who, she later remembered, "was really astonished" by the anti-Semitism she describes. "It never occurred to him that anybody in beautiful Swarthmore could suffer that kind of disability." Transfers to Radcliffe College, where her field of concentration is History and Literature, although history becomes her chief love. ("Widener Library," she will say in a 1963 lecture at Radcliffe, was "the single most formative experience in my career. . . . I could roam at liberty through the rich stacks, taking whatever I wanted. The experience was marvelous, a word I use in its exact sense meaning full of marvels. The happiest days of my intellectual life, until I began writing history again some fifteen years later, were spent in the stacks at the Widener.") Takes classes in literature with Irving Babbitt and John Livingston Lowes and in history with Charles Howard McIlwain. Escapes injury in a September 1929 automobile accident near Westerly, R.I., that kills the car's driver, another Radcliffe student. Works for Franklin D. Roosevelt's campaign in the summer of 1932; is introduced to Roosevelt by her grandfather Morgenthau on election night at campaign headquarters at the Biltmore Hotel in New York City. (Her cousin, Henry Morgenthau Jr., will serve as Roosevelt's Secretary of the Treasury, 1934–45.)

1933 At Radcliffe, submits honors thesis, "The Moral Justification for the British Empire" ("an unattractive title," she later recalls, "and, besides, inaccurate, because what I meant was the moral *justifying* of empire by the imperialists"). Graduates with a BA but decides not to do graduate work; later reflects that she "wanted to be, in some vague way, a writer; I did not know just how or in what form, but I was sure the form would not develop from more academic study." Travels to London to attend World Economic Conference with grandfather Morgenthau. Begins unpaid work for the American Council of the Institute of Pacific Relations (IPR), with offices in an annex of the East 52nd Street YWCA in Manhattan, and assists with research for *Economic Handbook of the Pacific Area*, a major institute project published the following year.

1934–35 Leaves for Japan in October 1934 upon being assigned to work in the IPR's Tokyo office; stays with the IPR's international secretary, William L. Holland, and his family for a few weeks before moving to her own apartment in downtown Tokyo. Assists with books about trade and commodity controls, and contributes articles to the Institute publications *Far Eastern Survey* and *Pacific Affairs*, which pays her $40—her first earnings as a writer—for "The Russo-Japanese Fisheries Controversy," published in June 1935. Spends a month in Peking, then returns to the United States via the Trans-Siberian Railway, Moscow, and Paris.

1936 Publishes short essay "Japan: A Clinical Note," in *Foreign Affairs* in April. Joins staff of *The Nation*, the liberal magazine that had been bought by her father to rescue it from bankruptcy the year before (he will sell it in 1937). Her first job is to clip items about currents events from various newspapers and magazines, then condense the information into two-hundred-word pieces that appear at the front of the magazine. ("The experience was invaluable.") Writes book reviews. Covers Roosevelt's re-election campaign.

1937–39 Is sent to Valencia and Madrid to report on the Spanish Civil War; is highly critical of the non-interventionist policies of the British and French governments in the face of open support of Franco's forces by Germany and Italy. "It was a somber, exciting, believing, betraying time, with heroes, hopes, and illusions." At one point she fires a gun, and many years afterward will keep the emptied cartridge on her dressing table. Moves to London, where in 1938 she publishes her first book, *The Lost British Policy: Britain and Spain Since 1700*, with an introduction by the English popular historian and biographer Philip Guedalla. The book, showing how Britain had traditionally tried to keep Spain free of control by continental powers, is intended as a warning of the dangers of a Spanish alliance with Germany and Italy. Writes for *War in Spain*, weekly bulletin subsidized by Spain's Republican government. Returns to the United States in the fall of 1938. Becomes American correspondent for the left-wing British weekly *New Statesman and Nation*. The defeat of the Spanish Republicans in early spring 1939 is "the event," she later recalls, "that cracked my heart, politically speaking, and replaced my illusions with recognition of *realpolitik*."

1940–42 Marries Lester R. Tuchman, a New York City internist, on June 18, 1940. "Not unreasonably," she later writes, Lester "felt at that time that the world was too unpromising to bring children into. Sensible for once, I argued that if we waited for the outlook to improve, we might wait forever, and that if we wanted a child at all we should have it now, regardless of Hitler." Daughter Lucy is born in 1941. Father becomes president of the American Jewish Committee and plays a key role in persuading it to drop its opposition to Zionism and to support the establishment of a Jewish state in Palestine. After the Japanese attack on Pearl Harbor, Lester joins the Medical Corps and is sent to Fort Rucker, Alabama, for training; Barbara and the new baby follow.

1943–45 Lester is sent overseas to serve in a U.S. military hospital in North Africa. Tuchman returns to New York and works for the Office of War Information on the Far East news desk, preparing broadcasts about the war in the Pacific and Asia to be transmitted to Europe. Her tasks include covering General Joseph Stilwell's campaign in Burma, and she develops an enduring interest in him. At war's end, Lester returns to New York and, as Tuchman later recalls, "domesticity for a while prevailed."

1946–55 The Tuchmans divide their time between Manhattan and Cos Cob residences, as they will for the next several decades. Daughter Jessica is born in 1946, daughter Alma in 1948. Inspired by the founding of the state of Israel, Tuchman starts work on book that will become *Bible and Sword: England and Palestine from the Bronze Age to Balfour*; it takes seven years to complete because of competing demands of being a wife and mother. ("When the children were very small," she says later in an interview, "I worked in the morning only and then gradually, as they spent full days at school, I could spend full days at work. I could never have done any of this work if I hadn't been able to afford domestic help.") Father dies in 1950; mother dies in 1953. New York University Press expresses interest in *Bible and Sword* and asks that she extend her treatment past the Balfour Declaration up through the present. Tuchman tries but the narrative "turned into polemic," as she recalled in the preface to the book's 1983 edition; British policy in Mandate Palestine from the 1920s through the 1940s she found "impossible to relate without outrage. This is not a suitable condition for a historian. The pages I produced were out of keeping with the rest of the book. . . . I tore them up and let the book terminate as originally planned, in 1918." In 1955 prepares a book proposal about the Zimmermann telegram, a secret German cable sent in January 1917 outlining an offer of support for the Mexican government if it will attack the United States; after the British decoded and passed it to the Wilson administration, it became one of the primary causes of America's entry into World War I. Tuchman is told by one publisher that she is interested in the "wrong war."

1956–57 *Bible and Sword* is published by New York University Press in 1956 and in England by Longman the following year. Works on *The Zimmermann Telegram.*

1958–59 *The Zimmermann Telegram* is published by Viking in 1958 and by Constable in England in 1959. Tuchman works on long essay on the 1904 kidnapping in Morocco of wealthy Greek-American Ion Perdicaris, whose abduction gave rise to an international incident; finding the material insufficient for an entire book, shortens her piece and publishes it as "Perdicaris Alive or Raisuli Dead" in *American Heritage* in August 1959. Wants to write a book about the crucial year of 1914, but is uncertain what the precise focus should be; is asked in December 1958 by Cecil Scott, editor at Macmillan, to consider writing about the Battle of Mons in August 1914. Counters with a proposal for a book about the pursuit of the *Goeben* and *Breslau*, also in August 1914, which her family had witnessed. Eventually the planned book takes shape in much expanded form as a narrative account of the first weeks of World War I. In addition to her usual extensive archival research, Tuchman travels to Europe and tours battlefields in France and Belgium. Takes notes, as is her invariable practice, on 4x6-inch file cards. In autumn 1959, begins first draft in longhand based on her notes, writing daily at the New York Society Library.

1960–61 Becomes Trustee of Radcliffe College in 1960. Works intently on her World War I book, initially using flashbacks in early chapters about the war's origins in England, France, Germany, and Russia; submits chapters to Cecil Scott at Macmillan, who responds that the flashbacks are confusing, and she agrees and opts for a straightforward chronological ordering (later remarks, "I have avoided razzle-dazzle arrangements ever since.")

1962 *The Guns of August* is published by Macmillan on January 29 to huge critical and commercial success; Tuchman becomes one of the best known historians of her time. A Book-of-the-Month Club choice, it remains on *The New York Times* best-seller list for forty-two consecutive weeks; it is also published in London by Constable (as *August 1914*), is serialized in the *Liverpool Daily Post* and *L'Aurore* in Paris, and appears in translation in several languages, including French, Italian, Spanish, and Dutch. President John F. Kennedy, deeply impressed with the book, asks that his aides read it and presents a copy to British Prime Minister Harold Macmillan in June. Tuchman's portrayal of European statesmen misunderstanding their opponents and blundering into war will influence his handling of the Cuban Missile Crisis; according to Robert Kennedy's memoir *Thirteen Days*, the president tells his brother on October 26, "I am not going to follow a course which will allow anyone to write a comparable book about this time, *The Missiles of October*." Tuchman reaches agreement for a documentary-film adaptation of *The Guns of August*, and is also involved in talks for a possible screen adaptation of *The Zimmermann Telegram*. Works on "La Belle Epoque," book about the years leading up to World War I that will become *The Proud Tower*.

1963 In April, delivers "In Search of History," Phi Beta Kappa Address at Radcliffe, the first of numerous addresses and essays in the years to come that consider the historian's practice. Wins Pulitzer Prize for general non-fiction for *The Guns of August*. Receives honorary doctorate from Bates College, the first of many such honorary degrees (from Yale, Columbia, Harvard, Brown, Smith, and Dartmouth, among others). Covers President Kennedy's funeral for the *St. Louis Post-Dispatch* (later finds fault with the article: "My piece, which took a rather cool view, was a disappointment to readers who wanted the grand tone").

1964 Publishes essay "When Does History Happen?" in *The New York Times Book Review* (it appears as "Can History Be Served Up Hot?" a title she dislikes) in March. Is honored by the Walden School in May. Publicly supports Republican incumbent Kenneth Keating against Robert Kennedy in the New York Senate race and Lyndon Johnson for president. Nathan Kroll's film version of *The Guns of August* is released in December to poor reviews.

1965–66 Tuchman publishes essay "History by the Ounce" in *Harper's* in July 1965. Completes *The Proud Tower*, her favorite among her books, which is published by Macmillan in January 1966; reviews are generally favorable if less enthusiastic than for *Guns of August*. Publishes essay "The Historian as Artist" in *New York Herald Tribune Book Week* in March, a defense of literary artistry and narrative history: "No one could possibly persuade me that telling a story is not the most desirable thing a writer can do." Addresses Chicago Historical Society in October with "Is History a Guide to the Future?" a speech skeptical of historians such as Arnold Toynbee and Karl Marx who see large patterns in history. Makes first visit to Israel and writes essay for *Saturday Evening Post*, published early in 1967, that is later used as the introduction to the Fodor guide to Israel. Delivers speech "The Historian's Opportunity" to the American Historical Association in December, urging historians to eschew jargon and use "everyday English, the language in use from Chaucer to Churchill," and warning that academic historians are in danger of failing to communicate outside their profession.

1967 Serves as member of the National Committee for an Effective Congress, group raising money for liberal candidates, particularly those who are critical of American policy in Vietnam. Addresses daughter Jessica's graduation at Radcliffe. Publishes essay "How We Entered World War I" in *The New York Times Magazine* in May. On May 28, amid mounting tension before the outbreak of the Six-Day War, speaks before a large demonstration on Manhattan's Riverside Drive in support of Israel, condemning the UN for withdrawing its peacekeeping troops from the Sinai peninsula and calling on the United States to take leadership in resolving the crisis (*The New York Times* describes her as the speaker who drew "the loudest and most persistent cheers"). Visits Israel after hostilities end in June and writes article for *The Washington Post* about the reunification of Jerusalem. Publishes essay about the Israeli victory, "the most nearly perfect military operation in modern history," and the Israel Defense Forces in the *Atlantic* in September.

1968 Expresses public opposition to the American involvement in the war in Vietnam; in March, publishes article in *Newsday* entitled "When, Why, and How to Get Out." Supports Eugene McCarthy's campaign for president and attacks Robert Kennedy for his "indecent rush" to enter the race in March after previously saying he would not run.

1969–70 Works on a project she will characterize as "like an egg with two yolks," a book about General Joseph Stilwell that combines biography and a history of Sino-American relations; it involves archival research, interviews, and, though she is unable to go to mainland China, a trip to Taiwan and Hong Kong.

1971 Macmillan publishes *Stilwell and the American Experience in China, 1911–1945* early in the year (English edition, entitled *Sand Against the Wind*, had been published late the previous year). It receives positive reviews, though is subsequently criticized for seeing Nationalist China and Chiang Kai-shek too much from Stilwell's perspective. Tuchman lectures on the writing of *Stilwell* to the National Archives Conference on Research in the Second World War in June. Testifies before the U.S. Senate Foreign Relations Committee in a televised hearing on June 25 urging the establishment of diplomatic relations with Communist China. Is elected president of the Society of American Historians.

1972 Publishes op-ed in *The New York Times* advocating the "unmentionable" option of charging users a modest fee for public library admission. Delivers address, "Generalship," at U.S. Army War College in April. Receives second Pulitzer Prize for *Stilwell.* Soviet officials hastily commission a Russian translation of *The Guns of August*, claiming that it provides a more "objective" account of the Battle of Tannenberg than Aleksandr Solzhenitsyn's recently published novel *August 1914*. In summer, a few months after Present Nixon's historic trip, Tuchman and daughter Alma travel to China for six weeks. Publishes series of articles via the Associated Press that form the basis of *Notes from China*, which also includes an essay published in *Foreign Affairs* in October, "If Mao Had Come to Washington," about what might have happened had U.S. officials taken up an offer made by Mao Zedong and Zhou Enlai in January 1945 to visit President Roosevelt.

1973–77 Delivers address "Why Policy-Makers Do Not Listen" to Foreign Service Association in January 1973. In the wake of the Watergate scandal argues for the impeachment of President Nixon in *The New York Times* and *The Washington Post.* Works on a history of Europe's middle ages examining the social impact of disasters such as the Black Death and the Hundred Years' War; book takes seven years to complete, and requires two extensive research trips, the first following the travels of Enguerrand de Coucy, the book's central figure, around Picardy and Normandy in France as well as the Swiss and Italian Alps, and the second tracing the path of the First Crusade down the Danube, across the Balkans, and through to Istanbul and Bursa, where Coucy died. Receives Radcliffe Alumni Recognition award in 1975. Gives lecture at American Historical Association meeting in December 1976, "The Assimilationist Dilemma: Ambassador Morgenthau's Story," which takes as its starting point her grandfather's appeal for aid to Jews in Palestine in 1914.

1978 Publishes *A Distant Mirror: The Calamitous 14th Century* (Knopf) to highly favorable reviews. Wins Gold Medal for History of the American Academy of Arts and Letters for History.

1979 Appointed president of American Academy and Institute of Arts and Letters, the first woman to be so honored. In interview with *The New York Times*, says she is grateful she never undertook a PhD: "It's what saved me, I think. If I had taken a doctoral degree, it would have stifled my writing capacity." Lester Tuchman retires from private practice after distinguished career as medical researcher and professor of clinical medicine at Mount Sinai School of Medicine. Tuchman delivers "The Book," Sillcox Lecture at the Library of Congress on October 17, in association with the library's recently established Center for the Book, on whose National Advisory Board she serves.

1980 Accepts invitation by the National Endowment for the Humanities to deliver its prestigious Jefferson Lecture. Delivers "Mankind's Better Moments," warning against undue pessimism, in Washington on April 24 and in London six days later. In May, publishes in *Esquire* "An Inquiry into the Persistence of Unwisdom in Government," germ of *The March of Folly.* Inducted into Belgium's Order of

Léopold, first class, and is named Trustee of the New York Public Library.

1981–83 In September 1981, gives paper "The American People and Military Power in an Historical Perspective" in Williamsburg, Virginia, at the annual conference of the International Institute for Security Studies. Knopf publishes *Practicing History*, a collection of her shorter writings dating back to the 1930s, in September 1981. With Lester, closes the Park Avenue apartment which has been their longtime Manhattan residence. In 1983, receives the Cosmos Club Award, presented annually by the prestigious Washington, D.C., social club. Tuchman is criticized by feminists for accepting award from a club that does not admit women; gives acceptance speech on folly in government and adds, "I take women's dignity for granted. I have never felt that I belonged to an inferior sex. . . . With regard to the Cosmos Club in particular, let me just say that, if as stated, the criterion of membership is 'achievement,' then the exclusion of women is the club's loss, not ours."

1984 Publishes *The March of Folly: From Troy to Vietnam* (Knopf), a best seller, that ends on pessimistic note that government is unlikely to be wiser in the future: "We can only muddle on as we have done in those same three or four thousand years, through patches of brilliance and decline, great endeavor and shadow." Gordon S. Wood, in *New York Review of Books*, writes, "Her history is no longer art: it is not written for its own sake. It is now science—popular political science—which she once said she would never write. . . . She is very eager now to find patterns or lessons in the past with which to teach us." Settles dispute with Robert Manning, a State Department official during the Vietnam War, who threatened legal action over claims that in *The March of Folly* Tuchman had misrepresented a memo he had written about government relations with the press; she agrees to change wording about the memo in subsequent editions.

1985–88 Opposes computerization of card catalogue at the Library of Congress: "When you don't write down your own list you lose contact with what you're doing." Writes *The First Salute*, in which she examines the American Revolution in its international perspective. Published by Knopf in 1988, it receives mixed reviews but becomes a best seller. With sister Anne, Tuchman contributes preface to catalogue of father's art collection, bequeathed to Harvard University's Fogg Art Museum after his death. Gives interview that appears on the PBS television program *World of Ideas with Bill Moyers*, September 30, 1988, in which she laments the "loss . . . of a moral sense" in America.

1989 Dies on February 6 after complications from a stroke suffered a few days earlier. Buried at Mount Hope Cemetery, Hastings-on-Hudson, New York.

Note on the Texts

This volume contains Barbara W. Tuchman's books *The Guns of August* (1962) and *The Proud Tower* (1966), along with, as an appendix, her essay "How We Entered World War I" (1967).

After publishing *The Zimmermann Telegram* (1958), a book about the secret German cable in 1917 outlining a German proposal for alliance with Mexico if Mexico would attack the United States, Tuchman sought to write another book about World War I, and specifically about events in 1914, although she was unsure what precisely to focus on. Over lunch on December 31, 1958, the Macmillan editor Cecil Scott asked her if she would write a book on the Battle of Mons in August 1914; shortly thereafter Tuchman proposed to Scott a book on the naval pursuit of the German warships *Goeben* and *Breslau* at the beginning of the war. At first Scott insisted that Macmillan was more interested in a book on Mons, but eventually the project was envisioned as an account of the war's first five weeks, excluding fighting on the Austrian front. As well as doing archival work in several libraries in the United States and Europe, Tuchman visited battlefields in Belgium and France as part of her research. In the fall of 1959, she began writing her first draft in longhand, working daily at the members' room of the New York Society Library. She typed the second draft at her apartment on East 78th Street in Manhattan, then made further changes by cutting out passages with scissors and taping them elsewhere in the manuscript and by making handwritten revisions. This revised version was typed by a professional typist, then corrected and edited by Tuchman before she sent it, one chapter at a time, to Scott at Macmillan. At first, she employed flashbacks in the early chapters in describing the diplomatic background that preceded the war's outbreak, but Scott advised her to abandon the technique, and she rewrote the material as a chronological account.

The Guns of August was published in New York by Macmillan in January 1962; the book was also brought out that year, under the title *August 1914*, by Constable in London. (Tuchman did not revise the text of *The Guns of August* for the English edition.) It soon appeared in translation in several European languages. In 1984 the Franklin Library published a limited edition of *The Guns of August*, reprinting the text of the 1962 Macmillan edition but commissioning new maps, by Rafael D. Palacios, to replace the original maps created by William A. Pieper; Palacios's maps, illustrating the same battles, are far more legible and detailed than Pieper's. The present volume prints the text of the 1962 Macmillan edition of *The Guns of August* but includes the maps from the 1984 Franklin Library edition. The photographs are taken from the 1962 Macmillan edition, which were obtained from Brown Brothers (1, 11, 13), the German Information Center (7), the Imperial War Museum (3, 4, 6, 8, 9, 10, 12, 15, 16), and the Radio Times Hulton Picture Library (2, 5).

Shortly after completing *The Guns of August*, Tuchman began "La Belle Epoque," a series of interrelated essays about the era leading up to the outbreak of World War I. She worked steadily on the book through 1965; prepublication excerpts appeared in *Atlantic Monthly* (May 1963), *American Heritage* (December 1962), *The Nation* (September 20, 1965), and *Vogue* (November 1, 1965). As *The Proud Tower: A Portrait of the World Before the War 1890–1914*, it was published by Macmillan in New York in January 1966 and in London that year by Hamish Hamilton (in an edition identical to the American edition except for the title and copyright pages). The text printed here is taken from the 1966 Macmillan edition. The illustrations in that edition, reproduced here, were obtained from Brown Brothers (5, 10, 11, 18, 21, 24, 27, 28); Country Life Publishing Co. (4); The Mancell Collection, London (29); the Museum of the City of New York (7); the Radio Times Hulton Picture Library (1, 26); The Royal Archives, The Hague (17); Dr. Franz and Alice Strauss (22); and unattributed sources. The following reproductions are printed by permission of the museums that currently own the originals: Lord Ribbesdale (Sargent), Copyright © National Gallery, London / Art Resource, NY; The Wyndham Sisters (Sargent), Copyright © The Metropolitan Museum of Art / Art Resource, NY; and Nijinsky as the Faun (Bakst), Wadsworth Atheneum Museum of Art / Art Resource, NY.

"How We Entered World War I" was first published in the *New York Times Magazine* on May 5, 1967, and reprinted in Tuchman's essay collection *Practicing History* (New York: Knopf, 1981). This volume prints the text of the 1981 Knopf edition.

This volume presents the texts of the original printings chosen for inclusion here, but it does not attempt to reproduce nontextual features of their typographic design. The texts are presented without change, except for the correction of typographical errors. Spelling, punctuation, and capitalization are often expressive features and are not altered, even when inconsistent or irregular. The following is a list of typographical errors corrected, cited by page and line number: 48.34–35, Mistinguette; 57.27, *eventuelle*; 96.18, Hotzendorff; 98.8, deeply"; 104.36, mobilization"; 112.27, attack"; 120.11, right"; 130.26, days; 175.32, Gloucester; 175.36, wave length; 179.7, in Aegean; 192.1, uniforms were; 194.3, Siegeskranz (and passim); 214.32, investigation the; 214.38, Hely (and passim); 219.17, Monk; 241.5, Liège was; 250.28, De Broqueville; 250.33, mission had; 283.22, felt; 312.19, Prittzwitz; 324.6–7, von François 1st; 332.17, Blagovestchensky "lost; 353.1, 1914.; 356.14, Davis's; 361.6, Germany; 363.20, expected,; 368.1, groups could; 371.28, voyage,"; 419.32, threshhold; 436.14, mistatement; 452.5, forego; 452.29–30, up"; 461.17, Mézieres; 462.37, number, of; 466.32, enemy"; 479.5, De Galbert; 481.1, Afterward; 481.6, the the war; 489.13, Generalstaab; 490.3, 1928; 501.2, Vienna, 1921–25.; 501.22, Haussman; 516.13, Kotzbue's; 517.5, by Living; 526.7–8, warships is; 532.15, de la France; 534.33, Sar-la-Bruyère; 535.42, take your clothes off; 537.27, friendly welcome"; 546.4, "He has a shout-Hurrah! mood"; 521.43, Kier; 550.19, Afterward; 563.38, heterogenity; 616.39–40, bimetalism; 664.13, miner's; 669.3, affair, which; 677.5, instantly,; 723.16, 1857, later; 726.15, excuse much; 730.22, Carribbean; 730.28, make a Cuba; 736.32, shoulder above the rest of us.; 738.30, Labor,; 768.21, Von Bülow; 768.33, De Rodays; 772.32, juive; 781.10, Republic in; 785.15, des; 812.40, l'Ameréе!",; 819.1–2, Casimir-Périer; 877.23, memtal; 882.38, H.M.S. Dreadrought; 895.28, did, not; 896.26, nation; 900.3, Social; 919.19, Verklärung.; 924.1, why Strauss; 964.16, Joseph to; 974.28, increasing; 995.20, veto; 1004.19, Ladies; 1018.11, "and; 1019.9, seamen's; 1024.28, Times; 1070.19, Socialists; 1088.9, Muller (and passim); 1091.37, Bells";; 1101.34, understanding Romain; 1112.32, Rhinehart; 1115.38, Day of; 1116.25, hatred and revolt"; 1128.23, Elizabeth; 1132.8, 1141.3, "The Waste Land."; 1141.28, humanizing war!; 1142.46, potent for; 1143.3, failures necessary; 1143.14, tendency toward; 1143.15, Landsowne; 1143.33, tentative, delicate; 1149.17, Eulenberg; 1160.35, Isvolsky.

Notes

In the notes below, the reference numbers denote page and line of this volume (the line count includes headings). No note is made for material included in standard desk-reference books. Biblical quotations are keyed to the King James Version.

THE GUNS OF AUGUST

13.22–24 Danilo . . . Merry Widow's lover] In the operetta *The Merry Widow* (1905) by Hungarian composer Franz Lehár (1870–1948), with a libretto by Viktor Léon (1858–1940) and Leo Stein (1861–1921), based on *The Embassy Attaché* (1861), stage comedy by French playwright Henri Meilhac (1831–1897).

15.1 *Roi Charmeur*] French: "Enchanting King," name bestowed on Edward VII by Lord Rosebery (1847–1929).

15.4 *Fashoda!*] In an attempt by France to expand its territory in east Africa, a small expedition led by Major Jean-Baptiste Marchand (1863–1934) reached the Nile at Fashoda in southern Sudan in July 1898, causing a diplomatic crisis with Britain. In September, a flotilla of gunboats led by British General Herbert Kitchener (1850–1916) arrived at Fashoda to confront the French garrison, which withdrew on November 3 under threat of war between the two nations. See also 630.29–33 in this volume.

15.21–22 *Vive notre Roi!*] French: long live our king!

16.37 *reise-Kaiser*] German: traveling Emperor.

17.22 Treitschke] German historian and politician Heinrich von Treitschke (1834–1896), advocate for unification and a powerful, expansionist German state. See also 843.9–15 in this volume.

17.35–37 Kaiser . . . Attila] See Wilhelm II's "Hun speech" of July 27, 1900, at Bremerhaven, addressing German troops about to leave for China to help quell the Boxer Rebellion: "As the Huns a thousand years ago under King Etzel made a name for themselves that has lasted mightily in memory, so may the name 'Germany' be known in China, such that no Chinese will ever again even dare to look askance at a German."

18.3 *Deutschland ganzlich einzukreisen*] German: Germany completely encircled.

19.13–14 Reinsurance Treaty] Secret treaty (1887) of alliance between Germany and Russia.

19.20 *un garçon mal elevé*] French: a badly brought-up boy.

24.2 heralded the Norman Conquest] Halley's Comet, visible over England in 1066, was taken to be an omen of the Norman Conquest, which began later that year.

25.23 Pickelhaube] Spiked helmet worn by members of the German military.

26.30 *Saul*] Oratorio (1739) by German-British composer George Frideric Handel (1685–1759).

32.22 Battle of Cannae] Battle (216 BCE) fought in northern Italy during the Second Punic War in which the Carthaginian general Hannibal encircled and destroyed a numerically superior Roman army led by Varro. At the start of the battle, the Carthaginian cavalry on Hannibal's left flank defeated the Roman cavalry facing it, then swung around behind the Roman army and drove the enemy cavalry on the opposing flank from the field. The Roman infantry, which had advanced and pushed back the center of Hannibal's line, was then enveloped on both flanks by his infantry and attacked from the rear by his cavalry. According to the historian Livy, 48,000 Roman soldiers were killed, about six times the losses of the Carthaginian forces.

43.5 Boulangism] Revanchist movement of the 1880s associated with Georges Boulanger (1837–1891), general and politician referred to as the "man on horseback" because he would often address Parisian crowds mounted on a black horse. Accused of conspiracy in 1889 amid fears that he would soon lead a coup d'état, he fled France, and committed suicide in 1891.

43.6 Dreyfus Affair] In October 1894, the French-Jewish artillery officer Alfred Dreyfus (1859–1935) was wrongfully accused of treason and sentenced to life imprisonment. The intense controversy that followed resulted in the case being reopened, and in September 1899 Dreyfus was pardoned by President Emile Loubet. He was fully exonerated by a military commission on July 12, 1906, and one week later publicly decorated with the Légion d'Honneur. See Tuchman's chapter on the Dreyfus Affair in *The Proud Tower*, 757–824 in this volume.

44.31–32 General Margueritte's . . . Sedan] After the Prussians completed their encirclement of French forces at Sedan, French General Jean-Auguste Margueritte (1823–1870) led a French cavalry charge and was fatally wounded.

45.19 *Victoire c'est la volonté*] French: victory is will.

47.29–30 Like the youth . . . "Excelsior!"] In "Excelsior!" (1841), poem by Henry Wadsworth Longfellow.

48.34–35 Mistinguett] French music-hall entertainer, born Jeanne Bourgeois (1875–1956), best known for her performance of "Mon Homme" (1916).

49.13–14 General Boulanger on horseback] See note 43.5.

49.28 *attaque brusquée*] French: surprise attack.

50.28 Agadir] The German gunboat *Panther* anchored at the North African port of Agadir on July 1, 1911, escalating the rivalry between France and Germany for economic and political influence in Morocco. Fears of war increased after Britain sided with France, but the crisis was resolved on November 4, 1911, when France ceded approximately 100,000 square miles of French Equatorial Africa to Germany in return for German recognition of a French protectorate over Morocco.

53.33 D'Artagnan, from Gascony] Charles Ogier de Batz de Castelmore, Comte d'Artagnan (c. 1611–1673), best known as the basis for the character in the novel *The Three Musketeers* (1844) by Alexandre Dumas (1802–1870), was born in Lupiac, a village in Gascony in southwest France.

59.10–11 Russian defeat at Mukden] In the Battle of Mukden, the final significant land battle of the Russo-Japanese War, February 19–March 10, 1905.

59.12–13 Kaiser's . . . March 31] Staged as a show of support for Moroccan independence, Wilhelm II visited Tangiers for a few hours as a challenge to French influence in Morocco, as established by the Anglo-French Entente (1904) and a Franco-Spanish treaty (1904) dividing Morocco into separate spheres of French and Spanish dominance.

72.14 siege of Plevna] In the Russo-Turkish War, Plevna (Pleven) held out for five months against a siege by Russian forces, July 19–December 10, 1877. The Turks inflicted heavy losses on the Russians and repulsed three assaults on the city before capitulating.

72.22 *mujiks*] Russian: peasants.

75.38 Tsushima] The Russian Baltic Fleet was destroyed by the Japanese in the battle of Tsushima Strait, May 27–28, 1905.

77.20–21 Levins . . . hope] Konstantin Levin, character in *Anna Karenina* (1877), novel by Leo Tolstoy; title character of *Uncle Vanya* (1899), play by Anton Chekhov (1860–1904) set on a provincial country estate in Russia.

77.27 Cherry Orchard] Chekhov's play (1904) set on a failing estate.

79.19–20 Provisional Government] The Russian Provisional Government, established after the abdication of Czar Nicholas II on March 2 (March 15, N.S.), was overthrown by the Bolsheviks on October 25 (November 7, N.S.), 1917.

83.7 famous Trakehnen stud] Horse-breeding center in East Prussia founded in 1732 by Prussian ruler Friedrich Wilhelm I (1688–1740).

92.14 *Lady Audley's Secret*] Popular novel (1862) by English writer Mary Elizabeth Braddon (1837–1915).

92.25 Algeciras and Agadir] Diplomatic conference at Algeciras in the Spanish zone of Morocco, January 16, 1906–April 7, 1907, to resolve disputes among European powers about Moroccan territory (see note 59.12–13). Agadir, see note 50.28.

96.8 anthroposophism] Anthroposophy, spiritual belief system founded by Austrian philosopher Rudolf Steiner (1861–1925).

103.5–6 Cyrano . . . gesture!] In *Cyrano de Bergerac* (1897), by French playwright Edmond Rostand (1868–1918).

107.20 *Evidemment*] French: obviously.

109.24–25 grasshopper . . . ant] In Aesop's fable, the grasshopper who fiddles and is left starving when winter comes is contrasted with the ant who has stockpiled food during the summer months.

111.21–22 paweth . . . Ha, ha] Cf. Job 39:21, 25.

114.39–40 *Et l'honneur? . . . l'honneur?*] French: and honor? Does England understand what honor is?

120.13 *Drang nach Osten*] German: drive toward the east.

134.35–36 Kitchener of Khartoum] Kitchener was celebrated as a British national hero after his victory over Mahdist Sudan's commander, Abdullah al-Taashi, and his 52,000 followers (known as the Ansar) at the Battle of Omdurman, in Khartoum, Sudan, on September 2, 1898.

135.7–8 Reservists and Territorials] Volunteer reserve soldiers; those in the Territorial Force could choose not to serve overseas.

141.25 *Corpsbrüder*] German: fellow members of a university student dueling society.

141.28–29 called each other *du*] Used the familiar form when addressing each other.

147.4–5 C'est . . . faut] French: It's Alsace and Lorraine / It's Alsace that we need.

147.15 *soixante-quinzes*] French: seventy-fives.

149.20–21 a "*Hoch!*"] German: a cheer.

150.14 *Sehr richtig!*] German: Hear! Hear!

150.24 gladiators' salute] "Hail, Emperor! We who are about to die salute you," recorded in Suetonius, *Lives of the Caesars*, ch. 21. The salute was offered not by professional gladiators but by condemned prisoners who were to be combatants in a mock sea-battle staged by emperor Claudius.

159.17–18 "Sick Man" of Europe] Phrase derived from Czar Nicholas I's remark to the British ambassador in January 1853: "We have on our hands, a sick man—a very sick man; it will be, I tell you frankly, a great misfortune if one of these days he should slip away from us."

180.19–21 among its passengers . . . Morgenthau] Tuchman herself as a two-year-old child, with her mother, father, and two young sisters.

184.4 sanguinary tragedy of Gallipoli] In the Allied defeat in the Gallipoli Campaign, April 25, 1915–January 9, 1916, British losses numbered 44,092 dead and 96,937 wounded, while Turkish losses amounted to an estimated 86,692 killed and 164,617 wounded.

185.23 Port Arthur] The Russian garrison at Port Arthur in Manchuria surrendered to the Japanese on January 2, 1905, after a siege lasting more than six months.

194.2–3 "Deutschland . . . Siegerkranz."] Patriotic German songs: "Das Deutschlandlied" ("Song of Germany"), words (1841) by August Hoffmann von Fallersleben (1798–1874), set to music (1797) by Franz Joseph Haydn (1732–1809), often called "Deutschland über Alles" ("Germany over all") after its first line; "Watch on the Rhine" (1840), words by Max Schneckenburger (1819–1849) and music by Karl Wilhelm (1815–1873); "Hail to Thee in Victor's Crown," words (1793) by Heinrich Harries (1762–1802) sung to the tune of "God Save the King."

194.27 *Man hat geschossen!*] German: someone has been shooting!

201.39–40 forty-nine . . . Toulon] During the siege of British-occupied Toulon, August 27–December 19, 1793, twenty-four-year-old Colonel Napoleon Bonaparte commanded an artillery brigade and played a key role in reclaiming the port for the French. His actions brought him national recognition and a promotion to brigadier general.

209.21 *poilu*] French: infantryman.

210.34 "Sambre et Meuse"] French patriotic song (1870) composed by Jean Robert Planquette with lyrics by Paul Cézano, later arranged as a military march. See 252.32–39 in this volume.

213.35 Jägers] German light infantry, used for reconnaissance and skirmishing.

216.1 *Les forts tiennent toujours!*] French: the forts are still holding!

219.17 General Monck] George Monck, 1st Duke of Albemarle (1608–1670).

234.28–31 two King Ludwigs . . . mad] Ludwig I (1786–1868) had an affair with the Irish dancer and actress Lola Montez, ennobling her and allowing her to exert political influence; he abdicated during the political unrest of 1848. His grandson Ludwig II (1845–1886), whose support for the operas of Richard Wagner was a consuming obsession, was deposed on grounds of insanity and committed to an asylum.

240.12 famous book] Edward L. Spears, *Liaison, 1914: A Narrative of the Great Retreat* (1931).

246.5–6 Blériot . . . Channel] On June 25, 1909, French aviator Louis Blériot (1872–1936) became the first man to fly across the English Channel in a heavier-than-air machine.

247.23 *Au fond*] French: basically.

260.14 *Je vous apporte . . . France*] French: I bring you France's kiss.

269.9–11 *Tout ça . . . zéro!*] French: that's sport, all that! . . . The airplane is nothing!

273.23 *En avant!*] French: forward!

278.31–35 Malplaquet . . . song] "Malbrouck s'en va-t-en guerre" ("Marlborough is going to battle"), sung to the tune of "For He's a Jolly Good Fellow," was supposedly written on the eve of the Battle of Malplaquet, September 11, 1709.

279.11 DSO] Distinguished Service Order.

286.23 General Allenby . . . Jerusalem] Edmund H. H. Allenby (1861–1936), commanded the British expeditionary force that defeated the Turks and occupied Jerusalem in December 1917.

288.21 no single Horatius] Horatius Cocles, Roman hero who in the sixth century BCE held back the Etruscan army of Porsenna from the wooden Sublician bridge until it could be demolished, then swam across the Tiber to safety.

288.26–27 V.C. and D.C.M.] Victoria Cross and Distinguished Conduct Medal.

291.27–28 Legends . . . Angels of Mons] In Welsh writer Arthur Machen's short story "The Bowmen," published September 29, 1914, phantom bowmen who had been at the Battle of Agincourt come to the aid of British soldiers during the retreat from Mons and kill German troops "by the thousands." The story was accepted by some as a true account, and popular variants of the tale included stories of warrior angels fighting alongside the British at Mons.

305.6 Twenty-one Demands on China] A list of aggressive Japanese demands presented to the Chinese president Yuan Shikai on January 18, 1915, including claims for territory in Manchuria, Shantung, and Inner Mongolia and the ceding of significant economic, military, and political powers to the Japanese.

325.6 traitor . . . Thermopylae] During the Battle of Thermopylae in 480 BCE, a local man named Ephialtes informed Persian King Xerxes of a path that led around a mountain pass that for two days had been defended by Greek forces, allowing the Persians to win the battle, despite the rearguard defense by a vastly outnumbered band led by Spartan King Leonidas.

353.19–20 *Schrecklichkeit*] German: terror, frightfulness.

354.14–15 *Die Franzosen . . . da!*] German: The French are there! The English are there!

357.1–2 Romain Rolland . . . Hauptmann] French man of letters Romain Rolland (1866–1941), author of biographical and critical studies of Beethoven, Michelangelo, and Tolstoy, plays, political tracts, and novels including the ten-volume *Jean-Christophe*; German playwright Gerhart Hauptmann (1862–1946), author of naturalistic plays such as *Vor Sonnenaufgang* (*Before Dawn*, 1889) and *Die Weber* (*The Weavers*, 1893).

358.2–3 Harnack . . . Roentgen] Theologian Adolf von Harnack (1851–1930), author of several volumes of church history; novelist and playwright Hermann Sudermann (1857–1928), whose works include the novels *Frau Sorge* (*Dame Care*, 1887) and *Das Hohe Lied* (*The Song of Songs*, 1908) and the play *Heimat* (*Homeland*, 1893); composer Engelbert Humperdinck (1854–1921), best known for his opera *Hänsel und Gretel* (1893); scientist Wilhelm Roentgen (1845–1923), physicist who discovered X-rays.

359.6–7 later Mandates . . . Nations] System established by the League of Nations in 1919 for the administration of former German and Ottoman colonies and territories after World War I.

360.11 Wells' novel] *Mr. Britling Sees It Through* (1916).

362.12–13 like the Russo-Japanese battle of Tsushima] See note 75.38.

366.14 yacht regattas of Cowes week] Yacht-racing festival held annually during the first week of August at Cowes, port on the northern tip of the Isle of Wight.

376.16–17 Hugo Münsterberg] German-born psychologist (1863–1916), a prominent pro-German apologist.

377.1 Casabianca on the burning deck of neutrality] Reference to "Casabianca," popular poem by Felicia Dorothea Hemans (1793–1835), often called, after its opening line, "The Boy Stood on the Burning Deck."

377.27–31 When Sherlock Holmes . . . Holmes] From "Silver Blaze" (1892), story by Arthur Conan Doyle.

381.38–39 *chasseurs à pied*] French: light infantry.

384.8 Battle of the Last Cartridge] At Bazeilles near Sedan, August 31–September 1, 1870, French marines barricaded themselves into houses to fight a much larger Bavarian force with the help of civilian snipers; one group, covering the French withdrawal from the town, fought until it ran out of ammunition.

387.31–32 Gallieni's . . . Lyautey of Morocco] Gallieni was sent to Madagascar in 1896 to crush an insurgency and succeeded in pacifying the island through a combination of military and political measures; Louis-Hubert Gonzalve Lyautey (1854–1934), who served with Gallieni in Madagascar, later implemented a similar campaign of pacification while colonial governor of Morocco, 1912–25.

387.34 *Erinnerungen . . . ragazzo*] German, English, and Italian: *Memoirs of My Boyhood.*

395.23 Green Mountain Men] Green Mountain Boys, militia commanded by Ethan Allen whose most famous exploit was their capture of Fort Ticonderoga, May 10, 1775.

403.5 *sous-préfet*] French: sub-prefect.

406.33 *chasseurs alpins*] French: mountain infantry.

406.35–36 Marchons . . . France!] French: let us march, march, march / Against the enemies of France.

410.34–35 *Eh bien . . . tranquille*] French: Well, my friend, now you can rest easy.

412.11–12 British Grenadiers and Tipperary] Marching song of the British Grenadiers; "It's a Long Way to Tipperary" (1912), British music-hall song by Harry Williams, words by Jack Judge.

427.39 *Taube*] German monoplane.

447.14 *ne veulent pas marcher*] French: do not want to march.

449.5 Blücher] Prussian field marshal Gebhard Leberecht von Blücher (1742–1819); the engagement at Brienne took place on January 29, 1814.

454.23–24 Puns . . . *Bordelaise*] A pun on the name of a steak dish prepared "in the style of Bourdeaux." *Tournedos* is a contraction of the phrase *tourne le dos*, "turn one's back."

454.26–27 *Aux gares . . . wagons!*] French: to the station, citizens! Climb into the train-cars!

462.28 Tarpeian Rock] Roman site of public executions in antiquity.

464.36 Sadowa] The Battle of Sadowa (also called the Battle of Königgrätz), July 3, 1866, Prussian victory over the Austrians in the decisive battle of the Austro-Prussian War, at Sadová in the present-day Czech Republic.

478.32–33 *arrière-pensée*] French: ulterior motive.

438.39 *Messieurs les Allemands . . . Noyon*] French: the Germans are still in Noyon.

487.33 *wie es wirklich war*] German: how it really was. Cf. Leopold von

Ranke, preface to *History of the Romanic and Germanic Peoples* (1824). (Ranke wrote "wie es eigentlich gewesen," which can also be translated as "how it really was.")

THE PROUD TOWER

562.3 *Grosse Politik*] German: great-power politics.

562.3 Isvolsky . . . Aehrenthal] Russian diplomat Aleksandr Izvolsky (1856–1919), foreign minister, 1906–10; Austro-Hungarian foreign minister Alois Lexa von Aehrenthal (1854–1912).

571.17–18 Casket Letters . . . Scots] Letters of uncertain authenticity said to be written by Mary, Queen of Scots (1542–1587), that were used as evidence of her alleged complicity in the murder of her husband Henry Stewart, Lord Darnley (1545–1567). The documents at Hatfield are contemporary copies of the original letters, which have disappeared.

574.10 "Pam" or "Dizzy" or the "Grand Old Man"] Nicknames for British prime ministers Palmerston, Disraeli, and Gladstone, respectively.

585.18 Marie Corelli] Pseudonym of Mary Mackay (1855–1924), popular English writer, whose best-selling novels, sometimes on spiritualist themes, include *A Romance of Two Worlds* (1886), *Wormwood: A Drama of Paris* (1890), and *The Soul of Lilith* (1892).

587.28 Cowes] See note 366.14.

589.7–9 famous picture . . . "*Floreat Etona!*"] British defeat in the First Boer War, February 27, 1881, in which a force of 550 soldiers led by General George Colley suffered heavy casualties; a popular illustration of the battle, *Floreat Etona!* (the school motto "May Eton flourish!"), was created by Lady Elizabeth Butler (1850–1933).

590.24 Chauncey Depew] American attorney, railway president, and politician (1834–1928), Republican U.S. senator from New York, 1899–1911.

596.20–21 *eau de Nil*] A pale green color (literally in French, "water of the Nile").

596.21 *mousseline de soie*] A lightweight, open-weave, sheer fabric of silk.

601.12 Uitlanders] Afrikaans: foreigners.

602.13 Dr. Jaeger's woollen clothing] Gustav Jaeger (1808–1871), professor of physiology and zoology at the University of Stuttgart, developed a line of undyed woolen undergarments and other clothing that he claimed would be more healthful than clothes made of silk, cotton, linen, or any material that had been dyed.

603.37 the Yellow Book] Periodical (1894–97) edited by Henry Harland, with Aubrey Beardsley as art editor, seen by many at the time as a magazine of decadent art; its contributors included Max Beerbohm, Henry James, and W. B. Yeats.

603.38 Mauve Decade] I.e., the 1890s, phrase popularized by Thomas Beer's book *The Mauve Decade: American Life at the End of the 19th Century* (1926).

608.30–31 General Gordon's . . . Sudan] British general George Gordon (1833–1885) was sent to Khartoum in January 1884 to oversee the evacuation of Egyptian forces at war with an Islamic insurgency led by the Mahdi (Muhammad Ahmad, 1844–1885). After a siege lasting nearly a year, Gordon was killed when Khartoum was captured in January 1885.

610.40–611.1 His son John . . . Tyler] Wat Tyler (d. 1381), leader of the 1381 Peasants' Revolt in England, was killed by Cavendish after being wounded in the neck by the Lord Mayor of London, Sir William Walworth (d. 1385).

611.36–37 mathematical tripos] Final honors examination at Cambridge.

612.30–31 Capability Brown] English landscape architect (1716–1783).

616.29 Mrs. Sidney Webb] Beatrice Webb (1858–1943), who with her husband Sidney (1859–1947) were English social reformers and prominent members of the Fabian Society, a socialist movement favoring incremental rather than revolutionary change.

620.13 *partie carrée*] French: foursome.

624.33–35 "to treat . . . entitled."] Cf. James Boswell, *Journal of a Tour to the Hebrides with Samuel Johnson, LL.D.* (1785), entry for August 15, 1773.

625.7 Macaulay] Thomas Babington Macaulay (1800–1859), English historian and essayist.

631.10 "Who never lost an English gun."] Cf. Alfred, Lord Tennyson, "Ode on the Death of the Duke of Wellington" (1852), l. 97.

632.36 distant predecessor] Canute I, eleventh-century Viking king of England and Scandinavia, legendary for commanding the waves to stop.

638.36–37 Paris Commune . . . general insurrection] In March 1871 a coalition of radical factions came to power in Paris in the aftermath of France's defeat in the Franco-Prussian War. The conservative national government, under Adolphe Thiers (1797–1877), suppressed the commune in May 1871, at the cost of 20,000–25,000 lives, most of whom were summarily executed after the fighting ended.

639.22 "Liberator" of the serfs] Alexander II's Emancipation Manifesto (1861) freed the Russian serfs.

640.3 Pinkertons] Operatives of the Pinkerton National Detective Agency.

644.24 Delectable Mountains] Pastoral locale in John Bunyan's *The Pilgrim's Progress* (1684).

647.40 Mrs. Potter Palmer] Chicago civic leader Bertha Honoré Palmer (1849–1918).

651.33 *passage à tabac*] French: beating.

654.16 the German Max Stirner] Pseudonym of Johann Caspar Schmidt (1806–1856), philosopher who influenced anarchism, author of *The Ego and His Own* (1844).

654.17 *culte de moi*] French: cult of myself.

660.35 *Guardia Civil*] Civil Guard, Spanish national police force.

661.9 *latifundia*] Latin: great estates.

661.24 defeated the Carlists] In the Third Carlist War, 1872–76 (sometimes called the Second Carlist War), against supporters of a Bourbon claimant to the Spanish throne.

663.36 William Rossetti] English essayist and editor (1829–1919), founding member of the Pre-Raphaelite Brotherhood.

688.36 Jane Addams] American social reformer (1860–1935), founder in 1889 of Hull House in Chicago, the first settlement house in the United States.

700.33 Charles Reade] English playwright and novelist (1814–1884), whose novels include *The Cloister and the Hearth* (1861) and *Put Yourself in His Place* (1870).

706.25–26 in 1910 . . . Cannon] Illinois Republican U.S. congressman Joseph Cannon (1836–1926), Speaker of the House, controlled the House Committee on Rules, which appointed other committees. To diminish his power, the House of Representatives passed a resolution in 1910 that enlarged the committee, excluded the Speaker from serving on it, and provided for the election of its members by the House.

714.8 Jomini] Swiss-born military theorist Henri Antoine Jomini (1779–1869), author of *Summary of the Art of War* (1836).

714.13–14 like M. Jourdain . . . knowing it] In Molière's play *The Bourgeois Gentleman* (1670).

714.39–40 oxygen . . . Priestley] English chemist Joseph Priestley (1733–1804) discovered oxygen in 1774.

724.32–33 Coxey's Army . . . Pullman strike] Ohio populist politician Jacob Coxey (1854–1951) led a protest march of unemployed men to Washington in 1894; Pullman strike, see 1051.32–1052.36 in this volume.

727.30–31 Lohengrin] Hero of German Arthurian legend, the titular character of Richard Wagner's opera (1850).

737.2 Mr. Dooley] Character created by the American humorist Finley Peter Dunne (1867–1936).

740.4 John Bright] English orator and reformist statesman (1811–1889), leading English supporter of the Union during the American Civil War.

744.20 *Deus Vult!*] Latin: God wills it!

751.1 Krag] Magazine-fed repeating rifle used by the U.S. army.

754.5–7 Secretary Hay . . . minds] U.S. Secretary of State John Hay (1838–1905) devised the American "Open Door" policy in 1899–1900, supporting free trade rights for all nations with China, recently divided into economic zones of influence by European powers and Japan.

754.8–9 American share in the relief expedition] In mid-1900 the United States sent a detachment of Marines to China for the relief of foreign diplomatic legations in Peking besieged by Boxer insurgents.

754.13 "full dinner pail"] Slogan of William McKinley's 1900 presidential campaign.

754.27–29 Dumdum bullets . . . before] See 865.5–35 in this volume.

764.9 Valmy] French victory against Prussian and Austrian forces on September 20, 1792, the first victory of French revolutionary forces against regular armies.

764.11 Marengo, Austerlitz and Wagram] Victorious French battles during the Napoleonic Wars.

764.14–15 Sebastopol and the Malakoff] In the Crimean War, French capture of a heavily defended Russian fortification, the Malakoff, September 8, 1855, ending the siege of the nearby city of Sebastopol.

764.15 Magenta and Solferino] French victories in its 1859 war with Austria, on June 4 and June 24, respectively.

764.18 Last Cartridges at Sedan] See note 384.7–8.

764.18–19 the wild cavalry charge] See note 44.31–32.

766.16 "*sale bête*" or "*ce salaud*"] French: "dirty beast"; "that bastard."

767.17–19 character . . . contempt] Farinata degli Uberti as described in *Inferno*, canto 10.

769.15–17 "Guermantes" . . . Swann] Aristocratic family in Marcel Proust's seven-volume novel *In Search of Lost Time* (1913–27); the wealthy stockbroker's son Charles Swann (769.17) is one of the novel's central figures.

769.19 married into the Faubourg] I.e., into the aristocracy, who resided in the Faubourg St.-Germain in Paris.

772.17 subsequent disabling May Laws] In the aftermath of anti-Jewish pogroms that were blamed on the Jews themselves, Czar Alexander III signed a group of anti-Semitic measures into law in May 1882, restricting Jewish residence to towns and villages and limiting Jewish ownership of property.

783.4 *l'Aiglon*] Play (1900) by Edmond Rostand, whose title role was first played by celebrated French actress Sarah Bernhardt (1844–1933).

785.14–16 epitomized decadence . . . Esseintes] Baron de Charlus, dissipated homosexual character in Proust's *In Search of Lost Time*; Des Esseintes, protagonist of *A Rebours* (*Against the Grain*, 1884), novel by French writer J. K. Huysmans (1848–1907).

788.19–20 Yvette Guilbert] Fashionable French cabaret singer and performer (1868–1944), painted and caricatured by Henri Toulouse-Lautrec.

790.26 Björnstjerne Björnson] Norwegian playwright and fiction writer (1832–1910), winner of the 1903 Nobel Prize in Literature.

791.37–38 Voltaire in the Calas affair] Voltaire wrote *A Treatise on Intolerance* (1763) in response to the execution of the Protestant French merchant Jean Calas (1698–1762), who was falsely convicted of murdering his oldest son, a suicide. His accusers claimed that he had committed the crime to prevent his son's conversion to Catholicism. Calas's family later proved his innocence.

794.35 Gabriel Monod] French historian (1844–1912) and professor at the Collège de France, author of *The Germans and the French* (1872).

795.40–796.1 Van Gogh's "Field of Iris"] I.e., *Irises* (1889), currently in the collection of the J. Paul Getty Museum, Los Angeles.

804.15 who led the Carmaux strike in person] See 1048.7–23 in this volume.

807.18 *France Quand Même*] French: France even so.

816.27 *A bas . . . l'assassin!*] French: down with the executioners! Down with the assassin!

817.6 Baudry] French painter Paul-Jacques-Aime Baudry (1828–1886).

817.8–9 *sabreur de la parole*] French: swordsman of speech.

817.26 *en brosse*] French: hair cut short and bristly.

820.11 G. A. Henty] British adventure novelist and journalist George Alfred Henty (1832–1902), whose books include *Under Drake's Flag* (1883), *With Clive in India* (1884), and *With Wolfe in Canada* (1887).

823.20 General André] French general Louis André (1838–1913), Minister of War from 1900 to 1904.

823.21 *fiches*] French: files.

829.33 *urbi et orbi*] Latin Papal blessing: to the city and to the world.

841.29 the point of *non possumus*] Impossibility, from Latin: we cannot.

846.30–31 "Bloody Sunday"] Violent suppression by the police of a mass demonstration in Trafalgar Square, November 13, 1887, in which three protesters were killed.

847.4–5 General Booth] English evangelist William Booth (1829–1912), founder of the Salvation Army.

847.32 Cardinal Manning] Henry Manning (1808–1892), Catholic archbishop of Westminster.

847.33 Mrs. Annie Besant] English theosophist, social activist, and author (1847–1933).

851.3–4 Generals von der Goltz and Bernhardi] Military leaders and historians Colmar von der Goltz (1843–1916), author of *The Nation at Arms* (1883), and Friedrich von Bernhardi (1849–1930), who argued for aggressive German expansionism in *Germany and the Next War* (1912; see 946.24–27).

857.24–25 *Frappez vite . . . l'audace*] French: strike quick and strike hard, audacity, audacity, always audacity.

867.22 *Mene, Tekel, Upharsin*] Hebrew: "Numbered, weighed, divided," the words written on the wall at the banquet of King Belshazzar in Babylon; see Daniel 5.

877.17–20 presumed American citizen . . . dead!] Roosevelt ordered warships to Tangier after the wealthy Greek-American Ion Perdicaris (1840–1925), a former American citizen, was kidnapped in Morocco on May 18, 1904, by the Berber insurgent Ahmed ibn-Muhammed Raisuli (1875?–1925). Perdicaris was released by Raisuli on June 24; the slogan "Perdicaris Alive or Raisuli Dead" became a rallying cry for the Republican Party in the 1904 election.

878.39–40 dispute over Venezuela's debts] After Venezuelan dictator Cipriano Castro (1858–1924) declared forfeit $12.5 million of debt to European creditors in 1902, Germany, England, and Italy blockaded Venezuela's ports. President Roosevelt sent the U.S. Atlantic Fleet to the Venezuelan coast, then persuaded the disputants to submit the case to arbitration by the International Court of Justice at The Hague.

879.12 Dogger Bank affair] On the night of October 21, 1904, during the Russo-Japanese War, Russian warships in the North Sea en route for the Far East fired on English fishing boats, mistaking them for Japanese torpedo boats.

Several trawlers were sunk or damaged and three British sailors were killed. The incident brought Russia and Britain to the brink of war.

913.24 Herr Geheimrat] German: privy counselor.

933.15 Krafft-Ebing] Richard von Krafft-Ebing (1840–1902), German psychiatrist, author of *Psychopathia Sexualis* (1886), a compendium of case histories of sexual perversion.

955.37 the Russian "Five"] Composers Mily Balakirev (1837–1910), Modest Mussorgsky (1839–1881), César Cui (1835–1918), Aleksandr Borodin (1833–1887), and Nikolai Rimsky-Korsakov (1844–1908).

957.3 *épatant! . . . Bis, bis!*] French: shocking!; more, more!

957.10 *de trop*] French: too much.

960.16 *Ras, Dwa, Tri!*] Russian: one, two, three!

974.22 Tangier Crisis of 1905] See note 59.12–13.

971.38–39 Roundheads . . . Charles] The "shipmoney" tax levied by King Charles I (1600–1649) without parliamentary consent was fiercely resisted by Puritan parliamentarians known pejoratively as "Roundheads." Part of the opposition was based on the belief that Charles was using ship money for purposes other than the navy.

973.5 Corn Laws] Laws imposing duties on grain imported into Great Britain that were repealed in 1846.

997.36 *Iolanthe*] Light opera (1882) by W. S. Gilbert (1836–1911) and Arthur Sullivan (1842–1900).

1013.9 Hilaire Belloc," as Wilfrid Blunt noted] Catholic English poet, essayist, and member of Parliament Hilaire Belloc (1870–1953), advocate of economic and social reform; poet, diplomat, and travel writer Wilfrid Scawen Blunt (1840–1922).

1014.5 Reform Bill] Act of Parliament (1832) that introduced major changes to the electoral system of the United Kingdom, increasing the size of the electorate by as much as 80 percent.

1015.15–16 "Diehard" . . . famous regiment] The 57th Regiment of Foot, famed for its stand during the Battle of Albuera, May 16, 1811, during the Peninsular War, when its commander Sir William Inglis (1764–1835) ordered his men, "Die hard, 57th, die hard!"

1017.37–38 Sir Thomas Lipton . . . grocers] Sir Thomas Lipton (1850–1931), Scottish merchant, founder of successful grocery-store and tea businesses.

1023.18 Erastians] Adherents of the ideas of Swiss theologian Thomas Erastus (1524–1583).

1023.40 "Redmond!"] John Edward Redmond (1856–1918), Irish member of Parliament, leading advocate of Home Rule for Ireland.

1043.35 Primrose League] English conservative organization founded in 1883.

1049.1 Mounet-Sully] Jean Mounet Sully (1841–1916), French actor.

1055.12 August Belmont] August Belmont, Jr. (1853–1924), banker and prominent horse breeder.

1060.3 "*Que sais-je?*"] French: what do I know?

1075.2 Paterson strike] Strike by silk workers in Paterson, N.J., February–July 1913, led by the IWW; it collapsed when ribbon weavers agreed to a separate settlement with the factory owners, and other workers soon followed.

1095.29 *Guerre à la guerre!*] French: war on war!

HOW WE ENTERED WORLD WAR I

1167.28–29 a place called Château-Thierry] In early June 1918 American troops helped stop a major German offensive in heavy fighting around Château-Thierry, a town on the Marne forty miles east of Paris.

1167.29 "Over There,"] Popular patriotic song (1917) during World War I, with words and music by George M. Cohan (1878–1942).

1167.29–30 form of transport called "40 and 8,"] French transport boxcars, so called because of their intended capacity of forty men or eight horses.

1169.12 New Freedom] Name of Woodrow Wilson's platform during the presidential campaign of 1912; also the title of a collection of his speeches, published in 1913.

1169.18–20 Neville Chamberlain's reference . . . nothing."] Cf. British Conservative prime minister Neville Chamberlain's remarks on BBC radio, September 28, 1938: "How horrible, fantastic, incredible it is that we should be digging trenches and trying on gas-masks here because of a quarrel in a far-away country between people of whom we know nothing."

1170.34 Declaration of London] Code of proposed rules governing naval warfare, based on deliberations of an international naval conference held in London, December 4, 1908–February 26, 1909.

1172.2–3 trial and execution of Edith Cavell] Edith Cavell (1865–1915), a British nurse who taught at a nursing school in Brussels, was shot by the Germans on October 12, 1915, for helping Allied soldiers escape to Holland.

Index

THE LIBRARY OF AMERICA SERIES

The Library of America fosters appreciation and pride in America's literary heritage by publishing, and keeping permanently in print, authoritative editions of America's best and most significant writing. An independent nonprofit organization, it was founded in 1979 with seed funding from the National Endowment for the Humanities and the Ford Foundation.

1. Herman Melville: *Typee, Omoo, Mardi*
2. Nathaniel Hawthorne: *Tales and Sketches*
3. Walt Whitman: *Poetry and Prose*
4. Harriet Beecher Stowe: *Three Novels*
5. Mark Twain: *Mississippi Writings*
6. Jack London: *Novels and Stories*
7. Jack London: *Novels and Social Writings*
8. William Dean Howells: *Novels 1875–1886*
9. Herman Melville: *Redburn, White-Jacket, Moby-Dick*
10. Nathaniel Hawthorne: *Collected Novels*
11. Francis Parkman: *France and England in North America*, vol. I
12. Francis Parkman: *France and England in North America*, vol. II
13. Henry James: *Novels 1871–1880*
14. Henry Adams: *Novels, Mont Saint Michel, The Education*
15. Ralph Waldo Emerson: *Essays and Lectures*
16. Washington Irving: *History, Tales and Sketches*
17. Thomas Jefferson: *Writings*
18. Stephen Crane: *Prose and Poetry*
19. Edgar Allan Poe: *Poetry and Tales*
20. Edgar Allan Poe: *Essays and Reviews*
21. Mark Twain: *The Innocents Abroad, Roughing It*
22. Henry James: *Literary Criticism: Essays, American & English Writers*
23. Henry James: *Literary Criticism: European Writers & The Prefaces*
24. Herman Melville: *Pierre, Israel Potter, The Confidence-Man, Tales & Billy Budd*
25. William Faulkner: *Novels 1930–1935*
26. James Fenimore Cooper: *The Leatherstocking Tales*, vol. I
27. James Fenimore Cooper: *The Leatherstocking Tales*, vol. II
28. Henry David Thoreau: *A Week, Walden, The Maine Woods, Cape Cod*
29. Henry James: *Novels 1881–1886*
30. Edith Wharton: *Novels*
31. Henry Adams: *History of the U.S. during the Administrations of Jefferson*
32. Henry Adams: *History of the U.S. during the Administrations of Madison*
33. Frank Norris: *Novels and Essays*
34. W.E.B. Du Bois: *Writings*
35. Willa Cather: *Early Novels and Stories*
36. Theodore Dreiser: *Sister Carrie, Jennie Gerhardt, Twelve Men*

37a. Benjamin Franklin: *Silence Dogood, The Busy-Body, & Early Writings*

37b. Benjamin Franklin: *Autobiography, Poor Richard, & Later Writings*

38. William James: *Writings 1902–1910*
39. Flannery O'Connor: *Collected Works*
40. Eugene O'Neill: *Complete Plays 1913–1920*
41. Eugene O'Neill: *Complete Plays 1920–1931*
42. Eugene O'Neill: *Complete Plays 1932–1943*
43. Henry James: *Novels 1886–1890*
44. William Dean Howells: *Novels 1886–1888*
45. Abraham Lincoln: *Speeches and Writings 1832–1858*
46. Abraham Lincoln: *Speeches and Writings 1859–1865*
47. Edith Wharton: *Novellas and Other Writings*
48. William Faulkner: *Novels 1936–1940*
49. Willa Cather: *Later Novels*
50. Ulysses S. Grant: *Memoirs and Selected Letters*
51. William Tecumseh Sherman: *Memoirs*
52. Washington Irving: *Bracebridge Hall, Tales of a Traveller, The Alhambra*
53. Francis Parkman: *The Oregon Trail, The Conspiracy of Pontiac*
54. James Fenimore Cooper: *Sea Tales: The Pilot, The Red Rover*
55. Richard Wright: *Early Works*
56. Richard Wright: *Later Works*
57. Willa Cather: *Stories, Poems, and Other Writings*
58. William James: *Writings 1878–1899*
59. Sinclair Lewis: *Main Street & Babbitt*
60. Mark Twain: *Collected Tales, Sketches, Speeches, & Essays 1852–1890*
61. Mark Twain: *Collected Tales, Sketches, Speeches, & Essays 1891–1910*
62. *The Debate on the Constitution: Part One*
63. *The Debate on the Constitution: Part Two*
64. Henry James: *Collected Travel Writings: Great Britain & America*
65. Henry James: *Collected Travel Writings: The Continent*

66. *American Poetry: The Nineteenth Century*, Vol. 1
67. *American Poetry: The Nineteenth Century*, Vol. 2
68. Frederick Douglass: *Autobiographies*
69. Sarah Orne Jewett: *Novels and Stories*
70. Ralph Waldo Emerson: *Collected Poems and Translations*
71. Mark Twain: *Historical Romances*
72. John Steinbeck: *Novels and Stories 1932–1937*
73. William Faulkner: *Novels 1942–1954*
74. Zora Neale Hurston: *Novels and Stories*
75. Zora Neale Hurston: *Folklore, Memoirs, and Other Writings*
76. Thomas Paine: *Collected Writings*
77. *Reporting World War II: American Journalism 1938–1944*
78. *Reporting World War II: American Journalism 1944–1946*
79. Raymond Chandler: *Stories and Early Novels*
80. Raymond Chandler: *Later Novels and Other Writings*
81. Robert Frost: *Collected Poems, Prose, & Plays*
82. Henry James: *Complete Stories 1892–1898*
83. Henry James: *Complete Stories 1898–1910*
84. William Bartram: *Travels and Other Writings*
85. John Dos Passos: *U.S.A.*
86. John Steinbeck: *The Grapes of Wrath and Other Writings 1936–1941*
87. Vladimir Nabokov: *Novels and Memoirs 1941–1951*
88. Vladimir Nabokov: *Novels 1955–1962*
89. Vladimir Nabokov: *Novels 1969–1974*
90. James Thurber: *Writings and Drawings*
91. George Washington: *Writings*
92. John Muir: *Nature Writings*
93. Nathanael West: *Novels and Other Writings*
94. *Crime Novels: American Noir of the 1930s and 40s*
95. *Crime Novels: American Noir of the 1950s*
96. Wallace Stevens: *Collected Poetry and Prose*
97. James Baldwin: *Early Novels and Stories*
98. James Baldwin: *Collected Essays*
99. Gertrude Stein: *Writings 1903–1932*
100. Gertrude Stein: *Writings 1932–1946*
101. Eudora Welty: *Complete Novels*
102. Eudora Welty: *Stories, Essays, & Memoir*
103. Charles Brockden Brown: *Three Gothic Novels*
104. *Reporting Vietnam: American Journalism 1959–1969*
105. *Reporting Vietnam: American Journalism 1969–1975*
106. Henry James: *Complete Stories 1874–1884*
107. Henry James: *Complete Stories 1884–1891*
108. *American Sermons: The Pilgrims to Martin Luther King Jr.*
109. James Madison: *Writings*
110. Dashiell Hammett: *Complete Novels*
111. Henry James: *Complete Stories 1864–1874*
112. William Faulkner: *Novels 1957–1962*
113. John James Audubon: *Writings & Drawings*
114. *Slave Narratives*
115. *American Poetry: The Twentieth Century*, Vol. 1
116. *American Poetry: The Twentieth Century*, Vol. 2
117. F. Scott Fitzgerald: *Novels and Stories 1920–1922*
118. Henry Wadsworth Longfellow: *Poems and Other Writings*
119. Tennessee Williams: *Plays 1937–1955*
120. Tennessee Williams: *Plays 1957–1980*
121. Edith Wharton: *Collected Stories 1891–1910*
122. Edith Wharton: *Collected Stories 1911–1937*
123. *The American Revolution: Writings from the War of Independence*
124. Henry David Thoreau: *Collected Essays and Poems*
125. Dashiell Hammett: *Crime Stories and Other Writings*
126. Dawn Powell: *Novels 1930–1942*
127. Dawn Powell: *Novels 1944–1962*
128. Carson McCullers: *Complete Novels*
129. Alexander Hamilton: *Writings*
130. Mark Twain: *The Gilded Age and Later Novels*
131. Charles W. Chesnutt: *Stories, Novels, and Essays*
132. John Steinbeck: *Novels 1942–1952*
133. Sinclair Lewis: *Arrowsmith, Elmer Gantry, Dodsworth*
134. Paul Bowles: *The Sheltering Sky, Let It Come Down, The Spider's House*
135. Paul Bowles: *Collected Stories & Later Writings*
136. Kate Chopin: *Complete Novels & Stories*
137. *Reporting Civil Rights: American Journalism 1941–1963*
138. *Reporting Civil Rights: American Journalism 1963–1973*
139. Henry James: *Novels 1896–1899*
140. Theodore Dreiser: *An American Tragedy*
141. Saul Bellow: *Novels 1944–1953*
142. John Dos Passos: *Novels 1920–1925*
143. John Dos Passos: *Travel Books and Other Writings*

144. Ezra Pound: *Poems and Translations*
145. James Weldon Johnson: *Writings*
146. Washington Irving: *Three Western Narratives*
147. Alexis de Tocqueville: *Democracy in America*
148. James T. Farrell: *Studs Lonigan: A Trilogy*
149. Isaac Bashevis Singer: *Collected Stories I*
150. Isaac Bashevis Singer: *Collected Stories II*
151. Isaac Bashevis Singer: *Collected Stories III*
152. Kaufman & Co.: *Broadway Comedies*
153. Theodore Roosevelt: *The Rough Riders, An Autobiography*
154. Theodore Roosevelt: *Letters and Speeches*
155. H. P. Lovecraft: *Tales*
156. Louisa May Alcott: *Little Women, Little Men, Jo's Boys*
157. Philip Roth: *Novels & Stories 1959–1962*
158. Philip Roth: *Novels 1967–1972*
159. James Agee: *Let Us Now Praise Famous Men, A Death in the Family*
160. James Agee: *Film Writing & Selected Journalism*
161. Richard Henry Dana, Jr.: *Two Years Before the Mast & Other Voyages*
162. Henry James: *Novels 1901–1902*
163. Arthur Miller: *Collected Plays 1944–1961*
164. William Faulkner: *Novels 1926–1929*
165. Philip Roth: *Novels 1973–1977*
166. *American Speeches: Part One*
167. *American Speeches: Part Two*
168. Hart Crane: *Complete Poems & Selected Letters*
169. Saul Bellow: *Novels 1956–1964*
170. John Steinbeck: *Travels with Charley and Later Novels*
171. Capt. John Smith: *Writings with Other Narratives*
172. Thornton Wilder: *Collected Plays & Writings on Theater*
173. Philip K. Dick: *Four Novels of the 1960s*
174. Jack Kerouac: *Road Novels 1957–1960*
175. Philip Roth: *Zuckerman Bound*
176. Edmund Wilson: *Literary Essays & Reviews of the 1920s & 30s*
177. Edmund Wilson: *Literary Essays & Reviews of the 1930s & 40s*
178. *American Poetry: The 17th & 18th Centuries*
179. William Maxwell: *Early Novels & Stories*
180. Elizabeth Bishop: *Poems, Prose, & Letters*
181. A. J. Liebling: *World War II Writings*
182s. *American Earth: Environmental Writing Since Thoreau*
183. Philip K. Dick: *Five Novels of the 1960s & 70s*
184. William Maxwell: *Later Novels & Stories*
185. Philip Roth: *Novels & Other Narratives 1986–1991*
186. Katherine Anne Porter: *Collected Stories & Other Writings*
187. John Ashbery: *Collected Poems 1956–1987*
188. John Cheever: *Collected Stories & Other Writings*
189. John Cheever: *Complete Novels*
190. Lafcadio Hearn: *American Writings*
191. A. J. Liebling: *The Sweet Science & Other Writings*
192s. *The Lincoln Anthology: Great Writers on His Life and Legacy from 1860 to Now*
193. Philip K. Dick: *VALIS & Later Novels*
194. Thornton Wilder: *The Bridge of San Luis Rey and Other Novels 1926–1948*
195. Raymond Carver: *Collected Stories*
196. *American Fantastic Tales: Terror and the Uncanny from Poe to the Pulps*
197. *American Fantastic Tales: Terror and the Uncanny from the 1940s to Now*
198. John Marshall: *Writings*
199s. *The Mark Twain Anthology: Great Writers on His Life and Works*
200. Mark Twain: *A Tramp Abroad, Following the Equator, Other Travels*
201. Ralph Waldo Emerson: *Selected Journals 1820–1842*
202. Ralph Waldo Emerson: *Selected Journals 1841–1877*
203. *The American Stage: Writing on Theater from Washington Irving to Tony Kushner*
204. Shirley Jackson: *Novels & Stories*
205. Philip Roth: *Novels 1993–1995*
206. H. L. Mencken: *Prejudices: First, Second, and Third Series*
207. H. L. Mencken: *Prejudices: Fourth, Fifth, and Sixth Series*
208. John Kenneth Galbraith: *The Affluent Society and Other Writings 1952–1967*
209. Saul Bellow: *Novels 1970–1982*
210. Lynd Ward: *Gods' Man, Madman's Drum, Wild Pilgrimage*
211. Lynd Ward: *Prelude to a Million Years, Song Without Words, Vertigo*
212. *The Civil War: The First Year Told by Those Who Lived It*
213. John Adams: *Revolutionary Writings 1755–1775*
214. John Adams: *Revolutionary Writings 1775–1783*
215. Henry James: *Novels 1903–1911*
216. Kurt Vonnegut: *Novels & Stories 1963–1973*
217. *Harlem Renaissance: Five Novels of the 1920s*

218. *Harlem Renaissance: Four Novels of the 1930s*
219. Ambrose Bierce: *The Devil's Dictionary, Tales, & Memoirs*
220. Philip Roth: *The American Trilogy 1997–2000*
221. *The Civil War: The Second Year Told by Those Who Lived It*
222. Barbara W. Tuchman: *The Guns of August & The Proud Tower*
223. Arthur Miller: *Collected Plays 1964–1982*
224. Thornton Wilder: *The Eighth Day, Theophilus North, Autobiographical Writings*
225. David Goodis: *Five Noir Novels of the 1940s & 50s*
226. Kurt Vonnegut: *Novels & Stories 1950–1962*
227. *American Science Fiction: Four Classic Novels 1953–1956*
228. *American Science Fiction: Five Classic Novels 1956–1958*
229. Laura Ingalls Wilder: *The Little House Books, Volume One*
230. Laura Ingalls Wilder: *The Little House Books, Volume Two*
231. Jack Kerouac: *Collected Poems*
232. *The War of 1812: Writings from America's Second War of Independence*
233. *American Antislavery Writings: Colonial Beginnings to Emancipation*
234. *The Civil War: The Third Year Told by Those Who Lived It*
235. Sherwood Anderson: *Collected Stories*
236. Philip Roth: *Novels 2001–2007*
237. Philip Roth: *Nemeses*
238. Aldo Leopold: *A Sand County Almanac & Other Writings on Ecology and Conservation*
239. May Swenson: *Collected Poems*
240. W. S. Merwin: *Collected Poems 1952–1993*
241. W. S. Merwin: *Collected Poems 1996–2011*

This book is set in 10 point ITC Galliard Pro,
a face designed for digital composition by Matthew Carter
and based on the sixteenth-century face Granjon. The paper
is acid-free lightweight opaque and meets the requirements
for permanence of the American National Standards Institute.
The binding material is Brillianta, a woven rayon cloth made
by Van Heek–Scholco Textielfabrieken, Holland. Composition
by Dedicated Book Services. Printing and binding
by Edwards Brothers Malloy, Ann Arbor.
Designed by Bruce Campbell.

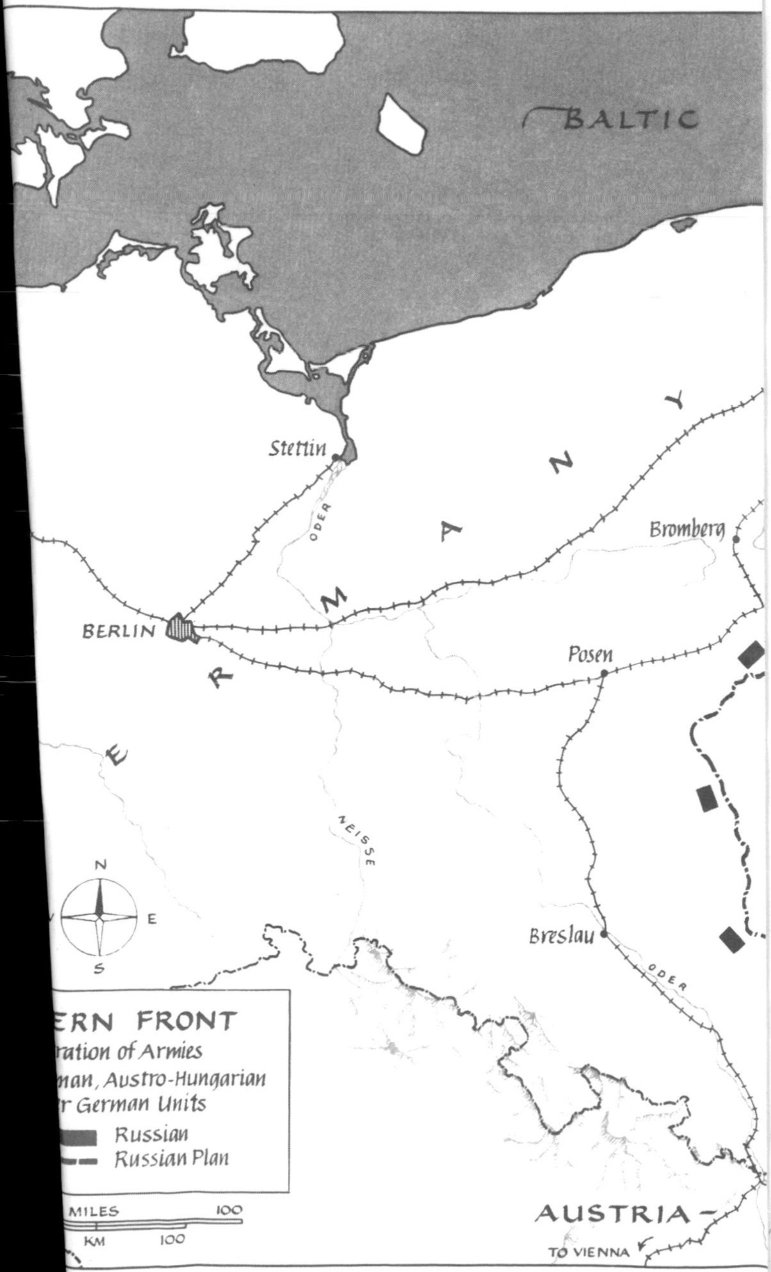

BALTIC
Stettin
ODER
Bromberg
G E R M A N Y
BERLIN
Posen
NEISSE
N
E
S
Breslau
ODER
ERN FRONT
ration of Armies
man, Austro-Hungarian
r German Units
Russian
Russian Plan
MILES 100
KM 100
AUSTRIA
TO VIENNA

TO HAMBURG
ELBE
EAST
palacios